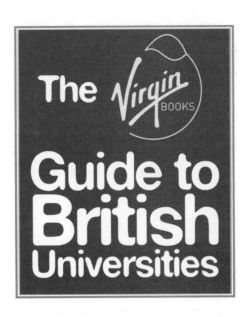

The *Virgin* BOOKS
Guide to British Universities

FOR
REFERENCE ONLY

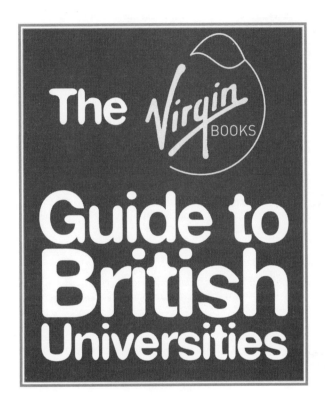

The Virgin BOOKS

Guide to British Universities

Piers Dudgeon

Published by Virgin Books 2009

2 4 6 8 10 9 7 5 3 1

First published in Great Britain in 2009 by
Virgin Books
Random House, 20 Vauxhall Bridge Road,
London SW1V 2SA

www.virginbooks.com
www.rbooks.co.uk

Addresses for companies within The Random House Group Limited can be found at:
www.randomhouse.co.uk/offices.htm

The Random House Group Limited Reg. No. 954009

A CIP catalogue record for this book
is available from the British Library

ISBN 9780753519516

The Random House Group Limited supports The Forest Stewardship Council [FSC], the leading
international forest certification organisation. All our titles that are printed on Greenpeace-approved FSC-
certified paper carry the FSC logo.
Our paper procurement policy can be found at www.rbooks.co.uk/environment

FSC

Design & Technical Consultant
Jonathan Horner, www.jonhorner.co.uk

Printed and bound in Great Britain by
CPI Mackays, Chatham ME5 8TD

'The best bar none... Most university guides tell you what grades are needed for entry, but fail to give any impression of what it's really like... *The Virgin Guide* bridges this gap. Amusing contributions from students already on their way to degrees detail the nitty gritty of student life at each institution, including accommodation, health, living on a shoestring, low- and high- workload courses, union life, societies, sports and — last but not least — watering holes and where to get a decent curry... The guide is based on thorough research [and] includes an official facts section, covering acceptance requirements to employment expectations.'
Times Educational Supplement

'Serious and honest' *Times Higher Educational Supplement*

'Glistening with success — a worthy contender for the best all-purpose buy for the aspiring undergraduate.' *Yorkshire Post*

'This is a very impressive piece of work... a serious and honest picture of student life at each major higher education establishment in the UK... *The Virgin Guide* looks set to take over as the nation's favourite antidote to the occasional excesses of the higher education marketing professionals.' *Careers Adviser*

'The value of this book lies in the info-crammed pages on universities, starting with Aberdeen and ending with York.' *The London Evening Standard*

'Lesson learned... Get studying this guide!' *Sun*

'Welcome to *The Virgin Guide*, an invaluable assessment... raw, earthy and direct.' *Wolverhampton Express & Star*

'It's the warts and all approach to help students make their choices.' *Leicester Mercury*

'Where you can believe what you read' *Cardiff Western Mail*

'Just the thing to make a truly informed choice' *Dundee Sunday Post*

CONTENTS

University Location Map	8
Introduction	11
Oxford and Cambridge	16
Admissions Tests	18
Recession Beating League Tables	19

A

Aberdeen University	33
Abertay Dundee University	36
Aberystwyth University	39
Anglia Ruskin University	43
Aston University	46

B

Bangor University	49
Bath University	53
Bath Spa University	58
Bedfordshire University	61
Birkbeck College	65
STUDENT BIRMINHAM - THE CITY	65
Birmingham University	67
Birmingham City	72
Bolton University	77
Bournemouth University	80
Bradford University	84
STUDENT BRIGHTON - THE CITY	88
Brighton University	89
STUDENT BRISTOL – THE CITY	93
Bristol University	94
Bristol West of England University	101
Brunel University	104
Buckingham University	109
Buckinghamshire New University	112

C

Cambridge University	114
Canterbury Christ Church University	126
STUDENT CARDIFF – THE CITY	129
Cardiff University	132
Uni Wales Institute, Cardiff (UWIC)	135
Central Lancashire University	138
Chester University	142
Chichester University	145
City University	148
Coventry University	152
Creative Arts, University of	155
Cumbria University	158

D

De Montfort University	161
Derby University	165
Dundee University	168
Durham University	173

E

East Anglia University	179
East London University	183
Edge Hill University	187
STUDENT EDINBURGH – THE CITY	190
Edinburgh University	192
Edinburgh Napier University	197
Essex University	200
Exeter University	204

G

Glamorgan University	209
STUDENT GLASGOW – THE CITY	213
Glasgow University	214
Glasgow Caledonian University	219
Gloucestershire University	222
Glyndwr	225
Goldsmiths College	228
Greenwich University	232

H

Heriot-Watt University	236
Hertfordshire University	240
Heythrop College	243
Huddersfield University	244
Hull University	348

I

Imperial College, London	253

K

Keele University	257
Kent at Canterbury University	262
King's College London	265
Kingston University	269

L

Lampeter University	274
Lancaster University	277
STUDENT LEEDS – THE CITY	281
Leeds University	282
Leeds Metropolitan University	288
STUDENT LEICESTER – THE CITY	291
Leicester University	292
Lincoln University	296
STUDENT LIVERPOOL – THE CITY	300

Liverpool University 301
Liverpool Hope University 305
Liverpool John Moores University 309
STUDENT LONDON – THE CITY 313
London Metropolitan University 315
London School of Economics
  & Political Science (LSE) 320
London South Bank 324
Loughborough University 327

M

STUDENT MANCHESTER – THE CITY 331
Manchester University 333
Manchester Metropolitan University 338
Middlesex University 342

N

STUDENT NEWCASTLE – THE CITY 345
Newcastle University 346
Newport University 351
Northampton University 354
Northumbria University 357
STUDENT NOTTINGHAM – THE CITY 360
Nottingham University 361
Nottingham Trent University 366

O

Oxford University 371
Oxford Brookes University 381

P

Paisley University 385
Plymouth University 389
Portsmouth University 393

Q

Queen Margaret University 393
Queen Mary, University of London 396
Queen's University, Belfast 400
STUDENT BELFAST – THE CITY 405

R

Reading University 406
Robert Gordon University 411
Roehampton University 413
Royal Holloway, London University 416

S

St Andrews University 420
St George's, University of London 425
Salford University 426
School of Oriental &
  African Studies (SOAS) 430
School of Pharmacy 431
STUDENT SHEFFIELD – THE CITY 431
Sheffield University 433
Sheffield Hallam University 437
Southampton University 441
Southampton Solent University 446
Staffordshire University 449
Stirling University 451
Strathclyde University 455
Sunderland University 459
Surrey University 462
Sussex University 465
Swansea University 469
Swansea Metropolitan University 472

T

Teesside University 473
Thames Valley University 476

U

Ulster University 479
University College London 481
University of the Arts, London 485

W

Warwick University 487
West of Scotland University 491
Westminster University 494
Winchester University 497
Wolverhampton University 500
Worcester University 403

Y

York University 506
York St John University 510

UK UNIVERSITIES

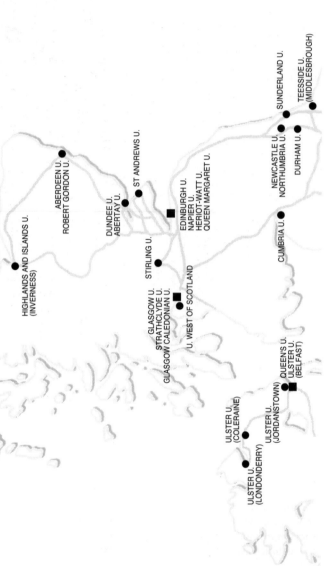

HIGHLANDS AND ISLANDS U.
(INVERNESS)

ABERDEEN U.
ROBERT GORDON U.

DUNDEE U.
ABERTAY U.

ST ANDREWS U.

STIRLING U.

EDINBURGH U.
NAPIER U.
HERIOT-WATT U.
QUEEN MARGARET U.

GLASGOW U.
STRATHCLYDE U.
GLASGOW CALEDONIAN U.

U. WEST OF SCOTLAND

ULSTER U.
(COLERAINE)

ULSTER U.
(LONDONDERRY)

ULSTER U.
(JORDANSTOWN)

QUEEN'S U.
ULSTER U.
(BELFAST)

CUMBRIA U.

NEWCASTLE U.
NORTHUMBRIA U.

SUNDERLAND U.

TEESSIDE U.
(MIDDLESBROUGH)

DURHAM U.

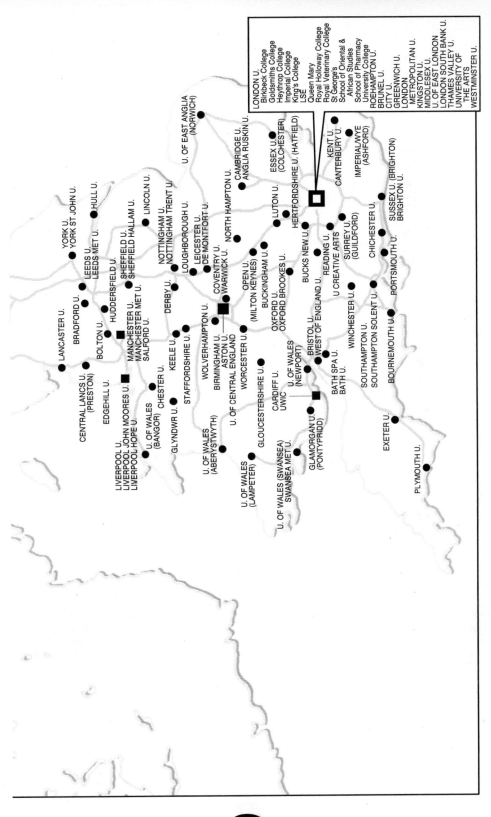

INTRODUCTION

INTRODUCTION — CHOOSING A UNIVERSITY

You are going to university at a time of recession. Some say it's the best place to be, given that jobs are at a premium. For sure, recession focuses the mind wonderfully on finding a degree with real job prospects and getting the best value out of the next few years.

Many Lower Sixth pupils thinking about university for the first time reckon they have a pretty good idea already where they want to go. Word has filtered down from the Upper Sixth. They know where the brightest went last year, where the sportiest went, and where those ended up who possibly should have accepted the offer of a year out coaching cricket at a school in South Africa rather than signing up to study PR because 'university' is what you do after school.

> *The first decision must be 'Which subject?', the second, 'Which university?' Bound up with the choice of university is the subtle distinction between a subject and a course.*

There are so many misconceptions, so much prejudice and lack of information, not only about the question of which university, but which subject to study. Time and again we listen to students who made the wrong choice of subject or course:

Misham Bhana, Edinburgh, reading Medicine: 'Don't do Medicine unless you're sure you definitely want to be a doctor. Sounds obvious, but there's a lot of clinical work in the course and if you don't enjoy talking to patients you'll probably hate it.' Garry Beardsworth, Leeds Met: 'Make sure you are completely certain about your university choice. I made the mistake of rushing into a degree in Architecture, and I didn't enjoy it at all. It's one of the most difficult and embarrassing things to admit to your parents, when they have ploughed vast amounts of money into it.' Aneesa Patel, Aberdeen: 'Make sure your course is the one you want to do. You would be amazed how many unhappy students are doing courses because their friends were, or their parents wanted them to.'

The first decision must be 'Which subject?', the second, 'Which university?' Bound up with the choice of university is the subtle difference between 'subject' and 'course'. A course is how a particular university, or department, delivers a subject. It may be delivered on its own or with another subject, or particular aspects of the subject may be the focus at the expense of others. You may be reading for a degree in English that focuses on 18th-century literature, which is a quite different experience to reading one that focuses on 19th-century literature, Some courses combine subjects from different faculties, which can be very effective. It is an axiom of research that looking at a subject from a different point of view, from 'outside the box' as people say, may lead to a Eureka! moment, a surprise discovery. As an undergraduate, looking at a science subject from a humanities point of view can give you a new slant on it. It may, for example, raise ethical issues that might otherwise not be dealt with. One course is very different from another. How a particular course deals with the subject of your choice determines how you benefit and develop, which in turn will influence you and your employability.

Of course you want a job when you graduate, but you should be looking for a course that offers more than motor skills in an area of work, skills that may in any case be better developed through hands-on experience at work.

Look closely at the job prospects of the department delivering your course. We rate university departments according to whether their graduates end up with real graduate jobs (that is, jobs they wouldn't have got had they not gone to university), and also how many of their students, looking back on the experience, are satisfied with their courses and the teaching.

You can attend a university like the London School of Economics, which boasts 90% and even 100% graduate employment at the end of many of its courses, and still end up wanting, as Lawrence Bushell did:

'In June I left the LSE (ranked fourth best university in the country) expecting to find myself slipping seamlessly into an Armani suit and munching a Pret sandwich as I admire the pencil-skirted receptionist across *the office. Instead, having searched for work for more than six months, I face another day hauling yet another wardrobe up umpteen flights of stairs as a removal man.'*

Lawrence wrote to the *Daily Mail* that he believes his problem is that he 'lacks experience'. Employers and employment agencies have told him so, and he has become convinced that he should not have gone to university at all, that he would have got a job and be further ahead than he can hope to be even if he got a job now.

Lawrence is wrong. Development at university is of a different order to work experience, which is why employers want top graduates.

THE STORY OF A BOY

Since the introduction of tuition fees, universities have been treating higher education as a business and students as consumers, which gives students the idea that the onus is on the universities to get them a good job at the end. But the fact is that university is only an opportunity provided you yourself are purposeful.

I am following a boy at the moment who is 17 going on 18 and taking A levels in June. Next year he will be supplying information for the *Guide* about Edinburgh or Glasgow University, the two universities that have offered him places, provided of course he makes the grade in the public examinations. He started thinking about what he would like to read at university last Spring, in the second term of the Lower Sixth. His subjects at A level are Maths, Biology and Chemistry. He liked Maths best back then but decided he wanted a course at university that was more 'real world' than Maths. There are doctors in his family. He wasn't passionate about being a doctor, but the pressure was there and he decided to go on a residential four-day MEDlink course at Nottingham University with a mate. He wasn't very impressed by the lectures and his mate fell asleep in most of them. He returned convinced that Medicine was not for him.

But one lecture did stay with him. It was given by a psychiatrist and made him interested enough to read *The Man Who Mistook His Wife for a Hat* by Oliver Sacks, an engaging book of case studies in Psychology which demonstrate the variety and ever-changing aspects of the subject, and the potential of the human mind.

The boy, his name is Edward James, had been going to get in touch with a surgeon friend of his father and ask whether he could observe him in theatre, but his growing interest in Psychology led him to arrange three weeks voluntary work with a local charity instead. Ryedale Special Families helps disabled children suffering from conditions such as Autism, ADHD, Cerebral Palsy and Downs Syndrome. The work was very hands-on, taking the children on outings to local beauty spots, swimming, and at the Centre there was plenty of opportunity to interact with them. He found this work challenging but was surprised how rewarding. He felt that he had gained some insight into the caring nature of Psychology, as well as the problems of children with these conditions. He enjoyed it enough to take up the offer of a paid position with them this summer.

Meanwhile, his reading continued. He found a copy of Jung's autobiography, *Memories, Dreams, Reflections*. Sounds deep, but it isn't. It tells the story of a man disillusioned with his pastor father's Christianity who rediscovers God and the Devil in his own mind, in the guise of Freud's conscious and unconscious. It is a great book for a beginner because you cannot fail to grasp many of the concepts of early psychology when they are delivered in the context of so extraordinary a life. Jung never quite lost his belief in the supernatural.

Subsequently, Edward was given Robin Skynner and John Cleese's *Families and How to Survive Them*, equally accessible, and his mother had Susie Orbach's *Bodies*, which is now on Edward's bedside table. At this stage he read no set books from the courses he had started to look at. He was following his own nose, discovering facets of this subject, so completely new to him, and found he was enjoying doing so.

Off his own bat, Edward had come across the first principle of university application: *it is important, above all, to choose a subject at university that you enjoy and to be clear what it is about it that you enjoy.*

Seeing this transformation taking place, Edward's father got in touch with an acquaintance of his, Marjorie Wallace, who founded the National Mental Health Charity SANE in Whitechapel, in the

University is an opportunity provided you yourself are purposeful.

The first principle of application is to choose a subject that you enjoy.

East End of London. She offered Edward unpaid work for two weeks last summer. It was hard, quite different to the Ryedale Centre. He was filing in the Fundraising department and the Media office. He worked out that if he did this ten hours a day for two weeks solid he would sort out one of the four filing cabinets that faced him, and probably go mad. But after the first week, when he had begun to get to know the staff, he found that he was given copy-typing to do, responding to routine letters, then phone work, dealing with all sorts of people in the business of raising money and spreading awareness of mental health in the community. The work required him to respond to direction and to work off his own initiative, to be methodical and systematic, and to have attention to detail. At the end, he was given a personal reference from Marjorie Wallace and was offered paid work, if he wanted it, in the future.

Most of all, this episode threw Edward on his own resources in a place that was quite foreign to him. He, a rural boy from the North of England, had to find his way alone around London from the house where he was staying (a member of his family's) to his place of work in Whitechapel every day, and look out for himself at lunch time, and explore this colourful and surprising part of the metropolis.

He, a rural boy from the North of England, had to find his way alone around Whitechapel every day, and look out for himself at lunch time, and explore this colourful and surprising part of the metropolis.

This had all happened within five months of his beginning to think about what he should study at university.

When it came to writing his personal statement for the UCAS application form that autumn he didn't have to look far for something to say.

At the same time he had begun to look at the courses on offer in Psychology and his interest had become increasingly tied to his interest in Biology, which had begun to develop in parallel. Maths had been his first love, now it was Biology. Thinking about Psychology had led to the change. He had found an interest in tying this science of the mind to what goes on in the brain and elsewhere in the human body.

That was the reason he made Edinburgh his first choice. In the BSc Biological Sciences (Psychology) at Edinburgh the biological bases of science are key and the department is currently expanding as a centre of excellence in Human Cognitive Neuroscience. In the first of four years you study a wide range of topics to help find your feet in what for many will be a new subject, not focusing solely on Psychology until years 3 and 4.

Edward was discovering the second principle of university application: *once you have decided what subject you want to study and understood what it is that interests you about it, you must look for a course that delivers it, a course that will stimulate you for three or four years.*

Edward then went to an Open Day at Edinburgh, loved the city and was swept away by one of the lectures he attended, in which the lecturer showed a film of two teams of two or three players each, one team dressed in white, the other in black. They were passing a ball to each other. The lecturer asked the 200 or so potential applicants in the lecture hall to count the number of times the ball was passed between the members of the teams. When the film ended almost everyone agreed that it had been passed fourteen times. They had all concentrated hard, many of them no doubt desperate not to fail at the first post by getting such a simple question wrong.

The lecturer then asked who among these potential Edinburgh undergraduates, cream of the Class of 2008-9, had seen a huge gorilla come into shot and walk right through the group of players as they were passing the ball.

Not a hand in the hall went up. The lecturer announced that she would replay the film, and this time her audience should not bother to count the number of times the ball was passed. And there was the gorilla, plain as daylight to the students now that they were not concentrating on the counting task she had given them.

Psychology is the scientific study of the mind and human and animal behaviour. Edward laughed at the lady lecturer's manipulation of his mind, and saw at once these people in the Psychology department at Edinburgh knew what they were about.

He also needed a back-up choice of course, and went about this with scientific precision. He chose another Scottish university — not because he is Scottish or has any Scottishness in his family — but he had heard that Scots were good teachers, and reasoned that Scottish universities, which don't charge fees to their own, could probably use the fees they do charge Sassenachs.

Right or wrong, he thought he'd probably get a good deal, and when he looked at Glasgow he was amazed to discover that in the most recent National

Student Survey (2008) the department was ranked 4th of all Psychology departments in the UK, and 1st in Scotland (i.e. actually higher than Edinburgh). Later in the year, as I began my research for this edition of *The Virgin Guide*, I was able to point out to him that also in 2008, in the first assessment of the research provision of British universities since 2001, 20% of the research at Glasgow's Psychology department was rated 'world-class', and 40% 'of international significance'. In the parlance of *The Virgin Guide* they had sizeable 4* and 3* ratings, which ranked them 7th in the UK.

Not only that, Glasgow made the World's Top 200 Universities in a league table published by the *Times Higher Education* magazine after soliciting information from the world's leading universities. It actually came 73rd, just below the LSE and above the likes of York, St Andrews, Nottingham, Durham, and Newcastle.

Edward had chosen Glasgow as a back-up because the department asked for less points than Edinburgh. He now found that it was one of the best value deals for Psychology going. He wouldn't have known had he not looked. And I was able to give him the low-down on the campus and city scene, which puts Edinburgh in the shade.

> *The second principle of application: once you have decided what subject you want to study, you must look for a course that delivers it, a course that will stimulate you for three or four years.*

No-one at Edward's school had any information at all about Glasgow. They were all queuing up for Edinburgh, Durham, Bristol, etc., because their parents, who knew nothing about the status quo, but wanted to boast about their children, advised them to, and their peers had gone to these places in droves last year. No-one had gone to Glasgow University from his school. There was a vague rumour that that the Academic Head's son had found himself there after finding he didn't enjoy his first choice. But that was it.

Edward visited both universities and obtained a detailed idea of what they and the courses were about, so that when he wrote his personal statement on the UCAS form he could make the match between his interests and what he knew they delivered in their courses.

The happy result was an offer of 3 Bs from Edinburgh and a B and two Cs from Glasgow, and he is now working hard because he has found two universities he wants desperately to attend.

I tell you the story not because I want to recommend Edinburgh or Glasgow, or reading Psychology, but to exemplify the sort of line you must follow.

STEP-BY-STEP TO UNIVERSITY

First, choose a subject. Are you choosing a subject because you're good at it? Are you choosing one that fits the career path your parents want for you? Are you choosing one that you actually want to study *for itself*? Do you have a real interest, or might it be worth considering alternatives?

Opt for something you really want to do, because that is absolutely fundamental. Not only because you are about to study it in depth for more years and at a higher level than you have ever worked before, but your future happiness may indeed be determined by it.

Second, when you know what it is you want to study, look at what you can realistically afford in terms of the points you are likely to accrue. Look at 'points required', and also at the employability of graduates from the department that delivers your subject. Employability is in everyone's mind these days, and we have a lot about it in the *Guide*. Some departments consistently turn out employable graduates, employable not as secretaries and admin men, but as graduate career people. The statistics are there for all to see. Look. Listen to what students who are there have to say. The USP of our *Guide* is that we listen to what students, who are actually at university, tell us.

Look, too, at what goes on beyond the lecture theatre. When I first wrote the *Guide* twelve years ago, many sixth formers chose universities almost completely on the basis of where the club scene was. People opted for Manchester because of the Hacienda, Liverpool for Cream at the Nation. Students today have a more real-world focus and they want university to make a deeper cut in their lives.

Student Unions — the bodies that represent students at University, manned by ex-students taking a year off before going out into the world — have for years operated as if pure hedonism is still the name of the game, filling freshers (first years) with massive amounts of alcohol and their goodie bags with condoms and sick bags. Only now are they waking up to the change, and to the fact that the whole extra-curricular scene that is funded by the Student Unions is as important to students as the work they do in the library, perhaps more so.

GOOD VALUE

A few freshers see at once how to turn Student Union funds to advantage. When that happens, suddenly the really extraordinary essence of what university is about becomes clear.

Nick Coupe, a Londoner in the first term of his second year at Leeds University, is reading English and Theatre:

'I'm doing my degree in English and Theatre, so it's sort of the theoretical side of theatre rather than performance or anything like that, but I'm involved with Theatre Group which is a Student Union Society and they take proposals from students of all years, first to third year can propose to direct a play and then they give you funding and the venue to put it on and the support that you need.'

Nick has just put on *The Changeling* by Thomas Middleton, playing to 300 people over the inside-period of a week. I found him because I have a friend who is a theatrical agent in London, who Nick works for in the holidays. Nick is serious about what he wants to do. He knows it's no good bleating about not getting a job as a graduate. He knows he will get a job. He doesn't worry about things like that, because he is passionate about what he is doing.

He chose Leeds because of the student theatre scene, which is vibrant. They just won three awards at the NUS Drama Festival, and they fund people like Nick to produce plays, even from the first year.

'For me the Union is massive, a massive, massive union, seriously into everything it does — really high quality student paper, student radio, student TV that you can get involved with really easily. One of my friends who has only been here the same amount of time as me, is already Vice President of LSTV so although it is massive you can still get very heavily involved in something.

'I applied for English at five universities and English and Theatre at this one and I came for the interview and the Open Day and sort of fell in love with it and decided this was definitely what I wanted to be doing. The first year you study what you are told to study, but then when you get into second year you can really choose absolutely what you want to be studying and how. I am doing modules on Harold Pinter at the moment which is what I'm really interested in, so it's great that I can be studying the stuff I'm reading in my spare time as well.

'There are only twenty-five people on my course in my year, so all the lecturers and all the teaching staff know you by name or say hello to you if you see them out and about, which is something... one of my friends does history, and he barely knows his lecturers' names. I think it's a great system here that you can just pop into someone's office and have an informal chat about essays rather than having to make an appointment and know exactly what you want to say and have ten minutes. You genuinely can go and have a cup of tea and a chat about the module which I would have thought was quite unusual.'

Quality of the extra-curricular scene is what makes for true value at university, as well as good teaching, of course:

'My daughter is in her final year as an undergraduate at one of the country's more distinguished universities. Her contact time with her lecturers and supervisors consists of precisely two group seminars a week for about eighteen weeks a year... That's seventy-two hours of teaching — the equivalent of two working weeks for ordinary people — each year. For this, we parents fork out several thousand pounds, and she has run up debts of several thousands more.'

I picked this up in January from *The Times*. One Richard Morrison was the scribe. It is unfortunately more typical than one might suppose. In a letter to the *Times Higher Education* magazine Professor Alan Gilbert, vice-chancellor of Manchester University, explained why. The whole emphasis in the so-called Russell Group of universities — those with the best reputations — has been on research, not teaching: 'We know what good teaching is, but everything that is happening in Russell Group universities is moving in a different direction...' he said in February 2008. Gilbert was launching a 'root-and-branch' review of the teaching at Manchester, with more interaction between lecturers and students, smaller seminar groups (no more than eight), learning mentors, student feedback, and a simpler programme of degrees featuring core subjects, at the heart of it.

This is the kind of information you should be looking for in *The Virgin Guide*, along with what the Student Union can make available to someone with your interests.

Read everything you can. Choose a subject. Choose a course. Choose a university. There is no best university. There is a best university for you. It may not be Oxford or Cambridge, or even Bristol or Durham or Edinburgh, but it is your choice.

The Virgin Guide hands this choice back to you.

OXFORD & CAMBRIDGE

In many people's minds Oxford and Cambridge are the pinnacle of achievement. I talked about this with Tim Morrison, the master responsible for Oxbridge entry at Oundle School near Peterborough, where 33/75 (44%) of the Upper Sixth were offered places at Oxford and Cambridge this year. Tim was himself educated at a day school in Essex and read Classics at St John's Cambridge from 1999 to 2002. I wanted him to tell me what was involved in studying at Oxbridge and how to overcome the ultimate application hurdle.

I had my own thoughts, some of which I delivered to Tim fairly provocatively: 'It seems to me that if you sit for Oxbridge you are sitting for a completely different experience than is on offer at any other university. They will expect you to rise to the challenge of one-to-one with dons who are working at the coal face of their subject, writing books about it. One can imagine that few of these suffer fools gladly, which is presumably why one hears about horrendous interview experiences where the don humiliates the applicant.

'Then, once you're there, there's no time to do anything but work. The terms are shorter and the work load is far greater than at any other university. If you are reading English you are going to have to read umpteen books and write a 3,000 word essay every week at a level that will engage one of the finest brains in Britain. Question, does this make for one-dimensional graduates? Answer, it makes for academically-minded graduates. If there is a limitation we should be clear to our readers what it is.

'The other thing that makes me wary is that Oxbridge graduates never tire of telling you where they studied. Old school tie, jobs galore. There is absolutely no doubt about the nepotism. Oxbridge graduates are the choice of Oxbridge graduate employers in virtually any sphere you care to mention — from publishing to politics, from theatre to media, from industry to the civil service. Yet, even so, I know that it is not true that overall Oxford and Cambridge have the best graduate job figures.

'The picture one gets from the statistics is that Oxbridge graduates are less prepared for the world of work than many from other universities, and that they make up for it with a certain overweening confidence derived from the myth. One suspects that is because there is simply no possibility of developing in the way that other undergraduates may. Both Oxford and Cambridge unions, who look after the extra-curricular development of their students, had very low ratings in the recent *Times Higher* Student Experience Survey...'

Tim was already back in the lap of his *alma mater*, and later put down his thoughts in the following piece:

Punting downriver, sipping champagne and discussing Wittgenstein, before waltzing into a top city job... Oxbridge exerts a powerful pull on the imagination, but the reality needs to be considered carefully before applying.

There is no doubting the advantages that the two universities offer. The surroundings are stunning: people travel across the world simply to visit a place that you could be calling home. Their degrees are also hugely respected by employers, and will open any number of doors after you leave. Perhaps most importantly, both are home to some of the finest minds in the world, who will push you to your limits, and will help you to discover enormous amounts about the subject that interests you most. That said the hugely competitive and academically-pressured nature of the universities will not suit everyone, and some may find the whole experience all too one-dimensional.

WHY DOES EVERYONE TREAT OXBRIDGE' SO DIFFERENTLY?

It is partly their amazing history and reputation that accounts for why Oxford and Cambridge are treated slightly separately from other top universities, but there is more to it than that. Not only do the two universities contain some of the world leaders in their fields, they also expect these top minds to teach undergraduates in very small groups (often one-on-one). For this reason they take a different approach to admissions from most other universities. First, they have a commitment to interview a huge proportion of applicants in all subjects, in order to discover who they want to spend the next three or four years working with. Second, there is the college system. The colleges are separate, self-contained institutions, and it is to one of these, rather than the universities themselves, that you will apply. The colleges usually have somewhere for undergraduates to live and eat, as well as their own bar, chapel and library. Often, particularly in arts subjects, much of the teaching is done here too, though lectures are given at a central faculty.

SHOULD I APPLY?

Before thinking about whether you have a chance of getting in you should think about whether it will suit you. The surroundings and quality of teaching are of course outstanding, and the teacher:student ratios are amazing. Often you will be taught in a group of one or two, meaning you get the close attention of one of the top minds in your field for at least an hour a week, and develop close relationships with the people who teach you. Although this can be intimidating at first, most people ultimately relish the opportunity. If you prefer to go about your work in quiet anonymity, however, you may wish to think carefully about whether it is for you.

OTHER COMMON CONCERNS

They are small, boring towns. There is an element of truth in this and, especially because of the small college-based nature of life, they can feel rather claustrophobic at times. There are a huge number of sports teams, societies etc. so there is always something to do, but if it is top clubbing you are after, look elsewhere.

They are full of posh public school boys. This is largely untrue. Admissions tutors just want the best people to teach, and choose the best people in the country (and indeed the world), with no prejudice whatsoever. There are a few of these kinds of characters around, and they tend to be rather high-profile, but you will find people from all sorts of backgrounds at all of the colleges.

I won't be clever enough. It is true that academic standards are high, and you will be asked to work very hard indeed. It can also be tough getting used to the fact that you are no longer the cleverest person around. Not everyone is a genius, however. They are just bright and enthusiastic people who are keen to learn.

The workload is huge. This is undoubtedly the case. In arts subjects in particular, the difference between what is expected at Oxbridge compared to other universities can be huge. Every week you will be expected to read a number of books and articles and produce at least one essay of between 2,000-3,000 words. This means that work has to be a priority for most of the time that you are there (which, incidentally, is only about half the year — there are two eight week terms, one four week term and exams for a few weeks). You are not allowed to get a job during term time, and taking on big extra-curricular commitments is very difficult indeed.

What do I do next? The incredibly focused nature of life at the two universities means that you do not really have as much time as you might like to plan your career. An Oxbridge degree may well be the best thing to put on a CV, but that is not to say that it offers the best preparation for the world of work.

WILL I GET IN?

The applicant:place ratio is relatively encouraging, particularly in some subjects, but the quality of candidates you are up against is generally very high indeed. There are no hard and fast rules about exactly how they will assess your application, but the following are important:

1. *A strong academic track record.* They will of course take your circumstances and education into account, but will nonetheless expect you to have performed very well, particularly in subjects relevant to the one you are applying for.

2. *Genuine enthusiasm for the subject.* This needs more than simply asserting how passionate you are about it — you need to prove it by reading around areas of interest, doing relevant work experience and so on. You can convey this both in your personal statement and at interview.

3. *Potential to develop further.* This is difficult to assess, but they want to know whether you will flourish when you are really pushed academically. This is the main reason for interviewing you.

HOW DO I CHOOSE A COLLEGE?

It can seem impossible choosing between colleges. There are a few factors that are important, but you should not get too worried about it — the significant minority of applicants who fail to get into the college of their choice end up perfectly happy. Some things you might like to weigh up include:

1. *Big or small* — do you like the idea of a small college, where you get to know everyone in your year, or somewhere bigger and more diverse?

2. *Location* — some of the colleges are in peaceful surroundings a little way out of town, others are very central and convenient for lectures, shops etc.

3. *Old or new* — while some of the older colleges are prettier from the outside, and more prestigious, their newer counterparts are often purpose-built and therefore more pleasant to live in.

4. *Your subject* — it is worth trying to find out how many teachers of your subject there are at the college (the answer is sometimes zero) and roughly how many undergraduates they take each year for it.

There are league tables published (known as the Tompkins Table at Cambridge, and the Norrington

Table at Oxford) of the undergraduate results, which may be of interest, but these reflect overall achievement – it could well be, for example, that everyone doing your subject got a First, but the average score at that college was low because of other results.

The number of applicants per subject at each college is also published in the prospectuses. Some candidates therefore apply to one where fewest people applied, in the hope that this will improve their chances. There is not really much point in this, since:

i.   The numbers vary hugely every year.
ii. The colleges communicate with each other, so that those with too many good candidates send them over to those with too few.

WHAT IS THE INTERVIEW LIKE?

Your personal statement, school/college reference, and public exam results will all be taken into account, and if these are of a good enough standard you will usually be called for interview. The two universities are beginning to take measures to cut down the proportion of candidates they interview, however. At Cambridge this can take the form of excluding you on the basis of your AS scores (if you apply to Cambridge you will have to declare your scores in a separate form, whether or not they have been mentioned in your reference).

Applicants to Oxford are often asked to sit a pre-test (usually at your school/college in October or November). Generally those who come in the bottom quarter are then told that they will not be interviewed. You can get information about pre-tests and practice papers from the university website, but largely speaking they are designed to be general tests of ability, that do not rely too heavily on specific knowledge or revision. You may wish to practise to ensure you understand how they work, and roughly how much time to spend on each question. As far as is possible, however, they are designed to be revision-proof: dons do not want to know who is the best-prepared candidate, but who is the best at understanding, assimilating and using new information, or getting immediately to the heart of an argument. Although they are looking for potential, they will want to see that you already have the ability to think and write clearly about difficult topics.

If you get over these hurdles you will then have an interview, usually in early December. There are a number of myths and anecdotes about Oxbridge interviews (dons standing on their heads, rugby balls thrown at you, etc.) but they are much more standardised and professional in reality. They are predictable in that they will usually ask you about your current A-level work, as well as interests mentioned in your personal statement. They will of course push you beyond what you are comfortable with, introducing concepts and ideas that are new to you and forcing you to justify every statement that you make. This can be an uncomfortable and very challenging experience, but also an exhilarating one: to discuss your favourite subject with some of the most knowledgeable and sharpest minds in the field should be something that excites you.

They will not expect you to understand everything, but they want to see how quickly you pick things up and how well you can apply them to what you already know. This will vary hugely from subject to subject (a new poem in English, a new topic in Maths, an unknown skull in Biology), but the principles do not vary: are you interested in, and capable of quickly picking up, ideas about the subject. You may well be asked to take some sort of written test in addition to just discussing things at interview – they will usually warn you about this in advance.

This may seem rather daunting, but the extra time that they put into choosing the right people for the course pays dividends: Oxbridge has comfortably the lowest drop-out rate of any university (just 1.2% against a national average of 9%).

There are lots of good reasons for applying to Oxbridge, and it is an amazing experience, but you need to go into it with your eyes open. Do not apply just because you have done well at school so far, and your teachers think you should, or your parents like the idea of it, often for their own reasons. The courses that Oxford and Cambridge offer are sometimes quite different from those at other universities, and the style of teaching and lifestyle are more intense than anywhere else. Equally, if you do think it will suit you, ignore silly prejudices and cliches and go for it. It is a unique opportunity to work closely with great minds, and push yourself to your academic limits. Anyone who really loves a subject will surely jump at that chance.

Tim Morrison, March 2009

ADMISSIONS TESTS, NEW DISCRIMINATORS

As Chris Conway, a seasoned careers teacher at Shrewsbury School, wrote in the last edition of the *Guide*: 'Clearly the Government view that the A Level system is the gold standard does not add up if the top end is not differentiating in the way the selective universities want it to and they are having to resort to tests of their own.'

The tests are with us. What are they? Who are they for?

UKCAT — UK Clinical Aptitude Test — is required by medical and dental schools at Aberdeen, Brighton & Sussex, Cardiff, Dundee, Durham, East Anglia (UEA), Edinburgh, Glasgow, Hull York, Imperial (graduates only), Keele, King's College London (KCL), Leeds, Leicester, Manchester, Newcastle, Nottingham, Oxford (graduates only), Peninsula (Plymouth & Exeter), Queen's, Sheffield, Southampton, St Andrews, St George's, Warwick (graduates only). See www.ukcat.ac.uk.

BMAT — the BioMedical Admissions Test — is required by the following medical and veterinary schools: Bristol Veterinary School, Cambridge, Oxford, Royal Veterinary College, UCL, and Imperial. See www.bmat.org.uk.

GAMSAT — the Graduate Medical School Admission Test — is required by St George's London, Nottingham, Peninsula School of Medicine & Dentistry, Keele, and Swansea. See www.gamsatuk.org.

MSAT — Medical School Admissions Test — is required by King's College London, Queen Mary, and Warwick. See msat@acer.edu.au.

LNAT — The National Admissions Test for Law — is required by Birmingham, Bristol, Cambridge, Durham, Exeter, Glasgow, King's College London, Nottingham, Oxford, and UCL. All candidates will sit the test at a computer terminal monitored at a test centre. See www.lnat.ac.uk/ and www.kaptest.co.uk for an online practice test.

HAT — History Aptitude Test — is required by Oxford. See www.history.ox.ac.uk/prosundergrad/applying/hat_introduction.htm.

MML — Modern and Mediaeval Languages Test — is required by Cambridge. See www.mml.cam.ac.uk/prospectus/undergrad/applying/test.html. Also, www.cam.ac.uk/admissions/undergraduate/courses/mml/tests.html.

STEP — Sixth Term Examination Papers — are required to read Mathematics at Cambridge. See www.maths.cam.

ELAT — Required by Oxford to read English.

HPAT — Required to read certain medical courses at Ulster.

TSA (Cambridge) — Thinking Skills Assessment required by most of Cambridge colleges. See tsa.ucles.org.uk/index. html.

TSA (Oxford) — Required by Oxford to read PPE or Economics & Management.

COURSES IN MEDICINE

Requirements at each of the medical schools are dealt with in the context of the universities with which the schools are associated. Recommended reading: *The Insider's Guide to UK Medical Schools* by Sally Girgis, and *The UK MedSchool Guide*, which can be downloaded from the Cardiff University website (www.cardiff.ac.uk).

SOURCES FOR STATISTICS

Information and figures used in the editorial boxes and drawn upon in the text entries of *The Virgin Guide* come from various sources: student populations and analyses from the university admission offices, the Higher Education Statistic Agency (HESA) and UCAS. Social demography and drop-out rates come from HESA, accommodation costs, etc. from the accommodation offices of the universities, research statistics from the Research Assessment Exercise (RAE) 2008 (see http://submissions.rae.ac.uk/results/) and *Times Higher Education*, teaching assessments from the Quality Assurance Agency (QAA) — see www.qaa.ac.uk — and from the universities.

Average points requirement for entry, overall student satisfaction rates, and the percentage of students into real graduate jobs at each university, emanate from the Higher Education Funding Council for England (HEFCE) — see www.unistats.com/.

Student views and ratings come of course from students themselves, but our ratings for helpful/interested staff, tuition in small groups, good social life and good student union are also informed by the ground-breaking national Student Experience Survey carried out by Opionpanel for the *Times Higher Education* magazine, which itself compiles the World's Top 200 Universities league table, remains the last word in insider knowledge in higher education in Britain, and has nothing to do with the *Times University Guide*!.

As ever at *The Virgin Guide* the most telling information is our students' views, but second to it is HESA's incredibly useful draw-down on the universities' own research into where everyone who gets a job after leaving university actually ends up.

I would like to thank all parties for their help and co-operation.

Applicants or students at university who would like to be interviewed for the next edition of *The Virgin Guide* — (payment is made) — should email me at janthony78@ymail.com.

Piers Dudgeon, April 2009

POINTS TARIFF FOR ENTRY

A full account of the UCAS points tarrif is given on the UCAS website. Last year, for the first time, UCAS pulled the International Baccalaureate into the tariff, and many felt that it gave it a very soft ride.

Basically, you have to study six subjects for the IB, three to a high level, three to a standard level. A pass earns you 4 marks. So, if you pass all six subjects you amass 24 marks, which UCAS have made equivalent to 280 points in the their tariff. As this is almost three B grades at A level, and many IB students expect to do much better than pass, you can begin to see why A-level diehards raised something of a stink.

A LEVEL POINTS TARIFF

A Level Grades	A level Points
A	120
B	100
C	80
D	60
E	40

AS Level Grades	AS Level Points
A	60
B	50
C	40
D	30
E	20

INTERNATIONAL BACCALAUREATE

IB Diploma Marks	IB Points
24	280
25	303
26	326
27	350
28	373
29	396
30	419
31	442
32	466
33	489
34	512
35	535
36	559
37	582
38	605
39	628
40	652
41	675
42	698
43	722
44	744
45	768

RECESSION BEATING UNIVERSITY LEAGUE TABLES

The following tables show the Higher Education Funding Council's Student Survey results for selected subjects. Three columns of figures ask: How many A level points on average were actually accepted? What percentage of graduates got real graduate jobs within six months of graduation? What was the level of student satisfaction?

Only universities were included which could show that 60% or more graduates (50% in the case of English, History, Philosophy, Politics, Psychology and Sport) obtained real graduate jobs within six months of graduation.

Abbreviations

Uni Arts = University of the Arts
UEA = University of East Anglia
UEL = University of East London
KCL = King's College London
UCL = University College London
LSE = London School of Economics
RAC = Royal Agricultural College
SOAS = School of Oriental & African Studies
UWIC = University of Wales Institute Cardiff
'ND' indicates 'No Data'.

Go to www.unistats.com and make your own choice.

	A Level Points Accepted	Real Graduate Jobs	Student Satisfaction
Accountancy			
Aberdeen	399	70%	88%
Anglia	210	65%	67%
Bath	420	92%	88%
Birmingham	390	80%	84%
Bournemouth	260	60%	95%
Bradford	250	60%	75%
Brighton	240	60%	ND
Cardiff	370	65%	91%
City	370	78%	95%
De Montfort	250	61%	87%
Dundee	428	70%	70%
UEA	325	85%	89%
Essex	280	60%	83%
Exeter	370	75%	100%
Glasgow	490	95%	94%
Glasgow Cal	277	70%	87%
Gloucester	240	67%	79%
Heriot-Watt	382	70%	91%
Hull	320	85%	76%
Kent	295	90%	95%
Kingston	240	60%	90%
Lancaster	410	65%	84%
Liverpool	370	80%	ND
Liverpool JM	240	65%	87%

	A Level Points Accepted	Real Graduate Jobs	Student Satisfaction
LSE	440	100%	82%
Manchester	400	75%	91%
Manchester Met	215	70%	80%
Newcastle	400	85%	92%
Northumbria	320	85%	100%
Nottingham Trent	220	86%	79%
Oxford Brooks	310	68%	89%
Queen's Belfast	400	85%	95%
Reading	345	90%	88%
Robert Gordon	330	100%	ND
Sheffield	350	82%	86%
Sheffield Hallam	260	75%	89%
Southampton	365	90%	89%
Staffordshire	260	70%	ND
Strathclyde	596	75%	98%
Ulster	330	77%	89%
Architecture			
Anglia	ND	95%	77%
Bath	480	100%	95%
Birmingham City	220	95%	80%
Brighton	300	96%	84%
Bristol UWE	260	85%	80%
Cardiff	480	95%	ND
De Montfort	260	100%	67%

	A Level Points Accepted	Real Graduate Jobs	Student Satisfaction
Dundee	474	98%	67%
Edinburgh Napier	290	98%	ND
UEL	ND	90%	80%
Edinburgh	472	95%	75%
Greenwich	240	95%	80%
Heriot-Watt	334	95%	67%
Huddersfield	250	85%	ND
Kingston	240	91%	58%
Leeds Met	280	70%	71%
Lincoln	280	90%	55%
Liverpool	400	95%	67%
Liverpool JM	290	95%	78%
London Met	ND	85%	ND
London South Bank	180	95%	54%
Manchester	380	94%	84%
Manchester Met	ND	99%	70%
Newcastle	450	99%	78%
Northumbria	290	100%	86%
Nottingham Trent	260	94%	80%
Oxford Brookes	380	95%	ND
Plymouth	330	85%	ND
Portsmouth	310	83%	88%
Queen's Belfast	360	95%	56%
Reading	330	95%	93%
Robert Gordon	324	95%	ND
Salford	280	90%	80%
Sheffield	460	98%	84%
Sheffield Hallam	300	100%	89%
Southampton Solent	180	70%	68%
Strathclyde	528	84%	80%
UCL	420	85%	88%
Ulster	320	100%	88%
Westminster	320	90%	76%

Biological & Related Sciences

	A Level Points Accepted	Real Graduate Jobs	Student Satisfaction
Aston	280	65%	89%
Bath	420	67%	92%
Bournemouth	260	77%	80%
Bristol	420	62%	96%
Brunel	295	75%	86%
Cambridge	540	75%	95%
Cardiff	370	60%	87%
Durham	470	63%	92%
UEA	350	60%	96%
UEL	180	63%	76%
Edinburgh	448	60%	92%
Edinburgh Napier	258	70%	ND
Exeter	330	60%	87%
Greenwich	200	61%	81%
Heriot-Watt	365	65%	89%
Imperial	430	70%	92%
Keele	280	65%	94%
Lancaster	340	65%	90%
Manchester Met	220	62%	88%
Middlesex	180	65%	72%
Newcastle	360	62%	91%
Northumbria	250	70%	77%
Oxford	480	62%	91%
Portsmouth	320	60%	94%
Royal Holloway	310	60%	88%
Sheffield	410	61%	96%
Sheffield Hallam	240	70%	94%
Staffordshire	240	64%	86%
St Andrews	400	60%	90%
Strathclyde	466	70%	74%
Surrey	300	75%	97%
Sussex	350	60%	95%
Ulster	280	70%	100%
Warwick	400	60%	95%
Wolverhampton	180	70%	63%

Business & Administrative Studies

	A Level Points Accepted	Real Graduate Jobs	Student Satisfaction
Aberdeen	399	70%	88%
Anglia	210	69%	66%
Uni Arts	520	64%	54%
Aston	380	77%	94%
Bangor	260	60%	86%
Bath	420	92%	88%
Birmingham	400	73%	91%
Bournemouth	280	76%	83%
Brighton	270	74%	83%
Bristol	410	95%	80%
Bristol UWE	240	68%	86%
Brunel	290	63%	72%
Cardiff	370	65%	88%
Central Lancs	270	72%	84%
Chester	260	75%	74%
City	370	80%	92%
Cumbria	220	70%	68%
Dundee	433	74%	69%
Durham	340	81%	85%
UEA	340	78%	88%
Edinburgh	482	70%	80%

	A Level Points Accepted	Real Graduate Jobs	Student Satisfaction		A Level Points Accepted	Real Graduate Jobs	Student Satisfaction
Edinburgh Napier	270	65%	ND	Birmingham City	180	65%	ND
Essex	300	62%	80%	Bournemouth	230	86%	83%
Exeter	380	80%	97%	Bradford	200	66%	55%
Glasgow	454	80%	90%	Brighton	230	77%	ND
Gloucestershire	240	70%	77%	Bristol	430	95%	75%
Heriot-Watt	328	70%	78%	Bristol UWE	220	85%	73%
Hertfordshire	240	75%	77%	Brunel	290	72%	72%
Hull	260	76%	94%	Cambridge	540	100%	82%
Kent	290	80%	92%	Cardiff	330	85%	ND
KCL	400	75%	77%	Central Lancs	240	79%	84%
Kingston	240	61%	88%	Chester	240	80%	83%
Lancaster	400	69%	91%	City	255	93%	79%
Leeds	400	74%	80%	Coventry	200	68%	ND
Leicester	310	75%	92%	De Montfort	180	67%	88%
Lincoln	230	72%	82%	Dundee	532	75%	87%
Liverpool	365	68%	83%	Durham	510	70%	90%
Liverpool Hope	200	60%	81%	UEA	300	85%	87%
Manchester	400	81%	82%	UEL	ND	90%	ND
Manchester Met	240	64%	73%	Edinburgh	440	90%	86%
Newcastle	380	86%	86%	Edinburgh Napier	247	73%	ND
Northumbria	300	82%	87%	Essex	290	80%	95%
Nottingham	400	80%	88%	Exeter	300	75%	75%
Nottingham Trent	260	79%	83%	Glasgow	411	85%	99%
Oxford Brookes	300	70%	83%	Gloucestershire	200	68%	76%
Plymouth	250	61%	88%	Glyndwr	ND	90%	ND
Portsmouth	260	62%	90%	Goldsmiths	190	65%	68%
Queen Mary's	320	75%	79%	Greenwich	160	66%	91%
Reading	340	60%	93%	Heriot-Watt	360	80%	90%
Robert Gordon	294	84%	ND	Hertfordshire	180	66%	80%
Holloway	340	80%	76%	Huddersfield	220	78%	67%
Sheffield	ND	75%	90%	Hull	240	92%	92%
Sheffield Hallam	260	71%	84%	Imperial	480	95%	96%
Southampton	370	83%	84%	Kent	280	91%	88%
Staffordshire	230	74%	90%	KCL	340	90%	70%
Stirling	311	70%	77%	Kingston	200	62%	81%
Strathclyde	534	70%	92%	Lancaster	340	80%	79%
Surrey	340	73%	82%	Leeds	360	86%	84%
Swansea	290	63%	82%	Leeds Met	200	64%	64%
Warwick	420	75%	90%	Lincoln	240	75%	75%
Worcester	ND	60%	89%	Liverpool	320	70%	80%
				Liverpool JM	200	81%	76%
				Loughborough	300	94%	91%

Computer Science

	A Level Points Accepted	Real Graduate Jobs	Student Satisfaction
Aberystwyth	250	70%	86%
Anglia	210	65%	66%
Aston	280	74%	81%
Bath	400	90%	84%
Birmingham	380	85%	86%

	A Level Points Accepted	Real Graduate Jobs	Student Satisfaction
Manchester	370	88%	74%
Manchester Met	220	68%	72%
Middlesex	160	80%	79%
Newcastle	320	90%	94%
Northumbria	260	81%	90%

	A Level Points Accepted	Real Graduate Jobs	Student Satisfaction		A Level Points Accepted	Real Graduate Jobs	Student Satisfaction
Nottingham	330	75%	83%	Central Lancs	260	68%	68%
Nottingham Trent	220	88%	70%	Cardiff	310	77%	63%
Oxford Brookes	230	75%	82%	Uni Creative Arts	ND	68%	70%
Plymouth	255	71%	84%	De Montfort	260	63%	70%
Portsmouth	240	70%	77%	UEA	370	60%	89%
Queen's Belfast	320	80%	80%	Edinburgh Napier	356	75%	ND
Queen Mary's	250	75%	63%	Glasgow School Art	385	60%	ND
Reading	320	90%	93%	Gloucestershire	280	60%	63%
Robert Gordon	249	85%	ND	Goldsmiths	370	75%	88%
Salford	210	66%	64%	Heriot-Watt	370	83%	82%
Sheffield	340	90%	ND	Hertfordshire	220	63%	48%
Sheffield Hallam	210	73%	66%	Kingston	280	73%	78%
Southampton	380	90%	94%	Leeds	380	64%	64%
Southampton Solent	180	70%	68%	Leeds Met	260	63%	77%
Staffordshire	230	80%	74%	Lincoln	260	67%	75%
Strathclyde	506	80%	94%	London South Bank	210	60%	70%
Surrey	340	90%	90%	Loughborough	370	69%	83%
Sussex	360	80%	82%	Manchester	420	60%	81%
Swansea	280	75%	82%	Newport	260	60%	63%
Swansea Met	190	70%	81%	Northumbria	290	77%	75%
Teesside	260	63%	76%	Nottingham Trent	300	75%	80%
Ulster	280	64%	80%	Reading	300	60%	73%
Warwick	440	91%	94%	Robert Gordon	284	65%	ND
Wolverhampton	160	71%	81%	Salford	200	61%	75%
York	440	90%	86%	Staffordshire	240	63%	81%
				UWIC	240	62%	82%

Dentistry

				Wolverhampton	200	61%	69%
Birmingham	430	100%	96%				
Bristol	445	100%	86%	**Economics**			
Cardiff	420	100%	83%	Aberdeen	399	65%	96%
Dundee	598	100%	93%	Anglia	240	76%	78%
Glasgow	527	100%	94%	Bath	440	86%	82%
KCL	450	100%	80%	Birmingham	400	75%	92%
Leeds	450	ND	100%	Bradford	240	72%	76%
Liverpool	420	100%	85%	Bristol	460	85%	77%
Manchester	470	100%	72%	Bristol UWE	260	80%	87%
Newcastle	470	100%	98%	Brunel	300	62%	78%
Queen's Belfast	455	100%	96%	Cambridge	540	90%	ND
Queen Mary's	400	97%	75%	Cardiff	400	65%	81%
Sheffield	445	100%	98%	Central Lancs	240	65%	80%
				Durham	460	94%	88%

Design Studies

				Edinburgh	480	90%	77%
Uni Arts	420	72%	59%	Essex	330	70%	84%
Bath Spa	260	60%	71%	Exeter	390	80%	95%
Bournemouth	270	89%	64%	Glasgow	466	80%	88%
Brighton	300	63%	88%	Kent	260	70%	93%
Brunel	340	82%	89%	Lancaster	400	65%	87%

	A Level Points Accepted	Real Graduate Jobs	Student Satisfaction
Leeds	420	75%	84%
Leicester	320	74%	96%
Liverpool	380	75%	ND
LSE	480	100%	77%
Loughborough	360	80%	84%
Manchester	390	78%	78%
Middlesex	180	62%	81%
Newcastle	390	85%	87%
Nottingham Trent	220	65%	97%
Oxford	510	80%	96%
Oxford Brookes	290	72%	86%
Portsmouth	240	65%	91%
Queen's Belfast	340	65%	86%
Queen Mary's	340	70%	75%
Reading	310	60%	74%
Royal Holloway	350	85%	81%
Salford	250	69%	79%
Sheffield	360	66%	95%
Southampton	390	75%	79%
Staffordshire	240	82%	80%
St Andrews	ND	90%	92%
Stirling	312	55%	92%
Surrey	270	65%	91%
Swansea	270	75%	92%
Ulster	260	71%	76%
Warwick	480	91%	87%
UCL	470	88%	80%
Manchester	400	85%	80%
Newcastle	340	95%	95%
Queen's Belfast	360	95%	83%
Sheffield	400	95%	94%
Strathclyde	540	90%	89%
Surrey	290	95%	94%
Swansea	300	95%	78%

Engineering (Aerospace)

	A Level Points Accepted	Real Graduate Jobs	Student Satisfaction
Bath	460	85%	95%
Bristol	440	100%	97%
Glasgow	432	70%	67%
Hertfordshire	250	70%	86%
Imperial	480	80%	69%
Kingston	200	75%	80%
Leeds	360	70%	72%
Loughborough	400	100%	87%
Manchester	420	80%	71%
Salford	220	60%	72%
Southampton	455	75%	100%

Engineering (Chemical)

	A Level Points Accepted	Real Graduate Jobs	Student Satisfaction
Dundee	500	100%	94%
Edinburgh	480	95%	90%
Glasgow	416	85%	60%
Heriot-Watt	424	93%	84%
Imperial	470	85%	94%

Engineering (Civil)

	A Level Points Accepted	Real Graduate Jobs	Student Satisfaction
Bath	440	95%	94%
Birmingham	350	90%	84%
Bristol	440	100%	90%
Cardiff	400	95%	93%
Dundee	500	100%	94%
Edinburgh	474	95%	90%
Glasgow	416	85%	60%
Heriot-Watt	424	95%	81%
Imperial	460	100%	ND
Kingston	195	85%	90%
Leeds	340	95%	88%
Loughborough	350	95%	95%
Manchester	400	100%	95%
Newcastle	340	95%	95%
Northumbria	260	95%	82%
Nottingham	400	91%	93%
Plymouth	270	85%	90%
Queen's Belfast	360	100%	85%
Sheffield	420	100%	100%
Southampton	460	95%	78%
Strathclyde	514	95%	71%
Surrey	310	95%	92%
Swansea	300	95%	78%
UCL	390	85%	86%

Engineering (Electronic and Electrical)

	A Level Points Accepted	Real Graduate Jobs	Student Satisfaction
Birmingham	ND	95%	90%
Birmingham City	220	73%	58%
Bristol	420	95%	85%
Brunel	ND	75%	87%
Cardiff	340	90%	79%
Derby	245	60%	78%
Edinburgh	480	95%	91%
Loughborough	325	95%	92%
Manchester	370	85%	83%
Northumbria	260	77%	81%

	A Level Points Accepted	Real Graduate Jobs	Student Satisfaction
Portsmouth	220	85%	93%
Queen's Belfast	350	85%	85%
Reading	300	85%	80%
Robert Gordon	303	95%	ND
Sheffield Hallam	180	75%	66%
Southampton	390	95%	94%
Strathclyde	512	90%	85%
Teesside	240	65%	86%
Warwick	380	90%	72%
York	360	80%	93%

Engineering (General)

Cambridge	540	93%	92%
Coventry	160	75%	ND
Durham	470	96%	90%
Edinburgh Napier	272	79%	ND
Glasgow Cal	321	65%	84%
Oxford	520	90%	89%
Ulster	240	85%	73%
Warwick	420	94%	73%

Engineering (Mechanical)

Aberdeen	364	85%	ND
Birmingham City	200	70%	ND
Bristol	460	97%	91%
Bristol UWE	230	70%	63%
Brunel	260	95%	69%
Cardiff	370	95%	88%
Central Lancs	ND	65%	88%
Coventry	210	71%	76%
Edinburgh	448	95%	63%
Edinburgh Napier	272	79%	ND
Glamorgan	200	65%	ND
Glasgow Cal	300	70%	ND
Heriot-Watt	419	90%	71%
Hertfordshire	250	71%	79%
Huddersfield	210	80%	ND
Leeds	340	77%	80%
Liverpool	320	70%	80%
Liverpool JM	220	65%	58%
Loughborough	360	93%	92%
Manchester	380	81%	57%
Manchester Met	220	80%	ND
Newcastle	320	95%	86%
Queen's Belfast	340	83%	82%
Queen Mary's	260	65%	85%
Salford	215	60%	74%

	A Level Points Accepted	Real Graduate Jobs	Student Satisfaction
Sheffield	380	95%	93%
Sheffield Hallam	200	80%	85%
Southampton	430	88%	96%
Strathclyde	528	84%	80%
Surrey	270	95%	90%

Engineering (Production & Manufacturing)

Aston	290	75%	66%
Bath	460	90%	92%
Birmingham	380	80%	69%
Bristol	471	95%	95%
Brunel	305	95%	69%
Cardiff	360	95%	90%
Coventry	240	67%	72%
Edinburgh	444	95%	63%
Glasgow	422	70%	77%
Harper Adams	300	95%	84%
Heriot-Watt	419	90%	71%
Hertfordshire	250	73%	81%
Huddersfield	220	80%	ND
Imperial	480	90%	ND
Leeds	340	79%	83%
Liverpool JM	220	70%	60%
London South Bank	ND	60%	38%
Loughborough	370	92%	93%
Manchester	420	80%	46%
Manchester Met	220	80%	ND
Newcastle	340	95%	86%
Nottingham	360	72%	92%
Portsmouth	220	76%	84%
Queen's Belfast	350	87%	78%
Sheffield	380	95%	94%
Sheffield Hallam	180	80%	88%
Southampton	420	100%	94%
Strathclyde	536	88%	78%
Swansea Met	190	75%	ND
Ulster	220	85%	73%

English

Aston	330	75%	87%
Bath Spa	300	50%	85%
Birmingham	410	57%	81%
Bristol	480	70%	91%
Cambridge	480	75%	ND
Cardiff	410	52%	93%

	A Level Points Accepted	Real Graduate Jobs	Student Satisfaction		A Level Points Accepted	Real Graduate Jobs	Student Satisfaction
Central Lancs	250	60%	83%	Durham (HS)	440	65%	86%
De Montfort	260	55%	95%	Durham (PG)	460	60%	95%
Durham	480	62%	94%	UEA (GS)	390	60%	92%
UEA	380	52%	90%	Edinburgh (HS)	471	65%	71%
Edinburgh	450	53%	93%	Hertfordshire (GS)	260	60%	85%
Essex	300	60%	93%	Hertfordshire (PG)	260	60%	84%
Exeter	420	56%	96%	Hull (PG)	280	60%	87%
Goldsmiths	350	50%	85%	KCL (GS)	350	70%	90%
Hertfordshire	250	50%	73%	KCL (HS)	360	65%	92%
Heriot-Watt	400	75%	97%	Kingston (GS)	220	65%	76%
Hull	320	55%	90%	Kingston (PG)	230	65%	77%
Kent	330	62%	95%	Leeds (HS)	380	65%	98%
KCL	420	75%	83%	Leeds (PG)	360	65%	88%
Kingston	240	50%	96%	Leicester (GS)	310	65%	94%
Leeds	440	56%	92%	Leicester (HS)	315	70%	95%
Leeds Met	280	50%	87%	Loughborough (GS)	360	64%	87%
Leicester	370	51%	91%	Loughborough (PG)	360	67%	86%
Loughborough	360	50%	96%	Manchester (PG)	380	62%	82%
Manchester	420	56%	76%	Newcastle (HS)	370	70%	85%
Newcastle	420	54%	79%	Newcastle (PG)	350	75%	92%
Nottingham	440	52%	79%	Nottingham (PG)	400	60%	90%
Nottingham Trent	260	51%	90%	Reading (PG)	340	65%	93%
Oxford	480	61%	95%	Sheffield (HS)	400	65%	86%
Oxford Brookes	270	55%	ND	Southampton (HS)	400	60%	95%
Queen Mary	360	59%	97%	Southampton (PG)	390	77%	94%
Royal Holloway	410	58%	87%	UCL (GS)	420	70%	92%
Sheffield	440	60%	93%	UCL (HS)	430	65%	90%
Southampton	380	53%	92%				
St Andrews	460	50%	94%				
Staffordshire	225	60%	83%	**History**			
Sussex	420	70%	78%	Birmingham	400	51%	87%
UCL	480	65%	98%	Bristol	440	71%	68%
Warwick	450	64%	91%	Cambridge	480	70%	97%
York	480	60%	86%	Central Lancs	260	57%	91%
				Durham	480	69%	95%
				Edinburgh	436	66%	84%
Geography				Kent	320	53%	94%
HS = Human & Social				KCL	460	65%	92%
GS = Geographical Studies				Leeds	400	56%	91%
PG = Physical Geography & Environmental				Leicester	360	51%	95%
Science				Lincoln	280	50%	85%
Birmingham (HS)	370	60%	100%	LSE	480	95%	77%
Bristol (GS)	440	85%	83%	Manchester	420	51%	75%
Bristol (PG)	440	75%	87%	Newcastle	400	59%	86%
Cambridge (HS)	500	80%	90%	Northumbria	300	50%	82%
Cardiff (GS)	310	65%	93%	Nottingham	420	53%	83%
Cardiff (PG)	310	65%	96%	Nottingham Trent	280	55%	91%
Central Lancs (GS)	ND	65%	93%	Oxford	480	69%	ND

	A Level Points Accepted	Real Graduate Jobs	Student Satisfaction		A Level Points Accepted	Real Graduate Jobs	Student Satisfaction
Oxford Brookes	340	55%	ND	UEA	400	70%	92%
Queen Mary's	360	60%	91%	Edinburgh	504	70%	80%
Royal Holloway	380	51%	93%	Glasgow	518	75%	82%
Lampeter	240	50%	88%	Greenwich	240	60%	86%
Sheffield	440	61%	95%	Hull	330	65%	91%
St Andrews	440	65%	98%	Keele	320	70%	90%
Sussex	380	60%	83%	Kent	360	67%	90%
UCL	430	57%	93%	KCL	440	62%	95%
Warwick	440	61%	91%	Leeds	460	60%	82%
				Leicester	400	73%	91%
Languages				Lincoln	240	60%	87%
Aston	350	80%	88%	Northumbria	360	89%	ND
Bath	410	76%	95%	Nottingham	480	60%	89%
Birmingham	370	65%	91%	Nottingham Trent	300	62%	87%
Bristol	420	74%	82%	Oxford Brookes	340	65%	88%
Cambridge	510	78%	93%	Queen's Belfast	410	74%	77%
Durham	440	75%	98%	Sheffield	410	65%	83%
Edinburgh	460	75%	74%	Southampton	410	70%	90%
Essex	300	62%	90%	Southampton Solent	160	65%	74%
Exeter	410	60%	89%	Staffordshire	260	65%	87%
Heriot-Watt	400	75%	97%	Strathclyde	588	60%	87%
Hull	300	65%	93%	Sussex	390	75%	93%
KCL	410	68%	83%				
Lancaster	360	80%	89%	**Management**			
Leeds	390	68%	92%	Aberdeen	362	65%	85%
UCL	420	67%	85%	Anglia	210	65%	67%
Manchester	420	65%	76%	Uni Arts	660	60%	63%
Newcastle	420	75%	84%	Bath Spa	220	60%	97%
Nottingham	390	65%	89%	Bournemouth	240	79%	78%
Nottingham Trent	240	60%	91%	Central Lancs	200	60%	79%
Oxford	480	73%	95%	City	ND	85%	93%
Queen Mary's	350	60%	96%	UEA	340	75%	88%
SOAS	340	75%	72%	Exeter	370	80%	97%
Sheffield	390	76%	91%	Gloucestershire	240	69%	82%
Southampton	420	65%	94%	Greenwich	170	70%	85%
Staffordshire	225	60%	84%	Hertfordshire	240	75%	77%
St Andrews	474	80%	90%	Hull	240	65%	92%
Sussex	400	75%	89%	Keele	290	75%	81%
Warwick	450	60%	95%	Kent	290	79%	92%
				KCL	400	75%	77%
Law				Leeds	400	74%	82%
Aberdeen	487	60%	98%	Lincoln	260	75%	80%
Birmingham	420	60%	92%	LSE	440	95%	77%
Bristol	450	70%	94%	Loughborough	300	80%	95%
Brunel	340	60%	79%	Manchester	400	73%	85%
De Montfort	240	60%	90%	Newcastle	380	86%	ND
Durham	480	70%	82%	Nottingham	400	80%	89%

	A Level Points Accepted	Real Graduate Jobs	Student Satisfaction
Oxford Brookes	310	68%	90%
Queen's Belfast	330	65%	ND
Reading	370	90%	89%
RAC	300	81%	76%
Salford	180	60%	ND
Southampton	370	80%	81%
Southampton Solent	ND	65%	81%
Stirling	300	75%	87%
Strathclyde	440	60%	87%
Surrey	340	72%	81%
Warwick	460	90%	85%

Marketing

	A Level Points Accepted	Real Graduate Jobs	Student Satisfaction
Uni Arts	380	65%	42%
Bedfordshire	ND	70%	86%
Bournemouth	320	70%	90%
Bristol UWE	250	75%	75%
Brighton	250	85%	ND
Central Lancs	240	85%	77%
De Montfort	250	65%	88%
Gloucestershire	240	75%	74%
Greenwich	180	60%	74%
Hull	280	71%	92%
Lancaster	380	87%	86%
Lincoln	260	68%	92%
Manchester Met	250	71%	72%
Newcastle	350	90%	ND
Northumbria	290	82%	85%
Oxford Brookes	300	70%	83%
Portsmouth	270	70%	85%
Southampton Solent	210	67%	83%
Swansea	290	63%	81%

Maths

	A Level Points Accepted	Real Graduate Jobs	Student Satisfaction
Bath	480	85%	89%
Birmingham	420	64%	93%
Bristol	480	79%	83%
Brunel	280	60%	75%
Cambridge	540	75%	93%
Cardiff	400	75%	91%
City	290	65%	87%
Durham	540	75%	81%
UEA	420	60%	98%
Edinburgh	460	75%	79%
Exeter	370	70%	87%
Glasgow	450	70%	96%
Imperial	480	74%	82%

	A Level Points Accepted	Real Graduate Jobs	Student Satisfaction
KCL	420	75%	83%
Leeds	410	67%	82%
LSE	495	95%	79%
Loughborough	360	75%	96%
Newcastle	390	75%	92%
Nottingham	440	68%	86%
Oxford	540	77%	92%
Queen's Belfast	360	60%	80%
Royal Holloway	370	70%	89%
Sheffield	400	80%	93%
Sheffield Hallam	230	80%	89%
Southampton	420	85%	84%
Strathclyde	556	60%	90%
UCL	480	70%	92%
Warwick	520	83%	88%
York	440	62%	85%

Medicine

Brighton Sussex, Hull York, Keele, and St Andrews medical schools provided insufficient data re: graduate employment and were not included.

	A Level Points Accepted	Real Graduate Jobs	Student Satisfaction
Aberdeen	554	100%	100%
Birmingham	480	100%	75%
Bristol	460	100%	79%
Cambridge	540	98%	ND
Cardiff	460	100%	66%
Dundee	606	100%	96%
UEA	440	99%	94%
Edinburgh	540	100%	93%
Exeter	390	100%	89%
Glasgow	520	100%	83%
Imperial	480	100%	88%
KCL	460	100%	81%
Leeds	460	100%	94%
Leicester	465	100%	84%
Liverpool	460	100%	75%
UCL	480	100%	92%
Manchester	460	100%	77%
Newcastle	480	100%	91%
Nottingham	480	99%	82%
Oxford	530	100%	94%
Plymouth	415	100%	82%
Queen's Belfast	420	100%	90%
Queen Mary's	400	98%	73%
Sheffield	470	100%	83%

	A Level Points Accepted	Real Graduate Jobs	Student Satisfaction
Southampton	420	99%	93%
St George's	440	100%	90%
UCL	480	100%	92%

Philosophy

	A Level Points Accepted	Real Graduate Jobs	Student Satisfaction
Birmingham	370	50%	76%
Bristol	460	65%	90%
Central Lancs	270	60%	91%
Durham	460	65%	90%
Edinburgh	440	60%	76%
Glasgow	440	50%	91%
Hull	290	55%	91%
Kent	300	50%	87%
KCL	390	55%	81%
LSE	420	95%	ND
Manchester	410	60%	87%
Newcastle	380	59%	88%
Nottingham	390	60%	88%
Oxford	520	75%	96%
Oxford Brookes	330	55%	ND
Queen's Belfast	340	55%	88%
Sheffield	430	60%	96%
Warwick	450	55%	89%
York	450	50%	90%

Physical Science

	A Level Points Accepted	Real Graduate Jobs	Student Satisfaction
Bath (Chem.)	370	70%	89%
Bath (Phys.)	420	75%	84%
Birmingham (Phys.)	420	65%	95%
Aberdeen	342	80%	95%
Uni Arts	330	70%	ND
Bradford	220	70%	78%
Bristol (Chem.)	390	75%	96%
Bristol (Phys.)	430	65%	85%
Central Lancs	290	63%	91%
Durham (Chem.)	480	75%	94%
Durham (Phys.)	500	75%	95%
Edinburgh (Chem)	460	70%	88%
Edinburgh (Phys.)	480	70%	82%
Exeter (Chem.)	350	65%	89%
Exeter (Phys.)	360	70%	92%
Glamorgan	220	65%	82%
Huddersfield (Chem.)	225	60%	84%
Imperial (Phys.)	500	75%	86%
Leeds (Chem.)	350	75%	85%
Leeds (Materials/Minerals)	ND	60%	76%

	A Level Points Accepted	Real Graduate Jobs	Student Satisfaction
Liverpool JM	200	60%	75%
Manchester (Chem.)	400	70%	85%
Manchester (Phys.)	440	69%	95%
Manchester (Materials/Minerals)	390	70%	75%
Manchester Met (Materials/Minerals)	260	73%	63%
Northumbria (Chem.)	260	75%	92%
Nottingham (Chem.)	350	75%	98%
Nottingham (Phys.)	440	62%	83%
Oxford (Chem.)	530	85%	90%
Oxford (Phys.)	540	69%	85%
Plymouth	240	64%	87%
Reading (Phys.)	310	60%	ND
Royal Holloway (Phys.)	330	75%	98%
Sheffield (Chem.)	380	75%	95%
Strathclyde (Chem.)	509	65%	ND
Strathclyde (Phys.)	490	65%	93%
Warwick (Chem.)	420	80%	89%
Warwick (Phys.)	480	70%	95%
York (Chem.)	410	80%	97%
York (Phys.)	400	60%	92%

Politics

	A Level Points Accepted	Real Graduate Jobs	Student Satisfaction
Aberdeen	371	50%	94%
Bath	410	70%	90%
Birmingham	390	63%	89%
Bristol	420	75%	62%
Brunel	300	60%	77%
Cardiff	380	55%	93%
De Montfort	210	50%	92%
Durham	460	70%	77%
Edinburgh	460	65%	83%
Essex	340	60%	90%
Exeter	400	60%	92%
Hull	320	70%	90%
Keele	310	55%	94%
Kent	280	59%	87%
Leeds	380	59%	82%
Leicester	320	60%	99%
Liverpool	350	60%	84%
London Met	ND	55%	85%
Loughborough	300	55%	94%
LSE	480	95%	77%
Manchester	420	61%	73%
Newcastle	380	70%	88%

	A Level Points Accepted	Real Graduate Jobs	Student Satisfaction
Northumbria	270	50%	87%
Nottingham	400	63%	81%
Nottingham Trent	ND	60%	90%
Oxford	510	85%	92%
Portsmouth	270	60%	99%
Reading	335	60%	91%
Sheffield	440	67%	94%
Southampton	360	65%	85%
St Andrews	530	85%	97%
Sussex	380	65%	91%
Warwick	460	60%	90%
York	440	55%	85%

Psychology

	A Level Points Accepted	Real Graduate Jobs	Student Satisfaction
Aston	360	63%	91%
Bath	460	55%	75%
Bedfordshire	ND	50%	77%
Bristol	420	65%	88%
Brunel	320	53%	88%
Cardiff	420	51%	80%
Central Lancs	290	58%	84%
City	330	65%	63%
Durham	410	63%	91%
East Anglia	360	55%	96%
East London	ND	63%	77%
Edinburgh	480	52%	82%
Edinburgh Napier	274	51%	ND
Essex	330	55%	88%
Glasgow	430	55%	94%
Greenwich	220	60%	74%
Heriot-Watt	360	55%	88%
Hull	320	64%	92%
Keele	320	50%	86%
Kent	340	71%	84%
Leeds	430	54%	88%
Leeds Met	300	50%	71%
Leicester	370	66%	92%
Lincoln	300	55%	92%
Loughborough	400	57%	91%
Newcastle	410	60%	78%
Northumbria	320	57%	95%
Oxford Brookes	340	50%	88%
Royal Holloway	380	65%	95%
Sheffield	420	59%	88%
Staffordshire	260	68%	86%
Surrey	370	60%	61%
Sussex	390	66%	85%

	A Level Points Accepted	Real Graduate Jobs	Student Satisfaction
Teesside	260	55%	89%
Warwick	420	55%	80%
York	470	60%	85%

Social Work

	A Level Points Accepted	Real Graduate Jobs	Student Satisfaction
Anglia	220	85%	71%
Bath	410	78%	85%
Bedfordshire	200	87%	79%
Birmingham City	220	95%	35%
Birmingham	340	85%	64%
Bournemouth	ND	95%	78%
Bradford	ND	95%	62%
Bristol	420	77%	77%
Bristol UWE	ND	100%	72%
Brunel	ND	85%	32%
Bucks New	160	70%	74%
Central Lancs	210	95%	74%
Chester	ND	100%	83%
Chichester	295	65%	82%
Coventry	ND	85%	77%
De Montfort	185	98%	67%
Durham	420	76%	86%
UEL	ND	61%	76%
Edinburgh	460	71%	77%
Essex	330	67%	88%
Gloucestershire	230	85%	76%
Goldsmiths	ND	95%	85%
Hertfordshire	ND	99%	61%
Huddersfield	220	78%	80%
Hull	220	95%	77%
Leeds Met	180	60%	74%
Lincoln	220	95%	80%
Liverpool JM	220	62%	79%
London South Bank	160	75%	81%
Manchester	400	61%	74%
Manchester Met	ND	95%	79%
Newport	160	60%	91%
Northumbria	ND	100%	66%
Nottingham Trent	ND	95%	71%
Portsmouth	220	90%	73%
Queen's Belfast	ND	94%	85%
Reading	ND	95%	83%
Robert Gordon	298	95%	ND
Royal Holloway	340	72%	72%
Salford	260	84%	67%
Sheffield	390	66%	90%
Sheffield Hallam	220	78%	65%

	A Level Points Accepted	Real Graduate Jobs	Student Satisfaction		A Level Points Accepted	Real Graduate Jobs	Student Satisfaction
Southampton	380	65%	83%	Greenwich	190	60%	83%
Staffordshire	ND	95%	76%	Heriot-Watt	360	55%	88%
Sunderland	200	63%	80%	Hertfordshire	270	52%	73%
Sussex	ND	95%	94%	Hull	260	69%	85%
Teesside	ND	100%	90%	Leeds	350	50%	85%
Ulster	300	90%	65%	Leeds Met	280	55%	70%
UWIC	ND	97%	87%	Lincoln	270	55%	92%
Wolverhampton	220	89%	65%	Liverpool Hope	200	50%	73%
York	420	52%	83%	Loughborough	410	52%	92%
				Middlesex	180	65%	72%
Sports Science				Northumbria	280	58%	85%
Abertay Dundee	358	60%	ND	Nottingham Trent	270	59%	92%
Bath	400	70%	88%	Oxford Brookes	280	51%	84%
Birmingham	380	52%	91%	Portsmouth	260	57%	90%
Bournemouth	270	83%	81%	Staffordshire	220	60%	90%
Brunel	300	54%	81%	Strathclyde	470	54%	83%
Central Lancs	260	55%	100%	Swansea	260	65%	95%
Chichester	210	54%	95%	Teesside	250	57%	82%
UEL	180	63%	76%	Ulster	340	60%	95%
Edinburgh	446	55%	89%	Wolverhampton	180	60%	82%
Essex	300	65%	93%	Worcester	240	54%	89%
Exeter	350	55%	95%				

UNIVERSITY OF ABERDEEN

The University of Aberdeen
Regent Walk
Aberdeen AB24 3FX

TEL   01224 273504
FAX   01224 272034
EMAIL sras@abdn.ac.uk
WEB www.abdn.ac.uk

Aberdeen University Students' Association
The Hub
Old Aberdeen AB24 3TU

TEL 01224 272965
FAX 01224 272977
EMAIL ausa@aberdeen.ac.uk
WEB www.ausa.org.uk

VAG VIEW

*A*berdeen is the oldest university outside Oxbridge, its Chair of Medicine was the first established in the English-speaking world, and King's College Aberdeen was founded in 1495. It is also one of only twenty-nine British universities in the World Top 200.

As one of four ancient universities in Scotland, the teaching is traditional, seminars, tutorials, etc, and some of the lecture rooms full of traditional character (and draughts). They are adamant that the industrialisation of higher education will not deter their principal aims: 'When we debate higher education, we tend to talk about student employability and how institutions contribute to the economy,' says Principal C Duncan Rice. 'But there is not so much talk about traditional liberal learning and about the role the humanities and social sciences play in society.'

What this means is masses of interested, helpful teaching staff with strong, often world-wide, reputations in their subjects, and small tutorial groups, plenty of one-to-one dialogue, delivering the enlightened idea that study at this level

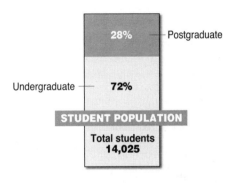

STUDENT POPULATION

Undergraduate — **72%**

28% — Postgraduate

Total students 14,025

might just be about something other than getting a job.

Not everyone is up to this. There's a high student satisfaction rate - 91% of them gave Aberdeen their vote in the latest survey, but also a high drop-out rate, of 10%.

FEES, BURSARIES

Non-Scottish UK student fees in year 2009-10: £1,820. If you are a Scottish-domiciled first degree student you are eligible for you tution fees to be covered by the Scottish Government. Aberdeen offers entrance scholarships worth £1,000 p.a., allocated on the basis of financial need or academic merit. Applicants must be resident in the UK, and have already applied to the university. See www.abdn.ac.uk/sras/undergraduate/ bursaries. shtml. There are a number of sports scholarships too, and awards made to talented musicians.

CAMPUS

Aberdeen is on the North East coast of Scotland, pretty much final step on the way to the Arctic (a couple of farms and the odd island notwithstanding). Easily reachable, if you've a bit of time on your hands, Aberdeen provides a safe haven for those trying to get as far away as possible from parents, and the rest of civilisation.

The Granite City, as it is accurately called, harbours a bit of a cosmopolitan atmosphere (there's some docks) and a very long beach. The

UNIVERSITY/STUDENT PROFILE	
University since	**1495**
Situation/style	**Civic**
Student population	**14025**
Total undergraduates	**10155**
Mature undergraduates	**17%**
International undergrads	**6%**
Male/female ratio	**45:55**
Equality of opportunity:	
state school intake	**82%**
social class 4-7 intake	**25%**
low-participation area intake	**2%**

climate is raw, as are the people, but when the sun shines, everything warms up and it's actually a beautiful city.

The city itself is framed around Union Street, with the main university campus about a mile (and a lung-busting hill) north of the main centre. This is King's College campus, the oldest part of the university, located in the imaginatively entitled Old Aberdeen.

There are other campuses: one in town which is not used anymore, except to keep dead bodies for first year medics to play about with, the hospital, where they keep the live bodies for the rest of the medics to play about with, the Hilton campus for Education, complete with its own halls of residence, and Foresterhill campus, where a new medical education and training centre is under construction. It will provide facilities for the teaching of anatomy and clinical skills to medics.

STUDENT PROFILE

There's a highish count of public school types (18%), but the successful completion of the Summer School for Access guarantees a place on most of the uni's degree courses. Writes Rob Littlejohn, 'The students come in eight distinct groups: Aberdonians, who talk smugly about pubs in other parts of town and watch quietly as we get lost; Country Teuchters (pronounced 'choochters' - there you know some local dialect already), very similar to Aberdonians,

> *A traditional uni without the stigma of being an Oxbridge wannabe like St Andrews or Edinburgh. Excellent reputation in subjects for the professions - Law, Medicine, etc.*

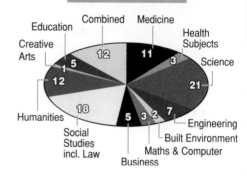

SUBJECT AREAS (%)

Education, Combined, Medicine, Health Subjects, Creative Arts 5, 12, 11, 3, Science, 12, 21, Humanities 18, 5 3 2 7, Engineering, Social Studies incl. Law, Built Environment, Maths & Computer, Business

but without the urban sophistication; Edinburgh Public Schoolers, a feature of most Scottish unis with better English accents than most of those south of the border and more money than sense; Other Scots - Scotland has a greater tradition of staying at home to study and we do get some Edinburghers keen to distance themselves from a public school education, Glaswegians pining for home, sectarianism and annoying accents, and Dundonians just happy to be somewhere else. There's also the Huge Bands of Others - Northern Irish, random English, foreign students and Greeks, the final lot warranting their own category for sheer number!'

ACADEMIA & JOBS

Eighty-nine per cent of Aberdeen's teaching was adjudged either Excellent or Highly Satisfactory in the assessments, and in the most recent examination in 2008 nearly 90% of research undertaken was recognised to be of international quality, with eleven subjects ranked amongst the top 25% in the UK: Health Services Research; Biological Sciences; Agriculture and Food Science; Pure Mathematics; General Engineering (including mining); Town and Country Planning; Anthropology; French; English Language and Literature; Theology, Divinity and Religious Studies; and History.

There are three 'Colleges': Arts and Social Sciences; Life Sciences & Medicine; and Physical Sciences, through which are taught more than 550 undergraduate degrees and 140+ masters degrees.

For the Medicine degree, AAB is required in 3

TEACHING SURVEY AT A GLANCE

Avg. UCAS points accepted	**392**
Acceptance rate	**18%**
Overall satisfaction rate	**91%**
Helpful/interested staff	★★★★★
Small tuition groups	★★★★
Students into graduate jobs	**76%**

Teaching most popular with undergraduates:
Medicine (100%), Law (98%), History, Archaeology (97-8%), Economics (96%), Geology (96%), Philosophy & Theology (96%), English (95%), Physical Science (95%), Languages (94-5%), Politics , Sociology (94%), Pharmacology (93%), Biology, Biological sciences (90-91%), Health, Zoology, Geography (91%).

Teaching least popular with undergraduates:
Architecture, Building, Planning (40-42%).

A levels, taken at the first sitting: Chemistry plus one of Maths, Biology or Physics. Most other subjects are acceptable for the third subject. The UK Clinical Aptitude Test (UKCAT) is also required.

Industrial placements combined with strong relationships with industry, major research centres and other leading international universities help ensure that courses are relevant to the requirements of the modern world and professional graduate jobs do certainly follow - 76% of graduates have them within six months of graduation. Mainly they become doctors or find themselves in social work, in the education sector (notably primary), in government administration, accountancy, banking, or in the retail sector or mining (especially gas and oil), and a lot go on to become lawyers, for Law is, along with Medicine, Divinity, and Engineering, one of the pillars of the Aberdeen establishment.

A new library is expected to open in 2011.

SOCIAL SCENE

September 2006 saw the completion of a renovation of catering and social facilities on campus. **The Hub** is now, they say, 'a one-stop shop for all your needs'.

The Students Association funds 100+ clubs and societies, counting sports ranging from football and karate to boxing and underwater hockey, and masses of cultural societies catering for the diversity of the international student body, plus a particularly busy University Music Programme - orchestra, choral society, chapel choir or concert band. The weekly student paper - free and run by students - is *Gaudie*.

Writes a Union wallah: 'The city boasts a huge variety of venues ranging from trendy clubs to old-world pubs full of atmosphere and everything in between. There is an eclectic mix of music for gig-goers, which regularly attracts major tour gigs by the biggest names around; and for committed clubbers there is a whole host of dance floors in and around the city centre, serving up sounds of hip hop, dance, chart classics, indie, rock, latin beats, soul, cheesy pop and lots more.

'For those who prefer a quiet drink and good conversation, there is a multitude of different settings, from hip wine bars and jazz clubs to cosy café bars and student hang-outs. And let's not forget our own Students' Union, the newest bar in town is everything a Union should be, a concoction of cheap drinks, ancient traditions, a cosy environment right in the city centre which offers all the standard things (pub quizzes, dj's, etc.). It's the Number One Venue for a night out.'

Yes, but it's off campus and they've taken away

	4*	3*
RESEARCH EXCELLENCE		
% of Aberdeen's research that is		
4* *(World-class)* or **3*** *(Internationally rated):*		
Hospital Based Clinical Med.	15%	60%
Epidemiology, Public Health	10%	50%
Health Services Research	25%	55%
Primary Care	25%	40%
Biological Sciences	15%	40%
Pre-clinical. Human Biological	5%	35%
Agriculture, Vet, Food Science	20%	35%
Earth Systems, Enviro. Sci.	10%	50%
Chemistry	5%	35%
Pure Mathematics	20%	45%
Computer Science	20%	50%
General Eng., Mineral, Mining	20%	35%
Town and Country Planning	20%	40%
Geography	10%	40%
Economics and Econometrics	20%	45%
Business and Management	10%	30%
Law	5%	30%
Politics	5%	20%
Sociology	15%	40%
Anthropology	30%	25%
Psychology	5%	45%
Education	5%	20%
Sports-Related Studies	5%	25%
French	20%	35%
German, Dutch, Scandinavian	0%	25%
Iberian and Latin American	10%	35%
Celtic Studies	0%	15%
English Language and Lit.	30%	35%
Philosophy	0%	25%
Theology	15%	65%
History	30%	30%
History of Art, Architec., Design	20%	35%
Music	5%	45%

all the student nightclubs and bars they used to have on campus! It happened all of a sudden, like a Palace coup, a few years back. The University moved in and that was that. Students were reduced to a bar in Education, and it's never been quite the same since. Very poor show.

SPORT The £28-million first phase of a new sports Village is due for completion this summer. Included in the complex will be a full size indoor football pitch, indoor running straight with throwing and jumping areas, large games hall, squash courts, large fitness suite and performance gym, exercise studios, sports science facilities and dining and conference areas. The current external running track and football/hockey pitch will be enhanced by a new stand with seating for 500. Plans for phases two and three include additional grass and artificial surfaces, and an Olympic-sized pool. The centre is base for the Sports Union's 54 affiliated clubs and Intra Mural sports programme.

WHAT IT'S REALLY LIKE

UNIVERSITY:

Social Life	★★★
Campus scene	**Small & friendly**
Student Union services	**Poor**
Politics	**Internal**
Sport	**54 clubs**
National team position	**28th**
Sport facilities	**Improving**
Arts opportunities	**Drama, music exc.; film good; dance, art poor**
Student newspaper	**The Gaudie**
Student radio	**Aberdeen Student Radio - NSR**
Bar	**Off-campus bar**
Union ents	**Guarded promise**
Union societies	**70+**
Most active society	**MedSoc**
Parking	**Some**

CITY:

Entertainment	★★★★
Scene	**Intoxicating**
Town/gown relations	**Good**
Risk of violence	**Low**
Cost of living	**Average**
Student concessions	**Average**
Survival + 2 nights out	**£60 pw**
Part-time work campus/town	**Good/excellent**

PILLOW TALK

Halls of Residence, on-campus or nearby, offer traditional single study bedrooms or self-catering flats. These and university-administered property in the city have trained wardens in residence.

GETTING THERE

☛ By road: from south, A92 and ring road where you'll pick up signs; from north, A96 or the A92.
☛ By rail: Edinburgh, 2:30; Dundee, 1:15; Newcastle, 4:50; London King's Cross, 7:00.
☛ By air: Aberdeen International Airport.
☛ By coach: London, 11.30; Birmingham, 12.35.

ACCOMMODATION

Guarantee to freshers	**100%**
Style	**Halls, flats**
Security guard	**All**
Shared rooms	**Some halls**
Internet access	**All**
Self-catered	**Most**
En suite	**Some**
Approx price range pw	**£72-£140**
City rent pw	**£65-£140**

UNIVERSITY OF ABERTAY DUNDEE

The University of Abertay Dundee
Bell Street
Dundee DD1 1HG

TEL 01382 308080
FAX 01382 308081
EMAIL sro@abertay.ac.uk
WEB www.abertay.ac.uk

Abertay Dundee Students' Association
1-3 Bell Street
Dundee DD1 1HG

TEL 01382 308950
FAX 01382 308326
EMAIL president@abertayunion.cac.uk
WEB www.abertaystudents.com/

VAG VIEW

*L*ocated on a modern campus in the centre *of Dundee, Abertay, formerly the Dundee Institute of Technology, resists the Higher Education Funding Council's interest in the opinion of its small, 4,000-strong body of students as to what goes on, boldly and possibly wisely electing not to be part of the National Student Survey.*

There is, in fact, a high local intake and sizeable mature and overseas student population, and a good and often idiosyncratic reputation for its courses in Computing, Business and Sport.

Its record for student employment is traditionally high, but a mere 51% have real graduate jobs six months after graduation,

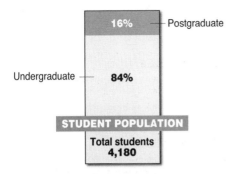

Postgraduate — 16%

Undergraduate — 84%

STUDENT POPULATION

Total students 4,180

which is very low. Nevertheless, students like it here. The drop-out rate is a tolerable 7-8%.

FEES, BURSARIES

Non-Scottish UK student fees in year 2009-10: £1,820. If you are a Scottish-domiciled first degree student you are eligible for you tution fees to be covered by the Scottish Government. There's a Sporting Excellence fund of £10,000, Centenary scholarships of £1,000 - students must submit an essay of 1,500 words, and a hardship fund, means tested. There's also a Mature Student bursary fund targeted at childcare, accommodation and travel costs. The Nine Incorporated Trades of Dundee fund seven scholarships for students in financial need. Meanwhile, the Robert Reid Trust has £1,000 for students from poor backgrounds.

STUDENT PROFILE

There's a 37% take from the lowest four socio-economic groups and 3% from 'low-participation neighbourhoods'. They get the largest access partnership grant from the Scottish Funding Council. Abertay has four academic schools: Computing, the Dundee Business School, Science & Engineering, and Social & Health Sciences.

ACADEMIA & JOBS

At the core of its provision is the International Centre for Computing and Virtual Entertainment (IC-CAVE). A defining mark of Abertay is that it was the first university to offer Computer Games Technology as a degree. An Abertay student, David Jones, created the legendary Lemmings and Grand Theft Auto. Among job areas consistently filled by Abertay students are software consultancy, games design, and the manufacture of computers, and a number of graduates go into related retail and telecommunications. Among the degrees, Ethical Hacking & Countermeasures is a world first, and Creative Sound Production, Mobile Entertainment, and Smart Systems are all new degrees this year.

In 2009 Abertay became the first accredited UK Centre for Excellence in Computer Games

UNIVERSITY/STUDENT PROFILE	
University since	**1994**
Situation/style	**Civic**
Student population	**4180**
Total undergraduates	**3500**
Mature undergraduates	**23%**
International undergrads	**18%**
Male/female ratio	**47:53**
Equality of opportunity:	
state school intake	**97%**
social class 4-7 intake	**37%**
low-participation area intake	**3%**

Education; this was supported by a government investment of £3 million. However, this area does not show up as significant in the recent world-wide research assessment exercise. More impressive, of significant world repute no less, was their faculty of Earth Systems & Environmental Technology.

As befits Scotland's top 'new' university for environmental research, the Centre for the Environment is a £4-million research and knowledge transfer centre, part-funded by the EU, designed to provide small and medium-sized

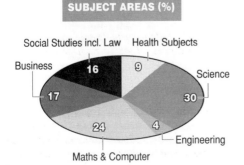

SUBJECT AREAS (%)

Social Studies incl. Law — Health Subjects

Business

16 — 9 — Science

17 — 30

24 — 4

Maths & Computer — Engineering

TEACHING SURVEY AT A GLANCE	
Avg. UCAS points accepted	**360**
Acceptance rate	**22%**
Overall satisfaction rate	**No data**
Helpful/interested staff	**No data**
Small tuition groups	**No data**
Students into graduate jobs	**51%**

Subjects most popular with undergraduates:
Computer Arts, Games Technology, Earth Systems & Environmental Technology, General & Mineral Engineering, Law, Psychology. No student satisfaction figures available.

RESEARCH EXCELLENCE

% of Abertay's research that is
4* (World-class) or **3*** (Internationally rated):

	4*	3*
Allied Health Studies	0%	10%
Earth Systems, Enviro. Sci.	10%	35%
General Eng.. Minera, Mining	5%	20%
Business and Management	0%	15%
Law	0%	20%
Psychology	0%	15%

companies in Eastern Scotland with expert help in devising more environmentally-friendly products, services and processes.

Sports trainers and coaches also flow out of Abertay in number, and there's a new sports science laboratory for their BSc Sport Coaching & Development and Sport, Health & Exercise, and a new degree this year: MBA Sports Development.

There are good resources, including a computer arts design studio, an £8-million library, fully networked for the digital age, and over 1,200 personal computers available.

Other popular employment areas are banking, local government, higher education, law, hospitals and the community. Nurses (SEN, SRN, RGN, etc) are a prominent feature, and there's a new MSc Sexual & Reproductive Health degree.

In the Law provision, Abertay are European LLB Specialists, but also consider their BSc Forensic Sciences degree and BSc Forensic Psychobiology. Bestselling crime writer Ian Rankin opened a gruesome scene-of-the-crime-house here. 2009 sees the official opening of a 'Scenes of Crime' bank, first of its kind on Scotland.

There's a good reputation, too, for placing graduates from their BSc Civil Engineering and Dip HE Civil Engineering Studies, and although there are no dedicated BSc degrees in Quantity Surveying there's a strong current of graduates finding employment in this area, too.

In the business sector Abertay founded Embreonix, Scotland's first graduate enterprise centre dedicated to helping students set up their own business. Watch out, too, for their Human Resource Management provision, another department which makes a solid showing in the job figures

SOCIAL SCENE

STUDENTS' ASSOCIATION As a result of the local intake, weekends didn't used to figure much in the Students' Association ents calendar, and the extra-curricular life was fairly lame. But now they have

a £6 million **Student Centre**, which opened its doors to students for the first time in Spring 2005, and was later opened again, officially, by Midge Ure. It includes bars, a bistro, shop, nightclub, theatre and exhibition space, as well as offices for the Students' Association and Welfare. Daytime obsessions are more or less satisfied this year by thirty-five clubs and societies (mainly sport).

SPORT Underway is an Elite Athletes Development Programme, which supports staff and students competing at national and international level. There's a good variety of sports/pursuits available at the recreational level, with intra-mural activities, club sports and institutional competitions available to the progressively more serious competitor.. besides their own gym facilities and £500,000 sports science laboratory (one of the best medicine facilities in the country), students must make do with free access to local facilities, walking distance or under 10 minutes by bus. These include Astroturf pitches and good swimming pools as well as the Caird Park Athletics Stadium, an International Sports Complex, and the

WHAT IT'S REALLY LIKE

UNIVERSITY:	
Social Life	★★★
Campus scene	**Local, friendly**
Student Union services	**Developing**
Politics	**Activity low**
Sport	**25 clubs**
National teamposition	**86th**
Sport facilities	**Building fast**
Arts	**Dance, music, film average; art, drama poor**
Student magazine	**None**
Nightclub	**Basement**
Bars	**Lounge/Bistro, Sports Bar, Rooftop garden**
Union ents	**Wednesdays, Playground; Fridays, Slinky**
Union societies	**35**
Most popular society	**Role-Playing**
Parking	**Adequate**
CITY:	
Entertainment	★★★★
Scene	**Pubs, good live**
Town/gown relations	**Average**
Risk of violence	**Low**
Cost of living	**Average**
Student concessions	**Good**
Survival + 2 nights out	**£60 pw**
Part-time work campus/town	**Excellent/average**

Olympia, Lynch, Lochee and Douglas Sports Centres. Thera are also two premier league football clubs, the Scottish National Golf Centre, and championship courses at St Andrew and Carnoustie all within minutes of Dundee plus, in the nearby mountains, the Glenshee Ski Slopes. With the success of their Sports Coaching degree, there is an awareness of sport which they hope will attract big investment in the future.

Town Pubs are the focus and the cost of living is low compared to Aberdeen, Glasgow and Edinburgh. See Dundee Uni entry.

GETTING THERE
☛ By road: M90, M85, A85, A972.
☛ By rail: Newcastle, 3:00; London Euston, 6:00.

ACCOMMODATION	
Guarantee to freshers	**100%**
Style	**Halls, flats**
Security guard	**Campus**
Shared rooms	**None**
Internet access	**All**
Self-catered	**All**
En suite	**Some**
Avg. price range pw	**£65**
City rent pw	**£60**

☛ By air: Dundee Airport for internal flights; Edinburgh International Airport is an hour away.
☛ By coach: London, 10:05; Newcastle, 6:05.

UNIVERSITY OF WALES, ABERYSTWYTH

The University of Wales, Aberystwyth
Aberystwyth
Ceredigion SY23 2AX

TEL 01970 622021
FAX 01970 627410
EMAIL ug-admissions@aber.ac.uk
WEB www.aber.ac.uk

Aberystwyth Guild of Students
Aberystwyth
Ceredigion SY23 3DX

TEL 01970 621700
FAX 01970 621701
EMAIL union@aber.ac.uk
WEB www.aberguild.co.uk

VAG VIEW

The University of Aberystwyth's location makes it a top choice for many applicants. 'Think Wales; think west; think coast,' write Pete Liggins and Kate Glanville. 'It is then slap bang in the middle, a lovely seaside town whose two main industries are tourists in the summer and students in the closed season.'

Its academic strengths are in niche areas such as countryside management, tourism, international politics, Welsh/Celtic studies, Irish, geography and earth sciences, equine science, marine & freshwater biology, information & library studies, theatre, film and TV (there's a £3.5-million centre for these).

The uni certainly has its specialities; its very Welshness can seem daunting to some, but it isn't long before you realise that what makes Aber a good bet is the way it delivers every aspect of student services right

through academia and into the social side of the Students' Guild, whatever your expectations.

Students love it. An incredible 90% of them gave it a thumbs-up in the nationwide survey, and the drop-out rate is low (6%). In

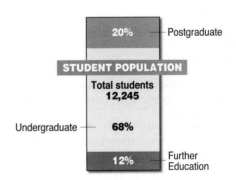

particular they like the interest shown in them by teaching staff and the small size tuition groups. Yet oddly, Aber always seems to show a poor graduate employment rate

UNIVERSITY/STUDENT PROFILE	
University since	**1872**
Situation/style	**Campus**
Student population	**12245**
Total undergraduates	**8255**
Mature undergraduates	**12%**
International undergrads	**11%**
Male/female ratio	**51:49**
Equality of opportunity:	
state school intake	**95%**
social class 4-7 intake	**28%**
low-participation area intake	**9%**

(real graduate jobs) after six months. Perhaps they just can't drag themselves off the beach until winter sets in.

FEES, BURSARIES

UK & EU Fees for 2009-10, £3,225. National Welsh entrant grants aside, there are bursaries of up to £1,000 p.a. available to UK and EU students, depending on residual household income, entrance scholarships and merit awards worth up to £1,200 p.a., bursaries of £667 a year in certain subject areas, and sports bursaries of £500 p.a. Then there are £500 discounts on the first year's accommodation fee, music bursaries worth £400 a year, and a specially nice touch are the care leaver bursaries worth between £1,000 and £1,800 a year. These are for students under 24 years of age, who have spent a period of time in care prior to their 16th birthday. Get the whole picture at www.aber.ac.uk/en/scholarships/aber-bursaries.

> *90% of students gave it the thumbs-up in the nationwide survey. Yet oddly, Aber shows a poor graduate employment rate (real graduate jobs) after six months. Perhaps they can't drag themselves off the beach until winter sets in.*

CAMPUS

Most of the university, including the main Students' Guild building, is contained within the Penglais campus, set on a hill above beautiful Cardigan Bay. But there is another campus at Llanbadarn, less than a mile away and home to the Department of Information and Library Studies, the College of Further Education and the Institute of Rural Studies. The sites are linked by a common telephone system, and there's a good bus service (if you're too lazy to walk).

STUDENT PROFILE

The student body is diverse. There are plenty of English here, though homage is paid to the Welsh hosts by their own countrymen, and the Students' Guild, or Yr Undeb as it translates in Welsh, plays a key role in supporting the native lingo: 'The unwritten rule is that you should accept anyone's right to speak in Welsh and not get paranoid that they are talking about you if you can't understand.' Relatively few public school types (5%).

ACADEMIA & JOBS

The best teaching, say students, is in Physical Sciences. In the Institute of Geography & Earth Sciences, there's Earth Planetary & Space Science, Environmental Earth Science (and with Education), Geography (there's a well-trod pathway for cartographers), and Water Sciences (see also the Marine Biology degrees). They took 'Excellent' in the assessments.

New this year is the Institute of Biological, Environmental and Rural Sciences, which brings together staff from the Institutes of Rural Sciences and Biological Sciences. It is set to play a major role in a £27-million initiative launched by the Biotechnology and Biological Sciences Research Council this year to develop clean, green and sustainable fuels. The aim is to provide the science to underpin and develop the important and emerging UK sustainable bioenergy sector - and to replace the petrol in cars with fuels derived from plants.

In the area of another strength - Politics - Aber has a history, which goes back to the 1960s when there were things called ideals hard fought for on campus. Now, there's a £5 million HQ for the world-renowned Department of International Politics. For graduates today, all this opens up a sound route into the Defence industry.

In-depth strength in Drama/Dance/Performing Arts also shows in the uni's employment figures. Arts administrators, managers, and stage managers come out of here in number.

There is a good administrative reputation all round, it seems, with managers and administrators of one sort or another heading Aber's graduate employment list. Would-be museum archivists, curators, librarians should look with respect at their BA Museum & Gallery Studies and BA Information & Library Studies. The latter can be combined with American Studies, Art History, Drama, Fine Art, languages, Film & TV, etc, and their Museum & Gallery Studies joins the same joint honours scheme. The whole mind set in this area favours research jobs in media (publishing is especially strong) and government.

Look, too, at the computer provision - software engineers dominate the employment figures. Courses include Artificial Intelligence and Robotics, Computer Graphics Vision and Games, Mobile and Wearable Computing.

Sports Science is among the most popular departments, with a 96% student approval rate of the teaching, and it has just been included in the London Olympics Organising Committee Pre-Games Camp Training Guide, as a training centre for elite athletes in mountain biking.

Accountancy & Finance degrees are another niche, with jobs in banking aplenty.

And note their specialist LLB Human Rights and European Law and Business & Commercial Law degrees. In 2005 they introduced a new degree

TEACHING SURVEY AT A GLANCE

Avg. UCAS points accepted	**300**
Acceptance rate	**24%**
Overall satisfaction rate	**90%**
Helpful/interested staff	★★★★
Small tuition groups	★★★★
Students into graduate jobs	**54%**

Teaching most popular with undergraduates:
Physical Science (100%), Human & Social Geography (99%), Sports Science (98%), Celtic Studies, Zoology (97%), European Languages, Physical Geography & Environmental Science (95%), Agriculture (93-4%), Biological Sciences, Law (92%), Accounting, Biology, Economics (91%), Politics, Business (90%),.

Teaching least popular with undergraduates:
Cinematics & Photography (80%).

SUBJECT AREAS (%)

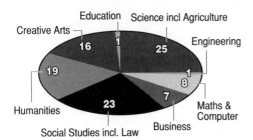

Education 1
Science incl Agriculture 25
Creative Arts 16
Engineering 1
8
Humanities 19
Social Studies incl. Law 23
Business 7
Maths & Computer

scheme in Criminology and new Legal Practice scheme (and new this year is BscEcon Criminology - single and joint honours. Law students can qualify now in Aber without needing to proceed to Law College, and the Law Dept allows non-Law graduates to take a 2-year full-time or 3-year part-time Senior Status law degree.

New degrees for this year include BSc Psychology (single and joint honours), and BA Childhood Studies. Besides the university's extensive library you will have access to the National Library of Wales (over six million books, maps and prints).

SOCIAL SCENE

The best times in Aber are had on those sun-shimmering days when there are half a dozen beach fire parties to chill out at. With students making up half the town's population, if you are out day or night then you are bound to bump into someone you know or someone you would sooner forget.

Students' Guild Llanbadarn has **Y Gwyllt - The Outback** bar, and entertainment facilities, discos and a pool room. Back at base camp, in the Penglais Guild building, there's **Bar 9** and the Joint, a nightclub, with **Cwrt Mawr Bar** the halls pub on this campus. Sadly, this isolated coastal resort is not a draw for big name bands, but 'live' is definitely part of the ents menu.

Guild facilities also include dance, art and drama workshop spaces, an art cinema, studio theatre and art gallery.

RESEARCH EXCELLENCE

% of Aberystwyth's research that is
4* (World-class) or **3*** (Internationally rated):

	4*	3*
Agriculture, Vet., Food Science	**10%**	**35%**
Physics	**5%**	**15%**
Pure Mathematics	**5%**	**35%**
Computer Science	**25%**	**45%**
Geography	**20%**	**45%**
Business and Management	**5%**	**25%**
Library and Infor. Mgt	**10%**	**40%**
Law	**5%**	**30%**
Politics	**40%**	**25%**
Sports-Related Studies	**0%**	**15%**
European Studies	**20%**	**15%**
Celtic Studies	**25%**	**40%**
English Language and Lit.	**10%**	**30%**
History	**10%**	**35%**
History of Art, Architec., Design	**5%**	**20%**
Drama, Dance, etc	**30%**	**30%**

WHAT IT'S REALLY LIKE

UNIVERSITY:

Social Life	★★★★★
Campus scene	**Contained, safe tight-knit & fun**
Student Union services	**Excellent**
Politics	**Top-up fees, Welsh education**
Sport	**Consistent**
National team position	**66th**
Sport facilities	**Good**
Arts opportunities	**Good Arts Centre**
Student magazine	**The Courier Yr Utgom**
Student radio	**Bay Radio**
Nightclub	**The Joint**
Bars	**Bar 9, Cwrt Mawr, Outback**
Union ents	**Comedy, cheese, clubnights beach parties**
Union societies	**40**
Parking	**Good**

TOWN:

Entertainment	★★
Scene	**Scenic seaside**
Town/gown relations	**Good**
Risk of violence	**Low**
Cost of living	**Average**
Student concessions	**Poor**
Survival + 2 nights out	**£60 pw**
Part-time work campus/town	**Good**

Student media is pre-eminent with *The Courier* (*Yr Utgorn* - www.thecourier.org.uk/), *Ur Ytgorn* - Welsh language magazine, and Bay Radio.

Traditionally, political activity is high compared to many, with, typically, active Welsh Language campaigning, and international human rights, and peace and justice issues to the fore.

The Guild also offers a range of courses to develop employment skills.

SPORT It's a big thing at Aber, American Football being among their areas of excellence. There are fifty acres of pitches and specialist facilities for water sports, including a boat house, an indoor swimming pool, two sports halls, an all-weather floodlit sports pitch, squash courts and indoor facilities for football, badminton, basketball, hockey and tennis. Cardigan Bay and nearby Snowdonia offer windsurfing and skiing opportunities respectively, and there is

orienteering, mountain-biking, rambling, sub-aqua and hang-gliding too.

TOWN There's a one-screen cinema, where films tend to be shown around two to three weeks after their actual release date. The flick makes up for this by being cheap, friendly and licensed - so you can have a pint while watching the film - and the programme sports some of the cheapest and best local advertising you will ever have the pleasure to view. The cinema's ethos seems to sum up the whole town; everything is more laid back here: the sun shines and things slow down; it's life without the big city stresses.

Aber is also blessed with a number of pubs, described by one student as 'beyond definition; every taste should be catered for somewhere. There is something of a worrying trend, however, towards refitting and furbishing with an emphasis

ACCOMMODATION

Guarantee to freshers	**100%**
Style	**Halls, flats**
Security guard	**All**
Internet access	**All**
Self-catered	**Some flats, no halls**
En suite	**No halls, some flats**
Approx price range pw	**£64.75-£96**
City rent pw	**£50-£75**

on American tack, for each of these is a true local - one in particular won't serve a pint of Guinness in less than five minutes.'

Safety is not an issue in Aberystwyth.

PILLOW TALK

Accommodation ranges from a twin room space (self-catering) to a single room in a catered residence - currently, £64.75 to £96.00, whereas in town, it's £50 to £75 per week for a single room (self-catering), with 50% retainer charged during the summer vacation.

GETTING THERE

☞ By road: A484 from north or south; A44 from the east.
☞ By rail: London Euston, 5 hours. Chart your route carefully or you'll end up on a slow local line through the mid-Wales countryside.
☞ By coach: London, 7:00; Newcastle, 11:00.

ANGLIA RUSKIN UNIVERSITY

Anglia Ruskin University
East Road
Cambridge CB1 1PT

TEL 0845 271 3333
FAX 01245 251789
EMAIL answers@anglia.ac.uk
WEB www.anglia.ac.uk

Anglia Ruskin Students' Union
East Road
Cambridge CB1 1PT

TEL 01603 593272
EMAIL info@angliastudent.com
WEB www.angliastudent.com

VAG VIEW

*A*nglia Ruskin is based in Cambridge city centre and in Chelmsford, Essex. The university comes out of Cambridgeshire College of Arts and Technology and the Essex Institute of Higher Education, which merged in 1989 to form Anglia Higher Education College. In 1991, this became Anglia Polytechnic, and Anglia Polytechnic University the following year. Its re-branding as Anglia Ruskin occurred a decade later.

In its student population it is very much a 'new' university. All but 2% are state school educated, and 16% are drawn from neighbourhoods for whom university is an unknown. Perhaps inevitably, the drop-out rate is higher than average (11%).

There is an effort, however, to institute manageable, decent size tuition groups, and although students don't rate staff interest and helpfulness especially highly, there is a good 'real graduate job' employment rate in the first six months after graduation (83%), boosted in particular by the primary teacher, nursing, midwifery, allied health professions (Radiography), and social work provisions.

Students vote Drama, Social Policy, Biology, Sociology, Philosophy, Music, History, English, Communications/Media among the best taught. However, Education Studies from which many graduates eventually enter the teaching profession, got the thumbs down. Only 40% of Anglia students rated the teaching of it.

CAMPUSES

Beyond the flagship campus in the city of Cambridge, Chelmsford campus is home to the School of Education and the Ashcroft International Business School. A sports hall and student centre was also opened here in September 2004.

FEES, BURSARIES

UK & EU Fees for 2009-10 entry: £3,225 p.a. There's a bursary for students in receipt of full HE Maintenance Grant £319 p.a.

UNIVERSITY/STUDENT PROFILE	
University since	**1992**
Situation/style	**City/town campuses**
Student population	**20300**
Total undergraduates	**16855**
Mature undergraduates	**50%**
International undergrads	**31%**
Male/female ratio	**33:67**
Equality of opportunity:	
state school intake	**98%**
social class 4-7 intake	**37%**
low-participation area intake	**16%**

STUDENT PROFILE

There's an eclectic mix of arty types, nurses, laddish engineers and teachers. This is a modern university. Many local and mature students come here more for Anglia's tickets into industry than anything else. Many are part-time, sponsored by employers.

Writes Jill Walker. 'We have lots of mature students, who make everyone work harder 'cos they are the only ones to do the reading. Lots of

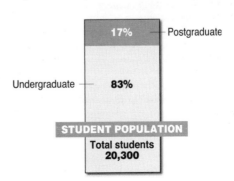

Postgraduate 17%

Undergraduate 83%

STUDENT POPULATION
Total students
20,300

TEACHING SURVEY AT A GLANCE

Avg. UCAS points accepted	**240**
Acceptance rate	**23%**
Overall satisfaction rate	**65%**
Helpful/interested staff	★★
Small tuition groups	★★★
Students into graduate jobs	**83%**

Teaching most popular with undergraduates:
Drama (94%), Social Policy (87%), Biology (86%), Sociology (85%), Philosophy (82%), Music, History (81%), English, Communications/Media (80%).

Teaching least popular with undergraduates:
Education Studies (40%).

students are local. Cambridge is far more international than Chelmsford.'

ACADEMIA & JOBS

Programmes are designed in collaboration with employers in the health sector, in local government, in the legal sector, in engineering, in science-based industries, in the ICT sector, and in media. There are work placements available with over 100 companies, and in-company, award-bearing courses for such as Marconi, Ford, and Suffolk County Council.

Their Employer Mentoring Scheme is intended to support second year undergraduates in thinking about and planning for the transition from study to work. Each student is matched with a mentor for their chosen career field.

Less well publicised is the heartening, in-depth academic expertise among lecturers revealed in the latest survey of research undertaken at British universities, which looks at work cited world-wide in academic papers. In particular, Anglia has a good record at world and international levels in History, Psychology, English Language and Literature, Social Work, and Social Policy & Administration.

There are eight Schools of study: Arts & Letters, Applied Sciences, Law, Languages and Social Sciences, Ashcroft International Business School, Education, Design and Communication Systems, Healthcare Practice and Community Health and Social Studies.

Training teachers is one of Anglia's core commitments, health is another defining strength. Look at their Pharmacy, Genetics, Health & Social Care degrees. In nursing, they offer Adult, Child, Learning Disabilities and Mental Health degrees, and BSc Midwifery.

They are also a big player in optometry and

ophthalmic dispensing, and in natural health therapy - acupuncture, reflexology and aromatherapy. Interesting, too, is the Vet Nursing degree they sponsor at the College of West Anglia.

For better or worse, in business they have recently developed a course with Barclays bank. Students are work-based, sponsored and salaried for all three years of their course.

In Forensic Science they are one of the nation's leaders and there is a new BSc (Hons) Information Security and Forensic Computing on offer.

Their long-term reputation for art and design was one of the points of excellence acknowledged in the research assessment. They offer Illustration as an integral part of the graphics course. A new Fine Art course was launched in 2004.

Look, also, at their programme of drama

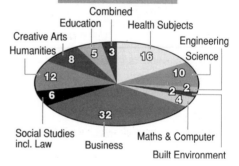

SUBJECT AREAS (%)

Combined
Education
Health Subjects
Creative Arts
Humanities
Engineering
Science
8
5
3
16
12
10
2
2
6
4
32
Social Studies incl. Law
Business
Maths & Computer
Built Environment

degrees, which sets the scene at the Mumford Theatre on Cambridge campus, and at a range of new degrees in the area of Performing Arts launched in 2004.

Again, the Music Technology degrees are a

RESEARCH EXCELLENCE

% of Anglia Ruskin's research that is
4* (World-class) or 3* (Internationally rated):

	4*	3*
Geography and Enviro. Studies	5%	15%
Health	5%	10%
Social Work, Policy & Admin	5%	25%
Psychology	5%	40%
European Studies	0%	20%
English Lang. and Lit.	15%	45%
History	20%	40%
Art and Design	5%	25%
Music	5%	10%

productive employment niche. There's also much activity in media, where publishing and journalism are real live employment possibilities.

Another significant graduate employment is opened up by the Sports Science degree, which has links with the English Cricket Board's local Centre of Excellence. Anglia is among the country's top producers of physical training instructors in Education.

Altogether there's been no shortage of money spent on academic facilities, which include a Forensic Science laboratory, complete with scene of crime workshops, four libraries, sound and recording studios, a Sports Science laboratory, an Optometry clinic, simulated hospital wards and operating theatres, a complementary medicine suite, counselling rooms, a theatre, art gallery, mock courtroom for Law students, and language laboratories.

SOCIAL SCENE

The Students' Union on Cambridge campus occupies the Helmore Building, complete with new Student Union office, music, arts and language laboratory facilities, bar (**Kudos**) and nightclub/venue (**Academy**). At Chelmsford it's the Tindal building, again with bar/venue (**Kudos**) and restaurant.

Ents - Cambridge: *Touch* club night on a Friday (cheesy tunes/disco); on Wednesday the union becomes pre-club venue for night out in the city's **Twenty Two - The Nightclub**; then there are open mic nights/comedy on a Tuesday. Sunday night has a quiz. They also showcase up and coming bands. At Chelmsford it's *Spanked* on Tuesdays - fun and games; *Funkin' Marvellous - Friday Night* clubnight; *Rock It* - rock night on a Saturday.

There is an award-winning student radio station shared with the University of Cambridge. It won 'Best National Student Radio Station' in 2007 and 'Best Presenter' in 2008.

SPORT There are tennis courts and a multigym on the Cambridge campus, and 100 metres away the Kelsey Kerridge Sports Centre with gym and nearby swimming pool. Half a mile north of the campus there are three football pitches, a rugby pitch and a cricket square. Ex-England Cricketers Mike Gatting and Peter Such helped to launch Anglia's new sports scholarships and bursaries. Rowing crews rack their eights at Cambridge Uni's Emmanuel College Boat House. At Chelmsford Campus, there's a new sports centre.

PILLOW TALK

No official guarantee, but in reality they can accommodate 95% freshers at Chelmsford and

WHAT IT'S REALLY LIKE	
UNIVERSITY:	
Social Life	★★
Campus scene:	**Diverse**
Student Union services	**Poor**
Politics	**Cambridge: interest high; Chelmsford low**
Most popular societies	**Camb: RAG; Chelm: Mission Croatia**
Sport	**55 clubs**
National team position	**119th**
Sport facilities	**Adequate**
Arts opportunities	**Drama, music exc; dance good; film, art average**
Student newspaper	**The Apex**
Bars	**Kudos**
Union ents	**New nightclubs + tie-up with town**
Union societies	**32**
Parking	**Poor. Student issue at Chelmsford**

90% at Cambridge. At Chelmsford there's a student village with en-suite rooms in flats of 3-6. At Cambridge there are en-suite and older style halls, along with uni-owned and leased houses. Newest accommodation is at Sedley Court, in Cambridge (150 en-suite rooms).

ACCOMMODATION	
Guarantee to freshers	**90-95%**
Style	**Halls, flats**
Security guard	**For some**
Shared rooms	**Some halls**
Internet access	**All**
Self-catered	**All**
En suite	**Some (most flats)**
Approx price pw	**£65-£120**
Cambridge city pw	**£70-£120**
Chekmsford town pw	**£70-£100**

GETTING THERE - Cambridge

☛ By road (from London): M25/J27, M11/J11, A10. From west or east: A45. From northwest: A604. From Stansted Airport: M11.

☛ By train: London's Liverpool Street, under the hour; Nottingham, 2:30; Sheffield, Birmingham New Street, 3:00.

☛ By coach: London, 1:50; Birmingham, 2:45; Leeds, 5:00; Bristol, 5:30.

GETTING THERE - Chelmsford
☛ By road: A12, A130 or A414.
☛ By rail: London Liverpool Street, 35 mins.

☛ By air: 10 miles from the M25 and access to Stansted Airport and Heathrow.
☛ By coach: London, 1:40; Norwich, 5:00.

ASTON UNIVERSITY, BIRMINGHAM

Aston University, Birmingham
Aston Triangle
Birmingham B4 7ET

TEL 0121 204 3000
FAX 0121 333 6350
EMAIL ugenquiries@aston.ac.uk
WEB www.aston.ac.uk

Aston Students' Guild
The Triangle
Birmingham B4 7ES

TEL 0121 204 4855
FAX 0121 333 4218
EMAIL guild.president@aston.ac.uk
WEB www.astonguild.org.uk

VAG VIEW

*A*ston University, Birmingham, is a small university slap bang in the eye of the urban vortex, yet sheltered from any of the city's urban excesses in an attractive, green-field campus bowl - a crisp and tasty morsel in Birmingham's tangled spaghetti junction. As a student said of its particular locus, 'The dual carriageway acts as a kind of natural barrier. You go under the flyover and suddenly, wow! It's Birmingham.'

Aston stands for business, science, health, and European studies. The worlds of work and academia are at no point distinct - 70% or more undergrads take sandwich courses, i.e. a year's placement in industry as part of the degree course. As a result there is a perennially high employment rate. Eighty per cent find a graduate level job in their discipline within six months, and with an overall student thumbs-up to the experience here of 89% and a drop-out rate of less than 4%, it is clearly a good and enjoyable deal, and in many ways quite its own sort of experience.

FEES, BURSARIES
UK & EU Fees, 2009-10: £3,225 p.a. Awards of £1,000 for all students on placement. Additional £500 for all students on year abroad or unpaid placements. Placement year fee is £1,610 for 2009, half the full fee of £3,225. For update visit www.aston.ac.uk/fees. Sports scholarships worth £500 p.a. are available.

UNIVERSITY/STUDENT PROFILE

University since	**1966**
Situation/style	**City campus**
Student population	**9555**
Total undergraduates	**7030**
Mature undergraduates	**13%**
International undergrads	**14%**
Male/female ratio	**51:49**
Equality of opportunity:	
state school intake	**92%**
social class 4-7 intake	**36%**
low-participation area intake	**9%**

CAMPUS
Aston is well defined, straightforward, scientific. You get what you see at The Triangle. The clean lines of this modern, high-rise, plate-glass, green-field Birmingham city campus (complete with artificial lake) brook no idle intent. Twenty-four hour CCTV and well-trained, friendly security staff are everywhere. Campus is also part of a recognised police beat and enjoys close relations with the local force for advice on prevention etc. Crime is extremely low. But above all, this is a determinedly close-knit community.

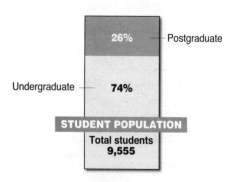

26% Postgraduate

Undergraduate 74%

STUDENT POPULATION
Total students
9,555

STUDENT PROFILE

More than a third of intake is working class, 9% from neighbourhoods where university is a novel idea. Public school kids are pretty thin on the ground.

Expect to find suits in the business section, and earnest, professional techies behind the superb lighting and sound systems in the Guild Hall, as they prepare for some serious Aston student nights.

There is a disarming, fresh-faced authenticity about the place. Aston is the only university where someone like me will be met by union and university executives around the same table. There are no divides, rather there is exuberance about their open, genuinely caring attitude, a contra-current to the traditional angst-ridden, existential flow of undergraduate life, and in an odd sort of way quite sweet and disarming. See what you think, sign up for Open Day.

One hundred and fifty volunteers elect to become Aston aunties and welcome freshers on the basis that Auntie knows best. Every year they have different slogans, like 'We are family!' or 'The cream of Brum.' For Fresher's Week they do city tours, campus tours, supermarket trips (?!), cultural crawls, canal cruises, fun things like go-karting and paintballing, an Alton Towers trip, and the departments all have other things organised, library visits and so on.

Said one union bod: 'We had a classic quote yesterday from a student whose parents had just left: ¡Oh, I haven't even been here for twelve hours yet and I feel at home already!¡'

If I'd heard this anywhere else I wouldn't have believed it, but at Aston what you see is what you get. You can thrust, you can parry, but 'you won't hear a thing against Aston from us,' they say. This is true all over campus.

ACADEMIA & JOBS

In-depth expertise lies in Business, Health, Engineering, and European Studies. Students praise the teaching of Ophthalmics, Chemical

TEACHING SURVEY AT A GLANCE	
Avg. UCAS points accepted	340
Acceptance rate	15%
Overall satisfaction rate	89%
Helpful/interested staff	★★
Small tuition groups	★★
Students into graduate jobs	80%

Teaching most popular with undergraduates:
Ophthalmics, Chemical Engineering (96%), Sociology, Social Policy (95%), Business, Health (94%), Psychology, French (91%).

Teaching least popular with undergraduates:
Mechanical Engineering (66%).

Engineering, Sociology, Social Policy, Business, Health, Psychology, and French, but there are a few murmurs of dissent when it comes to Mechanical Engineering. Also, one has to say that in spite of the care taken of students outside the lecture hall, Aston students do not rate staff highly for their academic interest in them, and small-

RESEARCH EXCELLENCE		
% of Aston's research that is		
4* (World-class) or 3* (Internationally rated):		
	4*	3*
Allied Health Studies	15%	35%
General Eng., Mineral, Mining	10%	25%
Business and Mgt Studies	15%	45%
European Studies	5%	15%

group tutorials are pretty thin on the ground, which is odd when one considers that this is more of a teaching than a research-led university.

Broadly, Aston consists of three faculties: Life & Health Sciences; Engineering & Applied Science (Civil Engineering, Chemical Eng. and Applied Chemistry, Mechanical & Electrical Eng., Electronic and Applied Physics, Computer Science and Applied Maths); and Management Languages & European Studies. The latter includes the Aston Business School and School of Languages and European Studies.

Teaching assessments accorded full marks to Pharmacy and its business and management courses, while Biological Sciences, Optometry, French, German, and Psychology were not far behind. Note that Spanish is now offered in addition to French and German, and English

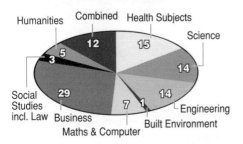

SUBJECT AREAS (%)

Humanities — Combined — Health Subjects — Science — Engineering — Built Environment — Business — Maths & Computer — Social Studies incl. Law

12, 15, 3, 5, 14, 29, 7, 1, 14

Language is also an option in that faculty.

Aston is heavy on workload, extremely well resourced and geared to top-class employment by means of industry contact, study-abroad programmes, language combinations and sandwich courses. Your friends, like you, are probably up for a four-year term, at the end of which a job is more or less unavoidable.

The University tells us: 'Over 200 companies and organisations visited us in 2008 to promote to and recruit our graduates.' Graduates find work in the health industry, particularly ophthalmics. Aston has around 27% of the graduate provision in this. If you have your eyes tested in England there's a good chance that it will be an Aston graduate doing it. Graduates also herd into business, banks, local government, computing, and the motor industry, and the Pharmacy department is another that shines job-wise: only Queen's Belfast turns out more pharmacists.

The Business School is one of the largest in Europe and one of only a handful in the world to have triple accreditation from the major European (EQUIS), American (AACSB) and MBA benchmarks of quality for business education.

Related courses tackle the behavioural side of enterprise, such as Organisational Studies, Human Psychology and Psychology with Management. See also the qualifying Law with Management Programme, new in 2008.

The school is a vital part of what this uni is all about. Note the 4-year sandwich BSc International Business & Economics (could add on French, Spanish or German), the International Business & Management degree, which offers the possibility of placement across the world. Look too at the 5-year sandwich Int. Foundation in Business/Business BScs. And for 2010 there's a new 4-year sandwich degree in Finance.

Six per cent of Aston's graduates are among the 4,500-odd graduates going into Banking each year, and the uni figures impressively in management consultancy, too.

A word too about the potential of their electronic engineering and computer provision. For would-be software engineers on the smaller-uni ticket, there are two key unis, Essex and Aston.

Finally, mooted for this year are 4-year QTS degrees in Secondary Science in partnership with nearby Newman University College. It's a way of picking up a teaching qualification while mainstreaming on an

Aston degree. Expect more graduate teachers to come through as a result. Presently they account for around 5% of the graduate passing out parade.

SOCIAL SCENE

STUDENTS' GUILD The no-nonsense efficiency of this uni far from cripples any desire for after-work pleasure, either at the Students' Guild or a walk away in the centre of Brum itself.

The Guild offers the three venues. **The Loft** is a social study area on the second floor, **Einstein's** a community style pub on the lower ground floor, featuring Karaoke and pub quizzes, with big screen and two man-size pool tables. Then there's the **Blue Room** and the **Guild Hall** (a café by day), which, together with the Blue Room, gives a max building capacity of 1,150 for evening events.

WHAT IT'S REALLY LIKE	
UNIVERSITY:	
Social Life	★★★
Campus scene	**Lively, caring suits & techies**
Student Union services	**Efficient**
Politics	**Interest low**
Sport	**35 clubs**
National team position	**89th**
Sport facilities	**40 clubs**
Arts opportunities	**Dance, music excellent; drama good**
Student newspaper	**The Aston Times**
Student magazine	**Wotsup?**
Nightclub	**Guild Hall**
Bars	**Einstein's, The Blue Room**
Union ents	**Twice weekly**
Union societies	**30**
Most popular societiy	**Fusion (dance music), Islamic**
Parking	**No**
CITY:	
Entertainment	★★★★★
Scene	**Excellent**
Town/gown relations	**Average**
Risk of violence	**Average**
Cost of living	**High**
Student concessions	**Excellent**
Survival + 2 nights out	**£120 pw**
Part-time work campus/town	**Good/Excellent**

> *Aston is mainly for science, engineering and business. It is very defined, very straightforward, very scientific. You get what you see at The Triangle, and students do seem to enjoy themselves.*

There are twice weekly events, featuring low priced drinks and national acts. They also feature fortnightly lunchtime acoustic sessions.

Astonbury Festival is a major highlight on campus in June when exams finish: 'The best gig of the summer,' according to Radio One's Zane Lowe.

SPORT Aston came 89th in the BUSA sports competitive rankings, not bad for a small university. New developments include an extended gym - now 75 stations, new all-weather pitch and additional facilities at the Outdoor Sports Centre 6 miles from campus - 40 acres of pitches, floodlighting, pavilion and all weather facilities. On campus there are two sports centres - **Woodcock** (with swimming pool) and **Gem Sports Hall**. It is sport for everyone, rather than club level; 'relaxed' is the word used, although the options are varied enough to include American Football, korfball and other alternative sports.

TOWN See *Student Birmingham.*

PILLOW TALK

Self-catering flats and houses, all on campus, all within 2 mins walk of each other and 5 mins walk from all other campus facilities. Flats vary in size from 4-12 students sharing. Freshers tend to be in larger flats. Convenient, friendly, safe. Fixed 'Wi-Fi' internet access for all; 80% of rooms en suite. Catered meal plan available for all - c. £300 per term for 2 meals a day in campus outlets.

ACCOMMODATION	
Guarantee to freshers	**100%**
Style	**Flats**
Security guard	**Police beat**
Shared rooms	**None**
Internet access	**All**
Self-catered	**All**
En suite	**80%**
Approx price range pw	**£68-£106**
City rent pw	**£45-£110**

They guarantee to find all freshers flats who hold Aston as CF/UF choice and apply for accommodation before the end of July. No guarantee for clearing and insurance students.

They are building 1,350 new, fully networked en-suite rooms ready for 2010 entry, green technologies to the fore, and the usual internet/data/digital connections and access and security features.

GETTING THERE

☞ By road: M6/J6, A38M 3rd exit, then first exit at Lancaster Circus roundabout.
☞ By rail: Bristol Parkway, Sheffield, 1:30; Euston, 1:40. New Street 12 mins' walk from campus.
☞ By air: Birmingham International Airport.
☞ By coach: London, 2:40; Bristol, 2:00.

UNIVERSITY OF WALES, BANGOR

University of Wales, Bangor
Gwynedd LL57 2DG

TEL 01248 382016/7
FAX 01248 370451
EMAIL admissions@bangor.ac.uk
WEB www.bangor.ac.uk

Bangor Students' Union
Gwynedd LL57 2TH

TEL 01248 388011
FAX 01248 388020
EMAIL undeb@undeb.bangor.ac.uk
WEB www.undeb.bangor.ac.uk

VAG VIEW

Setting the whole deal in context for a semi-final of University Challenge, Jeremy Paxman described the natural environs of Bangor, which is in North Wales, just across the Menai Strait from the Isle of Anglesey, as 'one of the most beautiful locations of any British university, between the beaches of Anglesey and the mountains of Snowdonia.'

Bangor started life on 18 October, 1884, in an old coaching inn, a promising beginning, particularly as half the student intake was female, which was swimming against the tide in those days.

Today the pendulum has swung and the student pop. is almost two-thirds female . While not overly demanding at entry (say

UNIVERSITY/STUDENT PROFILE	
University since	**1884**
Situation/style	**Rural bliss**
Student population	**14020**
Total undergraduates	**8500**
Mature undergraduates	**18%**
International undergrads	**7%**
Male/female ratio	**38:62**
Equality of opportunity:	
state school intake	**96%**
social class 4-7 intake	**33%**
low-participation area intake	**11%**

280 points should see you in), it has risen to be one of the most popular unis with its own students. There's an 86% satisfaction rate, and a fair chance of getting a graduate type job after six months: 70% do.

The biggest job-take is in the health sector. Bangor has nurses aplenty: adult, child, learning disability and mental health nurses; but these are far from alone in the medicine cupboard. The College of Health & Behavioural Sciences has the schools of Healthcare Sciences, Psychology, Sport, and Health & Exercise Sciences, and no less than The Institute of Medical & Social Care Research. Even that isn't all: the North West Cancer Research Fund Institute at the School of Biological Sciences conducts fundamental research into the causes of cancer.

So, nursing sits alongside social work, community and counselling, and other human health and medical practice activities in forming the biggest single job-of-work category here, with Education (notably but far from exclusively primary teacher education) not far behind.

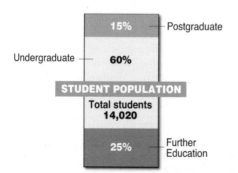

Postgraduate 15%
Undergraduate 60%

STUDENT POPULATION
Total students 14,020

25% Further Education

Interestingly, however, the students praise different areas. Favourite teaching is in Environmental Science, Finance & Accounting, Geography, History, Heritage, Archaeology & & History, and Law. While Business Studies barely raises a whisper of approval, with only 67% students rating it.

Not surprisingly, with so much going for Bangor, the drop-out rate (7%) is considerably lower than the national average.

FEES, BURSARIES
2009-10 fees are £3,225 p.a. for non-Welsh students, but the Bangor Bursary means you could receive up to £1,000 a year on top of any state-funded maintenance grants and loans, or any other University bursaries (sport and academic entrance, merit, and excellence scholarships) you may be eligible for. It depends on household income, of course. See www.bangor.ac.uk for more details.

CAMPUS
North Wales is different from the rest of Wales: they're the real Welsh up here and Welsh is still the natural language over much of Gwynedd. It is a small, town-size 'city' community that manages not to protest at the regular incursion of a student population which more than doubles the local population at the start of each term. While not exactly a campus university, all the buildings, with the exception of the School of Ocean Sciences, which is a few miles from the Menai Bridge, are within walking distance of one another.

It is also cheap and safe.

STUDENT PROFILE
There is a sizeable Welsh population, largely female, and a number of mature students. Precious few come from public school (4%), indeed many inhabit areas new to the idea of sending to university. However, they have in place one of the UK's longest established peer guide/'student mentoring' programme, ensuring a fine welcome and continuing student care.

Cutting-edge cool it is not, however. If you come to Bangor, you'll likely be sporty, interested in outward bound perhaps, maybe a classical music lover (there is an international reputation for music here). This is no place for the club loon. As one student put it, 'you'll probably find more night life in a tramp's vest.'

None of this stems the flow of students from abroad, and the uni goes out of its way to help them settle. The International Welfare Unit assists and advises, and orientation days are arranged to help international students get acclimatised to the country. The ELCOS (English Language Courses for Overseas Students) Unit provides instruction for those whose language skills need polishing. There's also an organisation (called 'Shekina') which offers help to wives and husbands of students and organises a range of activities, including English language courses.

For all freshers, Bangor has one of the largest welcoming schemes of any university.

ACADEMIA & JOBS

The academic structure delivers six 'colleges', each a federation of schools.

The College of Arts & Humanities schools are English, Welsh, History & Welsh History, Linguistics & English Language, Modern Languages, Music, Theology & Religious Studies, NIECI (National Institute for Excellence in the Creative Industries), ELCOS (English Language Centre for Overseas Students), and WISCA (Welsh Institute for Social and Cultural Affairs).

The College of Business, Social Sciences & Law has the Bangor Business School and schools of Law and Social Sciences.

The College of Education & Lifelong Learning has schools of Education and Lifelong Learning.

The College of Natural Sciences incorporates schools of The Environment & Natural Resources, encompassing Geography and Regional Studies, the schools of Biological Sciences and Ocean Sciences, the Welsh Institute of Natural Resources,

> *It has risen to become one of the best universities academically... and, even if you accept a student's claim that you'd find more night life in a tramp's vest, Bangor, because of its geographical position, makes a plausible case.*

TEACHING SURVEY AT A GLANCE	
Avg. UCAS points accepted	**280**
Acceptance rate	**22%**
Overall satisfaction rate	**86%**
Helpful/interested staff	★★★★
Small tuition groups	★★★★
Students into graduate jobs	**70%**

Teaching most popular with undergraduates:
Environmental Science (98%), Finance & Accounting, Geography, History, Heritage, Archaeology & History (96%), Law (92%).

Teaching least popular with undergraduates:
Business Studies (67%).

encompassing the CAZS - The Natural Resources and the BioComposites Centre.

The College of Physical & Applied Sciences incorporates the schools of Chemistry, Electronics, and Computer Science. Finally, the College of Health & Behavioural Sciences is described above, under 'VAG View'.

A 4-star rating for helpful/interested staff and decent-size tutorials underpins the teaching, which benefits from a wide range of in-depth research. In psychology and music in particular a fifth to a quarter of their work has been adjudged world class, and more or less half of the research in these areas gained a 3-star international rating. The same is true of the Agriculture, Environmental, Celtic Studies, and Accounting & Finance provisions.

A new £10 million Business and Management Centre houses Bangor's School for Business and Regional Development, though this clearly fails to cheer up the 33% of students who did the teaching down at the student survey.

There's an employment niche for turning out museum archivists, curators, and librarians. They come from across the academic board - from Humanities, Languages, Biological Sciences, and Law. Look also at the Information Technology degrees.

There's also a preponderance of translators sufficient to make the Language Department a highflyer in this area nationally.

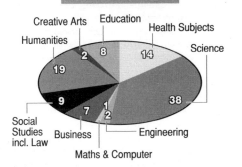

SUBJECT AREAS (%)

Creative Arts — 2
Humanities — 19
Education — 8
Health Subjects — 14
Science — 38
Engineering — 2
Maths & Computer — 1
Business — 7
Social Studies incl. Law — 9

Another notable feature of the academic provision generally is that it favours students with disabilities - there are study support centres which house CCTVs, scanners and braille embossers. They also have induction loops and infra-red transmission equipment to help those with hearing difficulties, and ramps and lifts in the main buildings to help those with mobility problems. A Dyslexia Unit is apparently internationally renowned.

New courses this year include Environmental Science MEnvSci, Cancer Biology, Zoology with Animal Behaviour, Zoology with Animal Ecology, Marine Science MMSci/MMBiol/MOcean, Information and Communications Technology, Information and Communications Technology for Business, and a whole host of Electronics degrees, as well as a couple of offerings that promise to shake you out of the rut of traditional academia - Law with Media Studies LLB, and English with Songwriting.

RESEARCH EXCELLENCE

% of Bangor's research that is
4* *(World-class)* or **3*** *(Internationally rated):*

	4*	3*
Health Services Research	**5%**	**20%**
Biological Sciences	**5%**	**20%**
Agriculture, Vet., Food	**5%**	**40%**
Earth Systems and Enviro.	**10%**	**50%**
Chemistry	**10%**	**35%**
Computer Science	**15%**	**35%**
Electrical and Electronic Eng.	**30%**	**40%**
Accounting and Finance	**15%**	**50%**
Social Work,l Policy & Admin.	**5%**	**25%**
Psychology	**20%**	**45%**
Education	**10%**	**20%**
Sports-Related Studies	**10%**	**25%**
European Studies	**5%**	**20%**
Celtic Studies	**10%**	**45%**
English Language and Lit.	**15%**	**30%**
Linguistics	**5%**	**30%**
Theology	**5%**	**25%**
History	**15%**	**35%**
Music	**25%**	**45%**

WHAT IT'S REALLY LIKE

UNIVERSITY:	
Social Life	★★★★
Campus scene	**Outdoor, cheap, close-knit, Welsh, and full of life**
Student Union services	**Good**
Politics	**Internal**
Sport	**Rising**
National team position	**73rd**
Sport facilities	**Good**
Arts opportunities	**OK**
Student newspaper	**Seren, Y ddraenen**
Student radio	**Storm FM**
Nightclub	**Amser/Time**
Bars	**Main/Prif Far, Jock's Bar**
Union ents	**Live acts, DJs, comedy**
Union societies	**25**
Most active societies	**Mountain walking, Football, Community Action**
Parking	**Good**
CITY:	
Entertainment	★★
Scene	**Scenic, fun**
Town/gown relations	**Average-poor**
Risk of violence	**Low**
Cost of living	**Low**
Student concessions	**OK**
Survival + 2 nights out	**£40-£50 pw**
Part-time work campus/town	**Good**

SOCIAL SCENE

STUDENTS' UNION They have made a £1-million investment in the Students' Union. There's a 1,000-capacity, award-winning **Amser/Time** nightclub (open to the public and students at a discount) and two bars: the 390-capacity **Main (Prif Far)** and the 100-capacity basement bar, **Jock's**. Prices are very low.

Typically, Wednesday is *Trash* @ **Main** (rock, metal, indie), Friday is Racubah, Saturday Elevate (hard house & hard trance); Friday is *Sugar & Spice* @ Amser/Time (chart hits). Otherwise, national tours - NME, orange, DJs: Rob Tissera, Mr Scruff, Scratch Perverts, Stanton Warriors, Norman J. Live music has brought Robert Plant, Toploader, Weetus, Hundred Reasons, Funeral for a Friend, Lamarr, Dreamteam, etc.

There are twenty-five student societies - Community Action (student volunteers) is probably the most popular, mountain walking and football close behind.

There's a Welsh-language student magazine called *Y ddraenen* and an English newspaper, *Seren*.

Political activity is high, but centred on such as Welsh language recognition. The drama soc, Rostra, is very popular.

The uni has its own professional chamber ensemble and student symphony orchestra, chamber choir, opera group, chamber ensembles and concert band.

SPORT Rock climbing, paragliding, mountain

ACCOMMODATION	
Guarantee to freshers	**100%**
Style	**Halls, flats**
Security guard	**All**
Shared rooms	**None**
Internet access	**All**
Self-catered	**All**
En suite	**All flats, not in hall**
Approx price range pw	**£66.50-£103.50**
Town rent pw	**£60**

biking, canoeing, sailing, and surfing are available as well as the usual team sports - rugby, hockey and football. Women's Rugby is traditionally strong. 1,500+ participate weekly in sporting activities. You will benefit from a Lottery-sourced, £4.5 million extension to the sports hall. There's great emphasis on sport, thanks to the Sports Science and PE courses. Outward-bound activities, such as mountaineering, are especially popular, as are rowing, sailing and canoeing. This is a small uni and so makes a poor showing in national team competitions, but it does its own thing with flair.

Town 'As far as towns go, we ain't no Liverpool or Birmingham,' says Becki Thurston, 'but that doesn't mean we're pants and boring. Although it's designated a city, it's diddy. The bonus is that we take over. There's nowhere doesn't feel like home.

Wherever you go, wherever you are, you'll bump into someone you know. Trouble is, people know who you snogged last night, even before you've sobered up enough to realise!'

A positive advantage of Bangor's size is that competition between pubs etc. is strong. So prices are low. Besides pubs - Irish, **Wether-spoons**, **Fat Cat** and late-night pub/clubs **Joot and Joop**, you'll find café bars, restaurants (Spanish, Italian, Greek, Chinese, Indian), and two more nightclubs - **Octagon** and **Bliss**.

For arts lovers the city offers a varied mix of classical concerts; there are regular visits from the BBC National Orchestra for Wales, other orchestras from afar, and from the Centre for Creative & Performing Arts.

PILLOW TALK

Six hundred and fifty new rooms opened in September 2008 and a further 450 in September 2009, all with en suite facilities. Nice, confident touch in offering summer-vacation halls accommodation to prospective undergraduates - with or without parents - to get a taste of the place. One hall exclusively for Welsh speakers.

GETTING THERE
- By road: A5, A55, A487; 90 minutes from M56.
- By rail: London Euston, 4:00; Birmingham New Street, 3:00; Manchester Oxford Road, 2:30; Liverpool Lime Street, 2:15.
- By coach: London, 8:00; Leeds, 6:15.

UNIVERSITY OF BATH

The University of Bath
Claverton Down
Bath BA2 7AY

TEL 01225 383019
FAX 01225 386366
EMAIL admissions@bath.ac.uk
WEB www.bath.ac.uk

Bath Students' Union
Claverton Down
Bath BA2 7AY

TEL 01225 386612
EMAIL sabbs@bath.co.uk
WEB www.bathstudent.com/

VAG VIEW

*B*ath is a small, happy science and business-based university with a huge, world-wide reputation built on its sandwich course provision, excellence in sport, and streamlined curriculum. Says Tom Alderwick, who is studying Politics and

Economics: 'The main reason I chose Bath is because of the sandwich degree. Most people here are doing sandwich courses.'

It is first choice for many capable of Oxbridge, although Bath's 3-star teaching rating for lecturers' support of students and small-size tuition groups (our star rating based on the Times Higher's Student

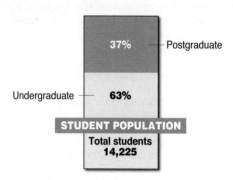

STUDENT POPULATION
Total students
14,225

37% — Postgraduate

Undergraduate — **63%**

Like so many at Bath, Tom's thing is not arts but sport. 'It stems from the reputation... Bath is one of the top three sports unis.'

Actually it came second only to Loughborough last year. It is a centre for International Sport, and the amazing facilities are used by many professional clubs. 'Bath rugby club use the gym up there at the Sports Training Village, and when there are events like the World Cup or Olympics, people come in and train as well.'

CAMPUS

The self-contained campus is situated 2 miles south-east of the city, at the top of Bathwick Hill. Being apart from the urban action is not considered a problem, as bright orange buses run regularly until 3 a.m., and facilities on campus are good. The buses are also cheap (£1.75 return; ten-trip and longer season tickets are also available).

A central building houses the Library and Learning Centre (with 24-hour access), the Careers Office and Students' Union, all set around The Parade, a walkway not unlike a shopping precinct.

Alas, the sixties concrete architecture does not look its best on a wet, wintry, foggy day. Tom's sentiments - 'I like the atmosphere of the campus, but the actual campus itself I just find so ugly' - are widely shared.

To Katie Mellors, a student of Business Administration from the North, even the famous Bath stone in town grates after a while: 'The City of Bath is in the South West of England, very close to Bristol. It is a beautiful city, lovely stone architecture, but after a while I craved to see good old fashioned red brick buildings. It is also very small, but if you take the time to look, there are little wonders around every corner. The train station is small but has good links with London and the rest of the country via Bristol, which is nearby and good for clubs and clothes shops cheaper than in Bath.'

Experience Survey) is a good deal lower than at either Oxford or Cambridge.

Nevertheless, overall student satisfaction is high - 88%. A similar proportion of the student body land graduate-level jobs within six months of leaving, and a very low drop-out rate (3%) completes the picture..

The complete absence of an Arts provision at Bath has an interesting effect. Says Tom: 'I wouldn't say that everyone is kind of like a science geek, but while I personally haven't had that much involvement with arts societies, people from my house last year were kind of involved,

UNIVERSITY/STUDENT PROFILE	
University since	**1966**
Situation/style	**City campus**
Student population	**14255**
Total undergraduates	**9030**
Mature undergraduates	**9%**
International undergrads	**15%**
Male/female ratio	**56:44**
Equality of opportunity:	
state school intake	**76%**
social class 4-7 intake	**18%**
low-particioation area intake	**4%**

and I guess science people here feel less restricted artistically than at a uni where the Drama Society is dominated by students who are studying the subject. We are not really worried about that at Bath, which is probably a plus. I think people are less scared about getting involved. I don't know personally how good the arts societies are, but I know people enjoy going along.'

FEES, BURSARIES

UK & EU Fees, 2009-10: £3,225 p.a. Bursaries are available for new students eligible for the full HE Maintenance Grant. For three decades Bath has offered sports scholarships. Also on offer are scholarships for students of chemistry, chemical engineering, modern languages and European studies.

STUDENT PROFILE

Thirty-four per cent are from public school, which is far greater than is the norm. There is also a preponderance of students from the South of

England, as Northerner Katie soon discovered: 'In terms of social groups and finding friends, I was a bit apprehensive about the amount of Southerners and how they already new lots of people here. However, everyone is so accepting and friendly, and they all love my Northern accent. Making friends here has been the easiest thing. Bath is an international university and caters for a wide range of cultures, hence they have an oriental shop and café, but they cater well beneath the surface too. Everybody mixes really well and you'll have lots of friends, no matter where you're from. The most noticeable social group is made up of sports types, but there is room for everyone. It is my experience that the sports socials are first class, Initiation and The Snowball being the most memorable.'

ACADEMIA & JOBS

Bath concentrates on seven areas - Sciences, Social Sciences (Economics, Politics, Psychology, Social Policy, Social Work, Sociology), Engineering, Pharmacy & Pharmacology, Business, Languages, and Sport.

The programmes are modular, consisting of self-contained units taught and assessed on a semester basis. The academic year is divided into two semesters.

'Lecturers are strict on the minor details, like punctuality,' says Katie. 'But in seminars you really feel close contact with them, and that they care about your progress. My work is not as pressurised as my friends', but be prepared to work hard. Bath has a reputation to uphold. The internet is key to your time here. Most communication is by email, and such as lecture slides are to be found on the net. There is a connection in each room in halls, which makes it all very quick and efficient, and the library is central to the campus, with excellent resources and help on hand when you need it.'

The benefits of the sandwich deal are clear, as Tom demonstrated when we asked what kind of placement a Politics and Economics undergraduate might expect: 'In my department you can either go for a political or a business placement. There's one offered by the House of Commons and the House of Lords, and there are quite a few in Brussels, political lobbying or doing something with the EU. Big accountancy firms offer work and some people go into banking. I've just recently sorted mine out. I have a year working for American Express.

'I'll be working in Victoria, in London, getting paid a salary of £18,000. I think it was Goldman Sachs offered a placement for £35,000, but most of them pay, I would say, between £15,000 and £20,000.

TEACHING SURVEY AT A GLANCE

Avg. UCAS points accepted	**420**
Acceptance rate	**12%**
Overall satisfaction rate	**88%**
Helpful/interested staff	★★★
Small tuition groups	★★★
Students into graduate jobs	**86%**

Teaching most popular with undergraduates:
Aerospace Eng., Architecture, Euro. Languages, Molecular Biology, Biochemistry, Pharmacology, Pharmacy (95%), Civil Eng. (94%), French, Iberian (93%), Automative, Mechanical, Manufacturing Eng. (92%), Politics (90%).

Teaching least popular with undergraduates:
Psychology (75%).

'American Express held first round interviews here on campus and then we went to the offices in London for further interview, and we had to give a presentation and have lunch. So yes, it's quite competitive.

'My house mate is doing Management with French and he has just sorted his placement to work in Paris for Barclays. My other house mate, she does Spanish, so for six months she is going to a university in Argentina and then for the next six months she is going to go to Spain, to a job there.'

Most popular teaching among students is in

RESEARCH EXCELLENCE

% of Bath's research that is
4* *(World-class) or* **3*** *(Internationally rated):*

	4*	3*
Pharmacy	**20%**	**40%**
Biological Sciences	**10%**	**40%**
Chemistry	**5%**	**55%**
Physics	**20%**	**50%**
Pure Mathematics	**25%**	**35%**
Applied Mathematics	**20%**	**50%**
Statistics	**20%**	**40%**
Computer Science	**25%**	**50%**
Electrical and Electronic Eng.	**25%**	**35%**
Chemical Engineering	**10%**	**45%**
Mech., Aero., Manufac. Eng.	**10%**	**45%**
Architecture/Built Environment	**25%**	**45%**
Business and Mgt Studies	**30%**	**40%**
Social Work, Policy & Admin.	**35%**	**40%**
Development Studies	**15%**	**30%**
Education	**15%**	**30%**
Sports-Related Studies	**15%**	**20%**
European Studies	**10%**	**35%**

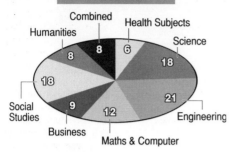

SUBJECT AREAS (%)

Combined — Health Subjects
Humanities — Science
Social Studies — Engineering
Business — Maths & Computer

Aerospace Engineering, Architecture, European Languages, Molecular Biology, Biochemistry, Pharmacology, Pharmacy, Civil Engineering, French, Spanish, Automative, Mechanical and Manufacturing Engineering, and Politics, in that order. No subject fell below a 75% positive student rating. Research is largely world class, or 3-star internationally rated by government inspectors, as our box on the previous page shows.

Students with disabilities and learning difficulties now have free access to state-of-the-art laptops that cater specifically for their learning needs. The Assistive Technologies Initiative enables students to use laptops containing software that can do everything from translating speech into written text, to helping people 'map' their thoughts and ideas.

The high 86% statistic of graduates into real graduate jobs after six months favours banking and accountancy, aircraft manufacture, the construction industry, architecture and engineering design, government, secondary and higher education, hospital and social work, pharmaceuticals, sport, and personnel.

Vectura, a company established by academics at the uni, is among the top four university spin-off companies in the UK. Now, a new Student Enterprise Centre gives students free access to the training, support and resources they need to turn their business ideas into reality. Based in the Students' Union, the Centre facilities include a suite of five computers, meeting rooms and two dedicated business support professionals as part of the Student Enterprise Team.

STUDENT SCENE

STUDENTS' UNION The Union's **Plug Bar** is open from 9 a.m. Monday to Friday, 12 p.m. at the weekend. There are six pool tables and games machines. Food includes the 2-minute Stone Willy's pizza and the 'All Day Champion' B.L.T. It's also the place to buy all your Union events tickets

such as *Score, Flirt!* and *Elements of Laughter* .

In Freshers' Week there's a different theme every night culminating with the infamous *Toga Party*, a rare opportunity to go out in public wearing just a bed sheet. The *Pub Crawl* is another highlight - the mission: to visit 20 of Bath's finest drinking establishments and, well, get drunk.

'Freshers Week was extremely well organised, which made settling in easier,' Katie recalls. 'Each kitchen group was assigned a crew to guide them through the first week and to life in Bath. The pub-crawl is legendary. Most fresher events were in the campus sports hall, and drinks were expensive, but with the drinking games with your freshers crew it soon became less of an issue. You will know at least 40 people before you even start your course.'

Nightclub **Element's** regular Wednesday night *Score* is followed on Friday by *Flirt!* and *4play* - the latter being four hours of preparatory fun (3-7pm). Regular theme nights include such as *Back to School, Fetish, Doctors and Nurses*.

Come Play is a new party night on Saturdays, the best chart, r&b and hip-hop dance tunes.

Besides the occasional comedy night, *Elements*

WHAT IT'S REALLY LIKE	
UNIVERSITY:	
Social Life	★★★★
Campus scene	**Busy, friendly**
Student Union services	**Professional**
Politics	**Union active**
Sport	**52 clubs**
National team position	**2nd**
Sport facilities	**Excellent**
Arts opportunities	**Good**
Student newspaper	**Impact**
Student radio	**URB**
Student Radio Awards	**4 in last 2 years**
Student TV	**CTV**
Nightclub	**Elements**
Bars	**Plug, Parade, Claverton Rooms**
Union ents	**Score, Funky Guppy, etc**
Union societies	**85**
Parking	**No 1st years**
CITY:	
Entertainment	★★★
Scene	**Average clubs, good pubs**
Town/gown relations	**Good**
Risk of violence	**Low**
Cost of living	**High**
Student concessions	**Good**
Survival + 2 nights out	**£75 pw**
Part-time work campus/town	**Excellent/good**

of Laughter, and one Thursday every month there's live bands or unplugged acoustic nights. Top D.J. nights occur on various Thursdays. Off campus it's **Po Nana/Down Town** on Mondays.

Then there's the Summer Ball, great bands, fairground attractions, street entertainment, jazz bands, sound systems.

TOWN Writes Katie of campus and city nightlife: 'I came to Bath from a large Northern city with a good nightlife, and I must admit it took a while to adjust to all that's worth going to in Bath. They only play cheese here, and I dare say that after four years I will think, if I never hear another cheese song again it will be too soon. But for now I am loving every minute of the social side to my degree. The clubs in town have cheap drinks and are safe. The main town night for students is on a Monday. Campus has its own nightclub for Wednesdays and Fridays, again playing cheese, and with fancy dress as a must!

'Despite the cheese and the small size of the clubs, Bath is a fantastic night out and this I put down to the people. You know almost everyone in the club and have such a laugh that you will not forget a single night out, either on campus or off.'

Says Tom: 'Student societies arrange socials, get buses to go to Bristol. The Economics Society arranges a bus and takes every one there and brings them home about 3 a.m.'

There are eighty-five societies on offer so it is really easy to get involved. The centre for arts is **The Arts Barn** - drama, dance, music, studio workshop space for visual arts and crafts. BUST is the drama society. There's a musicals society, opera, a choral society - 'not quite so elitist as the chamber choir'. They also have student bands and orchestras.

Media-wise, there's a weekly newspaper, *Impact*, a radio station, URB, which won two Bronze gongs in the 2008 student awards, and a TV station, CTV, with monitors installed in the Plug Bar. Politics brings societies for the three main parties, and the popular Debating Soc., into action.

SPORT There are fantastic sports facilities on campus, ranging from an Olympic size swimming pool, 8-lane athletics track, squash, badminton and tennis courts. They attract the sporting elite, but all the sports facilities are free to students. Right on campus there's a generous range of team pitches and no facility is more than a stroll away. The sports village complex, partly built with Lottery money, offers the floodlit running track; 50-metre and 25-metre pools; a 4-court tennis hall; 16 hard tennis courts; 2 synthetic grass pitches; a shooting range; sports hall; squash courts; a performance testing lab; weight training rooms; a physio centre.

Nor does all this professionalism keep the keen amateur away. Though it can be challenging getting a tennis court, a statistic, much bandied, is that 80% of students make use of what's on offer (there are 52 sporting clubs).

> **'Despite the cheese and the small size of the clubs, Bath is a fantastic night out and this I put down to the people.'**

PILLOW TALK

October 2008 saw the completion of Woodland a new complex of 355 premium en-suite rooms, including 24 large fully accessible study bedrooms for students with special requirements. A refurbishment programme of several campus residences reaches completion this year, the majority with newly fitted kitchens and updated bedrooms, the more expensive offering flat screen monitors and IP telephony.

Writes Katie: 'Once you have settled you can literally roll out of bed and go to lectures (I have been in my pyjamas). Houses in town are cheaper and more spacious, and they have a lounge of course, which is something I definitely miss.'

ACCOMMODATION	
Guarantee to freshers	**100%**
Style	**Halls**
Security guard	**Campus 24/7**
Shared rooms	**None**
Internet access	**All**
Self-catered	**All**
En suite	**Some**
Approx price range pw	**£70-£105**
City rent pw	**£65-£75**

GETTING THERE

☞ By road: M4/J18, A46.
☞ By rail: London Paddington or Southampton, 1:30; Birmingham, 2:15; Cardiff, 1:50.
☞ By air: Bristol Airport.
☞ By coach: London, Birmingham, 3:15

BATH SPA UNIVERSITY

Bath Spa University
Newton St Loe
Bath BA2 9BN

TEL 01225 875875
FAX 01225 875444
EMAIL enquiries@bathspa.ac.uk
WEB www.bathspa.ac.uk

Bath Spa University Students' Union
Newton St Loe
Bath BA2 9BN

TEL 01225 875588
FAX 01225 876151
EMAIL www.bathspsu.co.uk
WEB www.bathspasu.co.uk

VAG VIEW

*B*ath Spa, a University College since 1999 and a uni since 2005, came out of Bath Academy of Art, Bath College of Education and Newton Park College, the last two being teacher training colleges.

There are four faculties, Applied Sciences, Art and Music, Education and Human Sciences, and Humanities, on two campuses: Sion Hill and Newton Park.

Its defining character seems at first sight to be traditional arts - creative writing, drama, dance, film, fine art, music, design, etc., but there is a clever mix with humanities, appropriate not only to its continuing drive to educate teachers, but also to the responsibility Bath Spa feels to the practical matter of paid work for its budding artists.

A joint honours provision attaches

> *'I arrived a timid, not-sure-why-I-was-leaving-home type of person... if you have a shell to come out of, you'll discard it within weeks of coming here.'*

seriously good Business, Management and Cultural courses to Performance Arts, for example, so that when you look at where graduates end up, besides the cream going into artistic creative work, broadcast and other mainstream media and artistic areas, there is a graduate force not just surviving but building a career base in specialist retail, publishing, printing, government administration, and community and cultural work.

Proof of the pudding comes in the results of the National Student Survey, where 97% gave the thumbs-up to their Business and Management courses - made most popular in the university by the vote of student artists.

Sixty-six per cent of Bath Spa graduates find real graduate jobs in the first six months after graduation. Sure, Education (in particular primary school) remains a mainstay, but in fact it only accounts for around 8% of graduates. Health and food (diet and the food industry), and environmental science, are also key focuses of the provision.

Another terrific recommendation is the low drop-out rate (6%), and according to the Student Survey, 84% of students are at least satisfied with what goes down at Bath Spa.

UNIVERSITY/STUDENT PROFILE	
University since	**2005**
Situation/style	**City campus**
Student population	**7110**
Total undergraduates	**4505**
Mature undergraduates	**15%**
International undergrads	**1%**
Male/female ratio	**32:68**
Equality of opportunity:	
state school intake	**95%**
social class 4-7 intake	**30%**
low-participation area intake	**10%**

FEES, BURSARIES

UK & EU Fees p.a. £3,225. Bursaries for students in receipt of HE Maintenance grant, Scholarships for eligible students on some science-based courses.

See www.bathspa.ac.uk/prospectus/moneymatters/getting-money/bursaries.asp.

CAMPUSES

Newton Park is 4 miles west of the city in a landscaped saucer of Duchy of Cornwall countryside, an original Capability Brown design, with a Georgian manor house at its administrative hub and a cash dispenser, recently installed by the Students' Union. There are half hourly and late-night buses to and from town. The most extensive building programme in Bath Spa's history, amounting to £11 million provides a new Students' Union, library and ICT suites, a Performing Arts arena with a 214-seat theatre, rehearsal spaces, associated technical accommodation and changing facilities, a refectory, and a Creative Writing Centre

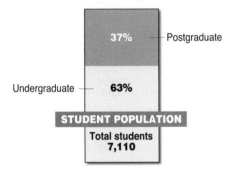

STUDENT POPULATION

Total students 7,110

- Postgraduate 37%
- Undergraduate 63%

housed in a 14th-century Gatehouse, renovated in collaboration with English Heritage.

Sion Hill (the Art and Design campus) is within walking distance of the city centre on the north side. It comprises a large modern building and the Georgian crescent Somerset Place, set in attractive grounds. A £3.5m scheme here promises new specialist workshops, art studios, library, refectory, etc.

STUDENT PROFILE

It is a small, quiet, supportive community, appealing particularly to females (68% of undergrads) and mature undergraduates (15%) One student told of its 'friendly, warming atmosphere.' She admitted, 'I arrived a timid, not-sure-why-I-was-leaving-home type of person... if you have a shell to come out of, you'll discard it within weeks of coming here.'

It is far from being some sort of specialist dumping ground for sensitive souls, however. Bath Spa comes out high in league table of new unis.

ACADEMIA & JOBS

Bath Spa University is a Centre for Excellence in Teaching and Learning for creative subjects, with particularly good resources and facilities. Course

TEACHING SURVEY AT A GLANCE

Avg. UCAS points accepted	**260**
Acceptance rate	**15%**
Overall satisfaction rate	**84%**
Helpful/interested staff	★★★★
Small tuition groups	★★★★
Students into graduate jobs	**66%**

Teaching most popular with undergraduates: Business, Management (97%), History, Food Studies (96%), Philosophy (95%), Education (93%), Biological Sciences, Geography, Sociology (91%), Enviro. Science, Psychology (90%).

Teaching least popular with undergraduates: Creative Arts (55%).

design displays individuality and flair. They are known for degrees leading to careers in the creative industries, and they are a major provider of teacher training.

There is a mix of seminars, lectures and workshops, also practical sessions in science subjects and performance-based subjects (music, performing arts, dance). Courses are modular in structure offering flexibility so that students can build up a programme of study to suit their particular interests and career aspirations. Full-time students take 120 credits each year (some core, some optional) from modules worth either 20 or 40 credits. Students have 12 hours formal contact time in Year 1. There is a 4-star rating for help and interest of staff and decent-size tutorials, quite a turn-round from the old days of poor student-staff ratios.

The Minerva virtual learning environment (using 'Blackboard' VLE software) allows students to access online teaching materials, and provides a range of other functions including announcements

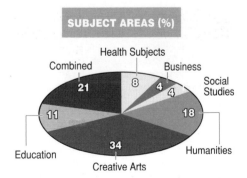

SUBJECT AREAS (%)

- Combined 21
- Health Subjects 8
- Business 4
- Social Studies 4
- Humanities 18
- Creative Arts 34
- Education 11

RESEARCH EXCELLENCE

% of Bath Spa's research that is
4* (World-class) or 3* (Internationally rated):

	4*	3*
Biological Sciences	**0%**	**0%**
Geography and Enviro. Studies	**0%**	**15%**
Psychology	**0%**	**5%**
Education	**0%**	**15%**
English Language and Lit.	**5%**	**25%**
Theology	**0%**	**10%**
History	**5%**	**40%**
Art and Design	**5%**	**15%**
Media	**10%**	**10%**
Music	**10%**	**20%**

from tutors, online discussion groups, an email tool, and other aids to communication.

By far the majority of the 30-odd per cent of Bath Spa graduates who find employment in Education do so as primary school teachers, some specialist music teachers among them, for music is another vital string to their bow.

At Newton Park, an academic interest in music is given a performance dimension at the **Michael Tippett Centre**, a 250-seater auditorium. But music technology is one of the fastest growing career opportunities.

Graduates are entering the recording industry, new media (web audio, sound design, game audio, VR), the broadcasting industry (composing for TV, film, radio, etc) and the music technology industry (product development, software design).

Bath Spa's relevant degree is the BA Creative Music Technology, and now new Foundation Degrees, many run in conjunction with partner FE colleges (eg Broadcast Media, Popular Music, Music Production) are available.

There are excellent facilities and well-used industry links. The degree is part of an impressive department, which includes a Foundation and BA degree in Commercial Music - performance and songwriting are key elements (students played their first live gig in January 2002) - a BA (Hons) Music and a BA Performing Arts.

Specialist facilities have been built for students of creative arts subjects as part of the Artswork project (Bath Spa's a Centre for Excellence in Teaching and Learning): MusicLab, DesignLab, BroadcastLab, FashionLab, PerformanceLab and PublishingLab.

All this sets the tone of the Bath Spa 'real world' approach throughout the curriculum, whether in arts courses or food, nutrition and health, from which graduates carve out careers in the food industry and the hotel and restaurant trade, and also in counselling, in hospital and in all sorts of human health activities.

New degree courses this year include Contemporary Circus and Physical Performance, Creative Media Practice, Further Education Management, Musical Theatre, and Professional Musicianship.

SOCIAL SCENE

New refectory, delicatessen, SU bar, lounge, shop and offices, as Bath Spa tooled up for life as a university: *Flirt!* on Wednesday, Friday and Saturday could be indie, metal, whatever - good nights, plus good jazz and live bands.

Said the SU: 'The campus estate is absolutely beautiful. Bath and Bristol are just a bus ride away. Small numbers create a real community aspect and a sense of belonging.

'The new SU is amazing - chill out in the afternoon over coffee and bacon sandwiches or get your groove on in the evening on one of the biggest dance floors and largest capacity clubs in Bath.'

PILLOW TALK

Seventy per cent of first year students can be accommodated in university accommodation, in self-catering halls located on or near campus. Off-

WHAT IT'S REALLY LIKE

UNIVERSITY:

Social Life	★★★
Campus scene	**Good scene**
Student Union	**Average**
Politics	**No**
Sport	**Feeble**
Arts opportunities	**Excellent**
Student magazine	**H20**
Bar/venue	**SU bar and lounge**
Union ents	**Cheese, jazz, live bands, karaoke**
Union societies	**25**
Most active society	**LGBT**
Parking	**None**
CITY:	
Entertainment	★★★
Scene	**Average clubs, good pubs**
Town/gown relations	**Good**
Risk of violence	**Low**
Cost of living	**High**
Student concessions	**Good**
Survival + 2 nights out	**£75 pw**
Part-time work campus/town	**Average/good**

site blocks between Newton campus and the city (both on a good bus route) are Waterside Court and Charlton Court. The off-site option for Sion Hill campers is Bankside House, although they too can opt for Waterside and Charlton Courts. Private rented houses are reserved for the unlucky 30% who don't make the cut. All accommodation is self-catered. Most have a security guard. Internet access assured.

GETTING THERE
☛ By road Newton Park: from London and east: M4/J18, A46, A4, A39 to Wells, turn left after 200 yards into Newton Park Estate. By road Sion Hill: M4/J18, A46, A420, first left to Hamswell, at second give-way take a right and second right into Landsdown Crescent, over crossroads, first right to Sion Hill on your right.

☛ By rail: London Paddington or Southampton, 1:30; Birmingham, 2:15; Cardiff, 1:50.
☛ By air: Bristol Airport.

ACCOMMODATION	
Guarantee to freshers	**70%**
Style	**Halls, flats**
Security guard	**Most**
Shared rooms	**Some**
Internet access	**All**
Self-catered	**All**
En suite	**Some**
Approx price range pw	**£75-£112**
City rent pw	**£65-£75**

UNIVERSITY OF BEDFORDSHIRE

The University of Bedfordshire
Polhill Avenue
Bedford MK41 9EA

TEL   01582 489286
FAX   01582 489323
EMAIL admission@beds.ac.uk
WEB www.beds.ac.uk

University of Bedfordshire Students' Union
Europa House
Luton LU1 3HZ

TEL 01582 743265
FAX 01582 457187
EMAIL [firstname.surname]@beds.ac.uk
WEB www.ubsu.ac.uk

VAG VIEW

*W*hen De Montfort University's Faculty of Education, Bedford campus, merged with Luton University in 2006 the new unit was re-named the University of Bedfordshire, and for the first time the county had its very own Centre of Higher Education.

De Montfort's Bedford campus had been spread across two sites - Landsdowne (Humanities) and Polehill (Sport and Education - the bit that is now Beds). There was an exceptional sense of community. It was a thriving, self-sufficient set-up, one we picked out as a model for larger institutions. And they were proud. They'd been national finalists in women's rugby at Twickenham, won the women's football, and were the first men's hockey finalists.

Luton Uni was a different story, beleaguered from the start. After they took university status in 1993, there were

associations with Exodus Collective, a free party movement running raves in disused warehouses to which 5,000 party people would flock, and someone joked that all you needed to get in to Luton was two Es, but now you needed two Es and a bag of amphetamine.

Then a Sunday newspaper tore into

UNIVERSITY/STUDENT PROFILE	
University since	**2006**
Situation/style	**Town campus**
Student population	**14550**
Total undergraduates	**12320**
Mature undergraduates	**54%**
International undergrads	**12%**
Male/female ratio	**38:62**
Equality of opportunity:	
state school intake	**99%**
social class 4-7 intake	**42%**
low-participation area intake	**10%**

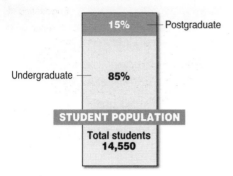

STUDENT POPULATION

- Postgraduate 15%
- Undergraduate 85%

Total students
14,550

them, calling them 'the lowest form of university life'. Quite unjust, we felt, and said so.

Today, the new set-up - the University of Bedfordshire - is putting its past behind it. In-depth academic flair is implicit in the recent 4-star and 3-star research ratings (world and international renown) for Earth Systems and Environmental Science, Computer Science, Business Management Studies (there are five new degrees in this area this year), Social Work, Sports-Related Studies, and English Language and Literature.

There is 80% student satisfaction, according to the National Student Survey, which is high, and their three stars for lecturer interest and helpfulness speaks of the revolution that is being undertaken here. 'Support,' they say, 'is one of our core values.'

No one at Bedfordshire is running away with thinking they have arrived at the summit. Teaching most popular with undergraduates is in Business, Complementary Medicine, Law, Marketing, Health, Computer, Social Work, and Social Psychology, but the highest rating is 89%, while the better universities have student appreciation well into the 90s for their top subjects. And the 12.6% drop-out rate still needs taming.

CAMPUS

Park Square is the main campus in the centre of Luton. It is home to a £5.5-million Media Arts Centre and a £7.8-million Learning Resources Centre. In 2010 it is undergoing a £74-million redevelopment, which will include new on-campus accommodation, and a new Student Centre. The new en-suite accommodation will

house 850 students.

There's a rural mansion a few miles away (Putteridge Bury), a conference centre and home to the Faculty of Management. Then there's a site in Castle Street in town for Humanities.

Bedford Campus is 20 miles away, 20 minutes by foot from Bedford town centre. Originally, this was the local sports college. Sixty million pounds has already been invested in new facilities - £20 million on student halls of residence, £8 million on a Physical Education and Sport Science Centre, and £6 million on a new Campus Centre, with a £4.5-million 280-seat theatre, studio, gallery and Fairtrade restaurant. The new accommodation - Liberty Park - has more than 500 en-suite rooms.

Students based at Luton & Dunstable and Bedford hospitals moved in to new teaching facilities at Butterfield Park campus in early 2008. Future developments will include simulation laboratories complete with fully functional theatres, ward, and clinic environments.

Students at Stoke Mandeville and Wycombe General hospitals are in the process of relocating to a new Buckinghamshire campus this year. These nurses mainly are welcome to enjoy the fun and games at the other campuses, but in reality they are out on their own. Says the university: 'The move will help consolidate our presence in Buckinghamshire and our commitment to delivering highly-commended quality courses.'

FEES, BURSARIES

UK & EU Fees, 2009-10: £3,225. There is a means-tested University Bursary of up to £842, and at the very least every student gets £319 p.a. If you get 280 UCAS points or more, with at least 200 at A2 level, you can apply to receive £1,050 a year. County and international standard sports scholarships (£320 and £1,050) are also available.

TEACHING SURVEY AT A GLANCE

Avg. UCAS points accepted	**220**
Acceptance rate	**24%**
Overall satisfaction rate	**80%**
Helpful/interested staff	★★★
Small tuition groups	★★
Students into graduate jobs	**78%**

Teaching most popular with undergraduates:
Business (89%), Complementary Medicine (88%), Law, Marketing , Health (86%), Business & Admin. Studies, Computer (83%), Social Work, Social Psychology (82%).

Teaching least popular with undergraduates:
Education Studies (58%).

Also, UK or EU applicants from one of their partner colleges may qualify for a scholarship of £320 per year. Finally, there are a number of 'special scholarships' to help defray the costs of being a student. See www.beds.ac.uk/money for more information.

STUDENT PROFILE

The student body is almost exclusively State School educated, with 42% coming from the traditional working classes and 10% from neighbourhoods that have never supplied undergraduates before. There is a 62% female population (largely nurses and primary school teachers and secondary PE with QTS), and 54% of undergraduates are 'mature'.

ACADEMIA & JOBS

Bedfordshire operates through six faculties: Business, Design & Technology, Health Care & Social Studies, Humanities, Management, Science & Computing, and Education. They are one of the largest providers of Initial Teacher Training in the UK. The School of Physical Education & Sport Sciences has 100 years teaching experience and a tradition of top marks at inspection.

> *Someone once joked that all you needed to get in was two Es, but now you needed two Es and a bag of amphetamine.*

Nursing is a large section of what the uni is about, and a popular route for non-hospital nurses is BSc Mental Health Nursing, and BSc Midwifery, which sit alongside other degrees like Health Science, Health Psychology, and BSc Psychology.

The top four career areas for graduates are primary education, social work, community & counselling activities, general secondary education, hospital and medical practice activities.

For many others, 'Media and sport are the big attractions,' as one student put it. They are indeed Top 10 providers to the radio/TV sector, and advertising, publishing, film and publishing take from Beds. in quantity.

Computer science, Business, and Management also feature strongly in the employments statistics, with one niche in particular in the travel operator provision. Graduates of the various Management degrees tend to become marketing managers and sales managers in large retail operations. Personnel is also a popular line via BSc Hons Human Resource Management.

Finally, there are jobs aplenty for graphic artists, designers and Illustrators, who follow their BA Graphic Design, Interior Design, and similar

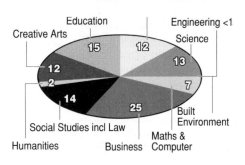

degrees

In total, there's a 78% rate of employment in real graduate jobs within six months of graduation.

SOCIAL SCENE

STUDENTS' UNION/LUTON Main Bar is the focal point, replete with all the usual trappings - arcade machines, a juke box, tellies and the like. An adjacent, courtyard, beer garden is very popular in the more clement months. The venue for most of the organised hedonism is **Sub Club,** in the basement of the building. Official student nights are *Cheeky Monkey Monday* @ town clubs **Liquid** and **Envy.** *Frenzy* is *Wednesday Sports Night* @ Sub Club (themed nights once a month). On Saturday, it appears, everyone goes home or to the **Hat Factory** for live bands. The brain-damaging effects of such revelry can be put to the test at the regular *Quiz Nights*, and students with bright ideas can also put the facilities to their own use if they can convince the powers that be that enough people will attend.

RESEARCH EXCELLENCE		
% of Bedfordshire's research that is **4*** *(World-class) or* **3*** *(Internationally rated):*		
	4*	3*
Earth Systems, Enviro. Sci.	5%	10%
Computer Science	0%	30%
Business and Mgt Studies	0%	15%
Social Work, Policy & Admin.	5%	45%
Sports-Related Studies	5%	15%
English Language and Lit.	15%	25%
Media	10%	40%

WHAT IT'S REALLY LIKE

UNIVERSITY:

Social Life	★★
Campus scene	**Urban good timers meet primary school teachers**
Student Union services	**Average**
Politics	**No**
Sport	**33 clubs**
National team position	**106th (Luton) 84th (Bedford)**
Sport facilities	**Good**
Arts opportunities	**Good drama; average art**
Student magazine	**Streaker**
Student radio	**Luton FM**
Nightclub	**Sub Club**
Bars	**Main Bar, Bar Soviet**
Union ents	**Sportsnight, themed nights, town clubnights**
Union societies	**26**
Most popular society	**Islamic (Luton), Dance (Beds)**
Parking	**Adequate**

TOWN:

Entertainment	★★★
Scene	**Pubs, clubs**
Town/gown relations	**Poor**
Risk of violence	**Average**
Cost of living	**Average**
Student concessions	**Good**
Survival + 2 nights out	**£32 pw**
Part-time work campus/town	**Average/good**

ACCOMMODATION

Guarantee to freshers	**95%**
Style	**Halls**
Security guard	**All**
Shared rooms	**Some**
Internet access	**All**
Self-catered	**All**
En suite	**None Luton, most Bedford**
Approx price range pw	**£80-£85**
Town rent pw	**£50-£65**

Galaxy Centre - with arcades, bowling, cinema - **Hat Factory** (theatre, UBSU Saturday band nights), and **Vauxhall Recreational Centre** for sports and gym access.

STUDENTS' UNION/BEDFORD The £14-million re-development brings a new Campus Centre with a 300-seat auditorium, in addition to sport facilities and accommodation. Bedford students spend a lot of their time at the union bar. Town club **Oxygen** and **Bar Soviet** are the official UBSU partners here. Wednesday nights are the stuff of legend. The official student night is Monday at **Oxygen**. It's **Esquires** for live bands like Guilly Mots and Electric Soft Parade, and the Corn Exchange for theatre, dance and orchestra. Bedford also traditionally has Freshers, Christmas and Summer balls.

Bedord town is a place for pubs and bars (more than clubs). **The Forresters** (traditional), **Pilgrims Progress** (excellent value with decent food), the **Bull Nosed Bat**, **The Bedford Lounge** (with dance floor), the **Litton Tree**, **The Rose** (pop venue with dance floor), **Venom** for r&b, **New York, New York** (bit cheesy). Late licensing to 2 or 3 a.m. is the thing. There are off-campus club nights at places like **Nexus**, and what was **Limehaus** is now a cool venue called **The Pad** - dance nights, big names, small but intimate. Nightclubs big with students are **Oxygen** (4 floors, masses of rooms, **Bar Soviet** (the student affiliated bar with themed nights), **Time Out** (small & funky, open till 5 a.m.) **Esquires** is a live music venue with a reputation for hosting new bands - even Cold Play and Oasis - before their time. **Corn Exchange** is a live venue for theatre, music and comedy.

SPORT The £8-million Physical Education and Sport Science Centre is set to train athletes for the 2012 Olympics at Bedford, so you'll be awed by the facilities. They feature regularly in the national student finals. Besides football, rugby and hockey, gongs in Mountain Biking and White Water Kayak Championships give the spread. The annual Rugby

Undisputed highlight of the year is the *May Ball*, which attracts thousands of the Luton faithful. The gowned and tuxedoed masses arrive in such numbers that the event is one of the country's largest. The likes of Prodigy, Tim Westwood, Jeremy Healy, Dodgy, Space and the Bootleg Beatles have rocked their world, while casinos, funfairs and top nosh add to the experience.

Most active societies, of which there are 26 in all, include Islamic, Darts, Christian Union, Creative Writing. Media-wise, there's magazine Streaker (student life laid bare) and radio station, Luton FM. Town/Luton 'Luton is a brilliant in-between town,' said Becky Hill. 'We have access to London in less than an hour, and Milton Keynes is brilliant for shopping.' If this sounds a bit of a back-handed compliment, it is. Luton is not a place you'd go out of your way to spend time in. But there are pubs galore and a handful of clubs. Most popular club is **Liquid**. Bars - **The Park**, **Riley's** for pool, The

Sevens is as famous as it is notorious.

PILLOW TALK

In Luton, the Student Village lies within staggering distance of the Union, town centre and lecture halls, and offers secure accommodation to 1,600 students in eleven separate halls, single-sex and mixed flats, each with shared kitchen, laundry facilities, and bathroom. Several flats are designed for students with disabilities. With around 25% of students living in uni-managed accommodation close by, the town centre feel almost like a campus.

Twenty million pounds has been invested in accommodation at the Bedford campus. Liberty Park now has upwards of 500 new, en-suite rooms. By September 2010, a further £40 million will have been spent on new en-suite accommodation for 850 students at Luton.

GETTING THERE

☛ By road: M1/J10t.
☛ By rail: King's Cross, 40 mins; Nottingham, 1:45; Oxford, 2:15; Birmingham New Street, 2:30.
☛ By air: London Luton Airport.
☛ By coach: London, 1:15; Manchester, 5-6:00.

BIRKBECK COLLEGE, LONDON

Birkbeck College
University of London
Malet Street
London WC1E 7HX

TEL 020 7631 6000
FAX 020 7631 6270
EMAIL admissions@admin.bbk.ac.uk
WEB www.bbk.ac.uk

Learn as you earn – Birkbeck College, founded in 1823 as the London Mechanics' Institution, became a school of London University in 1920. It provides part-time degrees for adults engaged otherwise during the day.

COLLEGE PROFILE	
College of London Uni since	**1920**
Situation/style	**City site**
Student population	**18480**
Undergraduates	**15055**
Accommodation	**Limited, in**
University of London halls of residence	
See www.halls.london.ac.uk	

FACULTIES/SCHOOLS:
English & Humanities; History, Classics & Archaeology; History of Art, Film & Visual Media; Languages, Linguistics & Culture, Law, Philosophy, Politics & Sociology

STUDENT BIRMINGHAM – THE CITY

Birmingham has shaken off its grey image to incredible effect in the last decade. Developments right across Britain's second city total hundreds of millions of pounds. Improved social and shopping facilities carry the bonus of better graduate job prospects and mean that whatever you're after from your student career, Birmingham can probably supply.

The most dramatic recent development has to have been Birmingham's **Bull Ring Centre**. There's been a market here at least since 1154, when Peter de Birmingham, a local landowner, obtained a Royal Charter for a cattle and food market. In 1964 a new concrete-smothered mixed market of indoor shops and outdoor stalls was built, a design unintegrated with the city that proved to be locked into its time and of questionable practical form. In 2000 it was reduced to a hole in the ground, and then recently it opened anew in spectacular form to public applause. The big name designers and retailers, like **Selfridges**, have flocked their in droves, and Birmingham Retail has been resurrected, the time the whole operation took to complete giving the rest of Brum's shopping world a chance to flourish, with such as **Mailbox** offering us a chance to drool at **Harvey Nichs**, Armani, DKNY, etc, even if many students will stick to the pedestrianised areas around New Street and the Pallasades, where every high street store you could want is juxtaposed with designer off-cut stores and street markets.

CAFES, PUBS, CLUBS

Aston students report, 'There are so many places

to go, and so much to do that you will always be spoilt for choice... Spend an evening in a canal-side café, pub or restaurant, take a trip to the cinema, theatre or ballet or laugh the night away at the **Glee Comedy Club**. The Broad Street, Brindley Place/Mailbox area is particularly popular with our students and has lots of places to eat and drink beside the canals, for example **The Works**, **Flares** (2 floors of cheese), **Hard Rock Café**, **Bar Epernay** (rotating piano), **Fifty Two Degrees North**, the pricier **Zinc** and Aussie-themes **Walkabout** (amongst many others). Rumour has it that there are 100 pubs and bars within a one-mile radius of the Aston University Campus – **The Square Peg** (Wetherspoons), **Bar Med**, **Chambers**, **Sack of Potatoes** (facing Aston Uni), **Gosta Green** (It's A Scream), the stylish **RSVP Bar**...the list is endless. Numerous pre-clubbers like **Poppy Red**, **Ipanema**, **The Living Room**, and **SoBar** are also open late, as you would expect from a real entertainment city like Birmingham. The bars, cafés and clubs at **The Arcadian Centre** (near the Chinese Quarter) are also popular with students.

Birmingham is bursting with clubs playing anything from dance, house, drum 'n' bass and jungle, to hard rock, 70s, 80s, lounge, soul, jazz and garage. **The Que Club** (one of the largest clubs in the UK) alas is no more, but clubs like **The Sanctuary**, **The Medicine Bar**, **Bakers**, new club **Air** (home to Godskitchen), **The Works** and **Bobby Brown's** play host to top DJs and attract clubbing aficionados from across the UK in their coachloads.

LIVE

The recently opened **Birmingham Academy** is the best local venue – it's one of the essential stops on any band's UK tour, its reputation boosted far and wide in 2001 by Radio 1's hosting most of its One Live in Birmingham events there.

The **Wolverhampton Civic**, just a short train ride away, is still seen as a main Midland live venue, and the **NEC** is equally popular with bands of U2 or S Club proportions. In the smaller venues expect massively varying music styles and quality. **Ronnie Scott's** offers more than just jazz, whilst the **Fiddle and Bone** is a pub with a plethora of acts for free – from tribute bands to student musos

through to Beethoven. Further into the backstreets you'll find a glut of pubs with fascinating (but sometimes frightening) live acts.

COMEDY, THEATRE, ARTS

Judging by the success of venues like the **Glee Club**, the new rock 'n' roll this may be. The venue attracts the best comic newcomers and the established talents of Eddie Izzard and Harry Hill – all for under a fiver if you go on a student night.

At the newly-revamped **Hippodrome** or **Alexandra Theatre** can be seen an array of Lloydesque and other West End shows, as well as the magnificent Welsh National Opera.

In the **Symphony Hall**, the renowned City of Birmingham Symphony Orchestra resides, playing host also to hundreds of international performers and offering a huge variety of classical music all year round.

For smaller fry the **Midlands Arts Centre**, or **MAC** as it is known, nestles comfortably on the edge of Cannon Hill Park near the University of Birmingham. With its combination of theatre, exhibitions, cinema and a damn fine bar it offers excellent choice and value. **The Electric Cinema**, showing arthouse, world and classic cinema in a charming setting, is the place to go if you want to see something different, although if it's Hollywood blockbusters you're after the **Odeon**, **UGC** and **Starcity** complexes offer about six billion different films, allegedly on twice as many screens.

For theatre **The Rep** in town has come in for a great deal of well-deserved praise lately with their showcase for new work, **The Door**, and also show fantastic productions in their main theatre. Stratford-upon-Avon is but a short train ride away, but watch out for the RSC's value for money student trips to productions there. For community productions (usually) as good as the professionals, check out the **Crescent Theatre**, offering Shakespeare and other productions.

For art you are spoilt in Brum, **The Barber Institute** on the University of Birmingham's campus is astounding. For more modern exhibitions head for **Ikon** or **The Angle** galleries.

Crucially all these places offer heavy discounts for students. Life with a 10% discount is what being a student is all about.

UNIVERSITY OF BIRMINGHAM

The University of Birmingham
Edgbaston
Birmingham B15 2TT

TEL 0121 415 8900
FAX 0121 414 7159
EMAIL admissions@bham.ac.uk
WEB www.bham.ac.uk

Birmingham Guild of Students
Edgbaston Park Road
Birmingham B15 2TU

TEL 0121 251 2300
FAX 0121 251 2301
EMAIL info@guild.bham.ac.uk
WEB www.guildofstudents.com/

VAG VIEW

*B*irmingham is the original 'red-brick' uni, with all that that entails beyond its masonry - none of the snobbery attached to Oxbridge and for many a reputation second only to it, though some from the softer south may recoil at the city. 'My first impression,' said Sorrel from the Garden of Kent, 'was that it didn't look to me to be very nice. I mean at home it's all countryside and really, really quiet and pretty, and then Birmingham is completely the opposite, especially where students live in their second and third years [Selly Oak].'

Nevertheless, she gave her approval of the campus itself, which is away from the urban hubbub: 'I think it is a very impressive campus. You know, it's all sort of red brick, old buildings. But then you have also really modern buildings, the sports science facilities have been recently built.' Sorrel is studying Sport. 'And right in the centre of the campus by the main library there is a nice sort of green area with lots of benches where you can sit and work on the grass, so it's quite communal.'

So much for the aesthetics. Birmingham took 75th place in the World Top 200 Universities, coming 12th among British universities, just behind Glasgow, but ahead of Sheffield, St Andrews and Leeds. It is a popular first choice and for the top flight candidate, a useful back-up. In the recent assessment of the research capabilities of British universities, it achieved yet again an impressive list of 4- and 3-star results - world class and international renown across the board from Epidemiology to English (see our Research Excellence box two pages on).

But chipping away at the coal-face of a

UNIVERSITY/STUDENT PROFILE	
University since	**1900**
Situation/style	**Campus**
Student population	**30415**
Total undergraduates	**18480**
Mature undergraduates	**11%**
International undergrads	**9%**
Male/female ratio	**43:57**
Equality of opportunity:	
state school intake	**78%**
social class 4-7 intake	**22%**
low-participation area intake	**7%**

subject by way of research is not teaching it, and when asked, students gave their lecturers only average applause for hands-on help and interest and personal tuition opportunity, while recommending the following among the best in the teaching: Human & Social Geography (100% gave this the thumbs-up), Dentistry, Biochemistry, Health subjects, Physics & Astrophysics, Maths, Law, Economics, Media, Business Studies, Physics, Sports Science, Electronic & Electrical Engineering, European Languages, and certain subjects allied to Medicine (there's Nursing and Physiotherapy on offer).

Less enthusiasm was forthcoming for the teaching of Medicine itself (72%), although aspects of the subject featured strongly in the recent research assessment. And, as frequently elsewhere, Social Work got caned. A mere 64% of undergraduates gave it the nod.

As a Birmingham graduate you've got a 75% chance of getting a graduate-level job within six months of leaving. The medics and nurses dominate the employment stats, with nearly 400 graduates going into hospital work of some sort. Then come jobs in the Civil Service - central and local government, in specialist retail occupations, social work, community & counselling activities, the hotel & restaurant industry (mainly through Biological Sciences), accounting, personnel, banking, primary, secondary and higher education, dental practice, software consultancy & supply, etc.

Overall, 85% of students said they were satisfied with the Birmingham experience, and there's only a 5% drop-out rate.

CAMPUS
The self-contained campus lies a couple of miles south of the city in leafy Edgbaston. Parking is not encouraged.

FEES, BURSARIES
UK & EU Fees, 2009-10, £3,225 p.a. for first degrees. Bursaries for all students whose family income is £32k or less. University scholarships are available for those who qualify for the HE Maintenance Grant and who have the requisite UCAS tariff points; also subject scholarships in e.g. physics, engineering, computer science.

STUDENT PROFILE
There's a high (22%) public school intake, though not as high as Oxbridge, Bristol, Durham. Says Sorrel: 'I'd say the student population is quite diverse. You have got people from all different races, and then you have got quite a few private school people, but also you have state school people. There is definitely a good mix.'

Southerners think that Brum is north enough, but not too far north. Northerners, bored with Manchester and Leeds, see it as the next best city without London's expense. Thanks to strong overseas links there's also a large international community. The gist is that there are loads of people with interests sympathetic to yours at Birmingham, and you'll meet them through lectures, accommodation or socialising.

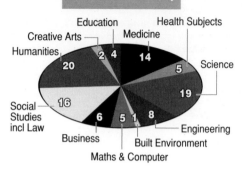

SUBJECT AREAS (%)

Education — 4
Health Subjects — 14
Creative Arts — 2
Medicine
Humanities — 20
Science — 5
Social Studies incl Law — 16
19
Business — 6
Maths & Computer — 5
1
Built Environment — 8
Engineering
Science — 19

In an effort to ease the plight of disabled students, the uni has an action plan to adapt and re-design facilities and access points, to increase disability staffing, expand the equipment pool, assistive technology in libraries, availability of specialist software, more support workers, etc.

For international students, there's now a 'Welcome Week' induction programme before the

TEACHING SURVEY AT A GLANCE	
Avg. UCAS points accepted	**400**
Acceptance rate	**13%**
Overall satisfaction rate	**85%**
Helpful/interested staff	★★★
Small tuition groups	★★★
Students into graduate jobs	**75%**

Teaching most popular with undergraduates:
Human & Social Geography (100%), Dentistry, Biochemistry, Nursing (96%), Physics & Astrophysics (95%), Maths (93%), Law, Economics (92%), Media, Business Studies, Physics, Sport (91%), Electronic & Electrical Eng., European Languages (90%).

Teaching least popular with undergraduates:
Medicine (71%), Social Work (64%).

start of term, and three full-time Student Advisers and free lessons in English during term time.

ACADEMIA & JOBS
Involvement with the world of work is an aspect of a number of courses, and the proximity of important industries and businesses, as well as artistic nuclei, is key to the academic provision. Even the Arts School non-vocational courses give special attention not just to what is studied, but how. Skills such as organisation, analysis,

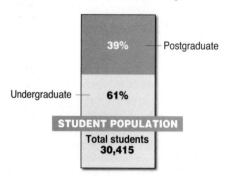

39% — Postgraduate
Undergraduate — 61%

STUDENT POPULATION
Total students
30,415

presentation, communication and problem-solving are to the fore.

The degree in Medicine is the 4/5-year MBCgB. There's a Black Country strategy in partnership with hospital trusts in Wolverhampton, Dudley, Sandwell and Walsall. 340 - 360 Tariff points (i.e. minimum AAB grades) normally achieved in Year 13 from three A levels or equivalent normally including two GCE science A levels - Chemistry and one of Biology, Maths, Physics. Biology at a minimum of AS is compulsory. For dentists, it's the 5-year BDS; entry ABB-AAB.

Birmingham is one of the few unis offering non-Law graduates a 2-year full-time or 3-year part-time Senior Status Law Degree. All candidates must sit the National Admissions Test for Law (LNAT).

It is not necessary to take a degree to become a qualified accountant any more than it is to become a solicitor, but Birmingham is the big graduate provider in this sector, with Warwick and Durham not far behind. At the Business School A level requirements are high, and conceptual, analytical, ICT and problem-solving skills are to the fore, as are communication/discursive skills and the ability to work on one's own. Birmingham also lead in getting graduates jobs as tax experts and consultants. For a job in banking, look at the BSc Money, Banking & Finance plus one year (well spent) to combine with French, German, Italian, Portuguese or Spanish.

Note this language interest; it's characteristic of all kinds of courses at Birmingham. The department is also high in the pecking order for graduates wanting jobs as interpreters, and leads many into the area of human resource management.

Would-be electrical, electronic and telecommunications engineers note that full marks in the old teaching assessments, high praise in the National Student Survey and a good reputation for research put the department high on any discerning applicant's list. And there's a Business Management orientation available for most of what's on offer.

Music is another niche area. An amazing 50% of their Music research is world-class (4 star), 35% of international stature (3 star). There's a Centre for Early Music Performance & Research, excellent rehearsal facilities and a brilliant Electro-Acoustic Music Studio, which is worth exploring in detail on the web. Five different degree routes are offered.

They are also up there with the best in Psychology and Sport, both of which enjoy 25% 4-star and 35% 3-star ratings. The sport degrees are Sport & Exercise Sciences; Sport, Physical

RESEARCH EXCELLENCE

% of Birmingham's research that is
4* *(World-class) or* **3*** *(Internationally rated):*

	4*	3*%
Cardiovascular Medicine	5%	35%
Cancer Studies	15%	65%
Infection and Immunology	10%	40%
Other Clinical Subjects	20%	55%
Epidemiology/Public Health	10%	50%
Health Services Research	15%	50%
Primary Care	35%	30%
Psych., Neurosci, Clin. Psychol.	5%	20%
Dentistry	10%	50%
Biological Sciences	10%	40%
Earth Systems/Enviro. Sci.	15%	50%
Chemistry	10%	50%
Physics	20%	40%
Pure Mathematics	15%	40%
Applied Mathematics	10%	35%
Computer Sci.and Informatics	30%	45%
Electrical and Electronic Eng.	10%	50%
Chemical Engineering	20%	45%
Civil Engineering	10%	55%
Mech., Aero., Manufac. Eng.	20%	50%
Metallurgy and Materials	15%	60%
Town and Country Planning	10%	40%
Geog. and Enviro. Studies	15%	40%
Archaeology	10%	40%
Economics and Econometrics	15%	50%
Business and Mgt Studies	20%	35%
Law	15%	45%
Politics/International Studies	5%	40%
Social Work, Policy & Admin.	15%	45%
Sociology	5%	25%
Development Studies	10%	25%
Psychology	25%	55%
Education	10%	35%
Sports-Related Studies	25%	35%
American Studies	20%	25%
Middle East and Afric. Studies	20%	40%
European Studies	20%	25%
French	10%	35%
German, Dutch, Scandinavian	15%	45%
Italian	15%	35%
Iberian and Latin American	5%	45%
English Language and Lit.	25%	35%
Classics, Ancient History, etc.	20%	30%
Philosophy	5%	40%
Theology	15%	45%
History	20%	40%
History of Art, Architec. Design	30%	40%
Drama, Dance, Perform. Arts	15%	50%
Music	50%	35%

Education & Coaching Science, Sports Science & Materials Technology. Says sporty Sorrel: 'I really liked the sound of the course at Birmingham. Also,

I do athletics and cross country and the coach for athletics at Birmingham is the Great Britain coach. He invited me to go and train with them and the athletes showed me around the uni. I decided that for my running it would be really good. I want ultimately to become a PE teacher.'

The specialist Applied Golf Management Studies assumes a handicap on entry of 4.4 or less (this is a PGA requirement). Coaching is a key element and you'll be expected to take up a summer placement in the community. Not a bad way to spend three years. You might consider their very strong student media as compatible in career terms.

SOCIAL SCENE

GUILD OF STUDENTS The main source of non-academic entertainment on campus is the Student Union. By day they offer numerous eateries and bars, from **Joe's**, the typical trendy student bar, to the delicious hot food of **Café Connections**.

There's the chance to join one of over 150 societies, and a huge range of student services (legal advice, local info from the ARC (Advice & Representa-tion Centre - currently in refurb.), part-time job info at the Job Zone, etc).

Media-wise Birmingham is top notch, everything together in the same spot - magazine, newspaper, radio and TV. GTV won two Bronze gongs in the NASTA awards this year. Radio & TV broadcasting and broadcast journalism are, like paper journalism, intensely competitive areas. Birmingham does well employment-wise for students, it has a good Media, Culture & Society degree in its Social Sciences faculty (which features, too, in Joint Hons), but the very fine student media set-up is also instrumental.

Some freshers prefer the hall bars to the Guild, before moving on to one of the city-centre clubs and bars. Students living in neighbouring Selly Oak or Harbourne frequent the many local student pubs and balti houses in those areas, as well as the most popular city club nights.

Guild nights are OK, however, and the nightclub, **The Underground** is legendary. There's also **Deb Hall**, used for full-building nightclub events, plays, dance shows and formal events, and the bars - **Joe's** and **Beorma**, and **Cybercity** - games room, pool, etc.

Typically, there's Curryoke Thursdays (karaoke for free curry for 2), theme party

> *Birmingham is a big, bustling, happening place and there is that self-same disinterested, confident air that you notice at all our best universities. If you don't enjoy a three-year spell here, it is unlikely to be Birmingham's fault.*

WHAT IT'S REALLY LIKE	
UNIVERSITY:	
Social Life	★★★★★
Campus scene	**Traditional, busy, cosmopolitan**
Student Union services	**Good**
Politics	**Activity high**
Sport	**Key; 43 clubs**
National team position	**3rd**
Sport facilities	**Very good**
Arts opportunities	**Film excellent; drama, dance, music, art good**
Student newspaper	**Redbrick**
Student magazine	**Bugged**
Student radio	**Burn FM**
Student TV	**Guild TV**
TV Awards 2008	**2 awards**
Nightclub	**The Underground, Deb Hall**
Bars	**Joe's, Beorma**
Union ents	**Theme nights, comedy, drum 'n' bass, old skool, live bands**
Union societies	**150+**
Most active society	**Rock Soc**
Parking	**Poor**
CITY:	
Entertainment	★★★★★
Scene	**Excellent**
Town/gown relations	**Average**
Risk of violence	**High**
Cost of living	**High**
Student concessions	**Excellent**
Survival + 2 nights out	**£75 pw**
Part-time work campus/town	**Average/excellent**

nights at Joes on Friday - Joe's Presents... (*Bad Taste, Tequila Night, 999 Emergency Services*, etc), and *Fab 'n' Fresh* at Joes and The Underground on Saturday.

On campus, artistic input is high. Across drama, dance, music and art, extra-curricular societies are very active. The Film Society is excellent. Musically, there's a chamber orchestra, an orchestra of 100 and a choir of 220. For art there's **The Barber Institute** - founded in 1932 it incorporates both Fine Art and Music departments and has been described as 'one of the finest small picture galleries in the world'. There's also a musical theatre group which nurtures, milks and dispenses talent that abounds among students. If you're into theatre, Birmingham is one of the places to be. There's a Guild group and a Drama Dept group in the uni's **Studio Theatre**; students perform all over the city (often before taking their productions to the Edinburgh Fringe), and there's a student humour night at the **Glee Club** in town.

If you do find yourself dipping into the overdraft it's easy to find a job at the Guild, where students are given decent wages for bar work, security, marketing, and other jobs. Alternatively, businesses around the city always want flexible, enthusiastic part-timers. Most of them advertise in the Guild's Job Zone.

SPORT Birmingham came 3rd in university sports last year. Only Loughborough and Bath did better. This is their usual position. **The Munrow Sports Centre's** mission statement 'to enhance the sporting experience of the university by providing opportunities at all levels' sums up the sporting situation. For the casual athlete the Active Lifestyles Programme offers weekly courses in martial arts, swimming, aerobics and team games.

The Athletic Union is made up of 40+ sports clubs, each with a qualified coach. Clubs exist also at inter-departmental and inter-hall levels. Interests are more than catered for by the 25m pool, two gyms, a climbing wall and full-size running track, as well as two floodlit, synthetic pitches, physiotherapy and sports science support, and a Fitness Services Unit for all levels.

Off-campus, 5 miles from home, there are seventy acres of pitches served by coaches and minibuses, and by Lake Coniston in Cumbria, 170 miles away, they have a Centre for Outdoor Pursuits (watersports, mountaineering, mountain biking, etc).

The university supports 30 sports scholarships at international level.

TOWN Says Sorrel: 'Birmingham is obviously known for good night life, so anyone here has a good social experience at university. The clubs are all on Broad Street. You quite often get bar crawls, and you can do that on the one street. Students from the Food College, Birmingham City University, and Aston University all tend to go to the same bars and clubs and integrate with one another.' The city does have less desirable areas (name a city that doesn't) but the average student has little contact with them, and if you're sensible about sticking in groups after dark and not flashing your cash around you shouldn't have any problems. As in all student areas there are complaints from disgruntled locals about kick-out time noise and student mess, but the Guild liaises with residents and police to keep the peace.

PILLOW TALK

'Halls are dotted all over the place,' says Sorrel. 'They are all reasonably close. I was in one called Tennis Courts which was about a ten minute walk onto campus, and the majority of them are about ten minutes away, but there are some in the city centre. One I went to - IQ5 - was really modern and nice, but you have to get a bus or train in. It's just behind Broad Street, so really close to the bars and clubs. For the first year definitely it's better to be close to campus, I would say.'

Which hall is most likely to appeal to a public school type? 'I would say Shackleton. Tennis Courts and Shackleton are quite close to each other.' However, there is also the ultra posh Jarratt Hall, boasting 620 en-suite bedrooms

Most freshers live in university accommodation. The main area is the Vale, a beautiful grassy bit set around a lake which houses catered and self-catered halls, and the Hub Centre (new in 2004) with two bars, eating areas, welfare and committee rooms. Other self-catered halls are either adjacent to the main campus or a bus journey away (The Beeches and Hunter Court).

ACCOMMODATION	
Guarantee to freshers	**100%**
Style	**Halls, flats**
Security guard	**CCTV, Security Centre, police.**
Shared rooms	**Some**
Internet access	**All**
Self-catered	**Most**
En suite	**Some**
Approx price range pw	**£72-£140**
City rent pw	**£85-£95**

GETTING THERE

☛ By road: A38. Avoid entry through suburbia from the M40; instead use M42/J1, A38.
☛ By rail: London Euston, 1:40; Bristol Parkway or Sheffield, 1:30; Liverpool Lime Street, Manchester Piccadilly,1:40; Leeds, 2:15. Frequent trains from New Street to University Station.
☛ By air: Birmingham Airport.
☛ By coach: London, 2:40; Bristol, 2:00; Manchester, 2:30.

BIRMINGHAM CITY UNIVERSITY

Birmingham City University
Franchise Street
Perry Barr
Birmingham B42 2SU

TEL 0121 331 5595
FAX 0121 331 7994
EMAIL choices@bcu.ac.uk
WEB www.bcu.ac.uk

Birmingham City Students' Union
The Union Building
Perry Barr
Birmingham B42 2SU

TEL 0121 331 6801
FAX 0121 331 6802
EMAIL students.union@bcu.ac.uk
WEB www.birminghamcitysu.com

VAG VIEW

*B*irmingham City University, as the old *Central England is now to be called (and let's not get into the £1.5-million-ish controversy about its re-naming) is a huge, urban conglomeration of sites, incorporating Business, Engineering & Technology, Built Environment, Law & Social Sciences, Computing, Health, the Birmingham Institute of Art & Design, the Acting School, and two little gems - the Jewellery School and the Birmingham Conservatoire.*

Student sabbaticals have always told us, 'We're a really friendly university, whichever campus you study on and wherever you live.' This is undoubtedly true, but the main campus, Perry Barr, where they do the whole cheesy student thing, is not the centre of the universe for everyone at BCU. If you are studying music at the world-renowned Conservatoire, for example, you tend to avoid Perry Barr like the plague, and have your own very good time doing so.

Says Tim Wilkinson: 'The thing is split up into so many different colleges, all quite far apart. A lot of the places I know of, but have never ventured anywhere near. Nor would I. We all have our own section.'

When you go to an Open Day you hear about 'the different Student Union clubs and stuff, but the trouble is that most of them are to do with Perry Barr.' The SU sabbaticals do a great job putting up posters at the various satellite campuses about what's happening at HQ, but it does little to bring the whole student body together.

So, what you have at BCU is a federation, and the character of the place is not about to change - £150 million has been

UNIVERSITY/STUDENT PROFILE	
University since	**1992**
Situation/style	**Civic**
Student population	**24460**
Total undergraduates	**19470**
Mature undergraduates	**46%**
International undergrads	**8%**
Male/female ratio	**46:54**
Equality of opportunity:	
state school intake	**98%**
social class 4-7 intake	**45%**
low-participation area intake	**15%**

allocated to the building of yet another city centre campus, in the Eastside district of Birmingham.

As a result, statistics which treat BCU as a single, unified item, may not be accurate for your campus.

At the Conservatoire, percussionist Tim gets an amazing 40 hours of 1-on-1 tuition in a year. His girlfriend Katie, who is a pianist, gets 35 hours with one tutor 1-on-1 and 5 hours with another. It is a very personal scene at the Conservatoire. 'You build up personal relationships with the teachers, they are happy for you to go and find them at any time, they know who you are, they know what you are doing.' This is not the rule across the whole university, which returned a very poor 2-star rating for interest and helpfulness of staff and size of tuition groups.

It is important, therefore, if you are considering applying to BCU, to research the particular subject and college to which you are applying, as if it was quite distinct from the rest.

FEES, BURSARIES

UK & EU Fees for 2009/10 £3,225. Students in lower income brackets will be eligible for grants for living costs, also bursaries are available to anyone receiving a full or partial maintenance grant. See www.bcu.ac.uk/prospective/finance.

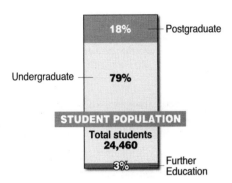

Postgraduate 18%

Undergraduate 79%

STUDENT POPULATION
Total students
24,460

Further Education 3%

STUDENT PROFILE

As diverse as its campus sites, but with the emphasis clearly on work-purpose and real-world living. Many are mature, many local and many from overseas, and UCE far exceed their Government benchmarks for recruiting from under-represented groups in higher education.

CAMPUS SITES & FACULTIES

A CCTV system covers each site. 150 cameras are constantly monitored and the system is key to supporting the work of a 70-strong security team to ensure a safe environment in which to study.

PERRY BARR Main campus. Location: north of city; approach via M6/M5 Junction 7 and A34 Walsall Road. Access to city: 15 minutes by bus plus rail link to Birmingham New Street. Accommodation: two halls for 850 students - the Coppice and Oscott Gardens (en suite); both self-catering. Bars: **Bar 42**, pub/food in daytime, nightclub/venue in the evening. Faculties: Business School; Education; Law, Humanities, Development & Society; and Health. The Department of Media and Communication, part of the Birmingham Institute of Art & Design (BIAD) is also here.

The Business School (www.business.uce.ac.uk Galton Building, Perry Barr Campus) provides single and joint programmes to over 4,000 students in such as Accountancy, Advertising, Business, Business Law, Business Psychology Computing, Economics, Finance, ICT Internet Systems, Human Resources, Management, Marketing, Multimedia, Network Technology, Software Engineering and Public Relations.

The Faculty of Education (www.ed.uce.ac.uk Attwood Building, Perry Barr Campus) proides both primary and secondary and operates in the multi-ethnic context of the West Midlands. The students who join its initial teacher training courses are also from diverse backgrounds.

The Faculty of Law, Humanities, Development & Society (www.lhds.uce.ac.uk Perry Barr Campus) might as well be called the School of Diversity. It delivers academic and vocational programmes in Construction, Criminal Justice, English, Housing, Law, Planning, Property, Psychology and Sociology; there is something for almost everyone.

There is a real practical bent. Law students may spend a summer in America, working on death row cases. The School of Law also boasts a 'highly commended' Legal Practice Course, and all law students can make use of a mock courtroom. Meanwhile, criminal justice students experience real prison visits.

At the National Academy of Writing, published authors, Jim Crace, Melvin Bragg, Jilly Cooper, Ian Rankin, Philip Pullman have been involved.

In the School of Property, Construction and Planning, professional accreditation is available for all would-be surveyors, town planners and

TEACHING SURVEY AT A GLANCE	
Avg. UCAS points accepted	**250**
Acceptance rate	**20%**
Overall satisfaction rate	**75%**
Helpful/interested staff	★★
Small tuition groups	★★
Students into graduate jobs	**76%**

Teaching most popular with undergraduates:
Politics, Sociology (90%), Initial Teacher Training (89%), Architecture (86%), Music (84%), Accounting (83%), Media Studies (82%), Building, Planning (80%).

Teaching least popular with undergraduates:
Social Work (35%).

construction managers. And so on.

The Faculty of Health (www.health.uce.ac.uk Westbourne and Perry Barr Campuses) attracts over 7,000 full and part-time students each year. They have partnerships with NHS Trusts and health and social care providers, and are the largest provider of qualified staff to the NHS and Social Services in the region. All undergraduate courses include practice placements.

In employment terms, BCU accounts for a large number of non-hospital nurses (adult, child, disabilities and mental health) and senior hospital

RESEARCH EXCELLENCE

% of Birmingham Citys research that is
4* *(World-class)* or **3*** *(Internationally rated):*

	4*	3*
Town & Country Plannig	10%	15%
Business & Management	5%	20%
Art & Design	30%	30%
Social Work,l Policy & Admin.	5%	15%
Education	5%	20%
English	5%	15%
Music	15%	25%

nurses (SRN, RGN), also for 12% of graduate midwives with their 3-year BSc (Hons) Midwifery. Other certainties in this sector are BSc (Hons) Diagnostic Radiography and BSc (Hons) Radiotherapy. Then there's a particular niche - BSc (Hons) Speech & Language Therapy.

MILLENNIUM POINT Location (Curzon Street, Birmingham B4 7XG) on the east side of Birmingham city centre, well served by buses, public car parks and New Street, Snow Hill and Moor Street railway stations. Faculties: a £114-million building housing tourist attractions, commercial and retail businesses, and UCE's Faculties: Technology Innovation Centre (tic) and Birmingham School of Acting (BSA).

Technology Innovation Centre (www.tic.ac.uk , Millennium Point) Tic is a key faculty of the university, offering a wide range of interactive media, ICT, design technology and advanced engineering courses.

Birmingham School of Acting (www.bssd.ac.uk, Millennium Point) merged with BCU in 2005. Formerly Birmingham School of Speech and Drama, it was founded in 1936. The main focus is acting. There's a BA (Hons) Acting and a one-year Graduate Diploma for postgraduate students. A

Musical Theatre course is planned for September 2007. The School's courses are accredited by the National Council for Drama Training.

WESTBOURNE Location: south city suburb of Edgbaston, on Westbourne Road, accessed via M5/J3, A456 or M5/J4, AA38. Regular, cheap and late-night bus service to and from city centre. Faculty: Health. There's been a major £25 million redevelopment of this campus including new classrooms, a suite of clinical skills facilities, lecture theatres, a Students Union complex - including a new shop, a coffee bar, a bar (The Lounge), and Student Activities centre. Accommodation: one hall - 245 single study-bedrooms and 34 shared (two bedrooms and joint study); self-catering.

GOSTA GREEN Birmingham Institute of Art and Design (BIAD) is one of the largest faculties of art, design and media education in the United Kingdom. Here you'll find Fashion, Textiles & 3-Dimensional Design and the Department of Visual Communication. But BIAD's Dept of Media and Communication is based at Perry Barr. At Gosta Green you'll also cop the School of Theoretical and Historical Studies. Students have access to adjacent Aston Uni union facilities.

Location: adjacent to Aston Uni campus, edge of city centre; accessed via M6/J6, A38M. Ignoring the signs to Aston Uni, leave the A38M at third exit and take the first exit at Lancaster Circus r/about.

BOURNVILLE CENTRE FOR VISUAL ARTS Location: 4 miles to the south of the city on the Bournville Village Trust, an urban village, built by the Cadbury family over a century ago. Two listed buildings, refurbished to the tune of £6 million.

THE ART DEPARTMENT Grade I listed Venetian Gothic property on Margaret Street, centrally sited.

THE JEWELLERY SCHOOL Recent refurbishment makes this the smartest, coolest site within BCU; also state-of-the-art workshops and technology. Location: Vittoria Street in the city centre - the famous old Jewellery Quarter, a walk from Birmingham New Street.

THE BIRMINGHAM CONSERVATOIRE This is the purpose-built Conservatoire, a little gem, a lively, creative environment, one of our best music colleges, it has been going in one form or another since 1859. Based in the heart of the city centre only a few minutes' walk from Symphony Hall, the Conservatoire has some of the finest performing and teaching facilities of its kind in the country,

SUBJECT AREAS (%)

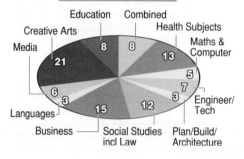

Education — 8
Combined — 8
Health Subjects — 13
Maths & Computer — 5
Engineer/Tech — 3
Plan/Build/Architecture — 7
Social Studies incl Law — 12
Business — 15
Languages — 3
Media — 6
Creative Arts — 21

including the recently refurbished 520-seat Adrian Boult Hall, 150-seat Recital Hall customised for performance with live electronics, four recording studios and a specialised music library, recently rebuilt from the ground up, with around 95,000 individual scores and parts and 10,000 sound recordings. There's both a BMus (Hons) and a specialised BMus (Hons) Jazz. The Conservatoire also works in collaboration with the Technology Innovation Centre to provide a BSc (Hons) course in Music Technology; with South Birmingham College to provide an HND in Popular Music; and with BIAD to provide a new MA in Digital Arts in Performance.

Location: Close to the Birmingham Rep Theatre and ICC & Symphony Hall, it is sited on a traffic island (Paradise Circus) a few minutes walk from Birmingham New Street station. It offers more of a challenge by car. From M6 South or North-West leave at J6 and follow the A38(M) and signs to 'City centre, Bromsgrove, (A38)', over a flyover and through Queensway tunnel (signposted 'Bromsgrove and Queen Elizabeth Hospital'). Leave tunnel left but stay in right-hand lane of exit road. No parking for you on Paradise Island. Unload and move on or seek car park close by: after exit for A456 (Broad Street), take left into Cambridge Street.

ACADEMIA & JOBS

The teaching most popular with undergraduates is in Politics, Sociology, Initial Teacher Training, Architecture, Music, Accounting, Media Studies, Building and Planning. The least popular teaching occurs in Social Work: only 35% of students thought their lecturers were doing a good job. Overall, student satisfaction is an unexciting 75%.

In what is well taught, however, there is plenty of optimism, and even where the teaching is not rated there are often good jobs at the end - especially in hospitals for those studying Nursing and Radiotherapy degrees. BCU graduates also turn up in number in central and local government (mainly from Social Studies - Politics included - and Education), in primary education, in retail (among them all those jewellers), in architecture & engineering, and social work.

Actors and musicians are of course among those who make a good showing in the artistic sector. A number of graduates in Computing become software consultants. Otherwise, the various faculties boost employment figures in particular in personnel, it seems, in miscellaneous business and management activities, in the hotel and restaurant trade, in building and civil engineering, banking, the Law, accounting, and the occasional niche area, like the rag trade, where dedicated degrees (Fashion, Textiles) point the way.

WHAT IT'S REALLY LIKE

UNIVERSITY:	
Social Life	★★★
Campus scene	**Diverse but friendly & focused**
Student Union services	**They try**
Politics	**Luke warm**
Sport	**24 clubs**
National team position	**112th**
Sport facilities	**Extensive**
Arts opportunities	**Good**
Student magazine	**Spaghetti Junction**
Student radio	**SCRatch**
Student TV	**UCEtv**
Venue	**Bar 42**
Bars	**Bar 42, ibar, Village Inn, Lounge, Pavilion, Conservatoire**
Union ents	**Very popular**
Union societies	**30**
Parking	**OK**
CITY:	
Entertainment	★★★★★
Scene	**Excellent**
Town/gown relations	**Average**
Risk of violence	**Average**
Cost of living	**Average**
Student concessions	**Excellent**
Survival + 2 nights out	**£75 pw**
Part-time work campus/town	**Good/excellent**

SOCIAL SCENE

Union HQ is **Bar 42** on Perry Barr Campus, where there's a well-planned programme for all the satellite campuses. Says Tim: 'It's really cheesy, sixties, seventies, eighties music. We do get told about these nights. Someone from the Students Union will come to the Conservatoire, put posters up so you know about them, but that's more than you ever want to know about them.'

ibar is the student bar at the prestigious Millennium Point. Then there's **the Lounge** at Westbourne Campus, and there's a small bar at the Conservatoire. In addition, there's the **Village Inn** at Hamstead halls (see *Pillow Talk*), and the **Pavilion** out at Moor Lane Sports Centre. Parties and events are held every term in the Village Inn and ibar. Come Wednesday, *Sports Night*, it's off to the **Oceana** nightclub in town.

Town Says Tim: 'Broad Street is the place to go out in town, because it's just lined with every different type of café and bar. There are even casinos, which is where most student loans end up. There is everything to do there, but because so many students do go there, you will often find on Friday and Saturday nights the more discerning students avoid it.'

The cooler brigade make their own music. 'Come Friday/Saturday night, when people from Perry Barr flock in, we and other students that live nearby, go elsewhere.

'Because Broad Street is so close we can go out there any night of the week, me and a couple of friends we will often find a place on Broad Street right by the canal, like **Pitcher and Piano** or the **Handmade Burger Company**. There is a big jazz section at the Conservatoire. Pretty much everyone has a group of friends that are in a jazz band. There is a place right at the bottom of Broad Street, the **Yardbird** (named after the Yardbirds), and every night they do different things, but Thursday they do live jazz, and most of the time that is the Conservatoire's night out. It's not very big, it can hold maybe 200 people, and that's the best place to go. Because basically you know everyone playing, it's all students playing there. But the biggest reason we go there is that we don't get Birmingham University or Birmingham City University students going there.'

Bohemia rules, and Tim and his friends are also to be found in the **Rag Market**: 'I will often go there to buy meat, it's so much cheaper than Tesco's. We bought half a goat for £15 earlier this year! And me and my flatmates cooked it up and made goat curries, I mean £15 for half a goat. So the rag markets are like what the Bullring used to be.'

Back at Perry Barr thirty student societies are now up and running. Student magazine is *Spaghetti Junction*. SCRatch Radio is the community radio station, and there's student TV too. Student Community Action (SCA), the Union volunteering project, passes on key skills that employers are always asking for, as well as making a real difference to the local community. A so-called LEAP campaign currently promotes sport for local children. Drama, Cheerleading, RAG (Raising and Giving) and ACS (Afro Caribbean Society) are highly active socs. Politically the Union has shown its teeth in campaigns like 'Sentenced to debt', against Top-Up fees, and in a Housing Accreditation Scheme to improve housing standards in the city.

SPORT The Union runs the massive Moor Lane Sports Centre, with extensive conference and banqueting and partying facilities attached, playing host, too, to the annual Frisbee tournaments. A new £7-million sport centre - comprising a sports hall and eighty-station fitness suite - is due to open at main campus Perry Barr later this year.

PILLOW TALK

Hamstead Campus is a 16-acre residential campus 2 miles from the Perry Barr Campus, with good bus services between the two and to city centre. They

ACCOMMODATION	
Guarantee to freshers	**100%**
Style	**Halls, flats**
Security guard	**All**
Shared rooms	**None**
Internet access	**All**
Self-catered	**All**
En suite	**No halls, some flats**
Approx price range pw	**£64-£95**
City rent pw	**£85-£95**

guarantee a place in halls for all freshers.

There is other accommodation (see www. bcu.ac.uk/accommodation/), the newest, swishest is to be had at Jennens Court in Jennens Road, Birmingham - 3, 4, 5 and 6-bedroom flats with lounge and kitchen area and en-suite bedrooms, plus laundry, parking spaces and bike racks.

All accommodation is self-catered, and has internet and security.

GETTING THERE

☛ By road: M1, M5, M6 and M40 all give ready access to the city. See also campus notes.
☛ By rail: Bristol Parkway or Sheffield, 1:30; London Euston, 1:40; Liverpool, 2:00; Leeds, 3:00.
☛ By air: Birmingham International Airport.
☛ By coach: London, 2:40; Bristol, 2:00.

UNIVERSITY OF BOLTON

The University of Bolton
Deane Road
Bolton BL3 5AB

TEL 01204 900600
FAX 01204 399074
EMAIL enquiries@bolton.ac.uk
WEB www.bolton.ac.uk

University of Bolton Students' Union
Deane Road
Bolton BL3 5AB

TEL 01204 900850
FAX 01204 900860
EMAIL BISU@Bolton.ac.uk
WEB www.bolton.ac.uk

VAG VIEW

In the beginning, in 1982, the old Bolton Institute was formed out of the Bolton Institute of Technology and Bolton College of Education (Technical), and subsequently Bolton College of Art became part of the picture too. They have had the distinction of being able to award their own degrees for some time, but in January 2005 they gained university status.

Student satisfaction is lowish at 77% , but rate of students into real graduate jobs six months after leaving is fairly impressive at 76%. They have a bad drop-rate of just under 18%.

CAMPUS

There were two campuses, Deane, on the west side of town, and Chadwick, on the east side. Now there is one. Chadwick Road campus has gone and its facilities moved to the main site at Deane Road.

In June 2005 they opened The Design Studio on Deane Campus, a £6-million remodelling of Deane Tower that has completely transformed the face of the campus. New corporate hospitality facilities adjoin it, including lecture theatre, boardroom and breakout rooms - the Deane Suite. This kicked off an extensive, phased landscaping

UNIVERSITY/STUDENT PROFILE	
University since	**2004**
Situation/style	**Town campus**
Student population	**8740**
Total undergraduates	**6375**
Mature undergraduates	**40%**
International undergrads	**10%**
Male/female ratio	**56:64**
Equality of opportunity:	
state school intake	**99%**
social class 4-7 intake	**46%**
low-participation area intake	**22%**

and refurbishment programme.

Last September they opened the £2.5 million Social Learning Zone at the heart of campus (see Social Scene below), next to the library.

Not content with this, they also opened a £1-million campus in United Arab Emirate, just 45 minutes from Dubai for around 150 students initially, to increase to around 700 five years. It offers undergraduate and postgraduate courses in Built Environment, Engineering, Business, IT and Art & Design. Bolton students can study at the new UAE campus for part of their degree course.

FEES, BURSARIES

UK & EU Fees for 2009-10, £3,225 p.a. Bursary for students on a HE Maintenance Grant. The Bolton Scholarship is also available to those progressing from a partner institution. There is also help for disabled students. See www.bolton.ac.uk/Prospec tiveStudents/Undergraduate/Finance/Home.aspx.

STUDENT PROFILE

Among undergraduates there is a large mature population (40%) and many are part-timers. Almost half come from families new to the idea of university, and there is a strong overseas presence. The diversity is impressive. Perhaps not surprisingly there is, at this stage, a very high drop-out rate; only Bell College (now part of West of

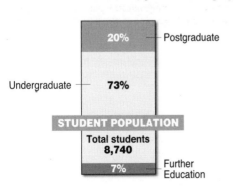

20% — Postgraduate
Undergraduate — 73%
STUDENT POPULATION
Total students 8,740
7% — Further Education

TEACHING SURVEY AT A GLANCE

Avg. UCAS points accepted	**180**
Acceptance rate	**11%**
Overall satisfaction rate	**77%**
Helpful/interested staff	**No data**
Small tuition groups	**No data**
Students into graduate jobs	**76%**

Teaching most popular with undergraduates:
Youth & Community Work, Social Studies (96%).

Teaching least popular with undergraduates:
Technology (43%).

Scotland with the old Paisley University), and UHI Millennium Institute in the Scottish Highlands have worse.

ACADEMIA & JOBS

Departments are Art & Design, Built Environment, Business Studies, Business Logistics & Info Systems, Computing, Cultural & Creative Studies (from English to Media, from Arts in the Community to stage and screen), Education, Engineering & Design, Health & Social Studies, Management, Product Design & Development, Psychology & Life Sciences, Sport, Leisure & Tourism Management.

They specialise in degree courses tailored to meet employer needs. Many are taught by professionals with industry experience. Key employment areas are the health industry, central and local government administration, the construction industry, miscellaneous business activities, secondary education, retail (food, etc), engineering design consultancy, architectural consultancy, personnel, community & counselling activities, computer and related activities, artistic & literary creation, banking.

Courses feeding graduates into jobs in these

areas include Human Sciences, which covers Biology, Environmental Studies, Psychology and Community Studies. Biology courses offer third year specialisation in such as Human Genetics and Sensory Physiology, and involve a placement. There's a series of Community Health and Community Studies degrees, and one in Youth & Community Work.

Then there are the Architectural Technology, Building, Quantity Surveying, and Building Surveying & Property Management courses.

Computing, Law, and Business Information Systems and Business Management degrees are also clearly effective job-wise. The artistic and literary creation employment element mentioned above puts their Creative Writing degrees in a good light, and the Fine Art provision.

New courses in Business Management this year include specialist emphases on Languages,

RESEARCH EXCELLENCE

% of Bolton's research that is
4* (World-class) or 3* (Internationally rated):

	4*	3*
General Eng., Mineral, Mining	**10%**	**15%**
Architec., Built Environment	**10%**	**30%**
Business and Management	**0%**	**10%**
Social Work, Policy & Admin.	**5%**	**40%**
Psychology	**0%**	**5%**
Education	**0%**	**15%**
English Language and Lit.	**0%**	**10%**
Philosophy	**0%**	**55%**
Art and Design	**0%**	**0%**

Marketing, Tourism, E-Business, and...Judaic Studies. It seems they do their research. There are also more in the areas of robotics, music, and visual effects. It is all very convincingly commercial.

In addition to the £6m Design Studio, two floors of adjacent state-of-the-art teaching space and a new Product Design Studio, costing £3.5m, opened in September 2006.

Keep an eye on their media courses. Bolton are part of a university consortium, headed by Salford University and called Northern Edge, involved with the BBC.

There is a flexible approach to entry. Typically, 180 points see you in.

SOCIAL SCENE

STUDENT UNION As well as new Students' Union offices and the stylish **Loft** bar, the **Social Learning Zone** (known as the **SLZ**) incorporates a

SUBJECT AREAS (%)

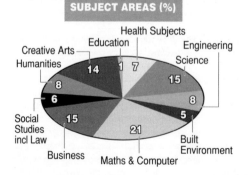

Health Subjects
Education
Creative Arts
Humanities
Engineering
Science
14 1 7
15
8
6
8
Social Studies incl Law
15
21
5
Built Environment
Business
Maths & Computer

laid-back student meeting area, which at night is converted into a venue for gigs, club nights and other student functions.

Ents-wise it's a quiz on Monday, pool and big screen footie on Tuesday. Mid-week Wednesday is Student Night at **McCauleys** ('Bolton's student friendly nightclub') after drinks warm-up at the **Venue Café Bar**. Thursday is open mic night and Friday live local bands.

Societies-wise it is again fairly undeveloped as yet: Christian Union, Students with Disabilities, Islamic Soc, Afro Caribbean Soc and Motorsports (Bolton are strong in automobile engineering and product design and offer degrees in Motor Vehicle & Transport.)

There's a newspaper, *Student Direct*, masterminded by Manchester University, and a radio station is promised. Other than that, it's the annual 3-Legged Fancy Dress race

SPORT They are nationally competitive in men's basketball, women's basketball, men's football, women's football, men's hockey, netball, men's rugby union, men's cricket, men's water polo, but sadly languished at 125th nationally last year. Compatible sports rehab., coaching, development and management degrees will help. The annual sports ball and award ceremony is already a high point of the social calendar.

TOWN Bolton's proximity to Manchester and to the Pennine Moors makes for a nice balance. A couple of nights of Mancunian debauchery, followed by a soul-searching chill on the wilderness of Tufton moor might be just the thing if you ever manage to tear yourself away from campus. Bolton itself offers a handful of clubs, but McCauley's is fave.

There's a cinema complex, the ground-breaking **Octagon Theatre** (modern interpretations of Shakespeare and equally at home with

WHAT IT'S REALLY LIKE	
UNIVERSITY:	
Social Life	★★
Campus scene	**Largely local, very loyal**
Student Union services	**Galvanising itself**
Politics	**Little interest**
Sport	**13 clubs**
National team position	**125th**
Sport facilities	**Promising**
Arts opportunities	**Few**
Student newspaper	**Student Direct**
Nightclub/bar	**The Venue**
Union ents	**Live, and light ents progr. + tie-ups with clubs in town**
Union clubs/societies	**5**
Parking	**Available**
TOWN:	
Entertainment	★★
Scene	**Clubs, pubs**
Town/gown relations	**Good**
Risk of violence	**Average**
Cost of living	**Low**
Student concessions	**Good**
Survival + 2 nights out	**£60 pw**
Part-time work campus/town	**Average**

Alan Bennett) and live music venue **Albert Halls**, which includes comedy, jazz, classical music. Buit it's nearby Manchester for the high life.

PILLOW TALK

There are two halls, self-catering, with security guard and car parking. The Hollins comprises two blocks with flats servicing six to nine, the Orlando Village is eight blocks, each with eight six-bedroom flats plus a common room. Both are close to the town centre. All freshers get a place. Rooms cost £65.00 per week. All are let on a 38-week contract. You pay £50 per year extra to have internet access in your bedroom. Competition in town costs about £40 per week.

GETTING THERE

☛ By road: M61/J3, A666 for Chadwick; M61/J5, A58 for Deane. Good map on web site.
☛ By coach: London, 5-7:00; Liverpool 2:00.
☛ By rail: Manchester frequent.
☛ By air: Manchester Airport 30 mins.

ACCOMMODATION	
Guarantee to freshers	**100%**
Style	**Flats**
Security guard	**All**
Shared rooms	**All**
Internet access	**Extra £50**
Self-catered	**All**
En suite	**None**
Approx price range pw	**£65**
Town rent pw	**£40**

BOURNEMOUTH UNIVERSITY

Bournemouth University
Talbot Campus
Fern Barrow
Poole
Dorset BH12 5BB

TEL 01202 524111
EMAIL enquiries@bournemouth.ac.uk
WEB www.bournemouth.ac.uk

Bournemouth Students' Union
Talbot Campus
Fern Barrow
Poole
Dorset BH12 5BB

TEL 01202 965774
FAX 01202 535990
EMAIL subu@bournemouth.ac.uk
WEB www.subu.org.uk

VAG VIEW

*B*ournemouth is a seaside resort with an unusually spectacular reputation for night life. It is also a university which has cut out for itself some individual niches in its undergraduate programme, and built quite a reputation for getting students real graduate jobs in places (especially media), which others fail to reach.

In December 2008 inspectors from the Quality Assurance Agency descended and exited stage right commending the uni for its Peer Assisted Learning Scheme, its development opportunities for student mentors, the additional support it provides for first year students, and generally the staff peripatetic roles for liaison, advice and support, which operate across the University. This is also recognised in the National Student Survey, where they won a 3-star rating for helpful/interested staff and 4 stars for small-size tutorial groups.

What's more, for a university known hitherto for its teaching rather than its in-depth research capability, it has done well in the recent research assessment. Indeed, it was the fourth most improved UK university in terms of research quality.

Fifteen per cent of the work going on in Art & Design and Media is world-class, and 55% and 35% respectively was of international significance. Architecture and Nursing did well too, with 10% world class and 25% and 30% respectively of international significance. Business and Computing also came through with distinction. The only dog was Law, which achieved nothing in the two top classes.

UNIVERSITY/STUDENT PROFILE	
University since	**1992**
Situation/style	**Campus**
Student population	**17670**
Total undergraduates	**15425**
Mature undergraduates	**20%**
International undergrads	**8%**
Male/female ratio	**51:49**
Equality of opportunity:	
state school intake	**95%**
social class 4-7 intake	**29%**
low-participation area intake	**8%**

There's a great time to be had on and off campus at Bournemouth. Student satisfaction is 79%, which seems a bit ungrateful, but the drop-out rate (6.7%), is way below average.

CAMPUSES

Talbot (2 miles from the town centre) is the main campus; the other, Bournemouth, or Town Campus, is more of a collection of town sites, with teaching facilities for Business, Health, Design, Engineering, Computing, Conservation. There's a no-parking rule within a mile. Students are also discouraged from bringing cars on to Talbot, though many do. There's a free bus service between campuses and halls.

FEES, BURSARIES

UK & EU Fees, 2009-10: £3,225 There's a means tested non-repayable cash bursary, also sport scholarships, music scholarships, an Academic Achievement scholarship for three Grade A's at A Level or an average of three Distinctions at BTEC National Diploma or equivalent, and the Endemol scholarships for third year TV Production students of minority ethnic origin (Black and Asian), which involve placement with a professional mentor from the industry in addition to financial support.

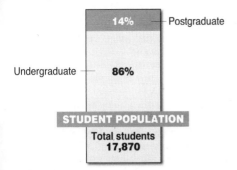

Undergraduate — **86%**

14% — Postgraduate

STUDENT POPULATION

**Total students
17,870**

Finally, Citizenship scholarships are offered to students who can demonstrate that they have contributed significantly to community-related projects outside formal education or work.

STUDENT PROFILE
The main campus is very studenty and unpretentious. This may be a career-orientated student body, but there's a relaxed scene both in the Union and in town. Only 5% of students come here from public schools. There are 20% mature undergraduates and 8% from overseas, beyond the EU.

ACADEMIA & JOBS
Courses include Accounting, Advertising, Software Engineering Computer and Creative Technology (product design, animation, etc), Film, TV, and Radio Production, Media, Social Work, Paramedic Science, Physiotherapy, Occupational Therapy, PR, Sports Management and Psychology.

The teaching reckoned among undergraduates to be best is in Journalism, Accounting, Archaeology, Marketing, Tourism, Communication and Media, the worst in subjects allied to Medicine, Nursing, and Geographical Studies.

Careers are carved out in associated areas, most popularly in health, but also in quantity in software consultancy & supply, advertising, HR (personnel), film, publishing, Defence, social work and counselling, sport, market research, tourism, banking, accountancy, architectural consultancy, and radio and TV, among other areas.

Close working relationships with business and industry shapes their courses and fuels research and consultancy interests. Forty-week professional placements are integral to their four-year undergraduate programmes. As a result, there's an 81% rate of students into graduate track employment within six months of leaving, which is excellent.

Typically, the uni's Advertising and Marketing Communications degree is twinned with an agency through the Institute of Practitioners in

Advertising. Six months work experience is part of it. As a result, around 4% of Bournemouth graduates become advertising account executives with major agencies, or execs in publishing companies, public relations consultancies, research consultancies or in the marketing departments of other large companies.

The Business School and School of Finance and Law are now one. They are specialists in commercial & business law, and have degrees combining Law & Taxation and Accounting & Taxation. You can also take the Common Professional Examination (CPE) here, which you'll need if you want to become a solicitor and don't have a law degree.

Of the many art colleges and universities with Animation degrees, few have as fruitful a line into

TEACHING SURVEY AT A GLANCE

Avg. UCAS points accepted	**280**
Acceptance rate	**19%**
Overall satisfaction rate	**79%**
Helpful/interested staff	★★★
Small tuition groups	★★★★
Students into graduate jobs	**81%**

Teaching most popular with undergraduates:
Journalism (96%), Accounting (95%), Archaeology (91%), Marketing, Tourism (90%), Communication & Media (89%).

Teaching least popular with undergraduates:
Subjects allied to Medicine (59%), Nursing (58%), Geographical Studies (57%).

the film as Bournemouth, who host the National Centre for Computer Animation. The recent back clap for Art & Design and Media in the research assessment suggests strength in depth in the area of visual image.

SUBJECT AREAS (%)

Creative Arts
Humanities **3**
Health Subjects **13**
Engineering Science **12**
9
3 **3**
22
Social Studies incl Law
35
Business
Maths & Computer

RESEARCH EXCELLENCE

% of Bournemouth's research that is
4* *(World-class) or* **3*** *(Internationally rated):*

	4*	3*
Clinical Subjects	**0%**	**20%**
Nursing and Midwifery	**10%**	**30%**
Computer Science	**5%**	**30%**
General Eng., Mineral, Mining	**5%**	**35%**
Geography & Environment	**10%**	**35%**
Archaeology	**10%**	**25%**
Business and Management	**5%**	**25%**
Law	**0%**	**0%**
Art and Design	**15%**	**55%**
Media	**15%**	**35%**

Recently the Media School unveiled a state-of-the-art Motion Capture facility. 'MoCap' tracks and records the movement of a human subject or object as computerised motion data so that three-dimensional images can be animated with realistic motion in real time - animating characters in computer games, film or TV. Look at their animation degrees. The Wallisdown Campus of The Arts Institute at Bournemouth, which is now a university sector institution, is adjacent. In 2006 the Bournemouth Screen Academy was launched as a joint venture between the Institute and the uni Media School and recognised as 'Centre of Excellence' in film education and training, one of only seven such institutions in the UK. In 2007 it became a Skillset Screen and Media Academy as one of Britain's key centres for filmmaking. Its Film Production BA enjoys an international reputation for excellence.

Meanwhile, Bournemouth's BA Hons Television Production offers practising TV producers, writers and technicians as your teachers. Great resources and top employment track record.

Activities are backed by good student media, Nerve Magazine, Nerve TV are regular award winners, but this year it was Birst Radio's turn: they took Gold and Silver in the Student Radio Awards. In the curriculum look especially at Scriptwriting for Film & TV. Those not making it straight into scriptwriting find work as script readers, editors, agents, production assistants, researchers, etc, or write for radio, magazines, corporate videos, even computer games. Recent figures showed that 18 out of 23 traceable graduates were in permanent employment. There is also a strong Creative Writing degree.

In sport, golf is a speciality. Student golfer Andy Shakespear returned from the 2008 world university golf championships with two bronze medals, while Caroline Atkins from Bournemouth's Sport & Recreation team flew the flag during the recent England ladies cricket tour of Australia and New Zealand.

SOCIAL SCENE

STUDENTS' UNION SU night club, **The Old Fire Station** (**TOFS** for short) is the envy of many a Student Union up and down the country. It's very cool and has three rooms to play in! The student special is a legendary Friday night out *Lollipop*, with more r'n'b and cheese than you can shake a stick at. Popular too are the funky fancy dress parties where themes include: *Back to Skool*, *Grease, Doctors and Nurses, Chav Party* and *Pyjama Party*. Wednesdays are live band nights, Monday nights are home to *Comedy Factory*, where doors open at 8, and Saturday nights sees *Maison* on

WHAT IT'S REALLY LIKE

UNIVERSITY:	
Social Life	★★★★
Campus scene	**Spin doctors & suits/up-beat ents**
Student Union services	**Good**
Politics	**Little interest**
Sport	**Competitive**
National team position	**36th**
Sport facilities	**Good**
Arts opportunities	**Available**
Student magazine	**Nerve**
Student newspaper	**Student Press**
Student radio	**Birst FM**
National Radio Awards	**Gold, 2006**
Student TV	**Nerve TV**
TV awards	**4 awards, 2006**
Nightclub	**The Old Fire Station**
Bars	**Dylans, D2**
Union ents	**Fancy Dress Mondays, Lollipop, Comedy Factory, RAG, one-off gigs**
Union societies	**40**
Parking	**Poor despite many with cars**
TOWN:	
Entertainment	★★★★
Scene	**Beach, shopping, night life vibrant**
Town/gown relations	**Good**
Risk of violence	**Average**
Cost of living	**High**
Student concessions	**Good**
Survival + 2 nights out	**£75 pw**
Part-time work campus/town	**Good**

monthly rotation.

Balls are frequent and memorable - Freshers, Christmas, Valentine's, Sport - and the Summer ball, the creme de le creme of the entertainment calendar in a large field just outside Bournemouth - more like a festival than a ball.

Talbot Campus is home to **Dylan's Bar**, with very cheap menu - pizza, burgers and healthier options like baked potatoes and omelettes. Evening entertainment includes quizzes, DJ's and live gigs. **D2** is a more relaxed sports bar where football is screened on the large projector screen.

> *Serious, specialist job opportunities are on offer, and its students are enjoying a Brighton-style seaside resort, bursting with hedonistic promise.*

Both on-campus bars are open seven days a week during term time.

What else is it good for? Well, media of course, and there's a vast array of clubs and societies, from diving to computer gaming, poetry to horse riding and music: there's a good orchestra and choir.

There are also numerous volunteering opportunities in which to get involved throughout the year with MAD days, Community Champions, etc.

SPORT With the arrival of the course in Sports Management, a brand new golf simulator has been installed in the Department of Sport and Recreation. This joins the south coast's premier climbing facility, the Hot Rocks climbing wall. Proximity to the sea encourages windsurfing, sailing, paragliding, jet skiing, etc. The uni provides full-time instructors and facilities for a wide range of other sports, and there has been a huge improvement in their national placing recently (36th). A sports hall includes squash courts and multigym. Cricketers play at the county-standard ground, Dean Park.

TOWN Dropped in the middle, where four roads meet, we found wall-to-wall pleasure, whatever your bent. There's no shortage of things to spend money on, and part-time opportunities for work are legion. It is an extraordinary place, a born-again English seaside resort, and if bar and club life proves too much, there's always the beach, and the New Forest is but a short drive away.

PILLOW TALK

Accommodation is guaranteed for first years, but the guarantee includes hotels and guest houses, so get in quick. Places in the student village on Talbot (3 to 7-bed en suite houses), and in Hurn House (single study bedroom with sink in central Bournemouth), Cranborne House (single en-suite study bedroom 5 mins from Hurn House; subsidised uni bus) and new Purbeck House (single, en-suite study bedrooms close to Cranborne House) are limited to 250, 152, 497 and 518 respectively. Rooms in Talbot are en suite. Abbotsbury House in Pokesdown, close to Bournemouth Hospital is the new residence (4-6 bed flats) for nurses. Most recently opened are the 308-bed Corfe House in Poole and a further 150 beds at Okeford House in Winton. A 400-room cluster flat complex at Lansdowne campus will also later this year.

All halls have good security and internet access. As in most seaside resorts, town accommodation is plentiful and good.

ACCOMMODATION	
Guarantee to freshers	**95%**
Style	**Halls, flats**
Security guard	**All halls, some flats**
Shared rooms	**None**
Internet access	**All**
Self-catered	**All**
En suite	**Many**
Approx price range pw	**£78-£82**
City rent pw	**£60-£80**

GETTING THERE

☞ By road: M3/M27/A31/ A338, The Wessex Way; at second r/about follow uni signs to Talbot. From west A35 then A3049 (Wallisdown Road). For Bournemouth campus, leave A338 at St Paul's r/about (Travel Interchange junction) on to St Paul's road and find a car park.

☞ By rail: London Waterloo, 1:45; Bristol, 2:30; Manchester, 5:37.

☞ By coach: London, 2:15; Bristol, 3:10.

UNIVERSITY OF BRADFORD

The University of Bradford
Richmond Road
Bradford BD7 1DP

TEL 0800 073 1225
FAX 01274 235585
EMAIL course-enquiries@bradford.ac.uk
WEB www.bradford.ac.uk

Bradford University Union
The Communal Building
Bradford BD7 1DP

TEL 01274 233300
FAX 01274 235530
EMAIL ubu@bradford.ac.uk
WEB www.ubuonline.co.uk/

VAG VIEW

A *university since 1966, Bradford came out*
of the local Technical College, which
itself grew out of the textile industry in the
1860s. Today the connection between higher
education and the workplace remains key.
Their slogan is 'Making Knowledge Work'
and they have erected a 5-metre high, bronze
sculpture to celebrate it. Sandwich courses
are their stock in trade.

Teaching most popular with students
delineates their individual taste for science
and technology: Ophthalmics, Mechanical
and Automative Engineering, Medical
Engineering, Cellular & Molecular
Pathology, Pharmacology, Toxicology,
Pharmacy, and other subjects allied to
Medicine. Least popular with
undergraduates is Computer Science - only
55% of the class give it time of day.

The clue to why may lie in the National
Student Survey, which suggests a less than
helpful/interested teaching staff, and
something of a dearth of small-size tuition
groups.

Departments with most high-powered,
world-renowned research going on are
Archaeology, Politics, Pharmacy, Nursing
and Midwifery, Social Work, and
Mechanical, Aeronautical, and
Manufacturing Engineering.

But it is the graduate employment picture
that identifies most clearly the academic
character of Bradford students. Far and
away the largest employment sector entered
into by graduates is health. Many go to work
in hospitals, some into the community as
social workers and counsellors, while yet
others go on to occupy themselves in

UNIVERSITY/STUDENT PROFILE	
University since	**1966**
Situation/style	**City campus**
Student population	**13600**
Total undergraduates	**9110**
Mature undergraduates	**30%**
International undergrads	**12%**
Male/female ratio	**51:49**
Equality of opportunity:	
state school intake	**94%**
social class 4-7 intake	**49%**
low-participation area intake	**16%**

specialist retail, the dispensing of spectacles,
pharmaceuticals, and other medical goods.
After these come Bradford's bankers,
graduates in Economics, Accountancy &
Finance, and Business Computing, and at
length those quite different creatures who
succumb to the lure of museum, library, and
other archival and cultural activities,
including, no doubt, some of those well-
taught archaeologists. Many graduates also
take up teaching posts in higher and
secondary education.

Real graduate employment is more or
less guaranteed, with 83% of all graduates
finding a real graduate-level job in six
months or less after graduating.

Of course, Bradford is not London, nor is
it Milton Keynes (thank god!), nor yet is it
Leeds. Bradford may challenge the
Southerner's picture of what he would like
the North to be, but what it offers all its
undergraduates, and always has done, is a
very studenty, close-knit, pub-based, curry-
central experience, uninhibited by issues of
wealth and class. To many a Bradford
student, the Southerner's picture of the

acceptable face of the North, namely Leeds (because of its premier-league nightclubs and Harvey Nichs) appears rather expensive and, well, just a tad outre.

Bradford students can easily partake of Leeds, as the city is just a few moments down the road, but few do.

Recently, there has been a huge investment in the Hub, the student focus of campus. Seventy-nine per cent of undergraduates say they are very satisfied with what goes on there, and yet the drop-out rate remains suspiciously high at 11%.

TEACHING SURVEY AT A GLANCE

Avg. UCAS points accepted	**260**
Acceptance rate	**22%**
Overall satisfaction rate	**79%**
Helpful/interested staff	★★
Small tuition groups	★★
Students into graduate jobs	**83%**

Teaching most popular with undergraduates:
Ophthalmics (93%), Mechanical. Automative Eng. (92%), Medical Eng., Cellular & Molecular Pathology (90%), Pharmacology, Toxicology, Pharmacy (89%), Subjects allied to Medicine (88%).

Teaching least popular with undergraduates:
Computer Science (55%).

CAMPUS

The main campus, a ten-minute stroll from town, is compact and bounded by roads on all four sides. All teaching, except for Business Studies, is carried out on site, and there are many halls of residence on and nearby it. The Hub opened its doors in March 2007.

FEES, BURSARIES

UK & EU Fees, £3,225. If in receipt of a Maintenance Grant, regardless of whether partial or full, you get a £500 bursary in the first year, £700 in your second, and £900 in your final year.

STUDENT PROFILE

They have an open access policy, and the intake from the lower socio-economic classes (4-7) is well over their government benchmark. Forty-nine per cent comes from the working classes, 16% from so-called 'low-participation neighbourhoods'. Only 6% public school kids successfully apply.

There is a particular welcome to overseas students and careful monitoring of all processes of integration. Most undergrads are scientists and techies, but life isn't too predictable.

ACADEMIA & JOBS

Broad study areas at Bradford are Archaeological Sciences, Chemical and Forensic Sciences, Computing & Informatics, Design &

SUBJECT AREAS (%)

Humanities
Social Studies incl Law
Combined
Health Subjects
13
34
1
18
10
6
12
6
6
Science
Business
Engineering
Maths & Computer

Technology, Engineering, Geography & Environmental Sciences, Health Studies, Humanities, ICT, Law, Life Sciences, Management and Business, Media Studies, Psychology, Social Sciences.

A Disability Office follows a proudly proactive strategy. An organisation called Impact targets ethnic students with a view to enhancing their employment chances.

Bacteriologists and microbiologists work with living organisms, an awareness of human health and environmental issues, food poisoning, drugs, viruses, bacteria and other bugs. It's an important field, and Bradford is a leader, one aspect of the health industry dimension which we have seen is their single biggest area of graduate employment, and

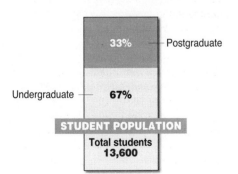

Postgraduate
33%

Undergraduate
67%

STUDENT POPULATION
Total students
13,600

RESEARCH EXCELLENCE

% of Bradford's research that is
4* *(World-class)* or **3*** *(Internationally rated):*

	4*	3*
Nursing and Midwifery	10%	25%
Medical Bioscience	5%	35%
Optometry	5%	35%
Pharmacy	15%	40%
Computer Science	5%	40%
Electrical and Electronic Eng.	0%	10%
Civil Engineering	5%	50%
Mech., Aero., Manufac. Eng.	10%	30%
Archaeology	20%	30%
Business and Management	15%	30%
Politics	15%	35%
Social Work, Policy & Admin.	10%	40%
Development Studies	5%	25%
History	5%	20%
Media	5%	15%

which includes a pioneering Clinical Science pathway into medicine. Biochemists, pharmacists, medical scientists (see their BSc Applied Biomedical Sciences), physiotherapists, medical radiographers and midwives all look carefully at what is on offer here. There is a £6-million Institute of Pharmaceutical Innovation. The uni is among the leaders, too, in producing ophthalmic opticians.

The Bradford graduate employment map is also studded with systems analysts, software engineers, computer/IT consultants and programmers. Look at the Computing and Cybernetics faculties. There is also a fine track record in film through its BSc Computer Animation & Special Effects degree, and the BSc Animatronics is especially interesting in that it teaches technology and skills to create, sculpt and animate motorised puppets - the 'live' monster that you see in movies.

Look, too, at another niche area - their Electrical and Electronic Engineering, Mobile Communications and Telecommunications degrees. Again, the Automotive Design Technology and Integrated Industrial Design (Eco Design, Sports Technology, etc) degrees make them leaders in careers for design and development engineers.

Would-be social workers and counsellors note that the Social Work degree is accredited by the General Social Care Council. There's also a fully fledged School of Law with an LlB, and BSc Internet, Law & Society.

Other key strands take us further into the ethos of the place, Bradford's famed Department of Peace Studies (studied from the standpoints of ethics, psychology, sociology, history), and such as International Relations & Security Studies and Conflict Resolution.

SOCIAL SCENE

Basement is the 1,200-capacity night club in the Union building. **Colours** is half of Basement for smaller events and live bands. **Escape** is the nightclub ideal for sports clubs, societies and individual students to run their own music nights. *Rez: Rock and Metal Night* is billed as 'a fantastic rock and metal night in Escape from 10pm'; *Hades* is another, entry £3. Courtyard is the pub venue.

There's no Arts faculty at Bradford, but they have three of the most pulsating Arts venues to be found. **Theatre in the Mill** is home to the Theatre Group, which puts on a show (student or pro) every week and has the cheapest bar (Scaff Bar) in the uni. **The Tasmin Little Music Centre** does similar stuff for a student jazz ensemble, choral society, chamber choir and three orchestras, and an amazing series of Music for Lunch at the **Alhambra Studio** in Great Horton Road. Then there's Gallery II for art.

Student cinema, **BSC**, happens three times a week - Art movies and the latest blockbusters, many only a few months after general release, all for a couple of quid. Showings are in Great Hall (capacity 1,300).

The Media Area is split into Ram Air (Student Radio); *The Bradford Student* (Newspaper), the BSC (Bradford Student Cinema) and ubuonline.co.uk (the website).

There's also a Societies Area. Among some fifty societies, Twirl Soc and Amnesty are the most popular. Amnesty International is of course the foremost organisation in defence of human rights. Twirl Soc, you may be intrigued to discover is about twirling, throwing, juggling anything that spins in a circle of motion. Politics spins left, activity average - war, racism, recycling.

SPORT There are 35 sports clubs - women's volleyball is a particular strength. An on-campus sports centre has a 25m swimming pool, sauna suite, solarium, Nautilus fitness suite, etc. There are squash courts and a dozen or so pitches for cricket, football and rugby, plus 9,000 square metres of artificial turf sand-grass for 5-a-sides, netball, and hockey. One site is behind the halls of residence, the other 4 miles from campus, where the pavilion has a bar.

In the city the Bradford Bulls rule.

City music and theatre are a big part of what Bradford is about - local bands and drama groups brighten local venues such as **The Priestley**, **Delius**, **St George's Hall** and **Love Apple**.

You may have heard there's also a large multi-cultural population, bringing with it a fantastic mix of art, culture and food.

Bradford is of course curry central. Students have curry locals; staff and dishes become firm friends. It is also one of the cheapest university cities in the country

PILLOW TALK

No guarantee for accommodation unless as a fresher you hold an unconditional offer as your firm choice. Most halls are on the main campus or a short five-minute walk away. Most, but not all, rooms have free Broadband access. Generally security is good. Some halls have wardens. There's no sharing. All rooms in hall are single study-bedrooms. Residence agreements are for 42 weeks (September to July) and therefore include the Christmas and Easter vacations. You may be able to stay over summer too if life's that tedious.

University and Bradford halls are on campus in close proximity to the Library, Sports Centre, Students' Union, teaching areas, social areas and events.

ACCOMMODATION	
Guarantee to freshers	**100%**
Style	**Halls**
Security guard	**Some**
Shared rooms	**Some**
Internet access	**Most**
Self-catered	**All**
En suite	**Some**
Approx price range pw	**£65-£84.55**
City rent pw	**£45-£50**

WHAT IT'S REALLY LIKE	
UNIVERSITY:	
Social Life	★★★★
Campus scene	**Close-knit, active, studenty**
Student Union services	**Good**
Politics	**Left – funding, war, racism, recycling**
Sport	**35 clubs**
National team position	**88th**
Sport facilities	**Good**
Arts opportunities	**Excellent drama dance, film, music; art avg**
Student magazine	**Scrapie**
Student radio	**RamAir**
Nightclub	**Basement,**
Small venue	**Escape**
Bars	**Steve Biko, Courtyard**
Union ents	**Live plus club-nights Rock Sox, Pop Sox, disco - FND, Allsorts (LGBT)**
Union societies	**85**
Most popular societies	**Twirl Soc/Amnesty**
Parking	**Good**
CITY:	
Entertainment	★★★
Scene	**Curry central/ rough in parts**
Town/gown relations	**OK**
Risk of violence	**Average**
Cost of living	**Low**
Student concessions	**Excellent**
Survival + 2 nights out	**£40 pw**
Part-time work campus/town	**Good**

They are organised into self-contained flats of 6 or 8 bedrooms, with a shared kitchen and dining area and bathroom facility.

Arkwright Hall is just over the road, with deluxe and standard en-suite rooms split into flats of 3, 4 and 5 bedrooms with shared kitchen and living accommodation.

Halls on Laisteridge Lane are 5 minutes' walk away, closer to the School of Health Studies and include the recently refurbished Dennis Bellamy hall - each floor has 21 rooms split into flats of 7 with a shared kitchen/dining area in each flat. Trinity B & C Halls are also on this site.

GETTING THERE

☛ By road: M62 and M606 connect with national motorway network; from north, A629/A650; from northeast, A1 or A19, then A59, A658.
☛ By rail: London King's Cross, Birmingham, 3:00; Edinburgh, 4:00; Manchester, 1:00.
☛ By air: Leeds/Bradford Airport.
☛ By coach: London, 4:30; Manchester, 1-2:30.

STUDENT BRIGHTON – THE CITY

It's often been said there is something a little bit cheeky about Brighton & Hove. Made popular by the flamboyant Prince Regent, Brighton has a reputation for naughtiness and frivolity. What you will find is a welcoming city full of diversity and tolerance, perhaps the most cosmopolitan place in the UK. It's multitude of clubs, shops, restaurants and vast range of entertainment make Brighton and Hove the 'city by the sea' that really does have everything for everyone, so it's no wonder so many students never leave and settle for good.

NIGHTLIFE

The town has a huge array of clubs and pubs. The place to be for students on a Wednesday is *Ave It!* at **Creation**, where Brighton and Sussex Uni students dance the night away fuelled by the cut price drinks.

Students head for the seafront clubs, including **The Beach** and **Concorde2**, home of the famous *Big Beat Boutique*. If it's drum and bass you're after, lesbian and gay clubs, reggae or salsa, you won't be disappointed; check local listings for info. If trash is your thing go to **Dynamite Boogaloo** and revel in cheesy and camp disco 'toons' and be astounded by the almighty Dolly Rocket and Boogaloo Stu's outrageous live cabaret.

Midweek madness continues with the Latino feel and many participate in the carnival-style nights. You could be forgiven for thinking that no one works in Brighton, as week-night events are often as packed as the big weekend events.

EATS

Brighton boasts cuisine from almost every country in the world. Entire streets, like Preston Street on the Brighton/Hove border are devoted to gastronomic indulgence, there are late-night and 24-hour restaurants, shops and supermarkets for the night owls. There are over 400 restaurants including Cordon Bleu, English, French, Indian, Mexican, freshly caught fish (and chips), Japanese, Thai, tapas, Greek, Spanish, Lebanese, Egyptian, American, Cajun, greasy spoon, vegetarian, places with beautiful views of the sea, sushi and take-away. The numerous Italian eateries situated in the **Lanes** are locked in a price war, each bending over backwards to offer pizzas and pastas at amazingly cheap prices, making it possible to have a filling meal and a pint for under a fiver in a decent restaurant.

It is said that there are nearly as many pubs in Brighton & Hove as there are days in the year, they range from sophisticated late-night-cocktail-bars, high street pub chains to small independent owned drinking dens.

Do head for the student friendly **Ali-Cats** which is good for cocktails and shows free early evening movies. **Mrs Fitzherbert's** offers a cosy drink regular and acoustic nights. For THE student pub experience seek out **The Druid's** where the insatiable landlord Chippy offers students a warm welcome, great food and regular drinks promotions to make everyone feel at home.

SHOPS

With the best shopping south of the capital, there are more than 700 independently owned shops to browse. For designer clobber and antiques The **Laines** will suit any wannabe David Dickinson, but the prices will not be 'cheap as chips'. The North Laine is the bohemian centre of the town: with feel-good veggie cafés, bars, great second hand emporiums and a mishmash of fabric and clothes shops there is not much you can't get your mitts on in this district. Kemp Town boasts a flea market, a second hand book shop and is home to Brighton's own Lesbian and Gay quarter, with bars, clubs and shops to attract the Pink Pound. Big name stores can be found under one roof at **Churchill Square**, and the **Marina** has designer outlet stores in addition to a gigantic Asda, bowling alley, cinema, casino and other attractions.

STREET/BEACH LIFE

Whether it is the middle of winter and you want to blow away the cobwebs, or top up the tan in the summer you will find the beach is a welcome respite from the hub bub of city life. Boasting two piers, the famous west pier now open again after the huge fire a few years ago, you can visit fortune tellers, play the penny falls, buy more rock than you can shake a stick at and kiss me quick, squeeze me slow to your heart's content.

Highlights of the many events include the month-long **Brighton Festival** held in May, both revellers and locals flock to the beach and streets to enjoy the food, drink, juggling, samba band processions, free film shows on huge screens, firework displays and annual events like the **Pride Parade** and the **Winter Solstice** 'Burning of the Clocks' extravaganzas mean you are never short of something to do. There is also talk of **Fatboy Slim** holding another of his legendary beach parties.

ARTS

All over the city, self-expression is the way. Brighton Uni's **Grand Parade Gallery** and the

Brighton Art Gallery in Pavilion Gardens feature regular innovative ever changing exhibitions.

Innovative, contemporary art is also displayed in a multitude of cafés, bars and often in the street. There are many live venues, which again cater to all tastes. The **Dome** concert hall has hosted diverse artists including the London Philharmonic, Beverly Knight and Air.

In terms of comedy, theatre and film, Brighton is incredibly spoilt. **The Paramount Comedy Festival** comes to town in October bringing big name talent like Jo Brand, Bill Bailey and Johnny Vegas. The **Komedia Cabaret** bar has two different productions simultaneously each night with deals for students. **The Dome**, **Theatre Royal** and the **Brighton Centre** get the big-name touring artists in addition to the snooker championships. **The Gardner Arts Centre** on the University of Sussex campus plays host to art, film, theatre, comedy and music, and is nationally acclaimed. If it all gets too much you can always nip to the flicks, The **Odeon** is the most student-friendly offering discounts; the **UGC** is part of the **Marina** multiplex, and the **Duke of York's** the only cinema with legs (no it's true they are hanging off the roof!), a Brighton treasure and the oldest purpose-built cinema in Britain shows art-house and classic films.

It is almost as if Brighton was made for students; you cannot ask for a much better place to study.

Harvey Atkinson

UNIVERSITY OF BRIGHTON

The University of Brighton
Mithras House
Lewes Road
Brighton BN2 4AT

TEL 01273 644644
FAX 01273 642607
EMAIL admissions@brighton.ac.uk
WEB www.brighton.ac.uk

Brighton Students' Union
Steam House
Pelham Crescent
Brighton BN2 4AF

TEL 01273 642896
FAX 01273 694060
EMAIL S.U.President@brighton.ac.uk
WEB www.ubsu.net/

VAG VIEW

*T*he University of Brighton can traces its roots back to 1877, when the School of Art opened on Grand Parade, opposite the Royal Pavilion. Since then, Brighton town has been re-born as a city, inevitable consequence of its long-term reputation as London-by-the-sea. It is an energetic, laid-back, imaginative, vibrant, artistic, commercial, alternative, innovative, refreshing coastal cocktail, and its very own university evinces some of these elements too, especially the Faculty of Arts & Architecture.

The cream of the art world strut their stuff on Grand Parade, while the business suits, techies and teachers, doctors and sporty types do their thing out of town, variously at the Moulsecoomb, Falmer, and Eastbourne campuses.

Eighty-one per cent of under-graduates claim to be 'satisfied', and the teaching is

UNIVERSITY/STUDENT PROFILE	
University since	**1992**
Situation/style	**Seaside campuses**
Student population	**21135**
Total undergraduates	**17085**
Mature undergraduates	**30%**
International undergrads	**6%**
Male/female ratio	**42:58**
Equality of opportunity:	
state school intake	**93%**
social class 4-7 intake	**29%**
low-participation area intake	**9%**

good: Brighton gets three stars for helpful/ interested lecturers and the same number for small-sized tutorial groups. Teaching most popular with students is in Medicine, Languages, Initial Teacher Training, Design, Architecture, Building, and subjects allied to Medicine (which include Nursing,

Complementary Medicine, Occupational Therapy, Osteopathy, and Podiatry). Least popular are Fine Art, unexpectedly, and Cinematics & Photography.

The end result is good, however, with 78% of graduates getting real graduate jobs within six months, and only 8% dropping out on the beach.

CAMPUS

Brighton University spreads through central Brighton and into the surrounding areas of Moulsecoomb, Falmer and Eastbourne. For Moolsecoomb go north up the Lewes Road from the arts campus on Grand Parade - (rail and bus links are good, parking is not). Here lie the Business School, the Faculty of Science & Engineering, which includes pharmacy, maths, engineering, the Faculty of IT, and Med. School.

Further on you find the Falmer Campus, actually bang opposite the University of Sussex campus.

While Grand Parade is the old art college and

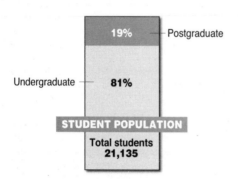

Undergraduate — **81%**

19% — Postgraduate

STUDENT POPULATION

**Total students
21,135**

Moulsecoomb the old technical college, the Falmer site was once Brighton's teacher training college and still offers teacher training today, along with health.

The Medical School teaching facilities are located on both the Sussex and Brighton/Falmer campuses.

Off to the east along the coast from Brighton, is the Eastbourne Campus, the uni's nationally renowned Chelsea School of Sports Science. They opened a £3-million sports centre there in November 2000. Outdoor pitches and indoor facilities are open to the public - widening access,

integrating with the community. It's what this uni is all about, in case you hadn't heard.

Along the coast to the west, the Brighton-backed University Centre Hastings is building on its reputation for media production with the opening of a new radio studio in autumn 2008. This includes a radio control room, a small voice booth and large studio area. Students will be able to access the latest technology to develop their broadcasting skills, be they a budding presenter or producer.

Find out which campus you're bound for and visit it - they are all very different.

FEES, BURSARIES

UK & EU Fees, 2009-10: £3,225. For bursary information, see www.brighton.ac.uk/studentlife/money/bursaries. Two hundred Academic scholarships, worth £1,000 each, are awarded to eligible students at the end of years 1 and 2, and year 3 of four-year courses, as well as years 1 to 4 of five-year Brighton and Sussex Medical School degrees.

There are also Elite Athletes scholarships (up to £1,500 per academic year), and ones for 'talented sports performers' (up to £300 per academic year). On the Eastbourne campus alone there are five bursaries of £1,500 for disabled athletes.

In addition, two Pestalozzi scholarships for ethnic students will be awarded this year, and for the three years of an undergraduate degree, to cover the full cost of tuition fees and also provide a financial bursary which meets half the recipient's living costs. See www.brighton.ac.uk/studentlife/money/scholarships/pestalozzi.

Finally, 75 International Scholarships, worth £2,000 off tuition fees for each year of a course, are awarded to outstanding degree applicants.

STUDENT PROFILE

International first degree undergraduates represent a mere 6% of the undergraduate body, so these scholarships may be useful recruiters. There is no typical Brighton student. It is all very disparate. Almost a third are mature students, few (only 7%) are from public school. Cutting-edge artistes may seem to be the most visible in town, but they are far from representative of the whole corpus.

> *The cream of the art world strut their funky stuff around Brighton, while the commercial, innovative and energetic bits find expression beyond its bounds in the Brighton Business School, the School of IT, the Chelsea School of Sport, and now the Brighton Sussex Med. School.*

ACADEMIA & JOBS

Brighton now has five faculties: Arts and

Architecture; Education and Sport; Health; Management and Information Sciences; Science and Engineering.

Brighton's strength in Art and Design has been recognised in the award of national teaching centres in design and creativity. Now the uni has a growing reputation in areas such as sport and hospitality, as well as scoring well in teacher education rankings. Health-related subjects have also grown strongly.

Today they have, besides the Fine Art (Painting, Printmaking, Sculpture), BA Fashion with Business. Successes in fashion and textiles have been both local and international and include employment with DKNY, Calvin Klein, Versace, Dolce & Gabbana, Valentino, Givenchy, Alexander McQueen, Hussein Chalayan and Julien MacDonald.

Graphic artists, designers, illustrators, sculptors, ceramists and set designers also fare well. Thirty-five per cent of research in Art & Design is world-class, and 30% of international significance.

From Interior Architecture, Product Design

TEACHING SURVEY AT A GLANCE	
Avg. UCAS points accepted	**280**
Acceptance rate	**16%**
Overall satisfaction rate	**81%**
Helpful/interested staff	**★★★**
Small tuition groups	**★★★**
Students into graduate jobs	**78%**

Teaching most popular with undergraduates:
Medicine (96%), Languages (92%), Initial Teacher Training (91%), Subjects allied to Medicine (89%), Design (88%), Architecture, Building (84%).

Teaching least popular with undergraduates:
Fine Art (66%), Cinematics & Photography (64%).

Biosciences, Nursing and even Acupuncture (Complementary Specialist Practice).

The degree at the Medical School is a 5-year BMBS (Bachelor of Medicine, Bachelor of Surgery). A small, personal school, they are looking for commitment and compassion in their applicants. You'll be based with the teacher trainees and other Health undergrads at the Falmer Campus, readily accessible by road/train and bang opposite the Sussex University campus. Chemistry and Biology is required at AS and at least one of these at GCE A level. Conditional offers of 340 UCAS tariff points are made from three A levels, if both Chemistry and Biology are among them. If Chemistry or Biology is only taken to AS level, grade B additionally is required. The UK Clinical Aptitude

SUBJECT AREAS (%)

(BSc), 3D Design, Music & Visual Art in the Art & Design Faculty to Civil Engineering, Design Engineering, Design Sports Technology in the Engineering Department, and BSc Architectural Technology in Science & Engineering, there is a strand which identifies the symbiotic nature of the uni's academic profile and weaves a colourful thread through the fabric of graduate employment nationally. What's more, entry is not demanding.

Further design suggestions are made by BEng Hons Automotive Engineering, a big strength, where would-be racing car designers will be pitted at the Moulsecoomb campus, the old techno college just north of the city. Easy ride by train.

In the vital health provision, there's a great reputation in Pharmacy, Biomedical Sciences,

RESEARCH EXCELLENCE		
% of Brighton's research that is		
4* *(World-class)* or **3*** *(Internationally rated):*		
	4*	**3***
Clinical Subjects	**5%**	**30%**
Biomedical Sciences	**10%**	**25%**
Allied Health Professions	**0%**	**15%**
Earth Systems, Environment	**0%**	**40%**
Physics	**0%**	**45%**
Applied Mathematics	**0%**	**15%**
Computer Science	**15%**	**40%**
Mech., Aero., Manufac. Eng.	**5%**	**65%**
Business and Management	**20%**	**25%**
Library and Infor. Management	**10%**	**30%**
Social Work, Policy & Admin.	**0%**	**35%**
Education	**10%**	**25%**
Sports-Related Studies	**10%**	**25%**
European Studies	**0%**	**10%**
Art and Design	**35%**	**30%**
Media	**5%**	**30%**

WHAT IT'S REALLY LIKE

UNIVERSITY:

Social Life	★★
Campus scene	**Individual**
Student Union	**Aimless**
Politics	**Average; student issues, anti-war**
Sport	**70 clubs, very competitive out at Eastbourne**
National team position	**38th**
Sport facilities	**Good**
Arts opportunities	**Drama/Dance OK**
Student magzine	**Jon Doe**
Nightclub	**None**
Bars	**Falmer Bar**
Union ents	**Ave It! @ Creation**
Union societies	**50+**
Parking	**Not good**

TOWN:

Entertainment	★★★★★
Scene	**Exceptional**
Town/gown relations	**OK**
Risk of violence	**Low**
Cost of living	**High**
Student concessions	**Good**
Survival + 2 nights out	**£100 pw**
Part-time work campus/town	**Average/excellent**

(UKCAT) test is also required.

Education is, of course, a major provision here - some 15% of Brighton's graduates will become teachers. For would-be physical training instructors (Education) Brighton you couldn't do better. See also the BA (Hons) Sport Journalism degree, which includes teaching for the National Council for the Training of Journalists certificate in magazine journalism. The BBC's director of sport, Peter Salmon, will be helping develop the broadcast aspect.

The Faculty of Management and Information Sciences, new in 2003, combines the Business School, School of Service Management and the new school of Computing, Mathematics and Information Sciences, together with the research group CENTRIM. It was created to adapt to changes in the business and management world where the integration of IT is key to success.

An interesting niche in the business provision is a dedicated series of International Travel/Tourism Management degrees, which score well for employment. New this year are Entreprenuership in Hospitality/Ttravel & Tourism, and foundation degrees - Travel & Tourism Marketing and Tourism Enterprise Management.

Note, too, the language provision at this uni,

which internationalises the business provision. Brighton had an international Grade 5 for research in European Studies, but actually slipped this year, 10% of its research work only being given the second string international award.

New degrees this year include English Literature, Environment and Media Studies, Globalisation: History, Politics, Culture, Humanities: War, Conflict and Modernity, Sport Coaching, Youth Work, Paramedic Practice, and four Engineering top-ups: Automotive, Aeronautical, Electronics, Mechanical and Manufacturing.

SOCIAL SCENE

STUDENTS' UNION The sad truth is that ents at Brighton have been flattened by a series of mishaps. First they had the **Basement**, a seriously good club/venue that was commandeered by the uni administration. Then they took over **Akademia**, a café bar and theatre on Manchester Street, which again was prised from them. Now they have **Falmer Bar**, and students make use of Sussex campus, and eat their heart out at **The Retreat Cafe** (Falmer) or **Cockcroft Café** (Moulescoomb), or go into Brighton. The Union promotes a clubnight on Wednesday nights at **Creation** on West Street.

Going out on the town can get expensive. Many of the jobs in Brighton are service sector based, so the wages reflect this, but there are opportunities for students to work in call centres and for local businesses where the rates of pay can be well above the minimum wage.

The Union claims 50 + societies and 70 + sports clubs, but it is impossible to pull the student scene together with so many outposts and such diversity.

PILLOW TALK

Accommodation for refreshers is guaranteed only to international students, students under 18, BSMS students, or students with disabilities.

It's all self-catered, mainly halls but also uni-leased houses/flats. They claim to be the

ACCOMMODATION

Guarantee to freshers	**80%+**
Style	**Halls, flats**
Security guard	**All**
Shared rooms	**None**
Internet access	**Most**
Self-catered	**All**
En suite	**Some**
Approx price range pw	**£70-£128**
City rent pw - Brighton	**£80**
Eastbourne, Hastings	**£70**

cheapest in the south of England.

New halls of residence on Falmer campus opened in 2003 - 162 en-suite rooms.

Last year at Eastbourne came Welkins Halls, the multi-million pound complex accommodating 354, groups of six rooms, en suite, sharing dining and kitchen areas.

GETTING THERE

☛ By air: Gatwick and Heathrow Airports.

☛ By road: M23 (past Gatwick), A23 to Brighton, A27 eastbound for Falmer, right turn (south on B2123) for Moulsecoomb. From east or west, A27. For Eastbourne, A27 and signs south on to A22.

☛ By rail: London Victoria, 1:10. Change at Brighton for Moulscoomb and Falmer (8 mins).

☛ By coach: London, 1:50.

STUDENT BRISTOL - THE CITY

Billed by many as the London of the South West, Bristol has a distinctly West Country feel and the moment you hear the regional accents you'll know you're a long way from the gold-paved streets of London. Despite this regional feel Bristol itself is a buzzing multicultural city with loads going on and so much to offer that you'll feel as though you're reaping all the benefits of living in a capital city.

ROCK ON

Hills, churches and water are abundant in Bristol and the city has many lush green parks to stroll in. The tastefully-developed Harbourside houses many restaurants and galleries/art centres and is home to much of Bristol's social scene, especially in the summer when the Grolsch musical festivals come to the city (Massive Attack, Basement Jaxx and Kosheen have performed in previous years).

In fact Bristol has a great music scene, born of the days when bands such as Massive Attack and Portishead made their name here.

Centres such as **Colston Hall** and the **Carling Academy** host an array of local, national and International bands. Recent acts in the city are Hard-Fi, James Blunt, Babyshambles, The Magic Numbers and K T. Tunstall. The Junction and The Croft at Stokes Croft showcase more alternative or folk music.

The Student Union's **Anson Rooms** have also hosted their own share of great acts; last year saw the Kaiser Chiefs and Franz Ferdinand, while The Rakes are scheduled for the forthcoming term.

Clubs and pubs fill the city, though some are rather expensive. There are plenty of studentier hang-outs though. **Evolution** on the waterfront hosts great nights such as *Wedgies* on Wednesday and Friday. **Bierkeller** and the **Carling Academy** have good student concessions and put on live alternative/rock music. A fledgling gay scene is to

be found at the **Queen's Shilling** or **Vibes** at the bottom of Park Street.

Ninety percent of Bristol's off-licenses and many pubs are located on Whiteladies Road, near the Clifton halls of residence. Ones worth a visit are **Bohemia**, **The Black Boy Inn** and the **Penny Farthing**. However, if you're looking for a stylish joint you should head for **Sloanes** or **Henry J Beans**. And if your parents are in town then a trip to the lovely **Avon Gorge Hotel** is recommended – for a good view of the famous Clifton suspension bridge.

ART

The revamped **Arnolfini** on the Habourside offers a wide range of arty events – from performance poetry to contemporary art. The city of Bristol **Museum** is free entry and currently houses the throne of weapons (installed by artists using de-commissioned weapons from Mozambique) and a rather random collection of pianos and pottery.

Hours can be spent sipping bottomless coffee in cafés around the University areas though particularly good are the **Boston Tea Party** on Park Street and **Toby's Deli Diner** just off Tyndall Avenue. **The York café** in Clifton should also be road-tested for its great fry-up.

THEATRE, FILM

Theatres such as the Old Vic run great deals once a week when students pay a minimum contribution of £3.50 for a ticket. Bristol's **Old Vic** is on a par with London theatres, in terms of variety and standard of drama on offer. Recent plays such as Christopher Marlowe's *Tamburlaine*, starring Greg Hicks, got great reviews from the national press.

For musicals and flashy shows the **Hippodrome** is the place to go though you won't get such cheap tickets. More avant-garde or obscure plays/ performances can be found at **The Cube**

Microplex (at Dove St South just off King Square). The art centre shows films and art exhibitions but also puts on all sorts of weird and wonderful events such as October's 'Ich bin ein Berliner' festival: a three day celebration of the said city showcasing electronic tunes, films and art.

If film's your thing then the city has a cinema to suit your every taste. **Cineworld**, **Vue**, **Showcase** and **Odeon** cinemas around Bristol show most Blockbusters and mainstream films while the **Watershed** and the Arnolfini on the Harbourside put on art house or International cinema.

The **Imax** centre, also on the Harbourside, is worth a visit to see some incredible 3D and special effects. There are also several film festivals on throughout the year, the best being the 'Brief Encounters' short film fest and the self-explanatory 'Animated Encounters'.

OTHER ENTERTAINMENT

Sport is important in Bristol, even though the city lacks a top-flight football club. Bristol City have a large following and have enjoyed success in recent years, unlike local rivals Bristol Rovers.

For rugby, however, though relegated in 2003 from the Zurich Premiership, they are setting new records, finding their way back (and safely so) with extraordinary ease. They can rely too on Gloucestershire County Cricket Club to put a smile on their faces. A visit to all these clubs is well worthwhile.

Laura Cattell

UNIVERSITY OF BRISTOL

The University of Bristol
Senate House
Tyndall Avenue
Bristol BS8 1TH

Bristol Students' Union
Queens Road
Clifton
Bristol BS8 1LN

TEL 0117 928 9000
FAX 0117 925 1424
EMAIL ug-admissions@bristol.ac.uk
WEB www.bristol.ac.uk

TEL 0117 954 5800
FAX 0117 954 5817
EMAIL communications-ubu@bristol.ac.uk
WEB www.ubu.org.uk/

VAG VIEW

*B*ristol University is a major player, once considered to be the choice of privilege, but for some time out to convince that its exclusivity is merely down to entry requirements that admit confident, ambitious and able students. Its Access to Bristol policy to tap the academic potential of a wider range of students is gradually persuading applicants from previously under-represented groups to apply. Now, time and again we hear from public school sixth formers that they are the ones being discriminated against. Has the pendulum, given momentum originally not by Bristol but by the Labour Government, really swung that far?

State school intake is 63% at Bristol, which is very low relative to most other universities. intake from the working classes is a mere 14% and from so-called 'low-participation neighbourhoods', 4%. So there

UNIVERSITY/STUDENT PROFILE	
University since	**1909**
Situation/style	**Civic**
Student population	**22780**
Total undergraduates	**15330**
Mature undergraduates	**7%**
International undergrads	**14%**
Male/female ratio	**48:52**
Equality of opportunity:	
state school intake	**63%**
social class 4-7 intake	**14%**
low-participation area intake	**4%**

is no evidence that they are discriminating against public school kids, even though there is plenty of evidence that they are trying to diversify.

The Access to Bristol scheme is a programme of events designed to encourage academically motivated local pupils from schools and colleges identified by the Widening Participation and Undergraduate

Recruitment Office to apply to the university, and they encourage such applications with Access to Bristol bursaries.

The work is purposeful and hardly threatening, but the complaints persist, and criticism spreads to accusations of discrimination against Northern applicants, too.

For years Northerners have thought of Bristol as 'a Southern poof's university,' as one student put it.

The undergraduate body of two universities far to the North, Durham and Edinburgh, is almost identical proportionally in terms of public school student intake, and both have been criticised by students in the past for the boorish behaviour of said public school kids, mainly from the South, who they refer to as 'chavs with money'. I put this to Hannah, a second year undergraduate at Bristol reading Mathematics, and asked her whether it was true of Bristol.

'Well definitely there are quite a few groups of you know, that sort of public school... actually not so much public school but loads of middle class "private" school students from London. There are so many people here from London and it is a bit sickening sometimes.'

Hannah is herself from London, where she attended a Roman Catholic day school. 'I have talked to a couple of friends at Durham, and they said basically everyone is from public school, or really posh sort of people. I think at Bristol you get more the street-wise student, it's much more kind of "alternative". There are lots of different types obviously, but these are the sort of people who would apply to a place like Bristol, where there's so much stuff going on, a really busy city and so many different music genres, a place which isn't just made up of students like Durham is.'

Hannah seemed to be saying that the Bristol student is intelligent cool, rather than boorish.

As at Oxbridge, there is also the sense that Bristol wants students who can hack the greater workload. 'I think you do have to do a lot of work if you want to get a good degree and there are some very hard-working people at Bristol. Certain degrees have different

reputations for working hard, like Dentistry is really hard, they work incredible amounts, it completely depends which degree you do.'

What about Hannah's course?

'In Pure Maths I think there's a good balance. You know how people always say arts students never have any work and people who do sciences do loads of hours, but Maths is kind of in between. It's really good because the homework is set. For each module, they give us the homework that we have to do for the next week. It's not like leaving it to you to do the work you think you should be doing.'

What about the teaching staff at Bristol? did she find them available when she needed to consult them? Do they have an interest in teaching, or are students a bit of a necessary evil?

'I think for Mathematics lecturers it's quite hard, because they are not generally really people! For some of them (and this is a bit of a generalisation), some of them would be more interested in their own work. But we have had a few lecturers who have been really, really good and really easy to access. It was much easier in first year because we had tutorials then and we don't now.'

In the National Student Survey Bristol is

TEACHING SURVEY AT A GLANCE

Avg. UCAS points accepted	**420**
Acceptance rate	**9%**
Overall satisfaction rate	**83%**
Helpful/interested staff	★★★★
Small tuition groups	★★★
Students into graduate jobs	**83%**

Teaching most popular with undergraduates:
Molecular Biology, Biophysics & Biochemistry (100%), Aerospace Eng., (97%), Medical Science & Pharmacy (94%), Biology& Related Sciences, Chemistry (96%), Mechanical, Production & Manufacturing Eng. (95%), Biology, Law (94%), Anatomy, Physiology & Pathology, Sociology (93%), Zoology (92%), English, Mechanically-based Eng. (91%), Philosophy, Physics, Civil Eng., Engineering & Technology (90%).

Teaching least popular with undergraduates:
Medicine (77%), History (68%), Animal Behaviour& Welfare (65%), Politics (62%), Drama (43%).

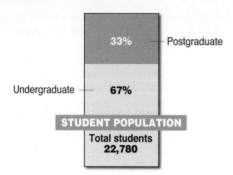

33% — Postgraduate

Undergraduate — 67%

STUDENT POPULATION
Total students
22,780

noted for its helpful/interested staff, but less
so for small-size tutorials. In her first year
Hannah had tutorials of four or five people
at least twice a week. Why did they stop?

'I don't actually know. Maybe because
they are too difficult to organise, because you
are allowed to choose different modules in
the second year, so everyone is doing a whole
range of different things, whereas in first
year everyone does the same one subject.'

I ask what modules Hannah is taking
and it emerges that she has chosen subjects
wholly unconnected with Maths.

'Well, actually this year I'm doing an
open unit in Social Anthropology, so I have
been using the library quite a bit, which I
don't need to do for Maths, and I'm doing
French as well.'

What made you choose these?

'Oh well, that was because I found Maths
really full on. I just wanted to try some
different things.'

Doing these three subjects, which involve
quite different modes of learning, Hannah
discovered made her much more interested in
all of them. It freshened her thinking about
Maths. In particular, Social Anthropology
involves a great deal of reading in the
library, Maths none. And French cleanses
her mind in another way. One can begin to
see why Hannah was accepted at Bristol.
There is interest in what she is doing and
self-awareness of how her mind works. She
also finds time to be ladies team Captain of
the Bristol University sailing team, a sport in
which Bristol University excels.

CAMPUS

Set a stone's throw from the city centre and near
the trendy Clifton area, Bristol University is a great
example of a city campus. It presents a safe but

lively environment within a beautiful and vibrant
city. University buildings such as the Gothic Wills
Memorial Building and the 18th century Royal Fort
House fit in well with the historic past of the city.
The row of Victorian houses which form the Arts
department is also a pretty place to spend your
undergraduate days.

FEES, BURSARIES

UK & EU Fees, 2009-10: £3,225 p.a. There's a
bursary for students in receipt of full HE
Maintenance Grant. In addition, bursaries to
students whose household income is £50,000 or
less. Local students, defined as living in the BA or
BS postal code at the time of their UCAS
application, will also be eligible for the Local 'Top-
up' bursary. See www.bristol.ac.uk/prospectus/
undergraduate/2009/moneymatters.

Vice-Chancellor's Scholarships, valued at
£3,000 per annum, are awarded to students with
exceptional musical, dramatic or sporting talent.
See www.bristol.ac.uk/vc-scholarships.

For details of the Access to Bristol Bursary, see
www.bristol.ac.uk/accesstobristolbursary

STUDENT PROFILE

Ten years ago Tony Dunkels wrote to us: 'Bristol
University has the reputation, especially among
some of its more northerly competitors, as being
a bit of a shandy-drinkin', southern poof's
university, comprising mostly ex-Oxbridge
wannabes and the like.'

Today, if you provoke union bods along these
lines they are genuinely hurt: 'The change has
occurred. It really isn't actively snooty any more.'

Writes Ruth Naughton Doe, a current Bristol
student: 'You will hear the negative "toff"
stereotyping, but I have found these to be untrue.
Like most other universities, Bristol attracts all
types - although the North is notably under-
represented and there are a lot of Londoners and
a high proportion of international students.'

SUBJECT AREAS (%)

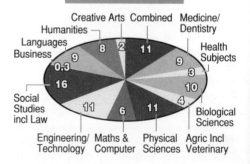

Creative Arts Combined Medicine/
Humanities   Dentistry
Languages   8   2   11
Business   Health
          9   Subjects
       0.3   9
     16   3
                           10
Social   4
Studies   11   6   11
incl Law   Biological
                            Sciences

Engineering/ Maths & Physical Agric Incl
Technology   Computer Sciences Veterinary

ACADEMIA & JOBS

Writes Laura Cattell: 'Cutting edge for Medicine and Veterinary Science, the uni is a Mecca for the Science and Technology subjects. However, there are over 34 subjects on offer, and over 20% study Humanities or Languages. The Arts and Social Sciences library is a bit dark and dingy, but there are plenty of good faculty libraries, and excellent access to online journals and resources. The IT provision is good, staff are very helpful and range from the old-fashioned tweedy types to more dynamic younger ones.'

Ruth Naughton Doe: 'Courses at Bristol vary. Sciences, Medical Sciences, Social Sciences and Law seem to provoke good reviews from the students I talk to, but the Arts Faculty does not. The library is severely lacking in resources (there is a 2-month ban on buying any new books, as I write) There have also been many debates about lack of contact time [with lecturers, tutors], most Arts students having only 6-10 hours a week. Talk to a student before choosing Bristol to do an Arts Degree. Despite all this, they are getting a new Arts and Social Sciences library by 2009.'

Teaching most popular with Bristol undergraduates is, according to the national poll, in Molecular Biology and Biophysics & Biochemistry. One hundred per cent of the class applauded the teaching in these. Then followed Aerospace Engineering, Medical Science & Pharmacy, Biology & Related Sciences, Chemistry, Mechanical, Production & Manufacturing Engineering, Biology, Law, Anatomy, Physiology & Pathology, Sociology, Zoology, English, Mechanically-based Engineering, Philosophy, Physics, Civil Engineering, Engineering & Technology.

Teaching least popular with undergraduates is in Medicine (only 77% gave it the thumbs-up, not surprising, perhaps, as the old teaching assessments only gave it 20 out of 24 points, relatively low), History (68%), Animal Behaviour & Welfare (65%), Politics (62%), Drama (a crushing 43%).

In spite of the students' view of the teaching of Medicine, doctors, dentists and vets account for more than a fifth of graduate jobs at Bristol.

For the 5/6-year MB, ChB, you'll need to be able to tell them what you expect from a career as a doctor, that you are aware of the levels of commitment and challenge, and what you in particular have to offer.

Candidates are encouraged to offer four subjects at AS, three being taken to full A level. Chemistry required at A level for course A100, plus one other science subject. AAB grades required at A level. Links are strong with special clinical academies in Bristol, Bath, Cheltenham,

Gloucester, Taunton, Swindon, where in years 3-5 you'll spend half your time.

RESEARCH EXCELLENCE

% of Bristol's research that is
4* *(World-class)* or **3*** *(Internationally rated):*

	4*	3*
Cardiovascular Medicine	10%	45%
Infection and Immunology	5%	45%
Other Clinical Subjects	5%	55%
Epidemiology, Public Health	35%	35%
Health Services Research	20%	60%
Primary Care	25%	45%
Psychiatry, Neuroscience, and Clinical Psychology	5%	55%
Dentistry	20%	40%
Biological Sciences	10%	40%
Biochemistry	20%	45%
Pre-clinica/Human Bio. Sci.	15%	40%
Agriculture, Vet., Food Sci.	0%	40%
Earth Systems, Environment	25%	50%
Chemistry	25%	50%
Physics	20%	35%
Pure Mathematics	30%	40%
Applied Mathematics	25%	45%
Statistics	25%	45%
Computer Science	30%	40%
Electrical and Electronic Eng.	10%	55%
Civil Engineering	25%	55%
Mechanical Engineering	20%	60%
Aerospace Engineering	25%	55%
Geography and Environment	30%	40%
Archaeology	15%	35%
Economics and Econometrics	30%	55%
Accounting and Finance	10%	45%
Business and Management	0%	30%
Law	15%	40%
Politics	10%	30%
Social Work, Policy & Admin.	20%	40%
Sociology	10%	40%
Psychology	10%	50%
Education	25%	35%
Sports-Related Studies	20%	35%
Russian, Slavonic, East Euro.	15%	45%
French	5%	30%
German, Dutch, Scandinavian	15%	35%
Italian	20%	35%
Iberian and Latin American	10%	20%
English Language and Lit.	20%	50%
Classics, Ancient History, etc.	20%	35%
Philosophy	30%	35%
Theology	15%	30%
History	15%	40%
History of Art, Architec., Design	15%	30%
Drama, Dance, etc.	45%	30%
Music	10%	75%

For dentists, it's the 5/6-year BDS. Entry AAB-ABB including Chemistry - the 6-year course allows entry with 2 non-science subjects. Teaching was rated satisfactory by 86% of students.

For vets, there's the 5-year BVSc. Candidates must sit the Biomedical Admissions Test (BMAT). Also a 3-year Veterinary Pathogenesis and a 4-year Vet Nursing & Practice Administration. Teaching was rated satisfactory by 80% of students.

Overall, 83% of all graduates can expect to land a real graduate-level job within six months of graduating from Bristol. In order of take-up, after medicine, dentistry and veterinary, Bristol trains you best for banking, business & management consultancy, social work, community & counselling, HR (personnel), the hotel & restaurant trade, software consultancy & supply, engineering design consultancy, central & local government, specialist retail, publishing, secondary, adult, higher and other education, security broking & fund management, accounting, defence, manufacture of aircraft & spacecraft, radio & TV, the Law, advertising, entertainment, sport, artistic and literary creation, telecommunications, architectural and engineering activities.

SOCIAL SCENE

STUDENTS' UNION Ruth writes: 'The Student's Union is housed in one of the ugliest buildings in Bristol and far from where most students spend time, but it is very lively.' Despite persistent rumours about plans to relocate it, there is regular expensive refurbishment of the interior. The **Epi** is the main student bar. There's also **AR2** (for small gigs and as a bar for larger gigs in the adjacent Anson Rooms) and the Avon Gorge room (for large society events and awards ceremonies). **Café Zuma** serves hot and cold meals throughout the day.

Says Hannah: 'Not many people go out in the actual Union. It has got a reputation for being really rubbish, but actually there are loads of really cheap gigs that play there which are amazing, like kind of alternative indie bands which normally if you went to see in London would be three or four times the price. Like you can go for about a tenner and that's really good I think.

'There is a bar in the Union which people go to sometimes, but again it doesn't have a good reputation. Oh, and it has just shut down apparently. I think they are trying to re-market it, trying to have a whole new revamp of the Union, because they have realised they are not making very much money. There are so many other places in Bristol to go to, so much choice. People realise that there are better places to go, particularly better locations, because the Union location isn't great.'

WHAT IT'S REALLY LIKE	
UNIVERSITY:	
Social Life	★★★★★
Campus scene	**Lively, rich student culture**
Student Union services	**Disappointing**
Politics	**Activity high, mainly student issues**
Sport	**54 clubs**
National team position	**12th**
Sport facilities	**Good**
Arts opportunities	**Excellent**
Student newspaper	**Epigram**
Student magazine	**Helicon**
Guardian Media Awards	**Two in 2008**
Student radio	**BURST**
Gig venues	**Anson Rooms, AR2**
Bars	**Epi, Avon Gorge**
Union ents	**Live, disco, etc**
Union societies	**183**
Most active societies	**Ballroom Dancing, Film-Making, BUMS (Music)**
Parking	**Poor**
CITY:	
Entertainment	★★★★★
Scene	**Full on waterfront and fringe**
Town/gown relations	**Clear differences**
Risk of violence	**Average**
Cost of living	**High**
Student concessions	**Good**
Survival + 2 nights out	**£80 pw**
Part-time work campus/town	**Good/Good**

Said a Union bod: 'Our Union is notable for its vast amount of student activities. In particular, our RAG (which raises over £100,000 a year) and Student Community Action (which organizes 36 volunteering projects within the local community and co-ordinates over 1,000 volunteers) are so big and popular that they each have individual union officers dedicated to them. Our Debating Society is one of the best in the world, and Ballroom Dancing one of the best in the country. We also have 10 performing arts societies that take 4 arts shows to the Edinburgh Fringe every year.'

Among the most active societies are Ballroom Dancing, UBFS (University of Bristol Film-MakingSociety), Dance soc, BUMS (Bristol University Music Society), STA (Stage Technicians Association), and International Affairs.

The Drama Society utilises two theatres: the 200-seater Winston Theatre, and the smaller Lady

Windsor Studio Theatre. Epigram is the student newspaper; student radio is BURST.

SPORT Says Laura: 'Sports-wise the University really does have something for everyone, from tennis to hang-gliding there are just so many societies. The flashy sports centre on Tyndall Avenue has a large gym and daily fitness classes, and though it's a bit hard to find, there is also a swimming pool on the ground floor of the Union building.' There are 54 sports clubs; the teams came 12th nationally last year.

Says Hannah: 'I've done quite a bit of sailing coaching, which I really enjoyed. Different universities have different reputations for different sports, but Bristol is definitely one of the best for sailing. Most universities have one or two teams and we have got six, and it's a really active club socially as well.'

TOWN Writes Ruth: 'The city is large enough to accommodate everyone's interests yet small enough for it to feel familiar. It is a hip, vibrant hub, catering for all interests and cultures, but also a beautiful city with spectacular views - and prepare to tone your thighs wonderfully from walking up and down its hills. It is also a safe place, bad areas being far away from where you'll be. It is hard to live here cheaply but it can be done. And if it all gets too much, take the Bristol-London 1 pound megabus to London for a clubnight out there.'

Says Hannah: 'There is the Triangle Area which has most of the mainstream bars and clubs. Usually people go out there, and if you go down towards Broadmead and the shopping area there are three clubs there which are quite big for students, the Syndicate, Panache, and Oceana. But it's a bit of an effort, much more of the big mainstream thing. On the weekend there are the local clubs, the more alternative ones in the Gloucester Road area. So, if you want to go for big mainstream nights out then you go to like Syndicate and Oceana. If you want to go to sort of cheesy fun, it's the Triangle. If you want the more alternative slightly more druggy, it's the Gloucester Road area.'

Are there any no go areas?

'Well, we have been told that St. Paul's Road is

ACCOMMODATION	
Guarantee to freshers	**99%**
Style	**Halls, flats**
Security guard	**Some**
Shared rooms	**Some**
Internet access	**All**
Self-catered	**Some halls, most flats**
En suite	**Some**
Approx price range pw	**£52-£152**
City rent pw	**£67 upwards**

a bit dodgy, but I've never actually been there.'

PILLOW TALK
Writes Laura: 'Most first year students get allocated a place in halls which means a choice of two locations: Stoke Bishop and Clifton. Stoke Bishop is about 40 mins from the University precinct, while halls based in Clifton are in one of the nicest parts of the city and just a 15 minute walk away. The best choice may seem obvious, but actually Stoke Bishop houses a larger number of students and possesses a vibrant campus atmosphere which halls in Clifton really lack.'

Ruth cannot agree: 'I have visited all the halls of residence and in my opinion Goldney Hall in Clifton is excellent, with a good JCR that organises great events and boasts beautiful gardens.'

Says Hannah: 'Stoke Bishop was really good. I definitely think that that area is better than living in Clifton, because there are six halls up there and it feels more like a campus. E ach hall has its own bar and the Howard Baker bar is really good, a real mix of people unlike some of the posher halls. They also have tennis courts and squash courts, and a big grassy area, which is really nice in the summer. Everyone goes and hangs out there.'

The choice is yours. Go and see.

GETTING THERE
☛ By road: M4/J19, M32 or M5/J17 and follow signs to the zoo (an elephant).
☛ By rail: London Paddington or Birmingham New Street, 1:30; Nottingham, 3:00.
☛ By air: Bristol Airport.
☛ By coach: Birmingham, 2:00; London, 2:20.

BRISTOL, UNIVERSITY OF THE WEST OF ENGLAND

Bristol, University of the West of England
Frenchay Campus
Coldharbour Lane
Bristol BS16 1QY

TEL 0117 32 83333
FAX 0117 32 82810
EMAIL admissions@uwe.ac.uk
WEB www.uwe.ac.uk

UWE Students' Union
Frenchay Campus
Coldharbour Lane
Bristol BS16 1QY

TEL 0117 32 82577
FAX 0117 32 82986
EMAIL union@uwe.ac.uk
WEB www.uwesu.net

VAG VIEW

*B*ristol West of England, or UWE as it is known, sees itself as a 'new' university, which is understood to mean 'positive, forward-looking, a real value university'.

UWE attracts a distinctive breed of student quite different to that of its neighbour. Forty per cent come from within a 40-mile radius, 21% of its undergraduates are mature. The result is that many have a mature real-world outlook on what they want to do and spread that ethos, which drives the university's strategy.

Frenchay, the main campus sited in the north of Bristol, is the hub, nestling in Silicon Gorge, with Hewlett Packard and Aardman's, the makers of Wallace and Grommit, on their doorstep, along with the NHS, organisations that characterise three of the university's academic concentrations - computer, film, and subjects allied to Medicine.

There is more. Environment Agency and Airbus are on hand, as is BBC TV's natural history base in Bristol. Producer Mike Salisbury is involved, as is Adam Hart-Davis, and the business guru, Charles Handy, and Sir Digby Jones, ex-head of the CBI, also come in to talk to students.

UWE employs lecturers who are practitioners. The ethos is practical. The ethos is practical, real-world. Health and social care hopefuls will find themselves in a real hospital, even on Open Day. Their future employment is on the schedule even before Day One. Industry designs the courses, refreshes the curriculum, assesses the students' work - student projects in Built

UNIVERSITY/STUDENT PROFILE	
University since	**1992**
Situation/style	**Campus/ city sites**
Student population	**29760**
Total undergraduates	**23930**
Mature undergraduates	**21%**
International undergrads	**6%**
Male/female ratio	**48:52**
Equality of opportunity:	
state school intake	**89%**
social class 4-7 intake	**29%**
low-response area intake	**10%**

Environment are considered locally by real architectural companies. Getting a job at the end is simply another step in a 3-4-year process as inevitable as the one before. Seventy-seven do so within six months.

Yet the vocational element is not at the expense of academia, as is shown by the rise of the Philosophy Department, which, only a short while ago, was a mere History and Politics adjunct. Says Charlotte, a second year student: 'It's only recently that they have become their own little department, but it's a really good course. I have got nothing but good things to say about it.'

This development is in fact astute vocationally too. Industry is waking up to the fact that philosophy graduates think creatively and productively about problems, whatever they may be, problems in the research laboratory and on the shop floor. All of a sudden employers are actively seeking philosophy graduates to work for their companies.

So, UWE is in the forefront right now, in

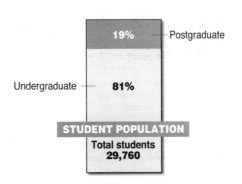

the National Student Survey enjoying three stars for helpful/interested staff and small-size tutorials. In the Philosophy Department they have given birth to a new mode of teaching they call 'a lectorial... For some parts of the curriculum,' says Charlotte, 'instead of having a separate lecture or seminar we just have a two-hour block where it's sort of a lecture and seminar combined, like a big discussion group almost. It works really well I think because for those modules where we are literally studying one text it's quite good to be able to have that opportunity to discuss it. There are never more than fifteen people, which is quite a good size I think.'

The problem with UWE, if there is one, is a lack of cohesion. There is a plethora of campuses. Charlotte, being a humanities student, attends the St Matthias Campus, one of a number of quite small satellites, and rarely sets foot in the main campus.

However, she sees this as a positive advantage: 'There is not so much cohesion as there would be if the entire university was on one campus, but I do think it's quite nice because at the little campuses there is more of a community feel than is possible in the larger situation. I do think that one of the best things about UWE is that it is a bit spread out, because you get the experience of living in Bristol as well as the university experience.'

> **'I do think that one of the best things about UWE is that it is a bit spread out, because you get the experience of living in Bristol as well as the university experience.'**

number of public school kids for a new university (11%), and at the same time 29% come from the lower social classes and 10% from homes in non higher education postcodes. International students amount to 6% of the population.

CAMPUS

There are four sites in Bristol itself, mainly around the north of the city, with regional centres in Bath, and Swindon concentrating on nursing. Only Bower Ashton, which houses Art, Media and Design, is in the south of Bristol. The main campus at Frenchay, close to Bristol Parkway station, but 4 miles out of the city centre, has the main body of students and includes the Centre for Student Affairs, which brings together the various non-academic services. The St Matthias site (Social Sciences and Humanities) and Glenside (Health) are more attractive, but less lively. Education now occupies a new, £16-million headquarters at Frenchay.

FRENCHAY (address above) Location: north of the city, near Bristol Parkway Station. Faculties: Applied Sciences, Business, Built Environment, Computer, Engineering & Maths; Education; Humanities, Languages & Social Sciences; Law. Library has recent £6.5 million extension. Campus security is good. CCTV and this is one of the only campuses to have its own bobby.

Bower Ashton Kennel Lodge Road, off Clanage Road, Bower Ashton, Bristol BS3 2JU; Tel: 0117 966 0222. Location: south of river, west but in easy reach of city centre. Faculties: Art, Media & Design. £4 million going into a complete redevelopment strategy, the first students to benefit going in this year. Ents

FEES, BURSARIES

UK & EU Fees 2009-10: £3,225 p.a. There's an income-assessed Bursary of £1,000 for students in receipt of the full HE Maintenance Grant. Other awards include an Access Bursary of £1,000 for undergraduates who have completed a recognised Access course, and a Care Leavers Bursary of the same amount for full-time undergraduates who have been in local authority care. See www.uwe .ac.uk/money.

There are also sports and music scholarships for up to £3,000 and £1,000 per year.

STUDENT PROFILE

The student body is a good mix. There's a healthy

TEACHING SURVEY AT A GLANCE	
Avg. UCAS points accepted	**260**
Acceptance rate	**23%**
Overall satisfaction rate	**83%**
Helpful/interested staff	★★★
Small tuition groups	★★★
Students into graduate jobs	**77%**

Teaching most popular with undergraduates:
Biology and related sciences (96%), Cinematics & Photography, Forensic & Archaeological Science, Physics (95%), Medical Science & Pharmacy, Anatomy, Physiology & Pathology, other Subjects allied to Medicine, Maths, Phys. Geography & Enviro. Science (94%), Accounting, Biological Sciences , Finance, Law, Psychology (93%), Geographical Studies (92%), History, Philosophy (91%), Creative Practices (90%).

Teaching least popular with undergraduates:
Design Studies (66%), Mechanically-based Engineering (63%).

facilities: opening hours short in Bower's Bar, but good, buzzy atmosphere.

St Matthias Oldbury Court Road, Fishponds, Bristol BS16 2JP; Tel: 0117 965 5384. Location: sometime monastery, northeast of city centre, near Glenside (see below), good bus service to city action. Faculty: Humanities, Languages & Social Science; Applied Science; Psychology. Accommodation: two halls. Learning resources: library. Sport facilities: cricket square, two soccer pitches, gym. Ents facilities: St Matt's bar.

Glenside Blackberry Hill, Stapleton, Bristol BS16 1DD. Tel: 0117 958 5655. Location: northeast of city centre, nearest to St Matthias, good bus service to city action. Faculty: Health & Social Care. Accommodation: purpose-built, self-catering. Learning resources: library. Sport facilities: space for aerobics, etc. Ents facilities: student/staff social club, good restaurant, not far from Frenchay.

The Hartpury Campus Hartpury House, Gloucester GL19 3BE. Tel: 01452 702132. www.hartpury.ac.uk/. An Associate Faculty since 1997, the college comprises 200 hectares of countryside, with woodlands, farm, lake and equine centre. Animal Science, etc. Students bring their own horses. Oh, and premiere division Gloucester Rugby Club train there.

ACADEMIA & JOBS

Teaching most popular with undergraduates is in Biology and related sciences, Cinematics & Photography, Forensic & Archaeological Science, Physics, Medical Science & Pharmacy, Anatomy, Physiology & Pathology, subjects allied to Medicine, Maths, Geography and Environmental Science, Accounting, Finance, Law, Psychology, History, Philosophy, and Creative Practices.

The following employment sectors account for 72% of those who get graduate jobs.

14% end up working in hospitals. Nursing is a big feature and the range of degrees is wide - Health & Community Practice, Learning Disabilities, Adult Nursing, Care of the Older Person, Cancer Care, Emergency Care, Critical Care, Palliative Care, Mental Health, Children's, etc. Check campus situation, many are at Glenside in Bristol, but Adult and Mental are also available at the Gloucestershire site, where there are also Learning Disabilities and Children's Nursing degrees. Also, Physiotherapy, Occupational Therapy and Radiotherapy score in this sector.

9% become teachers, mainly, but far from exclusively, at primary level. After that, jobs are found in social work, community & counselling (see the BSc Social Work), in central & local government administration (a steady stream via Social, Economic & Political Studies departments, Business Administration, and such as BSc Public Health), and in miscellaneous business activities, banking, insurance, and accountancy.

UWE's top-rated Business School dropped only one point at inspection. Same was true of Economics. There are plenty of jobs in retail, business & management consultancy, human resource management, and the transport industry, and a range of dedicated Accountancy degrees with interesting add-ons - from Business, Finance, Economics, Law, Tourism and Maths to Drama

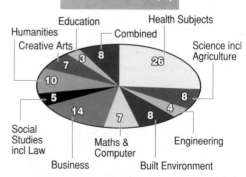

SUBJECT AREAS (%)

Education, Health Subjects, Humanities, Combined, Creative Arts, Science incl Agriculture, 3, 8, 26, 7, 10, 8, 5, 14, 7, 8, 4, Social Studies incl Law, Maths & Computer, Engineering, Business, Built Environment

RESEARCH EXCELLENCE

% of UWE"s research that is
4* *(World-class) or* **3*** *(Internationally rated):*

	4*	3*
Nursing and Midwifery	5%	35%
Allied Health Professions	15%	50%
Agriculture, Veterinary, Food	5%	40%
Applied Mathematics	0%	10%
Computer Science	10%	35%
Engineering,Mineral, Mining	10%	45%
Architecture, Built Environment	5%	40%
Town and Country Planning	5%	45%
Geography and Environmental	0%	20%
Accounting and Finance	10%	30%
Business and Management	0%	30%
Law	5%	15%
Politics	0%	15%
Social Work, Social Policy	0%	25%
Sociology	0%	15%
Education	5%	10%
English	5%	25%
Linguistics	10%	35%
History	5%	35%
Art and Design	10%	50%
Communication, Media Studies	15%	45%

campus. Always this practical, real-world emphasis. There is also a car crash scene for forensic science students, and participation with the local Bristol police force, and the UWE course is one of only a handful to be accredited by the Institute of Forensic Science.

Millions have been spent on new studios, suites and facilities for Art, Media and Design students at the Bower Ashton campus, widely known for its fashion, and of course the Animation courses, source of the outflow into the film industry. Peter Lord, one of the producers of Aardman, teaches there. Sixty UWE students appeared in the list of credits for Chicken Run.

It is also good for Fine Art. The Royal West of England Academy, based in Bristol, has close links and UWE's Dean of Creative Art is a well-known artist in his own right.

Finally, they have a range of Animal Science degrees (even Equine Dental Science), and a popular development has been Veterinary Nursing Science, and Veterinary Practice Management.

and Early childhood. In the insurance/pension sector, UWE is again a leading force, as they are for would-be investment analysts.

Jobs in the hotel & restaurant industry flow in number from Business, Biological Sciences, and Design.

Architectural Technology and Engineering degrees steer graduates into architectural consultancy, building, and town planning. And in the field of engineering, their record for employment in aeronautics is second only to Loughborough. See their Aerospace Design Engineering degrees.

There are also estate agents aplenty - see the Real Estate (Valuation & Management) degree, and many go into publishing, computing, the Law, sporting activities (there's a big range of coaching degrees, among others), and films.

Principal employment strengths in computing include the computer games sector, and systems analysts.

In Law, they are specialists in European and commercial & business law. They also offer a Legal Practice Course (LPC), essential step to becoming a solicitor, and are one of only eight unis where the BVC (Bar Vocational Course, essential to becoming a barrister) may be undertaken. Bristol University Law students take their law practice and bar vocational courses here. There is a mock court on

WHAT IT'S REALLY LIKE

UNIVERSITY:	
Social Life	★★★
Campus scene	**Diverse mix**
Student Union	**Active**
Politics	**Average**
Sport	**Strong**
National team position	**35th**
Arts	**Drama very good**
Student magazine	**Westworld**
Student newspaper	**Western Eye**
Student Radio	**Hub**
Nightclub/venue	**Venue**
Central campus bar	**Escape**
Other campus bars	**St Matthias, Glenside, Bower**
Union ents	**Clubnights, good live bands**
Union societies	**40**
Most active societies	**Comets Cheerleaders**
Parking	**Poor**
CITY:	
Entertainment	★★★★★
Scene	**Full on waterfront and fringe**
Town/gown relations	**Good**
Risk of violence	**Average-high**
Cost of living	**High**
Student concessions	**Good**
Survival + 2 nights out	**£70-£100 pw**
Part-time work campus/town	**Good/Excellent**

SOCIAL SCENE

STUDENTS' UNION Escape is the main bar on Frenchay. Big cheesy Friday nights - a multiplicity of events. There's also **Red** - café culture by day, and another main venue for club nights, bands, etc. - and a number of cafés - **Street Café, One Zone, Faz**, plus one in the sports hall - attract additional custom.

The bar at St Matts is reputedly the friendliest bar at Uni, where everybody knows your name. They put on Friday-night events, karaoke nights and even pantomimes. Glenside is the perfect place for a pint before a big night out, and Bower's bar is uniquely the students own.

The media set-up is good. There's *Westworld* (magazine), *Western Eye* (newspaper) and Hub (the radio station). 'We also have a very active Drama society, linked with the centre of Performing Arts which the university run, and the standard of our shows is very high.

ACCOMMODATION	
Guarantee to freshers	**100%**
Style	**Flats, houses**
Security guard	**Some**
Shared rooms	**None**
Internet access	**Most**
Self-catered	**All**
En suite	**50%**
Approx price range pw	**£87-£133**
City rent pw	**£70**

SPORT There is a friendly rivalry with Bristol University, a varsity match (rugby), a boat race (the biggest outside Oxford and Cambridge, they claim), and the new sports centre at Frenchay really is all that it's cracked up to be, with an eight badminton court sports hall, aerobics studio, large fitness room with masses of machinery, and two glass back squash courts. There are 43 clubs - everything from sky diving to American football - and they came 35th nationally last year.

PILLOW TALK

All the beds at Frenchay (1,932 of them for first years) will have been snapped up by May, so if you want a part of the new student village, get in quick. Security is superb. Besides CCTV, you have to unlock four doors before you get to your en-suite, broad-banded room, six of which make up a flat. The rest of student accommodation is in the city. Very wide range of flats and houses, including harbourside city centre accommodation.

GETTING THERE

☞ By road to Frenchay, Glenside, St Matthias: M4/J19, M32 or M5/J16, A38; Bower Ashton, M5/J19, A369.
☞ By rail: London Paddington, Birmingham New Street, 1:30; Nottingham, 3:00.
☞ By air: Bristol Airport.
☞ By coach: Birmingham, 2:00; London, 2:20.

BRUNEL UNIVERSITY

Brunel University
Uxbridge
Middlesex UB8 3PH

Union of Brunel Students
Uxbridge
Middlesex UB8 3PH

TEL 01895 269790
FAX 01895 203102
EMAIL admissions@brunel.ac.uk
WEB www.brunel.ac.uk

TEL 01895 269269
FAX 01895 462300
EMAIL su.president@brunel.ac.uk
WEB www.ubsonline.net

VAG VIEW

*B*runel, known as the University of West London, is based close to the M25, M40 and M4 confluence. Heathrow Airport is just around the corner. Students are fifty minutes by tube and thirty minutes by overland train from central London.

Out of a 19th-century, technical background, Brunel established itself in the late 1960s as a science/technology/engineering uni, which was 'all well and good if you had long oily hair, wore AC/DC T-shirts and had the personality of a walnut,' recalls Satiyesh Manoharajah. However, things have been a-changing these past few years. The Social Sciences, Arts and Media faculties have greatly expanded, bringing an influx of generally more exciting students and, indeed, women!

There is now an almost equal male/female ratio, but while there are a few arty types, 'the general mix is still of engineering, computing and sporty types,' according to Ollie Wright.

The change is more noticeable perhaps in the students' declaration of their favourite teaching, which is in Languages, English, Sociology, Anthropology, Design Studies, Psychology, Electronic & Electrical Engineering, Biology and related sciences, Media Studies, Sports Science, Cinematics & Photography. Least popular is Social Work, a department in which only 32% are satisfied with what is on offer.

One thing that hasn't changed is the preponderance of sandwich courses - paid placements in industry, which are incorporated into many of the courses, from Aviation Engineering to Psychology & Anthropology, from Business & Management to Biomedical Sciences.

Brunel was a pioneer of the sandwich course. You may take a one-year block (for a 'thick-sandwich' course) or in some cases two six-month periods (for a 'thin-sandwich' course). Many students subsequently gain employment with their placement companies on graduation.

Employment is constantly on their minds, and success in the graduate employment league tables goes back decades. However, currently, the 74% figure for real graduate jobs gained within six months of graduation is hardly trail blazing, and one is bound to be cautious, armed with the national student survey, which shows only 77% student satisfaction.

One wonders whether the poor stats on helpful/interested lecturers and size of tutorials (2- and 1-star respectively in our 'Teaching Survey At A Glance' box) might have something to do with it. The statistic is at odds with Brunel's performance on another level. Student support last year merited an award from the Times Higher Education magazine, in this case it was support for for disabled students, however. Meanwhile the physically able students are taking the responsibility for their future very

UNIVERSITY/STUDENT PROFILE	
University since	**1966**
Situation/style	**Suburban campuses**
Student population	**15510**
Total undergraduates	**10350**
Mature undergraduates	**18%**
International undergrads	**8%**
Male/female ratio	**52:48**
Equality of opportunity:	
state school intake	**93%**
social class 4-7 intake	**38%**
low-participation area intake	**5%**

much on their own shoulders. Their Entrepreneurship Society is the fastest growing student-led group at Brunel and has recently won 'the title Best Entrepreneurial Society 2008', so they tell us.

CAMPUSES

Everything is now centred on the Uxbridge campus. Packed with bizarre, grey, concrete buildings, it has undergone a huge facelift in recent years, the main excitement being created by a £6.5-million outdoor sports complex, a £7-million indoor athletics facility, and a £9-million Health Services and Social Care Building. Says Olly Wright: 'The library building, called the Bannerman Centre, the refurbished pubs and club, Indoor Athletics Centre and four new halls have made big changes to the landscape.'

FEES, BURSARIES

UK and EU Fees 2009-10: £3,225 p.a. There are bursaries for students in receipt of full HE Maintenance Grant, see www.brunel.ac.uk/ugstudy/finance/support/brunel. Awards are also available for elite performance athletes (e-mail sports-scholarships@brunel.ac.uk for further details). There are academic and music scholarships too. See www.brunel.ac.uk/ugstudy/finance/support/brunel. For musicians, auditions are held at the beginning of each academic year (see www.brunel.ac.uk/about/pubfac/artscentre/awards).

Awards are also available to students from low socio-economic background. See www.brunel.ac.uk/ugstudy/finance/support/brunel.

STUDENT PROFILE

There is a 93% state school take, and 38% of undergraduates are drawn from among the four lowest socio-economic classes (4, 5, 6 & 7).

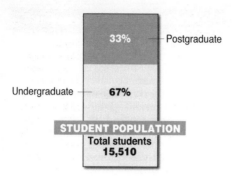

STUDENT POPULATION
Total students
15,510

67% Undergraduate
33% Postgraduate

International students account for 8% of total. The International Pathway Centre facilitates entry with an appropriate orientation strategy, language preparation, and support.

ACADEMIA & JOBS

Brunel provides degree courses in Design, Systems, Electronic, Computing and Mechanical Engineering, Education, Health and Social Work, the Humanities, Social Studies, the Creative and Performing Arts, and Sports Science. Sandwich placements and strong links with industry and business are to the fore.

Student satisfaction (77%) is not especially high. Nor indeed, as mentioned above in VAG View, is the real graduate job rate, though there are promising pockets.

The teaching most popular with undergraduates is in fact in Languages and English, where tuition groups are relatively small, but neither groups propsers particularly job-wise at Brunel. Then comes Sociology, Anthropology, Design, Psychology, Electronic & Electrical

Engineering, Biology and related sciences, Media, Sports Science, and Film. Least popular with undergraduates is the teaching of Social Work, where only 32% in the class gave it the nod in the National Student Survey.

Health and Social Work courses are a prominent part of what is being delivered. Near enough 10% of Brunel graduates take jobs in hospitals. The Biomedical Science degrees (Genetics, Human Health, Immunology), and courses like Occupational Therapy and Physiotherapy, account for this. Many also go into the manufacture of pharmaceuticals and medicinal chemicals. While others become social workers in spite of the unpopular teaching, and there's a fair drift into the community from graduates of the Youth and Community degree.

Meanwhile, a host of degrees in Business & Management, Business Economics, Economics & Finance, Finance & Accounting and Financial Computing pave the way for large numbers of graduates into banking, accountancy, etc.

Engineering fares less well. All those sexy Aerospace, Aviation and Motorsport degrees, along with the more traditional Civil and Mechanical Engineering degrees, lead in relatively small number merely to boosting the figures of graduates finding work in software consultancy and Engineering Design Consultancy from the Computer division.

Brunel's graduates of Computer and Electronic Systems, and Games Design find work in well over forty categories of the Higher Education Statistics Agency's graduate employment record, but especially in software consultancy & supply.

Arts are also to the fore in the curriculum - from English to Film/TV Studies, from Drama to Creative Writing. The novelist, Fay Weldon, teaches creative writing here. Brunel is also up among the best for turning out actors, rivalling specialist colleges. Their Performing Arts Department, which includes the Rambert School of Ballet & Contemporary Dance, is a centre for Film & Television Studies as well as for Drama and Music.

The Antonin Artaud building, a venue to support the teaching and research in performing arts, was recently opened by director and playwright Steven Berkoff. Graduates find work in the film industry, in radio and television, and in the creative arts. But the number that do is relatively small.

The line into radio and TV is clearer via their Broadcast Media and Communications & Media degrees. Publishing is also a popular sector.

In the Law Department they are specialists in Business & Commercial Law. Other social sciences

---

TEACHING SURVEY AT A GLANCE

Avg. UCAS points accepted	**300**
Acceptance rate	**14%**
Overall satisfaction rate	**77%**
Helpful/interested staff	★★
Small tuition groups	★
Students into graduate jobs	**74%**

Teaching most popular with undergraduates:
Languages, English (93%), Sociology (92%), Anthropology, Design Studies (89%), Psychology (88%), Electronic & Electrical Eng. (87%), Biology and related sciences (86%), Media Studies (83%), Sports Science , Cinematics & Photography (81%).

Teaching least popular with undergraduates:
Social Work (32%).

show strong emphasis on Politics, Sociology, and Social anthropology. Psychology has a good reputation here, both for world-class research and teaching. Graduates spread into a host of different areas with the skills and knowledge they accrue. Labour recruitment and personnel, and the Civil Service, are strong areas, fed by a number of different departments.

Brunel are among the leaders in finding jobs for graduates in Sport. The tradition of sport goes backack through the mists of time to Brunel University College, which was the Loughborough of its day, its song the Borough Blazer (after the college's original name, taken from its position on Borough Road). Today athletes, team players and would-be officials revere their modern Sports Science degrees - Coaching, Administration and Development, Fitness, PE, and Technology. They make their mark in the National University Championships too, coming 21st last year.

STUDENT SCENE

The Students Union has undergone a huge refurbishments of the bars, nightclub and food hall, and there are new shops, a balcony café and central atrium.

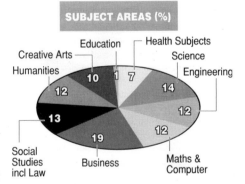

SUBJECT AREAS (%)

Education — 10
Creative Arts — 1
Humanities — 12
Health Subjects — 7
Science — 14
Engineering — 12
Maths & Computer — 12
Business — 19
Social Studies incl Law — 13

'The nightclub is the **Academy**,' writes Olly. 'No extra space has been gained, which would have been useful as some nights it does fill up and some are turned away. The new design is better than before, there's lots of stainless steel creating more light and space-age feel. It is open seven days a week from 9 or 10 pm till 2am, apart from Sunday when it shuts at 12.30am, but not to townies, as all entrants are checked against Brunel photographic identification on the door. Students may bring guests as long as they are students and have signed in at the student union reception.

'There is the regular cheesy night every Wednesday. Most other days are themed nights, with Monday open to societies to put something on.

RESEARCH EXCELLENCE		
% of Brunel's research that is **4*** *(World-class) or* **3*** *(Internationally rated):*		
	4*	**3***
Health Services Research	15%	50%
Allied Health Professions	10%	15%
Environmental Sciences	10%	30%
Applied Mathematics	5%	55%
Statistics	15%	35%
General Eng., Mineral & Mining	5%	45%
Mechanical, Aeronautical, Manufacturing Eng.	10%	40%
Geography	5%	20%
Economics and Econometrics	10%	50%
Business and Management	10%	35%
Library, Info. Management	20%	30%
Law	5%	45%
Politics	5%	20%
Social Work, Social Policy	5%	30%
Sociology	10%	40%
Anthropology	20%	30%
Psychology	5%	30%
Education	5%	10%
Sports-Related Studies	15%	20%
English	15%	30%
Art and Design	0%	35%
Drama, Dance, Performing Arts	15%	25%
Communication, Media Studies	10%	25%
Music	15%	30%

Tuesdays are sport teams' night. Thursday is generally when any famous names would appear, for example Coolio, The Heartless Crew. Friday is *Elements*, a regular DJ who plays r&b, hip-hop, house, garage, dancehall, trance and drum and bass. Saturday starts off with comedy then moves to a retro disco, and Sunday is rock night. Some examples of themed nights I went to last year are *Pimps & Prostitutes, James Bond Night, Doctors & Nurses*, and the traditional 1st night for all freshers, *Pyjama Party*. One night the Union hired out a couple of poker tables, a blackjack table, a roulette wheel and some croupiers and put on a *Casino Night*, which was free and no real money was gambled, but still fun nonetheless.

'The bar is still **Loco's** and has also been refurbished, like something out of *Star Trek*, with all new leather sofas, chairs and tables, a no- smoking section, many plasma's covering the walls, three pool tables, a table football table, two fruit machines and a couple of monopoly machines. For a uni bar, the drinks are expensive, but compared to London prices they are cheap. Prices rise about 5% in the Academy. Again, Loco's is not open to townies and there is security on the doors from

WHAT IT'S REALLY LIKE

UNIVERSITY:

Social Life	★★★
Campus scene	**Lively, trecky, sporty**
Student Union services	**Good**
Politics	**Average**
	Student issues
Sport	**Good**
National team position	**21st**
Sport facilities	**Good**
Arts opportunities	**Excellent drama, film; good art, dance, music**
Student magazine	**Route 66**
Student radio	**B-1000**
Nightclub	**Academy**
Bars	**Loco's Bar**
Union ents	**Good clubnites & live bands**
Union societies	**120**
Parking	**Good**

CITY:

Entertainment	★★★★★
Scene	**Cheesy local club, good pubs, cinema. Mainly London beckons**
Town/gown relations	**Good**
Risk of violence	**Average**
Cost of living	**High**
Student concessions	**Good**
Survival + 2 nights out	**£100 pw**
Part-time work campus/town	**Average/Excellnt**

'The local London students certainly do desert the uni at weekends, and their exit is noticeable by Friday afternoon when all the car parks empty, apart from one or two lonely cars. But there is still a good amount of students around and the Academy is certainly never lacking people on a Friday night.'

The Arts Centre is the platform for musical concerts throughout the year. Student groups include The Brunel Singers, an orchestra, guitar, brass, wind and string groups; all are professionally trained and music bursaries are awarded annually. Classes in photography and various visual art forms are given on a weekly basis by visiting professionals. There are several student drama groups.

SPORT Fourteen million pounds has been invested in a world-class sports complex, which includes an indoor athletics and netball centre, an outdoor athletics arena and floodlit turf, and all-weather pitches and courts. The gym and free-weights room have also been refurbished. Hurricanes Superleague netball are based here, and UK Athletics use it as a training faculty for elite athletes.

'Many of the students are doing sport science and related subjects,' says Olly. They are indeed one of the top unis for sport, coming 24h overall last year and with many championship finals to their credit. You can dabble, satisfy curiosity or take up fanatically more or less what you want to, even become part of a university team.

TOWN 'Mmm...the lovely town of Uxbridge... There are two shopping centres, The Chimes and The Pavilions, containing all the shops one could ever need. There is even an Odeon on the top floor of Chimes. Uxbridge also has a few nice student-happy pubs, like The Hog's Head, The Zanzi Bar, The Metropolitan. There's also a nightclub, Royale's, not recommended, plays cheesy pop and there is a guaranteed fight at 3am when everyone leaves, the only positive being the cheap drinks.

'Generally, the locals must be used to living with students as there is peace between us. There are many takeaways - if you go a day without a menu coming under your room door in halls then there is something wrong - four pizza houses, a few Indians and Chinese.'

7pm. They also have a typical pub food menu until 7pm.

'Another pub on campus - **Bishops Bar** - is not run by the Union, and generally the drink prices are lower. This is the place to go to watch football, while Loco's generally shows rugby. Bishops has also been newly refurbished and they are still in the process of finishing the balcony. Then there's the **Zest Bar**, located above the gym, a nice place to go to after a workout, smaller and generally quieter than the other two pubs, but still worth checking out if only for the San Miguel bottles. There is also a café which opened recently on the ground floor of the new library, always full of students and lecturers getting their caffeine hit, or a croissant.

> *Out of a 19th-century, technical background, Brunel has become seriously good at Social Sciences and the Arts, bringing an influx of generally more exciting students and, indeed, women!*

PILLOW TALK

Their accommodation has been transformed in recent years. In 2008, they completed a £250-million campus redevelopment pro-gramme, which saw the refurbishment of existing halls and the construction of the Isambard Complex. See www.brunel.ac.uk /life/accommodation.

All bedrooms (halls and flats) have internet and are self-catering. The flats are all en suite. Prices range from £81.41 - £99.96 p.w.

GETTING THERE

☛ By Underground: **Uxbridge** – Metropolitan line and Piccadilly during peak hours. Then bus, U3 or U5.

ACCOMMODATION	
Guarantee to freshers	**100%**
Style	**Halls, flats**
Security guard	**Some**
Shared rooms	**None**
Internet access	**All**
Self-catered	**All**
En suite	**Some halls, all flats**
Approx price range pw	**£81.41-£99.96**
City rent pw	**£65-£90**

UNIVERSITY OF BUCKINGHAM

The University of Buckingham
Hunter Street
Buckingham MK18 1EG

TEL 01280 820313
FAX 01280 822245
EMAIL admissions@buckingham.ac.uk
WEB www.buckingham.ac.uk

Students' Union
The University of Buckingham
Hunter Street
Buckingham MK18 1EG

TEL 01280 822522
FAX 01280 812791
EMAIL student.union@buckingham.ac.uk
WEB www.buckingham.ac.uk/life/social/su/

VAG VIEW

*N*ame a university which engenders greater student satisfaction than Cambridge (indeed, has the highest rate of student satisfaction in the country), almost exactly the same percentage of students into real graduate jobs after six months of graduation as Cambridge, rates as highly for helpful/interested staff and decent-size tutorials, and is available to a far wider section of the public than Cambridge at almost exactly half the number of A level points.

The answer is Buckingham, Britain's only independent university. They have one member of staff for every 8.4 students, whereas the average is 1:17.6. What's more, the norm is tutorial groups of no more than six.

The big news this year is the inception of a new School of Medicine.

TEACHING SURVEY AT A GLANCE	
University since	**1976**
Situation/style	**Town campus**
Student population	**840**
Total undergraduates	**610**
Mature undergraduates	**30%**
International undergrads	**61%**
Male/female ratio	**50:50**
Equality of opportunity:	
state school intake	**80%**
social class 4-7 intake	**NIL**
low-participation area intake	**3%**

The undergraduate course (see Academia below) is not yet up and running, but graduates are being sought for the Clinical MD degree.

CAMPUS

The three sites - Hunter Street, 8-acre Verney Park and the more recently developed Chandos Road complex, are walking distance apart and within the town boundaries.

FEES, BURSARIES

UK and EU Fees 2009-10: £8,340 p.a., high, but there is a saving on attendance. The logic is as follows. The time it takes to complete a degree at Buckingham is eight terms, the duration of which is two years. So, total fees = £16,680 + two years of living costs, estimated at £7,460 p.a., making a grand total of £31,600. You can expect to pay £3,225 annual fees for a 3-year (9-term) degree course at most other English universities, plus 3 years living costs at £7,460 p.a., making a grand total of £32,055, which is actually £455 more than at Buckingham.

Their argument is stronger in comparison to the fees at a decent public school, which are in the order of £22,000 p.a.

STUDENT PROFILE

Many undergrads are mature and 61% come from

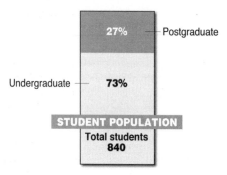

overseas. 'Each student mixes with 79 other different nationalities,' they say, and since there are only 730-odd Buckingham students in total, that is quite a mix. The male/female split is 50/50. Eighty per cent are state school educated.

ACADEMIA & JOBS

Buckingham has specialised in two-year degrees since its inception thirty-one years ago. The degrees operate on a four-term per year basis. What elsewhere is a long summer holiday is at Buckingham a term of teaching.

New this year is the Medical School. Two degrees are mooted, a Clinical MD for those who have already qualified but who want to study in more depth a series of medical sub-specialities, and the MBBS, the undergraduate medicine programme. Still under construction, it will be a 4-year course for students coming from any discipline.

The course will be fully GMC accredited and lead to a Foundation Year post within the UK National Health Service.

Other departments include Accounting, Business, Economics, English Language Studies (EFL), English Literature, Financial Services, History, History of Art, Information Systems, International Hotel Management, International Studies, Law, Marketing, Politics and Psychology. Also available, and paired with English are degrees in Multimedia Journalism and Media Communications. They say that for A level candidates they ask for three passes, but combinations of A and/or AS levels are also considered.

As this is an independent institution, it is not obliged to be assessed by the Quality Assurance Agency for Higher Education. However, in November 2003, it submitted itself voluntarily for an Institutional Audit by the QAA and was awarded a judgement of Broad Confidence in the quality of its programmes and the academic standards of its awards. The new-style QAA Institutional Audit process introduced in 2002, does not award scores at subject level, but departmental audits (Discipline Audit Trails) undertaken during the Institutional Audit confirmed that the standard of student achievement was appropriate to the titles of the relevant awards in the subjects scrutinised.

Areas of particular strength - Buckingham's Law and Business Schools are very popular and highly regarded. 2006 saw the introduction of the Bachelors in Business Enterprise, which offers students the chance to set up their own business as part of the degree. The Aylesbury Vale Enterprise Hub also opened in 2006 and offers advice and space to start up businesses in the Vale, incorporating a hatchery space for entrepreneurs who are at the 'pre-start' stage of their business plan.

Other new degrees include an MA in Global Affairs, BA degrees in Business Enterprise, Journalism with English Literature, Journalism

---

TEACHING SURVEY AT A GLANCE

Avg. UCAS points accepted	**260**
Acceptance rate	**8%**
Overall satisfaction rate	**96%**
Helpful/interested staff	★★★★★
Small tuition groups	★★★★★
Students into graduate jobs	**87%**

Teaching most popular with undergraduates:
Business, Business Studies, Economics (100%), Business & Administrative Studies (98%), Social Studies (97%), Law (94%), Languages (92%).

Teaching least popular with undergraduates:
English Studies (90%).

with Communication Studies, Journalism with International Studies, and a BSc in Economics with Business Journalism.

The international nature of the university (the opportunity to study with students from so many different countries) also sets students up well to work abroad after they graduate. There is an excellent alumni network. Graduates' close contact with fellow graduates offers unique mentoring for their future careers.

There are libraries at each site, a language centre and a networked IT set-up (a computer suite at Verney Park is accessible 24/7). There's a trained teacher of the dyslexic, who works with students from the minute they arrive. Degree courses are very concentrated, however. The intensity of the academic experience leaves little time or desire for the worst excesses of student fun and games.

SOCIAL SCENE

STUDENTS' UNION At one-tenth of the average size of a British university, Buckingham provides a cosy enough environment. The Union, located in the **Tanlaw Mill** on the Hunter Street site (refectory and George's Bar, pool tables, video games, lounge with Satellite TV), organises discos on Fridays and a Graduation Ball. Then there's the **Franciscan Building** (Verney Park) for private-hire cellar parties. There are currently eleven societies, mainly cultural or departmental, quite a few organised trips and a series of concerts and lectures.

The most active student society is Bahamian. There's a magazine called Cygnet, and in November 2005, a cinema opened on campus. Films are shown over the weekend, and often one mid-week showing. For escape, there are various restaurants and traditional country pubs in Buckingham, or Milton Keynes (14 miles), Oxford (23 miles), London (58 miles). Bring a car.

WHAT IT'S REALLY LIKE	
UNIVERSITY:	
Social Life	★★
Campus scene	**Small, friendly, multi-cultured, mature**
Politics	**Internal**
Sport	**Local & BUSA**
Arts opportunities	**Few**
Student magazine	**Cygnet**
Union ents	**Functions, films, discos, balls**
Union venue	**Tanlaw Mill**
Union Societies	**11, mainly cultural**
Parking	**Permit required**
TOWN:	
Entertainment	★★
Scene	**Trad pubs**
Risk of violence	**Low**
Student concessions	**Some**
Cost of living	**Average**
Survival + 2 nights out	**£50-£80 pw**
Part-time work campus/town	**Poor/Excellent**

SPORT Four all-weather tennis courts, one all-weather five-a-side pitch, a swimming pool, gym complex and sports field; other playing fields a mile away. There are riding schools in the vicinity. The uni teams are mainly locally competitive. Matches played against alumni and staff are also regular features. There is a campus fitness programme - aerobics classes, martial arts - and a well-equipped fitness centre. They are currently raising funds to build a Sports Hall.

PILLOW TALK

Guaranteed first-year, self-catered accommodation in mixed halls of residence at Hunter Street and Verney Park, or shared flats at Hunter Street. Security is tight on campus. All bedrooms have internet access.

GETTING THERE

☞ By road: M40/J9 from the south, then A41, A421. Also A422, A421. A413 from the north.
☞ By rail: Buckingham has no station, the nearest are at Bicester and Milton Keynes. London Euston, 1:00; Birmingham New Street, 1:20.
☞ By air: Heathrow or Gatwick.
☞ By coach: London, 1:20.

ACCOMMODATION	
Guarantee to freshers	**100%**
Style	**Halls, flats, houses**
Security guard	**Security**
Shared rooms	**None**
Internet access	**All**
Self-catered	**All**
En suite	**Some**
Approx price range pw	**£66-£111**
Town rent pw	**£90+**

BUCKINGHAMSHIRE NEW UNIVERSITY

Buckinghamshire New University
Queen Alexandra Road
High Wycombe HP11 2JZ

TEL 0600 0565 660
FAX 01494 605023
EMAIL admissions@bucks.ac.uk
WEB www.bucks.ac.uk

Bucks Students' Union
High Wycombe
Buckinghamshire HP11 2JZ

TEL 01494 610600
FAX 01494 556195
EMAIL union@bucks.ac.uk
WEB www.bucksstudents.com/

VAG VIEW

*B*uckinghamshire New University can trace its history back to a School of Science and Art founded in 1893 and to Buckinghamshire College of Higher Education, formed in 1975 out of High Wycombe College of Technology and Art and Newland Park College of Education.

From 1992 Brunel University validated its degrees. Then, in 1999, four years after it had been given powers to award its own degrees, the college was confirmed by the Privy Council as Buckinghamshire Chilterns University College. Finally, in October 2007, it gained university title and another new name.

Today it is celebrating a 33.7% increase in applications for its full-time undergraduate courses, the second highest increase at a UK university. They put this down to the reorganisation of their degree portfolio, the 're-branding', and the commitment they have made to enhancing the student experience through a package they call 'the Big D£al' (see Social Scene below).

This is an unashamedly 'new' university, unfolding on a wave of PR directed at students, whom they perceive as consumers in the modern fashion.

Business and Sports courses, Music Management, and Film and TV Production proved most popular amongst applicants for September 2009.

The National Student Survey shows that the best teaching is actually in Law, Management, Sociology, Social Studies, Music, Psychology, Business &

UNIVERSITY/STUDENT PROFILE	
University since	**2007**
Situation/style	**Campus sites**
Student population	**9045**
Total undergraduates	**8295**
Mature undergraduates	**29%**
International undergrads	**4%**
Male/female ratio	**49:51**-
Equality of opportunity:	
state school intake	**97%**
social class 4-7 intake	**36%**
low-participation area intake	**9%**

Administrative Studies. While least popular are Film, Photography, Technology, Languages, PR & Marketing - Mass Communications.

Now they are enjoying an opportunity to 'do' the PR and marketing rather than teach it.

The reality lies before them.

LOCATION

Until recently they were sited at three locations: two - High Wycombe and Wellesbourne campuses - within the market town of High Wycombe itself, one - Chalfont campus - some 10 miles to the east, centred on an eighteenth-century mansion and set in 200 acres close to the village of Chalfont St Giles. The hub of the new university - The Gateway, as the main campus is known - is under construction on Alexander Road in the centre of High Wycombe, and was a building site when we visited. Students from the old Chalfont and Wellesbourne campuses are moving lock stock and barrel to the new site for September 2009.

The Gateway will provide student facilities and the majority of the teaching provision, with Nursing courses delivered at another new location: 106

Oxford Road in Uxbridge. Facilities at High Wycombe will, in the first instance, include a sports and fitness suite, music studios, video production/TV studios, drama and dance studios, a

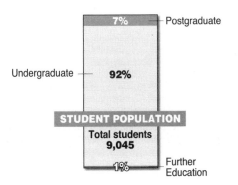

STUDENT POPULATION
- Postgraduate 7%
- Undergraduate 92%
- Further Education 1%

Total students
9,045

lecture theatre and conference room, a library, study rooms, and study 'hot spots' with wired & wireless access, a range of computer labs - IT/CAD/Networking & Communications, and a café.

STUDENT PROFILE

There is a large mature population. Ninety-seven per cent are state school educated. More than a third come from social classes 4-7, and 9% from neighbourhoods new to sending their people to university.

ACADEMIA & JOBS

There has been a complete reorganisation of departments into three new faculties.

Creativity & Culture is the umbrella for four schools: Arts & Media (Creative Writing, Drama, English, Film, Journalism, etc.), Design & Craft (Art & Design, Ceramics & Glass, Furniture, Jewellery, Product Design, Spatial Design), Visual

& Communication Arts (Advertising, Graphic Arts, Animation, Fine Art, Textiles), and Music, Entertainment & Moving Image (Music Management and Production, TV & Film).

Advertising degree graduates pour out of the Design school. Others find work as graphic artists, designers and illustrators, in media & government research, and textiles. Also, they are sector leaders in furniture design. High Wycombe has been associated with the craft for more than a century and Bucks New delivers the largest range of furniture design programmes in the world. There is also a Jewellery degree, which brings graduates into the Fashion industry.

Media degrees, which include Film & TV Production, Radio Production, Journalism, Sports & Events Broadcasting, Music Management, Production, etc. Evidence of degrees leading to jobs in the radio and television industry is strong, and there is a visible presence in the publishing industry too.

The Enterprise & Innovation faculty delivers Business & Management, Computing & Advanced

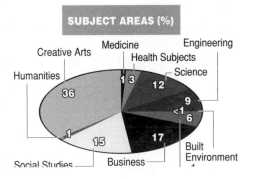

SUBJECT AREAS (%)
- Creative Arts
- Medicine 3
- Engineering
- Health Subjects 12
- Science 9
- Humanities 36
- <1
- 6
- 1
- 15
- 17 Built Environment
- Social Studies
- Business

Technologies, and Sport, Leisure & Travel. All are important elements in their graduate employment portfolio. There's an interesting niche in Air Transport & Pilot Training - two degrees that yield around 3% of their graduate employment provision.

Finally, Society & Health delivers Nursing, Community Health & Social Care, which looks after around 10% of the graduate employment provision), and Human Sciences & Law. They are specialists in commercial and business law, and have a strong employment track record with their police degrees.

SOCIAL SCENE

It's too early to say what will occur. But the Big D£al promises free access to a range of activities and events, in addition to a £500 non-means-tested bursary. What this means is that tickets for all of their gigs, club nights, comedy events, theme parties and events will be totally free for Bucks students.

PILLOW TALK

There are two halls at High Wycombe - Brook Street and John North Halls, with self-catering accommodation for 500. As part of their ambitious redevelopment plans for the town, they are

ACCOMMODATION	
Guarantee to freshers	**100%**
Style	**Halls, flats**
Security guard	**Some**
Shared rooms	**Some**
Internet access	**Most**
Self-catered	**All**
En suite	**Some**
Approx price range pw	**£60-£80**
City rent pw	**£60-£80**

building new accommodation at Hughenden Road - en-suite student rooms with communal facilities, rooms for disabled students and larger rooms for mature students. The first phase of this build is underway, with 234 student rooms scheduled for completion this year.

Accommodation is guaranteed to all freshers. All is self-catering, most with internet access. Rents range from £60 to £80 per week.

GETTING THERE

☞ By road to High Wycombe: M40/J4, A4010.
☞ By rail to High Wycombe: London Marylebone, 35 mins.

UNIVERSITY OF CAMBRIDGE

Cambridge Admissions Office
The University of Cambridge
Kellet Lodge
Tennis Court Road
Cambridge CB2 1QJ

TEL 01223 333308
FAX 01223 366383
Email admissions@cam.ac.uk
WEB www.cam.ac.uk/admissions

Cambridge University Students' Union
11/12 Trumpington Street
Cambridge CB2 1QA

TEL 01223 356454/333313
FAX 01223 323244
EMAIL info@cusu.cam.ac.uk
WEB cusu.cam.ac.uk

VAG VIEW

*T*he University of Cambridge, which stands at No. 3 behind Harvard and Yale in the latest Times Higher Education table of the Top 200 Universities Worldwide, is celebrating its 800th anniversary.

It began life early in the 13th century, more than 100 years after Oxford. Its colleges have always been self-governing, with their own property and income, and tradition continues to be an important dimension of the Cambridge experience.

Things do occasionally change, however. This year there is a new degree (see Academia), and New Hall, founded in the 1950s has changed its name.

STUDENT PROFILE

Cambridge students are bright: 'If you're thinking of applying to Cambridge: congratulations!' writes Caroline Muspratt, a student of Modern &

Medieval languages at Christ's. 'Why do I say that? Because even to consider applying, you must be a straight-A student, from a private school, with a white, middle-class background and parents who earn nearly £100K a year. Right?

'Wrong! It's a common misconception that state school students, ethnic minorities, poor people, etc, don't get in. None of this matters. It won't affect your application, it won't change the friends you make, the societies you join, or the grades you get. I'm from a state school, I have working-class parents, and I'm the first person in my family ever to go to university. And yes, there are people here who went to Eton and have spent their whole lives being groomed for Cambridge, but students are students and the public-state divide is little more than a media fabrication. The university is extremely welcoming to overseas students and ethnic minorities: CUSU (the students' union) recently won a national award for ethnic diversity and its publication, The Little Black Book.'

Loyalty flies in the face of the facts. Cambridge fails to meet its benchmarks for attracting applicants from the lower classes and families new to the idea of university, but perhaps they have other, more interesting reasons for selecting their students. Perhaps it is exclusive not because it deliberately excludes applicants from state schools or working-class families, but because its dons are looking for young people with whom they can work on a one-to-one basis and push forward a bit,

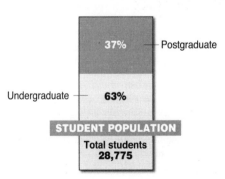

STUDENT POPULATION
Total students
28,775

not back into the hopeless class struggle of yesteryear.

Katie Lydon went to school at Bolton comprehensive and is 'more than fulfilled,' and quite unable to identify the typical Cambridge student or dominant group, only the caricature: 'Cliques grow up around sports, drama and other activities, as well as drinking societies and simple friendship groups. Although there is the odd example of the elitist stereotype, they are in the

UNIVERSITY/STUDENT PROFILE	
University since	**1209**
Situation/style	**City collegiate**
Student population	**28775**
Total undergraduates	**18185**
Mature undergraduates	**7%**
International undergrads	**11%**
Male/female ratio	**51:49**
Equality of opportunity:	
state school intake	**58%**
social class 4-7 intake	**12%**
low-participation area intake	**4%**

minority. Some groups, like sports teams and drinking societies, can dominate bar areas and seem intimidating, but this only tends to happen a few times a term, or after sporting victories.'

FEES, BURSARIES
UK & EU fees 2009-10: £3,225 p.a. Bursary for students in receipt of full HE Maintenance Grant falls under the Cambridge Bursary Scheme. See www.cam.ac.uk/admissions/undergraduate/finance/support.html#bursary.

For sport awards, see www.sport.cam.ac.uk/bursaries/, including their Talented Athlete Scholarship Scheme. Individual colleges offer financial support, which may include scholarships and prizes for academic achievement. For awards to disabled students, see www.cam.ac.uk/cambuniv/disability/support/ financial.html. For music awards (choral awards, organ scholarships and instrumental awards) see www.cam.ac.uk/admissions/undergraduate/musicawards/.

ACADEMIA & JOBS
A big event, a new degree, Linguistics BA Honours, will be available as a full course from 2010 entry.

Last year Cambridge submitted 2,040 researchers for assessment, and 31.7 of submissions were in the 4* category (world-leading), while 39.2% were adjudged 3* (internationally excellent).

All Cambridge undergraduates study for the BA degree, whether they are reading an arts or science subject. There are three graduate colleges not profiled below, which do take the odd bod for undergraduate studies if they have already done a degree elsewhere or are over 21 at entry. These are: Hughes Hall, CB1 2EW. Tel 01223 334 897. WEB www.hughes.cam.ac.uk. St Edmund's CB3 0BN. Tel 01223 336 086. WEB www.st-edmunds.cam.ac.uk. Wolfson CB3 9BB. Tel 01223 335 918. WEB www.wolfson.cam.ac.uk.

'The work ethic is very strong throughout the university,' warns Caroline. 'You'll be expected to study hard, and to achieve a lot in a short time... it can initially be intimidating, and I wasn't the only one who spent the first few weeks convinced that the interviewers had made a mistake. After a few alcohol-aided evenings out with other freshers, you realise that you are on a level pegging with most of them.

'Teaching is done through supervisions and lectures. Supervisions are given by fellows or research students to one or two students. It's a very intensive way of learning, and the short teaching term (eight weeks) means that there isn't much let up. This can take its toll, especially in the stressful summer exam term. Libraries are excellent, but...it can be difficult to get hold of books when the entire year is doing the same paper.'

The most popular sector for Cambridge graduates is health. The leading Medicine degree is the 5/6-year MB, BChir. AAA is required at A level, including Chemistry, and at least one further A level and one AS level (preferably two A levels) in two of Biology, Maths and Physics. You will also have to sit the Biomedical Admissions Test (BMAT) test (see bmat.org.uk). The test is being used to assess scientific aptitude, not fitness to practise medicine (which will continue to be assessed in interview) and focuses on scientific abilities relevant to the study of medicine.

The MB, BChir involves heavy science-based pre-clinical in first two years, core subject study (Anatomy through to Psychology) the speciality. A number of graduates go into full-time laboratory research. For those who don't there's the chance to do the PRHO at top Addenbrooke's Hospital.

The veterinary degree is a 6-year MB and not available at Peterhouse or King's colleges.

Law is another key Cambridge profession. All candidates must sit the National Admissions Test for Law (LNAT). Non-Law graduates may apply for a 2-year Senior Status Law degree here.

Finance is, though, after health the most popular job sector for graduates from Cambridge. Among routes into investment analysis, banking, merchant banking and share dealing, Economics leads, engineering comes next. In that faculty specialisms such as Information & Computer Engineering and Management Studies are available. Languages are also a well-trammelled route. From Occitan to Hebrew-Biblical, the choice is wide. Then again, the mind-train of Classics is much sought after in the City of London, and interestingly Cambridge are levelling the playing field socially by introducing a four-year classics degree for students with little knowledge of Latin or Greek from school.

Software consultants and engineers are popular areas for employment, too. Graduates come to them from Computer Science and Engineering in almost equal proportion, significant numbers (though less) through Mathematics. The Publishing industry takes a shine to Cambridge language graduates in particular. Humanities is another route to publishing; and journalists and editors come out of Engineering and Social Sciences, and of course student media - the magazines are *Inprint*, *May Anthologies*, etc; the newspapers *Varsity* and *Cambridge Student* - are regularly award winning, as is CUR and CUTE (radio and TV).

From student activity in drama come the new generations of directors, producers and theatre managers (there being no vocational drama degree at Cambridge University). Arts administrators and

SUBJECT AREAS (%)

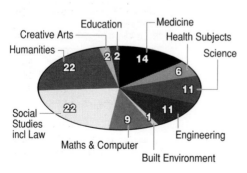

Education — Medicine
Creative Arts — Health Subjects
Humanities — Science
22 — 2 2 — 14
6
11
Social Studies incl Law — 22 — 9 — 1 — 11
Maths & Computer — Engineering
Built Environment

managers are also legion.

The Music Tripos involves history, analysis and compositional technique - intellectual and practical skills with an increasing amount of freedom to develop. There is a good record in employment for musicians, conductors, composers.

Humanities graduates also become charity officers in quantity. Languages are again to the fore as preparation for lecturers in Adult Education, and in social work. Languages and Social & Political Sciences graduates find ready access to research jobs in media and government.

There are two Education routes, one where Education Studies is a complementary but subsidiary focus of Biosciences, English & Drama, English, Geography, History, Maths, Music or Religion; and the other available only at Homerton College, which recently gained full recognition as an undergraduate college but where there is still an emphasis on Education Studies.

SOCIAL SCENE

STUDENTS' UNION 'Fresher's Week is organised by college JCRs (Junior Common Rooms), involving pub crawls and ents,' writes Katie. 'What I found especially encouraging was the willingness of the different year groups to mingle, and the fact that you are assigned ìcollege parentsî in different years to help you settle in.'

The Cambridge Union boasts more than 400 student societies for the few with time on their hands. Drama Society is big on tours to America and Europe every year, and a high number of productions go to the Edinburgh festival. Media-wise, the student papers, Varsity and Cambridge Student, and radio station CUR are award-winning, and positions like May Ball President, Union President and those on the JCRs are awarded after strenuous public hustings, since they develop the communication, teamwork and leadership skills sought by employers.'

There is no central nightclub, but CUSU run popular student nights at local clubs and live acts or many and various.

SPORT 'Sports facilities are abundant,' writes Katie, 'but vary between colleges. If sport is your thing, check out the college facilities, where exactly the playing fields and so on are before you apply. All have, or share, a boathouse and operate a novice rower training programme, which can be a really good way of getting to know people if you can hack the early mornings.

The university came 14th in the National University Team Competitions last year.

TOWN 'If you're looking for somewhere with 24-

RESEARCH EXCELLENCE

% of Cambridge's research that is
4* *(World-class)* or **3*** *(Internationally rated):*

	4*	3*
Cardiovascular Medicine	35%	50%
Cancer Studies	35%	45%
Infection and Immunology	35%	45%
Hospital Clinical Subjects	35%	45%
Laboratory Clinical Subjects	45%	40%
Epidemiology, Public Health	40%	45%
Primary Care	20%	45%
Psychiatry, Neuroscience, & Clinical Psychology	40%	40%
Biological Sciences	20%	40%
Agriculture, Veterinary, Food	5%	40%
Environmental Sciences	40%	50%
Chemistry	40%	40%
Physics	25%	40%
Pure Mathematics	30%	45%
Applied Mathematics	30%	45%
Statistics	30%	45%
Computer Science	45%	45%
General Eng., Mineral, Mining	45%	45%
Chemical Engineering	30%	55%
Metallurgy and Materials	40%	55%
Architecture, Built Environment	30%	50%
Town and Country Planning	30%	45%
Geography	30%	40%
Archaeology	30%	30%
Economics and Econometrics	30%	45%
Business and Management	35%	40%
Law	25%	35%
Politics	20%	30%
Sociology	20%	35%
Social Anthropology	35%	35%
Biological Anthropology	35%	25%
Psychology	35%	50%
Education	30%	35%
Middle Eastern/African Studies	35%	40%
Asian Studies	15%	35%
East European Languages	25%	30%
French	20%	35%
German, Dutch, Scandinavian	25%	30%
Italian	45%	35%
Iberian and Latin American	30%	40%
Celtic Studies	45%	30%
English	40%	25%
Linguistics	20%	30%
Classics, etc	45%	25%
Philosophy	35%	30%
Philosophy of Science	25%	40%
Philosophy	35%	25%
Theology	40%	25%
History	40%	25%
History of Art	10%	50%
Music	45%	40%

WHAT IT'S REALLY LIKE

UNIVERSITY:	
Social Life	★★★★
Campus scene	**Bright, exclusive, focused, fun**
Student Union services	**Poor, but socs good**
Politics	**Active**
Sport	**Huge**
National team position	**14th**
Sport facilities	**Good**
Arts opportunities	**Drama/dance excellent, rest good**
Student magazine	**Inprint, May Anthologies, etc**
Student newspaper	**Varsity, Cambridge Student**
Student radio	**CUR**
Student TV	**CUTE**
Nightclub	**None**
Union ents	**College JCRs**
Bars	**All colleges**
Union societies	**400+**
Parking	**Buy a bike**
CITY:	
Entertainment	★★★
Scene	**Cheesy clubs, great pubs**
Town/gown relations	**Average-poor**
Risk of violence	**Low**
Cost of living	**Average**
Student concessions	**Good**
Survival + 2 nights out	**£60 pw**
Part-time work campus/town	**Expellable offence**

scientists, all the scary chemicals are provided, and for arts students, the libraries are amazingly well-stocked. Travel costs should be zero: you'll soon find that everything in Cambridge is within walking distance (unless you're at Girton).'

PILLOW TALK

Students at Cambridge are provided with College accommodation. Sometimes this is in the main College grounds, alternatively it can be in a purpose-built block outside the main College or a College-owned house. The style of accommodation varies a lot but most students will have a room of their own. Some accommodation has en suite facilities where as others has shared WC and bath/shower facilities. Students have access to the College caféteria as well as self-catering facilities and most rooms have Internet access. Colleges also have Porters' Lodges staffed 24 hours a day.

Students are provided with accommodation for three years of undergraduate courses and in many cases a fourth year as well. Room rents are subsidised by the colleges and they are increasing,

ACCOMMODATION

Guarantee to freshers	**100%**
Style	**College, hall or house**
Security guard	**Porter's Lodge**
Shared rooms	**None**
Internet access	**Most**
Self-catered	**Plus college**
En suite	**Some**
Approx price range pw	**£70-£100**
City rent pw	**£70-£120**

hour opportunity, forget Cambridge; take a 45-minute train ride to London.

'Club fare in town ranges from cheesy, sweaty through the slightly nicer smaller, more chilled and alternative. There is a student night every weeknight.

'What the city lacks in clubs, it makes up for in pubs. There are dozens in the town centre, ranging from cosy locals to trendy wine bars. New restaurants are springing up all the time, and Cambridge is,' says Katie, 'a very safe place to live,' but what does it all cost?

'Cambridge is a relatively cheap city,' writes Caroline. 'If you're trying to work out a budget, allow about £80 per week for food, going out two nights a week, and all the other bits and pieces you'll need. I tend to get through about £800 per eight-week term, not including room rent. Books and equipment usually come free of charge: for

but you can currently expect to pay from about £70 to £100. Every college has a normal canteen and a Formal Hall. You'll pay about £2 per meal. In Formal Hall, you'll pay about £5, but for this you get a three-course meal with coffee, served by waiting staff as you sit on long, candlelit tables. Grace is said in Latin and vast quantities of wine and port are consumed.

GETTING THERE

☞ By road: M25/J27, M11/J11, A10. From west or east, A45. From northwest, A604.
☞ By rail: London's Liverpool Street, under the hour; Nottingham, 2:30; Birmingham, 3:00.
☞ By air: Stansted Airport, M11.
☞ By coach: London, 1:50; Birmingham, 2:45; Leeds, 5:00; Bristol, 5:30.

COLLEGE CAMEOS
by Katie Lydon

CHRIST'S
Cambridge CB2 3BU
Tel 01223 334 953
WEB www.christs.cam.ac.uk

Founded in 1448, Christ's is a beautiful college situated in its own extensive grounds in the centre of town. It has a strong academic reputation, regularly tops the Tompkins Table, and there's a strong atmosphere of study. Library access is 24-hour access and computer facilities, including room connections, are available. Christ's also makes 'easy offers' to around a third of its intake.

The balance of north/south and state/independent school students is relatively good, with 49% of the 2000/01 intake coming from the state sector. Women are under represented, but not drastically.

Uniquely, there are two bars, though one closes at 8.30pm. The ents committee puts on around four themed nights a term, and there is a formidable biennial May Ball. The JCR publish an alternative prospectus (see web site).

The college sporting reputation has become good and the drama society, CADS, is well known and respected across the university. The college has a squash court and boathouse - sports pitches are twenty minutes away - and use of its own theatre; there is a cinema that puts on both recent releases and classic films.

Writes Christ's Caroline Muspratt of the accommodation: 'The rooms are generally very good apart from the 'typewriter', a horrible building at the back of Christ's. You may be lucky enough to get an en-suite bathroom; otherwise you can be sharing with anything from three to twelve people. The kitchens are usually very small and ill-equipped: the college wants to encourage everyone to eat in Hall. Upper Hall opens for breakfast, lunch and dinner, and the food ranges from excellent to mediocre. Formal Hall, which starts later in the evening, is particularly good: you can book in guests, and the three-course meal is served in a medieval dining hall.'

CHURCHILL
Cambridge CB3 ODS
TEL 01223 336 202
WEB www.chu.cam.ac.uk

Churchill was founded in 1960. The distance (five-minute cycle) from town is more than compensated for by the extensive grounds, proximity to sports facilities and the relaxation of being off the tourist trail. Academically it is strong and dominant in Computing, Natural Sciences and Engineering

The state school presence is high (around 70%), and men are the dominant sex (around 77%), though Churchill was the first all-male college to admit women (1972). While very different from and less photographed than its older, town centre counterparts, Churchill's modern architecture is Grade I listed and popular for its functionality.

College ents are regular and popular with students throughout the university, as is its huge bar. All rooms have network and phone connections, and there are extensive sports facilities on site.

CLARE
Cambridge CB2 1TL
Tel 01223 333 246
WEB www.clare.cam.ac.uk

Founded in 1326, Clare is the second oldest college. It occupies extensive grounds that begin in a town-centre huddle of other colleges, and stretch to straddle the River Cam across to the University Library and arts faculties. It is friendly, academically successful and is continually over-subscribed. Students are quite evenly divided between the arts and sciences. English and Engineering applicants are encouraged to take a gap year.

Clare choir is famed in Cambridge and throughout the country, and Clare is also home to some of the best alternative ents in the university. Its hugely popular cellar based venue hosts regular live band sessions ranging from jazz to drum 'n' bass, attracting names such as the James Taylor Quartet. Its May Ball is renowned and tickets sought after.

The drama and art societies are particularly good, and Clare sports teams, especially rugby and hockey (men's and women's) and boat club are strong.

Accommodation is usually very good, with most first years living together in the same court, many in en-suite bathrooms. In later years there is the opportunity to move out to the large houses that constitute Clare Colony, a short walk along the river.

CORPUS CHRISTI
Cambridge CB2 1RH
Tel 01223 338 056
WEB www.corpus.cam.ac.uk

Founded in 1352, Corpus is situated right in the centre of Cambridge, opposite Kings (popular myth claims that Corpus actually owns Kings' land and that the lease is soon to expire, to the amusement of the inhabitants of the smaller college). Small but friendly, Corpus' architecture is as pretty as that of its bigger neighbours, but the college is better than most at protecting its students from the constant tourist invasion that can be a liability of a central college.

Corpus places a strong emphasis on academic pursuits, and presents an incentive to achievement in the form of its controversial academic room ballot. Strengths are mainly in the arts, especially History and English, but it is also strong in Engineering.

Traditionally enthusiasm is the only pre-requisite here for sport, and the college offers a wide range of facilities, including on-site squash and a strong boat club. There's an annual sports 'Challenge' with Corpus Christi, Oxford.

The JCR is active and the bar a central feature, though its opening hours are variable. The film society puts on a regular mix of classic and new titles, and the drama society (The Fletcher Players) is well known and has links with the intimate, adjacent venue, **The Playroom**.

DOWNING

Cambridge CB2 1DQ
Tel 01223 334 826
WEB www.dow.cam.ac.uk

Downing is one of the newer town centre colleges, founded in 1800 just off Cambridge's main shopping street, close to the science, architecture and engineering faculties (the Sidgwick arts site is a little further). Once through the gates one finds an array of unusual neo-classical architecture and large, open, green spaces. It's a peaceful retreat, brilliant in summer. The atmosphere is friendly and lively, politically neutral and relaxed.

Academically, Downing is always in the Top 10; all subjects are well represented; Law and Medicine are particular strengths. The library is well stocked and pleasant, with an especially good law section. The JCR organises a good Freshers' Week; bar, common room and TV room are excellent. Termly events usually attract big name DJs and are popular across the university. They are perennially successful in sports; particular strengths are rowing, rugby and athletics. There are network connections in all rooms.

EMMANUEL (EMMA)

Cambridge CB2 3AP
TEL 01223 334 290
WEB www.emma.cam.ac.uk

Emma is a relaxed, open college founded in 1584 in the centre of town, opposite the arts cinema and the largest pub in the country. Emma students come from a wide range of backgrounds. It offers scholarships and hardship funds; financial status should never be a barrier to entry.

Emma is also outstanding academically, consistently featuring among the top five colleges. Arts are a particular strength, and it is often the most popular choice for English applicants.

The bar runs weekly funk and cheese events and is the best and most popular in Cambridge. Sport is strong, especially women's rowing and football. There's a squash court and an outdoor swimming pool. The municipal (and indoor) pool is close by, as are most of the shops and both cinemas. Drama and film societies are prominent, and a May Ball happens every other year.

Most rooms have network connections; unusually, Emma offers a free, weekly laundry service.

FITZWILLIAM (FITZ)

Cambridge CB3 0DG
TEL 01223 332 057
WEB www.fitz.cam.ac.uk

Founded in 1969, Fitz is one of the newest colleges in the university, occupying modern, spacious, award-winning buildings - the oldest date from 1963, very different from the classical architecture elsewhere but regarded as functional and user-oriented in a way older colleges often aren't.

Being a five-minute bike ride away from the town centre in open, generally quiet grounds, students have a reputation for being relaxed and sociable. The college is good academically, comes about mid-Tompkins Table, but is not as frenzied as some. A high proportion of its intake comes from state schools.

Tradition isn't as prominent as in other colleges, though there is just enough to remind you that you are at Cambridge. The bar is well-loved and is the centre of social activity, and what are widely thought of as some of the best ents in Cambridge are put on twice a term.

Sport, especially football, is strong, and the college has its own squash court and gym.

GIRTON

Cambridge CB3 0JG
TEL 01223 338 972
WEB www.girton.cam.ac.uk

Girton was founded as a women's college in 1869, began to admit men in 1979, and now the latter slightly outnumber the former. It sits on a beautiful 50-acre site a couple of miles out of the city centre and, uniquely, has its own student car park. Architecturally impressive and undisturbed by tourist invasion, the distance encourages a close-knit community and strong collegiate atmosphere; there's a 24-hour garage across the road for bits and pieces, and Girton village isn't far.

Girton isn't the most academic of colleges, the atmosphere is unpressured and relaxed. The **Cellar Bar** is the social focus and ents venue. The formal hall food is famed across the university for its quality, so much so that the boat clubs and drinking societies of other colleges strive to get themselves invited for dinner. Sport is popular at Girton, and facilities include an on-site indoor heated swimming pool. The boat club is popular and does well.

Students initially live in college, then move out to nearby houses or Wolfson Court - much more central, near the University Library and Sidgwick site.

GONVILLE & CAIUS
Cambridge CB2 1TA
TEL 01223 332 447
WEB www.cai.cam.ac.uk
Founded as Gonville in 1348, 'Caius' (pronounced 'Keys') was added to the name in 1558. It occupies a convenient city centre site, but tourist traffic is less than might be expected as it sits between Trinity's famous Great court and King's Chapel.

Caius is academically strong, always in the top half of the Tompkins Table, and its particular strengths are in Economics, Law, History and Medicine. The always accessible library is excellent, as are the computer rooms, and most student rooms are connected. Drama and music are popular, and Caius Films has become a prominent presenter of varied movies, drawing a cross-collegiate audience.

Sport is taken fairly seriously, with the boat club very successful. Squash, netball, football, hockey and racquet facilities are within a few minutes walk of college and served by a licensed pavilion.

Uniquely its students are compelled to buy forty-five dinner tickets per term at around £4 each. While this may seem a little expensive, the result is a stronger college atmosphere.

The college can accommodate all undergraduates well, though again, quite expensively.

HOMERTON
Hills Rd, Cambridge CB2 2PH
TEL 01223 507 252
WEB www.homerton.cam.ac.uk
Homerton was founded in 1695 as a College of Education and moved to its present site in 1894. It still specialises in Education, but offers other

subjects too, including Archaeology and Anthropology, Computing Science, Economics, Engineering, English, Geography, History, History of Art, Land Economy, Music, Natural Sciences, Oriental Studies, Philosophy, Social & Political Sciences, and Theology & Religious Studies.

Situated a bit out of the town centre, close to the railway station, Homerton tends to cultivate a fairly close community. There is a relatively high proportion of mature students, and women outnumber men. They recruit mainly from state schools, though students are drawn from all backgrounds.

Participation in university activities, such as journalism, drama and politics, is strong. Facilities are excellent - Homerton's on-site sound and dance studios are the rehearsal venue for many university productions. It also boasts its own gym, squash court and sports field. Men's rugby and women's rowing are both strong.

Students initially live in college, but there is the opportunity to move out into houses scattered around the town in later years.

JESUS
Cambridge CB5 8BL
TEL 01223 339 495
WEB www.jesus.cam.ac.uk
Jesus was founded in 1496 and, 'greener' and more open than some of its neighbours, overlooks the common and river from its spacious grounds, five minutes from the city centre.

Academically Jesus is relatively strong, and takes its students from a variety of backgrounds. The JCR bar is a popular social hub, but ents are few because of lack of room. Music and drama are strong, and the college offers exhibitions to organ and choral scholars.
Sport is very strong, and the college's location means that all of its facilities, which include pitches for soccer, American football, cricket, rugby and hockey, and squash and tennis courts, are on site. The boat club is a short walk across the common.

Accommodation for all undergraduates is in college or houses across the street - some of the latter have been recently refurbished and a new on-site block of en-suite accommodation opened.

KING'S
Cambridge CB2 1ST
TEL 01223 331 417
WEB www.kings.cam.ac.uk
Founded in 1441, King's and its famous chapel are most popularly representative of Cambridge. Its public perception, however, as the epitome of

prestige and tradition, contrasts sharply with the reality. It takes over 80% of its students from the state sector and is reputedly obsessed with being politically correct. Its students aren't required to wear gowns at formal dinners or elsewhere - in fact, there are no formal arrangements for meals.

King's fame attracts more tourists than any other college, but most come only to visit the chapel, and careful controls ensure that this doesn't impinge on study too much.

Academically King's is average, but its students are the most diverse bunch in the university. The atmosphere is relaxed and while students work hard, they make time for other activities - university drama, politics and journalism all feature high numbers of King's students.

Ents, based in their Cellar, are among the best in Cambridge, with queues forming long before the tickets for their famous termly Mingle events go on sale. The choir is of course world famous, making several recordings a year, and choral and organ scholarships are offered. Sport isn't a King's strength, perhaps something to do with the fact that its rowers wear purple lycra?

LUCY CAVENDISH
Cambridge CB3 0BU
TEL 01223 330 280
WEB www.lucy-cav.cam.ac.uk
Lucy Cavendish was founded in 1965 as a college for mature women. It is placed in a pretty cul-de-sac behind St John's, five minutes from the city centre.

Academically, Medicine, Law and Veterinary Science are strong. Sport isn't a particular strength, although the first Lucy Cavendish rowing crew hit the river a couple of years ago. Having had to start at the bottom, its reputation has yet to rise to the surface. The college has its own gym and access to squash and badminton courts. There's a summer ball after the festivities of May Week have died down and its own students are still around.

A recently built block of rooms with en-suite facilities has increased the on-site accommodation available to students.

MAGDALENE
Cambridge CB3 0AG
TEL 01223 332 135
WEB www.magd.cam.ac.uk
Magdalene (pronounced 'Maudlin'), founded in 1542, straddles Bridge Street, alongside the river on the north side of the city. Its grounds meet those of St John's and allegedly trespass on its land, which why students of the former refer to Magdalene students as their 'villagers'.

You'll hear that there is an overwhelming public school presence, and that tradition is paramount, with a nightly, formal candlelit dinner. But Magdalene students claim no atmosphere of elitism or arrogance. Most regard the dinner (non-compulsory) as a pleasant social occasion rather than an imposed tradition.

Academically not outstanding, but its students participate widely in university sport, drama and journalism, and have recently had a heavy involvement with the Cambridge Union.

Facilities are good - the college shares playing fields with St John's - and it has its own Eton Fives court. Most impressive facility is its music room, with grand piano, two harpsichords and an organ. The bar and other social facilities are good, and well complemented by the adjacent **Pickerel Inn**.

NEW HALL
Huntingdon Rd, CB3 0DF
TEL 01223 762 229
Ten minutes walk from the city centre, Murray Edwards was founded as New Hall in 1954 to increase access to Cambridge for women. It is still a women-only college, but Ros Smith (a New Hall graduate) and Steve Edwards have given the college two transforming gifts, an endowment of £30 million and a new name.

Indisputably, many Murray Edwards students are pooled here as second choice, but many others chose to be there, and the two 'groups' cohere to form a pleasant and sociable community.

Academically the college is continually close to the bottom of the Tompkins Table. Particular strengths are Medicine, Physics and Economics. The college hosts the largest contemporary exhibition of women's art in permanent residence.

Its futuristic **Dome** houses a famed rising kitchen, applauded when it appears at meal times, and is generally thought of as one of the best ent venues in the university, hosting large events with big-name DJs - including the respected termly Vibrate - and yes, men are allowed in. No May ball, but a garden party is held.

Sports facilities are good, including tennis, squash and netball courts, and the college is close to playing fields. Murray Edwards rowers are feared by other colleges' women crews.

College accommodation is available to all undergraduates.

NEWNHAM
Cambridge CB3 9DF
TEL 01223 335 783
WEB www.newn.cam.ac.uk
Newnham, founded in 1871 as an all-women college, continues to admit female students only,

and, like Murray Edwards, is anything but insular - guests of both sexes are welcome around the clock...as long as they are accompanied.

The college is situated close to the river and Sidgwick arts site, in attractive grounds with extensive gardens (where, uniquely, you may walk on the grass). Students are from a mix of backgrounds, though predominantly state school. Unspectacular academically, Newnham's strengths are in the arts.

Sport facilities include cricket, hockey, lacrosse, football and rugby pitches, a croquet lawn and tennis courts. Newnham's is the oldest women's boat club in England. Newnham students are also heavily involved in life outside college, particularly in drama and journalism.

PEMBROKE

Cambridge CB2 1RF
TEL 01223 338 154
WEB www.pem.cam.ac.uk
Pembroke was founded in 1347 and enjoys the benefits of a central location without the hassle of being on the tourist trail. It has pretty gardens, hidden from the roads by high walls.

Academically strong, computer facilities are good, and student rooms are mostly connected to the network. Pembroke also has busy dramatic, musical and journalistic interests. The Pembroke Players and the musical society are known across the university, and the college has its own newspaper, Pembroke Street. They also have a popular bar and regular ents, a sports ground and boat club, and enjoy high-level participation and reasonable success in rowing, rugby, football, netball and hockey.

Accommodation is good and either in college or nearby houses; a new block has just been completed.

PETERHOUSE

Cambridge CB2 1RD
TEL 01223 338 223
WEB www.pet.cam.ac.uk
Peterhouse is the oldest and smallest college in Cambridge. Founded in 1284, the buildings are attractive and close to Pembroke and the engineering and science faculties.

Reputed to be more stringent than most in its interviewing and admissions procedures, Peterhouse has particular strengths in Classics, English, History, Law, Engineering, Maths, Medicine and Natural Sciences. Its stereotype - oft denied - is that of a staunchly right-wing, public-school environment. Men outnumber women significantly, but allegations of a sexist culture appear unfounded as girls from other colleges

choose to join Peterhouse choir and other activities. (the college has its own theatre). Sports are actively pursued, particularly rugby, football and rowing. The college also has its own magazine and many of its students are involved in university newspaper journalism.

QUEENS'

Cambridge CB3 9ET
TEL 01223 335 540
WEB www.quns.cam.ac.uk
Founded in 1448, in pleasant grounds straddling the river, and close to most faculties, Queens' is open, pleasant, and students say the most people-based college in Cambridge. Certainly its students come from staggeringly different backgrounds. Around the top of the academic league tables, strengths are in natural sciences, medicine, engineering, languages and law.

Facilities are fantastic, including a hall that hosts some of the biggest ents in Cambridge (such as the famed cheesy Jingles); it doubles as theatre or sporting venue. The entertainment schedule is the envy of the university, and there is a huge May Ball every other year. The drama society puts on some of the most innovative and controversial plays in Cambridge, there's a thriving gossip magazine, the film society provides a college cinema two nights a week, and the sporting ethos, while placing emphasis on enjoyment, embraces success at university level (there are squash courts and playing fields). Yet, Queen's still manages to remain a genuinely friendly, relaxing, unpretentious, but inspiring place to be.

College can accommodate all students, and all rooms are connected to the internet.

ROBINSON

Cambridge CB3 9AN
TEL 01223 339 143
WEB www.robinson.cam.ac.uk
Robinson is the newest Cambridge college, founded in 1979 and based in red-brick buildings behind the University Library and arts faculties, next to the uni rugby ground - slightly out of town (five-minute cycle), but close to sports facilities. Its 'new' status means tradition is kept to a minimum. Here, Cambridge stereotypes are despised and disproved.

Academically average, the emphasis is on personal freedoms and development. Robinson draws the majority of its intake from state schools; the atmosphere between staff and students is very open and respectful, with meetings open to everyone.

Ents are well attended and include karaoke and music nights featuring anything from cheese to jazz. The JCR publishes its own alternative prospectus - check the web site.

Accommodation is comfortable, functional and available to all undergraduates.

ST CATHERINE'S (CATZ)

Cambridge CB2 1RL
TEL 01223 338 319
WEB www.caths.cam.ac.uk

Catz is a small college on the main street, along from King's, almost opposite Corpus Christi, and within ten minutes' walk of the main arts, science and engineering faculties. Founded in 1473, its relatively small size makes for an inclusive community. There's a good social mix, though women are a minority (usually around 40%).

It has a tradition of academic excellence. Strengths are in Natural Sciences, Geography and Medicine. The library is new and well stocked.

Even though its ents are generally poor, Catz has a good social tradition: Freshers' Week is legendary, recently the bar and common room have been refurbished, and its formal dinners are popular and over-subscribed.

Music and drama are strong, and Catz has its own 150-capacity theatre in the Octagon buildings. The literary Shirley society is the best known in Cambridge. Sport is strong, notably rugby and athletics.

The boathouse is a short cycle away, and facilities are generally good - there's an Astroturf pitch, courts for racquet sports, and pitches for field sports. Swimming is a Catz strength, and though it doesn't have its own pool, the excellent, new town facility is close.

Students live initially in college, moving out to the Octagon colony of flats near the Sidgwick site in the second year.

ST JOHN'S

Cambridge CB2 1TP
TEL 01223 338 703
WEB www.joh.cam.ac.uk

St John's was founded in 1511 in the centre of Cambridge, next to its long-standing rival, Trinity. It is the second largest college in Cambridge and so is able to house all its undergraduates. Architecturally impressive, its buildings chart varied and increasingly modern styles, culminating in the listed Cripps Building, seen as ugly by some, but functional and popular accommodation for first years.

Academically, John's is very strong (fourth in the tables for the last couple of years, and generally in the top five) and boasts an impressive and very well-stocked new library. Its beautiful Old Library houses many ancient manuscripts.

Computing facilities are excellent, with two main computer rooms and terminals scattered around the library and in the JCR. All student rooms in college have internet connections. Book grants are automatic; travel grants and hardship loans are generous.

St John's choir is respected globally, the college chapel providing a beautiful setting, and the jazz Society is famed across the university. Drama - the Lady Margaret Players - is a great tradition, the freshers' play a big draw, and they have their own venue in the **School of Pythagoras**, apparently the oldest university building in the country. The film society operates twice a week, and there are disco clubnights three times a term in the underground **Boiler Room**, noted for its drum 'n' bass, hip hop and cabaret. Sport is strong, especially rugby, football and the famous Lady Margaret Boat Club. There are extensive pitches at the back of college and a new boathouse just down the river. There are also squash, badminton, tennis and netball facilities. Finally, John's formal hall is arguably the best (and best value for money), and tickets for their May Ball are among the most sought after.

SELWYN

Cambridge CB3 9DQ
TEL 01223 335 896
WEB www.sel.cam.ac.uk

Selwyn was founded in 1882 and sits in pleasant grounds close to the Sidgwick site of arts faculties. The college's proximity to green fields and 15 mins distance from the bustle of the city centre gives it an atmosphere less claustrophobic than most.

Not noted for its academic reputation, though usually in the top half of the Tompkins Table, Selwyn's strengths include engineering, history and natural sciences.

There is an even mix between arts and science students and between men and women, and students come from a wide variety of backgrounds.

Facilities are good - the library is satisfactory. For arts students, faculty libraries are on the doorstep and can be equally accessible. Most student rooms are connected to the internet, and communal computer facilities are good.

Drama (The Mitre Players) have their own venue in the **Diamond**, and the music and film societies are also active.

Sport is not a major strength, except rowing, where in recent years Selwyn has become a force. The bar is popular, and there are several student run ents. The impressive May Ball is biennial.

All undergraduates can be accommodated either in college or in nearby houses.

SIDNEY SUSSEX

Cambridge CB2 3HU
TEL 01223 338 872
WEB www.sid.cam.ac.uk
Sidney was founded in 1596 on what is known to today's students as 'Sainsbury's Street'. The modern world beyond the gates may be extremely busy, but once inside you'll find architecture dating back 400 years and a relaxed and unpressured atmosphere.

Accommodating a balance of arts and science students, with an even ratio of women to men, Sidney isn't the most academic of colleges, although it is currently pushing its way up the Tompkins Table.

The bar is good and run by students, with a sound system better than that of most other college bars, pool table and table football. The frequent ents are well attended

College food has allegedly improved since it was voted second worst in Cambridge in 1993. Sport isn't strong. A sports ground, a short cycle away, is shared with Christ's; the boathouse is close.

Students are accommodated either in college or in nearby houses.

TRINITY

Cambridge CB2 1TQ
TEL 01223 338 422
WEB www.trin.cam.ac.uk
Founded in 1546, Trinity is the largest college in Cambridge. Situated centrally with beautiful views onto the river and the Backs and next to St John's, Trinity is its (friendly) rival in almost everything.

The college architecture is much admired, notably the Wren Library and Great Court, whose 'run' was made famous in Chariots of Fire (though actually filmed at Eton).

There is an impressive academic record - they are rarely out of the top four or five in the Tompkins Table - particularly in sciences. Contrary to popular belief, it recruits a significant majority from the state sector; women are, however, poorly

represented (around 40%).

As befits the richest college in Cambridge, facilities are excellent, the library well stocked and computer facilities first class. Book grants are available to all students, room rents are among the lowest in the uni (although rooms have varying facilities, due to the age of the buildings, all are comfortable).

Ents aren't particularly notable, but the bar is well used, if a bit small. Extra-curricular activities are fervently pursued, and sport is strong. The boat club has recently listed several impressive victories, facilities are superb and nearby.

TRINITY HALL (Tit Hall)

Cambridge CB2 1TJ
TEL 01223 332 535
WEB www.trinhall.cam.ac.uk
Trinity Hall was founded in 1350 and nestles in pretty riverside grounds next to Trinity, its bigger and richer rival.

There is a popular myth about Trinity porters phoning their Tit Hall counterparts to ask them to turn the music down at some gig - the reply came that Trinity Hall was 'there first' and so would do as it pleased. This anecdote sums up the atmosphere - it's a close, strong community that refuses to be overshadowed by its neighbours simply because of its size. There's a good mix of students and of men and women.

Tit Hall is, according to the Tompkins Table, academically average, but its traditional strength is Law. The new library, overhanging the river, is well stocked, if a little noisy in the summer, when it's a feature on guided punt tours.

Bar and JCR are lively and ents often referred to as the best. They face tough competition from King's, but are enjoyed for their individual style, the quality that best represents Tit Hall's students.

Sport and sporting facilities are good, and drama and music societies active.

CANTERBURY CHRIST CHURCH UNIVERSITY

Canterbury Christ Church University
North Holmes Road
Canterbury
Kent CT1 1QU

TEL 01227 782900
FAX 01227 782888
EMAIL admissions@cant.ac.uk
WEB www.canterbury.ac.uk

Canterbury Christ Church Students' Union
Canterbury
Kent CT1 1QU

TEL 01227 782817
FAX 01227 458287
EMAIL ccsu@canterbury.ac.uk
WEB www.ccsu.co.uk

VAG VIEW

*B*efore Canterbury Christ Church achieved university status in 2005 it excelled for a decade as a university college, awarding its own degrees. Founded by the Church of England in 1962 (and currently boasting the Archbishop of Canterbury as Chancellor), it is located in modern buildings on part of St Augustine's Abbey (built in AD 597). It began as a teacher training college, but expanded and diversified impressively, with undergraduate applications up 20% this year.

A £40-million development plan underwrites its new status, to include a £30-million learning resource centre, with a café, two garden terraces, and an atrium, at Augustine House in the city, and £10 million worth of sport and music facilities.

Overall there's a high level of student satisfaction (83%), with a good 3-star rating for helpful/interested staff and decent-size tuition groups. Within six months of graduation, 77% of students are in real, graduate-level occupations. Along the way 10% drop out, which is average.

CAMPUS

Canterbury is a good place to be, small and friendly, if not exactly jumping with action. It is just big enough to hold a cathedral, some run of the mill shops and a fair range of pubs - and on first visit you might wonder that there's room for two degree-awarding institutions. The more widely known of these is the University of Kent (UKC), a traditional

UNIVERSITY/STUDENT PROFILE	
University since	**2005**
Situation/style	**City campus**
Student population	**14945**
Total undergraduates	**11360**
Mature undergraduates	**7%**
International undergrads	**11%**
Male/female ratio	**51:49**
Equality of opportunity:	
state school intake	**97%**
social class 4-7 intake	**35%**
low-participation area intake	**13%**

campus university situated up what has become known to the thousands of UKC students who trundle up and down it daily as Mount Everest. Canterbury Christ Church's campus is situated on the east side of the city.

There are other campuses, too: nearby Broadstairs Campus (Northwood Road, Broadstairs, Kent CT10 2WA; 01843 609120) - business, computing, digital media, education, health, commercial music, performing arts, policing), Chatham Campus (30 Pembroke Copurt, Chatham Maritime, Kent ME4 4UF; 01634 890800 - education, health and policing: Greenwich and Kent universities are, with Canterbury Christ Church partners in the Universities at Medway Students' Association (UMSA) - see the Kent entry). Finally, Salomans Campus is for postgraduate study.

And now, there's University Centre Folkestone, developed with the University of Greenwich, with higher education facilities for the Performing Arts, Business and IT, and Fine Art with Digital Media.

FEES, BURSARIES

UK & EU Fees 2009-10: £3,225 p.a. Bursaries worth £860 are available to students with a household income of less than £25,000. Bursaries worth £510

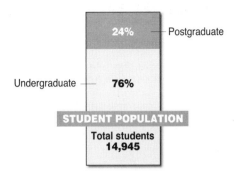

STUDENT POPULATION

Total students
14,945

Undergraduate — **76%**

24% — Postgraduate

(11%), with graduate jobs spread across a wide spectrum of activities, and Creative Arts, which incorporates the very popular Music and Performing Arts and produces 10% of Canterbury's job share, again pretty widespread, the biggest group in teaching, and very few as creative artists in their field, at least in the first instance. Opening soon is a new £8-million Music Centre with a 350-seat concert auditorium, a suite of fully equipped rehearsal and practice rooms, and flexible space that can be used to provide additional areas for teaching and workshops.

Biological Sciences (the well-taught Sports Science included) accounts for 7% of graduate jobs

are available to students with a family income of between £25,001 and £49,305. Six Sport Scholarships valued at £2,000 a year and 7 of £500 a year, and Music Scholarships valued at £25-£1,500 a year are also offered.

ACADEMIA & JOBS

The uni is the largest centre of higher education in Kent for the public services - notably teacher education, policing, health and social care, including clinical psychology - and is a significant provider in a wide range of academic and professional areas.

There are four faculties, Arts & Humanities, Business & Sciences, Education, and Health. This year a new learning and library resource centre opened as part in Augustine House in central Canterbury.

The initial problem facing an applicant is the sheer volume of courses on offer - four pages on the UCAS web site! Most new universities start off in this way before rationalising their list of degrees to show clearly what they are about. Canterbury's degree list is daunting, to say the least.

We will start with the subjects that students say are well taught, which include Geography (100% of undergraduates in the department gave Geographical Studies and Human & Social Geography their unqualified approval), History, Media, Business Studies, Computer Science, Biological Sciences, Sociology, Sports Science, Music, Initial Teacher Training, Business & Administrative Studies, Marketing, and Creative Arts & Design.

Least popular are Social Work and Fine Art - only 56% and 49% of the students of these subjects expressed themselves satisfied.

Teacher Training is highly rated - and 24% of graduates end up as teachers. Social Studies, which includes Geography and Sociology, are the next biggest employment area - 13% of Canterbury's graduates, more than half of whom fiund jobs as teachers, or in community and counselling activities, or government admin istration.

Business is another healthy employment area

TEACHING SURVEY AT A GLANCE

Avg. UCAS points accepted	**230**
Acceptance rate	**21%**
Overall satisfaction rate	**83%**
Helpful/interested staff	★★★
Small tuition groups	★★★
Students into graduate jobs	**77%**

Teaching most popular with undergraduates:
Geographical Studies, Human & Social Geography (100%), History (97%), Media (92%), Business Studies, Computer Science (91%), Biological Sciences, Sociology, Sports Science, Music (88%), Initial Teacher Training, Business & Administrative Studies, Marketing, Creative Arts & Design (85%).

Teaching least popular with undergraduates:
Social Work (56%), Fine Art (49%).

---

here, Historical Studies about the same (which is high). But when it comes to the nitty gritty, their popular media courses - Film, Radio & TV, and reams of Media & Cultural Studies - muster only 5%, and Computer Science only 2.5%.

More certain are subjects allied to Medicine -

SUBJECT AREAS (%)

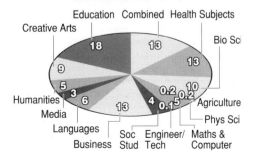

RESEARCH EXCELLENCE

% of Canterbury's research that is
4* (World-class) or 3* (Internationally rated):

	4*	3*
Allied Health Professions	0%	5%
Education	10%	25%
Sports-Related Studies	0%	20%
English	0%	20%
Theology	0%	20%
History	0%	30%
Music	10%	20%

Nursing, Health Studies, Occupational Therapy, Operating Department Practice, Optical Dispensing - which are not among the best taught, but are a better bet job-wise. As ever in the health industry, most everyone gets a job anyway. Likewise, Law is less popular with students, but secure. Besides the two Law degrees (LlB or BA) there are masses of Legal Studies and Applied Criminology courses, an international degree, a Forensic attachment, and a strong, traditional link with the police expressed in a series of Police Studies degrees. All these lead to jobs, around 5% of the graduation total. Around the same quota attaches to Languages too - French is a speciality, , and there's a European Business degree.

STUDENT SCENE

In the SU it's classic anthems and old school cheese: quizzes, promotions, giveaways, fancy dress nights - Pimps & Hookers - parties, balls. 'Also we have partnership deals with clubs in town (**Chicago's**, a favourite for male students, given the uni's strong female lean).' At the Union there's something pretty cheesy on every weekday night. Tuesdays are either karaoke, live comedy or quiz nights. Wednesday is Sports Fed night, where all the teams get horrifically drunk in the SU. Thursday is *Frame 25*, the student cinema, which shows recent movies on a weekly basis. There are balls all year round - Freshers', Halloween, Graduation, Christmas - the climax being the Summer Ball with fairground and bands.

Ents at Medway are held at **Coopers**, the bar at the heart of it all - same fare, theme nights, etc. At Broadstairs, it's **Horizons Bar**.

The media provision at HQ in Canterbury had been a bit pathetic of late, given the focus on media in the curriculum, but now they have *Unified*, a monthly newspaper, CSR, a readio station that broadcasts on 97.4FM across the city, and CCTV, which broadcasts through the website (www.ccsu.co.uk) and via the SUB screens in the Canterbury SU.

TOWN Writes Dominic Conway: 'Nice big cathedral, old cobbled streets, strong whiff of history in the air and a two hour walk to the beach. That is Canterbury. To accommodate the evident wealth of students there are two clubs (plus some secret ones) and plenty of good bars. Most pubs have music, a dj, or jukebox. **The Penny Theatre** in Northgate has good atmosphere, good music. If you keep your ear to the ground local groups will put on authentic unpretentious rock shows and Whitstable on the coast hides a number of world class musicians playing jazz, blues, and Turkish folk music that will content even the most selective muso. There is also a wide variety of shops and supermarkets to take your pick from! The toughest thing is avoiding the temptation to spend money in one of the many restaurants and café bars that line the streets. Apart from that everything is very simple and easy to find. If you come here you will have everything really: countryside and seaside, but still be near to London:; entertainment and nightlife, but still a calm working environment.'

SPORT A new £5-million pounds sports centre opened recently, with eight badminton courts, a fitness centre and studio. They have 20 acres of sports fields with four football pitches, four tennis courts,

WHAT IT'S REALLY LIKE

COLLEGE:	
Social Life	★★★
Campus scene	**Lively, local**
Student Union	**OK ents & media**
Politics	**Left of Centre**
Sport	**Sport-for-all**
National team position	**102nd**
Arts opportunities	**Excellent**
Student radio	**CSR**
Student TV	**CCTV**
Union ents	**Theme nights, balls**
Live venue capacity	**450**
Union societies	**17**
Parking	**Very poor**
CITY:	
Entertainment	★★★
Scene	**Touristy, historic, very studenty; pubs OK**
Town/gown relations	**Good**
Risk of violence	**Average**
Cost of living	**High**
Student concessions	**Adequate**
Survival + 2 nights out	**£80 pw**
Part-time work campus/town	**Average/Good**

and lacrosse and rugby pitches.

PILLOW TALK

Style of accommodation includes catered halls (some en suite), self-catered flats (again, some en suite), and self-catered houses. First years are prioritised for halls. On the Canterbury Campus main site, Davidson, Lang and Temple are en suite, Fynden and Thorne are single rooms with washbasins and catered, but rent quoted does not include meals. Canterbury-based self-catered residences at College Court and Holmes Court are 2 mins from campus. Lanfranc and Oaten Hill are farther, but the latter is a refurbished oast house and much in demand. Newest is the Parham Road Student Village, a 10-min walk from campus, with houses and flats for 3 to 7 students and a new block this year, Amandos Court. Finally, there's Pin Hill, 15 mins away from campus, a development of 5 halls, Ramsey, Coggan, Runcie and Carey (all very episcopal) and Benson House (which has 40 en-suite rooms). Broadstairs and Chatham cmpuses both have self-catered residences.

ACCOMMODATION	
Guarantee to freshers	**100%**
Style	**Halls, flats**
Security guard	**Campus**
Shared rooms	**No data**
Internet access	**No data**
Self-catered	**All flats, no halls**
En suite	**Some**
Approx price range pw	**£70-£105**
City rent pw	**£65-£75**

GETTING THERE

☞ By road: M2 and A2 connect Canterbury to London and beyond.

☞ By coach: London Victoria, 1 hour 45 mins.

☞ By rail: two or three times an hour from London Victoria, Charing Cross and Waterloo East stations. The fast service takes 1 hour 20 mins.

STUDENT CARDIFF - THE CITY

Cardiff is one of the best places to study in Britain. As well as three universities, it has well-situated, cheap housing, lively nights out, friendly people, great shops and hundreds of miles of countryside just a little to the north. It is all that any right-thinking fresher could desire in a college town.

And, if there's one thing Cardiff has in its bag of tricks that almost all others in the UK haven't, it is its status as a capital. As a result, a medium-sized city with a similar population to Coventry is loaded with amenities, arts venues, stadia, beautiful civic parks, a world-class research university and everything else you, a naive 18-year-old from the backwoods of some distant shire, could want. And cos it's so small, most of it is easily walkable - result.

SHOPPING

If you ignore the Victorian splendour that marks out many of Cardiff's city centre shops and focus on the dull plastic high street facades of Queen Street you could be in Newcastle, Manchester or any city in the UK. But, if you're willing to wander a bit Cardiff has some of the best shops in the UK. From **Spillers** in the Hayes (Britain's oldest record shop don'tcha know), to **Madame Fromage**, a wondrous land of cheeses and continental meats, in the Castle Arcade, the city has more than

enough to entertain, after a few cursory glances at Top Shop and Debenhams anyway.

As any Cardiffian with an ounce of sense will tell you, it's the **Arcades** that house most of Cardiff's best stores. The narrow alleys that splinter various city centre streets are filled with secondhand book shops, vintage and designer clothes stores, cafés and shoe shops. You could live here for years and still discover shops you're sure you've never seen before.

Away from the fun of the arcades, the **Capitol Centre** and **St David's Centre** (and forthcoming **St David's 2** in the Hayes) house most of the dull chemists, opticians and department stores that you can blow your novelty-sized loan cheque on.

FILMS

The best cinema in Cardiff is **Chapter Arts** in deepest, darkest Canton. Canton's actually a lovely part of the city, but it's a good 20-minute walk from the city centre, so 90% of students won't bother with it. You should; this converted school-turned arts complex has one of the best bars in the city and shows films that wouldn't get near a multiplex.

More conventionally there is the huge, and dependable, **Cineworld** megaplex which has 3 floors of screens, 2 bars, and means to sate any culinary desires you have, as long as they involve hot dogs and gulp-sized colas. Ditto **Vue**, which is lodged in some godawful leisure complex glued onto the **Millennium Stadium**. There's a big **UCI** down in the Bay too. So Cardiff, if you're one for the motion pictures, is super.

ARTS

Cardiff's capital status means it gets more arts money pumped into it than a Tracey Emin cash machine exhibit. With too many art galleries to mention, it's probably best you stop by the **National Museum and Art Gallery** (which is free) and let them point you in the direction of other galleries in the city.

The New Theatre is a good stop for standard touring fare and the occasional big budget local show but the city is also home to smaller local theatres like the **Sherman** on Senghennydd Road, which put on shows by local companies as well as small tours and comedy.

Ah, stand-up, a great place for you to show-off that new found campus wit in front of a crowd of literally hundreds with a heckle or too. The Sherman and New Theatre have tonnes of comedy shows throughout the year, but your best bet is **St David's Hall**, which has recently been host to student favourites like Dylan Moran, The Mighty Boosh and Paul Merton. There's also the weekly stand-up show in the students' union as well as **The Glee Club** in the Bay which is host to many a promising chortle merchant.

EATING OUT

Although it has no Michelin stars, Cardiff has many a restaurant for you and your friends to go and have one of those big group meals where one person inevitably doesn't pay and everyone else has to stick an extra quid in. The new Brewery Quarter off St Mary's Street is home to **La Tasca**, **Nando's**, **Hard Rock Café** and many others. It's as safe a bet to take your society chums as it is your parents on a rare visit.

Of course there are plenty of smaller, independent eateries; enough curry houses to smelt you tastebuds (try **Chillis** on Whitchurch Road), enough pub grub to feed a league's worth of hungry rugby players (try the Sunday roast at the **Blackweir** on North Road) and vegetarian options to suit the most hardened carrot muncher (**The Greenhouse** on Woodville Road, for example).

The Bay also offers everything from **Pizza Express** to Turkish to **Harry Ramsden's**. You can stuff yourself before trekking around the fancy new Welsh parliament building or visiting Roald Dahl's old gaff, the **Norwegian Church**.

PUBS

There are, thank goodness, enough pubs to sooth the insistent needs of every kind of student. There are rowdy discount card pubs like the **Woodville** (Cathays Terrace) and the **George** (Macintosh Place), small slightly-traditional, but not quite, pubs like the **Pen & Wig** and **Rummer Tavern**, a smorgasbord of **Wetherspoons**, as well as a few choice, if pricey, city centre watering holes like **Floyds**.

St Mary's Street is the natural home of all the pile 'em high, sell 'em cheap pubs that cause Cardiff to resemble Baghdad on a weekend night. If that's your kind of thing then you'll be thrilled, but if not take the time to explore bars out of the city centre like **Bar En-Route** on Cathays Terrace, the aforementioned Chapter Arts bar and plenty more pubs that aren't full of people dressed for a round of pub golf. Suffice to say, if one of your key aims in exploring higher academia is to consume vaultloads of booze, then Cardiff will service you as well as anywhere.

CLUBS AND LIVE VENUES

Thanks to having venues of almost every size, Cardiff is one of Britain's best cities to catch a gig. Whether it's the noisy and new at **Barfly** and **Clwb Ifor Bach** (or **Welsh Club** as it will quickly become known), the mid-sized rock of the students' union (recent gigs include Bloc Party, Kaiser Chiefs, Panic! At The Disco) or the pomp of the **Cardiff International Arena**, you'll be well catered for. St David's Hall is mainly a classical venue but occasionally hosts the likes of Morrissey. **The Point** at the Bay is a converted church that is probably the city's best small venue, local heroes Super Furry Animals and Stereophonics have played warm-ups there in the not-so-distant past.

If sweaty rock music isn't your thing, and frankly there are better things to do on a Friday night than get your shoes stamped on by Strokes fans in Barfly, you won't struggle to find somewhere to spend your dimes.

All the plastic chain nightclubs are here, **Liquid**, **Jumpin' Jaks**; you name it... But if you check out the likes of super-trendy **Soda**, where Wales's golden couple Charlotte Church and Gavin Henson are regulars, and which is so trendy it doesn't have a sign on the door, you can have a night as good as any in Britain.

Keep an eye out for monthly nights by LAmerica and Cool House which switch residences around the city.

Will Dean

CARDIFF UNIVERSITY

Cardiff University
Cardiff CF10 3AT

TEL 029 2087 4455
FAX 029 2087 4457
EMAIL prospectus@cardiff.ac.uk
WEB www.cardiff.ac.uk

Cardiff Students' Union
Cardiff CF1 3QN

TEL 029 2078 1400
FAX 029 2078 1407
EMAIL studentsunion@cf.ac.uk
WEB www.cardiffstudents.com

VAG VIEW

Cardiff is a tip-top uni academically, with a 4-star rating for staff interest in its students and a place in the Times Higher Education's *World's Top 200 Universities, yet its average entry requirement (380 points) is not as demanding as some.*

It is also hugely popular with its students, who run a breathlessly active extra-curricular scene.

Unsurprisingly it has a drop-out rate of only 5%, while its application acceptance rate (14%) is generous enough to encourage even average students to apply. It also makes the cut for.

Is Cardiff perhaps the best kept secret among Britain's universities?

CAMPUS

Cardiff is a campus in the city, an academic precinct, separate and yet part of the city. A short walk from the classical lines of the main university buildings brings you to the fastest growing capital in Europe (see Cardiff City, above). Yet, when you go there what you notice is its compactness and accessibility, its clean lines and the way they have maintained the airiness of a wide open space. The city is also still a cheap place to live and the crime rate is livable with and minimal on campus since the introduction of CCTV.

FEES, BURSARIES

UK & EU Fees 2009-10: £3,225 p.a. Welsh students get the £1,940 fee grant from the Welsh Assembly Government. UK/EU students awarded NHS-funded places for Dental Therapy/Hygiene, Nursing, Occupational Therapy, Physiotherapy, Radiography, will be paid by the NHS, who may also pay tuition fees for medical and dental students from the fifth year of study. All students are eligible to apply for a tuition fee loan which covers the full cost of the fees. You only begin to repay this loan once you have graduated and your income exceeds £15,000 per annum. Repayments would then be a minimum of 9% of the difference between £15,000 and what you are earning.

Bursaries are available to students from lower income backgrounds on top of state-funded maintenance grants and loans, the value dependent on household income, at either £1,050, or £500 per year.

See www.cf.ac.uk/sport/performance/bursary and www.cardiff.ac.uk/scholarships for notice of sport and academic scholarships respectively.

STUDENT PROFILE

Writes Lisa Andrews: 'it's all rain, rugby and sheep, right? Wrong. Okay, so if you opt to study at Cardiff, chances are that 9 times out of 10 you'll get

UNIVERSITY/STUDENT PROFILE	
University since	**1883**
Situation/style	**Civic**
Student population	**30930**
Total undergraduates	**21800**
Mature undergraduates	**15%**
International undergrads	**22%**
Male/female ratio	**41:59**
Equality of opportunity:	
state school intake	**86%**
social class 4-7 intake	**22%**
low-participation area intake	**6%**

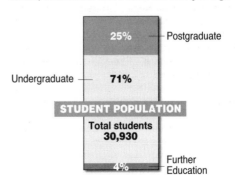

Postgraduate 25%
Undergraduate 71%

STUDENT POPULATION
Total students 30,930

Further Education 4%

TEACHING SURVEY AT A GLANCE

Avg. UCAS points accepted	**380**
Acceptance rate	**14%**
Overall satisfaction rate	**87%**
Helpful/interested staff	★★★★
Small tuition groups	★★★
Students into graduate jobs	**79%**

Teaching most popular with undergraduates:
Philosophy (100%), Chemistry, Music,
Ophthalmics, Physical Geography & Enviro.
Science, Pharmacology, Toxicology & Pharmacy
(96%), Geology (95%), Subjects allied to
Medicine, Theology (94%), Geographical Studies,
Civil Eng., English, Communications & Information
Studies, History, Politics, Sociology, Social Policy,
Anthropology (93%), Physics & Astronomy (92%),
Journalism, Languages, Maths, Accounting
(91%), Finance, Mechanical, Production &
Manufacturing Eng., Media (90%).

Teaching least popular with undergraduates:
Medicine (64%).

Communications & Information Studies, History, Politics, Sociology, Social Policy, Anthropology, Physics & Astronomy (recently they opened the UK's first Centre for Astrobiology, which links the study of Biology with Astronomy), Languages, Maths, Finance, Mechanical, Production & Manufacturing Engineering, and Media (notably Journalism).

Least popular was the teaching in the School of Medicine. Only 64% regarded it as satisfactory, which is a pity because a £3-million teaching facility has just been opened. The College of Medicine merged with the university only recently, do politics lie at the bottom of the vitriol?

The College of Medicine campus has a 920-bed hospital. The 5/6-year MB BCh degree combines academic study well with clinical and communication skills. There's even a pre-med Foundation for Arts A level candidates or those with one Science and Arts. They require AAB at A Level and a minimum of a grade C in a fourth AS subject. The A-Levels must include two science GCE A level subjects out of Chemistry, Biology, Physics and Maths (one being Chemistry or

soaked on the way to lectures and spend the next hour dripping puddles in your pew. And on match days, it's hard to avoid the Welsh rugby spirit, if only because your quiet local is heaving with red-shirted fans. But with 22,000 undergraduates of 100 nationalities, Cardiff is nothing if not culturally diverse.' The statistics support Lisa's case. There is also a high-ish independent school intake (14%), balanced by a consistent 22% recruitment from the lower socio-economic groups. It's a well-balanced picture.

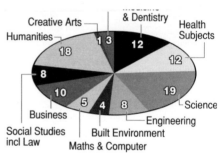

ACADEMIA & JOBS

The recent assessment of research in our universities showed Cardiff at its world-renowned best in Psychiatry, Neuroscience & Clinical Psychology, Computer Science, Engineering, Planning, Law, Sociology, Psychology, and especially in English. Many other Cardiff departments achieved 4-star ratings, but in these, world-class research is being undertaken between 20% and 35% of the time.

Students regard teaching to be at its best in Philosophy, which achieved 100% student approval. Then it's Chemistry (millions have been spent on their Chemistry Department, creating a new laboratory and a 500-seater lecture theatre and resource centre), Music, Ophthalmics, Physical Geography & Environmental Science, Pharmacology, Toxicology & Pharmacy, Geology, subjects allied to Medicine, Theology, Geographical Studies, Civil Engineering, English,

Biology at grade A.) Chemistry or Biology required at AS, with a grade B, if not at GCE A level. If applicants offer two or more Maths subjects at AS or A level, only one will count towards meeting the conditions of an offer. General Studies is not acceptable at AS or A level, nor is Critical Thinking acceptable at A level. You will be required to sit for UKCAT.

When one looks at Cardiff's graduate employment figures, a massive 35% find work in the health industry (doctors, dentists, nurses, social workers, therapists, radiographers, etc), dwarfing the 7% who go into teaching, for example.

Other important elements of Cardiff's presence in the health industry are its biologists

RESEARCH EXCELLENCE

% of Cardiff's research that is
4* *(World-class) or* **3*** *(Internationally rated):*

	4*	3*
Cardiovascular Medicine	5%	35%
Cancer Studies	10%	55%
Infection and Immunology	10%	40%
Hospital Clinical Subjects	0%	25%
Primary Care	5%	60%
Psychiatry, Neuroscience, & Clinical Psychology	20%	60%
Dentistry	15%	50%
Nursing and Midwifery	15%	30%
Allied Health Professions	20%	35%
Pharmacy	15%	40%
Biological Sciences	15%	40%
Environmental Sciences	15%	55%
Chemistry	10%	50%
Physics	5%	45%
Pure Mathematics	5%	35%
Computer Science	20%	50%
Electrical and Electronic Eng.	10%	40%
Civil Engineering	25%	65%
Mechanical, Aeronautical & Manufacturing Engineering	20%	45%
Architecture/Built Environment	20%	45%
Town and Country Planning	30%	35%
Archaeology	15%	40%
Business and Management	35%	35%
Law	25%	35%
Sociology	25%	30%
Psychology	25%	45%
European Studies	15%	30%
Celtic Studies	15%	40%
English	35%	25%
Philosophy	5%	25%
Theology	5%	30%
History	10%	35%
Media	45%	30%
Music	15%	55%

practice placement, followed by a 2-year BArch. Cardiff is the seventh largest provider of architectural consultants in the UK.

Another strength is in Banking and Accountancy. There is a whole host of international courses in Accounting, Economics, and Business Administration, and the Business Management Human Resources degree yields excellent job figures in the industry. The curriculum makes more than a few tax experts and consultants too.

Defence is another key graduate employment area, and recruits from a wide range of subjects.

Computer Science degrees feed graduates into software consultancy in particular, Media and Languages into Radio and TV in particular, though by far the most Language students from Cardiff end up in the Civil Service, and in publishing, specialist retail, the hotel and restaurant trade, personnel, higher education, and work in our diverse British communities.

In Journalism they have one of a handful of industry-respected postgrad degrees that many careers advisers will recommend you take before you begin the search for full-time employment. Meanwhile, their BA Journalism, Film and Broadcasting degrees are good enough to make them an attractive proposition in journalism anyway. Student media helps. They have a newspaper, magazine, radio and TV stations, see Social Scene below.

There's also a fair smattering of graduates going into artistic literary areas, again from the Languages Department and Historical & Philosophical Studies, a department which also creates a steady flow of graduates to archival work in libraries and museums.

In Law Cardiff is one of eight institutions where the Bar Vocational Course (BVC) may be undertaken (essential for barristers). Also, non-Law graduates may opt for a 2-year full-time or 3-year part-time Senior Status Law degree here. There's also a strong line into the Police.

SOCIAL SCENE

STUDENTS' UNION The union is a top-class venue under continual enhancement. The **Taf bar** has recently been extended and changed from 'olde worlde' style to a stylish modern design. Evenings there inevitably lead to nights in **Solus**, the union's 1,800-capacity, custom-built nightclub with an immense dance floor and state-of-the-art sound and lighting systems. With an eclectic music policy crossing the spectrum from big beat to cheese, few would dispute that Solus offers some of Cardiff's best nights out.'

Currently the ents programme includes *Lush*

and pharmacists, occupational therapists and ophthalmic opticians. There's a new £20-million teaching facility for the School of Optometry and Vision Sciences.

Another impressive element of graduate employment lies in the Civil Service and government administration, where Social Studies (Politics, Economics, etc), the Town & City Planning degrees, and Languages, and Historical & Philosophical Studies are the departments that feed.

Cardiff is also strong employment-wise in Architecture, Engineering Design, Construction and Civil Engineering. Becoming an architect is a 6-year commitment, a 3-year BA Hons, a year's

WHAT IT'S REALLY LIKE

UNIVERSITY:

Social Life	★★★★★
Campus scene	**Vibrant premier scene**
Student Union services	**Top-rated**
Politics	**Activity high**
Sport	**60 clubs**
National team position	**17th**
Sport facilities	**Good**
Arts opportunities	**Excellent**
Student newspaper	**Gair Rhydd**
Student radio	**XPress Radio**
Student Radio	**CUTV**
Student magazine	**Quench**
Guardian 2008 Awards	**Mag. of the Year**
Nightclub	**Solus**
Live venue	**Great Hall**
Bars	**Taf, CF10**
Union ents	**6 nights a week**
Union societies	**150**
Parking	**Adequate**

CITY:

Entertainment	★★★★
Scene	**Buzzing**
Town/gown relations	**OK**
Risk of violence	**Low**
Cost of living	**Low**
Student concessions	**Excellent**
Survival + 2 nights out	**£80 pw**
Part-time work campus/town	**Excellent**

(Friday, £3); *Comeplay* - party tunes in the main room, *Traffic*, the students own DJ and Clubbing Soc, plays house music in the other (Saturday, £3.50); *Fun Factory* - Cardiff's alternative night, featuring bands, a heavy rock room and a generally sweaty, rocked out scene (Monday, free); *Comedy Club* (Tuesday, £4), *The Rubber Duck* (Wednesday, £2); *Drink the Bar Dry* (Thursday, £5); and so it goes on right through the summer until the Summer Ball (June 12, £39).

For the more discerning, there's **Great Hall**, a major concert hall with top-line acts. The adjoining all-day café-bar used to transform itself into Seren Las, an intimate club by night. It still has a stage area, but is now called **CF10** and acts much the same after hours - as a chill-out room during club and gig nights, as well as being a popular haunt for club and society ents.

Otherwise, get down to favourite superclub **Tiger Tiger** in town , or **Jazz Café** (Monday's *Jazz Attic* has a 10-year pedigree). See also the films and rootsy music at Chapter Arts Centre, comedy, music and other stuff at St David's Hall and Sherman's Theatre.

The Union, which has had an amazing facelift recently - a 3-phase programme costing some £6 million - is not just popular for its bargain booze and carefree clubbing. Writes Lisa. 'Besides the regular 6-night ents programme, it is home to 60 sports clubs and 150 societies. High on the list are the Film Society, Act One, for drama, LGB, the lesbian/gay group, SHAG, sexual health awareness group, etc. There's the aforesaid student newspaper, *Gair Rhydd* and Xpress Radio, both award-winning in past years, and the magazine *Quench*, which won *Magazine of the Year* at last year's *Guardian* Awards, and now a new project CUTV. Finally, Act One, the drama soc is especially popular, putting on productions at the **Sherman Theatre** next door.

SPORT Sporty students at Cardiff, despite the boasts of the university prospectus, have, according to the Union, been badly served. Action works. The Athletic Union President wrote a paper about it and got a £350,000 all-weather pitch. Now they are going for a new swimming pool and other facilities. All traditional sports are catered for and the uni is a major contender in the BUSA leagues - overall 17th nationally in team sports last year. The Talybont Sports Centre has a £2 million multi-purpose sports hall and there are 33 acres of pitches. In town an International Sports Village is under construction which will offer first class facilities close to the centre of Cardiff for swimming, canoeing, white water rafting, skiing, snowboarding and climbing. And Sophia Gardens Cricket Ground has been redeveloped ready to stage Ashes Test Cricket later this year.

PILLOW TALK

The university's biggest hall, Talybont, is student paradise, en suite, own bar and comprehensive sports facilities. It opened in Sept 2005. It's also next to a 24-hour Tesco: perfect for those midnight munchies and obligatory trolley snatches!

The lazy should avoid University Hall. Although recently subject to a £4-million refurbishment, it's a good half-hour away and the

ACCOMMODATION

Guarantee to freshers	**100%**
Style	**Halls, flats**
Security guard	**All**
Shared rooms	**Some**
Internet access	**All**
Self-catered	**Most**
En suite	**Most**
Approx price range pw	**£55-£84**
City rent pw	**£54+**

free bus service isn't so free - Uni Hall rent is a few hundred pounds extra to subsidise it. All other halls are a walk away. Newest to their portfolio is Allensbank, likewise en-suite. All residences come with internet access and security.

GETTING THERE

- ☞ By road: M4/J32, A470 signposted Cardiff or M4/J29, A48(M)/A48 and A470 signposted City.
- ☞ By rail: London Paddington, 2:30.
- ☞ By air: Cardiff airport for USA and inland.
- ☞ By coach: London, 3:00; Manchester, 5:40.

UNIVERSITY OF WALES INSTITUTE, CARDIFF

University of Wales Institute, Cardiff
PO Box 377 Western Avenue
Cardiff CF5 2SG

TEL 029 2041 6044
FAX 029 2041 6286
EMAIL uwicinfo@uwic.ac.uk
WEB www.uwic.ac.uk

UWIC Students' Union
Cyncoed Road
Cardiff CF23 6XD

TEL 029 2041 6190
FAX 029 2076 5569
EMAIL studentunion@uwic.ac.uk
WEB www.uwicsu.co.uk

VAG VIEW

The University of Wales Institute Cardiff (UWIC for short) is big on sport - they get more graduates into the industry than any other university, though it has to be said they dropped to 15th place last year in the National Student Competitions - a good position for any other university with around 10,000 students, but a poor showing for UWIC.

But, hey, 'social life here, combined with Cardiff city life make an amazing combination, guaranteed to turn your three years studying into an experience that you will never forget!' says Jon Ruch.

That, at least, has not changed in the dozen years we have been publishing the Virgin Guide. 'When a Cyncoed student hits the bar, anything goes,' says Rob Blunt

INSTITUTE/STUDENT PROFILE	
University College since	**1996**
Situation/style	**Civic**
Student population	**10910**
Total undergraduates	**7605**
Mature undergraduates	**25%**
International undergrads	**5%**
Male/female ratio	**42:58-**
Equality of opportunity:	
state school intake	**95%**
social class 4-7 intake	**39%**
low-participation area intake	**10%**

sagely, musing on 'one of life's unanswered questions: why the essay that was researched, drafted, redrafted and put in a week early always got a lower mark than the one scribbled at 4 in the morning, assisted by six pints of Caffreys?'

Thoughts of academic work may often enough flow out on a river of beer from Taffy's Bar, but in fact both Art & Design, the School of Management, and the Cardiff School of Sport were adjudged world-class for between 5% and 10% of their research recently, with 60% of Art & Design being adjudged internationally excellent.

Odd, then, that the students themselves voted the teaching of Fine Art (though not Design) and Management Studies as least good.

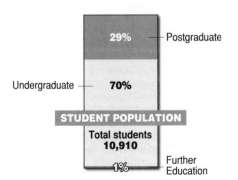

29% — Postgraduate

Undergraduate — 70%

STUDENT POPULATION

Total students 10,910

1% — Further Education

Teaching the Ruchs and Blunts of this world may not fit into every world-class researcher's idea of a good time, but it should be said that both subjects, whilefaring least well in the National Student Survey of Teaching, actually satisfied more than 70% of their student clientele, making them the highest-rated, least popular subjects in the whole of Britain!

Overall, there's an 81% satisfaction rate for UWIC's teaching, which is good, but a drop-out rate of almost 12%, which is higher than average. Perhaps the sporty ethos and six pints of Caffrey's brigade are too much for some.

CAMPUS LIFE

There are four campuses.

Cyncoed Campus, Cyncoed Road, Cardiff CF2 6XD, is central. Faculties: Education and Sport. Ents & Ambience: Teachers and wannabe sports stars, and the highest concentration of first years. **Taffy's Bar** (capacity raised to 500 since recent refurb) is the main Student Union ents venue, with £15,000 sound and light system.

SPORT First-class facilities and National Indoor Athletics Centre sit alongside rugby, football and cricket pitches, indoor and outdoor tennis courts, gym, indoor cricket nets, swimming pool, volleyball, netball, basketball, badminton and squash courts, and a dance studio. As the Wales Sports Centre for the Disabled is also here, they've got some of the best resistance-training equipment available anywhere.

Colchester Avenue Campus Colchester Avenue, Cardiff CF3 7XR. Faculties: Business, Leisure and Food. Ents & Ambience: Workaday, daytime scene - Sky TV, darts and PlayStation, but no evening ents or bar at Colly Ave, as it's known. So it's off up the hill at Cyncoed, where you're likely to be housed, too, or across the road to the **Three Brewers**.

Howard Gardens Campus Howard Gardens, Cardiff CF2 1SP. Faculty: Fine Art. Ents & Ambience: Couldn't be more different from, more alternative to, the sporting scene that dominates the personality of UWIC. **Tommy's Bar** is the focus. Eclectic ents - see Social Scene below.

Llandaff Campus Western Avenue, Cardiff CF5 2YB. Faculties: Art, Design & Engineering and Community Health Sciences. Ents & Ambience:

TEACHING SURVEY AT A GLANCE	
Avg. UCAS points accepted	**240**
Acceptance rate	**22%**
Overall satisfaction rate	**81%**
Helpful/interested staff	**No data**
Small tuition groups	**No data**
Students into graduate jobs	**69%**

Teaching most popular with undergraduates: Initial Teacher Training (93%), Media Studies (90%), Sports Science, Food & Beverage Studies (88%), Social Work, Biological Sciences (87%), Psychology (86%), Tourism, Business & Administrative Studies, Subjects allied to Medicine (83%), Design (82%).

Teaching least popular with undergraduates: Fine Art (72%), Management Studies (71%).

Complete makeover gives us The Loft bar. Also - a first for UWIC - an Advice & Representation Centre (ARC) with an educational & welfare officer and full-time welfare adviser. Thursday and Saturday are disco nights.

TOWN See *Cardiff Student City,*.

FEES, BURSARIES

UK & EU Fees 2009-10: £3,225 p.a. Welsh students get the £1,940 fee grant from the Welsh Assembly Government. There are also means-tested bursaries in place and sports and academic scholarships. See www.uwic.ac.uk.

ACADEMIA & JOBS

Academic studies are conducted through five schools: Art & Design, Education, Health Sciences, Management, and Sport

UWIC puts some 62% of its Education graduates into primary school teaching, Education accounting for more than a fifth of all graduate jobs here. Nevertheless more graduates come successfully off the production line into the job market from Health, Business, and Art & Design.

Health Sciences deliver Biomedicine , Applied Social Sciences, Complementary Therapies, and embrace the Centres for Dental Technology , Nutrition Dietetics & Food Science, Psychology, Speech & Language Therapy, Podiatric Studies, and Public Protection. Few escape a job after running with one of these carefully aimed degrees. Public protection concerns environmental health, consumer and trading standards, health and safety and environmental protection. For Dental Technology graduates a job in NHS or private

RESEARCH EXCELLENCE		
% of UWIC's research that is 4* (World-class) or 3* (Internationally rated):		
	4*	3*
Allied Health Professions	5%	10%
Business and Management	0%	10%
Education	0%	0%
Cardiff School of Sport	5%	20%
School of Management	5%	20%
Art and Design	10%	60%

practice is assured; nearby Cardiff and Bristol Dental Schools offer employment to one third of UWIC's students before they even graduate.

There is a healthy graduate employment situation in Biological Sciences, too, whence almost a quarter of UWIC's graduate jobs flow. Counted here by the Higher Education Funding Council, who hold the employment secrets of all universities, are the sporting degrees, but also Biomedical Sciences, honours degrees accredited by the Institute of Biomedical Science and designed to maximise career choices in clinical laboratory investigation, research and enterprise.

One key to the Art & Design employment figures is the focus on Architecture, always a good employment bet, at least in good times.

The UWIC Business degrees tend to get you a job in accountancy, the restaurant and hotel industry, tourism, retail and marketing. UWIC managers and administrators proliferate in these areas and in the leisure and sport industries.

SOCIAL SCENE

STUDENTS' UNION **Taffy's Bar** is next door to the Sports Hall at Cyncoed, so the venue is awash with full fancy dress cheesy disco nights, stand up comedy, live team socials, live sport, pool and darts competitions, drinking games, quiz romps and DJ sets.

Tommy's Bar at Howard Gardens has excelled in recent years as UWIC's best venue for live bands, some of the best in rock and acoustic music to the SU, and a geat alternative to the dance scene of the city. They've also had live circus acts, open deck DJ nights, poi, BBQs in the courtyard, and even fire eaters.

Crazed nites in town are Digital @ **Oceana** every Monday, Get Lost every Tuesday at **Liquid** (drinks for just 80p)... Shotgun Rules @ **Revolution** every Wednesday.

Specials currently on the menu are the Easter Rave at Taffy's, the *Dissertation Hand-in Party* at Oceana - 'Celebrate Sacking That Diss!', and of course the highlight in the UWIC social calendar, the Athletic Union Annual Sports Awards Presentation Dinner.

There's a student newspaper, *Retro*, and some quite amazing societies, like Believers Loveworld Campus Fellowship, Carbon Neutral Society, Cheerleading Squad (natch), Cymdeithas Cymraeg, Egyptian Society, Electronic Music Society, Water Sports Society, etc, and four that suggest UWIC's international contingent is finally finding a voice: Islamic Society, Indian Society, Silat Club (surely Sylhet?), and Omani Society.

PILLOW TALK

UWIC has nearly 1,000 study bedrooms located at the Cyncoed and Plas Gwyn campuses, and also allocates just over 250 private en-suite rooms in Evelyn Court. But they cannot guarantee all freshers accommodation.

They have 528 single study-bedrooms on Cyncoed, of which 165 are self-catered and en suite, and 50 are self-catered with shared bathroom facilities. The remaining 312 rooms are catered (meals provided centrally). Students resident at Cyncoed are well placed to take advantage of the sports facilities located at the campus, including the indoor swimming pool, Tommy's Bar, indoor tennis centre and fitness suite.

WHAT IT'S REALLY LIKE	
COLLEGE:	
Social Life	★★★
Campus scene	**Sports crazy**
Politics	**Interest low**
Sport	**Key**
National team position	**15th**
Sport facilities	**Excellent**
Arts	**Film good**
Student newspaper	**Retro**
Nightclub	**Chilli's**
Bars	**Taffy's, Tommy's**
Union ents	**Cheesy, boozy**
Union clubs/societies	**7**
Most active society	**Christian Union**
Parking	**Just adequate**
CITY:	
Entertainment	★★★★★
Scene	**Brilliant**
Town/gown relations	**OK**
Risk of violence	**Average**
Cost of living	**Low**
Student concessions	**Excellent**
Survival + 2 nights out	**£80 pw**
Part-time work campus/town	**Average/excellent**

ACCOMMODATION	
Guarantee to freshers	**55%**
Style	**Halls, flats**
Security guard	**Secure**
Shared rooms	**Some**
Internet access	**Most**
Self-catered	**Some**
En suite	**Some**
Approx price range pw	**£70-£97**
City rent pw	**£54**

Plas Gwyn is set in landscaped grounds in the small cathedral 'city' of Llandaff, two miles from Cardiff. There are 391 rooms, self-catered, en suite.

Recently, UWIC have acquired private sector Evelian Court - 253 self-catered, en-suite hall-style rooms, a few are doubles, a few are self-contained flats.

All at Plas Gwyn and Evelian Court have internet access. Hall managers are present at each of the campuses and are supported by a team of trained student wardens.

GETTING THERE

- ☛ By road: M4/J29, A48(M)/A48.
- ☛ By rail: London Paddington, 2:30.
- ☛ By air: USA and inland destinations.
- ☛ By coach: London, 3:00; Manchester, 5:40.

UNIVERSITY OF CENTRAL LANCASHIRE

University of Central Lancashire
Preston
Lancs PR1 2HE

TEL 01772 201201
FAX 01772 894954
EMAIL uadmissions@uclan.ac.uk
WEB www.uclan.ac.uk

Central Lancashire Students' Union
Fylde Road
Preston PR1 2TQ

TEL 01772 893000
FAX 01772 894970
EMAIL suinformation@uclan.ac.uk
WEB www.uclansu.co.uk

VAG VIEW

*T*he University of Central Lancashire (UCLan) traces its origins back to 1828, when Preston Institution for the Diffusion of Knowledge was founded. Growth in student numbers makes it one of the largest universities in the country, with some 30,000 students in total and over 25,000 undergraduates.

They are known as a caring university. 'The i' is a one-stop-shop (info centre), a first point of contact for such as financial support, council tax enquires, international student guidance, to NUS card distribution, accommodation and disabled student advice.

A fourth-year health student, confined in a wheelchair since infancy, went out of her way to praise its accessibility to the disabled, the helpfulness of staff, and for the chance they gave her of the 'few wild years' she had enjoyed there.

Wild indeed, for UCLan's approach to the social side of things is legendary. More than a decade ago the nightclub was hailed

UNIVERSITY/STUDENT PROFILE	
University since	**1992**
Situation/style	**Civic**
Student population	**29845**
Total undergraduates	**25415**
Mature undergraduates	**69%**
International undergrads	**15%**
Male/female ratio	**44:56**
Equality of opportunity:	
state school intake	**97%**
social class 4-7 intake	**38%**
low-participation area intake	**13%**

by media as diverse as The Observer and DJ Magazine as, 'Best student dance club in the UK,' and 'One of the Top 30 clubs in the country,' respectively.

Ultimately, however, the uni is a modern university dedicated to getting graduates jobs, and recruiting from social groups new to the idea of going to university. One result of its open access policy has been a wild drop-out rate, which, at 14%, remains untamed.

Nevertheless, among the students serious enough to stay, there was an 82% expression of satisfaction about the teaching in last year's National Student Survey. They get 4 stars for helpful/interested staff and small-size tuition groups. Seventy-eight per cent of UClan graduates get real graduate jobs within six months of leaving.

CAMPUSES

Having divested themselves of the Penrith Campus at the head of the Eden Valley, where the Faculty of Land-based Studies was based, and Carlisle, home of their business, computing, travel and tourism degrees, all now part of Cumbria University, they are investing £120 million at the main Preston campus, and in new campuses at Burnley, West Lakes and Llangollen.

FEES, BURSARIES

UK & EU Fees 2009-10: £3,125 p.a. A UCLan bursary worth £500 is available to all UK, full time undergraduate students who come from homes where principal earner's gross salary is less than £60,000 per year. If students qualify for maintenance grant, they will receive £319 on a means-tested basis in years 2 and 3.

There are also sports scholarships worth £4,000 over the length of a course, and UCLan rewards for good performance throughout a course. The Harris Bursary Fund is available to support local students in financial hardship, a maximum of £1,000 is paid to any individual student in one year. The Gilbertson Scholarship is for postgraduate study after taking a first class degree. All UCLan students who continue on to postgraduate study at UCLan will be eligible for 20% off the cost of their postgraduate tuition fees.

See www.uclan.ac.uk/information/prospective _students/fees_and_finance/scholarships_bursarie s.php.

STUDENT PROFILE

None of the Radley/Eton brigade are to be found here. UCLan is a 1992 'new' university recruiting a large number of undergraduates from the state sector (97%) and from social groups who haven't traditionally benefited from a university education - 35% from SEC classes 4-7 (what was once called 'unskilled working class') and 13% from 'low-participation neighbourhoods'. No-one cares a damn either way. It is a well-balanced, friendly scene.

ACADEMIA & JOBS

Faculties are now Arts, Humanities and Social

TEACHING SURVEY AT A GLANCE

Avg. UCAS points accepted	**260**
Acceptance rate	**25%**
Overall satisfaction rate	**82%**
Helpful/interested staff	★★★★
Small tuition groups	★★★★
Students into graduate jobs	**78%**

Teaching most popular with undergraduates:
Sports Science (100%), Tourism & Travel (94%), Geographical Studies, History, History & Archaeology, Philosophy (93%), Forensic & Archaeological Science, Physical Science, Combined honours programme (91%).

Teaching least popular with undergraduates:
Journalism, Marketing (77%), Social Work (74%), Art & Design (66%), Architecture, Building, Planning (61%), Performing Arts (59%), Cinematics & Photography (55%).

Sciences Management including the Lancashire Business School), Health and Social Care Management.

In last year's nationwide research assessment they were adjudged world-class for between 5% and 15% of a whole range of subjects, such as, Physics, Architecture (Surveying also part of the degree provision), Archaeology, Business, Social Work, Psychology (they offer Neuropsychology and Neurosciences degrees as well), Linguistics (this got the highest praise), History, and Media.

In the undergraduate provision Media is a traditional strength at UCLan, as is Sport: they have more graduates going into the sports industry than any other university bar Cardiff UWIC. But what do students think?

In the National Survey, 82% were satisfied with the teaching at UCLan. One hundred per cent gave their approval to the teaching of Sports Science. After that they rated Tourism & Travel, Geography, History, Philosophy, Forensic &

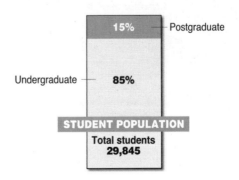

15% — Postgraduate

Undergraduate — 85%

STUDENT POPULATION

Total students
29,845

RESEARCH EXCELLENCE

% of Central Lancashire's research that is
4* *(World-class) or* **3*** *(Internationally rated):*

	4*	3*
Nursing and Midwifery	10%	40%
Allied Health Professions	10%	10%
Physics	5%	35%
General Eng., Mineral, Mining	0%	30%
Architecture/Built Environment	5%	35%
Archaeology	5%	15%
Business and Management	5%	25%
Law	0%	15%
Politics	0%	5%
Social Work, Policy & Admin.	10%	30%
Psychology	5%	15%
Education	0%	5%
English	0%	20%
Linguistics	15%	25%
History	10%	25%
Art and Design	0%	15%
Media Studies	15%	20%

Health Informatics, Paramedic Practices, Deaf Studies, Human Biology, Acupuncture, etc., then account for 11% of graduate output, mainly to hospitals.

The next most prolific employment-wise is Creative Arts and Design, which accounts for the hiring of 10% of UCLan's talented graduates. One shouldn't be surprised, for besides the usual fare - Fine Art, Ceramics, Acting, Music (Practice, Production, Theatre), etc. - UCLan offers degrees in such as Creative & Cultural Industries, Advertising, Asian Fashion, Creative Fashion Knit, and Fashion Promotion: all carefully aimed at making their graduates busy in the world of work.

The well-known Journalism and other Media degrees, such as Media Production and TV Production, account for about 5% of graduate jobs, in publishing (mostly), television of course, advertising, and a whole host of other sectors.

The sport degrees that score so well are of a wide variety, including Coaching, Development, Management, PR, Technology, Therapy, and degrees with names like Adventure Sports Coaching and Strength & Conditioning.

SOCIAL SCENE

STUDENTS' UNION Step into the award-winning, £6.5-million Student Union building. Enjoy all that the new £15.3 media Centre promises. In these two areas - hedonism and media - UCLan have always reigned supreme.

Source is the Student Union bar in the centre of campus, open Monday to Thursday 10 am until 12 midnight; Friday till 2 am; Saturday noon till 3 am; Sunday noon till midnight. **53 Degrees** is the venue and club, Brook Street, Preston (01772 893000).

Rescuing you from *Okey Dokey Karaoke* quiz nights, toga parties, *Aftershock Frenzy*, and compelling comedy from Silky and the like, is *Thursday's Premo*, the place to be (drinks £1 each) before the big night out at *Promo*, at 53 Degrees. Friday is *Crash @ Source*, wheeling and dealing as the prices of drinks rise and fall throughout the night - 'if the Crash happens you can be quids in for your favourite drink!'. Saturday is *The Mash Up*, a mix of pop, indie, retro, '90s, dance and r'n'b tunes.

Yet bigger news is *The Worx* - 'everything old skool to suit all needs, acid, hardcore, Italian, piano and uplifting anthems'. Coming soon are *Pendulum* live at 53 Degrees, and when the *Radar Tour* takes to the road in the summer, the NME's annual showcase of new sounds.

Meanwhile, headlining the downstairs room is Justin Robertson, current resident at **Turnmills** and founder of the **Black Rabbit** club with Ed from

Archaeological Science, Physical Sciences, and the UCLan Combined Honours Programme. This last has always been a feature of the curriculum and is worth a careful trawl.

Least popular were Performing Arts and Film, which found almost 50% of their classes dissatisfied.

Of all the faculties, the Lancashire Business School puts most graduates into employment, mainly in manufacturing (notably the aircraft industry), in retail (often specialist), in the hotel and restaurant industry, in travel, and in building societies, government administration, higher education, hospitals, and in the business side of sporting and other recreational activities.

Nursing (including Mental Health), Midwifery,

SUBJECT AREAS (%)

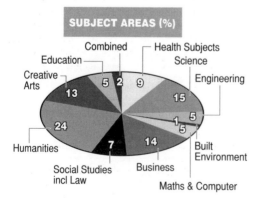

the Chemical brothers - experimental electronic, techno. On the current 'downstairs' menu is Lee Coombs (breakbeat).

In addition, theatre, music, dance and art all go on in **St Peter's Church** and the **Grenfell Baines Gallery**, the uni's Arts Centre in town.

There are 19 student societies. Student media currently includes Preston Student Television (PSTV), an internet-TV station, and of course *Pluto*, the award-winning student newspaper that's been around for more than 25 years.

SPORT Thirty clubs (counting Cheerleading). They came 45th position nationally with their teams. A £12-million outdoor multi-sport complex is sited two miles from campus.

The **Preston Sports Arena** has 8-lane athletics track, 5 grass pitches, 2 floodlit all-weather, 4 floodlit netball and tennis courts, 1.5 km cycling circuit, 7 floodlit training grids, plus 18-station fitness suite. There's also the on-campus, recently refurbished **Foster Sports Centre** for badminton, tennis, basketball, volleyball, soccer, fencing, martial arts, etc.

TOWN 'With something like 40- 50 pubs within 5 mins walk of the university,' writes Neil Doughty, 'there's always somewhere to hide away out of the rain. Some might contest that with so many pubs you'd need to be careful to avoid the ïlocals onlyï places where the only use for sawdust is mopping up the blood after a fight. Not so! With 20,000+ students making up a sixth of the in-term residents of Preston, the locals are well aware of the benefit of students to the local economy, and are very accommodating - loads of student discounts, tons of shops, a range of restaurants and two large-screen cinemas mean that there's always something to do when the workload lessens. Staff in venues all over town are always friendly.

'Even the nightclubs are relaxed both in terms of

WHAT IT'S REALLY LIKE

UNIVERSITY:	
Social Life	★★★★★
Campus scene	**Local, diffuse, mature but lively**
Student Union services	**Top-rated**
Politics	**Interest low**
Sport	**Competitive**
National team position	**79th**
Sport facilities	**Good**
Arts	**Drama, dance, film, music, all good, art excellent**
Student newspaper	**Pluto**
Student radio station	**Frequency 1350**
Nightclub	**53 Degrees**
Bars	**Source**
Union ents	**Massive club and live events**
Union societies	**33**
Parking	**Adequate**
CITY:	
Entertainment	★★★
Scene	**Good clubs, excellent pubs**
Town/gown relations	**Good**
Risk of violence	**Low**
Cost of living	**Average**
Student concessions	**Good**
Survival + 2 nights out	**£50 pw**
Part-time work campus/town	**Good/average**

atmosphere and prices. With no dress code in the week, and drinks prices fair, the town is ideally suited to students.'

PILLOW TALK
They guarantee to assist all freshers to find accommodation either in uni-owned halls and houses or privately owned ones. None of the uni residences are catered, there's a top-up smartcard that students can use to pay for their meals at refectories around campus. Leighton Hall, a private hall with 350 en-suite rooms and studios, opened in 2006. Get on to it quick.

GETTING THERE
☛ By road: travelling south, M6 (J32/M55), exit 1 (A6); travelling north, M6/J31, A59.
☛ By rail: London, 3:00; Manchester Oxford Road, 50 mins; Lancaster, 23 mins.
☛ By coach: London, 5:15; Liverpool, 1:00.

ACCOMMODATION

Guarantee to freshers	**No**
Style	**Halls, flats**
Security guard	**All**
Shared rooms	**Some**
Internet access	**All halls, some flats**
Self-catered	**All**
En suite	**Some**
Approx price range pw	**£45-£81**
Town rent pw	**£40-£65**

UNIVERSITY OF CHESTER

The University of Chester
Parkgate Road
Chester CH1 4BJ

TEL 01244 511000
FAX 01244 511260
EMAIL enquiries@chester.ac.uk
WEB www.chester.ac.uk

Chester Students' Union
University of Chester
Chester
Cheshire CH1 4BJ

TEL 01244 513399
FAX 01224 392866
EMAIL csupres@chester.ac.uk
WEB www.chestersu.ac.uk

VAG VIEW

Established by William Gladstone in 1839 as the first teacher-training college in the country with a Church of England foundation, Chester University comes out of Chester College, which became University College Chester in 1996, before being granted full university status in 2005.

Chester is a Roman town in the north west of England, with a picturesque centre, a thriving tourism industry and a lowish cost of living.

The university's curriculum has expanded beyond teaching education into Health Care, Applied Sciences, Humanities, Social Sciences, Performance Arts & Media, and Business & Management.

They were given a fillip in the National Student Survey when 80% of their students declared themselves satisfied with the teaching.

Equally, in the Times Higher Education's *Student Experience Survey, their lecturers scored well for their helpfulness and interest in their students and the size of the tuition groups.*

The teaching leads to 77% of graduates getting graduate-style jobs within six months of leaving. The drop-out rate of just below 11% is, albeit high, not the worst on the university map.

CAMPUS

The uni is a two-campus beast. Chester campus is a 32-acre site, 5 mins walk from the city centre, and

UNIVERSITY/STUDENT PROFILE	
University since	**2005**
Situation/style	**City campus**
Student population	**15095**
Undergraduates	**11655**
Mature undergraduates	**16%**
International undergrads	**2%**
Male/female ratio	**34:66**
Equality of opportunity:	
state school intake	**97%**
social class 4-7 intake	**36%**
low-participation area intake	**13%**

has undergone a variety of developments over the last 18 months. New facilities include a high-tech fitness suite, a modern School of Health and Social Care building, a large state-of-the art multi-purpose building featuring a brasserie, computer suite, conference facilities and high specification teaching areas. Next to campus is a newly built block of self-catered apartments, offering en-suite rooms.

Warrington campus is set on a 35-acre site a short bus ride away and has recently benefited from general improvements and refurbishments, including a modern dining area, new facilities within the Department of Media and a brand new Students' Union building. There is also a new Lifelong Learning Centre, incorporating new learning resources (libraries etc), learning support services and CITS (computer management/support etc), together with a café, lounge area and seminar rooms. A site has also been cleared for a new £2.9 million Business Management and IT Centre.

An impressive reputation has been built at Warrington Campus with production courses and links to a range of media organisations including the BBC and Granada Television. In addition, Business,

Computer Science, Media, and Sport & Exercise Sciences are all at least part-based at Warrington.

FEES, BURSARIES

Fees 2009-10: £3,225 p.a. There is a University of Chester Bursary (£1,000) for students in receipt of full HE Maintenance grant. Two-thirds of the student body receive it. There's also the Chester Sports Scholarship Scheme, sport being a defining element of student life at Chester. They also offer an organ scholarship, and two music scholarships/'Director's Assistant' posts based around the choir, and two similar positions based around the orchestra. Alto, tenor and bass choral scholarships are also available for positions in the Chester Cathedral Choir, tenable for one year in the first instance. See www.chester.ac.uk/undergraduate/moneymatters.html.

STUDENT PROFILE

The stats tell us that there is a high number of undergraduates (36%) from backgrounds not traditionally associated with going to university, and many are mature (i.e. over-21 at registration). Very few, only 3%, come here from the independent school sector. It is also a largely female

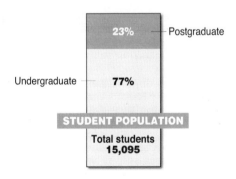

STUDENT POPULATION

Total students
15,095

undergraduate population, once described by the uni as an 'overwhelming majority', but if you're a bloke you may find you'll be able to cope.

Says Alastair Coles: 'If you are considering coming to Chester, you are most likely white, Northern, female, not the sort of person who got two As and a B at A level, and probably sporty.'

The lean to female is down to the numbers studying Nursing, Midwifery and Education - Primary.

Finally, very few of Chester's undergraduates come from outside the EU. It is a notably local scene. When it was a mere university college, this was just as true, but always notably a tight, compact unit, with a friendly and relaxed atmosphere. This is unlikely to change.

ACADEMIA & JOBS

The uni has been re-organised into seven schools of study: Applied & Health Sciences; Business, Management & Law, Arts & Media, Education, Health & Social Care, and Social Sciences.

Departments are Biological Sciences, Business, Computer, Education, English, Fine Art, Geography, Health & Social Care, History and Archaeology, Law, Leadership & Management, Maths, Media, Modern Languages, Performing Arts, Psychology, Social & Communication Studies, Sport and Exercise Sciences, Theology & Religious Studies, Work Related Studies.

In the recent countrywide survey of Britain's research provision, Chester managed four subjects in the world-class category. History did best, with 15% of its research accorded world-class status, and 30% of international significance. The others were Performing Arts, English, and Sport.

Teaching most popular with undergraduates is in Geography (100% of the class were in accord on

RESEARCH EXCELLENCE		
% of Chester's research that is **4*** (World-class) or **3*** (Internationally rated):		
	4*	**3***
Allied Health Professions	**0%**	**15%**
Applied Mathematics	**0%**	**15%**
Geography & Enviro. Studies	**0%**	**10%**
Social Work,l Policy & Admin.	**0%**	**15%**
Sports-Related Studies	**5%**	**20%**
English	**5%**	**15%**
Theology	**0%**	**30%**
History	**15%**	**30%**
Art and Design	**0%**	**5%**
Drama, Dance, Performing Arts	**5%**	**25%**

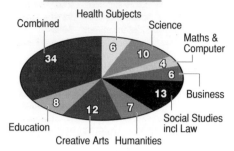

SUBJECT AREAS (%)

Combined — 34
Health Subjects — 6
Science — 10
Maths & Computer — 4
Business — 6
Social Studies incl Law — 13
Humanities — 7
Creative Arts — 12
Education — 8

the Drama Department and Society putting on frequent productions. Altogether, there are thirty-six societies and thirty-seven sports clubs.

SPORT Sport is of obsessive extra-curricular interest on the Chester campus, and there are constantly evolving facilities to support it, including a refurbished all-weather hockey pitch, a 25m pool, a fitness suite and sports hall - all part of a £5-million development. Chester is one of 90 educational establishments across the country delivering sporting services to a variety of Talented Athlete Scholarship Scheme (TASS) athletes. Chester Campus came 74th nationally in the BUSA team sports last year, which is excellent for the size of the university - Warrington came 140th.

TOWN Moving away from the campus into Chester itself, you'll find one of the prettiest historic city centres in the country. A big plus is that in comparison to most, it is also relatively cheap. Popular student haunts are the Odeon cinema, the Gateway Theatre, and over sixty pubs, most in walking distance. There are various student nights in town.

this). After that, it's English, Mathematics, and Theology, the original core subject of this Church of England Foundation. Teaching least popular was in Communications & Information Studies, and in Journalism.

Law is a relatively new part of the curriculum, offered both as single and combined honours. The department has close links with the Chester Centre of the College of Law, where LPC and Graduate Diplomas can be studied for - the College of Law is the largest legal training and education establishment in Europe.

The School of Health and Social Care is the major provider of pre-registration nursing and midwifery education across Cheshire and the Wirral. It also offers a wide range of undergraduate and postgraduate programmes for nurses, midwives and other health care professionals.

SOCIAL SCENE

STUDENTS UNION There are two Union centres, one for each campus. The new bar at Warrington (Wazza) is **Fu Bar** (was Scholars). It hosts live bands and *T.P.I. Wednesday* (beach party time, grass skirts at the ready, with DJ Paul Webber, 8pm-1am); also games and quiz nights, and there's a re-launch of classic alternative night, *Deckheadz*. There's also **Padgates** club night on Saturday.

At the Chester campus there is a fractious history attached to the fun and games. Some years ago the so-called Small Hall venue had to be closed down. It was so popular that massive queues would form outside, and it fell victim to noise-pollution protestors. These problems still characterise student life on campus, judging by the SU's 'Shhh' campaign to highlight problems caused to neighbours.

Still, students have now moved into a new phase with the opening of a £2-million, purpose-built Student Union building.

Society activity is as busy as you want to make it, though don't expect radical politics. Arts are well provided for, especially music and drama, with both

WHAT IT'S REALLY LIKE	
UNIVERSITY:	
Social Life	★★★
Campus scene	**Active**
Student Union services	**Average**
Politics	**Little interest**
Sport	**Key**
National team position	**74th (Chester)**
	140th (Warrington)
Sport facilities	**Good**
Arts opportunities	**Music, drama excellent**
Student newspaper	**Collegian**
Student Radio	**The Source**
Nightclub	**Max 250, Fu-Bar**
Bars	**As above**
Union ents	**Cheesy**
Union clubs/societies	**Mainly sport**
Parking	**Adequate**
CITY:	
Entertainment	★★★
Scene	**Pubs cheesy, clubs OK**
Town/gown relations	**Complaining**
Risk of violence	**No**
Cost of living	**Average to low**
Student concessions	**Good**
Survival + 2 nights out	**£90 pw**
Part-time work campus/town	**Good/excellent**

PILLOW TALK

There is a variety of accommodation available to freshers: halls, flats, houses, on-campus, off-campus, etc, but look in particular at a modern, high-specification, block of self-catered flats for freshers, completed three years ago. It's situated directly opposite the Chester campus.

Internet access is not available in many of the rooms. Hall security goes no further than normal campus security.

GETTING THERE

☛ By road: the uni is situated at the junction of the A540 and Cheyney Road.
☛ By rail: London Euston, 2:45; Sheffield, 2:25;

ACCOMMODATION	
Guarantee to freshers	**950 rooms**
Style	**Halls, flats**
Security guard	**None**
Shared rooms	**Some halls**
Internet access	**Most**
Self-catered	**Some**
En suite	**Some**
Approx price range pw	**£55-£115**
Town rent pw	**£41-£55**

Birmingham New Street, 1:45; Liverpool Lime Street, 40 mins; Manchester Oxford Road, 1:00.
☛ By coach: London, 6:00; Sheffield, 3:00.

UNIVERSITY OF CHICHESTER

The University of Chichester
Bishop Otter Campus
College Lane
Chichester PO19 4PE

TEL 01243 816002
FAX 01243 812104
EMAIL admissions@chi.ac.uk
WEB www.chiuni.ac.uk

Chichester University Students' Union
Bishop Otter Campus
College Lane
Chichester PO19 6PE

TEL 01243 816390
FAX 01243 816391
EMAIL c.woodwood@chi.ac.uk
WEB www.chisu.org

VAG VIEW

*S*ituated between the South Downs and the sea at Chichester and at nearby Bognor Regis, Chichester University was once known as the West Sussex Institute of Higher Education, then as Chichester College of Higher Education. In 1999 it became University College Chichester and gained the power to award its own degrees. Forty-nine per cent of its graduates go into Education, and Sports Science is the popular specialisation, but more recently they have built a reputation in the schools of Visual and Performing Arts, and Cultural Studies.

It became a fully fledged university in 2005 and last year had an overwhelming vote of confidence from its students in the National Survey - 87% declared themselves satisfied with what they are up to. We award their staff a maximum five stars for the interest and help they give their students and four stars for the small tuition groups they manage to organise.

You get all this attention for a meagre

UNIVERSITY/STUDENT PROFILE	
University since	**2005**
Situation/style	**Coastal sites**
Student population	**4930**
Undergraduates	**3715**
Mature undergraduates	**35%**
International undergrads	**4%**
Male/female ratio	**37:63**
Equality of opportunity:	
state school intake	**96%**
social class 4-7 intake	**40%**
low-participation area intake	**4%**

260 points at entry. It's no wonder the drop-out rate is so small - 5%.

CAMPUSES

The Bishop Otter Campus, in name at least, takes us back to 1839 when Bishop Otter College was founded by the Church of England as a teacher training establishment. There is, today, a striking modern chapel in the campus grounds, which lie within this walled cathedral city, widely known for its annual Festival of Music and Arts.

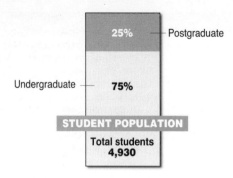

STUDENT POPULATION
Total students
4,930

25% — Postgraduate

Undergraduate — **75%**

The less imaginatively named Bognor Regis Campus is located five miles away. Bognor is, as she sounds, a seaside resort long in the dying.

Bishop Otter is the bigger of the two campuses, though Bognor has most of the Teacher Training provision. The campuses are far enough apart to cause something of a psychological split, and the Student Union has been preoccupied with getting the bus service between the two improved.

FEES, BURSARIES
UK & EU Fees, 2009-10: £3,225 p.a. There are bursaries for students receiving the Maintenance Grant on a sliding scale, according to income. There's also the 'Talented Sports Performer' Bursary Scheme, which makes annual payments to outstanding sports persons.

STUDENT PROFILE
Lots of students are local, mature, and from neighbourhoods and socio-economic groups with little hope of going to university until a few years ago, when places like Chichester rose to the fore.

TEACHING SURVEY AT A GLANCE

Avg. UCAS points accepted	**260**
Acceptance rate	**18%**
Overall satisfaction rate	**87%**
Helpful/interested staff	★★★★★
Small tuition groups	★★★★
Students into graduate jobs	**73%**

Teaching most popular with undergraduates:
Historical & Philosophical Studies (97%), History (96%), Biological Sciences, Business, Business Studies, Sports Science (95%), Media Studies (94%), Imaginative Writing, Academic Studies in Education (92%), Initial Teacher Trainig (91%).

Teaching least popular with undergraduates:
Music (77%), Dance (75%).

There is a strong female presence, great sporting prowess, and a sense that no lack of family experience of going to university is going to hold them back in any way.

ACADEMIA & JOBS
There are six schools: Teacher Education; Physical Education; Sport, Exercise & Health Science; Cultural Studies; Visual & Performing Arts; and Social Studies.

Undergraduates may study for single honours, joint or major/minor programmes, or BA (QTS). Degrees include a range of Business degrees, Dance, Creative Writing, Music, Fine Art, Events Management, Human Resource Management, Media, Sport, and Social Work - all of which, along with the Teaching, find expression in the graduate employment picture, while a range of Theology

RESEARCH EXCELLENCE
% of Chichester's research that is
4* *(World-class)* or **3*** *(Internationally rated):*

	4*	3*
Sports-Related Studies	**5%**	**15%**
English	**0%**	**25%**
Theology	**0%**	**15%**
History	**0%**	**30%**
Drama, Dance, Performing Arts	**0%**	**40%**

degrees maintain continuity with the college's Church of England past.

Seventy-three per cent of graduates get graduate-style jobs within six months of graduation, 82% of these as primary and secondary school teachers, in community and counselling activities, in sport, specialist retail, the hotel & restaurant industry, recruitment and personnel, government admin., business, publishing, entertainment, and artistic pursuits.

A smattering also get jobs in radio & TV, film, and in arts management.

Teaching most popular with undergraduates is in Theology, History, Sports Science, Business, Media, Creative Writing, Education and Initial Teacher Training. Even the less popular subjects - Music and Dance - appealed to 75%.

Out of the lecture theatre there is a strong tradition in jazz and classical music, and regular student music society performances and workshops (the college and Chichester Cathedral are regular venues). Dance (ballet, jazz and tap) is supported by the Studio, and, like music and art, involves public performance/exhibition at both student and professional level.

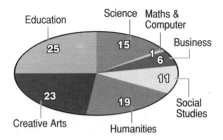

SUBJECT AREAS (%)

Education — 25
Science — 15
Maths & Computer — 1
Business — 6
— 11
Social Studies — 19
Humanities
Creative Arts — 23

There's a Learning Resources Centre at Bishop Otter - a library (200,000 items), a media and computer facility, and art gallery. A similar centre at Bognor Regis has recently been refurbished.

SOCIAL SCENE

STUDENT UNION A new Union building opened at Chichester campus recently, with a 650 capacity **ZeeBar**. At Bognor, it's **The Mack**. The majority of students are local, so weekends are not that big, but ents are impressive for so small a clientele, and

WHAT IT'S REALLY LIKE	
UNIVERSITY:	
Social Life	★★★
Campus scene	**Female, sporty, closed weekends**
Student Union services	**Very good**
Politics	**Active**
Sport	**Key**
National team position	**67th**
Sport facilities	**Good**
Arts opportunities	**Music, dance, drama excellent**
Student newspaper	**The Clash**
Nightclub	**ZeeBar**
Bars	**ZeeBar, The Mack**
Union ents	**Cheesy. 6 nights, not Saturday**
Union societies	**7**
Most popular society	**Business & Management Soc**
Parking	**Poor**
CITY:	
Entertainment	★★
Scene	**Arts good**
Town/gown relations	**Good**
Risk of violence	**Average**
Cost of living	**Low**
Student concessions	**Average**
Survival + 2 nights out	**£70 pw**
Part-time work campus/town	**Good/**

as cheesy as you like. *Big Wednesday* is Sports Night in Chichester, while down in Bognor it's *The Alternative* (live music and DJ's). There were also Comedy Nights, and 4 balls a year - Freshers, Graduation, Christmas and Summer.

There are alternative music societies, arts societies, a role-playing games, society even an English literature appreciation society. Oh, and an LGB (gay) Society flourishes, regularly holding events on campus and in a gay pub in the town. 'There's been a big growth,' says a bod at the union, which, for a moment, sounded a tad alarming.

Level of political activity has recently been impressively high, with a focus on Drink Awareness, Anti-Bullying, Mental Health Awareness, and a campaign for better inter-site transport and washing facilities.

SPORT Sport is key; last year their teams came 67th nationally, which is good for a uni of less than 5,000. There are 13 sports clubs, all, except netball, with both men's and women's teams.

PILLOW TALK

There is catered accommodation in halls at both sites, and higher capacity and en suite at Bognor. New self-catering halls of residence opened at the Chichester Campus in September 2006, with 124 en-suite rooms with communal kitchens and lounges. They have also acquired 93 extra shared facility rooms close to the university, bringing total accommodation provided to 675 students. This allows them to guarantee accommodation to all

ACCOMMODATION	
Guarantee to freshers	**100%**
Style	**Halls**
Security guard	**Campus**
Shared rooms	**Some**
Internet access	**All**
Self-catered	**Some**
En suite	**Most**
Approx price range pw	**£73.50-£127**
Town rent pw	**£65**

freshers. Remaining accommodation is allocated on a 'first come, first served' basis.

GETTING THERE

☛ By road: to Bishop Otter campus, A286 from the north. From east and west it's the A27. The road between Chichester and Bognor is the A259.

☛ By rail: London Victoria, 0:45; Birmingham, 4:00.

☛ Frequent trains from Gatwick Airport.

☛ By coach: London, 4:40; Birmingham, 6:00.

CITY UNIVERSITY

City University
Northampton Square
London EC1V OHB

TEL 020 7040 5060/8028/8716
FAX 020 7040 8995
EMAIL ugadmissions@city.ac.uk
WEB www.city.ac.uk

City University Students' Union
Northampton Square
London EC1V 0HB

TEL 020 7040 5600
FAX 020 7040 5601
EMAIL studentunion@city.ac.uk
WEB www.citysu.com

VAG VIEW

City received its Royal Charter in 1966. The university is, as its name suggests, very much at the hub of life in the City of London and occupies a singular place in the world of higher education. It has a fine reputation in professional education and staff pride themselves on close contact with professional institutions, business and industry. Many of the programmes are accredited by professional bodies, and there is a very healthy graduate employment track record. But the social scene is hopeless. Go to City and you go to London and attend a university during the day, as you might a job - albeit with high, and wholly justified, expectations. Campus life has been on hold, largely because for some reason a decent licence has been hard to get, This year, although there is still no late licence, there's a new venue, and 75% of the student population are very happy with the singular character of City University.

CAMPUS

City Uni inhabits the famed City of London, but is only fifteen minutes from the West End, a dawdle from Islington, with its theatres, cinemas, fashionable restaurants, trendy bars, clubs and traditional pubs, and a short way (in the opposite direction) from Clerkenwell, once-artisan London and now a fashionable area for cool, young, City-mile workers.

The main university buildings form part of Northampton Square. Main library, lecture theatres and Students' Union are here. The Department of Arts Policy and Management are nearby in the Barbican Centre. The Dept. of Radiography and halls of residence are also within walking distance. The St Bartholomew School of Nursing is some way away in West Smithfield and Whitechapel in the East End. The Business School now occupies new premises in the heart of the city (see Academia below).

UNIVERSITY/STUDENT PROFILE	
University since	**1966**
Situation/style	**City sites**
Student population	**23835**
Undergraduates	**14655**
Mature undergraduates	**24%**
International undergrads	**20%**
Male/female ratio	**44:56**
Equality of opportunity:	
state school intake	**89%**
social class 4-7 intake	**40%**
low-participation area intake	**4%**

'City University is located within walking distance of no less than four tube stations (Barbican, Angel, Farringdon, Old Street), but strangely very few people can ever find it!' writes Catherine Teare. 'Tasteful, grassy Northampton Square, which supports a sizeable bandstand and water trough, has been the site for many an adventure for students - a place to chill in summer and the bandstand a place to shelter when raining. The men's rugby team used to use it for their initiation ceremonies - something

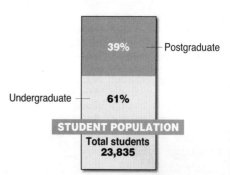

about running round it in the buff!'

FEES, BURSARIES

UK & EU Fees 2009-10: generally £3,225 p.a., but the University charges tuition fees which vary between programmes, as well as between UK/EU and other students. There are bursaries for students in receipt of full HE Maintenance Grant, and school-based scholarships in specific subjects. For further details on fees and funding, visit www.city.ac.uk/study.

STUDENT PROFILE

Full-time, first-degree undergraduates, many of whom are mature and from overseas, make up an unusually small percentage of the student body. Many more students are part-timers and there is a large number of postgraduate students. Says Catherine: 'City University is like nowhere else. The mixture of cultures and personalities makes it one of the most diverse university communities in London.'

ACADEMIA & JOBS

Great emphasis is placed on links with industry and the professions - Journalism, Law, Banking. However, its showing in the *Times Higher Education* magazine's Student Experience survey was dire for lecturer interest in students, support, and small-size tutorial groups.

Eighteen per cent of City graduates go into banking, financial activities, accountancy, or business. The Cass Business School is a £50-million building which provides, so they say, 'a state-of-the-art resource for management education in the 21st Century'.

There are dedicated degrees in Actuarial Science. Half the staff in the Actuarial Science & Statistics Department are Fellows of the Institute of Actuaries. There's a high 'ask' at A level, but a 4-year degree with a first-year Foundation course looks inviting, as does a study abroad option.

The health provision is massive. They have a School of Nursing (including degrees in Mental Nursing, and Midwifery), and there is a strategic link with University of London Queen Mary's School of Medicine & Dentistry (see entry), boosted by a recent £10-million investment.

Now there's a new School of Allied Health Professions, which brings together Optometry & Visual Science, Language & Communication Science (speech therapy), Radiography (the Saad Centre for Radiography Clinical Skills Education is the new teaching facility), Health Management, and Food Policy (postgrad. only).

Nineteen per cent of graduates go on to work in hospitals, fifteen per cent as dispensing opticians,

---

TEACHING SURVEY AT A GLANCE

Avg. UCAS points accepted	**310**
Acceptance rate	**12%**
Overall satisfaction rate	**78%**
Helpful/interested staff	★★
Small tuition groups	★
Students into graduate jobs	**85%**

Teaching most popular with undergraduates:
Civil Engineering, Finance (96%), Accounting (95%), Management Studies (93%), Business & Administrative Studies (92%), Business Studies (90%), Ophthalmics (89%).

Teaching least popular with undergraduates:
Social Work (35%).

---

for which there is the dedicated 2-year Foundation in Dispensing Optics, and then the BSc Optometry.

There are two BSc Radiography degrees, Diagnostic and Therapeutic, also well-trod pathways into employment. See, too, the dedicated BSc route into Speech and Language Therapy, another certainty in terms of employment.

Law graduates (who will have been particularly well schooled in performance skills) have, in City's Inns of Court School of Law, one of the few institutions validated to run LPCs (Legal Practice Course), essential for solicitors.

The passage from graduate to barrister is smooth, as The Inns of Court School of Law is also one of the few places where you can study for the Bar Vocational Course (BVC). There's also a LLB Law & Property Valuation alongside a degree in Real Estate Finance & Investment.

Location favours would-be journalists, too - you are in the very heart of British media, and you will be lectured by practitioners. The portfolio of degrees espouses the idea of combining journalistic skills with knowledge in a particular subject area -

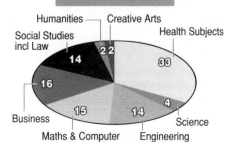

SUBJECT AREAS (%)

Humanities — Creative Arts
Social Studies incl Law
Health Subjects 33
Business 16
Maths & Computer 15
Engineering 14
Science 4
14 2 2

Economics, Psychology, or Sociology.

They get their graduates jobs aplenty in this area, and in publishing and advertising.

Note, too, City's renowned postgraduate journo provision: International Journalism Diploma/MA is practically orientated with a focus on both print and broadcast - very hands on, very productive employment-wise. There is also a PhD for mid-career practitioners, who will submit a piece of work and undertake supervised research to produce a thesis.

The department, part of the School of Arts, is internationally respected and has trained the likes of Kirsty Lang (BBC), Dermot Murnaghan (BBC), Gary Younge (Guardian/Observer), Sharon Maguire (Director of Bridget Jones's Diary), Gillian Joseph (Sky News) and Samira Ahmed (Channel 4 News).

City is also traditionally strong in engineering. Racing car enthusiasts should note an interesting niche, the 3-year BEng and BSc Automotive & Motorsport Engineering (4/5-year B/MEng degrees as well). Aeronautical and Air Transport degrees also look interesting, as do the Civil Engineering Degrees, which come with either Surveying or Architecture on the side. There are good job lines into Construction, Architecture, or Town Planning.

The BSc Computing Science degrees with AI/Distributed Systems/Games Technology/Music Informatics add-ons have a fine reputation. There's a particularly strong line into software consultancy.

SOCIAL SCENE

STUDENTS' UNION The renowned Journalism course provides welcome support to the extra-mural media side of life. The monthly glossy *Massive* has been replaced this year by *City Offline*, which keeps students well informed of forthcoming events and current hot topics. The radio station (Divercity) and TV station (SUBtv) have gone, but plans are afoot to revive the radio at least.

The Student Union has tried to give a stable base for the disparate and scattered student body, but frankly, other than the sound community life in one of the halls, student life at City has been on a seemingly unstoppable dive into oblivion for quite a few years. You should be aware that you are not joining a student scene that you'd find at some other London universities.

In an attempt to halt the slide they just spent £1.5 million on new facilities. There's a new venue, **Ten Squared**, and dear old **Saddlers Bar** has been given a new lease of life and now fills one entire floor of the main building, providing space for 160 diners during the day, an HD multi-screen TV system, air-hockey table, table football and pool tables. Students may book it for up to 400 people. There's a sophisticated multi-zone sound and lighting system, but it is rarely used. How about employing an ents manager, having a good time, and making some money?

Weekends are a washout and although

RESEARCH EXCELLENCE		

% of City's research that is
4* *(World-class)* or **3*** *(Internationally rated):*

	4*	3*
Health Services Research	0%	5%
Nursing and Midwifery	30%	40%
Allied Health Professions:		
Language and Communication	10%	30%
Optometry and Visual Science	10%	20%
Applied Mathematics	5%	15%
Computer Science	15%	40%
General Eng., Mineral, Mining	10%	35%
Economics and Econometrics	10%	45%
Business and Management	15%	40%
Library and Infor. Management	15%	50%
Law	5%	30%
Social Work,l Policy & Admin.	20%	45%
Sociology	15%	30%
Psychology	5%	45%
Art and Design	5%	40%
Music	30%	35%

Wednesdays are Student Club and Society Night, the whole scene frankly needs a bit of inspiration.

'Does City have a campus life? Yes and No,' writes Catherine. 'Students use a number of sites dotted around London, which makes it hard for us to feel like we belong.' They've no late licence at the Union. They are, in effect, virtually closed to ents, but hey, you're in London and can make your own scene. As for societies, there is little to shout about either, though they claim to have upped the number by 25 in the current year (if so, the total is 55). There have also been some effective student campaigns on Racism, Women's Safety and Islamophobia, and they raised £1k for Comic Relief.

> *Strong lines into the professions – business, finance, law, health – and very much a London experience. But what have they done to the fun and games at the Student Union?*

In 2007 a Student Centre opened at Northampton Square where students can go for help and advice on a wide range of topics including

WHAT IT'S REALLY LIKE	
UNIVERSITY:	
Social Life	★★★
Campus scene	**Closed weekends**
Student Union services	**Uninspired**
Politics	**Avoided**
Sport	**Unfocused**
National team position	**115th**
Sport facilities	**Average**
Arts opportunities	**Some**
Student magazine	**Massive**
Nightclub	**Ten Squared**
Bars	**Saddlers**
Union ents	**Limited**
Union societies	**50**
Most popular society	**Law, Islamic**
Parking	**Non-existent**
CITY:	
Entertainment	★★★★★
Scene	**Excellent local pubs, clubs, arts**
Town/gown relations	**Good**
Risk of violence	**High**
Cost of living	**High**
Student concessions	**Good**
Survival + 2 nights out	**£100 pw**
Part-time work campus/town	**Excellent**

ACCOMMODATION	
Guarantee to freshers	**No guarantee**
Style	**Halls, flats**
Internet access	**All**
Self-catered	**All**
En suite	**Some**
Approx price range pw	**£103-£111**
City rent pw	**£100**

Road, Oxford Street and Camden.'

SPORT Interest may be high but levels and facilities are not impressive, and now they no longer have Sports Night at Saddlers. There are pitches in Walthamstow; a small rowing club is based, of course, on the Thames; the Saddler's Sports Centre, with badminton, football, netball, tennis, aerobics and yoga and a good martial arts programme, a couple of squash courts; and some Islington facilities are popular nearby.

PILLOW TALK

All applicants over 18 living outside Greater London who firmly accept an offer of a place at City and submit an accommodation application form by 15 May are guaranteed a place in halls. There are two, both within walking distance of the main site. The first, Finsbury & Heyworth, are linked by a bar/common room; fees include an evening meal and late breakfast on Saturdays and Sundays. Walter Sickert Hall, which overlooks the Regents Canal, is more plush, with en-suite, single study-bedrooms. Next to Finsbury/Heyworth is a block of purpose-built self-catering flats, 3-6 single study-bedrooms, living room/kitchen and showers. Newly available to first years are self-contained flats (single study-bedrooms with shared facilities) at Francis Rowley Court, about ten minutes' walk from the uni.

'Popular private housing student areas,' reports Catherine, 'include Hackney, Stoke Newington and Shoreditch.'

GETTING THERE
☛ All sites are well served by buses.
☛ Parking is difficult and expensive.
☛ Nearest Underground stations to main sites: Angel (Northern line), Farringdon and Barbican (Hammersmith & City, Metropolitan and Circle).
☛ For the School of Nursing, it's either District or Metropolitan, depending on the station you choose. All is accessible from City.

housing, financial support, visa and immigration advice, fee payments, course registration and graduation enquiries.

TOWN Location is all. Never was that more true - you'll be 5 mins walk from the attractions of Angel, Old Street, Shoreditch, Hoxton and Farringdon, and just a short bus ride from the West End.

If you walk north towards Angel you come to Upper Street, which must have the most bars and restaurants in any one area of London after the West End. There is something for everyone, cheap and expensive. It has a friendly, safe atmosphere and a 24-hour Sainsbury's on Thursday to Saturday.

If you walk west down Roseberry Avenue, you come to Exmouth Market and its surrounding area. This offers pretty much the same as Upper Street, but on a smaller scale. Exmouth Market has some of the best sandwich shops in London and, especially in the summer, a really welcoming atmosphere.

Camden is a mere 10-minute tube ride away, while the West End is twenty minutes on the bus. Many clubs offer discounts to students with an NUS card, but you must make sure you go on the right night. The nearest places to shop are Holloway

COVENTRY UNIVERSITY

Coventry University
Priory Street
Coventry CV1 5FB

TEL 024 7615 2222
FAX 024 7615 2223
EMAIL studentenquiries@coventry.ac.uk
WEB www.coventry.ac.uk

Coventry University Students' Union
Priory Street
Coventry CV1 5FJ

TEL 024 7679 5200
FAX 024 7655 5239
EMAIL suexec@coventry.ac.uk
WEB www.cusu.org

VAG VIEW

*A*fter devastating bombing during the Second World War, Coventry rose from the ashes to become a major industrial force. Elements of what later became the university evolved during this time, and in 1970 the Coventry College of Art merged with Lanchester College of Technology and Rugby College of Engineering Technology to form Lanchester Polytechnic. In 1987 the name was changed to Coventry Polytechnic. Then, in 1992, the poly became a university.

There was a 79% student satisfaction rate in the Higher Education Funding Council's latest National Student Survey, and 72% find real graduate jobs within six months of graduating from the university. The drop-out rate is about average at 10%.

UNIVERSITY/STUDENT PROFILE	
University since	**1992**
Situation/style	**City campus**
Student population	**19415**
Undergraduates	**16430**
Mature undergraduates	**43%**
International undergrads	**8%**
Male/female ratio	**29:71**
Equality of opportunity:	
state school intake	**97%**
social class 4-7 intake	**39%**
low-participation area intake	**10%**

There are scholarships for Sport: up to £4,000 p.a., depending on level of performance, and up to £2,000 p.a. for achieving 320 points from a variety of qualification sources. Then there's the Enterprise Scholarship: £2,000 p.a. and a Creative or Performing Arts Scholarship: again £2,000, and STEM (the Science, Technology, Engineering and Mathematics Scholarship) to the value of the tuition fee paid.

CAMPUS

The modern precinct campus is directly opposite the bombed-out ruins of the original cathedral. Looking around the ecclesiastical shell is a thought-provoking experience. Students from Cov were sketching it at the time we visited. Especially memorable is a sculpture of reconciliation (two figures embrace to express forgiveness for the Luftwaffe's devastation of Coventry) created by Josefina de Vasconcellos and, as it happens, given by Richard Branson. An identical sculpture stands in the Peace Garden at Hiroshima, Japan.

FEES, BURSARIES

UK & EU fees 2009-10: £3,225 p.a. There's a bursary for students in receipt of full HE Maintenance Grant, indeed of any partial Maintenance Grant - £320 p.a. See www.coventry.ac.uk/studentfinance.

STUDENT PROFILE

There is a large mature student population, bent on vocational training. Many undergrads come via the state sector from the locality, but also a lot

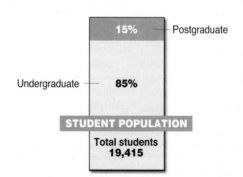

15% — Postgraduate

Undergraduate — 85%

STUDENT POPULATION

Total students
19,415

from overseas. A third of first degree undergrads are part-timers. The uni has been diligent in its open access policy, giving many families their first taste of a university education.

Generally overlooked is the massive preponderance of females in the Coventry demography. We think of the university speciailising in all those traditionally male degrees, Automative and Aerospace Engineering and Design, Civil Engineering, Motorsport, Motorcycle, and Powertrain Engineering, Building, and those odd little apparently masculine niches associated with this university, Disaster Management, and Natural Hazards. And yet, 71% of undergraduates are female.

ACADEMIA & JOBS

Of course the female of the species has been taking degrees in Engineering for years. I have the distinction of knowing the first female under-graduate to study Engineering at Nottingham University. But overlooked at Coventry is the fact that the largest single graduate employment sector is not engineering at all, it is hospital and human health activities - around a fifth go into these areas from degrees Physiotherapy and other employer-friendly health science degrees, which include Nursing (Adult and Mental Health), Dietetics, Midwifery, Occupational Therapy, Paramedic Science, Operating Department Practice, and Biomedical Science degrees, all dovetailing into community degrees in Social Work, Welfare, and Youth Work.

While the motor vehicle manufacturers are the fourst biggest employment sector, they account for only 5% of grautae output here, however significant a contribution that may be relatively nationwide.

There are two schools: Lifelong Learning and Art & Design, and three faculties: Health & Life Sciences; Business, Environment & Society; Engineering & Computing.

A school's careers master told us, 'They have deliberately gone for the vocational - that was their background. We have students for whom Coventry is exactly right.'

For cars and planes, Coventry is still among the leaders. Would-be engineers and manufacturers come bounding out of here. Less well known are low-cost offers for the design of boats, bikes, toys, indeed, all sorts of product design in the developing Art & Design faculty.

But this city is the home of car manufacture, and the car industry is central to its calling. There are BA hons degrees in 3D Design Representation, Automotive Design, and Automotive Design & Illustration, as well as the range of BEng hons. Racing car designers and team managers note: the

degrees in Motorsports Engineering are not demanding at entry.

Design also favours graphic artists, designers and illustrators (often the advertising industry or journalism as destination). BSc Architectural Design Technology favours the would-be town planner, while jobs in the construction industry are very much available to Cov's Built Environment graduates - Building, Surveying and Quantity Surveying.

Would-be solicitors will observe that Coventry are European, commercial and business law specialists, and non-Law graduates may opt for a 2-year, or 3-year part-time, Senior Status Law degree

---

TEACHING SURVEY AT A GLANCE

Avg. UCAS points accepted	**240**
Acceptance rate	**21%**
Overall satisfaction rate	**79%**
Helpful/interested staff	★★
Small tuition groups	★★
Students into graduate jobs	**72%**

Teaching most popular with undergraduates:
Languages (97%), Economics (94%), Sociology (88%), Biological Sciences, Business Studies, Performing Arts (84%), Psychology (83%),

Teaching least popular with undergraduates:
Media Studies, Mass Communications & Documentation (57%).

RESEARCH EXCELLENCE

% of Coventry's research that is
4* *(World-class) or* **3*** *(Internationally rated):*

	4*	3*
Allied Health Professions	5%	5%
Applied Mathematics	0%	20%
Computer Science	5%	20%
Electrical and Electronic Eng.	5%	45%
Mechanical, Aeronautical & Manufacturing Engineering	0%	25%
Metallurgy and Materials	0%	20%
Town and Country Planning	0%	20%
Business and Management	0%	20%
Library and Info. Management	5%	35%
Law	0%	5%
Politics	5%	5%
Social Work, Policy & Admin.	5%	20%
Psychology	0%	0%
Education	0%	20%
Sports-Related Studies	0%	15%
Art and Design	5%	55%

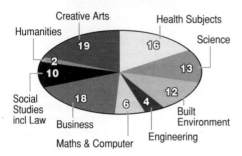

SUBJECT AREAS (%)

Creative Arts — 19
Humanities — 2
Social Studies incl Law — 10
Business — 18
Maths & Computer — 6
Engineering — 4
Built Environment — 12
Science — 13
Health Subjects — 16

here. There are also degrees in Forensic Science.

Computer and Games Technology degrees translate into jobs in software consultancy and supply. If you have an adventurous streak and purposeful outlook, rifle through their Disaster Management degrees and the one in Natural Hazards. This is a genuine niche. Coventry has ten years' experience teaching such subjects. Where might they lead you?

Generally the points ask at admission is low, around 240 points. Coventry lecturers fared less well than most in the *Times Higher* Student Experience Survey, however, and earn a mere 2 stars for interest in their students, and the size of their tuition groups.

In the National Student Survey the teaching most popular with Coventry undergraduates was in Languages. They are hot on French and Spanish and there are a number of degrees in European Business/Construction/Engineering/Entrepreneurship.

Next most popular were Economics, Sociology, Biological Sciences (including a whole range of degrees in Sport), Business Studies, Performing Arts (including Music Practice, Dance and Theatre), and Psychology.

The only dogs were the Media and Journalism degrees. Only 57% of students gave them time of day.

SOCIAL SCENE

STUDENT UNION The most recent addition to the campus is a new student centre, which offers a 'one-stop' service. Students can get help on a range of issues including finance, registry, accommodation, international office, recruitment and admissions and student services.

The campus is a hive of activity revolving around the café/bar, **Revolution**, located on the top floor of the Union building in Priory Street and known for its hot chocolate. It serves breakfast through to late-night munchies and screens all the top sporting fixtures. There's also a Premier convenience store, a café called **Coffee**, a computer cluster, hairdresser's and the Union's main offices.

Artie and indie types will be found in the **Golden Cross** and **Fads** caféteria in the art block. Language and engineering students will be found in the library. Sporting people will be found at the Union bar or slumped in the corner somewhere. International students seem to be everywhere.

Much of uni social life is dominated by societies, which are particularly sporty, though the sometime award-winning media, *Source* (newspaper) and Source Radio, appeal too. Most societies have their local haunts: the **Hope and Anchor** is frequented by 'The Lanch' Rugby Union team, for example. Sporting societies often organise theme-night fund-raising events - Man 'O' Man, The Full Monty, Slave Trade, etc. - and these are high on the student social calendar.

What was once **The Planet** on the corner of Cox Street - a revolution in its day - is now **Studio 54**. Here there is a Friday diet of cheese - *Flirt* - a dedicated ents manager, and entertainment throughout the week, including various jam nights, and open deck and rock nights. During the day you can grab a snack and a drink at Studio 54 - there's a **Subway** sandwich shop and a concession for jacket potatoes. It's but a short walk from campus.

SPORT The uni muscled its way to 70th in the overall BUSA ratings for team sports last year. It's had its Olympic swimmers and pumped-up boxing champs. **The Sports Centre** is campus central, with fitness suite, injury clinic, 4-court and 2-court halls and dance studio. Thirty-seven acres of uni playing fields are at Westward Heath, 4 miles away, and cater for rugby, soccer, hockey and cricket. There's also a 9-hole golf course.

TOWN The compact city centre has a much-loved traditional indoor market. The £33-million **Sky Dome** complex houses a multi-screen cinema, bars and café bars, two nightclubs, restaurants, and there is a 4,000-seat arena, a popular concert venue that doubles as an ice rink.

The **Herbert Art Gallery** and **Museum** and **Belgrade Theatre** provide the cultural dimension. Sport is, however, the thing, with the £60-million **Coventry Arena** no longer a dream. The **City**

> *'They have deliberately gone for the vocational - that was their background. We have students for whom Coventry is exactly right.'*

Sports Centre has an Olympic-sized swimming pool.

Cost of living is quite low, and there are lots of student discounts. Wednesday nights is student

WHAT IT'S REALLY LIKE	
UNIVERSITY:	
Social Life	★★★
Campus scene	**Busy, diverse, Good ents scene**
Student Union services	**Average**
Politics	**Internal**
Sport	**Much vaunted, but average**
National team position	**70th**
Sport facilities	**Good**
Arts opportunities	**Film, art exc.; dance, music popular; drama improving**
Student newspaper	**Source**
Student radio	**Source FM**
Venue, bar	**Studio 54, Revolution**
Union ents	**Eclectic**
Union clubs/societies	**50**
Parking	**Poor**
CITY:	
Entertainment	★★
Scene	**Clubs 'n pubs**
Town/gown relations	**Nothing special**
Risk of violence	**Variable**
Cost of living	**Low**
Student concessions	**OK**
Survival + 2 nights out	**£60 pw**
Part-time work campus/town	**Average/Good**

night at **Lava Ignite**. Other city nightclubs include **Jumpin Jacks**, **Coventry Kasbah**, and **Colisseum**. There's also **Escape Coventry**, a bar and mini venue. See also the Student Union at nearby Warwick University.

Otherwise, 'Most pubs in Cov are of the Rat,

Parrot and Firkin ilk,' says Andrew Losowsky, 'but **The Golden Cross** and **The Hand and Heart** are worth a look for something different.'

PILLOW TALK

'Priory Hall is the largest of the student residences over 600 rooms,' writes Jennifer Johnston. 'It is dominated by lads who haven't yet discovered how to open a tin of beans. Singer Hall is organised into flats and is self-catered. Caradoc Hall is a tower block of self-contained flats and is just out of the city centre. There are lots of suitable student houses in the Stoke, Earlsdon and Radford areas of the city, with good low rents.'

New-ish accommodation includes university-owned Sherbourne House and Lynden House and non-university Liberty Park and Trinity Point. Raglan House was completed for occupation in September 2007 - self-catered, en-suite cluster flats.

GETTING THERE

☞ By road: from London M1/J17, M45, A45, signs for City Centre. From the south, M40/J15, A46, signs for City Centre. From the southwest, M5,

ACCOMMODATION	
Guarantee to freshers	**88%**
Style	**Halls, flats**
Security guard	**Some**
Shared rooms	**Some flats**
Internet access	**All**
Self-catered	**Some**
En suite	**Some**
Approx price range pw	**£84-£115**
City rent pw	**£70**

M42/J6, A45. From Northwest, M6/J2, City Centre signs. From north, M1/J21, M69, City Centre.
☞ By rail: London Euston, 80 mins; Manchester Piccadilly, 2:30; Nottingham, 1:45; Bristol, 2:30.
☞ By air: Birmingham Airport.
☞ By coach: London, 1:20; Leeds, 4:00.

UNIVERSITY FOR THE CREATIVE ARTS

University for The Creative Arts
Farnham
Surrey GU9 7DS

TEL 01252 892696
FAX 01252 892624
EMAIL admissions@ucreative.ac.uk
WEB www.ucreative.ac.uk

University for the Creative Arts Students' Union
Farnham
Surrey GU9 7DS

TEL 01252 710263
FAX 01252 713591
EMAIL rhayes@ucreative.ac.uk
WEB www.uccasu.com/

UNIVERSITY/STUDENT PROFILE	
University since	**2007**
Situation/style	**Confederacy**
Student population	**7460**
Total undergraduates	**5035**
Mature undergraduates	**22%**
International undergrads	**4%**
Male/female ratio	**35:65**
Equality of opportunity:	
state school intake	**98%**
social class 4-7 intake	**34%**
low-response area intake	**9%**

VAG VIEW

*I*n 1987 three Kentish art colleges - *Canterbury, Maidstone and Medway -* merged , and the result, known as KIAD, became the third largest higher education Art & Design college in the UK. Alone among such colleges, they had a School of Architecture. Kent University awarded their degrees, and proximity to Europe, a 13% overseas student population, and strong links abroad gave them an international flavour. They also had accommodation. But even the three of them together were a small unit (2,000 odd), and when the work was done, the scene for students was not exactly overpowering.

Then in 2005 they met the Surrey Institute of Art & Design, a like-minded of higher education organisation, founded in 1969 with a 16-acre campus in leafy Farnham, Surrey, and a small site in Epsom.

The Institute was also small - around 2,500 undergraduates - youthfully minded, a groovy set-up with a fast-track reputation for

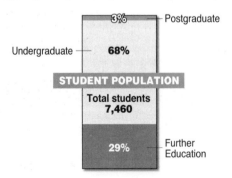

getting graduates jobs in interesting artistic and media areas, in subject specific degrees - from producers and theatre managers to graphic artists, from advertising account executives to animators, from fashion journalists to interior designers, from clothing & textile designers to photographers, from TV & film cameramen to archivists and librarians. But could it face the future alone?

It was about then that KIAD spent millions on new Fine Art studios, art gallery, library, computer suites and a 90-seat lecture theatre, making the Canterbury campus in particular an even more attractice proposition. And so the merger was mooted, the knot was tied, and they took the title of University soon after.

Together, in spite of their scattered base, they cut an impressive figure in the higher education world of Art and Design. Five per cent of their research was last year adjudged world-class in the national research assessment, 5% of it of international significance.

In the old Surrey Institute the real-world spirit was amazing, their principal aim to get their students into work, and this is part of the mix too. High on the agenda are integrating processes and disciplines in the courses which need to be second nature in an artist's work. They put the onus on students on certain courses to 'produce' their own projects, find sponsors for film work, for example, organise their own work placements.

UCA is constantly involved with the industries and agencies on which their students' livelihoods will depend.

Sixty-three per cent of graduates can expect to be in work within six months of graduation, which is great, considering how long it takes an artist to establish a career. Ten per cent go straight into the artistic scene for which they have been training. About the same numbers start their own businesses, and set up in specialist retail outlets.

Blocks of about 6% then go into advertising and architecture, the rag trade, film, publishing, and education (higher, adult, and secondary). Two per cent find work in radio and TV, and around the same *number in museums and archives. It's all tailor-made to what they have been studying, an impressive real-world creative set-up that works.*

FEES, BURSARIES

UK & EU fees 2009-10 p.a. £3,225. Minimum Standard Bursaries for students in receipt of the full Maintenance Grant. Creative Scholarships are awarded to up to 160 students in each year group (£1,000 p.a.). Only students from households with a family income of under £39,305 may apply.

STUDENT PROFILE

Almost a quarter are mature students and two-thirds are female. Artistic types predominate obviously. There's a fairly low intake from beyond the EU, but there are enough EU students from beyond the English Channel for them to run a pre-Session course in English at the Canterbury campus.

CAMPUS

CANTERBURY CAMPUS New Dover Road, Canterbury Kent CT1 3AN. Tel: 01227 817302. Undergraduate courses - Foundation Degree in Architectural Technology. BA (Hons) degrees in Architecture ARB/RIBA Part 1, Architectural Technology, Fine Art, Interior Architecture & Design, plus a pre-Session course in English for the Creative Arts.

Accommodation: Ian Dury House is a nine-flat en-suite development situated on campus; each flat houses six students. No parking. Rent a little over £90 per week. If you want to create a little space between yourself and campus at the end of the day, go for Hotham Court, a new, 107-room block of en-suite and shared facilities in flats of two, four, five and six single study bedrooms about half an hour away rent depends on whether you get an en-suit

apartment, but in any case it's also around the £90 mark. You'll be in good company, for not only is Hotham Court close to another UCA block of four flats, Riverdale House, but it's in amongst Canterbury Christ Church student village All Riverdale is en-suite. Rent's the better side of £90.

EPSOM CAMPUS Ashley Road, Epsom, Surrey KT18 5BE. Tel: 01372 728811. Undergraduate courses - BA (Hons) degrees in Fashion, Fashion Journalism, Fashion Management & Marketing, Fashion Promotion & Imaging, Graphic Design, Graphic Design: New Media, Music Journalism.

Accommodation: Woodcote Side is a block of twelve flats, 2 to 6 beds per flat, situated about a mile from campus. Pretty basic, but you can expect to pay upwards of £90 a room, depending on size. Room size, that is. Alternatively it's Worple Road on campus - three blocks of flats into which they squeeze 54 students. But here you get en-suite and there are flats with wheelchair access. Rent is just over £90 per week.

FARNHAM CAMPUS Falkner Road, Farnham, Surrey GU9 7DS. Tel: 01252 722441. Undergraduate courses - Foundation degrees in Creative Advertising Production, Hand Embroidery (delivered by the RSN at Hampton Court), and Music Video Production. BA (Hons) degrees in Advertising & Brand Communication, Animation, Arts & Business Management, Arts & Media, Computer Games Arts, Digital Film & Screen Arts, Film Production, Fine Art, Graphic Communication, Graphic Storytelling & Comic Art, Interior Architecture & Design, Journalism, Leisure Journalism, Motoring Journalism, Photography, Product Design Sustainable Futures, Sports Journalism, Textiles for Fashion & Interiors, Three Dimensional Design (Ceramics, Glass, or Metalwork & Jewellery).

Accommodation: Main Hall is situated on campus and was built for the purpose of accommodating students in 1976, so don't expect ultra modern tic-tac. There are seven flats with four or five beds in each flat, including some 'same gender' twin bedrooms. Twenty years newer is the campus village - 343 students occupy single bedrooms, each with its own washbasin. Each house or flat accommodates up to 8 students. Some have en-suite bedrooms, and some wheelchair access. Rent varies - around £70-£90 per week.

MAIDSTONE CAMPUS Oakwood Park, Maidstone, Kent ME16 8AG. Tel: 01622 620000. Undergraduate courses - Foundation degrees in Broadcast Media and Graphic Media. BA (Hons) degrees in Animation Arts, Broadcast Media, Graphic Design: Visual Communications, Graphic Media, Illustration, Photography & Media Arts, Photography & Video, Printmaking, Video Arts Production.

Accommodation In Maidstone it's Westree Court - 134 study bedrooms arranged in flats of 4, 6 and 7 persons less than a mile from campus. Students have their own rooms with en-suite shower, toilet and wash-basin. Rent is about £90 per week.

ROCHESTER CAMPUS Fort Pitt, Rochester, Kent ME1 1DZ. Tel: 01634 888702. Undergraduate courses - Foundation Degree in Art & Design: Creative & Technical Practice. BA (Hons) degrees in Art & Design: Creative & Technical Practice, Applied Arts, CG Arts & Animation, Contemporary Jewellery, Contemporary Photographic Practice, Creative Arts for Theatre & Film, Design, Branding & Marketing, Fashion Atelier, Fashion Design, Fashion Management, Fashion Promotion, Fashion Textiles, Modelmaking, Product Design, Silversmithing, Goldsmithing & Jewellery, Style Futures.

Accommodation The Doust Way student flats are about five minutes from campus, close to the river - 214 rooms mostly arranged in flats of six. Students have their own room with an en-suite shower, toilet and wash basin. Rent £90+ per week.

SOCIAL SCENE
There are bars at all the campuses, and as they say,

'You can be sure of a creative angle on the action.' Freshers' Week, Graduation Ball. For a fledgling university what more could you want than artistes teaching you to break dance, or pulling you in to a bit of life drawing, before getting down to some serious poker? You can do all these things in societies - also Cinema, Drama, Musicians, Tech Crew, and more - yes the old LGBT is here and Salsa, and an international club for the Greeks and Turks. There's even a student magazine and eleven sports clubs, including, of course, Capoeri, Snow Sports, and Yoga.

In the old Surrey Institute they always had a good time at the pubs in leafy Epsom, trips to the Brixton Academy, or to clubs in Guildford, or Kingston - the **Works** may no longer be trading, but it's not all **Oceana** at Kingston: **Bar-Eivissa** becomes **Studio 48** on Friday and Saturday night, then there's gay club **Escape**, alternative basement club **Bacchus** offers everything from indie and punk to hip hop and house. Poised they are in Surrey - on the edge - and in Epsom itself there's the 400-seater **Playhouse** (plays, films, alternative comedy, jazz).

In Canterbury, you're spoiled for fun. Pubs and clubs keep two universities satisfied already, and there's the **Venue** and **Lighthouse** at Kent Uni, and the CCC Uni nites at **Chicago's** (cheap bottles on Thursdays).

GETTING THERE
☛ By road: Rochester: M20/J4, A228. Maidstone: M20/J6, A229. Canterbury: from the west, M2, A2; from the south, A28 or A2; from the east, A257; from the northeast, A28; from the northwest, the A290.
☛ By rail: London to Canterbury, 90 mins; to Maidstone, under the hour; Rochester, 40 mins.

UNIVERSITY OF CUMBRIA

The University of Cumbria
Fusehill Street
Carlisle
Cumbria CA1 2HH

TEL 01228 616234
FAX 01228 616235
WEB www.cumbria.ac.uk

University of Cumbria Students' Union
Lancaster
Lancashire LA1 3JD

TEL: 01524 65827
FAX 01524 841924
EMAIL info@su.ucsm.ac.uk
WEB thestudentunion.org,uk/

*T*he University of Cumbria was formed officially on 1st August 2007 from an amalgamation of St Martin's College,

Cumbria Institute of the Arts, and the Cumbrian campuses of the University of Central Lancashire. The University has

UNIVERSITY/STUDENT PROFILE	
University since	**2007**
Situation/style	**Confederacy**
Student population	**8027**
Total undergraduates	**4735**
Mature undergraduates	**31%**
International undergrads	**4%**
Male/female ratio	**76:24-**
Equality of opportunity:	
state school intake	**99%**
social class 4-7 intake	**28%**
low-participation area intake	**7%**

campuses in Carlisle, Penrith, Ambleside and Lancaster and a specialist teacher-education centre in London, all of which have featured in the Guide before. It is a courageous attempt to put higher education on a sound footing in one of our most beautiful, but relatively lightly populated, counties. HQ is in Carlisle.

CAMPUS

These institutions bring with them campuses in Carlisle, Penrith, Ambleside and Lancaster, and a specialist teacher-education centre in London. The uni will also have strong links and close partnership working with 4 FE Colleges in Cumbria (Lakes Colleges, Furness College, Carlisle College and Kendal College).

ST MARTIN'S COLLEGE

St Martin's is a teacher training college with a Church of England foundation (1964), but it is also the base for a number of courses leading to employment in health and the caring professions - nursing, midwifery, occupational therapy, radiography - in the Church, in the worlds of art, design and imaging science, in drama, dance, music, in media, in business and in the sports and leisure industries. Degrees have been awarded by nearby Lancaster Uni since 1967.

The main St Martin's campus is a mile or so from the central shopping area of Lancaster, and offers teacher training, primary and secondary, and degrees in business, sport, arts, humanities, social sciences, health (including nursing). There are also smaller campuses in Ambleside (Lake District) and Carlisle, and Health/ Nursing training centres at Whitehaven and Barrow-in-Furness. Ambleside specialises in Early Years QTS, 3 and 5-11, with drama and PE among the options, and three degrees in Adventure Recreation Mgt and Outdoor Studies. Carlisle is also for Early Years QTS, but with music and religion among the options, and various degrees in social sciences, health (including nursing, radiography, occupational therapy and physiotherapy), and business and info technology. Finally, in Tower Hamlets, London, there's a centre for teacher training, primary years.

CUMBRIA INSTITUTE OF ARTS

Located on 3 sites in Carlisle, the main green-field campus overlooking Rickerby Park and the River Eden - paradise indeed - Cumbria is a cracking college academically, with teaching assessment

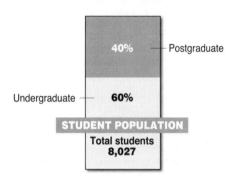

40% — Postgraduate

Undergraduate — 60%

STUDENT POPULATION
Total students
8,027

scores of 21 out of 24 for Art & Design and 19 for Communication & Media. It is also exceptionally well resourced with electronic and media production facilities and a £4.5-million development incorporating a new library, theatre and dance studio, and improved teaching accommodation. Courses focus on creative writing, drama, dance, film, journalism, and fine art and design.

TEACHING SURVEY AT A GLANCE	
Avg. UCAS points accepted	**260**
Acceptance rate	**21%**
Overall satisfaction rate	**79%**
Helpful/interested staff	**No data**
Small tuition groups	**No data**
Students into graduate jobs	**83%**

Teaching most popular with undergraduates:
Geographical Studies, Physical Geography &
Envior. Studies (91%), Social Studies (85%),
Social Work (84%), Initial Teacher Training (82%),
Education (81%)

Teaching least popular with undergraduates:
Mass Communications & Documentation (51%),
Biological Sciences (48%).

RESEARCH EXCELLENCE

% of Cumbria's research that is
4* (World-class) or 3* (Internationally rated):

	4*	3*
Education	0%	5%
English	0%	10%
Theology	5%	10%
History	0%	20%
Art and Design	0%	10%

CENTRAL LANCASHIRE UNIVERSITY CAMPUSES

The old Cumbrian campuses of Central Lancashire University (UCLan) are at Newton Rigg (Penrith) and Carlisle. Newton Rigg has 250 hectares at the head of the Eden Valley, where a faculty of Land-Based Studies had been quietly doing its thing as Newton Rigg Agric College until, in 1998, UCLan took it over. UCLan's Carlisle campus used to be part of Northumbria University, which ran great courses - business, computing, travel, tourism, etc - at generous entry rates, for which many an applicant put his name down before realising to his horror that he wasn't going to be based in Newcastle. It has been well shepherded by UCLan since then and as the Cumbria Business School boasts 'a significant number of international students from a wide variety of countries, including China Nigeria and the USA'.

FEES, BURSARIES

UK & EU Fees, 2007: £3,070 p.a. As yet not fixed for 2008. There are grants, scholarships, teaching bursaries to accompany the Government Maintenance grant (if your parents' earnings are low enough). For students on NHS-funded full-time courses, fees paid are by the strategic health authority. Extra allowances are available for older students and students with dependants. There is also a range of support people studying part-time.

ACADEMIA

The uni has four faculties. Arts, Design & Media will enjoy a £6 million redevelopment programme. Education is delivered across 3 campuses (Lancaster, Ambleside and Carlisle) and at 2 sites in London (Tower Hamlets and Greenwich). Health, Medical Science & Social Care offer training as a nurse (adult, child, learning disabilities or mental health branches), midwife, occupational therapist, physiotherapist, radiographer or social worker. And there's a degree in Child, Young Person and Family Studies.

Meanwhile, Lancaster University is leading the way in a collaboration with UCLan, Cumbria and Liverpool universities, and the University Hospitals of Morecambe Bay Trust in recruiting teaching and research staff to meet the terms of a government decision to allow 50 extra places a year for Liverpool medical students to be based full time at the Lancaster campus.

Finally, there is a Faculty of Science & Natural Resources.

Student satisfaction with the teaching in the Higher Education Funding Council's National Student Survey was, at 79%, not high, but the figure of 83% students into graduate-level jobs within six months of graduation is impressive.

The teaching most popular with undergraduates is in Geographical Studies (besides Geography, there's Forestry & Woodland Science), Social Studies (including Youth and Community degrees), Social Work, Initial Teacher Training, and Education (which comes in a whole host of joint honours degrees - Art & Design, Childhood Education, English, History, Maths, PE, RS, Science, etc.).

Least popular are the media and journalism degrees and Biological Sciences (including some of the Sports degrees), where only around half the class gave the thumbs up.

STUDENT UNION

In Carlisle, the **Calva Bar** is open daily from 10.30a.m. to 11 p.m., and stages live bands, hypnotists, comedians and theme nights.

In Ambleside, the Overdraught Bar is central to student social life. Regular theme nights and music genre nights make up the programme. There's a 280 capacity and the bar is open seven days a week from 7pm.

The **JCR** is the social heart of Lancaster and offers a programme that dovetails with **Liquid**, a local club with student nights on Monday and Wednesday.

In the JCR, it's 'quality music and pound-a-pint night' on Monday, and *Music Corner* - a live band showcase on Tuesday. *Wild and Wacky*

ACCOMMODATION

Guarantee to freshers	**98%**
Style	**Halls**
Security guard	**Halls**
Shared rooms	**Ambleside**
Internet access	**Planned**
Self-catered	**Some**
En suite	**Many**
Approx price range pw	**£45-£75**
Town rent pw	**£45-£60**

Wednesdays is the pre-Liquid party night.

Then there's *Thursday Night Lite* - chilled night - and *Bar FTSE* on a Friday. On Saturday, it's *Chillout* in the JCR, and the *BIG Quiz* on Sunday.

ACCOMMODATION

They offer only 1,200 rooms across the various campuses, so apply early. Internet access is 'planned' but not yet delivered. Some rooms in Ambleside are twins, though many elsewhere are a modern enough conception to be en-suite even.

Town accommodation is plentiful, and the uni office will help you get something. There are 'house hunting help days, where you can meet other students, receive guidance from a buddy (a second or third-year student), view accommodation and question prospective landlords.'

North West England is inexpensive.

● ●

DE MONTFORT UNIVERSITY

De Montfort University
The Gateway
Leicester LE1 9BH

TEL 0116 255 1551
FAX 0116 250 6204
EMAIL enquiries@dmu.ac.uk
WEB www.dmu.ac.uk

De Montfort Students' Union
Mill Lane
Leicester LE2 7DR

TEL 0116 255 5576
FAX 0116 257 6309
EMAIL dsureception@dmu.ac.uk
WEB www.mydsu.com

VAG VIEW

*L*eicester's *De Montfort University (DMU) has emerged from a period of shrinkage, when it lost some eight sites or campuses to Lincoln and Bedfordshire universities, to build, if not the new Jerusalem, new Centres of Excellence, the material expression of a new order.*

The principles on which they are moving forward seem sound. They have decided that the future will be ever so much easier if their students take responsibility for it themselves in a spirit of entrepreneurship. There is good precedent for this. Communities have always needed entrepreneurial spirit to grow.

DMU students on sandwich courses can now chose to start their own businesses instead of taking work placements with established employers. As a result, graduates of the university now lead the region in starting businesses and are in the Top 20 of self-starters in the UK: 138 of their most recent graduates are self-employed, more than at any other university in the Midlands.

The Higher Education Funding Council for England saw what they were doing and threw money their way. With it they have set up Enterprise Inc., which will provide

UNIVERSITY/STUDENT PROFILE	
University since	**1992**
Situation/style	**City campus**
Student population	**21210**
Total undergrads	**17125**
Mature undergraduates	**16%**
International undergrads	**7%**
Male/female ratio	**42:58**
Equality of opportunity:	
state school intake	**97%**
social class 4-7 intake	**42%**
low-participation area intake	**10%**

seventy-five enterprise opportunities for students during the next three years.

The principle also inspires DMU's Student Union, which, as of this year, has become a limited company and Institute of Leadership and Management, bent on spreading the word to other Unions. They have already trained sabbatical officers, ex-students who are taking a year out to run their Student Unions, at ten universities up and down Britain.

Meanwhile, massive modern buildings have sprung up on campus to celebrate the new emerging DMU order - a Performance Arts Centre of Excellence building, an award-

winning £9-million Campus Centre, a suite of Creative Technology Studios, and now the £35 million Business and Law building, which is opening this Autumn.

In the same period, the university as a seat of learning has never had better press. Forty-three per cent of its research activities across nineteen subject areas have been rated world-class (4 stars) or internationally significant (3 stars). Some subjects, like English, Civil Engineering, Business, Nursing & Midwifery, Drama, Dance & Performing Arts, Media Studies, and Music have knocked the competition into a cocked hat. In the last assessment they had only a couple of near-

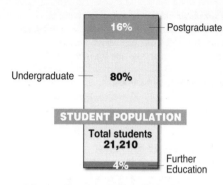

STUDENT POPULATION

Postgraduate 16%
Undergraduate 80%
Further Education 4%

Total students
21,210

TEACHING SURVEY AT A GLANCE

Avg. UCAS points accepted	**240**
Acceptance rate	**21%**
Overall satisfaction rate	**83%**
Helpful/interested staff	★★★
Small tuition groups	★★★
Students into graduate jobs	**74%**

Teaching most popular with undergraduates:
English (95%), English-based Studies (94%), Music, History, Business Studies, Politics (92%), Aural & Oral Sciences, Drama, Education (91%), Law (90%), Teacher Training (89%), Media Studies, Marketing, Computer (88%), Pharmacology, Toxicology & Pharmacy, Mass Communications, Finance & Accounting (87%), Management (86%), Psychology (85%).

Teaching least popular with undergraduates:
Forensic Science (56%).

---

miss world-class results (for Politics and English). Now, their 2008 results seem to suggest they could be taken seriously in the upper echelon.

Success in this area does not mean that DMU lecturers are becoming research boffins for whom students are a necessary evil, as they have been in research-led institutions like LSE for years. For the Higher Education National Student Survey shows that 83% of DMU's students are satisfied with the teaching they receive, and their lecturers earn three stars for support and interest, not only in what but in whom they are teaching. There is definitely a sense of DMU going somewhere.

The Student Union has always been in the forefront when it comes to extra-curricular societies and pleasure zones. They still are, but now they are listening to a new voice among their students and acting upon a new kind of call... for space in the Union building not to celebrate the pound-a-pint ethos, but for a 'Nasa', a 'non-alcoholic social area'. The tide is turning. DMU's Nasa is the most used area in the Union.

FEES, BURSARIES

UK & EU Fees 2009-10: £3,225 p.a. There's a bursary for students in receipt of full HE Maintenance Grant, value at £500, and academic scholarships worth £1,000 - you'll need at least 280 UCAS tariff points from A2 level subjects only, achieved in a single academic sitting. The Creative Industries Scholarship awards students £2,000 for 320 UCAS points, and the Opportunity Scholarship (200 of these available) awards £1,000 to applicants with an Access to Higher Education qualification. There is, in addition the Looked-After Children Bursary, valued at £1,000. See www.dmy.ac.uk for further details.

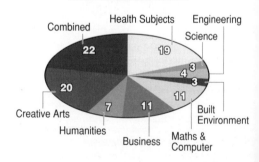

SUBJECT AREAS (%)

Combined — 22
Health Subjects — 19
Engineering — 3
Science — 4
Built Environment — 3
Maths & Computer — 11
Business — 11
Humanities — 7
Creative Arts — 20

STUDENT PROFILE

There's a 16% mature undergraduate population and an open-access policy that brings in many who might not have gone to uni a few years ago - 42% from the lowest socio-economic groups, 10% from 'low-participation neighbourhoods' - and such a fun-loving crew that neighbouring Leicester Uni students time and again crash in on their excellent ents.

ACADEMIA & JOBS

Faculties are Art and Design; Business and Law; Technology (new name for Computer & Engineering); Health and Life Sciences; and Humanities.

Health produces most jobs - 19% of DMU graduates go on to do something to do with health, around 13% into hospital work. There's a host of degrees - Biomedical Science, Dental Technology, Medical Science, Audiology (all course fees are paid by the NHS, and a year-long work placement commands a salary), Pharmacy, Health Studies, Social Work, Nursing, and Midwifery. See also the BSc Human Psychology - there's a history of employment in psychotherapy from DMU, and this degree is accredited by the British Psychological Society as first step towards becoming a chartered psychologist.

From the Business Faculty, with its degrees in Creative Management & Enterprise, Economics & Finance, Business, Accountancy (BA Accounting and Finance course also offers the maximum exemptions from Association of Chartered Certified Accountants and CIMA qualifications - you can't get more exemptions from an undergraduate degree in the UK), and Human Resource Management, graduates find work easily in banking, business management, accountancy and personnel. Also, their Marketing degrees, with Media and Psychology add-ons, have strong relationships with Chartered Institute of Marketing: www.cim.co.uk and IDM: www.theidm.com. Students get exemptions from professional qualifications of both these bodies through study of certain marketing modules.

DMU is also a leader in Public Policy research. Look at the BA Public Policy, Government & Management. The Local Governance Research Centre is internationally recognised.

In Technology, they have useful degrees in Animation, Games Programming, Electronic Games Technology, Game Art Design, and Software Engineering - all of which are made for the employment market.

In Media they have Business & Media, Digital Video & Broadcast Production, Journalism, Media Production, Film, Music production, Radio production. There's a strong tradition of student radio at DMU (see Social Scene below). BSc Media Production includes a practical component with the BBC Training and Development unit in Wood Norton. BSc Radio Production gives hands-on experience of producing programmes. In November 2007 one of the most advanced recording and broadcast studio facilities in a UK university was launched, the £3.7-million Creative Technology Studios, with video, audio and radio production suites set up to replicate the workflow of a professional studio environment.

Two years earlier DMU were given 'Centre of Excellence in Teaching and Learning' status in the Performing Arts. Two years on, the Centre took shape, a base for pioneering new approaches to teaching dance, drama and music technology. Yjere is, too, interest in their job-friendly BA Arts Management degree.

> *DMU is moving forward in a spirit of entrepreneurship: students on sandwich courses can now chose to start their own business instead of taking a work placement with an established employer.*

RESEARCH EXCELLENCE		
% of De Montfort's research that is **4* (World-class)** or **3* (Internationally rated):**		
	4*	3*
Nursing and Midwifery	10%	20%
Allied Health Professions	5%	20%
Pharmacy	5%	40%
Computer Science	10%	35%
Electrical and Electronic Eng.	5%	30%
General Eng., Mineral, Mining	5%	45%
Civil Engineering	25%	45%
Mechanical, Aeronautical & Manufacturing Engineering	5%	45%
Architecture/Built Environment	15%	50%
Business and Management	10%	25%
Law	0%	20%
Politics	5%	15%
Social Work,l Policy & Admin.	5%	25%
English	40%	20%
History	0%	45%
Art and Design	5%	40%
Drama, Dance, Performing Arts	20%	30%
Media Studies	25%	35%
Music	15%	40%

Fashion is another key area at DMU - Clothing with Design, Contour Fashion (the only degree in the world to specialise in lingerie, bodywear, swimwear, performance sportswear, 'structured' eveningwear and bridalwear, established apparently in 1947 at the request of the corset industry), Fashion Design, Textile Design are among the degrees. Students visit underwear manufacturers throughout Europe and Asia, after Hong Kong businessman Andrew Sia set up the Ace Style Institute at the university.

Design altogether is strong - Product Design, Interior Design, Design Crafts/Management/Innovation/Products. Yhe Architecture degrees keep architectural consultancy a perennially important graduate job destination for DMU students, while teaching jobs in Further Education tend to mop up a number of graduate strays from Creative Arts, Engineering, Computer Science, Social Science, and Business.

ACCOMMODATION	
Guarantee to freshers	**100%**
Style	**Flats**
Security guard	**Some**
Shared rooms	**None**
Internet access	**All**
Self-catered	**Most**
En suite	**Most**
Approx price range pw	**£74-£90**
City rent pw	**£35-£160**

SOCIAL SCENE

STUDENTS' UNION The Campus Centre building has restaurants and a bar, the Students' Union administration, a dance theatre and performing arts studios. The venue is called **Level 1** - DJ booth, laser lighting, amazing effects: 'We now have comfy leather sofas and funky chairs,' they say, 'a quadrant of bars, more drinking stations on your nights out.'

Regular ents nights are a mix of activities from comedy to film previews, from karaoke to live gigs.

Monday is Students and Societies Night, where any club or society puts on ents and enhances their resources. Tuesday is *Quiz Night*. Wednesday is *Univibe*, a year-old night of r&b flava musik, ranging from desi beats, ragga, bhangra to hip hop. Thursday is *Kinky*, a 21st-century disco night. Friday is *Death at the Stairs*, an indie/rock night. Saturday is *The Big Bad Cheese* - two rooms, one r&b, the other cheesy tunes.

Besides all this they have a lot of local independent bands, DJ sets and the like. Among the many societies there is a great reputation for media. Radio station Demon Fm has won awards for many years and built up a huge reputation within the industry. This term it has been awarded a community licence, which means transmission 24/7. There's also Demon TV and the *Demon* newspaper of course. In the old days they were always up among the annual media awards, nut not recently.

TOWN See *Student Leicester*

SPORT There's an emphasis on fun rather than serious competition. There's the John Sandford Sports Centre, a fitness studio, solarium, weight training and gym. Basketball team the Leicester Riders have strengthened their ties with DMU and are now known as the De Montfort University Leicester Riders. There's swimming, athletics and cycling close to campus.

WHAT IT'S REALLY LIKE	
UNIVERSITY:	
Social Life	★★★
Campus scene	**Unpretentious, fun-loving, studenty**
Student Union services	**Good**
Politics	**Active**
Sport	**30 clubs**
National team position	**94th**
Sport facilities	**Good**
Arts opportunities	**Theatre, music & film good**
Student newspaper	**Demon**
Student radio	**Demon FM**
Student TV	**Demon TV**
Nightclub	**Level 1**
Bars	**Bars 1 to 4**
Union ents	**7 days a week**
Union societies	**30**
Most popular society	**Chinese Soc, Hindu Soc**
Parking	**Poor-adequate**
CITY/TOWN:	
Leicester Nightlife	★★★★★
City scene	**Top town - clubs, pubs, curries**
Town/gown relations	**OK**
Risk of violence	**Average**
Cost of living	**Average**
Student concessions	**Good**
Survival + 2 nights out	**£50-£80 pw**
Part-time work campus/town	**Good/Excellent**

PILLOW TALK

Most accommodation is in cluster flats with 4-6 students sharing. Other units 7-10 share. All accommodation has internet access. 1,800 of rooms for freshers have been built in the last two years.

GETTING THERE

☛ Leicester by road: M1/J21 or M6 then M69.
☛ By rail: London St Pancras, 75 mins.
☛ By air: Birmingham International Airport or East Midlands International Airport.

UNIVERSITY OF DERBY

University of Derby
Kedleston Road
Derby DE22 1GB

TEL 08701 202330
FAX 01332 597724
EMAIL askadmissions@derby.ac.uk
WEB www.derby.ac.uk

Derby University Students' Union
Kedleston Road
Derby DE22 1GB

TEL 01332 591507
FAX 01332 348846
EMAIL info@udsu.co.uk
WEB www.udsu-co.uk/

VAG VIEW

*T*he University of Derby is situated at the southern edge of the Peak District, 10 miles west of Nottingham. It has been a diffuse conglomeration of as many as twelve sites scattered across the city, but is now much more clearly concentrated at the main Kedleston Road Campus and the relatively new Buxton Campus 50 minutes away.

In the Higher Education National Student Survey, overall satisfaction with the university was relatively low (76%), and in the most recent analysis, although most of its graduates entered employment, the instance of real graduate-level jobs six months after leaving is also low (60%).

Nevertheless, there was student approval of the teaching in a number of areas, specifically in Law, Education, English, Languages, Biological Sciences, Electronic & Electrical Engineering, Psychology, Business, Physics, and Management.

Least popular was Computer Science, a subject also among the least productive as a means to a real graduate job.

Generally, there is evidence to suggest that the lecturers at Derby are helpful and interested in their students, and that much of the teaching is undertaken in decent size tuition groups.

As for life outside the lecture hall, Derby undergraduates have always had a good

UNIVERSITY/STUDENT PROFILE	
University since	**1992**
Situation/style	**City campus**
Student population	**21875**
Undergraduates	**12275**
Mature undergraduates	**53%**
International undergrads	**2%**
Male/female ratio	**41:59**
Equality of opportunity:	
state school intake	**98%**
social class 4-7 intake	**38%**
low-participation area intake	**17%**

time, and now, besides the city scene at venues like the **Rockhouse** and **Zanzibar**, they have at Kedleston Road a new Union bar and venue, the **Academy**, conceived by their own Architectural Design students.

There is also a Student Union out at Buxton, the second campus, with the **Boiler House** and the **Hub** serving the students' every need.

CAMPUS

The main site at Kedleston Road is 10 minutes walk from the city centre. Buxton Campus became part of the scene after the merger of High Peak College with the university. From there they deliver both further and higher education. The idea is that you can move through the various levels within the university, from NVQs and BTECs, to Foundation Degrees and Higher Level qualifications. The first cohort of students graduated from here in 2006/7.

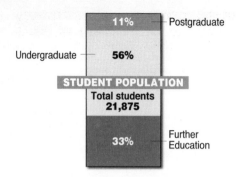

Postgraduate 11%

Undergraduate — 56%

STUDENT POPULATION
Total students
21,875

33% — Further Education

There is also a presence at Markeaton Street in Derby, where most of the Arts, Design and Technology courses are taught, and at Britannia Mill they have the School of Social Care and Therapeutic Practice. Finally, 35 minutes away to

TEACHING SURVEY AT A GLANCE

Avg. UCAS points accepted	**240**
Acceptance rate	**19%**
Overall satisfaction rate	**76%**
Helpful/interested staff	**★★★**
Small tuition groups	**★★★★**
Students into graduate jobs	**60%**

Teaching most popular with undergraduates:
Law (97%), Education (96%), English, Languages, Biological Sciences (81%), Electronic & Electrical Eng. (78%), Psychology, Business (77%), Physics (74%), Management (73%).

Teaching least popular with undergraduates:
Computer Science (60%).

the north, in Chesterfield, there's a campus for nurses and other healthcare professionals.

FEES, BURSARIES

UK & EU Fees, 2009-10: £3,225. A high proportion of Derby students are eligible for bursaries. There's a sliding scale bursary for those eligible for the HE Maintenance Grant, depending on parental income. Also, if you're from Derby itself, or your immediate family has a DE postcode, or you come from one of the fifty-three local schools and colleges in Derby's Compact Scheme, you'll get an extra concession.

STUDENT PROFILE

Derby is at the forefront of the 'new university' revolution, which released higher education to the masses in 1992, when so many of the old polytechnics were redefined as universities. Its open access policy has attracted a very large mature undergraduate population (53%). There are also many part-timers and many from traditional working-class families (38%), and from postcode areas which have never before supplied to the university sector (19%). Inevitably this has also resulted in a high drop-out rate (just under 13).

ACADEMIA & JOBS

Derby's schools are Art, Design & Technology; Business, Computing & Law; Education, Health & Sciences; and the further and higher education provision out at Buxton - a joint honours curriculum delivering such as Hospitality, Spa Therapies (Buxton is a spa town), Public Services Management, Public Relations, the Culinary Arts, Sports, Travel & Tourism, Events Management, Countryside Management, etc. The main academic aspiration is to make teachers and healers out of its students. Education (principally Primary School) and Health (mainly hospital work) together account for more than a quarter of Derby's graduate employment.

The Health degrees include Nursing, Healing Arts, Diagnostic Radiography, and Occupational Therapy. On Chesterfield Campus there's a fully-functioning Clinical Skills Suite with hospital beds, drug trolleys, hoist and other medical equipment, and SimMan, an electronically programmed robot, simulates ailments for treatment by the student

SUBJECT AREAS (%)

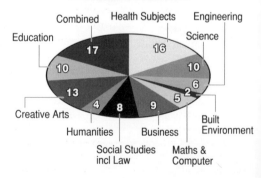

Combined · Health Subjects · Engineering
Education · Science
17 · 16
10 · 10
6
13 · 5 · 2
Creative Arts · 4 · 8 · 9 · Built Environment
Humanities · Business
Social Studies incl Law · Maths & Computer

nurses. The BSc in Occupational Therapy is recognised by the College of Occupational Health and the Health Professions Council.

There are various related strands in the curriculum - for example, many a pathologist comes off their biological/forensic science provision, and their Pharmacy degree scored full marks in the old teaching assessments. Finally, some 6% of Derby graduates go into community and counselling work in the community from such degrees as Allied Community & Youth Work, Applied Social Work, Social Care Health in Community settings, Children's & Young People's Services,

Arising out of Maths, Computer Science, but mainly out of Design & Technology, is a particular niche in graduate employment - they send a sizeable cohort each year into aircraft manufacture. Design is productive of jobs in other areas too, notably Architecture Design, and Creative Design Practices, where advertising is a popular destination for many.

Derby's in-depth expertise in design was recognised in the recent nationwide assessment of research, in which 25% of their research was adjudged either world-class or internationally significant.

The other area of success in the research assessment was Media, where 25% was accorded world class status and 15% of internationally significance. Look at the Broadcast Media, Film & TV, and sound production provision. There are jobs in radio, television, and film for the best graduates each year. About the same number find work from the artistic/creative degrees, Theatre Arts, Dance, and Creative Writing. On the business side, the vocational validity of BA Human Resource Management is to be recommended. There are also well-trod pathways into catering and tourism, transport planning and distribution, sales management, retail management, and accomm-odation management.

SOCIAL SCENE

STUDENTS' UNION The new facility at Kedleston Road is the **Academy Bar** - two levels and decking outside which looks out over Markeaton Park.

They've had live acts here - We Are Scientists, Scouting for Girls - but mainly it's themed nights at **Level 2**, like the recent Union Blue, or use is made of the 40-foot screen for *Popcorn* - 'an afternoon of the greatest movies ever made'. T are pre-party games and activities all afternoon on a Wednesday, leading to

WHAT IT'S REALLY LIKE	
UNIVERSITY:	
Social Life	★★★
Campus scene	**Friendly mix, good ents**
Student Union services	**Good**
Politics	**Interested, but 'non-engaging'**
Sport	**29 clubs.**
National team position	**109th**
Sport facilities	**Poor**
Arts opportunities	**Drama OK**
Student magazine	**Dusted**
Newsletter	**The Word**
Student radio	**D:One**
Nightclub	**Level 2**
Bars	**Academy Boiler House**
Union ents	**Rock, hiphop, cheese & big balls**
Union societies	**29**
Most active societies	**D:One, LGBT**
Parking	**Poor**
CITY:	
Entertainment	★★★
Scene	**Small, friendly, pub rock/indie**
Town/gown relations	**Good**
Risk of violence	**Low**
Cost of living	**Average**
Student concessions	**Good**
Survival + 2 nights out	**£70 pw**
Part-time work campus/town	**Excellent**

the big night at **Zanzibar** in town - *Spank* (10pm till 3). Tuesday tends to be spent at the First Floor in **Rockhouse**, also in town - 'the official rock night of Derby SU' - two rooms of rock, all the classics, metal, nu-metal, industrial, punk, ska. Society nights are also popularly organised at **Walkabout**.

There are somewhat lighter musical goings-on at the **Boiler House** at Buxton, but they all come together in the May Ball, a five stage affair at Kedleston Road, live acts on the Main Stage, *Godskitchen* @ the **Academy**, indie and acoustic stages, and the *Silent Arena* (headphone disco, the new rave). The ball runs from 9pm till 6 am, but there are three pre-bars - **Varsity**, **Barracuda**, and **Sun Lounge** in town, and an *After-Party* at **Zanzibar** from 6am. There's a theory that Derby isn't a 53% mature

As for life outside the lecture hall, Derby undergraduates have always had a good time, and now, besides the city scene at venues like the Rockhouse and Zanzibar, they have a new Union bar and venue.

student population, they're just amazingly tired.

The Source is the Independent Student Advice Centre at Kedleston Road. It's the Hub at Buxton. They have a student magazine - *Dusted*, a radio station - D:One, 15 societies, including one - International - at Buxton, and 29 sports clubs (9 at Buxton), including American Football, Basketball, and Dodgeball.

Students tend to be 'slightly non engaging' when it comes to NUS campaigns, 'but we are working on that!'

SPORT Not a serious contender on the national stage - they came 109th (Derby) and 134th (Buxton) last year. On-site facilities include a gymnasium and pitches.

TOWN Derby is nicely poised between 'friendly town' and 'sprawling metropolis'. Says Asam Rashid: 'There are many student-friendly bars in Derby that are safe, fun and not so expensive.' Besides the clubs, mentioned above, there's a large variety of pubs, and the **Derby Playhouse** (with which the SU secure good discounts) three cinemas, two of which are multiplexes and require a short trip by taxi. The third is in the town centre and dispenses arthouse fare.

PILLOW TALK

Halls with flats, lodges, and houses are of a good

ACCOMMODATION	
Guarantee to freshers	**100%**
Style	**Halls**
Security guard	
Shared rooms	
Internet access	
Self-catered	**All**
En suite	**Some**
Approx price range pw	**£65-£80**
City rent pw	**£65-£140**

standard at various locations around the city; none is catered; 50% are en suite (all rooms at Peak Court are en suite). All the halls are wired up so you can subscribe to telephone and free internet use. Freshers are guaranteed accommodation if their applications are received by August 31.

GETTING THERE

☛ By road: Kedleston Road campus is just off the A38, the main southwest/northeast thoroughfare which goes south to Exeter and meets the M1 at Junction 28. M1/J25 for access from the east, A6 from the southeast (Loughborough way).

☛ By rail: rail links with Derby are easy. London is two hours away.

☛ By coach: London, 3:15.

UNIVERSITY OF DUNDEE

The University of Dundee
2 Airlie Place
Dundee DD1 4HN

TEL 01382 344160
FAX 01382 348150
EMAIL srs@dundee.ac.uk
WEB www.dundee.ac.uk

Dundee Students' Association
Airlie Place
Dundee DD1 4HP

TEL 01382 386060
FAX 01382 227124
EMAIL dusa@dundee.ac.uk
WEB www.dusa.ac.uk

VAG VIEW

*F*ounded in 1883 as University College Dundee, seven years later it became part of St Andrews University and remained so until it gained independence in 1967.

Today, Dundee is a traditional, premier-league university, but unusually relaxed and friendly. It has a history, but isn't steeped in

it. Nor does it feel bound by tradition to repeat itself.

Generally, however, teaching is in the traditional, tutorial-based mould: lecturers are top-rated (5 stars) for their interest in students, and 4-starred for their small-size tuition groups.

Long before it was fashionable, support was undertaken here in an online environment, with 24/7 internet-based access to resources, timetables, lecture enhancements, assessments, assignment submission, discussion boards and collaborative working opportunities.

They claim to have been the first university in Scotland to engage with an online Personal Development Planning programme, which acts to ensure that a student's academic education occurs in concert with their personal and career development. Students create portfolios to illustrate their personal development, and these are being utilised for external appraisal such as for job applications. The results are there to see - 84% student satisfaction overall; 83% get real graduate jobs within six months of leaving.

UNIVERSITY/STUDENT PROFILE	
University since	**1967**
Situation/style	**City campus**
Student population	**18225**
Total undergraduates	**12250**
Mature undergraduates	**28%**
International undergrads	**8%**
Male/female ratio	**39:61**
Equality of opportunity:	
state school intake	**88%**
social class 4-7 intake	**26%**
low-participation area intake	**3%**

fees in year 2009-10: £1,820, more for Medicine.

CAMPUS

"Dundee lies on the East Coast of Northern Scotland, a couple of hours away from Glasgow, Edinburgh and Aberdeen,' writes Sameen Farouk. 'Next door is St. Andrews. Dundee is one of a handful of genuine get-away-from-it-all universities. The scenery up here is breathtaking.

> *Dundee is a traditional, premier-league university, but unusually relaxed and friendly. It has a history, but does not feel bound by tradition endlessly to repeat itself. Lecturers have 5 stars for their interest in their students and 4 for decent-sized tuition groups.*

'The main campus, with compact teaching facilities, IT centre, the main libraries, the art college, sports facilities, the union, the dental hospital, John Smith Bookshop, Bonar Hall, the famous Wellcome Trust building (all within 5 mins walk of each other), is located on the edge of the town centre. It is safe, clean and increasingly accessible to the disabled community.

'The medical campus is located in the town's main hospital, Ninewells. Other sites, the nursing college (Kirkaldy in Fife, 35 miles from Dundee) and Northern College - the Faculty of Education & Social Work (Gardyne Road) are a little further out.'

FEES, BURSARIES

UK & EU fees, 2009-10: if you are a Scottish-domiciled, first degree student you are eligible for your tution fees to be covered by the Scottish Government. Students from England, Wales and Northern Ireland pay a flat-rate tuition fee for each year of their programme. Non-Scottish UK student

STUDENT PROFILE

'Without being steeped in outmoded tradition,' writes Hannah Hamilton, 'the university retains a strong self-image, and the students form a very real community around the central core of campus.'

Dundee attracts students from all walks of life and from all areas. The inevitable scattering of public school types joins a healthy dose of students from Ireland and a very strong international community.

'Dundee could never be criticised for being a quaint English retreat,' agrees Sameen. 'The university recruits internationally and has strong Arab, Chinese, Malaysian, Korean and Hispanic communities. There is also a substantial South-Asian population. The local communities are also targeted keenly, and there is a growing population of mature students.'

Once among the elite in the context of the

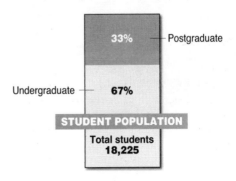

33% — Postgraduate

Undergraduate — 67%

STUDENT POPULATION

Total students 18,225

Government's as pirations to level the socio-economic playing field in Higher Education, Dundee meets its Government benchmark for student intake from the four lower classes, but not for intake from the so-called 'low participation neighbourhoods'. But this is no ex-poly ,asquerading as a 'new' university, bent on matching course to job. It is a university for the professions: medicine, dentistry, nursing, architecture, finance, and the law. Dundee sends more graduates into the professions than any other university in Scotland, and it is well balanced socially, classless, with its eye on other things.

ACADEMIA & JOBS

There are four colleges: College of Art & Design, Architecture, Engineering & Physical Science; College of Arts & Social Sciences; College of Life Sciences; College of Medicine, Dentistry and Nursing. 'I suppose, if you are a Scot, and you want to study medicine,' said a sixth-form careers mistress, 'Edinburgh would have to be high on the list, but people have had very good experiences of Dundee.' In fact, Medicine at Dundee was the second most popular in Britain, with 97% of its students applauding it. It tied with St Andrews. Only Aberdeen created greater enthusiasm. England could produce nothing like it.

The requirements are straightforward: AAA at A level (A2) to include Chemistry and one other science. You will also sit UKCAT.

The degree is the 5/6-year MBChB. Integrated med school and hospital. Course problem/community-based, i.e. clinical experience from Year 1. For dentists it's the 5/6-year BDS. Entry AAA.

There were some interesting developments in the 2008 research assessment of our universities. Dundee did well, as out Research Excellence box shows, but perhaps not always in the areas it

---

TEACHING SURVEY AT A GLANCE

Avg. UCAS points accepted	**478**
Acceptance rate	**16%**
Overall satisfaction rate	**84%**
Helpful/interested staff	★★★★★
Small tuition groups	★★★★
Students into graduate jobs	**83%**

Teaching most popular with undergraduates:
English, History, Politics (99%), Medicine (97%), Languages, Medical Science & Pharmacy (95%), Civil, Chemical Engineering (94%), Biology and related sciences (90%), Philosophy (94%), Dentistry (93%), Engineering & Technology, Initial Teacher Training (92%), Subjects allied to Medicine, Geography (90%).

Teaching least popular with undergraduates:
Architecture (67%).

---

expected. Seven years earlier the university had leapt eleven places nationally, with medical and biological research achieving the highest accolades. Now, Biological Sciences maintained its position - 25% of its research is world-class, 40% internationally significant, but Clinical Medicine showed only 5% world-class.

The Biosciences degrees here are key. They include such as Anatomical Sciences, Biochemistry, Biological Chemistry, Biomedical Sciences, Microbiology, Molecular Biology, genetics, Neuroscience, Pharmacology, Sports Bioscience.

Altogether, 47% of all Dundee graduates find work in health and social work. But it is the Biosciences, subjects allied to Medicine, that put as many as 24% of Dundee graduates to work in hospitals, while Medicine account for only 16%.

Nine per cent of Dundee graduates become teachers, 5% of them in Primary Education, and in the National Student Survey appropriately enough 92% of the students studying Initial Teacher Training applauded the teaching of it. The first cohort of secondary school teachers graduated in 2005 on a course which allows distance learning and part-time study.

Five per cent of all Dundee graduates also go into Architectural Consultancy, which is a relatively large number and interesting not least because the teaching of Architecture was slammed by its students - only 67% of them approved of it, which is low for a university of the stature of Dundee. Also, the department merited the world-class tag for only 5% of its research work, whereas its sister department, Civil Engineering, where the

SUBJECT AREAS (%)

Creative Arts — 13
Education — 5
Medicine & Dentistry — 13
Health Subjects — 20
Humanities — 8
Social Studies incl Law — 13
Business — 5
2
5
Built Environment — 5
Science — 11
Maths & Computer
Engineering

teaching was applauded by 94% of students, was adjudged world-class for 15% of its research and internationally significant in 70%, which is very high. It would be as well to look closely at both these departments' courses and, always assuming you know the career path you want to follow eventually, see precisely where - in which department, which course - you want to study.

Art & Design also demands our attention - 35% of its research is world-class, 20% internationally significant. Textile Design (the city's industrial inheritance) was always rated highly in the old teaching assessments. Companies like Nike and Calvin Kline queue up to employ Dundee graduates. Bang in the middle of the city's new cultural quarter with its pubs, clubs and gallery shops, the Art/Design College, through its reputation in the fashion and design industries, provides a global dimension to what has been called 'Dundee-chic'. A £9-million, Lottery-funded collaboration between uni and city has resulted in Dundee Contemporary Arts, a centre for visual arts with the university's Visual Research Centre at its hub, an art laboratory equipped with cutting edge facilities for producing design prototypes, videos, prints, artists' books, etc. Artists, designers and media types should look closely at the College. Jobs for graduates are diverse, from graphic designers and illustrators to printers, publishing production managers, set designers and jewellery designer-makers. Encouragingly, real live artists account for a whopping 3% of Dundee's entire army of satisfied graduate job hunters. There is also a consistent line from this College into the motor industry, via the Innovative Product Design degree.

In Law, they're internationally rated for research, European law specialists and the only uni to offer both Scots and English Law. Non-Law graduates may take a 2-year full-time or 3-year part-time Senior Status Law degree here. Now a new International Water Law Research Institute is to open, it's the first of its kind in the world, and is set to train future leaders to arbitrate water conflicts.

SOCIAL SCENE

STUDENTS' ASSOCIATION There are 2 nightclubs: **Mono** (900 capacity), **Floor 5** (350 capacity) and 2 bars: **Air** (300 capacity) and **The Liar** (650 capacity), plus a huge games room with pool tables, games machines, and a **Food on 4** catering outlet. Ents offer *Skint* in Mono on Tuesday and Saturday. Friday is *Perfect 10* - ten different drinks priced £1; special events include theme nights (like neds and emos), and society fundraisers (like Graphic Design Department's *90s Rave*).

RESEARCH EXCELLENCE		
% of Dundee's research that is **4*** (World-class) or **3*** (Internationally rated):		
	4*	*3**
Laboratory Clinical Subjects	5%	60%
Primary Care Clinical Subjects	5%	40%
Dentistry	10%	40%
Nursing and Midwifery	10%	40%
Biological Sciences	25%	40%
Applied Mathematics	10%	35%
Computer Science	15%	50%
General Eng., Mineral, Mining	5%	30%
Civil Engineering	15%	70%
Architecture/Built Environment	5%	35%
Geography	15%	45%
Economics and Econometrics	5%	40%
Accounting and Finance	5%	35%
Law	5%	45%
Politics	10%	20%
Social Work, Policy & Admin.	5%	30%
Psychology	5%	30%
Education	5%	15%
English	10%	35%
Philosophy	10%	35%
History	15%	50%
Art and Design	35%	20%

At Liar and Air on Saturday there's £-*Stretchers Tennents*, vodka, whisky, gin and white rum £1 each. It's the warm-up for Mono or Floor 5. On Thursday it's *Thumbcandy* - game tournaments on the Xbox - Pro Soccer 09 and the like. Air runs *X-Factor Karaoke*. At Floor 5 it's Bass Orgy's *Farfletched* and the Public House of Dub, plus James Coull of Concrete Streets fame and some BeatRepeat freak called Matt Small.

Just as typical is *Spice Up Your Life* - classic 80s and 90s, from grunge to house, hip hop to Brit-pop. Well, they are all medics here.

There are some 50 societies. 'Most active,' says a union wallah, 'Lip Theatre, Islamic Society, DARE (Development and research expeditions) People and Planet. A large cross section of international students makes for very mixed campus culture. SRC and many societies push campaigns on global warming, nuclear disarmament, etc.' *The Magdalen* is the student magazine, which distributes around 1,000 copies a month.

SPORT The particularly popular activities are mainstream team sports like hockey, rugby, football (not cricket), boxing and the water sports. Most sports have strong societies. Around Dundee there is also a well-established martial arts scene.

The Institute of Sport and Exercise has recently undergone a £3.5 million development and now includes a 400 metre-square gym over two levels, international competition standard squash courts, swimming pool, several aerobics studios and 2 games halls.

This year a £1.65-million upgrade of the outdoor sports facilities will begin. Two artificial surfaces will be installed, existing grass pitches renovated, and a new tennis court and changing accommodation built.

There is a Regional Strength Performance Centre and laboratories for sports science, performance assessment and research activities.

The Institute was accredited in 2008 by the London 2012 Olympic Organising Committee as an official Pre-Games Training Camp venue. It is one of six national centres which form the Scottish Institute of Sport network supporting elite athletes in Scotland.

Town Dundee, which already ranks among the world's most intelligent cities for its scientific expertise, has been voted Scotland's sexiest city by the *Scotland on Sunday* newspaper. 'For many years

ACCOMMODATION	
Guarantee to freshers	**97%**
Style	**Flats**
Security guard	**Most**
Shared rooms	**None**
Internet access	**Most**
Self-catered	**All**
En suite	**Most**
Approx price range pw	**£76-£105**
City rent pw	**£60**

Dundee has seemed to play second fiddle to Aberdeen, Glasgow and Edinburgh,' writes Michael Sheldon. 'However, if you scratch the surface of the City of the 3 J's (Jute, Jam and Journalism) you will find one of Scotland's most progressive and desirable cities.

'Tired tourist touts will tell you that it is the birthplace of *The Beano* and *The Dandy*, home to the RRS Discovery (made famous by Scott of the Antarctic), and to the Mills Observatory (the only full-time public observatory in the UK). And then direct you to the Verdant Works Museum, where the history of Dundee's textile industry is documented and non-Dundonians learn what "an ingin ene inna" means!' But this city is not stuck in the past. Recently, it has reinvented itself.

'Two unis - Abertay and Dundee - means two modern centres of entertainment. The Abertay building houses two bars, a night club and a cinema. Across town at Dundee's Student Association, as it likes to be known, there are another two bars, two nightclubs, a huge pool room and regular big name DJ and comedy acts. There are also three cinemas at Camperdown, Douglas and in the DCA, an Ice rink, loads of Parks and Coffee Shops.'

The Perth Road and West Port areas are probably best for pubs, with establishments such as **The Speedwell Bar**, with a huge selection of whiskies, the **Art Bar** and **Tally's**, to name but few. Club-wise, there's **Fat Sam's**, open seven days a week, **Underground**, which is not so much a club as a bar open till 2.30 a.m., and for something different, **The Reading Rooms**, host to acts such as Biffy Clyro and Mr. Scruff. 'The new meets the old close to the university in **The Cultural Quarter**, where lie the **Dundee Rep Theatre**, the multi-million-pound **Dundee Contemporary Arts Centre**, **The Sensations Science Centre**, a hands-on science museum for the big kid inside you. All this and the city's multiple-floor shopping centres, **The Wellgate** and **The Overgate**.'

WHAT IT'S REALLY LIKE	
UNIVERSITY:	
Social Life	★★★★★
Campus scene	**Diverse culture**
Student Union services	**Top-rated**
Politics	**Society-based**
Sport	**45 clubs**
National team position	**43rd**
Sport facilities	**Good**
Arts opportunities	**Music, film, art excellent; drama good; dance avg**
Student magazine	**Magdalen**
Nightclubs	**Mono, Floor 5**
Bars	**Air, The Liar**
Union ents	**Full on**
Union societies	**50**
Most popular	**Lip Theatre, Islamic Society, DARE**
Parking	**Poor**
CITY:	
Entertainment	★★★★
Scene	**Scotland's sexiest**
Town/gown relations	**Average**
Risk of violence	**Low**
Cost of living	**Low**
Student concessions	**Good**
Survival + 2 nights out	**£70 pw**
Part-time work campus/town	**Excellent/Good**

PILLOW TALK

There are five residence sites, each comprising between 30 and 90 self contained flats, all single rooms Four sites offer en-suite facilities. Not all would agree that halls were the best option: 'Personally, I found hall a bit of an expensive option.,' says Sameen.

However, over 1,000 new en-suite rooms opened in 2006, relatively expensive (see Accommodation box), but very nice.

GETTING THERE
☞ By road: M90, M85, A85, A972.
☞ By rail: Newcastle, 3:00; London Euston, 6:00.
☞ By air: Dundee Airport for internal flights; Edinburgh International Airport is an hour away.
☞ By coach: London, 10:05; Birmingham, 10:05; Newcastle, 6:05.

UNIVERSITY OF DURHAM

The University of Durham
Old Shire Hall
Old Elvet
Durham DH1 3HP

TEL 0191 334 6128
FAX 0191 334 6055

EMAIL admissions@durham.ac.uk
WEB www.dur.ac.uk

Durham Students' Union
Dunelm House
New Elvet
Durham DH1 3AN

TEL 0191 334 1777
FAX 0191 334 1778

EMAIL student.uniont@durham.ac.uk
WEB www.durham21.co.uk

VAG VIEW

*F*ounded in 1832, Durham is, like Oxford and Cambridge, a collegiate university, although unlike Oxbridge its colleges are purely residential. Academically, it is faculty based. It offers all the advantages of the best of British universities and is demanding at entry, shamelessly going after Oxbridge rejects, delaying its selection until after those two more ancient universities have taken their pick. But it combines this policy with another, designed to net applicants from elsewhere, particularly from non-traditional higher education heartlands, 'low participation' neighbourhoods and social classes. It has been known for sixth formers to get in to Durham with one AS level and a GNVQ. As a result, the percentage of undergraduates from these non-traditional backgrounds is greater than at Oxford or Cambridge, or indeed Bristol, and closer to Nottingham, Bath and Leeds.

But all said, state school intake is only 62%, which is very low compared to most other universities, and intake from the working classes is a mere 15% and from so-called 'low-participation neighbourhoods',

UNIVERSITY/STUDENT PROFILE	
University since	**1832**
Situation/style	**City collegiate**
Student population	**17410**
Undergraduates	**11995**
Mature undergraduates	**6%**
International undergrads	**5%**
Male/female ratio	**48:52**
Equality of opportunity:	
state school intake	**62%**
social class 4-7 intake	**15%**
low-participation area intake	**5%**

5%. So there is some way to go for the population of Durham University to resemble that of the country at large, if that is, or even should be, its aim.

More significant than all this demographic massage is a change coming, we detect this year, not quite for the first time, from the ground: there's an 'alternative' strain in the Durham camp. Two years ago, Rik Fisher told us: 'In what is almost a knee-jerk reaction against 'rah culture' there is more of an effort to express personal style *and individuality.' Now, an Alternative Society is gathering at the **Angel** pub (see Social Scene below).*

Contentment among students is widespread - 86% gave the thumbs-up to the university in the National Student Survey. Also, teaching staff get four stars for interest in their students and for decent sized tuition groups.

Around 90% of Durham staff undertake research of international significance, as well as being active teachers, but they are insistent that research and teaching are never seen as distinct, let alone mutually exclusive, and there is a cross-faculty, interdisciplinary ethos in both. 'You will find experts from across many subjects joining together to discuss themes of research that transcend traditional subject areas,' they say.

The happy result of their strategy is that 80% of graduates get real graduate jobs within six months of leaving, and the drop-out rate (2.6%) is one of the lowest in the country.

CAMPUS

Durham is a small, stunningly beautiful city, 16 miles south of Newcastle. The nucleus of the medieval city, where the five Bailey colleges and the Arts and Social Sciences Departments are located, is formed by a bend of the River Wear around a rocky peninsular, dominated by the 11th-

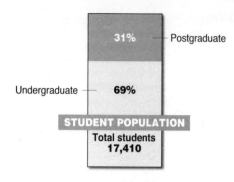

STUDENT POPULATION

Postgraduate 31%

Undergraduate 69%

Total students 17,410

century cathedral and castle. Sixty million pounds is about to be invested in a new student services building, library extension, Law School, refurbishment of the Bailey and Palace Green and catering facilities across the university.

Another campus, officially known as The University of Durham Queen's Campus, Stockton, lies south down the A1(M), on the banks of the River Tees. There are two colleges, John Snow and George Stephenson. Infrastructure and resources are good, from en-suite accommodation to library and IT resource centre, lecture rooms, laboratories and student recreational facilities. The campus is at the heart of a planned £300-million investment in the surrounding North Shore area.

FEES, BURSARIES

UK & EU Fees 2000-10: £3,225 p.a. The Durham Grant Scheme awards £1,300 to students with a household income of less than £25,000. Further details at www.durham.ac.uk/undergraduate/finance/dgs. There's also the Vice-Chancellor's Award for Sport, Music and the Performing Arts. See www.durham.ac.uk/undergraduate/finance/vc_scholarships for a range of modest funds to assist with participating in extra curricular activities.

STUDENT PROFILE

Writes Alex Pharaoh: 'I came to Durham from a grammar school in North Yorkshire, aware that it had a reputation of being a haven for public schoolers and Oxbridge rejects, and, yes, a lot of people here do fall into one of these categories.'

Says Martha Wright: 'I feel it's really mixed. My friendship group is very varied. We have a Harrow boy, but also state school people like me, so we don't really notice the difference that much. We have someone from Newcastle, Reading, Scotland, London, Yorkshire. You have got your central bar in College, and all the events that happen in College, and you tend to meet people from all the years there.'

TEACHING SURVEY AT A GLANCE

Avg. UCAS points accepted	**450**
Acceptance rate	**12%**
Overall satisfaction rate	**89%**
Helpful/interested staff	★★★★
Small tuition groups	★★★★
Students into graduate jobs	**80%**

Teaching most popular with undergraduates: Education, Theology (96%), History, Physical Geography & Envior. Science, Physics & Astonomy (95%), Archaeology, Chemistry, English (94%), Physical Science (93%), Biology & related sciences, Classics, Business & Administrative Studies (92%), Psychology (91%), General Engineering, Philosophy (90%).

Teaching least popular with undergraduates: Music (78%), Politics (77%).

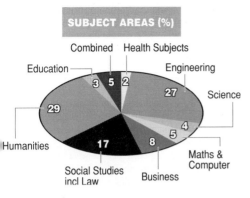

SUBJECT AREAS (%)

Combined — 5
Health Subjects — 2
Education — 3
Engineering — 27
Science — 4
Humanities — 29
Maths & Computer — 5
Social Studies incl Law — 17
Business — 8

ACADEMIA & JOBS

According to the National Student Survey, the most popular teaching lies in Education, Theology, History, Physical Geography & Environmental Science, Physics & Astronomy, Archaeology, Chemistry, English, Physical Science, Biology & related sciences, Classics, Business & Administrative Studies, Psychology, General Engineering, and Philosophy.

Even the least popular Music and Politics kept more than three-quarters of the class amused. Most graduates become teachers, then accountants and civil servants, or they go into business and management consultancy, personnel/recruitment, banking, social work, or community counselling, business and management, health, Defence, publishing.

There is a medical faculty, shared with neighbours Newcastle, but it is primarily aimed at mature students, with a special Pre-med programme for applicants without the necessary scientific background for Stage 1 entry. The course (MBBS) has two years at Stockton before transfer to Newcastle, where in years 3, 4 and 5, students will be assigned a regional clinical unit. Requirements are AAA at A level. Subjects should include Chemistry and/or Biology at AS or A level. If only one of Biology and/or Chemistry is offered at A or AS level, the other should be offered at GCSE grade A (or Dual Award Science grade A). You must also sit UKCAT.

This is a uni with great contacts in the City. In Accountancy they are one of the big three providers, along with Nottingham and Warwick. They have first-class links with the major firms. There's a dedicated degree and Foundation degree. Defence is another strength in employment, taking graduates largely through Modern Languages, Physical Sciences, and Social Studies.

Physics, Physics with Astronomy, etc, are very strong. In the Institute of Computational Cosmology there's a £1.4-million supercomputer capable of making ten billion calculations a second and 'recreating the entire evolution of the universe'.

Civil servants come through Modern Languages, Social Studies, Physical Sciences, and History & Philosophy. Jobs in human resources and recruitment come through Modern Languages and Biological Sciences, as well as Social Studies.

Subjects within Social Studies and Modern Languages account for 33% of the entire employment provision at Durham, it is worth knowing.

DURHAM COLLEGES

Each college has its own distinct identity. The system promotes great loyalties and sporting rivalries. The Durham college stereotype is described in the rivalry between the so-called Bailey colleges (John's, Chad's, Cuth's, University - known as Castle - and Hatfield), situated in the Bailey area of the medieval city, and the Hill

RESEARCH EXCELLENCE		
% of Durham's research that is **4*** *(World-class) or* **3*** *(Internationally rated):*		
	4*	3*
Biological Sciences	10%	40%
Environmental Sciences	15%	55%
Chemistry	20%	45%
Physics	20%	40%
Pure Mathematics	20%	40%
Applied Mathematics	15%	60%
Statistics	5%	45%
Computer Science	20%	45%
General Eng., Mineral, Mining	10%	50%
Geography	30%	40%
Archaeology	35%	40%
Business and Management	15%	40%
Law	30%	35%
Politics	15%	35%
Social Work, Policy & Admin.	15%	45%
Anthropology	20%	35%
Psychology	15%	45%
Education	20%	35%
Middle Eastern, African	20%	45%
East European Languages	5%	35%
French	15%	35%
German, Dutch, Scandinavian	20%	40%
Italian	5%	20%
Iberian and Latin American	20%	45%
English	30%	30%
Classics, etc.	25%	40%
Philosophy	15%	40%
Theology	40%	25%
History	20%	40%
Music	30%	30%

WHAT IT'S REALLY LIKE

UNIVERSITY:

Social Life	★★★★
Campus scene	**Great fun, serious opportunity**
Student Union services	**Good**
Politics	**Active**
Sport	**Key; 46 clubs**
National team position	**4th**
Sport facilities	**Good**
Arts opportunities	**Good**
Student newspaper	**Palatinate**
Student radio	**Purple Radio**
Nightclub	**Fonteyn Ballroom**
Bars	**Kingsgate, Vane Tempest, Riverside Café**
Union ents	**Planet of Sound + dance & cheese**
Union societies	**124**
Most prominent socs.	**Big Band, Durham Revue, Ballads**
Parking	**Poor**

CITY:

Entertainment	★★★
Scene	**Historic city, cheesy clubs, good pubs**
Town/gown relations	**Poor**
Risk of violence	**Low-avg.**
Cost of living	**High**
Student concessions	**Good**
Survival + 2 nights out	**£60-£150 pw**
Part-time work campus/town	**Average**

colleges (Trev's, Van Mildert, Mary's, Collingwood, Grey's and Aiden's), situated southwest of the Bailey.

Sophie urges: 'Pick your college carefully. Within a couple of days you'll have learned your college songs and rituals, and feel a strange affiliation with this set of buildings, which will manifest itself loudly on many a river bank or touch line throughout your life as a Durham student. The stereotypical image we have is of Rahs on the Bailey and Plebs on the Hill. And then there's St Hild & St Bede, the biggest college, a minute or two further out, perhaps with a more diverse mix than some of the others. Don't go entirely by the stereotypes though; be sure to visit.

'The Hill colleges are more like a campus, all a drunken stagger from one another. Next to the Science site, computers and library too, but what you gain in convenience you lack in history and surroundings. The Bailey colleges are also near enough for a bar crawl, and the cobbled streets and cathedral backdrop make it far more aesthetically pleasing. Chad's and John's bars are barely big enough to swing a cat, however, and you may be more likely to stumble upon Evensong than a pint of lager in St John's. Hild Bede bar resembles an airport lounge.

'Colleges also differ in facilities. Hild Bede has a newish multigym, an abundance of tennis courts, squash courts, gyms, and beautiful if basic accommodation. Castle, on the other hand, offers third years the chance to live in a castle, while Collingwood gives you en-suite shower rooms and kettles. The choice is yours!'

'Trevs is very representative of the whole student body,' writes Eleanor. 'It is also friendly and has strong college spirit. There are loads of social events, two balls a year and one of the larger, and more tasteful bars. We are fairly standard when compared to other colleges. Our accommodation is decent, not as nice as Collingwood, however. Bailey accommodation tends to be the worst, as it is the oldest and they also room some students far from the main building, Cuth's is worst for this. Hill Colleges have purpose built accommodation blocks. John's is very religious, Van Mildert is good for music opportunities, Cuth's is famed for having a bar with proper opening hours!'

Says Alex: 'My college, Collingwood, is known as one of the best. We have the most modern accommodation, more en-suite rooms, more IT networked rooms, less room sharing, better central facilities, such as bar and gym, and allegedly, better food than others. We are one of the newest colleges, and have less tradition than those on the Bailey, which can be seen as a good or bad thing. We have a great social calendar - bar theme nights, "megaformal" dinners, bops, trips, sporting events and the legendary Summer Ball.'

From October, 2006, applicants have been able to opt for a new Durham-based college, the first for more than 30 years, named after the Northumberland-born writer, pioneer of women's education and social reformer, Josephine Butler. The 400 rooms are en suite and self-catering - 6 to a flat - on the southern edge of the city, close to the Science Site and main University Library. Special student rate buses are frequent. There's a bar, a launderette, an IT Suite, a music practice room, a large hall, a variety of smaller rooms available for events, and special provision for the disabled, especially students with special dietary requirements. Flats are available from October to June, including the Christmas and Easter vacations.

Down at Stockton, John Snow and George

Stephenson Colleges look quite inviting in the prospectus pictures, but they are going to have to do something to liven things up a bit. Like many, Lawrence Mantini, an Oxbridge wannabe, found himself there when his public exams didn't quite go the way he planned. He put what seemed to us, a brave face on his lot:

'It's kind of like your own little community. You see everyone because you are living so close to one another. There are about six different halls [within John Snow], three floors and each floor is split into three different flats: six rooms share a kitchen. My whole floor knows one another, so we just go from side to side really. After the first year they encourage you to go out and find a house, which I have got to do in the next couple of weeks. It tends to either be Thornaby or Stockton. It's not the prettiest town, but it has everything you need, and the water is very nice, you get the rowers coming by and everything. Thornaby and Stockton have kind of merged into one, as far as I can tell.

'John Snow is about ten minutes away from the actual teaching base and then Stephenson is right next door to it. Pub-wise there are one or two places that are student friendly, Weatherspoon-type places. It's one of the downsides, I guess. There is only one student night in Stockton, it's good but it can get repetitive going to the same place every Monday night.'

'There's the **Arc**,' I suggest.

'I've been there once or twice. They show a constant round of drama productions and comedians and stuff. I actually tried to go, but it was sold out. It's a nice looking place. I think there is a small cinema.'

'So, what does a student do at Stockton Campus?'

'There's the college bar. It's a waterside bar and it's a really nice, modern, big kind of bar. They show sports there and have events there, all different drinks and food. John Snow and Stephenson share that bar. It's quite a highlight of the whole campus. Otherwise, I'm either doing my assignments or I go into town quite a lot, but apart from that there is not a whole lot to do to be honest.

'There is opportunity to do sport. I just haven't taken it up. John Snow have their own boat club and they have got a wide range of sports clubs, they use the water well, and there are the university teams at Durham, which is a half an hour bus ride away. The bus is free if you have your campus card. Mainly people go to Durham for sporting things and on Friday nights there is a student night.

'What kind of people are students at Stockton?'

'There is a fair amount of mature students on my course, I'd say. On my floor I'm the only Londoner, but apparently there are quite a lot. There are not that many Northern people here, it's more Midlands and Southern, I would say. I applied for main Durham campus, but because of my grades they offered me a course here. It's not as pretty as Durham, but I'm happy to be here, yeah.'

'Where else did you apply?'

'I applied to Oxford, Warwick, York and Bristol.'

'There is no doubt that the [Applied Psychology] course at Stockton is a very good one,' we say.

'Yeah, I would highly recommend it. Tonight I'm going to go up to Durham to the student night there.'

Can you blame him!

SOCIAL SCENE

STUDENTS' UNION The social scene in Durham is better. The SU building and main bar, **Kingsgate**, have had a facelift, and **Pitstop**, a shop, has opened at the entrance to the building. Kingsgate is the union bar with balcony overlooking the river. Food is served in the nearby **Riverside Café** until 11 pm (waitress service). Venues remain **Vane Tempest Hall** and the **Margot Fonteyn Ballroom**, though everyone knows it all simply as **'the DSU'**, the Durham Student Union.

Martha put me neatly in the picture: 'On a Friday all of it is open, like different rooms for different music. So you have got *Planet of Sound* downstairs in the big hall, and there's a cheese room for *Twisted*, which on Saturday makes way for drum and base. And *Revolver's* on Saturday, which is indie.

'On a Wednesday most people go to **Loveshack** in town. That's the new nightclub, it's really good. It's got a VW Van inside as a sofa. Yeah, Loveshack's best on a Wednesday, when all the sports teams generally go out.

'The Student Union is probably best on a Tuesday, when there's a one-off night for *Twisted*. There is so much competition at the moment with all the clubs trying to promote themselves.

> *Has Durham found its 'alternative' side at last? 'There is a big alternative scene. Fishtank put on all the alternative things. Basically we just have a good rock...'*

ACCOMMODATION	
Guarantee to freshers	**96%**
Style	**Halls, flats**
Security guard	**All**
Shared rooms	**Some halls**
Internet access	**All**
Self-catered	**Some halls, all flats**
En suite	**Some halls, most flats**
Approx price range pw	**£99.32-£142.10**
City rent pw	**£66-£74**

Loveshack is about £3 entry, the most you will ever pay to get in anywhere in Durham is about £5.50 for *Planet of Sound*. Also every college has a Social Committee and every club will contact the Social Chair, like me for Aiden's. They offer you deals all the time. I think lots of the Bailey colleges get free entry for **Klute**, but it's all up to your Social Chair where you are going to get free entry.

'Then there's the **Loft**. I think Loft is more used when a college rents it out for a night. It isn't the best, but it's still quite good. **Studio** is probably better than Loft now. Studio has two floors of different music and every night they have a different night going.

'The **Reform** is good, that's the pre-club place opposite Studio. I don't go to **Chase**. I'm not really sure what sort of people go to Chase. I think it might be quite expensive. **Fishtank** is a little alternative, it's a house that has been renovated into a club and they do alternative nights. There is quite a big alternative scene, and they do *Dove Step* as well. Like it's really big in London, *Dove Step*, and drum 'n' bass, and Fishtank put on all the alternative things that maybe Durham doesn't promote as such. That is just round the corner from the Viaduct [landmark on the Durham scene], usually free entry unless it's a big night. Then **Fabio's** does jazz, and you can eat there and then go upstairs to a little bar, quite pricey but really nice - quite a classy night always.

'And there is a new promoter in town... He rented out Loveshack but before that I think he was trying to promote **The Fighting Cock**, which is a pub which used to be totally local, he's been trying to get it up, but I don't know how popular it will be. That's a student doing that, and his rival is Russell Cowie - Russell Cowie Entertainment. He's a music student and the other one is an Anthropology student. They're in their third year and both run their own like businesses. I met the Anthropology guy, we were both paying in to the bank... I helped

him promote his *Hot Chip* set. He is going to help us find a band, maybe, or a DJ, for the Summer Ball.'

Martha aligns herself to the Alternative Society, the bohemian alternative to what goes on up the Bailey, an unthinkable proposition at Durham only a few years ago: 'I know the people who were like the execs on the Alternative Society and I think it must have been going for a while, but they requested that I join the group. Well, they do like live music, they do band nights and I'm always quite interested in that. Basically they just have a good rock, usually at the Angel pub.'

Among other societies, student media is first class, with *Palatinate* and Purple FM proving to be a worthy claw sharpener for the real thing. The Union is active on welfare (Advice Centre, Nightline, etc) and politics extend into high profile - national media - fees campaign. In student politics, Labour, Conservative and Lib Dem socs are all active, as well as People & Planet and Fight Racism, Fight Imperialism. The Union has an active policy of independence from all political parties. Most debate sadly restricted to issues directly affecting Durham students. Others of their 124 societes include Pagan Witches, Bellydancers, Medieval Warmongerers and the Chemistry Society.

TOWN/GOWN When term begins, students herd in and outnumber locals. In the past it has proved to be a recipe for disaster. Writes Eleanor: 'Locals are generally friendly, and students are normally safe. Weekends are more dangerous, however, as country locals invade and they are more inclined to indulge in the favourite sport of student bashing.' Says Alex, 'There is some tension. Trouble is easily avoided if you shun the pink shirt/ bodywarmer/scarf, and don't talk in a loud southern accent on your mobile phone at 3 am, drunk, in the middle of the road, wearing a DJ.' They have a university security patrol that goes round the city every night. They also have a night-bus which picks up all around town and drops off at all the colleges.

SPORT Durham is very sporty, they came 4th last year, and the beautiful river is a temptress to hundreds of novice rowers. Academic concessions for sporty types are apparent, though not admitted. High standards are encouraged by inter-college rivalry, Castle vrs Hatfield (rugby), Castle vrs Hild Bede (rowing). College rowing crews are often better than other university crews. Sixty acres of playing fields are maintained to first-class standard.

GETTING THERE

- By road: A1/J6. Well served by coaches.
- By rail: King's Cross, 3:00; Edinburgh, 1:00.
- By air: Newcastle, Teesside Airports (25m).
- By coach: London, 5:30; Birmingham, 4:00.

UNIVERSITY OF EAST ANGLIA

The University of East Anglia
Earlham Road
Norwich NR4 7TJ

TEL 01603 591515
FAX 01603 591523
EMAIL admissions@uea.ac.uk
WEB www.uea.ac.uk

Union of University of East Anglia Students
Union House
Norwich NR4 7TJ

TEL 01603 593272
FAX 01603 250144
EMAIL su.comms@uea.ac.uk
WEB www.ueastudent.com

VAG VIEW

Set apart in rural Norfolk, and yet only 15 minutes by road from the centre of Norwich, East Anglia University (UEA) was founded in 1964 and reaches out to the world with innovation and flair.

It is among the best on virtually any grounds you care to mention, and perhaps because it is so cut off from the world, the student body seems more reflective, more worldly wise perhaps than most.

In the National Student Survey, 91% of them said they were satisfied with what they get. Based on the Times Higher's *unique national survey, we give lecturers 5 stars for helpfulness and interest in their students (what else is there for them to do? you may ask), and 4 stars for the small size of their tuition groups.*

The Student Union scores high, too, for maximising extra-curricular opportunity for those it represents. It puts on a blinder ents-wise too.

If there is a niggle it is that you are there on campus with everything you need and much of what you want, but no means of going elsewhere to discover it for sure. Perhaps that's the reason why an ungrateful 7% of undergraduates do not see the whole experience through to the end.

UNIVERSITY/STUDENT PROFILE	
University since	**1964**
Situation/style	**Campus**
Student population	**19585**
Undergraduates	**15190**
Mature undergraduates	**15%**
International undergrads	**7%**
Male/female ratio	**46:53**
Equality of opportunity:	
state school intake	**87%**
social class 4-7 intake	**24%**
low-participation area intake	**9%**

CAMPUS

The campus, built on a 320-acre, sometime golf course, has won awards for its architecture - Denys Lasdun's ziggurats (glass-fronted buildings, tiered upwards like garden terraces after the ancient tiered mounds of Babylonia) continue to amaze. It revolves around the Square, a student rendezvous, transformed into an open-air disco at the end of the academic year. But, as student Daniel Trelfer declares, self-containment isn't to everyone's taste:

'Everything you need is on campus, but while some people are happy to live for twelve weeks inside a square quarter mile, others go insane and have to run to town to feel free again.' Yet even that is no solution, for 'the campus and the city of Norwich are strangely similar in that both are somewhere in the wilderness miles from anywhere. The fact that the nearest town is 45 mins away by train, and even then it's only Ipswich, gives you some idea of how remote Norwich is. If you drive there you will see nothing but flat lands, tractors and trees for the last half hour of your journey.'

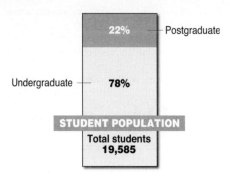

STUDENT POPULATION

Postgraduate 22%

Undergraduate 78%

Total students
19,585

FEES, BURSARIES

UK & EU Fees 2009-10: £3,225 p.a. Sliding-scale bursaries for students in receipt of HE Maintenance Grant are available, dependent on parental income. There are awards for sport and music, and a range of scholarships for academic performance. See www.uea.ac.uk/mac/aao/courses/UG/Fees/.

STUDENT PROFILE

UEA has a well-balanced student population for a pukka uni, with an 87/13 split between state and public school types, 24% from the lower socio-economic classes and 9% from postcodes new to the idea of going to university. There is a fair-sized mature intake (15%) and a few more girls than boys, owing to the nursing degrees.

ACADEMIA & JOBS

UEA is made up of 23 academic departments known as Schools of Study, which are grouped into the Faculties of Arts & Humanities, Social Sciences, Science and the Institute of Health.

The 2008 Research Assessment of British universities places UEA's History of Art, Film Studies, American Studies, and International Development in the top three in the country, with Environmental Sciences and Pharmacy in the top ten. Over 50% of its submissions were deemed world-class or internationally excellent.

Top teaching, students say, is in Pharmacy, Pharmaceutical Chemistry, Maths, History, Archaeology, Biological Sciences, American Studies, Physical Science, Medicine, Politics, Economics, Geographical Studies, Law, Philosophy, English, Film, Languages, and Social Studies.

Graduate employment poses a few question marks. Seventy-seven per cent get graduate-level jobs within six months of leaving, which is OK, if not top of the tree. An awful lot more get rpetty average sort of jobs to begin with, which is often the case (one thinks of St Andrews) with unis that specialise in humanities and languages . Graduates

have to start somewhere, and many who start as clerks no doubt find success in the end. Indeed, UEA has itself conducted surveys that show this. This year they have a drop-in centre on the Square 'to help students and graduates find student jobs, volunteering opportunities, graduate level jobs and much more,' as they put it to the Guide.

Possibly uniquely, Language graduates find it easier to get jobs than graduates of any department other than Health. They are wanted by employers across the board, in particular in publishing, the civil service and government administration, in personnel recruitment and the hotel/restaurant trade, in business, radio and television, and in

TEACHING SURVEY AT A GLANCE

Avg. UCAS points accepted	**360**
Acceptance rate	**21%**
Overall satisfaction rate	**91%**
Helpful/interested staff	★★★★★
Small tuition groups	★★★★
Students into graduate jobs	**77%**

Teaching most popular with undergraduates:
Pharmacy, Pharmaceutical Chemistry (100%), Maths (98%), History, Archaeology (97%), Biological Sciences (96%), American Studies, Physical Science (95%), Medicine, Politics (94%), Economics (93%), Geographical Studies, Law, Philosophy (92%), English, Film, Languages, Social Studies (90%).

Teaching least popular with undergraduates:
Anatomy, Physiology, Pathology (77%)..

secondary education.

Far and away the most jobs for UEA graduates are, however, in the health industry. Physiotherapy is particularly productive and directs attention to an expanding aspect of UEA's curriculum -

SUBJECT AREAS (%)

Education — Medicine
Creative Arts — Health Subjects
Humanities — 21 · 7 — Science 15
30 — 16
Social Studies incl Law — 15 · 7 · 7 — Maths & Computer
Business

Midwifery, Nursing (Adult, Children, Learning Disability, Mental Health), Operating Department Practice, Occupational Therapy, Physiotherapy, Biochemistry, Biomedicine, Pharmacy, Pharmaceutical Chemistry, and of course the programme in Medicine. The MBBS Medicine with a Foundation Year was recently introduced to widen participation in Medicine from under-represented groups. Theory and practice is integrated throughout in the 5-year MB BS, and clinical experience is yours from the outset, thanks to extensive collaboration with close-to-campus Norfolk & Norwich University Hospital. They consider a wide range of qualifications, but you must have a background in to at least A Level equivalent. Grades AAB at A2 level, including Biology/Human Biology, plus additional grade B in fourth AS level subject.

> *The LCR has been voted the best student venue in the country by the music industry's Live! magazine. Each year more than 50 live bands grace its stage; gigs are sold out months in advance.*

Community youth workers and social workers also come out of here in abundance. Naturally they come through Social Sciences (from the dedicated Social Work degrees), from Biological Sciences, but also via Languages.

UEA also enjoys particular success in the literary firmament. There are twice-yearly literary festivals, a writer in residence, and it is here that Sir Malcolm Bradbury set the literary firmament alight with his creative writing school, out of which came Ian McEwan and Kazuo Ishiguro, among others. Look at English or American Literature with Creative Writing (also Scriptwriting & Performance). There is also a fine reputation for the 4-year American Studies, which scored full marks in the assessments. Campus is home to the Arthur Miller Centre for American Studies. Arts graduates are given a ringing endorsement by UEA's MA in creative entrepreneurship, which supports artists, writers and musicians in practical business skills.

Another clue to the uni's academic identity is its concern for the environment. They pride themselves on being at the forefront of green awareness and aim to have their own energy needs met by an on-campus biomass generating plant due to be completed this year. They are also among the top suppliers of graduates to the environmental sector. There's a sheaf of Ecology and Environmental Sciences BSc degrees, with options for European and North American experience (the same for Geophysical Sciences). There's also a BA and a BSc Development Studies (one with Overseas Experience). The climatic research unit is a world authority, and the uni is home to the Tyndall Centre for Climate Change Research. The Jackson Institute, with the largest environmental research programme in the UK, has also set up here, and there's a new Institute for Connective Environmental Research - an attempt to bring together science, industry, politics, business to make real steps forward in the area of environmentalism.

Finally, they are European and American law specialists. All candidates must sit the National Admissions Test for Law (LNAT).

RESEARCH EXCELLENCE

% of UEA's research that is
4* *(World-class)* or **3*** *(Internationally rated):*

	4*	3*
Epidemiology, Public Health	5%	40%
Health Services Research	5%	40%
Nursing and Midwifery	10%	30%
Allied Health Professions	0%	15%
Pharmacy	15%	40%
Biological Sciences	10%	40%
Environmental Sciences	25%	45%
Chemistry	5%	50%
Pure Mathematics	15%	45%
Applied Mathematics	5%	40%
Computer Science	20%	45%
Economics and Econometrics	15%	50%
Business and Management	10%	35%
Law	5%	35%
Politics	10%	15%
Social Work, Policy, Admin.	10%	45%
Development Studies	25%	35%
Psychology	0%	15%
Education	15%	35%
American Studies	20%	30%
English	20%	45%
Philosophy	5%	30%
History	20%	40%
History of Art	50%	20%
Media Studies	50%	40%
Music	0%	40%

SOCIAL SCENE

STUDENTS' UNION The **LCR** (Lower Common Room) has been voted the best student venue in the country by the music industry's *Live!*

ACCOMMODATION	
Guarantee to freshers	**100%**
Style	**Flats**
Security guard	**Campus-wide**
Shared rooms	**Some**
Internet access	**All**
Self-catered	**All**
En suite	**Most**
Approx price range pw	**£60.20-£95.55**
City rent pw	**£50-£80**

magazine. Each year more than 50 live bands grace its stage; gigs are sold out months in advance. Union bars feature **The Union Pub** - all-day opening, pool tables, table footie, arcade machines, jukebox and large screen TV. Then there's **The Union Bar (Blue Bar)**, **The Hive** (redeveloped a few years ago, creating a light, more spacious environment), and **The Grads Bar**. Live in the Hive includes (free) local bands, as well as karaoke, quizzes, games and comedy shows. Besides the LCR, the uni has its own venue in Norwich - **The Waterfront**. There are 3 bars and 2 rooms of music. There's a lively reputation for journalism - their TV station is Nexus TV, their radio station, Livewire. *Concrete* is the newspaper, which incorporates *The Event* entertainment magazine and often wins national awards. There is a track record for graduate careers in radio/TV and publishing, and top ratings for teaching in media/communications.

They boast 70 societies and 40 sports clubs. It is a highly developed student culture and has to be because campus is so cut off. Politics is a scene. The 3-weekly Union Council meeting is a passionate event. Gays get a good deal: LBG is among the most active societies, along with *Concrete*, Livewire, and Rock Gospel Choir which seems to have performed everywhere. **The Studio** is the UEA theatre, drama a top-rated course.

SPORT Good, though not top notch, they came 62nd in the national league last year. Great facilities. The purpose-built and soon to be extended Sportspark includes a 50-metre pool, athletics track, indoor arena, squash and tennis courts, a climbing wall, a fitness centre, dance studios and 40 acres of playing fields and pitches. Women's hockey is very strong. Other big deals are football, tennis, trampolining, rugby, athletics, kerfball and American footie.

TOWN Apparently, Norwich has a pub for every day of the year. It also has the **Theatre Royal** (touring companies, RSC, National), **The Maddermarket**, a smaller, amateur but vibrant venue. The bohemian

King of Hearts rules for music, art, jazz, literature readings, and **The Norwich Arts Centre** for live music, from rock and jazz to chamber music, exhibitions, dance workshops and comedy - David Baddiel, Frank Skinner, Lee & Herring and The Fast Show's Simon Day all played here. There are three cinemas, the **ABC** and the **Odeon** (in the heart of the excellent Magdalen Street curry scene, and Cinema City for arthouse.

PILLOW TALK

Accommodation is guaranteed to all first year undergraduates who live over 12 miles from UEA. Students live in their own study bedrooms within 8-12 person flats. There are standard and en-suite rooms on campus, in the adjoining university village, and in the city centre. New and refurbished flats just opened on campus.

GETTING THERE

☞ By road: A11(M), A47.
☞ By rail: London Liverpool Street, 2:00; Birmingham New Street, 4:00; Sheffield, 3:50.
☞ By air: Norwich Airport.
☞ By coach: London, 2:50; Birmingham, 6:00.

WHAT IT'S REALLY LIKE	
UNIVERSITY:	
Social Life	★★★★
Campus scene	**Lively**
Student Union services	**Excellent**
Politics	**Active**
Sport	**40 clubs, but not obsessional**
National team position	**62nd**
Sport facilities	**Good**
Arts opportunities	**Excellent**
Student newspaper	**Concrete**
Student radio	**Livewire 1350**
Student TV	**Nexus**
Nightclub	**LCR, Waterfront**
Bars	**Union Pub, Blue Bar, Hive, Grads**
Union ents	**Massive**
Union societies	**70**
Most popular society	**Livewire, Concrete, Rock Gospel Choir**
Parking	**Poor**
CITY:	
Entertainment	★★★
Scene	**OK pubs, clubs**
Town/gown relations	**Average**
Risk of violence	**Low**
Cost of living	**Average**
Survival + 2 nights out	**£70 pw**
Part-time work campus/town	**Good/excellent**

UNIVERSITY OF EAST LONDON

The University of East London
Docklands Campus
4-6 University Way
London E16 2RD

TEL 020 8223 2835
FAX 020 8223 2978
EMAIL admiss@uel.ac.uk
WEB www.uel.ac.uk

The University of East London Students' Union
Docklands Campus
4-6 University Way
London E16 2RD

TEL 020 8223 7025
FAX 020 8223 7508
EMAIL students.union@uel.ac.uk
WEB www.uelsu.ac.uk

VAG VIEW

In UEL we have the former East London Polytechnic, now University of the People in London's East End, traditionally the soul cultures of the Metropolis, which has for the past 250 years taken into itself a diverse immigrant population.

Today, it is as lively an evolutionary culture as it ever was, and the Uni is an integral part of it. UEL's stated mission is 'to provide the highest possible quality of education in order to meet...' not the needs of the country or Europe or the world, but '...the needs of individuals and of the communities and enterprises in our region.'

Its mission is no less ambitious for its narrow geographical focus, for in many ways UEL has its doors more widely open to the real world than most of its competitors, what with its high intake from beleaguered areas, its Refugee Bursaries, its low entry requirements and, against all odds, a fierce determination to hang on to its students for the full term of their courses and equip them for a world that many off to Bristol and Durham universities can barely imagine.

Following a full-scale institutional audit by the Quality Assurance Agency in 2005, UEL was praised for its culture of equality and diversity, its equitable approach and support for its part-time staff and students, the effectiveness of its staff development, and the integration into the curriculum of skills

UNIVERSITY/STUDENT PROFILE	
University since	**1992**
Situation/style	**City sites**
Student population	**19305**
Undergraduates	**14230**
Mature undergraduates	**55%**
International undergrads	**9%**
Male/female ratio	**44:56**
Equality of opportunity:	
state school intake	**99%**
social class 4-7 intake	**46%**
low-participation area intake	**10%**

development for students, particularly through the Skillzone programme (see Academia below).

Clearly they are doing something right. There is confidence aplenty, as they concentrate their efforts now on two campuses: Docklands and Stratford.

On Feb 16, 2007, the Queen opened the new Business School and Knowledge Dock Centre on the waterfront of the Royal Albert Dock, in the presence of HRH Prince Turki of Saudi Arabia and Lord Rix, Brian of Whitehall farce fame, who is UEL's Chancellor.

But no farce here. The event followed the successful completion of a £110-million investment and development programme, which also saw an overhaul at Stratford, too.

It's only when polls like the Times Higher Education *'Student Experience' Survey come along that UEL just does not do itself justice. It was bottom on all counts, but in a very real sense there is no fair comparison with most other* universities on most counts.

When it comes to research expertise staff acquit themselves well. In the first national assessment of the research performance of our universities for seven years, UEL leapt from one plaudit in 2001 to 78% of its research submission being rated as at least of 'internationally recognised' quality, with a significant percentage rated world-class in terms of originality, significance and rigour. The uni jumped 28 places to be placed among the Top 3 post-1992 universities in London for research, and in the Top 10 post-1992 universities in the UK.

CAMPUSES

DOCKLANDS CAMPUS 4-6 University Way, London E16 2RD. Located on the waterfront of the Royal Albert Dock, it serves 7,000 students focused on the new economy, cultural and creative industries. The Architecture and Visual Arts facility was completed in 2003, and a new Business School and Enterprise Centre opened in 2007. Here, too, are the School of Computing and Technology, the Learning Resource Centre and Knowledge Dock, a restaurant, bar and cafés, and a Student Union development. Also accommodation of course; see Pillow Talk below.

STRATFORD CAMPUS Romford Road, London E15 4LZ. Tel 020 8223 3000. Close to the London 2012 Olympic Park, the Stratford campus is now expanding rapidly. A new Centre for Clinical Education in Podiatry, Physiotherapy and Sports Science - areas of significance in their graduate employment profile - was opened last year by

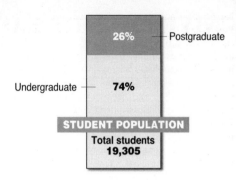

STUDENT POPULATION
Total students
19,305

HRH the Duchess of Cornwall. A new £16-million Cass School of Education and a Conference and Computing Centre with landscaped gardens will open this year.

As at Docklands, there are brand new Student Union facilities here, and work is now being undertaken on new buildings for the Schools of Law and Education.

FEES, BURSARIES

UK & EU Fees, 2009-10: £3,225. There are bursaries for students in receipt of full HE Maintenance grant, a Progress Bursary to all who complete the first semester and progress to a second, and 200 Achievement scholarships to first-year students for sport, academic excellence, citizenship, and voluntary work. See www.uel.ac.uk/studentlife/moneymatters/bursaries.htm.

STUDENT PROFILE

UEL have large ethnic, overseas, and mature student populations (55% of the latter), and welcomes many from the lower socio-economic orders and those neighbourhoods where people have never thought about university for themselves before. There is a friendly, laid-back feel to the place. Students are getting on, and will do provided they're not bound fast by politically correct red tape, as some feel they are.

ACADEMIA & JOBS

The uni's Skillzone is a learning support and employment service. They are good at raising money for this sort of thing; their mission is in line with Government policy; they are good at speaking the language of the times in which we live, and they know their way around the forms.

Today, the Knowledge Dock (formerly the Thames Gateway Technology Centre) works with over 2,000 companies and entrepreneurs across the region. It provides a range of business services, training, consultancy, and funded programmes including the DTI flagship Knowledge Transfer

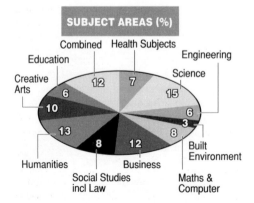

SUBJECT AREAS (%)

Partnerships and the Shell Technology Enterprise Programme, for which it was named best new agency. UEL invests among the highest per student for library and learning resources. It is also a leader in disability and dyslexia support. Facilities include a regional Access Centre offering dyslexia screening and tutoring, technology training, exam support and an RNIB Resource Centre for blind and visually impaired students on physiotherapy programmes.

At UEL, look for degrees in Health, Psychology, Culture, Art, Dance, Music, Computer and Sport, and you will find jobs at the end of them. More graduate jobs come to UEL in the area of social work, community and counselling than anywhere else. Also high up the employment list are artistic jobs, employment in the media, and in sport.

Media (including Journalism), Art & Design, Performing Arts, Sociology and Social Work all contributed to their success in the recent research assessment exercise, and it is in these areas that the uni fulfils its mission to meet 'the needs of individuals and of the communities and enterprises in our region.'

For their Cultural Studies series (courses like Third World Development) and their Playwork series, as well as in degrees like Dance: Urban Practice and the Early Childhood Studies series, UEL proclaims its distinctive identity, which feeds into the artistic endeavour in such courses as Community Arts, Music (theory and production), Psychosocial Studies and in their brand of Journalism. For these courses they want students from diverse social, intellectual, and cultural backgrounds, and they find a number of them on their doorstep.

'The course,' said one student of a BA (Hons) Cultural Studies degree, who went on to edit Sky Magazine, 'gives fuel to things you're already

---

TEACHING SURVEY AT A GLANCE

Avg. UCAS points accepted	**200**
Acceptance rate	**18%**
Overall satisfaction rate	**73%**
Helpful/interested staff	★
Small tuition groups	★
Students into graduate jobs	**71%**

Teaching most popular with undergraduates:
Finance (95%), Accounting (94%), Law (81%), Architecture (80%), Medical Science, Pharmacology (78%), Psychology (77%), Social Studies, Sociology, Anthropology, Biological Sciences (76%), Subjects allied to Medicine (75%).

Teaching least popular with undergraduates:
Fine Art (56%).

---

thinking about and puts them in context.'

A high percentage of graduates finding employment out of UEL do so as social workers, probation officers or community youth workers. Their psychologists deal with real issues of the community in which they live and work. UEL's School of Psychology dropped only one point in the old teaching assessments and is now one of the leading schools in Britain for undergraduate and professional diploma programmes. They run a range of postgraduate programmes in partnership with Relate, the Psychosynthesis and Education Trust, and the Tavistock Clinic (the UK's leading centre for post-graduate training in mental health).

Physiotherapy is another major career field, as is Sport.

In 2003, they brought together the Schools of Architecture and Art & Design to form the School of Architecture and the Visual Arts, located in a new 6,000 sq m purpose-designed studio building at Docklands. UEL is rated highly for the teaching of architecture, and there's a strong pathway into the profession. They are one of a few Schools to be awarded unconditional validation by the Royal Institute of British Architects (RIBA) and the Architects Registration Board (ARB).

SOCIAL SCENE

Political awareness is the most notable aspect at student level, and a culturally rich ents programme, including dedicated and *Mixed Flavour* discos - indie, soul, swing, '70s/'80s, jungle, hip hop, ragga, bhangra, reggae, old school, cheese, pop, rock n roll, triphop, hip hop and dub - comedy nights, cabaret, live bands, video nights and the odd society 'do'. One-offs include Spring

---

RESEARCH EXCELLENCE

% of UEL's research that is
4* (World-class) or 3* (Internationally rated):

	4*	3*
Allied Health Professions	10%	20%
Law	5%	30%
Social Work, Policy & Admin.	0%	35%
Sociology	10%	30%
Psychology	0%	20%
Education	5%	20%
Art and Design	10%	30%
Drama, Dance, Performing Arts	5%	30%
Media Studies	20%	60%

ACCOMMODATION

Guarantee to freshers	**100%**
Style	**Halls, flats**
Security guard	**All**
Shared rooms	**Some halls**
Internet access	**All**
Self-catered	**Most**
En suite	**Some**
Approx price range pw	**£72-£140**
City rent pw	**£65-£140**

windsurfing, skiing, sub-aqua, riding, and weekend and vacation courses are arranged.

With the Olympics setting up stall around the corner, it's a good bet sport is going to be a major focus in the future, and indeed there are plans to develop sports coaching, working with local authority partners to deliver sports programmes for young people, facilities and event management training, engaging and empowering local communities through voluntary action, disability sport in partnership with the National Paralympic Association, and support for elite performers at their new sports science laboratories.

Ball, Valentine Bash, Diwali Rave, Hallowe'en Night, Christmas Rave.

They number 31 societies this year (including Respect) and 13 sports clubs (from Rowing to Black Star). A lot of bar activity/events are laid on by students through cultural societies, like *Reggae Nite with DJ Freestyle,*

There's a culturally rich ents programme, including dedicated and Mixed Flavour discos - jungle, hip hop, ragga, bhangra, reggae...but Islamic Soc has the largest membership.

TOWN 'Well it's London, so all bets are off,' said our informant. 'Cost of living is high, general things (food etc) are fairly priced compared to other places. It's the social side of things that costs so much. Start saving now. Risk of violence is,

Wheel of 4 Tunes, Good Friday Society Nite, Calender (sic) Club Nite, DJ's r&b, hiphop, catwalk, samba band. Hard to tell which iof the societies s the most active, but Islamic has the largest membership. Student media includes a magazine, *re:fuel,* and that's about it.

At Stratford campus the new facilities include an internet café and bar. In the political arena, they are one of a handful of universities capable of organising a decent sit-in, getting together with Goldsmiths to do a *Rough Guide to Occupation* at one stage. Currently they describe the level of activity as 'average, meaning less people compensate with great awareness and enthusiasm!' Campaigns traditionally include Anti-racism/fascism and Free education for all. Speakers have been Neville Lawrence, Ken Livingstone and Glenda Jackson. Ken Livingstone and Glenda Jackson.

SPORT Relaxed attitude, twenty teams, not nationally competitive. Teams make use mainly of council pitches and halls that offer student discounts. A swimming pool is used for water polo, sub-aqua and canoeing; there are two gyms, facilities for aerobics, dance, badminton, table tennis, karate, circuit training, volleyball, basketball, indoor football, a squash court, four tennis courts, a fitness centre. Playing fields are a few miles away, at Little Heath. Badminton is available near the Stratford campus and there are other recreational activities on offer - golf, sailing,

surprisingly random. Arguably, people would say London is prone to greater violence. But really it's

WHAT IT'S REALLY LIKE

UNIVERSITY:	
Social Life	★★★
Campus scene	**Authentic, urban culture**
Student Union services	**Average**
Politics	**Anti-racism & free education**
Sport	**Relaxed/13 clubs**
National team position	**None**
Sport facilities	**Average**
Arts opportunities	**Some**
Student magazine	**Refuel**
Bars	**Each campus**
Union ents	**Rootsy**
Union societies	**31**
Most popular society	**Islamic**
Parking	**Poor**
CITY:	
Entertainment	★★★★★
Scene	**Local clubs 'n uptown flavours**
Town/gown relations	**Poor**
Risk of violence	**Random**
Cost of living	**High**
Student concessions	**OK**
Survival + 2 nights out	**£60 pw**
Part-time work campus/town	**Good, must travel**

all quite random. You'll need about £80 to live on if you want to go out at least two nights. Chance of part-time employment is high. Both within the Students' Union and wider a-field.'

PILLOW TALK

Allocation priority is given to students with special needs, and then to students entering their first year at the university from outside the local area. A number of rooms are reserved for applicants whose normal place of residence is outside the UK. What can you expect? At Stratford, university house or flat-share at landscaped Park Village nearby.

New accommodation at Cedars Road for this year. At Docklands, self-catering study-bedrooms and flats. The waterfront Student Village opened spring 2007 with 800 studio flats, café-bar, shops, SU facilities.

GETTING THERE

☛ **Stratford** by Underground, Central Line; closest overland rail station is Maryland (connect London Liverpool Street).
☛ **Barking** by Underground, City & Hammersmith and District lines; Goodmayes overland station.
☛ **Docklands** via the Docklands Light Railway.

EDGE HILL UNIVERSITY

Edge Hill University
St Helens Road
Ormskirk
Lancashire L39 4QP

TEL 0800 195 5063
FAX 01695 584355
EMAIL enquiries@edgehill.ac.uk
WEB www.edgehill.ac.uk

Edge Hill University Students' Union
St Helens Road
Ormskirk
Lancashire L39 4QP

TEL 01695 575457
FAX 01695 577904
EMAIL enquiries@edgehill.ac.uk
WEB www.edgehill.ac.uk

VAG VIEW

*E*dge Hill was founded in 1885 as the UK's first non-denominational teacher training college for women. Initially based in the Edge Hill district of Liverpool, the College moved 12 miles to the north, to Ormskirk, in 1933. In 1960 it became co-ed, and diversified into health in 1968. In the 1970s it became a partner college of Lancaster University and in time offered a broad range of degree courses.

In 1980 it took into itself Chorley College of Education and in 1993 the Sefton School of Health Studies. Thirteen years later the college achieved university status. Edge Hill has always been an unusually slick set-up, whose boss used to call himself a Chief Executive and who always had a team of marketing and communications executives following close behind.

It has embarked upon an ambitious building programme. Last year a £14-million Faculty of Health building, which is also a facility for Online Teaching, opened. Already

UNIVERSITY/STUDENT PROFILE	
University since	**2006**
Situation/style	**Town campus**
Student population	**18735**
Undergraduates	**12370**
Mature undergraduates	**25%**
International undergrads	**1%**
Male/female ratio	**36:64**
Equality of opportunity:	
state school intake	**98%**
social class 4-7 intake	**40%**
low-participation area intake	**21%**

this year, an £8-million Business School has opened its doors.. which includes a mock court room for Law and Criminology students. Teaching is good here. In the National Student Survey, 83% of their students gave the thumbs-up to what they are doing. In the Times Higher Education magazine's Student Experience Survey they were praised for their supportive and interested staff, and small sized tuition groups.

CAMPUS

Writes Peter Cooper: 'The campus is about 10 minutes walk from the centre of Ormskirk, a small market town. If you like a small community where you are likely to get to know everyone then this is a good campus. It is a relatively safe place and although it may not have all the facilities of a larger university, it compensates with its friendly atmosphere. Liverpoool, Preston, and even Manchester, are readily accessible.'

The main Ormskirk campus consists of 75 landscaped acres, with lake, theatres and sports centre. In addition, they have campuses at Aintree and Chorley. The Faculty of Health is based at the former, which is known as University Hospital Aintree, and the Faculty of Education's continuing professional development (CPD) work is located at the latter, known as Woodlands Campus.

In addition, there are uni sites in Liverpool, Silkhouse Court where a part-time BSc (Hons) in Information Systems is studied, and in Manchester, Shrewsbury, Winsford (Cheshire) and the Wirral.

FEES, BURSARIES

UK & EU Fees 2009-10: £3,225 There's a bursary of £500 if family income is less than £25,000 p.a.; £1,000 for siblings of Edge Hill undergraduates, a £200 Learning Support bursary, £750 for care leavers, £1,000 bursaries for disadvantaged students, and others for certain vocational courses in teaching, health and social work. See www.edgehill.ac.uk/study/fees

In addition, there are over 70 entrance, on-course, and online scholarships for excellence and achievement in Sport, the Performing Arts, the Creative Arts, etc. And the first Jesse Jackson Scholarship will be awarded for academic year in 2009/10 to support a student, who has overcome disability or disadvantage to progress in higher education at the University.

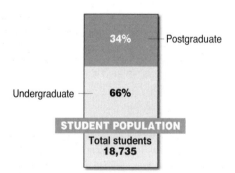

TEACHING SURVEY AT A GLANCE

Avg. UCAS points accepted	**240**
Acceptance rate	**18%**
Overall satisfaction rate	**83%**
Helpful/interested staff	★★★★★
Small tuition groups	★★★★
Students into graduate jobs	**73%**

Teaching most popular with undergraduates:
Law (100%), Psychology (95%), Social Studies (93%), Social Work, Creative Arts & Design, Biological Sciences (92%), English (91%), Management Studies, Drama, Nursing (80%).

Teaching least popular with undergraduates:
History (51%).

STUDENT PROFILE

Edge Hill easily surpasses its Government benchmarks for encouraging under-represented socio-economic groups into higher education. Virtually all their undergrads come from state schools, 39% from the four lowest socio-economic classes and a quarter from so-called 'low participation neighbourhoods'. There is also a large local and mature student population and, mainly on account of the Nursing provision, numbers of women greatly exceed those of men. None of these stats give a feel of the place, however, which is lively enough. When, a few years ago the college was taken to court by a neighbour for the regular early hours clamour of students enjoying themselves, the judge commented, 'It's like Brideshead Revisited meets St Trinians, isn't it?', as the prosecution itemised the complainants' 5-year 'noise diary'.

ACADEMIA & JOBS

There are three faculties: Education; Health; and Humanities, Management, Social & Applied Sciences, within which fall the Business School, English: Language, Literature, Creative Writing and Film Studies , History, Law and Criminology, Media, Natural, Geographical and Applied Sciences, Performing Arts, Social and Psychological Sciences, Sport and Physical Activity.

More than 40% of all graduates become primary or secondary teachers or go into hospital work of some sort. Other defining areas of graduate employment are social work, community & counselling activities, regional & local government administration, and recreational, cultural & sporting activities in the community. These destinations point us to the core courses at Edge Hill.

By taking a BA or BSc degree with qualified teacher status (QTS), you can study for a degree and do your initial teacher training at the same time. A BA or BSc with QTS is an honours degree that also incorporates teacher training. Edge Hill is the largest provider of Initial Teacher Training for secondary education in the UK. Nineteen per cent of their student teachers take the Biological Sciences route, which includes Sport (PE & School Sport, Therapy, Coaching, Psychology, Development, Science, etc.).

Languages (there is an interesting niche in Chinese), Maths, Computer Science, Physical Sciences, and the Creative Arts (Art, Creative Writing, Drama, Dance, Design) also pave the way principally to jobs in teaching.

The community health destinations of Edge Hill graduates - hospital and beyond - arise from their degrees in Nursing, Midwifery, Operating Department Practice, Assisting Professional Practice, Child & Youth Studies, Counselling, Social Work, Playwork, Working with Families & Communities/with Vulnerable Adults, Complementary Medicine, Women's Health, Nutritional Health, and so on.

Added to this area in 2009 are MSc Evidence Based Practice/Medicine, MCh Master of Surgery: Otorhinolaryngology, and MCh Master of Surgery: Trauma & Orthopaedics.

The sports degrees also take graduates into recreational jobs in the community, while jobs in local and regional government administration come principally from the degrees in Biological Sciences once again, but also from Creative Arts, Languages, Law, and Business. Law and the Creative Arts are leading routes into counselling and community activities, but Edge Hill Business graduates (Accounting, Management, Marketing, PR) mainly find work in retail.

They boast that they are one of only fourteen

RESEARCH EXCELLENCE		
% of Edge Hill's research that is 4* (World-class) or 3* (Internationally rated):		
	4*	3*
Nursing and Midwifery	5%	25%
Geography	0%	5%
Social Work, Policy & Admin.	0%	15%
Education	0%	5%
English	0%	20%
History	10%	15%

institutions to have National Council for the Training of Journalists accreditation for the undergraduate Journalism programme. The Media department also includes Film & TV, Advertising, Music & Sound, and Production Management. But few graduates actually find work in these areas.

The teaching that received the greatest praise from students was in Law, Psychology, Social Studies, Social Work, Creative Arts, Biological Sciences (including Sport), English, Management, Drama, and Nursing.

SOCIAL SCENE

Ten years ago a student described Edge Hill to us as 'a small, friendly community that caters for the basics'. Now, it is less small, but just as friendly, and there is a great deal more on campus than the college bar and dining room. The **Venue** is the place for live music, dance nights, themed discos, sports nights, resident and visiting DJs, quizzes, pool, video games, and big screen TV. **Sages** is the original 1930s dining room, but that has now been joined by the **Terraced Café**, **The Diner** (fast food), **Grinders** (coffee bar), and **Water's Edge** (restaurant with cyber café). Still not satisfied students opt for club-loon outings to Manchester, Liverpool and Preston, or slip into Ormskirk, heaven forbid, and sample **The Styles** or **Disraeli** bars. With some 50 societies on offer, the extra-curricular scene is better here than in many a more mature university. **The Rose Theatre** and **Studio Theatre** on campus are used for student theatre and music events, and by visiting companies - more than 100 films, theatre and musical performances are staged every year. Community Action has 150 volunteers. And then there are the sports clubs.

SPORT Which brings us to Sporting Edge. There is a sports crazy element at Edge Hill, and the facilities are good, thanks to a £1.9-million Lottery Grant and additional funds made available to afford the

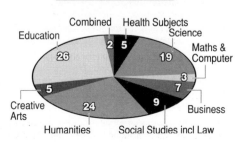

SUBJECT AREAS (%)

Education 26
Combined 2
Health Subjects 5
Science 19
Maths & Computer 3
Business 7
Social Studies incl Law 9
Humanities 24
Creative Arts 5

£3.9 million it all cost - a 4-court hall, a fitness suite, squash court, 7 floodlit tennis courts, 4 soccer pitches, 2 rugby pitches, 5 netball pitches, a 5-lane athletics track and an 8-lane straight, a cricket square, gymnasium, swimming pool, synthetic hockey pitch and 5-a-side area. On top of this there's the **Wilson Centre** - specialist labs to measure sporting performance.

Some of these facilities are used by Premiership football squads and professional rugby league sides, and they have earned Edge Hill a place in the official Guide to potential training camps for the London 2012 Olympics and Paralympics.

Finally, a fully-equipped dance studio with sprung floor hosts a varied programme of exercise classes, including aerobics, yoga and pilates.

PILLOW TALK

There are 19 halls on Ormskirk campus, satisfying 669 freshers (half of them catered, a fifth en suite). Rooms are allocated on a first come first served basis, although priority will be given to students with disabilities, care-leavers, and/or to those who live outside a 10-mile radius of the university. New

ACCOMMODATION	
Guarantee to freshers	**75%**
Style	**Halls, flats**
Security guard	**All**
Shared rooms	**None**
Internet access	**All**
Self-catered	**Most halls, all flats**
En suite	**Some halls, most flats**
Approx price range pw	**£51-£82**
Town rent pw	**£55-£75**

self-catered, en-suite accommodation will be available from September 2009.

GETTING THERE

☛ By road: M6/J26, M58/J3, A570 to Southport. The uni is 2 miles along on the right.
☛ By rail: Northern Line Merseyrail train connections from Liverpool Central and Preston Stations. Alight at Ormskirk, not Edge Hill.

STUDENT EDINBURGH - THE CITY

Edinburgh has a worldwide reputation for being one of the most interesting and exciting places to live and study. It is a city of contradictions. On the one hand it is an ancient city, with dramatic architecture and a rich cultural history. On the other hand it is a cosmopolitan capital and a critical financial and political centre. It is also a 24-hour city with an eclectic range of bars and clubs to suit any taste. Edinburgh, with consummate ease, combines ancient with modern, and work with play, making it one of the most vibrant and exciting cities in Europe.

CITY SCAPE

Edinburgh is centred round the beautiful castle that heads up the tourist filled Royal Mile complete with ancient cobbled streets and historical landmarks aplenty. The city is compact making it easy to get around simply by walking, although if you do get tired feet, the extensive bus network is ready and waiting. The town is essentially split into two with the ancient splendour of Old town, which houses the University, and the Georgian New Town separated by the stunning Princes Street gardens. Pay a visit in the festive season and

you will find an outdoor ice rink and huge Christmas market. This is also the site of the famed Edinburgh Hogmanay party that leads the world in celebrating the New Year.

COFFEE CULTURE

Edinburgh is typified by its coffee culture. You are never more than 5 minutes away from a good coffee and a comfy seat. Many of the best can be found around George Square, conveniently close to Edinburgh's central campus. **Assembly** and **Negociants** on Teviot place provide good lunches and tasty cocktails. The **Human Be-In** offers chic upmarket surroundings whilst the American style diner, **Favorit**, offers good food at good prices until early in the morning. **Bean Scene** on South Clerk Street offers a comfy haven away from the hustle and bustle. It also boasts its own record label of up and coming talent, and regular live performances from its artists. For those who are star struck, the **Elephant House** is famed as J.K.Rowling's favourite coffee spot. It is where she wrote some of *Harry Potter*. It, and its smaller cousin, **Elephant and Bagels**, offer excellent food and friendly original decor. Those of you with a serious addiction to chocolate won't be disappointed with the range available in Edinburgh. **Plaisir du Chocolat** on the Royal Mile offers the best hot chocolate money can buy, but it will cost you a small fortune. **Chocolate Soup** in Hanover Square offers fabulous hot chocolates in a huge variety of flavours, served in the biggest cups known to man.

SILVER SCREEN

The city excels in cinemas. At the **Cameo** in Tollcross there's thematic music before the credits roll and the pleasure of enjoying a pint in its enticingly comfortable seats. **The Cameo** features a range of unusual films that you won't find at the big chain cinemas. It isn't arthouse cinema, but it is a break from the one-dimensional Hollywood blockbusters. **The Filmhouse** serves the more arty audience, excelling at foreign films. For Hollywood, head to the **UGC Multiplex** at Fountainpark or **Vue** cinema at the top of Leith Walk.

The city also holds an annual International Film Festival in August. The uni's Film Society offers membership at a bargain price of £15 and gets you entry to a massive range of great films throughout the academic year.

SPOTLIGHTS

Due mainly to the Edinburgh festival, the city has an excess of theatres. **The Playhouse** at the top of Leith Walk hosts all the major touring musicals. There are often generous student discounts. **The Lyceum** offers Shakespeare or post-modern avant-garde. The world famous **Traverse**, nestling nearby amongst high-class eateries, dishes up excellent experimental Scottish drama as well as having one of the hippest bars in Edinburgh. If you're into more mainstream theatre or opera, head to the **King's Theatre** or **Festival Theatre**. Then there's the only student-run pro theatre in the UK, **Bedlam** on Bristo Place. Regular favourites are the Improverts, who run a 'whose line it is anyway' style show, and perform every Friday in term time.

Edinburgh is also steeped in comedy grandeur due to the famed festival, but the laughs don't stop there: comedy continues all year round. Edinburgh University Students' Association hold one of the most famous venues, the **Pleasance**, which plays hosts to the Comedy Network every fortnight. Everyone, from Harry Hill to Frank Skinner, has played here on their way to fame. So, there is plenty of, 'I saw them before they were famous' boasting potential. **The Stand**, in York Place, is the city's only purpose-built comedy venue. It serves up good food and a great ambience in a cosy basement. **Jongleurs** comedy club in the **Omni Centre** is another venue. Although the comedy is average, there are usually good deals on the door.

RETAIL RELIEF

If you fancy some retail therapy, head down to Princes Street, which houses nearly all the major high street brands. If you fancy really splashing out, then George Street has all the fine boutiques, stuffed with luxury goods aplenty.

If retro is the requirement, **Armstrongs** and **The Rusty Zip** deliver the goods, while **Flip** on South Bridge is good for flares, cords and comedy seventies gear. For the ultimate in budget retailing, check out the numerous charity shops on Nicholson Street. Skaterkids are well-serviced in Edinburgh, with both **Cult Clothing** and **Odd One Out** especially popular with the baggy-trousered contingent.

For music, head to Cockburn Street, home to the capital's Number 1 music shops, **Fopp** and **Avalanche**, both of which are infinitely better value than their mainstream Princes Street rivals.

Edinburgh has the largest collection of second-hand book stores in the world. So, for all you book worms, there are plenty of places to spend your days. **Till's** on Buccleuch Street, **Armchair Books** at West Port, **McFeely's** on Buccleuch Street and **MacNaughtons** at Gayfield Place are but a few of the delights in store for you.

PUB IT

Like so much of Edinburgh the key word is variety. Edinburgh's pubs and bars have the benefit of staying open until 1am every night. If a pint in a traditional pub is your aim, head to the **Blind Poet** or the **Pear Tree**. The latter boasts an impressive beer garden and many a late night can be spent clutching a pint in the cold Scottish air. If you are looking for a cheap pint then try one of the Scream pubs such as the **Tron** or **The Crags**, conveniently located next to the main Student Union halls. If you are looking for something a little more fancy then head over to New Town and enjoy the delights of **Prive Council** or **Beluga** on Chambers Street.

Both offer upmarket chic surroundings and not unreasonable prices. The Royal Mile offers a plethora of bars, but often more expensive. Head to the Cowgate where you will find a virtual tunnel of bars. Of particular note is **Bannermans**, which holds live music nights for unsigned bands nearly every night of the week.

IN THE CLUB

Edinburgh has more clubs per head than anywhere else in Britain – fact. This means that you have a massive choice of venues and a huge variety of styles to choose from. For those looking for a traditional chart club night out then **City**, with its excellent lighting and sound, **Faith**, with its impressive décor and **Why Not?**, with its clean crisp image are all favourites. For the more chic amongst you, head to **Opal Lounge** or **Po Na Na** for stylish surroundings and swanky drinks. Beware the price tag that comes with the venue! Goth and Rock are catered for by **Opium** on the Cowgate and **Citrus** on Lothian Road. **Honeycomb** puts on an awesome funk night on Tuesdays, and the unique design of the club, with its literal honeycomb structure, is worth seeing anyway. **Bongo Club** offers the best hip hop and reggae in town. **Liquid Rooms** offers an excellent venue and a huge variety of nights, although it can be pricey. **Ego** on Picardy Place offers nights tailor made for gay clubbers, especially Tuesdays. With two floors of music, dirt cheap drink, and a young crowd this is an excellent night out. **CC Blooms** is the only permanent Gay Club with **Planet Out** and **Habana** providing the best of the bar scene.

Venues chop and change their nights each week, so for complete up-to-date listings pick up a copy of *The List*.

Iain Walters

UNIVERSITY OF EDINBURGH

The University of Edinburgh
57 George Square
Edinburgh EH8 9JU

TEL 0131 650 4360
FAX 0131 651 1236
EMAIL sra.enquiries@ed.ac.uk
WEB www.ed.ac.uk

Edinburgh University Student Association
Student Centre House
5/2 Bristo Square
Edinburgh EH8 9AL

TEL 0131 650 2656
FAX 0131 668 4177
EMAIL eusa.enquiry@eusa.ed.ac.uk
WEB www.eusa.ed.ac.uk

VAG VIEW

If you are looking at parents' perceptions, it's Oxbridge then Durham and Bristol, and Edinburgh is the Scottish equivalent of these. Edinburgh, they know, is the place to be.

An Edinburgh degree is a very good degree to have. It is still considered to be part of a Scottish person's birthright. Indeed, Edinburgh sits at No. 23 in the World Top 200 Universities League Table, and at No. 6 among UK universities in that table, ahead of Durham and Bristol.

In the Higher Education Funding Council's National Survey, 83% of its students gave the uni the thumbs-up, and more than 95% of them will see their course through to the end, 80% getting real graduate-level jobs within six months of leaving.

But, as elsewhere, Edinburgh University is a distinctive experience, which may or may not be the right one for you.

UNIVERSITY/STUDENT PROFILE	
University since	**1583**
Situation/style	**Civic**
Student population	**24225**
Undergraduates	**16980**
Mature undergraduates	**14**
International undergrads	**7%**
Male/female ratio	**44:56**
Equality of opportunity:	
state school intake	**68%**
social class 4-7 intake	**16%**
low-participation area intake	**2%**

CAMPUS

'The University is primarily divided into two main campuses, two miles apart,' writes James Lumsden. 'George Square (with its central city location) for Arts & Social Science, and KB (King's Buildings) for Science and Engineering. Recently, the university has spent wads of cash reinventing KB into somewhere that you no longer want to leave before you arrive. The result reminds some of a cross-channel ferry.

'George Square, meanwhile, has its own brand of ugliness, in the shape of Appleton and David Hume towers. For a beautiful city that's known as "the Athens of the North", Edinburgh University

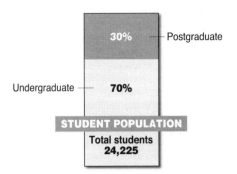

30% — Postgraduate

Undergraduate — 70%

STUDENT POPULATION
Total students
24,225

STUDENT PROFILE

'Often represented by a myopic media as a toffs' university,' writes James Lumsden, 'the true diversity of student and university life at Edinburgh goes misrepresented; there are more than 20,000 students from a wide variety of backgrounds and circumstances.'

Nevertheless, in the modern context, the uni does have its share of rahs. Jamie Scattergood is in his first year, up from a Yorkshire public school himself, a sportsman and academic, who got three A grades at A level. We spoke to him when things were still shaking down for him socially, as happens with almost every first year everywhere.

'It wasn't how I was expecting it, but I am enjoying it.'

'What's different?'

'I was fully aware of the public school contingent etc., but there is a huge, huge public school contingent here, and the Radley, Eton boys are very insular. When I first got here, the best way to integrate socially, I thought, is to join the rugby team. There is a boy from Radley... just because we are not from Radley or Eton he's quite hostile. I would say there are about 40 or 50 people here like that. But in general it is pretty easy to make friends, people seem to be very friendly. I don't like the fact that the rugby club is so cliquey, so literally people won't socialise outside the club. I'm not playing rugby next year, put it like that. Recently I have made a conscious effort to meet more people and already I have met 20/30 really good people. Also, my advice would be, don't come to Edinburgh with a friend. Make new ones...'

seems to have done its damnedest to flout convention.'

Actually, it is impossible not to be impressed by the gothic beauty of the University Precinct, as you walk up to it from the railway station for the first time, high above the city. One thinks of Scott and Robert Louis Stevenson, and not a little of 'The Strange Case of Dr Jekyll and Mr Hyde', which is all as it should be, for Stevenson was an undergraduate here. He founded the student newspaper in 1887.

The old Moray House Institute of Education is the uni's Faculty of Education. Founded in 1835, there are two campuses, Holyrood in the heart of the Old Town, adjacent to the university's central premises and, 6 miles away on the northwest edge of the city, a campus hitherto known as the Scottish Centre for Physical Education and home to PE, Leisure Studies and Applied Sports Science. The sporting facilities put Edinburgh in the Top 10 for sports trainers and coaches.

FEES, BURSARIES

UK & EU Fees, 2009-10: non-Scottish UK student fees in year 2009-10: £1,820 (more for Medicine). If you are a Scottish-domiciled first degree student you are eligible for your tution fees to be covered by the Scottish Government.

If you are in receipt of the full UK Maintenance Grant you will automatically receive a bursary from the University. All eligible first year students will be contacted by Scholarships and Student Finance staff following the start of the academic session.

Over 180 other bursaries will also be awarded for undergraduate study to UK students. The minimum value of each award is £1,000 p.a.

Up to 90 Accommodation Bursaries of £1,000 are also available - online application available.

The RUK Bursary is offered to English, Welsh and Northern Ireland undergraduate students who enter a Scottish University. There are also Sport and Academic scholarships. See www.scholarships .ed.ac.uk/bursaries/index.htm.

TEACHING SURVEY AT A GLANCE

Avg. UCAS points accepted	**460**
Acceptance rate	**9%**
Overall satisfaction rate	**83%**
Helpful/interested staff	★★★
Small tuition groups	★★★
Students into graduate jobs	**80%**

Teaching most popular with undergraduates:
Geology (98%), Linguistics (97%), Theology (95%), English, Medicine (93%), Biology & related sciences (92%), Engineering, Accounting (91%), Veterinary, Physical Geography & Enviro. Sciences, History, Archaeology, Computer Science (86%), Classics, Chemistry (85%), Politics (83%), Psychology, Physics & Astronomy (82%), Social Studies (81%), Law, Business & Admin. Studies (80%).

Teaching least popular with undergraduates:
Iberian Studies (52%).

On a wildly different wicket, the uni, in its efforts to spread the word throughout society, has recently been awarded the Frank Buttle Trust Quality Mark for Care Leavers in Higher Education. You get this for encouraging children in care to apply. Wonder what the Radley-Eton brigade would make of that.

The statistics are that 32% of undergraduates at Edinburgh are from public school. That compares with 37% at Bristol, 38% at Durham, and 42% at Cambridge. But of course there are different sorts of public school kid, and different universities exert their cultural influence on them in different ways and to different degrees, as Hannah at Bristol eloquently describes in that university's entry.

ACADEMIA & JOBS

The Scottish degree structure differs significantly from those in the rest of the UK. The fourth year leads to a breadth and depth of study much sought-after by employers. However, Jamie questions whether it is as heavy a workload as it might be.

'I'm doing Economics and Politics. Very happy with the course. It is pretty much as expected. I think the organisation is pretty good. Certain things take a bit of time. I don't think the relationship between the lecturers and students is that brilliant, but it works. It's not put on a plate for you, but in general it's pretty good. You get some lecturers who are brilliant. Quite a few in the Politics classes are American and they are really passionate about Politics. The tutorial size is about 12, it ranges between 10 and 20. The library is huge, absolutely huge, and you can't really expect them to stock 100 of each book, so I think in general they are pretty good. But the thing that I found quite frustrating, and I know this may sound silly, but I'm so *un-busy* at the moment. I'm doing a lot of extra-curricular stuff just to keep myself busy. What I'm trying to say is that Edinburgh should *up* its entry standards. All I did last term was two essays. Do you see where I'm coming from? It's quite frustrating.'

The *Times Higher Education* Student Experience Survey backs up some of what Jamie says. They are not the most helpful and interested staff at Edinburgh, and tutorial groups are not the smallest you will find by a long chalk. This is odd, because the uni boasts a guardian angel Director of Studies trained to guide each student through his or her course.

Lack of availability of books in the library for essays is a perennial problem. There is an incredible 2,275,000-vol library at Edinburgh, and excellent computer facilities and language laboratories, but we have heard before that there can be a problem in getting to use some of these resources. 'Queues for the Crisis Loans are lengthening ... study resources are being stretched to the limit,' said one student. When this is accompanied by a less than supportive staff, it can lead to great frustration.

Doubtless, Edinburgh will be inspired by the *Times Higher*'s survey to get their lecturers to look up from their research and talk more to their students, though perhaps they too are intimidated by these southern rahs, for many of the world-class research areas are also where the best teaching

RESEARCH EXCELLENCE

% of Edinburgh's research that is
4* *(World-class)* or **3*** *(Internationally rated):*

	4*	3*
Hospital Clinical Subjects	40%	40%
Psychiatry, Neuroscience & Clinical Psychology	10%	55%
Biological Sciences	15%	45%
Agriculture, Veterinary, Food	20%	35%
Environmental Sciences	15%	55%
Chemistry	30%	40%
Physics	20%	45%
Pure Mathematics	25%	45%
Applied Mathematics	15%	50%
Statistics	10%	35%
Computer Science	35%	50%
General Eng., Mineral & Mining	15%	40%
Architecture/ Built Environment	25%	45%
Geography	20%	35%
Economics and Econometrics	25%	45%
Business and Management	10%	40%
Law	30%	25%
Politics	10%	45%
Social Work, Policy & Admin.	30%	35%
Sociology	30%	25%
Anthropology	25%	35%
Psychology	15%	45%
Education	15%	30%
Middle Eastern, African	25%	45%
Asian Studies	10%	25%
East European Languages	5%	35%
French	10%	45%
German, Dutch, Scandinavian	25%	25%
Italian	0%	25%
Iberian and Latin American	15%	35%
Celtic Studies	20%	30%
English	40%	30%
Linguistics	30%	30%
Classics etc.	10%	35%
Philosophy	20%	45%
Theology	30%	30%
History	25%	35%
History of Art	15%	45%
Music	20%	45%

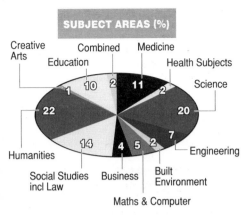

SUBJECT AREAS (%)

Creative Arts — 1
Education — 10
Combined — 2
Medicine — 11
Health Subjects — 2
Science — 20
Humanities — 22
Social Studies incl Law — 14
Business — 4
Built Environment — 5
Maths & Computer — 2
Engineering — 7

here is to be found. Students say the best taught subjects are Geology, Linguistics, Theology, English, Medicine, Biology & related sciences, Engineering, Accounting, Veterinary, Physical Geography & Environmental Sciences, History, Archaeology, Computer Science, Classics, Chemistry, Politics, Psychology, Physics & Astronomy, Social Studies, Law, and Business. The worst, they say, is Iberian Studies - only 52% of undergraduates were happy.

The degree in Medicine is the 5/6-year MB ChB. They promise 'early clinical contact' and deliver it in Year 1, together with case-based learning tutorials using problem-based learning methods. You will need three A levels and one AS in four subjects, Grades AAAb achieved or predicted. Non-science VCE AS and A levels may replace non-science GCE AS and A levels. Only one Maths will be considered. Chemistry plus Maths or Physics or Biology at A Level and Biology at least at AS.

> 'I know everyone is supposed to fall in love with their university, but Edinburgh just makes it so easy.'

The veterinary provision actually scored better than Medicine at the teaching assessments.

Graduate jobs are not a problem for Edinburgh graduates. Health and education are the two single largest destination sectors, and jobs also proliferate in community & counselling activities, banking, accounting, the hotel/restaurant trade, veterinary, the Civil Service, personnel, publishing, software consultancy & supply, retail, management, museum/library/archive, engineering design, sport, architecture, advertising, media, Defence, and much else besides.

On the curriculum, Languages, Historical & Philosophical Studies, Social Studies, and Biological Sciences are especially strong in graduate job

placement for students at Edinburgh.

SOCIAL SCENE

One hears that Edinburgh is an expensive place to enjoy four years. Jamie agrees: 'I think the comment about needing money to enjoy yourself at Edinburgh is pretty much true. I spend £60-£80 a week. It depends on the week. In Freshers Week I spent £500, but I suppose I could survive with £20-£25.' He might in Pollock Halls, where most freshers live, as it's catered.

The Pleasance has the **Cabaret Bar** (capacity 175), which hosts parties, discos, live bands, acoustic nights, theatre/dance/comedy. For society nights they can provide djs, sound and lighting technicians. **The Theatre** on the first floor is the principal performance space in the Pleasance, and the **Highland Room**, with lino floor and mirrored wall, is used for dance classes, meetings, rehearsals (capacity 70). Tea, coffee, buffets can be supplied. The **Ochil Room** is another space much-used for classes and meetings, and there are nine other, slightly smaller rooms available too.

Teviot Union, the oldest, purpose-built Students' Union building in the country, has 5 levels of possible entertainment. The **Underground** is a great little club (capacity 410) and theatre venue, most commonly used for club nights, band nights, discos and parties. The **Terrace Bar** is a split level affair. The **Mezzanine** can seat 300 for dinner, and is another club night, band night, disco or party venue. Then there's the **Debating Hall**, sounds a bit stodgy, but no stranger to the odd ceilidh. Capacity depends on the event, for discos it's 400. The **Loft Bar** boasts a roof terrace. The **Balcony Room** is a small bar perched at the top of one of Teviot's gothic turrets.

For night-time pleasure it's **The Potterow**, where the venue has 1,200 capacity, regularly reached on weekends. The newly refurbished **Bristo Lounge** has its own bar and is ideal for acoustic gigs or informal parties.

Down at King's Buildings, there's a £3.4 million student facility for the 7,000 science and engineering campus - catering and bar facilities, a games room, squash courts, a multi-gym, a sports hall and advisory and welfare services. KB get quizzes, pool comps and film nights by way of ents.

Meanwhile the University Theatre Company draws crowds for its many productions at **Bedlam Theatre**, the site of Bristo Bedlam, where 'the mad, manic and mental' were once locked away. Now

ACCOMMODATION	
Guarantee to freshers	**100%**
Style	**Halls, flats**
Security guard	**All halls. some flats**
Shared rooms	**Some**
Internet access	**All**
Self-catered	**All flats, no halls**
En suite	**Most halls, no flats**
Approx price range pw	**£56-£215.61**
City rent pw	**£55-£92+**

Bedlam's the UK's only student-run theatre.

Holly Crane, who threw herself into extra-curricular media when she was up had a hugely positive view of this aspect of the university: 'I know everyone is supposed to fall in love with their university, but Edinburgh just makes it so easy,' she writes. 'It's the ideal advert for higher education: a place where you learn not only facts and formulae from your academic studies, but also about what you can do, what you want to do - and what you don't want to do - with the rest of your life.'

Holly was sensitive to 'a discernible buzz about the university, a condensed feeling of potential, and energy. This is partly due to the city itself: there's just enough of the "ivory tower" atmosphere to leave you inspired but not oppressed by your impending academia. But it's also to do with the type of students. With many doing four-year (or longer) degrees, there is, if not more time, then more reason, to get up off your arse and do something a bit different.'

There is opportunity aplenty to do so - loads of clubs and societies, 200 of the latter alone, centred on the Pleasance, the most popular being Film Soc, The *Edinburgh Student* (newspaper) took Critic of the Year at the Guardian Media Awards this year. There's also a mag. called *Hype*, a radio station, Fresh Air fm, and Nightline (welfare). *Edinburgh Student* is Britain's third biggest student newspaper, with a weekly circulation of 12,000 copies distributed to all the universities and higher education colleges around Edinburgh.

SPORT The university is pre-eminent in sport, came 5th in the UK last year. Besides its twenty-five acres of playing fields and residential centre on Loch Tay, there's a sports centre with conditioning gymnasia, a fitness and sports injury centre, and a wide range of team and individual activities. Says Jamie: 'The gym is amazing. Recently I was on a bench press next to the South African rugby team! They were all using our gym,

it was surreal!' Sports bursaries are offered through the PE Department.

TOWN 'When you do step out, the city offers everything,' writes James Lumsden. 'There are enough bars and pubs to see you from this life into the next, and plenty of theatres, cinemas, clubs, and 'cultural stuff' to stop at, en-route. See *Student Edinburgh* above.

PILLOW TALK

Freshers from outside Edinburgh are guaranteed a place in uni accommodation provided they apply by September 1, and that UCAS has guaranteed their place at Edinburgh by that date. There's a mix of traditional full board halls, student houses, and flats. Main accommodation for first years is Pollock Halls, a complex of houses, together with a bar, shop and dining rooms, which take around 2,000 first years. All rooms are single, but, if you pay extra, you can upgrade to a double bed and en-suite

WHAT IT'S REALLY LIKE	
UNIVERSITY:	
Social Life	★★★★★
Campus scene	**Diverse, active, self-assured**
Student Union services	**Good**
Politics	**Active**
Sport	**Key**
National team position	**5th**
Sport facilities	**Good**
Arts opportunities	**Good**
Student magazine	**Hype**
Student newspaper	**Edinburgh Student**
Guardian Media Awards	**Critic of Year**
Student radio	**Fresh Air FM**
Nightclub	**Potterow**
Bars	**Sportsman's, Teviot, The Pleasance**
Union ents	**Cheese, comedy, Indie**
Union societies	**200**
Most popular societies	**Amnesty**
Parking	**Poor**
CITY:	
Entertainment	★★★★★
Scene	**Seething**
Town/gown relations	**Good**
Risk of violence	**Low**
Cost of living	**High**
Student concessions	**Excellent**
Survival + 2 nights out	**£150+ pw**
Part-time work campus/town	**Good/excellent**

shower. Most people go for full board; breakfast and supper in the week and three meals at the weekend. However, each house has a kitchen area where you can test out your culinary talents (toast). Another residential area is Robertson's Close which consists of self-catering flats. There are also uni-run student houses.

Says Jamie: 'Pollock Halls is where freshers begin. The one I'm in is typical of halls, about 50/60 years old. I didn't get very lucky, but it's en-suite. The Chancellors Court holds about 700 people and the rooms are like 3-star hotel rooms. They are currently making new accommodation for more people at Pollock. Unfortunately my window is right by the construction site. I think I'm going to get compensation for that.'

The new hall is John Burnett House, due to be opened this year.

GETTING THERE
☛ By road: M90 or M9 or A1 or M8.
☛ By rail: London King's Cross, 4:30; Glasgow Central, 50 mins; Newcastle, 1:30.
☛ By air: Edinburgh Airport.
☛ By coach: Glasgow, 1:10; London, 9:10; Birmingham, 8:10; Newcastle, 3:10.

EDINBURGH NAPIER UNIVERSITY

Edinburgh Napier University
Craiglockhart Campus
Edinburgh EH14 1DJ

TEL 08452 60 60 40
FAX 0131 455 6464
EMAIL info@napier.ac.uk
WEB www.napier.ac.uk

Edinburgh Napier Students' Association
12 Merchiston Place
Edinburgh EH10 4NR

TEL 0131 229 8791
FAX 0131 228 3462
EMAIL nsa@napier.ac.uk
WEB www.napierstudents.com

VAG VIEW

In 2009, Napier University changed its name to Edinburgh Napier University, thereby rushing up the alphabetical order in the Guide, and, more purposefully in its pursuit of student applicants at home and abroad, clarifying and capitalising on its location in Scotland's beautiful capital city. Given its generous but clearly necessary 31% acceptance rate of all-comers, it seems like a good idea.

Edinburgh Napier saw fit to eschew the Higher Education Funding Council for England's National Student Survey, which, as it is one of a very few universities to do so, is bound to make one wonder what they have to fear. Fortunately, they are still talking to us.

Napier has a good reputation for getting its graduates jobs. In 2008 the Higher Education Statistics Agency (HESA) named it Scotland's No. 1 university for employability, with 97.5% of its graduates in employment or further study within six months of graduating. Even if 15% should be shaved off that when you are looking only at real graduate jobs, it is a good result.

Its difficulty has always been that it is a bit split up, with no central focus. There has been

UNIVERSITY/STUDENT PROFILE	
University since	**1992**
Situation/style	**Civic**
Student population	**14540**
Undergraduates	**11260**
Mature undergraduates	**62%**
International undergrads	**10%**
Male/female ratio	**47:53**
Equality of opportunity:	
state school intake	**96%**
social class 4-7 intake	**33%**
low-participation area intake	**6%**

no one place where Napierites congregate, and very little going on outside the lecture theatre to amuse or interest its students.

Whether the slothful social scene is partly down to the less-than-frisky 62% mature undergrad. population is not clear, but being without much of a social or extra-curricular scene will surely have done little to encourage a younger crew, or stem the whopping drop-out rate, which is a careless sounding 18%.

The problem, it seems, is not so much the social life, which it would be difficult to nullify completely in Edinburgh, rather it is the

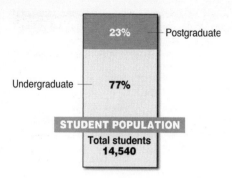

STUDENT POPULATION

Total students
14,540

23% — Postgraduate

Undergraduate — 77%

lacklustre performance of the Student Association, which has failed to galvanise the student body and shake it into action. Napier has been like a day college that closes down after lectures.

Now they are at least moving in a positive direction by rationalising the split-campus format, and when the Times Higher Education *managed to find a way in to ask questions of their undergraduates for the Student Experience Survey, it fell clear that what Napier does have is an excellent rapport between lecturers and students. The teaching is good here. The lecturers are helpful and interested in their students. What might be possible if the got the extra-mural societal side together too?*

CAMPUS

Long-term policy is to have one campus per faculty with state-of-the-art facilities, student accommodation and a proper Student Association presence. The first step was completed with the opening of the Craiglockhart Campus, home to the Business School. Their sights are now on redeveloping the Sighthill campus for the Faculty of Health, Life & Social Sciences - due to be completed in the academic year 2010-2011. There are also plans to refurbish the campus at Merchiston, where the Faculty of Engineering, Computing & Creative Industries is based, to include 'a social learning space'. It won't stop there, for there are, in addition, half a dozen other sites spread out mostly through the south and west of Edinburgh.

FEES, BURSARIES

UK & EU Fees, 2009-10: In line with other Scottish higher education institutions, Edinburgh Napier expects the 2009/10 tuition fee to be around £1,830. For information on bursaries and awards, see http://www.napier.ac.uk/napierlife/money/Pages/default.aspx.

TEACHING SURVEY AT A GLANCE

Avg. UCAS points accepted	**280**
Acceptance rate	**31%**
Overall satisfaction rate	**No data**
Helpful/interested staff	★★★
Small tuition groups	★★
Students into graduate jobs	**79%**

Teaching most popular with undergraduates:
No data

Teaching least popular with undergraduates:
No data

STUDENT PROFILE

The student profile shows a fairly typical 'new' university student population, but the most noticeable statistic is the mature student population of 62%.

ACADEMIA & JOBS

There are 3 faculties: Business; Engineering, Computing & Creative Industries; and Health, Life & Social Science.

In the old days, health was the big graduate employment destination, swelled by Nursing, which is now off the curriculum. There are other dimensions to the provision, however, including Biomedical Sciences, Immunology & Toxicology, Applied Nutrition, Social Sciences with Health, Complementary Medicine, Herbal Medicine, and the well designed Vet Nursing top-up and BSc (Hons) degrees.

These contribute to a fine showing for so small a university in last year's assessment of Napier's

SUBJECT AREAS (%)

Social Studies inc Law — 5
Creative Arts — 12
Health Subjects — 22
Science — 12
Engineering — 9
Built Environment — 4
Maths & Computer — 11
Business — 25

research provision. Alongside Health Professions, adjudged world-class and of international significance, were Architecture, Civil Engineering, Information Management, and English.

The uni is known for business, too, and recently they got together with Paris-based business school IPAG to offer an MSc in International Marketing and Tourism. Languages, Marketing and Tourism are features of other Business degrees, as is Hospitality Management, and all are rich seams in Napier's graduate employment field. They also have dedicated degrees in Accounting and a good reputation for jobs in banking and finance.

Architecture sits alongside courses in Building and Quantity Surveying, Built Environment, Construction & Project Management, and again, all these are strong areas of graduate employment, as is Civil Engineering, which teams up with Transport Engineering and sits alongside Transport Management, and Civil & Timber Engineering, which finds a cosy niche forestry as a career path - the whole picture is one of academia and jobs dovetailing neatly, the one into the other.

Computer Science is a major contributor to their employment figures, as are other less prominent features of the curriculum, like Sport, Publishing, Advertising, all dedicated degrees proven for employability over time. Now they also have a series of 'Customised' degrees, which allow

RESEARCH EXCELLENCE		
% of Napier's research that is **4*** (World-class) or **3*** (Internationally rated):		
	4*	**3***
Nursing and Midwifery	5%	35%
Health Professions	5%	5%
Environmental Sciences	0%	20%
Computer Science	0%	20%
Civil Engineering	5%	25%
Built Environment	5%	30%
Business/ Management	0%	15%
Information Management	10%	50%
Law	0%	5%
Sociology	0%	10%
Psychology	0%	5%
English	5%	15%
Art and Design	0%	25%
Music	0%	5%

you to get involved in the game of curriculum design they play so well. You can pic 'n' mix from virtually any subject area you care to choose.

But Napier's success in the job market isn't just down to curriculum design. 'Confident Futures' is its programme of personal development available to all students and designed to promote confidence, improve self-awareness, so to enhance their employability. How much more holistic would it be if the Student Association got more involved in some areas of the curriculum, like Media, Music, Film and Entrepreneurship, as tends to happen elsewhere.

SOCIAL SCENE

The **Union Bar**, 12 Merchiston Place, is round the corner from Merchiston Campus. Sports night is on Wednesday, sponsored by *Cool It* Events. *Open Mic* nights feature every other Thursday. Friday is *Cocktails Night*. And that's about it. There are 11 student societies on offer and 21 sports clubs. Their teams came 65th nationally last year, which is a massive improvement. There is a student newspaper, *Veritas*, and the most active student society is the Drama Club. Recent political campaigns of interest have included Student Retention, Access to Top Quality Sports Facilities and the Student Experience - which shows just how overdue it is for the authorities to give Napier students a decent deal.

Town See Student Edinburgh.

PILLOW TALK

Uni accommodation in apartment develop-ments

WHAT IT'S REALLY LIKE	
COLLEGE:	
Social Life	★★
Campus scene	**Friendly**
Student Union services	**Very poor**
Politics	**Interest low**
Sport	**21 clubs**
National team position	**65th**
Sport facilities	**Improving**
Arts opportunities	**Average**
Student mag/news	**Veritas**
Bars	**Union Bar**
Union ents	**DJs**
Union societies	**11**
Most popular society	**Drama**
Parking	**Poor**
CITY:	
Entertainment	★★★★★
Scene	**Seething**
Town/gown relations	**Good**
Risk of violence	**Average**
Cost of living	**High**
Student concessions	**Excellent**
Survival + 2 nights out	**£50+ pw**
Part-time work campus/town	**Poor/excellent**

in the city centre is guaranteed to freshers coming 'outwith a 30-mile radius of Edinburgh'. There is no catered accommodation. Four-person flats have one shared bathroom; five-person flats have two shared bathrooms. Developments are all centrally located, modern, purpose built student accommodation, all within easy access of Napier's campuses.

Says Gareth: 'Napier provides housing for over 1,000 students, it's quite expensive but is quickly snapped up. Edinburgh has an abundance of reasonably priced flats, so it should be easy to find one in an area that suits you and your pocket. Areas to consider include Tollcross, Gorgie/Dalry, Marchmont and Bruntsfield. You may see cheaper areas, but they may not be student-friendly.'

GETTING THERE
☛ By road: from north, M90; from Stirling, M9; from Newcastle, A1; from Glasgow, M8.
☛ By rail: London King's Cross, 4:30. Glasgow Central, 50 mins; Newcastle, 1:30.

ACCOMMODATION	
Guarantee to freshers	**60%**
Style	**Flats**
Security guard	**Some**
Shared rooms	**None**
Internet access	**All**
Self-catered	**All**
En suite	**None**
Approx price range pw	**£85-£86**
City rent pw	**£75-£90**

☛ By coach: Glasgow, 1:10; London, 9:10.

UNIVERSITY OF ESSEX

The University of Essex
Wivenhoe Park
Colchester
Essex CO4 3SQ

TEL 01206 873666
FAX 01206 873423
EMAI admit@essex.ac.uk
WEB www.essex.ac.ok

Essex Students' Union
Wivenhoe Park
Colchester
Essex CO4 3SQ

TEL 01206 863211
FAX 01206 870915
EMAIL su@essex.ac.uk
WEB www.essexstudent.com

VAG VIEW

*E*ssex University is based in Wivenhoe Park, Colchester. It was launched around the same time as York, Sussex and Warwick in the mid-'60s. Yet, after it had briefly marked its card as main seat of student revolution, it disappeared from public consciousness, partly one suspects because it will never win any prizes for beauty. It is a grey, drab institution, made almost entirely of concrete.

It is, however, one of the very best Social Science universities in the country. This was confirmed last year in the assessment of the research provision of all UK universities. The inspection placed it in the UK Top 10 in 8 of its 14 submitted subject areas, marking it out as the leading university in the Social Sciences, with Politics and Sociology ranked

UNIVERSITY/STUDENT PROFILE	
University since	**1965**
Situation/style	**Town campus**
Student population	**11660**
Undergraduates	**8355**
Mature undergraduates	**5%**
International undergrads	**25%**
Male/female ratio	**50:50**
Equality of opportunity:	
state school intake	**95%**
social class 4-7 intake	**32%**
low-participation area intake	**14%**

in first position, Economics in third, and Linguistics in fourth.

There are other good reasons for applying, the extra-curricular sport, ents and student media among them. Essex is also, of course, convenient for London.

Now they are launching an additional university operation at Southend-on-Sea, and with the University of East Anglia, they're fathering University Campus Suffolk, a centre on Ipswich waterfront.

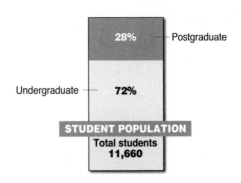

Postgraduate — 28%

Undergraduate — **72%**

STUDENT POPULATION
Total students
11,660

CAMPUS

The campus comprises 200 acres of landscaped parkland, 2 miles from the centre of Colchester, capital of Roman Britain and now commuter and garrison town, and a regional centre for commerce, light industry and high technology. It is an hour away from London by train.

Perhaps a subliminal need for aesthetic redemption has drawn them to the coast. For, as of 2007, Essex has been up and running with Southend-on-Sea, about 40 miles south of Colchester, on Elmer Approach, Southend-on-Sea, Essex SS1 1LW. Tel: 01702 328200. The plan has been hatching since further education college South East Essex's move to a new £52 million building there two years ago. Essex are taking over the old Odeon cinema and teaming up with SEEC for everything from library to student sport facilities.

Since 2000 the famous drama school, East 15 in Loughton, has also been part of Essex University. East 15 has been providing professional training in theatre, film, TV, radio and related fields for more than 45 years. The School has a campus in Loughton, on the borders of East London, and shares Essex's new campus in Southend-on-Sea.

Essex has launched a £250-million capital investment plan to build a new £25-million student centre and additional library, computing, teaching and learning space for the Colchester Campus, plus a range of student services and facilities. The Southend Campus will benefit from new student accommodation and the Acting School from new studio and performance facilities.

FEES, BURSARIES

UK & EU Fees 2009-2010: £3,225 p.a. A bursary of £319 p.a. is available to students with a household income of less than £25,000. Students whose families can call on between £25,001 and £34,000 p.a. will receive bursaries to bring their overall maintenance support to £3,225. Full details of awards are available at: www.essex.ac.uk/student finance/ug/.

STUDENT PROFILE

Nick Margerrison notes the mixed student profile as 'one of the best features - it is a small, friendly university; you will enjoy your time here, along with Sharon, Tracey and Wayne.' Mixed socially,

economically and nationally - people come to Essex University from almost every conceivable part of the known world, either to study full time or as part of their course elsewhere.

ACADEMIA & JOBS

In Colchester there are five Schools - Comparative Studies (Humanities, but with a cross-cultural, international approach), Social Sciences, Law, Maths & Computer Sciences, Science & Engineering - and consistently good teaching assessments recently - full marks for Electronic Systems Engineering and 22 out of 24 for Psychology, Sociology and Art History. While we're on the subject, a History of Modern Art degree includes a ten-day subsidised visit to New York.

The new Southend-on-Sea campus has the School of Entrepreneurship and Business, which delivers BSc programmes in Business and Service Industry Management, International Enterprise and Business Development, Marketing and Innovation, New Technology and Digital Enterprise Management, and New Venture Creation and

TEACHING SURVEY AT A GLANCE	
Avg. UCAS points accepted	310
Acceptance rate	17%
Overall satisfaction rate	88%
Helpful/interested staff	★★★★
Small tuition groups	★★★
Students into graduate jobs	67%

Teaching most popular with undergraduates:
History (99%), Philosophy (98%), Archaeology (96%), Computer Science (95%), English, Sports Science (93%), Sociology (92%), Social Policy, Anthropology (91%), Languages (90-92%), Politics (90%), Law (89%), Psychology (88%), Performing Arts (86%).

Teaching least popular with undergraduates:
Management Studies (75%).

Enterprise Management.

Then there's the School of Health & Human Sciences, which delivers BSc programmes in Nursing, Health & Human Sciences, and Social Psychology & Sociology, and BA programmes in Health Studies and Health Studies & Sociology.

Finally, the drama school East 15 has BA programmes there in Acting and Stage Combat, Physical Theatre, World Performance, and Community Theatre. The Loughton campus delivers East 15 degrees in BA programmes in Acting, Acting & Contemporary Theatre, and Community Theatre.

Graduate destination surveys show that the particular areas of study in which Essex has the greatest percentage of students going into full-time employment are: Art History, Computing and Electronic Systems, Entrepreneurship and Business, Health and Human Sciences, and US Studies.

At Essex the first year is thrown open to a study of four or five courses to enable you to investigate your chosen subject from a variety of points of view. This might involve studying Sociology from an Economics point of view, History from a Psychology pov. Then in the second year you move forward to a single or joint honours degree with deeper understanding.

Students say that the best-taught subjects are

> *Essex is seriously underrated. Eleventh best in the country for research. Consider it for social sciences, for biosciences, for sport, and much else, but close your eyes to campus architecture.*

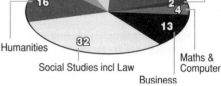

SUBJECT AREAS (%)

Combined Health Subjects — 1
Creative Arts — 6
7
Science — 19
Engineering — 2
4
13 Business
16 Humanities
32
Maths & Computer
Social Studies incl Law

History, Philosophy, Archaeology, Computer Science, English, Sports Science, Sociology, Social Policy, Anthropology, Languages, Politics, Law, Psychology, and Performing Arts. Least popular is Management Studies, but even that got three-quarters of the class applauding.

In computing, degrees in Software Engineering, Embedded Systems & Robotics, Internet Technology, Artificial Intelligence, Computer Engineering, Electronic Engineering turn out software engineers, consultants and manufacturers, and computer games designers (there's a dedicated degree for this) by the score. Among smaller unis, Essex is the giant in this sort of thing.

Law is another high point. It finds its way into all sorts of courses, and Law graduates from Essex are in demand by Government for Defence and admin. posts. Essex are European law specialists (and very good at languages too), and there is an interesting programme of Human Rights degrees, and a Human Rights Centre on campus. The programme represents a significant pioneering development in undergraduate education in the UK and draws on the expertise of members of the Centre, many of whom hold, or have held, posts at the UN.

As said, all the Social Sciences are key. Finally, Essex makes employment waves in sport, too. It was one of the few unis to receive 24 points (full marks) in the old teaching assessments, and has led to some very good sporting facilities.

SOCIAL SCENE

STUDENTS' UNION The Union nightclub is **Sub Zero**, refurbished and rebuilt recently at a cost of £1.25

RESEARCH EXCELLENCE

% of Essex's research that is
4* *(World-class)* or **3*** *(Internationally rated):*

	4*	3*
Biological Sciences	5%	35%
Computer	15%	50%
Electrical/Electronic Eng.	20%	40%
Economics	40%	55%
Accounting and Finance	10%	45%
Law	5%	45%
Politics	45%	30%
Sociology	35%	25%
Psychology	10%	45%
English	10%	45%
Linguistics	25%	35%
Philosophy	20%	55%
History	35%	35%
History of Art	25%	50%

million; capacity 1,200, fully DDA compliant, draft products, luxurious seating areas and dancing stage. Last year Sub Zero capped an impressive first year by winning the Smirnoff BEDA award for 'best student club in the country'. Watch out for big name events on Saturday nights, the next instalments of *Flirt!* on Fridays, special one-off events to celebrate Chinese New Year and St Patricks Day, and much, much more...

Smaller is **Level 2**, an intimate 300-capacity venue that hosts regular week night events, such as *Vibez*, International night, Sports Fed, Alternative night, many a society night, and even Tango classes on Thursdays. Lords of Level 2 include Trevor Nelson, Masterstepz, Mista Jam and Shortee Blitz. Then there's **Mondo** next door - pizza joint by day and a 250-capacity venue, which can run in conjunction with Level 2 to form a 550-capacity club, by night.

Then there's laid-back **Top Bar** - juke box, real ale, big screen sports, and the option of ordering hot food from Sizzlers next door. And **SU Bar**, of course, the main, pub-type bar, with a full programme of footy and curry, karaoke nights, mini Flirt!, SU Bar disco, and the *Sunday Pub Quiz*.

In addition they tot up 120 societies and 43 sports clubs, a student newspaper called *The Rabbit*, SX:TV and Red Radio. Winner of last year's Society of the Year Award was the Law Soc, but very popular are Islamic Soc, Indie Soc, RnB Soc, Human Rights Soc, all of which run regular events for their members and the rest of campus.

TOWN 'Colchester suffers from its relative proximity to other major venues in attracting big names in entertainment,' writes Stephen Peters. 'Some occasionally grace us with their presence, but for the real stars get on the train to Cambridge or London. New talent can be seen at the local **Arts Centre**. But if you like a drink, Colchester and its environs can provide.

'Most tolerate students as long as you don't share your dinner with their toilet floor. *The Wivenhoe Run* is infamous, and has to be experienced if you reckon you can down a few. But Colchester is a garrison town. Students, squaddies and alcohol are a volatile mix. Most of the time, though, you wouldn't know they are there. Find out where not to go in town when you get here (most notably the squaddie pubs).

'The nightclubs are pretty useless. Stick to the university nightclub, and only venture to town clubs for student nights.

'Local transport links are average. Buses are frequent and not too expensive. Have the right change though, or the bus drivers, notoriously

WHAT IT'S REALLY LIKE	
UNIVERSITY:	
Social Life	★★★★
Campus scene	**Diverse, fast developing**
Student Union services	**Top notch**
Politics	**Activity high**
Sport	**43 clubs**
National team position	**49th**
Sport facilities	**Excellent**
Arts opportunities	**Good**
Student newspaper	**The Rabbit**
Student radio	**RED AM 1404**
Student TV station	**SXTV**
Nightclub	**Sub Zero**
Bars	**SU, Level 2, Mondo, Top Bar**
Union ents	**Full on**
Union clubs/societies	**120**
Parking	**No parking if you live on campus**
CITY:	
Entertainment	★★★
Scene	**Clubs 'n pubs**
Town/gown relations	**Average**
Risk of violence	**Low**
Cost of living	**Low**
Student concessions	**Adequate**
Survival + 2 nights out	**£50 pw**
Part-time work campus/town	**Excellent/good**

miserable, get a bit shirty. Trains to London are quick and reasonably reliable. And if you have a bit of money to spend, Lakeside and Bluewater are just down the road.'

SPORT The student union website has run a poll as to how many applicants chose Essex for its sport facilities. They are among the best anywhere There's a hall with six badminton courts, fitness room, sauna, sun-bed, squash courts, table tennis, climbing wall, plus a sportsturf pitch, floodlit tennis courts, three cricket pitches (one artificial wicket) plus nets, Squirrel Run circuit, 18-hole disc/frisbee-golf, grass and synthetic pitches, and a watersports centre. There are coaching courses in badminton, pilates, squash and tennis, and a relatively new Master's degree in Sports Science (Fitness and Health) is a sign of uni commitment.

City clubs offer sailing, windsurfing, canoeing.

PILLOW TALK

More new rooms have recently been built on campus for first years. More than half of students live in uni accommodation, the majority of which is

ACCOMMODATION

Guarantee to freshers	**100%**
Style	**Flats**
Security guard	**On campus**
Shared rooms	**None**
Internet access	**All**
Self-catered	**All**
En suite	**Most**
Approx price range pw	**£63-£93**
City rent pw	**£65**

All accommodation is networked, so you can use your computer to access the internet and uni network from your rooms free of charge. It has become an essential for all uni accommodation. Each room also has a telephone at Essex, which provides free use of the internal telephone system.

The uni is developing plans for new accommodation at its Southend Campus.

Students at the Loughton Campus live in house shares, often found with the assistance of East 15 Acting School.

on campus. Tesco is within walking distance of campus, so shopping is easy.

Accommodation ranges from flats for 13 to 16 in the famous Towers (tower blocks) to smaller, en-suite flats for six people - South Courts, Houses and University Quays have smaller flats containing 4 to 8 rooms, all of which have en suite facilities.

GETTING THERE
☛ By road: A12. Well served by coach services.
☛ By rail: London Liverpool Street, 1:00, every half-hour; Birmingham New Street, 3:30; Sheffield, 4:00. Ten-minute taxi run to campus.
☛ By coach: London, 2:10; Norwich, 6:15.

UNIVERSITY OF EXETER

The University of Exeter
Northcote House
The Queen's Drive
Exeter EX4 4QJ

TEL 01392 263035
FAX 01392 263857
EMAIL ug-ad@exeter.ac.uk
WEB www.ex.ac.uk

The Students' Guild
Exeter University
Devonshire House
Exeter EX4 4PZ

TEL 01392 263536
FAX 01392 263376
EMAIL info@guild.ex.ac.uk
WEB www.exeterguild.org

VAG VIEW

*E*xeter lies in South Devon, at the end of the M5 motorway. The main campus is beautifully set on a hill 15 minutes walk from the centre of the cathedral city, which itself lies close to the sea on one side and the wild open spaces of Dartmoor on the other.

It became a university in 1955 out of the University College of the South West, first established in 1922. Before that it was the School of Art (est. 1855). In the 1970s Exeter took St Luke's College of Education into the fold, and by the time Margaret Thatcher ruled the waves in the 1980s and '90s, it had a reputation as something of a haven for the green wellie brigade: the Students' Guild's web site address used to be gosh.exeter.ac.uk.

Home County hoorays invaded by the

UNIVERSITY/STUDENT PROFILE

University since	**1955**
Situation/style	**Campus**
Student population	**15720**
Undergraduates	**10815**
Mature undergraduates	**11%**
International undergrads	**6%**
Male/female ratio	**46:54**
Equality of opportunity:	
state school intake	**73%**
social class 4-7 intake	**17%**
low-participation area intake	**4%**

Porsche-full, future city slickers out for a last taste of freedom in the soft folds of the South Hams, before being tethered to their workstations to make millions.

More recently, Exeter has divested itself of

all caricature and become the University of the Year. Today it is still cresting that wave.

2008 saw an impressive 37% increase in the number of UK/EU students who made it their first choice. International recruitment was double that of the previous year. Applications to the new Cornwall Campus rose by 156% and the number of entrants by 40%.

For 2009 entry, as we go to press, UK/EU applications are 18% up, compared with a national growth of 7%. International applications are up by 82%.

In short, Exeter has become a lot of sixth formers' first choice, for the courses certainly and the interest the lecturers show in their students, and because it gives its students a very good time. In the latest Higher Education Funding Council for England's National Student Survey, 91% of Exeter's students expressed complete satisfaction, and all but 3.5% of undergraduates see their courses through.

However, in the quest for real graduate jobs six months after graduation, Exeter can report only 73% success, which does not ultimately put them among the high flyers.

CAMPUS

'The university is very easy to fall in love with,' writes Jo Moorhouse. 'It has one of the most beautiful campuses in the country, in one of the most beautiful counties in Britain.'

'Students at Exeter have the best of both worlds,' writes Julie Moore, 'a cathedral city with the countryside right on the doorstep.

'Being near the beach makes the surfing society a popular choice, and with Newquay just down the road the summer terms are filled with weekend trips and beach parties.

'Many people, myself included, made Exeter their first choice uni after one tour of the campus. A lush green settlement dotted with ponds and famous sculptures, campus has a relaxed atmosphere with some perfect spots for chilling out with friends in the sun. Everything is within walking distance, which means if you have a lecture at 9am you can get up ten minutes before and still make it. There is no shortage of shops, cafés and bars, and you have no real need to leave.

'The only thing they forget to tell you is that flat roads are a rare luxury in Exeter, and some of the student halls are at the bottom of Cardiac hill, and definitely not advised for anyone with a heart condition! The other side is that you do get used to it, but tend to laugh less at the ongoing joke about "the Exeter thighs".'

St Luke's Campus The schools of Education, Sport and Health Sciences and the Peninsula Medical School are based at St Luke's Campus, about a mile away from the main Streatham Campus. A regular bus service operates between the two.

The Cornwall Campus is the £100-million campus at Tremough, a 70-acre estate deep in Cornwall overlooking the Fal estuary. Since 2004 Exeter's dominion over the South West has been celebrated in the Combined Universities of Cornwall, a collaborative partnership with the University of Plymouth and the Peninsula Medical School, Falmouth College of Arts, the Open University in the South West, the College of St Mark & St John near Plymouth, and Cornwall's Further Education colleges - Cornwall College, Truro College and Penwith College.

The campus offers the very latest in academic, research and residential facilities. The Fal is one of the most beautiful aspects of nature in all England and worth the trip on its own.

FEES, BURSARIES

UK & EU Fees 2009-10: £3,225 p.a. There is a sliding scale bursary for students in receipt of the full HE Maintenance Grant. There are also 30+ Sports Scholarships each year, including a tailored scholarship of up to £1,000. Smaller Elite sports awards totalling £500 are also available, as are sports specific bursaries in Golf and in Men's Rugby. Performers from any sport recognised by the Athletic Union will be considered, but emphasis is placed on High Performance Target Sports - Cricket, Golf, Hockey, Rugby, Sailing and Tennis.

Ten Vice-Chancellor's Excellence Scholarships are worth £5,000 per year each; 25 Jubilee and Millhayes Science Scholarships (£2,000-£3,000 p.a.); 30 Music Scholarships, and a number of

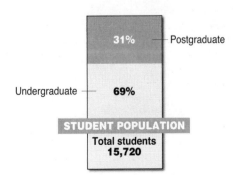

31% — Postgraduate

Undergraduate — 69%

STUDENT POPULATION
Total students
15,720

International Scholarships. See www.exeter.ac.uk/ scholarships/undergraduate and www.exeter.ac. uk/scholarships/international.

STUDENT PROFILE

For some time now Exeter has made a concerted effort to diversify its student population. The most recent national statistics show that participation of state schools is around 73%, a figure that has risen by about 4% in seven years. The take from lower socio-economic orders is some 17%, and from neighbourhoods altogether new to the idea of university, 4%. The number of international students applying is also certainly rising. But this massaging of the student population figures in the name of equality of opportunity, which is such a strange, time-consuming and expensive obsession of this Labour Government, and a job which would be far better done by schools than universities, has made little noticeable difference to campus.

ACADEMIA & JOBS

In September 2007 the first dental students joined the Medics at Peninsula, making it henceforth the Peninsula College of Medicine & Dentistry. The Dentistry course, operating on sites in Plymouth, Truro and Exeter, is a 4-year Graduate Entry Hon BDS. The programme is designed for those with a good honours degree in a biomedically related or health care professional subject, or with relevant experience of working as a health care professional. The Graduate Medical Schools Admissions Test (GAMSAT) will be required.

The Peninsula College is of course Exeter's collaboration with Plymouth University and the NHS in Devon and Cornwall, the NHS hand ensuring a strong clinical element in course design. The BM, BS degree focuses on the biological mechanisms that produce disease and its social impact. It looks very hands-on. First undergraduate intake occurred in 2002, half in

TEACHING SURVEY AT A GLANCE	
Avg. UCAS points accepted	**380**
Acceptance rate	**15%**
Overall satisfaction rate	**91%**
Helpful/interested staff	★★★★★
Small tuition groups	★★★★
Students into graduate jobs	**73%**

Teaching most popular with undergraduates:
Finance & Accounting (100%), Drama (98%), Business Studies, Management (97%), English, History, Philosophy, Theology (96%), Classics, Archaeology, Economics, Geology, Sports Science (95%), Human & Social Geography (94%), Languages (93%), Physics with Astrophysics, Politics (92%), Law, Creative Arts & Design, French, German (91%)

Teaching least popular with undergraduates:
Iberian Studies (78%), Computer Science (75%).

Exeter (at St Luke's), half in Plymouth. Both unis already had successful postgraduate medical schools. One of the key points about the new College is that it binds them tighter into the regional community. Students work initially with patients in Plymouth and Exeter, then in Truro in Cornwall, finally up with the hillbillies above Dartmoor.

You will be required to achieve 370 points from 21 units. At least 320 points must come from 3 full GCE A subjects, including at least one science and preferably one non-science subject. A minimum of C grades must be achieved at A/AS level and an A grade in a science at A-Level. A Level subjects should not overlap, e.g. Maths and Further Maths. General Studies is not included at AS or A Level.

The teaching of Medicine gets approval from 89% of its students. Far more excitement was expressed over Finance & Accounting (100%), Drama (98%), Business Studies, Management (97%), English, History, Philosophy, Theology (96%), Classics, Archaeology, Economics, Geology, Sports Science (95%), Human & Social Geography (94%), Languages (93%), Physics with Astrophysics, Politics (92%), Law, Creative Arts & Design, French, and German (91%).

Languages are especially productive of graduate jobs at Exeter - publishing, business and management, the hotel/restaurant industry, the Civil Service, and secondary education are some of the many employment areas - 19% of the total graduate employment figure - commanded by Languages. Then Social Studies looks after a further 15% of jobs (notably in accountancy, retail, estate agency, the Civil Service, travel agency,

SUBJECT AREAS (%)

Education — Combined 3
Creative Arts — 3
Medicine & Dentistry — 2
Health Subjects — 5
Science — 1
24
18
6
6
21
11
Humanities
Social Studies incl Law
Business
Maths & Computer
Engineering

recruitment & personnel, social work, community & counselling, and banking). Biological Sciences produces around 12%, adding sporting and hospital activities and jobs in higher education to the picture. There is a growing reputation at Exeter for getting graduates jobs in the world of sport. Engineering & Technology and Architecture establish the vital construction and architectural consultancy dimension; business leads into the field of insurance, among much else; computer science into software consultancy and supply; and there is a media/information technology influence, which further strengthens the muscle Exeter flexes in the publishing industry. Whether the latter is all down to Creative Media & IT, which also reaches out to advertising, is unclear, but Exeter has always had a strong extra-curricular presence in student media, which serves students well in employment.

Another particular string is a speciality in things Arabic. 'It has had a lot of inward investment from that direction,' we were told. 'It is very good on Middle Eastern languages, there's a large teaching/library facility on that side.' Arab & Islamic Studies continues to be a growth area at Exeter with rising undergrad. and postgrad. numbers and an expanding range of courses, including the introduction of Kurdish and Persian options.

'I did politics and there was quite a cross-over with Arab/Islamic, history of the Middle East, Middle East politics, etc,' said a graduate Guild officer, 'and the resource [the Institute of Arabic & Islamic Studies] is really good: letters, firsthand evidence... A lot of people don't realise that you don't have to know Arabic to study there. With the building of the institute - fantastic building! - we have got the largest Arabic Library and Middle East resource outside the Middle East and America. That may seem a bit random, here in Exeter, but the fact is that we are in the forefront on this thing, and it has a knock-on effect.'

In Law, there's an international Grade 5 for research, and they are European law specialists with LLB French Maitrise/ German Magister as well as Law with European Study/International Study.

At the Cornwall Campus they are opening an Environment and Sustainability Institute to tackle climate change and sustainability by bringing together researchers

RESEARCH EXCELLENCE		
% of Exeter's research that is		
4* *(World-class)* or **3*** *(Internationally rated):*		
	4*	3*
Hospital Clinical Subjects	5%	60%
Health Services	5%	45%
Biological Sciences	10%	40%
Physics	15%	45%
Pure Mathematics	10%	45%
Applied Maths	10%	50%
Computer Science	15%	50%
General Engineering	10%	45%
Minging, Minerals	5%	30%
Geography	20%	40%
Archaeology	15%	50%
Economics	20%	55%
Accounting	10%	45%
Business/Management	15%	45%
Law	10%	35%
Politics	20%	35%
Sociology	20%	35%
Psychology	15%	40%
Education	20%	40%
Sports	10%	25%
Middle Eastern/African	15%	25%
East European Languages	5%	55%
French	15%	35%
German	15%	40%
Italian	10%	25%
Iberian/Latin American	15%	30%
English	45%	20%
Classics	30%	30%
Theology	10%	40%
History	20%	40%
Performing Arts	35%	40%

across science, engineering and technology, the arts and humanities and the social sciences. This enlightened cross-faculty approach will also forge new BA and BSc degrees and modules.

It's difficult to see why Exeter's graduate job record is not as good as Durham's, for example. Both specialise in Languages, Social Studies, Biological Sciences, yet Durham's 80% real graduate jobs is measurably better than Exeter's 73% in the latest available statistics.

When Margaret Thatcher ruled the waves Exeter had a reputation as a haven for the green wellie brigade. More recently, it divested itself of all caricature and became University of the Year. Today it is still cresting that wave.

Everything one hears about Exeter suggests an enlightened approach, from the one-stop job-shop, **The Works**, in the Student Guild to what students say: 'Exeter is known as a university that produces students with a wide range of skills, not merely academically sound,' writes Julie Moore.

They produce a booklet outlining what you will require besides a degree to get a job at a worthwhile level in a competitive industry. There's a team of trainers to enable you to take those skills and training on board, and two recruitment fairs a year in Great Hall, plus a Law Fair because of strength in that area.

An Innovation Centre on campus provides start-up homes for small businesses, usually hi-tech. Funding is available in the region. Careers advice is given by alumni through the 'Expert' scheme, on how to get into hard-to-enter sectors like media, and non-profit organisations (charities).

Finally, the Exeter Award is an achievement award designed to enhance students' employ-ability by providing them with official recognition and evidence for future employers of extra-curricular activities that they've undertaken while at Exeter. In its first year, nearly 3,000 students signed up for the award in Exeter and Cornwall. Students can also go on to complete the Exeter Leaders Award which focuses on leadership and outstanding achievement. www.exeter.ac.uk/exeteraward.

STUDENT SCENE

THE STUDENTS' GUILD The Students' Guild Union watering holes are **The Ram**, **The Long Lounge**, **The Lemmy** nightclub. 'In the summer of 2005,' they say, 'the surrounding rooms of The Lemon Grove/Cornwall House were refurbished at a cost of £1.25 million to include state of the art sound (Funktion One) and lighting systems (as used in Ibiza clubs), a DJ booth to go with them and a state of the art air conditioning system amongst various cosmetic and structural fixes.

On quieter evenings there are open mic nights (Tuesdays or Wednesdays) and a *Cash-giveaway* quiz (every Sunday). It's also home to Big Screen Sport, with two projectors and a host of plasma screens. But the Lemmy is one of the main live venues in the South West and comes alive Friday and Saturday. 'Last year you could have seen the Kooks supporting the Subways in the Lemmy while Rooster were headlining in the Great Hall. Previous bands have included Blur, Radiohead, Coral, Muse and Keane.'

The gigs are usually public events, but the weekend 'Lemmy' is student only. Entscard holders get free admission.

Then they have the university orchestra and choral society, in the Great Hall. There's also a tradition of musicals in the Northcote Theatre, the

WHAT IT'S REALLY LIKE	
UNIVERSITY:	
Social Life	★★★★★
Campus scene	**Out-going, well-heeled, lively**
Student Union services	**Good**
Politics	**Student issues**
Sport	**Key**
National team position	**12th**
Sport facilities	**Excellent**
Arts opportunities	**Excellent, esp. theatre**
Student newspaper	**Exposé**
Student radio	**Xpression fm**
Student Radio Awards	**2005 winner**
Student TV	**XTV**
2006 Student TV Awards	**3 runners-up**
Nightclub	**The Lemmy**
Bars	**Ram, Long Lounge**
Union ents	**Lemmy disco + live acts**
Union societies	**105**
Parking	**Good; permit**
CITY:	
Entertainment	★★★
Scene	**Good pubs; average clubs**
Town/gown relations	**Average**
Risk of violence	**Low**
Cost of living	**Average**
Student concessions	**Good**
Survival + 2 nights out	**£80 pw**
Part-time work campus/town	**Average/good**

part-'pro' campus theatre. Footlights, Exeter Theatre Company and the Gilbert & Sullivan Society perform there, and the Exeter University Symphony Orchestra puts on termly concerts.

There is massive interest in media here. 'The weekly newspaper (*Expose*), currently 'Publication of the Year' following the *Guardian* Media Awards, the TV station (XTV, winner of two national awards in 2008) and student radio (Xpression fm - 2 Silvers in the 2008 nationals) have brought countless Exeter undergraduates into the business.

Someone reels off a list: 'Nick Baker, the wildlife presenter, Emma B from Radio 1, Thom Yorke of Radiohead who was a D, Isobel Lang, the weather presenter, people on the production side, like Paul Jackson who produced Red Dwarf - he came back to do a creative writing thing with the students in English, Stewart Purvis, chief exec of ITN.'

Around 400 freshers attend the Welcome to the Media event in freshers weeks. Those who stick with it are subjected to a period of training by the Exepose team.

SPORT Their £8-million facilities definitely get the thumbs up from students. New indoor tennis facilities to LTA standards opened in 2004. Said Julie: 'This uni is full of sports fanatics, excellent opportunities to join very competitive teams - it's all a very serious business. Also so many surfing, windsurfing and beach bum type societies to join.'

All major team games are well represented, also martial arts, watersports (rowing, canoeing, sailing - six Lark dinghies on the Exe Estuary) and ultimate frisbee. On-campus facilities include sports hall (basketball, netball, volleyball, tennis - there's a new LTA standard indoor/outdoor tennis centre - badminton, indoor cricket net), a climbing wall and traversing wall, rooms for fencing, martial arts, weights, etc. Pitches include 2 all-weather pitches, large grass pitch with nets area, and there are sixty off-campus acres of playing fields nearby.

TOWN 'There are certain pubs that you shouldn't really go into,' warns Juliet Oaks, 'and during Freshers Week the Students' Guild does advise you which to avoid. Also, although Exeter is a city, it is in the West Country: clubbing is not exactly the best.

;However, there is at least one student night at a club every night of the week. Entry before 10:30 is usually free or very cheap. Some of the clubs distribute tickets beforehand and these are definitely worth getting. A night out can cost around £40 if you push the boat out.

'For shopping there's enough diversity for anyone, from skaters to Goths.'

PILLOW TALK
Wide choice of good catered and self-catered accommodation. The majority of freshers take the

ACCOMMODATION	
Guarantee to freshers	**100%**
Style	**Halls, flats**
Security guard	**All**
Shared rooms	**Some halls**
Internet access	**All**
Self-catered	**Halls none, flats all**
En suite	**Some**
Approx price range pw	**£70-£171.50**
City rent pw	**£70-£85**

catered option, but 250 self-catering rooms are reserved for them too.

All the accommodation is either on campus or close by. There are en-suite rooms at ground level in the newer halls and flats suitable for disabled students, as well as some specially adapted rooms in the older residences.

With the exception of a small number of rooms in the older residences, study bedrooms have a high-speed connection to the University data network, which can be used for e-mail and Internet access. There is a modest fixed charge for this facility.

Two new self-catered residences opened in 2008 and 2009 in the city. £150 million is being spent on continuing upgrades to on-campus accommodation and the building of new residences at our Cornwall Campus.

See www.exeter.ac.uk/accommodation.

GETTING THERE
☞ By road: M5/J30.
☞ By rail: London Paddington, 2:30; Birmingham, 3:00; Plymouth, 1:15.
☞ By air: Exeter Airport is 15 mins from campus.
☞ By coach: London, 4:00; Birmingham, 4:30.

UNIVERSITY OF GLAMORGAN

The University of Glamorgan
Pontypridd
Mid Glamorgan CF37 1DL

TEL 0800 716925
FAX 01443 654050

EMAIL enquiries@glam.ac.uk
WEB www.glam.ac.uk

Glamorgan Students' Union
Pontypridd
Mid-Glamorgan CF37 1UF

TEL 01443 483500
FAX 01443 483501

EMAIL rdavies3@hotmail.com
WEB www.glamsu.com

VAG VIEW

*G*lamorgan University lies at Treforest in the Taff Valley, South Wales, a sometime coal mining village off the M4, not pretty but there are stunning views over the valley, a friendly atmosphere, and it's only 25 minutes from Cardiff's dens of iniquity by road (or you can go by train from the railway station near campus - trains run every 20 minutes).

But let's not leave before we have arrived. 'Living up here is nice,' writes Fiona Owen. 'It's nice to belong to a close-knit community. The area is scenic and there are lots of places to go for lovely walks with your friends or your new squeeze.'

There's even the odd lecture. Glamorgan lecturers get 3 stars for helpful interest in their students, which is not bad, and 3 too for small-size tuition groups. But overall only 78% gave the university their approval at the last National Student Survey, and according to statistics only 61% will get real graduate-style jobs when they leave.

A sense that this will be the case may lie behind the decision of 17.5% of them to drop out before graduation. Not many student retention rates are as poor.

However, as 2009 dawned, so a corner may have been turned. Glamorgan saw an amazing 18.4% increase in applications, smashing the UK average of 7.3%. They say this followed an impressive result in the Research Assessment Exercise 2008, 'where more than 70% of the uni's research activity was assessed as being of a quality recognised internationally for its originality, significance and rigour.'

UNIVERSITY/STUDENT PROFILE	
University since.	**1992**
Situation/style	**Rural campus**
Student population	**25465**
Undergraduates	**18280**
Mature undergraduates	**36%**
International undergrads	**7%**
Male/female ratio	**51:49**
Equality of opportunity:	
state school intake	**98%**
social class 4-7 intake	**42%**
low-participation area intake	**16%**

CAMPUS

Main campus is a couple of miles from the market town of Pontypridd. There is a new campus in Cardiff for the Creative Industries. ATRiuM, in the heart of the city centre opened in September 2007. The £35-million development brings together subjects like Animation, Film, TV and Radio, Design, Drama, Music Technology and Culture & Society.

FEES, BURSARIES

UK & EU Fees 2009-10: £3,225 p.a. Students from Wales and the EU will be eligible for a non-means tested grant (£1,940) from the Welsh Assembly Government towards the cost of tuition fees, and there's a Welsh National Bursary available to UK students with household incomes below threshold of £18,370. In addition, Entry Scholarships worth £3,000 are available to students with 300 or more UCAS tariff points, and there's a residential allowance worth £1,500 for students who come from more than 45 miles away. Then there's a Sports Scholarship for athletes who are competing at national and international level in their sport. See http://money.glam.ac.uk/.

STUDENT PROFILE

The student body is largely local, and in higher education speak, 'non-traditional'. Thirty-six per cent of undergraduates are over 21 at inception, 42% from the lowest socio-economic orders, 16% from low participation neighbourhoods.

Once on board, there's genuine warmth - 'Glamorgan University is small enough to generate real warmth and a sense of close-knit community, but large enough for you to be inconspicuous when that's what you want/need,' writes Beth Smith.

ACADEMIA & JOBS

Glamorgan's results in the National Research Assessment were indeed a considerable improvement on those of the last assessment in

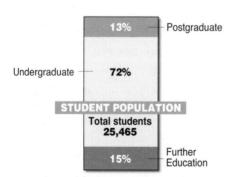

Postgraduate 13%

Undergraduate 72%

STUDENT POPULATION
Total students
25,465

Further Education 15%

2001, where they had no world-class research at all. On this occasion, part of the research in sixteen subjects was found to be either world-class or of international significance. In Nursing & Midwifery, Computer Science, Engineering, Built Environment, Business, Sport, English, History, Performing Arts, and Media between 5% and 15% of the research was world-class. English came out best, with 15% of its provision world-class and 30% of international significance.

When it came to the students turn to comment on the teaching, as opposed to the research, provision, they found the best classes were in Business, Psychology, Forensic Science, Sociology, Accounting, Biological Sciences, Computer, English, and Physical Sciences, and the worst actually in Media, where almost half the class gave it the thumbs down.

SUBJECT AREAS (%)

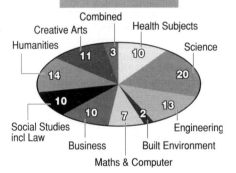

Combined **3**
Creative Arts
Health Subjects **10**
Humanities **11**
Science **20**
14
10
13
10 **7** **2**
Social Studies incl Law
Engineering
Business
Built Environment
Maths & Computer

The Computer job provision is equally disappointing, accounting for only 6% of jobs, which is surprising, as this is usually a good job area.

There are some useful occupational niches, like social work, community counselling, where degrees like Applied Psychology and the other social sciences come to play; and police work (the Forensic degrees and also Police Sciences - there's even a student society!); architectural consultancy, where the building and design degrees find jobs; and the degree in Substance Misuse, which

The sheer number of student nurses (Adult, Child, Mental Health, and Learning Disabilities) and midwives means that they dominate the graduate employment picture, with 20% of Glamorgan's graduate job share. But also contributing were degrees such as Chiropractic, Health Sciences, and Care Practice. Glamorgan's Chiropractic course is one of only 2 in the UK. The course has been accredited by both the General Chiropractic Council and the European Council on Chiropractic Education.

Next most productive of jobs is Engineering & Technology, with 16% of the share and most jobs in Defence, then in building, and in local and regional government administration.

The third most productive area is Business, which accounts for 14% of jobs, these three areas amounting to 50% of all graduate jobs at Glamorgan. The Business School is the largest in Wales.

Creative Arts & Design in Cardiff account for only 8% of the job total, and virtually none end up in artistic occupations, although it's early days.

RESEARCH EXCELLENCE

% of Glamorgan's research that is
4* (World-class) or 3* (Internationally rated):

	4*	3*
Nursing/Midwifery	**10%**	**25%**
Allied Health	**0%**	**0%**
Biological Sciences	**0%**	**10%**
Applied Mathematics	**0%**	**20%**
Computer Science	**5%**	**35%**
General Engineering	**5%**	**55%**
Built Environment	**10%**	**40%**
Business/Management	**5%**	**10%**
Law	**0%**	**15%**
Social Work	**5%**	**40%**
Psychology	**0%**	**10%**
Education	**0%**	**20%**
Sports	**5%**	**15%**
English	**15%**	**25%**
History	**10%**	**40%**
Performing Arts	**5%**	**25%**
Media Studies	**10%**	**20%**

WHAT IT'S REALLY LIKE

UNIVERSITY:	
Social Life	★★★
Campus scene	**Chummy, sporty**
Student Union services	**Good**
Politics	**Some internal**
Sport	**Competitive**
National team position	**63rd**
Sport facilities	**Good**
Arts opportunities	**Good**
Student newspaper	**Leek**
Radio station	**GTFM**
Nightclub	**Shafts**
Bars	**Baa Bar, Smiths**
Union ents	**Chart & party**
Union clubs/societies	**50**
Most popular society	**Chiropractic, LesBiGay**
Parking	**Adequate**
OFF-CAMPUS:	
Entertainment	★★
Scene	**Pubs or Cardiff**
Town/gown relations	**Mostly OK**
Risk of violence	**Average**
Cost of living	**Low**
Student concessions	**Average**
Survival + 2 nights out	**£60 pw**
Part-time work campus/town	**Average/good**

ACCOMMODATION

Guarantee to freshers	**80%**
Style	**Halls**
Security guard	**All**
Shared rooms	**None**
Internet access	**All**
Self-catered	**All**
En suite	**Most**
Approx price range pw	**£64-£82**
City rent pw	**£40-£60**

There's an active student media set-up, the student newspaper, *Leek*, and award-winning radio station, GTFM, offer plenty of challenge and opportunity, and a new society has just been set up to get Glam TV transmitting on campus and on the Internet. Besides other societies, which include the popular Chiropractic and Lesbian, Gay & Bi-sexual, Hellenic, Police Sciences and Christian Encounter - an eclectic mix - there's the uni concert band and big band, and a 40-member mixed choir. Something for everyone, you might say, but students will be students, as Stephen Harley observes: 'There are only three things that dominate every student's life: money, alcohol and sex. But if you come to Glamorgan there is a fourth thing, the mountain on which they built the university. Whenever you go down the hill from the halls of residence you should do as much as possible while you're at the bottom. The first time you go out for the evening and forget your wallet will, I promise you, be the last.

'The second point, important to note, is that the nightlife in Treforest is... well it isn't. There is a handful of good pubs which have the expected student buzz and the ents at Shafts make up for the short hours. Generally, life in Treforest is peaceful enough.' (See Student Cardiff.)

couldn't be more carefully aimed.

Again, quantity surveyors cost building projects and must have the care for detail of an accountant. Each year nationally more than 300 graduates find employment as quantity surveyors. Glamorgan has a part of that through its dedicated BSc degree.

SOCIAL SCENE

STUDENTS' UNION 'If you're a disco queen and demand that you put your spangly dancing trousers on at least a couple of times a week, the union has a formidable entertainment schedule to tease and tantalise you,' Fiona reassures.

There's **Smiths** bar/café, which serves food, snacks and drinks, accompanied by MTV, pool and arcade machines, and the gorgeously aromatic, freshly baked cookie and baguette bar. Then there's the bar - **Baa Bar**, and **Shafts** nightclub, where there's something on every night of the week, with special participation events, talent nights, etc.

> *'If you're a disco queen and demand that you put your spangly dancing trousers on at least a couple of times a week, the union has a formidable entertainment schedule to tease and tantalise you.'*

SPORT A major part of university life, in particular rugby, though in recent years, students in karate, football, hockey and basketball have also gone on to gain success at national and international level. Facilities are of a professional standard. There's a **Sports Centre** with six badminton courts, climbing wall, all indoor sports, but no swimming pool. There's a smaller hall for keep-fit, table tennis, martial arts, fencing, plus four squash courts (one glass-backed), two conditioning rooms, sauna/solarium suite, and 30 acres of floodlit pitches - football, rugby and hockey, plus trim trail, cricket pitch, archery - and one of the UK's only FIFA approved 3 'G' rubber crumb pitches. Coaching and a sports scholarship scheme are available for students at national/international level. Nearby you'll find swimming pools, golf courses, running tracks, and the Brecon Beacons for horse riding, canoeing, mountaineering, hang gliding, walking. Also sailing and windsurfing.

PILLOW TALK

Students at Cardiff Campus occupy new, privately owned halls of residence located opposite the campus. The majority of accommodation on the Treforest campus (halls) is reserved for first year students. New halls of residence will be built there in 2010.

The uni also lets houses close by, and a meal voucher service is available. New rules allow students to stay over Christmas and Easter vacs at no extra cost. Many students live in private rented accommodation locally; others in Cardiff.

GETTING THERE
☛ By road: M4/J32, A470. Exit Llantrisant, A473.
☛ By rail: London Paddington, 2:45; Birmingham, 2:15; York, 5:00.
☛ By air: Cardiff Airport.
☛ By coach: London, 4:00; Birmingham, 3:40; Bournemouth, 6:00.

STUDENT GLASGOW - THE CITY

'Glasgow - the only place in the world where you can get a free fish supper at 9 in the morning just by picking it out of the hands of a drunk who's passed out in the street the night before.' So said Rab C Nesbitt of his beloved home town, but - while there are still pockets of the city where the claim probably holds true, he neglects to mention the hundreds of other factors that make Glasgow one of the country's most popular student destinations.

Though not the capital, Glasgow is regarded by many as the only proper city in Scotland. Edinburgh may have the Parliament, Aberdeen has the oil, Dundee... is also a city, apparently, but Glasgow is where the fun is to be had. This is where the clubs, the shopping, the music venues, the theatres, Europe's (formerly the world's) tallest cinema building are. Sure, it may rain more than in any other city in Europe, but Glasgow's famous sense of humour more than makes up for that. Perhaps that's why the city now hosts Europe's largest annual comedy festival, and is the home of Scottish TV and media.

With relatively cheap rents and centrally located universities and colleges, Glasgow seems purpose-built for student living. Would-be applicants may be put off by perceived crime rates, but according to local police violent incidents are increasingly rare, and students are generally unlikely to fall victim.

In recent years the city has been changing at an incredible pace. Formerly downtrodden areas are undergoing regeneration, in keeping with a city aiming to be at the forefront of the modern Europe, while the historic sites of the old town - including one of the oldest universities in the world - are preserved as a link to the past.

Of course, should you ever find a reason to leave the city - perhaps, after the inevitable excesses of freshers' week, you just want to go and die in a field somewhere - picturesque Loch Lomond is only half an hour away.

Just remember to at least attempt to get a degree while you're here.

CITY SCENE
The Glasgow scene has launched countless stars in recent years, from Franz Ferdinand (not the one who invented World War One) to the outrageously low-camp Shahbaz, who crashed out of TV's *Big Brother* to widespread local amusement. The city boasts clubs for both extremes and all in between, from the achingly hip **Arches** and **Subclub** to student favourites the **Garage** and sticky-floored, pound-a-drink flea-pit **Jumpin' Jaks**. Glasgow is a highlight of many UK music tours, and generally the only stop in Scotland for bigger name acts. The gay scene is just as lively and varied as the rest of the city, with the **Polo Lounge** a staple and nights like **Utter Gutter** catering to the more 'extreme'.

ARTS & ENTERTAINMENT
Glasgow's arts scene is unparalleled outside of London, with a mind-boggling array of theatres,

galleries, cinemas and concert halls.

Many of the 14 major theatres offer student tickets for a fiver, bringing a night at the shows within almost any budget. All tastes are catered for - those seeking cutting-edge writing and performance need look no further than the **Arches** or the **Tramway**, more traditional fare is on offer at the **Citizens'** in the Gorbals, and shameless panto-afficionados should check out the **Kings**, or perhaps seek psychiatric advice.

Opera, ballet and classical performances can be found at the **Theatre Royal**, and the **Glasgow Film Theatre** showcases a variety of independent and classic films, complementing the blockbusters at the massive **Cineworld** complex.

The newly refurbished **Kelvingrove Art Gallery and Museum** has a wonderfully eclectic mix of exhibits, and the **Centre for Contemporary Arts** showcases the latest in design and concept art.

SPORT

Home to both of Scotland's football teams,

Glasgow affords the unique opportunity to witness the Irish troubles re-enacted weekly on the pitch, though the sectarian clashes which have marred the cityís sporting reputation have, receded in recent years. Rugby fans are still within an hour of Murrayfield by train, and those interested in more minority sports should be well served by some excellent university clubs.

PUBS

Glasgow has a thriving pub scene. Some of the lowest drinks prices in the country have cost students many a degree. Central to the life of any West End dwelling student will be Byres Road and the more upmarket Ashton Lane - try **Nude** or **Radio** for £1 cocktails, or **Uisge Beatha** for a proper pint. Those in the city centre may prefer **O'Neills'** mock-Irish charm or the classy appeal of **Royal Exchange Square**, while the **Pot Still's** world-class range of whiskies makes it well worth the trip from any part of town.

Chris Watt

● ●

UNIVERSITY OF GLASGOW

The University of Glasgow
University Avenue
Glasgow G12 8QQ

TEL 0141 330 6062
FAX 0141 330 2961
EMAIL ugenquiries@gla.ac.uk
WEB www.gla.ac.uk

Glasgow University SRC
University Avenue
Glasgow G12 8QQ

GUU: 0141 339 8697
QMU: 0141 339 9784
EMAIL enquiries@src.gla.ac.uk
WEB www.src.gla.ac.uk

VAG VIEW

*G*lasgow University was founded in 1451. *It started life on the east side in the heart of the medieval city, close to the Cathedral, which was founded only 250 or so years earlier. It moved to Gilmorehill on the more fashionable west side in 1870, where today it takes breath over beautiful Kelvingrove Park just north of the Clyde.*

Glasgow is 11th among UK universities included in the ultimate league, the World's Top 200 Universities. Its performance in a recent assessment of the UK's research provision was staggering, with between 5% and 45% of its provision across forty-one subjects rated 4-star world-class. In the

UNIVERSITY/STUDENT PROFILE	
University since	**1451**
Situation/style	**City Campus**
Student population	**25300**
Undergraduates	**18960**
Mature undergraduates	**15%**
International undergrads	**8%**
Male/female ratio	**43:57**
Equality of opportunity:	
state school intake	**87%**
social class 4-7 intake	**22%**
low-participation area intake	**3%**

HEFCE's Student Survey it commanded an 86% satisfaction rate with its students, and in the Time Higher Education's *Student*

Experience Survey it achieved the equivalent of a 4-star rating for the helpful, interested approach of its lecturers, and small-group tuition.

Alone among universities it has two Student Unions delivering second-to-none ents menus, and a third body, a Student Council, overseeing the vital area of extramural activities, in which it also excels.

Finally, the 5-star social life is carried from campus into a city whose pub, club and arts scene has been the envy of those in the know for longer than most of your parents can remember. Edinburgh has three or four clubs, Glasgow has hundreds. Above all, there is warmth, humour and a buzz on the street, an artistic energy absent on the Protestant east side of Scotland. It is, in essence, the New York of the North.

CAMPUS GLASGOW

'Glasgow itself has some wonderful sites,' writes Sharon Gaines - 'but the West End, by the university, has its own unique atmosphere. Ashton Lane winds round cobbled paths leading to the trendiest pubs in this safe and friendly part of town, while Byres Road facilitates the most extensive pub crawl - each within spitting distance. If the opulent Merchant City is the heart of the city, Great Western Road is its lungs. An old church looms over small quaint shops while half a mile of animal-like headlights shuffle slowly towards the flyover and three colossal tower blocks stand triumphantly in the distance. An awesome sight.

'If the more tranquil appeals to you, imagine gliding through a collage of a thousand colours of trees winding down a path passing two city heroes, dodging squirrels and birds until you land on a nineteenth-century bridge where the rain crashes down into the River Clyde, gushing downstream. This is the university's Kelvingrove Park - glorious in the autumn, brimming with smiling faces in the summer as everyone collates from across Glasgow on the hills.'

There are other, less widely-known Glasgow Uni campuses. St Andrew's College is the Faculty of Education, based since summer 2002 on Glasgow Caledonian Uni's old campus on Park Drive, where the West End starts. The Vet school and outdoor sports facilities are located at Garscube, with an £8-million development that includes a swimming pool, cardio-vascular suites and a wide range of gym facilities. To the south, in Dumfries, is Crichton campus, which offers

innovative study programmes to a mixture of full-time and part-time students, the first of whom are about to graduate.

FEES, BURSARIES

Fees for English: approx. £1,820 p.a. (£2,895 p.a. for Medicine). EU Fees: none to pay. Home and EU undergraduate scholarships include the BUTEX Scholarship For UK Students, the GU68 Engineers Trust, the Scottish - Italian Scholarship, the Stevenson Exchange Scholarships, and Undergraduate Talent Scholarships. There are also Sports Bursaries. See ww.gla.ac.uk/scholarships/homeandeuscholarships/.

STUDENT PROFILE

You'll not find the Southern rah brigade here that you'll find at Edinburgh. Its social balance is almost exactly that of Sussex University, Southampton, or Sheffield. There are no social divisions on campus. As one student commented, 'There's a sense of community - you cannot fail to walk down University Avenue without bumping into someone who wants to nick your lecture notes.'

ACADEMIA & JOBS

The high flyers on the world stage in the research assessment were Medicine, Computer, Economics, Library & Information Management, Psychology, Physics, English, History, History of Art, Architecture & Design, Performing Arts, Music.

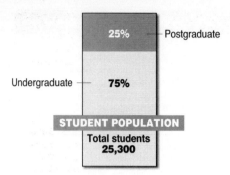

25% — Postgraduate

Undergraduate — **75%**

STUDENT POPULATION
Total students
25,300

Students' choice of best-taught subjects here are Geology, Biology, Biochemistry, Computer, Geography, Sports Science, Nursing, Comparative Literary Studies, Maths, History, Psychology, Archaeology, Finance, Accounting, Chemistry, Dentistry, Electronic & Electrical Engineering, Environmental Science, Pharmacology, Theology, Business, French, Philosophy, and subjects allied to Medicine.

Seventy-eight per cent of graduates find real graduate level jobs within six months of graduation. The areas of the curriculum most productive of these are Medicine & Dentistry (hospital, general practice), Biological

> *Eleventh among UK universities in the World's Top 200, and with a 5-star extra-mural scene that's carried from campus into a city alive with a sort of artistic energy you'll rarely find this side of New York.*

Sciences (counselling, higher education, retail, hotel/restaurant, banking, also sport and the Civil Service), Social Studies (social work, community counselling, Civil Service, hotel/restaurant, banking), and Languages (hotel/restaurant industry, specialist retail, Civil Service, community counselling, also adult/higher education, publishing and radio/TV). Graduates go into many other areas, but typically these provide 50% of the jobs Glasgow graduates get.

The degree in Medicine is a 5-year MB, characterised by clinical scenarios from Year 1, and IT featured instruction (all students are required to qualify for a Cert of Basic IT Competence). Requirements include three A level subjects - Chemistry and one from Biology, Maths or Physics. Three sciences are not required. General Studies is not acceptable. If Biology is not studied at A level it should be taken at AS or GCSE. You must have a minimum of AAB and UKCAT will be required.

For dentists, it's a 5-year BDS. Entry ABB. The Royal Veterinary College, Glasgow's 5-year BVMS Veterinary Medicine captures most of the graduate job market and is slightly lighter on entry, though still AAB.

They also have a Veterinary Nursing degree.

In addition to employment areas already mentioned, Glasgow graduates find large numbers of jobs in education, accountancy, engineering design, and sport.

For Education, it's both primary and secondary, and they turn out more adult education lecturers than anyone else. Languages are far and away the surest route in, perhaps because shortly after the acquisition of St Andrew's College of Education came the new School of Modern Languages & Cultures, which gives an international dimension to many degrees through six departments - Celtic, French, German, Hispanic, Italian and Slavonic. There's a very high research rating for the School of English & Scottish Language.

The accountancy provision comes through various dedicated degrees. Note Accountancy with International Accounting in particular, but there are others - Accountancy with Finance looks tempting. The uni is also a proven launch pad for actuaries - look at the Applied Maths degrees. Engineering and Technology degrees lead, in particular, to jobs in defence. Aeronautical, Audio & Video, Avionics, Electrical Power Engineering, Electronic & Software Engineering, etc, all pull weight in this direction and links are close with the Royal Air Force and the Royal Navy. The faculty has expanded in collaboration with Strathclyde Uni over a series of Naval Architecture degrees. There are also various BEng/MEng Aeronautical, Civil, Electronics & Electrical, Mechanical Design, Mechanical (also joint with E&E, Aeronautics, Music, etc) and Product Design.

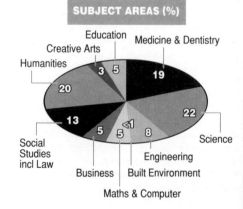

SUBJECT AREAS (%)

Education
Creative Arts
Humanities — 3 5
Medicine & Dentistry
19
20
22
13
5 <1 5 8
Science
Social Studies incl Law
Business | Built Environment
Engineering
Maths & Computer

Fighting its corner among other biological sciences for approval by the research assessors and the students is Sport. Glasgow lead in turning out physical training instructors (Education). Law also fared well in the research assessment and comes at undergraduate level with a number of language combinations. A traditionally difficult but successful area for employment is Archaeology, available single hons/joint as part of the Science Group, or as an arts degree in the popular joint hons programme.

There are masses of MA joint hons possibilities, featuring Classical Civilisation, History of Art, Archaeology, Celtic Civilisation, Scottish History, Islamic Studies, etc. History of Art, Architecture & Design came out top in the research assessment, with 45% of its provision world-class and 40% of international significance.

SOCIAL SCENE

Glasgow University Union (GUU) was founded in 1885. It is accommodated in an impressively scary-looking building at the foot of University Avenue. Both the organisation and the building were often referred to as the 'Men's Union' before women students were permitted to join in 1980. They have 6 bars: the **Beer Bar** (traditional, with the names of the campus's fastest drinkers immortalised round the bar), **Altitude**, **Deep 6** (pseudo-trendy basement music bar - live bands, karaoke, juke box - open till 2am Fridays, half price cocktails, etc.), the **Playing Fields**, **Balcony Bar**, the **Hive** (the nightclub - *Lollypop* on Thursday; *Brie* (a higher class of cheese) on Friday).

Then there is Queen Margaret's Union (QMU), which operates out of **Jim's Bar** (one of the main bars on campus), the **Games Room** (6 pool tables, masses of gaming machines and sofas), the bottle bar and **Qudos**, the 1,100 capacity nightclub, home to legendary club night **Revolution**, it has also seen awesome live acts such as Nirvana, Red Hot Chili Peppers, Franz Ferdinand, Primal Scream, Gary Numan, The Fratellis and The Dykeenies.

Qudos's main event is, however, the massively long-running *Cheesy Pop* - Fridays, 10pm - 2pm. Says one who knows: 'No two ways about it. Since 1993, when we invented the genre, *Cheesy Pop* has been the biggest and best student night in Scotland. Copied by many, but never equalled, the experience is still unique. Others interpret "cheesy" to mean crass, crap and often just down-right offensive, whereas *Cheesy Pop* is really about music which is fun. Imagine S Club, Rage Against The Machine, Abba, 2 Unlimited, Kylie and Stevie Wonder, all mixed up, then wonder why you ever considered going anywhere else.'

RESEARCH EXCELLENCE		
% of Glasgow's research that is **4*** *(World-class)* or **3*** *(Internationally rated)*:		
	4*	**3***
Cardiovascular Medicine	15%	50%
Cancer Studies	25%	50%
Infection & Immunology	5%	65%
Clinical Subjects	10%	25%
Epidemiology	10%	45%
Psychiatry%	0%	25%
Dentistry	15%	45%
Allied Health	15%	45%
Biological Sciences	15%	40%
Veterinary	5%	50%
Environmental Sciences	5%	50%
Chemistry	10%	60%
Physics	20%	40%
Pure Mathematics	15%	40%
Applied Mathematics	10%	40%
Statistics	15%	35%
Computer Science	30%	50%
Electrical/Electronic Eng.	20%	45%
Civil Engineering	15%	40%
Aeronautical Engineering	10%	35%
Marine Engineering	10%	45%
Town/Country Planning	15%	45%
Geography	10%	40%
Archaeology	10%	40%
Economics	25%	50%
Accounting	10%	35%
Business	10%	45%
Information Management	25%	30%
Law	15%	40%
Politics	15%	30%
Social Work	5%	35%
Sociology	10%	30%
Psychology	20%	40%
Education	10%	20%
European Studies	5%	35%
East European Languages	0%	5%
French	15%	30%
German	10%	25%
Italian	0%	40%
Iberian/Latin American	5%	25%
Celtic Studies	10%	50%
English	35%	35%
Classics	10%	15%
Philosophy	5%	50%
Theology	10%	35%
History	25%	35%
History of Art	45%	40%
Performing Arts	40%	45%
Music	35%	30%

WHAT IT'S REALLY LIKE

UNIVERSITY:	
Social Life	★★★★★
Campus scene	**Lively, diverse, fantastic fun**
Student Union services	**5-star**
Politics	**Activity average Student issues**
Sport	**45 clubs**
National team position	**29th**
Sport facilities	**Good**
Arts opportunities	**Drama, music, art exc; dance good; film average**
Student newspaper	**GU Guardian**
2006 Guardian Award	**Features**
Student magazine	**GUM, Qmunicate, GUUi**
Student radio	**SubCity Radio**
2008 Radio Awards	**Sikver award**
Student TV	**G.U.S.T.**
TV Awards	**2006 runner-up**
Nightclubs	**Qudos, Hive**
Bars	**Jim's Bar, Beer Bar, Deep-6, Altitude, Playing Fields**
Union ents	**Cheesy Pop rules + rock & indie, live**
Union societies	**120**
Most active society	**Dialectic or LGBT (lesbian, gay, bi- & transgender)**
Parking	**Poor**
CITY:	
Entertainment	★★★★★
Scene	**Very cool**
Town/gown relations	**Good**
Risk of violence	**High**
Cost of living	**High**
Student concessions	**Poor**
Survival + 2 nights out	**£80 pw**
Part-time work campus/town	**Poor/good**

Tuesday is *Revolution*, the ultimate night for lovers of rock, metal, punk, and emo. Last year in Freshers Week they brought Hayseed Dixie, the alt-bluegrass-hillbilly-country hard rock cover band to the stage - AC/DC, Motorhead, Aerosmith and Queen all got the banjo-and-washboard treatment. The set also featured the Kazoo Funk Orchestra and DJ Martin Bate.

The Students Representative Council (SRC) is the political arm of the Union and administers 120 student societies, supports volunteers and class representatives and is the official voice of the students on campus, constantly running Environment & Sustainability campaigns and the like.

Mention must be made of the lively journalistic scene: Subcity Radio the SRC-run *Guardian* (newspaper), the *Glasgow University Magazine* (*GUM*, oldest student magazine in Scotland), the two Union publications, *GUUi* and *Qmunicate*, and GUST (oldest student TV station in the UK).

Then there is GUSA, the Sports Association founded in 1881.

SPORT Excellent facilities, including a 25m pool, steam room and sauna, two activity halls with sprung flooring, basketball, volleyball, five-a-side soccer; a fitness and conditioning area, fully equipped. Bursaries are offered in squash, athletics, rowing, and golf. There are some forty golf courses in the area. The university came 29th in the national student team sports last year.

PILLOW TALK

Catered or self-catered halls of residence and self-catered student apartments are available, 7% catered, 23% en suite. See Accommodation box for prices and look out for Queen Margaret Residences - 400 places all new, all en suite.

ACCOMMODATION

Guarantee to freshers	**100%**
Style	**Halls, flats**
Security guard	
Shared rooms	
Internet access	
Self-catered	**Most**
En suite	**Some**
Approx price range pw	**£74-97**
City rent pw	**£85-£110**

GETTING THERE

☞ By road: M8/J19 or J18. Good coach services.
☞ By rail: Edinburgh, 50 mins; London King's Cross, 5:00. Main campus Underground Station is Hillhead.
☞ By air: Glasgow Airport.
☞ By coach: London, 8:20; Birmingham, 6:20; Newcastle, 4:20.

GLASGOW CALEDONIAN UNIVERSITY

Glasgow Caledonian University
70 Cowcaddens Road
Glasgow G4 0BA

TEL 0141 331 3000
FAX 0141 331 3005
EMAIL helpline@gcal.ac.uk
WEB www.caledonian.ac.uk

Glasgow Caledonian Students' Association
70 Cowcaddens Road
Glasgow G4 0BA

TEL 0141 331 3886
FAX 0141 353 0029
EMAIL student.association@
glasgow.caledonian.ac.uk
WEB www.caledonianstudent.com

VAG VIEW

*G*lasgow Caledonian is located on the
east side of the city on Cowcaddens
Road, opposite the Bus Station and close to
Buchanan Street shopping mall and George
Square, where famously the military once
met a strike of 80,000 as if it were a
Bolshevik uprising, with troops, tanks, a
howitzer, and machine gun nests around
the city centre.

Things have changed since 1919, when
Lenin was pin-up boy in the shipyards.
Glasgow Caledonian takes no noticeable
political line, but it is in some way a
university of the people.

Founded in 1971, it took title in 1992,
along with all the nation's polytechnics.
Since then they have centralised operations
on one site instead of five, opened new
accommodation, a Sports Centre, a £17-
million Health building and a new
Learning Centre called the Saltire Centre.
Their promise of a new Student Union
building has been fulfilled and perhaps we
will see a more concentrated effort to get an
extra-curricular, student culture together.

It is a large student body, some 17,000
souls, 85% of whom expressed themselves
satisfied with what the uni is up to in the
recent National Student Survey. It is a real-
world institution, with close links with
industry and the public sector, and a savvy
approach to drawing up a curriculum.

They get 77% of their students real
graduate jobs within six months of leaving.
There's a 13% drop-out, but that, it seems,
is part of the profile.

UNIVERSITY/STUDENT PROFILE	
University since	**1992**
Situation/style	**City campus**
Student population	**17450**
Undergraduates	**13920**
Mature undergraduates	**43%**
International undergrads	**3%**
Male/female ratio	**40:60**
Equality of opportunity:	
state school intake	**96%**
social class 4-7 intake	**35%**
low-participation area intake	**4%**

CAMPUS

City campus is part of an amazing con-centration
of some 50,000 students. Close to Caley are
Strathclyde University, the College of Building and
Printing, the College of Food & Technology, and
the College of Commerce are in the immediate
vicinity.

FEES, BURSARIES

Fees for English: approx. £1,820 p.a. EU Fees: none
to pay. Look out for the £5,000 p.a. Magnus
Magnusson Awards, the £3,600 p.a. Moffat
Scholarships, the £1,000 p.a. Masterton
Undergraduate Bursaries in Civil Engineering, and

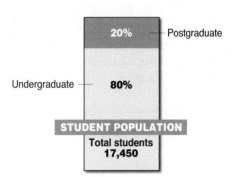

TEACHING SURVEY AT A GLANCE

Avg. UCAS points accepted	**298**
Acceptance rate	**17%**
Overall satisfaction rate	**85%**
Helpful/interested staff	★★★
Small tuition groups	★★★
Students into graduate jobs	**77%**

Teaching most popular with undergraduates:
Anatomy, Physiology & Pathology, Medical Science & Pharmacy (96%), Biology & related science, Law, Social Studies (95%), Psychology (92%), Medical Technology (91%), Complementary Medicine, Nursing, Ophthalmics (90%), Computer (89%), Finance (88%), Accounting, Built Environment (87%), General Engineering (84%), Business, media (80%).

Teaching least popular with undergraduates:
Marketing (76%).

the sports bursaries programme. See www.gcal.ac.uk/arc/bursary.html and www.moffat centre.com/scholarships/index.html and www.gcal.ac.uk/giving/magnusscholarship.html.

STUDENT PROFILE

'Most of Caley's recruits,' writes Rachel Richardson, 'are home-based students looking for a more vocational course.' Statistically, 43% of undergraduates are mature. Many are local, but the university is putting that right with a convincing appeal beyond the EU. It took first place in the *Times Higher Education* Awards in 2008 for Outstanding Support for Overseas Students, and for the third time in a row, it was rated Scotland's best international student experience in the International Student Barometer survey, carried out by independent research specialists' i-graduate.org.

Its home contingent is all but 1% state school educated; 35% come from the lower socio-economic bracket, 4% from neighbourhoods which until recently, we are told, never dreamt of taking a degree. Caley has been awarded the Frank Buttle Trust quality mark for support to students who come to university from public care.

ACADEMIA & JOBS

In the recent assessment of all our universities' research provision, Glasgow Caledonian was ranked first in Scotland in subjects allied to Medicine and second in Built Environment. In the UK at large it figured in the Top 10 and Top 20 respectively in these areas for research.

These are its great strengths. Forty per cent of graduate jobs come out of degrees in subjects related to Medicine (Nursing, Operation Department Practice, Occupational Therapy, Physiotherapy, Podiatry, Radiation Oncology Science, Biomedicine, Diagnostic Imaging Science, Food

RESEARCH EXCELLENCE

% of Glasgow Cal's research that is
4* *(World-class) or* **3*** *(Internationally rated):*

	4*	3*
Vision Sciences	**5%**	**25%**
Allied Health Professions	**15%**	**45%**
Applied Mathematics	**5%**	**5%**
Computer Science	**0%**	**15%**
General Engineering	**0%**	**20%**
Buikt Environment	**15%**	**45%**
Accounting/Finance	**0%**	**15%**
Business/Management	**0%**	**25%**
Law	**0%**	**15%**
Sociology	**5%**	**5%**
Psychology	**0%**	**10%**
Education	**0%**	**25%**
History	**10%**	**25%**
Media Studies	**10%**	**15%**

Bioscience, Human Biology, Nutrition Dietetics). The university's School of Nursing Midwifery and Community Health is one of the biggest nursing education providers in Scotland. But besides the Nursing, principal wage earners on the curriculum are Optometry and Ophthalmic Dispensing - Biomedical and Vision Science also got them world-class recognition in the research assessment. Caledonian's Department of Vision Sciences is the only vision science teaching establishment in Scotland.

Second star in the graduate employment firmament is Business. A dedicated Accountancy

SUBJECT AREAS (%)

Combined
Humanities
Social Studies incl Law
Health Subjects
Science
6
3
1
28
30
10
Business
9
6
7
Maths & Computer
Built Environment
Engineering

degree is a good prospect. Otherwise, Business steers graduates primarily into specialist retail, the hotel and restaurant industry, government administration, banking, security broking, fund management, and personnel.

The next most successful employment providers at Caledonian are Engineering & Technology and Built Environment. As for Health, so for Built Environment: 15% of their research work was found to be world-class, 45% of international significance. This and Engineering find jobs in construction, in government planning departments, and in all sorts of architectural and engineering activities. Engineering also trains students up for jobs in design consultancy. As such, it is completely compatible with Built Environment's degrees in Surveying and Quantity Surveying, Building Services and Construction Management. Together they account for 16% of all jobs for graduates at Caledonian.

Now there's a media niche emerging. Again this department did well at the research assessments, and is a popular one with students - degrees in Journalism, Interactive Media Creation /Design, Audio Technology, and this year MA Multimedia Journalism and MA Television Fiction Writing, although as yet employment figures are a bit bleak here. A few go into publishing, one or two into radio, TV, and film. Otherwise it's into teaching, the hotel industry and other less clearly related fields. But these are early days and maybe, as elsewhere among universities, it is an area that could be encouraged by extra-curricular student enthusiasm.

The trouble is that Caledonian has never been very active extra-murally. The large mature, local and part-time population is suggested as the reason for the relatively low level of action. The challenge is that after nightfall and at weekends the place is deserted, while in the day, the bars can be full to overflowing. Might all this be about to change?

SOCIAL SCENE

STUDENT ASSOCIATION Media-wise *Re:Union* is the student magazine, and Radio Caley is their brand new radio station, launched in February 2009.

Meanwhile, the SA has moved lock, stock and barrel to a newish building the other side of campus (previously used by Human Resources!).

The **Hanover Students Union Bar** is, as if you would never guess, the Student Union bar in the North Hanover Street Building. Typical fare - pub quizzes, *Superstar Karaoke*, comedians, Hypnotist Hugh Lennon and the Hypnodog. But Friday evening is live from the city that gave you all from the Sensational Alex Harvey Band through to Glasvegas and the Fratellis.

WHAT IT'S REALLY LIKE	
UNIVERSITY:	
Social Life	★★
Campus scene	**Friendly**
Student Union services	**Average**
Politics	**Activity low**
Sport	**On the rise.**
National team position	**81st**
Sport facilities	**Average**
Arts opportunities	**Slim**
Student magazine	**Re:Union**
Venue	**The Bedsit**
Bars	**SUB Bar**
Union ents	**Quiz, Caleyoke, cheesy disco, live acts**
Union clubs/societies	**Handful**
Parking	**Poor**
CITY:	
Entertainment	★★★★★
Scene	**Cool**
Town/gown relations	**Good**
Risk of violence	**Average**
Cost of living	**Average**
Student concessions	**Good**
Survival + 2 nights out	**£70 pw**
Part-time work campus/town	**Good.**

On the night we were there six bands with some interesting talent emerged: Daniel Wylie who fronted Cosmic Rough Riders, the Castlemilk boys who sold over 130,000 copies of an album called The Melodic Sunshine, the support shows with U2, the Black Crowes, and Led Zeppelin's Robert Plant. The Meatmen feature ex-Ronelles guitar men Del Meade and Richard Anderson, who not only played with the likes of Kings of Leon and the Zutons, but topped the charts in Japan. Local to Glasgow, just an ordinary old Friday 13th.

Then there's **the Hub**, info and resource centre for sports clubs and societies. Students use it to organise student activities for socs like Alpha for Students, Amnesty International, Chinese Students Association, Christian Union, Music Soc, Muslim Soc, GT Events, Hellenic Society, International Students, Lesbian, Gay, Bisexual Society, SSOS. There are now 27 societies, many more than there were. A Faith and Belief Centre, 'where our many religious and philosophical-belief based student groups can worship together', opened last year.

Finally, **Arc** gives access to health and fitness services and facilities, including a gym, a place to relax and de-stress at a yoga or t'ai chi class, to work out, play badminton or book in for a therapeutic massage session.

See also Student Glasgow.

ACCOMMODATION

Guarantee to freshers	**No guarantee**
Style	**Halls, flats**
Security guard	**All**
Shared rooms	**Some**
Internet access	**All**
Self-catered	**All**
En suite	**Most**
Approx price range pw	**£75-£85**
City rent pw	**£85-£110**

SPORT Investment in sport facilities has been rewarded with great success in the British Uni Sport Association (BUSA) league. They have zipped up from the depths to take 81st position. There are 26 sports clubs: American football, rugby, soccer (male and female), athletics catered for alongside such as snowboarding, hillwalking and table tennis. It's the Bearsden dry ski slopes for GCU Club Ski and the real white stuff for weekends in semester two. The Hillwalking and Mountaineering Club is the largest - weekends away in Glen Coe.

PILLOW TALK
For lucky first years, it's Caledonian Court, adjacent to campus, 6-8 bedroom flats.

GETTING THERE
☞ By road: M8/J19 or J18. Good coach services.
☞ By rail: 50 minutes Edinburgh, 5 hours London.
☞ By Underground: Cowcaddens and Buchanan Street Stations are nearby.
☞ By air: Glasgow Airport.

UNIVERSITY OF GLOUCESTERSHIRE

The University of Gloucestershire
Park Campus
Cheltenham
Gloucestershire GL50 4BS

TEL 01242 714501
FAX 01242 543334
EMAIL admissions@glos.ac.uk
WEB www.glos.ac.uk

Gloucestershire Uni Students' Union
PO Box 220
The Park
Cheltenham GL50 2RH

TEL 01242 714360
FAX 01242 261381
EMAIL union@glos.ac.uk
WEB www.yourstudentsunion.com

VAG VIEW

*G*loucestershire University was born out of Cheltenham & Gloucester College of Higher Education in 2001, following a merger between the College of St Paul and St Mary and the higher education section of Gloucestershire College of Arts and Technology. No need to ask where it is based.

It fared so-so at the hands of its students in the 2008 National Survey: 70% are happy with what they do, 72% get real graduate jobs within six months of leaving.

But when asked by the Times Higher Education *magazine about their lecturers, the students were much more forthcoming. There is clearly a good rapport. This is a teaching university, where personal help and interest in you will be an important part of the deal. So no surprise that the drop-out* rate is a relatively tame 7%.

UNIVERSITY/STUDENT PROFILE

University since	**2001**
Situation/style	**Campus**
Student population	**8745**
Undergraduates	**6730**
Mature undergraduates	**20%**
International undergrads	**4%**
Male/female ratio	**43:57**
Equality of opportunity:	
state school intake	**95%**
social class 4-7 intake	**32%**
low-participation area intake	**8%**

CAMPUS
There are three sites in Cheltenham. Park Campus is the main site, then there's Francis Close Hall (FCH) and Pittville. When you turn up at Park,

don't confuse it with the nearby Gloscat, monstrous further education establishment in crying need of a facelift. No, this is the one up the road that copped the dosh. The main campus is leafy, white, with everything (halls, bars, lecture theatres) close to hand and spanking new it seems, though many of the buildings must have been here for some time. It was once a botanic garden.

The newer £15-million Oxstalls Campus has opened in the nearby city of Gloucester. It was part of their remit that they would open up there. It is being used by the schools of Sport and Nursing, but will be developed and the subject base widened. There's a Student Union building, halls of residence for completion this year, a refectory and astroturf, a sports science building and learning resources centre. .

FEES & BURSARIES

UK & EU Fees 2009-10: £3,225 p.a. Relief on a sliding scale for those meeting the conditions of the Higher Education Maintenance Grant. There is an Open Sport Scholarship worth £500 - see resources.glos.ac.uk/faculties/shsc/recoutreach/scholarships/index.cfm. Full-time students who either sing in the University choir, or play in the Orchestra may be entitled to a bursary. See resources.glos.ac.uk/music/index.cfm.

Eligibility for a £500 Academic Scholarship turns on a student gaining 360 UCAS tariff at A level, BTec or equivalent, in one sitting.

STUDENT PROFILE

Broadly, Pittville attracts interesting/arty-types, Park be-suited-&-booted business management-types. Like Oxford Brookes, and unusual in a new-uni demography, there was once a lean to independent school types. Now, on the Government's say-so, the intake of the lower socio-economic orders has risen to 32%, and they take 9% from so-called low-participation neighbourhoods, while public school types have dwindled to only 5%. Despite big changes, students talk of the 'really great sense of community', unusual for a multi-campus institute.

ACADEMIA & JOBS

First degree subjects fall under 3 faculty heads: Arts & Education (split between Park and Pittville), Business & Social Studies (Park), Environment & Leisure (FCH and Oxstalls). The programmes (BA/BSc Hons) are modular and very broad based. There is a choice of single, joint or major/minor courses, each of them composed of more than twenty modules with often less than clear synergy between subjects.

Hundreds of main subject combinations are offered, from which you will build your course. It

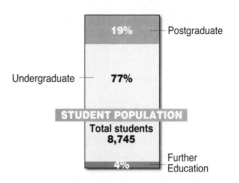

STUDENT POPULATION

Undergraduate — **77%**

19% — Postgraduate

Total students
8,745

4% — Further Education

can be quite daunting.

In last year's national assessment of all our universities, Gloucestershire's research provision was found to be world-class in 5% of four subjects subjects submitted - Planning, English, History, and Art & Design, and in 10% of Education.

Subjects Glos students say are best taught are English, Languages, Law, Geographical Studies, Geography, Environmental Science, Initial Teacher Training, Sports Science, History & Philosophical Studies, Management Studies, Film, Education. Students are least happy with the teaching in Media Studies and Journalism (the research provision didn't attract the assessors much either), but this has little effect upon the graduate employment picture, as we will see.

Subjects most productive of graduate jobs are Business (20%), Education (17%), Biological Sciences (including Sport) (12%), Art (12%), Media (10%), Computer Science (10%), Social Studies (7%).

The Business degrees earmark their students for particular employment areas - marketing,

TEACHING SURVEY AT A GLANCE

Avg. UCAS points accepted	**250**
Acceptance rate	**22%**
Overall satisfaction rate	**79%**
Helpful/interested staff	★★★★
Small tuition groups	★★★
Students into graduate jobs	**72%**

Teaching most popular with undergraduates:
English (93%), Languages, Law (92%), Geographical Studies (91%), Physical Geography & Enviro. Science (90%), Initial Teacher Training (89%), Sports Science (84%), History & Philosophical Studies (83%), Management Studies (82%), Cinematics & Photography, Education (80%).

Teaching least popular with undergraduates:
Media Studies (59%), Journalism (54%)...

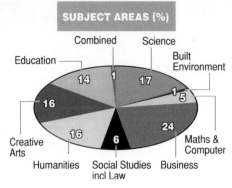

SUBJECT AREAS (%)

- Combined 1
- Science 17
- Built Environment 5
- Education 14
- Maths & Computer 24
- Creative Arts 16
- Humanities 16
- Social Studies incl Law 6
- Business

human resources, etc., but 10% of them end up in the hotel and restaurant business, which suggests that the Hospitality Management degree has muscle, and there's a niche in sport through the Business Management & Sports Development/ Sport & Exercise Science degrees.

Among those studying Education, well over half become primary school teachers. Again, sport is a favourite alternative destination, as is community work, government administration, and the ubiquitous hotel and restaurant trade.

Of those studying Biological Sciences, which includes the many Sports Science degrees, 16% get jobs in the sports industry, but many more go the teaching route, or into the hotel/restaurant industry. Some find work as sports gurus in the community, youth work, etc, but Glos graduates who find work in the community as carers tend to progress through Social Studies/Sciences. There is a whole range of degrees, like School, Youth & Community

Work, Youth Work, Social Work, and the BSc Psychology. Other degrees, Applied Theology, Children & Family Work & Practical Theology, for example, remind us that Glos was fathered by two church colleges, and that Lord Carey, former Archbishop of Canterbury, is University Chairman.

For graduates seeking work in the creative arts or media (significant destinations for Glos graduates), there are well-directed named degrees in Advertising, Film Management/Production, Radio Production, TV Production, Broadcast Journalism, Publishing (Books and Magazines), also Photojournalism.

SOCIAL SCENE

'Cheltenham & Gloucester is a fab, mad, lovely place,' I was told and didn't find much to contradict it. There are four bars, one on each campus. A workmanlike ents programme makes good use of the large, airy **Park Bar**, in Cheltenham, with stage and seriously provocative sound and lighting systems.

Fancy dress parties proliferate, with *Drink Around The World* events, a different country represented at each of the three bars. There's karaoke, fun and games type *Open-the-Box* drink promo nights, Bingo, various balls (the Summer Ball sells

---

RESEARCH EXCELLENCE

% of Gloucestershire's research that is
4* *(World-class) or* **3*** *(Internationally rated):*

	4*	3*
Planning	5%	35%
Geography	0%	15%
Business/Management	0%	10%
Social Work	0%	10%
Psychology	0%	10%
Education	10%	15%
Sports	0%	10%
English	5%	30%
Theology	0%	40%
History	5%	20%
Art and Design	5%	5%
Media Studies	0%	0%

WHAT IT'S REALLY LIKE

UNIVERSITY:	
Social Life	★★★
Campus scene	**Middle of the road, local**
Politics	**Interest low**
Student Union	**Good**
Sport	**Very competitive**
National team position	**40th**
Arts opportunities	**OK, film good**
Student newspaper	**Space**
Student Radio	**Tone Radio**
Nightclub	**Sub:Mission @ Park**
Bars	**Park, Pittville, FCH and Oxstalls**
Union ents	**Cheesy + huge Balls**
Union societies	**70**
Parking	**Poor**
TOWN:	
Entertainment	★★★
Scene	**OK clubs, pubs, good shopping**
Risk of violence	**Average**
Cost of living	**High**
Student concessions	**Excellent**
Survival + 2 nights out	**£70-£80 pw**
Part-time work campus/town	**Good**

upwards of 7,000 tickets, then there's Christmas Ball, Freshers Ball, Graduation Ball) and the odd *Doctors & Nurses* night, with *Sub:Mission* the big Saturday night attraction. Also some local live bands do their thing. Sports bar, **Oxtalls**, at the Gloucester campus is big on match days, of course.

It is fair to point out, however, that the emphasis is on club-nights in town with the local SU bar providing a kind of pre-club, warm-up session, and at weekends it's quiet.

Nevertheless, there is a sense of the society scene maturing. *Space* is the excellent fortnightly newspaper, Tone Radio the student radio station, and they were runners-up for a Guardian/Sky News Broadcaster of the Year Award in 2008. The Film Society is also very active. PDS (The Pittville Degree Show Society) puts on charity fund raisers throughout the year. The Art Society delivers fine shows at the end of each year in Pittville.

SPORT They do well in the BUSA leagues (40th nationally last year). It's their big thing. There is a swimming pool, sports hall, pitches (known as The Folley), a fitness suite, and at Oxstalls a sports science lab and astro turf pitch.

TOWN Cheltenham itself has fantastic shops (classy, unique and your high street shops too), some good pubs, the Arts Centre and a few clubs. 'Gold Cup Week brings the Irish to town and loadsa money,' a student confides, 'a great week for all the girls to go out. You get plied with drink after drink. This week is RAG week, just the best week of the academic calendar!! Tons of fun and misbehaviour, being on a

ACCOMMODATION	
Guarantee to freshers	**85%**
Style	**Halls, flats**
Security guard	**All**
Shared rooms	**Some**
Internet access	**All**
Self-catered	**Most**
En suite	**Most**
Approx price range pw	**£69-£102**
City rent pw	**£60-£80**

float, driven in front of crowds of people, drunk in charge of a water pistol by 9am, expecting a lot of "cheek" from the rugby boys. And all for charity!.' Is it always so...baby doll? we wonder. 'Well, Christmas carols in FCH chapel are always a laugh...specially with all that mulled wine in you.'

PILLOW TALK

Apply early for the luxurious-looking, mixed, self-catered or half-board halls at Park. Priority goes to first years and overseas students. New halls in Gloucester and 100-room Regency Halls in central Cheltenham opened in September 2006.

GETTING THERE

☛ By road: M5/J11 or M40/A40 or M4/J15, A419. Good coach service.
☛ By rail: Bristol Parkway, 45 mins; Birmingham, 1.00; London Paddington, 2:30.
☛ By coach: London, 2:35; Birmingham, 1:10.

GLYNDWR UNIVERSITY

Glyndwr University
Plas Coch
Mold Road
Wrexham LL11 2AW

TEL 01978 293439
FAX 01978 290008
EMAIL sid@glyndwr.ac.uk
WEB www.glyndwr.ac.uk

Glyndwr Students' Guild
Plas Coch
Mold Road
Wrexham LL11 2AW

TEL 01978 293226
FAX 01978 293227
EMAIL guildbar@newi.ac.uk
WEB www.newi.ac.uk

VAG VIEW

*G*lyndwr is a new university, located on the north western side of Wrexham in North East Wales. Wrexham is on the borders of Wales and England within easy motoring of Chester and Liverpool.

We know it of old at the Virgin Guide, *before the founding of so many new universities precluded the anomalous FE colleges that also offered degree courses. Now, NEWI, as it was called then, has made it into the upper echelons.*

NEWI stood for the North East Wales

Institute. It was a small college of the University of Wales, founded in 1975, of about 4,200 souls, very much part of the local community, which has a sound artistic tradition. Theatre Clwyd, at nearby Mold, for example, is a draw to top-flight theatre and opera companies, and the International Eisteddfod is held at Llangollen.

Now NEWI has almost doubled its student population, still projects itself as part of the local scene, but is reaching out to the world, and to that end has adopted a new name, and not any name.

Glyndwr is the name of a celebrated Welsh warrior chieftain with a touch of magic at his fingers.

Owain Glyndwr, anglicised by Shakespeare as Owen Glendower, was in fact the last native Welsh person to hold the title Prince of Wales, before it was yielded to the British Crown. He was the man behind the Welsh Revolt against Henry IV of England. When it was put down, he disappeared. Never captured or tempted by Royal Pardons, nor ever betrayed, Glyndwr was last seen in 1412. His final years a mystery, he passed into Welsh myth.

The name is an excellent choice, so long as they're not counting on tempting too many English across the border.

They run a tight ship at Glyndwr and thoroughly deserve the chance to develop into a university. It is all before them.

CAMPUS

There are two main sites within five minutes' walk of each other.

Plas Coch is headquarters. It may be found along the Mold Road, between Wrexham's Racecourse football ground and a retail park containing a supermarket, a multi-screen cinema, and a number of restaurants and other shops.

Plas Coch houses most of the programmes. Techniquest Glyndwr, the Science Discovery Centre, is based here, as is William Aston Hall, the key venue in Wrexham for concerts and live entertainment. The 900-seat hall stages plays and concerts - classical and pop/rock, and has a bar. The BBC National Orchestra of Wales plays here, and it has also attracted the likes of Billy Bragg, and Buddy Holly's Winter Dance Party 2009.

Also on site are a number of excellent places to eat and drink, including the **Scholar's Rest** refec-

UNIVERSITY/STUDENT PROFILE	
University since	**2008**
Situation/style	**Campus**
Student population	**7603**
Undergraduates	**2500**
Mature undergraduates	**70%**
International undergrads	**3%**
Male/female ratio	**40:60**
Equality of opportunity:	
state school intake	**99.7%**
social class 4-7 intake	**46%**
low-participation area intake	**18%**

tory and three coffee shops. The Glyndwr University Student Village is situated at the northern edge of the site, a short distance from the library, supermarkets and the Students' Guild.

The **Terry Hands Theatre** also opened here in 2006, following a £130,000 investment in NEWI's Theatre and Performance facilities. It is named after the man who founded the famous Liverpool Everyman Theatre in 1964, and is now the Director of **Clwyd Theatre Cymru**.

The second site, the North Wales School of Art & Design, is 10 minutes' walk away in Regent Street, in the centre of town. Not much more to say about Regent Street campus except that it has apparently developed 'its own artistic culture, obvious as soon as you enter the building. Murals and exhibitions show the remarkable talent that exists in art and design at Glyndwr University'.

There are also plans to develop facilities for land-based education on the 91-hectare site of the Welsh College of Horticulture, in Northop, Flintshire.

FEES, BURSARIES

UK & EU Fees, 2009-10: £3,225 p.a. Welsh students receive a Welsh Assembly Government fee remission grant of £1,940. In addition, the Glyndwr

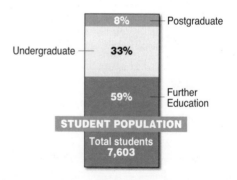

Postgraduate 8%
Undergraduate 33%
Further Education 59%
STUDENT POPULATION
Total students
7,603

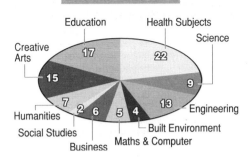

University bursary is available to those in receipt of the full HE Maintenance Grant, the exact amount awarded dependent on family income. They also offer the £1,000 Excellence scholarship for applicants with 300 UCAS Tariff points. Then there's the Gifted Athletes Scholarship, worth £1,800. And the Care Leavers Scholarship, for those who were once in Care.

STUDENT PROFILE

As expected, most of the students come from the locality at this stage, and 70% of them are mature. There are more women than men (60/40), as is usual when there's a Nursing and Primary Education provision, as here.

The student profile is in every way 'new' university, most students are local, 57% part-timers. Their local college turned into a university, and suddenly they found they were university undergraduates.

ACADEMIA & JOBS

The academic portfolio includes Art & Design, Built Environment, Business, Communications

TEACHING SURVEY AT A GLANCE	
Avg. UCAS points accepted	**220**
Acceptance rate	**17%**
Overall satisfaction rate	**80%**
Helpful/interested staff	**No data**
Small tuition groups	**No data**
Students into graduate jobs	**77%**

Teaching most popular with undergraduates:
Sports Science (96%), Biological Sciences (85%), Initial Teacher Training (84%), Architecture, Building (83%).

Teaching least popular with undergraduates:
Design Studies (59%).

Technology, Complementary Medicine, Computing, Education, Engineering, Health & Social Care, Humanities, Information Management, Languages, Science & Environment, Social Work & Criminal Justice, Sport & Exercise Sciences, Youth & Community.

Art & Design actually produces more employed than any other department, a very healthy 26% of them actually going into artistic creative work, which is unusual. There are courses like Animation, Fashion, Illustration, Fine Art, and Digital Media Design & Production - so traditional and new. The employment sector that attracts most of Glyndwr graduates, however, is hospital work, mainly but far from exclusively drawn from the Health School, which offers Occupational Therapy as well as Nursing. There are degrees in Complementary Medicine and Complementary Practice too, supported by an 8-bed Chinese Medicine Clinic with its own herbal pharmacy.

Primary teaching and social work, community

RESEARCH EXCELLENCE		
% of Glyndwr's research that is		
4* *(World-class)* or **3*** *(Internationally rated):*		
	4*	**3***
Nursing & Midwifery	**0%**	**25%**
Computer Science	**5%**	**35%**
Metallurgy & Materials	**5%**	**30%**
Social Work	**0%**	**20%**
Education	**0%**	**5%**
Art & Design	**0%**	**5%**

and counselling activities are other common employment destinations for graduates from a number of departments, notably of course from Education and Social Studies. Thirty-eight per cent of people who study in the Education school become primary school teachers. Among the Social Study degrees are Social Work, Addictive Behaviours (Substances), and Youth & Community.

The Engineering school is another key element, with degrees in Aeronautical & Mechanical Engineering, Automotive Engineering, and Motorsport.

There is also a multiplicity of media degrees. Television, Music Technology, Radio Production, Studio Recording & Sound Technology, Broadcast Journalism, etc. There are relatively few making it into the professional media yet, however: a handful into the film industry and radio and TV.

SOCIAL SCENE

STUDENTS UNION The new Students' Guild offers the usual ents, discos, quizzes in the bar. The main eaterie is the **Scholar's Rest**. Other outlets at Plas Coch include **Fellows Café Bar**, **Chapters Retail & Café Bar** (an 'essentials' shop), and **Café Darganfod**.

SPORT There is a Sports Centre at the heart of the main campus. It is one of North Wales' premier sporting venues. They have two floodlit artificial pitches, one a water-based international hockey pitch, the other sand-based for football. Adjacent is a Human Performance Laboratory. Other facilities include a 1,000 sqm wooden sprung floor, a dance studio, fitness suite, sun shower and spectator facilities. They run classes for such as yoga, pilates, kick boxing and step., and the centre supports the main teams: hockey, football and basketball.

PILLOW TALK

Almost all first years get a place in the Student Village, which has been in development for almost a decade. There's also a range of University-managed accommodation in Wrexham.

GETTING THERE

☛ By road: A483.
☛ By rail: Birmingham, 2:12; Cardiff, 3:40; Manchester, 1:30.
☛ By coach: Birmingham, 3:20.

ACCOMMODATION	
Guarantee to freshers	**80%**
Style	**Halls, flats**
Security guard	**24-hour**
Shared rooms	**Some**
Internet access	**Most**
Self-catered	**All**
En suite	**Some**
Approx price range pw	**£50-£75**
City rent pw	**£50**

GOLDSMITHS COLLEGE, LONDON

University of London Goldsmiths College
New Cross
London SE14 6NW

TEL 020 7919 7766
FAX 020 7919 7509
EMAIL admissions@gold.ac.uk
WEB www.goldsmiths.ac.uk

Goldsmiths Students' Union
Dixon Road
London SE14 6NW

TEL 020 8692 1406
FAX 020 8694 9789
EMAIL gcsu@gold.ac.uk
WEB www.gcsu.org.uk)

VAG VIEW

*G*oldsmiths is a college of the University of London, famous for its postmodern art department, ents programme, and for the active commitment of its students to fairness and justice. It is located in south-east London, and was listed as 'cool brand leader' (with MTV) by the Brand Council in 2004.

'Ours is one of the most exciting colleges in the country,' I was told. 'It's unpretentious [Oh, right], set in London and neatly poised between a bad-ass ents programme and radical action. We have one of the most politically active Students' Unions in the country.'

In the teaching provision there is richness and depth, evinced in its top, 4-star grades in the recent nationwide research assessment.

UNIVERSITY/STUDENT PROFILE	
College of London Uni since	**1904**
Situation/style	**Campus**
Student population	**7620**
Undergraduates	**4775**
Mature undergraduates	**56%**
International undergrads	**26%**
Male/female ratio	**34:66**
Equality of opportunity:	
state school intake	**92%**
social class 4-7 intake	**30%**
low-participation area intake	**6%**

Goldsmiths came an impressive 9th and was placed joint 1st in Sociology and in Media, where 80% of the college's research activity is rated either world-class or of international significance.

CAMPUS

At Goldsmiths almost everything is together on one site, so there's a strong campus feel to life here: they are big enough to offer some good facilities, but not so big that things seem impersonal and unfriendly. That's the university line, anyway.

'So, you want to know about Goldsmiths?' said Siobhan Daly. 'Well, don't come here looking for the architectural splendours of Oxbridge or the serenity of Durham. This is south-east London: bold, brash and full of embodiments of Delboy Trotter. One of my friends cried when she arrived, saying that it looked more like Grange Hill than a university.'

Writes Laura Cattell: "'Oh brave New Cross that has such people in it..." Just a bleak 7-minute train ride from London Bridge will deliver you to New Cross. Although not one of the best parts of London, estate agent rhetoric is beginning to convince some that this is "an up-and-coming urban area". I wouldn't go that far, but plans are indeed underway to build a Health and Culture Centre in New Cross.

'Cost of living is cheaper than in many parts of the capital and Campus is open, safe and welcoming. The buildings aren't outstanding, but the students are and this former Arts College has a great, friendly atmosphere. It's one of the most local universities in London, in that it really encourages local people to enrol and also has good links with the community.'

FEES, BURSARIES

UK & EU Fees 2009-10: £3,225. A Goldsmiths Bursary worth up to £1,000 p.a. is available to students from low household income backgrounds. See www.goldsmiths.ac.uk/ug/costs/funding/uk/bursaries.

There's also a series of scholarships awarded for academic achievement/potential. The Mayor's New Cross Award is worth £11,000 and available if you studied at a secondary school/college in Lewisham.

The Warden's Scholarship (£5,000) is awarded to two students who achieve 3 A grades at A Level. Sixteen Excellence Scholarships (£500) are awarded to others who excel at A Level.

Then there's the London Student Access to Goldsmiths Scholarship Scheme: 32 awards (£500) awarded to students who demonstrate high achievement/potential despite difficult personal circumstances.

You are advised to visit www.goldsmiths.ac.uk/ug/costs/funding/uk/scholarships and check with your admitting departments for additional funding opportunities.

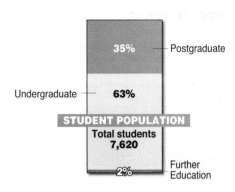

STUDENT POPULATION

Postgraduate 35%
Undergraduate 63%
Further Education 2%

Total students 7,620

STUDENT PROFILE

You don't need me to say this. Damian 'pickledcows' Hirst, Placebo, Julian Clary and Blur all strutted their stuff here. 'This doesn't, however, mean that you have to conform to the general "I'm-finding-myself" principle of dressing,' Siobhan reassures. 'Just do whatever you want; be yourself. If you are a heterosexual man, you'll love it here. If you are a homosexual woman, you'll also love it here. Goldsmiths is 66% women. The competition is hot!

'That said,' writes Laura, 'students here are a diverse crowd - masses of international students [26%], mature students [56%], "non-traditional" students [30%] - its widening participation scheme is one of the best in the country.'

ACADEMIA & JOBS

The research assessment was indeed a tremendous result for Goldsmith. Forty-five per cent of their

TEACHING SURVEY AT A GLANCE	
Avg. UCAS points accepted	300
Acceptance rate	17%
Overall satisfaction rate	82%
Helpful/interested staff	★★
Small tuition groups	★★
Students into graduate jobs	77%

Teaching most popular with undergraduates:
Design Studies (88%), Media studies (87%), Psychology (86%), English, Anthropology, Social Work (85%), History, Languages, Music, Social Studies (83%), Sociology (82%), Education (80%).

Teaching least popular with undergraduates:
Drama (70%), Computer Science (68%).

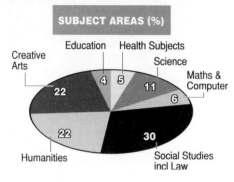

SUBJECT AREAS (%)

Creative Arts 22
Education 4
Health Subjects 5
Science 11
Maths & Computer 6
Social Studies incl Law 30
Humanities 22

research work in Media is world-class, 35% of international significance. In Music, it's 30%/40%; Sociology, 35%/35%; Computer, 20%/40%; Anthropology, 25%/30%; Art, 35%/20%, and so on. Right through Design, Psychology and History of Art the results were world-class and far better than outsiders expected, given their showing in the last assessment seven years ago.

But then along came the *Times Higher Education* magazine and put some salient questions to Goldsmiths' students and discovered that the one-to-one communication between lecturer and student is not always as generous as the student would like. We give them only 2 stars out of a maximum 5, based on the survey's findings: helpful/interested staff and small group tuition are not a main feature here. Instead, the picture one has is of a serious-minded academic staff, intense, but not always the most approachable.

RESEARCH EXCELLENCE

% of Goldsmith's research that is
4* *(World-class)* or **3*** *(Internationally rated):*

	4*	3*
Health Professions	0%	0%
Computer Science	20%	40%
Politics	10%	20%
Social Work	10%	25%
Sociology	35%	25%
Anthropology	25%	30%
Psychology	10%	40%
Education	10%	20%
English	15%	50%
History	10%	20%
Art	35%	20%
Design	20%	35%
History of Art	20%	30%
Performing Arts	20%	45%
Media Studies	45%	35%
Music	30%	40%

Two years ago Laura wrote of the excellent results Goldsmiths attained in the old teaching inspections, but added: 'Personal tutors often leave a little to be desired,' anticipating that matters would improve with the creation of a Peer Assisted Learning scheme. But the *Times Higher* survey took place at the end of 2008. So, clearly things haven't got better.

The truth may be that Goldsmiths is unusual, individualistic, even a tad eccentric, and that it is up to the individual to find his or her way into its culture. There is no change without pain. It is not Goldsmiths' place to pamper or coddle. That's not only true of Goldsmiths, but of Oxford and Cambridge too and reveals the weakness of 'flat playing field surveys', the rigor of which can sometimes iron out what is interesting in such as the lecturer-student relationship.

Says the uni: 'Our distinctive approach to learning encourages students to explore ideas that challenge and push preconceived boundaries, meaning that they are stretched intellectually and creatively to investigate fresh new ways of thinking.

'Goldsmiths is all about the freedom to experiment, to think differently, to be an individual. That's why our list of former students includes names like Antony Gormley, Julian Clary, Damien Hirst, Mary Quant, Bridget Riley, Vivienne Westwood, Graham Coxon, Malcolm McLaren. We bring creative and unconventional approaches to all of our subjects, but everything we do is based on the highest academic standards of teaching and research.'

Students rate most highly the teaching in Design, Media, Psychology, English, Anthropology, Social Work, History, Languages, Music, Social Studies, Sociology, and Education. But there is no real area of discontent. Even in the least popular courses, Drama and Computer Science, 70% and 68% of the class respectively gave their approval.

2005 saw an ambitious new Arts Complex open. The new Centre for Cognition, Computation & Culture houses studios and teaching facilities for the Visual Arts Department. Fine Arts has the lowest work load. The word is, never arrange to meet art students in the library, they'll never find it. If they did, they'd discover some 230,000 vols and 9,500 music scores. Investment has also been directed to music practice rooms for solo and ensemble work.

At the end of it all, however, it is all too easy to lose sight of the fact that Goldsmiths, the hip college of London Uni with its cutting-edge, cool appeal, gives most of its graduates to primary school education, and to the hard reality of life as clerks, sales assistants, accounts and wages clerks,

WHAT IT'S REALLY LIKE

COLLEGE:

Social Life	★★★
Campus scene	**Trendy, radical**
Student Union services	**Average**
Politics	**Anarchy**
Sport	**Fun**
National team position	**131st**
Sport facilities	**Getting better**
Arts opportunities	**Excellent film, theatre**
Student magazine	**Smiths**
National Media Awards	**Best Design 2006**
Student radio	**Wired**
Club venue + bar	**The Stretch**
Bar & café	**The Green Room**
Union ents	**OK disco**
Union societies	**21**
Most popular societies	**Respect**
Parking	**Non-existent**

CITY:

Entertainment	★★★★★
Scene	**Wild, expensive, but locally not**
Town/gown relations	**OK**
Risk of violence	**Average -high**
Cost of living	**High**
Student concessions	**Good**
Survival + 2 nights out	**£100 pw**
Part-time work campus/town	**Excellent**

Student societies range from Respect to Capoeira. In politics, anarchy rules. Students love to campaign here, religious awareness and equality being of particular importance. There's also a strong culture of altruism. They piloted a prison visiting scheme, and were nominated for a National Student Volunteering Award.

Student magazine *Smiths* regularly features in the national student media awards. 'The SU is very active,' concludes Laura. 'There's nearly always a student play on and most days you'll find a free lunchtime recital or musical performance on campus. Welfare is key and support services are accessible, mentoring schemes are well organised and available. They're also a good provider of part-time jobs about campus. A good way of earning is to become a Student Ambassador, assisting in a local school, helping out at a Widening Participation event or a school careers fair.'

TOWN 'The local pubs are great - not a pretentious wine bar in sight. **New Cross Inn** is worth a try as is the **Amersham Arms** - particularly on a Monday when you can enjoy top comedy for just a few pounds.

'Cinema is good; nearest is Peckham Multiplex or **Greenwich Picturehouse/Odeon Theatre** - in general a good arts scene locally, and very close to London's theatreland. Night clubs average/good, but local Venue is pretty awful.

ACCOMMODATION

Guarantee to freshers	**80%**
Style	**Halls, flats**
Security guard	**Most**
Shared rooms	**None**
Internet access	**Most**
Self-catered	**All**
En suite	**Most**
Approx price range pw	**£85-£114**
City rent pw	**£85-£140**

etc. The glamourous fashionable end of things, it seems, is highly competitive and will never be open to all. What's for sure is that you will change and develop at Goldsmiths, and remember that the 77% graduate employment figure was recorded just six months after graduation. It takes time to ply your talent as an artist.

Goldsmiths say simply, 'Graduates find employment in the arts, humanities, social sciences, computing and education sectors.'

SOCIAL SCENE

STUDENTS UNION Their building is called Tiananmen, **The Green Room** is the bar, and **The Stretch** is the bar/club venue - recent visitors are Roni Size, Goldie, Athlete. 'Our Students' Union may be a concrete monstrosity, but there's a fab nightlife hidden inside and rather outstanding alcohol prices,' writes Siobhan.

Writes Laura: 'The Student Union shuts down at the weekend, which is a bit of a shocker, but it does make up for it in the week by putting on plenty of cheap nights such as *Club Sandwich* - pop/dance/indie/r&b on Wednesday, *Sidebag* disco on Friday; also bingo, *Superquiz* and karaoke.'

'There are several cheap ethnic restaurants. If you're fed up with New Cross and Deptford then Greenwich is a 10-minute bus ride away - lovely with plenty of great restaurants and trendy bars. Best ones are the Gipsy Moth or the Spaniard.'

SPORT Not sporty, but there's a new fitness centre (**Club Pulse**). Around £20 or so a month gets you use of gym, all exercise classes for free, but no swimming pool. 'They have a good women's football team and their basketball team aren't bad either,' says Laura. 'Playing fields, as on most University of London campuses, are pretty far away, but they do exist.'

PILLOW TALK

They have 1,000 places within walking distance of the campus (most less than 15 mins away), flats, houses, and purpose-built residences. Halls here are quite reasonable for London, £85-£114 per week.

Decent en-suite hall development sees Loring now satisfying 400 students and Dean House 95. 'The on-site Loring Hall is the best on offer in my opinion,' Siobhan confirms, 'every room has an en-suite bathroom, personal telephone (you will be grateful for it!) and you can get cable television.' Internet is available in 'most' student rooms. You'll need it; check you have it.

Otherwise it's London. Writes Laura:

'Goldsmiths seems to own all the streets around campus, so students pour out of every corner, though they merge pretty well with the locals. Shared private accommodation is a little cheaper than the London average and you can find some decent places in the £65 price mark. Areas such as Brockley, New Cross, Deptford and parts of Peckham are popular with students. Lewisham can be pretty awful in parts, so look carefully. Greenwich and Blackheath are the best and safest parts, but reflect this in the rental prices.'

GETTING THERE

☛ By road: at the junction of A2 and A20.
☛ By rail: New Cross Gate or New Cross Underground and overland.

UNIVERSITY OF GREENWICH

The University of Greenwich
Old Royal Naval College
London SE10 9LS

TEL 0800 005006
FAX 020 8331 8145
EMAIL courseinfo@greenwich.ac.uk
WEB www.gre.ac.uk

Students' Union University of Greenwich
Cooper Building
Greenwich SE10 9JH

TEL 020 8331 7629
FAX 020 8331 7628
EMAIL J,Chan@greenwich.co.uk
WEB www.suug.co.uk/

VAG VIEW

A university since 1992, Greenwich came out of Woolwich Polytechnic, Avery Hill College of Higher Education, Dartford College of Education, and Garnett College. Ten years later Dartford and Woolwich were closed and it concentrated its resources at three campuses, its flagship the £50-million headquarters at Greenwich Maritime Campus, the old Naval College on the south bank of the Thames opposite the Isle of Dogs, a setting described by the London Evening Standard *as 'one of the grandest of any university in the world'. It is regularly used as a film or TV location, last year for* The Duchess, Young Victoria, Wolf Man, Dorian Gray, Sherlock Holmes *and* Little Dorrit.

What students dislike most about Greenwich University is the disparate nature of the place, the lack of community and dearth of student activity. The Student

UNIVERSITY/STUDENT PROFILE	
University since	**1992**
Situation/style	**City sites**
Student population	**24915**
Undergraduates	**17990**
Mature undergraduates	**69%**
International undergrads	**26%**
Male/female ratio	**50:50**
Equality of opportunity:	
state school intake	**98%**
social class 4-7 intake	**46%**
low-participation area intake	**10%**

Union has been poor. It came off very badly in the 2008 Times Higher Education's *Student Experience survey.*

But, on the up-side, 81% of its students are satisfied with the teaching. There's a strong study ethic on most campuses, and in spite of huge reservations on the extra-curricular side, one has to admit that the drop-out rate is relatively low at 7%, well below its Government benchmark.

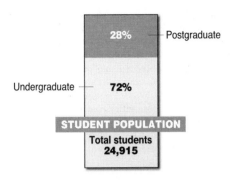

28% — Postgraduate

Undergraduate — 72%

STUDENT POPULATION
Total students
24,915

FEES, BURSARIES

UK & EU Fees 2009-10: £2,900 p.a. Lower than at most, and there is still the Mature Student Bursary and the Greenwich Partnership Bursary. See www.gre.ac.uk/students/finance/uni_support/bursaries. There are also sport, music and academic bursaries, and cash scholarships for UCAS point scores in excess of 300 (excluding AS levels). For sport, there's the £1,000 Gravesend Rugby Football Club Bursary; for music, the £1,000 David Fussey Choral Exhibition.

STUDENT PROFILE

Students vary from campus to campus, but what many have in common is a passion for technical and vocational courses.

Medway and Avery Hill have a high proportion of mature and live-at-home students. But across all campuses Greenwich is a safe haven for international students . The university provides immigration info concerning visas, working and health, and academic assistance: English classes, study skills, personal tutors and social events geared to integrate into the British and uni communities.

Statistics show that 69% of Greenwich's students are mature (as a result there are good childcare facilities), 46% are drawn from the lower socio-economic orders, and 10% from the so-called 'low participation neighbourhoods'.

It is in every sense very much a 'new' university, taking higher education out of its privileged past into the community.

CAMPUSES

GREENWICH CAMPUS has Humanities, Business, Law, Computing, Maritime Studies, and Maths. Designed by Christopher Wren in the 17th century, the building is now a UNESCO World Heritage site. Only a 20-minute train ride finds you in central London, but Greenwich is a lovely part of the city so you may just find yourself content to stay there.

There's a library, computing facilities of course, some postgrad. accommodation, conference centre

and the Greenwich Maritime Institute (a research/ postgrad. teaching facility).

There's also **Bar Latitude** and an excellent party atmosphere, by all accounts, but light on ents. Drinks promos, pool competition nights, karaoke, comedy. Greatly enhanced campus catering facilities opened in March 2007.

Nearby there are a number of pubs, among them **The Gipsy Moth**, **The Spaniard**, and a cheesy club called **The North Pole**). There are also bars, restaurants and takeaways, and downriver is the **02 Arena**, which last year was the world's best attended music venue.

Nearby Deptford has a great market on Wednesdays and Fridays. Cost of living is reasonable for a London university, particularly in areas surrounding Avery Hill and Medway (see below). Greenwich is definitely the pricier of the three, but worth it.

Accommodation is 10-15 minutes walk away: Binnie Court and Devonport House halls, and new Cutty Sark and McMillan Student Village en-suite residences. The most expensive but plush accommodation is found in the McMillan student village, but this luxury is reflected in the prices - £108 per week for a room, or £139-£163 for a studio flat. Binnie Court and Devonport House are almost as nice and much cheaper. Student accommodation is improving, but apply early for the best.

AVERY HILL Bexley Road, Eltham, London SE9 2PQ, and Every Hill Road, Eltham, London SE9 2HB. It delivers Health & Social Care, Social Sciences, Education, Architecture, Landscape, and Construction. A £14-million building project features a multi-purpose sports hall, a 220-seat lecture theatre and 4 clinical skills laboratories, which replicate real NHS wards.

Close by is the not so lovely New Eltham, but connections to London are good. Waterloo is just 30 mins away by train. The campus is pleasant - 86

SUBJECT AREAS (%)

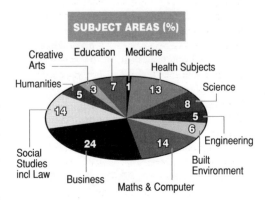

TEACHING SURVEY AT A GLANCE

Avg. UCAS points accepted	**200**
Acceptance rate	**14%**
Overall satisfaction rate	**81%**
Helpful/interested staff	**★★★**
Small tuition groups	**★★★**
Students into graduate jobs	**77%**

Teaching most popular with undergraduates:
Paramedic Science, Pharmaceutical Science,
History & Archaeology (96%), Philosophy (94%),
Accounting (93%), Finance & Accounting, Media
Studies (92%), Computer Science (91%),
Economics, Nursing (90%).

Teaching least popular with undergraduates:
Tourism Management (60%).

acres of parkland - but a little quiet and with, for
some time, a dwindling Student Union, reflective
perhaps of the student demographic: mature or
live-at-home.

However, new catering and fitness facilities

RESEARCH EXCELLENCE

% of Glreenwich's research that is
4* *(World-class)* or **3*** *(Internationally rated):*

	4*	3*
Nursing/Midwifery	**5%**	**25%**
Pharmacy	**5%**	**20%**
Horticulture, Animal Science	**5%**	**25%**
Statistics/Operational Research	**0%**	**40%**
Computer Science	**0%**	**20%**
General Engineering	**0%**	**20%**
Civil Engineering	**5%**	**30%**
Mechanical, Aeronautical, Manufacturing Engineering	**30%**	**40%**
Architecture/Building	**10%**	**30%**
Business/Management	**5%**	**15%**
Law	**0%**	**5%**
Politics	**0%**	**0%**
Development Studies	**0%**	**25%**
Psychology	**0%**	**15%**
Education	**5%**	**5%**
English	**0%**	**25%**
Linguistics	**0%**	**20%**
History	**10%**	**25%**
Media Studies	**0%**	**10%**

have recently been established, following a £3 million project to remodel the **Dome**, the student
nightclub. This is still the liveliest SU venue at the
uni. It holds 1,000 punters and has put on big-name
music acts, though the events calendar has been
pretty abstract of late. There's now an upgraded
café, contemporary dining area and a relaxed social
space, with comfortable soft furnishing and Wi-Fi
access throughout.

A new gym offers modern fitness facilities,
showers and changing rooms at the heart of campus. Village accommodation is open to all students
from the main campus, which is 40 mins away by
bus - there's a regular peak-time service. Shared
flats and maisonettes, some en suite.

MEDWAY Pembroke, Chatham Maritime, Kent ME4
4AW. Has Engineering, Science, Pharmacy,
Nursing, some Business, and incorporates the
Natural Resources Institute. There's a sports hall
with badminton and basketball courts and a weights
room. A new library, converted from a naval drill
hall and shared with the University of Kent, cost
£15 million and has 370 PC study spaces, 400 open
study spaces, more than 157,000 books and pamphlets, and 2.7 miles of shelves. Computer equipment and the latest software are available on an
open access basis, so you can log in and connect to
the resources you need.

There's a friendly traditional pub-style bar,
Coopers, with adjacent nightclub, **Purple** - resident DJs and regular ents. Medway students get
dual membership of Greenwich SU and the
Universities at Medway Students' Association - Kent
and Canterbury Christ Church universities (see
entries). Ents include karaoke competitions and
club nights.

Medway halls - shared en-suite flats - are close
to campus. A new one, for 140 students, opened in
September 2008.

Over all the campuses, the student balls are
best: Fresher's Ball, Football Dinner and Dance,
Christmas Dizzy, Valentine's Ball, and the biggest,
the May, or Summer, Ball. London's **Café Royal** in
London and **Alexandra Palace** have provided
glamourous settings for this black tie evening. The
location changes each year. Rag Week tends to pre-
cede it, in the nick of time bringing the student
body together in charity slave auctions and fancy
dress parades to raise money for charity.

There's a range of societies on offer across the
university, many indicative of the diverse student
body: Afro-Caribbean, Chinese, Cypriot, Hellenic,
Malaysian, Mauritian, Nigerian, to name but a few.

ACADEMIA & JOBS

Greenwich is a university of vocational courses, led

WHAT IT'S REALLY LIKE

UNIVERSITY:

Social Life	★★
Campus scene	**Ents-focused, disparate**
Student Union services	**Very poor**
Politics	**Interest low**
Sport	**Small interest**
National team position	**104th**
Sport facilities	**Good**
Arts opportunities	**Interest low**
Student magazine	**Sarky Cutt**
Nightclubs	**Dome, Purple**
Bars	**Bar Latitude, Coopers, Sports Bar**
Union ents	**Good club nights & comedy**
Union societies	**19**
Most popular society	**Gaelic**
Parking	**Mostly good**

CITY:

Entertainment	★★★★★
City scene	**Go to London**
Town/gown relations	**Average-good**
Risk of violence	**Avery Hill worst**
Cost of living	**Invariably average**
Student concessions	**Locally not much**
Survival + 2 nights out	**£80-£100 pw**
Part-time work campus/town	**Good/Average**

ACCOMMODATION

Guarantee to freshers	**100%**
Style	**Flats**
Security guard	**Most**
Shared rooms	**None**
Internet access	**All**
Self-catered	**All**
En suite	**Most**
Approx price range pw	**£74-£108**
City rent pw	**£65-£110**

in their design by the needs of the workplace.

The schools, or faculties, are Architecture & Construction; Business; Chemical & Life Sciences; Computing & Mathematical Sciences; Education & Training; Engineering; Health; Humanities; NRI (Earth & Environmental Sciences); Social Sciences & Law (Social Science subjects).

In the 2008 research assessment, Nursing, Pharmacy, Food Science, Engineering, Architecture, Construction, Business, and History were all found to be world-class to some extent. Notably, 30% of research work in Mechanical and Manufacturing Engineering was world-class and 40% of international significance. The figures were 10% and 40% respectively for Architecture and Construction.

Both are crucial areas to the curriculum at Greenwich. The Medway School of Engineering offers a wide range of programmes that includes mechanical, manufacturing, electrical and electronic, computer and communications engineering and engineering design. The Avery Hill schools of Architecture and Construction account for 9% of graduate employment at Greenwich.

Teaching most popular with students is in Paramedic Science, Pharmaceutical Science, History & Archaeology, Philosophy, Accounting, Finance & Accounting, Media Studies, Computer Science, Economics, and Nursing.

Seventy-seven per cent of graduates have proper graduate level employment within six months of leaving. For Greenwich Business graduates optimum employment areas are retail, banking, personnel, accounting and insurance, with dedicated degrees for some of these. Next most jobs come out of Education, principally primary school teaching. The Computer Science provision then accounts for 10% of Greenwich's graduate employment, principally again in retail, and software consultancy and supply. Then its health and social work that dominate the employment figures, the province of both Avery Hill and Medway: Biomedical Science, numerous Health degrees, Medical Sciences, Nursing, Midwifery, Osteopathy, Paramedic Science, Pharmaceutical Science, Social Work, Counselling, and so on.

Environmental health is another popular employment destination, engineered by such ast Environmental Sciences, Human Nutrition and a BSc in Public Health, which may be extended to include industrial placement.

Disabled and dyslexic students benefit from a dedicated Resource Centre.

SPORT Most sporting life goes on at Avery Hill (see Campus entry above). Football, rugby, hockey, netball, American football, basketball, cricket, and tennis are played at inter-university and inter-southeast club standard, and the boat club trains to a very high standard.

GETTING THERE

☞ By road from M25, join A2 (J2) and follow signs to Woolwich Ferry, thence Greenwich.

☞ By rail to main Greenwich site: trains to Greenwich or Maze Hill overland stations, or Docklands Light Railway from Bank.

☞ By coach: Bristol, 2:20; Birmingham, 2:40; Newcastle, 6:05; Manchester, 4:35.

HERIOT-WATT UNIVERSITY

Heriot-Watt University
Riccarton Campus
Edinburgh EH14 4AS

TEL 0131 451 3451
FAX 0131 451 3630
EMAIL admissions@hw.ac.uk
WEB www.hw.ac.uk

Heriot-Watt Students' Association
Riccarton Campus
Edinburgh EH14 4AS

TEL 0131 451 5333
FAX 0131 451 5344
EMAIL admissions@hw.ac.uk
WEB www.hwusa.org

VAG VIEW

*B*ased in Edinburgh, Heriot-Watt is a
research-led, technological university, high
on academic, industrial and business collaboration; many of its courses are accredited by
professional bodies, and relevant to employers'
needs.

It is small but achieves big results, a university strong on teaching, with lecturers
praised for their help and interest in the students. Equally, they moved up nine places in
the national research assessment results, published at the end of 2008. They were strongest
research-wise in Mathematics, Petroleum
Engineering, Physics, Computer Science,
Business & Management, the Built
Environment, and Art & Design (notably in
Fashion).

Moreover, it is a very good social life here,
and there's a decent Student Union, with
much to do extramurally.

It is no surprise therefore that 85% of the
students are satisfied with what they get, and
81% of them will be in real graduate jobs within six months of leaving.

CAMPUS

The main campus at Riccarton, 6.5 miles southwest of Edinburgh city centre is an attractive 380-
acre campus in a huddle with a number of independent research companies. There's a modern,
almost space-age, feel to it: smart buildings are set
in pleasant grounds, with trees, playing fields, an
attractive artificial loch, squirrels, ducks and
swans.

'The sense of seclusion at leafy Riccarton campus definitely aids study,' writes Richard Biggs, 'and
has given rise to a community spirit that doesn't exist
at inner city universities. However, the LRT buses
that run to and from campus tend to be erratic - not
fun in winter.'

UNIVERSITY/STUDENT PROFILE	
University since	**1966**
Situation/style	**City campus**
Student population	**10560**
Undergraduates	**5315**
Mature undergraduates	**6%**
International undergrads	**14%**
Male/female ratio	**61:39**
Equality of opportunity:	
state school intake	**92%**
social class 4-7 intake	**28%**
low-participation area intake	**5%**

Since the merger with The Scottish College of
Textiles in '99, H-W also has a Scottish Borders
campus. Situated in a small town in the Scottish
Borders called Galashiels, Gala, as the campus is
known), is only 33 miles/90 minutes by bus from
Edinburgh, but unfortunately (if you are in a
hurry) some two and a half hours by train, which
detours via Berwick-upon-Tweed.

FEES, BURSARIES

Fees for English: approx. £1,820 p.a., but the uni offers
UK domiciled students a number of scholarships. See
www.scholarships.hw.ac.uk/. There are also sports
scholarships, funded jointly by the university, the
Alumni Fund, the Royal & Ancient Golf Club of St
Andrews, and the Scottish Physical Recreation Fund.
See www.hw.ac.uk/sports/sports-scholarships.htm.

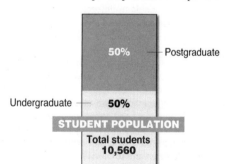

STUDENT PROFILE

'Though entry requirements can now be fairly steep (385 points is average), they throw a wide net for applicants, and claim a dogged policy of targeting 'pupils from schools where applications to university are low, students who have no family background or cultural experience of higher education and mature students with no formal qualifications who maybe want a second chance to enter university via an access course.'

They are, they say, committed to equal opportunities for all and go out of their way to pull in a diverse mix of student.

In the past they have been named as one of the elite universities who show that open access can be made to work by focusing on ability and potential, rather than on points scores at Scottish Highers or A level.

However, the fact remains that on average successful applicants to study at Heriot Watt actually attain 385 points, and while state school intake runs at 92%, intake from lower socio-economic groups (28%), and low-participation neighbourhoods (5%) is not that special, though either equal to or surpassing Heriot's Government benchmarks.

International students meanwhile make up 14% of the undergraduate body, which is large, and a new International Study Centre opened in 2008 to help prepare these undergraduates.

Recruitment overseas is definitely a focus here, and there are many foreign exchange students, the study of languages and a year abroad being a special feature of many of Heriot's courses.

ACADEMIA & JOBS

The schools are Engineering and Physical Sciences; Life Sciences; Built Environment; Mathematical & Computer Sciences; Management & Languages; and Textiles & Design.

Students rate the teaching best in Languages, Chemistry, Physical Science, Accounting, Maths, Computer Science, Finance & Accounting, Biology & related sciences, Management, Business & Administrative Studies.

Not mentioned is Architecture, which is in fact the second best area of graduate employment from Heriot-Watt. The degree is Architectural Engineering, which may be taken as BEng or BSc, and there's Structural Engineering & Architectural Design (BEng and MEng), so Heriot graduates come at it from every angle; many too (in fact 44% of students studying in the area of Architecture and Building & Planning) end up in estate agency.

There are also Engineering/Technology degrees to take you into gas and oil extraction - 22% of Heriot's engineers end up in that.

Meanwhile, a quarter of all success Heriot job-hunters come off a Business course and find work in banks, accountancy, management, and personnel. You'll find degrees dedicated to these. They also find their way from Business into the Civil Service, who also smile on Heriot's Language graduates, though they like their Computer, Planning & Housing, and Maths graduates too.

But more of Heriot's mathematicians find jobs in banks than in anything, and in pension work, financial consultancy, security broking and fund management. There are also dedicated degrees in Actuarial Science, and other niches in other disciplines, for example in brewing and distilling (there's a dedicated BSc), in photonics, and in translating and interpreting - the popular Heriot linguists again.

'Modern languages are an outstanding strength,' one sixthform adviser confirmed, and certainly their employment figures for translators and interpreters are good. 'You can walk straight out of

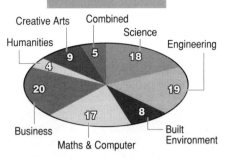

SUBJECT AREAS (%)

Creative Arts — Combined Science — Humanities — Engineering — 9 — 5 — 18 — 4 — 20 — 19 — 17 — 8 — Business — Maths & Computer — Built Environment

RESEARCH EXCELLENCE

% of Heriot-Watt's research that is
4* (World-class) or **3*** (Internationally rated):

	4*	3*
Food Science	5%	35%
Environmental Sciences	0%	25%
Chemistry	10%	40%
Physics	15%	40%
Pure Mathematics	25%	45%
Applied Mathematics	15%	50%
Statistics	10%	35%
Computer Science	15%	45%
General Engineering	10%	45%
General Eng./Petroleum	20%	45%
Chemical Engineering	10%	35%
Civil Engineering	5%	50%
Architecture & Building	10%	50%
Planning	20%	30%
Business/Management	10%	35%
Psychology	0%	5%
Sports Studies	10%	15%
European Studies	10%	20%
Art and Design	15%	35%

Heriot-Watt into a job in the EC.' Also, for foreign students, the School of Management and Languages now offers a range of language support classes (MA Foreign Languages and TESOL). Equally, there is also a big foreign exchange programme - all students can choose to study abroad at some point during their course.

In spite of all the science, Creative Arts account for 9% of graduate output, 34% of whom go into specialist retail. If you are interested in fashion and design, you are interested in retail.

Heriot graduates of dedicated degrees in Fashion, Textiles and related areas, including Management, Marketing and Promotion are much in demand.

The uni merged with the Scottish College of Textiles in 1999. There's collaboration with industry and business in the design of the courses. They offer the employment-oriented BA Fashion Design for Industry and BSc Clothing Design & Manufacture or Textiles & Fashion Design Management.

It has been in partnership with George Davies of 'Next', 'George at Asda' and the 'per una' collection for Marks & Spencer. They have the George Davies Centre for Retail Excellence at Heriot-Watt.

> **'There is a community spirit that doesn't exist at inner city universities. Modern languages are an outstanding strength. You can walk straight into a job in the EC.'**

There'll be in-company projects and master classes from leading academics and retailers, including George. The first postgrad. course in International Fashion Marketing ran from autumn 2005.

Heriot's strength is in the close relationship it has with industry, business and national support networks. In cahoots with the Scottish Institute for Enterprise they deliver an enterprise-training programme, bringing entrepreneurial skills to science and engineering from the first year of studies.

SOCIAL SCENE

STUDENTS' ASSOCIATION The Union on Edinburgh campus is a lively, campaigning body. In fact it won 'NUS Campaign of the Year' at the national student awards in 2008/9, its constant refrain an environmental one, again applauded in 2009 when it was presented with a Bronze award at the Sound Environmental Impact Awards.

The Union has three main venues: **Geordies** (bar) - the Heriot-Watt local with hustlers pool area: 3 pool tables and arcades, big screen and plasma screens, and home to the ever-popular and entertaining Monday night pub quiz. Then there's **Liberty's**, a café-bar with free wireless internet access, and Zero° nightclub (capacity 450). Its stage is also used for live music and *Comedy Club*.

Friday is *JAM* in **Zero**°: pop, chart, cheese and legendary student anthems; also *Night Train* in Liberty's: diverse range of 'quality music'. Every other Tuesday is *Comedy Club*: 'Well-established laughter session offering a changing line-up of some of the best local comics around. A bargain at only £3,' says The List. Saturday is *Lounge* in Liberty's - 'chillout to the sound of DJ's playing an eclectic mix of cool tunes" says the Student Association. 'Crayons to play with too!' Thursday in Zero° brings live music and, 'Often attracts Scotland's hottest band talent.' - *The List*. Thursday is *Traffic*, a crossroads of indie and alternative tunes. Every other Sunday in Zero°, alternating with *Your Turn* (open mic night) in Liberty's is *Have you got the S-Factor?*

See also Student Edinburgh.

Down at Gala, they are also getting some sort of scene together. There are newish Union premises, a full ents programme, a musician-in-residence and lashings of sponsorship from North Sea oil, which has led to COMA - not a state of unconsciousness due to inebriation, but the name for a network of groups available for gigs.

WHAT IT'S REALLY LIKE

UNIVERSITY:

Social Life	★★★★
Campus scene	**Like clockwork**
Student Union services	**Good**
Politics	**Low level**
	Student debt
Sport	**30 clubs, hockey strong**
National team position	**46th**
Sport facilities	**Good**
Arts opportunities	**Music, film good; dance, art average, drama poor**
Student newspaper	**Watts On**
Nightclub	**Zero°**
Bars	**Geordies, Liberty's**
Union ents	**JAM (cheese) heads big ents**
Union Societies	**30**
Most popular societies	**Poker Society**
Parking	**Poor**

CITY:

Entertainment	★★★★★
Scene	**Seething**
Town/gown relations	**Good**
Risk of violence	**Low**
Cost of living	**High**
Student concessions	**Excellent**
Survival + 2 nights out	**£60-£85 pw**
Part-time work campus/city	**Excellent**

ACCOMMODATION

Guarantee to freshers	**100%**
Style	**Halls, flats**
Security guard	**None; campus patrols**
Shared rooms	**None**
Internet access	**Edinburgh campus only**
Self-catered	**Most halls, all flats**
En suite	**Most halls, no flats**
Approx price range pw	**£57-£94.50**
City rent pw	**£55-£92+**

SPORT The Edinburgh campus boasts the impressive National Squash Centre, but also has a number of large playing fields (five football, two rugby, one cricket), a floodlit training area, jogging track, three tennis courts, three sports halls, climbing wall, two multigyms, golf driving nets, weights and fitness rooms and indoor sports courts. Membership is spilt into Gold, Silver and Bronze tariffs (year, academic year and term), ranging from around £20. The Heart of Midlothian Football Academy opened recently and includes pro-quality facilities and floodlit and indoor synthetic pitches. The city of Edinburgh has many golf courses, a large swimming pool, ice rink and the Meadowbank Stadium. Half the city is made of parks and open spaces .

PILLOW TALK

Catered and self-catered study bedrooms and self-catered flats, all a short stroll away from everything else. Of the 1,800 study bedrooms, more than 1,000 have their own shower and toilet, and there are never more than five sharing a kitchen, which comes with fridge freezer, cooker, kettle etc. Bring your own crockery, cutlery, pots and pans. Catered students have access to a pantry for snacks and hot drinks. For a small subscription, you can have access to a phone, the Internet and the Heriot-Watt Intranet. There is, in any case, free room-to-room and incoming calls, and voicemail. Each Hall of Residence has a warden to help students settle in and sort out any problems. There are patrols by Security Patrol Officers at night. These Officers can be called by students.

GETTING THERE

☛ By road: A71 or A70; if the latter, turn off at Currie on to Riccarton Mains Road.
☛ By rail: London King's Cross, 4:30; Glasgow Central, 50 mins; Newcastle, 1:30.
☛ By air: nearby Edinburgh Airport for inland and international flights.
☛ By coach: Glasgow, 1:10; London, 9:10; Birmingham, 8:10; Newcastle, 3:10.
☛ To Gala, A7 south from Edinburgh.

UNIVERSITY OF HERTFORDSHIRE

The University of Hertfordshire
College Lane
Hatfield
Hertfordshire AL10 9AB

TEL 01707 284800
FAX 01707 284870
EMAIL admissions@herts.ac.uk
WEB www.herts.ac.uk

Hertfordshire Students' Union
College Lane
Hatfield
Hertfordshire AL10 9AB

TEL 01707 285000
FAX 01707 286150
EMAIL uhsu@herts.ac.uk
WEB uhsu.herts.ac.uk

VAG VIEW

Hertfordshire University is among the most impressive of the 1992 unis in rate of growth and learning resources, but neither the student response to its teaching in the Higher Education Funding Council's National Student Survey (78%) nor the figure of 71% graduates in real graduate jobs after six months, is exactly electrifying.

The uni's close contact with industry and with the capital city, only strengthened by their strategically advantageous location (on the A1, minutes from the M25 and M1, and within striking distance of four airports: Luton, Stansted, Heathrow and Gatwick,) suggests that the employment figure should be better.

One must, however, complete the picture, for Herts's student population is diverse (see Student Profile below), very much a 'new' university demographic picture.

The evidence is that Herts is working with its student base exceptionally well, managing to maintain a drop-out rate of 7%, which is not only below their Government benchmark but also below the average for the nation.

A part of what the uni is doing right was suggested in the national research assessment at the end of last year, in which over 85% of the research Herts submitted was judged to be of international quality in terms of originality, significance and rigor.

Herts' take on research is not that it be something undertaken in an ivory tower. It places a high priority on research that is applied and used to develop leading-edge programmes for students. This integration of the research and teaching provisions is key, and carries with it the approval of industry.

UNIVERSITY PROFILE

University since	**1992**
Situation/style	**Suburban campuses**
Student population	**23725**
Undergraduates	**19170**
Mature undergraduates	**24%**
International undergrads	**9%**
Male/female ratio	**45:55**
Equality of opportunity:	
state school intake	**98%**
social class 4-7 intake	**40%**
low-participation area intake	**8%**

CAMPUSES

The uni is based at Hatfield and St Albans. The main Hatfield site comprises the original campus and the new de Havilland Campus, half a mile away, the two made one by cycleways, footpaths and shuttle buses.

DE HAVILLAND The £120-million campus houses the Business School and schools of Education and Humanities. There's a learning resources centre, a £15-million sports centre open to the public - its 3-year membership target met in the first month - an amazing 60-seater auditorium and student residences.

COLLEGE LANE The main campus is College Lane, where the original Learning Resources Centre is based. This autumn the doors will be opened for the first time on the Forum - a new student venue. The Forum is a joint venture between the University of Hertfordshire and the Students' Union.

It is designed to accommodate student needs not only for a social scene, but quiet areas for study and reflection, a nursery, a convenience store, and a multi-storey car park. Central to the student experience, it will cover 8,000 square metres and include

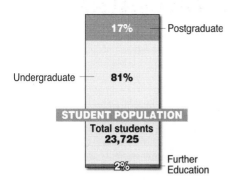

Undergraduate — **81%**

STUDENT POPULATION
Total students 23,725

17% — Postgraduate

2% — Further Education

an auditorium for live gigs and club nights, a balcony bar, style bar, refurbished student bar, mini club, a restaurant, a coffee bar and a convenience store.

Currently among student societies are the radio station, Crush, and the *Horizon* newspaper. The most active of 17 student societies are Christian Union, Drama and Alternative Music.

Town There's a 9-screen **UCI** in the Galleria Centre, and a pub that offers cut-price drinks. The union make merry with a student night at **Pub2Club**, but generally the nightlife is poor. London beckons.

St Albans The third campus is in St Albans, a small campus for those studying Law, easily accessible from Hatfield, where most first years are normally housed There is a refectory and a Students' Union area - TV and a pool table. The town has the oldest pub in the UK, **Ye Old Fighting Cocks**.

FEES, BURSARIES

UK & EU Fees 2009-11: £3,225 p.a. There's a bursary of £1,000 for those in receipt of the full HE Maintenance Grant. In addition there are two types of Chancellor's Scholarship: the Chancellor's Entrepreneurial and Excellence Scholarship, worth £3,000 a year and the Chancellor's Gifted and Talented Scholarship, worth £2,000 a year. Science and Engineering Scholarships (worth up to £3,000 over 3-4 years) are also available on certain science and engineering degrees for achievers of 280 UCAS points. Finally, they offer 135 externally funded scholarships, sponsored by companies such as Tesco and T-Mobile. See www.herts.ac.uk/courses/fees-bursaries-scholarships/bursaries-and-scholarships/scholarships/home.cfm.

STUDENT PROFILE

There is a very large student body of just under 24,000, 98% of which is drawn from the state sector, and 40% from the lower socio-economic groups. Twenty per cent of undergraduates are local part-timers, 24% are mature, and 9% are international students.

ACADEMIA & JOBS

Students say that the best taught subjects are Biomedical Science, Medical Technology, Initial Teacher Training, Law, Maths, Paramedical Science, Pharmaceutical Science, History, Philosophy, Aerospace Engineering, Geographical Studies, Accounting, Music. But when votes came in for Art & Design, more than half of the class gave it the thumbs down.

This seemed odd, as Art & Design is one of its research strengths. What's more, 12% of all graduate jobs at the uni are actually coming from Creative Arts, far more than from either Computer Science or Engineering, and not much less than from Business or Medicine.

> *Herts places a high priority on research that is applied and used to develop leading-edge programmes for students. This integration of the research and teaching provisions is key, and carries with it the approval of industry.*

Business accounts for 18% of graduate employment, subjects allied to Medicine another 18% - three-quarters of students of Nursing, Pharmacy, Physiotherapy, Radiography, Paramedic Science, etc) finding work in hospitals. Jobs galore take graduates from Aerospace Engineering into the aircraft industry and defence. Similarly, Computer Science graduates pour into software consultantcy and the like.

Traditionally, Herts is seen as a university

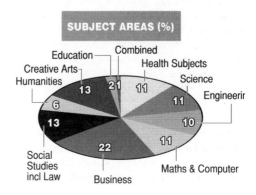

SUBJECT AREAS (%)

Education — Combined
Creative Arts Humanities — Health Subjects
Science
Engineerin
Social Studies incl Law
Business
Maths & Computer

13 · 21 · 11 · 6 · 11 · 13 · 10 · 22 · 11

TEACHING SURVEY AT A GLANCE

Avg. UCAS points accepted	**240**
Acceptance rate	**18%**
Overall satisfaction rate	**78%**
Helpful/interested staff	★★★
Small tuition groups	★★
Students into graduate jobs	**71%**

Teaching most popular with undergraduates:
Biomedical Science, etc (94%), Medical Technology, Initial Teach Training, Law, Maths, Paramedical Science, Pharmaceutical Science (92%), History (89%), Philosophy (87%), Aerospace Engineering (86%), Geographical Studies (85%), Accounting, Music (84%).

Teaching least popular with undergraduates:
Art & Design (48%).

associated with Business, subjects allied to Medicine, Physics, Engineering, and Computer Science. In the research assessment these subjects brought home the bacon, but then so did Art & Design.

Art & Design is in fact Hertfordshire's special focus, one made keener in 2005 with the launch of a School of Film, Music and New Media. Two years later a £10-million Media Centre opened at College Lane, housing the latest technology for the teaching of music, animation, film, television and multimedia.

On the one hand Creative Arts at Herts means what you might expect it to mean: Fashion, Fine Art, Graphic Design,Interior & Spatial Design, Photography. On the other, it means Industrial Design, Product Design, and, uniquely, Model Design & Model Effects.

This last - Model Design & Model Effects - is they say, 'the only course of its kind in the UK - possibly the world, as nowhere else has three interrelated degrees like this working alongside each other... You can spend up to half the second year working in industry with companies such as Artem, Asylum Models & Effects, Hothouse Models & Effects, Machine Shop Special Effects and internationally renowned companies such as Seymour Powell design consultants, the architects Foster and Partners and the Richard Rogers Partnership.' At Herts, Creative Arts is industry, the distinction between Art and Technology, Art and Science, has all but disappeared. And that is where the jobs are coming from - a 21st-century, cross-faculty approach that makes Creative Arts at this business-orientated, medicinally-minded university special. What's more, your teachers are all leading

experts in their field with industry experience & all the visiting lecturers are professionals currently working in the Film & TV industry. And you are part of that team. Its unique quality is something the survey managed completely to overlook.

The award-winning Learning Resources Centre at College Lane and its twin at adjacent de Havilland are open 24/7. Both make use of a computer system, StudyNET, their 'Managed Learning Environment', a personalised academic workspace for students on which appears information relevant to programmes of study, as well as a range of personal information management tools linking students to course databases.

Recently opened on College Lane is an Innovation Centre to provide incubation resources to spin out new companies, and a new Automotive Centre, dedicated to bring together academia and industry.

Is it any wonder that at Herts there are 6 applicants this year lining up for every place?

SPORT There are 17 degrees in Sport, and jobs in Sport account for more than 1% of the graduate job provision at the university. They came 52nd in the BUSA inter-university national team league last year. Base is the big new, £15-million sports complex, a 12-court sports hall, 3 artificial turf and 4 grass pitches, squash courts, a cricket hall and an aerobics studio, an 8-lane swimming pool, indoor cricket nets, and a 100-station fitness suite. The Sports Village hosted 2008 Olympians for their pre-Beijing training.

RESEARCH EXCELLENCE

% of Hertfordshire's research that is
4* *(World-class)* or **3*** *(Internationally rated):*

	4*	3*
Nursing/Midwifery	**25%**	**30%**
Pharmacy	**5%**	**30%**
Physics	**15%**	**40%**
Computer Science	**10%**	**45%**
General Engineering	**15%**	**35%**
Business/Management	**5%**	**30%**
Social Work	**0%**	**15%**
Psychology	**5%**	**25%**
Education	**0%**	**20%**
English	**10%**	**35%**
Philosophy	**0%**	**35%**
History	**25%**	**45%**
Art & Design	**10%**	**50%**
Music	**5%**	**10%**

PILLOW TALK

Halls are self-catering: 1,600 en-suite at the de

Havilland campus, all with broadband internet access and refrigerator. There are 1,400 new rooms

WHAT IT'S REALLY LIKE	
UNIVERSITY:	
Social Life	★★★
Campus scene	**Lively community, bit spoddy**
Student Union services	**Good**
Politics	**Average: Fees**
Sport	**29 clubs**
National team position	**57th**
Sport facilities	**New/excellent**
Arts opportunities	**Good**
Student newspaper	**Horizon**
Student radio	**Crush 1278 AM**
Nightclub	**Font Bar**
Bars	**Elehouse**
Union ents	**Bonk, Naughty, Swanky**
Union societies	**17**
Parking	**Average**
CITY:	
Entertainment	★★ – ★★★
Scene	**London beckons**
Town/gown relations	**Average**
Risk of violence	**Low**
Cost of living	**High**
Student concessions locally	**OK**
Survival + 2 nights out	**£70 pw**
Part-time work campus/town	**Excellent/poor**

ACCOMMODATION	
Guarantee to freshers	**100%**
Style	**Halls, flats**
Security guard	**All**
Shared rooms	**Some halls**
Internet access	**All**
Self-catered	**All**
En suite	**Some flats**
Approx price range pw	**£66.15-£101.50**
Town rent pw	**£69-£110**

on the College Lane campus, where they also have houses located in the Roberts Way student Village, which are shared between 8 people, communal bath/shower facilities, 6 single rooms in each house and 1 double room, shared kitchen/diner and internet access in all rooms. The Student Union runs a letting agency for private lets, a professionally run, student-friendly service.

GETTING THERE

☞ **Hatfield** by road: A1(M)/J3. By rail: London King's Cross, 22 mins. ☞ By coach: London, 1:00. ☞ **St Albans** by road: M25/J22, A1081. By rail: London (Thameslink), 25 mins.

HEYTHROP COLLEGE, UNIVERSITY OF LONDON

Heythrop College
Kensington Square
London W8 5HQ

TEL 020 7795 6600
FAX 020 7795 4200
EMAIL a.charles@heythrop.ac.uk
WEB www.heythrop.ac.uk

Heythrop College Students' Union
Kensington Square
London W8 5HQ

TEL 020 7795 6600
FAX 020 795 4200
EMAIL enquiries@heythrop.ac.uk

VAG VIEW

*H*eythrop is an independent college within the University of London specialising in Theology and Philosophy and with a refreshingly evolutionary concept of higher education. For their inspiration they turn to

the Swiss psychologist Jean Piaget, noted for his revolutionary work on the cognitive functions of children. Piaget wrote that 'the principal goal of education is to create people who are capable of doing new things, not simply of repeating what other generations have done... The second goal of education is to form minds which can be critical, can verify, and not accept everything they are offered.' Trawling through all that the higher educational establishments of this country can offer, such a breathtakingly simple statement seems almost unutterably bold. Their teaching is the traditional university method of tutorials and small-group seminars. They possess one of the finest collections of theological and philosophical literature anywhere to be found, their 250,000 volumes available to every one of their students without queue.

COLLEGE PROFILE	
College of London Uni since	**1971**
Total student population	**850**
Full-time undergraduates	**355**
- mature	**11%**
- overseas	**5%**
- male/female	**60/40**
ACCOMMODATION:	
Availability to freshers	**100%**
Style	**Halls**
Approx cost p.w.	**£100-£130**
City rent pw	**£100+**

STUDENT SCENE

'Ideally situated in the centre of Kensington, Heythrop projects an atmosphere of elegance and solemnity, but this really is the most friendly of colleges,' writes Clare Barker, 'quite impressive given the great diversity among Heythrop students. A huge number are either mature undergraduates or postgrads; then there's the diversity of religions and interests, and the proximity of **Lamda** – its drama students share one of our common rooms and make more unorthodox the already bizarre crowd milling around the corridors... And then there are the nuns. Campus is owned by nuns – and they keep rabbits. The nuns (and their rabbits) are very amiable and don't seem at all fazed at having leery students sharing their home. However, their presence leads to Heythrop having a prevailing feeling of a religious institution – strange, considering the vast number of philosophy students who are not diplomatic in the expression of their beliefs.'

GETTING THERE

☛ The college is tucked behind High Street Kensington, a short walk from Kensington Palace. High Street Ken station gives access to Piccadilly, Circle and District lines.

UNIVERSITY OF HUDDERSFIELD

University of Huddersfield
Queensgate
Huddersfield HD1 3DH

TEL 01484 473969
FAX 01484 472765
EMAIL admissionsandrecords@hud.ac.uk
WEB www.hud.ac.uk

Huddersfield Students' Union
Queensgate
Huddersfield HD1 3DH

TEL 01484 538156
FAX 01484 432333
EMAIL: students.union@hud.ac.uk
WEB www.huddersfieldstudent.com/

VAG VIEW

*H*uddersfield University traces its history back to the Young Men's Mental Improvement Society, founded in 1841. It was awarded university status in 1992 after two other incarnations, first as a technical college then as a polytechnic. Today it has a city-centre campus (Queensgate), Holly Bank campus, 2 miles to the north, and Storthes Hall, 4 miles to the south-east.

Huddersfield town, just 20 miles south west of Leeds, is an unusual mix. Its roots in the industrial revolution are not in doubt, but it is also known far and wide for its annual poetry festival, with famously the Albert pub as artistic font; folk and jazz are equally present. Sometime Heritage minister Stephen Dorrell once famously remarked that Huddersfield was the Paris of the North. One can't pretend this didn't raise a few eyebrows, but he did have a *point of sorts. The uni and the town are of a similar weave.*

There is this traditional, industrial, people-culture, but the academic spectrum is wide and its character modern. When you hear that it has the largest Music Department of any UK university, and that in the recent research assessment exercise it was announced that 20% of the department's research is world-class and 55% of international significance, you begin to wonder what other gems are lurking.

Now, with new Drama and Media facilities, it is also developing a strong Performing Arts, Broadcast and Humanities cluster of degrees, aided by the high profile of the University's Chancellor, the film actor Patrick Stewart, who drops by to give drama workshops.

In the recent National Student Survey, the 76% approval rating by their own students is certainly not the highest of a university, and the 79% employment rate - graduates into real graduate jobs six months after leaving - is not amazing either. But Huddersfield attracts a diverse student population (see Student Profile), *and the figures, including the drop-out rate of around 10% (in fact only a little over the national average), should not be seen outside that demographic context.*

CAMPUS

Storthes Hall campus is set in 350 acres of parkland 4 miles away from the main campus and connected to it by a subsidised bus service.

'I can't remember a more depressing view,' wrote student Tim Wild, a film-maker who came up to Huddersfield from Brighton as an undergraduate, about the initial culture shock.

'Most people only have the vaguest idea where the bloody place is, so I'll attempt to clear up the confusion. Smack bang in the middle - three hours away from London by car, and about three thousand light years away in attitude. That's why this place is special - they really couldn't give a toss whether you're from Taunton or Timbuktu, as long as you can hold your ale and laugh at yourself.

'If it's glamour and sophistication you're after, then stay away, because you'll only spoil it for the rest of us. I won't pretend it's paradise, but that's part of the appeal, in an odd way. Because it's the middle of nowhere, there are no cliques, no elite to try and be part of. It's just cold and grey and everyone here's in it together. Like the blitz, without the Germans.'

UNIVERSITY/STUDENT PROFILE	
University since	**1992**
Situation/style	**Town campus**
Student population	**19740**
Undergraduates	**16175**
Mature undergraduates	**33%**
International undergrads	**13%**
Male/female ratio	**44:56**
Equality of opportunity:	
state school intake	**98%**
social class 4-7 intake	**42%**
low-participation area intake	**16%**

The university has recently also opened up centres in Oldham and Barnsley to encourage participation in Higher Education in both towns.

FEES, BURSARIES

UK & EU Fees 2009-10: £3,225. Bursaries are available to those in receipt of the full HE Maintenance Grant.

STUDENT PROFILE

More than 5,000 of the undergraduate student body are part-timers and 33% mature. Intake from classes and neighbourhoods not traditionally represented at university are 42% and 16% respectively. As Tim Wild suggests above, social climbers need not apply.

ACADEMIA & JOBS

The academic schools are Human and Health Sciences, Applied Sciences (Transport & Logistics, Chemical and Biological Sciences, Geographical and Environmental Sciences), Computing and Maths, Design Technology (Textiles, Architecture), Education, Engineering, Business, Music and Humanities.

Students say that the teaching is best in History, Initial Teacher Training, Medical Sciences, Business, Food & Beverage Studies,

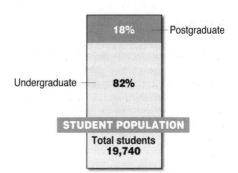

Postgraduate 18%

Undergraduate 82%

STUDENT POPULATION
Total students
19,740

TEACHING SURVEY AT A GLANCE

Avg. UCAS points accepted	**240**
Acceptance rate	**22%**
Overall satisfaction rate	**76%**
Helpful/interested staff	**★★★★**
Small tuition groups	**★★★★**
Students into graduate jobs	**69%**

Teaching most popular with undergraduates:
History (99%), Initial Teacher Training (96%),
Medical Sciences (97%), Business (82-89%),
Food & Beverage Studies (88%), Complementary
Medicine, Law, Music (87%), Biology (84%),
Chemistry, Physics (84%), Electronic & Electrical
Engineering, English, Languages,
Social Studies (83%), Psychology (82%).

Teaching least popular with undergraduates:
Sports Science (55%), Media Studies (50%).

Complementary Medicine, Law, Music, Biology, Chemistry, Physics, Electronic & Electrical Engineering, English, Languages, Social Studies, Psychology. About half the class was least happy with Sports Science and Media Studies.

Generally, the lecturers are extremely helpful and interested in their students, and tuition groups are well sized for the purpose. Huddersfield scored high on these points in the *Times Higher Education*'s Student Experience Survey.

The subjects that provide most graduate employment are the Creative Arts, Business, subjects allied to Medicine, Biological Sciences, then Social Studies, and so on. It is seldom that the Creative Arts cause such a storm - the faculty accounts for 23% of all graduate jobs at Huddersfield.

Behind it are degrees like Architecture and Interior Design (a 4 to 5-year BA/BSC), the foundation for 6 more in a similar vein, and Product Design, Transport Design, Digital Arts Practice, Digital Film and Visual Effect, and 5 Music Technology degrees (an area that got full marks at inspection), and of course the Fashion and Textiles courses: Fashion & Textile Buying/Managing/Retailing, 6 Fashion Design degrees, and Fashion Media & Promotion.

Students wanting to become fashion, clothing

Huddersfield University traces its history back to the Young Men's Mental Improvement Society, founded in 1841. Now its Chancellor is X-Men and Star Trek film star Patrick Stewart, who drops by to give drama workshops.

and textile designers should look no further. As befits a uni in the heart of the old woollen/textile industry, this is where it's at. There's high energy and superb employment results in this niche area at Huddersfield.

There is a £14-million 'flagship' Creative Arts building at the entrance to the Huddersfield campus, home to students studying music and music technology, fashion, creative imaging, multimedia, and business design awareness.

A tradition of vocational education dates back to its roots in 1841. Don't let its long-established reputation for such as textile design and engineering obscure the fact that its arts, health, and social studies courses have the same vocational slant.

Politics includes a 6-week work placement, which often takes students to the House of Commons. A third of the students in all subjects take sandwich courses, one of the highest proportions in Britain. Subjects allied to Medicine (Nursing, Midwifery, Occupational Health, Operating Department Practice, Podiatry, etc.), and Psychology with Counselling or Criminology, Social Work, 6 Sociology degrees, Youth & Community Work (an area of the research provision that was awarded a 4 star, world-class rating) and the Sports degrees all carry the same vocational momentum.

There's 24-hour computer access, and support for disabled students.

The Huddersfield Business Generator has created over 80 start-up businesses, half of them operated by Huddersfield graduates.

They are also among the giants for the catering industry with dedicated degrees in Hospitality

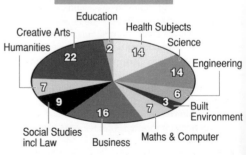

SUBJECT AREAS (%)

- Education
- Creative Arts
- Humanities — 22
- Health Subjects — 2
- Science — 14
- Engineering — 14
- Built Environment — 6
- Maths & Computer — 3
- Business — 7
- Social Studies incl Law — 16
- 7
- 9
- 7

RESEARCH EXCELLENCE

% of Huddersfield's research that is
4* *(World-class)* or **3*** *(Internationally rated):*

	4*	3*
Chemistry	0%	25%
Computer Science	5%	20%
General Engineering	5%	30%
Accounting/Finance	0%	30%
Politics	0%	0%
Social Work	10%	35%
Sociology	0%	25%
Education	5%	10%
English	5%	15%
History	5%	40%
Media Studies	0%	0%
Music	20%	55%

Management mixed to your taste with Tourism & Leisure. Transport is another rich seam. Said a careers master, 'I have seen more enthusiasm among the staff at Huddersfield - both in the departments of Transport and Logistics and in Hotel & Catering - than at any other university in the land. I had thought, Oh, Huddersfield, can I really afford the time to go? And I was surprised, very surprised. They've looked at the market very carefully and where there's a gap they have gone for it.'

Finally, they are commercial & business law specialists, scoring 'Good' in a recent assessment by the LPC Board.

SOCIAL SCENE

STUDENTS' UNION There is a new £4-million Student Union building, the current one having been converted to studio space for drama and media. There are both alcoholic and non-alcoholic social areas, space for bands performing and administrative areas for student societies.

The advent of X-Men and Star Trek: The Next Generation star, Patrick Stewart, as the University's Chancellor has seen him take a keen interest in the Drama and English courses.

The **Venue** is the multi purpose bar which plays host to a variety of events including club and band nights. UHSU has two regularly scheduled club nights: Friday night is *Grrrr*, an indie, rock and metal night; Saturday night plays host to *Quids In*, with drinks offers and a 'party' DJ playing disco, pop and some dance music. There are also one-off DJ events, like recently Hed Kandi played.

Student media is consistently good - the newspaper is *Huddersfield Student*, Student radio is Ultra

FM. Generally students are pretty apathetic. The SU occasionally attempts to get the student body into a more political frame of mind, but politics rarely run beyond campus concerns. They also launched a *Give It A Go* programme to galvanise more interest in societies. Islamic Soc remained the preferred choice.

SPORT Facilities are not extensive. There's a sports hall on campus, with a newish fitness centre and playing areas elsewhere, which provide for football, rugby (league and union), hockey, cricket and tennis. There is also a new Astroturf pitch and two new top-quality soccer pitches. Students have a discount at an Olympic standard sports centre with swimming pool in town. Rugby League players enjoy a sponsorship arrangement with Huddersfield Giants

PILLOW TALK

The uni no longer owns any accommodation, but recommends as its preferred and approved accommodation, the Storthes Hall Park Student Village and Ashenhurst Houses. These are privately-

WHAT IT'S REALLY LIKE

UNIVERSITY:	
Social Life	★★★
Campus scene	**Laid-back, authentic**
Student Union services	**Good**
Politics	**Interest low**
Sport	**Regional force**
National sporting position	**100th**
Sport facilities	**Average**
Arts opportunities	**Music, film; art, drama**
Student newspaper	**Huddersfield Student**
National Media Awards	**Commended**
Student radio	**Ultra FM**
Nightclub & bar	**Venue**
Union ents	**2 club nights and DJ events**
Union societies	**38**
Parking	**Non-existent**
TOWN:	
Entertainment	★★★
Scene	**Pubs, music, poetry, drama**
Town/gown relations	**Good**
Risk of violence	**Low**
Cost of living	**Average**
Student concessions	**Good**
Survival + 2 nights out	**£50 pw**
Part-time work campus/town	**Good**

ACCOMMODATION

Guarantee to freshers	**None**
Style	**Halls/flats**
Security guard	**24 Hour**
Shared rooms	**Some**
Internet access	**All**
Self-catered	**All**
En suite	**All**
Approx price range pw	**£66.95**
City rent pw	**£60-£75**

owned and operated by Ubrique Investments Limited trading as 'digs'. See www.campusdigs.com for further information.

Other hall-type accommodation and private shared houses are available around the town with rents from around £60 per week.

GETTING THERE

☞ By road: M62/J24, M1/J38-40.
☞ By rail: London via Wakefield, 3:30; Liverpool Lime Street, 1:45
☞ By air: Leeds/Bradford, Manchester Airports.
☞ By coach: London, 5:00; Leeds, 1:10.

UNIVERSITY OF HULL

The University of Hull
Cottingham Road
Kingston upon Hull HU6 7RX

TEL 0870 126 2000 (prospectus)
    01482 466100 (admissions)
FAX 01482 442290
EMAIL admissions@hull.ac.uk
WEB www.hull.ac.uk

Hull University Union
University House
Cottingham Road
Hull HU6 7RX

TEL 01482 445361
FAX 01482 466280
EMAIL [initial.name]t@hull.ac.uk
WEB www.hullstudent.com

VAG VIEW

*H*ull city's most famous literary son, the late poet and librarian Philip Larkin, described the city of Kingston upon Hull as 'in the world, yet sufficiently on the edge of it to have a different resonance.'

For centuries it was cut off from the rest of the country to the south by the Humber, to the north by the glorious, wide open Yorkshire Wolds (now home to David Hockney), and to the west by a large expanse of nothing. Then all the way from Liverpool on the opposite coast came the M62, meeting on its way the A1(M)), and suddenly Hull became part of the rest of the world, though as student Adam Ford told us, 'You'd be surprised at the number of people in Liverpool who still think that the M62 stops in Leeds.'

The essence of Hull is that it is distinct, not just because it has its own telephone system and white phone boxes, 'It is distinct culturally,' a sixthform careers master said to me in hushed tones. He teaches just an hour away and still he can't find his way into it; he sends pupils to Newcastle (two hours to the north), to York (an

UNIVERSITY/STUDENT PROFILE

University since	**1954**
Situation/style	**Campus**
Student population	**22275**
Undergraduates	**18710**
Mature undergraduates	**22%**
International undergrads	**10%**
Male/female ratio	**49:51**
Equality of opportunity:	
state school intake	**93%**
social class 4-7 intake	**31%**
low-participation area intake	**16%**

hour to the west), to Sunderland, to Teesside, but rarely, if ever apparently, to Hull.

The point, then, is that in its insularity, Hull has developed this 'unique resonance'. For the same reason, it is a cheap place to live, more than 2% below the national average: you can buy a three-bedroom house there for what it costs to send a child to public school for two years; parents do and sell it when their darling leaves. But perhaps more important than all this is that academically the University of Hull is very strong, with high scores in teaching assessments, the Queen's Anniversary Prize for Social Work and Social Policy, a first class reputation for arts & social sciences - politics and languages especially - for health, for science and for business. The joint Hull York medical school is the jewel in the crown.

Finally, the campus is a friendly and creative place to be, and there's a great Students' Union - 88% of students gave it their approval in the National Student Survey; drop-outs are a mere 6%, which, given their access policy, is a triumph.

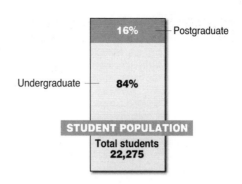

STUDENT POPULATION
Total students
22,275

16% — Postgraduate
Undergraduate — 84%

CAMPUS

'The university is situated on Cottingham Road, about half an hour's walk, or a fifteen minute bus ride, from the city centre,' writes Albertina Lloyd. 'Cottingham Road connects Beverly Road and Newland Avenue, and you will come to know these three roads very well - Newland Avenue for shops (one claimed to sell "everything but the girl" and gave the band their name) and cafés, Cottingham Road for takeaways and Beverly Road for pubs. So, all that a student needs is situated within a short distance of the campus itself.'

Writes Laura French: 'It's close enough to the centre of town to satisfy both shopping and partying appetites, whilst being far enough away to provide some peace and quiet when you decide it's actually time to get some work done/sleep.'

'Hull prides itself on being one of the friendliest campuses in the country,' notes Danny Blackburn. 'It is a genuinely warm and welcoming environment, in which everyone feels as if they belong. The bars, corridors and lecture theatres all emanate a tremendous feeling of one-ness; it is apparent from day one. Hull's campus is, on a human scale, large enough always to be fun and exciting, but small enough to be personal, comfortable and unimposing.'

Now, Hull has expanded into the old and neighbouring Lincoln & Humberside Uni campus, locating Health Education there and the new Hull-York Medical School.

There is, too, Hull's Scarborough Campus, 40 miles north up the coast, which is known for Drama, and is indeed the seat of the National Student Drama Festival (NSDF), its patron Sir Alan Ayckbourn, whose plays are always premiered in the town's Stephen Joseph Theatre, which he runs.

FEES, BURSARIES

UK & EU Fees 2009-10: £3,225 p.a. If in receipt of HE Maintenance grant there's a bursary on a sliding scale. For Sir Brynmor Jones/Ferens Scholarships for Academic Excellence, see

www.hull. ac.uk/money.

STUDENT PROFILE

The uni has always been seen as one of the 'access elite', in that it enjoys a pukka academic reputation, but has been able to bring in a number of undergrads from poorer areas/classes.

Currently 31% fall into this category, and 16% come from neighbourhoods new to the whole idea of going to university. Hull developed its policy by motivating 16-year-olds with conditional offers and running clubs for 11 and 12-year-olds.

Once ensconced on campus, Hull students become stereotypical (beer, beer and more beer), or sign up as members of one of the healthy subgroups, clubbers, metallers, crusties and skaters.

All intermingle without any trouble.

ACADEMIA & JOBS

'Students say the best teaching at Hull is to be had in Philosophy, History, History & Archaeology, American Studies, Business Studies, Education, European Languages, Computer Science, Management, Marketing, Psychology, Chemistry, Economics, Human & Social Geography, Law, Theology, Physics, English, Politics.

The results of the nationwide assessment of the research provision across all our universities sug-

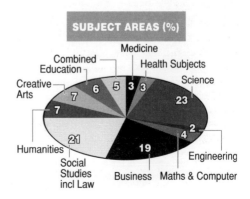

SUBJECT AREAS (%)

Medicine
Combined Education — Health Subjects
Creative Arts — Science
6 5 3 3
7 — 23
7
Humanities — 21 — 2
Social Studies incl Law — 19 — 4
Business Maths & Computer — Engineering

TEACHING SURVEY AT A GLANCE

Avg. UCAS points accepted	**290**
Acceptance rate	**26%**
Overall satisfaction rate	**88%**
Helpful/interested staff	★★★★
Small tuition groups	★★★
Students into graduate jobs	**78%**

Teaching most popular with undergraduates:
Philosophy (8%), History, History & Archaeology (97%), American Studies (96%), Business Studies (94%), Education, European Languages (93%), Computer Science, Management, Marketing, Psychology (92%), Chemistry, Economics, Human & Social Geography, Law, Theology, Physics (91%), English, Politics (90%).

Teaching least popular with undergraduates:
Social Work (77%), Finance, Accounting, Initial Teacher Training (76%), Engineering & Technology (74%).

gests in Hull's case that there's an in-depth knowledge bank to be drawn on in fifteen subjects praised as world-class, in particular health subjects like Biomedical Science, Nursing, and Operation Department Practice, 20% of which were adjudged 4 star, world-class. Geography & Environmental Studies, History, and Drama were also up there, and Politics, Social Work, and English too. Substantial amounts of the research in these subjects (between 25% and 40%) were also assessed as internationally significant.

Putting these results together with the students' assessment of the teaching is a worthwhile exercise, as it highlights History, Geography, English and Politics as especially strong at Hull.

The Politics Department is particularly well known for its Westminster-Hull Internship Programme established by Professor the Lord Norton of Louth, who teaches at Hull, whereby students have the unique opportunity to work on a placement with high-profile MPs. As a result, a high number of Hull graduates are working in Westminster.

The recent success in the research assessment of English reminds one of the distinguished array of poets that the University has either educated or employed, men such as Philip Larkin, Andrew Motion and Roger McGough. Kinship between English and Drama draws us to another great strength of the curriculum. There are currently five Theatre degrees and eleven Drama degrees at Hull. Recently, playwright Alan Plater opened the Anthony Minghella Drama Studio on campus in memory of the former Hull student and lecturer who went on to become an internationally acclaimed film director. Now there are plans for a multi-million pound dedicated Creative Arts Centre.

Small surprise then that Hull students win awards regularly at the NSDF, most recently in 2008 for the prestigious Mackinosh Cameron Award.

Business makes a notably large contribution to graduate jobs, particularly to employment in accountancy and the hotel and restaurant industry. There are numerous dedicated degrees in Accountancy at Hull, and Management and Tourism degrees relevant to the hotel industry. Biological Sciences makes almost as big an impact on the graduate employment figures, with jobs in hospitals for students of such as Human Biology and Biology with Molecular Sciences, and other Biology degrees taking their students into secondary education in number, while degrees in Sport, Psychology and Social Work, play their part in creating jobs in the community. 'Social Work, community and counselling activities' are in fact the third largest employment category for Hull graduates.

The degree in Medicine at the Hull York Medical School is a 5-year BMBS (Bachelor of Medicine, Bachelor of Surgery). You may be based at either Hull or York Uni campuses (it's a dual effort, both follow the same curriculum). Hull has a decade's experience in Medicine through its Postgrad. Medical School, while York's Biosciences and Health departments are top rated for teaching and research. Small-group clinical contact from Year 1. Equal emphasis on physical, psychological and social aspects. A low student-teacher ratio promised. You will need AABb at A-level (to include A Level Biology at grade A, and also A Level Chemistry - may tie the second grade A to Chemistry - applicants should check the website). They do not accept General Studies at A2 or AS or Critical Thinking at A-Level. You will need to sit for UKCAT. Caring experience and interpersonal skills will be a significant separator.

> *'One of the friendliest campuses in the country. All my lecturers operate an open door policy, and are never too busy to help out. Many of them use the all-important currency of humour in lectures.'*

RESEARCH EXCELLENCE

% of Hull's research that is
4* *(World-class)* or **3*** *(Internationally rated):*

	4*	3*
Health Professions	20%	40%
Biological Sciences	5%	10%
Chemistry	5%	45%
General Engineering	0%	40%
Geography	15%	40%
Business/Management	5%	40%
Law	5%	40%
Politics	10%	25%
Social Work	10%	30%
Psychology	5%	30%
Education	5%	20%
Sports Studies	0%	10%
English	10%	45%
Philosophy	5%	30%
History	15%	50%
Performing Arts	15%	30%
Music	5%	35%

New this year is BSc Global Health and Disease, designed for those wanting to work in development or humanitarian aid. This new HEFCE-funded course uses expertise across the uni, teaching modules from a range of disciplines, including Geopolitics of the Developing World, and Microbiology and Parasitology. It has been developed with help from NGOs Save the Children, Medecin sans Frontieres, and Oxfam GB.

Also offered for the first time this year are BA (Hons) Education, Social Inclusion and Special Needs, and BA joint honours in Education and Early Years. Primary school teachers account for 65% of graduate jobs in Hull's Education provision.

'All of my lecturers operate an open door policy, and are never too busy to help you out,' writes Joe Whinam. 'Many use the all-important currency of humour in lectures. The Brynmor Jones Library is absolutely huge, and I have never had problems getting a book from there. Seven floors packed full of books, great views, quiet work places and gorgeous exchange students. The computer network is surprisingly reliable and allows you to access your private account from any computer off campus, as well as course information, lecture notes, e-mail and all the programs you'd ever need.'

Finally, there is a good reputation for Law - they are European law specialists (French, German) with a Grade 5 rating for research. There's also a good line into the police. Note the BA

Criminology, Criminology with Psychology, and Criminology with Law. There's also Social Policy & Criminology and now Citizenship & Social Justice, and an intriguing bunch of Chemistry with Forensic Science & Toxicology degrees.

SOCIAL SCENE

STUDENTS' UNION 'Hull Union offers so much that you actually needn't venture off campus for a good night out,' writes Laura French. 'You'll hear third years tell how the newly refurbished bar, **The Sanctuary** is not as good as the **Rez**' (the old bar in the union). Just ignore them, a change is as good as a rest. Another bar, the **John McCarthy**, and a full-sized club, **Asylum**. Asylum is great fun; you will grow to love it, and its predictable soundtrack (mostly 80s/90s cheese and current pop).

They have different nights on every night, but the most popular are the Athletic Union nights on a Wednesday. Buy your tickets in advance. They even sometimes play films up on the big screen, which is cool. Like going to the cinema but cheaper and with a pint. Whilst Hull itself, unfortunately, does not attract a great many live acts, the union is getting increasing numbers of reputable bands to come and play there, The Feeling and We Are Scientists being recent examples. There's always loads going on, including karaoke, open mic nights, a quiz and much more.'

The on-campus **Gulbenkian Theatre** is the focus of the student drama scene mentioned in *Academia* above. There is a newspaper, *Hullfire*, and a student radio station, Jam 1575, again often award-winning. The Techincal Committee is a parallel organisation heavily into sound and lighting systems and gets its performance kicks at the Friday and Saturday discos.

Politically the union is averagely active. 'The Union Council is largely left wing and campaigns are well supported,' says Peter Bainbridge. Campaigns have supported Third World First, Animal Rights and Amnesty International, and there's a particularly active Women's Committee and Lesbian and Gay Society. 'Though the locals aren't the most tolerant of folk,' says Peter, 'there are gay-friendly places.'

TOWN Hull has undergone a major facelift in the form of the **St Stephen's Development**, a £200 million project at the heart of the city. There's a huge retail centre, a state-of-the-art transport interchange, a hotel, modern residences and a new home for the legendary **Hull Truck Theatre**.

WHAT IT'S REALLY LIKE

UNIVERSITY:	
Social Life	★★★★
Campus scene	**Friendly, lively, cheap**
Student Union services	**Cracking SU**
Politics	**Average: fees**
Sport	**47 clubs**
National team position	**64th**
Sport facilities	**Good**
Arts opportunities	**Drama excellent; music good; dance, film avg; art poor**
NSDF Drama Award	**Cameron Mackintosh 2008**
Student newspaper	**Hullfire**
Student radio	**Jam 1575**
Nightclub	**Asylum**
Bars	**McCarthy, Sanctuary**
Union ents	**Discos, live bands**
Union societies	**48**
Most popular societies	**Drama, Business, Afro Caribbean, Med Soc**
Parking	**Poor**
CITY:	
Entertainment	★★★★
Scene	**Good clubs**
Town/gown relations	**Poor**
Risk of violence	**High**
Cost of living	**Low**
Student concessions	**Average**
Survival + 2 nights out	**£50 pw**
Part-time work campus/town	**Excellent**

one. There's no shortage of nice pubs around the uni itself - **The Old Grey Mare** directly opposite does good, cheap food, **The Gardener's Arms** is a popular hangout for sports teams (whether you like rugby, or just rugby players) and **The Haworth Arms**, a little further down the road is a good place to hang out with friends.'

SPORT Writes Laura: 'Facilities are great. There is a relatively new sports centre with squash courts, halls etc and loads of pitches, both grass and Astroturf across the road from the uni. If, like me, team sports aren't your thing, but you still want to get fit, there is an excellent gym in the fitness centre.'

PILLOW TALK

Not before time, the uni has spent £16 million on refurbishments to halls over the last few years. Writes Joe: 'The three halls, Needler, The Lawns and Thwaite are in the village of Cottingham, a couple of miles from campus, great for pubs (karaoke at the Hallgate = winner), takeaways and

ACCOMMODATION

Guarantee to freshers	**100%**
Style	**Halls, houses**
Security guard	**All/Campus**
Shared rooms	**Some halls, not flats**
Internet access	**All**
Self-catered	**Most**
En suite	**Some**
Approx price range pw	**£54.29-£122**
City rent pw	**£50-£75**

Hull's Old Town is home to some of the city's traditional pubs and a fine Museum Quarter. The area near the University, Newland Avenue and Princes Avenue, has seen a lot of recent investment.

Writes Laura: 'Newland Avenue and Princes Avenue provide everything from greengrocers to convenience stores to café bars. They are slightly bohemian in feel, and, being in Hull, are much cheaper than their equivalents in other cities.

'Whilst Hull may not have the diversity of night life that you would get in other, bigger cities, there is nonetheless something for every-

shops. Regular buses run. Lawns is absolutely huge, has its own bar and police station. Thwaite is a posh version of Needler, but it is out of the way of everyone else.' Plans are afoot for more student accommodation in the near future.

GETTING THERE

☛ By road: M62, A63, A1079, B1233.
☛ By rail: Leeds, 1:00; Manchester, 2:15; London King's Cross, 4:30; Birmingham New Street, 3:00.
☛ By air: Humberside, Leeds/Bradford Airports.
☛ By coach: London, 5:10; Manchester, 3-4:00.

IMPERIAL COLLEGE LONDON

Imperial College
South Kensington
London SW7 2AZ

TEL 020 7594 8001
FAX 020 7594 8004
EMAIL admissions@imperial.ac.uk
WEB www.imperial.ac.uk

Imperial College Union
Prince Consort Road
London SW7 2BB

TEL 020 7594 8060
FAX 020 7594 8065
WEB www.imperialcollegeunion.org

VAG VIEW

*T*he Imperial College of Science,
Technology and Medicine is based
*principally in South Kensington,
London. Formerly a constituent college
of the University of London, Imperial
became independent of the University in
July 2007, on the 100th anniversary of
its founding.*

*Mergers have formed its character
since the beginning, where, in 1907, it
arose out of the marriage of the prestigious Royal College of Science, the Royal
School of Mines and the City & Guilds
College. The RCS gave Imperial pure
Science, the RSM gave it Mining (and
related fields, such as Geology) and the
City & Guilds College, Engineering.
Mergers with three London teaching hospitals leave it with a massive medical
provision. There are other influences.
Wye College in Kent brings the food
industry, agriculture, the environment
and business management into the
equation.*

Last year the Times Higher
Education *magazine placed Imperial
5th in the World's Top 200 Universities
table, behind Harvard, Yale, Cambridge,
Oxford, and the California Institute of
Technology.*

*However, in the recent Research
Assessment they slipped from second to
sixth place in the UK, and in the
Student Experience Survey Imperial's
lecturers get only an average-looking 3
stars for the help and interest they show
their students. Indeed, overall Imperial
only managed 60th place in the UK in
that survey.*

UNIVERSITY/STUDENT PROFILE	
School of London Uni since	**1908**
Situation/style	**City campus**
Student population	**13410**
Undergraduates	**8350**
Mature undergraduates	**46%**
International undergrads	**8%**
Male/female ratio	**46:54**
Equality of opportunity:	
state school intake	**13%**
social class 4-7 intake	**40%**
low-participation area intake	**65%**

*Nevertheless, Imperial has one of the
lowest drop-out rates in the country
(2.8%), which suggests that feeling
wanted is not much of a priority for its
students.*

CAMPUSES

'The main campus is situated in South Kensington,
Zone 1, Central London,' writes Saurabh Pandya.
'We are right next to the Victoria & Albert, Science
and Natural History museums (and are granted
free access to them). Travel is easy, the nearest
tube is a ten-minute walk away. Generally, it is a
low crime area, well lit and pretty safe for students,
especially as the uni, the union and most uni

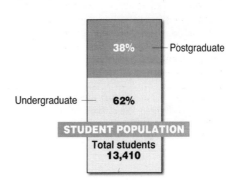

38% — Postgraduate

Undergraduate — 62%

STUDENT POPULATION

Total students
13,410

TEACHING SURVEY AT A GLANCE

Avg. UCAS points accepted	**480**
Acceptance rate	**16%**
Overall satisfaction rate	**85%**
Helpful/interested staff	★★★
Small tuition groups	★★★
Students into graduate jobs	**88%**

Teaching most popular with undergraduates:
Computer Science (96%), Molecular Biology, Biochemistry (95%), Chemical, Process & Energy Engineering (94%), Electronic & Electrical Engineering, Materials & Minerals Technology (93%), Sciences related to Biology (92%), Biology (90%).

Teaching least popular with undergraduates:
Aerospace Engineering (69%).

accommodation are all within 5 mins of each other.'

Says Sarah Playforth, 'This has got to be the best situated college in london, probably in England and perhaps even in the world. If you come from a small town like I do, you'll be blown away by it. Now, the negative. If daddy doesn't own half the oil fields in Texas you are likely to hit a major financial crisis if you eat out at anywhere other than McDonalds. Yes, central London is an extremely expensive place. By the time you graduate you'll probably have acquired an overdraft equivalent to the annual budget of a small country.'

There is a satellite campus, Wye College in Ashford, Kent. Tel 01233 812401, the sometime

> *'This has got to be the best situated college, probably in England, perhaps even in the world. If you come from a small town like I do, you'll be blown away by it. Now, the negative. If daddy doesn't own half the oil fields in Texas you are likely to hit a major financial crisis.'*

agricultural arm of London University. Imperial bought it and now it's home to an important Applied Business Management course, taught, it seems rather oddly, by Kent University. You get a Kent degree and an Imperial Associateship.

FEES, BURSARIES

UK & EU Fees, 2009-10: £3,225 p.a. All students in receipt of the full Government HE Maintenance Grant will receive a student support bursary up to a maximum of four years. There's also an award at the midpoint in a year for those in receipt of a partial HE Maintenance Grant.

STUDENT PROFILE

There is a sense of privilege in the air. They take around the same number of public school kids as Durham - only this lot are quieter. Another factor is the gender imbalance 65% male, though it seems even worse: 'The male:female ratio here is about 100:1,' said a student, 'but blokes have practically no chance of getting a woman, ever, and consequently Imperial is the sexual frustration capital of Britain!'

Sarah Playforth agrees, but feels for the girls: 'What you pull is not guaranteed to be human, but the good thing about the student body is that the college's international reputation leads to a large cultural diversity and you can make friends from all over the world.' It does indeed, 40% of undergraduates were international students at the last count. There's also a large mature student population - 13%.

ACADEMIA & JOBS

Students say the best teaching is to be had in Computer Science, Molecular Biology, Biochemistry, Chemical, Process & Energy Engineering, Electronic & Electrical Engineering, Materials & Minerals Technology, Sciences related to Biology, Biology. Least popular is Aerospace Engineering, the teaching of which had the approval of only 69% of its undergraduates.

'The work is hard, let's get that straight from the outset,' writes Saurabh. 'Most successful applicants have AAB or higher at A-level, and so a high standard will be expected of you. But help is always at hand should you fall behind. There are plenty of tutorials, one-to-one time with the lecturer; lecture

SUBJECT AREAS (%)

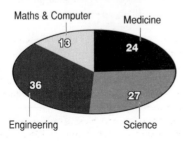

Maths & Computer **13**
Medicine **24**
Engineering **36**
Science **27**

% of Imperial's research that is
4* *(World-class) or* **3*** *(Internationally rated):*

	4*	3*
Cardiovascular Medicine	20%	45%
Cancer Studies	15%	60%
Infection & Immunology	30%	40%
Other Hospital Clinical	30%	45%
Epidemiology	40%	30%
Psychiatry	10%	50%
Biological Sciences	20%	45%
Chemistry	20%	55%
Physics	20%	45%
Pure Mathematics	40%	45%
Applied Mathematics	20%	45%
Statistics	25%	50%
Computer Science	35%	50%
Electrical/Electronic Eng.	20%	55%
Bioengineering	25%	50%
Earth Science and Eng.	25%	45%
Chemical Engineering	30%	55%
Civil Engineering	40%	55%
Mechanical, Aeronautical & Manufacturing Eng.	30%	50%
Metallurgy and Materials	20%	35%
Business/Management	35%	50%
History	40%	40%

notes are always on the web, and if you e-mail a particular lecturer they will always meet with you and explain anything that you don't understand. Most subjects have a representative, a student in your year, chosen by your vote, whose responsibility it is to ensure that you know what's going on, that the web notes are of a satisfactory standard, and so on.

AAB is rarely going to be enough. The ask is becoming ever more demanding. With the A* grade at A Level coming into effect this year, the Departments of Computing and Electrical & Electronic Engineering are expected to ask A*AA for 2010 admission, while Mathematics & Computer Science is expected to reach A*A*A*, the highest requirement in the country.

'The library occupies five floors and is shared with the Science Museum. It is pretty comprehensive, and as you would expect at a science and technology uni, the computing facilities are also first rate. There are plenty of PCs, and these are upgraded every eighteen months. Staff tend to be leading figures in their field, and regardless of subject you will get a world class education by coming here.'

The Medicine degree in this, the largest med.

school in the country, is a 6-year MB BS.

There's a special route in via a foundation year at Thames Valley Uni. Otherwise, the requirement is AAB in three A levels and grade B in a fourth subject at AS level. AS levels must include Biology and Chemistry and A levels must include two sciences, at least one of which must be Biology or Chemistry. General Studies is excluded and Maths cannot be offered with Further or Applied Maths as two individual subjects. BMAT is also required. All learning is in a clinical context. Traditional, but with special emphasis on communication skills. law, and information technology.

Imperial graduates become doctors, bankers, accountants, higher education lecturers, software consultants, engineering design consultants, manufacturers (especially of aircraft), or they go and work in Defence, or for a construction company. Jobs in oil extraction, mining, etc, also proliferate. Getting a job for an Imperial graduate is hard to avoid, 88% of them have one within six months of leaving.

Finally, the question of Wye is answered by the college in this way: 'The future of our rural environment and how we use it to produce safe and healthy food is of critical importance in this new millennium. The Department, already widely known for its interdisciplinary approach (integrating science and management) to new technologies, strategies and policies affecting rural development worldwide, has modern laboratories and facilities, including an award-winning learning resources centre and working farm on a 350-hectare estate.'

SOCIAL SCENE

STUDENTS' UNION Imperial is great at isolating itself and perhaps at alienating itself as well. It has left London University and it has left the National Union of Students. Students will barely notice the latter. ICU cards are accepted at most places in London, but they might miss the University of London Union (ULU) card, which is also widely recognised and allows use of some great facilities.

Imperial's facilities feature **Da Vinci's**, a modern-style café bar - trivia nights, cocktail nights and live jazz, big screen sport, Wednesday club-nights for the sports crowd (with recent additional barbecue facilities), Saturday pre-club and a non-stop succession of Friday clubnights.

The wood-panelled **Union Bar** is a more typical pub, with reputedly the largest pewter tankard collection in Europe. The Beit Quad bars are in the ground floor of the Union building in Beit Quad. Then there's the Charing Cross (med) Bar, Fulham, and the **Union Bar**, out at Wye.

In addition, a **Concert Hall** is used for bigger events and there's a smaller venue, **dBs** (rarely

one 'Angry Geek' was runner-up for Columnist of the Year.

Down at rural Wye, your average Wye-guy can be found done up in a penguin suit on his way to a ball, or one of their eccentric clubs, including the mysterious Druids, which take over the Union in a whirl of practical jokes, initiation ceremonies and over-consumption of alcohol.

SPORT Besides national competition in the uni leagues, where Imperial came 22nd last year, they excel in the London University league. But in rowing - the big thing at ICS - you're talking international levels. The boathouse is at Putney bridge.

A sports centre, Ethos, recently opened at the South Kensington campus - a 70-station fitness gym, 25m deck-level swimming pool, a sauna/steam room and spa, a five-badminton-court sports hall, a state-of-the-art climbing wall, exercise studio, and a sports injury unit.

Another at Prince's Gardens (Exhibition Road) includes a 25m swimming pool, four squash courts, a gym, a 25m rifle range, a training studio, sauna, steam room and poolside spa bath. Nearby there are tennis and netball courts, and a weights room. The 60-acre pitches are at Harlington, near Heathrow. Facilities include a floodlit multi-purpose surface and a pavilion with bar. There are a further 15 acres at Teddington (four pitches and a cricket square), 22 acres at Cobham, the boathouse at Putney and a sailing club at Welsh Harp Reservoir in North West London. In addition, its site at Charing Cross Hospital has a 25m swimming pool and squash.

PILLOW TALK

You are guaranteed a place in either Imperial College or London University intercollegiate accommodation for the first year of study. Imperial accommodation is self-catering except Linstead Hall on the South Kensington campus and the Wye campus halls. 'If you are lucky,' writes London-based Saurabh, 'you'll get into one of the halls right next to campus, and you can spend all year per-

known by its full name **Decibels**) or dB's **Club Bar** which is open Wednesday and Friday nights, again with big screen. Another attraction of the union is the cinema - 'the biggest student cinema in the country and the sixth biggest screen in London. It shows films much later than elsewhere but only go if you think the film is worth getting a sore bum for,' says our reporter.

The number of student societies at Imperial is pretty overwhelming - not far short of 300 from which to choose, everything from Chess to E-commerce, to Rugby to Juggling. And just because they are a techno-based uni, it doesn't mean they don't have any arty clubs - Opera, Drama, Art, Dance, etc., are all very active.

Film is rated excellent by students. Media, too, is very active both from a techno and literary pov. There's the student newspaper, *Felix*, and IC radio and STOIC, the TV arm, also the arts newsletter - *Phoenix*, and the science mag. - *I, Science*. In 2008 *Felix* won Best Journalist and Newspaper of the Year at the Guardian Media Awards. Meanwhile, *I, Science* was runner-up for Magazine of the Year, and

fecting your "get up at 8:55 and be in time for 9:00 lecture" technique. These are the Southside, Northside and Beit halls. If you are especially lucky, you will be placed in Beit Hall, which has Ikea-style kitchens and every amenity you could possibly want. There are other halls in Evelyn Gardens (15 minutes from campus) or Pembridge Gardens (40 minutes, or 20 by tube).'

GETTING THERE
☞ By Underground: South Kensington (Circle, District and Piccadilly lines).

UNIVERSITY OF KEELE

The University of Keele
Keele
Staffordshire ST5 5BG

TEL 01782 621111
   01782 584005/583994
FAX 01782 632343
EMAIL undergraduate@keele.ac.uk
WEB www.keele.ac.uk

Keele Students' Union
Keele
Staffs ST5 5BJ

TEL 01782 733700
FAX 01782 712671
EMAIL sta15@kusu.keele.ac.uk
WEB www.kusu.net

VAG VIEW

*K*eele *University is situated in Staffordshire, in an area known as the Potteries, whose most famous literary son, Arnold Bennett (Clayhanger,* Anne of the Five Towns*) couldn't get away fast enough, though to be fair he had been under pressure from his father to settle down and become a solicitor, and the place did certainly inspire him to write.*

The Uni was founded in 1949 with a coherent educational philosophy to provide a broadly based undergraduate education, in sharp contrast to the (then) heavy emphasis on the high specialised single honours degree. This strategy is today clearly visible still in the dual honours degree, which Keele pioneered and which offers a rare opportunity to cut across traditional faculty lines. Ninety per cent of Keele's students opt for this type of degree, so have a good look at what's on offer. Nearly all undergraduates, irrespective of the subject combination they are studying, have the opportunity to spend a semester at one of the uni's partner institutions in North America (American Studies modules encourage this), Australia, South Africa or Europe. Keele has been awarded the European Quality Label for mobility. Bennett would have liked that.

Students are passionate about the uni-

UNIVERSITY/STUDENT PROFILE	
University since	**1962**
Situation/style	**Rural campus**
Student population	**12345**
Undergraduates	**8950**
Mature undergraduates	**15%**
International undergrads	**7%**
Male/female ratio	**38:62**
Equality of opportunity:	
state school intake	**91%**
social class 4-7 intake	**27%**
low-participation area intake	**11%**

versity, almost as if they are part of a cult rather than a campus commune - 89% of them made their feelings known in the recent National Student Survey. Dropping out (of a degree course that is) is not something many contemplate, and only 6% ever do.

CAMPUS

Keele was the first complete new University after the Second World War, and the prototype of the green-field campus university. Today the majority of academic activities are still located on campus, with the exception of parts of the Faculty of Health, which are located on the nearby hospital site.

Campus is in fact a 617-acre country estate with lakes and woodland, just north of the A525 and west of Newcastle-upon-Lyme: 'The centre of England and the middle of nowhere,' write Mark

TEACHING SURVEY AT A GLANCE

Avg. UCAS points accepted	**310**
Acceptance rate	**15%**
Overall satisfaction rate	**89%**
Helpful/interested staff	**★★★★**
Small tuition groups	**★★★★**
Students into graduate jobs	**80%**

Teaching most popular with undergraduates:
**Biomedical and Forensic Sciences, Human
Biology, Medical Science, Pharmacy (100%),
Computer Science, Geology, Physical Science
(97%), Chemistry (96%), Biology, Human & Social
Geography, Politics (94%), Maths, Music (93%),
History, Social Policy (92%), Medicine (91%),
Law (90%).**

Teaching least popular with undergraduates:
Finance & Accounting (71%).

Holtz and Gareth Belfield. 'Keele University's self-contained campus is a stone's throw from Stoke-on-Trent, a constant worry for those students without protective headgear. In theory, the university is set within tiny Keele village, but the campus has grown over such a large area that saying it is part of Keele village is akin to saying that London is part of Westminster. The campus is on a hill top and is so exposed you expect a policeman to come along and arrest it for indecency. Nearby Newcastle-under-Lyme, Hanley (Stoke) and Crewe can be reached by the bus service called (joyfully) PMT. Train-wise, Manchester is only 30 minutes away, as is Birmingham. London direct can be done in around two hours. The M6 is within earshot of the campus, and sounds like the sea if you are drunk enough.'

FEES, BURSARIES
UK & EU Fees 2009-10: £3,225 p.a. There's a minimum bursary of £319 to students in receipt of a full maintenance grant. Most students in receipt of the full grant will receive £800. See www.keele.

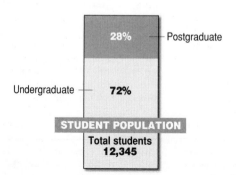

Postgraduate 28%

Undergraduate 72%

STUDENT POPULATION
Total students
12,345

ac.uk/undergraduate/bursaries. There's a programme for Elite Athletes who compete nationally or is particularly recognized for recent achievements, worth £300 and includes free gym membership, help with coaching and nutritional advice. Applicants who attain three A grades at A level or equivalent tariff points could be eligible for a £1,000 Keele Scholarship. Keele Link Bursaries - £500 for each year of study - are awarded to students from schools and colleges in the KeeleLink partnership. See www.keelelink. co.uk. Finally, there are Study Abroad Bursaries (£500) and Care Leaver Bursaries. Write to bursaries@ keele.ac.uk or call 01782 734240.

STUDENT PROFILE
'Take a generous measure of "traditional" students, two heaped tablespoons of mature, nursing, international and local students, heavily season with postgraduates, add a dash of complete weirdoes and you have the recipe for the most diverse and

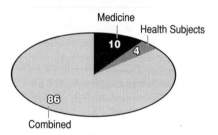

SUBJECT AREAS (%)

Medicine
Health Subjects
10
4
86
Combined

interesting concoction of a university anywhere in the world. It's impossible not to fit in at Keele, with over half the students living together on campus, you're never really in danger of running out of people to borrow sugar from.'
Female students abound (62% of undergrads).

ACADEMIA & JOBS
Students say that the teaching is best in Biomedical and Forensic Sciences, Human Biology, Medical Science, Pharmacy, Computer Science, Geology, Physical Science, Chemistry, Biology, Human & Social Geography, Politics, Maths, Music, History, Social Policy, Medicine, and Law.

But even the worst taught subject, Finance & Accounting, got 71% of the class vote. Lecturers get 4 stars for help and interest in their students and for the small size of tuition groups. No doubt it helps that everyone is trapped together on campus.

The dual honours degree is a multi-disciplinary strategy which promises more than a one-plus-one benefit - at best, new, enlightening points of view on a shared subject focus. Employers seem to like this, 80% of students get real graduate jobs within six months of leaving.

RESEARCH EXCELLENCE

% of Keele's research that is
4* (World-class) or 3* (Internationally rated):

	4*	3*
Clinical Subjects	0%	15%
Primary Care Clinical	15%	25%
Physics	5%	35%
Applied Mathematics	15%	45%
General Engineering	10%	40%
Business/Management	10%	35%
Law	10%	40%
Politics	10%	20%
Social Work	15%	50%
Psychology	0%	25%
Russian	15%	20%
English	10%	40%
History	20%	35%
Music	20%	45%

Social Studies prepare graduates for employment most effectively - 22% of the jobs come from this area of the curriculum. It takes them into the community and local government, specialising in such as social security, counselling, law and order... Degrees such as Psychology, Law or even Marketing with Social Science, Social Work, Politics, all count here.

Then subjects allied to Medicine work their magic turning graduates into human biologists and medicinal chemists and pharmacists in hospitals and elsewhere, and making nurses and midwives, pharmacists (a School of Pharmacy opened in 2006), physiotherapists and the like out of sixth-form hopefuls. These degrees (and one working with the visually impaired) now account for around 20% of the total graduate jobs at Keele.

They also offer the opportunity to study Medicine, a 5-year MBChB or 4-year fast track programme with direct entry to Year 2. There is, in addition, Medicine with Health Foundation Year, designed to provide an entry to Medicine for those without the conventional science A-level subjects normally required for direct entry. Continuation after the Foundation Year is subject to achieving specified grades.

Normal requirements to read Medicine at Keele are 2 Sciences at A level, one of which must Chemistry or Biology plus one other rigorous subject, with grades AAB. (Chemistry must be taken at AS Level grade B if not offered at A2.) Sciences not offered at A/AS Level must be offered at GCSE. You will also be required to sit the UKCAT test.

The School of Medicine is on three sites: on the main campus, at the University Hospital of North Staffordshire 3 miles away, and at Keele's Associate Teaching Hospital at the Shrewsbury and Telford Hospitals in Shropshire.

Banking is a major destination from the Business school, with dedicated degrees also taking large numbers into accountancy and recruitment/ personnel (the Human Resources degrees). Combinations with Computing take many others into software consultancy and supply.

A third of first years at Keele are studying a language or a related cultural module, and the degree orientation facilitates a wide range of graduate employment options.

Law is also worth a particular mention. Part of the multi-subject curriculum, but also a single honours subject, there's an international reputation and if you want to work as a solicitor and you already have a degree in another subject, you can take the Common Professional Examination (CPE) here.

STUDENT SCENE

STUDENTS' UNION Sam's Bar opens up to the Ballroom to take around 1100 on big live act nights. Apparently the KUSU building was originally designed to look like a ship with the Ballroom at the heart of the vessel. In the good old days the Rolling Stones used to use it as a rehearsal room and even now, on a still winter's night, faint echoes can be heard of the Eurythmics, UB40, Oasis and a young Jarvis Cocker, who graced the stage. More recent visitors were Fun Lovin' Criminals, Idlewild, Mis-Teeq, Liberty X, Atomic Kitten, Toploader, Reef, The Pet Shop Boys, Levellers, The Proclaimers.

The Lounge is - surprise - a lounge bar. K2, formerly The Club, is now KUSU's 'premier Entertainment Venue', having undergone a £250k refurbishment three years ago. With a top-specification PA & lighting system, it features a permanent 6m x 4m stage. Here, on a Monday is pop, chart & dance with resident DJ Chris; alternate Tuesdays is Comedy Club - Mark Lamarr, Peter Kay, Ed Byrne, Paul Tonkinson, Adam Bloom, Richard Morton and more. On other Tuesdays you might have Stella Screen - box office smashes before general release. Wednesdays - whole building is R-wind (retro - 80s, 90s) and indie/alternative from resident DJ The Rich. They also do

ACCOMMODATION	
Guarantee to freshers	**70%**
Style	**Halls, flats**
Security guard	**Halls, not flats**
Shared rooms	**Some halls**
Internet access	**Halls only**
Self-catered	**All**
En suite	**Some halls**
Approx price range pw	**£64-£105**
Town rent pw	**£40-£62**

WHAT IT'S REALLY LIKE	
UNIVERSITY:	
Social Life	★★★
Campus scene	**Isolated**
Student Union services	**Good**
Politics	**Average**
Sport	**Not impressive**
National teamposition	**69th**
Sport facilities	**Good**
Arts opportunities	**Excellent**
Student newspaper	**Concourse**
Nightclub	**K2**
Bars	**Sam's Bar, Ballroom, Lounge**
Union ents	**Cheesy + live**
Union societies	**80**
Most popular society	**Drama**
Parking	**Good**
TOWN:	
Entertainment	★★
Local (Stoke) scene	**Pubs/clubs**
Town/gown relations	**OK**
Risk of violence	**Average**
Cost of living	**Below average**
Student concessions	**Average**
Survival + 2 nights out	**£50 pw**
Part-time work campus/town	**OK/poor**

monthly fancy dress nights and, in The Lounge, Quiz and Cocktail evenings and Sunday karaoke competitions.

There's a variety of restaurants, bars, cafés and retail outlets on campus. The Comus offers a Five Day Meal Plan.

There are a number of societies on offer. Student radio, KUBE, is particularly active at the moment. It won Best Internet Only station at the European Radio Awards against non-student opposition, such as the BBC, Emap, Gcap media and many other national and commercial radio stations from across Europe. Six months later they won the gold award for online radio at the international Radio Awards in New York.

Finally, Keele has a history of political turbulence, but you wouldn't notice now: 'In the '70s,' write Mark and Gareth, 'Keele pre-empted Wales and Scotland by attempting to gain independence from Britain. Passports were issued, border patrols were set up, a national anthem created, and an unsuccessful attempt to enter the Eurovision Song Contest was made. More recently, they were the first university to reject the Government's tuition fees proposals.'

Sport In 2006, the AU won Most Improved University in the annual BUSA Awards, climbing the BUSA Championship ranking by an impressive 49 places - lifting them to 61st place out of 149 competing universities. Last year they managed 69th. Facilities include a gym, sports hall, floodlit synthetic pitch, 50 acres of grass pitches, tennis courts, fitness centre, squash courts, etc.

Town 'Aaarghh! Keele, the Potteries, where the main industry is not so much in decline, as plummeting down a precipice of bankruptcy. Locals refer to you as "duck" if they like you. If they don't like you they'll just try to run over you.'

PILLOW TALK

'There is something inexplicably nice about campus accommodation,' sigh Mark & Gareth, 'even if the cleaning ladies have mastered the art of knocking, unlocking your door, opening it, coming in, and saying, "Ooh, I'll come back when you've had time to put some clothes on," all in two seconds.'

Newest accommodation comprises 131 en-suite rooms in 2 blocks, arranged in 6-person flats. The HallsNet Service allows all students direct access to the Internet. In response to student demand last year a social space has been created in halls with alcohol-free facilities.

GETTING THERE

☞ By road: from the north M6/J16, A500, A531, right on to A525, right through Keele village; from south, M6/J15, A5182, left on to A53, right at Whitmore following signs.
☞ By rail: good service more or less everywhere, London 1:30 to Stoke-on-Trent station, then taxi.
☞ By coach: London, 4:00.

UNIVERSITY OF KENT AT CANTERBURY

The University of Kent at Canterbury
The Registry
Canterbury CT2 7NZ

TEL 01227 827272
FAX 01227 827077
EMAIL recruitment@ukc.ac.uk
WEB www.kent.ac.uk

Kent University Students' Union
The University
Canterbury CT2 7NW

TEL 01227 824200
FAX 01227 824204
EMAIL union@kent.ac.uk
WEB www.kentunion.co.uk

VAG VIEW

*T*he University of Kent at Canterbury (UKC)
*is, in a nutshell, a friendly, rather political-
ly correct campus, where it is easy to work
hard, play hard, or do a little of both.*

*Writes Dominic Conway: 'If you come to
this Uni you will have everything really, countryside and seaside, but still be near to London;
entertainment and nightlife, but still a calm
working environment. For the more hardcore
among you it may seem a little too relaxed, but
with the facilities and the high teaching standards you should definitely get a good education, and if you don't have enough fun, it's
more likely to be your fault than theirs.'*

UNIVERSITY/STUDENT PROFILE	
University since	**1965**
Situation/style	**City campus**
Student population	**18385**
Undergraduates	**14610**
Mature undergraduates	**15%**
International undergrads	**7%**
Male/female ratio	**38:62**
Equality of opportunity:	
state school intake	**92%**
social class 4-7 intake	**25%**
low-participation area intake	**9%**

CAMPUS

Canterbury Campus is situated on top of an alarm-
ingly steep hill about a mile out of the main city.
You will be assigned a residential college, Keynes,
Rutherford, Darwin or Eliot. You can be more or
less self-sufficient on campus, you could spend
your entire first year without visiting the city, and
many do.

Says Laura Budd: 'I like Canterbury because it
is not too big and not too wild and you are not too
far away from the coast - Whitstable, Hearne Bay
and Dover. I was hoping to go to Exeter University
and there was a lot of disappointment when I got
my results and didn't quite make it. But I have
always liked Canterbury ever since I first came,
especially with the Cathedral. It's just a really
friendly place to be. When we first had a look round
it, me and my parents - we missed the Open Day
and it was a self guided tour - people were coming
up to us: "Oh, are you OK? Do you need to know
where to go?" You know, really approachable.'

Medway Campus Twenty-five years ago the
Royal Navy left Chatham, North Kent, ending over
400 years of Naval history. The docks and the
northern part of Chatham Maritime, an island surrounded by the River Medway and a new marina,

have today been transformed into a thriving community, including campuses for Kent, Christ
Church Canterbury, and Greenwich universities.

Kent has invested millions of pounds in purpose-built facilities. The flagship Medway Building
has won awards for design excellence and houses
lecture theatres and seminar rooms, specialist studios and rehearsal rooms for the Music Technology
programme and facilities for the Centre for Sports
Studies. The Gillingham Building has other facilities, including a multimedia newsroom for the
Journalism programme. The Drill Hall Library,
shared with Greenwich University, cost £15 million
and has 370 PC study spaces, 400 open study
spaces, more than 157,000 books and pamphlets,
and 2.7 miles of shelves. See also 'Student Scene',
'Sport', and 'Pillow Talk' below.

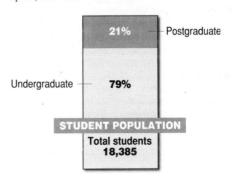

21%	Postgraduate
Undergraduate 79%	

STUDENT POPULATION
Total students
18,385

FEES, BURSARIES

UK & EU Fees: £3,225 p.a. If in receipt of HE Maintenance grant there's a bursary. There are bursaries too for applicants proceeding from less privileged backgrounds, and scholarships for sport and academic achievement.

STUDENT PROFILE

Intake from poorer socio-economic groups (25%) and neighbourhoods beyond the traditional university heartlands (9%) has risen sharply over the last few years in line with Government policy, and there are strong mature and overseas flavours, too - 16% of undergraduates are mature, but 20% are 'international'. Kent's position in the south east of England makes it easy to slip over to France or for the French to slip over here.

Said student of French Laura Budd, who had just returned from the Continent: 'You get a lot of students from Europe. With doing French I come across a lot of French students, like I've just met a French Erasmus student and we have become quite good friends. Some of them come over for a few months and some come over for their whole degree. There are three options for my year out. You can go to a French university and study, you can be a language assistant and teach in schools, or you can do a work placement. I want to be a primary school teacher so I'm going to France to teach. You know we are supposed to be called the European University!'

Indeed, Kent even has a campus in Brussels, the 'capital' of Europe, which offers specialist courses related to the study of international affairs. But their interest isn't simply in Europe. In recent years it has attracted students from over 50 countries

around the world. Catherine Robertson goes so far as to suggest that the reason why 'many British people haven't even heard of UKC is the uni's dedication to attracting overseas students,' but concludes 'what you will find is a friendly student body, and lecturers and tutors who pursue their own work as energetically as they do yours.'

ACADEMIA & JOBS

By 'lecturer's own work' Catherine meant their research. That of Kent University was up for

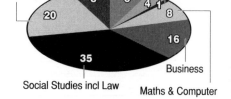

SUBJECT AREAS (%)

- Creative Arts
- Engineering
- Science
- Built Environment
- Humanities — 8
- 8
- 4
- 1
- 8
- 20
- 16
- 35
- Business
- Social Studies incl Law
- Maths & Computer

assessment at the end of 2008, along with the research of all other UK universities, and Kent did very well, coming 29th nationally. Great success was achieved in world-class rated Law, Social Work, Social Policy & Administration, English, History, and Drama (see Research Excellence box).

But what about the teaching? As Catherine said, there is the lecturers' work (the research) and the student's, which is to learn. Good researchers do not necessarily make good teachers. Are they helpful/interested in your work? In the National Student Survey undertaken by the Higher Education Funding Council the answer was a resounding 'Yes' - 89% of Kent students are satisfied, and we give lecturers at Kent 4 stars for helpfulness and interest, and for decent sized tuition groups, based on the results of the Student Experience Survey undertaken for *Times Higher Education* magazine.

Says student of French Laura: 'Usually you would have about two hours a week with your lecturers, depending on what you are studying. They are always really quick to reply to e-mails and are happy to meet you in their office at any time. But the system is actually changing at the moment. Your tutor is meant to be contacted only for academic matters. If you have a personal or pastoral matter then you can contact them in the first instance, and they will then pass you on to someone else. I had to do this last term actually for pas-

---

TEACHING SURVEY AT A GLANCE

Avg. UCAS points accepted	**300**
Acceptance rate	**20%**
Overall satisfaction rate	**90%**
Helpful/interested staff	★★★★
Small tuition groups	★★★
Students into graduate jobs	**70%**

Teaching most popular with undergraduates:
Anthropology, Finance, subjects allied to Medicine (98%), Accounting, English (95%), History (94%), Economics, History & Archaeological Studies (93%), Business & Administrative Studies, Management Studies, Social Policy (92%), Sciences related to Biology, Maths, Social Studies (91%).

Teaching least popular with undergraduates:
Sports Science (70%).

RESEARCH EXCELLENCE

% of Kent's research that is
4* *(World-class)* or **3*** *(Internationally rated):*

	4*	3*
Psychiatry	10%	20%
Biological Sciences	5%	30%
Environmental Sciences	5%	50%
Physics	0%	30%
Pure Mathematics	0%	35%
Applied Mathematics	10%	35%
Statistics	20%	45%
Computer Science	15%	50%
Electrical/Electronic Eng.	15%	25%
Metallurgy and Materials	25%	55%
Economics	15%	60%
Business/Management	10%	45%
Law	30%	35%
Politics	0%	35%
Social Work	30%	40%
Anthropology	20%	30%
Psychology	10%	30%
French	15%	35%
German	5%	15%
Iberian	5%	20%
English	30%	35%
Classics	5%	5%
Philosophy	10%	25%
Theology	10%	30%
History	35%	35%
Performing Arts	35%	35%

toral care. You go through the system. You fill out a form and you talk to various like senior tutors who are specialists in pastoral care. But now the system is changing and there are to be fewer tutors covering more students for academic matters. Hopefully, there are plenty of tutors for each subject, so if I have a problem with French, I won't end up seeing someone from Philosophy!'

Kent's commitment to the assimilation of European culture goes far and wide in the curriculum. They are European law specialists, for example, and many other courses are extended by study in Europe, by taking a European language and imbibing the culture, as in the European Arts course. 'Academically the university has a strong reputation for Modern Languages,' Catherine acknowledges, 'thanks to it's proximity to Europe and the

> *'Nice big cathedral, old cobbled streets, strong whiff of history, a two hour walk to the beach - that's Canterbury. Two clubs, plenty of bars, but one thing that's clearly missing is an exciting music scene.'*

encouragement to students to study abroad for a year.'

But it is not just about learning a language. Says Laura: 'My department isn't just French, it's one of six in the faculty of Humanities called the School of European Cultural Languages, and includes nine subjects. It's got all the languages, but also Philosophy, Religious Studies, Classics, Archaeology and Comparative Literature; it's quite mixed, and obviously French is just a section of that department. You learn a lot about other subjects and you expect to. At Kent French is a very literature-based course. I did Linguistics last term which was a nice break, but even so last year alone I studied 27 plays and novels in French. I'm getting up to the 50 mark now! I'm doing three literature modules this term, so it's about three novels a week!' I asked what effect this was having. 'It has developed the way I think about the country, and it has developed the way I think. Like studying Molliere, the French equivalent to Shakespeare... A lot of their writers are very sort of philosophical, so you end up thinking philosophically. And that's how all different subjects tie in, even though you are apparently only studying a language.'

There are other clear strengths in the curriculum. Drama not only scored full marks at the teaching assessments, but was a success at the research assessments. Focus for both student and professional theatre companies is the campus-based Gulbenkian Theatre.

In social sciences UKC are pre-eminent, with Social Policy, Economics, Anthropology and Psychology rated world-class for research.

SOCIAL SCENE

STUDENTS' UNION 'First years tend to remain on campus to socialise,' writes Catherine, 'simply because it is cheaper and more convenient. There are 5 main bars: **Origins** is in Darwin College (trendy-type bar, good fajitas); **Rutherford Bar** - guess where that is (a drinker's bar, good juke box); **Mungo's** is in Eliot (should be better than it is, no atmosphere); and then there's Keynes Bar (concrete garden, popular in summer). **Woody's** at Parkwood is more of a pub than a bar and haunted by the more cliquey sports clubs (you'll see what I mean). For those of you who don't want to spend all your time drinking alcohol, there is also the **Gulbenkian Theatre** coffee bar and 2 **Wicked** coffee shops.

ACCOMMODATION

Guarantee to freshers	**90%**
Style	**College halls, houses, flats**
Security guard	**All**
Shared rooms	**Some**
Internet access	**All**
Self-catered	**Some**
En suite	**Some**
Approx price range pw	**£72-£127**
City rent pw	**£65-£75**

WHAT IT'S REALLY LIKE

UNIVERSITY:	
Social Life	**★★★★**
Campus scene	**Friendly, southern but weekday**
Student Union services	**Good**
Politics	**Student issues**
Sport	**50 clubs**
National sporting position	**39th**
Sport facilities	**Good**
Arts opportunities	**Film, drama exc, music art good**
2008 NSDF Awards	**Acting**
Student newspaper	**KRED**
Student radio	**UKCR**
2008 National Awards	**Bronze award**
Nightclub	**The Venue**
Bars	**Lighthouse, Mungo's, Origins, Woodies**
Union ents	**Good but few live bands**
Union societies	**80**
Parking	**Poor**
CITY:	
Entertainment	**★★★**
Scene	**Touristy, historic, v. good pubs**
Town/gown relations	**Good**
Risk of violence	**Average**
Cost of living	**Average**
Student concessions	**Adequate**
Survival + 2 nights out	**£80 pw**
Part-time work campus/town	**Good**

'Now, what to do with your new-found friends once the bars have thrown you out into the cold, cold, night? Generally, people head onto **The Venue**, the campus club with a capacity of 1200, open six nights a week, and a café bar, **The Lighthouse** (200). Regular nights are Mondays, Sports Fed Night, where each sports club takes a turn as host. Thursdays are Retro nights Friday is dance, Saturday anything goes, from garage to pop, dance to r&b.'

Writes Dominic Conway: 'The Kent mentality is not a wild one. Although the 5 bars on campus will serve refreshingly cheap drinks nightly it is more common to see students sharing a few drinks at a comedy night or a salsa party than pushing the boundaries of alcohol consumption. The cultural diversity means that there is no obvious campus consensus, and the ever growing list of societies means that any student will feel well catered for.

'One thing clearly missing is an exciting music scene, the campus bands are sporadic and little talent tours these parts because there aren't any good venues for a live band. If you keep your ear to the ground, however, local groups will put on authentic, unpretentious rock shows and Whitstable (on the coast) hides a number of world class musicians playing jazz, blues, and Turkish folk music that even the most selective muso will be content with.

'Many students however don't make it as far as Whitstable and don't even trouble themselves with town very much, because the campus alone has so much to offer. The shops are a tad over priced but will stock all the essentials and some more exciting ingredients if you have a sudden urge to cook a lavish dinner. The Gulbenkian Theatre on campus hosts some remarkable shows, the manager is in close communication with the Drama department and is very well informed on the acts that students want to see. Its stage is open to comedy and music, as well as some bright lights in the world of modern theatre. The multitudinous societies keep freshening up the nightlife by hiring out the various venues for evenings for a more specific audience.

The hip-hop, drama and rock societies have put in the most effort so far in terms of catering for the uni as a whole. Safety on campus is ensured by Campus Watch, who offer an escort service for anyone walking around late at night on their own. '

The student radio station (UKCR) broadcasts 24/7 on 1350 AM. There are 2 studios. The student monthly magazine is *KRED*, an acronym derived from the initial letter of each of the colleges.

If campus gets too much, 'Canterbury is just a 20 minute walk away (or 10 minutes by bus, which comes regularly),' writes Dominic. 'Nice big cathedral, old cobbled streets, strong whiff of history in the air and a two hour walk to the beach. Although it is quite a quaint place, it is very lively and friendly - the locals never seem to mind or complain about the amount of students!'

Says Catherine: 'One thing it does not lack is pubs, and many of my friends have spent a happy drunken evening in the enchantingly named Bishop's Finger (the nun's delight apparently!).

After the pubs shut, things get a bit tricky, as Canterbury is not renowned for its club scene.'

UMSA/MEDWAY CAMPUS The scene here is run by the Universities at Medway Students' Association - Kent, Canterbury Christ Church and Greenwich universities. Coopers is the bar at the heart of it all. There are regular themed nights and you can party the night away, as it has a late licence. Nearby there are pubs and clubs, notably Tap'n'Tin for live music (Pete Doherty, The Bees and The View), and a multiplex cinema.

SPORT/CANTERBURY There are 50 clubs, all the usual stuff plus Choi Kwang Do, Taekwondo and Kendo (one of only five unis to offer this) and American Football (UKC Falcons). It's highly competitive. Various sports offer bursaries, some in cahoots with UKC alumni. UKC does well nationally at all the team sports, coming 39th in the national team league last year.

SPORT/MEDWAY CLUBS include football (women's and men's), rugby, cricket, netball, hockey, golf, rowing, tennis, canoeing, snow sports, badminton basketball, and the annual Medway Boat Race between Kent, Canterbury Christ Church and Greenwich unis is the major fixture of the year. Medway Park, an £11-million regional sports centre, is due to complete the picture. Already it has been approved as a pre-Games training camp venue for 13 Olympic and eight Paralympic sports. liquey. **The Works** is another favourite!'

PILLOW TALK

Canterbury Campus Writes Dominic: 'A lot of money has recently gone into accommodation, so the standard is fairly high. The new halls are the most spotless, but can be a little sterile. I would urge new students to brave a shared toilet for the sake of their social life.'

Most first years opt for halls in one of the 4 colleges or their posher extensions, or in Park Wood student village, made for the purpose. The colleges tend to be the easiest way to make friends as there are usually seven people randomly thrown together in a corridor and you all just mix and match.

The colleges, Eliot, Darwin, Rutherford and Keynes, are where the majority of first years end up, although you can get a place in Tyler Court or Becket Court, both new sets of accommodation.

A problem with the colleges is that they are semi-self-catered, i.e. you get breakfast included in the rent, but only until 9.30 am

Park Wood, the student village, is just off the main campus and made up of groups of houses for 4-to-6 students.

The problem here is that it is generally favoured by third years and foreign students, and they seem to get priority. The houses can leave you feeling freer, but a bit detached.

MEDWAY CAMPUS ACCOMMODATION at Liberty Quays is part of the new 'waterside village' set on the banks of the River Medway. The flats are for 6 to 8 students, each sharing a fully-equipped kitchen. The development has its own social area, launderette and Tesco Express store.

GETTING THERE

☞ By road: from west, M2, A2; south, A28 or A2; east, A257; northeast, the A28; northwest, A290.

☞ By rail: London Victoria, 85 mins; London Charing Cross or Waterloo East, 90 mins.

☞ By air: Heathrow and Gatwick.

☞ By coach: London Victoria, 1 hour 45 mins.

KING'S COLLEGE, LONDON

King's College, London
Waterloo Bridge House
London SE1 8WA

TEL 020 7836 5454
FAX 020 7836 1799
EMAIL enquiries@kcl.ac.uk
WEB www.kcl.ac.uk

King's College Students' Union
Surrey Street
London WC2R 2NS

TEL 020 7836 7132
FAX 020 7379 9833
EMAIL president@kclsu.org
WEB www.kclsu.org/

VAG VIEW

*K*ing's College London (KCL) is one of London University's oldest and most prestigious colleges, founded by George IV in 1829 and one of the federal university's original colleges in 1836. In the course of its history it has developed

UNIVERSITY/STUDENT PROFILE	
College of London Uni since	**1836**
Situation/style	**Civic**
Student population	**21230**
Undergraduates	**14010**
Mature undergraduates	**19%**
International undergrads	**10%**
Male/female ratio	**40:60**
Equality of opportunity:	
state school intake	**71%**
social class 4-7 intake	**22%**
low-participation area intake	**4%**

through many mergers, most recently, in the summer of 1998, with United Medical & Dental Schools of Guy's Hospital (where medical teaching began in the 1720s) & St Thomas's (where medicine has been taught since the 16th century). The full name for the new merged medical school is King's College London Medical School at Guy's, King's College and St Thomas's Hospital.

KCL stands at No. 22 in the table of the world's Top 200 universities (fifth highest among UK universities), and found the same position in the recent assessment of the research provision of all UK universities, where 60 per cent of its research activity was deemed world-class or internationally excellent. In total 91% of research activity entered was rated of international significance.

It is above all a health orientated university - 29% of graduates become doctors or dentists and a further 25% graduate in subjects allied to Medicine and find work in hospitals, or become pharmacists, or civil servants in the health area. There is, too, a strong presence of KCL graduates in banking and accounting, and in all areas of the civil service, and in the media, especially in publishing, advertising, radio and television, and its scholars in Ancient History and Classical Studies, and graduates of the Information Management and Language degrees run our museums, libraries and other archival institutions.

KCL's students are intensely loyal, 84% came out in wholehearted support of it in the Higher Education Funding Council's Student Survey (2008). Its lecturers get 4 stars for helpfulness and interest in their students, and 86% of graduates find real graduate jobs within six months of leaving. Not finishing a course here is rare; the drop-out rate is a tidy 5%.

Word on the ground is that KCL succeeds not in spite of, but because of its location in the Capital: 'Want to live and work smack in the centre of London?' write Ben Jones and Chris Wilding. 'Want high frequency bus and tube links with a 30% discount? You got it. Clubs? Pubs? Venues? Theatres? Museums? Galleries? Shops? Yeah, got them too. In fact, by nestling snugly and unassumingly within the heart of the capital, KCL appears to its students a seventh heaven.' But, as with all London colleges, at a price.

CAMPUSES

There are now five campuses, four of which cluster around the Thames, close to the centre of town. With the Students' Union **Macadam** building at its core is the **Strand campus**, on the north bank, close to Covent Garden. KCL is in the final stages of a £550-million redevelopment programme which is transforming their campuses; most recently Strand has had a £40-million facelift. Here are the schools of Humanities, Law and Physical Sciences. Just over the river across Waterloo Bridge is the newer **Waterloo Campus**, incorporating Education, Management, Health & Life Sciences, Nursing & Midwifery and the Stamford Street apartments with the basement gym, K4.

Three bridges to the east lies Guy's campus. Students of Medicine and Dentistry entering KCL

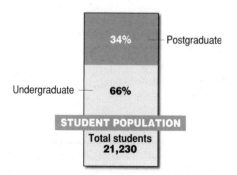

STUDENT POPULATION	
34% — Postgraduate	
Undergraduate — 66%	
Total students 21,230	

in 1999 were the first to study at this purpose-built centre close to London Bridge. The campus incorporates a new SU building with bar, swimming pool, ballroom, shop and welfare centre, as well as accommodation.

And then there's St Thomas's campus (Continuing Medical & Dental teaching), which overlooks the Houses of Parliament north across the river at Westminster Bridge, and Denmark Hill campus, south of the Oval.

The only site a little out on its own, Denmark Hill is base for clinical teaching at King's College Hospital and the Dental Institute, and home to the Institute of Psychiatry.

FEES, BURSARIES

UK & EU Fees 2009-10: £3,225 p.a. If in receipt of full or partial HE Maintenance Grant, KCL will award a bursary on a sliding scale according to level of grant. See www.kcl.ac.uk/funding/ for

TEACHING SURVEY AT A GLANCE

Avg. UCAS points accepted	**410**
Acceptance rate	**10%**
Overall satisfaction rate	**84%**
Helpful/interested staff	★★★★
Small tuition groups	★★★★
Students into graduate jobs	**86%**

Teaching most popular with undergraduates:
Classics (98%), Law, Music (95%), History (92%), Geographical Studies (90%), Biological and Physiological Sciences, Neuroscience, Politics (87%), Mechanical, Production & Manufacturing Engineering (86%).

Teaching least popular with undergraduates:
Theology (78%), Business Management, French Studies (77%), Linguistics (74%), Iberian Studies (70%).

SUBJECT AREAS (%)

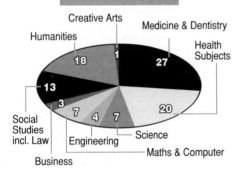

details of all new bursary and scholarship awards.

STUDENT PROFILE

Both King's and University College, London, the mother of all London University colleges, have a high public school intake, UCL's being higher than King's. There is, at King's, what one student described as a 'friendly competitiveness' with UCL. I have heard a KCL student refer to UCL students as 'godless scum', while UCL routinely call KCL the Strand Poly. In apparent contravention of this public school profile, the uni has been digging around and found quite a healthy percentage of applicants

> *Music is as strong as medicine and can be found in harmony with applied computing; war studies combines with theology, and there's an international centre for prison studies within the Law School.*

from less traditional classes and neighbourhoods - 22% of their undergraduates now come from the lower socio-economic orders. There is also a large mature contingent (19%), which they are encouraging in particular in their medical faculty (see Academia below).

ACADEMIA & JOBS

Students say that the best teaching at KCL is to be found in Classical Studies, Law, Music, History, Geographical Studies, Biological and Physiological Sciences, Neuroscience, Politics, Mechanical, Production & Manufacturing Engineering. Interestingly, Medicine finds less favour than any of these, but still gets 81% of undergraduates' support.

The degree in Medicine is the 5-year MBBS. There is full integration of medical science and clinical teaching, plus a wide range of special study modules. Fifth year includes an opportunity to study abroad. For entry there's a special Graduate/Professional programme for mature students.

Otherwise, you will be required to attain AAA at A Level with B in a fourth AS level subject. Chemistry and Biology must be included, one at A level and at the other to at least AS-level. UKCAT is also required.

The fifth-year study abroad option in Medicine (and Dentistry, as it happens, destinations range

RESEARCH EXCELLENCE

% of KCL's research that is
4* *(World-class)* or **3*** *(Internationally rated):*

	4*	3*
Cardiovascular Medicine	20%	60%
Cancer Studies	5%	50%
Infection/Immunology	15%	55%
Hospital Clinical Subjects	25%	50%
Lab. Clinical Subjects	5%	30%
Health Services	10%	40%
Neuroscience	15%	40%
Dentistry	30%	40%
Applied Biomedical Sciences	5%	30%
Nutritional Sciences	30%	35%
Pharmacy	15%	40%
Biological Sciences	20%	45%
Human Biological Sciences	20%	35%
Physics	10%	40%
Pure Mathematics	20%	50%
Applied Mathematics	15%	50%
Computer Science	15%	45%
Electrical/Electronic Eng.	5%	35%
Mechanical, Aero., Manufacturing Eng.	10%	35%
Geography/Environment	20%	50%
Business/Management	30%	40%
Information Management	35%	30%
Law	15%	35%
Politics	15%	30%
Education	30%	35%
American Studies	15%	35%
French	25%	40%
German	25%	35%
Portuguese	30%	35%
Spanish	20%	45%
English	15%	55%
Classics Studies	30%	35%
Philosophy	35%	40%
Theology	10%	55%
History	25%	35%
Performing Arts	40%	45%
Music	45%	40%

encouragement of students to take a Language module in their course. Almost all students may take modules at the Modern Language Centre, which again count towards the final degree. Currently on offer are Arabic, French, German, Greek, Italian, Japanese, Mandarin, Panjabi, Russian and Spanish. More specialised modules, e.g. business, culture and linguistics, are available in some languages.

Traditional, small tutorial and seminar teaching methods are one source of the levels of academic achievement at KCL, which, after Medicine and Dentistry, translates most successfully into graduate jobs in other areas of Health, such as pathology, pharmacy, nursing, physiotherapy and more jobs in hospitals for graduates in Biochemistry, Biomedical Sciences, Human Sciences, and Physiology. Thereafter, Languages lead to banking, publishing and museum-archival work, and Social Studies (Politics - including the trail-blazing War Studies, and Economics) lead to recruitment into Defence, banking, and the civil service.

Behind all the science lies excellence also in subjects like Philosophy, Theology and Music (the 4-year BMus, a collaboration with The Royal Academy of Music, which combines intellectual and practical approaches), which give not just balance to the curriculum but reveals the breadth and depth of character of higher education at KCL, epitomised in 'The AKC', the Associateship of King's College, a course unique to them (originally awarded in 1835), which provides lectures on aspects of ethics, philosophy and theology, and can be taken by all students alongside their degree.

STUDENT SCENE

In keeping with many student unions' apparent assumption that they can educate the masses by naming bars after prominent politicians, the showpiece attraction of King's Strand campus is its airy venue, **Tutu's**. Blessed with a stage, bar, café, dance floor and spectacular views of the South Bank, this offers an in-house retreat for the col-

from the United States to Papua New Guinea) is symptomatic of many courses at KCL, which has exchange programmes with some of the most prestigious universities in 15 countries across Asia, Australia, Europe and North America. Some exchange programmes are a compulsory part of the curriculum, while others are not. All can be counted towards the degree. Each department has an academic adviser who will guide you through the exchange process.

Thoroughly compatible with this is KCL's

ACCOMMODATION

Guarantee to freshers	**62%**
Style	**Halls, flats**
Security guard	**Some**
Shared rooms	**Some**
Internet access	**Some**
Self-catered	**Some**
En suite	**Some**
Approx price range pw	**£79-£180.60**
City rent pw	**£100-£180**

WHAT IT'S REALLY LIKE

UNIVERSITY:	
Social Life	★★★★
Campus scene	**Cosmopolitan, conservative**
Student Union services	**Average**
Politics	**Average: student issues**
Sport	**44 clubs**
National team position	**54th**
Sport facilities	**Poor**
Arts opportunities	**Good**
Student mag/news	**Roar**
Nightclub	**Tutu's, Inverse**
Bars	**The Waterfront, Guy's Bar, Tommy's Bar**
Union ents	**Phase, The Hop, Collide-a-Scope, Fuse, Score**
Union societies	**94**
Parking	**None**
CITY:	
Entertainment	★★★★★
Scene	**Wild, expensive**
Town/gown relations	**Average-good**
Risk of violence	**London v. high**
Cost of living	**High**
Student concessions	**Abundant**
Survival + 2 nights out	**£100 pw**
Part-time work campus/town	**Excellent**

bottles are £1.50, pints £1.90. What else could you want from a Saturday night?

Tommy's Bar and **Guy's Bar** look after the medics at their campuses, the latter apparently especially active on the karaoke and live music menu.

Clubs and societies are legion, with salsa, debating and the King's Players (theatre), popular choices. A further popular activity (although one without its own notice board) was reported by irreverent and controversial student tabloid, Roar. 'Basement Boys Use Bogs for Buggering' ran the headline. Roar, incidentally, is regularly nominated for its reporting. All in all, the Union keeps its flock busy - but with the bright lights of the West End topping the list of countless distractions, it will only ever deter a relatively small proportion of its students from finding ways to get deeper in debt.

At Guy's the uni's subterranean nightclub, **Inverse**, rules with its powerful sound system and fully integrated lighting system.

SPORT There are four sports grounds in Surrey and south London, rifle ranges at the Strand, the aforesaid K4 fitness club, a swimming pool and gym at Guy's, and highly successful boat and sub-aqua clubs. Nationally, KCL's teams came 54th last year in the national BUSA team league.

PILLOW TALK

All residences - halls (catered or self-catered), apartments or student houses (mainly for mature students) - are within London Travel Zones 1 or 2, and close to one or more of the campuses.

GETTING THERE

☞ **Strand campus**: Temple (District Line, Circle), Aldwych (Piccadilly), Holborn (Piccadilly, Central). **Waterloo campus**: Waterloo/Waterloo East overland; Waterloo Underground (Bakerloo, Northern). **Guy's campus:** (Northern) and overland. **St Thomas's campus**: as Waterloo or Westminster (Circle, District, Northern, Bakerloo). **Denmark Hill campus**: Denmark Hill overland.

lege's loose-livered and free of fancy. A bust of the venue's namesake presides with piously disapproving glare over a feast of comedy nights, discos, live acts and all the other student malarkey.

Fave nights are *Truffle Shuffle* (80s fancy dress), *The Final Fuse* (urban conflagration of r&b, Bhangra, hip hop, and UK garage), and Friday night's legendary *Phase* (party classics). On Saturday on the third floor is **The Waterfront**, which acts as a perfectly pleasant preamble and afterparty to its big brother, Tutu, upstairs. Open till 3 am, food till 1 am, live DJs from 10 pm, beer

KINGSTON UNIVERSITY

Kingston University
40-46 Surbiton Road
Kingston upon Thames KT1 2HX

TEL 020 8547 7053
FAX 020 8547 7080
EMAIL admissions-info@kingston.ac.uk
WEB www.kingston.ac.uk

Kingston Students' Union
Penrhyn Road
Kingston upon Thames: KT1 2EE

TEL 020 8517 2868
FAX 020 8547 8862
EMAIL studentsunion@kingston.ac.uk
WEB www.kusu.co.uk

UNIVERSITY/STUDENT PROFILE

University since	**1992**
Situation/style	**London sites**
Student population	**23135**
Undergraduates	**18200**
Mature undergraduates	**21%**
International undergrads	**8%**
Male/female ratio	**49:51**
Equality of opportunity:	
state school intake	**96%**
social class 4-7 intake	**37%**
low-participation area intake	**6%**

VAG VIEW

*K*ingston *is in Surrey, off the A3,
London's outflow to the south west.
Whatever they tell you about it being the oldest Royal borough, the place where Saxon
kings were crowned (the Coronation stone
lies in the Guildhall - King's Stone, geddit?), it
is, in the cold light of reality, a shopping cen-
tre/housewife's paradise, a lace-curtained,
wife-swapping suburbia 25 mins from central London by train.*

*Shoppers come from miles to the mall,
the market and the endless chain-shops,
while its pubs and clubs attract streams of
youthful revellers and the sometime Kingston
Poly delivers higher education to its many
thousands of students.*

*We're talking vocational at the university,
'even those courses that don't on the surface
appear to be vocational,' says the marketing
department. 'The transferable skills that students gain while they're here make them very
employable.' Students say that London being*

*only 15 minutes away facilitates the career
process further.*

*In the Higher Education Funding
Council's National Student Survey (2008)
81% of Kingston's students expressed themselves satisfied with the deal on offer here. In
the* Times Higher's *more recent Student
Experience Survey there was less enthusiasm
about the size of tuition groups, but a general
murmur in support of the helpfulness and
interest of the teaching staff. And while their
lecturers are not among the leaders in the
field of research, last year, in the first
research assessment since 2001, 96% of the
work submitted was rated as being of at least
national significance, and there was evidence
of a fair measure of world-class research
going on in Nursing, Business, English,
History of Art, Architecture and Design.*

*The undergraduate population is fluid
and challenging. There are around 2,500*

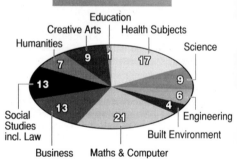

SUBJECT AREAS (%)

Education 1
Creative Arts 9
Health Subjects 17
Humanities 9
Science 9
7
13
6
13 4
Social Studies incl. Law 13
Business 21
Maths & Computer
Built Environment
Engineering

*part-timers, 21% mature students and not
far short of 40% from the lowest socio-economic groups, yet Kingston gets 75% of them
real graduate jobs within six months of leaving, and as creditably keep all but 9% of
them until the end of the course.*

CAMPUS SITES

The uni is based at four campuses near the A3,
London's south-west outflow - Penrhyn Road,
Kingston Hill, Knights Park and Roehampton Vale.
Current plans include a £20 million, 6-storey teach-
ing building and landscaped courtyard at the main
Penrhyn Road campus, and extensions to library
and teaching facilities at Kingston Hill and
Roehampton Vale.

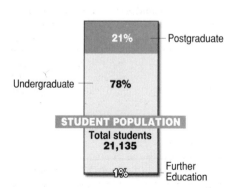

21% — Postgraduate

Undergraduate — 78%

STUDENT POPULATION
Total students
21,135

1% — Further Education

PENRHYN ROAD Kingston upon Thames, KT1 2EE. Tel (all sites): 020 8547 2000. Faculties: Science and some Technology.

KINGSTON HILL Kingston upon Thames, KT2 7LB. Faculties: Business, Education, Music, Law, Social Work, and Healthcare Sciences.

KNIGHTS PARK Kingston upon Thames, KT1 2QJ. Faculties: Art & Design, Architecture, Quantity Surveying, Estate Mgt.

ROEHAMPTON VALE Kingston upon Thames, KT1 2EE. Faculties: Mechanical, Aeronautical and Production Engineering.

FEES, BURSARIES

UK & EU Fees 2009-10: £3,225 p.a. Bursaries of between £300 and £1,000 awarded to HE Maintenance grant holders, depending on level of grant.

STUDENT PROFILE

They attract a mix of customer, from engineers to trendy artists, from nurses to would-be lawyers and City types, most notably a mature undergraduate body. Generally it's a 'new' university audience at Kingston. Writes Paul Stephen: 'It's an easy place to make friends, and the best time to start is freshers week. Although the events aren't really up to

TEACHING SURVEY AT A GLANCE

Avg. UCAS points accepted	**230**
Acceptance rate	**17%**
Overall satisfaction rate	**81%**
Helpful/interested staff	★★★
Small tuition groups	★★
Students into graduate jobs	**75%**

Teaching most popular with undergraduates:
English (96%), Languages, Maths (95%), Media, Journalism (94%), Medical Science, Pharmaceutical Science (93%), Drama, Politics (91%), Accounting, Civil Engineering, History, Initial teacher Training (90%), Law (89%), Business (88%),Imaginative Writing, Social Studies (87%), Sciences related to Biology, Economics (86%), Forensic Science, Sociology (85%).

Teaching least popular with undergraduates:
Fine Art, Music (67%), Mechanical. Production & Manufacturing Engineering (61%).

much, due to the limited space, the Students' Union makes a real effort to welcome you. Freshers' angels work round the clock to show you around, introduce you to others and generally force you to have a good time. Each year it's different, but last year's Freshers Ball featured ice-skating, Laserquest and mechanical surfing. My freshers week was awesome, and I made some friends then that I still hang out with now.'

There's a special welcome programme for the many international students they attract: a course, 'Understanding Britain', an international scholarship programme worth up to £300 per year; and fun events, parties and trips.

ACADEMIA & JOBS

Kingston says: 'Our courses are extensive and wide-ranging - from human rights to computer games programming, and from animal management to maths and stats, with many more in between.' Their students say that the best teaching is to be found in English, Languages, Maths, Media, Journalism, Medical Science, Pharmaceutical Science, Drama, Politics, Accounting, Civil Engineering, History, Initial teacher Training, Law, Business, Imaginative Writing, Social Studies, Sciences related to Biology, Economics, Forensic Science, and Sociology.

We say that there are enough courses at Kingston - 3 pages on the UCAS site - to confound a genuine interest in what at bottom they are about. Kingston clearly is aware of this, but

RESEARCH EXCELLENCE

% of Kingston's research that is
4* *(World-class)* or **3*** *(Internationally rated):*

	4*	3*
Nursing and Midwifery	15%	30%
Health Professions	5%	20%
Computer Science	5%	30%
General Engineering	5%	20%
Town/Country Planning	0%	10%
Geography/Environment	5%	25%
Economics	5%	15%
Business/Management	10%	35%
Law	0%	10%
Psychology	0%	20%
Education	0%	25%
European Studies	5%	15%
English	10%	30%
History	5%	25%
Art and Design	0%	30%
History of Art	10%	40%
Performing Arts	5%	30%
Music	0%	10%

WHAT IT'S REALLY LIKE

UNIVERSITY:	
Social Life	★★★
Campus scene	**London**
Student Union services	**Average**
Politics	**Student issues**
Sport	**31 clubs**
National team position	**75th**
Sport facilities	**Could do better**
Arts opportunities	**Drama, music, film, art good; dance poor**
Student newspaper	**SUblime**
Student radio	**Stone Radio**
Nightclub	**Bar Zen**
Bars	**Hannafords, Knights Park**
Union ents	**Eclectic**
Union societies	**32**
Most popular society	**Islamic/Afro-Caribbean**
Smoking policy	**Gannets, Hannafords OK**
Parking	**Adequate**
CITY:	
Entertainment	★★★★
Local scene	**Club scene OK**
Town/gown relations	**Average**
Risk of violence	**Low**
Cost of living	**Very high**
Student concessions	**Average**
Survival + 2 nights out	**£80 pw**
Part-time work campus/town	**Excellent**

instead of rationalising the programme they've handed the job over to applicants:

'From March 2009 the University will offer potential students the opportunity to build their own prospectus by visiting the University's website (www.kingston.ac.uk/build) and ticking the relevant boxes to indicate where they are based (local, national, international) and the courses they are interested in. The University will then send a tailor-made, personalised prospectus. For those students who aren't sure which course they would like to study, we are also offering an online questionnaire to give them an idea of the courses best suited to their interests.'

Sounds like a lot of hard work when the competition has got it all sorted. It might help for their essentially vocational clientele to know what the employers think of the various aspects of the curriculum. Kingston is markedly vocational, into finding jobs for its graduates. Sandwich courses, employment-enhancing language schemes for non-language undergraduate, a Teaching & Learning Support scheme, which supplies individually or group-designed study skills programmes, EFL courses for overseas students and a 'peer assisted' learning scheme for first years with advice sessions from second years.

The leading edge employment-wise lies in Creative Arts & Design (which produces 17% of graduate jobs at Kingston), Business (also 17%), Computer Science (12%), Engineering & Technology (9%), Social Studies (8%), subjects allied to Medicine (6%), Biological Sciences (6%), Building & Planning, Education, Languages, and the Law (all about 5%). After that come the media courses we hear so much about.

Besides Fine Art in Art & Design, they offer Graphic Design, Illustration, Interior Design, Product & Furniture Design, and Fashion. Kingston's BA Hons Fashion produces the second largest number of graduates into the industry. There's a 21-points assessment rating, which is good. Meanwhile, the BA Interior Design scores highly on the employment graph, producing the fifth largest number of graduates into the industry. And a new BSc(Hons) Product Design Engineering combines traditional art and design modules with those offered by engineering-based programmes.

Kingston excels in getting graduates into software engineering too. They produce computer programmers and IT consultants in quantity, and a handful of systems analysts. The computer course provision is wide and interesting.

Student engineers flock to Kingston to study BEng Civil, Aeronautical, Mechanical, Electronic, Automotive, Motorcycling and Motorsport degrees., and there is a BSc(Hons) Automotive Design taught jointly with Kingston's talented design department. There are jobs aplenty for Kingston graduates notably in engineering design, and in air transport, Defence, construction, and the manufacture of motor vehicles and aircraft.

In Building and Planning there are also real jobs in quantity in architectural consultancy and engineering, in the construction industry, in estate agency, property development and town planning.

The undergraduate Health provision produces senior hospital nurses, midwives and social workers by the score. See also the Exercise, Nutrition and Health degree, and FdSc Pharmacy Services, designed for people who want to work as pharmacy technicians, and BSc(Hons) Forensic Biology, which explores the biological subjects and techniques related to biological materials associated with criminal investigations.

Note, too, a niche for probation officers in the BA Criminal Justice Studies, which includes a diploma in Social Work. There's also BA Social Welfare Studies and various Psychology and Sociology combinations. Finally, at Kingston they are European law specialists, and if you do not have a Law degree, but want to become a solicitor, you can take the Common Professional Examination (CPE) here.

SOCIAL SCENE

STUDENTS' UNION Writes Paul Stephen: 'The Students' Union runs 3 bars on different campuses. **The Space**, based at the Penryhn Road, was refurbished last summer, giving it a café bar vibe with the addition of comfy leather sofas, a juice bar and "fair trade" coffee and tea. There is also a **Subway** sandwich counter. It's a good place to chill after lectures or to have a game of pool, but can easily be arranged for pre-club nights or live music.

'Then there's **Hannaford's** on the Kingston Hill campus. From the outside it's just an old bomb shelter, but inside it's a fairly modern bar, with Subway again. Seeing as it sits right next to the halls of residence on Kingston Hill, Hannaford's has the vibe of a 'local', with regular quiz and pool comp nights.

'Finally, there's **Knights Park Bar** on the artsy Knights Park campus. The bar has a patio, which sits on the side of the Hogsmill River, making it the perfect place for a beer on a sunny day. The small bar has a bohemian feel and offers a variety of ents. Three Saturdays a month it is home to Dickfest - unsigned bands and artists. The fourth hosts Preflex, a straight-friendly gay night - cheesy pop, sparkly house and glam indie. Non stop erotic dancing features every other Friday - sleazy electronica, post punk, punk, quality old school indie, dodgy cover versions and Johnny Cash! For the hard-core drinkers among you, ask the bar staff about Drunk Thursdays.

'The Afro-Caribbean society and the Islamic society are the busiest on campus, but there are many more, ranging from People and Planet to Circus skills societies. '

TOWN 'In town there is something on offer every night of the week. There are loads of pubs and Oceana is Kingston's superclub - 5 bars and 2 nightclubs. Then there's The Works, home to R&B, hip hop and garage until the recent arrival of New

ACCOMMODATION	
Guarantee to freshers	**No guarantee**
Style	**Halls, flats**
Security guard	**All**
Shared rooms	**None**
Internet access	**All**
Self-catered	**All**
En suite	**Most**
Approx price range pw	**£87.50-£109.75**
City rent pw	**£80-£120**

Slang - Thursday's indie and alternative club night, with signed bands and guest DJs. **McCluskey's** is on the river bank and offers cheap drinks and cheesy tunes.

Bacchus is an alternative basement club playing everything from indie and punk to hip hop and house. **Bar Eivissa** is also worth a visit on a Monday or Wednesday, the atmosphere is always good. And gay friendly club **Reflex** was the inspiration for Preflex at Knights Park. An average night out will cost you about £20.'

SPORT From football, rugby and hockey to Gaelic football and snowboarding, some 30 sports clubs fulfil most needs. Much of the activity takes place at the uni's sports facility at nearby Tolworth Court. There are also fitness facilities at Penrhyn Road. Kingston runs an Elite Athlete scheme to encourage students to compete at top levels in their sport. There's rowing on the Thames.

PILLOW TALK

First years have the 'comfort' of halls. If you live in hall at Kingston, you'll have a single room in a flat shared with other students. You'll share the kitchen with between 2 and 9 others. Kingston Hill campus has on-site, en-suite facilities. There are 4 other residential sites including Middle Mill Hall, self-catering flats opposite Knights Park Campus. Most are now en suite. Rooms are also available in a newly built, privately owned, student halls development in central Kingston, which have been leased by the uni's Accommodation Services.

GETTING THERE

☞ By road: M1/J6a, M25/J13, A30, signs to A308 (Kingston). From London: A3 to Robin Hood Roundabout, then A308.
☞ By rail: frequent trains from London Waterloo to Kingston. No Underground this far out, but well served by buses.
☞ By air: Heathrow.

UNIVERSITY OF WALES, LAMPETER

University of Wales, Lampeter
Lampeter
Ceredigion SA48 7ED

TEL 01570 422351
FAX 01570 423423
EMAIL recruit@lamp.ac.uk
WEB www.lamp.ac.uk

Lampeter Students' Union
Ty Ceredig
Ceredigion SA48 7ED

TEL 01570 422619
FAX 01570 422480
EMAIL president@lampeter.ac.uk
WEB www.lamp.ac.uk/su/

VAG VIEW

The classical lines of Lampeter University speak of its well-rooted traditions. It has been awarding degrees for longer than any institution in England and Wales, other than Oxbridge. The other thing about Lampeter is that it is situated in a very beautiful and inspirational place, not far from the Preseli Mountains where the gigantic stones of the innermost sacred circle of pre-historic Stonehenge - once Britain's national necropolis - are supposed to have been cut.

This is mythic Wales, celebrated in the oldest story in the Mabinogion, a magical collection of eleven stories sustained orally since earliest times and written down in the 14th century. The story which comes from this area (Pwyll, Lord of Dyved [Dyfed]) is probably the oldest of all, maybe as old as the second millennium BC.

There is much in the University of Lampeter that reflects this historical backdrop. Its spiritual aspirations for a start. For years it was a Theological college, the gradual change into its present state as university spurred in the 1940s and '50s when Anglican Canon Henry Archdall was Principal and brought it into the 20th century. Today, its courses still include Theology, Divinity, Religious Studies, Church History, alongside such as Ancient History, Latin, Classical Studies, and Archaeology. The area is littered with burial mounds and cromlechs redolent of civilisations long past. Nothing could be more apt.

But there is a new Lampeter evident in its courses too. Not only has Islamic Studies joined the Christian curriculum, which many of the old school would have found an exciting opportunity, but Business, Film and Media, and Information Technology.

It cannot have been easy to make the passage into the 21st century, and it is significant that in the Higher Education Funding Council's National Student Survey, it was the old Lampeter that the students applauded. The best teaching, they say, is still in Ancient History, Archaeology, Philosophy, Theology, and Religious Studies. What's more, in the more recent research assessment of our universities, Lampeter is found to be doing world-class research in Ancient History and Classics, in Theology, Divinity, and Religious Studies, and especially in Archaeology. The modern additions to the curriculum were not even submitted.

Students like studying at Lampeter - 85% of them declare themselves satisfied, which is high. The lecturers at Lampeter get 4 stars for their small tuition groups and maximum five stars for the helpful interest they show in their students. To grouse that only 67% of students get graduate level jobs within six months of leaving seems somehow to miss the point. And now there is a new threat. The ever present need to survive has brought upon it a merger with the old Trinity College Carmarthen, now called Trinity University College - see Academia below.

UNIVERSITY/STUDENT PROFILE	
University College since	**1971**
Situation/style	**Rural campus**
Student population	**8925**
Undergraduates	**7090**
Mature undergraduates	**34%**
International undergrads	**4%**
Male/female ratio	**48:52**
Equality of opportunity:	
state school intake	**93%**
social class 4-7 intake	**39%**
low-participation area intake	**10%**

CAMPUS

Writes Rachel Extance: 'Don't be surprised if you have only just heard of the place, it is set in the heart of mid-west Wales and its train station was removed by Beeching in the 1960s. Clearly its isolation will be a consideration. Looking at a map, you may note the distance between Lampeter and the nearest towns with more than ten houses, a post office and possibly a branch of Spar, but be advised that it is quite easy to get out of Lampeter if you know exactly when the two-hourly bus service runs.

'The theoretical advantage of being away from the shops is that your money will last longer. In practice you may spend as much money as your friends in the city because Lampeter contains fourteen pubs within a mile radius, with a cash point next to practically all of them.'

FEES, BURSARIES

UK & EU Fees - 2009-10. Fees £3,225 p.a. Statutory £1,800 grant for Welsh residents plus various scholarships and bursaries. See www.lamp.ac.uk/scholarships/index.htm.

STUDENT PROFILE

"The student population is incredibly diverse,' writes Rachel Extance. 'A high percentage is mature students; there is also a sizeable band of foreign students (Greeks, Italians, French, and Americans, to name just some of many nationalities you will encounter). There's a wide variety of religious groups, too. The place is simply too small for people not to get on with each other. Being in a small community, miles from anywhere is a great way of bonding people.'

It is a close-knit community, a small, cosy university. You will enjoy your time here if, as Rachel writes, 'your idea of the perfect university looks like an Oxbridge college, is peaceful, friendly, tucked away in the country, and a little bit out of the ordinary.'

ACADEMIA & JOBS

All courses are modular in scheme and taught in small groups. A fully equipped IT facility joins a library (170,000 vols), developed over 150 years and the Founders' Library (20,000 vols printed between 1470 and 1850).

The graduate employment figures show that a number of graduates find their way into education, mainly as instructors, further education, university and higher education lecturers, and as special school teachers.

There is also a showing of care assistants, welfare, community and youth workers, which one can imagine arises as much out of the culture of

TEACHING SURVEY AT A GLANCE	
Avg. UCAS points accepted	**240**
Acceptance rate	**26%**
Overall satisfaction rate	**85%**
Helpful/interested staff	★★★★★
Small tuition groups	★★★★
Students into graduate jobs	**67%**

Teaching most popular with undergraduates:
History, Archaeology (88%), Philosophy, Theology, Religious Studies (81%).

Teaching least popular with undergraduates:
Languages (73%).

(Most subjects insufficient data.)

the place as any vocational degree.

Otherwise, in the short period of six months post graduation, a great number take work as sales assistants, managers, administrators, and clerks, bar staff, local government officers and the like.

RESEARCH EXCELLENCE		
% of Lampeter's research that is		
4* (World-class) or 3* (Internationally rated):		
	4*	3*
Archaeology	**15%**	**35%**
Celtic Studies	**0%**	**5%**
English	**0%**	**15%**
Classics	**5%**	**15%**
Theology	**5%**	**30%**

It is as if Lampeter has somehow managed to opt out of the commercial pressures that other universities claim they have to deal with. Perhaps there is an optimum size for doing just that.

There is a constant rethinking of the curriculum, but the traditional courses are the ones that remain. Now they are bringing an entire college of new courses to the party:

'The University of Wales Lampeter and Trinity College Carmarthen have agreed to work together on creating a new university in Wales. This is early days and the new university (no name as yet) is not likely to come into existence before August 2010. A final decision is likely to be made in April 2009.'

Trinity College Carmarthen was a teacher training college that some time ago moved into degrees in all sort of subjects, such as Acting,

WHAT IT'S REALLY LIKE

UNIVERSITY:	
Social Life	★★★
Campus scene	**Small, friendly, relaxed, rural**
Student Union services	**Good**
Politics	**Active**
Sport	**18 clubs**
Sport facilities	**Improving**
National team position	**143rd**
Arts opportunities	**Drama, music, film good; art, dance average**
Student news/magazine	**1822**
Nightclub	**The Extension**
Bars	**Old Bar**
Union ents	**Discos + live acts**
Union societies	**29**
Most popular society	**Arts/Crafts, Rock, Underground, Wargames**
Parking	**Good**
TOWN:	
Entertainment	★★
Scene	**Scenic, boozey**
Town/gown relations	**OK**
Risk of violence	**Average**
Cost of living	**Low**
Student concessions	**Average**
Survival + 2 nights out	**£50 pw**
Part-time work campus/town	**Poor**

ACCOMMODATION

Guarantee to freshers	**100%**
Style	**Halls, flats**
Security guard	**Campus patrol**
Shared rooms	**None**
Internet access	**All**
Self-catered	**Most halls, all flats**
En suite	**Most**
Approx price range pw	**£59-£70**
City rent pw	**£45-£55**

Theatre Design & Production, Business, Management, Computing, Tourism, Creative Writing, Film, Fine Art and other Media, and Sport. They are now in fact called Trinity University College, but in their dark past they were quite a handful. Word reached the Guide of some 60 pubs, 4 nightclubs, a cinema and a Bingo hall servicing a mere 15,000 population in Carmarthen. As one might imagine things sometimes got a bit rough on a Saturday night, a situation exacerbated by the college crew being heavily into sport, notably rugby - that's men's and women's rugby. There is, however, a logic of sorts to the marriage with Lampeter, for Trinity College was established 150 years ago b y the Anglican Church, and through it all it has hung on to its religious convictions - on their curriculum are Christianity & Community Studies, Religious Education, Community Development and Youth & Community Work.

STUDENT SCENE

STUDENTS' UNION At the hub, **Old Bar** is the small, warm and friendly watering hole and host to Band in the Bar on Tuesdays and occasionally to karaoke nights. **The Extension** is the club venue, holds the latest licence in Ceredigion on a Saturday night, and is scene of discos on Wednesdays, Fridays and Saturdays, also big bands, comedy, games and more. The alcohol is cheap and plentiful, but interestingly the union is looking very seriously at meeting what it detects to be a need for an alcohol-free environment for students in the evenings. 'The union also houses a catering outlet called **Dewi's**,' adds Rachel, 'a TV room, pool tables, a games room, and, all importantly, the pigeon holes for post.'

The summer term President's Ball is a biggie. Live acts, various guest DJs, a 20-piece jazz band and firework spectacular. It's the culmination of a year that has seen such as Annie Mac from Radio 1 and the Queens of Noize from NME, bands like The Hazey Janes, and Kid Carpet, plus student acoustic nights, school disco and cheesy toons.

There are 18 sports clubs and 29 societies, the most popular are Arts & Crafts, Rock, Underground, Wargames. There's also a very active film society (commercial and arthouse). They are not overly political, but equal rights are something they take seriously. A satirical student newspaper, 1822, carries basic union news - 'very popular, always causes a stir,' I am told. Both are always on the look-out for writers, and they are in the process of setting up a radio station. This is the brainchild of an ever-growing Media Department, working closely with the Student union.

With an eye to the sizeable mature undergraduate population (34%), the union has set up a nursery. There is even a Welsh language playgroup. All round there's a strong welfare service, including Nightline and two 'pro' counsellors.

For part-time work, the union is the main source. There are jobs available in the bar and Extension, the union shop, security and with Union Entertainments. Working for Ents can mean anything from setting up the Extension for a gig, taking money on the door, or deejaying.

SPORT The 12 clubs range from surfing to tae kwon do. The national uni sports organisation, BUSA, gave it a special 'most improved' award recently. 'Being small, there are brilliant opportunities for everyone to have a go,' said a student, 'and if you're half good at anything, chances are you'll get in a team. Cricket and football are particularly successful.'

TOWN 'Lampeter town itself is compact,' writes Rachel, 'with two supermarkets, a Boots, and a couple of new Age clothing shops. The crime rate is practically non-existent! But unlike in the big cities, entertainment is not handed to you on a plate. Of the fourteen pubs, some are famed for their lock-ins, the Ram Tavern is noted for its food, the Cwmann for its bar quiz and live music, the Quarry for its disco, and the Kings Head as the main haunt of the football team.'

PILLOW TALK

Two mainly first-year halls are full board. Most are en suite. All are on campus. Living out in the second year and third year, you can get a nice place for around £40 a week, and you don't have to pay for the summer holidays. The size of the town means you're never living too far away.

GETTING THERE

☞ By road: A485; the M4 is about 45 mins away.
☞ By rail: London Euston, 5:00; Cardiff Central, 1:30; Birmingham New Street, 4:10.
☞ By coach: London, 5:55; Birmingham, 7:25.

UNIVERSITY OF LANCASTER

University of Lancaster
Lancaster LA1 4YW

TEL 01524 65201
FAX 01524 592065
EMAIL ugadmissions@lancaster.ac.uk
WEB www.lancs.ac.uk

Lancaster Students' Union
Slaidburn House
Lancaster LA1 4YA

TEL 01524 593765
FAX 01524 846732
WEB www.lusu.co.uk

VAG VIEW

*L*ancaster University, founded in 1964, is far away from the Lancashire industrial towns of popular imagination. It sits to the north of the county, sandwiched between the sea and the Forest of Bowland, a huge open fell space giving life to myriad becks. Lancaster itself is a city certainly, but it is small and has cobbled streets and well-maintained historic buildings.

A well-thought-out curriculum, a good chance of ending up with a first or upper second, consistently good teaching assessments, a recent £50-million capital expenditure on resources (art gallery, libraries, union, music buildings, halls, etc.), a popular college structure, good student ents (they own their own nightclub in town), an active media, drama scene and sporting tradition, and a beautiful 250-acre, landscaped campus within sight of the Lakes - all this contributes to Lancaster remaining a special kind of choice.

UNIVERSITY/STUDENT PROFILE	
University since	**1964**
Situation/style	**Rural collegiate campus**
Student population	**17410**
Undergraduates	**13865**
Mature undergraduates	**8%**
International undergrads	**15%**
Male/female ratio	**46:54**
Equality of opportunity:	
state school intake	**90%**
social class 4-7 intake	**22%**
low-participation area intake	**8%**

Students love it here - 89% of them said so in the Higher Education Funding Council's National Student Survey, and the drop-out rate, at 4%, is among the lowest in the country.

CAMPUS

'The university has a beautiful countryside location at Bailrigg, on the outskirts of Lancaster,' writes Lis Maree. 'It is 3 miles from Lancaster city centre and set in acres of landscaped woods and parkland. On a clear day the view can extend as far as the Lakeland fells. Lancaster is just 10 minutes away by bus, a friendly, bustling place which has all the amenities of a larger city, while retaining the unique charm of its antiquity.'

COLLEGE LIFE

The essential element of the Lancaster experience is the collegiate system. Virtually everything is done with or for your college

Writes Lisa: 'The colleges of the university are a very distinctive feature of campus life. Even staff are members, many of them active in collegiate life. The colleges vary considerably in atmosphere and size, but each is a busy centre of social, recreational and educational activity. All on-campus accommodation is located within college, which makes it easy to get to know people and quickly to gain a sense of belonging in this kind of supportive community.'

You might think, with campus being a small, all-encompassing 'city' miles from anywhere, it could get a bit claustrophobic in time, but that is not the experience of students. By your second year you will probably be ready to break out, but the urge is satisfied by leaving your college residence rather than the uni as a whole. For in your second year renting accommodation in town is actively encouraged, while continuing allegiance to your college is ensured by both sporting and course activities.

The result of this very successful organic experiment is that when you ask students what it's like at Lancaster University, the words that crop up time and again are 'friendly', 'relaxed', 'unintimidating'. In fact, I can't imagine that Lancaster's system of 'personal advisers' - a 1:5 staff to student welfare and educational advice service, has much to do.

FEES, BURSARIES

UK & EU Fees 2009-10. There are sliding-scale bur-

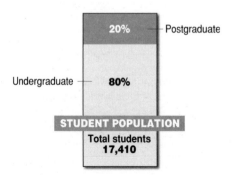

TEACHING SURVEY AT A GLANCE	
Avg. UCAS points accepted	**380**
Acceptance rate	**17%**
Overall satisfaction rate	**89%**
Helpful/interested staff	★★★★
Small tuition groups	★★★★
Students into graduate jobs	**63%**

Teaching most popular with undergraduates:
Mathematical Sciences (98%), Human & Social Geography (98%), French (96%), History, Biomedicine, Biomedical Sciences, Social Work (94%), English Studies, Media Studies (93%), Physics (92%), Physics & Astronomy, Physical Geograhy & Environment, Business Studies, Languages, Philosophy (91%), Biology and related sciences, Law (90%).

Teaching least popular with undergraduates:
Fine Art (74%), Music (66%)..

saries for students in receipt of HE Maintenance Grant. All courses carry an academic scholarship - see www.lancs. ac.uk/ugfunding/, and they operate a Talented Athlete Scholarship, £3,000 p.a.: see www.tass.gov.uk.

STUDENT PROFILE

'The best thing about the uni is the warm, friendly atmosphere created by the students in their somewhat wind-chilled and rainy environment. The student body comprises a wide cross-section of people, including large percentages of privately educated and overseas students.'

The independent school intake is around 10%, and although they had been among the UK's 'access elite' in the matter of taking classes of student new to the idea of university, others have now overtaken them.

ACADEMIA & JOBS

Students say that the best teaching is in Mathematical Sciences, Human & Social Geography, French, History, Biomedicine, Biomedical Sciences, Social Work, English Studies, Media Studies, Physics, Physics & Astronomy, Physical Geography & Environmental Science, Business Studies, Languages, Philosophy, Biology and related sciences, and Law.

No subject was slammed by its students, and there were even greater plaudits in the research assessment exercise, where all 22 of the subjects submitted were found to have produced some world-class research. Physics came top nationwide. Computer Science and Art & Design were both

80% world-class (4 star) and internationally excellent (3 star). Business and Management and Environmental Science were similarly rated 75% and 70% respectively.

In the *Times Higher Education* magazine's Student Experience survey they came 20th nationally and students pointed to small size tuition groups and the high degree of help and interest accorded students by Lancaster lecturers.

The disappointing 63% figure relating to graduates who find real graduate jobs concerns the period of six months after graduation. Interestingly, the three subjects - Physics, Computer, and Art & Design (which at Lancaster includes Music, Film, Theatre, and New Media) which got the great plaudits in the research assessment lead to relatively few jobs on graduation - 4%, 3%, and 6% of the total graduate output respectively. Much greater volume of jobs come out of Social Studies (20%, Business and Management (17%), Languages (15%), Historical & Philosophical Studies (13%), and Biological Sciences (11%).

They have re-named their Careers Service the Centre for Employability, Enterprise and Careers, better to reflect the extensive range of services delivered: careers education, enterprise skill development for budding entrepreneurs, business support services to increase the number of opportunities available to students and graduates of the university, and host one of the largest independent career fairs in the country held every autumn.

Perhaps the will come with the newly established School of Health and Medicine, traditionally a big graduate job provider. New developments include a research centre specialising in Bipolar disorder and a new Centre for Organisational Health and Wellbeing. The School of Health and Medicine is due to see its first medical students graduate in 2009.

Admission to the 5-year MBChB at Lancaster is managed jointly with Liverpool University. On your UCAS form specify the Liverpool code and code name (L41 LIV), then use the course code: A105, which is a unique code reserved for studying the Cumbria and Lancashire consortium medical degree at Lancaster. Requirements are AAB plus B in a fourth subject at AS. The AA must be in Biology and Chemistry.

Generally at Lancaster the system is that your first year is a kind of taster year. They've woken up to the fact that a number of students study subjects at degree level that they haven't studied at school. In Part One (your first year) you take three subjects. One of these has to be what you intend to major in, but the other two can be completely off the wall. If you registered to do Politics, but, after

RESEARCH EXCELLENCE

% of Lancaster's research that is
4* *(World-class)* or **3*** *(Internationally rated):*

	4*	3*
Health Professions	20%	40%
Environmental Sciences	15%	55%
Physics	25%	45%
Pure Mathematics	10%	40%
Statistics	15%	45%
Computer Science	25%	55%
Electrical/Electronic Eng.	10%	45%
General Engineering	10%	40%
Business/Management	25%	50%
Law	5%	40%
Politics	5%	15%
Social Work	20%	40%
Sociology	35%	25%
Psychology	10%	30%
Education	15%	30%
European Studies	5%	30%
English	20%	40%
Linguistics	20%	25%
Philosophy	10%	30%
Theology	15%	40%
History	15%	40%
Art and Design	25%	55%

a first year studying Politics, Law and Computing (for instance), you decide that you really should have applied to do Law all along, then so long as you get the required marks in your first year exams, transfer between departments is easy. This flexible programme in Part One is very popular.

They also have secret weapons in their educational armoury, like the Active Learning Unit, to which everyone is encouraged to submit. Special modules can be worked into your course-mix which will develop skills that employers want. And there's a first-class exchange scheme with

SUBJECT AREAS (%)

Combined — Engineering
Education | Health Subjects
Creative Arts — Science
5 1 3
15 1
18
3
4
28
23
Humanities
Social Studies incl. Law
Business
Maths & Computer

WHAT IT'S REALLY LIKE	
UNIVERSITY:	
Social Life	★★★★
Campus scene	**Healthy, lively, college-based**
Student Union services	**Good**
Politics	**Active, not Left: fees, welfare**
Sport	**31 clubs**
National team position	**47th**
Sport facilities	**Good**
Arts opportunities	**Art, drama, music, film good; dance poor**
Student newspaper	**SCAN**
Student radio	**Bailrigg FM**
2008 Radio Awards	**Bronze Award**
Nightclub	**Sugar House**
Bars	**College bars**
Union ents	**Indy/Alternative, r&b, hip hop, cheesy pop, live and comedy**
Union societies	**65**
Most popular society	**Theatre group**
Parking	**No first years**
TOWN:	
Entertainment	★★★
Scene	**Excellent pubs, main uni club**
Town/gown relations	**Good**
Risk of violence	**Low**
Cost of living	**Average**
Student concessions	**Average**
Survival + 2 nights out	**£60 pw**
Part-time work campus/town	**Poor/average**

many Lancaster students attending European and US institutions during their degree.

Clearly, languages are strength here. Note, too, that in Law they are European specialists.

SOCIAL SCENE

'Each of the colleges also has its own JCR (Junior Common Room), complete with bar and pool table,' reports Lisa. 'Many universities have only one union bar and the nine we have on campus provide perfect venues for bar crawls that last all night long. At the end of the academic year each college has its own entertainment event, affectionately named the extrav, which usually results in farcically ridiculous antics and the presence of Chesney Hawkes or Abba and Elvis tribute bands.'

A poll puts **Pendle Bar** in first place in a college league of bars, followed closely by **Grizedale** (Shite disco on Friday) and **Lonsdale.** most col-

leges organise subsidised fortnightly trips to clubs - Liverpool and Manchester are just over an hour away.

Sugar House is the union nightclub in town. It opens on Thursday, Friday and Saturday for indie, alternative to r&b, hip hop and also cheesy pop, and on other nights for live ents - bands, comedy, etc. - this year the Thrills, Fun Loving Criminals and the Dream Team.

The high-scoring Drama Department (full marks on inspection) empowers a studio theatre and the on-campus **Nuffield Theatre**, used for both student and 'pro' touring companies. The Lancaster Theatre Group is their most active society. Media-wise they are full strength with newspaper *SCAN*, radio station Bailrigg FM (BFM as it is known) and the student web site. All have been award-winning in the national student competitions over the last few years.

'There is a huge variety of societies,' writes Lisa. 'including alternative music, taekwando, photography, kickboxing, floorball, debating and juggling.

'If politics is your passion, the union is one of the most pro-active at the moment, campaigning for just about everything from abortions to AIDS. The Film Society is the largest society, and very popular are Bailrigg fm and Scan.'

SPORT Investment has just been approved for the development this year of a new on-campus sports centre.

Inter-college rivalries mean that if you enjoy sport, but aren't good enough to play at inter-university level, you will certainly be good enough to play at college level. A very high proportion of students enjoy competitive team sport, even those that aren't that good, but the place really comes alive at Roses - Lancaster vrs York Uni, a huge weekend of sport and socials.

TOWN 'The social life at Lancaster should not be underestimated,' writes Guy McEvoy. 'Lancaster town itself has been transformed over the past five years by massive investment from the major brewers. Trendy pubs are now displacing the traditional Northern watering hole in the centre of town (though these can still be found on the edges if that is your thing). The union-run Sugar House remains the most popular club.'

Writes Lisa: 'If you are on a very tight budget I would suggest drinking in the college bars before going out into Lancaster and then clubbing dry.

'Student friendly pubs include **The Merchants, The Firkin, The Walkabout,** Paddy **Mulligan's, The Waterwitch** and **Blob Shop.** Recommended nightclubs are Sugar House, of

ACCOMMODATION	
Guarantee to freshers	**100%**
Style	**Halls, flats**
Security guard	**All**
Shared rooms	**Some**
Internet access	**All**
Self-catered	**All**
En suite	**Most**
Approx price range pw	**£66.50-£91**
Town rent pw	**£66**

PILLOW TALK

All campus accommodation is located within undergraduate colleges, and most of it is very new: 4,400 new campus rooms have been delivered since 2003. The majority are en-suite, but there are some rooms with shared facilities. There are also brand new Eco-residences, townhouses for 12 students, with a living room, and a shower room for each 2 students.

GETTING THERE

☛ By road: M6/J34, A683 or M6/J33, A6.
☛ By rail: London Euston, 3:30; Newcastle, 3:00; Sheffield, 2:30; Leeds, 2:30; Manchester, 1:30.
☛ By coach: London, 5:50; Leeds, 3:55.

course, and **Liquid**, **The Carleton** (host to Chesney Hawkes in the past), **Elemental**, and **Tokyo Joe's** in Preston.

STUDENT LEEDS – THE CITY

Leeds is one of the most prosperous cities in Europe, conveniently placed in the middle of the country, where two main motorways, the M1 and the M62, intersect. It has an international airport and the busiest train station outside London, but 'the Jewel of the North' is dominated by its 50-odd thousand students to the extent that it really does seem to die when they go in the vacations.

CULTURE

Leeds is the clubbing capital of the North, but has a fantastic variety on offer, from the **West Yorkshire Playhouse** (Sir Ian McKellan, Ben Elton and Irvine Welsh have all premiered productions here) to **Opera North** to **Back 2 Basics** and **Speed Queen**, with the main nocturnal student activities being based in three areas of the city, Headingley, the Union and the City Centre. The re is, too, a fantastic gay scene, it is home to some of the best urban music nights and altogether it is truly multicultural in nature.

For art truly on the cheap, there are many free galleries, some of which showcase student work. The best of these are **The Henry Moore Institute** and **The Leeds Art Gallery,** which stand next to each other in town. A quick mention must be given to **The Royal Armouries** which was given to Leeds ahead of London and contains 8,000 exhibits for under a fiver.

FILM

In the age of the futuristic multiplex the best thing about film in Leeds is that the cosy independent cinema has survived. Like most places everything is student friendly price-wise, but real value and satisfaction can be found in the cinemas, which are dotted around studentland and cost around £2.50 a pop.

The Hyde Park Picture House is eighty-five years old and the height of cool. Cult and independent films, as well as the occasional blockbuster, can be found here, and its location slap bang in the in the middle of Hyde Park ensures that it's a student favourite. Headingley has two lovely cinemas – **The Cottage Road** and **Lounge** – both quite plush and with a lovely retro feel to them. Finally **ABC** in town plays the latest that Hollywood has to offer for prices that seem to be stuck in 1987.

PUBS

A must in these parts is completing the fabled Otley Run, involving a drink in every establishment from **Boddington Hall**, four miles north of campus, to Leeds Met's **Met Bar** on the outskirts of the city centre – four miles, twenty-odd pubs and a lot of drinking. All these pubs are geared towards students and the best remain the same year in, year out. **The Original Oak** and **The Skyrack** in central Headingley are pretty much the busiest pubs in the world. No space to move, but forever popular – go on your own and you'll soon bump into someone you know. Also cheap and cheerful 24/7 are the union bars: at Leeds Uni, it's **The Old Bar** (rumoured to be the longest in Europe) and now **Stylus** (1000 capacity), and down the road, the aforementioned **Met Bar**.

CLUBS

A massive explosion. Just down from the uni are **Majestyk** (massive) and **Jumpin' Jaks** (cheap), **Space (mid-week)**, **The Cockpit** (indie), **Tiger Tiger** (wrinklies) Wherever you turn in the city centre there seems to be a new club springing up. Whatever you're looking for is here. Itchy recommends student bars and pubs **Headingley Taps**, **Hyde Park** (both leaving you no doubt where they might be, **Original Oak** and **Skyrack** (both Headingley).

If you're into largin' it at every opportunity then **The Afterdark** in Morley is without doubt the best techno club north of London, with a galaxy of stars playing. Deeply fashionable and just off Leeds University campus is **The Faversham**, a pub in the week but a club on Thursday to Saturday with a crowd that is there to be seen. Situated in Call Lane, the redlight district, **The Fruit Cupboard** hosts the best R&B night in the city and is great for chilling out. Finally, no sampling of Leeds clubland can go by without mentioning the renowned hard house night *Speed Queen*, attracting an up for it gay/straight/TV crowd – was at **The Warehouse**, then at **Strinky's Peephouse** and now rumoured to be on the way back to **The Warehouse**, and *Back*

2 Basics – was at **Rehab**, then at **Peephouse**, a club now re-emerging appropriately enough as **My House** in February 2006. Yet there are many, many gems, many, many facets to explore before you'll find your favourites. Events details can be found in the weekly edition of *Leeds Student*, the newspaper for all students in Leeds.

SHOPPING

Leeds is often called the 'Knightsbridge of the North', but many up here think that Knightsbridge is the 'Briggate of the South'. In fact, from charity shops to **Harvey Nichols** your budget can be catered for. The main areas are in town and the best is **The Victoria Quarter**. Under a stained glass arcade independent and designer labels compete for your loan, but be prepared to spend. **The Corn Exchange** is another big hall much along the same lines, and for value, range and sheer presence the huge, Victorian, covered Kirkgate market is a joy to behold. If strapped for cash go to Hyde Park Corner and Headingley. Both have smaller independents and charity shops at the cheapest prices possible.

Karl Mountsfield

UNIVERSITY OF LEEDS

The University of Leeds
Leeds LS2 9JT

TEL 0113 343 2332 (prospectus)
    0113 343 2336
FAX 0113 244 3923
EMAIL admissions@adm.leeds.ac.uk
WEB www.leeds.ac.uk

Leeds University Union
PO Box 157
Leeds LS1 1UH

TEL 0113 380 1234
FAX 0113 380 1205
EMAIL comms@luu.leeds.ac.uk
WEB www.luuonline.com

VAG VIEW

*L*eeds is England's second city for the legal profession and banking. Of course many Law graduates leave Leeds University, founded in 1904, for further study, and the greatest number of students leave here to become doctors, dentists and bankers. But this is no specialist institution. It is a massive place - there are more than 33,000 students - and the culture runs rich and deep, so that graduate leavers immerse themselves in a culture of work reflective of society as a whole - artistic, scientific, creative, the top 50% going into health, finance and banking,

UNIVERSITY/STUDENT PROFILE	
University since	**1904**
Situation/style	**City campus**
Student population	**33315**
Undergraduates	**24510**
Mature undergraduates	**8%**
International undergrads	**6%**
Male/female ratio	**45:55**
Equality of opportunity:	
state school intake	**73%**
social class 4-7 intake	**20%**
low-participation area intake	**6%**

education, and the civil service, community work and artistic and literary creation, business, management and advertising, architecture and engineering, software and media (especially radio and TV, and publishing). The buzz that you get when you drop into the Union is this in pupation.

Do not expect the prevailing atmosphere at Leeds to be like that of any other university. It is on its own. 'What Leeds Uni has to offer, which I doubt anywhere else could match,' observed a recent graduate, 'is the students themselves. There's a real atmosphere about the place. You can do whatever you want without being criticised for it. You can really get involved. And students do. You don't come to a place like Leeds if you're an introvert.'

'The Union is never inactive. There is almost something on 24/7,' writes Zoe. They have so many student societies (210) that they split them into 10 groups just so you can absorb what's on offer: Faith & Culture, Departmental, General Interest, Martial Arts & Dance, Media, Outdoor Activities, Performance, Political & Campaigning, Sports, and Volunteering.

But there is a downside. 'Student life in Leeds can lack the close-knit community feel of a smaller uni. It can also be a somewhat overwhelming experience. Can be overwhelming because there is so much going on you don't know what to get involved in, especially in Fresher's week... People are everywhere... and you have to accept the good with the bad. It can sometimes be quite cliquey in societies and halls...'

CAMPUS

The campus is a mix of differing architectural styles, ranging from neo-gothic to '70s concrete to modern glass and steel, situated just to the north of the city centre before you get to the bulk of student housing areas.

Everything's within easy walking distance, and 'it's relatively safe,' writes Londoner Amy Shuckburgh. 'On the whole it doesn't have an intimidating feel to it. The same precautions should be taken as in any city: it is inadvisable to walk around late at night on your own; use taxis if possible; union night bus services are provided for girls along all routes, both girls and boys are strongly advised not to walk through Hyde Park at night.'

The union has an arrangement with a taxi service - any student can travel free on production of

their union card, which is then presented by the driver to the union for payment. The union settles with the student later.

FEES, BURSARIES

UK & EU Fees, 2009-10: £3,225 p.a. If in receipt of the HE Maintenance grant, there's a sliding-scale bursary according to parental income. They also have bursaries to encourage applicants from poorer postcodes and through outreach arrangements with feeder institutions.

STUDENT PROFILE

'There is a left-wing, anti-Capitalist stance at Leeds,' says Jude Corrigan. 'It is very prevalent here.' Nothing wrong with that, except that when you look at the student body, you see anything but true socialist flesh and bones on it. Compare it with neighbouring Leeds Met. Leeds has one of the lowest intakes from the state school sector (73% as against Met's 93%). Numbers of students from the four lowest socio-economic classes are likewise minimal (20% against Met's 32%). Again, intake from traditionally 'low participation' neighbourhoods is unusually low (6% against Met's 14%). So, it is anything but a working-class (or indeed particularly socially varied relative to some) student body, and when you look at its student politics closely you have a kind of Champagne socialism at Leeds, undergraduates with gusto born of privilege playing at real life, and leaving the socialist playground as soon as they get their well-paid professional jobs. I asked Nick Coupe how he found it.

'You can categorise people quite easily here. The most popular newspaper by a long way is the Guardian. Then there's what they call the Devonshire type - Devonshire are the halls of residence where you get the public school, very very Abercrombie and Fitch kind of people. There are probably more of them than I would imagine at other universities, but they are not typical. There was a protest here the other week when some anti-war students took over one of the university buildings to protest against [what Israel is doing in] Gaza. There's a lot of things like that where their demands are that the University should be affiliated with Gaza, but there are also jokes going around about the authorities in the Middle East sitting up and saying, "Oh wait, Leeds University!! We'd better get out!" You do sometimes feel that people are being overly political and overly campaigning, you know, for the sake of it. But our Union is very very student dominated so I guess that is a good thing.'

Perhaps the answer is, don't be held in thrall by those in control here; 9 times out of 10 they are not who they think they are (or give you the impression they are). Opt for Leeds, but do your

Teaching most popular with undergraduates:
Dentistry, Zoology (100%), Human & Social Geography (98%), Medical Sciences, Pharmacology (97%), Medicinal Chemistry, Neuroscience, Natural Sciences, Linguistics (96%), French (95%), Microbiology (94%), Genetics, Journalism (93%), English, European Languages, Medicine, Sociology (92%), History, Music, Philosophy (91%), Classics (90%).

Teaching least popular with undergraduates:
Creative Arts & Design (68%), Drama (66%), Fine Art (58%).

own thing and demand the money from the Union to allow you to do it in whatever type of society you choose to set up, even if it doesn't agree with their politics. Leeds is not a place to follow dumbly behind anyone.

ACADEMIA & JOBS

Students say that the best teaching is in Dentistry, Zoology, Human & Social Geography, Medical Sciences, Pharmacology, Medicinal Chemistry, Neuroscience, Natural Sciences, Linguistics, French, Microbiology, Genetics, Journalism, English, European Languages, Medicine, Sociology, History, Music, Philosophy, and Classics.

They had a tremendous result in the 2008 research assessments, rising from 26th to 14th place nationally, with research from all 46 subjects submitted world-class to some extent, and 80% of the research in Cancer, Computer, Electrical & Electronic and General Engineering, Minerals & Mining being either world-class or internationally excellent. Researchers don't always make good teachers, they say - note the absence of Engineering in the teaching students like. But overall Leeds do get 4 stars for helpful, interested staff, and where small tuition groups are feasible, as in English & Drama, which Nick is studying and which also did well at the research assessments (60% world-class and internationally excellent), and which moved into a £5-million performance complex at the heart of the Leeds campus in the summer of 2007:

'I personally really really enjoy my course. I

was quite nervous, I applied for English at five universities and English & Theatre at Leeds. I came for the interview and the Open Day and sort of fell in love with it and decided this was definitely what I wanted to be doing. The first year is quite rigid, you study what you are told to study, but when you get into second year you can really choose what you want to be studying and how. I am doing modules on Harold Pinter at the moment which is what I'm really interested in, so it's great that I can be studying the stuff I'm reading in my spare time as well. I've had a very different experience to all my friends because there are only 25 people on my course in my year, so all the lecturers and all the teaching staff know you by name, or say hello to you if you see them out and about, which is something. One of my friends does history and he barely knows his lecturers' names. I think it's a great system here that you can just pop into someone's office and have an informal chat about essays rather than having to make an appointment and know exactly what you want to say and have ten minutes. You genuinely can go and have a cup of tea and a chat about the module which I would have thought was quite unusual.'

The new Performance Centre includes a 180-seat theatre, the Alec Clegg studio theatre, a dance studio, and all the facilities associated with a public licensed venue, but the point that Nick made about lecturer interest was what struck a chord with fresher Susan Green: 'What's best about this uni is the very approachable lecturers. There's always someone around to help out.'

The Arts Faculty joint honours courses distinguish the curriculum. The range of these two-main-subjects programmes is wide and challenging, with Chinese, Japanese and Arabic joining the language provision, while Economics, Accounting, the Law and Politics provide some of the overt vocational elements against a rich worldwide cultural backdrop of Russian, Jewish, Roman and other civilisations. It is a heady mix. Leeds prides itself in offering some 375 of these, involving 58

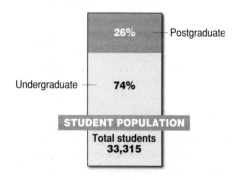

RESEARCH EXCELLENCE

% of Leeds' research that is
4* *(World-class)* or **3*** *(Internationally rated):*

	4*	3*
Cardiovascular Medicine	5%	40%
Cancer Studies	15%	65%
Hospital Clinical Subjects	5%	25%
Epidemiology	10%	50%
Health Services	20%	40%
Dentistry	20%	40%
Nursing/Midwifery	25%	35%
Biological Sciences	15%	45%
Food Science	20%	35%
Environmental Sciences	15%	55%
Chemistry	20%	50%
Physics	15%	35%
Pure Mathematics	10%	45%
Applied Mathematics	15%	40%
Statistics	25%	40%
Computer Science	25%	55%
Electrical/Electronic Eng.	30%	50%
General Engineering	20%	60%
Civil Engineering	10%	45%
Mechanical, Aero., Manufac. Eng.	20%	55%
Town/Country Planning	20%	45%
Geography/Environment	25%	45%
Business/Management	20%	50%
Law	15%	40%
Politics	5%	10%
Social Work	35%	30%
Psychology	10%	40%
Education	20%	40%
Sports	10%	20%
Asian Studies	5%	40%
Russian	5%	10%
French	15%	40%
German	25%	25%
Italian	25%	50%
Iberian	20%	40%
English	35%	30%
Linguistics	5%	45%
Classics	5%	25%
Philosophy	20%	45%
Theology	15%	30%
History	15%	50%
Art and Design	15%	40%
History of Art	25%	20%
Performing Arts	20%	50%
Media Studies	15%	35%
Music	20%	45%

subjects taught across 32 departments. First-year students divide their time equally between three subjects: the two named subjects and a third or 'elective' subject. Thereafter, they normally con-centrate on two of the three. Employers take a keen interest in graduates with two named subjects from Leeds.

There's particular mention by sixth form careers teachers of languages - 'One reason we recommend Leeds is that you can do exotic languages, Arabic,' said one. They are high placed in a league of graduate interpreters and translators (a difficult field), but languages find graduates a whole range of careers, in advertising, market research, media & government research, publicity, PR, government administration and the Civil Service, and it seems more likely than not that a graduate of Leeds will leave with a language or cultural studies course in tow.

The Leeds degree in Medicine is a 5-year MB ChB with its 3-phase focus on the fundamentals of clinical practice, clinical practice in context, professional competence. Communication skills, ethics, health & prevention of disease, community-based medicine, medical info & management are recurring themes. AAB grades are required at A level, only Chemistry is mandatory provided sciences and maths were passed at grade B at GCSE level. UKCAT is also needed. There's also Dentistry, and a nursing provision (child, adult, and midwifery), Midwifery, and BSc Radiography - Diagnostic.

In England's Second City for Finance, Economics holds much appeal here, and investment advisers/analysts, actuaries, tax experts/consultants, stockbrokers, sharedealers and bankers flood out of this uni on graduation, as do accountants. BA Accounting comes with Finance or Management, or as joint - both subjects main - with Law. BSc Accounting-Computing or Accounting-Info Systems can be taken as a 4-year course with one year in a European university.

There are more barristers in Leeds than any other city outside London, and it is an equally important element of the curriculum. There are 2 and 3-year LLBs and a 4-year French edition.

They are, too, among the leading unis on which the publishing industry draws, indeed they are a contender wherever media is mentioned. Again it's the joint hons programme, with languages to the fore, that appeals, with the award-winning student media providing some of the expertise. Look also at BA Broadcast Journalism or BA Broadcasting, and BA Creative Writing, which covers prose, poetry and scriptwriting, but turns out journalists, too.

SOCIAL SCENE

'Leeds is sort of the right size for me,' says Nick. 'I'm from London and Leeds is just a really nice varied city, which is what I was looking for. I feel

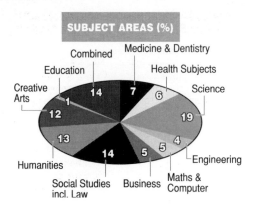

SUBJECT AREAS (%)

Combined — Medicine & Dentistry
Education — Health Subjects
Creative Arts — Science
Medicine & Dentistry 7
Combined 14
Health Subjects 6
Science 19
Education 1
Creative Arts 12
Humanities 13
Social Studies incl. Law 14
Business 5
Maths & Computer 5
Engineering 4

the city can be whatever you want it to be. There are libraries and benches and quiet little bookshops where you can just go in and keep yourself to yourself, but equally there are these massive clubs and huge shopping areas. One of the things when it came to making an application was that Leeds has a really good night life. But also for me the Student Union is massive, a massive, massive Union, really high quality student paper, student radio, student TV that you can get involved with really easily. One of my friends who has only been here the same amount of time as me, is already Vice President of LSTV, so although it is massive you can still get very heavily involved in something.'

The Union won the Equality and Dibersity Award at this year's NUS ceremony, and it was runner-up to the Student Union of the Year Award, actually won by Sheffield. Students picked up awards at the National Student Drama Festival and in the Media awards too.

Ents are good too. A £4.8m extension added 40% more shopping and meeting space for students and gave the city a new music venue. The nightclub is called **Stylus** (capacity 1,000), which is adjacent to **Pulse** (capacity 290; has been done out really nicely; in general the Union doesn't get too shabby before they refurbish). There are then two bars jointly known as **The Terrace** (complete with sun-terrace and disabled access), **Old Bar,** a traditional pub really, down in the basement, and a new food bar called **Mine**. That leaves the **Riley Smith Hall** (capacity 600) to host productions from the students' performing societies and **The Refectory** (capacity 2,000) as the biggest venue in Leeds, which has hosted more of the world's biggest bands that we'd care to mention. There's also a nightclub opened at Bretton campus. In addition, the union now has 6 shops, including Leeds' second largest newsagent, an off-licence, a card and ticket shop, a copy shop, one selling past exam papers and the last union-run bookshop in the country.

Ents can be as cheesy as at any other uni, like Old Bar Idol/Old Bar Karaoke. Friday is Fill up for Fruity (urban dance and eclectic dance floor grooves); every first Saturday of the month is Rock of Ages (rock and metal madness). Various events on all academic year include New Slang: Live Bands, and Lazy Dayz (Sunday lunch with live acoustic music).

They are good at much more than ents. They pride themselves on their student welfare services. Main political issues in recent years have been tuition fees, Stop The War, participation and diversity, and health, along with perennial ethical, environmental and international issues.

'At Leeds we are very, very strongly two separate institutions, the university and the union,' they tell us. 'Everybody knows that. But there's mutual respect. Community issues, drug and alcohol policy, things like that we work together on, but politically we like to be independent.'

There's an award-winning track record in media. The radio station is LSRfm.com, the weekly student newspaper, *Leeds Student*, a magazine called *Lippy* (women's welfare magazine) and Leeds Review (a new interdisciplinary arts society; they publish an arts journal which provides a platform for students to circulate their work), and TV station LSTV. At the 2008 National Media Awards both LSR and LSTV won awards.

Then there are the arts, and fund-raising, sport and Community Action (over 600 students are involved in this) societies. 'For drama, we've got **The Raven Theatre**. It seats a couple of hundred. The Theatre Group does three or four plays a term. The really big shows, musicals - *Grease, The Whizz, Hair* - are in The Riley Smith Hall.

'There's modern dance (they run jazz, tap, contemporary lessons), there's ballroom and salsa every Wednesday in the Refectory, which is packed out. You can barely move in there.

'The Symphony Orchestra and Symphonia and the chorals are all involved in the Leeds concert season, and then there's dance big bands - they've been on tour, had a CD out, played gigs in the city.

'The Film Society is very big, and the Film Making Society has really taken off. For art we've got all the resources in the city - Henry Moore Institute and the galleries and the gallery exhibition in the Parkinson Court.'

Small wonder that, 'Nightline is very high in demand... very heavily subscribed. It isn't any one thing that drives people to use it. You've got financial pressures, academic pressures, and then you've got the social pressures - to conform, to party, to pull in the grades, and then you've got other problems like housing. There's pressure from all sides.'

SPORT 'The rivalry between the two unis is friendly and good-humoured,' writes Zoe Perkins. 'Once a year it comes to a head in the Varsity Sports Day where respective teams compete at some 20 different sports for the Varsity Cup. The Met always wins. Leeds are always sore losers.' But overall nationally Leeds came 14th; Met 16th. There are facilities to match attainment - two sports halls, one large enough to take 1,500 spectators. Playing fields are 5 miles from campus; there are also cricket squares, a floodlit synthetic pitch and 6 floodlit tennis courts. There's rowing in Leeds and York, sailing on nearby lakes and reservoirs, hiking, climbing, canoeing and caving in the Yorkshire Dales. Students use the city's international swimming pool, and golf courses in the area.

PILLOW TALK

Says Nick: 'Accommodation is quite a tricky one because there are many different types. I was in Bodington Halls, which is half an hour's drive from campus really, but when you get there, there are thousands of people and it's a really great atmosphere. I did a play last year when I was in Bodington and I found that pretty tough rehearsing until quite late and then you have to get that much further home. But you get on with it really. I didn't mind being that much further out, but I know people who would only ever be on campus. I think that wherever you end up it's fine. I don't know anyone who had bad accommodation or any problems like that. The main issue is proximity to campus, apart from... Devonshires are quite separate. Devonshire Halls is in Hyde Park, about a 15 minute walk, but there is a Devonshire type of person and it's sort of renowned. All the other halls compete against Devonshire and turn their nose up at the Devonshire types, because they are very Abercrombie and Fitch.'

You can download an Accommodation Guide on www.leeds.ac.uk/accommodation/.

ACCOMMODATION

Guarantee to freshers	**100%**
Style	**Halls, flats**
Security guard	**Some**
Shared rooms	**Some**
Internet access	**Some**
Self-catered	**Most**
En suite	**Some**
Approx price range pw	**£40-£110**
City rent pw	**£55-£70**

WHAT IT'S REALLY LIKE

UNIVERSITY:

Social Life	★★★★★
Campus scene	**Great, if a bit self-conscius**
Student Union services	**Excellent**
Politics	**Campaigning**
Sport	**34 clubs**
National team position	**13th**
Sport facilities	**Good**
Arts opportunities	**Excellent**
2008 NSDF Awards	**2 Costume and Creative awards**
Student magazine	**Lippy**
Student newspaper	**Leeds Student**
Student radio	**LSR FM**
2008 Radio Awards	**Bronze**
Student TV	**LSTV**
Nightclubs	**Stylus, Pulse**
Bars	**Terrace, Old Bar**
Union ents	**Funky house & chart, drum n bass/old skool, r&b**
Union societies	**210**
Parking	**Poor**

CITY:

Entertainment	★★★★★
Scene	**Wild**
Town/gown relations	**Average**
Risk of violence	**Average**
Cost of living	**High**
Student concessions	**Abundant**
Survival + 2 nights out	**£90 pw**
Part-time work campus/town	**Good/average**

Private city accommodation is reasonable and certainly plentiful. Most people live in shared houses in the Headingley and Hyde Park areas of the city, the ghetto LS6. For people in the private rented sector there is a union and university backed housing standards authority, UNIPOL, for peace of mind. 'Burglary can be a problem,' notes Amy Shuckburgh, 'most student houses have window bars, door grates or alarms as deterrents.'

GETTING THERE

☛ By road: M62/J39, M1; or M62/J27, M621; or A1, A58; or A65, A650.
☛ By rail: Newcastle, 1:45; London Euston, 2:30; Birmingham New Street, 2:20.
☛ By air: Leeds/Bradford Airport.
☛ By coach: London, 4:00; Edinburgh, 6:00.

LEEDS METROPOLITAN UNIVERSITY

Leeds Metropolitan University
Calverley Street
Leeds LS1 3HE

TEL 0113 812 0000
FAX 0113 283 3129
EMAIL course-enquiries@leedsmet.ac.uk
WEB www.lmu.ac.uk

Leeds Met Students' Union
Calverley Street
Leeds LS1 3HE

TEL 0113 209 8400
FAX 0113 234 2973
EMAIL [initial.name]@leedsmet.ac.uk
WEB www.leedsmetsu.co.uk

VAG VIEW

*I*s *Leeds Metropolitan University (LMU), founded in 1970, a provider of higher education or a sponsor of sports? Certainly the latter has been its major focus in recent years, a public expression of which was the university taking a controlling interest in May 2007 in the local rugby club, Leeds Tykes, re-named Leeds Carnegie after the university's faculty of teaching and sport, and now coached brilliantly by former England open side, Neil Back. More recently, in January 2009, the Leeds Carnegie Rugby Club even sent a DVD to lecturers of all disciplines urging them to show it to students. Said one lecturer: 'We are academics, not salesmen for the v.c.'s pet sports projects.'*

There are steeper downsides. In its report to July 2008, LMU had to admit that it had failed to meet its student number target for the year, which resulted in a £1.5 million shortfall.

What does this mean for you? Well, an end certainly to the lowest tuition fees in the country. With the resignation of its Vice Chancellor, LMU is likely to discontinue the uniquely low rate of £2,000 p.a. in 2010-11.

UNIVERSITY/STUDENT PROFILE	
University since	**1992**
Situation/style	**City sites**
Student population	**39310**
Undergraduates	**23340**
Mature undergraduates	**46%**
International undergrads	**8%**
Male/female ratio	**46:54**
Equality of opportunity:	
state school intake	**93%**
social class 4-7 intake	**32%**
low-participation area intake	**14%**

Resigned to the next few years in debt, it is 'unlocking the growth in the capital of obsolete land', cashing in a few chips in other words.

We think they will be better for the experience. There was a sigh a relief among staff when the VC walked, and no gnashing of teeth when his wife left with him. In November last year she dictated an Etiquette and Style Guide, which explained the right way to eat peas, pricking them with a fork. In the Met's staff canteen, scooping them up wholesale is once more de rigueur, and the word is there's more time left for teaching.

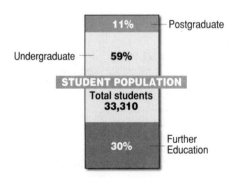

CAMPUS

City campus, close to Leeds Uni campus, has recently undergone a £100-million development. There are teaching facilities both here at Calverley Street and at nearby Queen Square. Headingley campus is 3 miles away in 100 acres of parkland (Beckett Park).

The cultures of the two sites differ as to the type of student. Sports, business and computing students colour Headingley, while City has a lot more arts, health sciences and engineering. 'Students who play sport go out there;' said a student. 'Students who want the library and the big

ents come down here.'

There is also a new campus in Halifax, a joint venture with Calderdale College

FEES, BURSARIES

UK & EU Fees 2009-10: Leeds Met has held its fee down to £2,000 for full-time home students but the word is that they are going up this year. As we went to press they still hadn't published their intentions. Plenty of scholarships for sport, academia and overseas students, see www.leedsmet.ac.uk/internat/scholarships_fees.htm.

STUDENT PROFILE

'The demographics are quite different to Leeds University,' says student Kate Denby. 'A large proportion [more than 7,000] students at our Leeds site are part-time. They'll come from the Yorkshire area, maybe do evening courses. The full-timers, who come from all over, tend to be more the mature type of student, people who have been out in the world. There are also lots of international students, many of whom come on exchange. It's a more cosmopolitan atmosphere than in Leeds University.'

There's also a low public school showing and a third come from the lower socio-economic groups, and 14% from neighbourhoods that until recently, when the Government began to push for their inclusion, never considered university as an option.

ACADEMIA & JOBS

There are six faculties. The Carnegie Faculty of Sport & Education is self-explanatory. Arts & Society includes Architecture, Landscape & Design; Contemporary Art & Graphic Design; Building & Quantity Surveying, Architectural Technology; Cultural Studies; Film, TV & Performing Arts; Social Sciences; Civil Engineering; Construction; Project Management; Planning, Human Geography & Housing; Youth & Community Studies. Business and Law incorporates all that you might expect, including Accounting & Financial Services. While Innovation North has Creative Technology, Music, Computing & IT. Then, there's the Faculty of Health, and lastly the Leslie Silver International Faculty, including Tourism Management, Hospitality Management & Retailing, Events Management, Applied Global Ethics, and the School of Languages.

The students say the best teaching is in Finance, Accounting, Languages, English, History, and Nursing. Support for Public Relations, Engineering & Technology, and Initial Teacher Training comes from around 60-65% of the class. The teaching of Fine Art, however, fails to thrill even half.

TEACHING SURVEY AT A GLANCE

Avg. UCAS points accepted	**250**
Acceptance rate	**20%**
Overall satisfaction rate	**70%**
Helpful/interested staff	★★
Small tuition groups	★★★
Students into graduate jobs	**68%**

Teaching most popular with undergraduates:
Finance, Accounting (89%), Languages (88%), English (87%), History, Nursing (82%)..

Teaching least popular with undergraduates:
Public Relations (65%), Engineering & Technology (62%), Initial Teacher Training (61%), Fine Art (42%).

In the *Times Higher Education* Student Experience Survey 2008 students criticised their lecturers for lack of help and interest in them, but a few may have been surprised when Sport, Media, Information Systems Technology, and some parts of the Art & Design portfolio caused small waves in the recent research assessment, all of them being assessed to some extent (15% in the case of Sport and Media) as world-class. Perhaps Leeds Met students don't see research as very important.

'This is a centre for applied learning,' said Kate. 'I'm doing a degree in Public Relations. It's hands on. What you generally find is a lot of students go on placement. They might have a year's placement or a day each week placement. I have no lectures on a Thursday and go into a company and work one day a week. You can do that sort of thing off your own bat or you can get placements via the placements office. People who come here have a goal. They know what they want to do. For example, we've got an Events Management course,

SUBJECT AREAS (%)

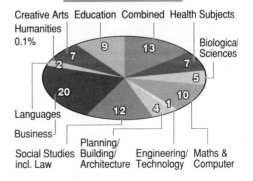

Creative Arts Education Combined Health Subjects
Humanities
0.1%
Biological Sciences
Languages
Business
Social Studies incl. Law
Planning/Building/Architecture
Engineering/Technology
Maths & Computer

RESEARCH EXCELLENCE		
% of Leeds Met's research that is **4*** (World-class) or **3*** (Internationally rated):		
	4*	3*
Allied Health Professions	0%	10%
Business/Management	0%	20%
Information Management	10%	35%
Education	0%	20%
Sports	15%	25%
Art and Design	5%	10%
Media Studies	15%	40%

very popular, been going for about five years. And Tourism Management and people going into leisure studies. It's across the board: sport, business, computing.'

The reality is that the Business and Economics degrees find most Leeds Met graduates jobs - in hotels and restaurants (the Hospitality degrees), in banking, personnel, local and regional government, accounting and sport. Computer graduates also go into banks, but mainly into software consultancy and supply and other related fields. The single largest job destination is health, graduates streaming out of Nursing and degrees in Biomedical Science, Osteopathy, Physiotherapy, Health care Sciences, Dietetics and the like. Education is important, too, mainly turning out primary teachers. And the Social Studies/Science degrees in such as Social Work, Psychology, Community & Youth Studies, Health & Social Care, and Public Health find quite a few jobs in local and regional government, social work, community.

Around 40 Leeds Met graduates end up with jobs in 'sport activities' on and off the field. That's out of a full graduate complement of over 2,000 and a nationwide graduate outpouring into the industry of around the same number. The uni comes 14th in this nationally.

Design degrees feed into advertising, and Architecture, Surveying, and Construction Management degrees into an employment niche in the building industry. It's some way down the list before you come across the handful of Media jobs.

SOCIAL SCENE

'LMU's **Met Bar** hosts legendary student events.' It is a huge area, a whole floor of the building which includes an enormous bar, café and the concert hall itself, which has a stage, decent dressing rooms and a built-in DJ studio block, besides formidable sound and lighting equipment. The whole thing is fully sound proofed, floating in plastic, the Learning Centre next door remains oblivious.

'Anyone who's anyone plays Leeds Met. Leeds Uni is better at things political,' is the considered student opinion. 'Ents is a totally professional area,' Kate Denby says. 'Everyone who works there is a paid professional, although we do have two students who work part-time for us in an events capacity, qualified to do lighting for example. We generally do 9 events a week across all three venues, so there's a lot to organise. Our main venue holds 1,500 people; it's the whole of the floor below us.

Regular Friday nights are STAR and most nights there are live bands. Recent live acts include Mark Owen, The Darkness, Damien Rice, Funeral for a friend, Athlete, Grandaddy, The Cooper Temple Clause, Electric Six, Shed Seven, New Model Army, Howard Marx.

Then there are the comedy and movie nights, big-screen footie and private parties, all adding up to an ents programme rarely surpassed elsewhere.

Among societies, CALM (Community Action at Leeds Met) is expanding rapidly with over 400 students participating in student-led student projects in the community. Two students are up for National volunteering awards.

> *There are completely different cultures in the two universities in Leeds. This is a centre for applied learning and the place with the reputation for nightlife. You'll find no middle-class socialism at Leeds Met.*

They have a presence on the production side of the award-winning Leeds Student newspaper. They also team up with Leeds University for radio - LSR. The Electric Press in Millennium Square is now home to the uni's School of Film, Television & Performing Arts. Joined to the Carriageworks Theatre on Millennium Square, it features fully-equipped studio spaces, editing rooms, a screening room and production offices. Perhaps this will boost the media societies' activities soon.

SPORT Students are enjoying the world-class facilities at the Carnegie Stand at Headingley Carnegie Stadium. The ground floor of the Carnegie Stand is home to a Helpzone and the Carnegie Café where students, visitors and guests can rub shoulders with champions. There is also a conference suite, seminar and meeting rooms, a conference and education centre and state-of-the-art coaching

WHAT IT'S REALLY LIKE

UNIVERSITY:

Social Life	★★★★★
Campus scene	**Sporty, spicy, action focused**
Student Union services	**Good**
Politics	**Student issues**
Sport	**50 clubs. Sport dominates**
National team position	**16th**
Sport facilities	**Excellent**
Arts opportunities	**Very little. Dance good**
Student newspaper	**The Met, Leeds Student**
Student radio	**LSR FM**
Nightclub	**The Met**
Bars	**Sugarwell, Kirstall Brewery, Becketts**
Union ents	**STAR, great live band prog.**
Union societies	**20**
Parking	**Poor**

CITY:

Entertainment	★★★★★
Scene	**Wild**
Town/gown relations	**Average**
Risk of violence	**Average**
Cost of living	**High**
Student concessions	**Abundant**
Survival + 2 nights out	**£90 pw**
Part-time work campus/town	**Good/average**

rooms, climbing wall, strength and conditioning room, gymnastics centre. Competition takes place in all sports, at all levels. 'There's also a Students Union out at Beckett Park,' informs Kate Denby, 'with a bar (Becketts), 450-500 capacity, sports theme, some accommodation.'

TOWN See Student Leeds.

PILLOW TALK

Uni-owned/managed halls or flats, self-catered houses, private lodgings. The £17-million residential development, Kirkstall Brewery, has 2 squash courts, a weight training and fitness centre, a two-floor bar complex (capacity around 1,000), regular weekly and one-off events, laundry and shop. Opal One and Two, a pioneering development in the heart of the student community on Burley Road, just outside Leeds City Centre has en-suite flats with on-site fitness suite, swimming pool, sauna and Jacuzzi.

ACCOMMODATION

Guarantee to freshers	**65%**
Style	**Halls, flats**
Security guard	**Campus**
Shared rooms	**Some**
Internet access	**Most**
Self-catered	**All**
En suite	**Some**
Approx price range pw	**£62.70-£120**
City rent pw	**£55-£70**

facilities, developed by Leeds Met, to allow players and students to use modern technology to analyse team play.

At Beckett Park you'll find three sorts centres: the Carnegie Indoor and Outdoor centres and the £multi-million Carnegie Tennis Centre - synthetic turf pitches, gyms, dance studio, swimming pool, sports halls, athletics track, grass pitches, squash courts, indoor and outdoor tennis courts, fitness

GETTING THERE
☛ By road: M1, A1 or M62. Good coach services.
☛ By rail: Newcastle, 1:45; London Euston, 2:30; Birmingham New Street, 2:20.
☛ By air: Leeds/Bradford Airport.
☛ By coach: London, 4:00; Edinburgh, 6:00; Bristol, 5:45.

STUDENT LEICESTER - THE CITY

The city is still sometimes unfairly seen as having little more to it than Walkers Crisps and its most famous son, Gary Linekar, but its profile is always on the up, be it through its football and rugby teams, Comedy Festival (nationally acclaimed comedians attract a 20,000+ audience), curries or nightclubs.

Leicester is compact enough to retain a strong community atmosphere, modern enough to combine this with what you want from a city, and there is always something going on.

Coming to university in a city like Leicester after growing up in a quaint market town could have been daunting, but for me, it was incredibly exciting.

To Londoners coming north perhaps Leicester

doesn't sound very glamorous, but you will soon discover behind the grey seventies buildings and run-down knitwear factories that this is a friendly and vibrant city with many hidden gems.

There are of course flaws, the biggest has to be the great big ring road around the city centre that can defeat even the most experienced navigator.

First, being a student in Leicester is great, because there are so many of us about. In term time, students make up a tenth of the population. Consequently there are always offers in bars and shops hungry for their disposable income.

Leicester is also a multicultural city and many different languages are spoken here. 'Diversity' is the buzz word here and on the whole it works very well. It's also the UKís first environmental city, with tons of bike routes and parks dotted about.

My favourite place in Leicester is Bradgate Park. Unfortunately I didn't discover this gem until my final year, so you will be one step ahead. The park is breathtaking and the perfect place to chill out, away from deadlines and other stresses.

Another reason why Leicester is so good for students is its aforesaid compactness. It is easy to cross on foot and both universities are within walking distance of the city centre, train and bus stations, which means you don't spend a fortune on bus fares or petrol. My halls of residence were within stumbling distance of the union bar and I could wake up 10 minutes before a lecture.

My other favourite place is the Narborough Road. This long road near De Montfort University defines being a student. Everything a student could possibly need is all on one road - taxis, kebab shops, a library, convenience stores, charity shops, internet cafés, trendy bars and banks. It's bustling, vibrant and loud, and I love it!

NIGHT LIFE

The nightlife in Leicester is excellent and varied. As well as the big clubs such as **Liquid** and **Zanzibar**, it has a variety of smaller late night clubs like **The Basement** or **Esko** for those who like to party until the early hours. There are also lots of alternative clubs, many with student nights such as **Mosh**, **Fan Club** and **Leicester Square**. The West End, close to De Montfort University, is an up-and-coming area filled with trendy cafés and cool bars. And of course both student unions are popular venues with legendary nights such as *Kinky* at DSU and LUSU's *Red Leicester*. For gigs, **The Charlotte** is the place to go. It's dingy and can get extremely hot, but is the perfect place to see the latest bands and get sweaty in the moshpit.

ART CULTURE

Leicester City Council is investing heavily in the arts and creating a cultural quarter with a new theatre and art-house cinema. Currently, cultural needs are catered for by various galleries, museums and theatres throughout the city. Leicester also hosts one of the UK's largest comedy festivals each February. This hugely successful festival started as a student project at DMU.

There are other festivals throughout the year, including the Summer Sundae - Leicester's answer to Glastonbury, the lively Afro-Caribbean festival and many religious festivals. It also hosts the largest Diwali celebration outside of India and it's really worth heading down to; as well as a whole area lit up with decorations and pretty lights there is also a magnificent fireworks display.

SHOPPING

The city has all the usual high street stores. Most important for students is the recent addition of a huge **Primark**. For those who want something unique, check out the **Leicester Lanes**. They aren't the equal of Brighton's Lanes, but they are filled with boutiques and independent shops, and are perfect for picking up something different.

There are big supermarkets close to both universities, but for bargains there is no better place then the Leicester market, the largest covered market in Europe. Where else can you buy 10 apples for a £1?

Nikki Slawson

UNIVERSITY OF LEICESTER

The University of Leicester
Mayors Walk
University Road
Leicester LE1 7RH

TEL 0116 252 2674
FAX 0116 252 5127
EMAIL study@le.ac.uk
WEB www.le.ac.uk

Leicester Students' Union
Percy Gee Building
University Road
Leicester LE1 7RH

TEL 0116 223 1203
FAX 0116 223 1112
EMAIL su-services@le.ac.uk
WEB www.leicesterstudent.org

VAG VIEW

*F*or successive years, Leicester University has been short listed for the prize of University of the Year by the Times Higher Education *magazine - the only university to have been so, and this year it made it! It is also featured in the World's Top 200 University league table.*

As significantly, a recent survey by NME placed it in the top 5 unis for social life. Students have a very good time here, which is why in the University Funding Council's National Student Survey 91% of its students gave it the thumbs up, and regularly it turns in a drop-out rate of less than 5%, which is very low.

We say it is a very good deal - small, per-fectly formed, not the hardest to get into, and with some interesting and important acade-mic specialities.

CAMPUS

'The main university campus is situated close to the city centre and within walking distance of all university halls of residence,' writes Christina McGear. 'But, unlike many inner city universities, everything you need is situated on campus includ-ing banks, restaurants, cafés, shops, the university library and union. This means that you never have far to walk between lectures.'

FEES, BURSARIES

UK & EU Fees 2009-10: £3,225. There's a Special Support Grant of up to £1,319 (2009 figure) for those on a full or partial HE Maintenance Grant. At least one bursary per term is awarded by the Sports Association to assist student sportsmen and women to pursue their chosen sport, and the uni-versity provides a non-repayable scholarship of

UNIVERSITY/STUDENT PROFILE	
University since	**1957**
Situation/style	**City campus**
Student population	**15495**
Undergraduates	**9250**
Mature undergraduates	**13%**
International undergrads	**9%**
Male/female ratio	**47:53**
Equality of opportunity:	
state school intake	**90%**
social class 4-7 intake	**26%**
low-participation area intake	**7%**

£1,000 to applicants who achieve AAB at A-level in certain subject areas.

STUDENT PROFILE

Student type? They'll tell you many are from the southeast - which is true, with a number from independent schools, good, white middle-class kids - and then they'll admit that there's a huge contingent from Wales. Why Wales? Because Leicester is far enough from Wales to make you feel like you are away and yet not too far for dis-comfort. And maybe that's as much of the truth as you are likely to get. For Leicester is the choice of students from more than 100 countries and has always been convenient to a wide cross-section of UK journeymen, including a large number from public schools.

ACADEMIA & JOBS

Students say the best teaching is in Geology, Electronic & Electrical Engineering, Politics, European Languages, Economics, Biological Sciences, Biochemistry, History, Human & Social Geography, Maths, Chemistry, Geographical Studies, Computer Science, Engineering & Technology, Physics, Business Studies, English, Psychology, Sciences related to Biology, Sociology, and Law.

They also give lecturers the highest praise for their help and the interest they show in students' work. With 82% of their teaching assessments either Excellent or scoring 18+ out of 24, Leicester's teaching record is first class and backed by an annual £3 million spend in the university library, a Student Learning Centre with workshops and self-learning materials designed to develop study skills and a well-equipped Language Centre supporting the uni's policy of 'languages for all'.

They also excelled did well in the recent research assessment, with the Museum section of their Communication, Cultural & Media provi-

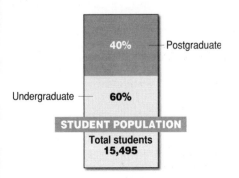

Postgraduate 40%

Undergraduate 60%

STUDENT POPULATION

Total students 15,495

TEACHING SURVEY AT A GLANCE

Avg. UCAS points accepted	**360**
Acceptance rate	**18%**
Overall satisfaction rate	**91%**
Helpful/interested staff	★★★★★
Small tuition groups	★★★★
Students into graduate jobs	**83%**

Teaching most popular with undergraduates:
Geology, Electronic & Electrical Engineering
(100%), Politics (99%), European Languages
(98%), Economics, Biological Sciences,
Biochemistry (96%), History, Human & Social
Geography, Maths (95%), Chemistry,
Geographical Studies (94%), Computer Science,
Engineering & Technology (93%), Physics,
Business Studies, English, Psychology (92%),
Sciences related to Biology,
Sociology, Law (91%).

Teaching least popular with undergraduates:
Not enough data available..

RESEARCH EXCELLENCE

% of Leicester's research that is
4* (World-class) or 3* (Internationally rated):

	4*	3*
Cardiovascular Medicine	10%	45%
Cancer Studies	5%	50%
Infection/Immunology	5%	25%
Hospital Clinical	5%	25%
Subjects	10%	50%
Epidemiology	10%	35%
Biological Sciences	10%	55%
Environmental Sciences	5%	35%
Chemistry	15%	40%
Physics	10%	40%
Pure Mathematics	5%	40%
Applied Mathematics	20%	45%
Computer Science	15%	30%
General Engineering	10%	30%
Geography/Environment	25%	40%
Archaeology	20%	50%
Economics	15%	40%
Business/Management	5%	35%
Law	5%	10%
Politics		
Criminology	5%	30%
Social Work	5%	20%
Sociology	10%	20%
Psychology	5%	10%
Education	5%	25%
French	0%	25%
Italian	10%	15%
Iberian	5%	45%
English	15%	45%
History	20%	30%
History of Art	10%	30%
Media/Communication	5%	55%
Museum Studies	65%	30%

sion. On assessment 65% of its work was found to be world-class (the top category) and 30% internationally significant. What degrees might shortly flow from this?

At the moment there are five teaching faculties - Arts, Law, Medicine, Science, Social Sciences. Top teaching assessments are in Economics, Sport, Psychology, Physics, Politics, History of Art, Maths, and Biosciences. They are widely targeted by employers. An on-line database keeps all students up to date with the latest job vacancies

The Faculty of Medicine, which, with Physics and American Studies, clocked 23 out of a maximum 24 points on inspection, would be a jewel in anyone's crown, and was one of three medical schools given the go-ahead to form new joint schools with other universities. Leicester's partner is Warwick. Part of the deal is a fast track medical degree for biological sciences graduates.

The 4/5-year MB ChB is in fact the backbone of Leicester's curriculum in terms of graduate employment. To get in you need four AS levels, including Biology and Chemistry, with three of them continued to A level, including Chemistry. If candidates take 2 Maths A levels, only one will count towards an offer. AAB grades required at A Level with a grade A in Chemistry. Also UKCAT is required.

The uni also has a world-class record in genetics - it was here that genetic fingerprinting was first developed. The career pathways of biological science graduates from Leicester are various, but in a given year 15% or so become biochemists,

SUBJECT AREAS (%)

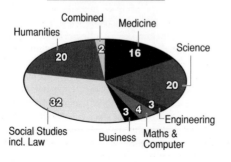

- Humanities 20
- Combined 2
- Medicine 16
- Science 20
- Engineering 3
- Maths & Computer 4
- Business 3
- Social Studies incl. Law 32

medical scientists, biological scientists or bio-chemists. Another strength is Pharmacology. BSc Psychology with Cognitive Neuroscience is new this year.

There is also a particular reputation in the fields of physics and astronomy. They claim the largest uni-based space research centre in Europe. The Beagle 2 Mars Probe, the UK's first mission to another planet, had its Operation Control Centre at Leicester. There is a Space Research and Multi-disciplinary Modelling Centre. Look at the BSc/MPhys degrees like Physics with Space Science/Planetary Science and Physics with Astrophysics.

Computer operators, software engineers, IT consultants and systems analysts flow in a steady stream from Leicester. See their Communications & Electronic Engineering degrees. New this year in a different but not unrelated field are the degrees in Aerospace Engineering.

They are, too, an employment leader in Archaeology. BA degrees only are available, though you can take BSc Geography. The department scored full marks in the teaching assessments and performed well in the 2008 research assessment - 65% of the work was either world-class or internationally significant. Geography is also hot at Leicester, BA and BSc degrees, and links with History or Geology as well as Archaeology.

Finally, there's an interesting Law provision; they are specialists in French law. Explore the difference between English & French Law (LLB/Maitrise) and Law with French Law and Language. The latter is of a four year duration.

SOCIAL SCENE

When the house scene was in its infancy their High Spirits club night travelled to **Es Paradis** in Ibiza, to the **Queen Club** in Paris and the **Venue** in Jersey. There must have been some energy around in the student union those days. Even today, Leicester maintains a full-time, non-student ents manager with two assistants, though, along with student taste, the focus has shifted.

WHAT IT'S REALLY LIKE	
UNIVERSITY:	
Social Life	★★★★★
Campus scene	**Lively, traditional, excellent vibes**
Student Union services	**Good**
Politics	**Involved**
Sport	**30 clubs**
National team position	**76th**
Sport facilities	**Good**
Arts opportunities	**All excellent**
Student newspaper	**Ripple**
Student radio	**LUSH FM**
Student TV	**LUST**
Nightclub	**Element**
Bars	**Redfearn**
Venue	**Venue**
Union ents	**Red Leicester, Madfer it, Brighton Beach**
Union societies	**100**
Parking	**Poor**
CITY:	
Leicester Nightlife	★★★★★
City scene	**Top town - clubs, pubs, curries**
Town/gown relations	**OK**
Risk of violence	**Average**
Cost of living	**Average**
Student concessions	**Good**
Survival + 2 nights out	**£70 pw**
Part-time work campus/town	**Excellent**

ACCOMMODATION	
Guarantee to freshers	**100%**
Style	**Halls, flats**
Security guard	**Some**
Shared rooms	**Some**
Internet access	**Some**
Self-catered	**Some**
En suite	**Some**
Approx price range pa	**£2549-£4197**
City rent pw	**£55**

Union ents happen at the **Venue**, at the beloved **Redfearn** pub, and at the **Lounge**, following a major refurbishment over summer 2007 - the Student Union's newest style bar and venue!

There's a Monday contract with **Zanzibar** in town (*Shag*). The best way to warm up for it is with a few drinks at the 'fearn, the 'hub' of student life. Then, on Tuesday, after *Pool Competition* there's the *Clever Fokker Quiz*.

The most popular union night they claim they've ever had is Wednesday's night, *Red Leicester*, which takes place in the Venue, '80s classics from Bon-Jovi to Brian Adams. Thursday is 60s and 70s night *Shampoo*, 'an intimate affair for party lovers' in the Lounge. *Madfer-it* is Friday's big deal, which takes over the entire building. Saturday is Brighton Beach - mods, rockers, pills and '60s sun, sea and sand...a chance for Leicester's perpetually drunk undergrads to escape the endless hell of '80s cheese and '90s pop. Actually, it's Room 1 classic soul, '60s, r&b and the newest guitar sounds. Room 2 has 60s Soul, Northern, Jazz & Freakbeat. There are also many special events.

There are around 100 societies and endless sports clubs (30), the former divided into 'academic, campaigning, performance, recreational, religious and cultural) to join,' writes Christine.'

Leicester University Theatre (LUT) is one of the largest and most active societies; the theatre has become recognised throughout the Midlands as a breeding ground for young talent, with many members finding employment after graduation. There's a good campaigning arm and lively media - *Ripple* is the newspaper, Lush FM the radio station. LUST, the TV, all always contenders for student media awards when they come round.

SPORT is big, though local competition is with Nottingham rather than international-level Loughborough, and developments are now afoot to lock horns more meaningfully with De Montfort University. There's a sports hall, Greenhouse 1, in the Charles Wilson Building on campus, and new rugby, lacrosse and football pitches at Stoughton Road, east of campus, close to Manor Road Sports Centre (Greenhouse 2) and halls.

TOWN See Student Leicester.

PILLOW TALK

'All halls are within walking distance,' writes Christine, 'and are served regularly by the number 80 bus. Beaumont Hall in Oadby is one of the most attractive, set amongst beautiful botanical gardens.'John Foster Hall is the newest, with high quality en-suite rooms, together with a number of older converted buildings offering self-catered accommodation. The university will support any student wishing to live in private accommodation. See www.le.ac.uk/accommodation for details.

GETTING THERE

☛ By road: M1/J21 or J22. Good coach services.
☛ By rail: London St Pancras, 1:20; Manchester Piccadilly, 1:30; Sheffield, 1:30; Birmingham New Street, 1:00; Nottingham, 0:30.
☛ By air: Bus from Birmingham International and East Midlands International Airports.
☛ By coach: London, 2:30; Leeds, 3:00; Cardiff, 4:10.

UNIVERSITY OF LINCOLN

The University of Lincoln
Brayford Pool
Lincoln LN6 7TS

TEL 01522 882000
FAX 01522 886041
EMAIL enquiries@lincoln.ac.uk
WEB www.lincoln.ac.uk

Lincoln Students' Union
Brayford Pool
Lincoln LN6 7TS

TEL 01522 886006
FAX 01522 882088
EMAIL (see website)
WEB www.lincoln.ac.uk

VAG VIEW

*L*incoln University has arrived. No-one can remember Humberside University or the fact that Hull was once its main base; and the bandwagon still keeps rolling on.

The university has invested over £100 million in its Brayford Pool campus in the heart of Lincoln - new library, performing arts centre, a media and technology enterprise centre - and now they have converted a former railway engine shed into a £6-million student union that looks set to make the Lincoln experience complete. The Engine Shed, as it is called, is, with a capacity of 1,500, one of the biggest concert venues in the East Midlands, and all extra-curricular

UNIVERSITY/STUDENT PROFILE	
University since	**1992**
Situation/style	**City campus**
Student population	**16705**
Undergraduates	**11295**
Mature undergraduates	**46%**
International undergrads	**3%**
Male/female ratio	**40:60**
Equality of opportunity:	
state school intake	**98%**
social class 4-7 intake	**36%**
low-participation area intake	**16%**

student activities will be focused here too.

In the National Student Survey 82% of students gave their approval; and there is a *drop-out rate of less than 7%, which for a 'new' university student profile is very encouraging indeed.*

CAMPUS

Brayford Pool Campus is situated on the riverside in this picturesque cathedral city. It's pretty impressive, although, reports Paula McManus, 'sometimes it feels more like an airport or shopping centre than a university: security guards are constantly on patrol to stop any damage being done to this sparkling new building.' How can they win!

A city-centre Hull Campus retains illustration, graphics, social work and community studies degrees, as well as computer games, animation and TV and film design and media technology degrees.

The agriculture and equine provision (once part of De Montfort Uni) is at the 1,000-acre Riseholme Park Campus, near Lincoln, while Lincoln's Art & Design is at the old pre-uni college site in the city.

FEES. BURSARIES

UK & EU Fees, 2009-10: £3,225. UK students who pay full tuition fees and qualify for the full HE Maintenance Grant will be eligible for a University of Lincoln Bursary - see www.lincoln.ac.uk/home/undergraduate/fees/bursaries_scholarships.htm. There's also a sports bursary scheme worth up to £1,000 p.a. See www.lincoln.ac.uk/home/undergraduate/fees/bursaries_scholarships.htm, The Blackburn Scholarship is £1,500 p.a. for students who have been in care.

STUDENT PROFILE

Recruitment has been successful among social groups that do not traditionally consider university. More than a third of undergraduate entrants come from the middle to lower end of the social spectrum and from new-to-uni social groups. Many are mature students; few arrive from the public school sector.

ACADEMIA & JOBS

Students say the best teaching lies in Finance, Accounting, Media Studies, Biological Sciences, Marketing, Psychology, Forensic Science, Social Policy, and subjects allied to Medicine, and the worst in Creative Arts, which failed to muster enthusiasm among even 50% of the class in the University Funding Council's National Student Survey, but is the side of things the university is pushing hard.

TEACHING SURVEY AT A GLANCE	
Avg. UCAS points accepted	**260**
Acceptance rate	**26%**
Overall satisfaction rate	**82%**
Helpful/interested staff	★★★★
Small tuition groups	★★★
Students into graduate jobs	**67%**

Teaching most popular with undergraduates:
Accounting (93%), Finance & Accounting (94%),Media Studies (93%), Biological Sciences, Marketing, Psychology (92%),Forensic Science, Social Policy (91%), subjects allied to Medicine (90%)

Teaching least popular with undergraduates:
Drama (63%), other Creative Arts (47%).

The research assessment at the tail end of 2008 suggests that at Lincoln in-depth strength may be found in Communication, Culture & Media, and in Computer Science. There are a number of Production degrees - Media Production (aimed at producing writers and producers), Multimedia, Audio, also Film & TV, and much Journalism - the BA Hons covers print, internet, radio and TV, but there are also Investigative and Community developments, and Journalism with Politics or PR.

In Computer it's Games, Information Systems, and here, in amongst these degrees, one begins to see why Creative Arts & Design, for all the students have to say about it, is actually the best employer at Lincoln - 23% of graduate jobs flow from a close brotherhood with Computer in the Design Department: degrees in Animation, Games Design, Architecture, Design for TV and Film, Interactive Design, as well as the more traditional Fine Art, Graphic Design, Illustration, Interior Design, and the specially employment friendly Fashion and Exhibition Design provision.

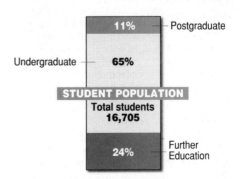

11% — Postgraduate
Undergraduate — 65%
STUDENT POPULATION
Total students 16,705
24% — Further Education

SUBJECT AREAS (%)

Science incl Agriculture Engineering <1
Health Subjects
Combined
Education
Built
Environment
17 1 11 2 4
Maths &
Computer
<1
19 14
Creative
Arts
21 11
Humanities
Social Studies incl Law
Business

The Lincoln Business School, the Lincoln School of Architecture and the Institute of Medical Sciences were launched as recently as 2003, yet they are now heavily subscribed, firm fixtures.

They were joined by the Lincoln School of Journalism in 2004, and the School of Performing Arts followed on the Brayford campus.

Language and cultural experience is an integral part of the whole academic recipe. Study abroad arrangements are made in Europe and Australia; formal exchange arrangements are made with sixty-two EU universities or colleges; 25% of first degree students take a language as part of their course and 15% spend six months or more abroad.

In the health faculty, Lincoln have teamed up with Nottingham to offer a certificate in Health Science to students from poor or deprived backgrounds who want to go on to study medicine at

RESEARCH EXCELLENCE

% of Lincoln's research that is
4* *(World-class)* or **3*** *(Internationally rated):*

	4*	3*
Health Professions	0%	10%
Agriculture	5%	5%
Computer Science	15%	35%
Architecture	5%	30%
Business/Management	0%	20%
Law	0%	10%
Politics	5%	15%
Social Work	5%	30%
Psychology	5%	20%
Education	5%	30%
History	0%	40%
Art and Design	5%	10%
Performing Arts	5%	15%
Media Studies	15%	55%

Nottingham. This is an amazing opportunity to study at one of the best medical schools in the country, with a bursary that gets you going.

Prospective animal health technicians should also be aware that Lincoln lead in this field since taking on De Montfort's Lincoln-based agric. Operation, and along with Bristol West of England, Aberystwyth and Leeds. Note, too, the degree in Bio-Veterinary Science

They also offer a track for probation officers through their Criminology degrees, which ties up interestingly with anything from Psychology to Journalism and Forensic Science.

A series of five sports degrees - one, Sport & Exercise Science, is being developed with nearby Lincoln College. Others include, Development & Coaching, Business Management, and Marketing. Around two dozen graduates find employment from these each year.

Finally, this year the National Centre for Food Manufacturing is opening at the Lincoln's Holbeach campus. It's a fully-functioning food processing factory, base for education and training, and no doubt the source of new degrees in the future.

SOCIAL SCENE

Students' Union **The Engine Shed** is the 1,500-capacity night club and live music venue. Within are a main room for live music and club events and 3 bars - the **Tower**, **Sport Bar** and **Pod Bar**. Regular club/disco nights include Wednesday night's *Fever Pitch* (the official Athletic Union club night), featuring a range of DJ's and regular themed events and guest appearances, like Ralf Little, Outhere Brothers and Roy Walker. *Saturday Essential* is the funky weekend club night. Live bands this year have included The Zutons, Ocean Colour Scene, Embrace, The Babyshamles, Dirty Pretty Things and the Kings of Leon.

The building is also home to the SU and a shop, and will soon house a job shop, activities centre and book shop. They claim to have 62 societies up and running, and 12 sports clubs, some with up to 70 members.

The student mag. is *Bullet Magazine*, newspaper *The Linc*, student radio station Siren Radio. Among the most active student societies are ACS, International Students, Equine, and Drama.

SPORT There's a sports centre with pitches and a gym. Five years ago a student could say, 'We are not major contenders yet against other universities.' Not so now. They have good sports teams for their size, coming 61st out of well over 100 nationally. Golf and football are specialities and badminton, volleyball and rugby made their way com-

WHAT IT'S REALLY LIKE

UNIVERSITY:

Social Life	★★★
Campus scene	**Expanding, diversifying**
Student Union services	**Good**
Politics	**Student issues**
Sport	**Good, 12 clubs**
National team position	**61st**
Sport facilities	**OK**
Arts opportunities	**Film OK**
Student magazine	**Bullet**
Student newspaper	**The Linc**
Student radio	**Siren**
Venue	**Engine Sheds**
Bars	**Tower, Sport, Pod**
Union ents	**Cheese**
Union societies	**62**
Most active society	**International, Equine, Drama**
Parking	**Poor**
CITY:	
Entertainment	★★-★★★
Scene	**Good pubs; average clubs**
Town/gown relations	**Average**
Risk of violence	**Low**
Cost of living	**Average**
Student concessions	**Average**
Survival + 2 nights out	**£50 pw**
Part-time work campus/town	**Average/good**

ACCOMMODATION

Guarantee to freshers	**100%**
Style	**Halls, flats**
Security guard	
Shared rooms	
Internet access	
Self-catered	**Most**
En suite	**Most**
Approx price range pw	**£75-£86**
City rent pw	**£60-£75**

swans paddle lazily, pausing only to let pleasure boats or brightly painted barges pass. And overlooking this pool...there are the university buildings...very modern.

'Basically, Lincoln is a safe, quiet town; perfect if you don't want to be in the centre of the action.'

The campus and all the bars/clubs are right in the middle of the city, based round the Waterfront - you won't use a taxi while in Lincoln, everything is central. The bars do great promotions - Double Vodka red Bull £1.75; food - £20 - two nights out £25 at the most.

For a cheesy night there are plenty of bars and clubs based around the Brayford Pool, right next to campus. Many find this a great spot to sit outside in the summer, enjoy the atmosphere and watch the boats pass by.

Visiting Nottingham for a night out is possible. Lincoln has no motorways, but you can meander mendably in the direction of finals. 'Our Volleyball Team,' they tell us, 'is made up predominantly of International players from Germany and Sweden.'

TOWN Think of the city of Lincoln, doesn't it remind you of Canterbury or York, both highly successful olde worlde cathedral seats of learning? To fresher Caroline Stocks, when she first set eyes on it, the place seemed promising if rather sedate: 'It's easy to see why so many pensioners flock to Lincoln during the summer, or why the annual Derby-and-Joan Christmas outing is to the town's festive market. There's the majestic cathedral and ancient castle, which sit on a hill overlooking the town, with its tiny old shops on cobbled streets. There are the visitors who stroll along the castle ramparts before taking a look at the 19th-century prison museum. There's the Brayford Pool, where round the country roads to Newark, Sheffield, or indeed Skeggie for a day by the sea.

PILLOW TALK

They offer only 39% of freshers university accommodation, but there are approximately 3,000 rooms in high-quality purpose-built private student residences just off campus, and they'll sort this out with you. Private developments near campus include The Junxion (569), Brayford Court (86), Brayford Quays (330), Hayes Wharf (224), and The Pavilions (2,200).

GETTING THERE

☞ By road: from north, A15; northwest, A57, A46 Lincoln by-pass.
☞ By rail: King's Cross, 2:00; Nottingham, 1:00.
☞ By coach: London, 4:10.

STUDENT LIVERPOOL – THE CITY

Visitors to Liverpool are constantly amazed by the rich tapestry of theatres, concert halls, museums, galleries, bars, shops and restaurants which the city centre has to offer. Liverpool also offers an abundance of parks and gardens, including Sefton Park with its beautifully restored Palm House. A short ferry journey across the Mersey will take you to the more rural surroundings of the Wirral.

The city celebrates its 800th Birthday in 2007 and becomes European Capital of Culture in 2008 with the special theme of *Performance* to highlight iys cultural and sporting achievements. As the birthplace of The Beatles, Liverpool is renowned for its musical talents. The *Mathew Street Festival*, *Liverpool Summer Pops* and *Creamfields* are some of the annual music events which take place around the city, with The Royal Liverpool Philharmonic Orchestra providing classical music performances throughout the year.

All three universities will be playing their part in this, as will cultural institutions like the **Playhouse** and **Everyman** theatres, **The Tate** and **Bluecoat** art galleries, the 4th Liverpool Biennial, The Royal Liverpool Philharmonic Society, FACT, the **European Opera Centre** and numerous smaller galleries and theatre companies, several of which are run by Liverpool graduates.

The city's thriving alternative student scene is clustered around three main epicentres: the city centre, Lark Lane and Penny Lane/Smithdown Road. Here's a whistle-stop guide to some of the hidden gems.

STAR PUB

Despite being part of the *It's a Scream* chain of pubs, the **Brookhouse** (Smithdown Road) is one of Liverpool's most popular student pubs, due to its proximity to the centre of student population. **Kelly's**, again on Smithdown, is a regular haunt for second and third years. **The Caledonia** on Catherine Street is always good for a few pints. Most decent nights have a pre-party here. **The Pilgrim** in Pilgrim Street offers cheap beer and passable Sunday lunch fare. It's quiet, safe and pleasant – a good place to chill the morning after the night before. Lark Lane's **Albert Hotel** is a busy, smoky student local with a friendly atmosphere and good draught beers.

STAR BAR

L'agos (or Lago's) is by far the star bar. Trendy decor, wonderfully cheap drinks, soulful music and a good mix of students and locals. **The Magnet** on Hardman Street co-exists with a restaurant, club and a vintage clothing shop. The food not always the best but the atmosphere is always brilliant, and the club is home to some very popular nights. **Hannah's Bar** on Hardman Street has an unpretentious atmosphere, live music or DJs most evenings and good looking bar staff. Fleet Street's **Rocomodo's** (**Modo's**) is suave and modern. It serves posh cocktails at decent prices, is often filled with beautiful people and opens until 2. Also in Fleet Street, is **Baa Bar**, which serves £1 cocktails called 'shooters' and is a common first stop on nights out in the city centre. **The Penny Lane Wine Bar** is friendly and small, with a good summer beer garden.

STAR EATERY

The new **Bluu Bar**, often with big queues (only a good thing?) has really tasty food, with a laid back atmosphere, leather sofas, perfect for a swish lunch.

The Everyman Bistro on Hope Street is attached to the famous theatre set up by graduates of the Liverpool Uni in the 1960s. At moderate prices the food is healthy, well presented and often veggie friendly. The adjacent bar was one of the first places in Liverpool to stock the legendary spirit absinthe – scourge of the Romantics and very trendy. **The Tavern Company** on Smithdown Road is a superb Mexican restaurant loved by students and parents alike. **Maranto's** (Lark Lane) is a large restaurant with a huge bar serving good, moderately priced international cuisine. More expensive is nearby **Viva**, but well worth it as a treat (or when the parents are in town). Best take-away in Liverpool is Smithdown Road's little-known **Pizza Parlour** – authentic pizzas at decent prices, with wine or Italian beer to drink at the counter while your order is prepared.

CLUBS

If it's clubbing you want then Liverpool is the place to come. **Cool Seel Street club The Masque was** started by 3 students 6 years ago and is intensely popular, full of beautiful people and attracts the biggest DJs around. It has won *Mixmag's* Club of the Year award.

Cream @ **Nation**? A distant memory... Today, **Nation** hosts *Bugged Out* on a Saturday, and the raucously fabulous student night *Medication* on a Wednesday (probably what it's most well known for now), as well as the drum 'n' bass fest *X*.

But the people behind Cream are back in a lounge bar/restaurant, **Baby Cream**, at Albert Dock.

At the other end of the spectrum is Tuesday night **The Blue Angel** (108 Seel Street) – 'even Johnny Vegas could pull here,' says Itchy. **The Raz,** as it is affectionately known, is Liverpool's cheesiest student dive, but alumni look back with tender memories – 'Best chat up line from a very pissed Welshman:' says Lotty. "I saw you coming down the stairs and I thought you were a vision of loveliness" – I did snog him and my mate snogged him the week after! Happy days...' Others can't imagine why you don't go looking for somethiung finer, like **Le Bateau** on Duke Street, known for its indie.

Look, too, at **L2** (The Lomax) for live and alternative dance nights, **Krazy Horse** for indie and hard rock, **Cavern Club** for Beatles nostalgia. Another outstanding club is the gay friendly **Garlands** (Eberle Street), also a winner of *Mixmag's Club of the Year Award*. Temporarily, **The State** is home to Garland's nights. Meanwhile, Monday's student night is *Double Vision* at **The Guild of Students**, Saturday's is *Time Tunnel* (city centre).

SHOPS

The one shop students couldn't live without is **WRC** (West World Retail Corp.) on Bold Street. For labels and good trainers for boys and girls visit **Open** (city centre) and **Drome** women (sorry lads). Hardman Street's **Bulletproof** is a good retailer of pretty much passé '70s clothing; it sells clothes by weight. Slater Street's **Liverpool Palace** and School Lane's **Quiggins** are *pot pourris* of student goods and services – from tatooists to African art. The University of Liverpool's *Monday Market* taps the same market for books, wall hangings and plants, but some stallholders provide products as diverse as PCs and collector's items.

THEATRE & MOUTH ART

The Everyman, Hope Street, is one of the most student-friendly venues around, is known for giving local writers a break, and has started the careers of several big-name Liverpudlian actors, like Pete Postlethwaite and Julie Walters. The more 'street level' **Unity Theatre** nearby does workshops and alternative theatre experiences. Currently, Hanover Street's **Neptune** is a cosy venue favoured by touring shows and comedy acts. **The Egg Café** (Newington, top floor) has bags of atmosphere and features open floor slots for local poets. **The Everyman Bistro** hosts the Dead Good Poets Society, a collective of performance poets, twice a month.

FILM, MUSIC & COMEDY

The new **FACT** centre – a gateway to the city's **Ropewalks** development, which is regenerating a sadly neglected area of the city – is an arts complex showing a wide range of films from quality blockbusters to the most obscure Eastern European cinema as well as media exhibitions and art installations. There are a few good chain cinemas on London Road, Switch Island and Edge Lane. **The Philharmonic**, Hope Street, shows classic films on its unique raising screen, with traditional organist.

Probably the two best venues for live music are **Liverpool Academy** at the University and **The Picket** (Hardman Street). The former has three venues with the largest having a 2,000+ capacity and has played host to many big names including Coldplay, Groove Armada, The Hives, Faithless. **The Picket** is famed for showcasing loads of local bands, but at present is under threat of closure.

The Rawhide Comedy Club at **Blue Bar** (the Docks) specialise in the field – essential to book ahead. With the **Everyman** they stage mainly established comedians. Sniggers Comedy at the Guild of Students hosts some decent comedians.

VISUAL ART

The Tate Gallery on Albert Dock has 3 floors featuring major touring exhibitions. **The Walker Gallery** (William Brown Street) offers traditional fare. Liverpool Uni has a small gallery by Abercromby Square. **The Open Eye** (Wood Street) exhibits touring photographic shows. Seek out also a plethora of little-known galleries, like the **Bluecoat Chambers** (School Lane).

Anne Fuell

UNIVERSITY OF LIVERPOOL

The University of Liverpool
Student Services Centre
150 Mount Pleasant
Liverpool L69 3GD

TEL 0151 794 5927
FAX 0151 794 2060
EMAIL ugrecruitment@liv.ac.uk
WEB www.liv.ac.uk

Liverpool Guild of Students
PO Box 187
160 Mount Pleasant
Liverpool L69 7BR

TEL 0151 794 6868
FAX 0151 794 4174
EMAIL guildcomms@liv.ac.uk
WEB www.guildofstudents.com

VAG VIEW

*E*stablished in 1881, Liverpool is the original redbrick university, a great big bustling traditional university, which far from feeling a need to keep up with the times seems somehow to absorb modern exigencies and move at its own pace.

Liverpool is a well-balanced university. They meet their Government benchmarks for widening participation with ease (and oddly they are not too testing). There are rising applications year on year, low-ish average points requirement for a top uni, and great 4-star ratings for helpful/interested lecturers and decent-sized tutorial groups.

85% of students there rate it, which is high, and they lose very few to wastage along the way.

CAMPUS

The campus Precinct is a few mins walk from the centre of this city, famous for football, the Beatles and the Mersey ferry. With Liverpool Uni, John Moores, and Liverpool Hope, this same city is now, also, one of the major centres of higher education in Britain - home to three universities.

FEES, BURSARIES

UK & EU Fees, 2009-10: £3,225 p.a. The Liverpool Bursary scheme awards on a sliding scale to those who are eligible for the HE Maintenance Grant. The Opportunity and Achievement Scholarship, worth £4,000, is also aimed at relieving hardship. Attainment Scholarships, worth £1,500 p.a., are made to applicants attaining outstanding entry qualifications (AAB). Departmental Scholarships are awarded on the basis of performance at the end of each university academic year. Sports Scholarships, of up to £2,000 p.a., are awarded to

UNIVERSITY/STUDENT PROFILE	
University since	**1661**
Situation/style	**City campus**
Student population	**20665**
Undergraduates	**16805**
Mature undergraduates	**16%**
International undergrads	**7%**
Male/female ratio	**50:50**
Equality of opportunity:	
state school intake	**85%**
social class 4-7 intake	**25%**
low-participation area intake	**9%**

talented athletes. There are also Alumni Awards (£2,000 p.a.), the John Lennon Memorial Scholarships (currently under review), the Hillsborough Trust Memorial Bursaries (also under review), and a discretionary Access to Learning Fund. For details of all scholarships and bursaries see

www.liv.ac.uk/study/undergraduate/money/future/scholarships-bursaries-2009.htm

STUDENT PROFILE

With two other universities in the city whose 'natural' clientele might be seen to fulfil the need to spread higher education through the lower socio-economic orders in the city, it is interesting that long before Government quotas existed Liverpool was running access courses for, and offering bursaries and access funds to, students without traditional academic qualifications. It is in the nature of the ethos of Liverpool to do so. Today, the university is popular with state and public school kids alike, and students from a whole range of backgrounds, including many from abroad. The perennially low drop-out rate (4%) shows that everyone is having a good time.

ACADEMIA & JOBS

Students say that the best teaching is to be had in Geography & Environmental Science, Pharmacology, English, History, subjects allied to Medicine, Anatomy, Physiology, Chemistry, Languages, Law, and Physical Sciences. Least popular was Architecture, but even that attracted 64% of the class vote.

However, in the research assessment in 2008, Architecture was among the very best performers - 75% of the work was adjudged either world-class or internationally excellent, an achievement shared by Computer Science, with Chemistry and history 70% and with 5% of their provision world-class.

When it comes to graduate employment, 75%

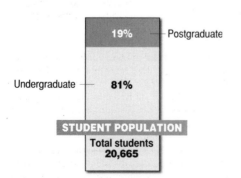

19% — Postgraduate

Undergraduate — 81%

STUDENT POPULATION
Total students
20,665

TEACHING SURVEY AT A GLANCE

Avg. UCAS points accepted	**370**
Acceptance rate	**13%**
Overall satisfaction rate	**84%**
Helpful/interested staff	**★★★★**
Small tuition groups	**★★★★**
Students into graduate jobs	**75%**

Teaching most popular with undergraduates:
Physical Geography & Enviromental Science
(97%), Pharmacology (95%), English, History,
subjects allied to Medicine (93%), Anatomy,
Physiology, Chemistry (92%), Languages (91%),
Law, Physical Science (90%).

Teaching least popular with undergraduates:
Architecture (64%).

RESEARCH EXCELLENCE

% of Liverpool's research that is
4* *(World-class)* or **3*** *(Internationally rated):*

	4*	3*
Cancer Studies	10%	30%
Infection/ Immunology	20%	45%
Clinical Subjects	5%	55%
Health Services	10%	45%
Dentistry	10%	30%
Health Professions	10%	30%
Biological Sciences	10%	30%
Human Biol. Sciences	10%	45%
Veterinary	5%	40%
Environmental Sciences	15%	60%
Chemistry	20%	50%
Physics	20%	45%
Pure Mathematics	10%	35%
Applied Mathematics	15%	45%
Statistics	0%	35%
Computer Science	30%	45%
Electrical/Electronic Eng.	15%	40%
Civil Engineering	5%	45%
Mechanical, Aero., & Manufacturing Eng.	15%	45%
Metallurgy and Materials	35%	35%
Architecture	30%	45%
Town/Country Planning	10%	40%
Geography Environment	10%	45%
Archaeology	25%	40%
Business/Management	10%	40%
Law	10%	45%
Politics	0%	15%
Sociology	5%	25%
Psychology	5%	25%
American Studies	15%	20%
European Studies	20%	20%
French	15%	25%
German	10%	35%
Iberian	15%	35%
English	30%	35%
Classics	10%	40%
Philosophy	0%	25%
History	35%	35%
Music	10%	50%

of all graduates have proper graduate-level jobs within six months of leaving 21% of these jobs come in the shape of hospital work, followed by veterinary, and then by...architectural consultancy. Other employment areas highly popular with Liverpool graduates are the civil service (some of those in town planning), then social work, community and counselling activities, and then the business finance brigade arrive, in banking, accounting, personnel recruitment, and then higher education, dental practice, and software consultancy, etc.

Faculties include Arts, Engineering, Law, Medicine & Dentistry, Science, Social & Environmental Studies, and Veterinary Science. There are some interesting inter-faculty combos, such as Maths & Philosophy.

Within Social & Environmental lie Accounting and Economics (BA and BSc) degrees.

The Medicine degree is a 4/5-year MC ChB with the simplest of requirements - AAB at A Level

(Biology, Chemistry plus one other subject) and B in a fourth AS subject. No mention of UKCAT even. Clinical skills are introduced in Year 1. Graduates with a 2:1 in an approved biomedical discipline or health/social care profession may also apply. The course focuses particularly on the ability to use and apply information in the clinical setting.

Liverpool has been allowed to recruit an extra 50 medical students and 32 dentistry students each year to enhance medical and dental provision in

SUBJECT AREAS (%)

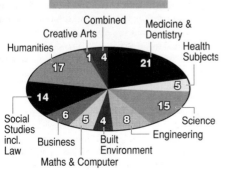

- Combined 4
- Medicine & Dentistry 21
- Creative Arts 1
- Humanities 17
- Health Subjects 5
- 15
- Social Studies incl. Law 14
- Business 6
- Built Environment 5
- 4
- 8
- Science
- Engineering
- Maths & Computer

Lancashire and Cumbria. The dental students will be based at Central Lancashire University and the medical students at Lancaster University.

Dentists go for the 5-year BDS - entry 360 points. Vets meanwhile opt for the 5-year BVSc, which requires relevant work experience. There's a 6-year BSc Intercalated Honours Year. Look also at the BSc degrees: Bio-veterinary Science and Veterinary Conservation Medicine.

> *The Students' Guild has four live music venues which go by the name of* Liverpool Academy. *This is the biggest capacity venue in the city. Annually, they run in excess of 180 live music events.*

There are healthy employment stats, too, for the degrees in Diagnostic Radiography, Radiotherapy, Physiotherapy and Occupational Therapy. Nursing struggled on its first teaching assessment, but came through with 22 points in the end.

Architecture's sister subjects extend the curriculum's planning theme into BA Urban Regeneration & Planning and MPlanning Town & Regional Planning - all of which make their graduate would-be town planners irresistible. Reliable pathways into the Civil Service are Law and languages. They are European specialists in Law See, too, their BA Legal & Business Studies.

For a career in the Royal Navy or RAF (a popular choice here), look at their Engineering Group of degree programmes, from Aerospace Engineering to Digital Signal Processing & Communications to Civil & Maritime Engineering. Teaching assessments range from 20 to 22 and there's a Grade 5* for research into Mechanical, Aeronautical and Manufacturing Engineering.

Consider, too, the BEng Materials, Design & Manufacture. This was another area that achieved a 70% world-class/internationally significant rating at the research assessment, as did Chemistry - the BSc/MChem Chemical Sciences comes with numerous combinations, such as Pharmacology, Industrial Chemistry, Industrial Management, Management, Materials Science, Oceanography or a European language.

SOCIAL SCENE

STUDENTS' GUILD The Guild has four live music venues which go by the name of **Liverpool Academy**, the biggest capacity venue in the city. Annually, they run in excess of 180 live music events. BLOC Party, Rooster, Subways, Motorhead, Texas, The Kills have all played here, as have Goldfrapp, The Coral and KT Tunstall within memory of those who tell us. They have two weekly club nights, called *Time Tunnel* (Saturday) and *Double Vision* (Monday) and the capacity for these is 2,600. In total, the Guild has nine bars, of which, **The Gilmore**, **The Liver Bar** and the **Saro Wiwa** are open throughout the day.

The student newspaper, *Liverpool Student*, like other top student city newspapers, *Leeds Student*, Manchester's *Student Direct* and *London Student*, has become a virtual passage into the media. If that's your thing, get involved. ICON is the radio station.

As elsewhere, there are all kinds of societies with which to get involved - 90 at the last count and 45 sports clubs. Among the former, the most popular are Islamic Soc, Drama, RockSoc, and LUST -

WHAT IT'S REALLY LIKE	
UNIVERSITY:	
Social Life	★★★★★
Campus scene	**Great time, unpretentious, rich opportunity**
Student Union services	**Excellent**
Politics	**Activity high: student issues**
Sport	**Strong**
National team position	**32**
Sport facilities	**Good**
Arts opportunities	**Excellent**
Student newspaper	**Liverpool Student**
Student radio	**ICON**
Nightclub venue	**Academy**
Bars	**9 bars, Gilmore, Liver Bar, Saro Wiwa...**
Union ents	**Time Tunnel, Double Vision, major live gigs**
Union societies	**90**
Most popular societies	**Islamic**
Parking	**Adequate**
CITY:	
Entertainment	★★★★★
City scene	**Fab**
Town/gown relations	**Good**
Risk of violence	**Average**
Cost of living	**Low**
Student concessions	**Excellent**
Survival + 2 nights out	**£70 pw**
Part-time work campus/town	**Good/Excellent**

that's Liverpool Uni Show Troupe.

The Guild runs LUSTI (Liverpool Uni Student Training Initiative) to train students in communication, assertiveness, time and stress management, meeting skills etc.

PULSE is a new job-centre service to help students find part-time jobs with local employers during term and more full-time during the vacations.

SPORT The Sports Centre - extended in 2004 - includes swimming pool, squash courts, weight training, indoor cricket nets, climbing wall, sun beds, facilities for aerobics, dance, trampolining. There's a hall at the gym for judo, fencing, archery, four additional squash courts, rifle and pistol range and a weights room. The main sports ground, near the halls, includes two floodlit artificial turf pitches for hockey, field sports, five rugby and six soccer pitches, four tennis courts, a lacrosse pitch, two cricket squares and two artificial wickets, bar and cafeteria. Two other grounds add a further six soccer pitches, and there's a base for climbing, walking, canoeing and field studies in Snowdonia, which accommodates eighteen.

TOWN See Student Liverpool.

PILLOW TALK

Most first years dwell in massive catered halls

ACCOMMODATION	
Guarantee to freshers	**100%**
Style	**Halls**
Security guard	**All**
Shared rooms	**None**
Internet access	**All**
Self-catered	**Some**
En suite	**Some**
Approx price range pw	**£80.50-£120.40**
City rent pw	**£40-£120**

(Greenbank or Carnatic) 3 miles out. All freshers who apply by August 31 are guaranteed a place. See *At A Glance* box for prices. If you're expecting luxury accommodation you'll be sorely disappointed, though the community spirit which grows up in halls like Rankin on the Carnatic site stand you in great stead. They have bars and ents, and are linked to uni and city centre by a regular bus service.

GETTING THERE

☛ By road: M6/J21a, M62, A5080, A5047. Well served by National Express coaches.
☛ By rail: Manchester, 40 mins; Sheffield, 1:45; Leeds, Birmingham, 2:00; London King's Cross, 3:00.
☛ Liverpool airports for inland/Ireland flights.
☛ By coach: London, 5:00; Manchester, 50 mins.

LIVERPOOL HOPE UNIVERSITY

Liverpool Hope University
Hope Park
Liverpool L16 9JD

TEL 0151 291 3295
FAX 0151 291 2050
EMAIL admissions@hope.ac.uk
WEB www.hope.ac.uk

Liverpool Hope Students' Union
Derwent House
Merseyside L16 9LA

TEL 0151 291 3651
FAX 0151 2913535
EMAIL union@hope.ac.uk
WEB www.hopesus.co.uk/

VAG VIEW

*L*iverpool Hope University has a reputation as a major provider in the field of Education, although this is anything but the whole story. For years they offered degrees in a variety of subjects, all of them awarded by Liverpool University. In those days, the Pro-rector's introduction - 'Hope is a great virtue with both sacred and secular connotations,' - sounded a bit like a sermon, and we should not be surprised, for Liverpool Hope, once the Liverpool Institute, has its roots in an ecumenical amalgamation of two colleges

with religious foundations - St Katherine's, an Anglican foundation, and Notre Dame, its Roman Catholic neighbour - a union championed years ago by the then Bishop of Liverpool - the cricketing David Sheppard. In 2005, when Hope became a university, its first Vice-Chancellor, Professor Gerald John Pillay, was fittingly a theologian.

Liverpool Hope offered Liverpool University course elements, such as Theology and Religious Studies, which it lacked. At the same time, Liverpool offered Hope top-notch facilities for its Sport, Recreation & Physical

UNIVERSITY/STUDENT PROFILE	
University since	**2005**
Situation/style	**Civic**
Student population	**7885**
Total undergraduates	**6190**
Mature undergraduates	**34%**
International undergrads	**2%**
Male/female ratio	**30:70**
Equality of opportunity:	
state school intake	**98%**
social class 4-7 intake	**41%**
low-participation area intake	**21%**

Education courses, which are still part of the syllabus today. It was a good marriage - made in heaven you might say.

But Hope was always bound to come good in its own right in these days of 'widening participation' because at the heart of its mission is a determination to make higher education more widely available, not for political correctness, but because it is an implicit in its ethos, and always has been. It was doing 'access' already - for real.

Springing from its religious roots is a determination to provide for 'those who have hitherto not had the most distinguished or easy path to academic honours.' Foundation courses prepare students without the required grades to study a degree course. Lecturers go out into the community and preach, sorry teach, those who for one reason or another can't take up a place at Hope. They called it their 'Reach Out' degree route long before Blair's Labour called it 'out-reach'. At Everton, a £15.5-million development was set up to house Hope's community-education strategy. More recently, they

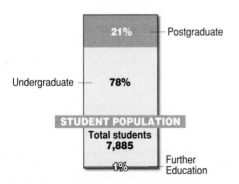

STUDENT POPULATION

- 21% — Postgraduate
- Undergraduate — 78%
- Total students 7,885
- 1% — Further Education

developed what they call a Network of Hope, a partnership with communities further afield that would otherwise not have had such a provision. It is now possible for students to undertake full- and part-time degree level study in Hope courses at colleges within the bounds of their local communities.

Characteristic of the Hope community ethos is Urban Hope, a wholly owned subsidiary company of Liverpool Hope University with expertise in the areas of widening access. It raised millions in the deprived Kensington area of the city, built the award-winning Life Bank building, which accommodates a 62-place nursery, the local Sure Start project and a primary care trust, as well as accommodating courses for the local community college. Urban Hope is has developed a 'community campus' nearby, which includes a £1.6-million Sports Centre.

Hope is running with a strong current in this vibrant, ever evolving city, and it was rewarded first with university college status and then university status because it is running with it rather well. In the National Student Survey, undertaken by the Higher Education Funding Council, 81% of Hope students declared themselves satisfied.

CAMPUS

With such an eternally optimistic agenda, how disappointing that its name comes from its location, Hope Park, Childwall, some 3 miles from the centre of Liverpool, the original buildings of the two constituent colleges forming the basis of a campus none too exhilarating architecturally.

This is the centre of operations, however, and where you'll find the student union HQ. Hope at Everton, a few miles away, has two Grade II Listed buildings, a hall of residence offering self-catering en-suite accommodation for 180 students and the refurbished St Francis Xavier's Church. It is well-established as one of the most important arts venues on Merseyside.

Here, students study Creative & Performing Arts subjects, Fine Art & Design, Film Studies, Dance, Drama & Theatre Studies and Music. Wholly appropriately, they share with the European Opera Centre, the Music Space Trust and The Cornerstone Gallery, with its continuous exhibition of professional art. Playwrights, artists and musicians, including Visiting Professors Willy Russell and John Godber, Alan Bleasdale, Julian

Lloyd Webber, Joanna McGregor and ex-Beatle Stuart Sutcliffe complete the scene.

The Reach Out Community Forum ties up with such as the Everton Development Trust, the Rotunda Community Arts Centre, local churches and secondary schools. The Hope Community Youth Theatre is based here, and The Royal Liverpool Philharmonic Orchestra, the 10:10 Ensemble and youth and community choirs all practise here.

FEES, BURSARIES

UK & EU Fees, 2008-10: £3,225 p.a. Bursaries are available on a sliding scale according to parental income. Academic scholarships worth £2,000 and £1,000 p.a. are awarded to high scorers at A level and £500 to applicants from Hope's partner schools and colleges. See www.hope.ac.uk/studentfunds/pages/2007-08/eng/scholarship.htm

STUDENT PROFILE

Around 34% of undergraduates are mature, 70% of them are female, which is apt, because its constituent colleges were both women's colleges; 27% are part time, 98% are from the state sector and 41% from the lower socio-economic classes and 14% from 'low-participation' neighbourhoods. Also, most, of course, are local. Beyond statistics, there is a spirit about the place - a relaxed, focused, community spirit - which is Hope's own, although campus can be a bit lonely at weekends. The drop-out rate - just below 12% do not complete the course - is above the Government benchmark.

ACADEMIA

Students say the best teaching is in History & Philosophy, Theology & Religious Studies, Social Studies, Sociology, Subjects allied to Medicine, Computer Science, Business Studies, Psychology, Law, Education Studies, Business & Administrative Studies, and Drama.

The least popular teaching were Sports Science

TEACHING SURVEY AT A GLANCE	
Avg. UCAS points accepted	**240**
Acceptance rate	**16%**
Overall satisfaction rate	**81%**
Helpful/interested staff	**No data**
Small tuition groups	**No data**
Students into graduate jobs	**70%**

Teaching most popular with undergraduates:
History & Philosophy, Theology & Religious Studies (92%), Social Studies, Sociology (90%), subjects allied to Medicine (87-88%), Computer Science (87%), Business Studies (86%), Psychology, Law (84%), Education Studies (83%), Business & Administrative Studies (81%), Drama (80%).

Teaching least popular with undergraduates:
Sports Science (73%), Performing Arts (69%).

and Performing Arts - Dance, Drama & Theatre Studies, music, which suggests the core areas are the thing and they don't quite get the modernising add-ons quite right. Interesting that the same is true at Lampeter. Even so, these two subjects satis-

RESEARCH EXCELLENCE		
% of Liverpool Hope's research that is ***4**** *(World-class) or* ***3**** *(Internationally rated):*		
	4*	**3***
Computer Science	**0%**	**20%**
Politics	**0%**	**0%**
Social Work	**5%**	**0%**
Psychology	**0%**	**5%**
Education	**0%**	**20%**
English	**0%**	**10%**
Theology	**5%**	**15%**
Performing Arts	**0%**	**0%**
Music	**0%**	**30%**

fied more than two-thirds of the class.

Generally, this is a teaching, not a research institution. Its showing in the recent nationwide research assessment was dire. They came fourth from bottom. Out of nine subjects submitted only 5% of two of them - Social Work and Theology - was rated world-class. But that was probably because they were getting on with them out there in the street rather than pouring over books and papers.

Subjects at Liverpool Hope are grouped into four Deaneries: Arts & Humanities, Education, Business & Computing, and Sciences & Social Sciences. All of the undergraduate programmes are

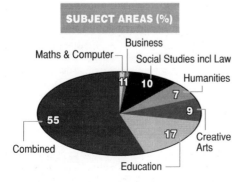

SUBJECT AREAS (%)

Business
Maths & Computer — Social Studies incl Law
11 10 Humanities
7
55 9
Combined 17 Creative Arts
Education

modular. There are BA and BSc single honours, BSc combined honours (major/minor), BA combined honours (major/minor), and equal weight combined honours for both BA and BSc subjects. There are also a load of 1-year Certificates in HE, the BA with QTS teacher training degrees, and a BDes (Design), the first year of which can be studied on the Isle of Man. Students are stimulated by the content and sympathetic delivery of the programme, and produce some imaginative work in response.

Theology is, of course, still on offer and scored 23 points at the teaching assessments and a Grade 4 at the research assessments. Business, however, scored full marks at the assessments and features in the BA single honours and widely throughout the 450 combination courses offered. There is also an apparently improbable course called Gaming Technology, which has in fact nothing to do with gambling, but computer games technology.

Teacher Training focuses on primary teaching - English Lang./Lit., Art/Design, Geography, History, Information Technology, Maths, Music, Special Needs, Sport Studies, Religion - and a series of Advanced Study of Early Years is part of the BA Hons combined course strategy.

Among social sciences, Psychology and Sociology both had good teaching assessments on inspection and are popular, and clearly their Childhood & Youth Studies, Social Work, Special Needs and Pastoral Leadership programmes are central to Hope's ethos. Sports Studies and Sports Development are add-ons to all kinds of subjects in the curriculum, which looks a bit odd. For true sport students they are available as single honours as Sport Psychology, Sport Studies, or Sport & Health Studies. There's an air-conditioned fitness suite, equipped with cardiovascular and resistance equipment.

The £5.3 million Sheppard-Worlock Library houses 250,000 books, many PCs and 500 study places. There is an on-site nursery that provides for children younger than two years, and the employment future prospects of both its many mature and more youthful students are encouraged by elective modules in languages and IT, and by modules which take students out into the workplace and community, both in the UK and overseas.

There's a 70% chance of real graduate employment for Hope graduates within six months of leaving.

SOCIAL SCENE

Student Union The two student bars are D2 (with video wall) on the ground floor of the Union, and the lounge-style **Derwent Bar** upstairs.

There is also a Union presence (and bar) at Everton. Ents are traditional fare - bands (of the

tribute variety), comedians (Jack Dee and Lee Evans have played here), karaoke, jazz nights, and a multitude of society thrashes. Tuesday takes students out to **The Blue Angel** in town (108 Seel Street) - 'even Johnny Vegas could pull here,' says Itchy. **The Raz**, as it is affectionately known, is Liverpool's cheesiest student dive, but alumni look back with tender memories - 'Best chat up line from a very pissed Welshman:' says Lotty. '"I saw you coming down the stairs and I thought you were a vision of loveliness" - I did snog him and my mate snogged him the week after! Happy days...'

Regular DJ Welsh Dave of the Derwent grooms Hope students for such antics. Wednesday is sports or societies night. 'It's always a popular night in D2 with each team coming up with a weekly theme to

WHAT IT'S REALLY LIKE	
UNIVERSITY:	
Social Life	★★
Campus scene	**Friendly, focused**
Student Union services	**Supportive**
Politics	**Caring**
Sport	**Easy going**
National team position	**96th**
Sport facilities	**Good**
Arts opportunities	**Excellent**
Student newspaper	**Liverpool Student**
Bars	**D2, Derwent**
Union ents	**DJs, cheese, karaoke, quiz**
Union societies	**45**
Parking	**Adequate**
CITY:	
Entertainment	★★★★★
City scene	**Fab**
Town/gown relations	**Good**
Risk of violence	**Average**
Cost of living	**Low**
Student concessions	**Excellent**
Survival + 2 nights out	**£70 pw**
Part-time work campus/town	**Good/Excellent**

ACCOMMODATION	
Guarantee to freshers	**100%**
Style	**Halls, flats**
Security guard	**24-hr security**
Shared rooms	**Some**
Internet access	**All**
Self-catered	**All**
En suite	**Some**
Approx price range pw	**£61.11-£88.75**
City rent pw	**£40-£120**

get ya involved.' On Friday comes 'The WORLD Famous all day party. Music and fun throughout the day in the Derwent bar from 12 with Karaoke and DJ's starting at 6. Getting you warmed up and in the mood for our Flagship night Reload, starting at 9.' It's DJ Welsh Dave again plus up and coming DJ's eager to fill his shoes. Saturday most people have gone home and it's live football and rugby on the screens. Then it's the Sunday Night Social - quiz, bingo, sing-a-long, 'with great acts every week'.

There are plenty of societies and an opportunity to be part of the team that produces the award-winning Liverpool Student newspaper that serves all 3 Liverpool universities.

SPORT They have recently installed a floodlit, all-weather Astroturf pitch for hockey, tennis, football; there's a gym, and the Athletics Union is involved in all the usual inter-Uni competitions, with not at all a bad record, given the size of the student population. They came 96th nationally last year.

Hope Park Sports is managed by Healthworks, an outside firm. Facilities include a multi-purpose sports hall for 5-a-side football, badminton, basketball and tennis, volleyball, netball and hockey. There's access to football and rugby pitches and squash courts and the new fitness suite mentioned under Academia above. There are exercise classes

and coaching courses for all abilities and levels of fitness.

Among a handful of unusual clubs is Kick Boxing, and the Mountaineering club is worth a mention not least because of Plas Caerdeon, Hope's Outdoor Education Centre. This old manor house in 18 acres of woodland overlooking the glorious Mawddach Estuary (Snowdonia) hosts field and study trips, but it's also a bolt hole for music students on Composition weekend, Drama students for rehearsals and anybody for simpler regenerative pleasures. There is good accommodation.

CITY See Student Liverpool.

PILLOW TALK
There's accommodation at the main Hope Park campus and at Aigburth Park, a satellite accommodation campus, and at The Cornerstone, where the Creative and Performing Arts courses are taught.

GETTING THERE
☛ By road: easy access M62 (east/west), which connects with M6 (north/south) at Junction 21a.
☛ Well served by National Express coaches.
☛ By rail: Manchester, 0:40; Sheffield, 1:45; Leeds or Birmingham, 2:00; London Kings Cross, 3:00.
☛ Speke Airport 5 miles away.

LIVERPOOL JOHN MOORES UNIVERSITY

Liverpool John Moores University
Roscoe Court
4 Rodney Street
Liverpool L1 2TZ

TEL 0151 231 5090
FAX 0151 231 3462
EMAIL recruitment@ljmu.ac.uk
WEB www.ljmu.ac.uk

Liverpool John Moores Students' Union
The Haigh Building
Maryland Street
Liverpool L1 9DE

TEL 0151 231 4900
FAX 0151 231 4931
EMAIL studentsunion@livjm.ac.uk
WEB www.l-s-u.com

VAG VIEW

*L*iverpool John Moores (LJMU) is Liverpool's metropolitan university, more part of the city than the older campus-based university. LJMU's many buildings are strewn all over the city, half its students come from Merseyside, and the university's roots run deep into the city's industrial history.

Origins go back to 1823 as the Liverpool Mechanics' and Apprentices' Library. As poly, the institution brought together the City

Colleges of Art and Design and Building, Commerce, and the Regional College of Technology, the City of Liverpool College of Higher Education, the IM Marsh College of Physical Education, the FL Calder College of Home Economics and the Liverpool College of Nursing and Midwifery - all of which give a good clue to the uni's academic profile today.

Finally, LJMU owes its name and ethos to one of the city's most famous entrepreneurs. Sir John Moores CBE (1896-1993) built Littlewoods - the football pools organisation - from scratch.

UNIVERSITY/STUDENT PROFILE

University since	**1992**
Situation/style	**Civic**
Student population	**24370**
Undergraduates	**20270**
Mature undergraduates	**10%**
International undergrads	**4%**
Male/female ratio	**47:53**
Equality of opportunity:	
state school intake	**96%**
social class 4-7 intake	**40%**
low-participation area intake	**18%**

'Sir John's business success was built upon his philosophy of the equality of opportunity for all,' the uni says. 'This fundamental belief...is a reflection of the university's commitment to higher education, to access, to flexibility and to participation.' Most of all, perhaps, it gives the clue to the underlying ethos - applied learning - they are very hot, across the board, on how what is learned and imbued here can be applied on graduation in the world of work.

Right now they have a problem, however, albeit quite a nice one. They are too popular. The uni is bound by a Government funding agreement limiting student intake, and the 17% increase last year has prompted a Government warning that if cuts to intake are not made, then LJMU will incur heavy fines.

CAMPUS

LJMU is roughly three main sites: Mount Pleasant, Byrom Street/Henry Cotton campus and IM Marsh. Each has lecture theatres, seminar rooms, laboratories, editing suites, individual study and computer rooms, as well as union bars, shops and sports facilities. Everything is in and around the city, accessible to public transport and in easy reach of the city centre and halls of residence.

Writes Emma Hardy: 'LJMU buildings are scattered across the city, many are impressive. The School of Media, Critical and Creative Arts, where I study, is one of the most impressive buildings in Liverpool. Located next to the Anglican Cathedral, the views from it are spectacular and the facilities are exemplary. The main library is a great glass structure of imposing stature and, like much of the rest of the university, likely to take your breath away when you first see it. But there are some grim high rise blocks too. Prospective students do well to bear in mind that what they see on Open Day are the best bits.'

FEES, BURSARIES

UK & EU Fees, 2009-10: £3,225 p.a. Students with a household income less than £25,000 qualify for a bursary. The Vice Chancellor's Award is awarded

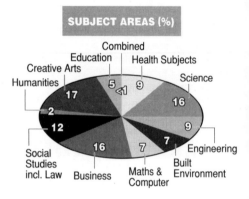

SUBJECT AREAS (%)

for academic - a maximum of six (£10,000 p.a.) awards are made each year. Dream Plan Achieve Scholarships (£1,000) are awarded to applicants with 360 UCAS points in three subjects. Achievers Awards - scholarships of £1,000 p.a. - are available to students who can show particular commitment, determination and achievement in areas such as the arts, sports, citizenship or volunteering. Sports Scholarships are also up for grabs.

STUDENT PROFILE

Forty-five per cent of LJMU students come from Merseyside, 37% of undergraduates are part-timers. Two thirds are eligible for a LJMU bursary, indicating they come from lower income households, as are over 65% of LJMU's scholarship winners. Students are recruited from around 106 countries and 11% are classified as a having a Black and Minority Ethnic background. There is also a high percentage of disabled (many dyslexic) students

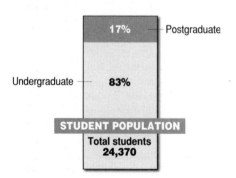

17% — Postgraduate
Undergraduate — 83%
STUDENT POPULATION
Total students
24,370

TEACHING SURVEY AT A GLANCE

Avg. UCAS points accepted	**240**
Acceptance rate	**21%**
Overall satisfaction rate	**78%**
Helpful/interested staff	**★★★**
Small tuition groups	**★★★**
Students into graduate jobs	**70%**

Teaching most popular with undergraduates:
Finance (93%), Animal Behaviour, Food &
Nutrition, Law, Research & Study Skills in
Education (91%), History (89%), Performing Arts
(89%), Drama, English, Biology (88%), Accounting
(87%), Pharmacy (85%), Languages, Subjects
allied to Medicine, Sports Science (83%),
Education Studies, Geography, Environmental
Science, Sociology (82%), sciences related to
Biology, Business, Social Studies (80%).

Teaching least popular with undergraduates:
Initial Teacher Training (69%), Engineering (58%-
66%). Fine Art (51%).

because they run a rigorous support programme.

Generally, LJMU's problem has not been getting students so much as hanging on to them: their drop-out runs at around 11%, quite high.

Asked to give us a profile from the ground, Emma concluded, 'Despite the huge diversity in matters of taste and style, your LJMU student is a mellow person, out to enjoy their time at university. The general atmosphere is far from snobbish, and with such a wide range of people studying here, friends are not hard to find, no matter what your age, or what your interests.'

ACADEMIA & JOBS

Writes Emma: 'LJMU are big on student feedback. Tutors are approachable and changes do get made. Questionnaires regarding each and every module taught are distributed to students and the uni does listen to complaints. The emphasis is on making the experience as enjoyable as possible.'

LJMU has three modern Learning Resource Centres, two of which are open 24/7. A virtual learning environment, Blackboard, links students to assignments, lecture notes, useful internet sites and other multimedia resources. Over 2,000 workstations are available in the LRCs and student open-access facilities. 100% of student rooms are wired for internet access.

Generally, there's a vocational bias, they're strong on sandwich courses and have good contacts with industry - professional associations offer direct employment routes, for example, in pharmacy, surveying and engineering. And now

they've established a business club for graduates called NEXUS, through which you'll be able to network and tap into uni-based expertise and resources. You also get lots of hands-on help in landing a job: a 'Ready for Work' programme is held weekly throughout the year - free, short, practical sessions and workshops designed to improve employability and prepare you for the first graduate job. All students are encouraged to develop skills and abilities like analysing and problem solving, team working and communicating, planning and organising, showing initiative, reasoning, and computing: 70% get real graduate jobs within six months of graduating.

They have six faculties: Business and Law; Education, Community & Leisure; Media, Arts & Social Science; Health & Applied Social Sciences; Science; and Technology & Environment.

LJMU students say the best teachings is in Finance, Animal Behaviour, Food & Nutrition, Law, Research & Study Skills in Education, History, Performing Arts, Drama, English, Biology, Accounting, Pharmacy, Languages, Subjects allied to Medicine, Sports Science, Education Studies, Geography, Environmental Science, Sociology, Sciences related to Biology, Business, and Social Studies. Least popular is Fine Art, where only half the class thought it was any good.

Biological Sciences produce the most jobs, then Arts & Design, Business, subjects allied to Medicine, Social Studies, Education, Architecture, Building & Planning, Engineering & Technology,

RESEARCH EXCELLENCE

*% of Liverpool JM's research that is
4* (World-class) or 3* (Internationally rated):*

	4*	3*
Nursing/Midwifery	**5%**	**35%**
Health Professions	**5%**	**20%**
Biological Sciences	**0%**	**10%**
Physics	**10%**	**35%**
Computer Science	**5%**	**45%**
Electrical/Electronic Eng.	**20%**	**40%**
General Engineering	**20%**	**40%**
Built Environment	**15%**	**45%**
Town/Country Planning	**5%**	**20%**
Accounting/Finance	**0%**	**5%**
Information Management	**5%**	**20%**
Anthropology	**10%**	**35%**
Education	**0%**	**20%**
Sports	**25%**	**25%**
English	**5%**	**25%**
History	**0%**	**15%**
Art and Design	**0%**	**35%**

Computer Science, and Media.

This year there's a new £24-million Art and Design Academy opened in January 2009, and a £22.5-million life sciences building is in prospect - including an indoor 70-metre running track and labs for testing cardio-vascular ability, motor skills and bio-mechanics functions. Sports Science is a big deal here. LJMU have the only Sport & Exercise Science department in the UK with a maximum teaching assessment rating of 24, and in the recent research assessment 50% of their work was either world-class or internationally excellent. See Science & Football, Sports Development & PE, Exercise Science, Sports Science/Technology, and Outdoor Education with PE.

Education is a defining provision - secondary and primary. There are also ESOL and TESOL courses - English for non-English speakers and courses for teachers of same.

In Art & Design, look for Creative Writing, Dance, Drama, Fashion, Fine Art, Graphic Arts & Interior Design, but also Creative Arts & Social Science, making the link to the Social Studies strengths. The degrees in Social Work and Applied Psychology keep LJMU in the top echelon of graduate providers in community work and counselling.

> *Students are requested to identify any disabilities including Dyslexia as early as possible, so as to take advantage of JMU's rigorous support programme.*

Drama students and local community groups make use of Black Box Theatre Company, Momentum Theatre Company, Liverpool Youth Service and Unity Theatre following a £200,000 refurbishment of the LJMU's Joe H Makin Drama Centre. Arts links to Media through Interactive Media Design, and Computer & Electronics via the Digital Broadcast degree. Radio & TV broadcasters and sound recordists love this uni, in particular their BSc Broadcast Technology. There's a Granada TV partnership status and great tie-ups with Sky TV. Look, too, at BA Hons Journalism, which includes practical TV Journalism (there's also International Journalism) and Media Professional Studies for TV production, business and management enterprise, info technology and media theory. The latter is run in partnership with Mersey Television (Brookside and Hollyoaks producer, Phil Redmond, is their Honorary Professor).

The uni's nursing and midwifery students now benefit from 'SimMan' - a high-tech 'universal patient simulator' mannequin, which is part of the new Clinical Practice Suite, developed in partnership with the Cheshire and Merseyside Strategic Health Authority: 6 rooms designed to function like real hospital wards. This is part of a strong health provision, including Paramedic Practice, Medicinal Biochemistry, Analytical/Medicinal Chemistry. Another related key area can be gleaned from the full-mark teaching assessment score (24 points) for Food & Nutrition, and Biosciences. See also BSc Nutrition, and Public Health. There's a good employment track record, too, for prospective chemists and those planning a career in Pharmaceutical Manufacture.

Animal health technicians, carers, nurses are trained here too. LJMU leaves the vet degrees to Liverpool Uni and positions itself instead with the likes of BSc Animal Behaviour and Zoology.

The Architecture and Property Management degrees (see also the Real Estate Management and BSc Quantity Surveying) are another great graduate employment focus. The in-depth knowledge bank evident from their 60% worlds-class and internationally excellent ratings at the research assessment.

In Law, they deliver the Legal Practice Course required for becoming a solicitor. There's a 'mock' courtroom to give law degree and legal practice students the chance to gain intensive trial practice. And, as is so often the case in a city university with Criminology, Forensic Science and Social Psychology degrees and a strong Sport provision, jobs come easy with the police.

SOCIAL SCENE

STUDENTS' UNION As a prospective student, bear in mind that it is up to you to make the most of your time at LJMU. This means finding out about what is going on and getting involved in what interests you. Radio stations, newspapers, clubs, societies and events need student support and make a return with interest through the character and abilities they impart.

The Union (LSU) has over 50 clubs and societies. Most of its organised activities take place in the main LSU building, the Haigh. Facilities include **Drift Café** - a place to relax with its fair-trade hot drinks, cakes and smoothies. There's free wi-fi and PC access. Scholars is the traditional student pub, with pool tables, jukeboxes and TVs. It serves quality bar food. The **Engine Room** serves lunch during the day and transforms into a nightclub at night. The ents menu is not quite what it was in the old days, with four nights a week culminating in *Time Tunnel* on Saturday, but there's plenty of variety: see calendar to download on www.l-s-u.com.

ACCOMMODATION	
Guarantee to freshers	**100%**
Style	**Flats**
Security guard	**All**
Shared rooms	**None**
Internet access	**All**
Self-catered	**All**
En suite	**Most**
Approx price range pw	**£64-£105**
City rent pw	**£40-£125**

WHAT IT'S REALLY LIKE	
UNIVERSITY:	
Social Life	★★★
Campus scene	**Local, top scene**
Student Union services	**Good**
Politics	**Active: safety, sex, housing**
Sport	**19 clubs**
National team position	**50th**
Sport facilities	**Good**
Arts opportunities	**Music excellent; drama, dance, film, art good**
Student magazine	**Re:Load**
Student radio	**Shout fm**
Nightclub Bars	**The Haigh**
Union ents	**Pop, retro, funky dance**
Union societies	**72**
Most popular societies	**Ski/Snowboard, Afro-Carribean, Christian Union**
Parking	**Poor**
CITY:	
Entertainment	★★★★★
City scene	**Fab**
Town/gown relations	**Good**
Risk of violence	**Average**
Cost of living	**Low**
Student concessions	**Excellent**
Survival + 2 nights out	**£70 pw**
Part-time work campus/town	**Good/Excellent**

Among the most successful student societies is the radio station, Shout fm, and now there's a magazine, Re:load, which in its previous incarnation as Shout figured in many a national awards ceremony.

Situated in the Haigh is UNITEMP, LJMU's own employment agency. It does offer some exclusive Unitemp related jobs, but doesn't beat getting the local newspaper, visiting the job centre, or simply asking around for vacancies.

SPORT The uni's sporting facilities include a swimming pool, all weather hockey and football pitches, fully equipped gym, dance studios, and climbing walls. Most facilities are based at LJMU's IM Marsh Campus, 3 miles from the city centre. LJMU's proudest boast is its Base Fitness Centre, well equipped and professionally staffed. There's a student sports pass for free/reduced price access to facilities - badminton courts, swimming pools, squash courts, athletics tracks.

TOWN See Student Liverpool.

PILLOW TALK

All freshers - even those who apply through Clearing - are guaranteed a place in city-centre halls: individual study bedrooms within shared flats alongside other LJMU students. Most rooms now also have private en-suite bathrooms. All accommodation is self-catering.

'Pretty much all university halls and LJMU residences are fine except Crete and Candia Towers, which should be avoided at all costs,' said a student. 'You have been warned.'

GETTING THERE

☞ By road: M62, M6/J21a. Well served by coach.
☞ By rail: Manchester, 40 mins; Sheffield, 1:45; Leeds, Birmingham, 2:00; London King's Cross, 3:00.
☞ Liverpool airports for inland/Ireland flights.
☞ By coach: London, 5:00; Manchester, 50 mins.

STUDENT LONDON - THE CITY

London is an expensive place to live. Everything from shopping to travel can bite huge chunks out of your student loan. Sometimes it can feel like the only thing you've achieved during your course is a hefty debt. That is unless you learn to flash your student card at every opportunity. Although you may face ridicule for being a 'bake bean loving, beer-swilling creature of the night', you will be the envy of every non-student when you get offered a rather nice discount just about everywhere you go.

With a population of over seven million, London is one of the most diverse cities in the world – 30% of residents were born outside England. Greater London not only covers a lot of multicultural ground, but also physical, as it spans 1584 square kilometres. That space is filled with so many interests and attractions that you could not visit them all in one lifetime; London plays host to more than 200 carnivals and festivals annually. With its mixture of historical landmarks and modern masterpieces, London is a great place to learn, and not just in the lecture theatre.

THEATRE

On an average day in London you will be able to watch one of 76 plays, 33 musicals, 19 operas or 16 dance performances. If you were to go to one a day starting on the first of January, you wouldn't be finished until the end of May. The West End is one of the UK's biggest attractions: the choice of plays and shows is superb, but you often end up paying more up there. **The National Theatre** (Southbank, Embankment tube, +44 (0)20 7452 3000) and **The Globe Theatre** (21 New Globe Walk, Mansion House tube, +44 (0)20 7902 1400) are two of the most popular repertory companies. Playing less commercial performances, they often have the best offerings. The NT is subsidised. Otherwise there are countless fringe theatres showing allsorts for allsorts.

TKTS is the place to go for theatre on a budget. As the only official half price and discounted theatre ticket operation in London, they offer tickets on the day of the performance only, and have no phone number, so you have to visit. They are based in both Leicester Square and Canary Wharf DLR Station. Many theatres offer student tickets with proof of ID, otherwise it can be worth waiting at the venue box office for returns or standby tickets before the performance.

DANCE

Whether you're up for a class or just sitting back and watching somebody else shake their thang, London is a great place for dance.

The Barbican Centre (Silk Street, +44 (0)20 7638 4141, Barbican tube) is Europe's largest arts venue and a key member of the dance scene, especially the unconventional. Students get half price tickets in advance for all Wednesday evenings. **The London Coliseum** (St Martin's Lane, +44 (0)20 7836 0111, Leicester Square tube) is home to the English National Opera and is the London base of the English National Ballet. Standby tickets are available to students. There are many more major venues including **The Place**, Riverside Studios, Royal Opera House and Sadler's Wells.

To get involved yourself, there are classes of many different styles held in many venues. **Dance**

Attic (Old Fulham Baths, 368 North End Road, +44 (0)20 7610 2055, Fulham Broadway tube) costs £50 a year for students to join, you then just pay per class. **Pineapple Dance Studios** (7 Langley Street, +44 (0)20 7836 4004, Covent Garden Tube) costs £70 a year, that's half price for students. For full Dance listings visit www.londondance.com.

COMEDY

A comedy club is a great choice for an evening out in London. There are dozens of great venues scattered around, but here are a few of the more student friendly offerings.

Backyard Comedy Club, 231 Cambridge Heath Road, +44 (0)20 7739 3122, Bethnal Green tube. This converted factory is now a club owned by comedian Lee Hurst, who quite often acts as host. There is also a restaurant and disco after the show for anyone wanting a full night out.

Chuckle Club, London School of Economics, Houghton Street, +44 (0)20 7476 1672, Holborn tube. For less than a tenner you can see a host of comedians, including household names. Being a student union bar the drinks are all fairly cheap.

The Cosmic Comedy Club, 177 Fulham Palace Road, Hammersmith tube. This club is free to get in. You just have to pay what you think it was worth afterwards. Also, every week the BBC makes comedy programmes for radio. It's free, so anyone can go along. Call BBC Radio Theatre +44 (0)20 8576 1227.

CLUBS AND VENUES

London has around 15% of all the clubs in Britain. That means that you are never lost for a place to go for a spot of late night drinking. The biggest clubbing nights are still Friday and Saturday, but any day is a good day. Some of the bigger names include **Fabric**, **Ministry of Sound** and **The Cross**, but there are hundreds of other venues catering for every taste. www.londonnet.co.uk has a great clubs section where you can select which day of the week you want to go out, or which style of music, and see complete listings. For free entrance into 25 London nightclubs, including **Café de Paris** and **Elysium**, become a Circle Club member, for just a £5 admin fee. It gives you free admission during the week and half price at weekends, and you can also purchase 2-4-1 drinks vouchers in advance. Visit www.circleclubcard.com for full details.

CINEMA

London has almost 500 cinema screens and a choice of over 100 films showing at any time. Leicester Square is the centre for cinema in London. Every year it hosts numerous star-studded premieres on the many huge screens. But it isn't particularly student friendly with rather expensive ticket prices, making London's independent cinemas the better option. The **Prince Charles Cinema** (7 Leicester Place, Leicester Square tube) is one such place. *Feel-good Fridays* cost just £1 and the most non-members have to pay for a regular performance is £4. Annual Membership is just £7.50. For a search that allows you to find a cinema by a particular postcode, tube location or where a certain film is showing visit www.viewlondon. co.uk. Alternatively most of the chain cinemas in Greater London offer student prices. **UGC** offers an unlimited monthly card for £13.99. Orange mobile customers can text FILM to 241 on Wednesdays and receive a code allowing them two tickets for the price of one.

ART

In London there are around 50 exhibitions open to the public each day. 17 national museums and galleries, as well as many other smaller, local galleries, allow free entrance. These include the **British Museum**, **National Gallery**, **Tate Modern** and **V&A Museum**. London exhibits countless works or all kinds, both permanent and temporary collections. For a list of all the contemporary exhibitions London has to offer at any time, visit www.newexhibitions.com. For more details about all the major London galleries go to www.londontourist.org/art.

MUSIC

There are 9 major concert halls in London – **Barbican** (where they often hold free events), **Purcell Room**, **Royal Albert Hall**, **Royal Festival Hall**, **Royal Opera House**, **Queen Elizabeth Hall**, **St John's Smith Square**, **Wembley Arena** and **Wigmore Hall** - as well as 47 major rock and pop venues, including **Astoria**, **Barfly**, **Brixton Academy**, **Forum and Garage**. From ultra-trendy to cheesy and trashy, international superstars to local legends, you will find whatever type of music you are after in London, and all of your favourite musicians will have played here, or will play here at some time. www.bbc.co.uk/music/whatson has regularly updated information covering all kinds of music. For the cheapest tickets go direct to the venue box office and avoid those booking fees, but for the best tickets visit www.gigsandtours.com or www.ticketmaster.co.uk

SHOPPING

Camden is a great place to shop. The cheap goods and cosmopolitan atmosphere make it a unique experience. You can find just about anything there and can easily spend a day wandering the many shops and stalls. The market is open seven days a week and the nearest tube station is Camden Town. Covent Garden market offers more specialist goods with many arts and crafts. This historic setting is full of street entertainers and is easily accessed from a number of tube stations including Covent Garden and Leicester Square. **Portobello Road**, in the trendy Notting Hill area , is also worth a mention (open on Saturdays). Then there' **Oxford Street** (**Selfridges**), Knightsbridge (**Harrods**), Regents Street. Most High Street stores offer a student discount, just remember, always flash your student ID, and don't be afraid to ask.

Paul Stephen

LONDON METROPOLITAN UNIVERSITY

London Metropolitan University
31 Jewry Street
London EC3N 2EY

TEL 020 133 4200
    020 7753 3272 (Campus North)
EMAIL admissions@londonmet.ac.uk
WEB www.londonmet.ac.uk

London Metropolitan Students' Union
2 Goulston Street
London E1 7TP

TEL 020 7320 2769
FAX 020 7320 3201
EMAIL d.everett@uni.ac.uk
WEB www.londonmetsu.org.uk

VAG VIEW

*L*ondon Metropolitan University was formed in 2002 by the merger of North London and London Guildhall universities. 'The new university is one of the biggest in the UK,' wrote John Shaw at the time. He was on the future strategy task group. With '13 main sites, grouped into two campuses (London North and London City),' it was Shaw's job to identify the two unis' very different histories and cultures and direct the

UNIVERSITY/STUDENT PROFILE	
University since	**1992**
Situation/style	**Civic**
Student population	**29495**
Undergraduates	**21955**
Mature undergraduates	**53%**
International undergrads	**21%**
Male/female ratio	**45:55**
Equality of opportunity:	
state school intake	**97%**
social class 4-7 intake	**43%**
low-participation area intake	**7%**

way forward.

It was not an easy commission. First there was the geographical problem. North London University, the old London Poly which took University title in 1992, was based in the Holloway Road, London Guildhall, one of the largest providers of part-time professional courses (mainly Business, but also Law, Psychology, Musical Instrument Technology and Art & Design)in the country was located in the East End of London.

Really the only way they came together was in the uniquely diverse character of their students.

London Guildhall boasted a handful of celebrity singers, Alison Moyet and Sonya from Echobelly, an MP (Kate Hoey), a pants-stroking comedian (Vic Reeves) and Margaret Thatcher's errant son, Mark. Said student Stuart Harkness of the main body: 'The resilience of the university stemmed largely from its streetwise clientele, devoid of opulent silver spoons and armed with a left wing, if slightly lethargic, political bias. They'll stand at the bar, or at the odd demo, but in general

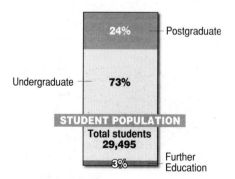

STUDENT POPULATION

Postgraduate 24%

Undergraduate 73%

Total students
29,495

Further Education 3%

the attitude is more down to earth than a rattlesnake's belly in a wagon wheel rut.'

Then there was the North London equivalent, soon to be suitor. The nearest they came to celebrity was having as the centrepiece of their theatre an organ that was once played by William Lloyd Webber, father of 'cello-playing Julian and musical impresario Andrew. As North London University from 1992 its students studied Business, but also Environment & Social Studies, Humanities, Education, Science, Computing, and Engineering. Sounds good, but it was all a bit of an uphill struggle. What the university was up against was what it called in 1995-6, 'the general difficulties faced by all graduates in gaining employment and University of North London graduates in particular. Reasons for this include the preponderance of mature students and a general misunderstanding of the quality and type of education provided here.'

The problem they had was that employers were not taking their graduates seriously. So they set about teaching their students to look at themselves closely, to analyse themselves, build up a picture of their strengths and weaknesses, and to develop personal skills, communication skills, and what they called in those days 'personal transferable skills'. When we spoke to student Maureen Okolo, however, it was far from clear that she had taken on board what the university intended by these personal transferable skills: 'UNL is in the right place for a great big, delicious slice of London's night life. Step outside and find yourself in the infamous Holloway Road... Uni life is great, if you like that sort of thing. Just expect constant rounds of socialising with chic, retro, funky, cool, funny individuals from all walks of life.'

I sometimes think back to those days and wonder whether Mr Shaw might have done better had he met Stuart Harkness and Maureen Okolo and really empathised with them before he set about the massive PR operation that still today markets London Metropolitan University as 'one of the foremost providers of undergraduate, postgraduate, professional and vocational education and training in Britain.'

Clearly, it is not. But it is a people's uni-

versity with masses of potential if only if it was managed from the bottom up rather than the top down, as indeed North London Poly used to be - a great place, with easy relations between lecturers and students, everyone part of the same scene, not teaching personality traits but encouraging their students simply to be. Then it wouldn't find itself in the pickle it did last year when recently it was ordered by the Higher Education Funding Council to investigate itself after allegations that one of its departments had leant on students to mark up its teaching so to improve its ratings in the National Student Survey.

Survey results, league tables, 'facts and figures' are the stock in trade of the top-down PR operation which simply doesn't suit certain higher education institutions. Why straightjacket its efforts in this way? Let them instead get on with what they are good at, or were good at before this union took place.

It has been a bad few months for London Met, for the funding council now also wanting to claw back millions overpaid to the university in past years owing to an apparent under-reporting of the number of student drop-outs. As we go to press hundreds of jobs are threatened, and a Commons motion signed by thirteen MPs urges 'a thorough exploration of all potential non-staff savings' for fear that it will undermine the viability of the university.

CAMPUS SCENE

It is an unusual set-up for a uni, with its umpteen sites, academic and residential in E1, E2, E9, E14, EC3, and N7.

CITY CAMPUS has the 12 sites in the City and the East End, which is a racially diverse area with, in particular, a thriving Bangladeshi community giving the cultural flavour to the eating and shopping delights of Brick Lane. The campus's main Moorgate site is built on what used to the most infamous insane asylum in England, the Bethlem Royal Hospital.

CAMPUS NORTH comprises a collection of sites around the Holloway Road, a student-friendly area packed with takeaways, cafés, restaurants and shops.

WHAT IT'S REALLY LIKE	
UNIVERSITY:	
Social Life	★★★
Campus scene	**Mature, local, urban, easy going**
Student Union services	**Average**
Politics	**Internal**
Sport	**Very competitive**
National team position	**25th**
Sport facilities	**Professional**
Arts	**Available**
Student magazine	**VerveZine**
Student radio	**Metsu Radio**
Nightclub venues/bars	**Sub Bar, Sub Club (Aldgate), Rocket (Holloway Road)**
Union ents	**Big Fish, etc.**
Union societies	**58**
Most active	**Islamic Soc**
Parking	**Non-existent**
CITY:	
Entertainment	★★★★★
Scene	**Wild, expensive**
Town/gown relations	**Average-good**
Risk of violence	**'Average'**
Cost of living	**Very high**
Student concessions	**Locally adequate**
Survival + 2 nights out	**£100 pw**
Part-time work campus/town	**Good/excellent**

So there we have it. Chapel Market and Camden Lock meet Aldgate, Petticoat Lane and Spitalfields.

FEES, BURSARIES

UK & EU Fees, 2009-10: £3,225. If in receipt of full HE Maintenance grant there's a bursary of £1,000; if in receipt of partial grant, bursaries are on a sliding scale as to parental income. They also have scholarships. See www.londonmet.ac.uk/scholarships

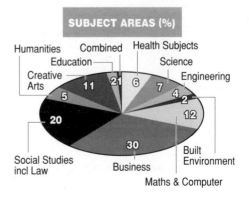

SUBJECT AREAS (%)

Humanities 11 · Combined 21 · Health Subjects 6 · Education · Science 7 · Creative Arts 5 · Engineering 4 · Maths & Computer 2 · Built Environment 12 · Business 30 · Social Studies incl Law 20

Avg. UCAS points accepted	**220**
Acceptance rate	**15%**
Overall satisfaction rate	**72%**
Helpful/interested staff	★★
Small tuition groups	★★
Students into graduate jobs	**62%**

Teaching most popular with undergraduates:
Mathematics (95%), Education (94%), Sociology (91%), Social Policy (90%), Drama, Performing Arts (86%), Accounting (82%), Politics (85%), Social Studies (84%).

Teaching least popular with undergraduates:
Film Studies (63%), Management Studies (62%), Marketing, Tourism (61%).

STUDENT PROFILE

A high proportion originate from London and the surrounding Southeast, but the melting pot is fuelled by those from farther afield, nearly 8,000 international students from 155 countries. The cosmopolitan flavour makes London Met a truly multi-cultural university. 'Multiple faiths are therefore evident and well catered for with prayer rooms at various university sites, a chaplaincy and numerous students' union-funded cultural societies, including Christian, Islamic, Muslim, Afro-Caribbean, to name but a few. All seem to respect each others' practices under the umbrella of LGU brotherhood.'

They run their own offices in China, India, Pakistan and Bangladesh, and provide a three-day orientation course for international students each September. There is also a successful peer support scheme, involving language support, a buddy system and subject area support. But all that aside, what we have is a cultural recipe with flavour, which is also what we have at Campus North, whose undergraduate body is to a large extent drawn from the local, notably ethnic population.

Statistics point to 21% international students and 53% mature; 43% from the lower socio-economic groups and 7% from 'low participation' neighbourhoods.

SOCIAL SCENE

Students Union London Met's **Rocket** has a fascinating history, worth a book of its own. It has been around since the inception of the North London Poly itself. It began as the Great Hall when the first students arrived in 1896. Some of their concerts were actually conducted by Proms inventor Sir Henry Wood. Since then it became a proscenium arch theatre, the arch picked up for a song from the old **Marlborough Theatre** down the road opposite the **Nag's Head**, after which it was used as a cinema, where William Lloyd Webber played the organ... And so the tale goes on. Today, the Rocket Complex, as it is known, is a meeting place of some style, cool enough for like-minded City students, used to their ground-floor **Hub Bar** in Goulston Street (where one of Jack the Ripper's victims was found) to get up and out, and go along.

Certainly the Rocket's entertainment list looks suitably enticing.

'The award-winning venue the Rocket Complex comprises a nightclub, live music venue (with the latest turbo sound floodlight system), 2 licensed bars, external courtyard, pool and games room, coffee bar and shop,' chirps a union wallah. 'The weekly events programme includes *The Big Fish* ("the best student night in London" - *Time Out*), *Pint Sized Comedy Club* and regular events showcasing music and culture from around the globe. Headliners include... Trevor Nelson, Jools Holland, Punjabi Hit Squad, Asian Dub Foundation, Kele le Roc, Ms Dynamite, Artful Dodger, Timmi Magic, DJ Hanif, DJ Luck + MC Neat, Jah Shaka, Latina Max + London's largest Brazilian Carnival.'

Sounds more enterprising than the ents down in City campus's **Hub** - Bar Footsie to One Ton Quiz, Big Fish again and, right now, the *Easter Eggstravaganza*. More up to the minute perhaps is the **Met Lounge**, also at Goulston Street, a smoke - and alcohol-free social space - wireless internet, newspapers, refreshments: it's the coming thing.

There's a new student magazine launched in December 2008, *VerveZine*, and a new radio station launched jointly by the Radio Soc and the Union - was to be called Verve Radio, but going out as Metsu Radio. There are internal media and arts awards aplenty and excellent departments in these areas. There is also political activity (and a tradition of that). Islamic Soc is the most active society.

Sport The sports teams do very well (25th nationally last year) on account of the excellence of the sports department, and good players are given scholarships. Sports facilities are shared with Arsenal FC and Essex CC. The new Arsenal stadium is right behind the old North London Uni buildings. Pitches, courts, sports halls, all the usual requirements are to a high standard. A new Sports Centre on North Campus has large sports hall and a fitness gym with a wide range of cardiovascular equipment and fixed weight machines, plus a free weights area. At Whitechapel High Street on City Campus there's a fitness gym with a range of cardiovascular equipment and fixed weight machines, plus a range of dumbbells. The Centre also has a therapy room offering massage and reflexology.

ACADEMIA & JOBS

Students say that the best teaching is to be had in Mathematics, Education, Sociology, Social Policy, Drama, Performing Arts, Accounting, Politics, and Social Studies.

Business (there is a particular strength in Accounting) and Architecture would almost certainly have been there, but the subjects were returned: 'Not enough data'. It is quite clear from the 2008 assessment of the nation's research provision that London Met has in-depth expertise in Maths, Architecture, Social Work, Social Policy etc., Education, American Studies, and Media - 10% to 15% of all these subjects were considered world-class. Social Work came out best with 50% of the provision either world-class or internationally excellent.

Around a third of Campus North students graduate in business subjects and there is a dominant but well thought-out joint degree series. Down at City around a third of students graduate in a very similar joint vocational degree system and more than a quarter graduate in business subjects. Some joint courses require travel to both campuses.

Then we have another important area - health, with degrees such as Herbal Herbal Medicine Science alongside Pharmaceutical Science and Pharmacology, and Biomedical Sciences, a programme that scores particularly strongly in the employment table. There is also a notable lean at North towards the therapeutic care side, with degrees in Social Work and BSc Psychology (Applied) & Health Studies.

Still on the professional front, look to either campus for LLB Law. While City are commercial & business law specialists, North have LLB (Social Justice).

RESEARCH EXCELLENCE		
% of London Met's research that is **4*** (World-class) or **3*** (Internationally rated):		
	4*	3*
Health Professions	5%	25%
Human Biological	0%	5%
Food Science	0%	5%
Pure Mathematics	10%	25%
Statistics	5%	20%
Computer Science	0%	10%
Metallurgy and Materials	0%	0%
Architecturet	15%	25%
Town/Country Planning	5%	30%
Economics	0%	35%
Business/Management	0%	15%
Law	0%	10%
Politics	5%	15%
Social Work	10%	40%
Psychology	0%	10%
Education	10%	40%
American Studies	10%	15%
European Studies	5%	30%
Art and Design	0%	10%
Performing Arts	0%	25%
Media Studies	15%	25%

movement. Writes Sam Hall: 'The university is gaining a reputation for artistic excellence, with well-respected jewellery-making and furniture departments, and many student-led initiatives leading to national awards.'

Jewellery design/making may be a small, specialist field, but City hits the spot employment-wise.

Furniture design and manufacture is another area of supreme confidence. North's response is with the BA Interior Architecture & Design, and a range of Architecture which achieves a sound employment record in architectural consultancy and construction.

PILLOW TALK

Students have access to over 1,300 rooms in halls, each situated close to either the London City or London North campuses. Accommodation is guaranteed for all first years who live more than 25 miles away and who accept a conditional or unconditional offer of a course and return their halls application by the 8th August.

ACCOMMODATION	
Guarantee to freshers	**35%**
Style	**Halls, flats**
Security guard	**Secure**
Shared rooms	**Some**
Internet access	**Most**
Self-catered	**Most**
En suite	**None**
Approx price range pw	**£82-£127**
City rent pw	**£100-180**

Another string to North's bow is sport, while a defining niche at City, for which they scored a near perfect score at the teaching assessments, is Fine Art, Design, Silversmithing, and Jewellery, including Fashion Jewellery, appropriate to the traditional strength of this area of London in the art and craft

GETTING THERE

☛ By Underground to City Campus: Aldgate (Metropolitan and Circle lines), Aldgate East (District and Hammersmith & City).
☛ By Underground to Campus North: Holloway Road (Piccadilly Line).

LONDON SCHOOL OF ECONOMICS & POLITICAL SCIENCE

The London School of Economics
& Political Science
Houghton Street
London WC2A 2AE

TEL 020 7955 6613
FAX 020 7955 6001
Email stu.rec@lse.ac.uk
WEB www.lse.ac.uk
LSE Students' Union

East Building
Houghton Street
London WC2A 2AE

TEL 020 7955 7158
FAX 020 7955 6789
EMAIL su.comms@lse.ac.uk
WEB www.lsesu.com

VAG VIEW

*T*he London School of Economics &
Political Science (LSE) is part of the federal University of London. It is famous the
world over for research. In 2008 it confirmed
its position as a world-leading research university, with outstanding success in the
national Research Assessment Exercise. LSE
has the highest percentage of world-leading
research of any university in the country,
though it came second to Cambridge overall.
Teaching inspection results have been high,
and the LSE is as secure as the British
Establishment, with which, despite the
school's history of '60s student revolt - ex-LSE
student Mick Jagger, Grosvenor Square and
the Vietnam War and all - it is, indeed, syn-
onymous.

LSE goes hand in hand with
Westminster, with Whitehall, with the City
and with the legal and the media sub-strata
too. In fact, its geographical position ensures
it closer contact with all departments of the
Establishment than either Oxford or
Cambridge, and its specialist areas -

UNIVERSITY/SCHOOL PROFILE	
University since	**1900**
Situation/style	**City campus**
Student population	**9030**
Undergraduates	**3825**
Mature undergraduates	**0%**
International undergrads	**40%**
Male/female ratio	**50:50**
Equality of opportunity:	
state school intake	**66%**
social class 4-7 intake	**18%**
low-participation area intake	**4%**

Economics, International Relations,
Government, Law, Finance - are what you
might call the active ingredients of the
Establishment. That is why many of its academic gurus are recognisable faces or by-
lines in the media. If analysis is required, it's
the LSE they call up. They even managed to
get 75% of Communications and Media into
the world-class and internationally excellent
class for research while not even offering it
as a named undergraduate degree.

It is difficult to see what better finishing
school you could find than this. Concludes
our student mole: 'The LSE is no Utopia, but
it is definitely one-up with its individual culture, school of thought, and world of opportunities.'

However, there is a downside. Only 77%
of their students gave it the thumbs-up in the
Higher Education Funding Council's highly
respected National Student Survey, and
when the Times Higher Education magazine
ran its Student Experience Survey, LSE came
87th. One of the problems seems to be that
LSE lecturers find students something of a

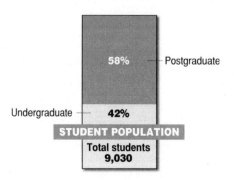

58% — Postgraduate
Undergraduate — 42%
STUDENT POPULATION
Total students
9,030

*necessary evil. In the 'helpful/interested' cat-
egory they scored very low, and tuition group
size pales in comparison to many other universities. Still, 95.5% of the undergraduates
stick it out to the end. And why not, statistics say they've got a 93% of a real graduate
job within six months, and not any job but
one with probably the highest starting salary
in the UK - an average of £27,000 a year to
begin.*

CAMPUS

'The LSE is the filling in a sandwich,' writes
Dominique Fyfe, a student from America. 'On one
side (the capital's financial and legal district) the
air is serious and the suits Armani, and the FT-
reading societal stress-set is on the go until long
after the sun is down.

On the other, west of Kingsway (hitherto the
dividing line, a road where all those who cannot
drive test their inabilities), lie the expensive, funky,
multi-purpose Covent Garden and London's theatreland and Soho, haven for sex addicts and non-
traditionalists, and the book lovers' paradise of
Charing Cross Road.'

To translate, LSE is situated between Kingsway
and the Strand, at the heart of London culture and
the legal establishment, and not far from the City
or Westminster either. It is a campus crowded with
buildings, the so-called Old Building being on the
site of the small hall, where it all began and from
which it has steadily expanded into buildings close
by - the East Building, Clare Market, St Clement, St
Philips, Clement House, all built on land which is
among the most expensive per square foot in the
world.

FEES, BURSARIES

UK & EU Fees, 2009-10: £3,225. If in receipt of
the HE Maintenance grant, there's a sliding scale
bursary according to parental income.

See www.lse.ac.uk/collections/studentServices
Centre/financialSupportOffice/,

STUDENT PROFILE

They come from all over the world. This is the
cream of students anxious to acquire the LSE
cachet, and there is a snobbery attached. It takes
only 66% from the state sector, but interestingly,
their take from the lower socio-economic classes is
quite a healthy 18%, and 4% from those unfortunately named 'low participation' neighbourhoods.

'Interesting conversation is one thing you will
not find a lack of at the LSE,' writes Dominique.
'The students here think critically in the classroom
but also have a point of view in friendly discussion

TEACHING SURVEY AT A GLANCE	
Avg. UCAS points accepted	**480**
Acceptance rate	**7%**
Overall satisfaction rate	**77%**
Helpful/interested staff	★★
Small tuition groups	★★
Students into graduate jobs	**93%**

Teaching most popular with undergraduates:
Accounting (82%), Law (81%), Maths (79%),
Economics, Management, Politics (77%), Human
& Social Geography (75%).

Teaching least popular with undergraduates:
Sociology (71%), Social Policy, Anthropology
(70%)., Finance (67%).

outside. Many are highly driven, always ready for
an intellectual challenge and very competitive.
However, not all are so intense; some don't even
find the library until summer exams!

'Naturally, most of the students you will meet
here are reading for a degree in Economics, but
what makes the school a fascinating place is that
there are so many studying other subjects, like
anthropology, finance, social psychology and philosophy, and you learn from everybody.

'The LSE is a breeding ground for global
nomads. In between lectures, the Houghton Street
hub of LSE activity overflows with student representatives of all races of our world. Languages you
will begin to learn in this global microcosm are
Indian, French, Italian, Spanish, Russian, German,
not to mention English of course. Not only do these
students of all cultures bring their traditions but
they also bring the trendy, money-sucking, modern
fashions, but don't worry if your wardrobe didn't
appear in the latest issue of *Cosmo* or *GQ*; nobody
really cares whether its Oxfam or Armani.'

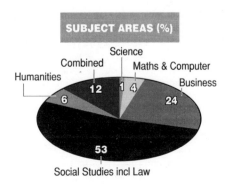

SUBJECT AREAS (%)

Science
Combined — Maths & Computer
Humanities
Business
6 — 12 — 1 — 4 — 24
53
Social Studies incl Law

% of LSE's research that is
4* *(World-class)* or 3* *(Internationally rated)*:

	4*	3*
Pure Mathematics	**5%**	**40%**
Statistics	**15%**	**40%**
Geography Environment	**20%**	**50%**
Economics	**60%**	**35%**
Business/Management	**30%**	**40%**
Law	**45%**	**30%**
Politics	**30%**	**30%**
Social Worn	**50%**	**30%**
Sociology	**20%**	**25%**
Anthropology	**40%**	**25%**
European Studies	**20%**	**45%**
Philosophy	**35%**	**30%**
History	**35%**	**30%**
Media Studies	**45%**	**30%**

ACADEMIA & JOBS

Writes Dominique, 'Lectures and classes are well enough taught. In fact I find myself wanting to go to them - a truly novel experience for me! Don't be surprised if the reading list for a class is more like a library's inventory record! The lectures are monologues, but the classes are interactive and "cosy" in size (maximum fifteen students). Essays are written for classes but not always formally assessed or given a definitive deadline, which can make procrastination seem dangerously attractive.'

The LSE library, the British Library of Political and Economic Science, founded in 1896, contains one million volumes, 28,000 journals (10,000 on current sub.), numerous specialist manuscripts - all totalling some three million items. Even so, it is not immune from student criticism: 'LSE's library is overwhelming and quite frankly I would not go there if I didn't have to. The process is as follows: when you reach the library half of the books you are looking for are not there and if they are, there is only one copy of the main text for about twenty to forty-plus students and are titled as set texts, which means that they can only be borrowed for twenty-four hours. Return it twenty-four hours too late and the librarians grow the devil's tail and horns and collect a large amount of your own precious money! If that seems a tough sentence, it is and is meant to be.'

> *The LSE is a breeding ground for global nomads. The Houghton Street hub of LSE activity overflows with student representatives of all races of our world.*

The top seven employment sectors that seek out LSE graduates are banking, which accounts for 23% of the total, accountancy (17%), financial activities (including the actuaries from the dedicated Actuarial Science degree, 7%), management consultancy (5%), the civil service (5%), community work/counselling (3%), and advertising (2%).

A Language Centre specialises in creating courses targeted to the particular needs of students and offers EAP, French, German, Italian, Japanese, Russian, Spanish, Arabic, Chinese, Portuguese, Norwegian, Basque, Turkish. Sixty-five per cent of the European Studies research provision was designated world-class or of international significance.

SOCIAL SCENE

STUDENTS' UNION **The Three Tuns**, **Underground Bar**, **Quad** and shop are all newly refurbished. 'Many students drift in the direction of the pub, The Three Tuns,' says Dominique, 'which has a "cool" atmosphere. The drinks are cheap, the company is friendly and the music plays at a level that doesn't reach eardrum-damaging decibels.

'The Students Union offers a wide range of societies at the Freshers' Fair! The Socialism Society and other political groups will attack in a desperate attempt to sway you, but other societies adopt a less obtrusive approach. There are plenty of opportunities to get involved, be it through the arts, politics, radio, religion (most religions and denominations are observed), business, or cultural groups. Sports teams exist, but I can give you little information about them, as I am motivationally challenged as regards any kind of physical activity.'

LSE claims the only weekly Students Union General Meeting in the country. More than 200 students regularly attend to hold union officers to account and to debate campus level, national and international issues. 'Those who get involved in the SU are usually left-wing,' says one who does; 'those who focus on careers are right-wing. Occasionally there are clashes.'

Excellent media: magazine *Script*, newspaper *Beaver*, radio station PuLSE fm, and TV LooSE TV.

LSE also has its own dedicated ents manager and the Friday night clubnight, *Crush*, is one of the most popular student nights in London every Friday. Other regular ents are *Mind the Gap*, and for LGBT students - gays - there's a gay salsa night, Exilo; *Afta Skool* (indie) is a Saturday clubnight at Quad. They can get 1,000 bodies in to the 3-room

SPORT In the basement of the Old Building there's a training room and multi-gym. The school also has its own sports grounds in South London. There are also netball, tennis courts and four large swimming pools within two miles of Houghton Street. The University of London Union has facilities for squash, basketball, rowing and swimming. LSE cricketers may use the indoor facilities at Lords. LSE sports teams came 53rd nationally last year in the national team league.

PILLOW TALK

All first year students are guaranteed a place in LSE or London University accommodation - basically halls and one block of self-catering flats. 'Residence halls are cheap and easy,' writes Dominique, 'but in my opinion the London University intercollegiate option is preferable. You will find the quality of food to be not much better than that of pig slop, but living next door to two vets, across the hall from a nurse, next door to a musician, down the hall from

club, made up of the Tuns, the Quad, with its sofa-strewn mezzanine, and the smaller venue, the Underground. There are also student nights at selected sites in London's clubland.

TOWN Top tip from Dominique: 'On arrival in London, buy the London A-Z (to avoid looking like a tourist only whip it out in times of emergency) and the student's bible, Time Out, essential to anybody's social survival kit. Manage limited finances by drinking your fill at the cheapest union bar before a night out.'

an opera singer, and one floor above a physiotherapist could only happen in an intercollegiate hall (see Introduction). This option definitely widens your social circle. Rooms are basic with a small single bed (not much room for two if you have big plans), a desk and a wardrobe. Your room is your home and you make it your own.'

GETTING THERE

☛ Holborn (Piccadilly, Central lines), Temple (District, Circle lines), Charing Cross (Jubilee, Northern, Bakerloo lines).

LONDON SOUTH BANK UNIVERSITY

London South Bank University
103 Borough Road
London SE1 0AA

TEL 020 7815 7815
FAX 020 7815 8273
EMAIL enquiry@lsbu.ac.uk
WEB www.lsbu.ac.uk

London South Bank Students' Union
Keyworth Street
London SE1 6NG

TEL 020 7815 6060
FAX 020 7815 6061
EMAIL hoggm@lsbu.ac.uk
WEB www.lsbu.org

VAG VIEW

*L*ondon South Bank University was once
South Bank Poly, and still the majority of
*students come from the locality, which
includes a rich tapestry of ethnic groups.
Much of it is clustered around a triangle
formed by Borough Road, London Road and
Southwark Bridge Road, just south of the
Thames at Elephant and Castle. The uni
projects you into the big city, where the
streets are paved with whatever you want
them to be paved with. You come to London
South Bank University (LSBU), you come to
London...for a bit of gritty realism.*

There was a poor showing in the Times
Higher Education *magazine's Student
Experience Survey. They came 94th, one of
the problems being the low level of
helpful/interested staff and decent-sized
tuition groups. Given the low ask of around
180 points at A level, which is bound to
attract students who need help, and the fact
that this is hardly a research-led university
which might detract lecturers' interest from
teaching, it is difficult to explain or excuse.
No surprise that applications fell by 19.6%
in 2008.*

UNIVERSITY/STUDENT PROFILE	
University since	**1992**
Situation/style	**City sites**
Student population	**23215**
Undergraduates	**15950**
Mature undergraduates	**70%**
International undergrads	**11%**
Male/female ratio	**58:42**
Equality of opportunity:	
state school intake	**96%**
social class 4-7 intake	**44%**
low-participation area intake	**7%**

CAMPUS

The good thing about the location is that it allows
easy access to more attractive elements, such as the
South Bank arts complex, the Tate Modern, Globe
Theatre and the London Eye. The West End is only
three stops away on the Underground, Whitechapel
and the East End is equally accessible, and the
nearby Thames is once again a main artery of the
Capital.

Writes Laura Cattell: 'LSBU is on London's cultural doorstep - The National Theatre, The Globe,
and the British Film Institute are a walk away from
the main campus. The City of London lies just over
the river with the Houses of Parliament and
Westminster Abbey is close by.'

'Location - prime,' agrees Lola Brown. 'Situated
in zones 1/2, the main campus is indeed ideally
located on the uber trendy South Bank, but
Elephant & Castle itself is a bit of a hole, though it
is improving rapidly with some major urban regeneration happening. It has its own tube station
(Bakerloo & Northern lines).'

The learning resources (including a library)
and the Students Union is currently on Keyworth
Street, where two years ago the brand new 9-storey
Keyworth Centre opened. There are yet two other
sites further away - the Faculty of Health & Social
Care at Harold Wood Hospital (Romford) and
Whipps Cross Hospital (Leytonstone) - a situation
rather optimistically 'solved' by calling these two

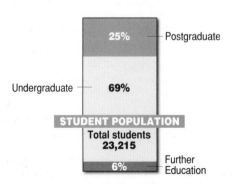

Postgraduate **25%**

Undergraduate **69%**

STUDENT POPULATION
Total students
23,215

Further
Education **6%**

distinct sites the Redwood Campus.

FEES, BURSARIES

UK & EU Fees, 2009-10: £3,225 p.a. See www.lsbu.ac.uk/fees for the latest info. There are bursaries and scholarships for sport and academic prowess, and support for ethnics.

STUDENT PROFILE

Seventy per cent of undergraduates are mature, some 6,000 are part-timers, almost a third come from the London Borough of Southwark, over half from ethnic minorities, and nearly 40% are from overseas (from more than 120 different countries). In socio-economic terms, 44% come from SEC classes 4-7, and 7% from 'low-participation' neighbourhoods.

'A real cross section!' exclaims Lola. 'Freshers here are not generally middle-class white kids, though there are a fair few of those too.'

In the context of the demography the loss of only 9% as drop-outs, which is more or less the national average, is quite an achievement.

ACADEMIA & JOBS

Students say the best teaching is in Sociology, Computer Science, Finance, Accounting, Business, Social Studies, Social Policy, the least good in Media Studies, Architecture, Building, and Engineering.

The criticism is a shame because Media and General Engineering were among the highlights of LSBU's submission at the recent national research assessment - 40% of the work LSBU does in Media was graded either world-class or internationally excellent. Engineering fared even better at 60%. So, the in-depth knowledge is there, it's the teaching that isn't. Social Studies/Social Policy seems the best bet, approved by students for teaching and actually the best showing in the research assess-

TEACHING SURVEY AT A GLANCE	
Avg. UCAS points accepted	**180**
Acceptance rate	**18%**
Overall satisfaction rate	**75%**
Helpful/interested staff	★★
Small tuition groups	★★
Students into graduate jobs	**80%**

Teaching most popular with undergraduates:
Sociology (89%), Computer Science (87%), Finance, Accounting, Business (83%), Social Studies, Social Policy (81%).

Teaching least popular with undergraduates:
Media Studies (56%), Architecture, Building (54%), Engineering (38%-47%).

ment, with 15% world-class and 45% internationally excellent.

However, the employment graph suggests otherwise. Far and away the most graduate jobs go to students of subjects related to Medicine at LSBU - students of Nursing (children's as well as adult),

RESEARCH EXCELLENCE		
% of London South Bank's research that is ***4* (World-class) or 3* (Internationally rated):***		
	4*	3*
Nursing/Midwifery	**5%**	**30%**
Computer Science/	**5%**	**25%**
General Engineering/	**5%**	**55%**
Business/Management	**5%**	**15%**
Information Management	**0%**	**15%**
Social Work	**15%**	**45%**
Psychology	**0%**	**20%**
Sports	**5%**	**20%**
Media Studies	**15%**	**25%**

Operating Department Practice, Theatre Practice, Therapeutic Radiography, Applied Science, Bioscience, Biochemistry, etc. These account for a third of all the jobs going on graduation from LSBU.

Employment in architecture, construction, planning is also a pretty good cert, from the Architecture and Built Environment degrees obviously, and Building Services Engineering, Quantity Surveying and the like.

The portfolio of degrees is markedly vocational. There's a taste of the workplace about much on offer.

Besides Built Environment, Engineering, Design & Technology, and Health & Social Care, faculties include Business & Management (by far

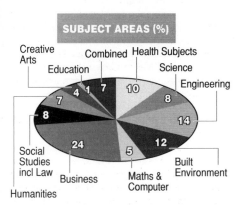

SUBJECT AREAS (%)

Creative Arts — 7
Education — 4
Combined — 1
Health Subjects — 7
Science — 10
Engineering — 8
— 14
Built Environment — 12
Maths & Computer — 5
Business — 24
Social Studies incl Law — 8
Humanities

WHAT IT'S REALLY LIKE	
UNIVERSITY:	
Social Life	★★
Campus scene	**More of a London than a uni scene**
Student Union services	**OK**
Politics	**Student issues, activity low**
Sport	**10 clubs**
National team position	**49th**
Sport facilities	**Improving**
Arts opportunities	**Music excellent, drama, dance, film good; art poor**
Student newspaper	**Scratch**
Nightclub	**Isobar**
Bars	**Rigg Bar**
Union ents	**Occasional**
Union societies	**7**
Most popular societies	**Afrikan, Islamic, Forensic Science**
Smoking policy	**Union, halls OK**
Parking	**Poor**
CITY:	
Entertainment	★★★★★
Scene	**Excellent**
Town/gown relations	**Average**
Risk of violence	**'Average'**
Cost of living	**Very high**
Student concessions	**Excellent**
Survival + 2 nights out	**£90-100 pw**
Part-time work campus/town	**Average/excellent**

ACCOMMODATION	
Guarantee to freshers	**75%**
Style	**Flats**
Security guard	**All**
Shared rooms	**None**
Internet access	**All**
Self-catered	**All**
En suite	**Most**
Approx price range pw	**£88.50-£106**
City rent pw	**£100-£180**

itself has a buzzing vibe every night and there are some fantastic restaurants in the Elephant - **Pizza Castella**, **Ivory Arch** (Indian cuisine) and **Tai Won Mein** (super cheap scrummy noodle bar). We're close to both the **Old Vic**, Shakespeare's **Globe** theatre and the famous **South Bank Arts Complex**, **National Theatre** and **Royal Festival Hall**, which'll inject you with culture. There's the **IMAX** cinema and it takes only about five minutes on the tube to get to Oxford Circus so the whole of London is your oyster.

'Elephant is not, however, the nicest of areas, but keep your wits about you and everything's cool.' On campus **The Rigg Bar** is at the heart of what the Union has to offer. At night it doubles as a club. Friday is the zenith of ambition, with live music and DJs at the heart of it and nothing else at the weekend. Monday, Tuesday & Thursdays the Rigg offers chilled out live music, karaoke, pub quiz nights and big screen sport.

the largest), Computing, Science, Humanities & Social Science.

The course programme is modular in structure. There are decent learning resources, a centre has 400 Pentium PCs with Internet facility and allows access to a CD-ROM network.

In addition, there are four libraries, one at each of the four sites, with a total of 300,000 books. The teaching picture is very good., while asking grades are low.

Business offers a less than certain employment pathway - some 19% of jobs are accounted for by Business graduates, but a large number enter employment as general administrators, sales assistants, and accounts and wages clerks. Accountancy, the hotel trade (there's a popular Tourism & Hospitality degree), advertising, recruitment, local government, but only then banking, are the more popular destinations.

SOCIAL LIFE

'It's London, innit,' exclaims Lola. 'Anything, anytime, whatever you like to do. The South Bank

Bar opens Monday to Friday 10.00am - 12.00 midnight, Friday nights open 'till late'.

A social life can also be lived through one of the sports clubs & societies. There are 22 societies, including LGBT and Socialist Worker Student Society. The most active student society is tabled as Arts & Media, but there is a grand tradition here of very successful cultural societies, such as the Afrikaan society with its hugely successful club night, Black Pepper. Islamic is also big - there are prayer rooms for Islamic students. There is also plenty of scope for students to get involved with the student magazine, or indeed to organise your own thing - as elsewhere, if you get a quorum, the union will fund it. 'Politically,' writes Lola, 'we're verging on the left wing, but the most political thing to happen is an occasional guest speaker or a meeting.'

SPORT There was a spectacular enhancement of the fortunes of LSB's Athletic union a few years ago when they finished 49th in the national leagues. The union was awarded the H G Messer Trophy for 'most improved university in 2003' from BUSA. They created an Academy of Sport, Physical Activity & Wellbeing, so that the indoor sports facilities on the main campus include a 40+ station fitness suite, weights room, sports hall and injury clinic. But, alas, now they are back at 90th.

The sports ground is a 21-acre site at Turney Road, Dulwich, with pavilion and bar. There are coaching courses and sports scholarships.

PILLOW TALK

LSBU has 1,400 single study bedrooms located across 4 residential buildings, both standard and en-suite. All are within a 10-minute walk of the main Southwark campus, are self-catered basis and located within self-contained flats. Flats accommodate between 2 and 9 residents. Every bedroom is equipped with a 'pay as you talk' telephone and internet access. See more at www.lsbu.ac.uk/halls.

GETTING THERE

☛ By Underground: Elephant and Castle (Bakerloo and Northern Lines) or mainline Waterloo station.

LOUGHBOROUGH UNIVERSITY

Loughborough University
Ashby Road
Loughborough
Leicestershire LE11 3TU

TEL 01509 223522
FAX 01509 223905
EMAIL admissions@lboro.ac.uk
WEB www.lboro.ac.uk

Loughborough Students' Union
Ashby Road
Loughborough
Leicestershire LE11 3TT

TEL 01509 635000
FAX 01509 635003
EMAIL union@lborosu.org.uk
WEB www.lufbra.net

VAG VIEW

*W*hen people think of Loughborough, which has been a university since 1966, they think of its engineering capability - it came out of Loughborough Technical Institute - and they think of sport, for today it is the best UK university at sport by such a long way that some of its teams can't find decent opposition on the university circuit and turn to professional clubs to sharpen their teeth on.

Surprise then that the weekly student magazine, Label, received a letter from a reader complaining that coverage favoured the arts at the expense of sport. Surprise that the official uni line is: 'Contrary to popular belief, sport does not pervade everything at Loughborough - couch potatoes are also welcome, and there are plenty of non-sporting activities for students to get involved in.' Surprise, too, that alongside aeronautical and electronic and electrical manufacturing, and sport, and defence, and the construction industry, we find artistic/literary, film/video and publishing as categories of graduate employment in which Lboro students excel.

UNIVERSITY/STUDENT PROFILE	
University since	**1966**
Situation/style	**Campus**
Student population	**18220**
Undergraduates	**11005**
Mature undergraduates	**5%**
International undergrads	**9%**
Male/female ratio	**61:39**
Equality of opportunity:	
state school intake	**84%**
social class 4-7 intake	**22%**
low-participation area intake	**6%**

The uni is now pre-eminent in social science, in English, in library & information management - these have been adjudged research areas of renown. Meanwhile, psychology, drama and art & design are among its top teaching subjects at inspection, and the student media is making waves in national competitions.

Loughborough also has strong environmental credentials. It is one of the partners in the Government's new £1 billion national Energy Technologies Institute (ETI), which will help accelerate the UK's transition to a

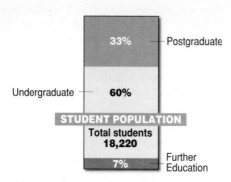

STUDENT POPULATION
Total students
18,220

33% — Postgraduate
Undergraduate — **60%**
7% — Further Education

The uni recently acquired the Holywell Technology Park on the edge of the campus, making it one of the biggest campus universities in the UK, with a total area of 410 acres. The new space is used to enhance its research portfolio and links with industry.

low-carbon economy. The headquarters of the ETI are now based on campus. In 2008 Loughborough was ranked 5th in the People and Planet Green League, and its Students' Union's was placed 7th in the Sunday Times Green List 2008.

The at the end of 2008 came the news that it had won the Times Higher Education Student Experience of the Year award for the third year in a row. And in the Higher Education Funding Council's National Student Survey, 91% of its students gave it their backing, with 4-star and 5-star rated lecturer commitment to its students.

All that apart, it IS good for sport. In fact, it is the very best. Loughborough did better at the last Commonwealth Games than 32 countries, including Malaysia, Singapore and Kenya, and almost equalled New Zealand's performance.

> *Loughborough did better at the last Commonwealth Games than 32 countries, including Malaysia, Singapore and Kenya, and almost equalled New Zealand's performance.*

FEES, BURSARIES

UK & EU Fees, 2009-10: £3,225. Bursaries for students aged under 21 on entry and in receipt of HE Maintenance Grant, there's bursary, the amount on a sliding scale according to income. See www.lboro.ac.uk/admin/ar/funding/ug/ukeu/index.htm. There are scholarships available for top sports performers, and £1,000 merit-based scholarships for top achieving students on certain science and engineering courses. Also, 2 music awards and mature students bursaries depending on income. See www.lboro.ac.uk/admin/ar/funding/ug/ukeu/scholarships/index.htm.

STUDENT PROFILE

'A typical Lboro student,' Vicky writes, 'is one who enthuses about sport and thrives on competition, and appears to be a walking advert for sportswear companies. There are students who are not like this, but they make less noise and therefore attract less attention. Sport at Lboro is impossible to ignore. This enthusiasm is not a bad thing, but if you don't share a love of sport it can become a tad irritating.'

There is a high-ish public school intake relative to most other universities , and a relatively low take from the lower socio-economic groups and 'low-participation' neighbourhoods. But none of this is very

CAMPUS

Loughborough is a campus university situated just off the M1 at Junction 23. 'It is one of the largest campuses in Europe,' writes Vicky Cook, 'and conforms to the stereotype of a leafy, green, self-contained campus. This has its advantages, everything is located within walking distance from halls (though the free campus bus is worth remembering on rainy days). There are bars, restaurants (although nothing gourmet) and three food shops to buy overpriced essentials when a walk into town is too great an effort. And, should campus and small market town become too claustrophobic, Leicester and Nottingham are mercifully close.

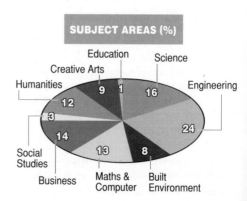

SUBJECT AREAS (%)

Education
Creative Arts
Science
Humanities
Engineering
Social Studies
Business
Maths & Computer
Built Environment

9, 1, 16, 12, 3, 14, 13, 8, 24

relevant. Students like it here, the drop-out rate (3.8%) is very low.low.

ACADEMIA & JOBS

Many of Loughborough's degrees are available with a sandwich (placement) option, allowing students to gain real-life working experience, a paid salary and valuable employer contacts.

Students say that you get the best teaching in Physics with Cosmology, Human Biology, Maths, Building, English, Languages, Accounting, Civil Engineering, Management, Materials & Minerals Technology, Sociology, Finance, Chemical, Process & Energy Engineering, Physics, Politics, Mechanical, Production & Manufacturing Engineering, Electronic & Electrical Engineering, Sports Science, Chemistry, Communication & Media Studies, Computer Science, Drama, Psychology, and Information Technology.

In the research assessment they came 28th nationwide: 85% of Design and Technology was found to be world-class or internationally excellent; in Architecture and Built Environment, it was 75%, in Aeronautical Engineering 70%.

Four years ago the university was awarded over £4 million in recognition of its excellent practice in linking industry and employers with engi-

---

TEACHING SURVEY AT A GLANCE

Avg. UCAS points accepted	**360**
Acceptance rate	**18%**
Overall satisfaction rate	**91%**
Helpful/interested staff	★★★★★
Small tuition groups	★★★★
Students into graduate jobs	**78%**

Teaching most popular with undergraduates:
Physics with Cosmology (98%), Human Biology (97%), Maths, Building, English, Languages (96%), Accounting, Civil Engineering, Management, Materials & Minerals Technology, Sociology (95%), Finance, Chemical, Process & Energy Engineering, Physics, Politics (94%), Mechanical, Production & Manufacturing Eng. (93%), Electronic & Electrical Eng., Sports Science. (92%), Chemistry, Communication & Media Studies, Computer Science, Drama, Psychology (91%), Information Technology (90%).

Teaching least popular with undergraduates:
Fine Art (85%), Creative Arts & Design (83%).

RESEARCH EXCELLENCE

% of Looughborough's research that is
4* *(World-class)* or **3*** *(Internationally rated)*:

	4*	3*
Public Health	0%	15%
Chemistry	0%	25%
Physics	15%	35%
Pure Mathematics	10%	45%
Applied Mathematics	10%	40%
Computer Science/ Electrical/Electronic Eng.	15%	40%
	15%	45%
Civil Engineering	15%	50%
Mechanical, Aero., Manufacturing Eng.	20%	50%
Architecture	25%	50%
Geography Environment	10%	40%
Economics	5%	40%
Business/Management	15%	45%
Information Management	15%	40%
Sociology	25%	20%
Education	5%	15%
Sports	25%	35%
European Studies	10%	30%
English	10%	40%
Art and Design	5%	30%
Design and Technology	55%	30%

---

neering teaching and learning. This funding was used to set up a Centre for Excellence to enhance teaching facilities.

For prospective aeronautical engineers it's got to be a preferred choice.

Automobile engineers are similarly well placed careers-wise by Loughborough's degrees, as are civil, mechanical and construction engineering graduates. Twenty-two per cent of jobs come out of the Engineering & Technology degrees, but then 15% come out of Creative Arts & Design.

Though known for engineering, business and built environment, the uni is pre-eminent in Art & Design, and in Social Sciences. In Art & Design, degrees such as Design with Engineering Materials and Product Design meet others such as Visual Communication: Graphic Communication or Illustration, and Textile Design (Multi-Media, or Printed or Woven Textiles). For a few years now the sometime largely female Art College down the road has been making a welcome impact on the largely male engineering/techno-based population, both socially and academically. The strength in textiles was awarded full marks at the teaching assessments, and these degrees and the Graphic and Communication degrees are telling too in the graduate employment figures.

In Social Sciences, the telling influences are the Economics degrees - with Accountancy, Geography, Politics, Social Policy, and Sociology, as well as all the single honours degrees in those subjects and in Psychology.

Look also at Computer Systems and Software Engineering orientations. Many graduates become software engineers and consultants - they are up there with Brunel as the largest suppliers to the sector. They come not only off the computer courses but also through Maths.

Meanwhile, aspiring bankers/merchant bankers come through Business Economics & Finance and, at Management Sciences, as well as the Economics, Languages and Computer areas.

Loughborough's Business School has the cornerstone 4-year sandwich degree, BSc (Hons) International Business, but they have an eye for business in every aspect of the curriculum, from engineering to fashion.

SOCIAL SCENE

STUDENTS' UNION The union club has much to offer, currently Tuesday is *Stupid Tuesday* (party tunes), Thursday is *Universal Thursday* (international flavour) and sometimes a pub quiz.

Mid-week is *Hey Ewe* after all the sports matches have been played (and usually won!) in the afternoon. Says Jennie Byass: 'We all meet up with our sports or social clubs for an hour or so for some social drinking, and then proceed onto Fusion, where the key theme to the night is cheesy music and lots of dancing. *Midnight Madness* happens between half 11 and half 12 at which time all drinks are only one pound!

'JC's is the sports bar, where everyone goes to celebrate victories. **Cognito** - bar - flashing dance floor, what more can I say? Live acts here have included Girls Aloud for the Freshers Ball, DJ Spoony, and Navi, a Michael Jackson impersonator, amazing!'

We asked an anonymous student about that hour's drinking on match night. 'There are certain rituals and traditions which we here in Loughborough have developed and institutionalised over the years,' I was told: 'The rugby shirt worn with jeans, AV's, collars up, Hey Ewe mayhem on a Wednesday evening, drinking games and of course Nasty...the Lufbra drink...' This latter, though increasingly at risk to the almighty Red Bull/voddie alternative (decried by purists as expensive and injurious to health), remains the people's choice.

Then Friday is *FND* (Friday Night Disco) - LSU's premier night out: 3 rooms of music, including just now FF Audition, a battle of the bands audition night - win the chance to play the Freefest on May 4. Saturday is *Pulse* (r&b). And through it all are scattered live bands - *Make Noise: Battle of the Bands 2009*, and such as Official Secrets Act, The Young Knives, and appropriately, Athletic.

There are 40 societies, the more traditional such as the International Students' Association and the LGBT Association, while quirkier ones, like the Hot Air Balloon club, the Breakdancing club and the circus society, Fever, show the possibilities. The Media Centre houses the 24/7 student radio station (LCR), which won Gold at the National Awards this year, the student magazine offices (*Label*) and a TV/video editing suite. LSUTV wins awards practically every year. The 'talk' studio and production studio (drum booth, guitar booth) beyond leave you in no doubt that these students have not been overcharged at £1.4 million. Sound, vision, print, web, all of it together on a single floor and serviced by student engineers who know their stuff.

The SU also has a student advice centre and employment exchange, and adjacent nursery with subsidised places for students' children.

SPORT Lboro teams beat everyone every year.

WHAT IT'S REALLY LIKE	
UNIVERSITY:	
Social Life	★★★★★
Campus scene	**Well resourced, sports crazy**
Student Union services	**Good**
Politics	**Light**
Sport	**Simply the best**
National team position	**Always 1st**
	53 clubs
Sport facilities	**Excellent**
Arts opportunities	**Very good**
Student magazine	**Label**
Student radio	**LCR**
2008 Radio Awards	**Gold award**
Student TV	**LSUTV**
2008 TV Awards	**1 award**
Nightclub	**Fusion + bar upstairs**
Bars	**JC's, Cognito**
Union ents	**FND (disco), Hey Ewe (cheese), Envy (r&b) + live**
Union societies	**40**
Most popular society	**International**
Parking	**No 1st years**
TOWN:	
Entertainment	★★
Scene	**Market town, good pubs**
Town/gown relations	**Good**
Risk of violence	**Average**
Cost of living	**Average**
Student concessions	**Excellent**
Survival + 2 nights out	**£70pw**
Part-time work campus/town	**Good/average**

Supportive of the effort is a huge investment in facilities on campus, including a 'super-gym' strength and conditioning centre, high-performance indoor and outdoor athletics centres and an Olympic-size swimming pool.

Says Jennie: 'The only problem that comes with such a high standard of facilities is the limited times non-elite athletes can use them. The focus here is undoubtedly on the elite athlete, and I've found it quite hard coming here after being towards the top standard of sports back home to being right at the bottom of the pile here.'

Town Loughborough is a small market town, pleasant, with all the basic shops you need, and plenty to offer, including a greater sense of security when compared to the majority of the big cities. But it is quite a different proposition to the other cities of sport, such as Manchester or Sheffield...

PILLOW TALK

'All freshers are guaranteed hall accommodation and it is usually possible to remain in hall throughout your time at Lboro, although a lot of people choose to spend a year in town. The halls are very varied. Don't set your heart on a particular one, the allocation process appears random.'

Says Jennie: 'I am in catered accommodation and my hall is situated in the heart of the student village, with food, washing rooms and leisure facilities all with in about a minute's walk. Some people are not so fortunate and I have seen some of the halls which could certainly do with some attention.'

A new student village is currently being built offering 1,000 additional bedrooms. The new development is a mix of 4- and 5- storey buildings, arranged around a courtyard, and has a combination of self catering facilities and flexible dining packages for the nearby restaurant and social centre.

Accommodation in town is more expensive, because of the utility bills, but it is quieter, less claustrophobic and less intrusive as you choose who you live with. All hall rooms are computer networked and carry phone sockets. There's something to suit every pocket, 'and the sense of loyalty and community spirit in these halls is of an intensity usually reserved for centuries-old universities.'

GETTING THERE

☞ By road: M1/J23, A512.
☞ By rail: London St Pancras, 1:45; Birmingham New Street, 1:30; Sheffield, 1:30; Nottingham, 0:20; Leicester, 0:15.
☞ By air: East Midlands Airport close by.
☞ By coach: London, 2:45; Exeter, 6:50; Newcastle, 8:10; Manchester, 4:30.

ACCOMMODATION	
Guarantee to freshers	**94%**
Style	**Halls, flats**
Security guard	**All**
Shared rooms	**Some**
Internet access	**All**
Self-catered	**Some**
En suite	**Some**
Approx price range pa	**£2644-£5746**
Town rent pw	**£50-£75**

STUDENT MANCHESTER - THE CITY

Writes fun-loving Alexandra Negri Not unlike London, Manchester is a city that never sleeps. Whatever day of the week or time of night, there is always somewhere to go, whether it is in the centre of town or the 'fields of fallow' - Fallowfield is the area of student residences at the furthest end of the Oxford Road corridor.

Oxford Road is of course student central. It sees tens of thousands of students pacing up and down it each day, whether it's to go to the various libraries, the lecture theatres, eateries, the infamous **Academy** (where the supremely tacky, yet unmissable *Torremolinos* is held every year), or the ridiculously cheap student bars (favourites including **Kro 1 & 2**, **The Footage**, **Sku Bar** and the Student Union of course.

The social scene in Manchester is endless and there is definitely something for everyone's taste and these are just a few suggestions and popular attractions.

Fallowfield is the perfect place to start for student nightlife. If you find yourself so far-flung and are not looking to venture far from your squalor, it's a passable destination for cheesy nights, stick-to-the-floor dance halls and cheap drinks. **Robo's** (popular on a Tuesday night), **Queen of Hearts** and the **Orange Grove** are a few of the famous haunts for students, all of which have their particular qualities; Robo's is a *Scream* bar, so with a yellow card you can gain even cheaper cheap drinks, and Queen of Hearts and Orange Grove are both pub-based, showing sports, serving pub grub and furnished with the odd pool table.

For first years, or those still clinging on to their youth, there is the infamous *Bop* held at **Owen's Park** every Friday. Don't be put off by the thousands that turn up hoping to be one of the lucky ones to enter the youth club come school gym. Turn up early, 10pm-ish, and either drink your wait away, or get legless inside for a tenner on Kermit's spunk, cheeky vimto's, snakebites or whatever other exotic tipple takes your fancy.

If you're feeling like breaking free of Fallowfield, then all the way down Oxford Road, right into the centre of town are places worthy of a visit. First hit the aptly named Curry Mile, either to start the night, or to satisfy the after-hours munchies - most curry house, kebab shops and pizzerias are open until the early hours.

If it is just a cheap meal you are after, then Rusholme is the place, as many restaurants here do BYOB (bring your own booze). Be careful though, because of the Muslim culture some restaurants do not allow alcohol at *All!!*

Through Rusholme and onto Oxford Road takes us past **Revolution**, **Space**, **Dry** and **Font**, a few other watering holes worth a visit.

Before you know it, you're in town and across the border between 'night out on a tenner', and tenner a drink'!! For the more hard-up students do not fear, there are still many establishments that cater for the tightest wallet.

If it's the clean cut, well chiselled, Cologne-smelling ladies man that takes your fancy then **42's** is definitely NOT the place for you. Long haired, scruffy t-shirt, skinny jeaned Indie boys fly the flag for 42's. Probably my, along with another 50% of the student population's, favourite place to be on a Thursday night. It's hot, it's sweaty, it's smoky, it's cheap, it's indie rock and roll, to quote one of the more frequently played artist there. Other Indie nights include **5th Avenue**, and **The Venue**.

The famous **Sankies** is host to some, if not all, the world's most famous DJ's, and after a recent re-vamp, promises to be worthwhile to those of you who do not fight shy of a good rave. Be sure to check the listings, as nights do vary, and in the summer, be prepared to stay til the break of dawn. Their boat parties, the 'Smugglers Run', down the Irwell (yes the Irwell!) are a real summer treat!

Or for the more elite who prefer to spend your student loan sipping Champers and gazing at footballers, try the bars on Deansgate, **Panacea** and **Coco Rooms**.

Northern Quarter has an eclectic mix of bars from live jazz and open mic nights at **Matt and Phredís** to soul and funk at **Bluu** bar and burlesque nights at **Mint Lounge** and the newly opened **Birdcage**. It is also home to the highly acclaimed **Affleck's Palace**, an eccentric shop where one can find anything from vintage classic to the best fancy dress.

Like most cities Manchester does have areas with a bad reputation, but in general, it's a safe city if you find yourself having to walk home, kebab in hand with not a penny to your name. For those in 4-inch stilettos I recommend a taxi. There are always black cabs around, and it will cost you around £7 to get back to Fallowfield, depending.

After a night out in the **Printworks** which holds **Tiger Tiger**, **Pure** and **Opus**, as well as one of the only 24 bars, a **Weatherspoons**, which I don't recommend, there is a late night bus service that stops right outside. An eventful ride home is usually guaranteed for those who prefer this mode of transport in the early hours.

Canal St., the home of 'pride' is defiantly worth a visit for some fantastic restaurants, happy hour deals, varied bars, and overall friendly fun, and sometimes bizarre service!

For the more refined there are two main theatres in Manchester, **The Palace Theatre** and **The Opera House**, which see many major productions. There are also a number of art galleries and exhibitions around town, a favourite of mine being in the **URBIS**, which recently displayed an exhibition on Graffiti Art and hosted the infamous 'Little Black Dress' design competition. **G-mex** is one of the larger exhibition centres which holds events like the ideal home show and career fairs.

THEATRE

Writes Elka Malhotra **The Royal Exchange Theatre** offers 2 stages (one in the round) and a combination of modern and traditional plays (all at student discounts). Situated in a rather nice area right in the city centre, it's also a good place to pop in for a cuppa during the day. **The Palace Theatre** in Oxford Road is designed for more family-friendly showings, they offer a good mix of shows and fairly big names. **The Contact Theatre** caters more to the student market and has occasional art exhibits as well as writing, DJ and drama workshops. **The Contact** also features the **Café Deluxe**, which makes hearty sandwiches and a mean cup of coffee. **The Green Room** is another avant-garde venue which, like **The Contact**, boasts its own nightclub nights, a small theatre and a small café-bar. **The Lowry** is also worth a mention here. Although a little more out-of-the-way than its rivals, it offers the largest stage outside of London, with Ferrari-designed seating! On a more low-key note, **The Library Theatre** offers a range of events from jazz to comedy, and traditional plays.

CINEMAS

Going to the cinema in Manchester costs about £4 pretty much everywhere. **The Filmworks** is by far the most popular, and despite seeming a little like an airport, boasts a ridiculous number of screens, some of which show IMAX 3D movies as well as arthouse and mainstream films. **The Odeon** is the city centre's only mainstream cinema, a quieter venue. In his days as Manchester United's captain, Eric Cantona used to get his French film 'fix' at the **Cornerhouse**, the best place for arthouse, foreign and small budget films. It also features a small but interesting art gallery and what is arguably the first modern-style bar in Manchester. Opened in 1985 it has an arty clientele and Belgium beers.

There is also the **AMC** situated in the Great Northern building on Deansgate, which usually shows all the latest releases. Although quite a way to travel out of the city and relatively expensive, **The UCI** at The Trafford Centre is also a nice little cinema complex (the outer facia has Islamic pillars beside the centre's themed food court).

COMEDY

Manchester knows how to have a laugh and **The Comedy Store**, situated on Deansgate Locks is definitely the best for doing that. *The Best In Stand-Up* on Friday and Saturday provide a fantastic night out and offer great student concessions, just make sure you buy tickets in advance the night is known to sell out. **The Frog and Bucket** is another popular comedy venue, although different in style, less slick and more traditional in its humour. They offer open mic nights on Mondays. **The Buzz** is possibly the longest running venue and has featured many a great, such as Jack Dee. **The Dancehouse Theatre** is also known to host occasional comedy nights, as is **The Contact**, known for its up-and-coming, very modern acts). Other popular comedy venues include **Bar Risa** and **Jongleurs**.

SHOPPING ON A LOAN

Affleck's Palace alone features more interesting little stalls than you can shake an oversized stick at, and is quite a Manc institution. A maze of a place it offers piercings, tattoos, t-shirts, CDs, vintage clothing, condoms, fancy dress, fetish wear and the ever popular rainbow-coloured hair extensions. **The Coliseum** is similar, situated behind **Affleck's**, on a smaller scale and with more of a gothic twist. **The Arndale Market** is handy for picking up cheap, fresh food as well as clothes, shoes and practical jokes – all fairly cheap.

The Student Market in the Academy sells bikes, clothes, hippie items, discount CDs and a variety of other stuff and is a favourite haunt on a Tuesday lunchtime. **The Trafford Centre** is the second biggest shopping centre in England and has literally miles of shops, but it's so big that your funky new purchases will probably have gone out of fashion by the time you leave.

Most chain shops can be found in the city centre. Student discounts are ubiquitous. A little more up market are **Harvey Nichols** and **Selfridges**, as well as the King Street area of the city centre which also features **DKNY**, **Max Mara** and **Hermes**.

UNIVERSITY OF MANCHESTER

The University of Manchester
Oxford Road
Manchester M13 9PL

TEL 0161 275 2077
FAX 0161 275 2106
EMAIL ug.admissions@manchester.ac.uk
WEB www.manchester.ac.uk

Manchester Students' Union
Oxford Road
Manchester M13 9PR

TEL 0161 275 2930
FAX 0161 275 2936
E: communications@umsu.manchester.ac.uk
WEB www.umsu.manchester.ac.uk

VAG VIEW

*T*he University of Manchester is the 29th best university in the world. So says the Times Higher Education *magazine's World Top 200 Universities*, which also puts it seventh best among the UK universities that make that league table of league tables.

Cambridge, Oxford, Imperial, UCL, KCL, and Edinburgh are above them, but we say that of all of these, Manchester has far and away the best university experience.

Manchester is cool and energetic in a way students from these other universities don't

UNIVERSITY/STUDENT/PROFILE	
University since	**1903**
Situation/style	**City campus**
Student population	**39165**
Undergraduates	**27310**
Mature undergraduates	**15%**
International undergrads	**19%**
Male/female ratio	**47:53**
Equality of opportunity:	
state school intake	**77%**
social class 4-7 intake	**21%**
low-participation area intake	**7%**

even begin to understand. If you don't believe me, forget Open Day, go to Oxford Road as the whole mighty monster awakens at the start of next academic year, and feel the vibes.

It is now one unit with the old Institute of Science & Technology (UMIST, as it was called) up the road. The Manchester Business School, just off Oxford Road, is part of the set-up too. In this feverishly studenty neck of the woods they are joined also by another Oxford Road university, Manchester Met, and with the Royal Northern School of Music here too, it must be the largest conglomeration of students anywhere in the world.

The whole area is, to all intents and purposes, campus. No one else gets a look-in.

Unable at first to take it all in, but aware that something special is going down, you, the wise fresher, will resist throwing himself frantically into the fray, as they encourage you to do at lesser universities until you wake up to the carnage, vomiting in the street. Nor will you retreat into your shell intimidated, as scores of them do at places like Imperial. You will imbibe, certainly, take it all in, but then consider how best it can serve you, and focus your

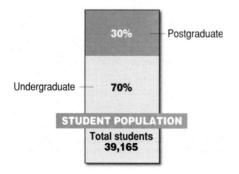

	30% — Postgraduate
Undergraduate —	70%

STUDENT POPULATION
Total students
39,165

mind on your own thing. For Manchester is a place for individuals, brilliant kids who like to do their own thing, in drama, in media, in whatever is their thing, and if you are ready it will release you to do the same.

Other people's scenes rarely impinge like they do on smaller campuses, like Loughborough where sport dominates all. Manchester focuses the mind of the adventurous wonderfully.

How long must we wait for Professor of Creative Writing Martin Amis to justify his salary of £80,000 for work that includes only twenty-eight hours a year of actual teaching, and write the campus novel and film, the latter-day Lucky Jim for which he was really, if possibly subconsciously, hired and which will put this much better than we can?

CAMPUS

North Campus is the old UMIST campus; South Campus, a few minutes away, is the original Manchester Uni campus, both on Oxford Road. The university has grown up with the city. The Wilmslow/Oxford Road runs right through the centre of campus, linking it at the top end with Manchester Met, Whitfield Street (gateway to the city's legendary Gay Village) and the old UMIST, and at the bottom end with the most populous areas of student residences - Rusholme, Fallowfield, etc. The whole street is campus, but it is also city. Manchester University has a theatre (Contact) and a premier gig venue (The Academy) and a museum (Manchester Museum) and an art gallery (Whitworth) which are all key sites of this city. City and university are absolutely inseparable, not least because they share the same vibe. It is an active, buzzing scene, a place some parents dread their children choosing.me parents dread their children choosing.

FEES, BURSARIES

UK & EU Fees, 2009-10: £3,225. If in receipt of full HE Maintenance grant there's a bursary. Scholarship-wise, there's the Talented Athlete Scholarship Scheme, The Manchester Advantage Scholarship, The Manchester Success Scholarship, The President's Award, and there are music scholarships, and accommodation bursaries. See it all on www.manchester.ac.uk/undergraduate/funding/.

STUDENT PROFILE

In general, they're an intelligent, resourceful, lively crew, not afraid or too lazy to lay themselves on the line and apply themselves, and not averse to letting their hair down either. Here's the advice of one of them, Alexandra Negri: 'For anyone going to a) a city as big as Manchester, b) leaving the tlc of your family, and c) being thrown into a world of slightly smelly, converse wearing, hard-up students, can be a bit daunting. However, the first days if not weeks could be the best you will ever imagine.'

The demographic picture is intriguing - 15% mature students, 19% from outside the EU, 23% public school, 21% from the lower socio-economic orders, 7% from the awe-inspiring 'low-participation' neighbourhoods. 'Uni really opens your eyes to different social groups, cultures and religions and this is especially the case in Manchester, where they have one of the biggest international student bases in the UK. Do not be put off by this, because you get to met even more weird, wacky and wonderful people than you ever hoped.'

ACADEMIA & JOBS

Students say the best teaching here is in Classics, Biology, Dentistry, Anatomy, Physiology & Pathology, Sciences related to Biology, Civil Eng., Geology, Biochemistry, Astrophysics, Accounting, Law, Maths, Pharmacy, Pharmacology, and Physical Science, the worst in Mechanical, Production & Manufacturing Engineering, where the lecturers don't even get half the student vote.

In the *Times Higher*'s Student Experience survey the students explain this with thumbs down to staff in general for their lack of interest in their students. As we say in the Introduction, Manchester has been aware that their lecturers have been doing their own thing too much. Research has taken over from teaching. They are addressing the problem.

The research is, however, very good, which means that you will have highly informed teachers, men and women working at the coal-face of your subject.

At the recent national assessment of the research provision of our research institutions they came 8th - 6th if you only count universities. Of course, this is where Ernest, First Baron Rutherford did the work which led to the splitting of the atom, and where the computer was invented, so there is some precedent.

· There are 4 Faculties: Engineering & Physical Sciences; Humanities; Life Sciences; Medical & Human Sciences.

With Medicine, Dentistry, degrees in subjects allied to Medicine, and Biological Sciences producing almost a third of all jobs that Manchester graduates get we should not be surprised to learn that they have created Europe's premier biomedical campus here, a series of linked scientific and hos-

---

TEACHING SURVEY AT A GLANCE	
Avg. UCAS points accepted	**410**
Acceptance rate	**13%**
Overall satisfaction rate	**81%**
Helpful/interested staff	★★
Small tuition groups	★★★
Students into graduate jobs	**78%**

Teaching most popular with undergraduates:
Classics (100%), Biology (98%), Dentistry, Anatomy, Physiology & Pathology, Sciences related to Biology (96%), Civil Eng., Geology, Biochemistry, Astrophysics (95%), Accounting, Law, Maths, Pharmacy, Pharmacology, Phsyical Science (91%).

Teaching least popular with undergraduates:
Mechanical, Production & Manufacturing Engineering (46%).

---

pital facilities on Oxford Road.

The 5/6-year MBChB scored full marks at the teaching assessments. Critical faculties and communication skills are to the fore, as is constructing a methodology of self-education. You will need a combination of Chemistry, plus one of Biology, Physics, Maths, plus a further rigorous academic subject at A level. Sciences not taken at AS/A level are required at

GCSE, ideally grade B or above. Equally acceptable are three sciences, or two sciences, plus one other rigorous subject. AAB grades at A level at the same sitting, but no grade is specified for the extra AS subject. You must also take UKCAT.

Among other degree subjects in this employment bonanza are Nursing, Midwifery, Optometry, Oral Health Science, Biochemistry, Biomedical Materials Science, Biotechnology, Cell Biology, Genetics, and Physiology.

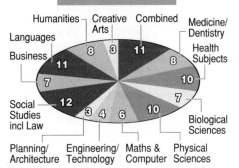

SUBJECT AREAS (%)

RESEARCH EXCELLENCE

4* *(World-class)* or 3* *(Internationally rated):*

	4*	3*
Cardiovascular Medicine	15%	60%
Cancer Studies	30%	60%
Hospital Clinical	10%	60%
Laboratory Clinical	5%	45%
Epidemiology	15%	45%
Community Clinical	40%	40%
Clinical Psychology	5%	45%
Dentistry	30%	45%
Nursing/Midwifery	50%	35%
Health Professions	20%	30%
Pharmacy	30%	40%
Biological Sciences	25%	40%
Human Biol. Sciences	20%	45%
Environmental Sciences	20%	50%
Chemistry	20%	45%
Physics	20%	35%
Pure Mathematics	20%	40%
Applied Mathematics	25%	35%
Statistics	20%	35%
Computer Science	30%	55%
Electrical/Electronic Eng.	25%	45%
General Engineering	20%	50%
Chemical Engineering	25%	60%
Metallurgy and Materials	20%	60%
Town/Country Planning	20%	40%
Geography Environment	15%	50%
Archaeology	15%	45%
Economics	25%	55%
Business/Management	25%	40%
Law	10%	40%
Politics	20%	30%
Social Work	15%	30%
Sociology	40%	20%
Anthropology	20%	30%
Development Studies	25%	40%
Psychology	10%	35%
Education	20%	35%
Middle Eastern/African	15%	45%
Asian Studies	10%	25%
Russian	35%	35%
French	15%	35%
German	20%	35%
Italian	20%	35%
Iberian	30%	45%
English	30%	45%
Linguistics	10%	45%
Classics	25%	30%
Philosophy	10%	35%
Theology	25%	40%
History	20%	40%
History of Art	40%	40%
Performing Arts	45%	40%
Music	50%	35%

In Social Studies, which accounts for 11% of graduate employment, jobs abound more in the political and economic arenas than in community work: the civil service, accountancy, banking and financial activities, recruitment and personnel, and only then social work/community counselling. A few more accountants come out of the Manchester Business School. 'The teaching standard at the Business School is high,' writes Alexandra. 'You will get the grades you deserve as long as you take courses you are interested in and are prepared to put the work in. Saying that a few slip-ups may be kindly overlooked in the haze of first year, and in general teachers are helpful and approachable if you are struggling. The workload is substantial but not great. You may find you have more lecture hours than fellow students on other courses. However, there will be less reading or coursework as a result. The Business School has its own library and computer clusters on hand, but you are still free to use any of the other resources around campus. The usual rush in the first weeks to secure text books from the library always occurs and it always seems to be the exchange students who get there first. Do not fear, either the books will be available at other libraries or you can purchase all set textbooks at Blackwell's located in the Precinct. Manchester Business School has a real sense of community because it is set aside from the rest of campus.'

Within Education, both adult and higher sectors are particularly well served. By far the most popular route into them is via the joint hons Languages, from which there's also a Top 10 provision of translators and interpreters. Note the Chinese and Japanese provision.

Architecture, town planning and property development are all rich employment seams out of Manchester. There's BA Architecture, but also an interesting series of MEng Structural Engineering & Architecture.

There is a good reputation for both English and Drama, the latter ably expressed extra-muraly.

Finally, Man Uni are European law specialists.

SOCIAL SCENE

STUDENTS' UNION It is an unadventurous soul who appears at the foot of MUSU's steps and resists propulsion inside - bodies hurry purposefully like ants, drawn irredeemably by the sights and sounds of the **Solem Bar**. 'Swedish sauna meets trendy metal,' sour-pussed someone, but actually it's a cosy place to hang out, and perhaps shoot some pool on the tables. It's open most nights till 11.

Up the road, is the old UMIST's **Harry's Bar** - Barnes Wallis Building, North Campus, perfect place to chill after lectures again, like Solem, there's pool, screens and surround sound. Nest door is **Paddy's Lounge**.

On the first floor is of the Steve Biko Building is **Biko's Café**, where there are several PCs with free internet and email access. The menu consists of healthy breakfast options and 'healthy choice' salad bar.

City and university are absolutely inseparable, not least because they share the same vibe. It is an active, buzzing scene, a place some parents dread their children choosing.

'Next door to the Union, South Campus, is the **Academy**, a 1,200-capacity live band venue,' Leonie Kenyon tells us, 'It pulls itself round in time for the Student Market during the day, a prime spot for posters, bikes, CDs, clothes and hippy items, a favourite haunt of students especially at lunchtime when the homemade chocolate cakes are rather popular! Another union nightclub is the **Cellar**, which features Horny on Friday, and plays a mixture of pop and cheese. On weekday afternoons it is also used as a café.'

Pangaea comes twice a year, a student-run, student-only, twelve-room mega event with a variety of headliners, genres and surprises, everything from Psi-trance to Mad Hatters and hopefully something a little weird. Meanwhile, students galvanise themselves into national prominence with their drama and media. Manchester's *Student Direct* is the city's No. 1 weekly student newspaper. With a readership of over 50,000, it serves the universities of Manchester, Salford and Bolton. Fuse FM (radio) and MSTV complete the picture. No surprise the uni is high in the employment league for editors, publishing and the like. In the area of drama, the uni is a major force, the annual springtime student festival still reigns supreme. And politically, the union's campaigning reputation still goes unquestioned.

SPORT The teams came 8th in the national uni team ratings last year. Facilities include a boat house on the Bridgewater Canal, Yacht Club at Pennington Flash, Leigh, 18 miles west of the city. Pitches (31 acres) for rugby, soccer, hockey, lacrosse, cricket, netball, are close to the student village at Fallowfield, also tennis courts, all-weather, artificial grass areas and pavilion. In Fallowfield, too, is the Armitage Centre with sports hall and squash courts close by. A further 90 acres lie ten miles south, below the M63, at Wythenshawe sports ground. On campus itself is the McDougal Centre, which has a swimming pool, indoor games hall, gym, squash and fives courts, an outside five-a-side court, rifle range, climbing wall, bowls carpets, sauna and solarium. The new Commonwealth Games swim-

ming pool is open to students. There are bursaries, two offered by the exclusive XXI, an elite sports club founded in 1932.

TOWN See Student Manchester.

PILLOW TALK

All freshers are guaranteed a place in halls and flats. The most populous areas of student residences - Rusholme, Fallowfield, etc - are at the bottom end of the Oxford Road corridor. Writes Leonie: 'Under the railway line and through Rusholme's Curry Mile - which, as the name would suggest, is full of curry houses and interesting Eastern-style shops. Although located next to the

WHAT IT'S REALLY LIKE	
UNIVERSITY:	
Social Life	★★★★★
Campus scene	**Big, busy, self-assured**
Student Union services	**Good**
Politics	**Active & widely representative: fees, war, housing, racism**
Sport	**Key**
National team position	**8th**
Sport facilities	**Good**
Arts opportunities	**Excellent; high profile drama, dance, film**
Student newspaper	**Student Direct**
Student radio	**Fuse FM**
Student TV	**MUSTV**
Nightclub and venues	**Cellar, Academy 1,2 & 3**
Bars	**Solem, Harry's, Paddy's Lounge**
Union ents	**Club Tropicana, Pangaea**
Union societies	**200**
Parking	**Permits**
CITY:	
Entertainment	★★★★★
City scene	**Legendary**
Town/gown relations	**Average-poor**
Risk of violence	**High**
Cost of living	**Average**
Student concessions	**Good**
Survival + 2 nights out	**£90 pw**
Part-time work campus/town	**Average/good**

infamous Moss Side, it's quite safe.

'Fallowfield is the ideal place to live as it is secure, lively, and features some very nice little houses. The student halls range from very nice to eyesore, and are backed by the university-owned Armitage Sports Centre, which offers student discounts on a range of sporty activities.'

Writes Alexandra: 'The slightly newer and nicer are Richmond Park with Willow Court and Poplar, built for residents when the Commonwealth Games were held in Manchester.'

Withington is a little quieter, a little more expensive, and that little bit further away from uni and the town centre, but has a good variety of pubs, shops and coffee shops. Similarly Didsbury (home of the 'Didsbury Dozen' series of pubs - a pub crawl classic) has a good deal to offer, but is more expensive than the wholly studenty Fallowfield area.

Victoria Park is seen as the posh alternative, probably because most of its halls are large, leafy, Victorian buildings. It's an area between Fallowfield and the main campus - approximately 15 minutes walk from the main university buildings. The Students' Union is located at the top of the Victoria Park area, as is Whitworth Park Hall, affectionately known as the Toblerone building and the perfect choice for Arts students, since you can stagger out of bed and be right outside the Faculty of Arts. These halls tend to be a tad more expensive because the rooms are nicer and most are catered.

There are also private halls of residence in the

ACCOMMODATION	
Guarantee to freshers	**100%**
Style	**Halls, flats**
Security guard	**24-hr security**
Shared rooms	**None**
Internet access	**All**
Self-catered	**Some**
En suite	**Some**
Approx price range pw	**£78-£130**
City rent pw	**£65-£75**

city centre Student Village, popular with students at Manchester Met since it is right on their doorstep. Victoria Hall is another privately owned student residence near the city centre.'

'Safety-wise, all the residence are patrolled 24 hours and there is secure parking in some of the residences,' concludes Alexandra. 'Taking a car to uni is not really necessary, as public transport is so good and you just end up being the local taxi service. It also costs extra for a parking permit.'

GETTING THERE
☛ By road: M63/J10, A34.
☛ By rail: London Euston, 2:30; Leeds, 1:45; Liverpool Lime Street, 0:50.
☛ By air: Manchester Airport for international and inland flights.
☛ By coach: London, 4:35; Bristol, 5:00; Newcastle, 5:00.

MANCHESTER METROPOLITAN UNIVERSITY

The Manchester Metropolitan University
All Saints
Manchester M15 6BH

TEL 0161 247 2000
FAX 0171 247 6871

EMAIL prospectus@mmu.ac.uk
WEB www.mmu.ac.uk

Manchester Met Students' Union
99 Oxford Road
Manchester M1 7EL

TEL 0161 247 1162
FAX 0161 247 6314

EMAIL mmsu@mmu.ac.uk
WEB www.mmunion.co.uk

VAG VIEW
*M*anchester Met, formerly Manchester Poly, is situated on various sites in Manchester and in Crewe and Alsager, two towns either side of the M6 between junctions 16 and 17.

People pick MMU for its reputation as a party-till-you-die university. When you visit, they do not disappoint: 'Everyone gets very focused on what's going here, which is massive,' confessed a student.

CAMPUS

The Manchester base is centred at the All Saints site on Oxford Road, very close to Manchester Uni, making, with UMIST and a couple of other colleges in the vicinity, a quite extraordinary concentration of students (around 100,000) within the square mile.

Crewe & Alsager are towns about 6 miles apart, some 35 miles south of Manchester, their semi-rural campus environments a million miles away in spirit from heaving Oxford Road.

'There's not a lot of contact with Crewe & Alsager,' my guide admitted. 'They always say there is, but in practice there's not. They have their own set-up down there. They're very sports and drama orientated. I think you still get some who enrol for C&A and are quite surprised that it's not just down the road and you can't always get up here on a Saturday night! I understand quite a few drop out over that.'

FEES, BURSARIES

UK & EU Fees, 2009-10: £3,225. If in receipt of the HE Maintenance grant there's a sliding scale bursary according to your means.

STUDENT PROFILE

At MMU 22% of undergraduates are mature and nearly 4,000 are part-time. Only around 5% hail from public school. Far greater are those from the lower socio-economic reaches. Bruce McVean sees only advantage in this. 'MMU is perceived to be the more dynamic university because it is not as staid as Manchester University.' Bruce was an engineering student at Manchester Uni and, seeking a course change to Geography, was turned down by Manchester and accepted by MMU. 'But I now know people doing Geography at Manchester and there's not a lot of difference between the two departments. When students are actually here, I don't think they perceive much difference between the two establishments.'

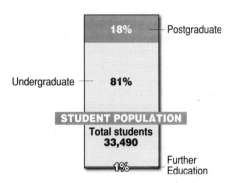

Postgraduate 18%
Undergraduate 81%

STUDENT POPULATION
Total students
33,490

Further Education 1%

ACADEMIA & JOBS

The modular courses have a practical emphasis, tracing a clear vocational line to jobs in industry, where their employment rate is good.

More than 400 courses are offered from within Art & Design; Community Studies, Law & Education; Food, Clothing & Hospitality Management; Humanities & Social Science; Management & Business; Science & Engineering.

At Alsager there's a range of sports science subjects available, plus the departments of Humanities & Applied Social Studies (Sociology scored an excellent 21 on inspection) and the Modular Office, which looks after all inter-departmental modular mixes. At Crewe, the Business & Management Department sits alongside the Department of Environmental & Leisure Studies with its own stream, woodland and conservation habitats. Other than that, there is the School of Education (PGCEs and Primary and Secondary degrees).

Students say that the teaching is best in Physical Science, Biology, Physical Geography & Environmental Science, Geography, Biological Sciences, English, Languages, Law, Accounting, Philosophy, and Social History.

In the research assessment they did best in Education, English, and Art & Design.

By far the greatest number of jobs come out of Business (note their Hospitality Management and Human Resource Management degrees in particular. Then it's Education, Art & Design (including Fashion, Textiles, Furniture, Advertising, Design & Art Direction, Graphics, Illustration, Animation, and Landscape Architecture). There is a sound track record, too, in Architecture, which can be combined with Structures, Construction, Environmental Studies, or with Humanities. Biological Sciences is a big provider, and of course includes Sport, the speciality of the out-of-town campuses. But there is also a massive presence jobs-wise in Education (50% Primary, then Secondary, Higher, and Adult), subjects allied to Health (Nursing, Dental Technology, Speech Therapy/Pathology and the like), Social Studies, which supplies graduates principally to community counselling and local & regional government), and Computer (software consultancy & supply, banks, and telecommunications).

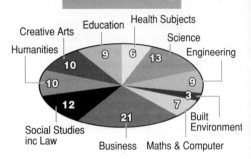

SUBJECT AREAS (%)

> *'It's true, we still have a really strong gay scene. Gays won't need to be told about Manchester's Mardi Gras... but the hub – day in, day out – is the Village: late licensing, all-night cafés and a huge choice of venues.'*

RESEARCH EXCELLENCE

% of Manchester Met's research that is **4*** *(World-class) or* **3*** *(Internationally rated):*

	4*	3*
Health Professions	5%	15%
Biomedical Sciences	5%	30%
Environmental Sciences	5%	40%
Computer Science	5%	30%
General Engineering	0%	35%
Metallurgy and Materials	0%	30%
Economics	0%	10%
Business/Management	5%	30%
Information Management	0%	20%
Social Work	5%	15%
Sociology	5%	30%
Education	20%	35%
European Studies	0%	20%
English	15%	20%
Philosophy	5%	35%
Art and Design	10%	35%
Performing Arts	5%	25%

SOCIAL SCENE

STUDENTS' UNION There are of course many collaborations between Manchester Uni and Manchester Met, the unions being but a walk apart on Oxford Road, the most visible of which is Student Direct, the paper which wins awards at national level. *Student Direct* and Manchester Met's *Pulp* magazine now get distributed to all Salford and Bolton too.

There are, nevertheless, marked differences between Manchester and the Met. There is great activity within student societies at Manchester Met - 70 all told, but, as one student said to me, 'Politics is a dirty word... We don't have a very political union. We have political groups - Socialist Workers and so on, but that whole scene is more active at Manchester University. It's a lot more that our Union here provides a service, it's more of a social and representational thing.

'It's true, we still have a really strong gay scene within the Union.' Gays won't need to be told about Manchester's *Mardi Gras*, an unforgettable weekend of parades and parties. But the hub - day in, day out - is the Village: late licensing, all-night cafés and a huge choice of venues, all within walking distance of one another and MU and MMU.

Watering holes at union headquarters on Oxford Road include **Blue Café**, open from 8.30 am Monday to Friday for breakfast, lunch. Then, there's **MancUnion Bar** with big screen TV and bar promotions. **K2** is the nightclub. They say that when K2 is open till 2, MancUnion is also open till 2, but then MancUnion has a licence till 2 every day except Sunday. Almost every major DJ has graced the K2 decks, so they'll tell you.

The MancUnion is a 450-capacity bar open 7 nights a week on the 2nd floor of the Student Union building on All Saints Campus, Oxford Road. K2's the 900-capacity nightclub downstairs, where after-match joys and blues are danced away on a Wednesday. Friday is *Double Vision* (party toons) - 2 floors of 'utter madness' - in the main room, commercial dance and chart stompers from past to present, plus r&b, soul and jazz upstairs and hip hop treats and laid back beats in the back room. On Saturday, it's *Rock Kitchen* and 'rock music played loud' through 2 rooms, 'hosted by DJs Stevie B, Adam, the Rock-It-Crew, and Boxer.' Plus specials like *Sex Lies and R&B*, and *Skool Disco* - 'free sweets, soggy school dinners and prizes for the best fancy dress', and live acts like Timmy Mallett and Pat Sharp. All of which culminates in the Summer Ball at the Palace Hotel, Manchester.

Down in Crewe + Alsager there is a Union presence, and bars, shops, clubs and societies at both campuses, and even a nightclub at Crewe. It is not Manchester, so don't come here if that's what you're after, but there are bus nights to city clubs and among a handful of societies may be found four - Live Music, Alternative Music, Music and Film - which suggest a commendable do-it-yourself artistry to life.

ACCOMMODATION

Guarantee to freshers	**54%**
Style	**Halls, flats**
Security guard	**Some**
Shared rooms	**Some**
Internet access	**All**
Self-catered	**Some**
En suite	**Most**
Approx price range pw	**£66.50-£96**
City rent pw	**£65-£75**

Alsager has an **Arts Centre** with a resident theatre company and a packed programme of performance and literary arts. There are two theatres (the Axis Theatre seating 500), a dance studio and an art gallery, and it is here that is run a Drama course so good that it was awarded 23 points out of 24 after a recent inspection. The mind/body balance is made at Alsager by one of the best sports outfits in the country. There are 32 acres of playing fields, an athletics track, swimming pool, indoor facilities galore and a 1,000 square metre laboratory complex, which features a 33 x 6m track for perfor-

WHAT IT'S REALLY LIKE

UNIVERSITY:	
Social Life	★★★★
Campus scene	**Huge, diverse happening place**
Student Union services	**Average**
Politics	**Low interest**
Sport	**Well equipped**
National team position	**71st**
Sport facilities	**Good**
Arts opportunities	**Music, film excellent; rest good**
Student newspaper	**Student Direct**
Student magazine	**Pulp**
Nightclub	**K2**
Bars	**MancUnion**
Union ents	**Double Vision**
Union societies	**70**
Parking	**Poor**
CITY:	
Entertainment	★★★★★
City scene	**Legendary**
Town/gown relations	**Average-poor**
Risk of violence	**High**
Cost of living	**Average**
Student concessions	**Good**
Survival + 2 nights out	**£90 pw**
Part-time work campus/town	**Average/good**

mance data collection, regularly visited by top professional athletes.

PILLOW TALK

The university halls are good for the first year, when you are wanting to meet people, but are not cheap and it is fairly difficult to get your first choice. The halls at All Saints have the best location; those at Didsbury require a considerable bus journey. See Manchester Uni entry, *Pillow Talk*, for city accommodation.

GETTING THERE

☞ By road: Manchester, M63/J10, A34. Coach services good. Crewe/Alsager, M6/J16.
☞ By rail to Manchester: London Euston, 2:30; Leeds, 1:45; Liverpool Lime Street, 0:50. Crewe, connections from Manchester Piccadilly.
☞ By air: Manchester Airport for international and inland flights.
☞ By coach: London, 4:35; Bristol, 5:00; Newcastle, 5:00.

MIDDLESEX UNIVERSITY

Middlesex University
Trent Park
London N14 4YZ

TEL 020 8411 5000
FAX 020 8362 5649
EMAIL admissions@mdx.ac.uk
WEB www.mdx.ac.uk

Middlesex University Students' Union
Trent Park
London N14 4YZ

TEL 020 8411 6450
FAX 020 8440 5944
EMAIL [[initial.name]@mdx.ac.uk
WEB www.musu.mdx.ac.uk

VAG VIEW

*L*ondon's strength derives from its unique *mix of cultures, as does Middlesex's, so they say. The capital's 9 million residents speak some 300 languages. Middlesex's student body includes students from all over the world.*

There are many impressive elements in Middlesex's strategy, not least their Able Centre, a disability support centre with recording studios turning out audio texts for blind students, a dyslexia support co-ordinator and a sign language bureau, which has appealed to thousands beyond campus too. But there is a huge locally based and mature student population and it would be a mistake to believe that this uni picks you up and takes you out of life in quite the same way as a traditional campus university like Nottingham, Kent or Sussex.

Most people who come to Middlesex are not that bothered that the extra-curricular scene at the Students' Union is second rate, or that much of what is on offer has been taken out of the hands of the students, but it may be that this aspect of a traditional university education is precisely what will be

UNIVERSITY/STUDENT PROFILE	
University since	**1992**
Situation/style	**Campus/city sites**
Student population	**23290**
Total undergraduates	**17755**
Mature undergraduates	**15%**
International undergrads	**17%**
Male/female ratio	**47:53**
Equality of opportunity:	
state school intake	**98%**
social class 4-7 intake	**48%**
low-participation area intake	**6%**

seen to be important to the applicant. The drop-out rate is certainly high.

CAMPUS

Getting to grips with this university has been like wrestling with a family of octopuses, so many tentacles are there reaching out across north London and beyond. At one time there were some 18 sites and campuses, but today they are based at 2 or 3 main campus sites, and offer 4 schools of study.

The School of Arts & Education is based at the Trent Park/Cat Hill campus. they concentrating their energies on 2 or 3 main-campus sites, pulling the whole operation together in a £100-million strategy. Trent Park Bramley Road, London N14 4YZ, is set in 900 acres of woodlands and meadows. Cockfosters or Oakwood tubes (Piccadilly line). Performing Arts, IT, Cultural Studies, Education Product Design & Engineering, Biological Science. For Cat Hill, Barnet, Herts EN4 8H, go to Cockfosters (Piccadilly line).

The Business School, the School of Health and Social Sciences and the old School of Computing Science (now re-named the School of Engineering and Information (EIS) and incorporating new Engineering courses) are based at the Hendon campus in North West London. Students in some health areas also study at the Archway campus,

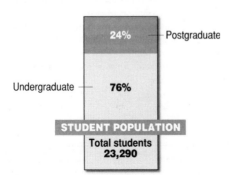

24% Postgraduate

Undergraduate — **76%**

STUDENT POPULATION
Total students
23,290

TEACHING SURVEY AT A GLANCE

Avg. UCAS points accepted	**180**
Acceptance rate	**15%**
Overall satisfaction rate	**75%**
Helpful/interested staff	★★
Small tuition groups	★★
Students into graduate jobs	**81%**

Teaching most popular with undergraduates:
Finance, Accounting (86%), Law (85%), Philosophy (83%), Social Studies (81%), Business & Administrative Studies, Dance (80%).

Teaching least popular with undergraduates:
Architecture (48%).

well placed for local hospitals and health care providers.

For Hendon, The Burroughs, London NW4 4BT, go to Hendon Central (Northern line). A new £17-million learning resource centre opened here recently.

FEES, BURSARIES

UK & EU Fees, 2009-10: £3,225. For those eligible for the HE Maintenance Grant there's also the Middlesex Bursary (see www.mdx.ac.uk/study/und ergrad/ugfees/bursaries.asp). Further awards include the Future Gold Scholarship, the Chancellor's Scholarships for sport and academic achievement, and awards to applicants for Academic Excellence. See www.mdx.ac.uk/study/ undergrad/ugfees/scholarships. Closing date for applications is 30th June 2009.

STUDENT PROFILE

Middlesex is a large university and has anything but a traditional university clientele. Many undergraduates are mature, many come from new-to-uni social groups. There is also a large number of part-timers among non-degree (HND) undergraduates. Where numbers have escalated since 1995 is in overseas recruitment. They have won awards for attracting students in from Europe and further afield. Language support is an essential requirement - there's a series of courses incorporating a Foundation year for non-EU international students. Coping with the high drop-out rate that their open-doors policy has helped create is clearly the thought behind the £1000 bursaries for applicants with 300 points at entry, mentioned in Fees, Bursaries above.

ACADEMIA & JOBS

Full-time courses are made up of 4 year-long modules, each worth 30 credits. A student needs to

RESEARCH EXCELLENCE

% of Middlesex's research that is
4 (World-class) or 3* (Internationally rated):*

	4*	3*
Nursing/Midwifery	5%	30%
/Health Professions/	5%	25%
Computer Science/	10%	25%
Geography Environment	5%	35%
Business/Management	5%	25%
Law	0%	15%
Social Work	5%	45%
Psychology	0%	10%
English	5%	30%
Philosophy	20%	45%
Art and Design	5%	20%
History of Art	15%	40%
Performing Arts	20%	35%
Media Studies	0%	45%

amass 120 credits in each year before progressing onto the next, and 360 in total to be awarded an honours degree. Examinations for each module take place at the end of the year. There is continual assessment, and coursework also contributes to the overall assessment result.

The 4 academic schools are Arts & Education, Computing Science, Health & Social Sciences, and Business.

Students say the best teaching is in Finance, Accounting, Law, Philosophy, Social Studies, Business & Administrative Studies, Dance, and the worst in Architecture (only 48% of the class raised a hand in support).

Business certainly pumps out most graduates into jobs, with accountancy and banking high on the list. Middlesex have plenty of Management degrees too, with such as Marketing, Business, Info

SUBJECT AREAS (%)

Education: 3
Combined: 7
Creative Arts: 15
Health Subjects: 9
Engineering <1
Science: 5
Maths & Computer: 15
Built Environment <1
Business: 25
Social Studies inc Law: 12
Humanities: 8

WHAT IT'S REALLY LIKE

UNIVERSITY:	
Social Life	★★
Campus scene	Friendly, mature, colourful, not campus focused
Student Union services	Average
Politics	Active
Sport	Competitive
National team position	78th
Sport facilities	Good
Arts opportunities	Excellent
Student magazine	MUD: Middlesex Union Direct
Nightclub	Enfield forum
Bars	1 on each campus
Union ents	Not a lot
Union societies	30
Parking	Poor
CITY:	
Entertainment	★★★★★
City scene	Wild, expensive
Town/gown relations	Average-good
Risk of violence	Average
Cost of living	Very high
Student concessions	Good
Survival + 2 nights out	£100 pw
Part-time work locally	Fair

Systems, and International-style biases, and their joint hons programme allows Management combinations in a whole host of areas. Sales managers proliferate in the end, most of them with an Art & Design bias - textiles, knitwear, jewellery, fashion providing the focus.

Art & Design is the next big job provider, with a massive 38% of their output actually becoming creative artists, rather than having to take second choice occupations.

In the recent national assessment of the research provision of our universities, Middlesex showed commendable world-class work in Performing Arts, History of Art, Architecture & Design, and Philosophy. There hadn't been an assessment for seven years, and on the last occasion the last two were top of the tree too. So, expect to find deep seams of knowledge in these departments. Look carefully at Philosophy at Middlesex, which came first among post-1992 universities and ahead of Durham, Warwick and Edinburgh, and also gets a strong rating from students for its teaching. On the History of Art, Architecture & Design front, be aware of the Interior Art & Design degrees.

Jobs for graduates in Art & Design proliferate for graphic artists, designers and illustrators, and elsewhere there's a dedicated BSc Computing Science Graphics & Games which puts them up there in the Top 10 for computer game design. Back in the arts area, among Fine Art, Fashion (also Knitwear and Textiles), Product Design, and Jewellery, the latter stands out as a good niche.

As for Performing Arts, musicians, composers, and would-be music industry managers are all well served here, and those interested in Dance and Drama. Be aware of the Jazz speciality in Music at Middlesex. For actors, directors, producers there are two BA degrees: Drama & Theatre Studies and Technical Theatre Arts.

Journalism, Publishing and TV Production also have dedicated degrees. Plans are afoot at Hendon for a new building for Art, Design and Media programmes.

Health is another strong area jobs-wise - Nursing, Pre-Registration Midwifery, and Veterinary Nursing, a joint course with the Royal Veterinary College (the best in the field). See, too, the Herbal Medicine and Traditional Chinese Medicine and Acupuncture, where Middlesex was a pioneer. The BSc Vet Nursing leads to the RCVS Vet Nursing Certificate.

There's also a strong line in psychotherapists at the graduate job bank. Look at the Social Sciences with Communication & Language Studies and the BSc Psychology, which carries British Psychological Society accreditation.

Finally, there is a discernable pattern of careers in environmental health and a whole range of Health & Policy Studies degrees in the BSc joint degree series, also Occupational Health & Safety and BSc Environmental Health.

They are also commercial and business law specialists incidentally, a subject that carries some useful management and other tie-ups.

SOCIAL SCENE

STUDENTS' UNION Shame, the bars and ents are now run by a private contractor (Scolarest); competitive sport directly by the university. This is no way to encourage a strong student culture.

The four bars - Enfield, Tottenham, Trent Park and Cat Hill - provide drinks promos and ents during the week, but they close at weekends. There's a Freshers' Ball, of course, and some tell of a Middlesex extravaganza, a 36-hour festival in the summer at Trent Park, and there's a student magazine called MUD - Middlesex Union Direct.

SPORT Gym facilities exist on all campuses. Sport is an area of continual investment, and students are good at it (came 55th nationally in 2006). Recent large projects include a £2.5m state-of-the-art gym,

ACCOMMODATION	
Guarantee to freshers	**75%**
Style	**Halls, flats**
Security guard	**All**
Shared rooms	**None**
Internet access	**All**
Self-catered	**All**
En suite	**Most**
Approx price range pw	**£82-£97**
City rent pw	**£90**

the Real Tennis Centre at Hendon, and two artificial hockey pitches at Trent Park. Students have access to uni swimming pools, indoor and outdoor, football and rugby pitches and a golf club.

PILLOW TALK

There are 2,400 places in halls, all of which are self-catering. Student union facilities and local supermarkets suffice. All students have a shared kitchen too. Most halls have been built over the past 6 years; all are within easy reach of their respective campuses. A security officer is on sight from 5pm to 9am Monday to Friday and all weekend. There's also an interactive website (studentpad) with details of private houses/flats to rent and also rooms within family homes.

STUDENT NEWCASTLE - THE CITY

The Toon is at the cutting edge of student life. Offering the very best in entertainment, its lively and vibrant atmosphere, progressive and diverse character make it an essential stop for any fun lovin' student. Ranked as the 7th best party city in the world, Newcastle is also heading up the field in all things cultural. Along with Gateshead, its neighbour on the Tyne, recent years have witnessed a massive boom for Newcastle Arts - the **Baltic Centre for Contemporary Art**, a 4- storey converted flour mill which houses numerous temporary exhibitions, and the **Sage Music Centre** on Newcastle's very own south bank.

NIGHTLIFE

Geordie attitude turns on the old adage, 'work hard, play hard', and be it the legendary **Bigg Market**, the swanky watering holes of the Quayside or the cosmopolitan bars of Jesmond's Osborne Road and the area around Central Station, there is opportunity for everyone to play as hard as they like, often at a price most students can afford.

When it comes to clubbing and live acts, both universities are up there with the best in live entertainment. The Darkness, Coldplay, Kosheen, Shed 7, Elbow, Starsailor, Mark Owen and Jools Holland are just a few of the big name acts to have played . **The Telewest Arena** attracts all the major national tours, from Justin Timberlake, Beyonce and Blue to Stereophonics and Craig David, while the **City Hall** has it's own share of the stars, the likes of Norah Jones and Travis The only downside is that our location means a lot of small tours do not visit. Don't expect to see everyone.

If you want to sample musical delights a little closer to home there are also smaller more intimate live venues such as **The Cluny** and **The Head of Steam** which showcase the cream of Newcastle's homegrown musical talent.

The city's club scene has rocketed to success in recent years with the launch of numerous highly acclaimed club events. Writes Katie Ashworth: 'When it comes to clubs, I generally go to alternative clubs and pubs, as opposed to ones that would play dance music. For indie buffs, I would recommend: **The Cooperidge** on a Monday, **The Cluny**, *Stone Love @* **Digital** on Thursdays, **The Forth** generally every night, **The Global** on gig nights, **The Head of Steam**, **The Hancock** pub any night, *Bulletproof @* **Carling Academy**... there's a lot more if you search around!

'For the rock/metal crowd: *Krash @* **Venue** on Thursdays, *Stone Love @* **Digital** on Thursdays, **Trillians** any night, **Legends**, *Red Room @* Northumbria, Uni. **The Hancock** pub upstairs any night, *Where Angels Play @* **Carling Academy**.. . Again, look around, keep your eyes and ears open for gigs and nights.

'For general drinking nights out: **Tiger Tiger**. **Sam Jacks** is always a laugh too, anywhere in **The Gate**, **Liquid**, **Flares** (a disco theme club), **The Goose**, *Solution @* Newcastle Uni on Fridays, *Wiggle @* Northumbria. **Blu Bambu** is ok, too.

'What does it cost? Night out anywhere from £10 to £50! I personally never spend more than about £15, but that's because I go to cheaper places and don't drink expensive things. Proper night out to "real clubs", anything around £30 or more. But I'd rather go to a pub, bar or gig, which are always cheaper. Entrance to clubs, anything from £3 to £12, although on average £4 is normal for the places I go to.'

SPORT

The whole city revolves around the fortunes of Newcastle United, so get informed. St James's Park is the most imposing landmark on the city skyline and the second largest stadium in the Premiership. Getting tickets can be a problem, however, despite the 52,000 capacity, but well worth trying for.

Elsewhere, Johnny Wilkinson (occasionally) and the rest of the Newcastle Falcons offer a student friendly environment for rugby fans, while the Newcastle Eagles do the same for basketball followers. Wherever you go, don't mention any allegiance to Northeast rivals Sunderland or Manchester United or you are liable to end up in a bit of bother.

CINEMA

The Odeon is the most central cinema and with its brand new multiplex having recently opened in **The Gate** on Newgate Street, you can enjoy all the top films at student prices right on your doorstep. Also in the city centre is a 12-screen **Warner Village**, while a short drive will take you to **UCI Silverlink** or **Metro Centre**.

For the more artistic, the **Tyneside Cinema** on Pilgrim Street is one of the best independent cinemas in the country.

THEATRE AND COMEDY

Newcastle is one of the Royal Shakespeare Company's second homes. In the autumn, it doth take over most of the city's stages for a month of highbrow entertainment. The major venue is the **Theatre Royal**, the poshest of Newcastle's theatres.

Try the maller, cheaper **Live Theatre**.

If it's a more relaxed, studenty atmosphere you're after you can't beat the **Playhouse** and **Gulbenkian Studio** to get the best in up and coming talent. Both theatres are housed in the same building at the edge of Newcastle University's campus, and are home to the more cutting-edge Northern Stage company.

For comedy look no further than the fantastic **Hyena Café**, open 12 months of the year, and the annual Newcastle Comedy Festival, which plays a number of venues across the city for a two-week spell. **Newcastle Student Union** also puts on a comedy night every Monday during term-time, in it's **Global Café** venue.

SHOPPING

The only major studenty shop is **Period Clothing**, with some fantastic stuff in store. Otherwise Newcastle blends high street stores with smaller designer boutiques well. On Northumberland Street you can check out all the high-street brands such as **H&M**, **Zara** and **Warehouse**, whilst **Eldon Square Shopping Centre**, just off Northumberland Street is home to **Top Shop**, **USC**, **Oasis** and all the major department stores. Grainger Town is where you'll find the 'trendier' and more expensive shops as well as some quality boutiques.

Check out **Mint**, just off Grey Street, it's a truly awesome shopping experience. A short journey will take you to the Gateshead **MetroCentre** and the major stores/labels. For music, **Steel Wheels**, **RPM** and **Flying Records** offer good independent options.

* *

UNIVERSITY OF NEWCASTLE

The University of Newcastle upon Tyne
Kensington Terrace
Newcastle upon Tyne NE1 7RU

TEL 0191 222 5594
FAX 0191 222 8685
EMAIL enquiries@ncl.ac.uk
WEB www.ncl.ac.uk

The Newcastle University Union Society
Kings Walk
Newcastle upon Tyne NE1 8QB

TEL 0191 239 3900
FAX 0191 222 1876
EMAIL president.union@ncl.ac.uk
WEB www.unionsociety.co.uk

VAG VIEW

*A*cademically, Newcastle is good right across the board. 'Those who live in the north perhaps understand how good it is better than those from the south,' said one Yorkshire-based school careers teacher, adding with weight, 'It is very popular among students who go there.'

Where Newcastle scores over London and, yes, over Manchester, is in its packing an incredible array of cultural, artistic and hedonistic power centres into a very small space (and at relatively low cost). So much is

UNIVERSITY/STUDENT PROFILE	
University since	**1963**
Situation/style	**Campus**
Student population	**19700**
Total undergraduates	**14060**
Mature undergraduates	**6%**
International undergrads	**5%**
Male/female ratio	**50:50**
Equality of opportunity:	
state school intake	**70%**
social class 4-7 intake	**20%**
low-participation area intake	**7%**

going on, and all of it so concentrated, that the buzz on the street at night is ten times what you will feel in the greater, but more dispersed metropolis.

In the Higher Education Funding Council's National Student Survey, 86% of Newcastle's students gave it the thumbs-up, and there's less than a 4% drop-out. Newcastle's undergraduates have a real and vibrant city to discover, but their loyalty is down to what goes on in the Students' Union. What you notice on campus is people doing, things happening, students in control...of themselves and what they are about. 'We actually own the whole set-up,' they say. They do - union building and all. Go there and see.

CAMPUS

Newcastle is a campus university situated right in the heart of this compact and compelling city, within walking distance of theatres, cinemas, shops, bars, pubs, restaurants, but equally only a short way from the eye-catching north-east coast.

FEES, BURSARIES

UK & EU Fees, 2009-10: £3,225 p.a., with bursaries on sliding scale if on the Government HE Maintenance Grant. You may also be eligible for an additional Achievement Bursary if you achieve high entry grades. See www.ncl.ac.uk/undergraduate/finance/bursary. They also award sport and academic scholarships. See http://www.ncl.ac.uk/undergraduate/finance/scholarships/index.htm.

STUDENT PROFILE

The student profile reveals a high proportion of public school entrants: 'The pink pashmina and boat shoe brigade do seem to claim the majority,' as a student put it, 'but people tend to separate into their own different groups according to individual taste. There is enough to do to keep all parties happy. Freshers Week tends to be the only time when you have to put up with people who aren't necessarily your kind of people.'

Writes Katie Ashworth: 'There is something that we call 'Rahs' in the halls where I live... they wear tracksuit bottoms and UGG boots, fake tans and all shout at each other in the halls. "Chavs with too much money" is a good description. They're all from down south. Apparently some duke's daughter came here a few years ago, so there's been an influx of the more posh crowd. However, in the rest of the accommodations, there has been more "normal people"; it's just the big self-catering hall that I'm in tends to attract the more sheltered types! I'm in the rock and indie societies, as well as music; there's a lot of music-obsessed people here, and also some people who would be "alternative". Apart from a few exceptions, I've got on with pretty much everyone I've met here. No one cares about what kind of person you are, as long as you're easy to talk to and friendly, everyone gets on.'

ACADEMIA & JOBS

'The general ethos seems to be work hard, play hard,' writes Geraldine England. 'The sta'The general ethos seems to be work hard, play hard,' writes Geraldine England. 'The standard of teaching is generally high, some lecturers being able to communicate with their students better than others.'

In fact, following the *Times Higher Education*'s Student Experience Survey, Newcastle's lecturers get 4 stars out of 5 for interest in their students, but only 3 for small-size tuition groups.

Katie Ashworth is doing English Language and Literature: 'The second semester is better it terms of content for me, as the first was full of fundamental language concepts that were pretty hard to grasp. Syntax could have been taught better, and my seminar leader assumed that we all were at the same starting level. Not true, as some people had

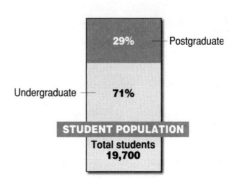

Postgraduate 29%

Undergraduate 71%

STUDENT POPULATION
Total students
19,700

TEACHING SURVEY AT A GLANCE

Avg. UCAS points accepted	**390**
Acceptance rate	**16%**
Overall satisfaction rate	**86%**
Helpful/interested staff	★★★★
Small tuition groups	★★★
Students into graduate jobs	**80%**

Teaching most popular with undergraduates:
Microbiology (100%), Dentistry (98%), Civil, Chemical and other Engineering, Medical Science & Pharmacy (95%), Finance & Accounting (93%), Computer Science, Accounting, Archaeology, Maths, Physical Geography & Enviro. Science (92%), Agriculture, Animal Science, Biology, Law (91%), Subjects allied to Medicine (90%).

Teaching least popular with undergraduates:
Architecture (78%), English Studies, Fine Art (76%), Classics (74%).

done A-level Eng Lang., but I hadn't!

'Tutorials are vital. They give you a chance to ask questions and share ideas. I always go to my seminars, even ones that I don't really have to go to. I think it's important that we all meet as a group every week. Seminars for me have a social side. A few of my tutors are postgraduates, so we sometimes have general chats before we start the academic side. I have met some of my best friends through my tutor groups!

Geraldine continues: 'There are two main libraries, the Robinson library and Medical library, both are well resourced, well staffed and fully computerised, but be prepared for a massive demand on books when it comes to exam time. Don't think that you will be able to pop into the library a day before the holidays and find all the books you need, because you won't. The geeks will have got there first.

SUBJECT AREAS (%)

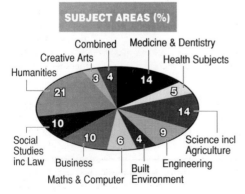

Combined — 4
Creative Arts — 3
Humanities — 21
Medicine & Dentistry — 14
Health Subjects — 5
Science incl Agriculture — 14
Engineering — 9
Built Environment — 4
Maths & Computer — 6
Business — 10
Social Studies inc Law — 10

'Computing facilities at Newcastle are excellent, each department having a number of its own computer clusters, all linked to the net, in addition to those available in the libraries. There is even a large 24-hour access cluster, a godsend because, though you might find it difficult to imagine now, you may well have to work through the night.'

In the teaching assessments, held some time ago, at the very height of academic excellence were Medicine, Physiological Sciences, Psychology, Molecular Biosciences, Pharmacology and subjects allied to Medicine. They scored full marks. Ore recently Newcastle's students voted that the best teaching was in Microbiology, Dentistry, Civil, Chemical and other Engineering, Medical Science & Pharmacy, Finance & Accounting, Computer Science, Accounting, Archaeology, Maths, Physical Geography & Environment Science, Agriculture, Animal Science, Biology, Law, and subjects allied to Medicine, which range from Biochemistry, Human Genetics, Medical Microbiology & Immunology to Speech & Language Sciences at Newcastle.

In the 2008 nationwide assessment of the research provision in our universities, Newcastle came 27th and the best of many world-class (4 stars) and internationally excellent (3 stars) results were Medicine (Cancer), Civil Engineering, Computing, English, Art & Design, and Music - 70% to 90% of the work in these was 4-star or 3-star.

In Medicine, besides the 6-year MB BS (with pre-med year for students without the necessary science background), there's a 4-year accelerated MB BS designed for graduates and a 5-year MB BS, Phase 1 of which can be undertaken here or at Durham Uni's Stockton Campus (south down the A1 on the outskirts of Middlesbrough); all come together at Newcastle for Phase II training in cahoots with the NHS. Clinical relevance is emphasised throughout. You will need AAA at A level. Subjects should include Chemistry and/or Biology at AS or A level. If only one of Biology and/or Chemistry is offered at A or AS level, the other should be offered at GCSE grade A (or Dual Award Science grade A). Neither General Studies nor Critical Thinking counts as an A level qualification. You will also need UKCAT.

Fifteen per cent of all Newcastle graduates get jobs in hospitals, most via a degree in Medicine. Then, it's the civil service, fed by graduates in Architecture, Languages, Social Studies, and Historical and Philosophical Studies; accounting largely from dedicated Accountancy degrees; architectural consultancy - again by the dedicated degree; and personnel recruitment: Social Studies and Languages.

In 2006, the university sought the views of hundreds of organisations to determine what skills they

RESEARCH EXCELLENCE

% of Newcastle's research that is
4* *(World-class) or* **3*** *(Internationally rated):*

	4*	3*
Cancer Studies	15%	75%
Hospital Clinical	15%	50%
Laboratory Clinical	15%	55%
Epidemiology	0%	40%
Health Services	10%	40%
Clinical Psychology	5%	35%
Dentistry	15%	45%
Biological Sciences	15%	45%
Agriculture	5%	40%
Environmental Sciences	15%	50%
Chemistry	5%	40%
Pure Mathematics	5%	30%
Applied Mathematics	15%	45%
Statistics	10%	45%
Computer Science	20%	50%
Electrical/Electronic Eng.	15%	45%
Chemical Engineering	10%	50%
Civil Engineering	20%	70%
Mechanical, Aero., & Manufac. Engineering	15%	50%
Architecture	25%	35%
Town/Country Planning	25%	40%
Geography Environment	10%	45%
Archaeology	15%	35%
Business/Management	10%	40%
Law	0%	40%
Politics	15%	25%
Sociology	15%	35%
Psychology	10%	30%
Education	10%	40%
French	15%	35%
German	20%	25%
Iberian	15%	35%
English	25%	45%
Linguistics	15%	25%
Classics	10%	35%
History	15%	25%
Art and Design	25%	60%
Music	35%	45%

the national final of the Graduate Enterprise Programme in Leicester this year.

Alongside the usual contact with employers and milk round, etc, 'Graduate Connections' is an online database of over 600 Newcastle graduates now employed in a wide range of jobs and professions. They give individual advice, information and insight about the work they do and how to get into a profession.

SOCIAL SCENE

STUDENTS' UNION By night the Union is transformed into one of Newcastle's premier scenes with an ents menu that's included world-class names, such as Lily Allen, Paul Oakenfold, Snow Patrol, The Killers, Coldplay, Arctic Monkeys, DJ Tiesto, Razorlight, Goldfrapp, and The Darkness. For main gigs it's The **Basement** and **Basement 2**, with 1,200 capacity. While for small sets it's the **Global Café** on the top floor, often opened out into the adjacent **Union Lounge** and **MLK Lounge**.

The **Mens Bar** - great pub atmosphere - is Union central, with nearby **Cochrane Lounge**. It gets its name from the Union's Latin motto, 'Men Agitat Molem', meaning, 'Mind Over Matter'. Mondays is *Home made Jam* in the Cochrane Lounge, and Big Screen Live Sport in Men's Bar; Tuesdays - *Union Quiz & Rock n Roll Bingo*; Wednesdays - *Get Your Kit Off*, the official post-sports £1-a-drink session from 6pm; Thursdays are *4 Play* - the official town pub crawl pre-bar, live DJ, £1-a-drink from 6.

Friday nights may be *2 Many Rooms*: Basement - Ben Yates *(Born in the 80's)*, Basement 2 - Sully *(Inertia)*, Green Room - NSR LIVE /RocSoc, Blue Room - *What's in the Box?* On a Friday in April we saw Bombay Bicycle Club. Then there's legendary once-a-month *Brighton Beach night*. Room 1 guitar-based rock & roll and soul classics, Room 2, a heady cocktail of 60's soul, northern soul, jazz, psyche and freakbeat, and new Room 3, the newest cutting edge indie tracks, some obscure classics and a smattering of local talent to boot.

There's a great student music scene, and this year they're opening large studios in a New Music Building, band rehearsal facilities and flexible studio spaces. Says the uni: 'This will be the main base for the loudest activities of the International Centre for Music Studies and will be available for use 24 hours a day.'

Writes Katie: 'Newcastle is MASSIVE! Although the SU night is alright, I'm very into music, so I'd prefer to go to a gig or something. I go to about 2/3 a week. Me and my friends went to a play last semester at the theatre, which is gorgeous, and directly opposite the Union. Nice restaurant, too.'

Once a term they have *Arcane* - all the proceeds

required of graduates. From this feedback, a skills framework was developed which will be used to embed skills development within the curriculum and throughout extra-curricular activities.

An Enterprise Centre turns ideas into action by creating new business, using public and private sector experts as mentors for students, brokering industry expertise in curriculum development and inviting entrepreneurs and other professionals to lecture to students. The culture enabled student companies from Newcastle to win four awards in

fund a student from some underprivileged area of the dark continent. Arcane lasts from about 8pm until 6am. As well as the two main dance floors (Basement, Global), there are specialist drum 'n' bass areas and chill out rooms.

> *Where Newcastle scores over London and, yes, over Manchester, is in its packing an incredible array of cultural, artistic and hedonistic power centres into a very small space (and at relatively low cost).*

'With all these great nights out, some extra cash is bound to come in handy,' writes Geraldine. 'The SU provides a job shop, advertising all kinds of part-time vacancies with accredited employers. It also offers welfare and advisory services in addition to supporting over 100 different societies and more than sixty sports clubs.'

Ents are, indeed, but the beginning. Much is done in the context of the real world outside. Student drama producers, for example, have to survive in real terms, are dependent on public audiences, arrange sponsorship and all the rest. Two or three student-produced plays appear each year either at **Northern Stage Theatre**, located in the centre of the campus, or at **The Gulbenkian**, a small, vigorously experimental studio-type place. There might be a production at **Live**, the theatre on the Quayside.

The *Courier* office (student newspaper) is a crammed galley of a room, space enough for the award-winning weekly to be committed to Quark. There's the award-winning radio station, NSR, too.

Writes Katie: 'There's a MASSIVE range of student societies. I fully recommend joining a few! I'm in English society, indie soc, rock soc and radio society. I participate mostly in radio society, as I interview bands, review gigs and cd's and go to meetings every Tuesday. I go to rock soc socials a lot, some indie and barely any English socs, as I see the English crowd every day anyway! My social life generally revolves around my course, and music. I've pretty much met all of my friends through English lectures and seminars, and gigs, and radio, and stuff like that. I like the girls in my corridor, but I don't have a lot in common with them. The people who I'm moving in with next year are actually from the corridor next to mine: 3 people who I've met here, and my best friend, who I sort of knew from home. I'm good friends with her brother, and he introduced us at a party in the summer holidays. Outside of lectures, I enjoy going to gigs, sleeping and wandering around Newcastle with my friends.'

SPORT The University Sports Centre incorporates a double-court sports hall together with a state-of-the-art 120-station Health and Fitness Suite, three large multipurpose activity halls, four squash courts and a dance studio. Pitches and courts for outdoor games including rugby, hockey, soccer, cricket, tennis and lacrosse are played at Cochrane Park, Heaton and Longbenton, all within 15 minutes by bus. The boat house is on the Tyne at Newburn. There's also an 18-hole golf course about 10 miles west of the city with preferential membership rates.

There's a Talented Athlete Sports Scholarship (TASS) scheme and 57 sports clubs on offer. The uni came 10th nationally last year.

WHAT IT'S REALLY LIKE	
UNIVERSITY:	
Social Life	★★★★★
Campus scene	**Lively, aware, middle-class**
Student Union services	**Good**
Politics	**Active, mainly student issues**
Sport	**57 clubs**
National team position	**10th**
Sport facilities	**Good**
Arts opportunities	**Drama excellent; rest good**
Student magazine	**Pulp**
Student newspaper	**The Courier**
Student radio	**NSR**
Nightclubs	**Global, Beats, Bassment**
Bars	**Mens Bar, Green Room, Cochrane**
Union ents	**Chart, dance, Indie, d'n b, live, & Arcane**
Union societies	**100**
Most popular societies	**NUTS (theatre), Cheerleading, Jazz**
Parking	**Adequate**
CITY:	
Entertainment	★★★★★
Scene	**Vibrant, fun**
Town/gown relations	**OK**
Risk of violence	**Low**
Cost of living	**Low**
Student concessions	**Good**
Survival + 2 nights out	**£70 pw**
Part-time work campus/town	**Average/excellent**

Town See Student Newcastle.

PILLOW TALK

Newcastle have a torturously worded test for uni accommodation, but as it allows first year undergraduates 'who will be coming alone to the University for the full academic year', the policy is effectively pretty inclusive. Local students will have more of a problem than those from afar, and be sure to get the application form in by 30 June.

Castle Leazes Halls and Henderson Hall are catered. Self-catered flats include: Richardson Road, Marris House, St Mary's College, Windsor Terrace, Leazes Parade, and Bowsden Court Shared Flats. There's also couple and family accommodation, and places adapted for students with disabilities.

Magnet Court opened recently, 3 and 4-bedroomed flats with en-suite shower rooms, situated in city-centre, just 5 min. walk from campus.

ACCOMMODATION	
Guarantee to freshers	**100%**
Style	**Halls, flats**
Security guard	**Team on rota**
Shared rooms	**None**
Internet access	**All**
Self-catered	**Some halls, all flats**
En suite	**Some**
Approx price range pw	**£69-£113**
City rent pw	**£45-£80**

GETTING THERE

☛ By road: A1, A167/A696; A167 exit.
☛ By rail: Edinburgh, 1:30; Leeds, 1:45; London King's Cross, 3:00; Manchester Piccadilly, 3:00; Birmingham New Street, 4:00.
☛ By air: Newcastle International Airport.
☛ By coach: London, 6:05; Birmingham, 4:25.

UNIVERSITY OF WALES, NEWPORT

University of Wales, Newport
Caerleon Campus
PO Box 101
Newport NP18 1YH

TEL 01633 432030, 432432
FAX 01633 432850
EMAIL admissions@newport.ac.uk
WEB www.newport.ac.uk

Newport Students' Union
College Crescent
Caerleon
Newport NP18 3YG

TEL 01633 432076
FAX 01633 432688
WEB www.newportunion.com

VAG VIEW

*U*niversity of Wales, Newport, came out of Gwent College of Higher Education. It became a University College in 1996 and a fully fledged university in 2003. During this period we watched it achieve huge success in a particular area, oblivious to Government assessment that most of its courses were merely Satisfactory. While the wheels of bureaucracy ground it down, Hollywood beckoned, and its students were nominated for Oscars and won BAFTA awards. Finally, in 2001, the Establishment had to take notice, and awarded its Art, Media & Design provision a top rating for research, recognising its international importance. Seven years on, the new assessment has found that 60% of its research provision is either world-class or internationally excellent. Engineering has even got a bit of a world-class reputation now too.

Overall, 76% of students like what's going

UNIVERSITY/STUDENT PROFILE	
University since	**2003**
Situation/style	**Campus**
Student population	**9780**
Total undergraduates	**7480**
Mature undergraduates	**39%**
International undergrads	**3%**
Male/female ratio	**45:55**
Equality of opportunity:	
state school intake	**99%**
social class 4-7 intake	**38%**
low-participation area intake	**16%**

TEACHING SURVEY AT A GLANCE

Avg. UCAS points accepted	**200**
Acceptance rate	**22%**
Overall satisfaction rate	**76%**
Helpful/interested staff	**No data**
Small tuition groups	**No data**
Students into graduate jobs	**73%**

Teaching most popular with undergraduates:
Social Studies (92%), Social Work (91%),
Business (87%), Business & Administrative
Studies (83%), Initial Teacher Training (80%).

Teaching least popular with undergraduates:
Creative Arts & Design (63%-65%), Film &
Photography, Design Studies (63%), Computer
Science (62%).

*down at Newport, and said so in the recent
National Student Survey. Only 9% fail to finish
their courses, which is about average and actually below the Government benchmark for
Newport.*

CAMPUS

Newport, Gwent, lies half way between Bristol and
Cardiff; it is the first town of any size you come to
travelling west along the M4 from England.
Activities are split between two campus sites:
Newport itself and, 10 mins to the north, Caerleon
- 'City of Legions and Court of King Arthur,' accord-
ing to Geoffrey of Monmouth. Caerleon is where
all the real stuff goes on.

The village of Caerleon, supposed site of
Camelot, takes us back into the mists of time.
There are still Roman baths and a fortress to be
seen, but the area is a tourist draw as much for its
beauty. To the east lies the Wye Valley and the Usk,
on whose banks lie the ruins of Tintern Abbey,

which inspired Wordsworth to write one of his
most important poems. To the west are the Welsh
valleys, industrial heartland of South Wales.

It is a safe and friendly campus, and typically
a guy from Gloucestershire reading documentary
photography said he had been won over by the
green fields as much as the course.

The Newport campus, known as Allt-yr-yn, is
home to the Newport Business School, to computing, engineering and the School of Health and
Social Sciences. It has none of the mystery of
Caerleon, but seems to be enjoying Newport's rise
just as much. There's an hourly shuttle between
the two.

All is soon to be complicated by the opening of
a new campus, first phase in a £50-million expansion. Being built as we write, down in the valley by
the river, opposite the Riverfront Arts Theatre,
which one hears so much about and which has its
own bar and independent film club and art gallery,
the new campus will house the glitzy School of Art,
Media and Design. With it, the uni is looking to
double its population within a year.

FEES, BURSARIES

UK & EU Fees for 2009-10, £3,225. Welsh entrants
are eligible for a grant of £1,800. There are scholarships available to students who have represented
their country or region in sport.

STUDENT PROFILE

As many as 56% of undergraduates are part-timers,
and 39% are mature. The Caerleon profile is not
easy to run to ground. You've got arty types and
rugger buggers and mysterious geeks with hobbit-
style goatees left to run wild. They are broadly a
new-university crew, 38% working class and 16%
from that nebulous 'low-participation' neighbourhood. The gender balance is pretty healthy (55%
female).

ACADEMIA & JOBS

The faculty or school that is causing all the fuss is
the Newport School of Art Media and Design. It
offers courses under the banners, Art &
Photography, Film and Animation, Performing
Arts, and Design.

Film is a big deal here. There are some of the
best art and design facilities in Europe, whose students are taking the world of film animation by
storm, with one film, Famous Fred, being nominated for a Hollywood Oscar, others, such as
Human Traffic and Waking Ned enjoying great
commercial success, and The Gogs winning its student makers a clutch of BAFTA awards. Not only
could the uni boast 60 of its graduates no less on
the credit list of the massive hit, Chicken Run, but

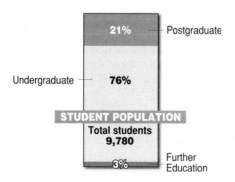

Postgraduate 21%

Undergraduate 76%

STUDENT POPULATION
Total students
9,780

Further
Education 3%

also *Women in Love* director Ken Russell (he late of Big Brother) is this year working closely with the department of film and video.

Camelot has become the International Film School, Wales, with BA (Hons) Animation, Cinema Studies & Scriptwriting, Computer Games Design, Documentary Film & Television, Film & Video, Performing Arts, MA Animation, and MA Film, BA Creative Sound & Music, Documentary Photography (BA and MA), Fine Art, Photographic Art, Photography for Advertising & Fashion, New Media Publishing, and MA Art.

If this is your bent, go for it, not least because they are among the top graduate providers to the film industry. Eight years ago, we wrote: 'What comes across is that Newport provides an imaginative environment. Subtlety, humour and creative thinking are to the fore.' We can find no reason to change that view.

Meanwhile, there's the Newport Business School, the School of Health & Social Sciences, the Centre for Community and Lifelong Learning, and Education - Primary Initial teacher training at the uni was designated as 'Excellent' by the Higher Education Funding Council for Wales in 2000.

Foundation courses leading to direct entry into the uni are available in Science, Technology, Info Technology (Computing, Business Studies, Statistics), Humanities (English, History, Media Studies), Labour Studies, Business Studies, Social Studies, Youth & Community Work and Politics.

SOCIAL SCENE

STUDENTS' UNION For ents, Caerleon is the centre of things, and students from Allt-r-yn flock to it. Halloween Ball in **Main Hall** (now 1,000 capacity) is the big deal. Otherwise, it's pretty limp, with 'Film Sundays', where two classic films are shown back to back, live music from up and coming indie acts, comedy nights, quiz nights, karaoke, bowling trips and *Bar FTSE* - beat the bar for the cheapest drinks before your Wednesday night in town, see

RESEARCH EXCELLENCE		
% of Newport's research that is 4* (World-class) or 3* (Internationally rated):		
	4*	3*
Mechanical, Aero. & Manufacturing Eng.	10%	15%
Social Work	5%	40%
Education	0%	0%
History	0%	20%
Art and Design	10%	60%

Student Cardiff. Saturdays are *Nebula*, which is basically a re-branding of the main venue into a nightclub scene.

Meanwhile, the Rathwell building is student central, and drawing big audiences among the student throng is live music in the **Clarence Bar**. There is also a refectory and café bar. We tried the vegetable curry, £2.30, at the café. The refectory meals looked better, but the rice was a well-advised solid base for a night's drinking at the Clarence, equipped outside front with one of those cash machines that charges you for use, a dirty touch. The bar hosts karaoke, Chris Tarrant-inspired 'Who wants to win a crate of beer?' and other quizzes. Also figuring large in students' lives is Newport's own **TJ's** - bar, disco and music venue.

As for student societies, up until recently Rugby was the deal, and maybe it still is, but there have been some dramatic changes in the society calendar, instigated by the founding of News Port, Radio Noize, and NTV, an online, on-demand station entertainment and information service for students, as well as a space to showcase their own work. *News Port* is a bi-weekly newspaper.

Jennifer Moran, who runs NTV, captured perfectly the real point of student societies: 'I realised this last year, that I wanted more. Not just more of what I was already doing. I wanted something else, something more to walk away with in my experience of University. When I was offered the role of manager for NTV, I knew this was the something. Of course I knew it would be challenging, it would be hard work from my spare time and definitely stressful at times. It was worth it without a doubt. I know this because when I look back at my time here, and imagine not having had this experience I feel like I have lost something. At the end of the day there were fun times, and its been a stepping stone in my self development.'

Think on, as you stagger down the road into Cardiff for another night out.

The Union is also active on student awareness

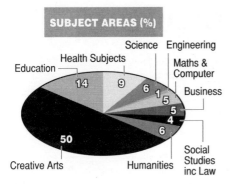

SUBJECT AREAS (%)

Science Engineering
Health Subjects
Education Maths & Computer
14 9 6 1 5 Business
5
4
6
50
Creative Arts Humanities Social Studies inc Law

WHAT IT'S REALLY LIKE

UNIVERSITY:	
Social Life	★★★
Campus scene	**Lively**
Student Union services	**Good**
Politics	**Active**
Sport	**Relaxed**
National team position	**121st**
Sport facilities	**Good**
Arts opportunities	**Good**
Student radio	**Radio Noize**
Student newspaper	**News Port**
Student online TV	**NTV**
Venue	**Main Hall**
Bar	**The Clarence**
Union ents	**Chees and live; good May Ball**
Union societies	**23**
Most popular society	**Rugby**
Parking	**Adequate**
TOWN:	
Entertainment	★★
Scene	**Pubs, clubs**
Town/gown relations	**OK**
Risk of violence	**Low**
Cost of living	**Average**
Student concessions	**Good**
Survival + 2 nights out	**£60 pw**
Part-time work campus/town	**Good**

concern (a student development officer is *in place*).

Sport There are 15 clubs, from Surf to Skiing, Rugby to Mountain Sports, boosted on Caerleon with a Sports Centre, hall, gym, fitness suite; also a rugby pitch and 2 floodlit tennis (there's a popular Tennis Academy) and netball courts. There is a need for more sports fields, and the athletic union eye one particular car park with degrees of envy and bitterness, as it was once a hockey pitch. There's no squash or swimming. For these it's off to public facilities in Newport, a centre where some champion Norwegian cyclist, who I should have heard of, does his stuff. They get involved with the Welsh Rugby Union and Cricket Association, and run courses to enable students to pick up nationally recognised coaching qualifications. Within easy reach are facilities for sailing and windsurfing, dry-slope skiing, caving, canoeing, mountain biking, rock climbing, orienteering and hill walking.

PILLOW TALK

They have 650 self-catered single study bedrooms on Caerleon. Every first year student who applies before September 1 will be satisfied. Traditional halls Abergavenny, Blaenavon, Camelot cost least, while Dolaucothi, more bog standard than most, comes in at £56.

GETTING THERE

☞ By road: M4/J25. If approaching Caerleon from Cardiff, there is no direct exit from the J25. Either exit at J26, or take J24 and U-turn at r/about to approach Junction 25 from the East.
☞ By rail: London Paddington, 1:50; Birmingham New Street, 2:00; Cardiff, 40 mins; Bristol Parkway, 25 mins.
☞ By coach: London, 2:45; Manchester, 5:15.
☞ By air: Direct coach from Heathrow, Gatwick.

campaigns, which have included breast cancer, access & equality, anonymous marking, sexual health and drug awareness. There is also a good focus on theatre, dance, etc, through the Performing Arts department, and Newport's **Riverfront Arts Theatre** figures strongly.

It is all a surprisingly eclectic and energetic mix, with regular art exhibitions vying with sporting nights, e-culture (**Cyber Café**) and student

UNIVERSITY OF NORTHAMPTON

The University of Northampton
Boughton Green Road
Moulton Park
Northampton NN2 7AL

TEL 0800 358 2232; 01604 735 500
FAX 01604 713083
EMAIL admissions@northampton.ac.uk
WEB www.northampton.ac.uk

Northampton Students' Union
Boughton Green Road
Moulton Park
Northampton NN2 7AL

TEL 01604 892818
FAX 01604 719454
EMAIL [firstname.surname]@ucnu.org
WEB www.northamptonunion.com

UNIVERSITY/STUDENT PROFILE

University since	**1999**
Situation/style	**Campus**
Student population	**10645**
Total undergraduates	**9065**
Mature undergraduates	**45%**
International undergrads	**5%**
Male/female ratio	**33:67**
Equality of opportunity:	
state school intake	**97%**
social class 4-7 intake	**36%**
low-participation area intake	**13%**

VAG VIEW

*U*niversity College Northampton became *Northampton University in October 2005. But it nearly didn't happen. Apparently, Henry III dissolved the original Northampton University in 1265, for no other reason than that it posed a direct threat to the University of Oxford - he had been advised by his bishops that many students from Oxford had migrated to it. A Royal command is law, but UCN put their legal beavers onto it, and the way was made clear. Oxford must be quaking in anticipation of the application backlash.*

In the Higher Education Funding Council's National Student Survey, 81% of students approved of what's going down at Northants, but to be honest it's very little on the extra-curricular side. The drop-out rate is nudging 11%, which is over the Government benchmark.

CAMPUS

The main Park campus, an 80-acre estate on the edge of town, has been well designed. What strikes the visitor immediately is the careful architectural

SUBJECT AREAS (%)

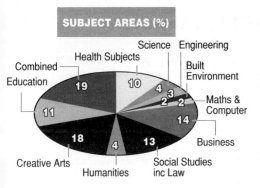

- Science: 10
- Engineering: 4
- Health Subjects
- Combined: 19
- Education: 11
- Built Environment: 3
- Maths & Computer: 2 2
- Business: 14
- Social Studies inc Law: 13
- Humanities: 4
- Creative Arts: 18

integration of facilities and services, none of which limit or indeed offend the eye. Halls are in among lecture theatres, sports centre by the nightclub, eaterie and bar; a rugby pitch in the centre of things gives a welcome sense of space and a reminder that rugby is a religion both here and in town, which has one of the best teams in the Premier League.

Close by is the intriguing Leather Conservation Centre - (Northampton is the centre of the shoe industry; the football ground is called The Cobblers). Some buildings are named after villages in the county, the halls after notable people of the area, including the tragic Northamptonshire

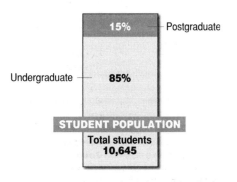

- **15%** — Postgraduate
- Undergraduate — **85%**

STUDENT POPULATION
Total students 10,645

poet John Clare, whose parents were illiterate, but who achieved national renown in his day by imbibing the spirit of this place before going insane.

Artistically, the focus is at UCN's Avenue campus in town, however. This 24-acre site - 20 mins away from Park and linked by a free bus service - houses Art, Design, Technology and Performance Arts. In particular there's quite a tradition for theatre.

FEES, BURSARIES

UK & EU Fees, 2009-2010: £3,225 p.a. Deal directly with the university about bursaries and scholarships.

STUDENT PROFILE

Most undergraduates are local; 45% are mature and 24% part-timers.

ACADEMIA & JOBS

There are three faculties. The Faculty of Applied Sciences includes schools of Leather Technology, Built Environment, Engineering & Technology, Environmental Science, Health & Life Sciences, and Nursing & Midwifery. Medical sciences have links with the General Hospital in Northampton and with Milton Keynes, 'Nursing courses are always over-subscribed,' I was told.

RESEARCH EXCELLENCE		
% of Northampton's research that is *4* (World-class) or 3* (Internationally rated):*		
	4*	**3***
Health Professions	**5%**	**5%**
Metallurgy and Materials	**0%**	**20%**
Business/Management	**5%**	**10%**
Education	**5%**	**10%**
Asian Studies	**0%**	**10%**
English	**0%**	**15%**
History	**5%**	**35%**
Art and Design	**0%**	**5%**
Performing Arts	**0%**	**25%**

The Faculty of Arts & Social Sciences includes Art & Design, Behavioural Studies (including a BSc in Psychology), Cultural Studies (such as a cross-cultural degree in Performance Studies - Drama, Dance, Music), Education (BA Hons QTS Primary), and Social Studies (American Studies, History, Sociology).

The Faculty of Management & Business includes the schools of Business, Information Systems, Law & International Business, Professional Studies (Finance and Accounting) and Management (MMB, MSc Management Studies).

A first this year is a degree in accounting, a foundation degree developed with the NHS and directed specifically at the Service's perennial problem in balancing its budgets.

Career strength in the health sector comes out of the occupational therapy and podiatry degrees. Countrywide, Salford and Northampton probably offer the best value - entry requirements to job satisfaction. There are strong links with the General Hospital in Northampton and Milton Keynes, a top notch teaching assessment result and a low entry requirement as well as the strong employment reputation makes it attractive.

Furniture design and manufacture is another niche employment strength. Northampton is in the heart of the leather industry, and furniture was probably always on the agenda for Product Design students. There is also a fast employment flow into these industries out of the Management & Business faculty up at Park (design being at Avenue Campus).

Graphic artists are particularly employable through BA Graphic Communication, and designers and sculptors also register with relatively strong prospects in the employment league.

In the business sector personnel officers/managers are particularly well served, the rush of graduates into the sector coming from a range of courses featuring Human Resource Management, like the 4-year sandwich BA Hons degree, Human Resource Management.

Most of the Education provision finds expression in primary school teaching. You'll be at Park.

SOCIAL SCENE

STUDENTS' UNION A new £1.65m 'Student Centre' has opened on Park Campus. But there's little going on by way of ents, students preferring **Lava Ignite** and the new club **Fever** in town on a Saturday. There are free buses from Park into town. The Union's become a bit of a place for hire, though *Lockdown* on Friday attracts some of the faithful.

Perhaps we shouldn't be surprised, most undergraduates are local, almost a quarter part-timers. In a spirit of loyalty they've kept the same names of bar and nightclub (by day a stylish diner) - **nn2**, and **Laidback's** still the café bar. The other bar, **Pavilion**, with views over games pitches and Sky TV, is now the university's and not the union's to run.

At **George's**, the hub of Avenue Union, a bar is open till 2 am Fridays for the regular clubnight, variously known as *Club Friday* and *Friday the 13th.* While we were there they had a hypnotist and comedian and Bar Footsie (Stock Exchange drinks promo).

The student newspaper *Wave* and newsletter *Xpress* have slipped into oblivion. Of 20 societies, Christian Union, kickboxing and Islam are most active. Twenty sports clubs play some 50 teams.

PILLOW TALK

Uni accommodation is guaranteed to 'first and firm choices' in halls or flats (some 67% are en suite).

GETTING THERE

☛ By road: M1/J15/15a/16; easy access to M5/6/25/40, A1 and A45.
☛ By rail: London and Birmingham, 1:00.
☛ By coach: London, 2:00; Birmingham, 1:35.

ACCOMMODATION	
Guarantee to freshers	**100%**
Style	**Halls, flats**
Security guard	**All**
Shared rooms	**Some**
Internet access	**All**
Self-catered	**All**
En suite	**Most**
Approx price range pw	**£36.20-£75.75**
City rent pw	**£45**

UNIVERSITY OF NORTHUMBRIA

University of Northumbria
Northumberland Road
Newcastle upon Tyne NE1 8ST

TEL 0191 243 7420
FAX 0191 227 4561
EMAIL ca.marketing@northumbria.ac.uk
WEB www.northumbria.ac.uk

Northumbria Students' Union
2 Sandyford Road
Newcastle Upon Tyne NE1 8SB

TEL 0191 227 4757
FAX 0191 227 3760
EMAIL su.enquiries@unn.ac.uk
WEB www.mynsu.co.uk

VAG VIEW

*T*he two universities in the city of Newcastle are situated within walking distance of one another. 'I think what is important about being a student in Newcastle is that the poly and the uni mix very well. There is little snobbery, rather a healthy competitive rivalry, especially when it comes to sport. Very often students find themselves living in a house with both uni and poly students, which is unheard of in places like Oxford. The poly has a far greater mix of people (the uni being overrun by people from public school). But don't be put off by this - Newcastle, as a city, caters for every taste and every person, and I have not heard of anyone who has not enjoyed it.'

So said Susannah Bell. Over the years the poly (Northumbria is not beleaguered by the distinction, any more than is KCL, when taunted with it by UCL) has held its own with Newcastle, often enough beaten it in sport, though last year Newcastle came 10th and Northumberland 16th in the overall national team positions. Sure there is an essential difference, Northumberland has 25% part-timers, Newcastle none, which places it firmly in the more local-college cate-

UNIVERSITY/STUDENT PROFILE	
University since	**1992**
Situation/style	**Civic**
Student population	**29850**
Total undergraduates	**22825**
Mature undergraduates	**30%**
International undergrads	**21%**
Male/female ratio	**46:54**
Equality of opportunity:	
state school intake	**91%**
social class 4-7 intake	**32%**
low-participation area intake	**14%**

gory, and while Northumberland's mature undergraduate population is 30%, Newcastle's is just 8%, and there is no contest when it comes to research - Newcastle stands at 27th in the country, Northumbria at 81st, though no subject submitted by Northumbria achieved less than 60% of its research rated at international level, and interestingly Northumbris rose 18 places this time, and Newcastle only 5.

Best of all, some of our ex-polys - Northumbria, like the others, took University title in 1992 - have not taken on board the significance of the student culture in student development. Northumbria did, and took big strides. Then it seemed to lose its head of steam. Now it's back on top again with more than 50 student societies and a refurbished Students' Union. In the National Student Survey, undertaken by the Higher Education Funding Council, which is answerable to the Government, Newcastle showed 86% student satisfaction and Northumbria 84%, and when it came to getting real graduate jobs within six months after graduation, Northumbria, with 81% graduates employed, pipped Newcastle by 1%.

All said, Northumbria is a powerhouse of a university, taking higher education into

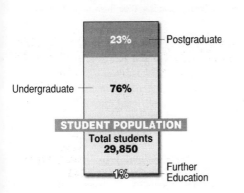

Postgraduate 23%

Undergraduate 76%

STUDENT POPULATION
Total students
29,850

Further Education 1%

areas Newcastle can never reach. That's two places ahead of Newcastle Uni.

CAMPUSES

CITY CAMPUS (address above) Student Union, library, sports centre, language laboratories, art gallery.

COACH LANE CAMPUS Coach Lane, Benton, Newcastle upon Tyne NE7 7XA. Tel: 0191 215 6000. Recent beneficiary of a £40-million development. Health, Social Work & Education are here. Coach Lane also has a Union, library and computing facilities, a sports hall, fitness suite, activity studio and all-weather hockey pitch.

FEES, BURSARIES

UK & EU Fees, 2009-10: £3,225 p.a. There are bursaries for those in receipt of the HE Maintenance Grant, and academic and sports scholarships. See www.northumbria.ac.uk/scholarships and www.teamnorthumbria.com/performancesport.

STUDENT PROFILE

Around 6,000 part-timers and half those are mature; meanwhile 32% of all undergraduates come from the lower socio-economic orders, and 14% from 'low-participation' neighbourhoods. It is hardly the traditional picture, but Northumbria makes it work. Only 7% of their undergraduates fail to complete the course (well below their Government benchmark), and 81% end up with real graduate jobs 6 months after graduating.

'Best thing,' said Jack Ford when he alighted there for the first time, 'was the relaxed atmosphere that enables students to bond and make lots of new friends.'

ACADEMIA & JOBS

Health is a crucial provision just as it is for the other uni. While Newcastle Uni has Medicine, Northumbria has Nursing (which achieved full marks at the teaching assessments), Midwifery, Physiotherapy, and Occupational Therapy. There are also some excellent Social Science degrees, including a key Law degree, a 4-year 'fast-track' Exempting degree. Another defining mark of Northumbria is its fashion department. They are even opening a School of Design in London - a new campus in Islington, offering fashion courses.

Students say the best teaching is in Accounting,

TEACHING SURVEY AT A GLANCE	
Avg. UCAS points accepted	**280**
Acceptance rate	**25%**
Overall satisfaction rate	**84%**
Helpful/interested staff	★★★
Small tuition groups	★★★
Students into graduate jobs	**81%**

Teaching most popular with undergraduates:
Accounting (100%), Psychology (95%), Human & Social Geography, Physical Geography and Environmental Science (93%), Chemistry, Initial Teacher Training (92%), Computer Science, Sociology (90%).

Teaching least popular with undergraduates:
Social Work (66%).

Psychology, Human & Social Geography, Physical Geography & Environmental Science, Chemistry, Initial Teacher Training, Computer Science, and Sociology.

Business is a dominant force at Northumbria, producing 16% of all graduate jobs here. Besides Accountancy, there's an excellent career niche degree is their 4-year sandwich BA Human Resource Management. Northumbria's health provision follows with only a few jobs less, and in third place, perhaps surprisingly, is Art & Design, a part of the curriculum that also showed up well in the research assessment. Of course the fashion element comes in here, and there are niche degrees like Apparel Design & Retail Merchandising, hardwired to employment, and there is Furniture Design, and Computer-aided Product Design, but also Dance and Drama, and together the whole thing explodes into an exceptional 300-odd jobs (that's 13% of total) at the end of the year.

Northumbria's School of Law is authorised by both the Law Society and the Bar Council to run the only 4-year Exempting LLB degree, in the UK

Contact with industry in the North East region is facilitated by all sorts of strategies, not least Northumbria's e.Business Centre, which dispenses advice and support to small and medium sized businesses, utilising uni expertise in law, technology, marketing and business.

Property developers, architects, construction managers, quantity surveyors and estate agents pour out of Northumbria too. There's a mix here of Business and Building/Engineering graduates boosting employment figures in Property

Development. The uni's Business & Management expertise is second to none - see the new 3-year Corporate Management degree, broken down into one year intensive learning, then two years on a work placement followed by a final six months to complete a dissertation.

In building, BA Architectural Design & Management sits alongside BEng Building Services Engineering, and BSc Architectural Technology, Building Design Mgt, Building Project Mgt, Commercial Quantity Surveying, Building Surveying, Construction Management, Estate Management, etc (foundation degrees available in many of these).

The School of Law, with its unique 4-year Exempting LLB degree, exempting the would-be solicitor from the need for further professional vocational training, has its own clear line, as do degrees in Politics, Social Work, and Social & Public Policy into the community and government administration (local, regional, and central), a destination that accounts for 198 graduates a year.

SOCIAL SCENE

WHAT IT'S REALLY LIKE

UNIVERSITY:

Social Life	★★★★
Campus scene	**Lively, less self-conscious**
Student Union services	**Average**
Politics	**Average**
Sport	**Key**
National team position	**16th**
Sport facilities	**Good**
Arts opportunities	**Drama, music, film good; dance, art average**
Student newspaper	**Northumbria Student**
Nightclubs	**New Bar, Stage 2**
Bars	**Reds, Bar One, Coach Lane**
Union ents	**Big club nights and live gigs**
Union societies	**53**
Parking	**Poor**
CITY:	
Entertainment	★★★★★
Scene	**Vibrant, fun**
Town/gown relations	**OK**
Risk of violence	**Low**
Cost of living	**Low**
Student concessions	**Good**
Survival + 2 nights out	**£70 pw**
Part-time work campus/town	**Average/excellent**

RESEARCH EXCELLENCE

% of Northumbria's research that is
4* *(World-class) or* **3*** *(Internationally rated):*

	4*	3*
Nursing/Midwifery	**15%**	**35%**
Health Professions	**5%**	**25%**
General Engineering	**5%**	**45%**
Built Environment	**5%**	**45%**
Business/Management	**0%**	**20%**
Social Work	**5%**	**30%**
Psychology	**0%**	**25%**
Sports	**5%**	**15%**
English	**5%**	**20%**
History	**0%**	**20%**
Art and Design	**15%**	**30%**
History of Art	**15%**	**15%**

At City Campus they recently opened a £2-million **New Bar**, an official warm-up bar for club nights on campus and in town. Then there's **Stage 2** with 'the largest student cinema screen in the country', so they claim. 'When we are not showing films or hosting live comedy, Stage 2 turns into one of the best music venues in the North.' Amy Winehouse, Maximo Park, and the Racounteurs have done their stuff here. Several bars in one, the venue's capacity is 3,000 and becomes everyone's favourite nightclub for *The Saturday Project* (10 till 3). Even so, **Reds Bar** (circular bar, capacity 500) is the main club venue, packed to the rafters all week long, from Alt Events such as *Get Yer Skates On* to *The Poundin'* and weekly cheese fest *Wiggle*. There's also **Bar One**, on the ground floor. Coach Lane campus has a big hall, one bar and one major club-night on a Thursday.

'We promote our own DJs in Reds.' There are also good opportunities for DJs to make the transition to city clubs. 'One of our DJs, who does Saturday night *Wiggle*, was a student here, and now he's working six nights a week in bars and nightclubs in town.'

There's also a decent drama society - 3 or 4 productions a year, a monthly newspaper, by name of *Northumbria Student*, looking for contributors, and they're totally involved with Newcastle Uni's LSR radio station.

Probably the most active of the 30 societies is Community Student Action. GLOBE - Gay, lesbian & Bisexual - get involved in national campaigns. Three years ago they invested £1 million in the Student Services department - the counselling, careers and study skills services.

SPORT Lots to offer, well-equipped sports hall, gym and indoor tennis courts, options to do anything from scuba diving to rugby, which has some very high-class teams and regularly trounces Newcastle Uni, good hockey, football and tennis. They run an Elite Athlete Programme - Team Northumbria - which offers practical and financial support to students with particular potential. Maybe too high class, one student complained that there's only 3 uni football teams and it's hard to get a trial date.

It won't get any easier once word gets around about the £26 million new sports facility opening in 2010.

PILLOW TALK

They guarantee only 57% fresher accommodation, but priority is given to non-locals. First-year accommodation consists of halls and flats. There are catered and self-catered halls, none en suite, no car parking, none with a security guard, but all on or pretty close to campus. Claude Gibb is the most popular hall, being in crawling distance of town and lectures - 'more of a public school crowd here,' said one. Lovaine, also on campus, is handy but poky. Of the flats a student recommended Glenamara and Stephenson, both with the advantage of a central location. See descriptions and clear map at www.northumbria.ac.uk/brochure /facilities/acc/halls/?view = Standard. The flats do look more likely, some are en suite, all are self-catering, most have internet access, and some even have car parking and security. Ask the right

ACCOMMODATION	
Guarantee to freshers	**57%**
Style	**Halls, flats**
Security guard	**Not halls, but some flats**
Shared rooms	**None**
Internet access	**Most**
Self-catered	**Some halls, most flats**
En suite	**Not halls, some flats**
Approx price range pw	**£65-£126**
City rent pw	**£45-£80**

questions of the Accommodation office as soon as possible.

GETTING THERE

☛ By road to Newcastle: A1(M) from the south and north; A19 from York; A69 from the west; M6 from the southwest.

☛ By road to Carlisle: A7 from the north; M6 from the south; A69 from Newcastle (the east).

☛ By rail to Newcastle: Edinburgh, 1:30; Leeds, 1:45; London King's Cross, 3:00; Manchester Piccadilly, 3:00; Birmingham New Street, 4:00.

☛ By air: Newcastle International airport.

☛ By coach: London, 6:05; Birmingham, 4:25.

STUDENT NOTTINGHAM - THE CITY

Nottingham is without doubt, the best city in the country for a student. Situated in the Midlands, it's never too far UK students to get home, and being in the middle of the country, you get a really good mix of both southern and northern students along with the grounded Nottingham locals themselves.

There are two universities and eight further education colleges in Nottingham, a bustling city that has come into its own, it almost seems, in the very process of catering for the huge number of students it attracts.

LIVE MUSIC

For its sheer size and the big names it attracts, the best venue for live music has to be the **Ice Centre**, situated in the **Lace Market**. The Strokes, Kelly Clarkson and the Little Britain Tour have all been there recently. The drinks are extortionately priced, but if you want to see the big names it generally does mean big bucks.

A venue for live music acts with more *cred.* is the less-commercial **Rock City**. City centre situated, and a lot more edgy, **Rock City** has hosted such as The Killers and Oasis in this small but very atmospheric club. With student club nights throughout the week, this is a *must* if you want to dodge the cheese and get heavily into eyeliner.

If its un-discovered talent you're after, then look no further than the **Rescue Rooms**, which is just round the corner and almost a pint-sized version of **Rock City**.

Live music is really taking off in Nottingham and even Trent's Student Union is jumping on the bandwagon, hosting its very own live music night with some great up-coming bands every second Friday.

CLUBBING

Nottingham is now seen as a bar city, not first and foremost club orientated. Yet, with the mix of clubs it has, catering for all wants and tastes, you will be hard pushed to find better elsewhere. The newlish **Oceana** is very popular with students – 5 rooms filled with different atmospheres and music – but again be prepared to spend a penny or two. The city also has **Mode** nightclub and **Lost Weekend**, both with great student nights, cheap drinks and cheesy tunes.

But the clubs of all clubs remains the mighty **Ocean** nightclub. Not to be confused with **Oceana**, it has just become solely a student nightclub every day of the week, with both universities holding nights. You're guaranteed a good night out, if drunken sportsmen, scantily clad ladies and cheap drinks and cheese is your cup of tea.

For an alternative night, try **Stealth**, **The Cookie Club** and **The Bomb**. The venues are slightly more intimate, a lot smaller, but by no less lively.

DRINKING

Nottingham Trent Students Union offers a fantastic place to drink with its **Glo** bar being well equipped for both chilling out and dancing, and its **Sub** bar to kick back and play some pool. **The Ark** at Nottingham Uni's Students Union is no way near as big, but still offers the usual guarantee of cheap drinks and cheese.

In the city centre, **The Horn in Hand**, **Varsity**, **Templars**, **Up and Down Under** and **Walkabout** are very student populated, give student discounts and offer a relaxed atmosphere. Each has a new deal each week.

For more sophistication, try Hockley and the Lace Market, where most of the following are situated – **Revolution** (over 100 different vodka shots can be tried and consumed), **Tantra** (you can hire out beds for the evening), **Quilted Lama** (with its enormous fish bowls), and the sometime church come bar, **Pitcher and Piano**. But be warned, it won't come cheap.

The Waterfront takes it home at the other side of town, and has 7 bars spread across 7 floors. In summer time, the canal-side terrace is packed.

SHOPPING

Prepare to spend, spend, spend when you come to Nottingham and hit the shops. It is worryingly easy to blow your student loan on the incredible shopping experience that Nottingham offers. There are all the chain stores, many cool trendy shops and it's rife with factory shops. Go to the **Victoria Centre** for day-to-day student favourites, the brand new **Topshop**, **La Senza**, **Republic**, and such as HMV, Boots... Along with its market, department store and supermarket, it caters for everyone. **The Broadmarsh** is at the other end of town and is again a shopping complex, but offers fair-priced **H&M**, **TK Max** and **New Look**. **The Broadmarsh** is very handy for fancy dress outfits at a cut rate, too.

If you want to spend that bit more, then walk down Bridlesmith Gate to **Flannels**, **Diesel** and **Kurt Geiger**. You really can get your heart desire, from retro gear at **Ice Nine** and **Wild Clothing** to everyday fashions at **Warehouse** and Zara.

EATING

Whether you are looking for quality (somewhere to drag your parents), quantity (eat all you want), or somewhere to bring your own wine, Nottingham does not disappoint. The **Corner House** in the city centre offers an array of different cuisine from Flaming Dragon, the Chinese buffet, to Bella Italia, a very fair priced and tasty Italian. American style diners proliferate around the city centre, including **Hard Rock Café** and **Frankie and Benny's**, while Hockley has **Fresh**, a great place to eat and very healthy, and some great bars that offer good, extravagant bar meals, like **Browns** and the **Hog's Head**.

For daytime snacking, it's **Subways**, the individual outlets scattered across the city, and you'll find a favourite dive among a whole host of small, reasonably priced city café's.

Whatever you're in the mood for, whatever your needs and requirements, Nottingham really does have something for everyone.

Annabel Woollen

UNIVERSITY OF NOTTINGHAM

The University of Nottingham
University Park
Nottingham NG7 2RD

TEL 0115 951 4749
FAX 0115 951 4668
EMAIL ugadmissions@nottingham.ac.uk
WEB www.nottingham.ac.uk

Nottingham Students' Union
University Park
Nottingham NG7 2RD

TEL 0115 846 8800
EMAIL studentsunion@nottingham.ac.uk
WEB www.su.nottingham.ac.uk

VAG VIEW

Nottingham is a top university with an 85% student satisfaction rate and an 80% chance of getting a top graduate job within six months of leaving.

I t is one of the most employer-friendly universities in the world, and students are happy here, only 3.5% don't last the course, which is very low.

Known, among much else, for its medical provision, the uni launched a School of Veterinary Science quite recently, a landmark - it was the UK's first new Vet School since the 1950s. Students will study 10 miles out, at Sutton Bonington.

This year there's a whole raft of new Chinese courses, as the uni has set up shop there, though there are as many new Russian and Spanish courses, and some interesting film and TV degrees, too. Nottingham students are hot on media. They win nearly everything at the nationals.

CAMPUSES

The 300-acre University Park, home to 3,000 students, workplace to a further 26,000 students and staff, and located just a short bus or bike ride from Nottingham city centre, is the main campus - huge lake, views over Trent valley, rolling Downs that sweep away into the distance, all a neat ten minutes by bus from town.

There is a 16-hectare satellite campus at Sutton Bonington, 10 miles distant, for the School of Biological Sciences, and now the new Vet School. Besides teaching and research facilities, the James Cameron-Gifford Library and student residences, there's a sports centre, bank and bookshop. A free shuttle-bus service runs between it and University Park during the day.

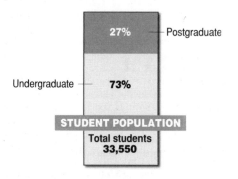

UNIVERSITY/STUDENT PROFILE	
University since	**1948**
Situation/style	**Campus**
Student population	**33550**
Total undergraduates	**24355**
Mature undergraduates	**8%**
International undergrads	**14%**
Male/female ratio	**51:49**
Equality of opportunity:	
state school intake	**98%**
social class 4-7 intake	**45%**
low-participation area intake	**15%**

The Jubilee Campus, on a site close to University Park, houses the Schools of Education, Computer Science and Information Technology, as well as The Business School. The site is also the home of The National College for School Leadership. Green in concept and design, an important feature is the series of lakes which, as well as being home to wildlife, provide cooling for the buildings in the summer and receive all surface water. Less visible - but equally important to this model of a sustainable campus - are the roofs which are, quite literally, green. A carpet of low-growing alpine plants helps maintain steady temperatures within the buildings throughout the year and is more effective than traditional insulation. Buildings also feature a super-efficient mechanical ventilation system, lighting sensors to reduce energy consumption, and photovoltaic cells integrated into the atrium roofs. The environmentally-friendly nature of the campus and its buildings have been a big factor in the awards that it has received, including the Millennium Marque Award for Environmental Excellence, the British Construction Industry Building Project of the Year, the RIBA Journal Sustainability Award and the Civic Trust Award for Sustainability.

'When I first visited the university, all fresh-faced and eager,' recalls Mark Tew, 'I couldn't help but be struck by the sheer size of the place. It's BIG.' Writes Phil Barnett: 'Walking through, with the river on one side and incredible architecture on the other, is an experience never to grow tired of. But, when the need arises, living away from main campus does mean a 20-minute walk or a free bus, which is supposed to leave every 15 minutes but always seems to be leaving as the bus stop is approached. The facilities are fantastic and all day to day necessities are available. It has its own shop and a sports centre with good facilities, but no gym (one occasion when a visit to main campus is necessary).

'Accommodation is all en-suite, fully catered,

and the food is more than satisfactory, with a choice of two cafés or the main hall.

'A lot of Jubilee students study business, of course, and can leave hall less than a minute before lectures begin. If you are one of these, living at Jubilee does means that a lot of your course friends are also the people you live with. However, a fair few Jubilee students do in fact study on the main campus, so there must be advantages in this. If you are visiting Nottingham, I'd advise you take a look around. New work to enhance the campus further began in February this year.'

FEES, BURSARIES

UK & EU Fees, 2009-10: £3,225 p.a. There's a sliding-scale bursary for those receiving the Government Maintenance Grant, and 'First in the Family' and Kevin B Malone Scholarships, open to students who live in the East Midlands and can satisfy certain other criteria. Also subject specific scholarships are awarded - see www.nottingham. ac.uk/financialestimator. Finally a Sports Bursary is available for students at regional or international level, or, in some instances, county level in any sport. See www.nottingham.ac.uk/sport/burstim. php.

STUDENT PROFILE

The uni has one of the lowest intakes from the state sector and from so-called non-traditional uni heartlands (lower socio-economic groups and neighbourhoods). However, they want to change this. To encourage applicants from poor areas of the local community with potential, they have an outreach programme offering summer schools, drama workshops, campus tours, coaching in study skills and interview techniques.

'I was told to expect a lot of bitter and twisted Oxbridge rejects with a big fat chip on the shoulder, but this hasn't been the case,' Mark recalls. 'The "rah-rah, sooo drunk!" toff brigade, however,

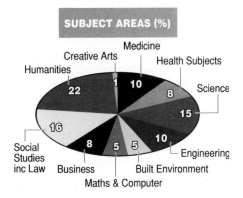

SUBJECT AREAS (%)

Area	%
Medicine	1
Creative Arts	10
Humanities	22
Health Subjects	8
Science	15
Social Studies inc Law	16
Business	8
Maths & Computer	5
Built Environment	5
Engineering	10

is definitely out in full force! Being from up t' North, it was a culture shock to say the least. But it's well worth being here if just to take the piss. "Another bottle of champers Roger?"'

ACADEMIA & JOBS

Students say the best teaching is in Chemistry, Music, Civil Engineering, Production & Manufacturing Engineering, Mechanically-based Engineering, Zoology, Agriculture, Archaeology, and Physical Geography & Environmental Sciences, while Iberian Studies was fingered as the worst by 36% of the class, which may be why the Department of Spanish, Portuguese and Latin American Studies is taking students back to the beginning. New this year will be Beginners' Spanish, which can be taken in combination with a range of subjects, including English, French, German, History and Russian.

The great thing about Nottingham is the help and interest shown in students by the lecturers. The students say this, and generally the tuition groups are manageable.

Other new degrees this year see a swathe of interest in China. The School of Contemporary Chinese Studies will offer: MSci Contemporary Chinese Studies (previously only BA Contemporary Chinese Studies); MSci Business and Economy of Contemporary China; MSci Global Issues and Contemporary Chinese Studies.

Over at Jubille, the medical degree, BMBS, is rigorous - 3 years to BMedSci, then 2 increasingly clinical years. They require AAB at A2, with Biology and Chemistry passed at grade A, and B in a third subject excluding General Studies and Critical Thinking. UKCAT too.

This year the School of Graduate Entry

RESEARCH EXCELLENCE

% of Nottingham's research that is
4* *(World-class) or* **3*** *(Internationally rated):*

	4*	3*
Infection/ Immunology	0%	25%
Hospital Clinical	5%	30%
Laboratory Clinical	5%	20%
Epidemiology	5%	35%
Primary Care	30%	40%
Clinical Psychology	5%	30%
Nursing/Midwifery	20%	35%
Health Professions	10%	30%
Pharmacy	35%	45%
Biological Sciences	10%	40%
Human Biol. Sciences	5%	35%
Agriculture, Veterinary	15%	45%
Chemistry	30%	55%
Physics	25%	40%
Pure Mathematics	15%	35%
Applied Mathematics	20%	45%
Statistics	20%	50%
Computer Science	30%	50%
Electrical/Electronic Eng.	10%	55%
General Engineering	25%	50%
Civil Engineering	25%	60%
Mechanical, Aero. & Manufacturing Eng.	25%	50%
Architecture	10%	30%
Environmental Studies	20%	40%
Archaeology	20%	40%
Economics	30%	55%
Business/Management	20%	50%
Law	30%	35%
Politics	15%	35%
Social Work	10%	40%
Sociology	15%	30%
Psychology	10%	50%
Education	20%	25%
American Studiess	25%	20%
Asian Studies	10%	20%
Russian	20%	40%
French	20%	35%
German	10%	30%
Iberian	30%	45%
English	35%	35%
Classics	10%	45%
Philosophy	25%	35%
Theology	20%	40%
History	15%	35%
History of Ar	20%	55%
Media Studies	5%	35%
Music	25%	60%

Medicine will offer BSc Healthcare Science and BSc Healthcare Science with a Foundation Year. The latter offers able students who do not have the traditional qualifications for a degree in healthcare science the opportunity to develop skills required for the full BSc degree. Both degrees eventually could ead to careers in pathology, immunology and haematology.

When the Nottingham Law degree was assessed by the LPC Board, it was among the very few to be rated Excellent. The 2008 research assessment found 65% of the Law submission either world-class or internationally excellent. All candidates must sit the National Admissions Test for Law (LNAT).

Finance, Accounting & Management degrees and Economics & Econometrics and the like prime graduates for one of the strongest areas of employment for Nottingham - accountancy, tax consultancy, banking. And the joint hons. Programme has BSc Maths & Economics, Maths & Management Studies, and BC Economics and Philosophy. Economics & Econometrics scored 85% world-class and internationally significant in the recent research assessment. Applied Maths and Philosophy scored 60% and 65% respectively

Industrial relations are good. Blue-chip companies that maintain ongoing research relationships include Powergen, Boots and GlaxoSmithKline. The Ford Motor Company and AstraZeneca have both been involved with the uni for over 30 years, and its relationship with Rolls-Royce includes hosting two Technology Centres in the areas of gas turbine transmission systems and manufacturing technology. They are also working together on a research programme aimed at improving the performance of aerospace engines for which the uni will receive £2.2 million.

Jobs also abound in forestry and agriculture through their degrees in Plant/Animal Science, Food Science/Microbiology, Zoology, Ecology, Botany, etc. Note, too, the Veterinary Medicine/Science degree and 1-year Pre-Vet Science Certificate.

Finally, Nottingham's top-rated BSc Psychology leads graduates into all sorts of areas, including market research, publicity and PR, choice too of many of Nottingham's sought-after graduates in languages, social studies, business and humanities.

SOCIAL SCENE

STUDENTS' UNION This is housed in the Portland Building, which overlooks the lake and which at long last has undergone a multi-million pound makeover, with a new SU shop, banks, Blackwells and Boots outlets, and a type of revolving door that spews students with armfuls of books out onto the steps.

A new bar and nightclub was recently created

here. The bar, **Mooch**, serves a range of food throughout the day and has an outdoor terrace. **The Venue** is an 800-capacity nightclub which hosts regular club nights and comedy nights.

In addition, the **D H Lawrence** bar can be found in the Lakeside Pavilion, where exhibitions and stage productions run as prolifically as in the **New Theatre**, which is elsewhere, tucked up behind Portland and as old as the hills.

There are also bars in the 14 halls of residence, and no difficulty in seeing how the drinking binge known as *Campus 14* became so popular. First-year social life spins off halls, off societies, off departments and off sport, rather more than off the Union: 'It still amazes me how such fine, upstanding, intelligent people, who clearly had the "right stuff" to get into Nottingham University, all seem mystically drawn to the Union on a Friday night,' writes Mark. 'Why? It's a dive! Maybe that's harsh. It's actually really nice during the day, its only real crime may be overcrowding on the weekend.'

Nottingham student radio URN is huge. The students have won more national awards than any other university. Last year, they won five Golds, two Silvers and a Bronze, if we didn't miss any. Including the Biggest Impact award. The magazine, also award-winning, is Impact. NUTS is a new TV station.

Nottingham has also long had an enterprising drama society. The **New Theatre**, which once exuded all the spit-and-sawdust appeal of true fringe theatre, now more suits its name. They write, produce and direct up to twenty plays a year and invariably take a production or two to Edinburgh. One of its productions (*Proof*) won five awards at the National Student Drama Festival last time. Theatre has always been big in this city, the **Playhouse**'s deep-rooted reputation to the fore, and **Malt Cross Music Hall** offers an eerie alternative with drama, music hall, comedy, jazz and folk, poltergeists in attendance and spooky goings-on that no one seems able to explain. Then there's the **Theatre Royal** of course (Gilbert & Sullivan, *Rocky Horror*, Arthur Miller, *My Fair Lady*, etc.), and music and dance at the **Palace Theatre**, Mansfield.

On campus, music societies proliferate, such as Blow Soc (wind, to be sure), and for music and art there's the **Arts Centre** - a superb art gallery (with artist in residence) and recital hall next door.

> *The New Theatre, which once exuded all the spit-and-sawdust appeal of true fringe theatre, now more suits its name. They write, produce and direct up to 20 plays a year there.*

WHAT IT'S REALLY LIKE

UNIVERSITY:	
Social Life	★★★★★
Campus scene	**Well-heeled, bright, sporty, creative**
Student Union services	**One of the best**
Politics	**Activity high**
Sport	**Key nationally & v. active inter-hall. 67 clubs.**
National team position	**6th**
Sport facilities	**Good**
Arts opportunities	**Drama excellent; music, art good; dance, film great**
Student magazine	**Impact**
Newspaper	**Grapevine**
Student radio	**URN**
2008 National Awards	**5 Golds, 2 Silver, 1 Bronze**
Venue	**Venue**
Bars	**Mooch, DHL, plus all halls**
Union ents	**Vibrant**
Union societies	**207**
Most popular society	**Christian Union, Cock Soc, Dance Soc**
Parking	**Adequate**
CITY:	
Entertainment	★★★★★
Scene	**Serious nightlife, good arts**
Town/gown relations	**OK**
Risk of violence	**High**
Cost of living	**Average**
Student concessions	**Good**
Survival + 2 nights out	**£90 pw**
Part-time work campus/town	**Good/excellent**

Students may come from comfortable backgrounds and rarely set the firmament alight with radical political action any more, but they have a caring nature apparently, expressed in the extraordinary agenda of Community Action: some 2,000 student volunteers getting involved in arts projects (drama, music), welfare projects (including prison visiting), health, education, housing, sport, environmental projects.

ACCOMMODATION

Guarantee to freshers	**100%**
Style	**Halls, flats**
Security guard	**Porters**
Shared rooms	**Some**
Internet access	**All**
Self-catered	**All flats**
En suite	**Some**
Approx price range pw	**£78-£173**
City rent pw	**£45-£80**

SPORT Nottingham teams came 6th nationally last year and claims the largest and most comprehensive inter-hall league. There is opportunity to participate at all levels in as many as 67 clubs. Facilities include three sports halls - a new sports centre was opened on the Sutton Bonington Campus in 2008, so there's now one on each of the three residential campuses. A second floodlit artificial pitch has been created at University Park. Boating (with boathouse) is undertaken on the tidal Trent. Bursaries are available.

PILLOW TALK

Freshers are guaranteed a place in halls if they receive your Preference Form by August 1. You're talking fully catered halls & self-catering flats. About a third are en suite. There's lots of other accommodation in flats, but catered halls it probably will be, unless you're at Sutton Bonington. Basic pantry facilities are available, but so is breakfast and dinner, and lunch on a flexible scheme which allows you to eat at any catering outlet on University Park or Jubilee campuses. There's not only internet access in all halls, but students can unsubscribe and will be refunded, if they wish. Porters and central site security is basic

There are 14 halls in total, home to approximately 4,000 students, across two sites - Jubilee Campus and University Park. Each hall offers great amenities - coin-operated laundry facilities, pantries to make snacks, chill-out areas like a bar, Junior Common Room, TV and games room, plus a mini library and computer suite.

Writes Mark: 'To be fair, all the halls are pretty nice. Being a former Lincolnite, my totally unbiased opinion is that it is by far the best hall in the world. Small, yet cosy bar, good food, big rooms, our very own library and even cheese and wine nights in the SCR! What more could you want? Ok, so Hugh Stu has the best bar, Derby has the best women and Sherwood has a slide shaped as a dragon. So what!'

If you have a disability and need accessible accommodation, you'll be guaranteed a suitable room. Email: disabilityadviser@nottingham.ac.uk

GETTING THERE

☛ By road: Nottingham, M1/J 25, A52. Sutton Bonington, M1/J24, A6, then left turn.
☛ By rail: London St Pancras, 1:50; Edinburgh, 4:30; Exeter, 4:00; Birmingham New Street, 1:30.
☛ By air: East Midlands Airport.
☛ By coach: London, 2:55; Birmingham, 1:30; Newcastle, 5:00; Exeter, 6:30.

NOTTINGHAM TRENT UNIVERSITY

The Nottingham Trent
University
Burton Street
Nottingham NG1 4BU

TEL 0115 848 2814
FAX 0115 848 6063
EMAIL admissions@ntu.ac.uk
STUDENT UNION TEL 0115 848 6200
WEB www.ntu.ac.uk

*C*entred on the building in Shakespeare Street where, in 1887, the foundation stone was laid by Gladstone for University College Nottingham, the institution later to become Nottingham University, this, the second uni in town began life as Trent Poly in 1970.

Writes Thomas Bell: 'As you may know, Trent is a former poly, now referred to as a "Modern Uni". We are often compared to the older, and by repute, better universities. This is not true across the board. For instance, my Law school runs some of the best courses around, and even Oxbridge postgrads are drawn to the department. Again, fashion and textiles courses are considered to be very good at Trent.

'We have a charity Varsity sports series with Nottingham University each year, which *attracts large crowds from both universities, and whatever happens nationally [Nottingham 6th; Trent 27th last year], we usually prevail, if not so regularly in rowing, where, for a number of reasons, we get our bums paddled. Despite this, in true "Trent" style, we still go out and celebrate like good underdogs should!'*

In the National Student Survey 83% of their students were satisfied with how things are going at the university. Less than 6% of them will not stay the course, which is well below Government expectations.

UNIVERSITY/STUDENT PROFILE	
University since	**1992**
Situation/style	**Campus in the city**
Student population	**24225**
Total undergraduates	**18640**
Mature undergraduates	**15%**
International undergrads	**4%**
Male/female ratio	**48:52**
Equality of opportunity:	
state school intake	**93%**
social class 4-7 intake	**36%**
low-participation area intake	**13%**

CAMPUS SITES

CITY CAMPUS Burton Street is the location of the central admin building, 'front' for a whole load of buildings in neighbouring streets, 2 mins from the action. Writes Thomas: 'The city site is by far the most exciting campus, as its right in the centre of Nottingham. A brand new tram line runs through 'Studentville', past the uni and into the town centre, terminating at the train station.'

The Students' Union HQ, with Byron Sports Hall, are here, along with the £13-million Boots Library, student residences and five of the uni's academic schools: Art & Design, Business, Law, Built Environment, and Social Sciences.

A £70 million regeneration of two buildings at City campus will be completed this year.

CLIFTON CAMPUS Clifton Lane, Nottingham NG11 8NS. This is a spacious, green field campus some 4 miles southwest of the city centre along the A453. It is wholly self-contained with its own SU, sports grounds and student village, and is home to Arts & Humanities, Education, Biomedical & Natural Sciences, and Computing & Informatics.

'Clifton is the smaller of the two campuses with around 5,000 students,' writes Daniel Ashley, 'and still thrives on the community atmosphere. Probably not a bad thing, as the Clifton locals are

not famed for their tolerance of us.'

The Student Village has a bar and diner, supermarket, bank, refectory and bookshop. The Student Union has an active programme here and as Clifton is home to Trent's sports department, there's a pro sports hall, all-weather floodlit sports pitch, a cricket pitch, and well-equipped gym

Clifton Hall, Clifton Village, is a Georgian manor house a few minutes walk from Clifton campus and includes lecture halls for use by the faculty of Education, a resource centre, dance studio and refectory.

BRACKENHURST COLLEGE is Trent's Department of Land-based Studies near the historic town of Southwell, 10 miles north east of Nottingham, which for years has offered Trent degrees and comes with a 200-hectare farm. There's a whole Student Union set-up here, bar, sports, ents, etc and special things with clubs in town.

FEES, BURSARIES

UK & EU Fees, 2009-10: £3,225 p.a. For students in receipt of the HE statutory maintenance grant there's a sliding scale bursary. In addition there the NTU Bursary for Grant eligible students whose permanent address is in Notts. There are also Academic Scholarships worth £2,000 p.a. - see www.ntu.ac.uk/financialsupport - and scholarships for Sport. See www.ntu.ac.uk/sport/elite_athlete/index.html.

STUDENT PROFILE

There are in fact fewer part-time undergraduates at the old poly than at Nottingham University, and far fewer international students, even though Thomas writes: 'Trent is a very diverse university, with a large Asian community. There is currently a banner outside our Student Union, which reads: "Proud to be diverse"'.

Trent does have the edge when it comes to

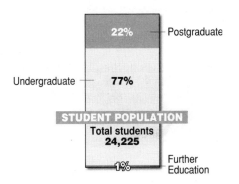

Postgraduate 22%
Undergraduate 77%

STUDENT POPULATION
Total students
24,225

Further Education 1%

TEACHING SURVEY AT A GLANCE

Avg. UCAS points accepted	**270**
Acceptance rate	**22%**
Overall satisfaction rate	**83%**
Helpful/interested staff	★★★
Small tuition groups	★★★
Students into graduate jobs	**78%**

Teaching most popular with undergraduates:
Education, Economics (97%), Chemistry (96%),
Sports Science (92%), History, Initial Teacher
Training, European Languages (91%), Biological
Sciences, English, Politics (90%).

Teaching least popular with undergraduates:
Social Work (71%), Film & Photography (68%).

maturity - 15% undergraduates registering after 21 years of age, to Nottingham's 8%. The public school intake is even more definitive: Nottingham takes 33%, Trent 8%, and Trent's take from the lower socio-economic brackets, at 36%, is far in excess of Nottingham's at 17%.

They would seem to share equally in enthusiasm and focus on what they are about, however. We had the impression that students make the most of their time here.

> *Nottingham Trent's strong links with employers, and students experiencing the real world of work as part of their courses, are together the basis of the uni's provision.*

'The socio-economic backgrounds of a large amount of our students differs from that of a university like Nottingham,' confirms Thomas. 'If you don't achieve your full potential at A-Level, coming to Trent may well be the best thing that's happened to you. Here you will meet and mix with many students from different walks of life, form a well-shaped outlook on the world, and develop skills and an understanding of people you would not get elsewhere.

'The one downside in my opinion is the lack of tradition and formality. Our annual Sports Excellence Ball, for example, seems to be simply an expensive lash-up, without any sort of real occasion - we gather at a hotel to eat and watch the award ceremony, perhaps throw some food about, then go on to the student union to do something you can do any other Saturday.'

ACADEMIA & JOBS

As rivals Nottingham gets into Veterinary Medicine, so a new Veterinary Nursing centre is completed by Trent on the university's Brackenhurst campus, where their land-based courses are studied. The unit will offer a Integrated Veterinary Nursing Foundation Degree course.

At Trent they claim more students on sandwich courses than any other uni, students experiencing the real world of work as part of their courses. This and the Trent's strong links with employers, is the basis of their provision and relative strength in graduate employment - 78% will have graduate-level jobs within six months of leaving.

Trent University and industry scratch each other's backs in a way that gets right to the spot. In particular, graduates from the School of Property and Construction attract some of the highest starting salaries in the country. With their Architectural Technology BSc they have the edge. It sits comfortably among their Building, Design and BSc Construction Management degrees. The architectural input brings social, political, economic, environmental features to the fore in an otherwise out-and-out technological degree. It can get you a job with an architectural practice, a building contractor, a local authority or a large property developer. There's now also BA Architecture. Look too at Planning & Property Development, Property & Management, Building Surveying, Quantity Surveying and Real Estate Management.

In government administration, local, regional, central Trent also have a strong pedigree. Look at their European Studies, Global Politics, Politics, Political Economy, and International Studies degrees.

In teaching, there's a primary school speciality, also advanced early years, and Design &

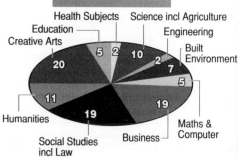

SUBJECT AREAS (%)

Health Subjects — 5
Science incl Agriculture — 2
Education — 10
Engineering — 2
Creative Arts — 20
Built Environment — 7
Humanities — 11 / 5
Social Studies incl Law — 19
Business — 19
Maths & Computer

RESEARCH EXCELLENCE

% of Nottingham Trent's research that is
4* *(World-class)* or **3*** *(Internationally rated):*

	4*	3*
Health Professions	20%	30%
Environmental Sciences	0%	5%
Computer Science	0%	30%
General Engineering	15%	40%
Built Environment	0%	30%
Archaeology	5%	25%
Business/Management	5%	25%
Law	0%	10%
Social Work	15%	45%
Psychology	0%	15%
Sports	0%	0%
French	0%	30%
English	10%	45%
History	5%	25%
Art and Design	5%	30%
Media Studies	25%	45%

student training centre in the UK to have access to authentic broadcasting facilities.

Finally, their sports provision produces more physical training instructors than any uni outside of Brighton.

SOCIAL SCENE

The Students' Union bar at City has undergone a £300,000 facelift, giving a new continental café bar and late-night (2 am at weekends) drinking spot, **Glo** bar, in addition to **Sub** bar, itself refurnished this year. At Clifton campus there's the **Point** bar and at Brackenhurst, the **Museum** bar.

'In the first week freshers rapidly form social groups. Freshers week is very well organised and provides an action-packed induction course in how to exploit the vibrant nightlife of Nottingham. The key to surviving the first term is eating well and sleeping, neither of which I did much of. My most memorable times were with the rowing team. Our weekly socials were well structured and action packed, if occasionally dangerous (beware

Technology (secondary), while graduates to further education tend to come mostly from Biological Sciences and Creative Arts, then Social Sciences. For aspiring environmental health officers, there's a dedicated degree in Environmental Health.

In the heady realm of pharmaceuticals, Trent jostles with others for top place as biggest graduate provider. Trent has a 3/4-year BSc/MSci Pharmaceutical & Medicinal Science, BSc Pharmacology & Neuroscience, BSc Physiology & Pharmacology.

For would-be bankers from the Business School, Barclays is sponsoring the country's first retail banking degree here. The BA (Hons) Business Management (Retail Banking) places employability and workplace performance at the centre of its course design. The bank and the Business School also run a BA (Hons) in Leadership. Computer Sciences is another popular route into banking.

In Law, students have a choice of eight institutions where the Bar Vocational Course may be undertaken, Trent's Nottingham Law School is one of them. The BVC course lasts for a year and is followed by a year's pupil age - practical training under the supervision of an experienced barrister.

Their Art & Design Faculty is renowned for its fashion and textile courses. It also leads many into advertising, Design for Television a particular niche.

For radio and TV broadcasting, Trent's Centre for Broadcasting & Journalism is housed in the old BBC studios in Nottingham, making it the only

WHAT IT'S REALLY LIKE

UNIVERSITY:

Social Life	★★★★
Campus scene	**Streetwise, fun**
Student Union services	**Average**
Politics	**Interest low**
Sport	**42 clubs**
National team position	**27th**
Sport facilities	**Average**
Arts opportunities	**Drama,art, music, good; dance avg; film poor**
Student newspaper	**Platform**
Student radio	**Fly FM**
National awards 2008	**2 Golds, 1 Bronze Broadcaster of the Year!**
Venue/bars	**Glo, Sub, Point, Museum**
Union ents	**Wild**
Union societies	**76**
Parking	**Clifton good, City campus poor**

CITY:

Entertainment	★★★★★
Scene	**Clubby, pubby, good arts**
Town/gown relations	**OK**
Risk of violence	**High**
Cost of living	**Average**
Student concessions	**Good**
Survival + 2 nights out	**£90 pw**
Part-time work campus/town	**Good/excellent**

ACCOMMODATION	
Guarantee to freshers	**70%**
Style	**Halls, flats**
Security guard	**Some**
Shared rooms	**Some**
Internet access	**Most**
Self-catered	**All**
En suite	**Some**
Approx price range pw	**£65-£104**
City rent pw	**£45-£85**

"the post-box challenge" - bones have been broken!). These socials end up at **Ocean** nightclub with all the other sports clubs. Ocean itself is pretty nondescript, but what really matters is who you're with.'

Explains Annabel Wollen: 'Once a month we have a legendary fancy dress night called Kinki at Ocean nightclub in town, each month with a different theme. It is somewhat infamous (a bit of a religion at Trent). Also at Ocean we have a Wednesday sports and societies night called Campus. Then there's a Thursday night called DV8 at **Walkabout**. Both these mid-week nights play mainly commercial music and a big dollop of cheese is always on offer. On Fridays we hold *Flirt!* at Clifton campus and alternate between *Assault* (a rock night) and *The Tone* club (live) at City, Sub bar being transformed into a late bar, chilled out and relaxed. Finishing the week is Saturday night - *Climax* - where our City site venue is transformed into a nightclub holding 2500 people. Music policy is cheese and golden oldies downstairs with a mix of r&b and garage upstairs. All our nights are NUS only, and packed to the rafters, but on a Saturday we do allow our members to sign townies in as guests.

Platform is the weekly paper, which the *Nottingham Evening Post* prints for them. 'They have nothing to do with editorial, well... they sort of peruse it, nick some of our stories.' It has won many awards. The Trent student radio station is Fly FM. In 2008, not only did they pick up a couple of Gold awards and a Bronze at the National Radio Awards, they got Broadcaster of the Year in the Guardian/Sky Awards.

The Students' Union is also proving that what it has long been doing for student entertainment it can do equally well for more serious pursuits: a Community Action Group was set up, an Employment Store has grown from one small office to two massive departments that together will deal with upwards of 9,000 placements in part-time employment this year, and the SU employment skills training programme, Stride, has broken all expectations, with every programme either full or over-subscribed.

TOWN The city is very popular with students - see Student Nottingham. Writes Thomas: 'Nottingham is regarded as a dangerous and unfriendly place to live. This, you will find, is not entirely fair. Every city can be dangerous, and part of being 'street aware' is learning to avoid the dodgy places, read and avoid potential situations when you're out. If you don't feel so sure, there's a number of bars and clubs that only let students in during the week.'

SPORT Their teams came overall 27th in the nation last year. They have many TASS athletes and also a handful who represent the country - in hockey, archery and canoe. There's £2-million sports hall plus all-weather pitch at Clifton, and 42 clubs offering everything from circus skills to rugby league, traditionally the most successful club in the university.

PILLOW TALK
They accommodate 70% of first years; 25% live in flats and shared houses in the private sector. Not sure where the residual 5% end up. All halls are self-catered, approximately 65% of rooms are en suite.

'City site freshers are likely to find themselves in one of the many halls scattered within a mile or so,' writes Daniel, 'so it is possible to get to college both on foot or by bike. Early enthusiasm for this does tend to wane as it gets a bit colder. However, the parking facilities in City are not brilliant, and a permit must be applied for. Do this as soon as you arrive.' At Clifton, the student village has 720 en-suite bedrooms with broadband access.

GETTING THERE
- ☛ By road: M1/J25/6. Good coach service.
- ☛ By rail: London St Pancras, 1:50; Edinburgh, 4:30; Exeter, 4:00; Birmingham New Street, 1:30.
- ☛ By air: East Midlands Airport 12 miles away.
- ☛ By coach: London, 2:55; Birmingham, 1:30.

UNIVERSITY OF OXFORD

The University of Oxford
Undergraduate Admissions Office,
Wellington Square
Oxford OX1 2JD

OUSU
28 Little Clarendon Street
Oxford OX1 2HU

TEL 01865 288000
FAX 01865 270708
EMAIL undergraduate.admissions@admin.ox.ac.uk
WEB www.admissions.ox.ac.uk

TEL 01865 270777
FAX 01865 270776
EMAIL info@ousu.org.uk
WEB www.ousu.org

VAG VIEW

*O*xford University, founded in 1096,
stands at No. 4 behind Harvard, Yale,
and Cambridge in the latest Times Higher
Education table of the Top 200 Universities
Worldwide. As a sixthformer, the great thing
is not to be fazed by the reputation. If you
fancy the trademark one-to-one tutor system
(and who wouldn't?), simply apply. So few
do apply that there's straightway a one-in-
four chance you'll get in, which is way better
than any other university but Cambridge.

UNIVERSITY/STUDENT PROFILE	
University since	**1096**
Situation/style	**City**
	Collegiate
Student population	**24640**
Total undergraduates	**16140**
Mature undergraduates	**5%**
International undergrads	**13%**
Male/female ratio	**53:47**
Equality of opportunity:	
state school intake	**53%**
social class 4-7 intake	**10%**
low-participation area intake	**3%**

FEES, BURSARIES

UK & EU Fees, 2009-10: £3,225 p.a. For those in
receipt of the HE Maintenance Grant, Oxford has
one of the most generous schemes in the country,
exempting eligible students from the whole fee on
a sliding scale until well in excess of an income of
£25,000. See www.oxfordopportunity.com for full
details. In addition, Oxford colleges offer various
financial awards and funds to their students,
including scholarships and exhibitions, awarded
after the first year for excellent academic achievement, etc.

STUDENT PROFILE

'Oxford as a vanguard of elitism and discrimination has made the headlines countless times in the
past few years. Personally, I haven't experienced
any discrimination,' writes history undergraduate
Rachel Cocker, 'but as a white, middle-class girl
from an independent school in the North West I
am not exactly a member of a minority group here.'
Rachel will tell us more, but perhaps Christabel
Ashby, from a different background, may have a
different story: 'I'm Christabel Ashby, I'm from
London. I went to a state school, and I'm a final-
year student at Keble, studying Theology. I'm not
going to lie; my first few days in Oxford were ter-
rifying. In Freshers week we were inundated with

information and events. There were both the university and the college fresher fairs [presentations
to freshers by sports clubs and societies], and we
were forced into going out and getting drunk by
well meaning second-year students. Despite this it
was really easy to make friends, and after two
weeks I felt as at-home and confident as if I'd been
there for years.

'The nice thing about the Oxford student scene
is that it is so inclusive. Whatever you're into, you
are bound to find people to hang out with. You will
probably meet a few people who are a bit elitist or
arrogant, but I suspect that is true of any university.'

ACADEMIA & JOBS

'The myth that Oxford students have no time for a
social life is false, but that we have a very heavy
workload is, however, perfectly true,' continues
Rachel. 'Eight weeks is a short period for a term
and a lot of work is packed into it. Scientists,
medics and lawyers have by far the most to do.
Historians get off relatively lightly. Still, it's hard
when you hear your mates at other unis talk of
two-month deadlines when you're going through
the weekly essay grind. It is stressful, but none of
my friends have, as yet, launched themselves off

Magdalen Bridge. Tutors are generally willing to give more guidance and leeway than you might

RESEARCH EXCELLENCE		
4* *(World-class)* or 3* *(Internationally rated):*		
	4*	3*
Cardiovascular Medicine	45%	40%
Cancer Studies	25%	50%
Infection/Immunology	45%	40%
Hospital Clinical	35%	35%
Laboratory Clinical	40%	35%
Epidemiology	40%	25%
Health Services	20%	45%
Community Clinical	45%	40%
Clinical Psychology	15%	45%
Plant Sciences	25%	40%
Zoology	15%	45%
Biochemistry	35%	40%
Human Biol. Sciences	30%	50%
Environmental Sciences	35%	50%
Chemistry	30%	45%
Physics	20%	35%
Pure Mathematics	35%	40%
Applied Mathematics	30%	45%
Statistics	40%	50%
Computer Science	35%	45%
General Engineering	25%	60%
Metallurgy and Materials	25%	55%
Environmental Studies	30%	40%
Archaeology	35%	30%
Economics	40%	55%
Business/Management	30%	40%
Law	35%	35%
Politics	35%	25%
Social Work	20%	50%
Sociology	25%	30%
Anthropology	25%	30%
Development Studies	35%	30%
Psychology	35%	45%
Education	30%	35%
Middle EasternAfrican	40%	30%
Asian Studies	25%	30%
Russian	35%	35%
French	30%	35%
German	25%	30%
Italian	30%	30%
Iberian	15%	45%
English	40%	25%
Linguistics	10%	30%
Classics	40%	30%
Philosophy	35%	30%
Theology	30%	35%
History	35%	35%
Art and Design	30%	35%
Media Studies	20%	35%
Music	50%	25%

imagine. At the end of every term you will be given a feedback form, and although for some this may be simply a faculty-proscribed exercise, for others students' comments have shifted the focus and structure of the course they teach.

'All colleges have computer facilities where you can type up your work or check your e-mail, an Oxford e-mail address is provided for everyone upon arrival.

Oxford has some of the best libraries in the world, the state of your college library depends on its personal wealth but as the Bodleian has a copy of every book ever written, or something like it, you don't have much of an excuse for not reading that "essential" item on the reading list.'

The uni is developing a rich diversity of online resources and course materials - full details can be found at http://www.online.ox.ac.uk/. There are also little known welfare resources - a disability service, for example, even grants available from such as the Dyslexia Fund. Again, the Oxford University Resources for the Blind provide tape recordings for students with a print impairment, including dyslexia sufferers. Note-takers or readers are also available.

To become a doctor at Oxford you will need the 4 or 6-year BM BCh. Oxford now stipulate that all candidates applying to read Medicine will sit the Biomedical Admissions Test (BMAT). The test is being used to assess scientific aptitude, not fitness to practise medicine (which will continue to be assessed in other ways, including interview) and focuses on scientific abilities relevant to the study of medicine. AAA (chem. + 1 from sci/maths). A 13% chance of getting in, a better application acceptance rate than most.

For the degree they have retained a 3-year preclinical course with small group tutorial teaching (often pairs). There are regular GP visits, too, and clinical experience. Nearly 20% of those who apply get in. Entry AAA: Chemistry with either Maths or Biology or Physics. Humanities subject welcomed. Teaching inspection 21.

The Law Faculty has a world-class Grade 5* for research. They are European Law specialists. Non-Law graduates may opt for a 2-year Senior Status Law Degree. All candidates must sit the National Admissions Test for Law (LNAT).

The appearance of Oxford University among the Top 10 providers to accountancy gives the lie to the proposition that vocational courses are what is needed in this area (in fact a degree is not needed at all). What they have is a small number of very high-powered courses in physical and biological sciences, which dispense skills of analysis so commanding as to question the wisdom of too early a specialisation. These, together with abilities honed

TEACHING SURVEY AT A GLANCE

Avg. UCAS points accepted	**500**
Acceptance rate	**23%**
Overall satisfaction rate	**92%**
Helpful/interested staff	★★★★★
Small tuition groups	★★★★★
Students into graduate jobs	**78%**

Teaching most popular with undergraduates:
Classics (100%), Creative Arts & Design,
Economics, Philosophy (96%), English, Most
European Languages, French, Music, Social
Studies (95%), Medicine, Theology (94%),
Molecular & Cellular Biochemistry (93%),
German, Scandinavian, Maths, Politics (92%),
Biology, Chemistry (90%).

Teaching least popular with undergraduates:
Geography (81%), Anatomy, Physiology &
Pathology (63%).

in departments of Modern Languages, Mathematics and even Humanities, provide 90% of Oxford's graduate accountants.

Likewise, analysing and understanding how people think, how communities respond, is what is required at the sharp end of market research, which is why 25% of Oxford graduates into this area have analytical minds honed in the study of biological sciences.

For anyone wanting to become an actuary three universities are head and shoulders above the rest in equating degree success with employment, namely Heriot-Watt, Warwick and Oxford. Again, there are no dedicated degrees, but look at maths, of course, and also the Physics Department, which is also where Oxford's actuaries come from.

It may seem strange to choose Oxford particularly if you want to be a management consultant, there being many more vocational courses elsewhere, but they are way out front in the stats for graduates into this sector. The degree that causes all the fuss is BA Economics & Management. There are also combinations with Engineering or Materials.

Bankers, merchant bankers, stockbrokers, sharedealers, investment advisers and analysts all proliferate out of Oxford. The Arts & Social Studies BA hons programme accounts for more than a third of them. This includes Economics & Management, but also a number of Classics combinations, and Oxford Classics graduates have always been much in demand in the City. Then it's Physics and Languages and Mathematics. Employers are after analytical and flexible thinking.

Plenty of their language graduates make it into

translating/interpreting, but how interesting, too, that Oxford language graduates get jobs as social worker/counsellors in number, and probably at levels higher than those reading Social Work degrees elsewhere.

At the same time, many of their language graduates are sought by advertising agencies - any European Language adjunct goes down well in this sector from Oxford. Languages are to the fore again in jobs for government and media research. As at Durham, there is an interesting focus here on European and Middle/Far Eastern Languages.

For jobs in publishing, Oxford is No. 1, and languages are again the most popular route, followed by the Arts & Social Studies combos (everything from English Language & Literature or Classics & English to Archaeology & Anthropology), followed by humanities.

They also turn out more graduate editors than most - nearly half are languages graduates again, then come students of humanities, biological sciences and law. Similar areas train a good number of those that take up journalism after Oxford - another powerful graduate employment area.

Languages and humanities graduates also find work in charities, and dominate the civil service and adult education sectors, and, as elsewhere, it's the arts & social studies joint degrees, languages, biological sciences and humanities that lead the way for lecturers into higher education .

Finally, Oxford is one of the top graduate providers to automobile engineering, with Loughborough, Oxford Brookes, Bath, Swansea Institute and Coventry University. Good to think of them hand in glove with the Swansea Institute. All engineering students here follow a general course for the first year before naming a MEng specialism.

SOCIAL SCENE

STUDENTS' UNION Once you've made your new-found friends, there is a reasonable social life to be had with them. A lot of it is college based; most have weekly bops. One thing Oxford seriously lacks is a central student venue, but once you venture outside the walls of your cosy college environment there are plenty of university-wide activities in which to get involved. Theatre, journalism, music, student politics and Anglo Saxon re-enactment (apparently) are all strong. *Cherwell* and *ISIS*, famous Oxford student magazines are not in fact published by the Union. *The Oxford Student* is the student newspaper, and Oxide, the student radio station, which won a Bronze award at the national media awards last year. Every year the Oxford University drama festival, 'Cuppers', sees around 30 productions performed, directed and often written by freshers. Hacks tend to gravitate towards the

UNIVERSITY:	
Social Life	★★★★
Campus scene	**Intense, challenging, satisfying**
Student Union services	**Well organised, but no venue**
Politics	**Active**
Sport	**Key**
National team position	**9th**
Sport facilities	**Good**
Arts opportunities	**Excellent**
Student mag/news	**Oxford Student**
2008 National awards	**Reporter of Year, Design of Year, Website of Year**
Student radio	**Oxide**
Nightclub	**None**
Bars	**College bars**
Union ents	**College-based**
Union clubs/societies	**200+**
Parking	**Buy a bike**
CITY:	
Entertainment	★★★
Scene	**Small, good pubs, OK clubs**
Town/gown relations	**Average**
Risk of violence	**Average**
Cost of living	**High**
Student concessions	**Good**
Survival + 2 nights out	**£70 pw**
Part-time work campus/town	**Good**

famed Oxford Union, where they can fine tune their debating and back-stabbing skills, and it is possible to infiltrate or avoid their number at will.

SPORT... 'is a big deal from football to ultimate fris-bee. There are college leagues for every sport you can think of; even pool. Most colleges have their own sports ground and of course there are the uni-versity facilities down Iffley Road, the 25-metre, eight-lane Rosenblatt swimming pool has now opened.

The pool is part of the training facilities for the OU Swimming and Water Polo Clubs, but it's avail-able for recreational use too. Most people try their hand at rowing at some point during their universi-ty career and many, many join the ranks of "boat-ies", consigning themselves to years of early morn-ing outings and gruelling weights sessions. All very rewarding, especially for all who get to cheer them to victory during Eights Week, while getting pissed on Pimms.

TOWN 'There are some great pubs; the most stu-denty of which are the **Kings Arms** and **The Turf**, both rammed to the rafters after exams. The city is also a haven for cocktail bars, and the **Duke of Cambridge** is immensely popular for its very happy "happy hour", which lasts from 5 till 8.30pm every single day of the week. Oxford also boasts some fantastic restaurants, although some of these are so fantastically priced you might have to wait until your real Mummy and Daddy come to take you home before sampling them.

'Oxford Brookes' Union hosts live touring bands and probably the best student nights to be had in the city on Fridays and Saturdays. College balls also feature largely in Oxford life and for an aver-age non-dining ticket you are looking at around £50. The larger balls, such as Merton in the winter and Magdalen, New, Trinity and Worcester in the summer can set you back up to £110 per person. Luckily, these only take place once every three years so a lot of people attend but one during their time here. Once you get in there, of course, every-thing is free.

'*Cost of living*: if you take into account that the average student here goes out at least twice a week (most people's workloads make it hard to manage more) then I would say someone with stronger self-discipline than myself might survive on £70.'

If you're a home/EU publicly-funded first-yea, you may be eligible for a bursary. Go to www.admissions.ox.ac.uk/finance/bursaries/index.shtml

'*Safety*: everything being just down the road encourages a feeling of safety, but there have been several attacks on students since I've been here. You do still need to be on your guard. Town/gown relations don't seem to be anywhere near as bad as in Durham, but there are a few unofficially desig-nated townie pubs and clubs, which students avoid, though not through fear for their lives.'

PILLOW TALK

All freshers are guaranteed college accommoda-tion for their first and at least one additional year. For freshers, most college rooms are single study-bedrooms, some of which have their own bath-room. Some colleges have 'sets', where two stu-dents share a study-living room but have their own bedrooms. All rooms are furnished; some have telephone and internet points. Car parking is not provided. Exact facilities vary between colleges but include a library, bar, common room, laundry facil-ities, computer room, sports ground and dining room, where three meals are offered every day. Costs vary from college to college - as a rough guide, £700 per term to include rent, cleaning, heating, water and electricity. If you were to take three meals a day in college, it might cost you an additional £350-£425 a term.

ACCOMMODATION	
Guarantee to freshers	**100%**
Style	**College**
Security guard	**Porters**
Shared rooms	**Some**
Internet access	**Most**
Self-catered	**Both facilities**
En suite	**Some**
Approx price range pw	**£111-£161**
City rent pw	**£100-£150**

COLLEGE CAMEOS
by Caroline Rowe & Sacha Delmotte

BALLIOL
Broad Street, Oxford OX1 3BJ
TEL 01865 277777
WEB www.balliol.ac.uk
Founded in 1263, Balliol has a claim to be the oldest Oxford college and is situated right in the centre of town, so access and convenience are optimum. Balliol has very high academic standards, and is proud to boast its 'effortless superiority'. Today its main strengths lie in Classics, PPE, Physics and Philosophy. The college used to be very left-wing, which is still evident today in one of the most active JCRs in the university, and the bar being entirely student-run (only Hertford does this as well). There is also a notable absence of Balls or even formal hall.

Balliol has, however, always been very liberal, and was the first college to admit international students (today it has the highest percentage of overseas students of all colleges), and the first to allow women into Oxford academia. There is a fairly high proportion of state-school students, and social elitism is not rife, despite the existence of the Annandale Society (a pretentious, all public school gentlemen's club of sorts).

Balliol provides a JCR Pantry, which is open all day, serving breakfast until 11:30, and provides colossal portions. College ents are of high standard, rent is second lowest in Oxford and the bar is small but relaxed. There is a long-standing feud between Balliol and Trinity, orchestrated by a (rather rude) song, the 'Gordouli'. College gossip is assured

instantaneous propagation via the *John de Balliol* bogsheet.

BRASENOSE
Radcliff Square, Oxford OX1 4AJ
TEL 01865 277510
WEB www.bnc.ox.ac.uk
Founded in 1509, BNC, as it is known, is renowned for its tourist-friendly location and its sporting exploits rather than for academic excellence. Rugby is very big and indeed sports in general tend to be edified, though to be fair it does have a good reputation for PPE and Law. The main social focus of the college is the infamous Gertie's Tea Bar, and it has a medium-size May Ball every summer term. BNC has a fairly low profile within the university, but is interestingly named after the brass door-knocker in hall.

CHRIST CHURCH ('The House')
St Allgates, Oxford OX1 1DP
TEL 01865 276150
WEB www.chch.ox.ac.uk
Founded in 1546, Christ Church is the biggest college (both in number of undergrads and in area), and still to this day has an (entirely undeserved) reputation of being a haven for rich Etonians and other public-school types. Typically, Christ Church students are fairly good at sport, and have the best kept and most central sports ground. The college does well academically and has a strong reputation for law with a specially dedicated library. Christ Church is also the second richest college after St John's and thus welfare and accommodation provisions are excellent, with rooms available for all your time in Oxford. The college is extremely beautiful, with extensive meadows, Oxford's mediaeval cathedral and an art gallery containing works by Leonardo da Vinci and Michelangelo. It holds a yearly impressive ball. Pembroke as its rival, not surprising as it technically owns the college. Film wise, while Magdalen has *Shadowlands*, Ch Ch can boast being the location for much of the new Harry Potter film!

CORPUS CHRISTI
Merton Street, Oxford OX1 4JF
TEL 01865 276693
WEB www.ccc.ox.ac.uk
Founded 1517, Corpus is tiny, really tiny, both in land area and in student number. This feature gives it a sense of intimacy that other colleges cannot claim, and accommodation is guaranteed for all students. Corpus excels academically and is quiet as a result of all the hard work. Recently it has introduced a new tradition, the Tortoise Race, where the Corpus reptile races against the demon

speed-machine from Balliol. Corpus puts on a small-scale Summer Event (advertised as the cheapest Oxford Ball) at the beginning of every Trinity term, but on the whole it has a low profile in the university.

EXETER

Turl Street, Oxford OX1 3DP
TEL 01865 279660
WEB www.exeter.ox.ac.uk

Founded 1314, Exeter is a compact college and is so close to the Bodleian Library it may as well be part of it. Public perception is that it contains rowdy, sport-playing types. This certainly appears to be the case as the bar is very active, with lots of cool, outgoing people, and intimate ents – the JCR is famously apathetic, and one rarely hears of political activism from within Exeter's walls. The college has a long-standing rivalry with its neighbour, Jesus, also on Turl Street.

HARRIS-MANCHESTER

Mansfield Road, Oxford OX1 3TD
TEL 01865 271009
WEB www.hmc.ox.ac.uk

Founded in 1786, there is very little to be said about this college since it only admits mature students, mostly to read an Arts degree. The college was founded in Manchester to provide education for non-Anglican students, who at the time were not allowed into Oxbridge. Following a move to Oxford, it was granted Permanent Private Hall status, and only recently (1996) become a full college. Currently the college faces long-term financial and governance problems. In 2003 they asked Derek Wood QC to review resources, particularly for history, PPE and related subjects. The upshot was to ditch history. Pleasant Gothic Revival buildings.

HERTFORD

Catte Street, Oxford OX1 3BW
TEL 01865 279400
WEB www.bertford.ox.ac.uk

Founded in 1740, Hertford has had a tumultuous past with various changes of name, owner and status over its 250-year history; it used to be a subdivision of Magdalen. Hertford is very central and opposite the ever-popular **King's Arms** pub. Hertford students really know how to party (their bar is rumoured to have the highest fiscal turnover in the university). Whether this is explained by its large population of state-school students, and the distinct Northern flavour of the undergrad body in particular, would not be PC to enquire. Altogether it is a progressive establishment and was one of the first all-male colleges to admit women and the first

to make the entrance exam optional. Students enjoy full accommodation, an excellent atmospheric JCR bar, which is entirely student run and concocts brilliant, toxic cocktails.

JESUS

Turl Street, Oxford OX1 3DW
TEL 01865 279720
WEB www.jesus.ox.ac.uk

Founded in 1571, Jesus is small, beautiful and wealthy, and has a reputation for being the 'Welsh College', which is perfectly fair since a not insignificant proportion of students come from Wales. The college bogsheet is *The Sheepshagger*. The college is quite insular and politically unmotivated. Jesubites have it easy: accommodation is excellent and hall food is cheap. Recently Jesus is feared in rugby circles, and does well in other sports too. It has a feud with Exeter.

KEBLE

Parks Road, Oxford OX1 3PG
TEL 01865 272711
WEB www.keble.ox.ac.uk

Founded 1870. Writes Christabel Ashby: 'Keble College is notable for being the only redbrick, Victorian college. It is ideally placed for town and most university facilities, and is right opposite the University parks. College facilities are good; we have phone and internet lines in every room, and all the rooms are nicely furnished. The college guarantees you two years accommodation.

'Keble is also rather traditional, there is formal hall every night, which means you wear your gown to dinner, which has waiter service. On the social side, there's a mixed bag. It has one of the largest undergraduate populations of Oxford colleges, which means there are lots of people with whom to make friends, but also means you will never know everyone, and seeing people you don't recognise all over the place can be a little disconcerting.

'Keble is sporty, there are lots of teams and clubs, and the bar is also fairly popular. Ents are predictable however, usually consisting of a live band or karaoke nights. These events happen once or twice a term. The JCR is well stocked with electronic games, pinball, table-footy and pool, and also has sky TV. Unlike some of the other colleges, however, there is no JCR shop.

'There is a strong sense of equality at Keble, both in terms of women's and men's rights and in gay/lesbian rights. The environment is welcoming and friendly to anyone and everyone, but at the same time its size means you are able to retain a degree of anonymity not possible in many of the other colleges.'

LADY MARGARET HALL
Norham Gdns, Oxford OX2 6QA
TEL 01865 274300
WEB www.lmh.ox.ac.uk
Founded 1878. LMH was the first college founded solely for women in the university. Since there was no vacant land in the centre of town, LMH is fairly far out of town, but this has resulted in the luxury of extensive gardens. The college began admitting men in the '70s, and since that day and age LMH has achieved an unparalleled male/female ratio of 1:1 at levels of college hierarchy. LMH is socially self-sufficient and has a low profile in the university. It is neither renowned for scholastic or sporting brilliance, and has no great political aspirations. Its sole reputation is for producing Thespians, who tend to hang out in cliques with other college actors (read 'actoars'). Otherwise unpretentious and not intimidating.

LINCOLN
Turl Street, Oxford OX1 3DR
TEL 01865 279800
WEB www.linc.ox.ac.uk
Founded in 1427, Lincoln is the smallest of the three colleges on Turl Street, but beautiful. The college is a rather wealthy one, which is evident from the extensive facilities provided to students: good accommodation, excellent sporting facilities, and allegedly the best hall food in the university. This comfort of college life means that very few Lincolnites emerge from their cushy environment to participate in university-wide activities, and thus charges of insularity are fair and merited. Overall, the college is a rather 'shy' one on the university scene, and is not really noted for spectacular achievement in any academic, political or sporting field. Tradition has it that on Ascension Day, Lincoln undergrads stroll around town in sub-fusc (formal wear) with the vicar of St Michael's in the Northgate and a gang of choristers 'beating the bounds', or thrashing at the town limits with canes. Then the students drink lots of ivy beer and toss hot pennies at the choirboys.

MAGDALEN
High Street, Oxford OX1 4AU
TEL 01865 276063
WEB www.magd.ox.ac.uk
Founded in 1458, Magdalen (read 'Maudlin') is a gorgeous college in every respect. It is one of the oldest, richest and most beautiful. Its buildings, extensive grounds (including the famous Deer Park), beautiful cloisters, and Magdalen Tower, and location on the banks of the River Cherwell are stunning, breathtaking. On May Day the choir sings from the top of Magdalen Tower and the tra-dition is to jump off the bridge into the river, although the police keep deciding to cordon it off. The film *Shadowlands* was shot there, and the money earned was spent on renovating certain college rooms. Accommodation facilities are second to none (everyone can live in throughout their whole student career), and some of the sets offered are simply amazing (bedroom, living room, and bath-room!). The college has a huge and lively bar, and puts on very good ents events, but is pretty insular (the **Lower Oscar Wilde Room** is often the site of debauched and drunken student carnage). Magdalen, like Christ Church, owns its own punt. It is academically successful and socially intense, but rather uninterested in political and JCR issues.

MANSFIELD
Mansfield Road, Oxford OX1 3TF
TEL 01865 270970
WEB www.mansfield.ox.ac.uk
Founded in 1886, Mansfield only obtained its college status in 1995; prior to that it was a Permanent Private Hall. It is among the smallest of colleges, only admitting about sixty undergrads every year. This leads to a very close-knit yet appreciably claustrophobic community. Due to the small size of the college many students explore extra-curricular opportunities in the university, and the college is famous for drama. The college is very poor and thus room rents are relatively high. Mansfield has a reputation for tolerance and is sometimes known as the LGB (Lesbian Gay Bisexual) college. Ents are diverse, with bops, karaokes, trips to the theatre, Laserquesting, and there is a triennial Venetian Masked Ball held in the seventh week of Michaelmas term.

MERTON
Merton Street, Oxford OX1 4JD
TEL 01865 276329
WEB www.merton.ox.ac.uk
Founded in 1264, Merton, along with Balliol and University, has a claim to be the oldest Oxford college, and is very rich and beautiful, containing the oldest surviving Oxford quad (Mob quad). The college has an undisputed reputation for being a centre of academic excellence, fuelled by SCR encouragement and a competitive spirit among the student population. Socially Merton appears to be fairly insular, and one rarely meets Mertonites around the university; in fact it would seem that Mertonites are quite dull. Nonetheless every year Merton puts on the only Christmas Ball in Oxford, on the last day of Michaelmas term, which is usually a roaring success. It is particularly popular with Freshers who are able to finish their first term at Oxford with style and panache (and a random

snog perhaps!). Merton's tradition, the Time Ceremony, has existed for barely fifteen years, but is now firmly implanted in the college calendar, and for a day lifts the veil of seriousness which rests upon the college. It involves students walking backwards around Merton's Mob Quad while continuously downing port, on a particular day of each year.

NEW COLLEGE

Holywell Street, Oxford OX1 3BN
TEL 01865 279590
WEB www.new.ox.ac.uk

Founded in 1379, here's another beautiful college, and very inappropriately named too! New is one of the oldest, largest and most impressive colleges in Oxford and takes in part of the city walls, as well as a few ancient plague-heaps. Widely accepted as having the best and most beautiful student bar, New puts on great ents: the bops are legendary, and the Long Room is as much a site of drunken mayhem as the Lower Oscar Wilde Room at Magdalen, with many different societies hiring the room to throw crazy parties. New also puts on a gargantuan Commemoration Ball every three summers, described by many as the best ball in Oxford. Scenes from the Bond film *Tomorrow Never Dies* were filmed at New College, and the college has a fair share of Bond-girl lookalikes. New is particularly accomplished in musical matters: the college choir is one of the best in Oxford. New has been described as 'one of Oxford's least stressful places to live'.

ORIEL

Oriel Square, Oxford OX1 4EW
TEL 01865 276555
WEB www.oriel.ox.ac.uk

Founded in 1326, Oriel is mostly famous for its monotonous and undeniable domination of the river: it's a boatie's college. Apparently Oriel brings in students from America especially for their rowing prowess, regardless of their academic (in)abilities, and provides them with the best en-suite rooms in college and lavish free meals. Every extra year that sees Oriel come out victorious of the Summer Eights rowing race, another of its old boats is religiously burnt in the middle of their quad (that's Oxford tradition for you!). Architecturally the college is something of a rabbit warren. The distinctive front quad sees a Shakespeare production every summer, and the college is strong musically, with its own orchestra and choir. Academically very relaxed, the college reveres sport: those who can participate, do, and those who can't, support from one of the best boat houses on the river.

PEMBROKE

St Aldates, Oxford OX1 1DW
TEL 01865 276412
WEB www.pmb.ox.ac.uk

Founded in 1624, Pembroke is one of the poorest colleges in Oxford, and allegedly the college Boat Club Trust Fund is richer than the rest of the college put together! This astonishing fact holds its currency in donations from rich alumni rowers. Thus Pembroke is very strong at rowing, and the only plausible pretender to Oriel's rowing crown. In fact in the fifteen or so years of Oriel dominance on the river, Pembroke has been the only college capable of beating them once, several years ago; now the college is regularly second behind Oriel. Socially Pembroke is rather insular, has a low profile in the university, and academically it is laid back. A college rivalry exists with Christ Church.

QUEEN'S

High Street, Oxford OX1 4AW
TEL 01865 279167
WEB www.queens.ox.ac.uk

Founded 1624. Despite having a very high-profile location, right in the middle of the High, the college has a very low profile in the University; one rarely meets students from Queen's. It has some of the most obviously dramatic architecture in Oxford, ranging from the classical cupola to the UFO-like Florey building off St Clement's. Queen's is very rich and is one of the cheapest colleges to attend, offering full accommodation for all your Oxford years. There is also a particularly good library. Excluded are undergrads wanting to read Single Hons English, however, a fact unconnected with the college being a home from home to Northerners. Quirkily, Queen's has an annual dinner to celebrate the survival of an undergraduate who in 1935 was viciously attacked by a boar and defended himself by driving a tome of Aristotle into the boar's mouth.

ST ANNE'S

Woodstock Rd, Oxford OX2 6HS
TEL 01865 274825
WEB www.stannes.ox.ac.uk

Founded 1879. St Anne's, very far away from the city centre, is atypical – laid back and unpretentious and lacking in the pomp and archaic traditions of older colleges. Isolation breeds self-sufficiency, and the college has a low profile in the university. A large proportion of the undergraduate community come from a state-school background, and the college is now one of the largest in terms of undergraduate numbers. Despite being a poor college, the library has around 100,000 volumes for current use, and is one of the two largest undergraduate college libraries in Oxford. The architecture is modern and unusual for Oxford, and the gardens are pleasant in the summer.

ST CATHERINE'S (St Catz)
Manor Road, Oxford OX1 3UJ
TEL 01865 271703
WEB www.stcatz.ox.ac.uk
Founded in 1963, St Catz possesses some breathtaking architecture, much of which is Grade 1 listed. Designed by Arne Jacobsen, the famous Danish architect, a spirit of openness infuses the place, with quads having no enclosing ends. It is located just outside the tourist-infested city centre, lending it some peace and tranquillity, but is still within a convenient distance of all central facilities. St Catz has exceptional resources, including the largest student theatre in Oxford, an extensive JCR building, and a moat. It is the youngest college, and, though obviously lacking traditions, has a very friendly atmosphere. Every summer St Catz has a Summer Ball which is a big success, and good bops are laid on regularly.

ST EDMUND HALL (Teddy Hall)
Queen's Lane, Oxford OX1 4AR
TEL 01865 279008
WEB www.seh.ox.ac.uk
Founded 1278. Teddy Hall, as it is informally known, is a very poor college, and rumours abound that it has been financially helped by its close neighbour Queen's. Its main reputation across the university is for being very good at sports: men excel at rugby in particular. Despite not being one of the highest profile colleges, Teddy Hall students still manage to get involved at most levels of university life, and are particularly good at drama and music. Teddy Hall is known for being the party college, where academia is not taken too seriously, and it puts on good ents.

ST HILDA'S
Cowley Place, Oxford OX4 1DY
TEL 01865 276816
WEB www.sthildas.ox.ac.uk
St Hilda's, all-female since its foundation in 1893, voted in June 2006 to accept male students. Up until then, the college was home to the notorious, roaming 'Hildabeasts', among the most active members of the university, getting involved in many sports, societies and other extra-curricular pursuits. College buildings are bland but pleasant, and the site is on the banks of the Cherwell, with beautiful gardens adding a colourful touch to the landscape. The college is fairly poor, and facilities are limited. St Hilda's is strong at rowing. Lots of ents are put on, with something to keep the lasses

happy every weekend. The bar is unexciting, despite being the cheapest in Oxford. Being next to the river, the college owns its own punts, which are free for use by St Hilda's students and their guests. The college is seldom visited by tourists, which is a good thing.

ST HUGH'S
St Margaret's Rd, Oxford OX2 6LE
TEL 01865 274910
WEB www.st-hughs.ox.ac.uk
Founded in 1886 St Hugh's is so far out (geographically) it may as well be part of another university, and the walk into the centre of town can be long and laborious, although buses are very frequent. This is both an affliction and an attraction: St Hugh's has huge grounds (including croquet lawns and tennis courts) and there is (unfortunately small and ugly) on-site space to accommodate all students. College facilities are good and social life is tumultuous and intense. Ents are good, with a large-scale bop including a bouncy castle and barbecue organised during the summer. Despite being so far out of town, St Hugh's students are reasonably involved across the university activities, especially in art and drama.

ST JOHN'S
St Giles, Oxford OX1 3JP
TEL 01865 277317
WEB www.sjc.ox.ac.uk
Founded 1555. This is the richest college in Oxford. St John's provides excellent facilities: there are financial rewards for the academically strong (1st, Norrington Table 1999): on-site accommodation (including luxurious sets and the strange honeycomb structures for Freshers) is guaranteed for everyone, there is a modern conference centre, and beautiful gardens adorn the quads. St John's is academically very strong and there is considerable pressure on students to work hard.

The college performs well in sports as well, at rugby and rowing in particular. On the social front St John's doesn't deliver quite as well: students tend to be quite dull, a fact reflected by the college bar which is very nice and spacious, but rarely alive and kickin'.

ST PETER'S
New Inn Hall Street, OX1 2DL
TEL 01865 278892
WEB www.spc.ox.ac.uk
Founded in 1929, St Peter's is a relatively new college in Oxford history, and covers very small grounds in the centre of town. Priorities here are much higher on social issues than on academic matters, and St Peter's doesn't excel at sports

either. Nevertheless students seem fairly involved around the university, and the JCR is very active. St Peter's is very poor, which is obvious from the blatant lack or inadequacy of certain facilities. The college has a reasonable bar and puts on good ents events. Every year a middle-size Summer Ball is organised.

SOMERVILLE

Woodstock Road, Oxford OX2 6HD
TEL 01865 270629
WEB www.some.ox.ac.uk
Founded in 1929, Somerville is the most recent of colleges to have gone mixed (1994) and is located just beyond the reach of annoying tourists, yet close enough to the city centre for convenience. The generally left-wing college [with some notable exceptions – this was Margaret Thatcher's college] has always been politically very active and JCR members voice their opinions loudly. Indeed, Somervillians are active in every respect of university life, and the college has a fairly high profile amongst university students. College atmosphere is easygoing though the number of political hacks and activists can sometimes be distressing. Somerville has good ents although the college bar is dull and bare.

TRINITY

Broad Street, Oxford OX1 3BH
Tel 01865 279910
web www.trinity.ox.ac.uk
Founded in 1554, Trinity is centrally located, next door to its arch-rival Balliol. The college has spacious and attractive grounds (which it leases from Balliol!) and elegant buildings. The undergraduate body is fairly small which lends to an intimate college atmosphere. Trinity used to be dominated by public-school types, but this has now changed. Accommodation provisions are good, and the college flats on Woodstock Road are regarded as among the best and poshest in Oxford. Trinity students have a high profile in the university, and are popular and involved in many activities. A Commemoration Ball is organised every three years in the summer and, on a more day-to-day basis, ents is good with fun bops, and Trinity men and women enjoy a lively and atmospheric bar.

UNIVERSITY

High Street, Oxford OX1 4BH
TEL 01865 276602
WEB www.univ.ox.ac.uk

Founded 1249. University is one of the colleges Oxford students hear the least about: it has an extremely low profile and is very quiet. This is despite the fact it is one of the oldest colleges (holding a claim, with Balliol and Merton, to being the oldest, although there is evidence that the college forged some deeds in 1381 to prove that it was founded in advance of Merton). The college is undeniably ancient, however, and very beautiful. Like St John's, it has a reputation for being full of bookworms who take life far too seriously and are unaware of the existence of the words 'fun' and 'enjoyment'.

College life is said to be a little slow, although the alleged existence of bops and a good bar do redeem it a little.

WADHAM

Parks Road, Oxford OX1 3PN
TEL 01865 277946
WEB www.wadham.ox.ac.uk
Founded in 1610, Wadham is a bastion of the left, with an even greater lefty image than Balliol. Getting involved in JCR and student affairs is a great springboard into the political limelight. It has always been liberal, and is very involved in LGB affairs: it hosts Queer Week, which culminates in an S&M and Fetishes Bop (where you get to see some quite outlandish costumes...). The college is also strong in music and drama (helped by the fact that Wadham has one of the university's only reasonably sized theatres), and the Saturday night bops are legendary.

WORCESTER

Worcester Street, Oxford OX1 2HB
TEL 01865 278391
WEB www.worcester.ox.ac.uk
Founded 1714. Worcester possesses huge and beautiful grounds, including tennis courts, sports grounds and a lake. Beautiful gardens decorate the college and provide a suitable backdrop to the medieval cottages and classic colonnade. All students are accommodated on the main college site. The college is presently enjoying some success at rowing and rugby, but is not known for any academic excellence. Lord Sainsbury was a Worcester student, thus hall food is very cheap and also very good. Every three years the college hosts a huge Commemoration Ball in the summer. Worcester is lively, fairly rich and somewhat self-contained.

OXFORD BROOKES UNIVERSITY

Oxford Brookes University
Gipsy Lane Campus
Headington
Oxford OX3 0BP

TEL 01865 483040
FAX 01865 483983
EMAIL admissions@brookes.ac.uk
WEB www.brookes.ac.uk

Oxford Brookes Students' Union
Helena Kennedy Student Centre
London Road
Headington
Oxford OX3 0BP

TEL 01865 484715
FAX 01865 484799
EMAIL obsu.president@brookes.ac.uk
WEB www.theSU.com

VAG VIEW

Oxford Brookes became the darling of the 'new university' league tables, and being based in 'that sweet city with her dreaming spires' soon found itself with a reputation and student clientele that defied placing it in the ex-poly category. If you are looking for a university still not overly demanding at entry, which offers a host of well-conceived modular courses in some interesting niche areas, and which enjoys the atmosphere of one of the world's great student cities, then Brookes might well be for you.

A stomping 86% of its students cheered for it in the National Student Survey; its support system is such that only 7% of them will not finish the course; and 80% will find themselves with a job they wouldn't have had otherwise within six months of leaving.

UNIVERSITY/STUDENT PROFILE	
University since	**1992**
Situation/style	**Campus**
Student population	**19070**
Total undergraduates	**13645**
Mature undergraduates	**22%**
International undergrads	**16%**
Male/female ratio	**47:53**
Equality of opportunity:	
state school intake	**73%**
social class 4-7 intake	**41%**
low-participation area intake	**6%**

the main Students' Union, is housed with teaching facilities and accommodation across the road from Gypsy Lane on the Headington Hill site, formerly the house of beleaguered tycoon Robert Maxwell, who called it the largest council house in England, which indeed it was. He never owned it.

CAMPUS

Brookes is based over three main campuses; two in Headington (approx. 1.5 miles from city centre) and one at Wheatley (5 miles away). A free inter-site bus service runs every half hour during the day. The Helena Kennedy Student Centre (HKSC),

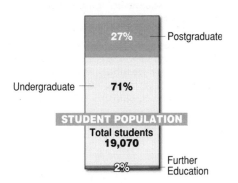

Postgraduate **27%**

Undergraduate **71%**

STUDENT POPULATION
Total students
19,070

Further Education **2%**

FEES, BURSARIES

UK & EU Fees, 2009-10: £3,225 p.a. If in receipt of the HE Maintenance grant there's a sliding scale bursary according to household earnings. See www.brookes.ac.uk/studying/finance/support/ug_home. The Brookes Academic Excellence scholarship is awarded to students attaining three A-grade A levels or equivalent and is worth £2,000 p.a. See www.brookes.ac.uk/studying/finance/support/academic_scholarships.

Community Scholarships of £1,000 p.a. are available to students of partner state schools and colleges.

STUDENT PROFILE

Oxford Brookes is uncharacteristic of most recently founded universities because of its high independent school intake (28% of undergraduates). This statistical lurch towards the middle class, unusual for an ex-poly, serves to prompt the stereotypical image of the uni as a hang-out for air-

TEACHING SURVEY AT A GLANCE

Avg. UCAS points accepted	**300**
Acceptance rate	**15%**
Overall satisfaction rate	**86%**
Helpful/interested staff	★★★
Small tuition groups	★★★
Students into graduate jobs	**80%**

Teaching most popular with undergraduates:
Education (100%), Physical Geography & Enviro. Science (97%), Initial Teacher Training (93%), Management Studies (90%), Social Work, Mass Communications, Business & Administrative Studies (89%), Law, Human & Social Geography (88%), subjects allied to Medicine, Media Studies, English (87%), Social Studies (86%).

Teaching least popular with undergraduates:
Music, Performing Arts (71%).

from a state school you will undoubtedly find "your type".

'There is also a large proportion of foreign students from a huge range of countries. Ethnic minorities from the UK are also very well represented and play a large part in the overall feel of the place.'

ACADEMIA & JOBS

There are 8 academic schools: Arts & Humanities, Built Environment, Biological & Molecular Sciences, the Business School, the Westminster Institute of Education, the School of Technology, Health & Social Care, Social Sciences & Law.

Students say that the teaching is best in Education, Physical Geography & Environmental Science, Initial Teacher Training, Management Studies, Social Work, Mass Communications, Business & Administrative Studies, Law, Human & Social Geography, Subjects allied to Medicine, Media Studies, English, and Social Studies.

Modular joint honours degrees characterise the curriculum, and an academic year-structure made up not of terms but semesters. Ground-breaking when first launched, the modular system can be made to work to your advantage, but individuals are left pretty much to design their own courses. The undergraduate programme offers 90 single honours degrees, which may be combined appropriately to form combined honours courses. Students may also add introductory modules.

Emily Waller says: 'All the rules and regulations can be confusing, so get help if you need it. The work load is manageable, but depends on the course that you are taking. Work placements both abroad and in Britain are common.'

On many a course they push study- and work-abroad options in Europe, USA, Canada or Australia, both to widen your take on life and earn credits towards your degree. Work placement programmes and grants are available in 27 EU countries. Language skills are another focus. Classes at all levels are available through the Modern Languages Unit. Modules are popular in French, Spanish, Japanese and Mandarin.

'Teaching staff are generally very helpful (if you can find them),' adds Emily. 'Each student is assigned a personal tutor for their years of study.'

They advertise a kind of second-layer support system called Upgrade, a confidential study advice service where you can solicit advice on issues such as planning and writing essays, assignments and dissertations. Upgrade tutors are there to highlight areas for improvement and help you understand what your subject tutors are looking for. Students can book a tutorial at advertised times. See www.brookes.ac.uk/services/upgrade/a-z.html.

head Sloanes who couldn't get a place at Durham. However, around 3,000 undergraduates are in fact part-time, 22% are mature, 41% come from the lower socio-economic orders, and 6% from the dreaded 'low participation' neighbourhood category. There is, too, a large (16%) overseas body of students. All of which prompted Giles Balleny to insist that whatever the statistics indicate re: the public-school brigade, on the ground the perception is of a rich tapestry of life.

'Brookes has an unusually varied cross section of students, which gives it a cosmopolitan outlook in everything it does. Among the more prominent groups, public-school student types are not as dominant as people suggest, although there probably is a larger public school contingent than at any other of the 1992 universities. Most ignore their fraternising and get on with doing their own thing. Whether you are from an independent school or

SUBJECT AREAS (%)

Health Subjects, Combined, Education, Science, Engineering, Built Environment, Creative Arts, Humanities, Social Studies incl Law, Business, Maths & Computer

27, 7, 5, 8, 10, 3, 19, 7, 5, 2, 7

RESEARCH EXCELLENCE		
% of Oxford Brookes' research that is 4* (World-class) or 3* (Internationally rated):		
	4*	3*
Health Professions	10%	20%
Biological Sciences	5%	15%
Applied Mathematics	0%	10%
Computer Science	15%	35%
General Engineering	5%	40%
Town/Country Planning	5%	35%
Business/Management	5%	20%
Law	10%	35%
Politics	0%	20%
Anthropology	5%	30%
Psychology	0%	25%
Education	5%	25%
French	5%	30%
English	5%	35%
Philosophy	0%	0%
History	25%	40%
Art and Design	15%	15%
History of Art	15%	40%
Music	15%	20%

Despite all this, in the *Times Higher Education*'s Student Experience Survey Brookes students suggest the actuality is not quite as amazing as it sounds. Brookes came out around middle table for helpful/interested staff and small-group tuition. We give them 3 stars out of 5.

Continues Emily: 'There are three libraries, well stocked with up-to-date and ancient texts and an easy-to-use computerised catalogue; friendly individual subject librarians are always willing to help. The main library has over 1,000 private study desks and some group study rooms (great for catching up on gossip, if not for study!). It is open until 10.00 pm weekdays. Every student has free Internet and e-mail access, and computers are accessible 24/7. Computer Services - in particular the help desk - are invaluable, as the network has an annoying habit of crashing (normally about five minutes before an assignment is due in!).'

They also advertise a Student Disability Service that assists with sensory and mobility impairments, dyslexia and other specific learning difficulties, mental health problems and medical conditions. A Support Worker Scheme can cover such as note-taking in lectures, reading onto tape and mobility support on campus. And there are specialist staff for deaf students. There's also extra time for exams, etc.

More than a quarter of graduates go into the health field. They educate a large number of graduate nurses, the majority SEN. There are BA and BSc degrees in Midwifery, and popular courses in Biomedical Science, Occupational therapy and Physiotherapy. Sixteen per cent of all Brookes graduates get jobs in hospitals. Public Health Nutrition, Environmental Biology, Environmental Science, and Public Health Nutrition are other degrees that take graduates into the public sector health area.

There's also a large primary teaching provision - BA Primary (Work-based) and BA Initial Teacher Training - which accounts for 9% of the graduate workforce.

In Engineering, their graduates are among the most popular with the automobile industry, and there's a particular niche in motor sport.

They are also renowned for a series of degrees in Publishing, having produced the prototype.

Estate agent/managers proliferate out of Brookes. Look at BSc Real Estate Management, also BA Business of Real Estate. Planning is big here, too: see BA Cities - Environment, Design & Development or BA City & Regional Planning. There are jobs aplenty in the construction industry from Brookes degrees. And they are management leaders in the catering and hotel trade, with such as the 4-year sandwich BSc Hotel & Restaurant Management and the two International Hospitality/Tourism Management, again 4-year sandwich BSc.

SOCIAL SCENE

STUDENTS' UNION There's an active ents programme with regular clubnights, film nights, comedy nights and termly balls. Wednesday is Playground (new themes and promos each week); Friday is Pleasuredome (9 pm-2 am) - 'the best sound system, lighting and dance tunes in Oxford', a mixture of styles at the main SU **Venue**, which has a capacity of over 1,200.

The main union bars based around the university are the **Harts** lounge bar, **Morals Bar** and the **Mezzanine**. Morals Bar is the home of Blitz (9 till 2 pop tunes), Chalk & Cheese (from live jazz to comedy) and the SU's rock and indie night Feedback - the best grunge, rock, metal, punk, alternative with resident DJs Sht Chaos and Hell. High above **The Venue**, the **Mez Bar** is the home of the Sunday Session.

'A free and confidential advice and counselling service is on offer, as is representation for all students on academic, personal and financial issues. Over sixty clubs and societies ensure that there really is something for everyone. Currently the most popular society is Cocktail.'

There's a monthly student paper and a TV stationthat just won two Batiobal TV Awards.

SPORT Facilities are excellent and include

WHAT IT'S REALLY LIKE

UNIVERSITY:

Social Life	★★★★
Campus scene	**Cross section**
Student Union services	**Good**
Politics	**Average**
Sport	**Competitive**
National team position	**41st**
Sport facilities	**Good**
Arts opportunities	**Drama, music, art excellent; film good; dance avg**
Student newspaper	**OBScene**
Student TV	**Brookes TV**
2006 NASTA Awards	**Two awards**
Nightclub	**The Venue**
Bars	**Morals, Harts, Mez**
Union ents	**Pleasuredome, pop, jazz, comedy**
Union societies	**60**
Most popular society	**Cocktail**
Parking	**Poor**

CITY:

Entertainment	★★★
Scene	**Small, good pubs, OK clubs**
Town/gown relations	**Average**
Risk of violence	**Average**
Cost of living	**High**
Student concessions	**Good**
Survival + 2 nights out	**£70 pw**
Part-time work campus/town	**Good**

Astroturf, squash courts, health suite, heavy weights gym, tennis courts, rugby, football, cricket and hockey pitches, fitness trails, two boat houses and a multi-purpose sports hall for aerobics, martial arts, women's boxing, circuit training, etc. The Centre for Sport is open from 7.30 am to 11.00 pm. The university teams came 41st overall last year.

TOWN 'The night life in Oxford, always busy and full of tourists and students, is varied but expensive, even with the student discount that most clubs, pubs, bars and restaurants offer.

There is a great music and theatre scene with lots of theatres, gig venues and cinemas, but the clubbing scene is definitely mediocre (unless you are a big cheesy '60s to '80s fan). Travel around the city is regular and simple, and for women the Students' Union runs a special Safety Bus from campus to doorstep. As long as 'home' is within the Oxford Ring Road, this is a free service. Coaches run every ten minutes to London, Gatwick, Heathrow and Cambridge. Student discounts are available.

PILLOW TALK

There are nine halls of residence, all with easy access to the university, and many, but not all, with an internet facility available in each room. Clive Booth Hall was opened last autumn, and Cheney Student Village in the spring. Although in practice most freshers live in halls, priority is given to those living farthest distant from Oxford.

ACCOMMODATION

Guarantee to freshers	**97%**
Style	**Halls, flats**
Security guard	**All**
Shared rooms	**None**
Internet access	**All**
Self-catered	**Most**
En suite	**Most**
Approx price range pw	**£88-£129**
City rent pw	**£100-£150**

Facilities generally accommodate both sexes, although single sex accommodation is available on request. With the exception of two halls, it's a condition of residency not to keep a car. Seventy new en-suite self-catered rooms opened this year.

GETTING THERE

☛ By road: from north, A423 or A34 or A43; London, M40; south, M4/J13, A34. Wheatley campus, M40/J8, A418. Good coach service.
☛ By rail: London Paddington, 1:00; Birmingham, 1:30; Bristol, 1:45; Sheffield, 3:30.
☛ By air: Heathrow/Gatwick; coaches/buses will stop outside Gypsy Lane campus on request.
☛ By coach: London, 1:40; Birmingham, 1:30; Leeds, 5:30; Bristol, 4:30.

UNIVERSITY OF PLYMOUTH

The University of Plymouth
Drake Circus
Plymouth
Devon PL4 8AA

TEL 01752 232 232
FAX 01752 232 141
EMAIL prospectus@plymouth.ac.uk
WEB www.plymouth.ac.uk

Plymouth Students' Union
Drake Circus
Plymouth PL4 8AA

TEL 01752 238500
FAX 01752 251669
EMAIL
presplymouth@su.plymouth.ac.uk
WEB www.upsu.com

VAG VIEW

The University of Plymouth has made a vigorous rise since gaining university status in 1992. Time was when its bits were scattered all over Devon, in Plymouth, Exmouth, Exeter, and Newton Abbot. Now all of a sudden everyone's at the heart of things, most recently Arts students moved into the new £35-million Roland Levinsky building on campus, which comes with a cinema, exhibition areas and a café. Meanwhile, Education has taken up residence in a £40-million development with residential accommodation, and Health & Social Work in a £10.75-million amenity, with 4-court sports hall, health and fitness centre, and another café.

None of this should give the impression that Plymouth's outlook is insular or its nest henceforth campus-bound, for among its 30,000 students are many based at partner colleges throughout the South West, and of course Plymouth is a partner - with the University of Exeter and the NHS in Devon and Cornwall - in the Peninsula College of Medicine and Dentistry.

Students love it here - 82% of them gave the uni their blessing in the National Student

UNIVERSITY/STUDENT PROFILE	
University since	**1992**
Situation/style	**Campus**
Student population	**30540**
Total undergraduates	**24490**
Mature undergraduates	**63%**
International undergrads	**4%**
Male/female ratio	**38:62**
Equality of opportunity:	
state school intake	**94%**
social class 4-7 intake	**31%**
low-participation area intake	**10%**

Survey, and a mere 6% don't last the course (2% below their Government benchmark). The strategy over the last few years has been weightily impressive, but let it not obscure the lighter, dreamier side of life available at Plymouth, which is widely known to specialise in Australian hunks, sand, sea and surf. There's even a Surf Science & Technology degree - believe it, dudes, this really does exist! They have been winning the national surfing championship held at Newquay's Fistral Beech for years. Perhaps that's why only 59% of graduates get a real graduate job from this university within six months of leaving.

FEES, BURSARIES

UK & EU Fees, 2009-10: £3,225 p.a. There's a sliding scale bursary scheme for those eligible for the HE Maintenance Grant. There are also sports scholarships, and academic ones and awards for students reading Chemistry, Civil Engineering, Theatre and Performance, and Modern Languages. There are also mature student and fieldwork bursaries available, and bursaries for students from university 'compact' schools/colleges, and anyone from the South West Peninsula region. See www.plymouth.ac.uk/money for details. those from the South West Peninsula region.

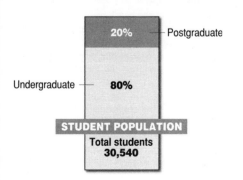

Postgraduate 20%

Undergraduate 80%

STUDENT POPULATION
Total students
30,540

TEACHING SURVEY AT A GLANCE

Avg. UCAS points accepted	**270**
Acceptance rate	**22%**
Overall satisfaction rate	**82%**
Helpful/interested staff	★★★★
Small tuition groups	★★★
Students into graduate jobs	**59%**

Teaching most popular with undergraduates:
Maths (100%), Tourism (96%), Geology (95%),
Human & Social Geography (93%), Physical
Geography & Enviro. Studies, Sciences related to
Biology, Initial Teacher Training (92%), Biology
(91%), Civil Engineering (90%), Business Studies,
Law (88%), Physics (87%), Anatomy, Physiology
& Pathology (86%), Engineering & Technology,
Languages, Management Studies (85%).

Teaching least popular with undergraduates:
Design Studies (67%), Creative Arts (65%),
Fine Art (43%).

STUDENT PROFILE

Applicants from the UK tend to be drawn from
below a line drawn south of the Midlands through
Wales, Bristol and London. Many are very local,
mature, and 7,500 are part-timers. Around 30%
come from the lower socio-economic orders and
only 6% from public schools. But the recruitment
effort is made in another area. There's a large
international draw from 100 countries, including
the surf cities of the world, and this year they are
establishing the Plymouth Devon International
College, with a range of one- or two-year, pre-uni-
versity courses designed to prepare overseas students for direct entry to courses at both undergraduate and masters level.

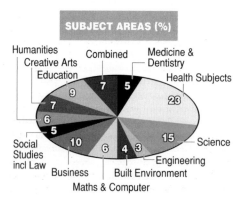

SUBJECT AREAS (%)

CAMPUSES

Plymouth looks south, out across Drake's Island
and the Sound to the English Channel. It is the last
big place before you tip across the Tamar into
Cornwall. South Devon is rich and creamy like its
cows, quite distinct from angst-ridden North
Devon, up beyond Dartmoor, with its leaner stock.
It is an enviable position in which to spend three or
four years, what with the city too, its shops, cafés
and Union Street bars and clubs. But in the end it is
Devon's 600 miles of coastline, the uni's proximity
to some of the country's most stunning beaches and
countryside, that make it such an ideal environment for study and leisure.

ACADEMIA & JOBS

Students say the best teaching at Plymouth is in
Maths, Tourism, Geology, Human & Social
Geography, Physical Geography & Environment
Studies, sciences related to Biology, Initial Teacher
Training, Biology, Civil Engineering, Business
Studies, Law, Physics, Anatomy, Physiology &
Pathology, Engineering & Technology, Languages,
Management Studies. Least popular is Fine Art,
which causes 57% of the class to yawn.

What's especially promising is the students'
commendation of the helpful/interested staff and
small-group tuition in the *Times Higher Education*
magazine's Student Experience Survey.

They are hot on study skills support programmes. There are disability services, support for
dyslexia, specialist assessment for students applying for the Disabled Student Allowance, and training in the use of specialist technical equipment.
They boast a higher percentage of disabled students than any other university.

But what is this degree in surfing? 'This is the
first academically rigorous surf science course in
the world,' boasts Dr Malcolm Findlay of the
Institute of Marine Studies. The first year dwells
on oceanography, surfing materials and business
studies. The second moves uncontroversially into
areas like human biology and human performance,
but in the third year you develop your own specialism. Head for the beach presumably.

Building on its worldwide reputation for excellence in marine skills and research, Plymouth will
this year launch its new School of Marine Science
and Engineering which, with 1,400 students and 85
staff, will be the largest of its kind in Europe.

There is all sorts of marine interest (the
Nautical School, the original fount of this uni, was
established in 1862, and marine courses account
for almost a quarter of Plymouth's undergraduate
programme - Aquaculture, Marine Biology, Marine
Navigation, Applied Marine Sport Science, Nautical

RESEARCH EXCELLENCE

% of Plymouth's research that is
4* (World-class) or **3*** (Internationally rated):

	4*	3*
Hospital Clinical	5%	60%
Epidemiology	5%	20%
Health Services	5%	45%
Nursing/Midwifery	10%	20%
Health Professions	0%	10%
Biological Sciences	0%	25%
Agriculture	0%	10%
Environmental Sciences	5%	45%
Applied Mathematics	0%	25%
Statistics	0%	30%
Computer Science	25%	50%
Electrical/Electronic Eng.	5%	15%
Civil Engineering	15%	30%
Mechanical, Aero., & Manufac. Eng.	0%	25%
Geography Environment	10%	40%
Business/Management	5%	25%
Social Work	5%	50%
Sociology	5%	30%
Psychology	5%	25%
Education	10%	20%
English	10%	20%
History	0%	25%
Art and Design	10%	45%
History of Art	5%	50%
Performing Arts	5%	15%

those with a good honours degree in a biomedically related or health care professional subject, or with relevant experience of working as a health care professional. The Graduate Medical Schools Admissions Test (GAMSAT) will also be required.

The Peninsula College is of course a collaboration with Exeter University and the NHS in Devon and Cornwall, the NHS hand ensuring a strong clinical element in course design. The BM, BS degree focuses on the biological mechanisms that produce disease and its social impact. It looks very hands-on. First undergraduate intake occurred in 2002, half in Exeter, half in Plymouth. Both unis already had successful postgraduate medical schools. One of the key points about the new College is that it binds them tighter into the regional community. Students work initially with patients in Plymouth and Exeter, then in Truro in Cornwall, finally up with the hillbillies beyond Dartmoor.

You will be required to achieve 370 points from 21 units. At least 320 points must come from 3 full GCE A subjects, including at least one science and preferably one non-science subject. A minimum of C grades must be achieved at A/AS level and an A grade in a science at A-Level. A Level subjects should not overlap, e.g. Maths and Further Maths. General Studies is not included at AS or A Level.

Plymouth also has degrees in Adult Nursing, Community Health Care, Mental Health, Midwifery, Physiotherapy and Podiatry, Dietetics, and Occupational Therapy.

Again, clinical psychologists abound from their BSc Psychology. The psychology and mental health provisions lead to an employment track record in psychotherapy.

Meanwhile, graduates in BSc combinations with their Criminal Justice Studies, Psychology, Social Policy, Social Research, Law, Sociology, Statistics, etc, find a variety of jobs, often probation officers.

The Faculty of Agriculture covers the whole gamut of courses, from Management to Nutrition, from Agriculture to Estate Management, and there's a Wildlife Conservation option too. A recent popular development has been the Veterinary Nursing & Management degree. Foresters also find jobs in quantity from Plymouth, and aspiring environmental officers enjoy a strong niche.

Cartography is another niche, which reminds us too of their popular Geography, Illustration, and Graphics courses. Meanwhile, Computer Science, which was adjudged either world-class or internationally excellent in 75% of its research provision at the 2008 nationwide assessment, accounts for about 7% of the university's graduate employment.

Studies and Ocean Science, Civil & Coastal Engineering, Geography or Geology with Ocean Science, Ocean Exploration. This year, degrees in Marine Studies appear with options to specialise in Ocean Yachting, Merchant Shipping or Navigation.

There's also a trio of Maritime Business degrees, and they have a BSc in Cruise Management, with support from Princes Cruises (hospitality, marine studies, business plus a year on a cruise liner!), directing our interest into their hospitality and tourism programme: Business & Tourism, Hospitality & Tourism, International Tourism Mgt, etc. Plymouth takes up the challenge from the Devon Riviera, excellent International and European Business degrees, plenty of sea air and extra-curricular encouragement.

In September 2007 the first dental students joined the Medics at Peninsula, making it henceforth the Peninsula College of Medicine & Dentistry. The Dentistry course, operating on sites in Plymouth, Truro and Exeter, is a Graduate Entry Hon BDS(4 years). The programme is designed for

SOCIAL SCENE

STUDENTS' UNION The Plymouth Students' Union has undergone a refurbishment and now boasts leather sofas, Sky TV and new games machines. A new DJ bar has met expectations.

They have a dynamic ents manager, digging out new local bands, and as a result Plymouth is featured in many a uni tour. The May ball, we are told, 'attracted 3,500 to a field', actually Newnham Park, the classical Georgian manor between the outskirts of Plymouth and the foothills of Dartmoor National Park.

Friday night's *Burn* sets the scene for the weekend on the main campus - two dance rooms, 1,450 capacity - cheese and party in **Ignition**; indie to rock, ska to punk in **Illusion**. Saturday is regulation SU fare: *Flirt!* in Ignition. Comedy nights (*Laughing Goldfish*) are especially popular, as are *Spin What You Bring* and *Open Mic Night*. *S.I.N.* is the official sports & societies DJ night, then it's on to C103 in town for more, where Wednesday is *Boogie Nights* (chart & cheese; Friday is *Total Rock* (Room 1: rock; Room 2: heavy metal).

They say the superclubs are closing down in Plymouth and students are going more for the pub music scene. The union still team up with clubs for student nights - **C103** in Union Street is the present choice, and the Plymouth **Walkabout** does good business with them.

When not clubbing and surfing, there are society activities, notably *Fly* magazine and SCAP, Community Action, which has BIG ideas, last year an international project in Thika, a small town in Kenya no less.

Now, in line with Plymouth's bid to become a 'European City of the Sea', they are planning to develop a 'cultural quarter'. The idea came simultaneously to Newcastle, and it's a good one - a conglomeration of galleries, cinemas, exhibition areas theatre space, and a café. The first building, due to open in 2007, will be a base for the Faculty of Arts and a new home for the Plymouth Arts Centre.

SPORT £850,000 has been invested in a new fitness complex with squash courts and resistance and cardiovascular training equipment, and over £70,000 has gone into new boats and dinghies for the University's own Diving & Sailing Centre. There's national/world-class water-sport - sailing, diving, surfing, windsurfing, power-boating, wakeboarding, canoeing and waterski. A fleet of dinghies and yachts provide sailing opportunities. Plymouth is the only UK uni to have its own diving and sailing centre. Students can learn to dive professionally as part of their course (selected disciplines only) or take a recreational diving course, which is open to all students.

WHAT IT'S REALLY LIKE	
UNIVERSITY:	
Social Life	★★★★
Campus scene	**Lively ents, water sporty**
Student Union services	**OK**
Politics	**Interest low**
Sport	**47 clubs**
National team position	**42nd**
Sport facilities	**Average**
Arts opportunities	**Drama, dance, music, art avg; film poor**
Student magazine	**Fly!**
Nightclub/bars	**Ignition, Illusion**
Union ents	**Party, cheese, indie**
Union societies	**78**
Most popular society	**Football**
Parking	**Non-existent**
CITY:	
Entertainment	★★★★
Scene	**Clubs, pubs OK**
Town/gown relations	**Poor**
Risk of violence	**Average**
Cost of living	**Below average**
Student concessions	**Average**
Survival + 2 nights out	**£70 pw**
Part-time work campus/town	**OK**

There's also the usual land-based team stuff. They came 42nd nationally last year - most popular club is soccer, though it was their American football squad that was named 'Team of the Year' by the British Collegiate American Football League last year.

TOWN Plymouth - destroyed during the war and rebuilt at a low point in British architecture - has been designated second poorest ward in Europe, but you wouldn't know it since it has won huge EU investment. There's a surfeit of accommodation which costs upwards of £40 per week, you can walk anywhere, it is a safe, friendly, smiley place. When the sun shines it is unbeatable, the beach is 10 minutes away, and when it doesn't shine, maybe the snow on the nearby moors is not so bad an option.

Like nearby Exeter, Plymouth has recently become more cosmopolitan. Think huge shopping centre and **Barbican**. The Barbican is, of course, waterside, the olde worlde bit of town - boats, fish and tourists, but more to the point, pubs, clubs and restaurants. Arts-wise, there's the **Theatre Royal**, which had the Royal Shakespeare Company in residence when we were there, and the alternative Drum Theatre for more progressive fare. If you're

ACCOMMODATION

Guarantee to freshers	**50%**
Style	**Halls, flats**
Security guard	**None**
Shared rooms	**None**
Internet access	**All**
Self-catered	**All**
En suite	**Most**
Approx price range pw	**£75-£120**
City rent pw	**£50-£100**

seriously into painting, why not cross the border into Cornwall - many do so as to chase the surf in Newquay (current international surf and clubland Mecca) - but continue west, down to St Ives, the 'Tate of the South West,' as it is known.

PILLOW TALK

You are guaranteed a room in halls if you come more than 25 miles away from the campus at which you'll be studying, provided it's your first choice uni and your application for a halls place is received before July 9. In fact, there are even more ifs and buts, so you'd better speak to them, or their lawyers, personally...and get in quick! Note, all medical students are guaranteed an offer of a place in halls for their first year of study. There are mixed-sex halls, flats and houses, all self-catering.

Mary Newman hall, with 157 en-suite rooms, opens in September 2007. In addition, 350 en-suite rooms are now available on campus in the new Faculty of Education development. Francis Drake Hall opened on campus in 2008, but it's not for exclusive use by freshers.

GETTING THERE

☛ By road: M5, A38 Exeter, Plymouth; Newton Abbot, A38, A383; Exmouth M5/J30, A376. Good coach services to Exeter and Plymouth.
☛ By coach to Plymouth: London, 4:40; Bristol, 2:30; Exeter, 1:05. Exeter: London, 4:00.
☛ By rail to Plymouth: London Paddington, 3:30; Bristol Parkway, 3:00; Southampton, 4:00; Birmingham New Street, 4:00. Exeter from London Paddington, 2:30; Bristol Parkway, 1:30; Birmingham New Street, 3:00.
☛ By air: Exeter or Plymouth City Airports.

UNIVERSITY OF PORTSMOUTH

The University of Portsmouth
University House
Winston Churchill Avenue
Portsmouth PO1 2UP

TEL 02392 848484
FAX 02392 843082
EMAIL admissions@port.ac.uk
WEB www.port.ac.uk

Portsmouth Students' Union
Cambridge Road
Portsmouth PO1 2ET

TEL 02392 843640
FAX 02392843667
EMAIL student-union@port.ac.uk
WEB www.upsu.net

VAG VIEW

Portsea behaves like an island, it has its own microclimate, slightly warmer than nearby Brighton or Bournemouth, as it sits snugly behind the Isle of Wight. For centuries, because of its strategic position, it was an important naval base, but now the focus is moving away from the military, the old naval dockyard giving itself to a pleasure zone of shops, nightclubs, bars, called Gun Wharf.

What once we detected as a military ethic in the university's 'Code of Student

UNIVERSITY/STUDENT PROFILE

University since	**1992**
Situation/style	**City campus**
Student population	**19860**
Total undergraduates	**15570**
Mature undergraduates	**27%**
International undergrads	**8%**
Male/female ratio	**56:44**
Equality of opportunity:	
state school intake	**95%**
social class 4-7 intake	**31%**
low-participation area intake	**9%**

TEACHING SURVEY AT A GLANCE

Avg. UCAS points accepted	**270**
Acceptance rate	**18%**
Overall satisfaction rate	**88%**
Helpful/interested staff	★★★★
Small tuition groups	★★★
Students into graduate jobs	**64%**

Teaching most popular with undergraduates:
Politics (99%), History, Human & Social Geography (98%), Maths, Management (97%), Sciences related to Biology, Physical Geography & Enviro. Science (95%), Biology, Civil and Chemical Engineering, English, Finance & Accounting (94%), European Languages, Sociology (93%), Electronic & Electrical Eng., Accounting (92%), Economics (91%), Business Studies, Law, Sports Science (90%).

Teaching least popular with undergraduates:
Medical Technology (78%),
Computer Science (77%), Social Work (73%).

Discipline' seems also to have slipped away - though there remains an active OTC (Officer Training Corps), and a high input of graduates into the defence arena from a variety of departments. Today, however, military-style disciplines seem to have been sublimated in a caring ethos, modern, civilian, and maybe a slip laden with PR. They describe themselves as 'a hands-on student university: we care that our students turn up at lectures.' There is no clock-watching, but they want to find out why a student's interest is dropping away, if it is.

The uni serves up vocational fare true to its roots. which lead us back to 1869, foundation year of Portsmouth & Gosport School of Science & Art. It was 100 years later that the college became Portsmouth Polytechnic, before receiving its Royal Charter as a university in 1992.

Students here love it - 88% gave it their unreserved recommendation in the National Student Survey last year.

CAMPUS

Guildhall Campus is the name they give to the collection of sites in the centre of town, which has a European, café-style feel to it, and there are so many students marauding about that it seems not so much town as university precinct. Indeed, it is now known as the University Quarter.

Within it there is now an almost entirely wireless campus, allowing students to communicate, research and work wherever they choose. The transition from desktop computer use to wireless has quadrupled usage to more than 6,000. All rooms in halls of residence have free, very high-speed broadband (10Mbps).

Two other campuses, Milton and Langstone, 2 and 3 miles away, are less and less significant.

FEES, BURSARIES

UK & EU Fees, 2009-10: £3,225 p.a. If in receipt of the full HE Maintenance grant there's a bursary of £900; if in receipt of a partial grant, it's £600. A bursary is available to 14 local feeder schools and colleges of £300. There's a Care-Leavers-Foyer-Sheltered Accommodation Bursary of £1,500, and eligible students can apply to the Access to Learning Fund and other hardship funds for financial assistance. See www.port.ac.uk/ bursaries, and for sport scholarships: www.port.ac.uk/sportscholarshipscheme.

STUDENT PROFILE

There's a part-timer body of about 2,500 undergraduates; 27% are mature and it has always been a predominantly male corpus - currently the gender split is 56-44. They tend to recruit from the south of England. For many, Portsmouth is the local university. There is a high state-school intake, and 31% of the undergraduate population come from sections of society new to university. Given the unpractised element, their drop-out rate of 6% should suggest there's something to stay for.

Support for the new uni intake is as good as they claim. 'There's a full-time counselling service,' a student tells me. Why? 'Students find it hard at this...at university, money problems, pressures. People think being at university is easy. It is not. I am the only child of five in my family to have gone to university. It wasn't part of the culture of my

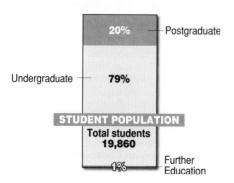

Postgraduate 20%
Undergraduate 79%
STUDENT POPULATION
Total students
19,860
Further Education 1%

family. I have struggled here, had to get jobs. People have this concept of university, students getting drunk all the time, having a good time...I have heard about that, but never experienced it.'

ACADEMIA & JOBS

Faculties are Humanities and Social Sciences; Science; Technology; Environment; and Business.

Says the uni: 'We are known for Science, particularly Sports Science, Biomedical Science, Psychology and Maths. The Faculty of Creative & Cultural Industries has particular strengths in Architecture, Animation, Film and Media Business, Management and Law Criminology and Forensics.

Say students: The best teaching is in 'Politics, History, Human & Social Geography, Maths, Management, Sciences related to Biology, Physical Geography & Environmental Science, Biology, Civil and Chemical Engineering, English, Finance & Accounting, European Languages, Sociology, Electronic & Electrical Eng., Accounting, Economics, Business Studies, Law, and Sports Science.'

A new £9m dental outreach building opens in 2010 to train dentists, dental technicians & dental nurses together as part of a team. There is an ever-increasing focus on health. Currently, a School of Professionals Complementary to Dentistry delivers dental nursing, hygiene and therapy. Housed in a purpose-built £4-million building, the school was, at its inception, the first new dental education facility in England for 50 years. In the recent research assessments, Portsmouth had 55% of its provision in the area of Allied Health Professions adjudged either world-class (4 stars) or internationally excellent (3 stars). A £4.5million ExPERT

> *Applied Maths scored highest in the research assessments and they are massive in software engineering and systems analysis*

RESEARCH EXCELLENCE		
% of Portsmouth's research that is **4*** (World-class) or **3*** (Internationally rated):		
	4*	**3***
Health Professions	**15%**	**40%**
Environmental Sciences	**5%**	**40%**
Applied Mathematics	**15%**	**60%**
Computer Science	**5%**	**20%**
Mechanical, Aero., & Manufac. Eng.	**5%**	**40%**
Geography Environment	**5%**	**25%**
Business\Management	**5%**	**30%**
Psychology	**0%**	**25%**
European Studies	**15%**	**30%**
Art and Design	**0%**	**10%**

Centre opened recently, manned by computerised mannequins, which breathe oxygen, drool, secrete fluids, blink, bleed and even react to drugs injected into their bodies. The centre trains students in biomedical sciences and healthcare professionals and has two simulation suites (operating theatre and hospital ward). There's a tie-up with Southampton University to train health care professionals to work together: trainee nurses alongside trainee pharmacists and trainee radiographers, and so on. Health subjects, such as nursing, radiography were all top scoring at the teaching assessments. The School of Pharmacy & Biomedical Sciences is recommended by both teaching assessments and employment data. There are degrees in Pharmacy, Pharmaceutical Science, and Pharmacology.

Clinical and educational psychologists also find jobs in number from here. The BSc Psychology is accredited by the British Psychological Soc., and if you get at least a second class degree you've taken the first step to becoming a chartered psychologist. There's also BSc Psychol. with Criminology. Many graduates find careers with the police and the probation service. One little gem is the Institute of Criminal Justice Studies, whose work on counter-fraud, benefits fraud and so on, has brought it links with TV's Crimewatch. Crime author PD James opened a library extension in January 2007.

The following summer a new School of Law opened, and a fully functioning mock court room is due to appear this year. They are commercial &

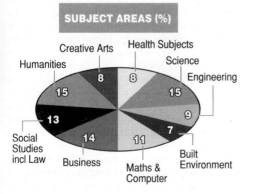

SUBJECT AREAS (%)

Creative Arts — 8
Health Subjects — 8
Humanities — 15
Science — 15
Engineering — 9
Social Studies incl Law — 13
Business — 14
Maths & Computer — 11
Built Environment — 7

business law specialists. The single honours degree is a 3-year or 4-year (sandwich) LLB with various possible adjuncts: Criminology, European Studies, International Relations, Business, and there are two BA degrees with Languages or Business English.

Generally, top recruiters from Portsmouth are the NHS, central and local government, National Probation Service, IBM (Applied Maths scored highest in the research assessments and their computing degrees are very strong, they are massive in software engineering and systems analysis).

Now the uni has Purple Door Recruitment, an agency working in collaboration with local and national business, which offers work experience and career opportunities.

Languages are another particular strength, useful in finding employment - 45% of research in European Studies was either 4-star or 3-star at the recent assessment; they shine at Russian/Slavonic/East European languages. One student in five takes a language course and around 1,000 go abroad for part of their course. French achieved a near perfect teaching score.

The Business School has moved into a new £12-million building on the main campus. Accountants do well here. There's a range of BA degrees with Business, e-Business, and Business Law. Then there's Accountancy Studies or Accountancy & Financial Management for students with sufficient experience or qualifications to miss out on Year 1 of a regular accountancy degree.

A recent addition to the degree portfolio is faculty of Creative and Cultural Industries, working out of refurbished facilities for media studies and art and design. There's even a facsimile newsroom to service a the Journalism degrees.

Graduates get jobs as designers, illustrators, set-designers and film/video producers from here. There are Photography, Video Production and various Film Studies degrees, and facilities include broadcast TV studios and a digital development laboratory.

They produce a number of architects, too. Causing a stir is the BA Hons Architecture which comprises 50% design projects and 50% taught courses. It earns exemption from Part 1 RIBA. Likewise, property and construction employment markets like employing Protsmout quantity surveyors in particular. A dedicated degree has been replaced by BSc Property Development with Quantity Surveying. There's also a good employment record for civil engineers and construction engineer/managers. The B/MEng Civil Engineering is accredited by the appropriate Institute.

There's a traditional tie-up with the navy,

WHAT IT'S REALLY LIKE	
UNIVERSITY:	
Social Life	★★★
Campus scene	**Good mix**
Student Union services	**Good**
Politics	**Average**
Sport	**50 clubs**
National team position	**37th**
Sport facilities	**Good**
Arts opportunities	**Plenty dance, music, film**
Student magazine	**Pugwash**
Student radio	**PURE FM**
Student TV	**UPSU TV**
Nightclub	**LUX**
Bars	**Waterhole, CO2, Embassy**
Union ents	**Rock, cheese, r&b, comedy**
Union societies	**40**
Most active societies	**People & planet, Breakdance**
Parking	**Poor**
TOWN:	
Entertainment	★★★
Scene	**Good: pubs, clubs**
Town/gown relations	**Good**
Risk of violence	**Low**
Cost of living	**Average**
Student concessions	**Excellent**
Survival + 2 nights out	**£70 pw**
Part-time work campus/town	**Average**

excellent career prospects with the army and a good number of jobs, too, for defence operatives and equipment engineers. The Institute of Maritime Heritage Studies preserves the tradition, it's based in an old boathouse in the naval dockyards area. Portsmouth is of course famous for being the site where the Mary Rose is docked.

Finally, there are BSc degrees in Sports Development, Sports Science, Water Sports Science. A £2.5 million sports science building houses labs, a swimming flume and two British Olympic Medical Centre accredited climatic chambers.

STUDENT SCENE

STUDENTS' UNION The SU building gives them a 2,500 capacity. The nightclub, **LUX**, alone can take in 1,100. Then there's the sportsbar **Waterhole** (500), chill-out bar CO2 (500) and international bar Embassy (400). Regular ents are *Purple Wednesdays*, *Kredit Crunch* and the live set *Portsmouth's Got Talent* (Fridays), *Pop Killer* (Saturdays).

Top of the ents menu are their mammoth balls - a new Presentation Ball for Purples (full/half colour awards: sport is big here), various societies' balls, Graduation, and so on.

Media-wise, students are active with monthly magazine, *Pugwash*, and Pure Radio has been enjoying its most popular year with daily Internet broadcasts. Now, too, UPSU TV is up and running online.

A nice recent touch is 'Money Doctors', a drop-in service to help students with their finances, help find a way to conserve or boost income.

SPORT Men's sports teams are consistently high in the BUSA league. Geographical position gives them special potential - sailing (larks and lasers), wind-surfing and canoeing. Applications for scholarships in hockey, rugby, swimming, water sports, gymnastics and netball are encouraged.

TOWN The new 170m Spinnaker Tower is already a major British landmark, looming over the buzzing **Gunwharf Quays** designer shopping area with its numerous restaurants, bars and nightclubs. The Historic Dockyard is one of the top 10 heritage attractions in Britain, while the city centre will soon be transformed by a £350m project to confirm its position as the south coast shopping and leisure choice.

Student and singer Genna Hellier says the nightlife was part of the reason she opted for Portsmouth: 'Also, it was a really nice summer's day and I saw the cafés lining the streets. It looked beautiful. I love it here. I came here shy and now I am going into PR! I never did any sport and now I work out every day. This union here provides amazing sporting opportunities.

'Gun Wharf is really nice,' Genna went on, 'all the London-based clubs are here. There is no rivalry between locals and students. It is a very safe place to live. Music is especially good here. More locally we have the **Wedgwood Rooms** and **The Pyramid**. There's a place called **Havana** for student bands, and we organise open mic nights at the union and so on. The local theatre is the **Theatre Royal**, nice little theatre in the **Guildhall**, often used for student productions. The uni also built **Wiltshire Studios**, where a lot of student productions are done.'

There's a bountiful supply of clubs, cafés and wine bars in the Guildhall area. Other student hang-outs, such as the **Havana Café Bar** and the **Frog on the Front**, are within walking distance. The club scene ranges from cheesy handbag to razor-tuned, techno beats. Then, of course, there's Premiership Football.

PILLOW TALK

Around 3,000 places are available. 710 en-suite, self-catered beds are now up for grabs at James Watson Hall, which opened recently. Every first year who makes the uni their first choice by end April will qualify for a place in hall. If you don't get a place with them, then the uni will sort you out: 'It is our philosophy to care all the way through.' All halls have free 10Mbps broadband.

GETTING THERE

☞ By road: A3(M), 2 hours from London.
☞ By rail: London Waterloo, 1:30; Bristol Parkway, 2:15; Birmingham New Street, 3:30; Sheffield, 4:45.
☞ By coach: London, 2:30; Exeter, 6:45.
☞ By air: Southampton Airport.

ACCOMMODATION	
Guarantee to freshers	**75%**
Style	**Halls, flats**
Security guard	**24-hr security**
Shared rooms	**Some**
Internet access	**All**
Self-catered	**Most**
En suite	**Most**
Approx price range pw	**£73-£111**
City rent pw	**£55-£75**

QUEEN MARGARET UNIVERSITY

Queen Margaret University
University Drive
Edinburgh EH21 6UU

TEL 0131 474 0000
FAX 0131 474 0001
EMAIL admissions@qmu.ac.uk
WEB www.qmu.ac.uk

Queen Margaret University Students' Union
Musselburgh
Lothian EH21 6UU

TEL 0131 317 3400
FAX 0131 317 3402
EMAIL union@qmu.ac.uk
WEB www.qmusu.org.uk/

VAG VIEW

*Q*ueen Margaret University set out in *1875 as the Edinburgh School of Cookery, when any sort of further education for women was unusual. The original lectures took place before huge audiences in the Royal Museum in Chambers Street, but it was in fact peripatetic in nature, teaching staff in those days went out with mobile gas and paraffin cooking equipment to give programmes of public lectures and demonstrations all over Britain, literally from the Shetlands to the Channel Islands.*

In 1930 a new name, The Edinburgh College of Domestic Science, gave it authenticity as a seat of academic learning . In 1972, following the introduction of a range of new courses, came the big break and it changed its name again, this time to Queen Margaret University College, the QM part a deliberate attempt to take it away from its image as a college of domestic science.

Soon it was located at four sites in Edinburgh. The main Corstorphine campus, out near Edinburgh Airport in the grounds of a former stately home, was home to Applied Consumer Studies, Communication & Information Studies, Hospitality & Tourism Management, Management & Social Sciences, Dietetics & Nutrition, Health & Nursing, and Speech & Language Sciences, which just shows how one thing can lead to another.

The second site lay to the northeast of the city centre, just off Leith Walk, in one of the most characterful parts of the city, to the northeast of the centre, just off Leith Walk, where, as a boy, Robert Louis Stevenson

UNIVERSITY/STUDENT PROFILE	
University since	**2007**
Situation/style	**Campus**
Student population	**5285**
Total undergraduates	**4130**
Mature undergraduates	**36%**
International undergrads	**11%**
Male/female ratio	**25:75**
Equality of opportunity:	
state school intake	**95%**
social class 4-7 intake	**30%**
low-participation area intake	**5%**

stood and stared at the great ships in the Western Harbour, listening to the sailors as they pulled on their ropes, his imagination fired with thoughts that would later produce the novels Kidnapped and Treasure Island. Queen Margaret even had a hall of residence named after him, possibly because one of the college's founders was one Louisa Stevenson, who may have been a relation. The Leith site was home to another academic dimension of the college, Occupational Therapy, Physiotherapy, Podiatry, and Radiography.

There was also a site near Edinburgh's Haymarket Station, a Business Development Centre, which provided a training and consultancy service to the business community, and the Gateway Theatre, actually on Leith Walk, once a repertory theatre and more recently the Edinburgh base for Scottish Television. This was to be its base for a degree in Drama, which looked at first like something of a tangent to an otherwise distinctive organic development, but drama is one of those interests which can also benefit students and impart personal skills that would be useful whatever a student's course. It was certainly a popular move: 'The opportunities for drama are excellent,' a student told us, 'now that we have our own Drama Department, theatre and studio.' It is still on the curriculum today.

In the late 1990s when we came upon Queen Margaret for the first time, sixth-form careers teachers said to us: 'People who choose QM mostly do so with a specific career in mind.' It was a vocational college, but with a wide range of subjects. Everyone was interested enough to wonder where next

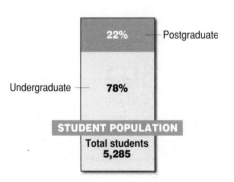

22% — Postgraduate

Undergraduate — 78%

STUDENT POPULATION

Total students **5,285**

it would go: 'Queen Margaret is making a big push towards Media and Business Studies,' said another; 'also the professions supplementary to Medicine, Physiotherapy and so on...'

Everything they did seemed to be done with purpose. The Business Development Centre now offered an ideal link to the industry for Business degree development and graduate employment. And that house of drama in Leith Walk had by this time become a major venue for the International Edinburgh Festival: a better shop window for QM would have been hard to find.

Thus did Queen Margaret, 132 years after its inception, come to the latest and most notable of its many transformations. In January 2007, it was granted full university title, and it changed its name to 'Queen Margaret University'.

CAMPUS

This latest transformation occasioned another, that of a 35-acre site at Craighall, East Lothian, from low grade farm land into landscaped parkland. QM has uprooted from Edinburgh. The new Musselburgh campus opened in Autumn 2007 and is located on the east side of the city, by Musselburgh. The site is bordered by the main east coast rail line to London and the A1. It also neighbours the city by-pass.

Campus is environmentally friendly and will leave less of a carbon footprint than Peter Pan. With its learning resource at its centre, it includes student residences, a Student Union building (social spaces, a café, an events area and a games room), indoor sports facilities and all weather surfaces, a variety of catering outlets, a shop and landscaped gardens.

It is a 15-min. walk to Musselburgh, which has a racecourse, a theatre, shops, bars and cafés. Also nearby is the Fort Kinnaird shopping complex, with a cinema and entertainment complex. Edinburgh is but 6 minutes away by train.

The relocation provoked a negative reaction after there was a delay in completion of the building of the campus and Drama students were stranded at the already sold Gateway Theatre for several months.

Students who studied at the Edinburgh college sites could be forgiven for feeling sad to uproot. The new campus, however friendly, has hardly had time to bed in. It is exceptionally well served by bus and rail from the city, but students are perched on farmland really nowhere, and the last train is at 11.15 p.m.

Still these ruffles are as nothing surely to what has been endured and overcome to get thus far.

FEES, BURSARIES
Fees for English: £1,820 p.a. EU Fees: none to pay.

STUDENT PROFILE
'IThirty-six per cent are mature students, 75% are female, and a quarter of undergraduates are part-time.

ACADEMIA & JOBS
What is on offer is what its history has been preparing it for: 'At Queen Margaret University,' they say, 'we offer a wide range of undergraduate and postgraduate courses in the areas of healthcare; drama and the creative industries; media, communication and sociology; and business and enterprise. We also have a number of continuing professional development (CPD) courses, which will be of interest to anyone who is wishing to update their current professional skills.'

Naturally the library is not extensive yet, more of a resource that will find books for you. But Edinburgh is at hand.

SUBJECT AREAS (%)

Creative Arts 11
Humanities 25
Business 20
Science 9
Health Subjects 35

RESEARCH EXCELLENCE

% of Queen Margaret's research that is
4* (World-class) or **3*** (Internationally rated):

	4*	3*
Health Professions	0%	5%
Business/Management	0%	5%
Linguistics	10%	30%
Drama	0%	0%
Media Studies	10%	30%

SOCIAL SCENE

It is all wonderfully new, the SU, its café a 'flexible venue', with a capacity of between 150 and 250 tops, but they have license problems: nothing later than 1 a.m. will be allowed. Freshers live in halls on campus, so there are people around, but no great ents yet, but there is work space for campaigns, sports, societies and welfare volunteers, once things get going.

A bar and the café are open Monday to Wednesday 11-11, Thursday to Friday 11am to 1am. Saturday and Sunday the bar is closed.

So what goes on of an evening? They say it's the usual pub quiz, themed events, live music, karoke, open mic nights, and big balls: Halloween, Christmas and the end of term Grand Ball.

Sport Alongside the SU is a multi-purpose sports

hall, a fitness suite, an aerobic studio and an outdoor all-weather sports pitch. In addition, a trim track runs around the site.

GETTING THERE

☛ By road: cars can access the campus via a slip road off the A1 southbound, between the exit for Newcraighall/Craigmillar and the Old Craighall Roundabout.

☛ By bus: the No. 30 Lothian bus goes directly from Princes Street into the campus and runs

ACCOMMODATION

Guarantee to freshers	**100%**
Style	**Halls, flats**
Security guard	**All**
Shared rooms	**Some**
Internet access	**All**
Self-catered	**All**
En suite	**All**
Approx price range pw	**£94.25-£99.50**
City rent pw	**£55-£92+**

approximately every 10 minutes.

☛ By train: the new campus is located right beside Musselburgh rail station. From Waverley Station to Musselburgh Station takes 6 minutes. Trains from West Lothian and Stirlingshire call at Newcraighall Station, which is 15/20 minutes walk from campus. For details, see www.firstgroup.com/scotrail/content/timetables/index.

● ●

QUEEN MARY, UNIVERSITY OF LONDON

Queen Mary, University of London
Mile End Road
London E1 4NS

TEL 020 7882 5511
Freephone: +44 (0)800 376 1800
EMAIL admissions@qmul.ac.uk
WEB www.qmul.ac.uk

Queen Mary College
Students' Union
432 Bancroft Road
London E1 8031

TEL 020 7882 5390
EMAIL president@qmsu.org
WEB www.qmsu.org

VAG VIEW

*Q*ueen Mary, a constituent college of the federal University of London, and once known as Queen Mary & Westfield, arose out of the merger (in 1989) of two colleges: Westfield College, a 19th-century pioneer in higher education for women, and Queen

Mary College, founded in 1885 and located at the People's Palace in Mile End Road, ideally situated for its essential purpose, namely to educate the East End poor. This is the uni's base in Mile End Road today. A later, medical foundation arose out of a merger in 1995 between the Royal London School of Medicine & Dentistry and St Bartholomew's

Hospital Medical School, now QMW's Medical School. Medical students undergo their clinical training at the Royal London in Whitechapel and Barts in West Smithfield.

QMW's location thus keeps it true to its roots, while its large overseas student contingent - they draw from some 100 countries worldwide - reflects the multi-cultural character of the area as it is today. Central to this strategy is a Study Abroad programme. Languages are to the fore throughout the curriculum, and have scored highly in both teaching inspections and research assessments.

FEES, BURSARIES

UK & EU Fees, 2009-10: £3,225 p.a. There are the usual bursaries for those eligible for the Maintenance Grant, and rewards for applicants who get three A grades at A level.

STUDENT PROFILE

'Integration between medical students and the rest of the college leaves a lot to be desired,' writes Kieran Alger, 'the two groups preferring to indulge in separate activities, the medical students enjoying their own bar, for example, and playing for separate sports teams while the main body of students mixes well, regardless of subject.'

As at other medical schools, the medical students sharply increase the public school quota and give QMW a state/public school ratio akin to Reading's or Southampton's, Warwick's or York's. The Mile End Road student population is another story. 'Queen Mary proper is a cultural melting pot,' agrees Kieran - 'a fascinating blend of overseas students, a large ethnic contingent and UK residents,' and a 31% draw last year from the new-to-uni social groups. There are also larger than average local and mature populations (they even have

UNIVERSITY/STUDENT PROFILE	
University since	**1915**
Situation/style	**Ciampus**
Student population	**12585**
Total undergraduates	**9350**
Mature undergraduates	**21%**
International undergrads	**12%**
Male/female ratio	**52:48**
Equality of opportunity:	
state school intake	**86%**
social class 4-7 intake	**33%**
low-participation area intake	**4%**

'mature student socials' at the student union), which serve to distinguish the clientele from what Kieran describes as 'the stereotypical beer and beans, lazy student'.

CAMPUS

'QM, with its modern architecture, is one of the few universities to combine the class of the well established with the youth, vigour and dynamism of an ex-polytechnic,' continues Kieran. 'Set in the heart of the multi-cultural hotchpotch which forms the East End, the student population reflects its intriguing surroundings. The East End, home of imports, the cloth trade, Phil, Grant and the Kray twins, has an illustrious history of intermingling races. From jellied eels at Spitalfield's Market to chicken balti in one of Brick Lane's curry houses, this area caters for a huge range of tastes. It is also asserting its own brand of sophistication in the stunning Docklands development. The combination of Canary Wharf Tower dominating on one side and the trendification of the E1, E2, and E3 postal areas is causing a surge in social and cultural activity. The East End, with its fashionable gangster land history and eerie Jack the Ripper connections, is the place London's affluent young professionals want to live. Neighbouring areas, such as Bow and Aldgate, are being inundated with new eateries, coffee houses, galleries and nightclubs.'

Clinical students head the new award-winning Medical School Building, a landmark building providing innovative research and laboratory facilities. Its Centre of the Cell for Bioscience Education Centre launched in March 2007 and is dedicated to inspiring curiosity and learning by connecting science to everyday life.

ACADEMIA & JOBS

The top areas of employment for graduates of Queen Mary are hospitals and other human health activities, banking, dental practice, specialist retail (could be anything from old books to pharmacy),

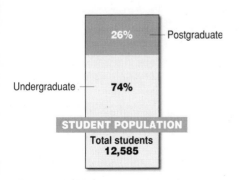

26% — Postgraduate

Undergraduate — **74%**

STUDENT POPULATION

Total students
12,585

publishing, recruitment and personnel, the civil service, accountancy, higher education, community & counselling activities, general retail, some sort of financial activities, hotels & restaurants, and telecommunications. Software consultancy and supply, radio and TV, and engineering design consultancy lurk not far behind. But really these do well delineate the Queen Mary graduate.

Mostly it's about health - 38% of all graduate jobs here come out of the Medicine and Dentistry degrees. Then, it doesn't much matter whether you are looking at Economics, Business, Maths, or even Physical or Biological Sciences, banking, accountancy, and financial activities of some sort crop up high in the pecking order of jobs that accrue to graduates in these areas. The software whizzes come, of course, through the Computer provision and the Design & Innovation degrees make their mark on the design front. But Publishing is interesting because it has no skill-feeding degree at its root. Few universities have it so high up on the employment agenda, and when you look, you see that the jobs are filled by QM graduates in Media certainly, but it's a Journalism & Contemporary History degree, and Languages and History graduates, the History degrees so well chosen to reflect the interests and deep knowledge bank that is at QM: history may be studied as a single hons of course, but then they offer you History & Comparative Literature, History & German Literature, History & German Language, History & Politics, and you just know you are going to get right inside the culture of the thing. With the language interest in particular (the selection of German so significant historically of course) they are offering you an opportunity to explore connections and interactions between cultural traditions at key moments in history.

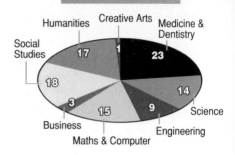

SUBJECT AREAS (%)

Humanities — Creative Arts 1 — Medicine & Dentistry 23
Social Studies 17
Social Studies 18
Business 3
Maths & Computer 15
Engineering 9
Science 14

QM is, in short, a rich cultural resource, ideally suited to serious publishing where a deep sense of the world pays dividends. It took the recent research assessment to remind us. Suddenly, from 48th position seven years ago, at the time of the last assessment, Queen Mary rose to 13th nationwide, with 60%, 70%, 80%, even 90% of the subjects submitted adjudged world class and internationally excellent.

For example, you read that 50% of their research into Drama is world-class and 40% internationally significant, and you wonder what happened to the other 10% - must have been an off day. And you scrabble around and wonder what fine shoots of an undergraduate course might grow out of this rich loam. Then you read: 'Drama at Queen Mary provides a study of performance in a variety of cultures and historical periods...[it] offers a practical and theoretical investigation into the ways in which drama can be used in different settings - art galleries, schools, prisons, warehouses and museums, as well as theatres, across the UK and internationally. Through a grounded exploration of the act of performance, you are encouraged to become a scholar-artist with your own interests and expertise.' It is then that you realise that this really is in itself performance art, not your usual skills course masquerading as such. It is the kind of module the best minds in the university - the future surgeons and financiers - would be interested to take for itself. For at QM 'vocational' has a more profound ring to it than at all our new universities, which bandy the word around so. There need be no rushing off to get a job in six months after taking a degree like this at QM. It is an education for life.

You'll be applying to Barts & the London School of Medicine if you plan to study Medicine at QM. The school's performance in the research assessment put it among the top five med. Schools

TEACHING SURVEY AT A GLANCE

Avg. UCAS points accepted	**330**
Acceptance rate	**16%**
Overall satisfaction rate	**84%**
Helpful/interested staff	★★★
Small tuition groups	★★★
Students into graduate jobs	**75%**

Teaching most popular with undergraduates:
English (97%), Languages, Law (96%), Drama (95%), Creative Arts & Design (94%), European Languages (93%), Biochemistry (92%), Politics, History (91%),

Teaching least popular with undergraduates:
Medicine (73%).

RESEARCH EXCELLENCE

% of Queen Mary's research that is
4* *(World-class)* or **3*** *(Internationally rated):*

	4*	3*
Cancer Studies	15%	70%
Hospital Clinical	15%	65%
Epidemiology	30%	50%
Health Services	30%	35%
Psychiatry	10%	30%
Dentistry	25%	50%
Biological Sciences	5%	35%
Human Biol. Sciences	20%	45%
Physics	15%	35%
Pure Mathematics	10%	50%
Applied Mathematics	10%	40%
Statistics	10%	30%
Computer Science	25%	50%
Electrical/Electronic Eng.	15%	35%
General Engineeringg	10%	35%
Metallurgy and Materials	15%	40%
Geography Environment	25%	50%
Economics	30%	55%
Business/Management	15%	40%
Law	20%	40%
Politics	5%	40%
Russian	20%	20%
French	10%	45%
German	5%	35%
Iberian	25%	35%
English	40%	30%
Linguistics	25%	55%
History	30%	30%
Performing Arts	50%	40%

in the country. The Medicine degree, a 5-year BM BS (Medicine, Surgery), stresses clinical method and communication skills and the experience of the patient in the community, and there's a significant element of problem-based learning (small-group explorations of particular scenarios). First 2 years at the Mile End campus, final three at the Royal London Hospital, Whitechapel Campus. There's a 4-year graduate entry, too. To get in you will need AAA from 3 A levels and a B in a fourth subject at AS. Chemistry and Biology also required at AS and one or other of them at A level. Two science A levels (out of Chemistry, Biology, Physics and Maths) required. One of them must be Chemistry or Biology. The third A level may be a science or a non-science (General Studies and Critical Thinking excluded). The AS and A levels must be taken within a two-year period. AS subjects taken on their own must be taken after one year, or two years if taken alongside A levels. If you

can understand that lot you deserve to get in. UKCAT will also be needed.

Of interest to would-be dentists, the dental schools with full marks at the teaching assessments are KCL, Manchester, Queen's Belfast and QM.

It's a 5-year BDS plus a B/MEng Dental Materials. Entry AAB including a science subject + Chemistry/ Biology. Once again, it made a fine showing in the research assessments - 75% of the work was adjudged world-class and internationally significant.

Safe ground, too, is Law. QM is a world-class European law specialist, and non-Law graduates may opt for a 2-year full-time or 3-year part-time Senior Status Law degree here. Recently QM Law students launched a Legal Advice Centre - unique in London as it is the first university-run centre to offer free legal advice to members of the public.

SOCIAL SCENE

The medics have their own union - SoMaD Students' Association. There are two bars: the **Clubs Union** bar at the Royal London Hospital (Whitechapel), and **Bart's Bar**, close to Bart's Hospital in Charterhouse Square (where there is also a swimming pool, squash, tennis and badminton courts). There's also a glass-fronted bistro bar, **BarMed**, in the Medical Science building looking out on to Library Square. Regular high jinks are the Association Dinner, the Christmas Show, Burn's Night and the sporting cup finals. There's a flourishing drama society - plays, a Christmas Show, a production for the Edinburgh Fringe - a Gilbert & Sullivan Society, a choir and orchestra, and of course Rag. Otherwise, they bounce around at Toga nights, Star Wars night, Austin Powers Night, and Mummies and Daddies Night. I guess Doctors & Nurses Night is simply 'too day-time' to compete.

In Mile End Road, the more dissipated wind up rather than down at looking for 'the best student nightclub in London' (the Union's boast) at **Club e1**. Complete with 12K JBL sound system and state of the art computer-controlled lighting rig it is open till 2 am from Thursday through Saturday. Then, there's **The Drapers Arms**. The e1 nightclub has a 750-capacity, top sound and lighting systems and a reputation built on the sometime, much-vaunted, Time Out-supported *Time Tunnel* ('60s to '90s) on Saturdays, a once regular Saturday pop ('70s to the present day) extravaganza, *ROAR*, and more recently, *FIZZ*, on Saturday night, *Gagging for it* on Tuesday, *Hail Mary* on Wednesday, *Now Music* on Thursday, *Take a Ride* on Friday... However, more recently there's been a more basic menu of *Flirt! Toga & Tequila Party*, Ann Summers Night followed

WHAT IT'S REALLY LIKE

UNIVERSITY:

Social Life	★★★★
Campus scene	**Lively**
Student Union services	**Average**
Politics	**Apolitical**
Sport	**19 clubs**
National team position	**82nd**
Sport facilities	**Average**
Arts opportunities	**Drama excellent**
Student newspaper	**Cub**
Nightclub	**Club e1**
Bars	**The Drapers Arms, Barts, Union Bar**
Union ents	**Flirt**
Union societies	**52**
Most active siocieties	**Islamic Soc, Friends of Palastine**
Parking	**Poor**
CITY:	
Entertainment	★★★★★
Scene	**Wild, expensive**
Town/gown relations	**Average-good**
Risk of violence	**London**
Cost of living	**High**
Student concessions	**Good**
Survival + 2 nights out	**£100 pw**
Part-time work campus/town	**Excellent**

SPORT Sports fields are at Chislehurst. 'Sports are abundant,' Kieran writes, 'from rock climbing, netball and fencing, to the somewhat more comfortable pastimes of rowing and rugby. The football club is of a particularly high standard, as is the women's football team. Collegiate London Uni delivers many an opportunity for battle.'

PILLOW TALK

For first years it's London University 'intercollegiate halls' (catered), where you could be with anyone, or QMU's own (self-catered) at the Mile End campus (2,109 places), where since last year there's a new Student Village - 995 rooms (15 for wheelchair users), all with computer connections, village shop, café bar... Mile End Park has single

ACCOMMODATION

Guarantee to freshers	**100%**
Style	**Halls, flats**
Security guard	**Secure**
Shared rooms	**Some**
Internet access	**Most**
Self-catered	**All**
En suite	**Some**
Approx price range pw	**£85-£114**
City rent pw	**£100-£180**

by *Flirt, Saints + Sinners Flirt, Flirt! Halloween, Mary's Cheese, Hail Mary. Flirt* is a national SU package, and the cheesy home-bred stuff suggests QM may have lost its way a bit. Mind you, they had a long way to fall, and they're feeling very defensive this year, what with Ismail Malik's article in London Student suggesting that 'a whole host of students who fail to get into other University of London institutions go to Queen Mary'. The pages of QMSU's newspaper, *CUB*, have been putting Ismail right.

No stranger to student media awards, CUB, founded in 1947, is one of the oldest student papers in London. There's a clubs and societies resource centre that pulls such things together.

rooms, en-suite facilities, arranged in flats - lawns, woodland courtyards. The older (pre-Village) accommodation at Mile End is the cheaper.

Fifty rooms are available at Dawson Hall, Charterhouse Square, close to Barts, and at Floyer House on the Whitechapel campus.

GETTING THERE

☞ By Underground: QMW, Stepney Green (District, Hammersmith & City) or Mile End (+Central line). The Royal London, Whitechapel tube (East London, District, Hammersmith & City lines); nearest Bart's is Barbican. St Paul's (Central).

THE QUEEN'S UNIVERSITY, BELFAST

The Queen's University of Belfast
University Road
Belfast BT7 1NN

TEL 028 9097 5081
FAX 028 9097 5131
EMAIL admissions@qub.ac.uk
WEB www.qub.ac.uk

Queen's University Students' Union
University Road
Belfast BT7 1PE

TEL 028 9097 3106
FAX 028 9097 1375
EMAIL studentsunion@qub.ac.uk
WEB www.qubsu.org

VAG VIEW

*T*he Queen's University Belfast, Northern Ireland's leading educational institution, has its origins in the Queen's College, Belfast, founded in 1845. There is a traditional Oxbridge-style reputation, with good lines into the professions, medicine, dentistry, the City and law.

Since 2005 Queen's has been implementing an ambitious Vision for the Future, beginning with a new academic framework, a £200 million investment in staff, students and facilities, including a £44-million library project, a £45-million student village, replacing the present high-rise catered tower blocks with self-catered three-storey villas in a village setting, and an extensive refurbishment to the Students' Union and the Physical Education Centre.

Students are a happy crew, 86% raised their hats to the university at the National Student Survey. Dropping out is virtually unheard of - only 7% do.

CAMPUS

Set a few kilometres from the city centre in a so-called 'safe' area of Belfast, the campus encompasses the Botanic Gardens and Ulster Museum. Areas around Queen's University, Stranmillis and Botanic Avenue are now busier than ever and spilling over into the once isolated city centre.

Writes Laura Cattell: 'The big red buses that pass by Queen's every few minutes are packed with camera-happy tourists snapping a shot of the redbrick Lanyon hall. The impressive building (apparently modelled on Oxford University's Magdalen College), is at the heart of the city campus and though few actual lectures take place in the building it's the focus for academic and cere-

UNIVERSITY/STUDENT PROFILE	
University since	**1908**
Situation/style	**Civic**
Student population	**24135**
Total undergraduates	**16700**
Mature undergraduates	**16%**
International undergrads	**6%**
Male/female ratio	**43:57**
Equality of opportunity:	
state school intake	**99%**
social class 4-7 intake	**35%**
low-participation area intake	**5%**

monial life at Queen's. Set in the southern and leafier part of Belfast, most of the departmental buildings are housed in the Georgian terraces along University Square, opposite Lanyon hall or in the larger more modern Ashby Hall further along Stranmillis Road. As a student, most of your social life will be based in this area - from Eglantine to Botanic Avenue. The Student Union is located opposite the Lanyon buildings and as with most 1960s university structures it's not architecturally stunning, but it has everything you need - from banks, second-hand bookshops, convenience stores and a laundry, to cafés, bars, toilets and a nightclub. Although much of Belfast has been affected by the troubles in recent years this part of the city remains largely untouched by sectarianism.'

FEES, BURSARIES

UK & EU Fees, 2009-10: £3,225 p.a. There's a generous system of means-tested support if in receipt of the HE Maintenance grant, also sports awards and entrance scholarships. There are also three Queen's Centenary Gold Medal Entrance Scholarships, worth £7,500, and Science, Technology Engineering and Mathematics Awards for three A-levels at 'A' grade. Travel Scholarships too. See www.qub.ac.uk/scholarships.

STUDENT PROFILE

Queen's claim to be 'one of the most socially inclusive universities in the United Kingdom. It consistently out-performs national benchmarks in attracting students from poorer backgrounds.' Perhaps they should do more for the beleaguered English public school boy and girl who, for example, find themselves victims of discrimination too. Certainly there are some opportunities for them here. For example, Queen's Uni's medical school is one of the best in the world, and the application acceptance rate is three times what you'll find in most English med schools.

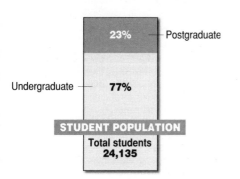

Postgraduate **23%**

Undergraduate **77%**

STUDENT POPULATION

Total students
24,135

The fact is that most of the student population is local, and 28% of undergraduates are part-timers. There is, however, a very low (5%) take from underprivileged so-called 'low participation neighbourhoods', but a high take (35%) from the lower socio-economic classes. Almost all that come here had a state school education, but this is not the land of the English public school after all.

ACADEMIA & JOBS

'Academically,' Laura continues, 'Queen's is Northern Ireland's best university and lies in the top three of Ireland's higher education institutions. It is still overlooked by many students in mainland Britain not only because of its location, but also because of its lowly ranking alongside U.K institutions. It is let down by a few weak departments, but this is counteracted by other world-class departments: Medicine, Engineering, English and Politics.

'There is a thriving literary scene, enlivened by the excellent teaching and research record of the English department. The School of English has some of the best academics in their field and is of course well-known for being the alma mater of Northern Ireland's most celebrated poets: Seamus Heaney and Paul Muldoon.'

Queen's is an artistic hub, home to Belfast's International Festival and to Northern Ireland's sole arthouse cinema in the Queen's Film Theatre, and to the region's newest museum, the Naughton

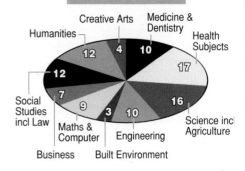

SUBJECT AREAS (%)

Creative Arts 4
Medicine & Dentistry 10
Health Subjects 17
Humanities 12
Social Studies incl Law 12
7
9
Maths & Computer 3
Business
Engineering 10
Built Environment
Science incl Agriculture 16

TEACHING SURVEY AT A GLANCE

Avg. UCAS points accepted	**360**
Acceptance rate	**17%**
Overall satisfaction rate	**86%**
Helpful/interested staff	★★★
Small tuition groups	★★★
Students into graduate jobs	**81%**

Teaching most popular with undergraduates:
Pharmacy, subjects allied to Medicine (98%), Anatomy, Physiology, Pathology (97%), Archaeology, Dentistry (96%), Accounting, English (95%), Anthropology (93%), Chemistry, Physics (92%), Agricultural Technology, Languages (91%), Finance, History (90%).

Teaching least popular with undergraduates:
Architecture (56%).

Gallery. The University runs a host of musical events, including an annual international festival of Contemporary Music. Courses in drama and film studies underpin its cultural contribution and the Seamus Heaney Centre for Poetry reinforces

the university's reputation as a world literary force.

'Famous-Seamus has also given his name to several buildings around campus and is an occasional visitor at the university,' writes Laura. 'The Heaney Centre, found at the back of the School of English, organises regular literary events - most of which are free and usually boast free wine as an incentive (if you need one!). Recent guests to the centre have been Jackie Kaye, Nick Laird, Ali Smith, Paul Durcan and Terry Eagleton. There's also a lively English Society and several reading and writing groups. Last year's poet-in-residence was Sinead Morrissey, who ran the writing group, while this year sees young poet Leontia Flynn as chair.'

The new academic framework consists of 21 large schools within 3 faculties: Arts, Humanities & Social Sciences; Engineering & Physical Sciences; and Medicine, Health & Life Sciences. It is too early to say how successful the reorganisation will be, though there have been criticisms about the organisational sense of the reshuffling of some schools into super-schools. The new library has 2,000 reader places and houses 1.5 million volumes. There's also an exhibition space, café, language laboratory, information points and multimedia resources.

Students are fairly complimentary about the helpfulness and interest of the teaching staff and about the size of tuition groups, and say the best teaching is in Pharmacy and in subjects allied to Medicine, in Anatomy, Physiology, Pathology, Archaeology, Dentistry, Accounting, English, Anthropology, Chemistry, Physics, Agricultural Technology, Languages, Finance, and History. Least popular is the teaching of Architecture, though it does well enough in the graduate employment stats. Architecture, Environmental Planning, Structural Engineering with Architecture, Civil Engineering, Environmental &

Civil Engineering are all B/MEng sandwich courses and there are decent teaching assessments and an international track record in research.

Queen's graduates end up mostly in hospitals, in social work in the community, in pharmacy retail, software consultancy, accounting, the civil service, banking, then architecture, building, dental practice, education (a fair number in higher education), and manufacture. Law is also an eventual destination for many.

The big initial outflow is into the health sector, and Queen's is about to take its medical school and dust it down to match its vision for a new school 'fit for the 21st century which will deliver an exciting educational and research environment that will attract good students, good staff and more externally funded fellowships'. In the meantime, in the 5-year MB, Scientific and Clinical Medicine is taught for each system of the body - system by system, and requirements are three A levels and one AS level to include Chemistry and at least one other science subject from Maths, Physics or Biology. If Biology is not the second science subject then it must be offered to at least AS Level. A non-science to at least AS Level is recommended but not required. A maximum of one VCE A level or GCE Applied A Level will be counted - Grades AAA at A Level plus A in the fourth AS Level. There is a pre-med year for applicants with broader based qualifications than A levels. In the Dental School, which scored full marks at the teaching assessments, the 5-year BDS requires AAB at entry.

Its reputation for engineering is world class: Mechanical, Aerospace and Manufacturing Engineering. Jobs are legion in the aeronautical department. Electrical and telecommunications engineers proliferate and benefit from Electrical & Electronic Engineering taking full marks in the assessment. There are good sandwich/professional experience opportunities.

Accountants are legion from the Management & Economics School, the named degree, Accounting, coming also with French, German or Spanish, and there's Economics with Accounting - 4% of all Queen's graduates become accountants. Also in the financial sector there's a dedicated Actuarial sandwich degree, which pays dividends.

Note another serious bunch of degrees, which includes Common & Civil Law with French/Spanish (4 years, and Law with Politics. Non-Law graduates may opt for a 2-year full-time or 3-year part-time Senior Status Law Degree here.

Computer programmers pour off a 4-year sandwich Business Information Technology BSc, there are BEng and BSc Computer Science, both 4-year sandwich, and a 4/5-year MEng Computer

RESEARCH EXCELLENCE		
% of Queen's Belfast's research that is 4* (World-class) or 3* (Internationally rated):		
	4*	3*
Cancer Studies	10%	40%
Hospital Clinical	10%	35%
Laboratory Clinical	5%	25%
Epidemiology	5%	35%
Dentistry	5%	60%
Nursing/Midwifery	10%	30%
Health Professions	15%	45%
Pharmacy	15%	40%
Biological Sciences	5%	25%
Agriculture	5%	25%
Chemistry	5%	40%
Physics	10%	40%
Pure Mathematics	5%	40%
Computer Science	15%	45%
Electrical/Electronic Eng.	20%	40%
Civil Engineering	20%	55%
Mechanical, Aero. & Manufacturing Eng.	15%	50%
Town/Country Planning	10%	20%
Geography/Environment	10%	40%
Archaeology	25%	30%
Business/Management	15%	40%
Law	25%	35%
Politics	10%	40%
Social Work	20%	35%
Sociology	20%	35%
Anthropology	35%	20%
Psychology	5%	25%
Education	10%	40%
French	5%	45%
German	5%	10%
Iberian	15%	40%
Celtic Studies	10%	20%
English	35%	30%
Classics, Ancient History	20%	10%
Philosophy	5%	60%
History	15%	45%
Performing Arts	15%	40%
Music	35%	35%

Science (the extra year in industry), also Games Design and Information Technology degrees.

SOCIAL SCENE

STUDENTS' UNION The Students' Union has had a £9 million refurbishment. There are various SU pleasure zones - the plush **Speakeasy Bar** with big screen sport, pub quizzes, Playstation challenge and hedonistic nights on the pull, the subterranean **Bunatee Bar** and intimate venue, **Bar Sub**, **Mandela Hall** (capacity: 1,000, one of the

WHAT IT'S REALLY LIKE

UNIVERSITY:

Social Life	★★★★
Campus scene	**Craic is good**
Student Union services	**Good**
Politics	**Yes**
Sport	**Competitive**
National team position	**97th**
Sport facilities	**Improving**
Arts opportunities	**Cinema excellent; theatre poor**
Student newspaper	**The Gown**
Venue/bars	**Speakeasy, Bunatee, Bar Sub, Mandela Hall, Varsity**
Union ents	**Shine (infamous house), Good Friday + live acts**
Live venue capacity	**1,000**
Union societies	**100**
Parking	**Adequate**

CITY:

Entertainment	★★★
City scene	**Clubs, pubs, arts**
Town/gown relations	**Generally OK**
Risk of violence	**Average-high**
Cost of living	**Low**
Student concessions	**Good**
Survival + 2 nights out	**£65 pw**
Part-time work campus/town	**Average**

offers, Tuesday Clubs & Societies Quiz, and

Pub Quiz Wednesday afternoon, Thursday nights *Flirt*, with drink offers.

Every so often the big Saturday night is *Shine* - infamous house night (non-Union run). Also watch website for gig listings. Recent live acts were Babyshambles and Fun Lovin' Criminals. Altogether the union building can take 2500 for entertainments.

The Snooker Room, which opened with the Union in 1967, is something else, and Queen's are the new British University Pool Champions this year, beating 70 UK university teams to get there (Durham in the final).

Once a favourite haunt of 'a young hustler named Alex 'Hurricane' Higgins, and exhibition venue of Jimmy White, Joe Swail and Peter Ebdon

Naturally students are highly politicised, with a strong focus on Northern Ireland politics, but also on student issues. The union is generally characterised as nationalist and left of centre.

Student media has been generally rather poor, but has suddenly risen phoenix like from the ashes. *SU Magazine* is a colourful freebie, four per year, 2,500 print, 5,000 downloads. It was judged 'Best Magazine of the Year' and 'Best Design and Layout' at the Irish National Student Awards in

Dublin 2008. Queen's Radio is the only student radio station currently operating in Northern Ireland and broadcasts 24/7 over 1134 MW (AM) and online at www.queensradio.org.

best live venues in Belfast, home to the *Underground* and the Comedy Network) and **Varsity** (just round the corner from the Union buidings).

Writes Laura: 'The Union is a hub of activity during term time and the long opening hours mean you can always pop in to grab something to eat or drink or even to buy some paper to print those essays on... Every night there is something going on.'

A typical offering at the Speak is Wednesday's *Franchise* (electro, funk, rock and roll: drinks £1.80), Thursday's *RADAR* gigs (local bands and talent - see www.qubsu-ents.com), and Friday's *Good Friday*, with DJs from the Friends of Jesus Sound System.

Bar Sub is open 7 days a week from 4pm to 1am. There are pool tables, plasma screens with live football, and a jukebox. They get involved with

Good Friday too. Saturday and Sunday are free entry, selected drinks 3 for £5.

At Bunatee it's paninis, pizzas, sandwiches etc, then Monday nights Connected, with great drinks

ACCOMMODATION

Guarantee to freshers	**80%**
Style	**Halls, flats**
Security guard	**All**
Shared rooms	**None**
Internet access	**All halls, some flats**
Self-catered	**All**
En suite	**Most halls, no flats**
Approx price range pw	**£63.56-£90.65**
City rent pw	**£50-£55**

Queen's clubs and societies are legion, but most of the Irish students clear off home at the weekend to get their washing done and to raid the family fridge. There's a very good cinema on campus - **Queen's Film Theatre** - which runs a film club, a short films festival, and lots of arthouse films every day of the week. See also the **Moviehouse** on Dublin Road - for all films.

SPORT They have two swimming pools (diving,

subaqua, water polo and canoeing facilities), conditioning rooms, squash courts, badminton, basketball, tennis courts, volleyball, handball, hockey, netball courts, two judo squares, cricket nets, a purpose-built mountain wall and facilities for gymnastics, athletics, fencing, golf, karate, bowls, yoga and archery, seventeen pitches for rugby, soccer, Gaelic, hockey, hurling, camogie and cricket, netball and tennis courts, a floodlit training area and an athletics arena where the Mary Peters Track is situated. Opportunities for golf at Malone Golf Club (3 miles away), sailing at Belfast Lough and Lough Neagh, waterskiing at Craigavon, gliding and parachuting at Magilligan, mountaineering in the Mourne mountains, caving in Fermanagh and rowing on the nearby River Lagan. Fifteen sports bursaries are available, sponsored by Guinness.

PILLOW TALK
Queen's has recently invested almost £45 million in building the Elms Student Village, which has a bistro, bar, convenience store and launderette. All rooms are self-catered, single study bedrooms. Students share kitchen facilities and make their own meals. There are standard rooms (with shared bathroom facilities) or en-suite rooms (which have a private shower room). Many of the residences are networked for internet access.

Says Laura: 'All the room facilities such as internet connections and en-suite bathrooms are excellent. If you're lucky enough to get a place in any of the university-owned houses then Mount Charles just off Botanic Avenue or Guthrie house on Fitzwilliam Street are the best of the bunch.

'In general, though, living in privately-owned accommodation is much cheaper so most students move out once they finish the first year. Most students live in South Belfast, along or off the Lisburn or Ormeau Road and rent per month varies from as little as £130 to £200 a month. Stranmillis, just a ten minute walk from the campus, is the most sought-after area, though naturally as a result it's a bit pricier - all to be expected if you want a BT9 postcode.'

GETTING THERE
☞ An hour by air from London, with at least 24 flights a day each way.

STUDENT BELFAST - THE CITY

TENSIONS
Town/gown relations are good and local businesses tend to recruit heavily from the university. Recent tension in the Holylands between students and residents has meant that the university comes down very hard on any students thought to be displaying 'anti-social behaviour'. Good community relations are very important and as such there are many local volunteering and work experience opportunities on offer at the uni careers service.

Belfast is one of those places that is stereotyped over and over again - descriptions such as 'divided', 'troubled', 'industrial' and 'the wettest place on earth' all come to mind. There are re-occurring sets of binaries that fracture the city: politically, socially and religiously. And whether you are from Northern Ireland or not, these fractures cannot be ignored, but this doesn't mean the city can't overcome such problems and enjoy itself.

Despite the tensions and occasional setbacks (the riots and fires of last October caused blockades and chaos around the city for several days), Belfast is a lively and great place to live. It's a small and compact city so you'll soon find your way around. The new bus system is cheap and efficient and as such you'll rarely find it necessary to get a train anywhere - they're far too pricey anyway. Unless you have a car already, don't get one to live in Belfast - driving around the city can be a nightmare.

Central and South Belfast is the focus for most of student life. Botanic gardens are a haven away from the busy city; the green is packed in the summer and there's often a brass band playing on the bandstand by the rose garden. Inside the gardens you'll find the pretty **Palm House** and also the **Ulster Museum**, which tends to show interesting contemporary art and houses the permanent 'Ireland in Conflict' exhibition. Botanic Avenue and Dublin Road lead the way from the city to the University area - a mere 15-minute walk.

Apart from the stunning white marble **City Hall** and several redbrick Victorian buildings (**The Linen Hall** and **Marks & Spencer**), the rest of the centre is fairly unspectacular. The waterside is still being developed although the **Waterfront Hall** and the **Odyssey Complex** are already good music and entertainment venues, and along and near Royal Avenue there are the usual High Street stores, lots of secondhand bookshops, plus, off Queen's Street, some pricier boutiques. But if you want to do any serious shopping, take the 2-hour train journey to

Dublin. It is well worth it.

CRAIC

As a newcomer to Belfast you'll soon learn the true meaning of the famous 'craic'. People really know how to go out and have a great time here. Bars and pubs are plentiful (though very smoky!) – from trendy 'sit-in-and-be-seen' cocktail bars, such as **The Apartment**, to traditional taverns such as **Whites**. In the city centre the Cathedral quarter contains the lovely **John Hewitt** pub (with an excellent choice of ales & beers) and **The Spaniard** – a great bar with quirky décor and fantastic music – serves tapas and light meals. **The Kitchen Bar** in the nearby **Cornmarket** is very classy and holds a jazz night every Monday. Going away from the city centre and leading towards the uni area, **Katie Daly's** and the **Limelight** are well known for their student-orientated theme nights. Closer to Queen's there's always a good atmosphere in **Auntie Annies** while **The Bot** and **The Egg** (off Eglantine Avenue) are convenient and cheap student dives (**The Egg** does a £5 Sunday roast). Though the variety of nightclubs doesn't really rival that of pubs, there are a couple worth checking out – **Milk** and **The Pothouse** being the best of the bunch. Although there isn't much of a gay/lesbian scene in Belfast there are a couple of sympathetic clubs in the cathedral quarter: **The**

Cremlin and **The Nest**.

ART

Belfast is full of poets and musicians and as such there's always a poetry reading or a band playing in a pub nearby. All music events are listed in the free pamphlet – *The List*, or you can find full entertainment listings in the *Belfast Telegraph* on a Friday. Traditional music sessions can usually be heard at **Whites**, **The John Hewitt** or **Kelly's Tavern**, while folk or rock bands often play in **Katie Daly's**, **The Empire** or **Auntie Annies**. **The Limelight**, **The Ulster Hall** and **The King's Hall** all host bigger bands – such as The Magic Numbers, K.T. Tunstall and Gabriel y Rodrigo.

Spring and autumn see lots of festivals in Belfast – such as the big Belfast Festival (all over the city), Between the Lines (literature & music – at **The Crescent Arts Centre**), Belfast Film Festival, the Cathedral Quarter Arts Festival and the new Holylands Arts Festival. Throughout the summer there are Irish festivals or fleadh held in West Belfast, and the **An Cultural Ann** (Culture Centre) on the Falls road has a lovely café and an Irish language book shop, where you can often hear local musicians.

Laura Cattell

UNIVERSITY OF READING

The University of Reading
Whiteknights
Reading RG6 6AH

TEL 0118 378 5439
FAX 0118 378 8924
EMAIL student.recruitment@reading.ac.uk
WEB www.reading.ac.uk

Reading University Students' Union
PO Box 230
Reading RG6 2AZ

TEL 0118 378 4100
FAX 0118 975 5283
EMAIL b.p.elger@reading.ac.uk
WEB www.rusu.co.uk

VAG VIEW

*T*he University of Reading is set on a campus a couple of miles from the centre of Reading, and 45 miles west of central London.

*The student body is far from being limited to the marauding agrics of popular legend. Its areas of academic strength cover a wider spectrum than many imagine - cybernetics, classics, environmental sciences, agri-*culture, meteorology, film & theatre.

Investment remains high - a Student Services Building opened recently, which provides a one-stop-shop for student support and welfare; the sports facilities have also been extended; and a new-look Student Union development was unveiled in the not too distant past.

Student media, often a barometer of cultural depth, has dwindled of late. Sport, however, remains a priority, but their performance in the graduate-track employ-ment league table has been erratic - 71% only can be assured of real graduate jobs six months after leaving, too many of them in estate agency. What, one wonders will they do now?

Still, students are happy at Reading, and the teaching and in-depth research is very good - a huge 88% gave their approval in the 2008 National Student Survey, organised by the Higher Education Funding Council for England, and less than 4% fail to last the course.

CAMPUS

Writes Laura Cattell: 'Set in the leafy Whiteknights grounds on the outskirts of the town Reading main-tains a close campus atmosphere while being only a stone's throw from the bright lights of London. One and a half miles from the town centre the University actually has two campuses - the larger Whiteknights where most undergraduates study and live and then the smaller Bulmershe, a further mile out of the city (home of Education faculty and unlucky Erasmus students who didn't get a place in halls on the main campus).'

FEES, BURSARIES

UK & EU Fees, 2009: £3,225 p.a. If eligible for an HE Maintenance grant there are bursaries available on a sliding scale, according to household earnings. There are also entrance and achievement scholar-ships for firm-choice applicants, and Music and Sports scholarships. See www.reading.ac.uk/stu-dentfinance.

STUDENT PROFILE

Life is relaxed and sport-orientated at Reading and the majority of students are southern and well-heeled, many of them from public schools. However, there is also a large take from overseas, and an increasing take (24%) from among families new to the idea of university. 'Nevertheless,' says Laura, 'despite the government's widening partici-pation scheme and a huge influx of international students, the uni still retains an upper to middle class/middle England feel.'

ACADEMIA & JOBS

Reading's reputation may be for agriculture, land management, cybernetics, food and soil sciences, but there's a huge range of arts, humanities, edu-cation, languages, and social studies courses.

Students rate the university for helpful inter-

UNIVERSITY/STUDENT PROFILE	
University since	**1926**
Situation/style	**Campus**
Student population	**14680**
Total undergraduates	**10640**
Mature undergraduates	**16%**
International undergrads	**13%**
Male/female ratio	**45:55**
Equality of opportunity:	
state school intake	**82%**
social class 4-7 intake	**24%**
low-participation area intake	**7%**

ested staff and say the best teaching is to be found in Archaeology, Initial Teacher Training, Architecture, Building, Business, Computer Science, History, Physical Geography & Environmental Science, Biology and associated sci-ences, Agriculture, Classics, Drama, English, Law, Politics, European Languages, and Finance.

In the recent research assessments Environmental Sciences, Architecture & Built Environment, Town & Country Planning, Archaeology and Philosophy came out best - all between 50% and 75% world-class and interna-tionally excellent.

Still, the sparkling exterior of the ISMA build-ing (Investment banking, International security, and finance - an extension sees a new 40-seat deal-ing room, the largest training facility of its kind in Europe) and the hi-tech Agri. Department domi-nate one's image of the place.

All undergraduates are matched with a per-sonal tutor, a constant for the duration. This can work well as long as you attend some lectures and meet with him/her when you're meant to. Within your undergraduate degree it's possible to take courses in other departments and taking on a free language class (part of the IWLP - Institution-wide Language Programme) is also a good way to sup-

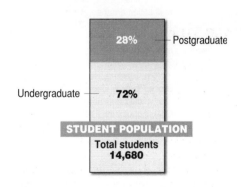

28% — Postgraduate

Undergraduate — 72%

STUDENT POPULATION
Total students
14,680

plement your studies and gain a further qualification. You can also take more free courses in the Library if you feel the need to update your computer skills or learn to use electronic databases more effectively.

They are big providers of graduates into accountancy - three degrees, two with Economics (one BSc), the other with Management, and there is great employment strength in both finance and business management. The uni just merged with the Henley Business College to create the Henley Business School at the University of Reading. Henley is the world's third largest supplier of MBA education and one of a few to be triple accredited by the major UK, US and European accreditation bodies (AMBA, EQUIS, AACSB). It becomes a faculty of the university.

Maybe the merger will raise the graduate employment profile for business graduates. Before banking and accountancy, estate agents still dominate the job market, with 45% of all business graduates going that way. Can't last in the recession. Real Estate and Building degrees also tend in that direction.

From the important research areas of Built Environment and Planning come BSc in Building Construction & Management and one in Construction Management & Surveying that gives you the entire construction process, from brief to architect through design, planning and project completion. The

> *The uni just merged with the Henley Business College, the world's 3rd largest provider of MBA education, which is bound to raise its graduate employment profile further for business graduates.*

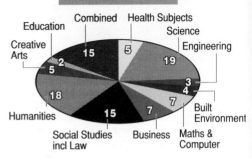

SUBJECT AREAS (%)

Subject	%
Education	
Combined	15
Health Subjects	5
Science	19
Engineering	3
Creative Arts	2
	5
	4
	7
Built Environment	
Humanities	18
Social Studies incl Law	15
Business	7
Maths & Computer	

Chartered Institute of Building (CIOB) grants membership after two years experience. There's also BSc Building Surveying.

All undergraduate courses include a Career Management Skills module, but Estate Agency is the single most popular job area, after which comes the civil service and government administration at all levels, fed in particular by Social Studies graduates, Languages, Historical and Philosophical Studies. There's an excellent series of both History and Philosophy degrees, and both did very well in the research assessment.

The third big employment area is hospitals, fed by Reading's degrees in subjects allied to Medicine, like Biochemistry, Biomedical Engineering, Primary Care Nursing (Public Health Nursing is also available) - and Biological Sciences: top scoring teaching assessments include Psychology, available actually in both BA and BSc degrees, pairing with such as Biology, Philosophy, Childhood & Ageing, Mental & Physical Health.

Farmers know this as the top-rated research establishment, and very strong on Agricultural Business Management, but also other sorts of management - Rural Resource, Landscape, Habitat & Soil. Also very big in Food Science, with Business, or as Food Technology.

Geography, Rural Environmental Science, Rural Resource Mgt, Land Mgt are all mainstream Reading. See the new BSc Applied Ecology & Conservation. This is a big area in research. A useful employment niche comes with Reading's BSc Meteorology, which sits alongside one with a year

TEACHING SURVEY AT A GLANCE

Avg. UCAS points accepted	**340**
Acceptance rate	**16%**
Overall satisfaction rate	**88%**
Helpful/interested staff	★★★★
Small tuition groups	★★★
Students into graduate jobs	**71%**

Teaching most popular with undergraduates: Archaeology (100%), Initial Teacher Training (94%), Architecture, Building, Business, Computer Science, History, Physical Geography & Enviro. Science (93%), Biolog and Sciences related to Biology (92%), Agriculture, Classics, Drama, English, Law, Politics (91%), European Languages, Finance (90%).

Teaching least popular with undergraduates: Economics (74%), Fine Art (66%).

RESEARCH EXCELLENCE		
% of Reading's research that is		
4* *(World-class) or* **3*** *(Internationally rated):*		
	4*	**3***
Pharmacy	**10%**	**35%**
Biological Sciences	**5%**	**30%**
Agriculture	**5%**	**40%**
Food Biosciences	**15%**	**40%**
Environmental Sciences	**30%**	**45%**
Chemistry	**0%**	**25%**
Applied Mathematics	**5%**	**35%**
Statistics	**5%**	**30%**
Computer Science	**5%**	**25%**
Electrical/Electronic Eng.	**5%**	**35%**
Built Environment	**25%**	**45%**
Town/Country Planning	**25%**	**35%**
Geography Environment	**10%**	**35%**
Archaeology	**40%**	**25%**
Business/Management	**10%**	**40%**
Law	**20%**	**40%**
Politics	**10%**	**25%**
Social Work	**5%**	**45%**
Psychology	**10%**	**50%**
Education	**10%**	**20%**
French	**20%**	**25%**
German	**5%**	**35%**
Italian	**25%**	**40%**
English	**25%**	**40%**
Linguistics	**10%**	**25%**
Classics	**10%**	**40%**
Philosophy	**30%**	**45%**
History	**10%**	**40%**
Fine Art	**15%**	**40%**
Typography/Graphics	**45%**	**35%**
History of Art	**15%**	**45%**
Performing Arts	**30%**	**25%**

in Oklahoma(!), and there's a Foundation year opportunity.

Cybernetics is also a defining influence on the curriculum. There's a new BSc Systems Engineering and BSc Robotics. Cybernetics also mixes with Computer Science (BSc or MEng). Reading scores highly with employers for software consultancy & supply and in IT consultancy.

Educational Studies to primary level (a major contributor to the graduate employment figures) is only part of the story for teachers. Language graduates find jobs as lecturers in further education, as do many graduates from the famous Faculty of Letters & Social Sciences with its unique set of arts and social science mixes.

Humanities pack graduates into libraries and museums as curators, librarians, archivists; archaeologists abound (the dedicated degree leaving few

hungry), and publishing is a very popular destination from Reading.

SOCIAL SCENE

STUDENTS' UNION 'The RUSU houses a student advice centre, large shop, off-licence, insurance outlet, student travel agency and three entertainment venues,' writes Laura. 'By day there are plenty of eateries and cafés open to grab a cheap lunch while by night the impressive Union offers up **Mojos**, **Café Mondial** and **3sixty** as watering holes/dance floors. Monday is Curry Night in Mojo's, sometimes a quiz, karaoke or comedy. Wednesday and Saturday are the biggest nights. *Extra Time* on Wednesday - cheesy chart music, r&b, retro '70/'80s hits - and all with a few rugby/hockey players covered in snake bite&black thrown in for good measure. There's *Rough Cuts* at 3sixty - live. The Union also occasionally attracts big bands such as Kosheen, Goldie Lookin' Chain and Travis, but regularly gets local bands to perform as well. *Candy Club* - a night of sweet tunes - sweeps them away every Saturday. A cheaper alternative is Friday night at the refurbished **Breeze Bar** on Bulmershe campus.

'The lively music department organises regular choir recitals and concerts. RUMS (Reading University Music Society) has a Choral Society, Gospel Choir and the also the more relaxed University Singers. There's also an orchestra, concert and jazz band, and it's home to the infamous *Reading Rock Festival* and the WOMAD world music festival, which liven up the town in the summer and offer up volunteer opportunities if you want a chance to see your favourite band for free.'

The HUB, within the Students Union is the central resource for students seeking any kind of advice or information, or backing/facilities for sports clubs and societies, the most active of which is Campaigns Forum. They also support around 1,500 volunteer groups of students working on projects within the local community. Despite Reading being a university focused on elite sportsmen and women at the expense of participation, students from around the campus have gained notable success in a wide range of activities from arts and music to firmly being at the heart of the student movement nationally.

Reading is now a very active community, demanding more from the student experience, though it's been a while since student media cut the mustard in the national awards.

The student newspaper - *The Spark* - is currently out of commission, but Junction 11, the student radio station, remains accessible on campus and in halls. If you are interested in media, the way is open at Reading for a bit of ingenuity.

WHAT IT'S REALLY LIKE	
UNIVERSITY:	
Social Life	★★★★
Campus scene	**Middle class, southern, sporty.**
Student Union services	**Average**
Politics	**Strong internal**
Sport	**52 clubs**
National team position	**26th**
Sport facilities	**Good**
Arts opportunities	**Good, esp. drama**
Student radio station	**Junction 11**
Nightclub	**3sixty**
Bars	**Mojo's, Breeze, Café Mondial,**
Union ents	**6 nights eclectic**
Union societies	**48**
Most active societies	**Campaigns Forum**
Parking	**Adequate**
TOWN:	
Entertainment	★★★
Scene	**Pubs, clubs OK**
Town/gown relations	**Average**
Risk of violence	**Average**
Cost of living	**High**
Student concessions	**Good**
Survival + 2 nights out	**£90 pw**
Part-time work campus/town	**Excellent**

river. Reading has bowed to the fashion for making every British town centre look exactly the same. There is the standard riverside development, known as the Oracle, full of chain restaurants and High Street stores. Look beyond the main High Street - to places like the Chinese supermarket or the Global café. In town, pubs and clubs-wise there's plenty of choice. And of course London and Oxford are only a short train ride away.'

PILLOW TALK

Sixty to 70% of first years are allocated catered hall accommodation, and if you want to make lectures in your first year, it's no bad idea. The best has to be Whiteknights, but equally fun and popular halls are Wantage, an Oxbridge-style building just off

ACCOMMODATION	
Guarantee to freshers	**95%**
Style	**Halls, flats**
Security guard	**All**
Shared rooms	**None**
Internet access	**All**
Self-catered	**Some**
En suite	**Some**
Approx price range pw	**£68.18-£160.10**
City rent pw	**£65-£75**

SPORT 'Sport is an integral part of life on campus. The sports facilities are excellent and most of the playing fields are on campus so whenever there's a big match there's a great atmosphere and everyone goes along to watch. The Wolfenden Sports Centre has a flashy gym and there are squash courts and several halls where most of the fitness classes and clubs/societies take place. £120+ for six months may seem a bit steep at the beginning of term, but it does entitle you to use all facilities in the centre at any time you like and you don't have to pay another penny after that.

Generally, team standards are pretty high, especially for women's netball and hockey. Overall they came 26th nationally last year.

TOWN 'Reading is set in picturesque countryside and pretty villages such as Sonning or Pangbourne are never far away if you fancy a walk along the

campus, but very close, St Patricks, and, for friendliness, Bridges. A redevelopment of St Georges Hall recently opened - 426 bedrooms, majority ensuite. If you're studying Education or Film & Drama you may be placed in modern Bulmershe halls, where there's a closer, friendlier, if quieter, atmosphere. The uni says, 'In the coming year, work on redeveloping some of our older Halls of Residences will start.'

GETTING THERE

☛ By road: M4/J11, A33. An express bus service to London leaves from outside the university.
☛ By rail: London Paddington, 0:30; Birmingham, 2:15; Oxford, 0:40; Bristol Parkway, 1:00.
☛ By air: Heathrow and Gatwick.
☛ By coach: London, 1:20; Brighton, 3:45; Exeter, 3-5:00; Leicester, 5:00.

THE ROBERT GORDON UNIVERSITY

The Robert Gordon University
Aberdeen AB10 1FR
TEL 01224 262105
FAX 01224 262185
EMAIL admissions@rgu.ac.uk
WEB www.rgu.ac.uk

Robert Gordon Students' Association
Aberdeen AB10 1JQ
TEL 01224 262294
FAX 01224 262268
EMAIL rgusa@rgu.ac.uk
WEB www.rgunion.co.uk/

VAG VIEW

*R*obert Gordon University is consistently
in the UK Top 20 for getting its graduates real, 'graduate track' jobs - 87% got
them last time around within six months of
leaving. It owes its foundation to philan-
thropist Robert Gordon, from whose estate
the Robert Gordon's Hospital was created in
1750, and which developed into a college half
a century later. It is also the beneficiary of
another Aberdeen entrepreneur, an architect
by name of Tom Scott Sutherland, who presented them with the grounds and mansion
where the Scott Sutherland School of
Architecture was based, a beautiful site overlooking the River Dee. Another of RGU's constituent parts is the Gray's School of Art,
named after Aberdeen engineer John Gray; it
was founded in 1885.

Now, they are investing £115 million over
ten years to create four 'academic precincts'
for art, business, health and technology -
what they call 'the best riverside campus in
Europe'.

CAMPUS

While the Students' Association and uni are based
at the Schoolhill site in Aberdeen, 75% of RGU students are now taught at the Garthdee Campus on
the south side of the city on the banks of the Dee,
which includes the mighty impressive Aberdeen
Business School, the Faculty of Health & Social
Care, and two schools - the Scott Sutherland School
and the Gray's School of Art - of the Faculty of
Design and Technology. Over £60 million has been
invested in the development of this campus in the
last four years.

The Schoolhill site encompasses the Schools of
Engineering and Pharmacy and the Student
Association. The St Andrew Street building is locat-
ed near Schoolhill and is home to the Schools of
Computing and Life Sciences, and a library that

UNIVERSITY/STUDENT PROFILE	
University since	**1992**
Situation/style	**Civic**
Student population	**12985**
Total undergraduates	**8880**
Mature undergraduates	**22%**
International undergrads	**4%**
Male/female ratio	**40:60**
Equality of opportunity:	
state school intake	**95%**
social class 4-7 intake	**33%**
low-participation area intake	**2%**

serves all the schools at the Schoolhill campus.

FEES

UK & EU Fees, 2009-10: Non-Scottish domiciled
students fees in year 2009-10: £1,820. If you are a
Scottish-domiciled first degree student you are eligible for your tuition fees to be covered by the
Scottish Government. A Sports Scholarship
Programme is currently supporting London
Olympic swimming hopeful, Hannah Miley, as she
trains for the 2012 Olympics. See www.rgu.ac.uk/
rgusport/scholarship/page.cfm?pge = 57572.
There's also a range of academic scholarships. See
www.rgu.ac.uk/learning/whyrgu/page.cfm?pge =
35752.

STUDENT PROFILE

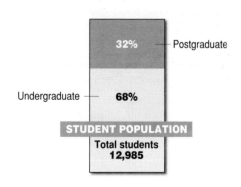

STUDENT POPULATION
Total students
12,985

TEACHING SURVEY AT A GLANCE

Avg. UCAS points accepted	**308**
Acceptance rate	**26%**
Overall satisfaction rate	**No data**
Helpful/interested staff	**No data**
Small tuition groups	**No data**
Students into graduate jobs	**87%**

Teaching most popular with undergraduates:
No data

Teaching least popular with undergraduates:
No data

There is a large undergraduate intake from the state sector, 22% are mature, many are local. and 24% are part-timers. There are also a number of participants in RGU's Virtual Campus courses (for info, visit www.campus. rgu.com).

ACADEMIA & JOBS

They offer degree programmes in Nursing, Business, Law, Engineering, Science, Computing, Art, Design, Architecture, Pharmacy and Health Sciences, and a well-balanced ethos with both academic and practical matters to the fore: 27% of the student body are on sandwich courses (fees for a placement year are £910, and a year abroad £1,820).

The traditional contribution to oil extraction and mining consultancy comes through Mechanical & Offshore Engineering, Mechanical & Environmental Engineering, etc, but that is no longer their defining area. There's now a major career focus in the area of health - nursing (adult, children, mental) radiography, nutrition, occupational therapy, physiotherapy are among the best from an employment point of view. See also their Biomedical Sciences degrees and the new MPharm Pharmacy; also Forensic Science (there's a tradi-

tional fast track into police work); and the BA and MSc (postgrad) Social Work.

In the Aberdeen Business School, they have great strength in the tourism and hospitality area - they are regularly No. 1 in Britain as graduate suppliers to the catering industry through dedicated degrees. Also, there's BA Retail Management, which accounts for a strong showing in retail, and BA Accounting & Finance.

Look, too, at their in-depth strength in Computing - Artificial Intelligence, Electronic Engineering, Robotics, Computing for Graphics & Animation, Computer for Internet, for Mobile Applications, for Business.

And then there's the traditional good showing employment-wise in Built Environment - BSc Architectural Technology, Construction Design, Surveying (Quantity Surveying, a dedicated degree, is a particular strength). Three degrees:

RESEARCH EXCELLENCE

% of Robert Gordon's research that is
4* *(World-class)* or **3*** *(Internationally rated):*

	4*	3*
Health Professions	**5%**	**15%**
Computer Science	**5%**	**40%**
General Engineering	**5%**	**15%**
Architecture	**10%**	**20%**
Accounting and Finance	**5%**	**15%**
Business/Management	**5%**	**35%**
Information Management	**15%**	**45%**
Law	**0%**	**5%**
Politics	**0%**	**25%**
Sociology	**0%**	**15%**
Art and Design	**5%**	**40%**

BSc Architecture, Architec. (European Practice) and Interior Architecture are recognised by RIBA. See, too, their Design for Industry programme - Digital Media, Graphic, Product Design degrees.

A longterm specialism in Law & Management has now been joined by a fully fledged LLB, recognised by the Law Society of Scotland.

Finally, there is now, too, a Sports Science degree, backed up by a multi-million pound sports and leisure centre at its new Garthdee Campus.

SOCIAL SCENE

STUDENTS' ASSOCIATION RGUnion has two bars at Schoolhill, which provide a wide range of entertainment 7 nights a week. Regular nights include: Open Mic, *Karaoke Idol*, r&b hip hop, *The Master Chill*, and everyone's disco favourite, *Thursday Night Fever*. The downstairs bar is available for pri-

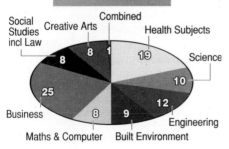

SUBJECT AREAS (%)

Social Studies incl Law — 8
Creative Arts — 8
Combined — 1
Health Subjects — 19
Science — 10
Engineering — 12
Built Environment — 9
Maths & Computer — 8
Business — 25

WHAT IT'S REALLY LIKE	
UNIVERSITY:	
Social Life	★★★
Campus scene	**Part-time, local but increasingly cosmopolitan**
Student Union services	**Poor**
Politics	**Interest low**
Sport	**9 clubs**
National team position	**77th**
Sport facilities	**New centre**
Arts opportunities	**Drama, dance, music good; film, art average**
Student magazine	**Cogno**
Nightclub/bars	**U-bar, Blue Iguana**
Union ents	**7 nights a week**
Union societies	**30**
Most active society	**Cogno**
Parking	**Adequate**
CITY:	
Entertainment	★★★★
Scene	**Intoxicating**
Town/gown relations	**Good**
Risk of violence	**Low**
Cost of living	**Average**
Student concessions	**Average**
Survival + 2 nights out	**£60 pw**
Part-time work campus/town	**Good/excellent**

used to develop the re-vamped student magazine, which goes by the name of Cogno.

SPORT The new sports centre will revolutionise things. There's hockey, athletics, rugby, rowing, football, archery, badminton, basketball, and of course all those outward bound activities - skiing, hill walking, etc, naturally available in this area.

PILLOW TALK
Accommodation is thin on the ground, and students' advice is to get in quick. There is a commendable lack of fuss, however, at the uni:

ACCOMMODATION	
Guarantee to freshers	**98%**
Style	**Flats**
Security guard	**Some**
Internet access	**All**
Self-catered	**Most**
En suite	**Some**
Approx price range pw	**£65-£68**
City rent pw	**£60-£100**

'Everyone who applies for accommodation,' they say, 'is usually allocated accommodation.' It consists of self contained, self-catering flats, six to eight sharing, all with own bedroom, 20% en suite. Price per week ranges from £65 to £80.

GETTING THERE
☛ By road: from south, A92, thence ring road for signs; from north, A96 or A92.
☛ By coach: London, 11.30; Newcastle, 7.35.

☛ By rail: London King's Cross, 7:00; Glasgow, 2:45; Edinburgh, 2:30; Newcastle, 4:30.
☛ By air: Aberdeen International Airport.

vate functions on Tuesdays and Sundays; students have recently used these nights for events such as speed dating and games like *Play Your Cards Right*.

The whole building has recently been refurbished and now provides a Volunteering Centre to help students gain recognition for unpaid work. The Union actively encourages students to get involved in university life by awarding recognised certificates for their volunteering efforts. A new Marketing and Communications Centre opened in January 2006, with up to date software that'll be

ROEHAMPTON UNIVERSITY

Roehampton University
Erasmus House
Roehampton Lane
London SW15 5PU

TEL 020 8392 3232
EMAIL enquiries@roehampton.ac.uk
WEB www.roehampton.ac.uk

Roehampton Students' Union
Froebel College
Roehampton Lane
London SW15 5PJ

TEL 020 8392 3221
EMAIL info@roehamptonstudent.com
WEB www.roehamptonstudent.com

VAG VIEW

Roehampton University, in south-west London, offers vocational courses in the Arts, Education, Social Sciences, Sciences and Sports areas, but with a rather attractive, artistic and caring ethos, which is part and parcel of the place.

Of its four constituent colleges, Digby Stuart College (Arts & Humanities) has a Roman Catholic foundation; Froebel College (Education) follows the teachings of Friedrich Froebel, the caring chappie who invented kindergartens; Southlands College (Social Sciences) has a Methodist base; and Whitelands College (Science) has a Church of England base.

They are not, however, in the business of shoving this down your throat. Now, with university status, they have fathered their sometime scattered colleges into one campus in south west London, and things are looking bright. In the National Student Survey, 80% said they were satisfied, though it has to be said that the 11% drop-out figure is some way above their Government benchmark.

CAMPUS

The uni's four colleges are cosily set together on the edge of Richmond deer park. Writes Becky Neaum: 'Roehampton University is situated in an affluent area of south west London, and within a 20-minute train ride of the central of the capital city. It is set within lush green grounds and only a few minutes from Richmond Park; a 9-mile deer park. So, if you are torn between choosing country and city, and if you love the bright lights of the city, but also the peaceful landscape of the country, then this University really is ideally located.'

'Roehampton combines the best aspects of liv-

UNIVERSITY/STUDENT PROFILE	
University since	**1992**
Situation/style	**City campus**
Student population	**8535**
Total undergraduates	**6720**
Mature undergraduates	**27%**
International undergrads	**13%**
Male/female ratio	**24:76**
Equality of opportunity:	
state school intake	**97%**
social class 4-7 intake	**36%**
low-participation area intake	**5%**

ing in London,' agrees Gina Wright. 'I cannot imagine a more perfect site - a peaceful green campus set in landscaped grounds with lakes and trees, yet near enough to buses and tubes to make the journey into central London in about half an hour.'

Digby College has the Belfry Bar, a Learning Resource Centre, self-catering flats and a warm, welcoming atmosphere. Froebel College is dominated by the imposing, Georgian Grove House, its period feel making it popular with students and TV productions such as Inspector Morse. It also has the music venue, Montefiore Hall.

Southlands, relocated from Wimbledon in 1997, is clean, modern and the musical pulse of the uni, with studios, a Steinway concert grand and a double-manual French harpsichord.

Whitelands founds its way here in 2004, and occupies an 18th-century Palladian mansion, Parkstead House, at the heart of campus.

FEES, BURSARIES

UK & EU Fees, 2009-10: £3,225 p.a. If in receipt of the Higher Education Maintenance grant, there's a bursary, and there are academic achievement scholarships.

STUDENT PROFILE

More than a third of undergraduates come from the lowest four socio-economic classes, and 5% from so-called 'low participation' neighbourhoods, for whom university is a new experience. Only about 4% come from the independent school sector.

ACADEMIA

Continues Becky: 'It being a small university, the lecturers have time for the students, and it's true that you feel a name, not a number here. Lecture and seminar groups are relatively small, which allows for more interaction and discussion.' This was confirmed by the Higher Education Funding Council's 2008 National Student Survey.

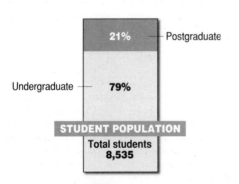

21% — Postgraduate

Undergraduate — 79%

STUDENT POPULATION

Total students
8,535

TEACHING SURVEY AT A GLANCE

Avg. UCAS points accepted	**220**
Acceptance rate	**18%**
Overall satisfaction rate	**80%**
Helpful/interested staff	★★★★
Small tuition groups	★★★
Students into graduate jobs	**69%**

Teaching most popular with undergraduates:
Mass Communications (93%), European Languages (91%), Education, Languages (87%), History, Philosophy, Theology, Religious Studies (85%), Anthropology, English (84%), Initial Teacher Training (83%), Biology & related Sciences, Social Studies, Social Anthropology (80%).

Teaching least popular with undergraduates:
Psychology (73%).

Roehampton lecturers are helpful and interested, and in the fields of Anthropology, Dance and Drama it has notched up some impressive recent research successes. Students say the teaching is best in Media European Languages, Education, Languages, History, Philosophy, Theology, Religious Studies, Anthropology, English, Initial Teacher Training, Biology & related sciences, Social Studies, Social Anthropology. Research in the Anthropology department was adjudged last December to be 15% world-class (4-star) and 65% internationally excellent (3-star). Meanwhile, Dance scored 55%-30%, an amazing result, which made them first in the country for Dance and second among all the universities providing any kind of Performing Arts. Drama wasn't far behind, with 15% 4-star, 45% 3-star.

'Workloads are not immense,' continues Becky. 'Pressure does build up towards the deadlines, but you are given plenty of time to do the work in.

There is 24/7 Internet access in the library and in most halls.'

When it comes to graduate supply to primary teaching, Roehampton mounts a very strong case. Output is almost totally Primary. They are renowned for their Drama and QTS courses in particular.

The religious background to the constituent colleges comes through in courses for the caring professions, such as healthcare and therapeutic work (and teaching too, under their particular educational regime). Look at the foundation course, Childcare and Early Years Education, and BSc Integrative Counselling, Counselling, Psychology & Counselling, Psychology, Psychology & Health, BA Early Childhood Studies, BSc Health & Social Care, Health Studies, and BA Human Rights.

They are also among the leaders in getting jobs for graduates in sport - as players or sport officials.

RESEARCH EXCELLENCE

% of Roehampton's research that is
4* *(World-class)* or **3*** *(Internationally rated):*

	4*	3*
Health Professions	**0%**	**20%**
Biological Sciences	**0%**	**5%**
Sociology	**5%**	**25%**
Anthropology	**15%**	**65%**
Psychology	**0%**	**20%**
Education	**5%**	**25%**
Sports	**0%**	**0%**
French	**0%**	**5%**
Iberian	**5%**	**25%**
English	**10%**	**25%**
Theology	**5%**	**15%**
History	**10%**	**25%**
Drama	**15%**	**45%**
Dance	**55%**	**30%**
Media Studies	**5%**	**30%**

The BSc Sport & Exercise Science is the prototype, a good balance of Physiology, Biomechanics and Psychology.

SOCIAL SCENE

'Unlike other universities in the London area, Roehampton has its own, very beautiful campus, and campus life is brilliant,' writes Becky. 'It is a small uni, but sizeable enough for footy games, summer sports day and an amazing annual Summer Ball. It is friendly as well, with a huge mix of people from all walks of life and of all ages. This is one of the first things that attracted me to Roehampton.

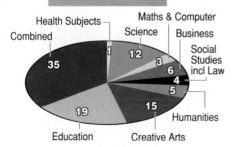

SUBJECT AREAS (%)

Health Subjects 1
Combined 35
Maths & Computer Science 12
Business 3
Social Studies incl Law 6
4
5
Humanities 15
Creative Arts
Education 19

WHAT IT'S REALLY LIKE

UNIVERSITY:

Social Life	★★★
Campus scene	**Diverse, friendly**
Student Union services	**Good**
Politics	**Apathetic**
Sport	**Keen**
National team position	**91st**
Sport facilities	**Poor**
Arts opportunities	**Excellent**
Student newspaper	**Fresh**
Venue	**Monte Hall, RSU Lounge, Belfry Bar**
Bars	**College bars**
Union ents	**Chav Night, Heaven or Hell + live bands**
Union societies	**25**
Most Active	**Open Mic**
Parking	**Poor (permit)**

CITY:

Entertainment	★★★★★
Scene	**Wild, expensive**
Town/gown relations	**Average-good**
Risk of violence	**High**
Cost of living	**Very high**
Student concessions	**Abundant**
Survival + 2 nights out	**£80 pw**
Part-time work campus/town	**Excellent**

nearby Putney. They have things with **Hammersmith Palais**, too, such as fashion shows, or the long-running *Roehampton Idol* might be held at **Monte Hall**. Of the balls, the infamous, extravagant Summer Ball is best. Froebel boasts the second largest ball after Oxford and Cambridge.

Societies tend to be transient. Large and long-standing socs are RIACAS, which promotes Afro-Caribbean and Asian culture, and top soc. Open Mic. There's a monthly newspaper, *Fresh*, and other societies spin off undergraduate courses.

Says Gina: 'The football battles between the Digby Lions and their "natural prey", the Froebel Zebras, are legendary!'

PILLOW TALK

ACCOMMODATION

Guarantee to freshers	**100%**
Style	**Halls, flats**
Security guard	**Some**
Shared rooms	**Some**
Internet access	**Most**
Self-catered	**Most**
En suite	**Some**
Approx price range pw	**£88-£135**
City rent pw	**£100-£180**

'Freshers Week was a fantastic experience here, although daunting at times. It was packed with things to do, day and night. Now the social scene off campus is rich and varied; with many student nights at nightclubs, such as **Oceana**, **Cheapskates** and **Hammersmith Palais**. Putney is our local pub haunt.'

Each of the four campuses has its own bar. Ents are OK. In the week this is being written, Thursday is Bands Night, featuring, for example, Last Gang In Town, Blue Mojo, Dancing Bears at Belfry Bar, Digby. Friday, at Froebel, is invariably *The Bop: Heaven or Hell*, or *Vicars and Tarts*, or some other theme. Monday might be comedy at the **Lounge**. Wednesday, Sports Night, is held at **Fez Club**, in

'Accommodation at Roehampton ranges from typical halls, with up to 25 or so people sharing a floor, and all facilities, to flats of 6 to 10 with private facilities,' Becky writes.

Two new student residences opened in 2004. All Colleges cater for vegetarians. There are some en-suite ground floor rooms for students with disabilities. They allocate rooms on a 'first come, first served basis', so get onto it fast.

GETTING THERE

☞ US Roehampton, Barnes British Rail station or No. 72 bus from Hammersmith Underground; No. 265 runs from Putney Bridge.

ROYAL HOLLOWAY, LONDON UNIVERSITY

Royal Holloway College
Egham
Surrey TW20 0EX

TEL 01784 434455
FAX 01784 473662
EMAIL liaison-office@rhul.ac.uk
WEB www.rhul.ac.uk

Royal Holloway Students' Union
Egham
Egham TW20 0EX

TEL 01784 486300
FAX 01784 486312
EMAIL reception@su.rhul.ac.uk
WEB www.surhul.co.uk

VAG VIEW

Royal Holloway, a college of London University, is situated on a 120-acre campus at Egham in Surrey, far enough to the south west of London's bright lights to favour a well-focused regime. Students almost uniformly mention the workload, although there is a lively campus social scene too. In the National Student Survey 85% approved of the way things go, and less than 4% fail to complete the course.

St George's, the University of London Med. School in Tooting, and Royal Holloway announced in October last year that they intend to form a single institution within the University.

CAMPUS

'Holloway, isn't that a women's prison?' says Sarah Toms with a sigh which suggests she has heard the jibe many times before. 'It is of course, but not here, it's in South London! You'll get used to that question. This is Royal Holloway, University of London - yes, the one with THAT building (Founders Hall). Located a train ride from central London - forty minutes on a good day, barring leaves on the line or the wrong kind of snow.'

It has been called 'London's Country Campus', and it is certainly a beautiful spot, made distinctive by Founder's Building, a copy of the Chateau de Chambourd in the Loire built by Thomas Holloway, who in 1886 founded a college for women there. Nearly a century later it merged with another all-female foundation, Bedford College, creating Royal Holloway and Bedford New College. It is a close, rather private, situation far from the bustle.

UNIVERSITY/STUDENT PROFILE	
University since	**1800**
Situation/style	**Campus**
Student population	**8335**
Total undergraduates	**9560**
Mature undergraduates	**15%**
International undergrads	**16%**
Male/female ratio	**43:57**
Equality of opportunity:	
state school intake	**79%**
social class 4-7 intake	**24%**
low-participation area intake	**4%**

FEES, BURSARIES

UK & EU Fees, 2009-10: £3,225 p.a. There's a bursary for those eligible for a HE Maintenance Grant, also the Founder's Scholarship and Bedford Scholarships. Other awards are made through the Lyell Bursaries in Geology, the Bioscience Entrance Scholarships and Physics Bursaries for freshers. There are also choral and organ scholarships, and instrumental scholarships/RCM exhibitions. Finally, they offer computer science scholarships, and sports persons are looked after through the Talented Athlete Recognition Scheme. See www.rhul.ac.uk/prospective-student/finance/ug.bursaries.

STUDENT PROFILE

The student body is small, little more than a third the size of King's College or University College, London, and largely female (57%). Public school intake is relatively high (31%), as it is from overseas (16%). The relatively new African-Caribbean society became an instant success.

ACADEMIA & JOBS

University of London degrees are offered in Biological and Physical Sciences, Maths, Computer Science, Humanities, Languages, Arts, Social Sciences and Management. Their success in the teaching assessments include full marks for Psychology and Biosciences, 23 points out of 24 for Drama, Physics and Classics, 22 for Maths, and 21 for languages, Sociology, and Business.

Students say that the best teaching is to be had in the following: Classics, Physical Sciences, Geographical Studies, Computer Science, Geology, Human & Social Geography, History, European Languages, Music, other Languages. All enjoyed 90% appreciation or more in the Higher Education Funding Council's National Student Survey last year.

It's a well balanced mix, more so when you see that they have developed a course unit method

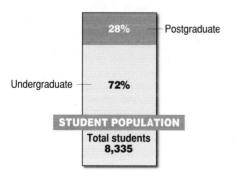

Postgraduate — 28%

Undergraduate — 72%

STUDENT POPULATION
Total students
8,335

TEACHING SURVEY AT A GLANCE

Avg. UCAS points accepted	**360**
Acceptance rate	**17%**
Overall satisfaction rate	**85%**
Helpful/interested staff	★★★
Small tuition groups	★★★
Students into graduate jobs	**68%**

Teaching most popular with undergraduates:
Classics, Physical Science, Geographical Studies (98%), Computer Science, Geology, Human & Social Geography (97%), History (93%), European Languages, Music (92%), other Languages (90%).

Teaching least popular with undergraduates:
Social Studies (72%), Media Studies (70%).

Resources degree too).

Management also hooks up with Marketing and with Information Systems and Technology & Operations. While the Computer Science facility produces numbers of software engineers, computer analysts/programmers, systems analysts, IT consultants, etc.

There are interesting History degrees, one with an extra 'International' year, and the graduates of these tend to gravitate towards jobs in higher education.

Highest score in the 2008 research assessment came from Music, 60% of its work world class (4-star), 30% internationally excellent (3-star). Media also did well - 20%-55% respectively, as did Theatre Arts - 35%-40%.

For Music there's a link with the Royal College of Music, and it can be studied as a single hons or with Maths or BA Psychology, or taken with a year abroad, a language thrown in. There's also an International Theatre (Australia) degree, so obviously the intention is to widen one's perspective by languages and travel as often as possible. The Drama & Media Arts provision lands graduates real jobs in such as publishing, radio, TV, film, advertising and market research.

Science is a big way forward here, with interesting developments in biological science - a degree in Molecular Biology & Genetics recently.

study that allows groupings of subjects across an often imaginative spectrum. For example, Latin is offered as a BA single hons, but also with English (a tantalising prospect for students of syntax and etymology). The Creative Writing course has benefited from the attentions of poet laureate Andrew Motion, Holloway's Professor of Creative Writing, and some of his students have achieved publication.

Those taking Languages actually took most of the graduate jobs last time - mostly in

> *The Creative Writing course has benefited from the attentions of poet laureate Andrew Motion, Holloway's Professor of Creative Writing.*

publishing, recruitment and personnel, business, community and counselling, banking, radio and TV. The International Building incorporates the English, French, German, Hispanic and Italian departments, a dedicated Japanese Studies section (including the Noh theatre - donated by the Japanese government), and a stylish café. Languages and European Studies, Literature, Culture are frequent course elements.

Principally at Royal Holloway students find jobs in banking, specialist retail stores, personnel and recruitment, civil service and government administration, social work, community and counselling, accounting, publishing, higher education and radio & TV. Social Studies Economics (highly rated for research) and Management courses find the accountants, Biological Sciences Psychology (again world class research) and Social Studies Social Work sort out careers in the community. Everyone bands together to swell the ranks of recruitment & personnel and government admin., perhaps sometimes as a second choice (though there's a dedicated Management & Human

Environmental Science fared well in the research assessments - 20% 4-star, 50% 3-star. There are degrees such as Ecology & Environment and Environmental Geography.

SOCIAL SCENE

STUDENTS' UNION The college is largely self-sufficient and most students spend their social hours on site, rather than succumbing to the distant twinkling lights of London. Frankly, the hour-long hike to the capital is seen as a hassle by most, as the last train back is at 11:30 pm, with no more links until 6 am the next day.

In contrast to the friendly, welcoming campus, the nearest town, Egham, remains aloof, a cultural and social pit of suburban blandness.

To compensate for the paucity of local entertainment, the SU serves up a social calendar of unprecedented fullness for an establishment of this size.

Every night is an ents night of some description, ranging from the usual pub quizzes on quiet Sundays to the late bars and DJs which dominate weekends and have a significant foothold in the working week as well.

There's a late licence five nights a week, main hall functions two to three times a week, bar ents every other night. How many unions boast two resident DJs poached from the brighter lights of London? Both Brandon Block and DJ Swing are employed to keep the body student moving, and the latter has been known to hurl the crispest of currency into the crowd too, enhancing popularity and drinks consumption in equal measure. Imported additions include Ministry of Sound, A1, Trevor Nelson, Apollo 440.

Tommy's is the newest bar in the union, and the most popular haunt of the socialites. Only Tuesday and Sunday see it shut before midnight, so the quiet beer with a friend at nine has a sneaky habit of turning into eight loud beers with a roomful of pissheads by kicking out time.

The **Dive Bar,** attached to Tommy's, isn't as seedy as it sounds, and offers a cosier venue. The **Union Bar** is a pretty standard affair, and it is these three which combine to hold 1,200 for the big function nights - it has its own in-house technical crew.

Also on campus is the **Stumble Inn** ('Stumble Out' would surely have been more appropriate), a pub to all intents and a popular one at that, ideal for those nights when aggravating your tinnitus shies you from Tommy's.

Holloway's Bar houses sixteen pool tables, dart boards and a host of ever-changing video games, a free Playstation for the deprived, and live sports courtesy of the ubiquitous Sky TV.

There is also the coffee bar, **TW20's**, a food and caffeine establishment that, according to some, is lamentable, but being dirt cheap and on campus attracts students like flies around the proverbial.

Every June they run a Summer Ball in the quads of Founders: 2,000 tickets are sold in exchange for big name acts, cocktail bar, champagne bar, Glastonbury stage, dance tent, fairground rides, hog roast - it runs from 7 until 7 all through the night.

Media, drama and entertainments in general, are of a high standard. The Musical Theatre Society goes to the Edinburgh Fringe. The radio station, 1287 Insanity and the student mag., Orbital. Are award winners. Politics, on the other hand, is less of a preoccupation.

SPORT The college has a reputation as the best sporting college in London University, and it does well in inter-LU leagues, though it languished at 70th position nationally last year.

A new sports complex has lifted it above its neighbours. Cricket, women's football have bossed the London indoor leagues for a few years, and

RESEARCH EXCELLENCE		
% of Royal Holloway's research that is 4* (World-class) or 3* (Internationally rated):		
	4*	3*
Biological Sciences	15%	55%
Environmental Sciences	20%	50%
Physics	10%	45%
Pure Mathematics	0%	25%
Computer Science	25%	40%
Geography Environment	20%	45%
Economics	20%	60%
Business/Management	15%	40%
Politics	5%	25%
Social Work	10%	35%
Psychology	15%	55%
French	15%	30%
German	20%	35%
Italian	5%	35%
Iberian	15%	30%
English	30%	35%
Classics	10%	25%
History	20%	40%
Performing Arts	35%	40%
Media Studies	20%	55%
Music	60%	30%

men's rugby supplies players to senior sides, such as Harlequins and London Welsh.

TOWN 'Sadly, the surrounding area, quaint little Egham, with as many useful shops as you are likely to see students at a nine o'clock lecture, fails to happen,' Sarah Toms reports, 'though it does have three supermarkets, a covey of takeaways, a bevy of student-friendly pubs, and The Staines Massive, which boasts not only a cinema, but wait for it... a nightclub! Those for whom the excitement proves too much, worry not. Royal Holloway is positioned a train ride away from the capital - deliberately, strategically even, to enable you to enjoy London life without paying a high price.

'Sure, the prices locally are higher than average, but not too damaging, and there is the advantage of the London loan rate and that both campus and surrounding area are fairly safe.

PILLOW TALK

'On the one hand, there is Founders Hall,' writes Sarah. 'Its rooms are fairly large and filled with an odd assortment of furniture from across the centuries. On the other, we have New Halls, built in the 1950s by an architect who won a prize for designing a Swedish prison! Affectionately known as 'Cell Block H', the rooms are, let us say, cosy...'

WHAT IT'S REALLY LIKE

UNIVERSITY:

Social Life	★★★
Campus scene	**Active, friendly, artistic, female**
Student Union services	**Good**
Politics	**Big right now**
Sport	**36 clubs**
National team position	**57th**
Sport facilities	**Good**
Arts opportunities	**Drama excellent; music, film good; dance, art avg**
Student magazine	**The Orbital**
Student radio	**1287 Insanity**
2008 National Awards	**Silver award**
Nightclub	**Union +Tommy's**
Bars	**Union, Tommy's, Stumble Inn, Holloway's, Dive**
Union ents	**Cheese, Spaced, Orgasmatron, etc**
Union societies	**99**
Most popular society	**James Bond Appreciation Soc**
Smoking policy	**No smoking**
Parking	**Adequate**

CITY:

London	★★★★★
Local scene	**Good pubs, but London beckons**
Town/gown relations	**Good**
Risk of violence	**Low**
Cost of living	**High**
Student concessions	**Average**
Survival + 2 nights out	**£40 pw**
Part-time work campus/town	**Good/poor**

ACCOMMODATION

Guarantee to freshers	**100%**
Style	**Halls**
Security guard	**All**
Shared rooms	**Some**
Internet access	**Most**
Self-catered	**Some**
En suite	**Some**
Approx price range pw	**£62.50-£125**
City rent pw	**£75-£150**

New-ish halls Athlone, Cameron and Williamson - are catered and come with common rooms, bar, snack bar (Times Square), and a good community spirit. Founder's comes with common rooms, TV rooms, bar/snack bar (Crossland Suite); it's hard to get a room here. Reid Hall, near New Halls, is catered with en-suite rooms. Runnymede is self-catered, flat-style around a central kitchen/social area, en-suite. The latest housing development (Tuke, Butler, & Williamson) opened in September 2007 - en-suite accommodation in self-catering flats.

Three halls - Beeches, Chestnuts, Elm Lodge - are converted Victorian houses, catered but with small kitchen/pantries and laundries. Kingswood is catered, off campus (but less than a mile away and with a free bus service to campus during the day) and has rooms and flatlets on a hillside overlooking the Thames at Runnymede with squash and tennis courts, TV/common room, tapas bar and dining room.

GETTING THERE

☞ By road: M25/J13, A30.
☞ By rail: London Waterloo, 35 mins; Reading, 40.

UNIVERSITY OF ST ANDREWS

The University of St Andrews
Old Union Building
St Andrews
Fife KY16 9AJ

TEL 01334 463324
FAX 01334 463330

EMAIL student.recruitment@st-andrews.ac.uk
WEB st-andrews.ac.uk

St Andrews Students' Association
St Mary's Place
St Andrews
Fife KY16 9UZ

TEL 01334 462700/1
FAX 01334 462740

EMAIL pres@st-andrews.ac.uk
WEB www.yourunion.net

VAG VIEW

*T*he University of St Andrews was founded in 1410, which makes it 41 years older than Glasgow and 173 years older than Edinburgh. It appeals almost as much to English students as to Scots as an alternative to Oxbridge. It is a small, very traditional university, set in the far north-east of Scotland, 13 miles south of Dundee and 45 miles north of Edinburgh.

Jargon is as prevalent here as in the great Imperial days of the public school system, whence many of its students come, but some of its practices earmarked as traditions are in fact only a few years old, so the tradition of being traditional is not about to change.

The sojourn here a few years ago of a future King of England as an undergraduate underlined that, as firmly as it may yet the statistic that more undergraduates of St Andrews get married to boy/girlfiends they meet there, than at any other university.

There's a spectacular chance to be happy here - in the recent Higher Education Funding Council's National Student Survey, 93% confessed they were blissfully so, and less than 2% of undergraduates fail to stay the course. However, some find it a bit of a jolt coming down after graduation - only 69% of them get real graduate jobs within six months of leaving, which is very low.

> **The most famous statistic about St Andrews is that more couples who meet here end up married than at any other university. Will it be the same for the Heir to the Throne?**

CAMPUS

St Andrews is a long way away from a lot of places, a small, ancient seaside town in north-east Scotland - beautiful, surrounded by open countryside and sea, and with one of the world's greatest golf courses on its doorstep.

FEES, BURSARIES

UK & EU Fees, 2009-10: Non-Scottish domiciled students fees in year 2009-10: £1,820 for all courses except Medicine, which they will be more. If you are a Scottish-domiciled first degree student you are eligible for your tuition fees to be covered by the Scottish Government. Subject-based scholar-

UNIVERSITY/STUDENT PROFILE	
University since	**1410**
Situation/style	**Campus**
Student population	**8965**
Total undergraduates	**6940**
Mature undergraduates	**9%**
International undergrads	**18%**
Male/female ratio	**44:56**
Equality of opportunity:	
state school intake	**59%**
social class 4-7 intake	**16%**
low-participation area intake	**3%**

ships are awarded on academic merit and made in the year of entry only. There are Purdie Chemistry Awards and Institute of Physics Bursaries, and Music and Sports Scholarships. See www.standrews.ac.uk/admissions/ug/Financialinformation/Scholarships/UKEUUniSupportedAwards/. Also, /UKEUExternalAwards/, and SportMusicAwards/.

STUDENT PROFILE

The student body is dominated by public school types, and for a Scottish university there is a surprisingly large percentage of English students. Most students are from the middle and upper classes. They fail hopelessly to make their quota for socio-economic classes 4-7, managing only a 16% take from them and a miniscule 2.5% from the so-called 'low-participation neighbourhoods'. Indeed, it would be a hopelessly one-dimensional scene if it did not have an unexpectedly high (18%) intake from countries beyond the EU.

It is a friendly community. 'You can almost

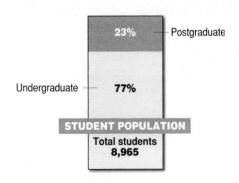

Postgraduate — 23%

Undergraduate — 77%

STUDENT POPULATION

Total students 8,965

TEACHING SURVEY AT A GLANCE

Avg. UCAS points accepted	**466**
Acceptance rate	**13%**
Overall satisfaction rate	**93%**
Helpful/interested staff	★★★★★
Small tuition groups	★★★★
Students into graduate jobs	**69%**

Teaching most popular with undergraduates:
Chemistry (100%), Ancient History & Arcgaeology (98%), History, Medicine, Politics (97%), Biology, Social Studies (96%), Maths, English (94%), Business Studies, Physics (95%), Economics, Human & Social Geography, Arabic (92%), Theology (91%), Sciences related to Biology, European Languages, Physics & Astronomy (90%).

Teaching least popular with undergraduates:
Physical Geography & Environmental Science (85%).

guarantee that every time you leave your front door, you'll see someone you know,' writes Melanie Hartley, though that has to be said to be true of most small universities. 'When you've just crawled out of bed for a 9am tutorial and you've only had four hours sleep, it's debatable whether that's a good thing or not! But St Andrews is a pretty close-knit society. Indeed, once people get here they don't tend to leave. They'll even tell you that one in three graduates end up marrying other St Andrews graduates!'

ACADEMIA & JOBS

When we look at graduate careers, we find an emphasis on analysis, management science and interpersonal skills, which St Andrew's clearly teaches well in whatever subject form.

But this is a small uni, with nearly a fifth of

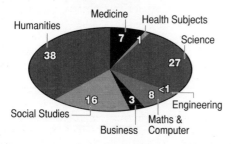

SUBJECT AREAS (%)

Humanities 38, Medicine 7, Health Subjects 1, Science 27, Engineering <1, Maths & Computer 8, Business 3, Social Studies 16

graduates on humanities degrees and another fifth on combined subject degrees, many of them involving languages and humanities, and one fears that job hunting, for some at least, might be a lottery.

The teaching is very good, the National Student Survey found terrifically helpful and interested lecturers and small tuition groups. It is, at the same time, highly regarded for research (14th nationally in the recent assessment), so they really shouldn't have time for students. But hey, what else is there to do?

However, can subjects like Mediaeval History, Hebrew, Biblical Studies, Classical Studies, Art History and the like find their graduates jobs, however well taught? After six months a tidy number of St Andrews graduates appear in the statistics as secretaries, sales assistants, clerks, bar staff and receptionists. But one has to be careful here, for the curriculum doesn't teach fast-fix vocational. This is a real university in the traditional sense. Like, for example, Queen Mary's in London University, a rich cultural resource, one that most of the brash new universities do not even attempt to emulate, nor could they. It is as if St Andrews is operating in a parallel dimension, one that transcends the Government's shorter-term policy-making. In that context, employment-after-six-months seems a less than appropriate yardstick.

Originally, the more vocational degrees were based in Dundee and became the curriculum of Dundee University, when the split came in the 1960s. Recently, the two have moved closer again with the launch of a joint degree in engineering - Microelectronics & Photonics (there had already been a parlay through their pairing of Art History with Dundee's excellent school of Art & Design). But there is evidence, too, that this very traditional university somehow gets behind the new-uni 'how-to' ethos into a kind of 'can-do', that in their hands the business of university is, as it was originally meant to be, a training of the mind per se, that far from being out-of-date, they are moving forward with insight. They show this not least in their inspired cross-faculty strategy.

Besides an increasing range of sciences with language degrees, there are some tantalising combinations such as Arabic-International Relations, Classics-Integrated Information Technology, Hebrew-Mathematics, and Economics-Social Anthropology. There is even the ultimate cross-faculty mesh - Integrated Information Technology and Theological Studies, which if not exactly offering a fast-track to the meaning of life, suggests a challenging examination of the traditional tensions between science and humanities.

End result is a sound training for whatever you

do, and a good record for jobs that do not require specific training at degree level - journalists and editors abound, for instance.

Elsewhere on the list, education and financial activities are to the fore. Instructors and secondary school teachers come from here in great number, the languages and humanities provision serving them well. For finance, it's the well-rated Economics, Financial Economics and Management degrees, some in combination with Russian (and including a year there), or with International Relations, European Languages, Mathematics, etc.

The medical degree asks AAB, including Chemistry and at least one

other of Biology, Mathematics or Physics at GCE A2 Advanced level. If either Biology or Mathematics is not offered at AS or A2 level, each must normally have been passed at GCSE grade B or better. Dual award

science is not acceptable in lieu of GCSE Biology. UKCAT will also be required. You will get a head start if you happen to attend Perth College, with which a new Pathway to Medicine initiative allows mature students from non-traditional backgrounds achieving an HNC in Applied Sciences to graduate to Medicine at the uni.

Clinical training for medical students takes place at Glasgow, Edinburgh, Aberdeen and Dundee universities. Work commenced in June 2008 on a new £45-million School of Medicine and the Sciences.

There's a good employment reputation for psychologists and care assistants, BSc Psychology providing the harder edge to what is offered in the MA joint hons system, where a good combo may be had with, say, Social Anthropology. Look also at physiology, Neuroscience, Medicinal Science, Medicinal Chemistry.

There is also a fair number of graduates getting jobs as software engineers, IT consultants, computer programmers, which shows that where they do go for a vocational dimension they can get it right. Computer Science comes with languages, Maths, Linguistics, Philosophy, Management, Physics, or Statistics. A new computer building opened in 2004.

Finally there's traditionally a close relationship with the army, and a big take-up in the civil service and defence.

A Learning and Teaching Support Unit (LTSU) works closely with the academic schools to co-ordinate and advise.

SOCIAL SCENE

STUDENTS' ASSOCIATION The student population makes up a large proportion of the town and the social life is created by students. Location denies

RESEARCH EXCELLENCE		
% of St Andrews' research that is 4* (World-class) or 3* (Internationally rated):		
	4*	3*
Laboratory Clinical	15%	25%
Biological Sciences	10%	40%
Chemistry	30%	40%
Physics	25%	40%
Pure Mathematics	5%	30%
Applied Mathematics	25%	45%
Statistics	10%	50%
Computer Science	15%	45%
Geography Environment	20%	40%
Economics	15%	40%
Business\Managements	10%	50%
Politics	10%	35%
Anthropology	25%	30%
Psychology	20%	45%
Russian	0%	20%
French	10%	50%
German	20%	40%
Italian	5%	25%
Iberian	10%	55%
English	35%	35%
Classics	15%	45%
Philosophy	40%	35%
Theology	20%	30%
History	20%	40%
History of Art	15%	60%
Performing Arts	50%	35%

them any big bands at the union.

Reports Melanie: 'There is no club as such; the union doubles up as a venue (**Venue 1** and **Venue 2**: 1,000 capacity), hosting events all through the week. Every Friday is the bop - a cheesy night [Red Not Bed], very reminiscent of your old school discos, but a particularly revered part of student life. Venue 2 hosts a range of different nights; Rock-soc, Bulletproof (alternative music) and Jazz-soc are regulars.' Saturday clubnights include *Squeeze* ('80s), Explosion (R&B), *Ebenezer* ('90s) or *Retro*.

'Pre-Sessional week - known as Freshers week everywhere else - is non-stop events, including some biggish acts: recent weeks have hosted Space, Toploader and Euphoria. There are lots of 2nd, 3rd and 4th years willing to make friends - (some a bit too willing!) - and to show you around. Some will become your academic parents, a tradition that involves a weekend of parties with them, some time in November, before you get dressed up - many wittily/ridiculously as bottles of wine, Care Bears or condoms - and are frogmarched to the Quad on the Monday morning for a huge shaving foam fight. So fondly do many look back on their

WHAT'S ITS REALLY LIKE

UNIVERSITY:

Social Life	★★★
Campus scene	**Conservative, traditional, uni by the sea**
Student Union services	**Good**
Politics	**Student issues; activity high**
Sport	**50 clubs**
National team position	**30th**
Sport facilities	**Excellent**
Arts opportunities	**Drama excellent; performing arts all very popular**
Student magazine	**The Vine**
Student newspaper	**The Saint**
Student radio	**Star FM**
Nightclub	**Venue 1**
Bars	**Main Bar, Venue 2**
Union ents	**Disco dance, retro, live acts massive & refined**
Union societies	**130**
Most popular society	**Breakaway (outdoor pursuits), Debating**
Parking	**Adequate**
TOWN:	
Entertainment	★★
Scene	**Pubs, coffee houses**
Town/gown relations	**Average**
Risk of violence	**Low**
Cost of living	**High**
Student concessions	**Average**
Survival + 2 nights out	**£100 pw**
Part-time work campus/town	**Poor**

Raisin experience that they try to recreate it every year. [It can in fact degenerate into a mass piss-up and/or an excuse to pull: "Remember not to be forced into anything ..." warns the SA's Alternative Prospectus.]

'Student life is very much centred around the pubs. There are reputed to be more pubs per square mile than in any other university town, which means you're never stuck for choice: **Broons** or **Bridges** if you want to hang with the yahs, **Ogstons** or **The Raisin** if you want large and loud, **Drouthy Neebors** or **The Cellar** if you're into Real Ale. Such is the pace of life that by the time you've been here a fortnight, you should have an encyclopaedic knowledge of what's available, and your weekly "happy hour'" schedule will be sorted!

'There are lots of ways in which this is a relatively cheap place to live, not least because it's small, though in fact taxis do a healthy business with flat fares anywhere in the town.

'For entertainment other than pubs, most students look to student societies. Everybody is a member of at least one, and most people more. Options range from academic to music to political. The International Politics society recently had Michael Douglas to talk on behalf of the United Nations. You might prefer the Tunnocks Caramel Wafer Appreciation society or Quaich (whisky appreciation). You could also get involved with The Saint (student newspaper), which often wins awards, or the new radio station: Star FM.'

The Union also has one of the oldest debating societies in the world, and drama is an active aspect of student life. Each year Mermaids, a sub-committee of the Students' Association, gives financial assistance to several productions, some of which go to the Edinburgh Festival.

Part-time work opportunities are poor, but, 'if you're looking for a bit of extra cash, the Dunhill Cup creates the possibility of a job washing up or directing traffic for the weekend,' Melanie reports. 'The attitude of most students is that term time isn't for working, but there are occasional jobs behind bars. Most of the shops, however, seem to favour 16-year-old Madras College kids over us students when it comes to weekend work.'

SPORT Golfers' paradise - the student team is one of the best in Britain. 'If this isn't your thing,' says Melanie, 'you still get to see the likes of Hugh Grant and Samuel L. Jackson strutting their stuff around town at the Dunhill Cup every October.'

In the national team championships they came 30th last year, which is very good for such a small uni. There's a sports centre with sports hall, gym, activities room, weight training room, squash courts, solarium. Extensive playing fields, jogging and trim tracks. Golf bursaries are funded by the Royal and Ancient Golf Club.

PILLOW TALK

Final phase of £35-million David Russell Apartments opened in September 2006. Environmentally-friendly (a grass and Sedum roof), award-winning en-suite single/twin rooms for 887 students in flats with shared living room/kitchen, grouped around man-made lake and central facilities.

'Most of the halls are in the centre of town, and are steeped in traditions,' writes Melanie. 'Most first years procure an undergraduate gown soon after arrival - a tasteful red fleece type-thing and a bit pricey. Although it varies from hall to hall, there will be occasions throughout the year when you can wear these - hall dinners, photographs,

ACCOMMODATION	
Guarantee to freshers	**100%**
Style	**Halls, flats**
Security guard	**Some**
Shared rooms	**Some**
Internet access	**All**
Self-catered	**Some halls, all flats**
En suite	**Some**
Approx price range pw	**£55.56-£168.29**
Town rent pw	**£50-£130**

Around half St Andrews students live in halls or other uni-owned accommodation Freshers are almost automatically given a place, but you must apply for it by May 31 in the year of entry. From then on there is no guarantee and the hunt for flats, particularly near the centre of town, can begin around the middle of January. Accommodation is quite expensive for such a small town - £80 per week - largely because students make up a high proportion of the population.

chapel. Most of the halls are catered, and the food is pretty reasonable, although you'd be well advised to avoid the universally acclaimed lemon "toilet duck" mousse. Self-catering accommodation can be found in Albany Park and in Fife Park, which provide some of the most economical student accommodation in the country. "Simplistic" isn't the word for these flats, but they're cheap."

GETTING THERE
☛ By road: Forth Road Bridge, M90/J3, A92 to Kirkcaldy, A915 to St Andrews; or M90/J8, A91.
☛ By rail: Nearest station on main line London (King's Cross) – Edinburgh – Aberdeen line is Leuchars (5 miles). Then bus or taxi.
☛ By air: Edinburgh Airport, airport bus to Edinburgh, thence by rail.

ST GEORGE'S, UNIVERSITY OF LONDON

St George's, University of London
Cranmer Terrace
Tooting
London SW17 0RE

TEL 020 8725 2333
FAX 020 8266 6282
EMAIL enquiries@sgul.ac.uk
WEB www.sgul.ac.uk

St George's, the University of London Medical School in Tooting, and Royal Holloway, another distinguished college of the federal University, announced in October last year that they intend to form a single institution within the University.

St George's entry requirements are four AS with three subjects continued through to A level: Chemistry and/or Biology at A level and two other subjects. Non-science subjects are encouraged. Grades between AAAb to BBCb - are considered in light of School Performance (see prospectus). UKCAT must also be taken. There's also a Foundation for mature students. Ten years ago, they were ahead of the game, wanting to bring clinical training in earlier, looking for problem solvers, allowing an Arts subject A level in.

Leisure-wise there's a Friday disco at the Med School Bar (650 capacity) and 42 clubs and societies, Rowing and Film being the most popular. Rootin' Tootin' itself has a colourful culture, plenty

COLLEGE PROFILE	
Founded	**1751**
Status	**Associate of London Uni**
Situation/style	**City site**
Student population	**3985**
Full-time undergraduates	**3460**
ACCOMMODATION:	
Availability to freshers	**100%**
Style	**Halls**
Cost pw (no food/food)	**£100**
City rent pw	**£100**

of curry houses, and - incomprehensibly to anyone not born of the London property boom - is now classed as a gentrified area.

The sports ground is in Cobham, Surrey - 9 winter pitches and 2 cricket squares, grass and hard tennis courts. They also keep an eight and a four in the London Uni boathouse and have facilities for sailing. Back at the hospital there's the Lowe Sports Centre, 6 squash courts, gym and areas for badminton, basketball, etc.

GETTING THERE
☛ Tooting Broadway Underground station (Northern Line), Tooting overland.

UNIVERSITY OF SALFORD

TheUniversity of Salford
The Crescent,
Salford,
Greater Manchester M5 4WT

TEL 0161 295 5000
FAX 0161 295 5999
EMAIL course-enquiries@salford.ac.uk
WEB www.salford.ac.uk

Salford Students' Union
University House
Salford,
Greater Manchester M5 4WT

TEL 0161 736 7811
FAX 0161 737 1633
EMAIL students-union@salford.ac.uk
WEB www.salfordstudents.com

VAG VIEW

Salford University is good for Built Environment, Science, Engineering, Computer and Business. Everyone knows that, but a closer look reveals a developing picture, in particular into the Arts, Languages and Media.

Salford itself is minutes from the centre of Manchester, and is famous for being the birthplace of L S Lowry. The Lowry Museum and Art Gallery is situated, together with the university at the renovated Salford Quays, the old docks where soon, on Pier 9 at the new Media City, the BBC will join them. The BBC is about to move five of its hitherto London-based departments into a building next door to the university, a move from which the Media department will benefit considerably.

There is a relatively low ask at Salford, around 250 points, and in some departments good teaching from interested lecturers. Eighty per cent of the students in the National Survey said they were satisfied with what goes on; 71% of them get real graduate jobs within six months of leaving; but the

ACADEMIC EXCELLENCE	
University since	**1967**
Situation/style	**Campus**
Student population	**19890**
Total undergraduates	**15505**
Mature undergraduates	**36%**
International undergrads	**6%**
Male/female ratio	**48:52**
Equality of opportunity:	
state school intake	**97%**
social class 4-7 intake	**40%**
low-participation area intake	**18%**

drop-out rate (12%) is high, far greater than its Government benchmark, even considering the number of students from families new to the whole idea of higher education.

CAMPUS

"The main campus, Peel Park, is 2 miles from Manchester City Centre,' reports Shauna Corr. 'There are 3 main campuses: Adelphi, Frederick Road and the main campus: which is known as Peel Park.'

'So what do you know about Salford? Well, have you ever seen the opening credits of Coronation Street? That's Salford,' informs Lindsay Oakes. 'It's where Corrie is set and filmed. You may also have heard that it's a rough area with a high car crime rate. Sadly, Salford is known more by its bad reputation than for any of its good points. Of course I'd be lying if I told you that there aren't any negative aspects to living here; it's like any suburban city area: if you're not sensible then it could be dangerous. But where better to spend three or four years of your student life than in the student capital of Britain - Manchester? Salford University actually lies closer to the centre of Manchester than Manchester University itself. It is only a fifteen-minute bus ride away, or five minutes in a taxi, the way they drive round here!

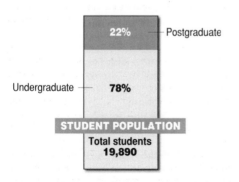

22% — Postgraduate

Undergraduate — 78%

STUDENT POPULATION
Total students
19,890

FEES, BURSARIES

UK & EU Fees, 2007: £3,225 p.a. Bursary for students in receipt of full HE Maintenance Grant is £320, as a proportion of the HEMG award. There are also the Vice-Chancellor's Scholarship and various subject, community and placement bursaries.

See www.salford.ac.uk/study/undergraduate/money_matters/bursaries/details/#gp. The total paid under these bursary and scholarship schemes will not exceed £1,000.

STUDENT PROFILE

This is an indelibly 'new university' student body. Around 40% are from the lowest socio-economic groups, 18% from so-called low-participation neighbourhoods. Many are mature students, and around 20% are part-timers.

'There are students from all walks of life here,' says Lindsay, 'and from practically every continent. There is a real international feel to Salford because of all the links we have with universities abroad [see Academia, below]. And it may be true of many universities, but there is a real community among Salford students,' in particular among freshers in the student village.

ACADEMIA & JOBS

The Government's 2008 Research Assessment Exercise found that 12% of Salford's research is world class (4 star) and 83% of international significance (3 star). Built Environment, Library & Information Management, and Media made the best showing.

Students say that these are not the best taught, however. Their vote goes to English, Biochemistry, Biomedical Science, Sociology, Aquatic Environments, Languages, Finance, Accounting, Music, Social Policy, Tourism, History, and Politics. Media Studies doesn't get a look in. Only 62% raised their hands in favour of the teaching. As this is now a

main commitment of the university, they'd better sort it out.

Salford is a pioneer of sandwich courses, work placement schemes, and their links with local firms are legendary. 'There are certainly strong links with industry,' says Shauna, 'and opportunity on many courses for industrial sandwich years, home and abroad.' The culture is fostered by Academic Enterprise their 'integrated third strand alongside teaching and research. Many students experience a work placement as part of their course and 50% of programmes offer the chance to work or study abroad. Our Business Enterprise Support Team (BEST) encourages staff and students to build upon their ideas for self-employment,' they say.

The School of Languages is especially impressive. Degrees such as Arabic/English Translation & Interpreting immediately catch the eye. There's also Chinese, Portuguese, Spanish, Italian, French, German... Not surprisingly translators and interpreters come in number from Salford. A new £1-million, campus-based Language Resource Centre offers advanced multimedia and language facilities. Many courses have an international dimension.

Meanwhile in the faculty's School of Media, which shone at the research assessments, there are degrees in Radio, TV (including Mobile & Internet TV), TV & Radio (theoretical elements married to practical modules, such as editing, producing, directing, a new Film degree, Journalism (with Broadcasting and other combinations, including War Studies), Professional Broadcasting, Professional Sound & Video Technology, Digital Broadcast Technology, Media Production and Media Technology (aimed at technical operators

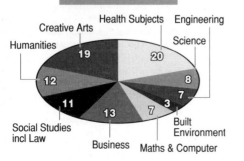

SUBJECT AREAS (%)

Health Subjects — 19
Engineering — 20
Science — 8
Built Environment — 7
Maths & Computer — 3
Business — 7
Social Studies incl Law — 13
Humanities — 11
Creative Arts — 12

RESEARCH EXCELLENCE

% of Salford's research that is
4* (World-class) or 3* (Internationally rated):

	4*	3*
Nursing/Midwifery	10%	30%
Health Professions	5%	30%
Statistics	0%	35%
Metallurgy and Materials	10%	40%
Built Environment	25%	40%
Geography, Environment	5%	25%
Business/Management	5%	25%
Info. Management	25%	20%
Law	0%	20%
Social Work	5%	45%
European Studies	5%	20%
English	10%	25%
Linguistics	5%	30%
Art and Design	5%	15%
Media Studies	15%	35%
Music	0%	25%

of high-tech facilities next to the BBC headquarters.

In the bedrock subjects, aspiring property developers still flock to Salford's world-class School of Construction & Property Management. In the research assessment last year Built Environment was something of a coup - 65% of the research was either 4* or 3*, which gave it lead position in the subject in at least one league table.

Salford's civil engineers also get jobs in number. One degree combines it with Architecture. Other sure-fire career hits are for aeronautical engineers. Salford places more graduates than most in the industry with its Aerospace courses. See also its Aviation Technology & Pilot Studies.

A group from the school of computing, science and engineering is involved with the British Quicksilver team attempt this year to break the land speed record of 317mph, being responsible for the aerodynamics of the craft to ensure it doesn't flip over, as it did in 1967, killing driver Donald Campbell at Coniston Water.

Note the Computer Science & Information Systems degree, a leading edge from the uni's suc-

and operational engineers), Audio Technology, Audio & Visual Systems, Design for Digital Media... Aspiring music producers should look at the BA Acoustics (Faculty of Science, Engineering & Environment), which prepares students for jobs with such as Philips (Holland) and Bang & Olufson (Denmark). There's a strong emphasis on practical work, industrial placement. Meanwhile, some find Popular Music & Recording the business.

Salford has recruited Smiths guitarist Johnny Marr as a visiting professor to teach students on the popular music courses. He joins other media and music visiting professors such as Shameless writer Paul Abbott, music journalist John Robb, and journalist Steve Hewlett.

Great student media - Shock FM and Channel M (TV) are the leisure-time expression of all this.

Salford was the first university to sign a partnership agreement with the BBC to develop degree courses. Last year marked the 10th anniversary of the university's partnership with Manchester's TV station, Channel M. The campus-based channel broadcasts to half a million people in the Manchester region with programmes developed and made at Salford's media facilities.

Students on media courses have the chance to work on making real programmes to be broadcast on terrestrial TV. Over 40% of the station's workforce is now made up of Salford graduates.

From 2011 the BBC will be moving five major departments, including Sport, Children's and Radio Five Live from London to MediaCity UK at Salford Quays, and the University will have a building full

WHAT IT'S REALLY LIKE

UNIVERSITY:

Social Life	★★★
Campus scene	**Friendly, boozy**
Student Union services	**Good**
Politics	**Interest low, but**
	SWSS & Anti-Nazi
	League
Sport	**19 clubs**
National team position	**98th**
Sport facilities	**Good**
Arts opportunities	**Excellent**
Student newspaper	**Student Direct**
Student radio	**Shock fm**
Student TV	**Channel M**
Nightclub	**The Pav**
Bars	**Lowry, Sub Club,**
	Wallness Tavern
Union ents	**Themed,**
	requests, tours
Union societies	**19**
Most popular societies	**Plastic Surgery**
Parking	**Adequate**
CITY:	
Entertainment	★★★★★
City scene	**Legendary**
Town/gown relations	**Average-poor**
Risk of violence	**High**
Cost of living	**Average**
Student concessions	**Good**
Survival + 2 nights out	**£90 pw**
Part-time work campus/town	**Average/excellent**

cess in the area of Library & Information Management at the research assessments. There's also Business Information Systems and Business Information Technology.

Serious employment strengths in the business sector include Finance, Marketing, Personnel, Human Resources, Economics, and Business Computing. There's also Gambling & Leisure Management, with study in North America, and Tourism Management. They are especially big in sales management. The Art Department, Product Design, Sports Equipment Design and Fashion also provide a subject focus for this.

They also score many a job in Government administration (local, regional and central) - degrees such as BSc Environmental Health helping graduates in. There's also Environmental Geography, Environmental Management, and Environmental Studies with Foundation Year.

Health care professionals are equally well served by courses in Radiography, Midwifery, Occupational Therapy, Physiotherapy, Podiatry, Prosthetics/Orthotics, Sport Rehab - all 22/24 points at assessment; they also offer a top-up degree in Acupuncture.

Among the uni's Biological Sciences, one of the most popular for its teaching is BSc Aquatic Sciences, which covers water resources, hydrology, glaciology, climate change, freshwater, estuarine and marine biology, and fisheries.

BBC TV is already involed with Salford's media courses. In 2011 five BBC departments are moving from London next door to the uni at Salford Quays.

Finally, a new Law School attracted almost 100 budding lawyers when it opened its doors in September last,- exceeding its target for the first academic year. A new £10-million building features a Law Society accredited library and mock-up court room.

SOCIAL SCENE

STUDENTS' UNION 'The union runs 4 bars (one being a nightclub-come-bar),' writes Shauna. 'The **Pav** (at Castle Irwell student village) has two main nights: Tuesday and Friday. Tuesday's *Flair*, '60s, '70s and '80's music, is a constant, and whatever they call Friday night when you get there, it won't be retro. The **Lowry** bar on Peel Park is situated in University House, it's a good day-bar. So far this year we have had a Ministry of Sound night, at which Youseff played, and we've had Jason Donovon, Timmy Mallet and Tymes four as well as student bands and DJs. We also have the Wallness Tavern, recently refurbished, open all day. The sub club, Frederick road, is a good day bar for stu-dents on site. All bars have games' machines and pool tables. Local pubs are a bit rough and not always safe for students.

'One thing I should point out,' writes Lindsay, 'is that unlike most unis, beer and food at Salford are not subsidised.'

Especially active among numerous sports clubs and societies is the LGB group - lesbian/gay. '*Student Direct* is our weekly publication,' Shauna continues, 'shared with both Bolton Uni and Manchester University.' The union rates most active societies as Plastic Surgery/Shock fm, both music societies: 'Plastic Surgery is the DJ soc, and Shock fm deals with the student radio station.'

Arts and media are part of the lives of the pre-dominantly scienctific student body. As the Arts provision has grown, so their interest in what is changing around them has galvanised the students, and extra-curricular Arts have become a reality. Recently, the **Robert Powell Theatre** was opened by namesake Salfordian actor, Robert Powell.

Salford Community Action Project (SCAP) is a student project involved with children in the locality, and senior citizens, the disabled, ex-offenders, and in giving English lessons to overseas students and others.

SPORT Writes Suzanne: 'The Union provides a swimming pool, climbing wall, weights room, badminton, tennis and squash courts, five-a-side football pitches, sun beds, sauna and Jacuzzi. There is a large sports hall with just about every indoor pitch marked down, facilities for trampoline, and sports pitches at Castle Irwell for rugby, football, hockey and cricket.' The annual Two Cities Boat race between Salford and Manchester University at Salford Quays is the North's answer to Oxford and Cambridge. There's a partnership with Salford City Reds Rugby League Club and Lancashire County Cricket Club whereby students on sports science and physiotherapy courses gain experience of treating professional athletes. The Salford Reds have also been coaching the University rugby teams and train on the uni's playing fields.

TOWN Cost-wise, as Suzanne Ashton points out, 'Salford has all the advantages of a town - cheap rent, everything close by, a friendly atmosphere - and yet still with the facilities of a city nearby.' See Manchester City article. 'There's part-time work in union bars, in ents, in the library and in Manchester,' notes Shauna, 'and a Job shop to help you find reliable and safe, part-time or holiday work. There are loads of part-time jobs to be had.

PILLOW TALK

They guarantee a place in one of the 4,000 study bedrooms to all freshers who have an unconditional offer and whose accommodation application form has been received by 12 noon on the September 1 in the year of admission.

The 3 main campuses (Peel Park, Frederick Road, Adelphi) are within walking distance of the residences. 'There is a good selection of accommodation ranging from Castle Irwell Student Village to blocks of flats and on-campus catered accommodation,' Shauna reports. 'Castle Irwell has 1,612 rooms and is 25 minutes walk from Peel Park campus. It boasts numerous playing fields, an Asrtoturf pitch, and The Pav. There is also a laundrette, taxi rank and a house with disabled access.'

Writes Lindsay: 'In the summer, the entire village turns out on to the playing fields to play sports, sunbathe or even have barbecues. In the winter, you'll find yourself having a snowball fight with someone you've never met before.'

Note that this year a company called Campus Living Villages is managing four accommodation blocks formerly owned by the uni. The deal includes a commitment to invest £2.6m in the refurbishment of two accommodation blocks over the next two years.

ACCOMMODATION	
Guarantee to freshers	**100%**
Style	**Halls, flats**
Security guard	**All**
Shared rooms	**Family rooms**
Internet access	**All**
Self-catered	**All**
En suite	**Some**
Approx price range pw	**£56-£78.54**
City rent pw	**£39-£75**

GETTING THERE

☛ By road: M62 (which connects with the M6, M63)/M602. Coach services good.

☛ By rail: Salford Crescent station is on-campus; Manchester Oxford Road is a few minutes away; Liverpool, 1:20; Sheffield, 1:30; Birmingham New Street, 2:30; London Euston, 3:30.

☛ By air: Manchester Airport,.

☛ By coach: London, 4:35; Bristol, 5:00.

SCHOOL OF ORIENTAL & AFRICAN STUDIES, LONDON UNIVERSITY

School of Oriental & African Studies
Thornhaugh Street
Russell Square
London WC1H 0XG

TEL 020 7898 4034
FAX 020 7898 4039
STUDENT UNION TEL 020 7898 4997
EMAIL study@soas.ac.uk
WEB www.soas.ac.uk

TEACHING SURVEY AT A GLANCE	
Avg. UCAS points accepted	**360**
Acceptance rate	**17%**
Overall satisfaction rate	**85%**
Helpful/interested staff	**No data**
Small tuition groups	**No data**
Students into graduate jobs	**74%**

Teaching most popular with undergraduates:
History (94%), Anthropology (93%), Economics (90%), Asian Studies (83%), Law (82%).

Teaching least popular with undergraduates:
Languages (76%), African & Modern Middle Eastern Studies (72%).

Part of the University of London, this exceptional school is situated in Bloomsbury and has a close working relationship with branches of the Civil Service, especially the Foreign Office, ahem! SOAS actually teach their staff.

Connections with the British and overseas governments, industry and commerce, facilitate, among other things, the college's study-abroad programmes.

There are more then 300 degree combinations available in the social sciences, humanities and arts, languages & Cultures. More than 24% of the programmes include a year abroad.

Whatever it teaches it teaches with reference to what goes on in Asia, Africa and the Middle East. Of necessity, it is strong on languages, from

Chinese and Japanese to a whole lot you may not have heard of, like Colloquial Cambodian, for example.

The SOAS bar, capacity 200, is 'home' to thousands of itinerant students and graduates of this eccentric, top-notch school. But now it is about to embark on the development of a major new building at the back of the terraces it owns on Russell Square. This will provide increased teaching and seminar space, new performance space, and increased social and workshop space. Let's hope it doesn't shake the character out of the place at the same time. Accommodation is available as single, en-suite study-bedrooms in cluster flats 15 minutes' walk away on the Pentonville Road. There are two squash courts on site and a sports ground at Greenford. London Uni Students' Union sport and fitness facilities are nearby.

ACCOMMODATION	
Guarantee to freshers	**Majority**
Style	**Halls, flats**
Security guard	**All**
Shared rooms	**None**
Internet access	**Most halls, all flats**
Self-catered	**No halls, all flats**
En suite	**Most halls, all flats**
Approx price range pw	**£120.89-£245**
City rent pw	**£100-£180**

GETTING THERE

☞ Underground: Russell Square (Piccadilly line).

SCHOOL OF PHARMACY, LONDON UNIVERSITY

School of Pharmacy
29-39 Brunswick Square
London WC1N 1AX

TEL 020 7753 5831
FAX 020 7753 5829
EMAIL registry @ulsop.ac.uk
WEB www.ulsop.ac.uk

The School of Pharmacy is another specialist school of the University of London. In 2008 the Government's research assessments confirmed its national and international reputation, with 25% of its research rated world-class and 40% of international significance. In the same year, in the Higher Education Funding Council's National Student Survey, 88% of its students said they were satisfied and 100% of them got jobs within six months of graduating. The mystery is that the school registered the worst drop in applications of any higher education institution in 2008: 28.1% fewer applicants chose it than in the previous year.

Situated within walking distance of the British Museum, the school has a small amount of its own accommodation, otherwise it's London University's intercollegiate halls. For sport, the school shares grounds out at Enfield with the Royal Free Hospital Medical School (now part of University College, London); closer to home are facilities for squash, badminton, swimming, etc., and the London University Union is close at hand. There is a union bar, a theme night on Friday, and facilities for table tennis, pool, etc..

GETTING THERE

☞ By tube: Russell Square (Piccadilly line); overland stations (King's Cross, St Pancras and Euston) are all within a short walk.

STUDENT SHEFFIELD – THE CITY

Steely Sheffield is a born-again cosmopolitan city offering pretty much anything you desire. For some it may never rival Leeds, Manchester or Nottingham, but come here and you will soon discover that it has its own inimitable charm. People are friendly to all, even if you are a student! And many students choose to stay after graduation, which proves that it is a place to live and work in, not just somewhere to pass through.

CLUBS

Sheffield placed itself in the vanguard of the club revolution with several big names – **Gatecrasher**: '**Gatecrasher One** has taken over *Skool Disco* duties, providing salivating perverts a new location to drool over girls in pigtails and pleated skirts,' writes Itchy, 'while *Blessed @* **Republic** on a monday night is absolute quality, if you like r&b and hip hop.' With major acts and DJ's plying their trade, there are no end of nights to check out and something to suit everyone's taste. Sheffield Hallam's **NMB** also provides, and sells out its *Stardust* and *Sheff 1* clubnights on a weekly basis.

The alternative scene is not to be missed though, with Sheffield University's Student Union offering a great live venue in the **Octagon** (yes, it has 8 sides) for touring bands. They are even kind enough to put on indie clubnights to fill the gaps between gigs. Look in particular for the *Fuzz Club* on a Thursday night.

Other venues include the popular indie haunt **Leadmill** (voted best venue outside of London a while back) and **City Hall** for the more 'cultured' acts. While Hallam's **Arena** and the **Don Valley Stadium** provide the capacity required by the really big bands, like recent Paul McCartney and Eric Clapton.

GALLERIES AND THEATRES

The Crucible and **Lyceum** are Sheffield's 2 major playhouse venues, they have shows running all year round, ranging from pantomime, to ballet to Shakespeare. Both offer discounts for students, who also have their own productions at the **Drama Studio** on Glossop Road.

Among major arthouses, the star attraction is the **Millennium Galleries**. **Graves Art Gallery** has smaller, but still great, exhibitions, a recent highlight the William Blake show from the Tate in London.

SCREENS

Film buffs love the **Showroom** on Paternoster Row, an arty cinema with bar attached; it even does a 'film and meal deal'. Cheap and cheerful in-town cinema is the 10-screen **Odeon**, while out at **Meadowhall** there's a 15-screen multiplex, where a film can be incorporated into a day out shopping. The **UGC, also** outside the city centre, boasts a huge 'Full Monty' screen, perfect for watching the latest blockbuster.

SPORT

Sheffield is home to 2 football teams – Sheffield Wednesday, who play at **Hillsborough**, and Sheffield United at **Bramall Lane**. Whatever you do, don't confuse the two. We also have ice hockey team and basketball teams. The Sheffield Steelers glide across the ice at **The Arena,** and the Westfield Sharks shoot the hoop there on non-ice days. Look, too, for the world-class swimming pool at **Ponds Forge**. And, of course, the **Crucible** is transformed once a year into a sporting venue, when it hosts the Embassy World Snooker Championship. Alternatively, many like a flutter at **Owlerton Greyhound Stadium** on Penistone Road.

STUDENT GHETTOES

As with most cities, students have monopolised a couple of areas. Broomhill, a paradise of pubs, take-aways, a supermarket and the ever popular **Record Collector** – whatever your taste in music, they'll stock it. Convenient for the Sheffield Uni campus – 10 minutes away on foot – it's reasonably cheap and pretty safe. Hallam students, meanwhile, tend to congregate around the Ecclesall Road area, or roads just off the city centre, being just a stone's throw away form their 3 campuses. Again, these areas have everything a student needs – supermarket, pubs and the odd bookshop or two.

There are endless pubs and bars, in particular in the student areas of Broomhill, Crooks and Ecclesall Road. Division Street also has a good dozen, while outside the city centre there are loads of vast watering holes.

CONSUMERISM

The debt-riddled student gets a lifeline from Broomhill's array of charity shops, also from **Castle Market** – brilliant for cheap veg, fish and meat. Those past caring visit Division Street, where all the latest trendy and alternative gear purveyed in chic boutiques and the **Forum Shopping Centre**. Chapel Walk is full of small shops with large price tags, and although Ecclesall Road is a student area, it, too, has shops generally far too expensive for a student's pocket.

Then there is the experience of **Meadowhall** (Meadow 'hell' on a Saturday) – shop after shop selling its wares, all under one roof, again sometimes at high prices.

Ellen Grundy

UNIVERSITY OF SHEFFIELD

The University of Sheffield
Western Bank
Sheffield S10 2TN

TEL 0114 222 1255
FAX 0114 222 1234
EMAIL www.sheffield.ac.uk/asksheffield
WEB www.sheffield.ac.uk ·

Sheffield University Students Union
Western Bank
Sheffield S10 2TG

TEL 0114 222 2000
FAX 0114 275 2506
EMAIL [firstname.surname]@sheffield.ac.uk
WEB www.sheffieldunion.com

VAG VIEW

Sheffield is a top university across the board. Whichever one of our statistical boxes you care to consult, it excels. And, as Student Profile shows (below) this is an exceptionally well balanced university.

Rose Wild writes: 'In today's cut-throat world, where new students have to pay just to enter this carnival of hedonistic abandon, and thereafter graduate to a future in which security is not guaranteed, it is probably worth choosing a university which gives you best value for your dosh and which has a reputation that will outshine the competition. That university is Sheffield.'

A resounding 89% of Sheffield student voices agreed with Rose in the National Student Survey, and 82% will have real graduate jobs within six months of leaving. It is also one of the top few universities in the country for extra-curricular opportunity and was voted Student Union of the Year in the 2008 National (NUS/Endsleigh) Student Awards. It is also a very happy place, which is why only 2.5% fail to finish the course.

CAMPUS

The city of Sheffield is roughly in the centre of England. The uni and student ghettoes are all on one side of it and there's a friendly community-feel, although Sheffield is most definitely not a campus university.

One word describes Sheffield, and that's 'hilly'. Most students walk everywhere, but public transport is reliable and cheap, and there's also Supertram, which runs from the centre to numerous places, including Meadowhall, the famous, out-of-town shopping centre. Having your own transport enables you to enjoy weekends, though. When you come here you'll be on the edge of the Peak District, one of the last great, beautiful wilderness areas of England.

UNIVERSITY/STUDENT PROFILE	
University since	**1905**
Situation/style	**Civic**
Student population	**25700**
Total undergraduates	**18480**
Mature undergraduates	**16%**
International undergrads	**18%**
Male/female ratio	**50:50**
Equality of opportunity:	
state school intake	**85%**
social class 4-7 intake	**21%**
low-participation area intake	**8%**

FEES, BURSARIES

UK & EU Fees, 2009-10: £3,225. There are Income Bursaries of between £430 and £700 for all UK tuition-fee paying undergraduates and PGCE students from households with incomes less than £35,515. There are also sporting and academic scholarships available, and other supportive bursaries. See www.sheffield.ac.uk/bursaries/.

STUDENT PROFILE

There are plenty of bright undergraduates, most of them capable of 400 points at A level. There's a good balance of public and state school types, far healthier than the Bristol-Durham-Edinburgh axis, and a fair number, too, of the old unskilled social groups (21%). As for mature students and groups

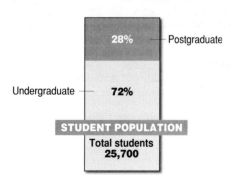

Postgraduate 28%

Undergraduate 72%

STUDENT POPULATION
Total students
25,700

TEACHING SURVEY AT A GLANCE

Avg. UCAS points accepted	**400**
Acceptance rate	**14%**
Overall satisfaction rate	**89%**
Helpful/interested staff	**★★★★**
Small tuition groups	**★★★★**
Students into graduate jobs	**82%**

Teaching most popular with undergraduates:
Civil Engineering (100%), Dentistry (98%),
Sciences related to Biology, Iberian Studies,
Philosophy (96%), Archaeology, Journalism,
Biology, Chemistry, Communications & Information
Studies, Economics, German & Scandinavian
Studies, History, Archaeology & History,
Astrophysics (95%), Civil, Chemical Eng.,
European Languages, Production &
Manufacturing Eng., Physics, Politics (94%),
Aerospace Engineering, Engineering &
Technology, English, Maths, Mechanically-based
Eng., Physical Geography & Enviro, Science
(93%), Linguistics (92%), French, Music (91%),
Aural & Oral Sciences, Business Studies,
Electronic & Electrical Eng., Social Studies (90%).

Teaching least popular with undergraduates:
Medicine (79%).

£23-million Sheffield campus learning resource opened its doors. It has over 500 PCs, wireless networking and IT equipped classrooms; well-equipped spaces for teaching, learning and study, 100,000 of the most in-demand books, and a 70-seat café.

Almost a fifth of graduates go into health. There's a £3.1-million Health Centre and £26 million was recently spent on the refurbishment of teaching and research facilities in the Medical School.

In the 5/6-year MB ChB there's an emphasis on self-learning and computer-aided learning packages. Wide clinical experience offered. The 6-year course includes a pre-med year for students with non-scientific backgrounds. Preferred subjects at AS level are Chemistry, Biology,

Mathematics or Physics, plus a fourth AS in any subject. At A level, you'll need Chemistry plus another science and any other subject which was also completed at AS, but excluding General Studies. Grades required are AAB.

A new £5.5 million extension has been built to the School of Clinical Dentistry, which offers the BDS/Dent for AAB, a course that achieved 98% student approval at the Higher Education Funding Council's National Student Survey.

Another noticeable career strength within the sector is BSc Psychology, fully accredited and first step to becoming a Chartered Psychologist. And speech therapists also thrive on the BMedSci Speech Science.

Accountancy is very big at Sheffield. Tax consultants also thrive, and aspiring actuaries get happy with their Maths degrees especially BSc Financial Mathematics.

Sheffield claim to attract more undergraduates in their School of Architecture than any other. There are a number of courses besides the single BA hons Architectural Studies, and various landscape and urban environment degrees, and MEng Structural Engineering & Architecture.

A new £25 million multidisciplinary science and engineering campus has recently been completed.

Engineering design consultants find their way from all over the Engineering faculty, but in particular there's Architectural Engineering Design, and such B/MEng Medical Systems Engineering, Computer Systems Engineering, Systems & Control Engineering. There's also Biomedical Engineering, which gets into design for prosthetics.

The Faculty of Engineering, which took full marks at teaching inspection and triumphed in the recent research assessment (especially Civil

from overseas, Sheffield is again far more open-minded than, say Durham, taking in 16% and 8% of mature and international students, as against Durham's 6% and 5% respectively. So, students come from a variety of backgrounds and together they are happy enough to achieve a 2.5% drop-out rate, which lower than Bristol's. Writes Rose: 'One of the most striking and pleasing things about the cosy little cocoon of life, which makes this university a very pleasant place to be, is that you will rarely - if ever - come across prejudice of any sort. The union's absolute tolerance of the sizeable gay community is but one reflection of this. Another striking feature is the high visibility of the university's religious community.'

ACADEMIA & JOBS

The research is good, they came 14th nationwide in the Government's recent research assessment. The teaching is also good, with the Times Higher Education's Student Experience Survey finding lecturers with an eye to students interests and decent sized tuition groups. Masses of subjects attracted 90% plus of the student vote for good teaching in the funding council's nationwide survey. Only Medicine fared relatively poorly.

In April 2007, Information Commons, the

Engineering, which also had 100% of the student

4* (World-class) or **3*** (Internationally rated):

	4*	3*
Cardiovascular Medicine	0%	25%
Cancer Studies	5%	55%
Infection/Immunology	5%	40%
Hospital Clinical	5%	55%
Health Services ScHARR	20%	35%
Medical Education	0%	10%
Clinical Psychology	10%	30%
Dentistry	15%	55%
Nursing/Midwifery	15%	35%
Health Professions	20%	30%
Biological Sciences	20%	50%
Environmental Sciences	15%	50%
Chemistry	15%	55%
Physics	20%	40%
Pure Mathematics	15%	40%
Applied Mathematics	10%	35%
Statistics	10%	50%
Computer Science	15%	50%
Systems Engineering	25%	40%
Electronic/Electrical Eng.	15%	45%
Chemical Engineering	15%	40%
Civil Engineering	20%	65%
Mechanical, Aero. & Manufacturing Eng.	30%	45%
Metallurgy and Materials	15%	50%
Architecture	35%	35%
Architecture/Landscape	20%	55%
Town/Country Planning	35%	30%
Geography Environment	20%	50%
Archaeology	25%	35%
Economics	15%	55%
Business\Management	15%	45%
Information Management	30%	35%
Law	15%	35%
Politics	45%	30%
Social Work	20%	45%
Psychology	15%	45%
Education	15%	25%
Asian Studies	5%	25%
Russian	25%	45%
French	25%	25%
German	10%	20%
Iberian	25%	30%
English	30%	25%
Linguistics	20%	40%
Philosophy	35%	35%
Theology	20%	45%
History	35%	30%
Media Studies	5%	50%
Music	45%	35%

vote for its teaching, which is exceptional), has established the Advanced Research Manufacturing Centre with Boeing and opened its third Rolls-Royce Technology centre in Advanced Electrical Machines and Drives. They are also collaborating with British Aerospace.

The Sports Engineering degree (introduced in 2004 and not to be confused with the Motorsports Eng.)is designed for those who want to gain mechanical engineering skills and apply them in a sports environment.

Sheffield's Faculty of Pure Science offers a whole range of 3/4-years BSc and Masters degrees, Chemistry, for example, coupling with Chemical Engineering, Maths, study in Europe or Australia or Japan or the US or in industry.

Computer Science (with Foundation year if you want it) has various language possibilities and Physics might come with Medical Physics, Maths, Study in Europe, or there's a 4-year MPhys in Theoretical Physics. There's also a BSc Science Foundation (4/5 years).

The Faculty of Social Sciences mixes social and political studies and reaches into China, Korea and Japan, and this is also where you'll find a raft of Economics degrees and Accountancy & Finance. Researchers for media & government come out of here, and out of language degrees. Aspiring translator/interpreters note the 4-year BA Modern Languages with Interpreting. A new Confucius Institute offers a valuable resource for Chinese-related studies, in partnership with Beijing Language and Culture University (BLCU) and Nanjing University.

Languages and Sciences produce editors, too, and look out for BA Journalism Studies (backed by superb student media). Sheffield is also a popular recruitment source for British publishing.

Instructors by the dozen come out of Sheffield and would-be adult education lecturers find a certain route via languages, where Russian is a particular strength.

SOCIAL SCENE

Fulcrum of the ents scene is **Bar One**, which recently had a £500,000 makeover. It serves over 30 varieties of beer and takes more in a night than most pubs do in a week. Bar One gives way to the **Raynor Lounge** - a venue for gigs and small club nights. Every Sunday it hosts *The Last Laugh Comedy Club*, and through the week is booked by students for parties and club nights.

Interval (600 capacity) is the continental style café bar - pasta, baguettes, pastries and cabaret acts. **Fusion** (600 capacity) is the intimate venue for live bands and clubnights. Then

WHAT IT'S REALLY LIKE	
UNIVERSITY:	
Social Life	★★★★★
Campus scene	**Diverse, lively, sporty, safe**
Student Union services	**Award-winning**
Politics	**High level**
Sport	**Key, 48 clubs**
National team position	**23rd**
Sport facilities	**Good**
Arts opportunities	**Film excellent, drama, dance music, art good**
2008 National Awards	**NSDF award**
Student magazine	**Stainless**
Student newspaper	**The Steel Press**
Student radio	**SURE FM**
Nightclub	**Fusion & Foundry, Octagon**
Bars	**Bar One, Interval + SU pubs in town**
Union ents	**Eclectic**
, Union clubs/societies	**188**
Parking	**Poor**
CITY:	
Entertainment	★★★★★
Scene	**Seriously good**
Town/gown relations	**Good**
Risk of violence	**Low**
Cost of living	**Low-average**
Student concessions	**Good**
Survival + 2 nights out pw	**£80**
Part-time work campus/town	**Good**

there's **The Foundry** (1,000), which, with Fusion, is host to an amazing series of club-nights. *Tuesday Club* is drum 'n' bass/hip hop, Wednesday's *Juice*, with top line DJs, Thursday's *Fuzz Club* (indie/metal in two rooms). Then there's Frouk's traditional roof-raising eclectic mix on Friday, and *Pop Tarts*, Saturday, the ultimate '60s/'70s retro party - which now employs two dance floors. The monthly *Climax* is LGB night, now a widely known favourite on the gay scene. Other mega nights are *Cuba Libre* (monthly), *Urban Gorilla* (one per term), and *End Of Year Carnival* (annually). **The Octagon Centre** is the major, national-circuit venue (1,600 capacity), feted as Club Mirror's 'Venue of the Year'. Gigs at the uni have included: Arctic Monkeys, Little Man Tate, the View, Automatic, Amy Winehouse, Ash, Brakes, Bat For Lashes, Rakes, Bloc Party, Milburn, Dirty Pretty Things, Charlatans, DJ Shadow, Beverley Knight, Paul Weller, Long Blondes, We Are Scientists, Orson, Russell Brand, Kooks, Maximo Park.

There's also Coffee Revolution, the Union's own eco-friendly 'Fair Trade' coffee shop.

Not all is ents, however. At the top of the Union building, you'll find the **Gallery**. Heart of sports clubs and societies, it consists of meeting rooms and work areas with telephones and computing facilities that members can use to contact each other, meet and organise events. One floor down is Source, information bank on the Union's 200 societies and sports clubs, and events across Sheffield. Currently the most popular societies are: Street & Breakdance, People & Planet, and Gospel Choir.

Here, you'll also find a multimedia computer suite, with digital cameras and camcorders available for hire. A recent initiative is the *Give It A Go* programme. The idea is to encourage you to dip in to a whole host of activities - suck it and see before making a long-term commitment to one society or another. In 2005/06 around 12,000 tickets were sold for *Give it a Go* activities.

Behind Source is Sheffield Volunteering, gateway to community projects in and around Sheffield. They won the Outstanding Project Award in the 2006 Volunteering Awards and again in 2008, and with students raising around £100,000 each year for charity, they also copped the Royal Mail Community Impact Award.

Societies cover almost everything, as Rose discovered: 'Whether you're one of the rare few who actually come here to learn, or you're one of the many who come to play rugby, edit a newspaper, watch bands, worship God, fight injustice, walk up big hills, practise politics, become an actor or do any number of diverse and often bizarre activities, you can not only do them here, but you can meet a load of people who'll do them with you.'

Sheffield is politically very active, with strong representation from across the political spectrum. Union Elections receive the highest turnout of any Union in the country and are hotly contested attracting a large number of high quality candidates for the eight positions. Below this there are a number of Committees and a strong Union Council, and numerous student political interest groups from the classic Socialist Students, through People and Planet to Conservative Future.

The Radio Society, Sure fm, started as an individual's idea and they're now broadcasting around the union from their own studio. Sheffield Base looks after the Website and the student newspaper, *Steel Press*, has won Newspaper of the Year at the *Guardian* Awards more times than one cares to remember (though not this year, it went to Imperial College).

The Union is one of only a few to boast its own 400-seat cinema, run by students, who picked up a Distinction at the 2006 British Federation of Film Societies Awards.

The Theatre Company uses the Drama Studio for productions ranging from Shakespearean tragedy to student-written plays and musicals. In 2008, at the National Student Drama Festival, they won the award for Promoting Student Theatre. A 400-seat auditorium, extension to the union, is used by the Film Unit as a cinema four times a week, showing films prior to release on video.

SPORT The Goodwin Sports Centre, which has a first-class (but cold) swimming pool, gym and numerous Astroturf pitches, has had major improvements to its facilities recently at a cost of £14 million. There are some 40 sports clubs with the policy 'sport for all', covering traditional sports like rugby, hockey and cricket and newer sports like frisbee, step and skiing. You can be as involved as you like, many aerobics classes work a 'pay as you go' system for example.

TOWN See Student Sheffield.

PILLOW TALK

Brand new accommodation at the Endcliffe Village opened in 2008. Located in leafy suburbs in the west of the city, 15 minutes walk to campus, the apartments have all mod cons. Students can choose catered or self-catering. The focal point is the Edge, a modern building at the heart of the village with a dining room, bar, café, support facilities, 24-hour IT

ACCOMMODATION	
Guarantee to freshers	**100%**
Style	**Halls, flats**
Security guard	**Most halls, some flats**
Shared rooms	**Some flats**
Internet access	**Most halls, some flats**
Self-catered	**All flats, some halls**
En suite	**Some**
Approx price range pw	**£70-£130**
City rent pw	**£43-£88**

space, WiFi, plasma screens, and launderette.

This has been built on the old site of its student residences (many of which were 40 years old), at a cost of £160 million. The first phase opened in September 2006, and the project - 38 new blocks of residences for up to 4,200 students - is now complete. The aim is to create thriving communities.

Construction of 'Ranmoor Village' is now underway. Once this is completed, this and Endcliffe Village will be home to over 4,000 students.

GETTING THERE

☛ By road: M1/J33, A630, A57.
☛ By rail: London, 2:30; Liverpool Lime Street, 1:45; Manchester Piccadilly, 1:00; Nottingham 1:00; Leeds, 30 mins.
☛ By air: Manchester Airport.
☛ By coach: London, 3:45; Newcastle, 4:45;.

SHEFFIELD HALLAM UNIVERSITY

Sheffield Hallam University
City Campus
Sheffield S1 1WB

TEL 0114 225 5555
FAX: 0114 225 4449
EMAIL: enquiries@shu.ac.uk
WEB www.shu.ac.uk

Sheffield Hallam Union of Students
The HUBS
Paternoster Row
Sheffield, S1 2QQ

TEL 0114 225 4124
FAX 0114 225 4140
EMAIL [initial.name]@shu.ac.uk
WEB www.hallamunion.com

VAG VIEW

*H*allam is big business. With almost 30,000 students, they turn over some £150 million a year. Its work-orientated courses suggest that it is bent on stoking the nation's economy. The courses are indeed worked out with the industries that will employ their graduates, but that is not all. Hallam, while coming out among the top 1992 universities in the recent Government Research Assessment, were also voted by their own students into a position above both Manchester and Imperial College in the Times Higher Education magazine's Student Experience Survey. One of the things that came out of that was that their lecturers show a real interest in the development of their students. This is a different Hallam to the one a Hallam student described for us 12 years ago: 'Your degree will find you a job, but you will need to be self-motivated. If you're after close-knit tutorials with tutors that take a thorough interest in you, you'd be better off at Sheffield University.'

Overall, 91% of Hallam students are satisfied with the deal on offer here, which extends to a mighty fine social life too. And hey, they beat Sheffield University for sport last year, taking 20th place nationally! Drop-out rate is 6.8%, well below its Government benchmark.

UNIVERSITY/STUDENT PROFILE	
University since	**1992**
Situation/style	**City campus**
Student population	**29700**
Total undergraduates	**21915**
Mature undergraduates	**23%**
International undergrads	**4%**
Male/female ratio	**48:52**
Equality of opportunity:	
state school intake	**96%**
social class 4-7 intake	**33%**
low-participation area intake	**16%**

CAMPUSES

SHU is based around 2 sites, City and Collegiate Crescent. Psalter Lane, with it's school-like corridors and grim exterior, has closed.

'Collegiate campus is really quite good,' writes Chris Gissing. 'It's a traditional, leafy campus, ideally placed on the revelation that is Ecclesall Road. Sheffield's Eccy Road is the hub of student ents, with about 830 bars and 6,000 coffee houses (well, maybe not as many as that, but after the first 5 pubs, who cares?).

'City Campus is excellent too, centrally located and based around 4 or 5 disparate buildings, connected by the stunningly designed Atrium. This glass/steel construction has masses of open space, and is like a cosmopolitan street café with tables and chairs and...well...a café. The Adsetts Centre is based here and offers 24-hour access to computers, Internet, books, photocopying etc. Fortunately, the library staff who seemed to fine me on a weekly basis don't work twenty-four hours.'

FEES, BURSARIES

UK & EU Fees, 2009-10: £3,225 p.a. There are bursaries for students in receipt of the HE Maintenance Grant. See www.shu.ac.uk/guides/studentfinance/getmoney.html. There is also a limited number of scholarships for first years based on academic achievement.

STUDENT PROFILE

'We have the whole range,' Chris continues, 'from working-class-kid-scraped-through-on-a-BTEC/through-

Clearing sort, to Mummy-and-Daddy-paid-for-my-flat-and-course-fees-darling sort. They're all here in this city - 12% of the city's population are students. Sheffield Hallam has more working-class students than Sheffield University does.'

Few come here from public school. They take 33% of their students from the lower socio-economic groups, 16% from the 'low-participation' neighbourhoods. More than 20% are part-timers and 23% are mature. Quite different to the student body at Sheffield University, but as Chris says, 'We all seem to get along fairly well, and we are of course allowed to use each others' union bars/women/blokes (delete as appropriate).'

ACADEMIA & JOBS

Students say the best teaching at Sheffield Hallam is in Physical Science (100% of the class gave it their unreserved approval), then in Nutrition, Planning Studies, Biology and related sciences, Food Marketing, Tourism, Biomedical Sciences, Forensic Science, and Film & Photography. Least popular Design Studies, which took a meagre 58% of the class vote.

Back-up resources are increasingly good, and Chris Gissing concludes: 'The teaching within my school (Computing & Management Science) was on the whole very good. I cannot fault the depart-

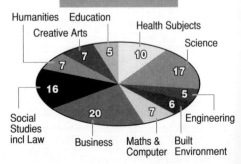

SUBJECT AREAS (%)

Humanities 7
Education 5
Creative Arts 7
Health Subjects 10
Science 17
Social Studies incl Law 16
Business 20
Maths & Computer 7
Built Environment 6
Engineering 5

ment for what they offer in terms of specialist knowledge and resources. On the IT courses there is a strong bias towards industrial placements and business skills, invaluable when going into the real world of work.'

More than 10% of graduates go into education - secondary and primary. Top scoring at the teaching assessments, it's not too difficult to get in, and Education is one of three subjects to score 23 points out of 24 for teaching. The others were maths and health.

Graduates of Computer Science, Health, Business, Social Science, and Creative Arts also march confidently into the higher education sector as lecturers.

Hallam is among the leaders for sheer number of graduates into banking, a 3/4-year sandwich BA in Banking & Finance requires 240 points only. A BSc Business & Finance is a top-up alternative. Hallam is again the place for insurance/pension brokers/underwriters.

Business scored 22 out of 24 points at the teaching assessments. They have an Enterprise Centre to imbue the whole uni with an enterprise culture. There are Finance, Human Resources Mgt, Marketing or Financial Services adjuncts and a series of International Business Studies (French, German, Italian, Spanish) and languages with e-Commerce degrees.

Employment figures show success in personnel in particular through the 4-year sandwich BA Hons Business & Human Resource Management. Look, too, at transport, where Hallam is out in front for graduate employment. BA Planning &

TEACHING SURVEY AT A GLANCE	
Avg. UCAS points accepted	**392**
Acceptance rate	**18%**
Overall satisfaction rate	**91%**
Helpful/interested staff	★★★★★
Small tuition groups	★★★★
Students into graduate jobs	**76%**

Teaching most popular with undergraduates:
Physical Science (100%), Nutrition (96%), Planning Studies (95%), Biology and related sciences, Food Marketing, Tourism (94%), Biomedical Sciences, Forensic Science (92%), Film & Photography (90%).

Teaching least popular with undergraduates:
Media Studies (68%), Computer Science, Electrical 7 Electronic Eng., Social Work (65%), Design Studies (58%).

Transport or Geography with Transport are the degrees. For the catering trade (another key graduate employment area) there's BSc Hons Hospitality Business Management with Conference/Events or Culinary Arts possibilities, or Leisure Events Management with Arts & Entertainments, Outdoor Recreation, or Tourism. They scored full marks at the assessments.

Marketing is also a strength and there is a steady flow of graduates into advertising. See the BA Communication and Information degrees - Communication Studies, and in the Art & Design Faculty, Information Design & Multimedia.

Engineering has always been a strength. For mechanical engineers they ask least at entry among the employment leaders. BEng Hons include Mechanical & Computer-Aided Eng and Mechatronics, and there's a major/minor route for Mechanical Engineering with minor options being Automotive, Control, Environmental Management, Business Management or Electrical Eng. 21 points at the assessments.

Again, like Bath Uni, they lead the way in guiding Electrical Engineering graduates into telecommunications. Look at the E & E and Computer Aided Engineering & Design degrees. There may be a low teaching assessment, but employers still love them.

Computer programmers come thick and fast off the Hallam production line with BSc Computing and its applications - Networks, Software Eng, Visualisation, Web Info. Systems & Services, or with Management Science.

BSc Pharmaceutical Sciences puts the uni into the Top 10 for finding graduates work in the pharmaceutical manufacturing industry. Meanwhile,

RESEARCH EXCELLENCE

% of Sheffield Hallam's research that is
4* *(World-class)* or **3*** *(Internationally rated)*:

	4*	3*
Nursing/Midwifery	10%	25%
Health Professions	0%	25%
Metallurgy and Materials	5%	30%
Built Environment	5%	40%
Town/Country Planning	20%	30%
Business/Management	5%	20%
Information Management	5%	20%
Law	0%	5%
Psychology	0%	10%
Education	5%	20%
Sports	10%	25%
English	5%	25%
History	10%	20%
Art and Design	20%	30%
Media Studies	5%	35%

WHAT IT'S REALLY LIKE

UNIVERSITY:

Social Life	★★★★
Campus scene	**Massive, diverse**
Student Union services	**Good**
Politics	**Activity high**
Sport	**35 clubs**
National team position	**20th**
Sport facilities	**Good**
Arts opportunities	**Few**
Student magazine	**SHU-Print**
Student radio	**RUSH**
Nightclub/bars	**Bar Phoenix**
Union ents	**Cheese, indie**
Union societies	**65**
Most popular society	**RUSH fm**
Parking	**Poor**

CITY:

Entertainment	★★★★★
Scene	**Seriously good**
Town/gown relations	**Good**
Risk of violence	**Average**
Cost of living	**Average**
Student concessions	**Good**
Survival + 2 nights out	**£80 pw**
Part-time work campus/town	**Good/excellent**

health subjects make a huge impact on their employment figures - degrees in Physiotherapy, Occupational Therapy, Radiotherapy, Oncology, Nursing... They have opted for areas where the other Sheffield university doesn't tread, and they dropped only one point at the assessments. The Diagnostic Radiography and Radiography & Oncology BSc degrees corner well over 4% of the national employment market in this sector at a low asking rate.

They're among the leading providers, too, for social workers/counsellors. The BA Social Work Studies hits the spot, but see, too, Social Policy, Social, Cultural and Psychology mixes.

See also the BSc Psychology, fully accredited by the British Psychological Society and first step to becoming a Chartered Psychologist.

Stats show, too, that BSc Architectural Technology or Architecture & Environmental Design are both solid lines into a career. Look also at Construction Management, Construction Commercial Management and Building Surveying. There is employment strength in-depth at Hallam for jobs in the construction industry and BSc Quantity Surveying is no exception. There's a track record, too, in property - look at BSc Property Studies.

Law also has a good reputation. Note the LLB /Maitrise En Droit (Francaise) - 2 years in Paris - and the joint degrees with Criminology, Business, Psychology. It is not difficult to see why more probation officers come out of Hallam than anywhere. You can study BA Criminology and Psychology/Sociology, Social Work Studies, Society & Cities, Social Policy, Social Policy & Sociology.

The Law is also a recognised pathway into Civil Service administration from here, while local and regional government administration call on Hallam graduates in such as Social Policy, Society & Cities, Urban Regeneration, Education, Architecture, Building & Planning, and Business & Administration. BA Business & Public Policy is clearly useful. Note also their BSc Public Health Nutrition, and the Planning & Transport BA.

Finally, they are employment leaders in sport, a fact which knits academia together with student leisure - they came 18th in the national sporting league last year. The department was among the few nationwide to score 24 points (full marks) in the teaching assessments.

SOCIAL SCENE

STUDENTS' UNION The stunning silver drums of the new Union Building (HUBs) beat a fanfare to what the uni describes as 'a unique and unrivalled welfare and social facility for 28,000 students'. It cost them £5 million, so we should allow them that.

There's a student advice centre and volunteering team, a shop, social space and activities area, plus 3 multi-functional entertainment rooms and a café/bar. **Bar Phoenix** is the focal point, downstairs from the club nights. Ents come on weekday nights in the shape of *Pounded, Flirt!, Sheff 1,* and *Last Laugh Comedy Club.* If it's Monday, it's *Pounded,* serving up a *Total Request Party.* Tickets really are £1, as are drinks (soft drinks only 50p). *Flirt!* is every Friday night, and offers up the best party tunes around, with 3 rooms covering modern chart hits through to retro classics and everything in between. Regular fancy dress themes add to the fun, like *Baywatch Party - Love the Hoff, 90s Rave Special,* or *Smirnoff Moulin Rouge Party* (free top hats and feather boas). Saturday night at Hallam is, and always has been, a night for the discerning clubber: *Sheff 1* is the chart and dance favourite choice of this city, and new for 2009 uDisco presents all the best in cutting edge and classic Electro Indie Anthems

There are 30 student societies, Media = the weekly *HUGE* - Hallam Union Guide to Events, also SHU-Print their monthly paper, and RUSH radio, 'with a brand new look and a brand new attitude!' There are 35 sports societies and thoroughly professional facilities are available.

SPORT In fact, the sports facilities have recently been

ACCOMMODATION

Guarantee to freshers	**95%**
Style	**Halls, flats**
Security guard	
Shared rooms	
Internet access	
Self-catered	**Most**
En suite	**Some**
Approx price range pw	**£79.15-£90.53**
City rent pw	**£55**

refurbished, with a £2-million gym and sports conditioning suite opening this very year. The new fitness suite spans 600 square metres and has more than 70 fitness stations, an array of the latest equipment, and an advanced weights and training area.

The changing facilities are fully equipped for the disabled, and there's also 'a sunbed, assessment rooms and full audio and satellite TV system' - they call that exercise? There's another suite on Collegiate Campus.

Hallam does well in sport. They came 20th this year nationwide. That's three places above their neighbouring university.

TOWN See Student Sheffield.

PILLOW TALK

Catered halls and self-catered purpose-built complexes are available. Some catered - about 10%. The Trigon is a newly developed site offering 361 en-suite rooms, CCTV, security patrols, on site office, laundry facilities.

UNIVERSITY OF SOUTHAMPTON

The University of Southampton
Highfield
Southampton SO17 1BH

TEL: 023 8059 5000
FAX: 023 8059 3939
EMAIL: prospenq@soton.ac.uk
WEB SITE: www.soton.ac.uk

Southampton Students' Union
Highfield
Southampton SO17 1BJ

TEL 023 8059 5201
FAX 023 8059 5252
EMAIL susu@soton.ac.uk
WEB www.soton.ac.uk/~susu/

VAG VIEW

Southampton has one of the finest academic records in the country, but in the past has suffered a poor reputation for student satisfaction beyond academia. Historically, the social side of things has been a bit limp. Now in the Times Higher Education magazine's Student Experience Survey (2008) they powered ahead of most of their rivals into 9th position nationally, their strength notably in extra-curricular activities and in the Student Union, and not bad either for social life. At the same time, students praise their lecturers for their help and interest in them and for the small size of their tuition groups, these accolades following hot on the heels of the Government's Research Assessment, which tied Southampton with Durham, St Andrews, Sheffield, Leeds, and Bristol in 14th place nationally, and labelled more than 25 % of their research world-class. It's an all-round deal on which few are

UNIVERSITY/STUDENT PROFILE

University since	**1952**
Situation/style	**Campus**
Student population	**24735**
Total undergraduates	**17120**
Mature undergraduates	**33%**
International undergrads	**11%**
Male/female ratio	**47:53**
Equality of opportunity:	
state school intake	**83%**
social class 4-7 intake	**20%**
low-participation area intake	**5%**

impolite enough to turn their backs. Only 3% dropped out last time.

CAMPUS

HIGHFIELD CAMPUS From east or west you rattle along the M27 until you hit Junction 5, whereupon you dive down south, following the uni signs, and suddenly, 2 miles from the centre of the city, there you are in it. You don't *enter* the main Highfield campus as you might Sussex campus or Nottingham. It is a campus split by University Road, a public road with uni buildings off to the left and right, so that you're not sure whether the city has wandered onto the campus or the campus has not yet quite commandeered its piece of the city (there is nothing of the excitement of Manchester's Oxford Road, where such questions would never occur).

There's a chemically, sciency feel to it. It's all rather laboratorial, claustrophobic, bursting at the seams, for such an eminent university. And then you are transported into some carefully landscaped botanical gardens with stream, and on, across The Avenue, eventually to be released onto the huge open acreage of Southampton Common, where you can...breathe!

Arts are at The Avenue Campus nearby. Finally, you arrive at their internationally renowned **Waterside Campus**/Oceanography Centre.

FEES, BURSARIES

UK & EU Fees, 2009-10: £3,145 p.a. There's a bursary for students in receipt of the HE Maintenance Grant. See www.soton.ac.uk/study/feesandfunding/financialsupport.html. In addition there are academic and sport scholarships and support for disabled, ethnic and other groups.

STUDENT PROFILE

The tradition is that, apart from a small scattering of minority groups and locals, Southampton students are middle-class, although the public school kid intake is in fact similar to that of Reading or Warwick, and less than at Bristol, Durham or Exeter. In a survey of student drug-taking habits by the Adam Smith Institute, they came out 'most abstemious'. The survey was undertaken before the opening of the new on-campus pleasure dome (see Social Scene below). It is as yet unclear whether students' habits have changed, only that everyone is having the time of their lives at

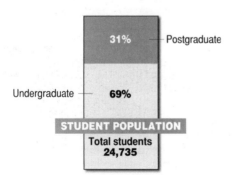

TEACHING SURVEY AT A GLANCE

Avg. UCAS points accepted	**400**
Acceptance rate	**14%**
Overall satisfaction rate	**86%**
Helpful/interested staff	★★★★
Small tuition groups	★★★★
Students into graduate jobs	**84%**

Teaching most popular with undergraduates:
Aerospace Engineering, Chemistry (100%), Geology (99%), Ocean Sciences, Sociology (97%), Mechanilly-based EngineeringHuman & Social Geography, Music (95%), Computer Science, Electronic & Electrical Eng., European Languages, production & Manufacturing Eng., Physical Geography & Enviro. Science (94%), Biology, Medicine, Physics with Space Science (93%), English, History, Archaeology & History, Language & Society, Labguage Learning (92%), Philosophy (91%), Engineering & Technology, Law (90%).

Teaching least popular with undergraduates:
Design Studies (54%), Fine Art (37%).

Highfield. What's more, against any charges of social elitism they can point to an impressive campaign recently, which saw Southampton students spend a week living rough on the streets of the city, with no access to money. The project was in aid of Student Action for Refugees, a campaign supported by two dozen other universities.

ACADEMIA & JOBS

In the Government Research Assessment, Engineering - Civil and Environmental Engineering in particular - scored especially well, as did Medicine, with primary care ranked 3rd in the country, and other community-based clinical subjects and cancer studies scoring particularly highly. Nursing and Midwifery, European Studies, Computer Science, Earth systems and Environmental Sciences, Applied Mathematics, and Statistics also scored highly, as did Music, Archaeology and History. Research at Southampton helped the British Cycling team win Gold in Beijing. The world-renowned Wolfson Unit for Marine Technology and Industrial Aerodynamics undertook wind tunnel testing to accelerate the development of track bikes and riders. Current projects include working on a blood test to spot early signs of breast cancer in women, and tackling hospital infections, such as MRSA.

Research is not teaching of course, but Southampton students rally in particular behind the lecturers in Aerospace Engineering, Chemistry

RESEARCH EXCELLENCE

% of Southampton's research that is
4* *(World-class)* or **3*** *(Internationally rated):*

	4*	3*
Cancer Studies	15%	60%
Hospital Clinical	10%	50%
Community Clinical	25%	60%
Nursing and Midwifery	45%	40%
Health Professions	0%	25%
Biological Sciences	10%	40%
Environmental Sciences	20%	50%
Chemistry	10%	50%
Physics	15%	40%
Pure Mathematics	5%	45%
Applied Mathematics	15%	55%
Statistics	15%	50%
Computer Science	35%	50%
Electrical/Electronic Eng.	25%	40%
Civil Engineering	25%	55%
Mechanical, Aero. & Manufacturing Eng.	15%	45%
Geography Environment	20%	35%
Archaeology	25%	35%
Economics	20%	60%
Business/ Management	15%	40%
Law	5%	45%
Politics	5%	25%
Sociology/Social Policy	35%	35%
Social Work Studies	0%	35%
Psychology	15%	45%
Education	10%	25%
European Studies	30%	25%
English	25%	40%
Philosophy	5%	35%
History	30%	40%
Art and Design	5%	20%
History of Art	15%	35%
Music	50%	30%

gy resources, significantly higher than the sector average of 81%.

The 5-floor Hartley Library on the main Highfield campus has recently undergone a massive refit, making it one of the most advanced university libraries in Britain. Access to resources has been improved and personal study areas have been restyled to allow more privacy.

The Medical Faculty was rated full marks in the teaching assessments. It's a 5-year BM with integrated course structure and clinical contact from first year. A 4th-year 8-week period of clinical experience may be had in subject and place of your choice (many opt to go abroad). It's more competitive than most to get in here, though the entry requirements are fair: AAB (340 points; subjects with overlap of material, such as Biology/Sports Studies, Maths/Further Maths, may not be considered in combination at A level; General Studies cannot be accepted. UKCAT is also required. They are looking for the committed, well-rounded applicant capable of approaching problems with a certain flair, not confined by speciality. Coursework is geared towards problem-solving; patient contact is made in the first term in order to develop communication skills.

Other departments that scored full marks for teaching are: Education, Philosophy, Economics, Electrical & Electronic Engineering, Archaeology and Politics.

If you look at another area in which the uni is renowned - Geography - you see a similar sort of picture. Analytical skills, problem-solving and written and oral expression are to the fore - it's an approach to which employers relate.

Physiotherapy, Occupational Therapy and Podiatry degrees further boost the health sector. There's also Nursing (Adult, Child, Learning Disability, Mental) and Midwifery. Psychotherapists also bound out of here. Look at their Applied Social Science degrees

(these both achieved 100% approval), Geology, Ocean Sciences, Sociology, Mechanically-based Engineering, Human & Social Geography, Music, Computer Science, Electronic & Electrical Engineering, European Languages, Production & Manufacturing Eng., Physical Geography & Environmental Science, Biology, Medicine, Physics with Space Science, English, History, Archaeology & History, Language & Society, Language Learning, Philosophy, Engineering & Technology, and Law. While they were a good deal less happy with Design Studies and Fine Art, the latter achieving only 37% of the class vote.

Overall, 87% of students said that they were satisfied with the quality of their course, and 89% with the library services and information technolo-

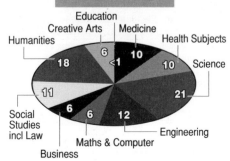

SUBJECT AREAS (%)

WHAT IT'S REALLY LIKE

UNIVERSITY:

Social Life	★★★★★
Campus scene	Active, impressive
Student Union services	Good
Politics	Tory heartland
Sport	70 clubs
National team position	125th
Sport facilities	Excellent
Arts opportunities	Drama, film excellent
Student newspaper	Wessex Scene
Student radio	Surge
New Student TV	SUSUTV
Nightclub	The Cube
Bars	Bridge Bar, Stag's Head
Union ents	Kinki, Generator, Fat Poppadaddys
Union societies	160+
Most active society	Theatre Group
Parking	No first years

CITY:

Entertainment	★★★
Scene	Pubs, clubs, water
Town/gown relations	Average-poor
Risk of violence	Average
Cost of living	Average
Student concessions	OK
Survival + 2 nights out	£80 pw
Part-time work campus/town	Good/excellent

(Anthropology, Criminology), as well as the BSc Psychology and BSc Social Work.

After health, the City claims most of Southampton's graduates. Accounting & Economics or Finance ensure good employment figures, and there's a leaning to careers for tax expert/consultants and actuaries. For the latter, look especially at Economics with Actuarial Studies and Mathematics with Actuarial Studies.

Southampton are hot on student enterprise. 'Spin out' companies have raised more than £20 million of private funds. More than 60 students enrolled with the Student Entrepreneurs Club. SETsquared is a dedicated support and mentoring facility for entrepreneurs and fledgling enterprises.

In the Oceanography Centre at Southampton's Dockside, Marine Science students again have access to exceptional analytical and research facilities. Ellen MacArthur's stunning performance in Kingfisher, in the Vendee Global Challenge, carried with it tank and wind-tunnel research work done by the university. The yachtswoman was closely involved in the design and testing processes.

Defence is clearly a priority. Like Portsmouth along the coast, Southampton has an active OTC. There's a University Air Squadron and Royal Naval Unit. Many Southampton graduates bound for the Defence industry come from the Faculty of Engineering & Applied Science, which gained world-class ratings in the research assessments, and Electronics scored full marks in the teaching assessments: Acoustical, Aerospace, Civil, Electrical & Electronic, Electromechanical and a number of Engineering Management degrees, also Computing Engineering. They regard themselves to be 'a golden triangle of Engineering research excellence' with Imperial College and Cambridge.

The Marine aspect is of course marked. Boat/ship designers/surveyors/brokers are all served well. Southampton satisfies through design, construction and operation. See in particular the B/MEng Ship Science, the MEng comes in various orientations: Yacht & Small Craft, Naval Architecture, Inter-Disciplinary, and the 4-year Advanced Materials. There's a 23-point assessment for Ship Science.

No mention of Southampton ever goes without a nod to Medicine, and in this context, some 8% of graduates going into Defence do so with some medical science background - Medicinal Chemistry, Biomedical Sciences, etc.

Computer programmers and software engineers also proliferate. They offer BSc Computer Science and various orientations - with AI, Distributed Systems & Network, Image & Multimedia Systems, Software Eng. There are also two MEng degrees: Software Engineering and the 4-year Computer Engineering, and a facility, too, study Computer Science for a BEng with Foundation year.

For would-be sound recordists Southampton leads the employment field with B/MEng Acoustical Engineering. Look at course links between their Institute of Sound & Vibration and the Dept of Music: BSc Acoustics and/with Music and the Acoustical Engineering Foundation course. Full marks and a world class reputation for Electronic Engineering and an 'Excellent' for teaching Music give one confidence.

For aspiring environmental officers the 4-year MEnvSci Environmental Sciences does the trick. Similar Masters degrees are available in Geology, Geophysics, and Oceanography, and then a whole range of BSc degrees variously offering French or German options, and there's an Environmental Sciences Foundation year too.

Meanwhile, their Sports Management & Leadership and Sport Studies degrees put them in the Top 10 for athletes, sportsmen, players and officials.

Finally, Law is also a big draw.

SOCIAL SCENE

STUDENTS' UNION A new Student Services Centre, site for SUSU's Advice & Information Centre opened in October 2005. There's also a new cinema and nightclub with three bars collectively known as **The Cube**, increasing capacity to 1,700. At the Friday night *Kinki* event - low drinks prices and music across three floors (from cheese, to dance, to indie) - it's heaving.

The Cube is open until 2 am, three nights a week. **The Stag's Head** is a pub-style bar with license until midnight, and runs events such as Karaoke and the Sunday Quiz.

There is also the **Bridge bar**, located at the top of the Union building and with a view of campus and stream below. The Bridge hosts the *Jazz Lounge*, the *Laughter Lounge*, and the chill-out **Living Room** events.

Fat Poppadaddys comes to town on Saturday (funk, 60s, hip hop, reggae, drum 'n' bass). Thursdays hosts *Generator* - their indie and rock night, which feature live bands, like Arab Strap.

Over the past couple of years, SUSU has also hosted big name DJs such as Dave Pearce, Carl Cox and Judge Jules. The Cut Up Boys kept the Grab Ball pumping, and Colin Murray took to the decks in Freshers' Week last year. Radio 1 Zane Low's In New Music We Trust tour came to the Union as well and Razorlight played live. More recently, Zane hijacked the student radio station, Surge, and took over the Saturday night show.

Societies have always been strong at Southampton. *Wessex Scene*, the student paper, and Surge Radio remain a feature, as does *The Edge*, the ents paper. Wessex Scene won the 2004 Guardian Media Award for Website of the Year and has been nominated in that category for 4 successive years. Surge, which has recently benefited from a new £20k studio, has had its share of awards too. Now, brand new, they have SUSU TV, and hosted the National Student TV Awards last year to show that they had truly arrived..

There are three internationally celebrated arts venues on campus, the **Turner Sims** concert hall, the **John Hansard Gallery**, and the **Nuffield Theatre**, where the Drama Society do their stuff, and there's a thriving Film Society, too, with a 320-seat cinema which shows second-release films through Dolby surround sound. There's also a tradition of student bands.

SPORT Sport is huge at Southampton. Last year saw the opening of a brand new sports centre on the campus, complete with Olympic swimming pool, gym, 8-badminton court sports hall and 140-station fitness suite. Three years ago the Wide Lane Sports Complex was opened by John Inverdale. This

ACCOMMODATION	
Guarantee to freshers	**100%**
Style	**Halls**
Security guard	**All**
Shared rooms	**Some**
Internet access	**All**
Self-catered	**Most**
En suite	**Some**
Approx price range pw	**£65.45-£145.60**
City rent pw	**£60**

£4.3m complex boasts 76 acres of pitches (including 2 floodlit synthetic pitches), 24 changing rooms, meeting rooms and a fully-licensed bar. There's also a boatyard for watersporters. The sailors have won the BUSA championship more times than Portsmouth care to recall.

TOWN While Southampton itself has neither the size nor vigour of Manchester or its football team, nor yet the groovy cuts of Brighton or even Bournemouth, it's a lively enough place to live. Having been a Regency holiday resort, the city centre has a large number of spacious parks and waterfront attractions.

'If Southampton were a person, it would be a dedicated alcoholic,' said a student. 'The city centre and waterfront have a network of colossal alcohol palaces (including Britain's largest pub, the Square Balloon), yet the city lacks a twilight zone, for, owing to a local statute, even nightclubs are not allowed to open later than 2.'

There are three cinemas and the Mayflower Theatre, which plays host to several major West End shows. Musically, it's often ignored by the larger acts: consult your Bournemouth train timetable.

PILLOW TALK

University accommodation (halls and flats) is guaranteed to all first year undergraduates who meet the terms of their offers, and name Southampton as their firm choice. Some halls have sports facilities, all have launderettes and many have shops and bars. Every room has a phone. Avoid Bencraft and Stoneham halls. Bencraft is miles from anywhere and Stoneham is Southampton's answer to the walled city of Kowloon apparently.

GETTING THERE

☛ By road to Southampton: M3/J 14, A33.
☛ By coach to Southampton: London, 2:30; Bristol, 2:45; Birmingham, 3:40.
☛ By rail to Southampton: London Waterloo, 1:40; Birmingham, 3:30; Sheffield, 4:45.
☛ By air: Southampton International Airport.

SOUTHAMPTON SOLENT UNIVERSITY

Southampton Solent University
Southampton SO14 ORT

TEL 023 8031 9039
FAX 023 8022 2259
EMAIL admissions@solent.ac.uk
WEB www.solent.ac.uk/

Solemt Students' Union
Southampton SO14 OYN

TEL 023 8023 2154
FAX 023 8023 5248
EMAIL supresident@solent.ac.uk
WEB www.solentsu.co.uk/

VAG VIEW

Southampton Solent University, out of Southampton's College of Art and College of Higher Education and the College of Nautical Studies at Warwash, showed a healthy 7.7 % increase in applications last year - fifth highest countrywide. There is an apparently innovative vocational portfolio, an enviable record of excellence in teaching assessments, a lively student scene, and it is not too demanding at entry.

Their mission is clear, 'accessibility and teaching strongly underpinned by research and community engagement. We will contin- ue to offer and develop innovative courses with an emphasis on preparing students for work.'

Accessible they certainly are. You need only 200 points to get in. At this stage the research is fairly patchy, and only 68% of those who were asked in the Student National Experience Survey said they were satisfied with the teaching. Solent has been packing the applicants in since they became a university in 2005, but are bleeding badly at the other end, the latest published figures show a near 12% drop-out rate, which is above the Government benchmark. Also, only 64% are finding real graduate jobs

UNIVERSITY/STUDENT PROFILE	
University since	**2005**
Situation/style	**Civic**
Student population	**17455**
Total undergraduates	**19990**
Mature undergraduates	**27%**
International undergrads	**13%**
Male/female ratio	**55:45**
Equality of opportunity:	
state school intake	**97%**
social class 4-7 intake	**36%**
low-participation area intake	**12%**

within six months of leaving.

FEES, BURSARIES

UK & EU Fees, 2009-10: £3,225 p.a. There are bur- saries for students in receipt of the HE Maintenance Grant on a sliding scale, according to parental income. Sports scholarships are available, as are the Lisa Wilson scholarship and Toft Scholarship for students 'who have overcome adversity or can demonstrate why he/she needs extra financial help with his/her studies'.

STUDENT PROFILE

Statistics show a student body made up 96% of state educated students, 33% from the lower socio- economic orders and 16% from the so-called 'low- participation' neighbourhoods. Writes Tanver Hussain. 'The blokes all look like fugitives from just about any boy band and the girls could form All Saints 100 times over. This excludes Art stu- dents and the rugby team, as you will find that they are in worlds of their own.'

ACADEMIA & JOBS

The faculties are: Business; Media, Arts and Society; and Technology. Besides Maritime (includ- ing yacht and powercraft design), departments include Design (Fashion, Fine Art, Graphic Design, Interior, etc); Built Environment (big strength in Architectural Technology degrees, Construction Management, etc); Business (Tourism

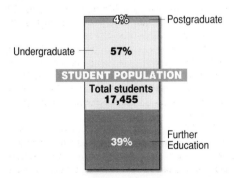

Postgraduate **4%**

Undergraduate **57%**

STUDENT POPULATION
Total students 17,455

39% Further Education

Management is new with options like Cruise and Travel Operations); Law (Commercial Law degrees); Media Arts (Film, Fiction, Journalism, Advertising); Social Science (Community Studies, Psychology, Criminology, Politics); Systems Engineering (masses of computer courses and a tasty specialist degree in Media Technology for the broadcast, film & entertainment industries).

Students say that the best teaching is in Sociology, Social Studies, Marketing, Publicity Studies, Management Studies, and Business Studies, and that the worst is Performing Arts and Fine Art, the latter getting a grudging 31% approval from the class.

Around 15% of the graduate workforce goes into retail or the hotel/restaurant industry. There are a number of Fashion degrees, and Interior Design, which may partly account for this. Thereafter it's government administration or business of some sort, before we get to the sexier end of the employment spectrum: advertising (there are dedicated degrees for this), publishing (a number of journalism degrees, such as Magazine Journalism & Feature Writing, with Language Foundation Year), artistic & literary expression, and film. But these, while impressive, for they are difficult employment areas to crack, account for relatively small percentages of total graduates as yet - around 4%, 4%, 2%, and 2% respectively.

In the past there has been good investment in music, media and broadcasting courses, upgrading studios, creating digital radio facilities and setting up a centre for professional development in broadcasting and multimedia production in collaboration with ITV Meridian, the local media set-up. Among the smaller student populations Solent, like Edinburgh Napier mount a strong challenge to the big boys in getting graduates into publishing, being right up there with universities that have double their number of undergraduates. Solent mounts its strategy not only through Journalism through Media Cultural Studies, Media

TEACHING SURVEY AT A GLANCE	
Avg. UCAS points accepted	**200**
Acceptance rate	**30%**
Overall satisfaction rate	**68%**
Helpful/interested staff	★★★
Small tuition groups	★★★
Students into graduate jobs	**64%**

Teaching most popular with undergraduates:
Sociology (91%), Social Studies, Marketing, Publicity Studies (83%), Management Studies, Business Studies (81%).

Teaching least popular with undergraduates:
Architecture (59%), Media Studies (58%), Music (42%), Performing Arts (32%), Fine Art (31%).

Communication, and through its Graphics, Design Studies, Product Design with Marketing, etc degrees. Its general Marketing, Management and Communications degrees are also a gateway.

It also claims a world first in its Comedy Writing and Performance BA, devised and run by academic and stand-up comic Chris Ritchie. Other institutions do run modules in comedy, often as part of drama courses. Kent is one.

In Advertising the emphasis is on developing the creative faculties by means of idea generation exercises and creative thinking workshops. Budding art directors or copywriters will also get genned up on campaign planning, media buying, targeting and brand positioning. Conversely, if you want to play a strategic role as account planner, handler, media buyer or brand manager, you get a chance to produce campaign concepts for a creative portfolio of work. There's a twinning with a London ad agency, and hands-on experience available from tutors.

There's constantly new things going on in art and design - a whole host of new fashion, fashion photography, interiors degrees last year - and recently Muti-media Design and Digital Imaging degrees have led to a big increase in jobs. BA Illustration with Animation also scores high in the world of computer games design.

BSc Mobile Web Technology was new last year, and Electronic Engineering is another big strength. Many come through the HND or Foundation years, their destination almost exclusively telecommunications. Employment figures are good.

Finally, boat/ship designer/surveyor/brokers find their way to courses dedicated to their interests - such as Maritime Business, Marine Operations, Yacht Manufacturing & Surveying and

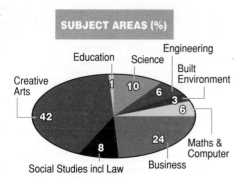

SUBJECT AREAS (%)

Creative Arts 42
Education 1
Science 10
Engineering
Built Environment 6
3
6
Maths & Computer 24
Business
Social Studies incl Law 8

WHAT IT'S REALLY LIKE	
UNIVERSITY:	
Social Life	★★★
Campus scene	**Active, diverse**
Student Union services	**Good**
Politics	**Not much**
Sport	**Sailing**
National team position	**59th**
Sport facilities	**Good**
Arts opportunities	**Available**
Student magazine	**Re:SUS**
Student radio station	**SIN Radio**
Nightclub	**In-town clubs**
Bars	**Top Bar, Bottom Bar**
Union ents	**Fat Poppadaddys, city student nights**
Union societies	**28**
Parking	**Poor, permiy**
CITY:	
Entertainment	★★★
Scene	**Pubs, clubs, water**
Town/gown relations	**Average-poor**
Risk of violence	**Average**
Cost of living	**Average**
Student concessions	**OK**
Survival + 2 nights out	**£80 pw**
Part-time work campus/town	**Good/excellent**

ACCOMMODATION	
Guarantee to freshers	**90%**
Style	**Halls, flats**
Security guard	**All**
Shared rooms	**Some**
Internet access	**All**
Self-catered	**All**
En suite	**Some**
Approx price range pw	**£50-£100**
City rent pw	**£50-£70**

Yacht & Powercraft Design. Foundation years are invariably available, if necessary.

SOCIAL SCENE

STUDENTS' UNION The union has two bars, renovated within the not so distant past, the imaginatively named **Bottom Bar** (downstairs) opens during the week, 11am-5pm, and on Saturday 7pm-11pm in concert with **Top Bar** (11am-11pm in week, 7pm-11pm Saturday). Saturday is the same here as it is at the other uni in Southampton – *Fat Poppadaddys* (funk, 60s, hip hop, reggae, drum 'n' bass). *Fridays @ Solent* are £1-a-shot funky house nights. Thursdays are *Paper Scissors Rock* (alternative). Wednesdays, there's *Loaded*, 9-10pm @ Top Bar, pre-club for *Cheeky Monkey* @ **Ikon Diva** or **Kaos** in town (with an Express Pass which beats the inevitable queue at these the biggest nightclubs).

This union/town tie-up is typical of the weekly ents menu. Tuesday is *Funkie Junkie* (mainstream r&b, house & party anthems) at newest club, **Junk**, on the London Road, again after a **Top Bar** warm-up. Monday, meanwhile, is *Acoustic Night* at Top Bar, a 'bring mates, bring a guitar' affair.

Media-wise there's SIN Radio and Re:SUS magazine. There are 28 societies in operation, not counting course-related efforts.

SPORT There were 31 sports clubs up and running this year, from Capoeira to roller hockey, and triathlon to taekwon do, as well as the more usual - rugby, rowing, American Football, and, as expected in a college dedicated to maritime subjects, water plays a key part. Sailing is the strongest sport - they've been national champions three times in the past four years (came second the other time) and three times in the top three in the world. Students come to the university because of its reputation in this sport. Sports scholarships were introduced to attract top performers in all sports. Ground-based sports facilities include a sports hall and fitness suite, sauna and solarium. Playing fields are 4 miles from the city. There's a licensed pavilion, the Budweiser Sports Bar.

PILLOW TALK

Cream of the halls crop would have to be Lucia Foster Welch, not only is it the biggest, but it has the advantage of having Ocean Village on its doorstep. The downside is that you are 15 minutes away from the main campus and there is no common room. The other halls all have their plus points, Kimber and its spangly new kitchens or Deanery, one of the newest. All have their own laundry, and all have recently been wired for intranet and intranet access, giving students 24-hour on-line access to the university's managed learning environment and email and internet. You can't choose where you live, but you can choose to have an en-suite bathroom or not.

GETTING THERE

- ☛ By road: M3/J 14, A33. Warsash: M27/J8, A27.
- ☛ By coach to Southampton: London, 2:30; Bristol, 2:45; Birmingham, 3:40.
- ☛ By rail: London Waterloo, 1:40; Bristol Parkway, 2:15; Birmingham, 3:30; Sheffield, 4:45.
- ☛ By air: Southampton International Airport.

STAFFORDSHIRE UNIVERSITY

Staffordshire University
College Road
Stoke-on-Trent ST4 2DE

TEL 01782 292753
    01782 292752 (prospectus)
FAX 01782 292740
EMAIL admissions@staffs.ac.uk
WEB www.staffs.ac.uk

Staffordshire Students' Union
College Road
Stoke-on-Trent
Staffs ST4 2DE

TEL 01782 294629
FAX 01782 295736
EMAIL theunion@staffs.ac.uk
WEB www.staffsunion.com

VAG VIEW

The sometime·Staffordshire Polytechnic has expanded enormously and has the necessary contacts with industry to sustain a strong vocational curriculum. There's also good sport, a strong local ents scene and plenty of student activities to widen your perspective on life.

UNIVERSITY/STUDENT PROFILE	
University since	**1992**
Situation/style	**Civic**
Student population	**15190**
Total undergraduates	**11795**
Mature undergraduates	**30%**
International undergrads	**4%**
Male/female ratio	**51:49**
Equality of opportunity:	
state school intake	**98%**
social class 4-7 intake	**39%**
low-participation area intake	**21%**

CAMPUSES

There are sites in Stoke and Stafford, 12 miles to the south, opposite the railway station. This is an area known as the Potteries, a borough incorporated in 1907 to include Stoke-on-Trent, Hanley, Burslem, Tinstall, Longton and Fenton. Its most famous son, Arnold Bennett (author of Clayhanger, Anne of the Five Towns – he preferred the sound of five, so left out Fenton) couldn't get away fast enough, but that had nothing to do with the university, which only gained its status in 1992.

FEES, BURSARIES

UK & EU Fees, 2007: £3,070 p.a. If eligible for a HE Maintenance Grant, there are bursaries on a sliding scale according to household earnings.

STUDENT PROFILE

The student profile is as you would expect. There's a sizable mature population and a sizable local intake. Most entrants are from state schools, and a third of non-mature entrants from social groups 4 to 7, while some 23% come from 'low participation neighbourhoods', i.e. new to the idea of university. The uni appeals to the region with a priority application scheme for locals.

ACADEMIA & JOBS

The faculties are Arts, Media & Design; Business & Law; Computing, Engineering & Technology; Health & Sciences; the Staffordshire University Business School; and the Staffordshire Law School. At Stoke there's Art & Design, Business, Law, Humanities & Social Sciences and Sciences. At Stafford, Computing, Engineering & Advanced Technology and Health. But what's novel is the HE-FE federation being developed with Tamworth & Lichfield College and other further education colleges. There is a Lichfield Campus for the purpose and a whole range of courses, degrees and HNDs with links to what's going on at the mother house.

There are top teaching assessments in Economics (full marks), Psychology, Philosophy, Art & Design, Physics, Sport, Biosciences, Nursing and other subjects allied to Medicine – the latter featuring midwifery and the nursing (adult, child and mental health). A new healthcare facility opened in 2004 at the Stafford campus to provide NHS care to students, staff and the community. There are doctors' consulting rooms, a practice nurse physiotherapy service and a retail pharmacy.

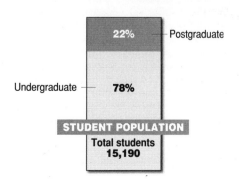

Postgraduate 22%

Undergraduate 78%

STUDENT POPULATION
Total students
15,190

TEACHING SURVEY AT A GLANCE

Avg. UCAS points accepted	**240**
Acceptance rate	**21%**
Overall satisfaction rate	**81%**
Helpful/interested staff	★★★
Small tuition groups	★★★★
Students into graduate jobs	**75%**

Teaching most popular with undergraduates:
Fine Art (91%), Business, Sports Science (90%),
Business Studies (89%), Law, Forensic Science
(87%), Biological Sciences, Psychology,
Performing Arts (86%), Sociology (85%).

Teaching least popular with undergraduates:
Social Work (76%), Computer Science (74%),
Technology (66%).

Meanwhile, Staffs' IT & Computing faculty is brimming with opportunity: Graphics/Imaging /Visualisation, Science, Systems, Applicable Maths, Internet Technology, Intelligent Systems, Software Engineering, Forensic, Mobile, computer Design, Games Design, Network Engineering... Aspiring computer programmers and IT consultants (they lead the employment field nationally) should go through it with a toothcomb, Staffordshire Uni is the top graduate supplier to this sector. Entry 240 points. Resources in computing are especially good – two IT centres, the £5-million Octagon centre being a central focus with 800+ workstations.

Graduates acquire accounting knowledge with computer-based analytical, management and design skills. The single honsBA Accounting is joined by combos with Business, Economics and Law.

There's a £1.25-million incubation business project at the Stafford Business Village, with 'high specification incubation' for 40 businesses. Marketing is one highly successful employment area at the Business School, which also explores management and entrepreneurship in areas such as personnel, travel and tourism, as well as having a clutch of degrees in business, computing and IT.

A large number of graduates go into welfare, community and youth work. Look at the Applied Social Studies top-ups, the Sport degrees and high-flying BSc Social Psychology, or the Psychology degrees, which can be done alone or with Criminology or Sport & Excercise. Also, BA Social Work.

The Sport & Leisure Department, which is up there employment-wise with the big boys at Brighton and Nottingham Trent.

The Law Society has awarded the University's LPC course an 'Excellent' rating, the highest accolade it can bestow. Staffordshire is one of only five to share this status. See their recent additions to the curriculum: LLB Sports Law/Human Resources Management/Human Rights/Business Law. A Crime Scene House provides simulated scenes for forensic students to develop detection skills. BSc Forensic Science can be studied alone or with Criminology or Psychology.

For niche employment areas, media is also to the fore. The BA degrees come in Journalism, Film, TV, Broadcast Journalism, Music Broadcasting, Sports Journalism, TV & Radio Documentary. While in Media & Entertainment Technology are the BSc degrees in technology in areas such as film, music, computer games design, 3D animation,, simulation, etc, etc.

Art & Design melds media with art – Animation, Media Production, Photography, for example, and BA CGI Animation & Special Effects..

SOCIAL SCENE

STUDENTS' UNION Students' Union There are three

WHAT IT'S REALLY LIKE

UNIVERSITY:	
Social Life	★★★
Campus scene	**Unpretentious fun**
Student Union services	**Good**
Politics	**Activity low: fees**
Sport	**Busy**
National team position	**87th**
Sport facilities	**Good**
Arts opportunities	**Drama, music excellent; dance, film, art good**
Student newspaper	**Get Knotted**
Student radio	**GK Radio**
Nightclub	**Legends**
Bars	**LRV, Ember Lounge**
Union ents	**Serious clubnights & live**
Union societies	**23**
Most active society	**Drama**
Parking	**Adequate**
TOWN:	
Entertainment	★★★
Town scene	**Pubs, clubs**
Town/gown relations	**Average**
Risk of violence	**Average**
Cost of living	**Average**
Student concessions	**Good**
Survival + 2 nights out	**£60 pw**
Part-time work campus/town	**Good**

bars – two at the Stoke campus, Leek Road Venue (LRV – 1800 capacity) and College Road's newly refurbished Ember Lounge (500) and one at Stafford, Legends, which goes forth as Sleepers during the day.

LRV stages some of the biggest student nights in the Midlands. There are two resident DJs and guest appearances by the famous (DJs and bands). There's also Comedy Club on Saturday. It's a busy, well-worked scene. 'We're not on the main gig circuit,' they admit, 'but the DJs and their agents now ring us!' There are also three balls a year, May in March, Summer in June and Graduation in November. May Ball's the biggest.

It isn't all music. There are in fact twenty-three societies at Stoke, and the most active is Drama – there's a good Drama & Theatre Arts degree; at Stafford there are a further ten. The uni newspaper is GK (Get Knotted) and the student radio station, GK Radio. The paper has received awards from the Guardian and the Daily Telegraph. Politics are low on the agenda, though they joined the national march on the tuition fees issue.

Sport Academic influence brings good facilities for all and fame for some. They have 41 clubs and came 99th nationally in the team ratings. Hockey is their sport. Cross country and badminton teams are also strong, and they have had their top-ranked swimmers, too.

Facilities include a sports centre, sports halls, squash courts, floodlit synthetic and grass pitches for football or rugby, fitness suites, gym with multi-gym, weights and fitness machines. There's also a dance and aerobics studio at the Sir Stanley Matthews Sports Centre in Leek Road.

Town Contrary to expectation Hanley, not Stoke, is the main man down among the potteries. There are pubs and clubs in both, however, to which you will soon feel like is home. Just outside Hanley is

ACCOMMODATION	
Guarantee to freshers	**100%**
Style	**Halls, flats**
Security guard	**Most halls, all flats**
Shared rooms	**All halls, some flats**
Internet access	**All**
Self-catered	**All**
En suite	**Halls none, flats most**
Approx price range pw	**£55-£95**
City rent pw	**£40-£50**

Festival Park – multi-screen cinema, Quasar, Water World, Super Bowl, etc. Stoke has a dry ski slope. Theatres include the New Victoria at nearby Newcastle-under-Lyme, the Rep Theatre (Stoke) and Theatre Royal (Hanley). Sundays and Wednesdays are film nights at Legends in Stafford; the Drama Soc. is forty strong and puts on four plays a year, including panto.

PILLOW TALK

Stoke: 6 on-campus halls of residence, 8 off campus. Student houses: 36-bedroom houses on Leek Road. Student Flats: blocks of flats, two thirds sharing, within two miles of Leek Road. Stafford: Stafford Court includes 249 en-suite rooms; an additional 307 rooms will be open by the time you get there and Yarlet House with fifty-one.

GETTING THERE

* By road: Stafford – M6/J14, A513. Stoke – M6 (J15 from south; J16 from north), A500.
* By coach: London, 4:00.
* By rail: Birmingham New Street, 40 mins; Manchester Piccadilly, 1:20; London Euston, 1:45; Nottingham, 2:00; Sheffield, 2:15.

UNIVERSITY OF STIRLING

The University of Stirling
Stirling FK9 4LA

TEL 01786 467044
FAX 01786 466800
EMAIL recruitment@stir.ac.uk
WEB www.stir.ac.uk

Stirling University Students' Association
The Robbins Centre
University of Stirling FK9 4LA

TEL 01786 467166
FAX 01786 467190
EMAIL susa@stir.ac.uk
WEB www.susaonline.org.uk/

VAG VIEW

The University of Stirling is a premier-league university with a reputation for leading the way. It was the first traditional uni to grasp the nettle of modularisation and reap the benefits of doing it in proper semesters - two blocks of fifteen weeks.

Physically it is a classic example of a campus university - typical 60s breezeblock buildings, but set in beautiful surroundings with a small loch in the centre, hills in the background, and more than enough ducks, rabbits, and squirrels to keep a nature lover happy. Situated a mile or so outside the city, it is so completely self-sufficient that you could, if you so desired, spend the whole semester there without leaving once.

Such is the lasting effect of the Stirling student experience that alumni line up to contribute to its development, while others return to work for its administration.

In the recent Higher Education Funding Council's National Student Survey, 86% of current students gave it the thumbs up, and the latest drop-out figures show fewer than 6% fail to complete the course, which is impressive enough.

CAMPUS

The 310-acre campus is was once part of the grounds of Airthrey Castle, base camp for the Highlands. As you approach, you see the Ochil hills in the distance, snow capped when we went in March. Think of Stirling as the apex of a triangle north-east of Glasgow, north-west of Edinburgh. It's an hour from either, give or take. Commonly, students hire a minibus for a night out in these cities. You need to escape occasionally

UNIVERSITY/STUDENT PROFILE	
University since	**1967**
Situation/style	**Campus**
Student population	**10510**
Total undergraduates	**7715**
Mature undergraduates	**13%**
International undergrads	**5%**
Male/female ratio	**43:57**
Equality of opportunity:	
state school intake	**94%**
social class 4-7 intake	**27%**
low-participation area intake	**5%**

from campus, for beautiful as it is, Stirling is also a bubble apart from the world.

The loch is the centrepiece of campus, with the Wallace Monument towering over it. You look out over the water from the halls of residence, enjoy summer and even Christmas barbecues beside it, and criss-cross it by bridge daily on the way to the Robbins Centre, Atrium and MacRobert Arts Centre in the Union facility, or for lectures in the Cottrell or Pathfoot buildings. The loch is the centre of everything: it gives itself to leisure pursuits (canoeing and fishing) and to academic experiment in Aquaculture and Marine Biology.

Chances are that you will already know from this description whether you are the kind of student that will suit Stirling. It has suited various writers (Iain Banks among them) and many golfers too, for Airthrey Golf Course is close. Some find it pleasantly secure, others slightly claustrophobic, but the spirit of the place espouses a student-centred ethos. One told us that he felt that Stirling had given him the kind of individual teaching and personal treatment that he imagined he might have enjoyed as a sixth former had he gone to a public school.

New facilities at a satellite campus in Inverness (Stirling's Highland Campus) offer up-to-the-minute training for student nurses.

FEES, BURSARIES

UK & EU Fees, 2009-10: non-Scottish domiciled students fees in year 2009-10: £1,820. If you are a Scottish-domiciled first degree student you are eligible for your tuition fees to be covered by the Scottish Government. Stirling offers no bursary to students eligible for the HE Maintenance Grant, but a hardship fund is available. There are scholarships in golf, swimming, disability swimming, tennis, triathlon, men's football, women's football), and the main academic award is the Carnegie Trust Scholarship.

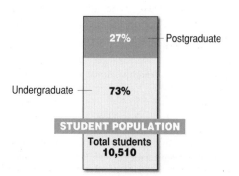

27% — Postgraduate

Undergraduate — 73%

STUDENT POPULATION
Total students 10,510

STUDENT PROFILE

Ninety-four per cent of Stirling undergraduates are in fact state school educated, 27% of its undergraduates come from the lower socio-economic groups, 5% from the so-called 'low-participation' neighbourhoods, and there is a keen focus on international recruitment. Already there are over 80 nationalities represented on campus, and its policy is to attract more. To that end, English language support is provided to help international applicants meet entry requirements, arrangements are made to meet students on arrival at the airport, and long before they arrive they will have corresponded with the International Society and taken a virtual tour of campus by means of a video available in Polish, Spanish, Russian, Japanese, Hindi, and Chinese. A story goes the rounds that when finally they reach campus, they have been known to greet the student stars of the video like long-lost friends, which gives a charming sense of the adventure they are on.

The small size of the student body (there are few more than 10,000 in all) and the seclusion of the situation at Stirling, dictate student experience. People get to know one another quickly across the years. As a fresher it won't be long before you know every second person. If this is what you like, you'll like Stirling. It certainly isn't an intimidating place: 'integration' is the administration's No. 1 buzz word.

RESEARCH EXCELLENCE		
% of Stirling's research that is		
4* *(World-class)* or **3*** *(Internationally rated):*		
	4*	**3***
Nursing/Midwifery	**20%**	**30%**
Aquaculture	**5%**	**45%**
Environmental Sciences	**5%**	**35%**
Computer Science	**5%**	**40%**
Economics	**15%**	**45%**
Accounting/Finance	**0%**	**45%**
Business/Management	**10%**	**30%**
Law	**5%**	**35%**
Politics	**5%**	**10%**
Social Work	**10%**	**45%**
Psychology	**5%**	**10%**
Education	**15%**	**40%**
Sports	**15%**	**25%**
European Studies	**5%**	**25%**
Englishe	**10%**	**45%**
Philosophy	**25%**	**45%**
History	**15%**	**35%**
Film & Media	**10%**	**60%**

TEACHING SURVEY AT A GLANCE	
Avg. UCAS points accepted	**312**
Acceptance rate	**15%**
Overall satisfaction rate	**86%**
Helpful/interested staff	★★★★
Small tuition groups	★★★★
Students into graduate jobs	**73%**

Teaching most popular with undergraduates:
Sociology, Social Policy (97%), Social Studies (92%), English (91%), Initial Teacher Training, Management (89%), History & Philosophy, Accounting, Sciences related to Biology (88%), Biology, Nursing (86%), History, Psychology (85%),

Teaching least popular with undergraduates:
Business (77%).

ACADEMIA & JOBS

At Stirling, your degree is built up of credits, accumulated through taking modules on a semester-by semester basis, rather than at the end of the academic year. The key benefit of modular study is flexibility. It is possible to start on one degree programme and graduate in something entirely different. In fact, around half of Stirling students change the focus of their degree in some way.

Stirling has scored high in the teaching assessments, partly due to this student-centred ethos which touches all faculties. In the Times Higher Education magazine's Student Experience Survey, Stirling undergraduates rated highly the helpful and interested nature of their lecturers and the relatively small-size tuition groups.

Students say the best teaching is to be found in Sociology, Social Policy, Social Studies, English, Initial Teacher Training, Management, History & Philosophy, Accounting, Sciences related to Biology, Biology, Nursing, History, and Psychology. These were the subjects that achieved 85% or more of the class vote in the National Student Survey.

The Stirling Management School has four divisions: Accounting & Finance, Business & Organisation, Marketing and Economics. The latter is an area of particular expertise. At the research assessments (2008) 15% of the submission was found to be world class (4-star), 45% internationally excellent (3-star).

Another subject that did well in the research assessment was Nursing and Midwifery, which achieved 20% 4-star and 30% 3-star. Seventeen per cent of all graduates jobs at Stirling involve employment in hospitals. An interesting development is a return-to-nursing-practice scheme after a period of absence - online learning, a dissertation and clinical practice.

Film and Media is another area in which the uni has been making waves. Again, in the research assessment 70% of the submission was either world class or internationally excellent. Out of this rich research culture comes a series of film and media degrees, and some convincing sounding Journalism joint courses. A few years ago a news room became part of the teaching resources. The Student Union is known for its award-winning media and has recently launched its own TV station.

In the wake of the uni's fortieth anniversary the library is being redeveloped, the idea to re-open it in summer 2010 more or less 24/7, if a pilot scheme succeeds. The computer labs are already open 24 hours a day.

SOCIAL SCENE

STUDENTS' ASSOCIATION To sustain life far from the city, SUSA puts on a fairly cheesy show from its base in the **Robbins Centre**, but no-one seems to mind. In fact, the SA won *Best Bar None* in 2005, 2006 and 2007 (for excellence in 'corporate social responsibility'). There are 3 bars: **Studio** is open from 9.30am for breakfast, and on into the small hours. Although it has its own programme of ents (pub quizzes, NFL Sundays), its main function in the evening is as pre-club for the nightclub downstairs, with capacity for up to 750. There are weekly live music nights, as well as frequent live comedy nights.

On campus too are the usual sports clubs and societies - 'SUDS, the Drama Society, aims to put on at least a couple of productions each semester,' writes Suzanne Bush, 'and there's a ready supply of theatre, cinema and music in the form of the MacRobert Arts Centre.'

The **MacRobert** is a multi-arts centre situated in the heart of campus, with a cinema, café bar restaurant, 468-seater auditorium, children's theatre, and arts crÉche. The complex also has rehearsal studio and gallery space. A mix of modern, arthouse and mainstream films are shown daily, and a mixed live programme in the main theatre. See www.macrobert.org.

Among non-sporting societies you can opt for anything from Chocolate Appreciation Society to Debating, Politics, or the award-winning media - *Brig* (the student newspaper), Air3 radio or Air TV - or, if you have 10 other people on board you can draw up a deal with the Union to found a society of your own.

WHAT IT'S REALLY LIKE	
UNIVERSITY:	
Social Life	★★★
Campus scene	**Small, friendly, beautiful scene**
Student Union services	**Average**
Politics	**Student issues**
Sport	**Very competitive, 37 clubs**
National team position	**24th**
Sport facilities	**Top notch**
Arts opportunities	**Excellent**
Student newspaper	**BRIG**
Student radio	**Air 3**
Student TV	**Air TV**
Nightclub	**The Nightclub**
Bars	**Studio, Nightclub, Long Bar**
Union ents	**Hip hop, cheese, retro**
Union societies	**40**
Parking	**Expensive permits**
CITY:	
Entertainment	★★
Scene	**Pubs, 3 clubs**
Town/gown relations	**Average**
Risk of violence	**Low**
Cost of living	**Low**
Student concessions	**Some**
Survival + 2 nights out	**£60**
Part-time work campus/town	**Fair**

Continues Suzanne: 'The student Musical Society works towards at least one big production every year. The University Choir brings together students and people from the community and puts on a big concert every December in Dunblane Cathedral. Politics is not a big issue until a big issue finds its way into this far-off campus, namely Car Parking! Some time ago the barriers went up and parking permits were required.'

SPORT Stirling has invested heavily in sport in recent years and has now been formally designated by the Scottish Government as Scotland's University for Sporting Excellence, not just in terms of high-performing students, but in research, education and sports science.

If you are interested in sport, Stirling is the place to be. The National Swimming Academy, with its 50 metre pool, is a designated Intensive Training Centre for the Olympics and Paralympics. It can be split into two and one of the 25 metre pools has a moveable floor, changing the water depth from 0 metres to 2 metres. There's a conditioning room next to the pool, as well as an Omega timing system and a full range of water polo fittings and equipment.

Next door, the National Tennis Centre recently expanded and has six indoor courts with more outside.

The **MP Jackson Fitness Centre** houses 3 sports science laboratories: athlete assessment laboratory, research laboratory, analytical laboratory, a fitness suite with 50+ pieces of cardiovascular and resistance equipment, and there's a strength and conditioning 'super centre' with 5 lifting platforms.

There are 23 acres of playing fields for football, rugby, athletics and hockey, with 2 all-weather pitches as well. In the sports hall are three squash courts, two basketball courts, and a loch for angling, sailing and canoeing. Finally, there's a Golf Centre with a short game practice area, three target greens and a nine-hole golf course. Jogging routes are situated around the campus.

They are sport mad up here, even the city of Stirling has just opened a sports village with swimming pool, curling and skating rink and ten-pin bowling.

PILLOW TALK

All freshers continue to be guaranteed university accommodation, though not necessarily on cam-

ACCOMMODATION	
Guarantee to freshers	**100%**
Style	**Halls, flats**
Security guard	**All**
Shared rooms	**None**
Internet access	**£15 extra**
Self-catered	**All**
En suite	**Some**
Approx price range pw	**£60-£88**
Town rent pw	**£65-£100**

pus. In Alexander Court there is self-catered, flat accommodation where kitchen and bathroom facilities are shared by 7 students. In Geddes Court and A K Davidson, the accommodation has communal bathroom facilities. In Andrew Stewart hall, the accommodation is en suite, and is probably the best for freshers. A K Davidson has also just been refurbished. Murray Hall is undergoing a refit, but will not be open until 2010-11. There are, in addition, university owned flats in town.

GETTING THERE

☛ By road: M9/J11, A9 or A91, A907, A9.
☛ By coach: London, 9:00; Edinburgh, 2:20.
☛ By rail: Glasgow/Edinburgh, 55 mins ;Aberdeen, 2:30; London King's Cross, 6:00.

UNIVERSITY OF STRATHCLYDE

The University of Strathclyde
Graham Hills Building
50 George Street
Glasgow G1 1XQ

TEL 0141 548 2814
FAX 0141 552 5860
EMAIL scls@mis.strath.ac.uk
WEB www.strath.ac.uk

Strathclyde Students' Association
90 John Street
Glasgow G1 1JH

TEL 0141 567 5000
FAX 0141 567 5050
EMAIL theunion@strath.ac.uk
WEB www.strathstudents.ac.uk

VAG VIEW

Strathclyde University's niche strengths are business and engineering. It had its beginnings in 1796 with Anderson's Institution, an equal-opportunity, science and technology college. John Anderson had been Professor of Natural Philosophy at Glasgow University and the institution that bore his name was founded under the terms of his will. University status came in 1964 following the merger of the Royal College of Science and the Scottish College of Commerce, which fact alerts us to Strathclyde's second largest faculty after Engineering, the Strathclyde Business School. In 1993, Glasgow's Jordanhill College joined the fold and became Strath's third largest faculty, Education.

CAMPUS

Today Strathclyde University occupies the same site as Anderson's Institution in the heart of Glasgow, just behind George Square and a walk

UNIVERSITY/STUDENT PROFILE	
University since	**1964**
Situation/style	**City campus**
Student population	**26000**
Total undergraduates	**16185**
Mature undergraduates	**—**
International undergrads	**8%**
Male/female ratio	**47:53**
Equality of opportunity:	
state school intake	**92%**
social class 4-7 intake	**27%**
low-participation area intake	**2%**

from either Central or Queen Street stations. The concentration of students in the immediate vicinity is extraordinary: Strathclyde and Caledonian universities, the College of Building and Printing, the College of Food & Technology, and the College of Commerce. The Jordanhill campus is in the west end of the city, close to Glasgow University. Jordanhill will close in 2010 and the Education Faculty move to a new building in the city centre.

FEES, BURSARIES

UK & EU Fees, 2009-10: Non-Scottish-based UK residents pay £1,820 p.a. for all courses at Scottish universities, except Medicine. For scholarships, see www.strath .ac.uk/scholarship.htm. There is a University Golf Programme and a Sports Bursary Programme. See www.strath.ac.uk/sport/sports-bursaries/bursaries/.

STUDENT PROFILE

Strathclyde is one of three unis in the city. 'Vibe wise, it has a more relaxed atmosphere in comparison with Glasgow University, which tends to have a more academic outlook,' said a student of Glasgow Uni. Peter Mann, a student at Strathclyde, suggested differences run deeper: 'Caledonian and Strathclyde have a similar kind of population.

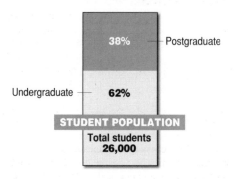

Glasgow is quite different and generally disliked because it is full of English people. There is not a tremendous amount of mixing.' A student of Caledonian offered this Pythonesque picture of the pecking order: 'Glasgow University looks down on Strathclyde as being John Street Poly, although it's been a university since 1964. And Strathclyde looks down on us as being the old Glasgow Technical College, the lowest of the low.'

There's a 92% state school population and a 27% take from non-traditional uni goers. Unlike Caledonian Strathclyde carries none of the poly cultural baggage, for it was the Royal College; Caledonian was the Poly. Nevertheless, a lot of the students are local. 'There's one guy in SUR [student radio],' said Peter, 'who's from Surrey, and he sticks out like a sore thumb.'

ACADEMIA & JOBS

It did well in the recent Government Research Assessments, coming 50th out of 132, its work at the coal face of knowledge apparently in Business, Engineering, Law and Science. Students say that the best teaching is to be had in Accounting, Forensic Science, Computer Science, European Languages (in particular French), Physical Sciences, Human & Social Geography, Business, English, Teacher Training, Pharmacology, Pharmacy, Politics, Finance, Maths, and Psychology. The worst teaching they said was in Biology, where only a few per cent more than half the class gave it time of day.

The single largest employment sector for Strathclyde graduates is primary teaching, which occupies around 9% of the total. Then come banking, social/community work of some sort, engineering design consultancy, specialist retail (pharmacy, etc), accountancy, the civil service, and higher education. Many go on to further training in the Law.

Key to the social and community work are degrees in such as Community Arts, Community Education, Outdoor Education in the Community, Social Work, Sport in the Community, but also Speech and Language Pathology, which may find its application in hospitals (for example with accident and stroke victims) and school, nurseries and special centres.

There is a fine academic reputation. Strathclyde's 92% Excellent and Highly Satisfactory rating in the teaching assessments actually puts it a nose ahead of Glasgow University. The key thing is the way they teach: audio-visual, video, visual materials, computer-assisted learning programmes are all to the fore. Very close links with industry and commerce ensure a real-world, highly practical emphasis.

They have a Learning Resources Base which, among other things, is there to help you in adjusting to study methods, curriculum design etc. Every student is assigned a personal tutor, and there's a built-in early-warning system to prevent any first year getting lost along the way.

The uni's Careers Service has received the National Charter Mark for excellence in customer service on more than one occasion.

Strathclyde graduates also find jobs as software engineers, and mechanical, process and production engineers, with jobs aplenty in manufacturing, as well as defence, telecommunications, etc - BEng Mechanical, Aero-Mechanical, Electrical & Mechanical, plus a series of MEng Mechanical with Aeronautics, Automotive, Biomedical or Material Engineering orientations, and one combo with Financial Management.

Mechanical Engineering is a major focus for Strathclyde.

The faculty has expanded in a collaboration with Glasgow Uni over Naval Architecture degrees. Besides the naval architecture degrees, there's the

RESEARCH EXCELLENCE

*% of Strathclyde's research that is
4* (World-class) or 3* (Internationally rated):*

	4*	3*
Health Professions	15%	45%
Pharmacy	15%	40%
Chemistry	10%	60%
Physics	5%	35%
Applied Mathematics	10%	40%
Statistics	10%	30%
Computer Science	15%	35%
Electrical/Electronic Eng.	15%	35%
General Engineering	15%	45%
Chemical Engineering	5%	35%
Civil Engineering	5%	35%
Mechanical Engineering	15%	35%
Naval Architecture & Marine Eng.	10%	45%
Built Environment	5%	35%
Business/Management	25%	40%
Law	20%	40%
Politics	0%	30%
Social Work	5%	35%
Sociology	0%	20%
Psychology	0%	30%
Education	5%	25%
European Studies	10%	10%
Italian	0%	20%
Iberian	0%	20%
English	15%	30%
History	5%	35%

traditional 4-year BSc Architectural Studies (with European Studies); also BEng Architectural Engineering.

Finally, there's a strong reputation for law - they are commercial & business and European law specialists, and have an LLB based on Scots Law too.

They are also leaders in forensic science. The Forensic Science Society (www.forensic-science-society.org.uk) take most of their members from Strathclyde and King's College London. Both offer MSc degrees in Forensic Science (KCL's is called Chemistry with Analytical Chemistry). The University of Strathclyde has MSc Forensic & Analytical Chemistry.

A new Centre for Forensic Science - the first of its kind in the UK - has built on the University's international reputation and provide a comprehensive range of educational, research and consultancy services to laboratories, police forces and other agencies.

SOCIAL SCENE

Strathclyde is Glaswegian not only because of the number of Glaswegians who attend, but in the very Glaswegian way students here go about having a good time. 'Their ents are marvelled at by other unions for their ability to bring in droves of students from rival unis, and give them just what they want – an excellent hangover for those on a budget!' reports Rachel Richardson. In fact, it is hard to assimilate the energy that is devoted to exciting pleasure in the students at Strathclyde. Whatever the legal capacity for the big night, it is not uncommon to find between 2,000 and 2,500 students here totally out of their heads. The legendary pleasure zone itself is 10 floors high, yet it is not the skyscraper you expect because in some extraordinary Alice-in-Wonderland fashion they have conspired to fit its ten floors, mezzanine-style, into the space of six or seven, leading this first-time visitor into utter confusion.

Last summer one of their bars was refurbished and rebranded into a Miller's sponsored bar. It's the ideal venue for small gigs, comedians and DJs, due to its intimate atmosphere. So, now the fun elements of the world-famous 10-floored Union are – Level 2: **Barony Bar** (main bar/club which is home to most of the regular nights); Level 3: **Gameszone** (Scotland's largest pool hall with 26 tables); Level 4: **The Scene** (eats); Level 5: **The Lounge** place to chill, relax; can consult support group Ask here too); Level 6: **The Priory** (relaxed café bar); Level 8: **Vertigo** (the larger gig space, where Girls Aloud, Fratellis, The View, and Vengaboys have played).

Ents include *12-hour Tuesdays*: 3pm-3am, all drinks 99p (**Barony**); *TFI Friday* is hosted by legendary, acerbic DJ Phil. This night has been running for 12 years and is the most successful student night in Glasgow. Cheap drinks and crazy antics, *TFI* is not for the faint hearted; Wednesday is touted as 'the only university gay night in Glasgow', every Wednesday comes with cocktails, and tunes from DJ Ricci.

Besides the live acts, guests DJs play here. Edith Bowman has graced the decks at Barony, and survived.

But it isn't all booze and sweat at Strath. There are 70 or more clubs and societies. Sport is excellent (see below) and media-wise they have a cracking set-up. 'It was a few years ago radio station SUR had its first restricted licence,' Peter Mann told me. 'It was funded from our *alumni* fund. Now we have more DJ talent than we could possibly use. We get DJs from all over, we don't restrict ourselves to students.' Now Strathclyde Fusion enables any student to get involved with all aspects of radio.

'Then we've got the *Strathclyde Telegraph*. There's a real professionalism around and that shows. There's no TV yet, but there will be. Basically, I started up Fusion and then took this sabbatical year to get it off the ground. TV will come later. I did a degree in marketing. I've learned the bits and pieces as I've gone along, electrocuted myself a few times. When I leave here I am going for a job connected with the Internet.'

You'd better believe it.

For drama, they have two theatres – the **Ramshorn** at John Anderson, the **Crawfurd** at Jordanhill; both offer courses in all aspects of theatre and there's plenty of opportunity, too, just to be involved in student productions. The Strathclyde Theatre Group puts on ten major productions a year. The **Collins Gallery**, also on campus, runs year-round exhibitions and workshops, and there's also a concert hall for the many musical productions. Choirs, bands, a symphony orchestra, ensembles, etc go to make up the Music Society, which presents weekly lunchtime recitals by visiting artists as well as by students in the National Trust for Scotland's **Hutchesons' Hall**.

See also Student Glasgow.

SPORT They came 44th in the national league last time. Successes: Rugby Men won British Unis' Plate; Football Men won British Unis' Vase. Badminton, Volleyball, Rugby, Hockey and Football all won their respective Scottish Leagues.

At John Anderson campus there are indoor facilities for basketball, netball, archery, volleyball, tennis, badminton, handball, martial arts, fencing, table tennis, gymnastics, circuit training, yoga, indoor training facilities for track & field, cricket, golf and hockey, a weight training & conditioning room, squash courts and swimming

WHAT IT'S REALLY LIKE

UNIVERSITY:	
Social Life	★★★★★
Campus scene	**City centre**
Student Union services	**Good**
Politics	**Student issues**
Sport	**38 clubs**
National team position	**44th**
Sport facilities	**Good**
Arts opportunities	**Drama, music, film, art good; dance poor**
Student newspaper	**Strathclyde Telegraph**
Student radio	**SUR**
Nightclub	**Vertigo**
Bars	**Barony, Darkroom, Lounge, Priory**
Union ents	**Club nights, cheese, live bands**
Union societies	**35-40**
Most active society	**SUPSA, SUDS**
Parking	**Poor/non-existent**
CITY:	
Entertainment	★★★★★
Scene	**Very cool**
Town/gown relations	**Good**
Risk of violence	**Average**
Cost of living	**Average**
Student concessions	**Poor**
Survival + 2 nights out	**£70 pw**
Part-time work campus/town	**Good/excellent**

ACCOMMODATION	
Guarantee to freshers	**100%**
Style	**Halls, flats**
Security guard	**All**
Shared rooms	**Some**
Internet access	**All**
Self-catered	**All**
En suite	**Some**
Approx price range pw	**£63-£85**
City rent pw	**£85-£110**

pool. Beyond campus there are grass pitches, artificial floodlit pitches, and a pavilion – team games include hockey, rugby, American football and soccer. Jordanhill has a similar range of indoor and outdoor facilities on campus. Proximity to river, sea and mountains enables a whole range of other sports – from mountaineering to sailing, from rowing to skiing. There are eight bursaries available for low handicap golfers from The Royal and Ancient.

PILLOW TALK
In the city, most uni accommodation is single or shared rooms in self-catering flats, some of it at a student village on JA campus, some of it a walk away. At Jordanhill it's on-campus, catered halls.

GETTING THERE
☛ By road: The John Anderson campus – M74, M8/J15 or A82, M8/J15 or M8/J15. Jordanhill – M74, M8/J19 or A82, M8/J19 or M8/J19.
☛ By rail: Edinburgh, 0:50; Newcastle, 2:30; Aberdeen, 2:45; Birmingham New Street, 5:30; London King's Cross, 6:00.
☛ By air: Glasgow Airport, 15-20 minutes' drive.
☛ By coach: Edinburgh, 1:10; London, 8:20; Birmingham, 6:20; Newcastle, 4:20.

UNIVERSITY OF SUNDERLAND

The University of Sunderland
Student Recruitment & Admissions
Edinburgh Building
Chester Road
Sunderland SR1 3SD

TEL: 0191 515 3154
FAX: 0191 515 3155
EMAIL: admissions@sunderland.ac.uk
WEB www.sunderland.ac.uk

Sunderland Students' Union
Wearmouth Hall
Chester Road
Sunderland SR1 3SD

TEL 0191 514 5512
FAX 0191 515 2441
EMAIL su.president@sunderland.ac.uk
WEB www.sunderlandsu.co.uk

VAG VIEW

Sunderland was an area robbed of its core industries a few decades ago, but has since been reborn and its uni with it. The poly became a university in 1992, the very year that Sunderland became a city. Since then they have been engaged in expansion.

Their niche areas are Media, Design, Law, Education, Business, Psychology, Pharmacy, Computing and Social Work.

This is a 'new university' student body. Undergraduates have a good time, 83% of them said in the National Student Survey that they were satisfied with what is on offer. But only 64% of them get real graduate jobs within six months of leaving. And the drop-out rate is nearly 13%, way above the Government benchmark.

CAMPUS SITES
The uni's Chester Road campus is in easy reach of the town centre and the newer, award-winning Tom Cowie Campus at St Peter's is but a stone's throw out at the mouth of the River Wear. They had been going to pull out of the city centre and bring everyone to St Peter's, but instead they built a multi-million pound 'Gateway' there, 'a one stop shop' for student services and information, and a Sports Science Centre with a range and quality of hi-tech equipment. Now they plan to develop it further, making provision for a 6-court sports hall, spectator gallery, fitness suite, catering and retail outlets, climbing wall, multi-purpose room, sports injuries service, and a large social space. They call the £12-million project City Space. Also at City is the Murray Library and the science complex, a modern range of laboratories for Science students.†

UNIVERSITY/STUDENT PROFILE

University since	**1992**
Situation/style	**Campus**
Student population	**20325**
Total undergraduates	**17020**
Mature undergraduates	**45%**
International undergrads	**10%**
Male/female ratio	**47:53**
Equality of opportunity:	
state school intake	**98%**
social class 4-7 intake	**48%**
low-participation area intake	**24%**

Tom Cowie at St Peter's fits unobtrusively into the landscape, as the ground falls away to the river. Wearmouth's iron bridge arches splendidly across the water like a young relation of Stephenson's famous iron bridge at nearby Newcastle; cranes complete the backdrop of the area's industrial past, against which the campus is heralded as an expression of the re-born character of the region. Jutting roofs and walkways on campus (a modern version of Oxbridge cloisters) keep students dry as they criss-cross University Square, to and from the Prospect Building. Rainwater plunges down huge chrome pipes from roofs topped with strange deckchair-shaped receivers, scanning the northern skies. Impressive, but the design never quite recovers from the creams and browns that make St Peter's look old before its time.

Business, Law and Psychology are here, as is the David Goldman Informatics Centre (Computing) and the David Putnam Media Centre, with studios, edit suites and a 200-seat cinema.

The uni is also associated with a £300-million film academy and studios at Seaham, a coastal town 10 minutes drive away. The plan is for a film studio complex, student campus, educational buildings, parkland, hotels and leisure facilities.

FEES, BURSARIES

UK & EU Fees, 2009-10: £3,225 p.a. For students in receipt of the HE Maintenance Grant, Sunderland's support package is £525 p.a. if you're earning less than £39,305 p.a. There is also a Success Scholarship, worth up to £965, and a scholarship of £525 p.a. for Foundation degree students. Finally, there is a £1,500 Bursary for Care Experienced Students.

STUDENT PROFILE

Sunderland are leaders in what is known as 'widening participation in higher education': 98% are from state schools, 48% are from the lower socio-economic orders, 24% from 'low-participation'

neighbourhoods, and 45% are mature students. International students are also attracted in increasing number.

ACADEMIA & JOBS

The University has four academic faculties: Applied Sciences; Arts, Design & Media; Education & Society; Business & Law. But when it comes to jobs, Education accounts for some 17% of graduate futures: 75% of school-teacher output is into secondary, which is the largest single graduate employment provision. The primary provision is also strong and there's a well-trod path into further education lecturing, particularly via the media and communications degrees and biological sciences, which scored full marks at the assessments.

Next most popular occupation is in pharmacy, which accounts for around 8% of graduates. There are foundation courses for both Chemical & Pharmaceutical Science and Pharmacology degrees. They do all in their power to wean you onto a course. The university has a strong Disability Support Team, offering a range of advice, including an outstanding learning support programme for dyslexic students.

Computing is another popular and successful employment pathway - AI, Business Computing, Forensic Computing, Intelligent Robotics, Network Computing and a strong Computer Studies presence on the joint honours scheme (a defining factor of the curriculum at Sunderland; most subjects figure). Graduates get jobs as IT consultants and software engineers in particular, as well as programmers and computer operators.

Graphic artists and designers also proliferate and a look into the art and design provision brings us unerringly to another defining aspect, the Glass,

TEACHING SURVEY AT A GLANCE

Avg. UCAS points accepted	**240**
Acceptance rate	**20%**
Overall satisfaction rate	**83%**
Helpful/interested staff	★★
Small tuition groups	★★
Students into graduate jobs	**64%**

Teaching most popular with undergraduates: English, Law (96%), History (95%), Psychology (92%), Initial Teacher Training, Languages, Media Studies (90%), subjects allied to Medicine, Pharmacology, Pharmacy, Pharmaceutical Sciences (86%).

Teaching least popular with undergraduates: Communications & Information Studies (67%), Computer Science (64%).

WHAT IT'S REALLY LIKE	
UNIVERSITY:	
Social Life	★★★
Campus scene	**Friendly, local**
Student Union services	**Good**
Politics	**Student issues**
	Activity low
Sport	**32 clubs.**
National sporting position	**92nd**
Sport facilities	**Improving**
Arts opportunities	**Film good; rest**
	'average'
Student magazine	**Degrees North**
Student radio	**Utopia fm**
New Student TV	**Sunderland TV**
2008 National Awards	**Winner TV Doc.**
Nightclub	**Campus**
Bars	**Wearmouth,**
	Bonded
Union ents	**Volume, Live**
Union societies	**51**
Parking	**Adequate**
CITY	
Entertainment	★★★
Scene	**Cheap fun**
Town/gown relations	**Poor**
Risk of violence	**Average**
Cost of living	**Low**
Student concessions	**Average**
Survival + 2 nights out	**£65 pw**
Part-time work campus/town	**Excellent**

with snooker table and big screen. Initial custom was 'a slow but steady stream,' then they started a series of comedy nights, which won them a decent audience. Now, with the halls up the road it is never quiet.

The main nightspot remains Campus, however. The club incorporates **Roker Bar** and operates as a daytime watering hole, food bar, pool and games room. For footie nights et al it boasts 'the biggest screen in Sunderland'. With no residents in the near neighbourhood the 3 am chuck-out time on Mondays, Tuesdays and Thursdays causes no grief. The club is cool, with good size stage, balcony and bar. It's a major town venue and they sort it so that whatever's on at Campus is not duplicated elsewhere.

Tuesday is Rock Night; Wednesday, *Juicy*; Friday, *Route 69* (dance and r&b); Saturday, *Volume indie* or *Bands Night*. Recent acts include Dead 60's, Arctic Monkeys, Golden Virgins, The Stranglers, The Subways. There's a Sunday Quiz in Wearmouth Bar, and a Karaoke Night on Friday in Bonded.

Besides all this, throughout the year, poets and musicians (roots, jazz, classical) perform on campus.

The Royal Shakespeare Company, Northern Playwrights and Ballet Rambert have done workshops with the drama and dance elements of the Faculty of Arts, Design & Communication. Also on campus is the uni's Screen on the River, based in the 400-seater Tom Cowie Theatre, a focus for weekend film festivals, and sister cinema to Newcastle's little Tyneside Cinema, renowned for its arthouse fare.

There are 19 societies and as many as 32 sports clubs, the most popular being Football, Netball, Rugby and CCSA. The student radio station has won awards in its time, and a new TV station took Best Documentary at the 2008 *Guardian* Media Awards. The magazine is *Degrees North.*

Architectural Glass & Ceramics degree. But see also the more modern dimension: the Photography, Video & Digital Imaging degree and those in Animation and Advertising & Design.

Business is always quoted as a big strength at Sunderland, and around 16% of students do leave with a business degree. There's Business & Administration/Human resource Mgt/Marketing/Enterprise/etc There's a Law degree with Business Studies, and indeed Sunderland are commercial and business law specialists.

On another tack, there is, too, a very strong showing in welfare and community care, and in nursing, where they dropped only one point at the assessments.

SOCIAL SCENE

STUDENTS' UNION The main student haunts are the **Wearmouth Bar** at City Campus, **Campus** nightclub at St Peter's and **Bonded**, a bar across the river from St Peter's at Panns Bank.

An early 19th-century marine store and smithy, Bonded has a shop and bar downstairs and right across the first floor is this large, beamed bar

SPORT Sports Centre has a 2-storey fitness and cardiovascular suite, a 25-metre swimming pool with canoeing facilities, and a sports hall for badminton, football and basketball.

Otherwise it's the city, which 'has a number of fitness clubs and sports centres – the Puma Tennis Centre, Nissan Sports Centre (brilliant football and basketball pitches), and Silksworth Sports Complex, with dry slope ski centre.

TOWN Masses of pubs around Chester Road and city clubs keep students happy. Cost of living is low. Every university wants to play down hassle in town, but Sunderland cannot be classed as the safest of the cities we visit, though uni properties seem to be well protected.

ACCOMMODATION

Guarantee to freshers	**100%**
Style	**Flats**
Security guard	**All**
Shared rooms	**Some**
Internet access	**All**
Self-catered	**All**
En suite	**Some**
Approx price range pw	**£37.31-£69.12**
City rent pw	**£40**

PILLOW TALK

They guarantee all first-years accommodation, whether or not you apply through Clearing. There are self-contained flats, a small number of family houses, and flats in halls. A Domestic Services Manager and a team of domestic staff manage the halls, all of which have 24-hour security. A team of resident tutors is on call during the evenings, throughout the night and at weekends to offer advice and support. 80% of the accommodation is designed and built post 1994. They also manage a range of private properties throughout the city, available to let. Halls are situated on both sides of the river, with the newest, Panns Bank and Scotia Quay, being close to the Bonded Warehouse.

GETTING THERE

☛ By road: A1(M), A690 or A19, A690.
☛ By rail: Newcastle, 0:25; Leeds, 2:15; Edinburgh, 2:30, Manchester, 3:30, London King's Cross, 3:45.
☛ By air: Newcastle International Airport.
☛ By coach: London, 6:20; Bristol, 6:25.

UNIVERSITY OF SURREY

The University of Surrey
Guildford GU2 7XH

TEL 01483 689305
FAX 01483 689388
EMAIL admissions@surrey.ac.uk
WEB www.surrey.ac.uk

Surrey Students' Union
Guildford GU2 7XH

TEL 01483 689223
FAX 01483 534749
EMAIL ussu.president@surrey.ac.uk
WEB www.ussu.co.uk

VAG VIEW

*T*he University of Surrey has roots in Battersea Poly. Its rise is a triumph of the career orientation of its courses and its very good teaching. It is many students' first choice.

In 2006 the Times Higher Education Student Experience Survey revealed at least one of its secrets, namely a body of lecturers who have the students' interests at heart, at least as much as they do their research work.

Since receiving a Royal Charter in 1966, Surrey has gone its own way, done its own thing, making the business of higher education seem almost clinically straightforward. Most recently, in the past two years, it has seen a 55% increase in applications, a reflection partly on its expansion in such as English, Accounting and Financial Management, Film, and Criminology.

UNIVERSITY/STUDENT PROFILE

University since	**1966**
Situation/style	**Campus**
Student population	**15705**
Total undergraduates	**9600**
Mature undergraduates	**11%**
International undergrads	**22%**
Male/female ratio	**49:51**
Equality of opportunity:	
state school intake	**91%**
social class 4-7 intake	**22%**
low-participation area intake	**6%**

In the Higher Education Funding Council's National Student Survey, 83% of Surrey's students applauded what they do, which with perfect symmetry is also the percentage of graduates who will get real graduate jobs within six months of leaving. The drop-out rate is less than 5%, well below their Government benchmark.

CAMPUS

Surrey's self-contained, concrete, in-fill, landscaped campus lies just off the A3 in the ancient city of Guildford, adjacent to the cathedral, 15 minutes walk from the city centre. writes Madeleine Merchant: 'The campus contains most first-year residences, all the teaching buildings, lecture theatres, library, computer labs, a sports centre, a shop, a health centre, a counselling service, a post office, a Nat West bank, many cafés, restaurants, and bars, the Students' Union building, picnic areas and a lake. It is in an attractive setting with many trees and shrubs, on a hill in the shadow of Guildford Cathedral. Many students complain of being woken up on Sunday mornings by the cathedral bells! A train line runs around a third of the perimeter, and the trains can also be heard in some of the residences.'

Much of the area is covered by CCTV cameras, and it is generally well-lit and perfectly safe, but three years ago, the Student Council debated whether more cameras should be put in for greater safety in off-campus paths nearby, which were deemed not so safe, even if the cameras might overlook some student residences. The Students' Union reported that the university had assumed responsibility of up-keep and maintenance from the council for some of these paths, and improved safety.

FEES, BURSARIES

UK & EU Fees, 2009-10: £3,225 p.a. If in receipt of the HE Maintenance grant there's a sliding scale according to household earnings. There are also academic scholarships and awards for sport.

STUDENT PROFILE

'The University of Surrey may be a depressing collection of ugly concrete monstrosities,' writes Alistair Gerard, 'but it's not the buildings that make a university, it's the people, and I wouldn't have chosen to be anywhere else. Campus is a cosmopolitan enclave in the whole middle-class Caucasian experiment that is Guildford. Besides the obvious lean towards science and engineering bods at Surrey, around a fifth of undergraduates are from overseas, nearly a quarter are mature students, and the state/independent ratio is well balanced. Students are saved from the male dominance that can affect science unis by the nursing provision and Human Studies. Everyone is happy.'

ACADEMIA & JOBS

Characteristically, Surrey graduates get jobs for which they have been educated - they enter employment not only at graduate level but in occupations directly related to their degrees. This is not typical through the length and breadth of the nation.

'In the third year, most students work for companies in placements, and earn lots of money,' Madeleine reports, 'and from what I've heard, most of these come back in the fourth year with clear ideas about whether they really want to continue working in that field, and many have definite job offers for when they graduate.'

Surrey leads the nation in producing computer programmers. See BSc Computer Modelling & Simulation and various alternative applications - Engineering, Communications, Info Technology. All are 4-5 years, depending on whether you take one of these professional years out, after which you are eligible to Associate Membership of the Uni. Look, too, at their BEng Electronics & Computer Eng, and the BSc/MPhys Physics with Computer Modelling.

Most students at Surrey graduate in business

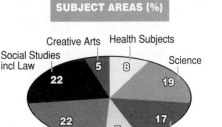

SUBJECT AREAS (%)

Creative Arts 5 — Health Subjects 8 — Science 19 — Engineering 17 — Maths & Computer 7 — Business 22 — Social Studies incl Law 22

and engineering subjects, and the manufacturing industry benefits by taking around a fifth of all those graduating from the uni.

Computer Science, Engineering and Business are the main routes into electrical and electronic manufacturing, with the occasional input from Surrey's sound recording courses. For electronic and aspiring telecommunications engineers, you're talking a world class (Grade 6*) department, with dedicated 4-5-year degrees like B/MEng Telecommunication Systems.

Aspiring sound recordists and technicians take note, there's also the 4-year BMus Music & Sound Recording (Tonmeister) for the performance spin. Teaching inspection 23 out of 24.

Civil engineers are the next most in demand in the engineering sector. They mix with Computing in the 3/4/5-year B/MEng programmes, or you can of course take the single hons. Again, there's an Associateship of the University in the offing.

Then there's mechanical, process & production, electronic and software engineers, all well serviced with dedicated degrees and interesting combo options relevant to these job sectors.

Note also the B/MEng Space Technology & Planetary Exploration degrees, remembering that both Physics and engineering achieved near full marks in the assessments.

WHAT IT'S REALLY LIKE

UNIVERSITY:	
Social Life	★★★★
Campus scene	**Efficient, techy**
Student Union services	**Good**
Politics	**Low interest**
Sport	**45 clubs**
National team position	**80th**
Sport facilities	**Good**
Arts opportunities	**Dance, music OK**
Student newspaper	**Barefacts**
Student radio	**GU2**
2008 Radio Awards	**Bronze**
Nightclub	**Rubix**
Bars	**Chancellors + 4**
Union ents	**Cheese, r&b, dance**
Union societies	**120**
Parking	**Non-existent**
TOWN:	
Entertainment	★★
Scene	**Rich man's clubs/pubs**
Town/gown relations	**OK-good**
Risk of violence	**Low**
Cost of living	**Very high**
Student concessions	**Good**
Survival + 2 nights out	**£70+ pw**
Part-time work campus/town	**Excellent/good**

RESEARCH EXCELLENCE

% of Surrey's research that is
4* *(World-class)* or **3*** *(Internationally rated):*

	4*	3*
Health Services	**0%**	**5%**
Health Professions	**20%**	**40%**
Physics	**10%**	**45%**
Applied Mathematics	**15%**	**55%**
Computer Science	**10%**	**40%**
Electrical/Electronic Eng.	**30%**	**40%**
General Engineering	**15%**	**60%**
Economics	**15%**	**50%**
Business/Management	**10%**	**40%**
Sociology	**30%**	**25%**
Psychology	**10%**	**30%**
European Studies	**5%**	**25%**
Performing Arts	**20%**	**40%**
Music	**15%**	**60%**

The health provision is next most productive, and is served by the European Institute of Health & Medical Sciences (Nursing, Midwifery, etc. A degree in Veterinary Biosciences is currently up for validation.In the business sector the Retail Management degree is singly the most productive

at point of employment, and the International Hospitality degrees lead unerringly to careers in the field of hotel management. Throughout the faculty, sales managers, marketing managers and management consultants are produced in quantity.

Graduates of Financial Mathematics and Business Economics degrees find their way, in number, into accountancy, and economists also proliferate.

A new Learning Resource Centre will be started this year and is due for completion in 2011.

SOCIAL SCENE

STUDENTS' UNION Chancellors bar, one of 5, can be found under Union House and opens as restaurant from 8.30am, transforming itself into a venue in the evening for Cocktail Nights, Chancellors Comedy, Pre *Citrus* and *Flirt* Drinks, Open Mic Night and Live Sky Footy on Saturdays. Nightclub is **Rubix**, with a capacity of 1600. Regular ents are *Flirt!* with Duncan Wilson – 'the cult of chav is with us, homage to world of Burberry, Elizabeth Duke & the Citroen Saxo' – and *Citrus* with Leroy Wilson. Then there are sell-out specials, which go under the name of *UNIFIED*, with such as 'Nicholas from X Factor, Master Stepz, Da Jump Off Ent, to mention a few', across 2 rooms.

Music and dance departments evolve their own series of concerts and the uni choir, orchestra, chamber orchestra and student Drama Society regularly perform.

There's a special relationship with nearby **Guildford School of Acting**. The uni validates its degrees in Acting and Stage Management. And an award-winning student radio station, GU2 (it took a Bronze award in the *Guardian* Media Awards in 2008), and newspaper *Barefacts*. There is also a film unit and many other societies in a Student Activities Centre, cultural, religious, political, course/interest-based. Lesbian/Gay is active, but generally, due to student apathy in this direction, political activity is low.

SPORT The Campusport Centre is the sports hall. The Varsity Centre is for field, squash and tennis, and pitches. Guildford's Spectrum Leisure Centre, home to ice hockey team, the Guildford Flames, provides facilities for swimming, ice skating and athletics, and the uni provides a bus linking Spectrum with other pick-ups in the city and the uni campus. Uni teams came 80th nationally last year. They had a world-class trampolinist apparently, and the gymnastic team was sent to the world championships in China, but that's about it. Sports bursaries are available. They need you.

Writes Madeleine: 'There are many clubs, both competitive - e.g. hockey, waterpolo - and non-competitive: mountain climbing, hiking, etc. Everyone gets Wednesday afternoons free of lectures as these are set aside for BUSA matches. If you aren't interested in sports, the university offers free language courses. As in sport, all levels are catered for.'

TOWN Writes Alistair. 'London is only 35 minutes away by train. Ergo, Guildford is very expensive. With the introduction of tuition fees, this must now be a consideration. There are sociological implications, too. It's a notoriously blue pocket of middle-class conservatism. Guildford shuts at 11 pm, with the exception of its nightclubs, where prices reflect this. The people who live in Guildford have done their partying; they have moved to a gilt-edged

ACCOMMODATION	
Guarantee to freshers	**100%**
Style	**Halls, flats**
Security guard	**All halls, most flats**
Shared rooms	**Some halls**
Internet access	**All**
Self-catered	**All**
En suite	**Some halls, most flats**
Approx price range pw	**£60-£104**
Town rent pw	**£75-£90**

ghetto to live in peace and tranquillity.'

Writes Madeleine: 'There is a mixture of the usual high street shops with student discounts, and the more expensive variety such as French Connection, Gap, House of Fraser etc, two theatres and a large Odeon, two or three nightclubs and many pubs and bars.

'For temporary ways to earn money, Guildford shops and businesses usually have positions available, and the university runs a Job Shop. The Union also employs many casual staff. Student nurses supplement their income by working at the local hospital as "bank" health care assistants, and for agencies.'

PILLOW TALK

Accommodation is in flats arranged in residential courts on campus. Many are en-suite. All freshers are guaranteed accommodation in these. None is catered, all have access to the internet. To keep pace with the uni's dramatic expansion, new fresher accommodation is to be made available this year and in September 2010, 568 rooms and 260 rooms respectively. Rent in town is anything from £75.00.

GETTING THERE
- ☛ Surrey Uni by road: A3, signs to University.
- ☛ By coach: London, 1:00; Birmingham, 4:30.
- ☛ By rail: London Waterloo, 30 mins.
- ☛ By air: Gatwick and Heathrow.

UNIVERSITY OF SUSSEX

University of Sussex
Brighton BN1 9RH

TEL 01273 678416
FAX 01273 678545
EMAIL ug.admissions@sussex.ac.uk
WEB www.sussex.ac.uk

Sussex Students' Union
Brighton BN1 9QF

TEL 01273 678555
FAX 01273 678875
EMAIL info@ussu.sussex.ac.uk
WEB www.ussu.co.uk

VAG VIEW

Sussex University first admitted students in October 1961. In its first decade or more it was the place to be - home of '60s radicalism, fighter of causes. Then all went quiet. Financial problems and a mouldering of relations between the uni and its students meant that 'any triumphs occurred despite rather than because of the powers that be,' as a student put it, endorsement to student satisfaction.

Recently they came back on top, but then in 2008 the university registered one of the worst drops (around 30%) in applications of any higher education institution. It is difficult to see why. In the Government's Research Assessment in 2008 it did very well, especially in subjects like History of Art, Media, Computer Science, American Studies, Music and Media. In the National Student Survey, 86% of its students said they were satisfied, and Sussex lecturers came out well as interested, helpful teachers. There is a good graduate job rate of 75% after six months, and the drop-out rate is a mere 5%. Even when the Student Union got a clobbering in the Times Higher Education magazine's Student Experience Survey, they were promptly runners-up for SU Campaign of the Year. Sussex is a close, community campus, with an unusually vigorous extra-curricular scene, and a great social life. We recommend you be there for its 50th anniversary celebrations in 2011.

CAMPUS

The Sussex campus is an 18th-century park desig-

nated as an area of outstanding beauty, on the Downs, 5 miles above Brighton. As at UEA, so here: 'At times being on campus can feel a bit isolated and claustrophobic,' writes Keren Rosen, 'but it is fifteen minutes to Brighton by bus and you are never more than ten minutes walk from the fields of the South Downs. Escape is always possible.'

FEES, BURSARIES

UK & EU Fees, 2009-10: £3,225 p.a. If in receipt of full HE Maintenance grant there's a bursary. And academic and sporting scholarships are available, as well as bursaries for applicants living in certain postcodes, and for ethnic minorities. Check out the details at www.sussex.ac.uk/scholarships_and_bursaries.

STUDENT PROFILE

'Owing to its strong international links, roughly a third of the student population comes from foreign parts and although the rest tend to come from London and the south of England, in general there is quite a nice mix of backgrounds,' observes Keren. 'There is also a large number of mature students studying at Sussex and although socially it is quite divided they definitely add a different perspective to study.'

ACADEMIA & JOBS

Sussex get the feedback from employers that they like the fact that their students are taught in seminars and are used to getting up and giving presentations and are articulate and confident, that they think on their feet, are analytical.

Two-thirds of Sussex students graduate in social studies, languages, humanities and biological sciences. More than a third enter the professions: health, education, finance and business management. There are also strong pockets of jobs in computing, media, publishing, drama and music, and there is something about this liberal, free-thinking campus that favours the generation

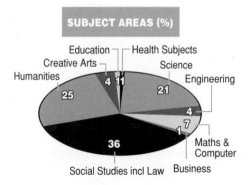

SUBJECT AREAS (%)

Education — Health Subjects
Creative Arts — Science
Humanities — Engineering
4 11 21
25
4
1 7
36
Maths & Computer
Social Studies incl Law   Business

and development of artistic ideas. They produce writers, and Sussex's student media is very active - newspaper Badger, magazine Pulse, radio station URF win awards frquently, most recently a Bronze in the 2008 Radio Awards. They act hurt when you point out that their courses are not all vocational. 'We have an Innovation Centre, where a number of outfits are student-started. It is an incubation centre rather than a money-making business park.'

Sussex constantly reassesses the curriculum, always has done. Right now it is restructuring its academic units for 2010, creating 12 specialist schools of studies, which will improve students' access to support. The newly created School of Business, Management and Economics will offer a new portfolio of undergraduate and postgraduate business and management programmes.

Computing was shown to be one of its great strengths in the Research Assessment of 2008: 20% of its work was ajudged world-class and 50% internationally excellent. Software engineers, IT Consultants and computer programmers come out

TEACHING SURVEY AT A GLANCE

Avg. UCAS points accepted	**380**
Acceptance rate	**15%**
Overall satisfaction rate	**86%**
Helpful/interested staff	★★★★
Small tuition groups	★★★
Students into graduate jobs	**76%**

Teaching most popular with undergraduates:
Physical Science (100%), Molecular Biology, Biochemistry (98%), Sciences related to Biology (95%), Biology, Social Work (94%), Economics, Law (93%), Medicine (92%), Politics (91%), Human & Social Geography, European Languages, Sociology (90%),

Teaching least popular with undergraduates:
Performing Arts (71%).

RESEARCH EXCELLENCE

% of Sussex's research that is
4* *(World-class)* or **3*** *(Internationally rated):*

	4*	3*
Hospital Clinical	**5%**	**30%**
Biological Sciences	**5%**	**30%**
Human Biol. Sciences	**20%**	**35%**
Chemistry	**10%**	**40%**
Physics	**15%**	**45%**
Applied Mathematics	**10%**	**40%**
Computer Science	**20%**	**50%**
General Engineering	**10%**	**50%**
Environmental Studies	**15%**	**50%**
Economics	**10%**	**50%**
Law	**5%**	**50%**
Policy Research	**20%**	**30%**
International Relations	**15%**	**40%**
Social Work	**15%**	**45%**
Sociology	**25%**	**30%**
Anthropology	**25%**	**30%**
Psychology	**15%**	**45%**
Education	**20%**	**35%**
American Studiess	**30%**	**30%**
European Studies	**15%**	**45%**
English	**20%**	**35%**
Linguistics	**0%**	**30%**
Philosophy	**10%**	**50%**
History	**25%**	**40%**
History of Art	**45%**	**25%**
Culture and Media	**15%**	**60%**
Music	**20%**	**45%**

of a fine range of degrees, including Computer Systems Engineering, AI, Robotics, Cybernetics & Process Automation, etc.

For biosciences they have a similarly fine track record for degrees and jobs. The BSc Psychology (with American Studies, Cognitive Science or Neuroscience) looks particularly attractive.

Now that the Brighton & Sussex Medical School has lift-off the 5-year BMBS is no different from the rest of the Sussex provision: they are looking for personal qualities, commitment, compassion in their applicants. Chemistry and Biology is required at AS and at least one of these at GCE A level. Conditional offers of 340 UCAS tariff points are made from three A levels, if both Chemistry and Biology are among them. If Chemistry or Biology is only taken to AS level, grade B additionally is required. The UK Clinical Aptitude (UKCAT) test is also required.

In Social Studies, Humanities and Languages they have done especially well in the teaching assessments: Philosophy and Sociology scored full marks, and Politics and American Studies 23 points out of 24; Linguistics and French 21. Their strategy here is to provide subject combinations that are more than the sum of their parts. The curriculum is indeed planned with flair.

The civil service is one significant employment destination for Sussex Law graduates and others in Social, Economic & Political Studies, Languages and Biological sciences, and there's a significant flow from these areas of the curriculum into adult education, too, and as one would expect, into social work and counselling.

What is interesting is that graduates entering the niche employment areas at which Sussex excel, such as publishing, radio/TV, journalism, come not

WHAT IT'S REALLY LIKE	
UNIVERSITY:	
Social Life	★★★★
Campus scene	**A freshers-only holiday camp**
Student Union services	**Average**
Politics	**Aware**
Sport	**Lightweight**
National team position	**66th**
Sport facilities	**Good**
Arts opportunities	**Drama, film excellent; dance, art, music good**
Student newspaper	**Badger**
Student magazine	**Pulse**
Student radio	**URF**
Nightclub	**The Hot House**
Bars	**Falmer Bar, Grape Vine, East Slope, Park Village**
Union ents	**Cheese**
Union societies	**200**
Parking	**Poor**
CITY:	
Entertainment	★★★★★
Scene	**Exceptional**
Town/gown relations	**OK**
Risk of violence	**Low**
Cost of living	**High**
Student concessions	**Good**
Survival + 2 nights out	**£80 pw**
Part-time work campus/town	**Average**

from departments dedicated to turning out media types - Media Studies and the like - but from across the scholastic board, out of a combination of application encouraged through the cross-faculty curriculum, and their own extra-curricular interest, which is exactly what you want from a university.

Sussex is a small university, but it has more extra-curricular clubs and societies (200) than many much larger. There is a vigorous student culture, and employers like to pick the fruits of that.

STUDENT SCENE

STUDENTS' UNION The focus is East Slope Bar: 'Live music, football, barbeques, but above all a great place to meet friends any night of the week,' says Tom Harle, 'and a great place to watch out for your next bus into town if the weather's not so good. Then there's Park Village Lounge: sea, sun, sand, well no, but a huge range of well-priced cocktails, wines and beers and a great place for a quiet evening chill-out. Get a free cocktail if it's your birthday! Falmer Bar is the place for a lunch time coffee, or your usual tipple on the way home, a

(veggie) burger or nachos to share. Meanwhile, The Hothouse is packed out every weekend, a great place to hide from over-priced central Brighton clubs.'

Every Friday at the Hothouse is EASY: hip-hop, r&b, garage, urban, 10pm till 2am, £3 entry. Saturday is YOOF CLUB: all the songs you love to hear', also till 2am.

What of student politics in the midst of all this middle-class reverie? I ask. Isn't Sussex all yesterday's '60s-student glory? Apparently not. 'Politics are as important today as they were in the late '60s.' Student politics at Sussex is 'doing the right thing', removing Coca-Cola from all Union outlets, presenting a motion of no-confidence in the University Council, campaigning on housing issues for first year students, campaigning about the Falmer (football) stadium project, on widening participation, encouraging a wider social mix among Sussex's privileged student clientele.

Student media is great: The Pulse (magazine), The Badger (newspaper) and URF, University Radio Falmer, which took a Bronze in the National Student Awards in 2008.

SPORT It's sport-for-all at Sussex, not too keenly competitive, yet they came 51st in the national team ratings last year. There are two large sports halls, a fitness room with multi-gym and training facilities, four glass-backed squash courts, sauna, solarium, café and bar. Elsewhere on campus are

ACCOMMODATION	
Guarantee to freshers	**100%**
Style	**Halls, flats**
Security guard	**All**
Shared rooms	**Some**
Internet access	**All**
Self-catered	**All**
En suite	**Some**
Approx price range pw	**£70-£108**
City rent pw	**£85**

the pitches, tennis courts, and five more squash courts.

TOWN "The town centre is small enough to be covered in its entirety on foot, but it manages to squeeze in a huge amount of clubs, pubs, bars and shops to suit every taste,' writes Keren. 'The theatre and art scene has a real emphasis on individuality. As the gay capital of England, Brighton has a laid back, party atmosphere and students and locals live in peaceful harmony. Brightonians do have a tendency to be a little self-consciously cool, verging at times on the pretentious, but it is possible to avoid that world completely if its not your thing.'

See Student Brighton for more.

PILLOW TALK
The majority of first years get housed on campus, but get in quick or you may have to share. It works on a first come, first served basis. Standard of accommodation is pretty high, all self-catering and varies between flats and rooms on corridors. In particular, check out 250 en-suite rooms in newly-

built Swanborough residence (self-contained flats in the centre of campus), and 463 en-suite rooms, plus 11 studio flats, in newly-built Stanmer Court, also on campus.

GETTING THERE
☛ By road: M23, A23, A27.
☛ By coach: London, 1:50.
☛ By rail: London Bridge/Victoria, 1:10; Portsmouth, 1:30; Birmingham New Street, 3:45; Leeds, 4:15; Manchester Piccadilly, 5:00.
☛ By air: Gatwick and Heathrow Airports.

UNIVERSITY OF WALES, SWANSEA

University of Wales, Swansea
Swansea SA2 8PP

TEL 01792 295111
FAX 01792 295110
EMAIL admissions@swansea.ac.uk
WEB www.swansea.ac.uk

Swansea Students' Union
Swansea SA2 8PP

TEL 01792 295466
FAX 01792 206029
EMAIL president@swansea-union.co.uk
WEB www.swansea-union.co.uk

VAG VIEW

If Swansea isn't a university that you would immediately consider, despite the evidence of the teaching assessments that the academic provision is excellent, do yourself a favour, go and see it - submit to the evidence of your senses.

'You can come here and never leave it,' a student said to us when first we asked. 'It's a bit like a black hole', a place of exquisite beauty and distinctly laid-back vibes.

CAMPUS
Singleton Campus is set in a glorious position with wide open Swansea Bay stretched out in front and parkland behind, just a couple of miles west of the town. Further west along the coast you come to the old fishing village of Mumbles (birthplace of Catherine Zeta Jones), its pubs, fish & chip and Indian restaurants a favourite trawl for students, and the Gower Peninsula, described by Dylan Thomas as 'one of the loveliest sea-coast stretches in the whole of Britain.' On a sunny day I didn't disagree, nor do Swansea's surfer dudes. 'It's all so easy, see; everything's in walking distance,' the same student opined. 'Students come to Swansea for that alone.' He was pointing at the surf.

Writes Maxine French: 'The Gower is a stretch of coastline incorporating bays such as Caswell, Port Eynon and Langland, the last a favourite spot

UNIVERSITY/STUDENT PROFILE	
University since	**1920**
Situation/style	**Campus**
Student population	**15525**
Total undergraduates	**11370**
Mature undergraduates	**16%**
International undergrads	**6%**
Male/female ratio	**45:55**
Equality of opportunity:	
state school intake	**93%**
social class 4-7 intake	**29%**
low-participation area intake	**10%**

for surfers and host recently to the Welsh leg of some mad, never-ending surf competition. During the summer term its almost compulsory to go to Caswell when the Geography Society holds its annual beach party. For those whose lives are not ruled by tide tables, the coast means the Mumbles, renowned for the "Mile", strictly non-athletic, a pub crawl to end all pub crawls, something Dylan Thomas might have liked too.'

He did. In 'Who Do You Wish Was With Us?' he wrote - 'Why don't we live here always? Always and always. Build a bloody house and live like bloody kings!'

The university is exploring options to expand onto a new site within the region in order to accommodate further increases in staff and students, and to relieve pressure on the Singleton Campus.

FEES, BURSARIES

UK & EU Fees, 2009-10: £3,225 p.a. Welsh students get the £1,940 fee grant from the Welsh Assembly Government. Swansea gives no bursary for students from outside Wales in receipt of a HE Maintenance Grant. There are sporting scholarships of course, which are now worth £1,000 p.a., and they also offer Excellence Bursaries to UK/EU undergraduate applicants who achieve 3 A grades at A-Levelor equivalent. Each is worth £3,000 over two years.

STUDENT PROFILE

Swansea was rated as one of the government's favoured 'elite access' universities, but now their figures of 29% intake from social classes new to the idea of uni, and 10% from 'low participation' neighbourhoods, are less than unique. The high mature-student intake (16%) is less than usual, and recently Swansea received an award for the 'Best Mosque Provision' from the Federation of Islamic Student Societies, but the real point is that campus is a very friendly sort of place. People are chatty, the scene a good deal less pressured than is the norm. 'There's a fantastic, multi-cultural community feeling at Swansea,' said one student.

ACADEMIA & JOBS

Academia is structured into 10 schools, Arts, Business & Economics, Engineering, Technology, Environment & Society, Health Science, Human Sciences, Humanities, Law, Medicine, and Physical Sciences.

Entry requirements are not overly taxing, and because Swansea is thought of as a bit off the beaten track the emphasis is more how on earth you'll ever get out. 'Once they are here, people do well,' a student said, adding rather languidly as he nursed a Sunday morning hangover, 'but I guess it comes down to nothing else to do but work.' It does strike one that it would be an easy place to settle, and not simply for the duration of a 3-year degree course.

Do not underestimate their expertise. Swansea's two great scores at the Government's Research Assessment (2008) were for Civil Engineering and Computer Science, the first adjudged 35% world-class and 60% internationally excellent, the second 25% and 45% respectively. Students say that the best teaching is in neither of these, but in English, Sports Science, Law, Human & Social Geography, Physical Geography & Environmental Science, Economics, French and other Languages, American Studies, History, and Philosophy. They praised the lecturers for their helpful and interested approach in the Tims Higher survey in particular.

Engineering is an enduring strength in the graduate employment market, civil engineers in particular. Also, Computing is highly productive of software engineers and programmers, and there's a fast track into telecommunications and defence from both Computing and Electrical/Electronic Engineering, with almost as many mechanical and chemical engineers following in their wake.

Languages (Celtic Studies included) are another important element, and every area of the curriculum benefits from them. They find their way in number into government administration, as do many from Social Studies, and social work, community and counselling activities are a strong draw for both these sorts of graduates, and graduates from Biological Sciences (both Sports Science and Psychology & Law (BSc) being helpful in their different ways). Aspiring social workers and counsellors should look at the BSc Social Work, another triumph in the Research Assessment: 10% world-class, 50% internationally excellent. In sport, extra-curricular interest is enormous, and employment stats for Sports Science graduates are good. There is both an HND and BSc Sports Science. See Sport below. Education also claims a large number of biological scientists, and Languages and Social Studies graduates from Swansea.

More definitive is Swansea's focus on Medicine and Health Sciences. Hospitals now claim the lion's share of Swansea's graduates, the Nursing degrees, Clinical Physiology, Audiology, Midwifery, all contributing strongly to the overall graduate employment record. Now Swansea has launched its own MBBCH/Med degree - graduate entry only, a fast-

WHAT IT'S REALLY LIKE

UNIVERSITY:

Social Life	★★★★
Campus scene	**Laid-back surfers**
Student Union services	**Good**
Politics	**NUS and national issues**
Sport	**70+ clubs**
National team position	**31st**
Sport facilities	**Good**
Arts opportunities	**Drama, dance excellent, music, film, art good**
Student newspaper	**Waterfront**
Student radio	**X-Treme**
Nightclubs/bars	**Divas, Idols, JC's**
Union ents	**Flirt!, Live & Wired; Time & Envy in town**
Union societies	**50+**
Parking	**Adequate**
TOWN:	
Entertainment	★★★
Scene	**Clubs, pubs, sea**
Town/gown relations	**Good**
Risk of violence	**Low**
Cost of living	**Low**
Student concessions	**Good**
Survival + 2 nights out	**£60 pw**
Part-time work campus/town	**Good**

track programme that will take students to graduation in 4 years. The Medical School is adjacent to Swansea's Singleton Hospital, but students will enter the University of Wales College of Medicine and the All-Wales Clinical Training Scheme for the final two years of their studies.

In the area of business, Finance is significant. Many graduates go into accountancy. There is also a BSc Actuarial Studies, with the option of an additional year abroad, and a new BSc Actuarial Studies with Accounting.

There are also BA media and screen studies degrees, and news of the opening of a Richard Burton Centre for Film and Popular Culture followed the handing over of the first of screen legend's diaries to the university by the actor's widow, Sally Burton. The diaries form part of an archive of her late husband's papers.

Finally, Law comes with a whole host of possible combinations, and an intercalary year in the US with Law & American Studies.

SOCIAL SCENE

STUDENTS' UNION There are 2 bars: **Idols** at Hendrefoelan student village - cosy atmosphere

with karaoke every Tuesday, and **JC's**, on campus - great pub with big screen for all sporting events, friendly and popular venue. **Divas** is the union nightclub - extremely popular, with a wide range of nights to cater for all tastes.

Time and Envy in the city centre hand over their club to the union on Mondays and Wednesdays - Monday is Student Night, and Wednesday is AU Night (Athletic Union). Besides karaoke at Idols every Tuesday, there's a pub quiz at JC's each Sunday, and in Diva's *Flirt!* on a Friday and *Live and Wired* (basically like an open Mike night) on Sunday.

There are 70+ sports clubs and 50+ societies up and running, RAG and Dance being the most active right now, though politics is a perennial interest, 'all parties represented, Lib Dem and Socialist and Respect,' they say. And the Tories? main issues this year have been about changes to the university, campaign against the arms trade, and student safety. *Waterfront* is the newspaper; X-treme Radio rules the airwaves.

There's an international Swansea Arts Festival every autumn. The Glynn Vivian Gallery in town, The Swansea Arts Workshop in the Maritime Quarter (the former docklands) and **The Taliesin Arts Centre** on campus, deliver year-round exhibitions and events, a constantly unfolding programme (for and by students and outsiders) of drama, dance, film and concerts from classical through jazz and rock. The building has a bar and a bookshop. For Swansea-based opera and comedy there's the **Pontardawe Arts Centre**; for comedy, rock, classical and musicals there's the **Penyrheol Theatre**, while **The Grand** delivers Welsh National Opera, Lily Savage, *The Pirates of Penzance*, Paul Merton and the *South Wales Evening Post* Fashion Show in quick succession.

SPORT Interest in sport is huge. Rugby is bigger than huge; Robert Howley and Dafydd James are alumni. Football and netball teams have been Welsh champions. The facilities in the £20-million Sports Village include a fitness centre, sports hall, squash courts, climbing wall, and physiotherapy and sports massage unit. Outdoors there are tennis courts, rugby, soccer, lacrosse and cricket pitches, and a new athletics track, all-weather pitches and indoor training centre. The 50m Wales National Pool Swansea (and its 25-metre warm-up pool) is home to one of British Swimming's High Performance Centres, which offers outstanding support for talented swimmers, including disability swimmers.

PILLOW TALK

Swansea provides accommodation on campus in

the Singleton Halls, off-campus in Hendrefoelan Student Village (approx 2 miles from the campus), and also runs a Managed Property Scheme of high quality housing in the surrounding areas of Uplands and Brynmill.

A range of options is available: en-suite, self-catering rooms arranged in flats of 8, en-suite part catering rooms 200 semi en suite, part-catering rooms (bathrooms shared by 2 rooms), standard rooms with shared kitchen and bathroom facilities. The Hendrefoelan student village has flats and houses for 4 to 11 students, with shared kitchen, dining and bathroom facilities. Two new student residential blocks opened on the Singleton Campus in September last year.

'Wherever you choose to live you'll find a community of really good friends,' writes Maxine. 'This is true even in private accommodation at Brynmill, an area close by but considered by many (though probably not by its long-term residents) as a second student village. There is this sense that everyone is linked in some way, friends, friend of a friend and so on. Students here are generally very

ACCOMMODATION	
Guarantee to freshers	**100%**
Style	**Halls, flats**
Security guard	**Some**
Shared rooms	**None**
Internet access	**All**
Self-catered	**Some**
En suite	**No halls, all flats**
Approx price range pw	**£72-£140**
City rent pw	**£65-£140**

laid back, and not just the surfers.'

GETTING THERE

☛ By road: M4/J42B.
☛ By coach: Cardiff, 1:10.
☛ By rail: London Paddington, 2:50; Bristol, 2:00; Cardiff, 0:50; Birmingham, 3:15; Manchester, 4:30.
☛ By air: Cardiff Airport.

SWANSEA METROPOLITAN UNIVERSITY

Swansea Metropolitan University
Mount Pleasant
Swansea SA1 6ED

TEL 01792 481000
FAX 01792 481085
EMAIL enquiry@smu.ac.uk
WEB www.sihe.ac.uk/

Swansea Met University Students' Union
Mount Pleasant Hill
Swansea SA1 6ED

TEL 01792 655 400
FAX 01792 460439Web:
http://www.metsu.org/
Email: su@sihe.ac.uk

Swansea Met, which has its roots in local colleges of Technology, Art and Teacher Training over 150 years ago, and was until recently Swansea Institute of Higher Education, achieved university status in 2008. Most of the students are local not only to Wales but to Swansea. A third are part-timers and 45% mature.

The point about Swansea Met is that all its courses are concerned with the application of knowledge to real-life situations, whether in the classroom, laboratory or workshop. For this reason, it has always had an impressive employment rate, which today translates into 77% of its graduates getting real graduate jobs within six months of graduation.

Its undergraduate faculties are three: Applied Design & Engineering, Art & Design, and Humanities. They operate out of various sites in Swansea. The Faculty of Applied Design and Engineering is located on Mount Pleasant campus,

UNIVERSITY/STUDENT PROFILE	
University since	**2008**
Situation/style	**City sites**
Student population	**5800**
Total undergraduates	**4415**
Mature undergraduates	**45%**
International undergrads	**8%**
Male/female ratio	**55:45**
Equality of opportunity:	
state school intake	**98%**
social class 4-7 intake	**43%**
low-participation area intake	**14%**

a short walk from Swansea city centre. Humanities, which includes Swansea School of Education, the Centre for Performance and Literature, and the Centre for Psychology and Counselling, are primarily on the Townhill campus, with spectacular views of Swansea Bay. Then there is the Dynevor Centre for Art, Design, and Media, again in the city centre.

Still within this employment powerhouse exist the original provisions of Art and Teaching. Fine Art (ceramics, painting, combined media), Illustration and Graphics have been joined by Photography, Photojournalism, Textiles for Fashion, and Performance Arts, Technical Theatre, and Video. And then there is this odd little niche for glass: Architectural Glass, Stained Glass, Restoration and Conservation, and this Centre for Lens Arts and Science Interaction, which dabbles in emerging lens-based practices such as photography, time-based media, performed photography, digital imaging, and electronic arts.

As for the Teaching provision, primary education is the principal destination for Swansea Met graduates: 15% of them end up in it.

But there are other dimensions to the curriculum. For years as Institute of Higher Education, Swansea was known as a major contributor of graduates to the automobile engineering industry by means of its degrees from Automotive Engineering or Design to Motorcycle Engineering or Motorsport Engineering.

There are other degrees clearly aimed at specific employment destinations, like Public Administration, Counselling, Psychology, Watersports & Adventure Activities Management. Then there are the Business degrees, for which its reputation is more visible: Finance, Tourism, Human resources, Information Technology, Leisure Management, Transport Management. And the Computer Science degrees, Web Design and so on. You suspect that David Warner has a clear idea where every single graduate of his will end up, that possibly he even knows the business personally

This is mainly a weekday university at present, but the Student Union is active enough and they've always had ents, currently either at the Metro Bar or at Oceans nightclub in town. But don't expect much mind - maybe Price Cut (pound-a-pint or whatever), Red Nose Eve Party, a visit from comedian Russell Kane, the Summer Ball. There are five Student Societies at present: Christian Union, Environmental Society, Outdoor Activities (from pony-trekking to paintballing), Volunteering, Dance Soc, and already there's a vibrant student newspaper, Swansea Eye. And this is Wales, so sport is on even if currently they occupy position 139 in the UK national student league. There's women's and men's football, hockey, rugby. Also netball and basketball, ultimate Frisbee and cricket. And alongside the team sports surfing, martial arts, karting, and kickboxing.

There's a bed for whoever wants one, 265 rooms in three halls, Gwyr Hall (en-suite shower cubicles, mixed accommodation toilets nearby), Dyfed Hall (mixed accommodation), Cenydd Hall (mixed; one flatlet for disabled use with en-suite facilities). Most single rooms have a fitted wardrobe and hand washbasin, with showers, toilets and bathrooms located on each floor. Dyfed alone has a coin-operated launderette on the ground floor, open daily. Then at Mount Pleasant there are 6 twin and 37 single study units all with en-suite toilet/shower facilities.

GETTING THERE
☞ By road: M4/J42B.
☞ By coach: Cardiff, 1:10.
☞ By rail: London Paddington, 2:50; Bristol, 2:00; Cardiff, 0:50; Birmingham, 3:15; Manchester, 4:30.
☞ By air: Cardiff Airport.

UNIVERSITY OF TEESSIDE

The University of Teesside
Middlesbrough
Tees Valley TS1 3BA

TEL 01642 218121
FAX 01642 342067
EMAIL registry@tees.ac.uk
WEB www.tees.ac.uk

Teesside Students' Union
Borough Road
Middlesbrough TS1 3BA

TEL 01642 342234
FAX 01642 342241
EMAIL enquiries@utsu.org.uk
WEB www.utsu.org.uk

VAG VIEW

*T*eesside call themselves the opportunity university and sit high in the league table of those that have widened access to higher education. What this means in their case is that entry requirements are not demanding, may well not include A levels, and that the undergraduate population, many of whom are mature, is largely drawn from the region.

Teesside is particularly strong in comput-

UNIVERSITY/STUDENT PROFILE	
University since	**1970**
Situation/style	**Campus**
Student population	**24160**
Total undergraduates	**20875**
Mature undergraduates	**35%**
International undergrads	**12%**
Male/female ratio	**46:54**
Equality of opportunity:	
state school intake	**99%**
social class 4-7 intake	**47%**
low-participation area intake	**25%**

er games design and animation, design, digital media, sport and exercise, forensic science and health-related courses such as physiotherapy and radiography.

Tens of millions have been spent on two new developments on campus - the Institute of Digital Innovation and the Centre for Creative Technologies. Both opened in 2007 and enhance Teesside's reputation as a leading university for digital innovation and design.

However, in 2008, after Thames Valley, Bolton, Bucks New, Chester, and of the old guard, Sussex, applications fell more than in any other university in 2008: by 19.7%.

CAMPUS
The campus is located within a few minutes walk of the centre of Middlesbrough, on the south bank of the River Tees, a short hop from the North Yorks Moors and Redcar and Saltburn beaches.

Students using the union building run a gauntlet of pubs on Southfield Road: The Dickens' Inn, licensed till midnight, The Star & Garter, offering

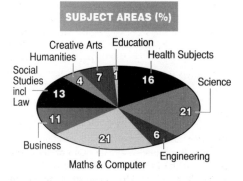

SUBJECT AREAS (%)

Creative Arts — Education — Health Subjects — Science — Engineering — Maths & Computer — Business — Social Studies incl Law — Humanities

'£1-a-pint, £2-for-2' and The Fly & Firkin. The architecture of the union and adjacent, £11-million, 5-storey Learning Resources Centre stuns - these delicately ribbed, green-tinted glass buildings glistening with seductive appeal.

FEES, BURSARIES
UK & EU Fees, 2009-10: £3,225 p.a. A bursary of £1.025 p.a. is available to students in receipt of the full Maintenance Grant. There are also Excellence or Subject Scholarships of £1,000 p.a. And finally they offer the Elite Athlete Bursary of up to £2,000.

STUDENT PROFILE
There's a large mature student intake and many come from non-traditional uni heartlands close by. They have a job-seeker's attitude to academia, i.e. serious, and a similar appetite for the hedonistic pleasures that Students' Union and town afford.In the 2008 National Student Survey 83% of Teesside's students were satisfied with the teaching they were receiving. Asked whether the library resources and services are good enough, the 91% vote in the affirmative placed the uni joint 3rd in the UK. Access to general IT resources brought even higher approval.

Teesside's two largest academic schools are Health & Social Care and Computing. Both have increased dramatically in size over the last five years. Together they account for half the student population.

Extensive use is made of the University's Virtual Learning Environment - E@T (Elearning@Tees). Each subject has its own support site for students and this contains a range of online learning tools, resources and links. The sites are accessible both on and off campus 24/7.

Significantly more than a quarter of Teesside students enter the health sector on graduation - by far the most becoming senior hospital nurses (SRN, RGN), then it's physiotherapists, community & youth workers, non-hospital nurses, occupational therapists, medical radiographers, social workers and midwives.

The uni is about to start work on a new £13m Sport and Health Sciences building on campus which will include a new Dentistry training school, Sports Therapy facilities, a series of laboratories and biomechanic and hydrotherapy facilities.

In the area of commmunity welfare they lead with BSc (Hons) Youth Studies and Youth Work, and the various Youth Studies combinations with Sociology, Criminology or Psychology, BSc degrees in Social Work, and Psychology, which comes on its own or with Counselling or Criminology.

The first subject at Teesside to be assessed Excellent for teaching was Computer Science and

TEACHING SURVEY AT A GLANCE

Avg. UCAS points accepted	**240**
Acceptance rate	**22%**
Overall satisfaction rate	**83%**
Helpful/interested staff	★★★★
Small tuition groups	★★★★
Students into graduate jobs	**74%**

Teaching most popular with undergraduates:
Media Studies (96%), Law (96%), History (97%),
Design Studies (94%), English, Social Work
(90%), Psychology, Sociology (89%), Social
Sciences (88%) Business Studies, Electronic &
Electrical Engineering, Physics (86%), Medical
Technology, Forensic Science (85%).

Teaching least popular with undergraduates:
Computer Science (76%), Anatomy,
Physiology & Pathology (53%).

this has been a crucial focus of investment. In the Government's Research Assessment of our universities in 2008, Teesside's work in Computer Science gained recognition as 10% world-class and 45% internationally excellent, which is very good. A significant niche area lies in computer games design. See their 3/4-year dedicated degrees (Animation, Games Art, Games Design, Games Programming, Games Science, Graphics Science). The Innovation Centre incorporates the unique Virtual Reality Centre, with large-scale VR development and viewing facilities.

Look also at BScs in Digital Forensics, Digital Music, Digital Music Creation, BA(Hons) Post-Production and Visual Effects, BSc (Hons) Technical Direction in Computer Animation. The uni is part of a plan to create a digital city in Middlesbrough. There'll be new teaching, learning and commercial facilities as well as opportunities for graduate start up-businesses.

Business-wise there's a strong lean towards information management and marketing, with BA degrees in e-Business, Business Information Systems, Accounting with Information technology, etc. See also vocational lines such as BA Marketing, and combinations with Retail Mgt, Advertising Mgt, Public Relations, and the new BA (Hons) Corporate Leadership and Management.

Their own business start-up scheme - Upgrade2 has assisted over 40 fledgling student companies. Collaboration with local and regional industry is the nub of their strategy in business and industry.

Note, too, that they are specialists in European and commercial law. There's a tie-up with Criminology, and a Senior Status LLB for graduates holding a non-Law degree. Links with Cleveland and Durham constabularies underwrite the pioneering BSc in Criminology. See also Crime Scene Science, Applied Science & Forensic Investigation, etc, and Fraud Management. They claim their Crime House Lab, where forensic science students put their investigative skills into practice, is the most elaborate facility of its kind in any UK university, and have just opened a Vehicle Examination Centre for forensic and crime scene science students to practise their skills. See the new BSc Digital Forensics, BSc (Hons) Forensic Investigation and Consumer Law, and BSc (Hons) Medico-Legal Death Investigation.

A significant graduate population find work as graphic designers, set and interior designers, and there are interesting interior design and advertising specialities. There's synergy, too, with Cleveland's TV & Film production degree. Web: www.ccad. ac.uk. Ther are, too, degrees in Digital Media, Radio Production, a Journalism foundation degree with specialist Darlington College, and BA (Hons) Multimedia Journalism Professional Practice, accredited by NCTJ. The Northern Region Film & Television Archive is housed on campus, providing a resource for students of history and media.

Finally, Teesside are among the top unis for turning out sports players and officials through their Coaching and Applied Sports Science/Exercise Science degrees. See also BA Sport and Leisure Management, BA Sport Management and BSc Sport and Exercise Psychology.

SOCIAL SCENE

There's **The Terrace Bar**, and the new second floor venue, **The Hub**, split level with 4 big screens and many plasma screens, a cool open space to relax through the day and let go on a Saturday night if SU put something on. The theory is that **Room 2 @ The Hub** works as a bookable meeting/training room during the day and in the evening as a second DJ room. There's a clubnight in one or other every Friday and Saturday, the first being current chart and r&b, and Saturday rotates with indie, retro, school disco and current chart.

On a good night the buzz is tangible. 'I've lived down south,' said Michelle, 'and I am not being biased, but the scene up here is great, one of the best in the North East. We've got far too many bars, people are just competing with each other, so it's great for students.'

Nor is it all night-time reverie. There are 20 societies and 40 sports clubs. Student media includes a monthly magazine, Cup of Tees. Most popular is the International Students Society with about 100 members. Then there are things like the

WHAT IT'S REALLY LIKE

UNIVERSITY:	
Social Life	★★★
Campus scene	**Lively, local scene**
Student Union services	**Good**
Politics	**Activity low**
Sport	**Keen**
National team position	**72nd**
Sport facilities	**Good**
Arts opportunities	**Dance, music excellent, rest OK**
Student newsletter	**Teesguide**
Student radio	**UTRN**
Nightclub	**Hub**
Bars	**Terrace Bar**
Union ents	**Chart, r&b, Indie, retro, disco**
Union societies	**60 (40 sport)**
Parking	**Poor**
TOWN:	
Entertainment	★★★★
Scene	**Pubs, big-time clubs**
Town/gown relations	**Average**
Risk of violence	**Average**
Cost of living	**Low**
Student concessions	**Good**
Survival + 2 nights out	**£50-£60 pw**
Part-time work campus/town	**Excellent/good**

ACCOMMODATION

Guarantee to freshers	**100%**
Style	**Halls, flats**
Security guard	**Campus**
Shared rooms	**Some halls, no flats**
Internet access	**All**
Self-catered	**All**
En suite	**Some**
Approx price range pw	**£45.50-£78**
City rent pw	**£40-£45**

radio station.

SPORT They have a £6.5 million Olympia Building with squash courts, floodlit artificial pitch and large sports hall, plus a range of up to the minute teaching facilities and the latest climate simulation facility - designed to test sporting performance in a range of temperatures. But they are languishing far down the national student team league (at 72nd).

PILLOW TALK

Campus residences are exclusively for first years. Allocations are made on a first come first served basis, so apply early. There are houses, halls, flats and managed housing off campus. Five mixed halls of residence all have self-catering facilities; 34% of campus accommodation is en suite.

GETTING THERE

- ☛ By road: A19, or A1/M, A66.
- ☛ By rail: Newcastle, 1:15; Leeds, 1:45; Manchester Piccadilly, 2:45; Liverpool Lime Street, 3:45; London King's Cross, 3:30.
- ☛ By air: Teesside International Airport.
- ☛ By coach: Birmingham, 3:15; York, 1:15.

Dilated Pupil Society, Dance Music Society, and Drama did a series of satirical sketches last Christmas. Said a Union wallah: 'Our Law society is very successful in the courtroom battles with high profile universities in the North East, Durham, Newcastle, etc.'

In January 2009, the University of Teesside Radio Network (UTRN) was launched via the internet. Students and staff can now tune into their own

THAMES VALLEY UNIVERSITY

Thames Valley University
St Mary's Road
London W5 5RF

TEL 0800 036 8888
FAX 020 8231 1353
EMAIL learning.advice@tvu.ac.uk
WEB www.tvu.ac.uk

Thames Valley Students' Union
St Mary's Road
London W5 5RF

TEL 020 8231 2276
FAX 020 8231 2569
EMAIL [firstname.surname]@tvu.ac.uk
WEB www.tvu.ac.uk

VAG VIEW

*F*ormerly West London Poly and incorporating the Ealing School of Art, where

Pete Townshend (the Who), Ronnie Wood (the Stones) and Freddie Mercury (Queen)... erm...studied, TVU works with local colleges on access programmes, allowing successful

STUDENT PROFILE

'The most positive point to be made about TVU concerns the diversity,' writes student Ian Draysey. 'Students of all ages come from all over the world, and studying there has given me the opportunity to meet people I never would have otherwise. The majority of universities make similar claims, but in this case it's true, honest!'

The student body is anything but like a traditional university. For a start 48% of the undergraduate population is part-time, 72% of it is mature. It is not especially diverse, for only 9% of undergraduates come from overseas, there is virtually no-one from public school and some 40% come from the lowest socio-economic orders.

ACADEMIA & JOBS

More than 40% of their students graduate in business and administration, and many find jobs in marketing and market research. There are BA Marketing degrees with Business or Advertising. See also the Public Relations provision.

There's also a particular slant towards the catering industry through the Hospitality Management and International Hotel degrees.

Advertising is itself a sound niche graduate employment area for TVU. There are well targeted degrees, and joint options ranging through Design, Radio Broadcasting, Video Production, Photography & Digital Imaging, and Marketing. There is altogether a strong career claim on the media sector. See BA New Media Journalism.

Smart music producers choose their 3-year Music Technology BA, which gives this uni one of its strongest employment records. Again there is the Specialist degree or one with options.

Statistics point to a track record for composers and musicians at TVU. See the BMus

completion of an access course as an alternative to usual entry requirements.

There was much optimism recently after their merger with Reading College and School of Arts & Design, and a tie-up with the mighty Imperial College London over a degree in Medicine. But the uni registered the second worst drop in applications of any higher education institution in 2008 - 26.4% fewer applicants chose it than in the previous year. Among current undergraduates, 76% are satisfeid with the teaching, and 71% will get a graduate-level job within six months of leaving.

CAMPUS

TVU is based on sites in Ealing (West London, where the Student Union is based) and Slough, at Reading and Brentford. Shuttle buses run between the campuses until late each night. There is no university-owned residential campus accommodation at Ealing or Slough, but they will sort you out.

The Reading Campus, Crescent Road, Reading RG1 5RQ (0800 371 434), was known as Reading College and School of Arts & Design before it merged five years ago with TVU. There is a Student Union presence, accommodation, an activities centre and football pitch.

Brentford Campus, off Boston Manor Road, is home to TVU's Faculty of Health and Human Sciences, with its many nursing and midwifery students. This is the largest healthcare faculty in the UK. It includes 849 study bedrooms, 221 key worker flats and 12,000 sq.m of teaching/office accommodation.

FEES, BURSARIES

UK & EU Fees, 2009-10: £3,225 p.a. If in receipt of a Government Maintenance Grant, there's a bursary.

WHAT IT'S REALLY LIKE

UNIVERSITY:

Social Life	★★
Campus scene	**London diversity, closed weekends**
Student Union services	**Average-poor**
Politics	**No interest**
Sport	**Local**
National team position	**134th**
Sport facilities	**Poor**
Arts opportunities	**Music, film, art**
Student newspaper	**The Voice**
Student radio	**Tube**
Nightclub	**The Studio**
Bars	**The Studio Bar**
Union ents	**Some**
Union societies	**11**
Most popular society	**Tube Radio**
Smoking policy	**None**
Parking	**Adequate**

CITY:

Entertainment	★★★★★
Scene	**London**
Town/gown relations	**Average**
Risk of violence	**Average**
Cost of living	**Very high**
Student concessions	**Good**
Survival + 2 nights out	**£80 pw**
Part-time work campus/town	**Average/excellent**

(Performance/Composition) and Popular Music Performance degrees.

Imperial College London and Thames Valley University have cleared a way for a collaboration. TVU's BSc (Hons) Human Sciences (Pre-medical Option) is a way of widening participation in Medicine for students who otherwise wouldn't have the opportunity to study at Imperial, one of the best medical schools in the world and normally extremely testing to get into. Students planning on applying must first apply via UCAS to TVU for the BSc (Hons) Human Sciences (B9C1). Those who meet the entry requirements for the Pre-medical Option will be invited to TVU for interview and a written exercise. Only Home/EU students who do not already hold a degree need apply, and they must have Grade C AS Level in Chemistry, plus A Level Grades C and D in 2 further subjects, plus GCSE Grade C in English and Maths. A Level equivalents are not accepted. Assuming all that, the following November they must sit the BioMedical Admissions Test (BMAT) and will be invited to interview at Imperial if they obtain a 60% aggregate result in their first semester modules.

Otherwise, TVU's health provision focuses on Nursing and Midwifery, and accounts for a huge proportion of graduate jobs here. There's also Health & Exercise Science, Health Studies, Sports Science & Medicine, a top-up Complementary Approaches to Health degree, and BSc Psychology with Counselling Theory, as well as the single hons accredited by the British Psychological Society.

The YVU Law degree recently got a fillip from the LPC Board (a Legal Practice Course is essential to becoming a solicitor) who pronounced it 'Good'.

Finally, there's a strong showing in financial administration. See their Accounting and Finance degrees and foundation year.

It is in line with their academic strategy to have help at hand for literacy, numeracy and IT skills.

SOCIAL SCENE

STUDENTS' UNION The **Studio** opens Monday to Friday, 11 am to 11 pm, the **Coffee Stop**, 8 am - 6 pm, Monday to Thursday, 8 am - 4 pm on Fridays. At the Ealing campus, traditional pool table and jukebox scenario is supplemented by Bhangra music and Hindi films. Ents include live bands, karaoke, DJs and drinking competitions. The uni's degrees in music (including Popular Music Performance) and its association with the London College of Music and Media provide input, and the fledgling Tube Radio, ambitiously aimed not just at students but at the wider community around Ealing, benefits from LCM's hardware.

The largest venue at TVU is **Artwood's**, with a capacity of 1,200. It has attempted to overcome its school hall demeanour with the installation of a bar to complement its livestock-bothering sound system, and has a good atmosphere when crowded.

Over at the Slough campus, the **Moon and Cucumber** bar, buffet bar, **Hamlyn Hall** and the smokeless **Studio Bar** offer alternative recreational facilities. Slough also houses a gym for those who'd rather build up their muscles than their beer guts.

They say that societies range from the Radio Society to the Asian Society and come under four categories, Cultural (Asian, Chinese), Religious (Christian Union, Islamic), Social (Radio, Music

ACCOMMODATION

Guarantee to freshers	**100%**
Style	**Halls, flats**
Security guard	**All**
Shared rooms	**None**
Internet access	**All**
Self-catered	**All**
En suite	**All**
Approx price range pw	**£89-£159**
City rent pw	**£90-£180**

Industry), and Academic (Law, Psychology). Sport at TVU has swung away from the more team-oriented stance of many universities, with activities such as badminton, fencing and aerobics gaining more members than football. There was no team placement in last year's national uni leagues.

GETTING THERE
☞ Ealing: Ealing Broadway Underground (Central and District Lines).
☞ Slough: By road: M4/J6, A4. By rail: London Paddington, 25 mins.

UNIVERSITY OF ULSTER

University of Ulster
University House
Cromore Road
Coleraine
Co. Londonderry BT52 1SA

TEL 028 7032 4221
FAX 028 7032 4908
EMAIL online@ulster.ac.uk
STUDENT UNION TEL 028 7032 4319
WEB www.ulst.ac.uk

VAG VIEW

*U*lster *is the largest of the 9 universities in Ireland. Spread across four sites (between seven and eighty miles apart) it is an enormous place in terms of students, 80% of whom are local.*

The uni came out of a merger in 1984 between Ulster Poly (now the Jordanstown campus) and the New University of Ulster (which was the old university, if you follow). Sites are at Belfast (art college), at Newtownabbey, in the hills above Belfast (the Jordanstown campus), at Coleraine (this is HQ, far northwest of Belfast, near the Giant's Causeway), and in Londonderry (Magee College campus, founded in 1865), yet further west.

To solve communications problems they have formed a wireless microwave network capable of transmitting data of Encyclopaedia Britannica proportions in a second. The Centre for Communications Engineering links them to Queen's Uni and Nortel Networks, and is a feature of their strategy for close working with industry.

There are plans afoot for massive improvements and expansion.

STUDENT PROFILE

There's a high mature undergrad percentage and an unusually high number of part-timers among the predominantly local student body; university strategy ensures that many, too, come from social groups with no great tradition of higher education. Together with this comes a high drop-out rate - 13%

UNIVERSITY/STUDENT PROFILE	
University since	**1964**
Situation/style	**Campus sites**
Student population	**23735**
Total undergraduates	**19170**
Mature undergraduates	**21%**
International undergrads	**8%**
Male/female ratio	**41:59**
Equality of opportunity:	
state school intake	**100%**
social class 4-7 intake	**48%**
low-participation area intake	**8%**

among non-mature entrants.

CAMPUS

BELFAST York Street, Belfast BT15 1ED. **Location:** close to city centre, part of the city's up and coming Cathedral Quarter, is traditionally considered the home of the School of Art and Design, though other disciplines are increasingly being taught there. **Faculty HQs:** Art & Design (including Interior Design and Textile & Fashion Design). Also American Studies, Architecture, Irish Literature, Chinese, English. **Accommodation:** none, but small number of Belfast students may use Jordanstown. A £30-million redevelopment of this campus was completed in 2008 and established a creative hub in the heart of Belfast City Centre. **Ents facilities:** Conor Hall (400-capacity venue). **Sports facilities:** 'What's sport?' said a student when asked. Arts facilities: foyer exhibition area, art shop, artist (writer, artist or musician) in residence. **Arts opportunities:** 'Second to none, vibrant, innovative, love it!' said our student contact. **Media:** monthly magazine, Ufouria.

TEACHING SURVEY AT A GLANCE

Avg. UCAS points accepted	**280**
Acceptance rate	**18%**
Overall satisfaction rate	**81%**
Helpful/interested staff	★★★
Small tuition groups	★★
Students into graduate jobs	**70%**

Teaching most popular with undergraduates:
Biology and related sciences (100%), Finance (96%), Sports Science (95%), Physical Geography & Enviro. Science, Marketing, Psychology (92%), English (94%), Politics, History, Accounting (89%), Architecture (88%).

Teaching least popular with undergraduates:
Medical Science, Pharmacy, Subjects allied to Medicine (57%-70%), Media Studies (67%), Design Studies (62%).

JORDANSTOWN Newtownabbey BT37 OQB. **Location:** seven miles north of Belfast on the shore of Belfast Lough; largest site. **Faculty HQs:** Business & Management (including Government, Law, Marketing), Engineering (including Biomedical Eng), Informatics, Social (economics, accounting, politics, social policy, sociology, counselling) & Health Sciences (nursing, physiotherapy, podiatry, speech & language therapy). Also architecture and construction, languages library management, sport. **Accommodation:** res. blocks, six-bedroom houses, flats & study-bedrooms in halls; self-catering. **Ents facilities:** Students' Union Bar (700 capacity), split level, two stages, tiered seating/standing; regular disco night is Monday. **Sports facilities:** two large sports halls, gym, fitness suite, six squash courts, eight-lane swimming pool and hydrotherapy pool, playing fields, synthetic training pitch, local water sports facility and River Lagan. **Arts facilities:** recital rooms, concert hall. Low key. **Media:** Naked is student newspaper.

ACCOMMODATION

Guarantee to freshers	**60%**
Style	**Flats**
Security guard	**Most**
Shared rooms	**Most**
Internet access	**Most**
Self-catered	**Most**
En suite	**Most**
Approx price range pw	
Coleraine	**£60-£97.80**
Jordanstown	**£47-£106.70**
Magee	**£51-£75**

COLERAINE (address with entry title) **Location:** market town close to north coast, 35 miles from Derry. The original uni, admin HQ and home to the Centre for Molecular Sciences. Biosciences, health (nursing, optometry), pharmacology, environmental science, dietetics, social sciences (psychology,), humanities (history, geography) languages and Euro studies, media (film, journalism, publishing), business, computer. **Accommodation:** residential blocks and student houses. Most students prefer to live out in coastal resort towns Portrush and Portstewart. **Ents facilities:** Biko Hall (venue) and recently rebuilt Uni-Bar; 550 capacity. Regular disco night is Monday. **Sports facilities:** Biko Hall is sports hall by day, five squash courts, fitness suite, solarium and steam room, playing fields, floodlit football pitch, pavilion, tennis courts, water sports centre on River Bann. **Arts facilities:** the Octagon (500-seat recital room), the Diamond (1,200-seat concert hall, prestigious Riverside Theatre, third largest pro theatre in Ireland, venue for drama, rock and classical concerts, ballet, opera, etc.

MAGEE COLLEGE Northland Road, Londonderry BT48 7JL. **Location:** residential quarter of Derry, Ireland's second largest city. A mixture of historical and new buildings and modern and traditional facilities, a small and tightly knit student population. New moves bring drama, music, dance and computing to the bedrock business, humanities, social sciences (psychology, law, politics, social policy, community youth work, sociology) & nursing. Languages are also to the fore, and Irish Studies. It is home to the Institute for Legal & Professional Studies. **Accommodation:** three halls of residence and student village (modern houses). **Ents facilities:** two bars, The Terrapin (known as 'the wee bar') and The Bunker (bar/nightclub, 400 capacity). **Ents:** bands and discos (Thursday); Derry wild with pubs. **Sports facilities:** sports hall, fitness suite and solarium; recent additions include sports pavilion, sand-carpet soccer pitch, synthetic training pitch; sailing at Fahan, rowing and canoeing on the Foyle. **Arts facilities:** the Great Hall.

GETTING THERE

☞ An hour by air from London, with at least 24 flights a day each way.
☞ Ulsterbus operates a fast and frequent service across Northern Ireland.

UNIVERSITY COLLEGE, LONDON

University College, London
Gower Street
London WC1E 6BT

TEL 020 7679 3000
FAX 020 7679 3001
EMAIL degree-info@ucl.ac.uk
WEB www.ucl.ac.uk/prospective-students

UCL Students' Union
25 Gordon Street
London WC1H 0AH

TEL 020 7387 3611
EMAIL mc.officer@ucl.ac.uk
WEB www.uclu.org

VAG VIEW

The college was the original University of London, the first in England after Oxford and Cambridge, inspired by the first principle of Utilitarianism, 'the greatest happiness of the greatest number'. It was a pioneering move by a group of thinkers, John Stuart Mill among them, for an alternative approach to higher education, which, in 1826, meant the privileged education dished out by Oxford and Cambridge.

The idea was to open the doors of education to the rising middle-classes and to free the educational establishment from the doctrinal prejudices of the Anglican Church. Roman Catholics, Jews and Nonconformists were barred from an Oxbridge education in those days. To ensure freedom from dogma, it was decided not to have subjects appertaining to religion taught at UCL.

UCL's research record is formidable and manages to combine this with helpful, interested teaching, a point made by its own undergraduates in the National Student Experience Survey. UCL is 7th in the country for research, 7th in the World's Top 200 Universities, and remains one of our foremost seats of learning.

UNIVERSITY/STUDENT PROFILE	
College of London Uni since	**1826**
Situation/style	**City campus**
Student population	**19385**
Total undergraduates	**11805**
Mature undergraduates	**16%**
International undergrads	**21%**
Male/female ratio	**48:52**
Equality of opportunity:	
state school intake	**67%**
social class 4-7 intake	**19%**
low-participation area intake	**3%**

CAMPUS
The location of UCL's main sites, just to the north of London's West End and hard by the University of London Students' Union building, provides students with amazing resource opportunity. What's more, most halls of residence are within walking distance.

SATELLITE CAMPUSES
ROYAL FREE HOSPITAL MEDICAL SCHOOL merged with UCL to form the Royal Free & University College Medical School. It is situated in Hampstead, one of the safest, most aesthetically pleasing areas of London.

SCHOOL OF SLAVONIC & EAST EUROPEAN STUDIES – SSEES (pronounced Cease) is an enigmatic institution specialising in the study of Eastern Europe, 'It holds the academically acknowledged best lecturers in their fields,' says Gideon Dewhurst, 'and the largest East European library in Britain. They have new purpose-built premises in Taviton Street.

FEES, BURSARIES
UK & EU Fees, 2009-10: £3,225 p.a. If in receipt of the HE Maintenance Grant, bursaries up to £2,775 are available, depending on household income. There are also academic scholarships, see www.ucl.ac.uk/scholarships.

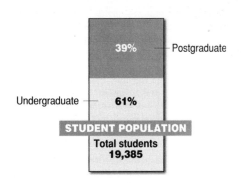

39% — Postgraduate

Undergraduate — 61%

STUDENT POPULATION
Total students
19,385

TEACHING SURVEY AT A GLANCE

Avg. UCAS points accepted	**430**
Acceptance rate	**11%**
Overall satisfaction rate	**88%**
Helpful/interested staff	**★★★★**
Small tuition groups	**★★★**
Students into graduate jobs	**83%**

Teaching most popular with undergraduates:
English (98%), Archaeology (97%), Anthropology,
biochemistry (96%), Architecture, Sciences relat-
ed to Biology (95%), Biology (94%), Anatomy,
Physiology & Pathology, Classics, History, Maths,
Medical Science & Pharmacy (93%), Medicine,
Civil Engineering, Geographical Studies (92%),
Chemistry, Human & Social Geography (90%).

Teaching least popular with undergraduates:
Economics, Business & Admin. Studies (80%).

STUDENT PROFILE

The relative imbalance in favour of public school
kids is ironic in the light of its history. Today, UCL
hardly fills the bill as 'Cockney College', the name
given in the 19th century by those who feared the
consequences of UCL's open-access stance. Few
universities take a smaller percentage of state sector pupils. However, judging by the recent concentration of activity in the areas of special needs and
academic counselling, what it's really after is good
minds.

ACADEMIA & JOBS

UCL places great importance on its tutorial system,
and its overall student-to-staff ratio is the best in
the country. All students are allocated a personal
tutor for consultation on academic or personal
matters. Further support is offered by departmental and faculty tutors and two advisers specialising
in women students. There's also a professional
counselling service and a Students' Union Rights &
Advice Centre to see you through any problems
academic, financial or emotional. Also, a special
educational needs IT suite was opened in
December 2001, offering computers and related
software and equipment. An IT trainer and a disabilities co-ordinator are at your disposal.

To become a doctor here, you'll need to be
accepted onto the 4/5-year MB BS. The approach of
the MB BS is lectures, tutorial and lab classes in
Phase 1, with a lot of computer-assisted learning
and problem-solving exercises. Only in Phase 2 do
you go out in small teams of consultants and doctors. Phase 3 offers intensive clinical experience.
AAB grades are required and BMAT. Also, four AS
levels in first year sixth form, including Biology

and Chemistry. Three subjects then to be taken on
to A
level, including Chemistry (excluding General
Studies). If candidates take two Maths A levels,
only one will count towards achieving an offer.
Chiropodists and speech therapists are part of the
picture too. BSc Speech Science has world-wide
reputation for research.

After Medicine, Languages (21 are offered),
and Physical and Social Sciences degrees are popular. A language GCSE, or similar, is now a compulsory qualification for acceptance at UCL. New
state-of-the-art language teaching facilities were
opened in February 2007 as part of the Centre for
Excellence in Teaching and Learning - Languages
of the Wider World. This is run in cahoots with the
School of Oriental and African Studies (see entry).

With the takeover of the School of Slavonic &
Eastern European Studies in 1999, the Language
options increased dramatically. This is a premier
route into Adult Education for would-be lecturers.

The BA degree in Language and Culture combines study of one foreign language to degree level,
plus one or two other languages, with a particular
focus in a chosen area of cultural studies - comparative literature, film studies, linguistics, history of
art or cultural history - giving students the opportunity to apply their language skills in deepening
their knowledge of different cultural fields from a
broader and comparative perspective.

UCL have recently teamed up with the famous
School of Oriental & African Studies (see entry) in
a Centre of Excellence in Teaching and Learning:
Languages of the Wider World, which 'recognizes,
promotes and develops the excellent teaching and
learning in less commonly taught languages'.

Physical sciences, humanities and language
graduates put UCL among the leaders at point of
employment for museum archivists, curators and
the like.

Geology, Geophysics, Earth & Space Science

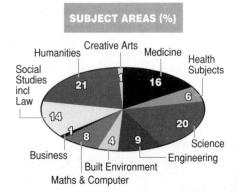

SUBJECT AREAS (%)

are cheek by jowl with History & Philosophy of

RESEARCH EXCELLENCE		
% of UCL's research that is **4*** *(World-class) or* **3*** *(Internationally rated):*		
	4*	3*
Cancer Studies	**25%**	**50%**
Infection/mmunology	**20%**	**60%**
Hospital Clinical	**40%**	**30%**
Epidemiology	**25%**	**35%**
Health Services	**5%**	**25%**
Community Clinical	**10%**	**40%**
Psychiatry	**15%**	**55%**
Dentistry	**15%**	**45%**
Nursing/Midwifery	**5%**	**40%**
Health Professions	**25%**	**35%**
Biological Sciences	**15%**	**40%**
Human Biol. Sciences	**35%**	**35%**
Environmental Sciences	**25%**	**55%**
Chemistry	**15%**	**50%**
Physics	**20%**	**40%**
Pure Mathematics	**20%**	**40%**
Applied Mathematics	**10%**	**40%**
Statistics	**10%**	**40%**
Computer Science	**35%**	**45%**
Electrical/Electronic Eng.	**25%**	**35%**
Chemical Engineering	**15%**	**60%**
Civil Engineering	**15%**	**40%**
Mechanical, Aero. & Manufacturing Eng.	**20%**	**35%**
Architecture	**35%**	**40%**
Town/Country Planning	**20%**	**40%**
Geography Environment	**25%**	**40%**
Archaeology	**30%**	**30%**
Economics	**55%**	**40%**
Information Management	**30%**	**25%**
Law	**35%**	**40%**
Politics	**20%**	**45%**
Social Workn	**15%**	**60%**
Anthropology	**30%**	**30%**
Psychology	**30%**	**45%**
Russian	**10%**	**35%**
French	**10%**	**45%**
Dutch	**5%**	**35%**
German	**25%**	**30%**
Scandinavian Studies	**10%**	**45%**
Italian	**20%**	**25%**
Iberian	**10%**	**35%**
English	**30%**	**35%**
Linguistics	**20%**	**30%**
Classics	**30%**	**35%**
Philosophy	**45%**	**30%**
Theology	**30%**	**40%**
History	**40%**	**25%**
Art and Design	**35%**	**35%**
History of Art	**30%**	**50%**

Science and Information Management, and what about Palaeobiology to set you up in a museum career?

UCL's BSc/MSci degrees in Natural Sciences combine science subjects into a structured and coherent degree, exploiting the increasing overlap of traditional science disciplines such as Biology, Chemistry and Physics which has created new and existing areas of scientific study.

See, too, the Faculty of Social & Historical Sciences, where you'll find Ancient History, Anthropology, Archaeology (Egyptian, General, Mediaeval), History of Art, and what about Archaeology, Classics & Classical Art?

Archaeology is an especially popular degree here. Besides the BA and BSc single hons, there's Mediaeval Archaeology, joint degrees with History of Art and a 4-year Classics & Classical Art.

Physics is a top flight department. Courses in Astronomy, Astrophysics, Chemical Physics, Theoretical Physics, Earth & Space Science seem to take one a million miles away from investment analysis - and they make their share of physicists and astronomers here - but Maths shares the faculty, and investment advisers and analysts are in fact drawn from here in equal quantity with those from economics.

In the context of Economics, note the single honours BSc degree and BSc Economics & Statistics, etc, as well as BA Economics & Business with East European Studies (in the School of Slavonic & East Euro Studies). They took full marks at the assessments and have a world-class Grade 6* rating for research. It's a launch pad for merchant bankers too, while others again came through maths and the largest group (28%) through Information Science.

As we have seen, they actively encourage you to add an international dimension to your degree programme. A growing number of courses now include a year abroad, and many more can provide an opportunity for students to spend some time abroad, for example as part of a Socrates exchange. A newly established Study Abroad Office advises students on the opportunities open to them, ensures that students going abroad are fully briefed, and also works to expand further UCL's links with overseas organisations.

UCL is of course renowned for Law, and their drive to promote the internationalisation of study now sees German Law sitting alongside English and French Law. You'll need LNAT to get in.

SOCIAL SCENE
Students' Union UCL obviously lacks the cosy feel of some campus universities, but not to its detriment. **Phineas** is the hub. The largest venue is the

WHAT IT'S REALLY LIKE	
UNIVERSITY:	
Social Life	★★★★★
Campus scene	**Affluent south-east dominates**
Student Union services	**Average**
Politics	**Activity average.**
Sport	**54 clubs**
National team position	**34th**
Sport facilities	**Good**
Arts opportunities	**Excellent**
Student magazine	**Pi Magazine**
Student radio	**Rare FM**
Student TV	**BTV**
Nightclub	**Windeyer**
Bars	**Easy J's. Gordons, 2econd Floor, Huntley, Phineas, SSEES**
Union ents	**SportsNite, 2Phat**
Union societies	**90**
Most active society	**Indian Society**
Parking	**None**
CITY:	
Entertainment	★★★★★
Scene	**Wild, expensive**
Town/gown relations	**Average-good**
Risk of violence	**Average**
Cost of living	**High**
Student concessions	**Abundant**
Survival + 2 nights out	**£100 pw**
Part-time work campus/town	**Good/excellent**

are as popular with lecturers as they are with students, sign that UCL is thriving intellectually and cutlurally.

Sport There are 54 active sports clubs, and UCL came 34th nationally last year. Facilities include two large grounds (with bars), a gym, fitness centre (with multi-gyms, squash courts, Dojo, aerobics/dance hall, sun beds & sauna) and a large sports hall. For those who want to swim, there is access to the University of London Union pool, next door to UCL.

Town See Student London.

PILLOW TALK

Accommodation is guaranteed to freshers if they firmly hold an offer of a place on a degree programme, apply for accommodation by the deadline (currently May 31 of year of entry), and have not previously been a degree student living in London.

There are two types of accommodation on offer: halls of residence (catered/breakfast and evening meal) and student houses (self-catering accommodation, some purpose built, others converted private houses). UCL has a rolling programme of upgrading its accommodation; a 100 bed extension at Ramsay Hall is due to be completed in 2008. Newer residences have en-suite facilities and computer points networked to the UCL system. Frances Gardner House is newly built – 215 single en-suite rooms, just 20 mins' walk from campus.

ACCOMMODATION	
Guarantee to freshers	**100%**
Style	**Halls, flats**
Security guard	**Wardens**
Shared rooms	**Some**
Internet access	**All**
Self-catered	**Most halls, some flats**
En suite	**Some**
Approx price range pw	**£68-£144**
City rent pw	**£100-£180**

comfortable **Windeyer**, with a capacity of 550, large dance floor and a variety of catering. Wednesday attracts *SportsNite* to the **2econd Floor** bar. Thursday's *2Phat* runs across **Phineas** and **Windeyer**.

The union oversees more than 144 clubs and societies, based, for the most part, in a specially created, open plan area with computers, phones, photocopy and TV/video facilities. The union's many arts societies fill a gap in UCL's academic curriculum. Drama Soc performs to professional level at UCL's **Bloomsbury Theatre, where** the New London Orchestra is a kind of orchestra-in-residence, and there's a smaller experimental **Garage Theatre** and a stage in Huntley Street.

Student media is active with *Pi Magazine,* the student radio station, Rare fm, and student TV – Bloomsbury Television (BTV).

Popular out-of-hours lectures (unusual speakers, boundary-breaking, often controversial) are generally free, but necessarily ticket events. They

GETTING THERE

☞ UCL: Euston Square (Metropolitan, Circle, Hammersmith & City lines), Warren Street (Victoria, Northern), Euston (Victoria, Northern). Royal Free: Belsize Park Underground (Northern line) or overland railway, Hampstead Heath.

UNIVERSITY OF THE ARTS, LONDON

University of the Arts
65 Davies Street
London W1Y 5DA

TEL 020 7514 6000
FAX 020 7514 8179
EMAIL info@arts.ac.uk
WEB www.arts.ac.uk

VAG VIEW

*G*ranted *University title in 2003 and re-named the following year, this is the old London Institute, Europe's largest university for art, design, fashion, communication and the performing arts, and one of the biggest arts institutions in the world. It showed a healthy 7.8 % increase in applications last year - fourth highest countrywide.*

Described by Newsweek *as 'the epicentre of London style', their glittering alumni include some of the most celebrated artists and designers of the past century, including Gilbert and George (artists); Alexander McQueen (fashion designer); Chris Ofili (artist); Rebekah Wade (newspaper editor); Mike Leigh OBE (director); Simon Callow (actor), Rankin (photographer); Sir Terence Conran (design entrepreneur), Stella McCartney and John Galliano (fashion designers), and Alan Fletcher (designer).*

UA offers a distinctive education in Art, Design, Communication and Performance in a range of distinct and distinguished Colleges across London, with roots that run as deep as 1842.

As elsewhere in the country students here live their interests as much outside class as in. Last year UA took the Design of the Year and was runner-up Photographer of the Year at the Nation Student Awards, for its work on the student magazine, Less Common More Sense. *See www.suarts.org/lesscommon.*

In class, learning is practice-based, creative and strongly linked with industry. Half the teaching is undertaken by Associate Lecturers, who combine teaching with their own practice and up-to-the-minute industry experience.

COLLEGE SITES

Camberwell College of Arts
TEL:† +44 (0)20 7514 6302
FAX: +44 (0)20 7514 6310
EMAIL: enquiries@camberwell.arts.ac.uk†

UNIVERSITY/STUDENT PROFILE	
University since	**2003**
Situation/style	**Collegiate**
Student population	**30885**
Total undergraduates	**12460**
Mature undergraduates	**62%**
International undergrads	**No data**
Male/female ratio	**30:70**
Equality of opportunity:	
state school intake	**95%**
social class 4-7 intake	**27%**
low-participation area intake	**16%**

WEB: www.camberwell.arts.ac.uk/
Camberwell College of Arts has an international reputation in the field of art and heritage conservation, with graduates working in some of the most important museums and galleries in the world. The undergraduate and postgraduate courses provide exceptional teaching in conservation practice, science, history and museology.

Each College has its own gallery space and this year Camberwell gets a new one, the Peckham Pier.

Central Saint Martins College of Art and Design
TEL: +44 (0)20 7514 7022
FAX: +44 (0)20 7514 7254
EMAIL: info@csm.arts.ac.uk†
WEB: www.csm.arts.ac.uk/
Work has begun on its new multi-million pound home in the heart of King's Cross. The move, which is due to take place in 2011, will see Central Saint Martins focus its world leading expertise in art, design, communication and performance on one site, forming a powerhouse of creative energy in the heart of London.Courses range from foundation to PhD. Fashion and Textiles, Media Arts, Fine Art, Graphic Design, Theatre and Performance, 3D Design, Interdisciplinary.

Drama Centre, part of Central Saint Martins, is one of only two drama schools to operate in Central London.

Chelsea College of Art and Design
TEL: +44 (0)20 7514 7751
FAX: +44 (0)20 7514 7778
EMAIL: enquiries@chelsea.arts.ac.uk
WEB: www.chelsea.arts.ac.uk/

TEACHING SURVEY AT A GLANCE

Avg. UCAS points accepted	**410**
Acceptance rate	**19%**
Overall satisfaction rate	**63%**
Helpful/interested staff	**No data**
Small tuition groups	**No data**
Students into graduate jobs	**73%**

Teaching most popular with undergraduates:
Drama (75%), Journalism (65%), Fine Art (64%),
Management Studies (63%), Communications &
Information Studies (62%),
Film & Photography (61%).

Teaching least popular with undergraduates:
Business & Administrative Studies (54%),
Marketing (42%).

In 2004, Chelsea moved to a single campus on Millbank by the River Thames, next to Tate Britain. Courses: Art and Design, Communication, Digital Arts and Media, Drawing, Film and Video, F i n e Art, Furniture, Graphic Design, Interactive Multimedia, Interior Design, Knitwear, Model Making, New Media, Painting, Photography, Printmaking, Printed Textiles, Screenprinting, Sculpture, Stitch/embroidery, Textile Design, Visual Design and Display.

LONDON COLLEGE OF FASHION
TEL: +44 (0)20 7514 7407
FAX: +44 (0)20 7514 7484
EMAIL: enquiries@fashion.arts.ac.uk
WEB: www.fashion.arts.ac.uk/
Courses: Accessories, Beauty Science and Beauty Therapy, Business and Management, Buying and Merchandising, Culture and Communication, Cosmetic Science, Costume, Curation, Design and Technology, Fashion Design, Footwear, Journalism, Make up and Hair Styling, Marketing, Media, Menswear, Millinery, Photography, Promotion, Styling, Tailoring and Garment Production, Technical Effects, Textiles for Fashion, Womenswear. Specialist facilities include a 3D body scanner, and the Archive of Mary Quant.

When Cordwainers College, a name in footwear, saddler and leathercraft since 1887, joined the University in 2000, it brought with it an expertise in footwear and accessories, two of the fastest growing areas in the fashion industry, and contact with the very roots of footwear craft skills.

LONDON COLLEGE OF COMMUNICATION
TEL: +44 (0)20 7514 6569
FAX: +44 (0)20 7514 6535
EMAIL: info@lcc.arts.ac.uk

WEB: www.lcc.arts.ac.uk/
Courses: Book Arts & Crafts, Film & Video, Interior Design, Photography, Print Media, Sound Arts, Surface Design, Graphic & Media Design, Advertising, Digital Media Production, Journalism, Magazine Publishing, Marketing & Advertising, Public Relations, etc, and foundation degrees in some of these and such as sports journalism and print and production.

Their specialist Printing and Publishing School is founded on 100 years of expertise and recently launched a unique MA course in Print Media Management, run in partnership with Heidelberg Print Media Academy in Germany. Students spend two intensive weeks at the Print Media Academy - the training centre for Heidelberg Druckmaschinen AG, in Heidelberg, Germany.

Specialist facilities include radio, TV and film broadcast studios, sonic arts studios, and a facsimile of a newsroom. Finally, the college is home to the extensive Archive of the Stanley Kubrick.

WIMBLEDON COLLEGE OF ART
TEL: +44 (0)20 7514 9641
FAX: +44 (0)20 7514 9642
EMAIL: info@wimbledon.ac.uk
WEB: www.wimbledon.arts.ac.uk
Wimbledon School of Art joined the uni as its sixth college in 2006. The merger saw it renamed Wimbledon College of Art. It enjoys a reputation for excellence in theatre design, boasting the UK's largest School of Theatre, home to the largest theatre centre in the UK offering undergraduate and postgraduate degrees in design and related studies for stage, screen, costume and special effects.

Drawing is also a key focus - the distinguished Jerwood Drawing Prize is offered here. The College has produced many of the greatest names in theatre design and the arts, including triple Oscar winning costume designer James Acheson, production designer Sarah Greenwood, fashion designers Georgina Chapman and Phoebe Philo, guitarist Jeff Beck, and Turner Prize winner Tony Cragg.

FEES, BURSARIES

UK & EU fees 2009-10: £3,225 p.a. From September 2009, students in receipt of the full Government Maintenance Grant of £2,906 p.a. will receive a bursary of £319 p.a. All students who receive a proportion of the Maintenance Grant will be eligible to apply for an Access Bursary of £1,000 p.a. In addition, scholarship provision is a priority. There is a £1-million-plus scholarship programme at London College of Fashion, established by fashion entrepreneur Harold Tillman. The Tillman scholarships are awarded annually to ten MA fashion students unable to finance an MA course; ensuring young talented designers are not lost through lack of support. London College of Communication has recently launched a Penguin Scholarship for MA Publishing students. Successful applicants receive a £3,000 scholarship funded by Penguin Books.

SOCIAL SCENE

There are student bars at the various colleges, of course, and quite frankly you are as much a part of London as you are of a college. Still, last year saw the uni trying to centralise things a bit, by opening the Student Hub at their headquarters in Davies Street, Mayfair, the heart of the West End of London.

It's a focus for student services and the idea is that it provides a central place for students to come together to work, learn, exchange ideas, be inspired, relax and socialise as part of a community. Besides the offices, there's an Arts Gallery which shows work by graduates and is open to the public, a cafe bar, an activities studio, computing facilities and the Learning Zone, with 'key library texts', PCs and Macs, laptops for use in the area, WIFI interactive and standard whiteboards, projectors, photocopiers and printers, spray mount booth, cutting tables and mats, trimmers, and light-box facilities.

ACCOMMODATION	
Guarantee to freshers	**No guarantee**
Style	**Halls, flats**
Security guard	
Shared rooms	**Some**
Internet access	
Self-catered	**All**
En suite	**Most**
Approx price range pw	**£72-£140**
City rent pw	**£100-£180**

PILLOW TALK

The University provides 2,243 places in 12 residences in north, south, southeast and east London. Approximately 65% of freshers who want to live in University accommodation are successful in securing a place. Disabled students and students under 18 at the start of their course are guaranteed accommodation. Priority is given to students who come from outside London. Accommodation includes self-catering halls, flats and self-contained studio rooms. New build residence Will Wyatt Court opened in September 2008 in the heart of London's Hoxton and close to Old Street tube station.

UNIVERSITY OF WARWICK

The University of Warwick
Senate House
Coventry CV4 7AL

TEL 024 7652 3523
FAX 024 7652 4649
EMAIL student.recruitment@warwick.ac.uk
WEB www.warwick.ac.uk

University of Warwick Students' Union
Gibbet Hill Road
Coventry CV4 7AL

TEL 02476 572777
FAX 02476 572759
EMAIL enquiries@warwicksu.com
WEB www.warwicksu.com

VAG VIEW

*W*arwick has exploded upon the university scene and there can be few who wouldn't want to have it on their UCAS list. 'I knew from the first time that I visited that it was the place for me,' writes Emma Burhouse. 'As far as I could see, it had the ideal balance of a good reputation, a sound education and excellent social life.'

Emma night have added that the extra-curricular scene here is also one of the best in the country, with student drama, media and even sport these days figuring strongly at national level. This year there is a new

UNIVERSITY/STUDENT PROFILE	
University since	**1964**
Situation/style	**Campus**
Student population	**30320**
Total undergraduates	**20375**
Mature undergraduates	**18%**
International undergrads	**16%**
Male/female ratio	**50:50**
Equality of opportunity:	
state school intake	**76%**
social class 4-7 intake	**18%**
low-participation area intake	**5%**

Student Union building to go with it.
Now is the time to take Warwick by

TEACHING SURVEY AT A GLANCE

Avg. UCAS points accepted	**460**
Acceptance rate	**11%**
Overall satisfaction rate	**88%**
Helpful/interested staff	★★★★
Small tuition groups	★★★
Students into graduate jobs	**84%**

Teaching most popular with undergraduates:
Comparative Literary Studies (96%), Sciences related to Biology, French, Media Studies, Molecular Biology, Operational Research, Physics (95%), Computer Science (94%), Classics, European Languages (93%), Biology (92%), Creative Arts & Design, English, German, History, Hist. & Arachaeology, Law (91%), Business Studies, Drama, Politics (90%).

Teaching least popular with undergraduates:
Medicine, Engineering & Technology (77%), Electronic & Electrical Eng. (72%).

storm. In the National Student Survey 88% of students gave the teaching their approval and 84% will find themselves with a real graduate-type job within six months of leaving. Unsurprisingly, the drop-out rate is less than 3%.

CAMPUS

Warwick, lovely little market town, big castle... And not a university within ten miles of the place. Don't be fooled, the University of Warwick is not in Warwick, it's in Coventry. The reason it's called Warwick is that it was part-funded by Warwickshire County Council.

'Campus architecture is entirely uninspiring,' reports Simon McGee, 'but the greyness of the endless car parks and square buildings is fortunately

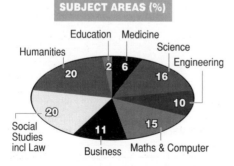

SUBJECT AREAS (%)

Education 2
Medicine 6
Humanities 20
Science Engineering 16
Social Studies incl Law 20
Business 11
Maths & Computer 15
10

balanced by hundreds of acres of surrounding grassland and forest.'

A second campus, ten minutes' walk away, houses the university's Education Institute and Westwood Halls of Residence. The point about Warwick is that like UEA, it is a campus apart from the town, and may seem to some a bit like living in a box.

'If you' re not paying attention, campus can feel a Doctor Seuss cartoon - you are surrounded by pointy concrete and sculptures straight off the set of Blake Seven. Some people take to campus life, and others quite frankly don't,' writes Andrew Losowsky.

FEES, BURSARIES

UK & EU Fees, 2009-10: £3,225 p.a. If in receipt of the HE Maintenance Grant there's a sliding-scale bursary dependent on household earnings.

STUDENT PROFILE

'You get the usual independent school boys and girls, for whom going to a university is the first time they haven't had to wear a uniform,' and, as Andrew points out, 'an unusually high mix of international students, meaning that, although most of the British students are from a middle-class background, there is still plenty of variety propping up the bar with you. The English - there are few Scots and Welsh - generally have the bland accentless tone of the home counties. Regional individuality may be gently mocked, but is in fact both envied and welcomed. Students on the whole are genuinely friendly here, and if you can't make any friends then you probably don't deserve to.'

ACADEMIA & JOBS

Warwick came 9th in the country in the recent Government Research Assessment, with powerful results in subjects such as Economics, where 40% of the work was rated world-class (4 star), and 55% internationally excellent (3 star). Business, Engineering, and History all fared well too, but it was Film & Tv Studies (60% 4* and 30% 3*) and Theatre, Performance & Cultural Studies (30 4*, 55% 3*) that made a special mark.

Students say that the best teaching is in Comparative Literary Studies, Sciences related to Biology, French, Media Studies, Molecular Biology, Operational, Computer Science, Classics, European Languages, Biology, Creative Arts & Design, English, German, History, History & Archaeology, Law, Business Studies, Drama, and Politics.

With Birmingham and Nottingham they recently founded the Midlands Physics Alliance, a joint School of Physics, with £3.9 million backing from the Government, delivering a subject to a new generation of students at a time when other universities are taking it off the curriculum.

Then there's the Leicester Warwick Medical School collaboration, an accelerated 4-year MB ChB for graduates of biological and health sciences. At the last count the application acceptance rate was 21, so there's a good chance of getting in.

The uni is heavily targeted by employers. Over 100 visit campus each autumn to give presentations and skills training sessions; many conduct first interviews with undergraduates on site. There are also five major recruitment fairs here each year.

In the matter of accountancy, there is nothing between Nottingham, Durham and Warwick. In the latest figures Warwick lies second to Nottingham and ahead of Durham in the matter of producing accountants. Together they are responsible for around 12% of the total number of graduates into the sector.

Education and finance dominate the graduate employment picture. After accountants it's investment analysts. Warwick's programmes stress business skills and enterprise 'working in interdisciplinary terms, just as they would in a corporate setting.' Tax experts and consultants also proliferate, as do actuaries. Three universities are head and shoulders above the rest in equating degree success with employment in actuarial science, namely Heriot-Watt, Warwick and Oxford. Warwick has BSc Maths-Operational Research-Statistics-Economics (Actuarial and Financial Mathematics). Together, the big three account for more than 20% of jobs in the sector.

Of the 5,000 + graduate teachers that spill onto the scene each year those destined for primary schools generally come through specialist colleges. Warwick is one very important exception, much to be recommended - as usual, they earned full marks in the assessments.

Warwick's Business School certificate in Applied Management is designed to develop the management skills of professional footballers who are in, or who want to take on, football management roles. Students include England players Les Ferdinand, Paul Ince and Steve Hodge.

There's also a strong English/creative writing scene - a whole raft of fascinating degrees that combine English with Theatre Studies, languages, American, even Latin, literature. And a useful employment niche in theatre. They have the national teaching centre with the Royal Shakespeare Company.

Finally, they are European law specialists, 2-4 years, including a year abroad. There are also Law degrees with Business and with Sociology.

RESEARCH EXCELLENCE		
% of Warwick's research that is 4* (World-class) or 3* (Internationally rated):		
	4*	**3***
Hospital Clinical	**5%**	**35%**
Health Services	**10%**	**55%**
Biological Sciences	**10%**	**40%**
Food Science	**20%**	**40%**
Chemistry	**15%**	**60%**
Physics	**15%**	**35%**
Pure Mathematics	**35%**	**45%**
Applied Mathematics	**30%**	**30%**
Statistics	**25%**	**45%**
Computer Science	**15%**	**50%**
General Engineering	**20%**	**50%**
Economics	**40%**	**55%**
Business/Management	**25%**	**50%**
Law	**10%**	**35%**
Politics	**20%**	**40%**
Social Work	**10%**	**50%**
Sociology	**30%**	**25%**
Psychology	**5%**	**60%**
Education	**20%**	**40%**
French	**20%**	**45%**
German	**15%**	**30%**
Italian	**30%**	**30%**
English	**35%**	**30%**
Classics	**25%**	**40%**
Philosophy	**15%**	**40%**
History	**30%**	**45%**
History of Art	**15%**	**55%**
Film & TV Studies	**60%**	**30%**
Theatre/Cultural Policy	**30%**	**55%**

STUDENTS' UNION

STUDENTS' UNION The two-phase Student Union rebuild is simply the biggest thing to happen on campus since anyone can remember. The stylish new glass-fronted, copper-roofed building is opening in two stages. By the time you get there it should all be complete. Central is the massive new first-floor **Terrace Bar,** which looks out from one whole side of the building over the entrance Piazza and has the **Island Bar** within. Behind it and below it is the Atrium, a light and airy covered space which runs right through the heart of the new Union, and takes in the cosy laid-back **Piazza café**. **The Graduate** pub remains, but has been extended and re-designed. The real jewel in the Union's new crown is the **Venue**, a split-level 3-floor space that provides a brilliantly equipped performance area and crowd space for 1,400, leading to the **Upstairs Club** (an additional 600 capacity; sound proofed it can be made separate or part of the Venue), and the

WHAT IT'S REALLY LIKE

UNIVERSITY:	
Social Life	★★★★★
Campus scene	**Good mix, non-elitist, vibrant**
Student Union services	**Excellent**
Politics	**Activity high, whole spectrum**
Sport	**74 clubs**
National team position	**19th**
Sport facilities	**Good**
Arts opportunities	**Drama, music, film, art excellent; dance good**
2008 Drama Awards	**3 @ NSDF**
Student magazine	**The Word**
Student newspaper	**Warwick Boar**
Student radio	**RaW**
2008 Media Awards	**2 Silver**
Student TV	**WTV**
Nightclub	**Venue**
Bars	**Terrace, Island, Graduate**
Union ents	**Top Banana, Score**
Union societies	**175**
Most popular society	**Cinema**
Parking	**None**
TOWN/CITY:	
Entertainment	★★★
Scene	**Local homely**
Town/gown relations	**Average**
Risk of violence	**Average**
Cost of living	**Average**
Student concessions	**Average**
Survival + 2 nights out	**£60 pw**
Part-time work campus/town	**Excellent/good**

Venue Bar, which runs the whole triple-staged height of the building.

Regular clubnights include *Top Banana*, party music; *Score*, Wednesday's after sports entertainment; Coalition, hip hop; *Pressure*, drum 'n' bass; *Heat*, international music; *Latin Night*, salsa rhythms; *School Dayz*, relive the best days of your life; *Vapour*, our very own house night; *Crash*, one of the biggest alternative nights in the Midlands; *Pure*, r&b; *Time Tunnel*, 60s, 70s and 80s music; *Metropolis*, the union gets turned into a major city for the night; and live music. Recent acts include: The Streets and Camera Obscura. Recently, too, they've been taking *Score* and *Top Banana* on the road, to clubs in the neighbourhood.

Strong in the student scene are not only ents but clubs & societies - there's an amazing 249 (74-odd sport), which must be a record, and they don't sustain them if interest flags. Encouraging them each year are their own society awards.

Media is especially strong - magazine (*The Word*), newspaper (*The Boar*), student radio (RaW), and WTV, the student television station. They are always in the national student awards. In 2008 it was the turn of RaW, which won two Silvers. Leo Robson also won Critic of the Year, an award made by the *Guardian* and *NME*. Strong, too, are arts activities - the **Warwick Arts Centre** is the second largest in the country, and has recently been refurbished thanks to a £33 million lottery grant. There is a concert hall, theatre, cinema, and art gallery. Student theatrical societies do well at the Edinburgh Festival and regularly get gongs at the National Student Drama Festival, where last year they took The Striker and won the Timothy West Award and two commendations for Acting and Direction. RAG and Community Action (13 projects in Coventry and Leamington Spa) are popular and the non-party political union works hard on ethical, human rights and environmental campaigns, though recently effort has been focused on anti-war and education funding.

SPORT Facilities are excellent - athletics track, games fields, artificial pitch and a recently completed £1-million sports pavilion. The Sports Centre, which also hosts Bear Rock, a rather vicious looking climbing wall for eager lemmings to try and scale, is free for students. Teams came 19th last year in the national student league. This year there's a new indoor tennis Centre.

TOWN 'Cov has a reputation for being dangerous,' writes Andrew, 'though in fact it's just like any other city. But even cities can be a shock after a year on campus, and few people spend time in Coventry. Which is a shame, as underneath the concrete nightmare is a friendly enough place, if you give it half a chance. Reasons to "brave" Cov practically quadrupled with the recent opening of **Skydome**, a huge multiplex with a sizeable gig venue, nine screen cinema, bars, restaurants and two outstanding clubs. It'll never quite beat the NEC, but a valiant effort nonetheless, and much closer to home. Most pubs in Cov are of the Rat, Parrot and Firkin ilk, but **The Golden Cross** and **The Hand and Heart** are worth a look for something different.

'As for Leam, it's a haven for trendy bars and homely pubs – don't miss **The Sozzled Sausage**, **Ocean** and **The Jug and Jester**.'

PILLOW TALK

From top quality en-suite halls to basic single rooms in shared accommodation with a lower rent, all study bedrooms have unmetered high-band-

ACCOMMODATION	
Guarantee to freshers	**100%**
Style	**Halls, flats**
Security guard	**All**
Shared rooms	**Some halls**
Internet access	**All**
Self-catered	**All**
En suite	**Some**
Approx price range pw	**£70-£115**
City rent pw	**£70**

width connection to ISP services. Everyone gets thrown out in their second year to live in Coventry or Leamington. The university owns plenty of houses, but most people end up going private. Leam is cheap, Cov even more so. If you can't handle a twenty-minute bus ride each day, then Leam is not an option.

GETTING THERE

☞ By road: M1/J21, M69, A46; or M1/J17, M45, A45, or M40/J15, A46; or M5/J4a, M42/J6, A45.
☞ By rail: Birmingham New Street, 30 mins; Manchester Piccadilly, 2:30; Nottingham, 1:45; Bristol, 2:30; London Euston, 1:20.
☞ By air: Birmingham International Airport.
☞ By coach: London, 1:20; Leeds, 4:00.

UNIVERSITY OF WEST OF SCOTLAND

The University of West of Scotland
Paisley Campus
Paisley, PA1 2BE

TEL 0141 848 3000
or 0800 027 1000
EMAIL uni-direct@uws.ac.uk
WEB www.uws.ac.uk

West of Scotland Students' Union
Paisley
Strathclyde PA1 2HB

TEL 0141 849 4157
FAX 020 7911 4158
EMAIL info@sauws.org.uk
WEB www.sauws.org.uk

VAG VIEW

*O*n 1st August 2007, the University of Paisley and Bell College merged to create Scotland's biggest modern university with campuses in Ayr, Dumfries, Hamilton and Paisley.

Paisley University came out of Paisley Technical College, founded in 1897. In the same year as it became a fully fledged university (1995) it began its development into Nursing and Midwifery, a faculty largely to be found at its campus to the south, in Ayr - Robbie Burns country. The main university campus is in Paisley itself, the largest town in Scotland and just a mile or so from Glasgow airport. Only a few years old is a third campus, a joint venture with Glasgow Uni and Dumfries & Galloway College, on an 80-acre parkland site half a mile from the centre of Dumfries, which is many miles to the south, close to the Solway Firth.

While most unis are struggling to meet Government targets to diversify their student body by delving into sections of the public that haven't traditionally gone to university, Paisley

UNIVERSITY/STUDENT PROFILE	
University since	**2007**
Situation/style	**Campuses**
Student population	**19550**
Total undergraduates	**17410**
Mature undergraduates	**46%**
International undergrads	**5%**
Male/female ratio	**40:60**
Equality of opportunity:	
state school intake	**99%**
social class 4-7 intake	**37%**
low-participation area intake	**6%**

has plenty of those and there's a very high drop-out rate.

Bell College in Hamilton was a Higher Education College founded in 1972, whose degrees were validated by Strathclyde University in Glasgow up until now. It lies 11 miles south east of Glasgow.

CAMPUS

PAISLEY CAMPUS takes getting to know: 'It would be really easy for a fresher, such as yourself, to mis-

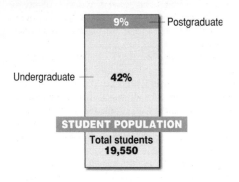

Postgraduate 9%

Undergraduate 42%

STUDENT POPULATION
Total students
19,550

take the main campus for a hospital wing in need of a cosmetic facelift,' writes Nausheen Rai. 'The "traditional" building has a blend of lino-type tiled floors, a supposed up-to-date glass "hamster" tunnel walkway (for fashion purposes darling), a surgical hospital smell that leaves one feeling oddly confused, and a brand new, £6-million, out-of-sync library with glass lift, plush pink carpets, novelty chairs and lots of space.'

AYR CAMPUS (known as 'Craigie') Tel 01292 886000. Opines Nausheen: 'This is definitely the more friendly campus (if that were to make the choice). Being smaller, it's more cosy. Males may count themselves fortunate to study in this sister campus tucked away on the west coast. There's an estimated ten women to every one of them.'

DUMFRIES CAMPUS Tel 01387 702060. It is situated beside the Crichton Business Park in eighty-five acres of parkland and gardens. A £1.8-million grant from the Scottish Funding Council is underwriting the development, which builds on franchise links which Paisley has had with Dumfries & Galloway College since 1994. The campus is an element in their open-access strategy, an attempt 'to widen the provision of higher education in the south west of Scotland.' It's worked.

HAMILTON CAMPUS Tel 01698 283100. This is the old Bell College, its higher education portfolio including business, accounting, law, journalism, sport (management, coaching, etc), social sciences, environmental sciences, engineering, product design, biosciences and computing. There is also a thriving further education provision.

FEES, BURSARIES
Fees for English: £1,820 p.a. EU Fees: none to pay. University bursaries are directed solely at international students.

STUDENT PROFILE
Many students are local, mature and/or part-timers and almost exclusively come to West of Scotland from the state sector, flooding in from neighbourhoods which haven't traditionally supplied universities.

ACADEMIA & JOBS
Faculties at Paisley include Engineering, Information Sciences, Science & Technology, Social and Management Sciences (and some midwifery and nursing). Faculties at Ayr are Education, Media Studies, Business, Nursing & Midwifery (apply through CATCH: 0131 220 8660). Subjects at Dumfries include Computing, Business & IT, along with Childhood Studies.

The big swell here is the increase in degrees in media, computing and technology. There has been a transformation at Ayr, where the largely female body of primary school teachers (Education is the most popular employment sector, 11% of graduates) and nurses have been getting cosy with the largely male students of BA Digital Art, BA Commercial Music, and BA degrees in Cinema, Media and Screen Practice. There are great media and broadcasting facilities at Ayr. They even run their own digital radio station.

Nevertheless, the real powerful computer and technology courses are still at Paisley, such as BSc Computer Games Technology, BA Computer Animation & Digital Art, BSc degrees in Computer-Aided Design, Digital Modelling, Computer Animation, Multimedia with Interactive Entertainment Technology, etc, and BEng degrees in Design and Product Design & Development, as well as BSc Music Technology.

Civil engineering is still a major focus, too, and they make as good a showing as Manchester Uni in the employment league. You get a BSc/BEng option in the single hons and three additional orientations for the BEng - Project Management,

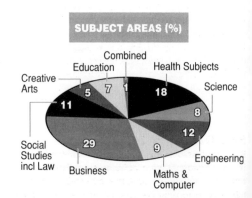

SUBJECT AREAS (%)

- Combined Education — 7
- Creative Arts — 5
- Health Subjects — 1
- Science — 18
- (Science) — 8
- Engineering — 12
- Maths & Computer — 9
- Business — 29
- Social Studies incl Law — 11

Environmental Mgt, Architectural Studies. Teaching inspection, Highly Satisfactory.

See also the Business IT & e-Commerce Department - BA Business Info Technology with either Accounting (there's an international Grade 5 in Accounting & Finance for research), Human Resource Management, Management or Marketing; or BSc with Multimedia or e-Business.

Note also an employment strength in social work, community and youth work - around 5% of graduates. See their Social Sciences faculty, which has a common first year before specialisation: Social Work, Sociology, Social Policy, Psychology, etc.

Bell was a well-organised operation. There are four faculties at the Hamilton Campus(Business, Engineering, Science, Health and Social Science) and Bell Innovations Ltd, a consultancy and training company that forges links with companies that help plan their courses and where students make profitable connections.

All degree courses at West of Scotland are designed with input from industry and commerce. Languages, IT training and work placements are key. IBM, M&S, BBC, Volkswagen, Standard Life and BAe all take Paisley undergrads on annual placements.

The University has a large network of companies across Europe for work placements. Placement companies have included Volkswagen, BBC, Siemens, British Aerospace, GlaxoSmithKline. There is also a tradition of celebrity lectures, workshops and seminars, most recently by such entrepreneur Chris Gorman, of Channel 4's 'Make Me A Million', who is an Honorary Professor of the University and provides an ongoing programme of business start-up and entrepreneurism workshops for students, and actor and director Peter Mullan, and Fran Healy of Brit Award-winning group Travis. Representatives from Sony Computer Entertainment Europe have also participated in student seminars, while motorsport students at the Hamilton campus have enjoyed workshops with rally and autosport experts.

Another boost to the degree portfolio recently has been the offer of a BSc Sports Studies, with its dedicated option routes. It's designed for students building on HNDs to degree level. Special focus areas are sports therapy, exercise, health and fitness, sports development, outdoor recreation administration.

STUDENTS' UNION

STUDENTS' ASSOCIATION UPSA have been campaigning for a proper union building since 1971. Now, following a new SU at Ayr - café-style, chrome tables, Chesterfield sofas, very slick - they have one, a £5-million town centre HQ.

Hitherto they have held comedy and home-grown theme nights, karaoke, quizzes and talent contests.

Now they do much the same, but with **Big Bar** the venue - a massive hanger of a place - and *Salamander* returns with resident DJs Brad and Anthony as the official Friday night extravaganza. Monday is pub quiz, *Universally Challenged*; Tuesday is Karaoke; Wednesday is Games Nights. A trip the six miles into the centre of Glasgow is a regular alternative.

At Craigie there are two or three discos, a Saturday party, quizzes, karaoke, etc, and a popular live act Acoustic Night. In town there's the **Wulf & Whistle** and **O'Briens,** virtually union property by adoption, and three cheesy nightclubs with weekly student nights.

Hamilton entertains with a few pubs and clubs, a wide range of sports facilities, and cinemas, theatres and museums are available locally. At the Students' Union there's ents throughout the year; clubs and societies range from sport to political and cultural groups.

SPORT The Robertson Trust Sports Centre is located in the student village in Paisley and has had a £1.5-million facelift. Some 1,500 students are members. Recent improvements include turf pitches for rugby and soccer and floodlit synthetic pitches. There are also facilities for squash, multi-gym workouts, badminton, hockey, netball, tennis, basketball, volleyball and table tennis.

There's not much sport in Ayr. At Hamilton there's a fitness studio and Sportsbarn.

PILLOW TALK

All accommodation at the Ayr, Hamilton and Paisley campuses is self-catered. In Ayr, halls of are on campus. At Paisley accommodation is at Thornly Park, 2 miles from campus. Costs are in the region of £65-£70 p.w.

GETTING THERE

☛ By road to Paisley: M8 - M74, A726, A737. For Ayr, M77/A77. For Dumfries, A76 or A701 from the north; A75 from the south.
For Hamilton, M74/J6.
☛ By rail to Paisley: Ayr, 45 mins; Glasgow Central, 15 mins. Glasgow to London, 6:00. For Dumfries: Glasgow, 2:00; Ayr, 1:50. For Hamilton: London, 5:27; Edinburgh, 2:04.
☛ By air: Birmingham International Airport.

UNIVERSITY OF WESTMINSTER

The University of Westminster
309 Regent Street
London W1B 2UW

TEL 020 7911 5000
FAX 020 7911 5788
EMAIL admissions@wmin.ac.uk
WEB www.wmin.ac.uk

Westminster Students' Union
32-38 Wells Street
London W1T 3UW

TEL 020 7911 5000 x 5454
FAX 020 7911 5793
EMAIL gensec@wmin.ac.uk
WEB www.uwsu.com

VAG VIEW

*T*he uni comes out of The Royal Polytechnic Institution, established in 1838 by (among others) Sir George Cayley, the North Yorkshire squire who invented the first man-powered flying machine, inveigling his unwilling butler to fly it solo down Brompton Dale.

On the surface, Westminster might appear to suffer all sorts of drawbacks characteristic of a new university in the metropolis - split sites, low entry requirements/high non-traditional student intake/high drop-out rate. Drop-out rate aside, because of its challenging commitment to an impressive curriculum, Westminster, in point of fact, flies higher than ever Cayley could have dreamt it would.

And right now they are giving their London campuses quite a shake-up, mainly to increase space for ex-curricular student activities.

UNIVERSITY/STUDENT PROFILE	
University since	**1992**
Situation/style	**Campus & city sites**
Student population	**24710**
Total undergraduates	**17850**
Mature undergraduates	**37%**
International undergrads	**12%**
Male/female ratio	**48:52**
Equality of opportunity:	
state school intake	**98%**
social class 4-7 intake	**44%**
low-participation area intake	**5%**

CAMPUSES

REGENT CAMPUS (address above). **Faculties** on four neighbouring sites: *Regent Street* (Social & Behavioural Sciences, including Psychology, some Business courses), *Little Titchfield Street, Euston Centre* and *Wells Street* (Law and Languages). **Academic resources:** Self-Access Language Centre, libraries, IT suites. **Leisure facilities:** Sport and Fitness Centre with cardiovascular and resistance equipment, saunas, solaria and indoor games hall; **Deep End Café** (Regent Street). The gym is on the way out and a bigger social space is in the making.

CAVENDISH CAMPUS 115 New Cavendish Street, London W1M 6UW (use main phone number above). The campus is undergoing a £25-million development, the first phase of which is due for completion this summer. **Courses:** Biosciences, Computing, Health. **Academic resources:** com-puter suites, science labs, library. **Leisure facilities:** bar and refectory. Soon to be the home of The Hub, see *Social Scene*, below.

MARYLEBONE CAMPUS 35 Marylebone Road, London NW1 5LS (use main tel. above). **Faculties:** Westminster Business School, School of Architecture and the Built Environment. **Academic resources:** library and laboratory. **Leisure facilities:** bar and **Café West**. A new venue is the big new gift to students. See *Social Scene* below.

HARROW CAMPUS Watford Road, Northwick Park, Harrow HA1 3TP. Tel: 020 7911 5936; Fax: 020 7911 5943. **Style:** well-designed, self-contained campus, close to horrendous looking hospital. **Faculties:** Harrow Business School, Computer Science, Media, Arts & Design. **Academic resources:** Information Resources Centre, including library, computers (1,000+ campus-wide), AV aids for presentations; also TV, radio, photography and music studios. **Leisure facilities:** venue (**Area 51**), open-air performance court, **The Undercroft Bar**, sports hall, fitness suite and playing fields close by.

FEES, BURSARIES

UK & EU Fees, 2009-10: £3,225 p.a. If in receipt of a HE Maintenance Grant there's a bursary of £319. In addition, Westminster has a wide range of scholarships for both undergraduate and postgraduate students, for both UK/EU and international students.

STUDENT PROFILE
In its student clientele, Westminster mirrors many other ex-polys. There's a sizeable mature, part-time, local and overseas population – they received a Queen's Award for Enterprise for their success in International Markets, and were the first post-1992 uni to have been so rewarded.

There's also a significant non-degree student population, and many students are the first in their families to experience university – 44% are from new-to-uni social groups.

ACADEMIA & JOBS
In their vocational, modular course planning they have taken advice from the professions and industry, and translated it into a strategy underpinned by an expert language provision. Their School of Professional Language Studies lays claim to one of the widest range of language teaching in the UK - they are particularly strong on Asian Studies. Russian, Arabic and Chinese also feature.

There's a reputation for finding students work in those most difficult areas of art, design and media. Though it would be wrong to suggest that these jobs come in a flood, relative to most other

TEACHING SURVEY AT A GLANCE

Avg. UCAS points accepted	**240**
Acceptance rate	**19%**
Overall satisfaction rate	**73%**
Helpful/interested staff	★
Small tuition groups	★★
Students into graduate jobs	**68%**

Teaching most popular with undergraduates:
Social Studies (91%), Psychology, Biology (86%), Sciences related to Biology (85%), Sociology (84%), Building (89%), English (79%), Architecture, Politics (78%), Languages (77%), Business, Electronic & Electrical Engineering (76%).

Teaching least popular with undergraduates:
Film & Photography (57%), Design Studies (51%).

RESEARCH EXCELLENCE

% of Westminster's research that is 4* (World-class) or 3* (Internationally rated):

	4*	3*
Community Clinical	10%	15%
Health Professions	10%	25%
Environmental Sciences	5%	30%
Computer Science	5%	20%
Electrical/Electronic Eng,	0%	15%
Built Environment	20%	40%
Town/Country Planning	5%	20%
Geography/Environment	10%	40%
Business/Management	5%	25%
Law	0%	35%
Politics	5%	15%
Psychology	0%	15%
Asian Studies	10%	20%
French	0%	25%
English	0%	20%
Linguistics	5%	5%
History	0%	15%
Art and Design	20%	55%
Media Studies	60%	30%
Music	10%	15%

unis they are areas in which Westminster enjoy success and have some very good courses.

In Art & Design they have graphic design, illustration, photography, animation, mixed media fine art and ceramics. In Communication/Design & Media they cover digital and photographic imaging, film and TV production, journalism, public relations, radio production, music informatics, and commercial music. The latter, for aspiring music industry managers, concerns music production, but also the business side, including the law. Strong industry links, good reputation in business management. You'll be based at the Harrow Campus. In the 2008 Research Assessment they had a spectacular result in media: 60% internationally significant, and 30% world class..

The majority of undergraduates read for degrees in business, many of them destined for jobs as accounts and wages clerks - at least in the first instance. Retail is a strength, as is marketing; there are dedicated degrees. See also their human resource business degrees, e-business, commercial law, etc, and the International degrees, making use of their excellent language provision. There are degrees in business at both central London and Harrow campuses, so be sure you know where you are destined.

In Law, they are commercial, business and European specialists, but with an interesting range of courses.

The computing provision is also strong and directs graduates along the clearest employment pathways: IT consultants, systems analysts, software engineers, analyst/programmers, etc.

There's enormous strength in architecture, town planning, and the building industry. The Architecture degrees are mostly technology, engi-

WHAT IT'S REALLY LIKE	
UNIVERSITY:	
Social Life	★★★
Campus scene	**Diverse, non-traditional**
Student Union services	**Average**
Politics	**Interest low**
Sport	**15 clubs**
National sporting position	**118th**
Sport facilities	**Improving**
Arts opportunities	**Drama excellent; film, music good; dance, art poor**
Student magazine	**The Smoke**
Radio Station	**Smoke Radio**
2008 media awards	**2 Silver, 1 Bronze**
TV station	**Smokescreen TV**
Nightclub	**Inter:Mission, Area 51**
Bars	**Dragon Bar, Undercroft**
Union ents	**r&b, bhangra, indie**
Union societies	**20**
Most popular society	**Law Soc, Dram Soc**
Parking	**Adequate**
CITY:	
Entertainment	★★★★★
City scene	**Wild, expensive**
Town/gown relations	**Average-good**
Risk of violence	**Average**
Cost of living	**Very high**
Student concessions	**Good**
Survival + 2 nights out	**£120 pw**
Part-time work campus/town	**Poor/excellent**

neering, and there are BA degrees in Interior Design and Urban Design. See, too, the Construction, Surveying and Property degrees, Urban Estate Management.

Then there is the health provision, with a full-marks teaching assessment score for BSc Psychology with Neuroscience. Note there is a foundation course into this, and a sound reputation for employment. There are nutrition and health degrees, physiology and pharmacology, sport and exercise, and complementary medicine degrees - they were one of the first to offer these and have made them a success. Westminster also award the degrees of The British College of Osteopathic Medicine.

SOCIAL SCENE

The Uni has revamped its central London campuses, so it's a pretty exciting time to be a student here. They've opened up a new venue, **Inter:Mission**, at the Marylebone campus (that's the one opposite Madame Tussauds) which is, well, white leather, mood lights, BOSE sound... alcoholic and alcohol-free sections, giant movable plasma screens and little TVs in every table.

This campus is envisaged as a major centre for the creative arts in London. **P3**, a vast new underground exhibition space opened here last year and has already hosted events in London Fashion Week, the launch of Architecture Week, and student degree shows. A new 3-year programme of events, Ambika at P3, will bring together artists, architects and creative practitioners from across the capital.

They are also moving the gym from Regent Street and creating a big new social space there too. Meanwhile, at New Cavendish Street, they are creating **The Hub**, a kind of central social space for West End students. They are also working on plans to improve the central London halls.

Out at Harrow, the self-contained campus close to the station, students already have their infamous nightclub, **Area 51**, and a cosy little bar, The Undercroft, as well as their typical Student Union dive-in central, the Dragon Bar.

Typical ents are *Happy Mondays* at **Undercroft**, *Candy Floss* on Thursday at Inter:Mission, and *Baby Shake*, a pre-party for *Milkshake* at **Ministry of Sound** on Tuesday. Says Rob: 'We've got a pretty full schedule of events at all these bars and clubs, including club nights and live music nights. We cater for most tastes, with the hugely successful FONO playing indie. The Freshers and May Balls bring in some of the best performers in the country. But because we cater for so many international and non-drinking students, we also provide activities around London.

'We're battling against student apathy, because many students in our central campuses live at home and don't get involved. We've a huge number of different nationalities and races here, and we have to try and cater for so many different interests, it's a big job.'

Some of the best society activity comes out of course disciplines (media, music), and you can't help wondering whether, if they really got this aspect of student life together, they might whittle down the drop-out rate. Clearly, with all these new social spaces in the West End, already showing in the autumn of 2006, that's what's in the mind of the uni, too.

The student media is excellent. Student newspaper *Smoke* has been up there at the national media awards in recent times, and in 2008 the student radio station, Smoke Radio, won three Silver awards and a Bronze. There is now, too, a student television station: Smokescreen TV.

SPORT The uni is not known nationally for its sporting prowess; they came 118th in the leagues last year, but their football and cricket teams are amongst the best in their more local leagues, and the Ju-Jitsu team wins tournaments up and down the country.

PILLOW TALK
There are halls, rooms or flats in Marylebone Road, Highgate Village and Victoria. The accommodation at Harrow is all en suite. There was recently a £11.2million refurbishment of the 21-storey Marylebone Road student halls, which reopened for the September 2008 intake.

GETTING THERE
☛ To Regent Campus: Oxford Circus Underground (Bakerloo, Central and Victoria).
☛ To Cavendish Campus: Warren Street Underground (Northern and Victoria lines).

ACCOMMODATION	
Guarantee to freshers	**60%**
Style	**Halls, flats**
Security guard	**All**
Shared rooms	**Some**
Internet access	**All**
Self-catered	**All**
En suite	**No halls, all flats**
Approx price range pw	**£73.50-£163.10**
City rent pw	**£80-£180**

☛ To Marylebone Campus: Baker Street Underground (Bakerloo, Metropolitan, Hammersmith & City, Circle, Jubilee lines).
☛ By road to Harrow Campus: A404 accessible via M25, M1 or M40/A40; by Underground – Northwick Park (Metropolitan line).

UNIVERSITY OF WINCHESTER

The University of Winchester
Winchester
Hampshire SO22 4NR

TEL 01962 827234
FAX 01962 827288
EMAIL course.enquiries@winchester.ac.uk
WEB www.winchester.ac.uk

Winchester University Students' Union
Winchester
Hampshire SO22 4NR

TEL 01962 827418
FAX 01962 827419
EMAIL SU_Pres@winchester.ac.uk
WEB www.winchesterstudents.co.uk/

VAG VIEW

*F*ounded as a Diocesan teacher training establishment, and until recently King Alfred's College, a university sector college with a range of Southampton University degrees and a speciality in producing primary school teachers, they are now, since 2005, a university.

They always had ambitions to be something other than what they were, and tried various things to hasten the process. In 1994, for example, they took over the Basingstoke and Winchester School of Nursing and Midwifery and began developing all sorts of multi-disciplinary courses in Health Care. But you'll not find a student nurse or midwife closer than Southampton today. Then, in September 2003, a 'new' Basingstoke campus opened with 'new earn-

UNIVERSITY/STUDENT PROFILE	
University since	**2005**
Situation/style	**Campus**
Student population	**5300**
Total undergraduates	**4250**
Mature undergraduates	**37%**
International undergrads	**4%**
Male/female ratio	**25:75**
Equality of opportunity:	
state school intake	**97%**
social class 4-7 intake	**32%**
low-participation area intake	**9%**

while-you-learn Foundation Degrees', a feeder site for a future university, the perfect thing to satisfy the widening participation requirement of all universities.

Meanwhile, one or two unusual specialities were emerging, a course in

TEACHING SURVEY AT A GLANCE

Avg. UCAS points accepted	**260**
Acceptance rate	**22%**
Overall satisfaction rate	**86%**
Helpful/interested staff	**★★★★**
Small tuition groups	**★★★★**
Students into graduate jobs	**57%**

Teaching most popular with undergraduates:
Sports Science (98%), Education (94%), Business & Administrative Srudies, History (93%), English, Management Studies, Psychology (92%).

Teaching least popular with undergraduates:
Dance, Drama (78%).

Biopsychology, another in Archaeology (taught by people actively involved on site work), an East Asian Studies course with Business Studies and BA hons combos with Japanese. All but Archaeology disappeared as magically as the nursing provision, but teaching assessments, after years of scoring 18-21 points at best, suddenly returned results of full marks for Archaeology and Education, and 23 out of 24 for bedrock Theology, and 22 points for Business and Sport.

After all, that was the way to go, and, following a swift baptism as University College Winchester, Alfie moved with all speed to achieve university status.

In 2008 Winchester climbed from 99th to 78th place in the Government's Research Assessment, with 5% of its research, including 15% of its History research, getting the highest, world-class, rating. At the same time 86% of its students told the National Student Survey that they were satisfied with the

teaching, and in the Times Higher's Student Experience Survey lecturers here were praised for their helpful and interested approach and for the size of their tuition groups. All of which tells why, with its distinctly 'new university' clientele, Winchester manages to keep its drop-out rate down to a manageable 8%. The 'real graduate job' figures are less enticing, however. Only 57% are successful within six months of graduating.

STUDENT PROFILE

There is a high proportion of mature students (37%), and the student body is overwhelmingly female (75%), as you would expect from a uni where many are studying to be primary school teachers. There are also many part-timers (20% of undergraduates), though that figure is on the decline, and locals. There is a kind of innocent cheery fun about the place, but big fish will find it something of a small pond.

FEES, BURSARIES

UK & EU Fees, 2009-10: £3,225 p.a. There are bursaries for those eligible for the Government Maintenance Grant, and ll UK domicile students are eligible to receive the Winchester Scholarship, a package of financial support specially designed to put money in your pocket during your study here at Winchester. All 4th-year BA Education undergraduates get a scholarship in recognition of the extra costs compared with the three year and PGCE qualified teacher status routes. There are also Winchester Partner Colleges Scholarships, and the King Alfred Scholarship of £2000 (one-off payment) for students under 25 at entry who have been 'looked after' for at least 13 weeks since the age of 14 and who have left care (as defined by the Children (Leaving Care) Act 2000).

CAMPUS

This is a campus uni overlooking the historic cathedral city of Winchester in Hampshire, 15 miles north of Southampton. It has its own theatre and dance studio, Student Union and accommodation.

ACADEMIA

Winchester offers undergraduate courses in American Studies, Archaeology, English, Creative Writing, Dance, Drama, Education, Film, Heritage, History, Horticulture, Journalism, Leisure, Management, Marketing, Media, Performing Arts, Psychology, Religious Studies, Social Care, Sport, Teaching, Tourism. There is a feeder site in Basingstoke, where you can get on degrees via

SUBJECT AREAS (%)

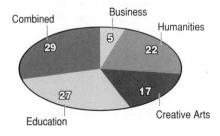

Combined 29
Business 5
Humanities 22
Creative Arts 17
Education 27

foundation courses.

The teaching assessments suggest their strengths lie in Education, Archaeology, Theology, Business, Psychology, Sport, while the research assessments point to Education, Media, and Performing Arts, all of which were adjudged world-class in at least 5% of the work, and a third internationally excellent.

Media and film courses at Winchester benefit from a link-up with the Asian Academy of Film and TV in the Bollywood city of Noida, near Delhi.

ACCOMMODATION	
Guarantee to freshers	**100%**
Style	**Halls, flats**
Security guard	**All**
Shared rooms	**Some halls**
Internet access	**All**
Self-catered	**Most**
En suite	**Some**
Approx price range pw	**£80-£90**
City rent pw	**£65**

SOCIAL SCENE

STUDENT UNION The Union provides three bars - **Bar 22**, **The Lounge** and **C2H** (Close to Home), recently refurbished at a cost of £100,000. Ents include club nights (*Timewarp* or *Club Tropicana*), bar quizzes, comedy evenings, live music, promotions, multi-venue events and theme nights, plus society nights, like *Indie Three Sixty* recently from *BFLP* Magazine. Bigger occasions are the Winton Reunion Weekend (sporty), and the Freshers, Christmas, Summer and Graduation Balls which traditionally play host to top name acts in the **Guildhall**, 'a great venue, with a main hall and lots of smaller rooms with jazz, karaoke, live music and a casino.'

The Stripe Theatre is the performing arts space and film studio on campus, hosting live productions by students and visiting professionals. In town, it's the **Town Arts Centre** and **Theatre Royal** for everything from stand-up comedy to children's theatre, music and dance to plays.

There's a year-round welfare-themed campaign called Play Mates, various societies, from Alternative Music to Ultimate Frisbee, and a media group that is causing something of a stir with *Big Fish Little Pond* magazine and Voice Radio.

SPORT They play in the national student leagues, but are happier in the Southern England Student Sports Association (SESSA), and in SUSC, a collection of local universities. There iare currently a rugby pitch and 2 football pitches a mile away; also a New Club House with bar. A sports hall hosts 5-a-side football, badminton, netball, hockey, volleyball, cricket, and is the home of the Knights and Angels Basketball teams. There are also 2 tennis courts (next to Alwyn Halls on campus), a squash court and fitness suite.

CITY There are nightclubs in nearby Eastleigh and Woodmancote, and 15 miles away in Southampton there's **Ocean + Collins** in Vincent Walk, with 1000 capacity, late bar, and a *Big Cheese* Student Night on Thursdays, but Winchester itself is fairly barren. Do not expect the *Brooks Experience* in the Shopping Centre to have anything to do with Jimi Hendrix. Pubs like **The Mash Tun**, the **King's Arms**, the **Forester** have music, and **O'Neills** has a big screen in the High Street, but watch out for squaddies from the nearby barracks. In general, they don't appreciate students, 'unless served on a plate with chips,' writes Stephanie Kirk, who in fact always feels safe here.

'If you have lived in a small town and feel threatened in a large city, Winchester may be the place for you. It is a city, not because of size, but because of its cathedral. It is quiet, picturesque and may prove to be a bit dull for some people.

'Winchester is steeped in history, not only due to King Alfred, but also to King Arthur. Allegedly his famous round table is housed in the city's Great Hall. the cathedral, where our graduation ceremony takes place, is the main focal point, along with Winchester boys' school, second only to Eton.'

There is also another side to the city, however. 'I follow Drama, Theatre and Television Studies, and a small group of us worked with a day centre. Most of the people were homeless, or on a very low budget, some are ex-offenders, some drug addicts. None of them wanted anything to do with drama! It took us ten weeks to get a workshop up and running, but the course was so satisfying in the end.'

PILLOW TALK

There are fewer than 1,000 study bedrooms available to students, self-catered at West Downs Student Village, catered on the main campus. Some specially adapted rooms are available for disabled students.

GETTING THERE

☛ By road: M3/J10; northwest, A272, B3041; southwest, A3090.
☛ By rail: London, 1:00; Bristol Parkway, 2:15; Birmingham, 3:15; Southampton, 20 mins.
☛ By air: Gatwick, Heathrow, Southampton.
☛ By coach: London, 2:00; Birmingham, 5:30.

UNIVERSITY OF WOLVERHAMPTON

The University of Wolverhampton
Compton Road West
Wolverhampton WV3 9DX

TEL 0800 953 3222
FAX 01902 323744
EMAIL enquiries@wlv.ac.uk
WEB www.wlv.ac.uk

Wolverhampton Students' Union
Wulfruna Street
Wolverhampton WV1 1LY

TEL 01902 322021
FAX 01902 322020
EMAIL president@wlv.ac.uk
WEB www.wolvesunion.org

VAG VIEW

The University of Wolverhampton was spawned by the Wolverhampton Poly following a merger with three teacher training colleges and West Midlands College of Higher Education. Operating on campus sites in and around Wolverhampton and in Shropshire, they have recruiting associations with dozens of colleges, and were the first to attract entrants via a high street shop. As many as 25,000 people a year visit the shop and more than 7% sign up.

UNIVERSITY/STUDENT PROFILE	
University since	**1992**
Situation/style	**Campus and city sites**
Student population	**23470**
Total undergraduates	**18935**
Mature undergraduates	**35%**
International undergrads	**14%**
Male/female ratio	**44:56**
Equality of opportunity:	
state school intake	**99%**
social class 4-7 intake	**51%**
low-participation area intake	**19%**

CAMPUSES

City Campus Location: a few minutes walk from Wolverhampton rail and bus stations. **Campus scene:** the busy centre of it all. **Courses:** Applied Sciences, Art & Design, Computing, Construction, Engineering, Health Sciences, Languages, Humanities and Social Sciences, including Law.

Compton Park Campus Compton Road West, Wolverhampton WV3 9DY. **Location:** mile or so west of main campus. **Courses:** Business Admin, Info Management, some Human Resourcing, Marketing, some Computing.

Walsall Campus Gorway Road, Walsall WS1 3BD. **Location:** six miles east of town centre. **Campus scene: known as** 'the concrete jungle', but strong community spirit. **Courses:** Education (incl. Sports Studies). New this year 350 study bedrooms, all en-suite. A £7.1 million Sports and Judo Centre includes a full fitness suite, coffee bar and crÈche, new tracks and all-weather pitches and the surrounding community will also have access to the facilities.

Shropshire (Telford) Campus Priorslee Hall, Shifnal Road Telford TF2 9NT. **Location:** 12 miles northwest of town. **Campus scene:** the International Students' Association thrives. **Courses:** Business, Computer-aided Product Design.

FEES, BURSARIES

UK & EU Fees, 2009-10: £3,225 p.a. There's a £300 to £500 'Start Right' bursary if eligible for HE Maintenance Grant.

STUDENT PROFILE

As many as 50% are from the lowest 4 social groups and 26% from 'low-participation neighbourhoods', families who have previously not considered uni an option. Perhaps that explains the persistently cheerful student scene at Wolverhampton, which was voted the friendliest university in the West Midlands via the Friends Reunited website.

More than 70% of its undergraduate intake is mature, a great number are part-timers, and the SU tells us that there is a high percentage of disabled students, too. There are certainly a number of very good special needs degree courses.

They are in that sense a modern university, playing an ambitious game. 'If there is any university with ambition, giving clear signs that it wants to play with academia's big boys,' said Mark Wilson. 'It may take a few years, but there is no doubt that it will get there. We are fortunate to have a 23,000-strong melting pot of cultures, skills, talents - sectors, like Lesbian, Gay & Bisexual (LGB), mature students or ethnic minorities, get people together and entertain them. It may take time to shake the wally poly stereotype, but the future is looking blinding from where I stand.'

ACADEMIA & JOBS

'The teaching is particularly good for the vocational courses on which we focus,' says Mark. 'Lectures and seminars, but also film screenings, guest speakers, hands-on activities and group work with assessments. The best thing may be that they teach subjects which lead to jobs, engineering, film, computer programming and many more.'

The Careers and Employment Service provides a specialist recruitment agency called The Workplace that will help students and graduates into all kinds of work: Local, national and international positions covering all careers are on offer. The Workplace has a database of over 9,000 companies from which vacancies are advertised.

Wolverhampton is taking the relationship between academia and industry to a new level by insisting that its teaching staff take part-time jobs in local industry under the aegis of 'staff development'. The deputy vice-chancellor said: 'Our staff already work in partner organisations. We have people working one day a week in the health service or people on secondments. We are now looking at joint appointments as well.'

Many courses are devised in consultation with businesses and the uni is committed to increasing the number of courses which offer accreditation or a licence to practice alongside a degree. However, the subject that attracted the highest mark - full marks, in fact - at the teaching assessments was Philosophy.

They have a newish £4.5-million Learning Centre - 967 study spaces, 130 IT spaces, 200,000 volumes - following the opening of a similar centre in Shropshire.

A close association with industry in this high density industrial area, as well as commerce and the professions, gives confidence, and their

TEACHING SURVEY AT A GLANCE	
Avg. UCAS points accepted	**180**
Acceptance rate	**23%**
Overall satisfaction rate	**76%**
Helpful/interested staff	★★★
Small tuition groups	★★
Students into graduate jobs	**75%**

Teaching most popular with undergraduates:
Languages (89%), English, Physics (88%), History, Philosophy (85%), Architectural Design, Visualisation, History & Archaeology, Sociology (84%), Engineering & Technology, Computer Science, General Eng., Initial Teacher Training (81%).

Teaching least popular with undergraduates:
Dance (57%).

employment record is good not only locally. A particular emphasis is on languages - students of all disciplines may study a language and the teaching assessments have been good: Russian scored 22 points out of 24, Spanish 20, French 19, German 17. There's a particular niche in British Sign Language Interpreting, the 3-year degree being pretty much a dead cert for getting a job. A foundation year is available.

Around a fifth of Wolverhampton students graduate in business subjects. The next most popular degrees may be found in Art & Design, although the employment picture for the latter is less sure in the first six months following graduation. Plenty of work for the graphic designers, artists and photographers, with some others finding jobs in further education as teachers, and in galleries.

The business/finance ticket is more certain. Accountancy, for instance go for the 3 or 4-year sandwich Accounting & Finance, or joint hons with Computing, Law or Marketing. Personnel - look at the Business & Human Resource Management combination. Sales and marketing, look for their dedicated degrees Marketing, Retail Marketing, Entrepreneurship, etc. Or explore the joint honours scheme for tie-ups between Marketing and such as Tourism or Media & Communication. Look also at their series of nine Tourism Management degrees.

There's are strong employment lines at Wolverhampton into the Civil Service through business and through the computer provision. And besides the expected computer engineers, analysts and programmers (4-year sandwich Computer Science/Software Engineering), there's a niche for games design - see the 4-year sandwich Computer

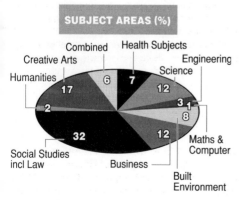

SUBJECT AREAS (%)

Combined — Health Subjects
Creative Arts — Engineering Science
Humanities
17 — 6 — 7 — 12
2 — 3 — 1 — 8
32 — 12
Social Studies incl Law — Business — Maths & Computer
Built Environment

RESEARCH EXCELLENCE

% of Wolverhampton's research that is
4* (World-class) or 3* (Internationally rated):

	4*	3*
Health Professions	5%	15%
Mechanical, Aero. & Manufac. Eng.	5%	25%
Built Environment	10%	40%
Business/Management	0%	20%
Information Management	25%	40%
Law	0%	25%
Education	5%	15%
European Studies	0%	25%
Linguistics	15%	40%
History	5%	25%
Art and Design	10%	25%

Floorcoverings & Interior Textile Design to Painting.

New Sound Production and Music Industry Practice foundation degrees are believed to be the first of their kind in the UK. See also new degrees in Music Technology, and Entertainment & Industries Management. Just how switched on they are to the power of entertainment media was shown last year when they produced a multimedia CD with local rock radio station Kerrang!, which included 16 tracks interspersed with promotional messages about Clearing and was distributed free from HMV stores throughout the West Midlands.

Finally, there's a good reputation for Law. Non-Law graduates may opt for a 2-year full-time or 3-year part-time Senior Status Law Degree, and recently the LPC Board assessed the department 'Good' on a scale of Excellent, Very Good, Good, Satisfactory or Unsatisfactory.

SOCIAL SCENE

STUDENTS' UNION At City Campus, it's **Fat Micks** (dance floor, food, pool tables, widescreen TV, 1,200

Science (Games Development). There's a Virtual Reality Centre in the School of Engineering. Look also for up-and-coming courses in Automotive Systems Engineering, Computer-Aided Engineering/Product Designs.

Certain, too, are the educational and health provisions. They produce primary and secondary teachers, physical education instructors, further education lecturers, and educational assistants - there are some good specialisms in the joint hons degree programme, such as Special Needs & Inclusion Studies and Deaf Studies .

In health, non-hospital nurses, nurses and midwives proliferate. There's also a Cancer Care top-up. There are also BSc degrees in Complementary Therapies and Health Sciences, and BSc Psychology and BSc Counselling Psychology - 21 out of 24 at the assessments.

Biochemists, biomedical scientists and pharmacists also come out of here in number - this department dropped only one point at the teaching assessments.

The 3% graduates joining the construction industry come out of BA Architecture or BSc Architectural Technology, Building or Quantity Surveying, Civil Engineering, Construction Management, Computer Aided Design (Construction), Interior Architectural Design, Project Management, etc.

Success in the creative arts/design and radio/TV industries directs us to their performance arts and media degrees, to the £2-million, Lottery-funded redevelopment of their Arena Theatre, and to the School of Art & Design's Gallery space, home to a range of courses, from Animation to Journalism & Editorial Design, from Computer-Aided Design to Sculpture, from

WHAT IT'S REALLY LIKE

UNIVERSITY:	
Social Life	★★★
Campus scene	**Local, lively**
Student Union services	**Average**
Politics	**Student issues**
Sport	**20+**
National team position	**83rd**
Sport facilities	**Good**
Arts opportunities	**Music, art excellent; drama, dance good; film average**
Student magazine	**Cry Wolf**
Nightclub	**Zone 34**
Bars	**Fat Mick's, Poly Bar, Bertie's, Auntie Rita's**
Union ents	**Chart and cheese**
Union societies	**50**
Most popular societies	**Qur'an & Sunnah, Christian Union**
Parking	**Poor**
TOWN:	
Entertainment	★★★
Scene	**Pubs, diverse studenty clubs**
Town/gown relations	**OK-ish**
Risk of violence	**Average**
Cost of living	**Low**
Student concessions	**Good**
Survival + 2 nights out	**£50 pw**
Part-time work campus/town	**Good**

capacity, licensed till midnight and till 2 am Wednesday, Friday and Saturday), the **Poly Bar** (a pre-club comedy or light entertainment venue) and now they also have **Zone 34** (**The Zone**, as it's known), replacement for the JL nightclub, which is now the Student Activities Hub. Yet, Tuesdays is student night in **Walkabout**, the new club in town - indie classics and alternative in main room, old skool in surfers paradise upstairs. Not until Wednesday does it warm up in the SU, when in parallel, at Fat Mick's and The Zone respectively, there's *Cut Loose* - indie, alternative, hip hop, soul, funk, and *BassSick* - RnB, hip hop, soul. Then Friday it's good old *Flirt!* - the student cliché that wows a nation - and Saturday, *FHUK* funky house.

There's much else besides, both in and out of the bars and clubs. Wolves has a strategy for developing an on-going programme of these to help students develop the skills they'll need. If you flip onto their web site you'll see the kind of helpful community this union is striving to create, whether it's revision classes, welfare or just plain fun.

At Telford, it's **Auntie Rita's** (capacity 250), licensed to 11 pm – 12 on Wednesday and Friday. **Berties Bar** (capacity 300) is on the third floor of Walsall Campus. Ents are theme nights, quizzes, movie nights, barbecues.

Sport There are sports hall, squash courts, fitness centre at Wolverhampton; sports hall, playing fields, running track, swimming pool, dance studio, tennis courts at Walsall, where judo hopefuls for the 2012 Olympic Games are using the uni's National Judo Centre of Excellence. This is also home to the town's basketball national league team, and at Telford, there's a new sports centre.

ACCOMMODATION	
Guarantee to freshers	**No guarantee**
Style	**Halls**
Security guard	**All**
Shared rooms	**Some**
Internet access	**All**
Self-catered	**All**
En suite	**Some**
Approx price range pw	**£61-£90**
City rent pw	**£45**

Town Wolverhampton can be unnerving, but the SU supplies advice, information, attack alarms. Clubland is good for house, garage, rock, indie, bhangra, jungle techno, acid jazz, folk. Cinemas include **The Light House** (mainstream/foreign); **Wolverhampton Art Gallery** for British and American Pop Art; the uni's own **Arena Theatre** for alternative, touring, student drama and music; the city's **Grand Theatre** for London shows.

PILLOW TALK

Walsall Student Village opened in 2005. All its rooms are fully furnished, with en-suite shower and wireless internet access. There is a safe courtyard with 24-hour security, CCTV and free parking. There are also specially-designed rooms for students with disabilities.

GETTING THERE

☞ By train: London Euston less than two hours;
☞ By road: M6/J10, M54/J2, M5/J2
☞ By coach: London, 4:00.

UNIVERSITY OF WORCESTER

The University of Worcester
Henwick Grove
Worcester WR2 6AJ

TEL 01905 855111
   01905 855141 (prospectus request)

FAX 01905 855377
EMAIL admissions@worc.ac.uk
WEB www.worcester.ac.uk
SU TEL 01905 855188

VAG VIEW

*W*orcester began as a teacher training college in 1946. In the '70s it became a college of higher education. In 1995 it merged with a college of nursing and midwifery, and in 2002 it was granted university college status, platform for their bid for full university status, which was secured last year.

Worcester University is the only Higher Education Institution in Herefordshire and Worcestershire, and has a largely female

UNIVERSITY/STUDENT PROFILE

University College since	**1999**
Situation/style	**Campus**
Student population	**7750**
Total undergraduates	**6149**
Mature undergraduates	**35%**
International undergrads	**3%**
Male/female ratio	**35:65**
Equality of opportunity:	
state school intake	**98%**
social class 4-7 intake	**34%**
low-participation area intake	**9%**

*student body (65%), owing to the primary
teacher training and nursing courses. It is
not a place for the faint hearted. University
of Worcester graduates, Joanne Yapp and
Mel Berry, were rival rugby captains a few
years back in the England and Wales
Women's Six Nations clash. Sport is another
of this uni's major preoccupations.*

CAMPUS

Headquarters is a parkland campus within walking
distance of the centre of this Cathedral city. On
campus there's a new Digital Arts Centre, a Drama
Studio, Sports Centre and Students' Union. Now,
flush with a £10-million grant from the Government
they have created an additional campus on a 5-acre
site in the city, which will include a new library
and Learning Centre, teaching and residential
accommodation.

FEES, BURSARIES

UK & EU Fees, 2009-10: £3,225 p.a. Eligibility for
the HE Maintenance Grant confers a bursary. Up
to 50 academic achievement scholarships of £1,000
are available after the first year of study. The uni
also works in partnership with Worcestershire
County Cricket Club and the Worcester Wolves

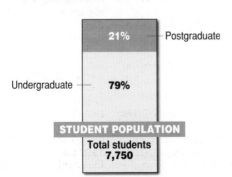

Basketball Club to award sports scholarships.

STUDENT PROFILE

Many of the mainly female undergraduates are
local and 35% are mature; a fair proportion (34%)
are from the lowest 4 socio-economic groups, new
to the idea of going to university, and 9% from
'low-participation neighbourhoods'. They have
partnerships with colleges in the region, in order,
they say, to widen participation further, though
widening into the upper socio-economic and overseas groups might seem to be more of a challenge.

ACADEMIA & JOBS

There's a modular course structure and 6 academic
departments: Applied Sciences, Geography &
Archaeology; Arts, Humanities & Social Sciences;
the Worcester Business School; Education; Health
& Social Care; Sport & Exercise Science.

A strong educational, nursing and sporting

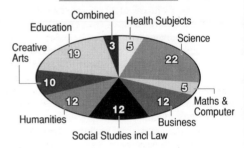

provision (their teams came 55th in the national
BUSA league last year, which is amazing for so
small a university), together with degrees in drama
and social welfare, make for a strong employment
record of great use to the health and welfare of the
community they serve.

Teaching inspections results have been fair.
Out of 24 points, Education did best with 23; then
Sport and Nursing scored 22; Sociology, Art &
Design; and Business 21; Biosciences and
Psychology, 20 (there is a BSc Psychology accredit-
ed by the British Psychological Society, first step to
becoming a chartered psychologist); and Health
19. In the National Student Survey, 84% said they
were satisfied with the provisions. Students say
that the best teaching at Worcester is in English,
History & Heritage Studies, Initial Teacher
Training, Sports Science, Business, History,
Creative Arts & Design, Biological Sciences.

Around 80% of graduates find real graduate
jobs within six months of leaving. Primary school

TEACHING SURVEY AT A GLANCE

Avg. UCAS points accepted	**240**
Acceptance rate	**21%**
Overall satisfaction rate	**84%**
Helpful/interested staff	**No data**
Small tuition groups	**No data**
Students into graduate jobs	**80%**

Teaching most popular with undergraduates:
English, History & Heritage Studies, Initial Teacher Training (91%), Sports Science, Business (89%), History (88%), Creative Arts & Design (87%), Biological Sciences (86%).

Teaching least popular with undergraduates:
Education (62%).

teachers account for almost a quarter of graduates; then there are educational assistants, welfare, community and youth workers, nursery nurses, physical training instructors, police, secondary school teachers, etc. There are also strengths in business, especially personnel, accounting and marketing. There are strong links with firms and organisations in business, creative, education and health.

Among their regional network of partner colleges, the following feed the uni with students on foundation degrees and HNDs: Evesham & Malvern Hills College, Halesowen College, Herefordshire College of Technology, Josiah Mason College, Kidderminster College, Pershore Group of Colleges, Stourbridge College, and Worcester College of Technology. Foundation degrees include Business in the Electronic Age, Commercial Web Development, Food Safety & Quality Management, Learning Support, and Adventure Tourism.

Writes Emma Aves. 'UCW gains greatly from the sense of intimacy which its size brings, you feel truly part of the institution, one that supports you throughout your course. The onus is on you to balance your interests and ensure academic requirements are fulfilled, but a personal tutor system is available to all and helps to compensate for the formal nature of lectures.' They also have a Student Advice Bureau and Employment Bureau, and are active in work-related skills training of undergrads.

SOCIAL SCENE

STUDENTS' UNION There are decent ents in the **Dive Bar**, cheesy fare but also a Battle of the Bands event and an active Alternative Music Society, which keeps people on their toes into the small hours. Birmingham is 45 mins to an hour away by train, with all its night-time distractions; a return fare without rail card costs £6.40 to £10.70. The

Student Birmingham.

'Activities such as RAG and Student Community Action are enthusiastically attended in order to establish that we are here for more than personal gain,' Emma continues. Indeed, English Student Sophie Nixon runs Kids Club in Dines Green, a local estate, and was recently presented with the Millennium Volunteer of the Year award for the West Midlands. With 15 other student volunteers, Sophie raises drama productions, discos, music lessons, arts & craft sessions, and organises trips out.

There are 33 clubs and societies at Worcester this year, from mountain boarding to the new dance soc. and Loco Show Co., the tried and tested musical theatre society. *The Voice* is the student newspaper, issued twice a semester.

SPORT There is a multi-million pound Sports Centre on campus and huge interest in sport, both through the sports courses and competitively across the board. They have all the traditional sports, and on, right through to Y'ai Chi. Worcester County Cricket Ground overlooks the River Severn – they list a Men's Cricket club only, odd that the women aren't interested. Worcester Rugby offers premiership rugby, its ground at Sixways a Centre of Excellence. The uni's close association with the

WHAT IT'S REALLY LIKE

COLLEGE:	
Social Life	★★
Campus scene	**Local, lively, largely female**
Politics	**Controlled**
Sport	**Competitive**
National team position	**55th**
Arts opportunities	**Excellent across the board**
Student magazine	**The Voice**
Nightclub/bar	**The Dive**
Union ents	**Cheese, live + 4 big balls**
Union clubs/societies	**33**
Parking	**Adequate**
CITY:	
Entertainment	★★
Scene	**Cathedral, arts, cricket, rugby, pubs**
Risk of violence	**Low**
Cost of living	**Average**
Student concessions	**Excellent**
Survival + 2 nights out	**£560 pw**
Part-time work campus/town	**Excellent**

ACCOMMODATION	
Guarantee to freshers	**100%**
Style	**Halls, flats**
Security guard	**Secure**
Shared rooms	**Some**
Internet access	**All**
Self-catered	**All**
En suite	**Some**
Approx price range pw	**£72-£115**
City rent pw	**£65**

club provides exceptional facilities and expertise.

TOWN Pubs and cheesy clubs predominate, but within a 30-mile radius there's Shakespeare country to the east, the Malverns Welsh borders and Wye Valley to the west, the Cotswolds to the southeast, and big city Birmingham an hour to the north.

Royal Worcester (porcelain) is their heritage, but the **Edward Elgar Birthplace Museum** points to another distinguishing mark, England's greatest composer. **The Swan Theatre** (for drama, comedy, dance) and **Huntingdon Hall** (seriously lively venue for jazz, folk, blues and classical), the **Odeon Film Centre**, the **Vue Cinema** complex, the **Worcester Arts Workshop**, and the recently reconstructed **Festival Theatre** at nearby Malvern complete the arts picture.

PILLOW TALK

Accommodation on campus ranges from ancient room-only halls to comfy, modern flats, but there are enough only for 90% of first years and international students.

GETTING THERE

☞ By road: M5/J7.
☞ By rail: Birmingham, 60 mins; Cheltenham, 24 mins; Hereford, 40 mins.

UNIVERSITY OF YORK

The University of York
Heslington
York YO10 5DD

TEL 01904 433533
FAX 01904 433538
EMAIL admissions@york.ac.uk
WEB www.york.ac.uk

Student Union
University of York
Heslington
York YO10 5DD

TEL 01904 433724
EMAIL few1@yusu.org
WEB www.yusu.org/

VAG VIEW

*F*ounded in 1963, York University is rela-tively small with a huge reputation for its teaching. Students are drawn fairly evenly from the Southeast, from the North and else-where.

Its academic strengths span a wide disci-plinary range within the arts, social sciences and sciences, and attract students with high career ambitions. It rose from 18th to 10th place in the 2008 Government Research Assessment. It came top in English Language and Literature, and in Health and Sociology it improved dramatically.

Whilst York offers perhaps fewer voca-tionally orientated programmes of study than some other universities, its graduates are highly sought after by employers. What's more, the university is very popular with its students, who are bright, fun-loving and notably unpretentious.

In the National Student Survey 85% said they were satisfied with the teaching, and in the Times Higher's Student Experience Survey their lecturers came out very well as helpful and interested in their students,

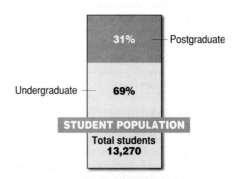

Postgraduate 31%
Undergraduate 69%

STUDENT POPULATION
Total students
13,270

unusual in an institution with so rich a life in research.

The drop-out rate, at less than 3%, is immaterial.

CAMPUS

It's a purpose-built campus at Heslington, on the south-east edge of the city: 'Very suburban, not at all monumental. It could get on the garden register,' mused Elaine Harwood of English Heritage. Student Gemma Thomas disagrees, 'Overall, the campus is a very pleasant place to live and along with York itself, one of the safest places. Heslington Hall, a gorgeous manor house on the edge of campus, provides an antidote to some of the bleaker aspects. It possesses extensive gardens, part of which, the Quiet Place, a collection of gigantic topiary knobs, is perfect for late-night games of hide-and-seek, or whatever else springs to mind.' The York Quakers, who were among those responsible for raising £70,000 for the Georgian gazebo and garden known as the Quiet Place will no doubt be pleased it is being put to such imaginative use. But, warns Gemma, 'Do NOT

UNIVERSITY/STUDENT PROFILE	
University since	**1962**
Situation/style	**Campus**
Student population	**13270**
Total undergraduates	**9105**
Mature undergraduates	**12%**
International undergrads	**9%**
Male/female ratio	**46:54**
Equality of opportunity:	
state school intake	**80%**
social class 4-7 intake	**17%**
low-participation area intake	**6%**

come here if you are anything less than tolerant of ducks. They are everywhere. On the lake, crossing paths, dive-bombing students wending their way to early morning lectures (or not).'

The university is a safe campus. Each college has a porter's lodge which is staffed 24/7. In the interests of ensuring a safe and secure environment, Security provide campus-wide patrols both on foot and in vehicles on a 24-hour basis.

FEES, BURSARIES

UK & EU fees, 2009-10: £3,145 p.a. There is a sliding-scale bursary for those in receipt of HE Maintenance Grant, according to parental income. Special awards and scholarships are available. See website (address above) for details.

STUDENT PROFILE

'After ducks, students form the most numerous campus species,' Gemma continues. 'No one type dominates, the balance between state and private sectors a surprise bonus in a university with this much prestige. York is a small, friendly, unpretentious university, which makes it incredibly easy to settle in. Also, student welfare is taken very seriously. Nightline, chaplains, a range of counselling services and equal opportunities are promoted heavily.'

ACADEMIA & JOBS

York is known for social sciences, technology, and science. The top 10 subjects at the teaching assessments lost only one point between them.

In the 2008 Research Assessment 12 departments were ranked in the Top 10 in the country, with almost all departments in the top 20. More than 90% of the uni's academic staff had their work submitted for consideration, so the results reflect quality and depth almost across the whole provision.

Students say that the best teaching is in Biochemistry, Chemistry, Archaeology, Biology and related sciences, Electronic & Electrical Engineering, Engineering & Technology, Physics with Astrophysics, Medicine, English, and Philosophy.

Computer Science & Engineering was top-rated for teaching at the assessments and has a world-class reputation for research. Computing is a significant graduate employment area; jobs in electrical and electronic manufacturing are also legion, and for electronic and telecommunications engineers York is a leader.

Social Sciences are also pre-eminent. Applied Social Work, Social Policy, Economics, Politics were all top-rated for teaching; Sociology scored 23 points out of 24 at the teaching assessments. The £4.2 million Alcuin Research Resource Centre (ARRC) now further enhances its research capacity in this area.

The single most popular employment pathway out of Economics is accountancy, though accountants also come through mathematics and physical sciences. Actuaries also proliferate in these disciplines too. This Economics bias and a Management and Industry axis in physical sciences (also full marks at the teaching assessments) encourage placements in business analysis, finance and investment consultancy, marketing management and management consultancy work.

Jobs also flow in welfare and youth work and care work in the community from the Applied Social Science - with its Crime, Health, Children &

Young People specialities. See also the BA/MA Social Work, and the newer Nursing degree programme: BSc Evidence-based Nursing Practice - Adult, Child, Learning Disability, Mental Health.

In Applied & Natural Science, biosciences (including a new BSc Bioarchaeology) scored full marks at the assessments and courses such as Chemistry: Biological & Medicinal Chemistry, Chemistry: Management & Industry, Chemistry: Resources & the Environment show the way, and, as in the Social Sciences, illustrate the widely varying ambitions of York's students. Look, too, at BSc Psychology, with its maximum teaching score and world-class reputation for research. Accredited by the British Psychological Society, it's the first step to becoming a chartered psychologist.

The launch of the Hull York Medical School in 2003 has been a great success. They offer a 5-year BMBS (Bachelor of Medicine, Bachelor of Surgery). You may be based at either Hull University campus (see entry) or York; all follow the same curriculum. Hull has a decade's experience in Medicine through its Postgrad. Medical School, while York's Biosciences and Health depts are top rated for teaching and research. There is a new Mother and Infant Research Unit (MIRU) at York.

An equal emphasis on physical, psychological and social aspects marks the syllabus. A typical offer will be AABb at A-level (to include A Level Biology at grade A, and also A Level Chemistry). They do not accept General Studies at A2 or AS or Critical Thinking at A-Level. The UKCAT test is also required, and caring experience and interpersonal skills are significant.

Well-trod pathways for humanities and language graduates include education and marketing, museum and gallery work, library and archival work, an area also favoured by graduates from the BA Archaeology degrees, Linguistics, Philosophy (again, full marks for teaching), History of Art, and History - the new £6.5 million, climatically-controlled building housing the Borthwick Institute is the home for more than seven centuries of North of England history.

Music was top-graded in the Research Assessment, with 50% of its work adjudged world class. There's a good track record both for musician/composers and music producers out of here. Jazz musicians Jonathan Eato and John Taylor are now part of the department, signalling new initiatives in undergraduate education and a new Master's degree in Improvised Music and Jazz.

Their English/Writing & Performance is another arts niche with a big performance in Research, a practical, contemporary course pulling directly on the experience of current actors, writers and directors.

SOCIAL SCENE

Each college has its own Junior Common Room

RESEARCH EXCELLENCE

% of York's research that is
4* *(World-class)* or **3*** *(Internationally rated):*

	4*	3*
Epidemiology	0%	30%
Health Services	35%	40%
Nursing/Midwifery	35%	35%
Biological Sciences	25%	35%
Environmental Sciences	10%	50%
Chemistry	15%	60%
Physics	15%	40%
Pure Mathematics	10%	35%
Applied Mathematics	10%	40%
Computer Science	25%	50%
Electrical/Electronic Eng.	10%	45%
Archaeology	25%	35%
Economics	15%	45%
Business/Management	10%	40%
Politics	15%	30%
Social Work	25%	40%
Sociology	30%	30%
Psychology	20%	45%
Education	15%	45%
English	45%	30%
Linguistics	20%	45%
Philosophy	15%	40%
History	25%	30%
History of Art	45%	25%
Music	50%	25%

(JCR) Committee, who run about two events per week per college and two or three big events per year. The Students' Union organises up to 5 large-scale club nights or other events per term.

The point about York is the interest and activity levels beyond mere ents. 'Students get involved,' said Helen Woolnough. 'The university has an excellent academic reputation, but its students don't work themselves into the ground twenty-four hours a day and they certainly don't take themselves too seriously.'

Student media: University Radio York (URY), launched by John Peel thirty years ago and now with fm licence, York Television (YSTV), and two fortnightly newspapers, *Nouse* (pronounced 'Nooze' after the River Ouse, which flows through York, and of course 'news', which is what it dispenses) and *York Vision*. Other publications appear occasionally - *Point Shirley*, a literary arts magazine; *PS...*, an arts review; *Havoc*, a miscellany of creative writing; *Matrix*, a women's issue paper; Christis, a Christian magazine, and Mad Alice, an on-line features magazine.

They win awards by the basket-full, but last year for a while it seemed they were picking up only runners-up awards: Reporter of the Year, Nouse Website of the Year, Sports Writer of the Year, Newspaper of the Year. But then the real stuff came through: Feature Writer of the Year, Best Live TV, and for URY a Gold and two Bronze awards, and a Creativity Award. At the National Student Drama Festival awards came just as thick and fast for the Drama Society's production of Metamorphosis: Stage Director of the Year, Best Actor, Lighting, Ensemble, and for Promoting Student Theatre. Among some 90 societies there are 8 active drama societies with three venues, the intimate Drama Barn, the large and versatile Wentworth College Audio Visual Studio and the aforementioned Central Hall, which is huge.

There is a tradition of political activity and a left-wing stance.

SPORT For such a small uni they do well at sport, and recently have leapt up the BUSA league table to 48th position. The Boat Club goes to Henley Royal Regatta, the Lacrosse team to the world championships, basketball is a bit a speciality and they have the best parachutists in the country apparently. There are forty acres of playing fields – rugby, football, hockey, cricket – floodlit artificial hockey pitch, all-weather (three floodlit) tennis courts, squash courts, a sports centre for archery, badminton (seven courts), basketball, climbing, cricket (five nets), fencing, five-a-side soccer, judo, karate, netball, sauna, table-tennis, tennis, trampoline, volleyball, a 400-metre, seven-lane athletics track. Rowing and sailing are on the Ouse about a mile from the University, golf at Fulford Golf Club, swimming at the Barbican Centre half a mile from campus. Gliding, hang-gliding, riding and other facilities also found locally.

Highlight of the year - both socially and sportswise is The Rose, when the white rose of York meets the red rose of Lancaster in sporting competition and two days of wild socialising that takes over the entire campus in May.

TOWN York itself is one of our most beautiful cathedral cities, a magnet for tourists from all over the world owing to the wealth of Viking and

WHAT IT'S REALLY LIKE	
UNIVERSITY:	
Social Life	★★★★★
Campus scene	**Bright, friendly, small and unpretentious**
Student Union services	**Excellent; galvanising**
Politics	**Activity high Student and world issues**
Sport	**50 clubs**
National team position	**39th**
Sport facilities	**Good**
Arts opportunities	**Drama, film excellent; dance, music, art avg**
Drama awards 2008	**6 awards**
Student newspapers	**Nouse, York Vision**
Press Awards 2008	**1 award**
Student radio station	**URY**
Radio Awards 2008	**4 awards**
Student TV	**YSTV**
Nightclub	**College-based only**
Bars	**1 in every college**
Union ents	**Club D, House Trained, Cooker, Dust**
Union societies	**140**
Most popular societies	**Media, Drama**
Smoking policy	**Bars, halls OK**
Parking	**Non-existent**
CITY:	
Entertainment	★★★
City scene	**Tourist haven**
Town/gown relations	**Good**
Risk of violence	**Low**
Cost of living	**Average**
Student concessions	**Good**
Survival + 2 nights out	**£50 pw**
Part-time work campus/town	**Excellent/good**

ACCOMMODATION	
Guarantee to freshers	**100%**
Style	**Halls**
Security guard	**Porters, patrols**
Shared rooms	**Some**
Internet access	**All**
Self-catered	**Can choose**
En suite	**Some**
Approx price range pw	**£72-£140**
City rent pw	**£65-£140**

Roman remains, as well as its mediaeval reso-
nances in the Minster, in streets like the Shambles
(where buildings lean inwards and over you as if
out of a fairytale), in street names like Whip-Ma-
Whop-Ma-Gate, and in the snickleways which
offer those in the know an alternative way to scut-
tle about. Then there are the waters of the Ouse,
lapping over green-field banks or warehouse walls,
redolent of the city's merchant past.

It is, however, far from being the clubbing capital of the North. If you are a hardened clubber,
take a 20-minute ride to Leeds.

For theatre, there's the **Arts Centre** and the
Theatre Royal (good rep), and the **Grand Opera**
has a full programme of touring companies and
performances, both theatre and music. There's a
multi-screen **Warner's** cinema out at Clifton Moor
Estate (on the north side of the city), **Odeon** and
independent **City Screen** in York, as well as **York
Student Cinema** on campus.

PILLOW TALK

All freshers are guaranteed a place in uni accommodation – halls, flats and houses. None is catered
– all pay-as-you-eat. Around 40% are en suite.

GETTING THERE

☛ By road: A1237 ring road; Heslington is on the
southeast side, 10 miles from A1/M1; 20 from
M62.
☛ By coach: London, 4:30; Edinburgh, 5:15.
☛ By rail: Leeds, 20 mins; Sheffield, 1:15;
Manchester, 1:30; London King's Cross, 2:00.
☛ By air: Nearest airport is Leeds.

YORK ST JOHN UNIVERSITY

York St John University College
Lord Mayor's Walk
York YO31 7EX

TEL 01904 624624
FAX 01904 612512
EMAIL admissions@yorksj.ac.uk
WEB www.yorksj.ac.uk

York St John Students' Union
Cordukes Building
York YO31 7EX

TEL 01904 629816
FAX 01904 620559
EMAIL su@yorksj.ac.uk
WEB www.ysjsu.com/

VAG VIEW

*F*ounded by the Anglican Church in 1841
as a teacher training college, York St
John now offers very much more.

In February, 2006, it was granted
University College status and the power to
award its own degrees, and on October 1
that year, full university status.

It is lucky to have Dr John Sentamu,
Archbishop of York and the most acute mind
in the Church of England, as its first
Chancellor.

It is appropriate that a university that
has risen to prominence partly on a reputation for pastoral care should have made the
invitation.

All that notwithstanding, applications
are up 11% and York St John have grasped
their new status with both hands. Campus is
a hive of activity and there is a freshness

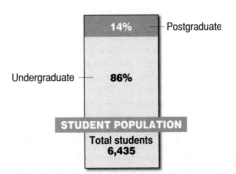

14% Postgraduate

Undergraduate — 86%

STUDENT POPULATION
Total students
6,435

and a buzz about the place. This is a new university, and you get the feeling it is going to lead the way in some interesting areas.

CAMPUS

The college is situated close to York Minster on a very attractive, newly re-vamped campus on this ancient site. The only worry is that there is nowhere for it to expand, as expand it surely must, in its present city-tight location.

FEES, BURSARIES

UK & EU Fees, 2009-10: Data withheld. 'Bursaries can be applied for without full HE Maintenance Grant: www.yorksj.ac.uk/bursaries'

TEACHING SURVEY AT A GLANCE	
Avg. UCAS points accepted	**392**
Acceptance rate	**18%**
Overall satisfaction rate	**91%**
Helpful/interested staff	★★★★★
Small tuition groups	★★★★
Students into graduate jobs	**76%**

Teaching most popular with undergraduates:
Theology & Religious Studies (95%), Initial Teacher Training (93%), Academic Studies in Education (91%), Subjects allied to Medicine (88%), History (87%), Languages (85%).

Teaching least popular with undergraduates:
Film & TV, Film Studies (42%).

UNIVERSITY/STUDENT PROFILE	
University since	**2006**
Situation/style	**Campus**
Student population	**6435**
Total undergraduates	**5505**
Mature undergraduates	**18%**
International undergrads	**1%**
Male/female ratio	**31:69**
Equality of opportunity:	
state school intake	**93%**
social class 4-7 intake	**29%**
low-participation area intake	**13%**

STUDENT PROFILE

This is a small, largely feminine student body, some 6,000 students, of which 72% are female. Some 20% are mature students, and a quarter of undergraduates are part-timers. Some 95% are recruited from the state sector, 3% more than demanded of them by the government, and 30% come from socio-economic backgrounds not traditionally drawn to university. In comparison, York University is positively rah: only 77% from state schools and 18% from the lower classes. state schools and 18% from the lower classes.

ACADEMIA & JOBS

There are four faculties. Arts incorporates performance, film and television, literature, media, history, American studies and art and design. They are hot on film. In February 2007 at City Screen two films by York St John student crews took the first ever BAFTA North event by storm.

'Performing arts, the therapies, Counselling Studies, and Linguistics I have heard very good reports about,' said one careers teacher. 'We had someone with straight A grades, could have gone anywhere, but chose York St John.'

In the Faculty of Education & Theology there's Teacher Education, Education Studies, Theology and Religious Studies, Theology and Ministry and Evangelism Studies. It is tempting to say that this is what attracted Sentamu, but he is as relaxed in the company of businessmen as he is clerics, which brings us to the third faculty: Business and Communication, which reflects the balance of the Archbishop with counselling and languages as well as business management and communication.

Finally, in Health & Life Sciences they have Professional Health Studies and Sports Science and Psychology. Degrees include Occupational Therapy BHSc and Physiotherapy BHSc, which underwent a thorough inspection in 2004, the results of which were top notch and can be read on the www.qaa.ac.uk web site. The BSc Psychology Specialist programme is the first step towards registration as a Chartered Psychologist.

In December 2008 the uni opened its new £15-million De Grey Court building, situated on the corner of Lord Mayor's Walk and Clarence Street, and housing new facilities for Physiotherapy and Occupational Therapy, and a Postgraduate research centre.

There's always been a practical spill into real life from the counselling programme: the Student Counselling Network employs a team of qualified and experienced counsellors for student use. It is just one example of healthy cross-fertilisation between academia and the real world.

Jobs-wise, Education (primary teachers) remains the strong bias, but hard on its heels comes the health industry, notably social work, and there is a fine showing in the area of archival/cultural jobs (galleries, museum, libraries, etc.), and in radio and TV of course. Every undergraduate programme

WHAT IT'S REALLY LIKE	
UNIVERSITY:	
Social Life	★★★
Campus scene	**Bright, friendly, unpretentious**
Student Union services	**Good**
Politics	**Aware**
Sport	**24 clubs**
National team position	**79th**
Sport facilities	**Adequate**
Arts opportunities	**Plenty**
Student newspaper	**The Saint**
Nightclub	**None**
Bars	**The Bar**
Union ents	**Theme nights**
Union societies	**32**
Most popular societies	**Welfare**
Parking	**Heavily patrolled**
CITY:	
Entertainment	★★★
City scene	**Tourist haven**
Town/gown relations	**Good**
Risk of violence	**Low**
Cost of living	**Average**
Student concessions	**Good**
Survival + 2 nights out	**£60 pw**
Part-time work campus/town	**Excellent/good**

has employment skills integrated into it.

SOCIAL SCENE

There is a bar with conservatory within the main hub of the Students' Union, and a programme of discos, live music, balls in summer and at Christmas. Also a coffee bar, a shop and The Crunch Bar, which is uni owned. Doesn't sound much, but this is a lively enough scene.

Happy Hours, pound a pint nights, Bar Footsie nights, live premiership matches, quiz machines, pool tables, table football, themed nights, quiz nights, acoustic nights are *de rigueur*. Saturdays you can get slewed all day for £1 pint and doubles-for-singles.

They have a weekly newspaper, *The Saint*, 8 societies, the most popular of which is Musical Productions Soc, and 24 sports clubs. With degrees in counselling, welfare is to the fore and the Education & Welfare Committee is one of the strongest in the union.

Just how even-handed are the students round here that when a controversy over the girlie Netball Calendar raged early in 2007 following a complaint to the Union's Women's Officer and then to the *Saint*, the complainant was invited to present her case to the Union Council, as well as representatives from the Netball Club. After the council had heard both sides of the story, a compromise was decided upon that advertising of the calendar would be text-only, limiting viewing of the photos to those who want to see it. Both parties exited content and the point of the calendar - to raise money for (appropriately) Breast Cancer Research - was achieved.

PILLOW TALK

Accommodation is on campus and on other city sites. Broadly, you can choose between catered, self-catered and en-suite halls and flats, 129, 599 and 124 respectively are available. Fifty-eight per cent of freshers can be accommodated. Percy's Lane opened in September 2008. (£90 - £125 p.w.). The accommodation - This is split into shared flats with en-suite facilities and self contained studio flats. Internet access is available from all bedrooms. A high level of security is provided by controlled access to all entrances and CCTV cameras linked to a 24-hour security office at Lord Mayor's

ACCOMMODATION	
Guarantee to freshers	**93%**
Style	**Halls, flats**
Security guard	**Most halls, all flats patrol**
Shared rooms	**None**
Internet access	**All**
Self-catered	**Most**
En suite	**Some**
Approx price range pw	**£69-£125**
City rent pw	**£60-£100**

Walk. The accommodation is situated inside the city's historic walls, 15 minutes walk to York St John's main campus and 5 minutes from the city centre. If you're unable to secure uni accommodation, they will help you find an alternative in York.

GETTING THERE

☛ By Road A1 into central York. Otherwise, see York University information.